THE BONHOEFFER READER

THE BONHOEFFER READER

Edited by
CLIFFORD J. GREEN AND MICHAEL P. DEJONGE

FORTRESS PRESS   MINNEAPOLIS

THE BONHOEFFER READER

Cover image: bpk, Berlin / Staatsbibliothek zu Berlin / Art Resource, NY
Cover design: Alisha Lofgren
Book design: HK Scriptorium, Inc.

Library of Congress Cataloging-in-Publication Data is available
Print ISBN: 978-0-8006-9945-1
eBook ISBN: 978-1-4514-3092-9

Manufactured in the U.S.A.
27   26   25   24   23   4   5   6   7   8   9   10

CONTENTS

Part 7: Theology from Prison: Worldly, Religionless Christianity

PREFACE

The recently completed *Dietrich Bonhoeffer Works English Edition* (*DBWE*), published by Fortress Press in sixteen volumes plus an index, makes available to English readers virtually all of Bonhoeffer's surviving writings. Both *DBWE* and the German critical edition it translates (*Dietrich Bonhoeffer Werke*, or *DBW*, published by Gütersloher Verlagshaus) are monumental achievements; decades in the making, they draw on the labor, expertise, dedication, and generosity of an international team of scholars, translators, publishers, and donors. They are maximally inclusive, incorporating not only those works of Bonhoeffer that were published during or soon after his lifetime but also previously unpublished works in a variety of genres, such as letters, diary entries, lecture notes, and reports. As such, these editions are the definitive resources for scholars from a number of disciplines who have reason to be interested in Bonhoeffer.

Of course, the very things that make *DBWE* the resource par excellence for scholars might not suit the general reader or beginning student of Bonhoeffer. *The Bonhoeffer Reader* is designed for such an audience. It collects in one place a significant and representative range of Bonhoeffer's theological writings. The *Reader* has considerable advantages over previously published collections of his works, since it draws on the numerous and significant advances in scholarship represented by *DBW* and *DBWE* while also conveniently directing the interested reader, through notes and other guides, to the resources of *DBWE*.[1]

Bonhoeffer's writings are interesting for many reasons, biographical, historical, and otherwise. This *Reader* is self-consciously a *theological* reader, however, in that it includes, above all, the writings that are of theological

---

1. In the *Reader*, marginal numbers indicate a given text's location in *DBWE*. (Furthermore, *DBWE* leads the student who wishes to consult the original German to the corresponding page in *DBW*.) The *Reader* takes as its source the electronic edition of *DBWE*. There are a few minor discrepancies (e.g., the numbering of footnotes, the correction of errata) between this electronic edition and the printed hardcover or paperback editions.

interest. This is not to say, of course, that Bonhoeffer's theology admits of neat abstraction from either his life or historical circumstances; indeed, the editorial introductions that precede the selections attempt, among other things, to set his writings in biographical and historical context. But it remains the case that a different range of texts would have been included if the *Reader* were about, say, Bonhoeffer the preacher, Bonhoeffer the person, or Bonhoeffer and the Church Struggle.[2] As it is, this *Reader* is about Bonhoeffer the theologian.

The main principle for selecting texts for inclusion in this *Reader*, then, has already been mentioned. But in addition to the criterion of theological interest, the editors strove for a selection of writings that represent the range of Bonhoeffer's career—from those written as a young student to those written in the weeks before his death—and a range of genres—from those academic monographs published during his lifetime to those fragmentary texts published soon after his death to the lecture notes and short pieces that, until *DBW* and *DBWE*, had not been widely available. Within the focus area of Bonhoeffer's theological writings, therefore, this *Reader* is quite exhaustive, including excerpts from every major text and every phase of Bonhoeffer's career. This *Reader* attempts to provide a picture of the whole of Bonhoeffer's theological work.

The wide range of texts protects this *Reader* to some degree from being unduly slanted by the interpretive interests of the editors. But it is also certainly the case that these interests informed their judgments regarding which of the minor texts and which sections of the major texts to include. The editors are comforted by the fact that the whole corpus stands available in *DBWE* for the enterprising reader.

The number of footnotes in the *Reader* is drastically reduced in comparison with *DBWE*, both for reasons of space and because of the different intended audience. In selecting which of the *DBWE* footnotes are reproduced here, the editors have generally observed the following guidelines. First, for footnotes that originated with Bonhoeffer himself, the *Reader*

---

2. For those interested in Bonhoeffer the preacher, *The Collected Sermons of Dietrich Bonhoeffer* (edited by Isabel Best) offers a selection of those sermons printed in *DBWE*. For those interested in Bonhoeffer's biography and the history during his lifetime, the most exhaustive resource remains *DB-ER*; a recent well-commended biography is Ferdinand Schlingensiepen's *Dietrich Bonhoeffer*. Many shorter biographies are available. For those interested in Bonhoeffer and the Church Struggle and resistance conspiracy, an appendix to this *Reader*, assembled by Victoria Barnett, lists the relevant Bonhoeffer works as well as recommended secondary sources.

retains references to "major" figures (such as Luther and Barth) but drops references to "minor" figures as well as footnotes that are not central to the given text's argument but could be characterized as learned asides. Bonhoeffer's own footnotes appear in the *Reader* without any brackets and in standard font. Second, *DBWE*'s editorial notes appear in the *Reader* when those notes are judged to be helpful for the intended audience's comprehension of the text in question or if they provide cross-references to other Bonhoeffer works. This means that footnotes which, for example, offer alternative readings of a passage or provide the manuscript history of a text have been omitted except when their omission would impede the reader's comprehension. *DBWE* editorial notes are indicated in the *Reader* by square brackets and the standard academic conventions for quoted material (quotation marks, ellipses for omitted material, and references to the original location). In some cases (e.g., formatting of citations, updating references from *DBW* to *DBWE*), the editors have made minor changes to these notes for the sake of consistency and for the reader's convenience in locating cited materials. Beyond Bonhoeffer's own notes and *DBWE* editorial notes, the editors of the *Reader* have on occasion contributed their own footnotes to aid comprehension and to provide cross-references. These notes are indicated by square brackets and italics. The *Reader* editors have also provided in-text biblical references as well as translations of foreign terms that either remained untranslated in *DBWE* or were translated there in footnotes. These are marked by square brackets and italics.

A note on using this *Reader*: while the texts are organized chronologically, the book can be used in flexible ways. An introductory course may begin with his very successful and accessible lectures like *Creation and Fall* or *Discipleship*. Advanced courses may choose to concentrate on a particular aspect of Bonhoeffer's theology such as his *Ethics*, his exegetical writings, his writings on the church, or his dissertations. Individual texts, or a group of texts, may be chosen for a course of short duration (e.g. Lent). The *Reader* may also be used to provide context for intensive study of a particular volume of *DBWE*. Or a course on the German churches during National Socialism could supplement texts in this volume with resources chosen from the Appendix; a course on ethics and the German resistance movement could do likewise. In short, the *Reader* is intended to be useful in a variety of imaginative ways.

As indicated earlier, this *Reader* relies heavily on *DBW* and *DBWE*. The editors therefore gratefully acknowledge the various editors, translators, and others who worked on them. We also thank Victoria Barnett for suggesting the contents of the appendix. Thanks also to Christopher King for kindly helping with formatting the manuscript.

ABBREVIATIONS

DB-ER	Eberhard Bethge, *Dietrich Bonhoeffer: A Biography.* English translation, revised edition.
DBW	*Dietrich Bonhoeffer Werke*
DBWE	*Dietrich Bonhoeffer Works English Edition*
LW	*Luther's Works*
WA	*Weimar Ausgabe* (Weimar edition), Martin Luther

PART 1
Student Writings:
Berlin, Barcelona, New York

1. PAPER ON HISTORICAL AND PNEUMATOLOGICAL INTERPRETATION OF SCRIPTURE

DBWE 9:285–300

After two semesters in Tübingen, the eighteen-year-old Bonhoeffer returned to Berlin, his home since age six, to continue the study of theology.[1] The 1925 summer semester at the Friedrich Wilhelm University (now the Humboldt University) was decisive.[2] He worked closely with the renowned Luther scholar Karl Holl, writing one of his several papers on Luther and the Lutheran tradition.[3] At the same time, he first seriously engaged with the work of Karl Barth and the new movement associated with him: dialectical theology.

In the following paper, which dates from that 1925 summer semester, Bonhoeffer examines the relationship between revelation and history, or, more broadly, the relationship between a pneumatological and a historical orientation toward scripture. More broadly still, this paper shows Bonhoeffer negotiating the often competing influences of Barth's theology of the word of God and the historical-critical approach to theology favored by Holl and others at Berlin. Barthian tones resound as Bonhoeffer emphasizes the self-authenticating nature of revelation and the limits of the historical-critical approach. But Bonhoeffer shows himself to be more than a slavish disciple of Barth, raising questions about the danger of removing revelation entirely from history. Thus this paper shows Bonhoeffer at the beginning of a process to find his theological voice in conversation with his Berlin teachers and Karl Barth, a process that continued through his doctoral dissertation, Sanctorum Communio, *and his postdoctoral dissertation,* Act and Being.

---

1. [*For historical background, biographical information, and a summary of texts from Bonhoeffer's student years 1924–1927, see* DBWE *9:1–11, editor's introduction, and* DB-ER, *45–96.*]
2. [DBWE *9:572, editor's afterword.*]
3. [*See* DBWE *9, part 2.*]

285

Can One Distinguish between a Historical and a Pneumatological Interpretation of Scripture, and How Does Dogmatics Relate to This Question?

Christian religion stands or falls with the belief in a historical and perceptibly real divine revelation, a revelation that those who have eyes to see can see and those who have ears to hear can hear. Consequently, in its innermost nature, it raises the question we take up here, namely, the relationship of history and the Spirit. With respect to the Bible this question refers to the letter and the Spirit, scripture and revelation, and human word and God's word. Methodologically we should not proceed historically but philosophically.

The Bible, translated quite simply "the ultimate book," narrates the most significant of events. They are more than just "accidental truths of history," and do not intend to be "eternal truths of reason," as rationalism wanted to see it. Certainly, one cannot prevent someone from considering this book as one book among others. Indeed, we all do this, for ordinary human beings wrote it. But it is the historian who expressly approaches the Bible with this sole presupposition that it is one book among others that has nonetheless gained a unique and incomparable significance above others. The 2000-

286 year history of the Christian religion rests on this book as the foundation for this approach. Without a doubt it is one writing among others—and one of extraordinary historical significance. It is no wonder that historical criticism found here its first and most enduring issue; no wonder that it here learned sharply to refine its best tools.

Its general principles are based on a scientific-mechanistic worldview. Its epistemological methods are, for that reason, those of the natural sciences. Every dogmatic connection is eliminated. This is the basic pillar upon which all historical research is built and must be built. Its knowledge should be attainable for every reasonable person by separating, in principle, the knowing subject and known object. Like science, it should be "universally valid." The growing interest in psychology, which brings with it new theories on the nature of understanding alien emotional life, could not bring about a decisive turning point in the understanding of the Bible. (One should mention in passing that when seen in relationship to the mechanistic method this is a powerful positive step beyond historical knowledge as such.)

Regarding the form of the Bible, with this approach the concept of the canon disintegrates and becomes meaningless. Textual and literary criticism are applied to the Bible. The sources are distinguished, and the methods of the history of religions and form criticism fragment the larger and even the remaining short textual units into little pieces. After this total disintegration of the texts, historical criticism leaves the field of battle. Debris and fragments are left behind. Its work is apparently finished.

The content of the Bible is leveled and made to match contemporary history. Parallels to the miracle stories are found. Yes, even the person of Jesus is stripped not only of the divine but also of human majesty. He disappears unrecognizably among various rabbis, teachers of wisdom, and religious visionaries. To be sure, even the critically reflective historian recognizes 287 that this book is concerned with unique and extraordinarily profound things, that here one catches sight of things of enormous significance. But if one did not, one would truly be an unsound historian, just as unsound a historian as if one believed that one could use such statements to prove that the Bible is God's word. One begins to see (recall Dibelius) that a certain final principle lies behind the synoptic tradition in spite of its fragmentation, as both Albert Schweitzer and Overbeck recognized. Yet our historical investigation stops here, and its work is completed. We will now continue our investigation.

First, we will compare unrelated types of pneumatological interpretation. Only one of these will pose a problem for us.

The first statement of spiritual interpretation is that the Bible is not only a word about God but God's word itself. In some way the decisive concept of revelation must be introduced here. When revelation is found, the extraordinary enters and its power is self-evident. The past is made present or—better—the contemporaneity and trans-temporality of God's word are recognized.

Let us review for a moment. Due to lack of insight into the relationship of revelation and scripture, nothing perplexed the early church more than the creation of the canon. With subjectively similar justification, orthodoxy and heresy quoted revealed passages in the discussion until the catholic church established a standard external to the Bible. This rule became the standard by which all catholic Christians were—and still are—supposed to interpret scripture. This was the regula fidei [*rule of faith*], i.e., the tradition, i.e., ultimately, the church.

This step was the first, most decisive, and yet most thorough misunder- 288 standing of the concept of revelation. In principle, all attempts to objectify and to tie down revelation as scripture follow from this misunderstanding. This includes attempting to grab hold of revelation in scripture by applying humanly introduced means external to scripture. This method was implemented by the mystics, the Anabaptists, and other groups up to and

including the establishment of Orthodoxy.[4] All seek to bring an external
standard to bear upon scripture, which is used to locate and interpret positive revelation within scripture. One cannot find such a standard within the
Bible itself. For the mystics and Anabaptists this might be found in the free
spiritual experience that is considered to be barely subordinate to scripture. For the orthodox, it might be the principle of verbal inspiration; other
groups would employ other approaches. In every case these methods sought
to locate and to objectify revelation from outside of scripture and thereby
to separate the source of truth and its verification. The difficulties that
arise out of this for the necessity and significance of scripture are generally overlooked. (1) Does God actually impart personal revelation so that
what God once clearly stated can still be confirmed? An example would be
the Anabaptists' spiritual experience. It ought to be confirmation enough
that God speaks. "Deus solus de se doneus testis est in suo sermone" [*God
alone is a fit witness of himself in his Word*] (Calvin). Is a double revelation
needed? (2) Do incorrect consequences result for interpretation? When
hermeneutical standards external to scripture are brought to bear, then
abuses are unavoidable. In order to force the text, particular methods that
permitted an incredible breadth of interpretation were in use for a considerable period of time. The method of allegorical interpretation completely
ignored historical reality. It used speculative and rationalistic methods that
could read into the text whatever one wished. Its history is as old as our
chronology. Protests against its arbitrariness rang out again and again.
289   Even the history of philosophy's much more profound typological treatment of the Bible led to exaggerations.

The doctrine of the fourfold sense of scripture[5] was authorized by the
Catholic church in order to be able to satisfy its demands on the Bible. This
is a principle that may be easier to justify sociologically than dogmatically.
With it progress was certainly made with respect to detailed exegesis, but
this is not significant for our principal question. Whether it is the enthusiasts' principle of spirit or the psychological understanding of liberalism, in
every case we find a humanization, i.e., a superficial reduction, of the con-

---

4. [*Bonhoeffer is referring to Protestant Orthodoxy, the late-sixteenth- and seventeenth-century movement within the Protestant traditions to codify and systematize the theologies of the first genera- tion of Reformers.*]

5. ["Historically, the church has understood that Scripture can be interpreted on multiple levels. Classically formulated, it resulted in a 'fourfold' approach, employing the literal, the allegorical, the moral, and the anagogical in recognition of the various ways that Scripture could be both interpreted and applied to the Christian life . . . ," *DBWE* 14:428, n. 78.]

cept of revelation. The divine was conceived in terms of the human in that a strict distinction was not made; the old maxim finitum incapax infiniti [*the finite is incapable of the infinite*] was forgotten.[6]

An energetic counterblow had to take place for independence in the sense of the deepening of the concept of revelation in relation to scripture.

Revelation for us can be found only in scripture. To the question why revelation is to be found precisely here the answer must simply be that this is where God speaks and this is where it pleases God to be personally revealed. Luther says, "If God gives me wooden apples and tells me to take and eat, I should not ask why." God's will cannot be given a basis but only experienced and proclaimed. Revelation is confirmed in scripture. Scripture uses the term "witnessed." Scripture itself belongs to a great complex of revelation as a *document that gives witness*. For us, it is its only remnant. Consequently, scripture is not revelation. If it were, one would once again objectify scripture by rational means. *Scripture* is not experienced as revelation, but the matter that it deals with. One can discover nothing a priori except that revelation is present where individuals hear it, where the human word becomes God's word, and where time becomes eternity. The single claim the scripture makes is that if it is to be understood it must be understood in the spirit of revelation. Where does this spirit come from? The paradoxical answer: it comes from scripture itself. We stand, therefore, before a circle. If we wish to understand and preserve the concept of revelation, one assertion cannot be true but both are necessary. There is only one revelation. A multiplication of revelations would amount to the humanization of revelation, and so revelation must be understood from itself.

This problem of consistent spiritual interpretation is one that the exegetes of the Catholic church and of the Anabaptists do not acknowledge. They both bring arbitrary standards external to scripture to bear on scripture. The *principle of interpretation* must derive from an already-understood scripture. Does God truly speak in scripture in such a way that only God and not humans can hear? The Spirit comes from the word and the word comes from the Spirit.

Is there a solution, or are we, along with the concept of revelation, plummeting further and further into darkness as we search for light and enlightenment? The solution lies in the fact God opens human eyes to receive revelation in certain indescribable and undetermined moments and words.

290

---

6. ["... This Reformed maxim is intended to emphasize the transcendence of God. It is directed at the Lutheran maxim, *finitum capax infiniti*, 'the finite is capable of the infinite,' which has in mind the becoming human of God in Jesus Christ," *DBWE* 9:289, n. 30.]

The object of understanding creates for its subject the means of recognizing in the act of knowledge. The object must become subject. God becomes the Holy Spirit.

This certainly occurs in the act which theologians might call "inspiration." In this concept one can see an actual commingling of both apparently circular assertions. Theological methodology cannot describe this in any other way than as successive and reciprocally consecutive. Only in this way can one speak of an objective, i.e., necessary *plainly literal,* understanding of scripture. This is true only when one considers the subject not externally but internally. Luther writes, "scriptura sacra est sui ipsius interpretes" [*holy scripture is its own interpreter*]. Like can be understood only by like. God can be understood only by God.[7] From this it can be concluded that the concept of revelation that emerges is to be conceived not substantially, but rather functionally. One does not encounter a being in scripture, but rather a judgment or God's will.

291

For this new way of knowledge (in cognitione sita est fides [*faith rests upon knowledge*], Calvin, *Institutes* 3.2.2), the implementation of historical temporality into contemporary existence, of the past into the present, is applied to the Bible. Directly associated with this is the fact that spiritual exegesis can relate the circumstances of the past and the present only if they exist in the same "dialectical" relationship. This is the only way, for example, that Karl Barth can justify as a completely literal translation his rendering of the Pauline "Israel" in Romans 9–11 as "church."

Let us also consider the issue of the so-called intuitive historical understanding. To be sure, it is difficult to interpret Goethe's lyrical poetry or ancient Indian Vedic poetry. The process here is different. It is to be understood in purely psychological terms and in terms of a reaching outward and a returning from the alien "I" to the self. This is a persistent, never completely possible advance toward the object. The final renunciation of the "I" in the understanding can never be perfected in this way. Even the most ingenious interpreter understands things from the "I." Faith, which is itself God's will, understands things from the subject matter itself. Faith, in particular, must not leave out what historical and psychological exegesis *must* leave out. Everything depends on the final renunciation of the "I." Here it is necessary to fend off another misunderstanding. Spiritual understanding is not to be identified with the a priori judgment of, for example, mathemati-

---

7. ["That like can be known only by like is a formula found in Aristotle's philosophy . . . It was taken up by dialectical theology and related to the knowledge of God . . . ," *DBWE* 9:291, n. 45.]

cal axioms. A divinely created a priori mental structure must be assumed here, which in spiritual understanding has to be created by God himself. God can be understood only from God's Spirit. This understanding is then 292 a most remarkable experience, not an a priori one. It is only here that illumination can be achieved, without which *all* this is *nothing*. Sine spiritus illuminatione verbo nihil agitur [*without the enlightenment of the Spirit the Word can do nothing*], Calvin's *Institutes* 3.2.33. Through this unique understanding, "inspiration" is received by the believer. Thus the believer comes to understand the category of revelation and uses it as the foundation for all further interpretation. Here we recall Augustine. "You would not seek me if you had not already found me."[8] To be sure, this does not nullify the fact that we always need the Spirit anew. We receive it to the same extent as we find Christ, just as we must always be renewed through God's will.

How does the Bible, as a historical literary classic, offer itself to this type of spiritual understanding? Now that we have understood the principles of historical-critical and pneumatological exegesis, we can address this question of how they relate to each other (the terminology originates with Beck). The question now centers on the relationship of the Spirit to the letter and of revelation to the written word.

Here we can, I believe, gain some important information from the analysis of the term "word."

On its dialectical side, a word is the finite and verbal form of an entity that, out of the infinitude of living things, occurs for the communication of the same. It occurs as a fragment of a whole that can never be completely represented. On the one hand, it is something that is finished and complete and is dead at the moment of conception. On the other hand, however, it is something that is open, unfinished, and alive. On the one hand, it is entity. On the other hand, it is power, life, and volition. But, of course, not every 293 word conceals eternity within it. This is true only of the word that has its origins in eternity. We can express this also in other ways. It belongs to the nature of the word that it expresses an *objective relationship* but not necessarily a *spiritual relationship*. The objective relationship is that part of the word that leads to an immediate a priori understanding. In this way, it is the *prerequisite* for the historical and psychological as well as the spiritual understanding and interpretation. At this point, we can already recognize that the historical and the spiritual do not relate to each other as cause and effect. Instead, they both have a common presupposition and only diverge later on.

---

8. ["Bonhoeffer falsely attributes this citation to Augustine. It comes from Pascal ...," *DBWE* 9:292, n. 57.]

In the Bible, we have the designation of Christ as the "Word of God" (John 1:1; Heb. 1:2). From God's perspective, for whom the terms "God spoke" and "it became so" are identical, Christ is the speaker and the doer of the word. Jesus existed in history. He was in the past and is not contemporaneous. Christ is the one who is born out of eternity through the Spirit of God. He is always living and present. In order, however, to be comprehended as Spirit, he must appear in verbal form. Jesus is one of the endless possibilities of God. Christ is the Spirit in personal form. If Christ is understood from the perspective of Jesus, then the past becomes present. This does not occur as a particular entity, a doctrine or a miracle, but rather through the particular as totality. The totality of Christ can be understood through one word. In this manner, every word is infinitely deep. It is not, however, flesh and blood that reveal the human Christ to be the Son of God. Instead it is the Spirit of the Father through the Holy Spirit.

Scripture is to be understood and interpreted on the basis of pneumatological interpretation in the sense that it was written by those to whom the Spirit had disclosed that revelation could be found precisely in this historical person, Jesus—fully human, appearing completely in the framework of ordinary events. Therefore, the biblical authors do not interest us as individuals but instead as apostles, prophets, and persons inspired by God. That is, it is not Paul whom we hear speaking but God. It is not we who hear but again it is God who hears in us. Still, the Bible remains a paradox. It will always remain the words individuals spoke to one person or to another. In order to transmit this realization they needed the proclaimed word, first as "good tidings and report," as Luther said, and then as a written record. Each of these written words of the Spirit, which mediate the understanding of the facts, is an incarnate image of the person of Jesus Christ himself. These are contained in a fully historical, insignificant, and unimposing husk, but behind that there is the other, what "inculcates Christ," where Christ is truly alive and present. For Catholics this occurs in the sacrifice of the Mass. In the word Christ is present—not as a substance, however, but as revelation, judgment, and will.

Such a view of the relationship between the letter and the Spirit, scripture and revelation, paves the way for a completely proper incorporation of historical exegesis into the general area of interpretation. We must say a priori that it is unacceptable for a pneumatological, faith-based interpretation to be dependent on historical methods of reading scripture with their shifting results. The difficulty rises from the fact that belief cannot free itself from the ὁ λόγος σάρξ ἐγένετο [*the Word became flesh*], nor does it want to. On the other hand, the historian's sense of truth cannot tolerate any patronizing by foreign methods. None of us can return to a pre-critical time. Both methods are used side by side by any pneumatological interpreter.[9]

Now, historical criticism is properly limited when it is placed in relationship to the pneumatological method. For a long time, liberal dogmatics was founded upon the leftovers of historical criticism. One was comforted by the thought that in the final analysis it really could not become dangerous. We have seen above where the historical-critical method can and must necessarily lead and—of course, not simply because of this negative reason—how it must follow another path.

For both the historical and the pneumatological methods the Bible is, first of all, writing, text, and the words of human beings. Both examine each context of meaning for its pure, external relationship to reality, i.e., its literal meaning. If there are problems here, then, after a precise reading of the manuscript's text, textual criticism plays a role. After the original text has been established, each of them goes its own way. If the contents are being examined, then the tradition at hand will be interpreted. We must pay attention to this. An examination of the *contents* can never be anything other than an *interpretation* of the tradition.

295

We will leave aside the consequences for a moment and turn to the analysis of the *form* of the tradition, which is sharply separated in principle from the results. That is, we remind ourselves of the field of ruins described above, bestowed on us by the critic. Insofar as the conclusions are true, they are *fully* recognized by pneumatological interpretation. Only when we are looking at these ruins do we see something else as well, something that holds everything together as a whole. To put it more precisely, it is not we who see, but instead our eyes are opened for us so that we can see what has been hidden, namely, the revelation to which the texts lay claim. The question of *genesis* can never touch the other question—of the thing itself. Therefore, there is no difficulty whatsoever in combining the two methods.

At first glance, it seems more difficult to take a position on the critique of the contents. We may not forbid the historical method to search for the actual events that lie behind the text and to examine them as sources. It must, however, investigate the uniqueness of the tradition, which is essentially not historical but cultic. If the results happen to be negative and even the person of Jesus slips out of reliable hands and disappears into the darkness, then one can assert that the pneumatological method seems to be completely at an end. We counter this statement: (1) If one remembers what

---

9. One thinks particularly of Calvin.

was established above, observing the content is interpreting the tradition. In our case this means that the person of Jesus in the Holy Scriptures can, at most, be *interpreted* as a free composition of the author. A conclusion regarding historicity is disallowed in principle. (2) Completely immersing oneself in the contemporary period in order to attain a pure historical perspective is symptomatic of the Christian concept of revelation. The God who entered history made God unrecognizable to the children of the world, from the manger to the cross. In extreme cases, the critic can contest the image of Jesus as a leader or a religious genius but never as *God's Son*. (3) It can be

296   positively stated that the pneumatological interpretation has its own plausibility for comprehending actual historical events. Because God speaks to people by means of the *authentic witness* of historical revelation through the Bible, God must personally also have spoken in historical events. This is, of course, true only of important historical events that are embedded in faith, such as those of the prophets and the historical person of Jesus Christ and his death on the cross for us. Individual accounts like the miracle stories, etc., are naturally not included here. Instead, they are included only insofar as the totality of faith directly depends on the factual truth of the historical events.

I intentionally did not include the "historical fact" of the resurrection. In my opinion, given all that has been said, it is senseless and clumsy to construe it as a naked historical fact. God wished to become manifest *in history*. The resurrection takes place within the realm of faith and revelation. All other interpretations seek to remove the decisive characteristic of *God within history*. In respect to the question of miracles, we can say with certainty that the laws of nature are not absolutely valid. They are, instead, statements about experience. However, to conclude from this that miracles are not break-throughs but are instead unknown forms of the laws of nature is also historically incorrect. We must accept them for what they claim to be in the Bible—true miracles. Neither history nor spiritual interpretation can give us information about the facticity of particular miracles. This is true because belief in Jesus Christ and historical revelation is not linked to the veracity of this or that miracle. Therefore, our concern with pneumatological interpretation is not, "Did the miracle in fact take place?" but rather, "What role does it play in the context of witness to revelation?" This is the case throughout. Scripture is only a *source* for history. For spiritual interpretation, scripture is a *witness*. In the final instance, this is based on the assertion that the inspiration of the biblical authors can never extend to the events. Instead, it can only extend to interpretation and knowledge. The question concerning the spiritual meaning of miracles and their ability to contain meaning, in spite of the complete immersing of the divine in history, belongs to exegesis itself.

Therefore, it is within this framework that historical criticism is put into play. The resulting tension is the necessary characteristic of pneumatological interpretation. At one point it is absolutely necessary that the noncontemporaneous, the historical, and the contingent be known and recognized. At the same time, however, the contemporaneous always emerges as the essential element. With this tension we find ourselves with our interpretation in exactly the same place as the writers of the Holy Scriptures themselves (cf. Luke l:lff.). It is absolutely necessary that we assure ourselves of the fallibility of these texts so that we can recognize the miracle that we really do hear God's words in human words.

297

The interpretation of the Synoptic Gospels has been compared to crossing a river on a thousand blocks of ice. One has to get across, but one cannot stop at any one point. One has to keep the whole picture in view. Yet we can be comforted by someone to whom we seldom go for advice. We have a model in the same tradition, who is a greater interpreter than we are. It is the apostle Paul himself.

The standard that must be preserved in the exegesis of scripture is handed to us along with the word that is the revelation and foundation of the Bible. This standard is taken from the Bible itself and is, as Luther noted, "what drives toward Christ." What the content of revelation does not have is not canonical.[10]

However, as far as the pneumatological method is concerned, the canon comprises only the highly striking evidence of the deep insight by which the significant writings were chosen from the great amount of literature of that time. Conversely, the canon can never be a proof of revelation. In principle, it must be acknowledged as open.

In principle, the Old Testament does not have a different status from the New Testament, although the Old Testament relates to the New as promise does to fulfillment, and Law does to Gospel. In both, the word of God is heard. "The same yesterday as today" (Barth).

Christian dogmatics, which has divine revelation in history as its subject matter, must hold upright the characteristic relationship of revelation and scripture as the representation of the entire complex of revelatory expe-

---

10. Here we are criticizing Calvin's Reformed principle of Scripture and its repristination by Barth, which places the concept of the canon above Luther's individual statement. We know that Luther is taking a very bold step, but we also know that it is in the interest of Protestant faith for us to take it with him.

rience. If the spiritual elements were to be suppressed, then dogmatics would become the presentation of New Testament piety. If the historical-critical method—not the historically factual element, which can never be suppressed—were to be suppressed, then it would take away some of the clarity of the concept of revelation. In principle, however, such a suppression would not necessarily change anything. The category of dogmatics is solely and alone the λόγος τοῦ θεοῦ [*the word of God*], insofar as it is in the proper sense "theology." Revelation is the source of truth for dogmatics at the same time as it is the confirmation of dogmatics. As the word of God, it has normative character.

The empirical representation of religion in the form of the church and congregation has the λόγος τοῦ θεοῦ [*the word of God*] as its source of truth and its norm. There is no independent church-community or church, as there is in Catholicism.[11] The sermon is the gift of grace for the proclamation of what has been made known.[12] Ἀνάγκη γάρ μοι ἐπίκειται οὐσαὶ γάρ μοί ἐστιν ἐὰν μὴ εὐαγγελίζωμαι [*and woe to me if I do not proclaim the Gospel*], 1 Cor. 9:16, cf. *WA* 53:252.

Its fate is the fate of interpretation and the fate of the scripture itself. It is the attempt to speak God's word with human words. This attempt will never go beyond the stage of experiment if God does not assent to it. Here we are at the very end, the most profound point. It lies buried in everything that had been said before. Every attempt at pneumatological interpretation is a prayer, a plea for the Holy Spirit, who alone determines, according to its pleasure, the hearing and understanding without which the most spiritual exegesis will come to naught. Scriptural understanding, interpretation, preaching, i.e., the knowledge of God begins and ends with the plea: "Veni creator spiritus" [*Come, Creator Spirit*].[13]

---

11. The famous objection of Bellarmine, in *De verbo Dei*, that the Reformers are dependent upon tradition simply through the reference to the Bible is blatant sophistry.

12. Cf. Jer. 20:9; Amos 3:8.

13. ["... the Pentecost hymn attributed to Hrabanus Maurus, although there is some debate about his authorship ... Cf. also the collection of sermons by Barth and by Eduard Thurneysen, *Come Holy Spirit*. Moreover, Adolf von Harnack's tombstone bears the inscription *veni creator spiritus* (Zahn-Harnack, *Adolf von Harnack*, 566)," *DBWE* 11:233, n. 288.]

2. Eulogy for Adolf von Harnack

DBWE 10:379–382

Adolf von Harnack—at various times rector of the University in Berlin, director of the Royal Library at Berlin, president of both the Academy of Sciences and the Kaiser Wilhelm Society—was the very embodiment of German culture and learning. He was a church historian of the highest order and the most distinguished member of the faculty during Bonhoeffer's tenure at the university. Bonhoeffer developed a close relationship with him, regularly attending his church history seminar and serving as his final seminar assistant. Bonhoeffer expressed his appreciation in a number of ways, including the eulogy printed below, which he delivered at Harnack's 1930 funeral as a spokesperson for the last group of students.

The eulogy is of theological significance as a witness to Bonhoeffer's complicated but enduring debt to liberal theology. Liberal theology "was theology under the imperative of freedom: freedom of thought and the pursuit of truth on every path it took, freedom from interference by those to whom authority had been given,"[1] and Harnack was its flag bearer. By the time Bonhoeffer delivered this eulogy, liberal theology had come under attack, most seriously from another of Harnack's students, Karl Barth, who found its scientific and historical approach inadequate to the "wholly other" subject matter of theology. As the previous selection shows, Bonhoeffer found Barth's critique persuasive and incorporated a version of it into his own theology. But unlike Barth, who publically debated Harnack,[2] Bonhoeffer remained deferential and grateful to him and the liberal tradition. In the last year of his life, Bonhoeffer wrote from his prison cell that he was still aware of the debt he owed to liberal theology.[3] With this confession, Bonhoeffer confirmed the foresight of his younger self, who, on the occasion of his graduation, wrote to Harnack, "What I have learned and understood in your seminar is too closely bound to my entire person for me ever to forget it."[4]

---

1. [*Rumscheidt, "Formation of Bonhoeffer's Theology," 54.*]
2. [*See Robinson,* Beginnings of Dialectical Theology, *165–187.*]
3. [DBWE *8:498–499* (Reader *810*).]
4. [DBWE *9:439.*]

379   Thousands of young theologians look back with me in this hour at their great teacher. Today his legacy is passed down to us, and we accept this legacy proudly and with a strong consciousness of the responsibility it brings. In so doing, however, we look to the future, to what Adolf von Harnack will continue to mean to the present generation of theologians.

380   Almost two generations separate us from him, whose original students have become our own teachers. We know him only as the aged master whose opinion the entire cultural world listened to attentively; who prompted everyone who met him to have reverence for a life led in the spirit and in the struggle for the truth; who, regardless of where he was, always brought an entire world along with him, a world that inevitably made an enduringly profound impression on whoever came into contact with it.

We young theologians who were fortunate enough to sense something of this world acknowledge it as something great, something that distinguishes us from all those for whom this world must remain something past.

He became our teacher; he became close to us the way true teachers become close to their students. He stood beside us with questions and across from us with superior judgment. The sessions of intensely serious work in ancient church history, for which he assembled us in his house during his latter years, allowed us to get to know his unerring striving for truth and clarity. Empty ways of speaking were alien to the spirit of his seminar. Clarity had to reign at all costs, though that did not exclude the possibility that questions of the most inward and personal nature also had a place and might expect to find in him an ever-ready listener and adviser who was always concerned with one thing: the authenticity of his response. But it became clear to us through him that truth is born only of freedom. We saw in him the champion of the free expression of truth once it was recognized, who formed his own free judgment each and every time, and expressed it clearly whatever the anxious inhibitions of the crowd. This made him the foe of all inauthentic academic loyalty, of all rigid pettiness; he was beyond all obsequiousness, so that he respected deeds and human beings, and this made him—something about which we are especially qualified to speak— the friend of all young people who spoke their opinions freely, as he asked of them. And if he sometimes expressed concern or warned about recent developments in our scholarship, that concern was motivated exclusively by his fear that the opinion of others might be in danger of confusing irrelevant issues with the pure search for truth.

Because we knew that with him we were in good and solicitous hands, we saw him as the bulwark against all trivialization and stagnation, against all fossilization of intellectual life.

But Adolf von Harnack—and this was the greatest thing for us—was a   381
theologian, a committed theologian, and we believed we could understand
him only from this perspective, and that is why this should be stated clearly
once more in this circle. Theologian—that means first of all not only that
he wrote a history of dogma. Theology means speaking about God. The
work of the theologian is concerned with nothing less. In Harnack the theologian we saw the unity of the world of his intellect; here truth and freedom
found the true unifying bonds, without which they become arbitrary. It was
consistent with his personality to speak few words here; better many words
too few than one word too many in such things. Here everything must be
completely truthful and completely simple. But what little he said sufficed
for us, whether he said it in the seminar or, better yet, outside, in the open
air, in Grunewald, where summer after summer he gathered his earlier and
later students. He believed that the zeitgeist was always determined through
the Holy Spirit of Christianity, and that the message of the Father God and
the Son of Man held eternal rights and thus also rights to us. It is here that
we find Harnack's legacy to us. True freedom of research, of work, of life,
and the most profound support by, and commitment to, the eternal ground
of all thought and all life.

I think it fitting that I should close with a statement that was one of his
own favorite sayings, one he passed along to us a year ago on a summer out-
ing of his old seminar: Non potest non laetari, qui sperat in Dominum [*who
hopes in the Lord cannot but rejoice*].

3. SANCTORUM COMMUNIO

DBWE 1:21, 34, 44–65, 107–116, 122–128,
130–134, 141–161, 184, 192–193, 198–200,
215–216, 226–227, 230, 246–247, 280–281

Though sometimes described simply as a treatise on the church, Sanctorum Communio *is much more—a far-reaching exploration of Bonhoeffer's conviction that theology must be approached from a social perspective. As he puts it in the preface, basic Christian concepts "can be fully comprehended only in relation to sociality." Already in his doctoral dissertation, Bonhoeffer strikes an independent and original course toward a theology of sociality.*

Driving Bonhoeffer's turn to sociality is his rejection of the epistemological subject-object relationship as a model for the relations of humans to one another and to God. Because the epistemological model ultimately reduces God and others to objects, "the attempt to derive the social from the epistemological category must be rejected." Viewed polemically, Bonhoeffer's argument for the sociality of theological concepts is an argument against their interpretation in merely epistemological terms.

Despite the technical vocabulary and complex argument, the organization of Sanctorum Communio *is straightforward, governed by Bonhoeffer's stated aim of displacing epistemological accounts of "'[p]erson,' 'primal state,' 'sin,' and 'revelation'" with social ones. After the first methodological chapter dealing with definitions of social philosophy and sociology, the theological argument proper begins in chapter 2 with the critical concept of the whole book, "the Christian concept of person." In contrast to the abstract and Kantian "epistemological concept of person," Bonhoeffer defines the person as intrinsically social, the "I" of the "I"-"You" relationship. This social-relational understanding of the person implies for Bonhoeffer that the individual person is essentially related to the community, and therefore that God's relationship to the individual is mediated through the community. Bonhoeffer's summary of this point is axiomatic for his whole theology: "The concepts of person, community, and God are inseparably interrelated."*

Chapter 3 examines this inseparable interrelationship in the context of creation, or the "primal state," and chapter 4 traces the changes to it that are caused by "sin."

Especially noteworthy is Bonhoeffer's analysis of sin in social terms. The interrelation-ship of individual and community allows Bonhoeffer to treat the traditional doctrine of original sin in a way that upholds both the culpability of the individual and the universality of sin: "Every deed is at once an individual act and one that reawakens the total sin of humanity." The consequences of sin, too, are understood socially as the degeneration of the community as found in the primal state: love becomes egotism, giving becomes demanding, and community becomes isolation.

Sanctorum Communio *culminates in the long fifth chapter on the church, which makes good on Bonhoeffer's opening statement that "revelation can be fully comprehended only in relation to sociality." Revelation is not a past historical hap-pening, nor information, nor doctrine, nor a holy book. Revelation is a person, Christ, who exists in social form as the church-community. The effect of revelation, then, is the creation of a new humanity. It is a new form of sociality "in Christ" that repairs the fallen form of sociality "in Adam."*

This social definition of revelation is Bonhoeffer's answer to an enduring theologi-cal question from the Enlightenment onward: how to speak about God, about divine transcendence. An epistemological subject-object approach to theology seems incapable of answering this question, since, Bonhoeffer argues, that model reduces God to an object. Bonhoeffer's social approach departs from this well-worn path to argue that the otherness of another person is the suitable model for thinking about the relation with the transcendent God. In the process, he redefines God's transcendence away from notions of remoteness and absence and toward the notion of presence in community.

There can be no doubt that "[u]nderstanding the theology of Dietrich Bonhoeffer requires a thorough understanding of Sanctorum Communio . . . *In this for-mative book Bonhoeffer articulates the concept of 'person' in ethical relation to the 'other,' Christian freedom as 'being-free-for' the other, the reciprocal relationship of person and community, vicarious representative action as both a christological and an anthropological-ethical concept, the exercise by individuals of responsibility for human communities, social relations as analogies of divine-human relations, and the encounter of transcendence in human sociality."[1]*

PREFACE   21

In this study social philosophy and sociology[2] are employed in the ser-vice of theology. Only through such an approach, it appears, can we gain

---

1. [DBWE *1:1, editor's introduction.*]
2. [*By* "sociology," *Bonhoeffer refers not to influential contemporaries such as Max Weber and Ernst Troeltsch but, rather, to a German school of* "systematic sociology," *which was concerned with*

a systematic understanding of the community-structure of the Christian church. This work belongs not to the discipline of sociology of religion, but to theology. The issue of a Christian social philosophy and sociology is a genuinely theological one, because it can be answered only on the basis of an understanding of the church. The more this investigation has considered the significance of the sociological category for theology, the more clearly has emerged the social intention of all the basic Christian concepts. 'Person', 'primal state', 'sin', and 'revelation' can be fully comprehended only in reference to sociality.[3] If genuinely theological concepts can only be recognized as established and fulfilled in a special social context, then it becomes evident that a sociological study of the church has a specifically theological character.

**

34
CHAPTER TWO:
THE CHRISTIAN CONCEPT OF PERSON
AND CONCEPTS OF SOCIAL BASIC-RELATION

A. Four Conceptual Models of Social Basic-Relation, and the Debate between These and the Christian Concepts of Person and Basic-Relation

Every concept of community is essentially related to a concept of person. It is impossible to say what constitutes community without asking what constitutes a person. Since the purpose of this study is to understand a particular concept of community, namely that of the sanctorum communio, in order to grasp it fully we must analyze its related concept of person. Thus the issue becomes concretely the *question of the Christian concept of person*. What one understands about person and community simultaneously makes a decisive statement about the concept of God. *The concepts of person, community, and God* are inseparably and essentially interrelated. A concept of God is always conceived in relation to a concept of person and a concept of a community of persons. Whenever one thinks of a concept of God, it is done in relation

---

the phenomenology of various social structures as based in different forms of will, purpose, and authority.]

3. ["The English term 'sociality' derives from Latin and French and dates back to the seventeenth century. In Bonhoeffer's usage it is a complex category comprising several specific views of person, community, and social relations. Its full meaning will become clear as he develops his argument below," *DBWE* 1:21, n. 2]

to person and community of persons. In principle, in order to arrive at the essence of the Christian concept of community, we could just as well begin with the concept of God as with that of person. And in choosing to begin with the latter, we must make constant reference to the concept of God in order to come to a well-grounded view of both God and the concept of community.

**

The term 'Christian concept of person' will now be used for the concept of person   44
that is constitutive for the concept of Christian community and is presupposed by
it. In theological terms this means not the person-concept of the primal human state, but that of the human being after the fall—the person who does not live in unbroken community with God and humanity, but who knows good and evil.[4] This Christian concept of person necessarily builds upon the fact of the human spirit, namely the structural, individual person-hood of this spirit, about which we will speak later. In this general concept of personal spirit we must also overcome the idealist concept and replace it   45
with one which preserves the individual, concrete character of the person as absolute and intended by God (cf. chapter 3 on this subject). For the present, we shall deal only with the specifically Christian concept of person in order to clarify how it differs from that of idealism.

The attempt to derive the social from the epistemological category must be rejected as a μετάβασις εἰς ἄλλο γένος [*change to a different category*]. *It is impossible to reach the real existence of other subjects by way of the purely transcendental category of the universal.*[5] How, then, can one arrive at the other as independent sub-ject? There is no cognitive way to reach this point, just as there is no purely cognitive way to know God. All cognitive methods of idealism are included in the realm of personal mind, and the way to the transcendent is the way to the object of knowledge. I bear within me the forms of the mind to grasp this object that, for precisely that reason, remains a mere object and never becomes a subject, or 'alien I'. To be sure, a subject can also become an object of knowledge, but then it leaves the social sphere and enters the epis-temological sphere. The epistemological and the social spheres can differ so greatly in principle, however, that *in spite of epistemological realism no social sphere is recognized, and on the other hand in spite of radical epistemological ideal-ism, i.e., solipsism, the social sphere is fully recognized.* This demonstrates that

---

4. ["On the knowledge of good and evil breaking community with God and others, and dividing the self, see *DBWE* 3:85–93, 121–126 (*Reader* 232–237, 255–257)," *DBWE* 1:44, n. 32.]

5. [*This paragraph alludes to Kant's epistemology.*]

neither sphere can be reduced to the other. What remains to be shown is what we mean by the social sphere.

As long as my intellect is dominant, exclusively claiming universal validity, as long as all contradictions that can arise when one knows a subject as an object of knowledge are conceived as immanent to my intellect, I am not in the social sphere. But this means that I enter this sphere *only when my*

46   *intellect is confronted by some fundamental barrier.* At first, of course, this can happen in the intellectual sphere, but not in the epistemological-transcendental sphere; idealism's 'object' is ultimately no barrier. What is important is not the nature of the barrier, but the fact that it is experienced and acknowledged as a real barrier. But what does it mean to experience and acknowledge a barrier as real? The point is the *concept of reality* that idealism did not think through thoroughly, and therefore did not think through at all. Essential reality for idealism is the self-knowing and self-active spirit, engaging truth and reality in the process. Persons have at their disposal their own ethical value. They have the dignity to be able to be ethical and, insofar as they are persons, they are obliged to be ethical. The boundary between 'ought' and 'is' does not coincide with the boundary of the person as a whole; rather, idealism divides the human being down the middle. Of course, to the extent that any serious imperative implies ethical transcendence, this should have been the point at which idealism could have had second thoughts. But with Kant's "You can, because you ought," the argument abandoned the realm of ethical transcendence for the immanence of a philosophy of spirit.[6] The necessary result of a one-sided epistemologi-

47   cal philosophy thus was rational persons deciding their own ethical value, having self-empowered entry into the ethical sphere, and bearing within themselves their own ethical motives as rational persons. So one came here to recognize the real barrier. This recognition is possible only within the ethical sphere. This does not mean, however, that the barrier itself can have only an ethical content. Rather, as I have mentioned, it can be purely intellectual, i.e., it can be experienced in the conflict of knowledge. Only the experience of the barrier as real is a specifically ethical experience. We have not yet described what we mean by reality over against and beyond idealism's understanding. The issue here is *the problem of time.*

Kant taught that continuously advancing time was a pure form of the mind's intuition. The result in Kant and in all of idealism is essentially a

---

6. Only when none other than God motivates and enters into the person can one speak in Christian terms of such an identification, and then of course only from the perspective of 'faith.'

timeless way of thinking. In epistemology this is evident; but even in ethics, too, Kant did not consciously move beyond this. The same starting points that could have led to recognizing the real barrier could also have led to overcoming the timeless way of thinking in ethics, without diminishing the absolute ethical claim. Fichte came closer to ethical reality in his view of individual duty, but he too remained far from the necessary transformation of thinking. In spite of the emphasis on the primacy of ethics in both philosophers, we see epistemology having a continual influence on ethics. *It is not my intention here to dispute the epistemological understanding of time as a pure form of intuition.* My starting point is different. Like Kant and Fichte, I am emphasizing the absoluteness of the ethical demand and now relate this to the person confronted with it. At the moment of being addressed, the person enters a state of *responsibility* or, in other words, of decision. By person I do not mean at this point the idealists' person of mind or reason, but the person in concrete, living individuality. This is not the person internally divided, but the one addressed as a whole person; not one existing in timeless fullness of value and spirit, but in a state of responsibility in the midst of time; not one existing in time's continuous flow, but in the value-related—not value-filled—moment. *In the concept of the moment, the concept of time and its value-relatedness are co-posited.* The moment is not the shortest span of time, a mechanically conceived atom, as it were. The 'moment' is the time of responsibility, value-related time, or, let us say, time related to God; and, most essentially, it is concrete time. Only in concrete time is the real claim of ethics effectual; and only when I am responsible am I fully conscious of being bound to time. It is not that I make some sort of universally valid decisions by being in full possession of a rational mind. Rather, I enter the reality of time by relating my concrete person in time and all its particularities to this imperative—by making myself ethically responsible. Just as sound lies in different spheres of perception for musicians and physicists, so it is with time for idealist epistemology and for a Christian concept of person, without the one sphere canceling the other.

Thus there follows from our concept of time an idea that is quite meaningless for idealism, that *the person ever and again arises and passes away in time.* The person does not exist timelessly; a person is not static, but dynamic. The person exists always and only in ethical responsibility; the person is re-created again and again in the perpetual flux of life. Any other concept of person fragments the *fullness of life* of the concrete person. In the last analysis the reason why idealist philosophy fails to understand the concept of person is that it has no *voluntaristic* concept of God, nor a profound concept of sin (as shall be demonstrated). This in turn relates to its position regarding the problem of history. The logical flaw in the formulation of

48

49 the idealist concept of person is no coincidence but is deeply rooted in the system. Idealism has no appreciation of movement. The movement of the dialectic of mind was abstract and metaphysical, while that of ethics is concrete. Further, idealism has no understanding of the moment in which the person feels the threat of absolute demand. The idealist ethicist knows what he ought to do, and, what is more, he can always do it precisely because he ought. Where is there room, then, for distress of conscience, for infinite anxiety in the face of decisions?[7]

But this brings us close to the problem of reality, the problem of the real barrier, and thus that of social basic-relations. It is a Christian insight that the person as conscious being is created in the moment of being moved— in the situation of responsibility, passionate ethical struggle, confrontation by an overwhelming claim; thus the real person grows out of the concrete situation. Here, too, the encounter lies entirely in the spirit, as in idealism. Spirit here, however, has a different meaning than it does in idealism. *For Christian philosophy, the human person originates only in relation to the divine; the divine person transcends the human person,* who both resists and is overwhelmed by the divine. Idealist individualism's notion of spirit as being-for-itself is unchristian, as it involves attributing to the human spirit absolute value that can only be ascribed to divine spirit. The Christian person originates only in the absolute duality of God and humanity; only in experiencing the barrier does the awareness of oneself as ethical person arise. The more clearly the barrier is perceived, the more deeply the person enters into the situation of responsibility. The Christian person is not the bearer of highest values; rather the concept of value can be related only to personal being, i.e., to the creatureliness of the person. Every philoso-
50 phy of value, even where it regards the value of the person as the highest value (Scheler), is in danger of taking away the value of persons as such, as God's creatures, and acknowledging them only insofar as the person is the 'bearer' of objective, impersonal value. But in so doing it closes itself off from the possibility of understanding personal-social basic-relations.

When the concrete ethical barrier of the other person is acknowledged or, alternatively, when the person is compelled to acknowledge it, we have made a fundamental step that allows us to grasp the *social ontic-ethical basic-relations of persons.*[8]

---

7. [*"Voluntarism" (from the Latin* voluntas, *will) refers to the centrality of will in Bonhoeffer's theological anthropology and doctrine of God. See further below,* DBWE *1:62, n. 3 (Reader 30, n. 13), and also in the Editor's Introduction,* DBWE *1:19.*]

8. ["For Bonhoeffer the Christian understanding of person at the ontological level is always that of the person in a social and ethical encounter with the other person; this is

Obviously, here the concept of barrier is decisive. Thus, its form and structure in personal experience must first be analyzed. The concept of barrier is not to be located in the relation between the individual and the universal. The person is not the individual per se, any more than the individual as such is intrinsically fallen and sinful (Schelling). But *the metaphysical concept of the individual is defined without mediation, whereas the ethical concept of the person is a definition based on ethical-social interaction.* From the ethical perspective, human beings do not exist 'unmediated' qua spirit in and of themselves, but only in responsibility vis-à-vis an 'other'. In this sense we call the ethical concept of the individual the social basic-relation, since one cannot even speak of the individual without at the same time necessarily thinking of the 'other' who moves the individual into the ethical sphere. One could object that so far 'other' has been understood as referring to God, whereas now a concept of social relation has suddenly been introduced, in which 'other' refers to another *human being.*

First of all, one should remember what was said at the beginning   51
about the interconnection of God, community, and individual. Thus the individual exists only in relation to an 'other'; individual does not mean solitary. *On the contrary, for the individual to exist, 'others' must necessarily be there.* But what is the 'other'? If I call the individual the concrete I, then the other is the *concrete* You. So what does 'You' mean in philosophical terms? At first glance, every You seems to presuppose an I who is immanent to the You, and without whom a You could not even be distinguished from an object-form. Thus 'You' would be identical to 'other I'. But this is only partially correct. Beyond the limit to epistemological knowledge there is a further limit to ethical-social knowledge, or acknowledgment. The other can be experienced by the I only as You, but never directly as I, that is, in the sense of the I that has become I only through the claim of a You. The You-form is fundamentally different from the I-form in the sphere of ethical reality. But since the You, too, stands before me as a person, as a thinking and acting mind, we must understand the You as an I in the general sense, i.e., in the sense of self-consciousness, etc. (see next chapter). These two I-forms should be strictly distinguished. The You as a reality-form is by definition independent in encountering the I in this sphere. In contrast to the idealist object-form, it is not immanent to the

the Christian basic-relation of I and You, self and other. It presupposes the theological axiom that the human person always exists in relation to an Other, namely God, and that human relations are in some way analogies of this fundamental relation," *DBWE* 1:50, n. 56.]

mind of the subject. The You sets the limit for the subject and by its own
accord activates a will that impinges upon the other in such a way that this
52   other will becomes a You for the I. If the objection is raised that the other
is also a content of my consciousness, immanent to my mind, then what was
said above about the distinctive spheres was not understood; *the transcendence of the You says nothing at all about epistemological transcendence.* This is a
purely ethical transcendence,[9] experienced only by those facing a decision;
it can never be demonstrated to someone on the outside. Thus everything
that can be said about the Christian concept of person can only be grasped
directly by the person who is facing responsibility.

I and You are not simply interchangeable concepts, but comprise specific
and distinct spheres of experience. I myself can become an object of my
own experience, but can never experience myself as You. Other persons can
become objects of my reflection on their I-ness, but I will never get beyond
the fact that I can only encounter the other as a You. I can never become
a real barrier to myself, *but it is just as impossible for me to leap over the barrier
to the other.* My I as a You-form can only be experienced by the other I, and
my I as an I-form can only be experienced by myself; thus *in the experience of
a You, the I-form of the other is never an unmediated given.* But this means that
I can be confronted with barriers by a You that has not yet become an I in
the sense of I-You-relations. Thus the You-form is to be defined as the other
who places me before an ethical decision. And with this I-You-relation as
the Christian basic-relation we move as a matter of principle beyond the
epistemological subject-object-relation. Likewise, it makes unnecessary the
concept of the You as the other I. Whether the other is also an I in the sense
of the I-You-relation is not something I can know. This is also applied to
the concept of God. God is an impenetrable You whose metaphysical personhood, which presupposes absolute self-consciousness and spontaneous
action, implies nothing at all about God being an I as described above.[10]

53   Doesn't the statement that the You is not necessarily an I militate against
54   the concept of community comprised of persons? Is the person not completely isolated, in effect? The person arises only in relation to a You, and

---

9. [*That "transcendence" as a key theological idea referring to God should be spoken about in
social-ethical terms, rather than metaphysically, is a hallmark of Bonhoeffer's theology. See this idea
finally reiterated in* Letters and Papers from Prison: *"Jesus's 'being-for-others' is the experience of
transcendence! . . . Our relationship to God is no 'religious' relationship to some highest, most powerful, and best being imaginable—that is no genuine transcendence. . . . The transcendent is not the
infinite unattainable tasks, but the neighbor within reach in any given situation,"* DBWE 8:501.]

10. This is not the place to discuss in what respects human beings are or are not
(because of sin) barriers for God.

yet the person stands in complete isolation. Persons are unique and thus fundamentally separate and distinct from one another. In other words, one person cannot know the other, but can only acknowledge and 'believe' in the other. Psychology and epistemology find their limitation here; the ethical personhood of the other is neither a psychologically comprehensible fact nor an epistemological necessity.

B. The Concept of God and Social Basic-Relations in Terms of the I-You-Relation

Our concern here is the relationship of the person, God, and social being to each other. The I comes into being only in relation to the You; only in response to a demand does *responsibility* arise. 'You' says nothing about its own being, only about its demand. This demand is absolute. What does this mean? The whole person, who is totally claimless, is claimed by this absolute demand. But this seems to make one human being the creator of the ethical person of the other, which is an intolerable thought. Can it be avoided? The person-creating efficacy of the You is independent of the personhood of the You. We now add that it is also independent of the will of the human You. One human being cannot of its own accord make another into an I, an ethical person conscious of responsibility. *God or the Holy Spirit joins the concrete You; only through God's active working does the other become a You to me from whom my I arises. In other words, every human You is an image of the divine You.* You-character is in fact the essential form in which the divine is experienced; every human You bears its You-character only by virtue of the divine. This is not to say that it is a borrowed attribute of God, and not really a You. Rather, the divine You creates the human You. And since the human You is created and willed by God, it is a *real, absolute, and holy You,* like the divine You. One might then speak here of the human being as the image of God[11] with respect to the effect one person has on another (cf. the later discussion of the problem of community of spirit and how one person becomes Christ for the other). Since, however, one person's becoming You for an other fundamentally alters nothing about the You as person, that person as I is not holy; what is holy is the You of God, the absolute will, who here becomes visible in the concrete You of social life. The other person is only a 'You' insofar as God brings it about. But God can make every human

55

---

11. [*Note here that the "image of God" is not an attribute of an individual person, such as reason, but a relationship of a "You" to an "I." In* Creation and Fall *(DBWE 3:65 [Reader 224]]), this will be stated as the* analogia relationis, *analogy of relationship.*]

being a You for us. *The claim of the other rests in God alone; for this very reason, it remains the claim of the other.*[12]

In summary, *the person is willed by God, in concrete vitality, wholeness, and uniqueness as an ultimate unity. Social relations must be understood, then, as purely interpersonal and building on the uniqueness and separateness of persons.* The person cannot be overcome by apersonal spirit; no 'unity' can negate the plurality of persons. *The social basic category is the I-You-relation. The You of the other person is the divine You.* Thus the way to the other person's You is the same as the way to the divine You, either through acknowledgment or rejection. *The individual becomes a person ever and again through the other, in the 'moment'.* The other person presents us with the same challenge to our knowing as does God. My real relationship to another person is oriented to my relationship to God. *But since I know God's 'I' only in the revelation of God's love, so too with the other person; here the concept of the church comes into play.* Then it will become clear that the Christian person achieves his or her essential nature only when God does not encounter the person as *You, but 'enters into' the person as I.*

Consequently, in some way the individual belongs essentially and absolutely with the other, according to God's will, even though, or precisely because, the one is completely separate from the other.

One could object, finally, that our argument has not come to grips with the real problem of idealism since (1) we did not inquire about the essence of the person as did idealism, but appeared to digress to the other question about the origin of the person; and since (2) when discussing content we were quite one-sidedly oriented toward the ethical and ignored the 'human spirit' that was at issue in idealism, as if it were not part of the person. To (1) we reply that it is no coincidence that we were led from the problem of the essence of the person to that of the origin of the person. Indeed, the Christian person alone exists in ever renewed coming-into-being. To (2) we reply that human 'spirit' with its moral and religious capacities is certainly an indispensable presupposition in order for the ethical person to come to be. This assertion has already been made above and will be elaborated further in discussing the doctrine of the primal state in the next chapter.

---

12. [*The following is found here in the original dissertation (italics Bonhoeffer's in the following):* ". . . it is a *Christian insight that God uses the social nature of human beings in order to act among them in every respect. God acts in history,* thus God's claim is mediated for us, essentially and primarily, by other people, and is bound to sociality. In concluding this reflection on the Christian concept of person we have arrived at an understanding of the profound relationship between God and community as regards the individual," DBWE *1:55, n. 77.*]

What follows is thus to be seen as presupposed by the preceding argument.

Chapter Three:
The Primal State
and the Problem of Community

58

A. Methodological Problems

The doctrine of the primal state cannot offer us new theological insights. In the logic of theology as a whole it belongs with eschatology. Every aspect helpful to its comprehension is imparted through revelation. Nothing about it can be ascertained by pure speculation. It cannot speak of the essence of human being, of nature, or of history in general terms, but only in the context of revelation that has been heard. The doctrine of the primal state is hope projected backward. Its value is twofold. It forces the methodological clarification of the structure of theology as a whole; then it renders concrete and vivid the real course of things from unity through break to unity.

59

60

61

62

Thus the concepts of person and community, for example, are understood only within an intrinsically broken history, as conveyed in the concepts of primal state, sin, and reconciliation. Neither concept can be understood theologically 'in itself', but only within a real historical dialectic—not a dialectic of concepts. In this respect we differ fundamentally from idealism, for which origin and telos [end or goal] stand in real, unbroken connection, the synthesis of which is expressed in the concept of 'essence'. There, sin and salvation are realities that do not alter the original essence of things. For us, though, the doctrine of the primal state is significant precisely because it enables us to grasp concretely the reality of sin, which infinitely alters the essence of things.

If the revelation in Christ speaks of the will of God to create from the old humanity of Adam a new humanity of Christ, i.e., the church, and if I know myself to be incorporated into this church of Christ, then it follows that we should project the idea of unbroken community with God and with human beings back to the doctrine of the primal state as well. This explains why we cannot essentially go further than what is said in teaching about the church, for example. But within the logic of the doctrine of the primal state itself, the doctrine of original community will be developed on its own terms, again just as an example.

Human beings, called by revelation to hear, know they are meant to be
63   active centers of intellect and will.[13] This is the formal presupposition for
what has been said about the Christian concept of person and what will be
said about the concept of person in the primal state. At the same time it is
obvious that to understand a person as nothing more than such a center
of acts is inadequate, because from a Christian-ethical, that is to say social,
point of view it is irrelevant and thus does not touch the sphere of reality
at all. Thus this formal and general metaphysical concept of person must
be thought of as having a different kind of fulfillment and purpose. The
Christian concept of person should be thought of historically, i.e., in the
state after the fall, for history in the true sense only begins with sin and the
fate of death that is linked with it. From this it follows that the concept of
person in the primal state must be understood differently, corresponding
to the idea of the new humanity which, in hope, overcomes the history of
sin and death. The formal and general concept of person should be thought
of as fulfilled by positive Christian content, i.e., established by God and
oriented toward God. Willing and thinking come from God and go toward
God; that is to say, community with God is completed in love and truth. The
miracle of the Christian concept of community is that love for God involves
submission, but that God's love, in ruling, serves.

Community with God by definition establishes social community as well.
It is not that community with God subsequently leads to social community;
rather, neither exists without the other. In the following we will show that
even the formal concept of person can be conceived only in terms of community. Thus unbroken social community belongs to primal being, in parallel to the eschatological hope we have for it in the church. This is expressed
clearly, if only indirectly, in the Genesis narrative. With their act of disobedience against God, human beings realize their sexual difference and are
ashamed before one another. A rupture has come into the unbroken community. Losing direct community with God, they also lose—by definition—
unmediated human community. A third power, sin, has stepped between
human beings and God, as between human beings themselves. Later this
is symbolized in the medieval representation of the fall. In the center is
64   the tree with the serpent coiled around it, man and woman on either side,
separated by the tree whose fruit they ate in disobedience.

---

13. ["'Will' is a key concept in Bonhoeffer's theological anthropology and also in his
typology of social forms. By speaking of human beings as 'willing' subjects or spirits, his
emphasis is not primarily on behavior as 'voluntary,' that is, uncoerced, but on decisions
that are intentional, purposeful, and responsible. This role of will is what he means when
speaking of 'voluntarism'. See *DBWE* 1:19," *DBWE* 1:62–63, n. 3.]

Thus we have sketched the archetype[14] of the church. While the theological problem presents little difficulty, *the methodological issues become more complicated by relating social philosophy and sociology* to the doctrine of the primal state. Here, too, it cannot be a matter of developing speculative theories about the possibility of social being in the primal state not affected by evil will. Instead, methodologically, all statements are possible only on the basis of our understanding of the church, i.e., from the revelation we have heard.[15] Thus social-philosophical and sociological problems can be dealt with in the context of theology not because they can be proved generally necessary on the basis of creation, but because they are presupposed and included in revelation. Only in this perspective can they be fully understood. Of course here, too, the reversed logic of the theological system applies to the description of what is known, in that the concept of the church only appears to emerge out of the amalgam of issues worked out in the doctrine of the primal state. This view of theological method must be kept in mind throughout the study, in order to maintain its theological character.

65

**

CHAPTER FOUR:
SIN AND BROKEN COMMUNITY

107

The world of sin is the world of 'Adam', the old humanity. But the world of Adam is the world Christ reconciled and made into a new humanity, Christ's church. However, it is not as if Adam were completely overcome; rather, the humanity of Adam lives on in the humanity of Christ. This is why the discussion of the problem of sin is indispensable for understanding the sanctorum communio.

The essential task of this chapter is to expose the new social basic-relations between I and You, as well as between I and humanity, that are inherent in the concept of sin. The concept of the Christian person presented in chapter 2 will be central to this discussion. The question of how these relations are connected to the natural forms can be treated much more briefly.

---

14. [*"Archetype" is not used in the Jungian sense.*]

15. ["In his theological interpretation of Genesis 1–3, Bonhoeffer similarly argues that 'only the church, which knows of the end, knows also of the beginning . . . It views the creation from Christ.' See *DBWE* 3:22 (*Reader* 211)," *DBWE* 1:65, n. 10.]

Whereas the previous spirit-form grew out of love, the fall replaced love with selfishness. This gave rise to the break in immediate community with God, and likewise in human community. With this change of direction the whole spiritual orientation of humanity was altered. Morality and religion in their proper sense disappear from human nature, and are now only formally visible in the structures of legal order and in natural religion.

108 Whereas in the primal state the relation among human beings is one of giving, in the sinful state it is purely demanding. Every person exists in complete, voluntary isolation; everyone lives their own life, rather than all living the same life in God. Now everyone has their own conscience. There was no conscience in the primal state; only after the fall did Adam know what good and evil are. Conscience can just as well be the ultimate prop of human self-justification as the site where Christ strikes home at one through the law.[16] Human beings, hearing the divine law in solitude and recognizing their own sinfulness, come to life again as ethical persons, albeit in ethical isolation. With sin, ethical atomism enters history. This applies essentially to the spirit-form. All natural forms of community remain, but they are corrupt in their inmost core.

But the recognition by human beings of their utter solitude in responsibility before God, and the utter uniqueness of their culpability, is met with another perception that does not cancel the first, but rather intensifies it, even while appearing to contradict it completely. This second perception is based upon insight into the qualitative nature of sin, that is, knowledge that the misery of sin is infinitely great. This implies, however, that sin must have a significance that is not only individual, but also supra-individual. Sin must be conceived as both a supra-individual deed and, of course, as an individual deed; it must be simultaneously the deed of the human race[17]

109 and of the individual. Thus recognition of one's *utter solitude* leads to the other insight, namely the *broadest sense of shared sinfulness*, so that by our very nature the 'one' is led to the 'other', without whom the existence and nature of the one would be unthinkable.

---

16. [*An allusion to the doctrine, strong in Lutheranism, of the law (God's commands) as a mirror or accusing judge that exposes sin.*]

17. ["'Human race,' meaning all human beings, the whole human species, is the translation for *Geschlecht*. The phrase 'human race' in English does not have the connotation of its German cognate *Rasse* (the latter can also mean 'breed' as in pedigree and selective breeding of animals). Bonhoeffer did not use the word *Rasse*, and he opposed any racist ideology, especially in the form of anti-Semitism. His theological concern is with all humanity, not with a biological ideology of race; see below, *DBWE* 1:114ff. (*Reader* 33ff.)," *DBWE* 1:108–109, n. 9.]

Two problems surface here. How should we understand the universality of sin in terms of the logic of theology? Simply regarding it as a fact is not enough. Second, how should the empirical spread of sin throughout humanity be conceptualized?

It was in the doctrine of original sin that the idea of the social significance of sin was elaborated theologically.

A. The Doctrine of Original Sin

This doctrine, which presupposes that sin has spread through all of humanity, investigates the manner of this spreading. It then details accordingly *how human beings belong together* and are bound together in status corruptionis [*state of corruption*]. But since ideas intended to prove the universality of sin in the first place were mixed into the inquiry about the proliferation of sin, the doctrine of original sin is one of the most difficult logical problems of all theology.

The culpability of the individual and the universality of sin should be understood together; that is, the individual culpable act and the culpability of the human race must be connected conceptually. When the human race is understood by means of the biological concept of the species, the ethical gravity of the concept of culpability is weakened. We must thus discover a Christian-ethical concept of the species. The issue is how to understand the human species in terms of the concept of sin. Previously the human species appeared to be comprehensively defined only in terms of nature. Young children, the mentally deficient, and normally developed people seemed to have to be conceived as equals. But this necessarily led to ethically indifferent views of sin, sacraments, and the church. It follows from this that the Christian concept of culpability is incompatible with a biological concept of the species. Thus the concept of the species should be based upon the concept of culpability, not vice versa. This would allow us to move on to an ethical collective concept of the human race, which alone can do full justice to the idea of the sin of the human race. The individual is then established as the self-conscious and spontaneously acting person, the prerequisite for ethical relevance, and the human race is conceived as consisting of such persons.

The idea of the sin of the human race and that of the individual must be discussed from the standpoint of the Christian concept of the human race, of humanity. How can one conceive of the individual culpable act and the guiltiness of the human race together without making one the reason for the other, that is, excusing one by means of the other? Augustine evidently thought of the sinful collective act as the basis for every individual act, and

Anselm and Thomas basically get no further than this. Ritschl moves in just the opposite direction by going from the sum of individual sins to arrive at the concept of the kingdom of sin, thus not sufficiently grounding the universality of sin. Everything obviously depends upon *finding the act of the whole in the sinful individual act*, without making the one the reason for the other. An ethical category must be related to the individual as a specific person. Precisely the social element, however, is thereby not excluded, but posited simultaneously. *The human being, by virtue of being an individual, is also the human race.* This is the definition that does justice to the human spirit in relation to the fundamental social category. When, in the sinful act, the individual spirit rises up against God, thus climbing to the utmost height of spiritual individuality—since this is the individual's very own deed against God, occasioned by nothing else—the deed committed is at the same time *the deed of the human race* (no longer in the biological sense) *in the individual person.* One falls away not only from one's personal vocation but also from one's generic vocation as a member of the human race. Thus all humanity falls with each sin, and not one of us is in principle different from Adam; that is, every one is also the "first" sinner. At the same time, this relationship

116   of individuals and human race corresponds to the monadic image presented in the section on social philosophy, where each individual monad 'represents' the whole world. Aware of this state of affairs, we connect consciousness of our deepest personal culpability with that of the universality of our deed. Every deed is at once an individual act and one that reawakens the total sin of humanity. This, then, establishes the universality of sin as necessarily posited along with, and in, individual sin.

**

122   # CHAPTER FIVE: SANCTORUM COMMUNIO

A. Basic Principles

1. Synthesis of the Previous Argument in the Concept of the Church: Retrospect and Prospect

The whole theological discussion thus far not only leads to the discussion
123   of the sanctorum communio, but is possible and meaningful only from the perspective of the sanctorum communio. Only from this vantage point are we justified to integrate philosophical considerations into the theological framework. It is not the case that the concept of the sanctorum communio would make everything that has been said about the peccatorum communio

[*community of sinners*] irrelevant; rather, it is precisely at this point that the meaning of the peccatorum communio first becomes relevant. True, the person who has been justified, who belongs to God's church-community,[18] has 'died to sin'.[19] "Whoever is in Christ does not commit sin." "The old has passed away, see, everything has become new." "For as all die in Adam, so all have been made alive in Christ," but the life of those who have been justified, that is, the new life, is "hidden in God." "I do what I do not want to do, and what I do want I do not do." "Nullum unquam extitisse pii hominis opus, quod si severo dei judicio examinaretur, non esset damnabile" [*There never existed any work of a pious human being which, if examined by God's stern judgment, would not deserve condemnation*]. The reality of sin and the communio peccatorum remain even in God's church-community; Adam has really been replaced by Christ only eschatologically, ἐπ' ἐλπίδι (in spe) [*in hope*]. So long as sin remains, the whole of sinful humanity also remains in every human being. In the concept of the church, therefore, all lines of thought pursued thus far converge; in this concept they are carried to their logical conclusion and are transcended.

Until now we have been pursuing two, or rather three, different lines of thought that must now be integrated conceptually—or better, we must reflect upon their union that already exists in the reality of the church. On the one hand, there was the line of thought about the ontic basic-relatedness of human beings to one another as persons. On the other hand, there was the discovery of the pre-volitional sociality of the human spirit, and the subsequent investigation of the forms of empirically existing communal relations, which always require intentional social acts in order to manifest themselves as personal social relations. The ontic-ethical basic-relations in the state of sin not only are fundamental for all personal social relations, but also condition even their empirical formation. When they are modified, or re-created, in the concept of the church, the concrete form of the community must change as well; indeed this provides the possibility and necessity of developing a unique empirical form of community. Since we recognized certain basic forms as belonging to the created order, we now

124

125

---

18. [*"Church-community," combining both theological and sociological aspects, is the standard translation in* DBWE *for Bonhoeffer's use of* Gemeinde *when it does not mean simply "congregation." For a detailed explanation of this translation, see* DBWE *1:14–17, editor's introduction.*]

19. [*In the following sentences, Bonhoeffer quotes from the Luther Bible translations of the following New Testament letters of St. Paul: Romans 6, 2 Corinthians 5, 1 Corinthians 15, 2 Corinthians 4, and Romans 7. This is followed in the original dissertation by his quotations from Calvin's* Institutes of the Christian Religion *and Luther's* Lectures on Romans. *See details at* DBWE *1:123–124 and notes thereto.*]

must ask about the extent to which the church as a social form participates in them, and even whether in it the synthesis of them all might be found. However, only later can this be discussed.

Sin remains even when the ethical basic-relations have changed, which means also that the old ontic relationships are not completely abolished; therefore every empirical formation is subject to the ambiguity of all human action. However, what is unprecedentedly novel is that the new basic-relations have their own unique form, that their sole function, as it were, is to produce such a form. In this we perceive a special will of God that we may not brush aside by condemning everything that has taken form as a merely human product. *Formally speaking, the necessary bond between the basic-relations and the empirical form of community, understood as a unique structure, constitutes the essence of the church.*

There are basically *two ways to misunderstand the church, one historicizing and the other religious; the former confuses the church with the religious community, the latter with the Realm of God.*[20] The former overlooks the fact that the new basic-relations established by God actually are real, and points instead to the "religious motives" that in fact lead to empirical community (the missionary impulse, the need to communicate, etc.). This view, however, plainly is condemned by the saying in John's Gospel that "You did not choose me, but I chose you" (John 15:16). The second misunderstanding does not take seriously the fact that human beings are bound by history; this means that historicity either is objectified and deified, as in Catholicism, or simply is regarded as accidental, as subject to the law of death and sin. Doing so, however, does not accept, but circumvents, God's will that all God's revelation, both in Christ and in the church, be concealed under the form of historical life. To put it differently, the much discussed 'seriousness' is carried so far that it loses its real character and becomes formalistic. It is almost impossible to avoid the first misunderstanding in a historical or sociological approach—a misunderstanding that is equally at home, however, in the religious-romantic circles of the Youth Movement. The second is found in theology. Both are dangerous, since both can be nourished by religious pathos and seriousness. Neither of them, however, understands the reality of the church, which is simultaneously a historical community and one established by God. Thus, the concept of the church, in our view, justifies and synthesizes the lines of thought that we have pursued thus far. The new ontic basic-relations are the foundation of a social entity that, viewed from

126

20. [*"Realm of God"* translates Reich Gottes, *the eschatological community of God's rule at the end of time, usually phrased "kingdom of God" or" kingdom of heaven" in the New Testament.*]

the outside, can only be called a 'religious community'. Now it is certainly possible to focus on the empirical phenomenon 'church' qua 'religious community' or religious society, to analyze it as a 'public corporation' and *to develop a sociological morphology* of it. In that case all theological reflection would be superfluous; or—and this is the other possibility—the claim of the church to be God's church is taken seriously. In this case one must focus on what this church acknowledges as constitutive, namely the fact of Christ, or the 'Word'. It will also be necessary to delineate the new social basic-relations, which are established by the fact of Christ, as constitutive in the deepest sense for a social body like the church. One premise, however, will not have to be justified further, namely that we take the claim of the church seriously, i.e., not as being historically comprehensible, but as being grounded in the reality of God and God's revelation. We do not want to employ external criteria for judging the church. Rather, the church can be understood fully only from within, on the basis of its own claim; only on this basis can we develop appropriately critical criteria for judging it. 127

With this, however, right from the very beginning we seem to fall into logical inconsistencies. We said we were taking seriously the claim of the church to be God's church; but naturally that does not mean, first of all, that we could assert this claim without examination. At issue is only the question, by which criteria do we examine the meaning of the assertion? In principle it is indeed possible to take the course of finding external criteria, which means deducing the truth of the proposition from the outside. This course basically does not lead beyond the category of *possibility*. From there one then necessarily arrives at the *concept of religious community*. The concept of the church is conceivable only in the sphere of reality established by God; this means it cannot be deduced. *The reality of the church is a reality of revelation, a reality that essentially must be* either believed or denied. Thus an adequate criterion for judging the claim of the church to be God's church-community can be found only by stepping inside it, by bowing in faith to its claim. Now, admittedly, faith is not a possible method by which to gain academic knowledge; rather, by acknowledging the claim of revelation, faith is the given prerequisite for positive theological knowledge. It would also be completely wrong to 'deduce' faith in the church, as a conceptual necessity, from faith in Christ. *Whatever is necessary conceptually is not thereby already real. Rather there is no relation to Christ in which the relation to the church is not necessarily established as well. The church, therefore, logically establishes its own foundation in itself*; like all revelations, it can be judged only by itself. What is to be found is presupposed. Knowledge and acknowledgment of its reality must exist before one can speak about the church. Precisely in this regard it proves itself to be a reality of revelation—not to an external observer,

128
but to the person who believes its claim. The legitimacy of this theological method can be acknowledged only by someone who already stands inside the church; then, however, the objective external position already has been surrendered. The logical stumbling block for the entire question of the church lies at this very point. People ask whether religious community—which is then also called church-community—is a necessary consequence of the Christian religion, or whether Christianity is essentially individualistic. They attempt to deduce a power that generates community from a concept of the 'holy', or they endeavor to prove from Christian ethics that human beings are ethically dependent upon one another. Or they try to infer a sociological category from the nature of a religion of revelation. But in no case is the starting point sought by acknowledging the reality of God's church-community as a revealed reality. And so it is certain from the outset that the concept of the church will not be reached. It becomes evident, further, in my view, that it is impossible to deduce from a general concept of religion, as a necessary consequence, the notion of a religious community. Two outstanding examples from the most recent Protestant and Catholic works on the philosophy of religion may illustrate this.[21]

**

130–31
132
There is in fact only *one* religion in which the idea of community is an integral element of its nature, and that is Christianity. Thus the two approaches just outlined are in our view unable to deduce the nature and necessity of religious community, let alone the necessity of the church. Of

133
course, this does not mean that the problem in philosophy of religion concerning the relationship between religion and community would be dismissed as such. In order to solve it, however, more distinctions are needed.

The general concept of religion has no intrinsic social implications. The idea of the holy in its general sense as religious category is actualized not in social interaction, but in the solitude of the soul with God. The mystic, too, is religious. If it is nevertheless a fact that religion is for the most part social in character, primarily due to psychological causes that are more or less accidental (the need to communicate, as in Schleiermacher, the receptive-active human nature, as in Seeberg), these causes demonstrate the possibility, but not the necessity, of religious community. This directs us back from the general concept of religion to the concrete form of religion,

---

21. [*Bonhoeffer illustrates his point with the views of Max Scheler and Heinrich Scholz*, DBWE *1:128–130.*]

which for us means the concept of the church. But here it is not possible to demonstrate that the communal form of the church is a general necessity; rather, such a demonstration is possible only where the Christian revelation is believed, that is, taken seriously. *Only the concept of revelation can lead*   134 *to the Christian concept of the church.* Once the claim of the church has been accepted, however, it is as superfluous as it is impossible to prove its necessity on general grounds. The situation here is not different from the case of the christological efforts that seek to demonstrate the necessity of redemption *after its reality has already been grasped.* Only when faith accepts the meaning of redemption does it become clear what makes this reality necessary. *In doctrinal theology necessity can be deduced only from reality.* This follows from the concept of revelation.

When works of doctrinal theology end by presenting the concept of the church as a necessary consequence of the Protestant faith, this must not imply anything other than the inner connection between the reality of the church and the entire reality of revelation. Only if the concept of God is understood to be comprehensible when exclusively connected to the concept of the church is it permitted, for technical reasons of presentation, to 'derive' the latter from the former. In order to establish clarity about the inner logic of theological construction, it would be good for once if a presentation of doctrinal theology were to start not with the doctrine of God but with the doctrine of the church.

Now in order to stand on firm ground in the positive exposition, we will give a brief outline of the New Testament teaching on the concept of the church, especially as a social phenomenon.[22]

**

B. Positive Presentation: Introduction   141
to the Basic Problems and Their Exposition

The church is God's new will and purpose for humanity.[23] God's will is always directed toward the concrete, historical human being. But this means that it begins to be implemented *in history.* God's will must become

---

22. [DBWE *1:134–141 presents this "brief outline" in eight points, under the heading "Major Themes in the New Testament View of the Church," the themes being based on biblical texts; the outline replaced in the published version the very considerable detail presented in the dissertation.*]

23. [*Contrary to the common misunderstanding that* Sanctorum Communio *is about a narrow "ecclesiology," this passage is additional evidence that Bonhoeffer's understanding of the church belongs to a concern for humanity and history as a whole.*]

142   visible and comprehensible at some point in history. But at the same point
       it must already be completed. Therefore, it must be revealed. Revelation of
       God's will is necessary because the primal community, where God speaks
       and the word becomes deed and history through human beings, is bro-
       ken. Therefore God must personally speak and act, and at the same time
       accomplish a new creation of human beings, since God's word is always
       deed. *Thus the church is already completed in Christ, just as in Christ its beginning
       is established.* Christ is the cornerstone and the foundation of the building,
       and yet the church, composed of all its parts, is also Christ's body. Christ
       is the firstborn among many sisters and brothers, and yet all are one in
       Christ; see Eph. 1:4f.: "just as he chose us in Christ before the foundation
       of the world to be holy and blameless before him. In love he destined us
       for adoption as his children through Jesus Christ"; 1:11: "in whom we have
       also become heirs, predestined by the decision which was made before by
       him, who works all things" (cf. 2 Tim. 1:9; John 15:16 in the Diatessaron).
       To be noted is the use of ἐν [*in*] throughout—"we are reconciled not only
       by him, but *in him.* Hence to understand his person and history properly is
       to understand our reconciliation properly." If we, the members of the Chris-
       tian church-community, are to believe that in Christ we are reconciled with
       God, then the mediator of this reconciliation must represent not only the
       reconciling divine love, but also at the same time the humanity that is to be
       reconciled, the humanity of the new Adam.

143   In order for the church, which already is completed in Christ, to build
       itself up in time, the will of God must be actualized ever anew, now no lon-
       ger in a fundamental way for all people, but in the personal appropriation
       of the individual. This is possible only on the basis of God's act in Christ.
       It also presupposes both being in the church, which is already completed
       in Christ, and the individual who is brought into the church—that is, into
       the humanity of Christ—only by the act of appropriation. The opposition
       of the concepts of revelation and time, completion and becoming, cannot
       be overcome logically. Revelation enters into time not just apparently but
       actually, and precisely by so doing it bursts the form of time. If, however, for
       this reason one regarded revelation only as beginning (potentiality), and
       not at the same time also as completion (reality), this would take away what
       is decisive about the revelation of God, namely that God's word became
       history.

           In order to build the church as the community-of-God in time, God
       reveals God's own self as *Holy Spirit.* The Holy Spirit is the will of God that
       gathers individuals together to be the church-community, maintains it, and
       is at work only within it. We experience our election only in the church-

community, which is already established in Christ, by personally appropriating it through the Holy Spirit, by standing in the actualized church.

Thus the line of argument falls naturally into the following parts. *First*, we have to inquire into the church-community established in Christ and already completed by God's act, the community-of-God; or, to express it in terms used earlier, we have to inquire into the life-principle of the new basic-relations of social existence. What we are dealing with is thus analogous to the basic-relations established in Adam and their preservation. These basic-relations are already completely established in Christ, not ideally but in reality. Humanity is new in Christ, that is, from the perspective of eternity; but it also becomes new in time. *Second*, we have to reflect on the work of the Holy Spirit as the will of God for the historical actualization of the church of Jesus Christ. But we must pay strict attention to the fact that here the counterpart of *actualization by the Holy Spirit is not potentiality in Christ, but the reality of revelation in Christ*. This is the foundation for the entire understanding of the problem of the church. The 'possibility' of the church not being actualized by the Holy Spirit simply no longer exists; the church that is established in Christ and already completed in reality must necessarily be actualized. Using the category of potentiality in Christ might seem very natural here. But this category virtually destroys the reality-character of redemption. For faith, the reconciliation and justification of the world are established in reality in the revelation in Christ, though faith is possible only within the actualized church. The church does not first become real when it assumes empirical form, when the Holy Spirit does God's work. The reality of the church of the Holy Spirit is just as much a revelational reality; the only thing that matters is to believe this revelational reality in the empirical form. As Christ and the new humanity now necessarily belong together, so the Holy Spirit must be understood as being at work only in this new humanity. It is evidently a mistake, therefore, to attempt to reflect on the objective work of the Holy Spirit independently of the church-community. The Spirit is only in the church-community, and the church-community is only in the Spirit. "Ubi enim ecclesia ibi est spiritus; et ubi spiritus dei, illic ecclesia et omnis gratia" [*For where the church is there is the Spirit; and where the Spirit of God is, there is the church and every kind of grace*]. But Troeltsch still thought it necessary to maintain that what matters in the Protestant concept of the church is not the church as community, but solely the word—that is, precisely the objective work of the Spirit. He maintained that where the word is, there is the church, even if there is no one to hear it. This is a complete misconception of the Protestant tenet of the importance of the word, which is still to be discussed.

144

145

It will then be necessary, *third*, to determine the relationship between the Holy Spirit of the church-community and the human spirit of the community that is brought about by the former. This then raises the problem of the empirical church. In this context the difference between the idealist and the Christian concept of objective spirit also will become clear.

1. The Church Established in
and through Christ—Its Realization

The reality of sin, we found, places the individual in a state of utmost solitude, a state of radical separation from God and other human beings. It places the individual in the isolated position of the person who confesses to committing the 'first' sin, confesses to being the one in whom all humanity fell. But the reality of sin places the individual at the same time, both subjectively and objectively, into the deepest, most immediate bond with humanity, precisely because everybody has become guilty. As a bond of those who are guilty it cannot take on empirical form; it is nevertheless experienced in each concrete relation. Now since in the individual guilty act it is precisely the humanity of human beings that has been affirmed, humanity has to be considered a community. As such it is also a collective person, but a collective person that has the same nature as each of its members.[24] In Christ this tension between isolation from, and bondage to, each other is abolished in reality. The cord between God and human beings that was cut by the first Adam is tied anew by God, by revealing God's own love in Christ, by no longer approaching us in demand and summons, purely as You, but instead by *giving God's own self as an I, opening God's own heart. The church is founded on the revelation of God's heart.* But since destroying the primal community with God also destroyed human community, so likewise when God restores community between human beings and God's own self, community among us also is restored once again, in accordance with our proposition about the essential interrelation of our community with God and human community.

In Christ humanity really is drawn into community with God, just as in Adam humanity fell. And even though in the one Adam there are many Adams, yet there is only one Christ. For Adam is 'representative human being', but Christ is the Lord of his new humanity. Thus everyone becomes guilty by their own strength and fault, because they themselves are Adam;

146

---

24. [*With the concept "collective person," Bonhoeffer uses his concept of the individual person in ethical relation and encounter as a model for social communities. For detailed commentary on "'Person' as a corporate concept," see Green,* Bonhoeffer, *36–45.*]

each person, however, is reconciled apart from their own strength and merit, because they themselves are not Christ. While the old humanity consists of countless isolated units—each one an Adam—that are perceived as a comprehensive unity only through each individual, the new humanity is entirely concentrated in the one single historical point, Jesus Christ, and only in Christ is it perceived as a whole. For in Christ, as the foundation and the body of the building called Christ's church-community, the work of God takes place and is completed. In this work Christ has a function that sheds the clearest light on the fundamental difference between Adam and Christ, namely *the function of vicarious representative*[25] (this will be discussed extensively later). Adam does not intentionally act as a vicarious representative; on the contrary, Adam's action is extremely egocentric. That its effect closely resembles a deliberately vicarious representative action must not obscure the *entirely different basic premises*. In the old humanity the whole of humanity falls anew, so to speak, with every person who sins; in Christ, however, humanity has been brought once and for all—this is essential to *real* vicarious representative action—into community with God.

Since death as the wages of sin (Rom. 6:23) first constitutes *history*, so *life that abides in love* breaks the continuity of the historical process—not empirically, but objectively. Death can still completely separate past and future for our eyes, but not for the life that abides in the love of Christ. *This is why the principle of vicarious representative action* can become fundamental for the church-community of God in and through Christ. Not 'solidarity', which is never possible between Christ and human beings, but vicarious representative action is the life-principle of the new humanity. True, I know myself to be in a guilty solidarity with the other person, but my service to the other person springs from the life-principle of vicarious representative action.

Now by encompassing the new life-principle of Christ's church-community in himself, Christ is at the same time established as the Lord of the church-community, which means his relation to the church-community is both 'communal' and 'governing'.

147

---

25. [*The role of "vicarious representative"* (Stellvertreter) *and the behavior of "vicarious representative action"* (Stellvertretung) *is central in Bonhoeffer's theology. Christ is* Stellvertreter *as the one who enters into the situation of humanity and acts on its behalf and for its sake. On this model, there is also a human ethical* Stellvertretung *when a person acts as a representative on behalf of, and for the sake of, a community or a people; examples would be Martin Luther King Jr. acting on behalf of African Americans, Gandhi and Mandela acting on behalf of their people, or Bonhoeffer acting on behalf of his church and his nation. For Bonhoeffer's own footnote on the ethical concept of vicarious representative action, see* DBWE 1:157, n. 17 *(Reader 49, n. 26).]*

Because, however, the entire new humanity is established in reality in Jesus Christ, *he represents the whole history of humanity in his historical life.* Christ's history is marked by the fact that in it humanity-in-Adam is transformed into humanity-in-Christ. As the human body of Jesus Christ became the resurrection body, so the corpus Adae [*body of Adam*] became the corpus Christi [*body of Christ*]. The former as well as the latter leads through death and resurrection; the human body—the corpus Adae—has to be broken, in order for the body of the resurrection—the corpus Christi—to be created. The history of Jesus Christ, however, is closed to us without his word. Only if we take both together will it be possible to read the past and the future of humanity in Christ's history.

Jesus Christ places his life under the law (Gal. 4:4); he takes his place within Israel's community-of-God. The baptism (Matt. 3:15) is the clearest example of this. What was Israel's community-of-God? It was the people,
148   as a collective person, whom God had chosen; it was constituted by God's law. The law of God for Israel is the calling properly heard. Law and calling belong together. Fulfillment of the law is the obedient realization of the calling. Because the people are called as a collective person, the fulfillment of the law is fulfillment of God's call to be a people, a holy community-of-God. Both ideas of God's call and of God's law, therefore, point toward community. To play off God's call against God's law—which means to invert the meaning of law and thus not to fulfill it—shatters the very core of the community that is constituted by the true correlation of calling and law. When taken under human control, the law becomes a claim of each individual on the God who calls. But at the same time the law reveals itself as a living force, becoming a power of wrath to those who misuse it, showing them the irreparable rift in the community, and isolating them completely. That, in brief, is the history of the community-of-Israel.

By placing himself within this community-of-Israel, Christ does not declare his solidarity with it, but in vicarious representative action for all he fulfills the law by love, thereby overcoming the Jewish understanding of the law. Whereas formerly only the willful transgressor of the law was excluded from the community-of-Israel, Jesus now declares the whole community-of-Israel to have essentially fallen away from God. Far from being the community-of-God itself, it belongs to the humanity-of-Adam, and must be reconciled with God. That is, it must be recreated into a new community. Whereas formerly each individual in the community faced the law in isolation, the person of Christ must now unite all individuals in himself, and act before God as their vicarious representative. The transformation
149   into a new-community-of-God is possible only if the deficiency of the old is recognized. To bring this about, Jesus calls to repentance, which means

he reveals God's ultimate claim and subjects the human past and present to its reality. Recognizing that we are guilty makes us solitary before God; we begin to recognize what has long been the case objectively, namely that we are in a state of isolation. With this recognition the old community-of-God, whose norm and constituting power is the law, is broken up. The law does not establish community but solitude—as a consequence of human sin, of course—for the law is holy and good and was meant to be the norm and pattern of life of a holy *people* of God. The law can only be fulfilled in spirit through the spirit, that is, an unbroken will to obey God, i.e., through perfect love. With the recognition that the strength to do this is lacking, the way is cleared for the gift Jesus gives, for the message of God's love and royal rule in God's Realm. Thus out of utter isolation arises concrete community, for the preaching of God's love speaks of the community into which God *has* entered with each and every person—with all those who in utter solitude know themselves separated from God and other human beings and who believe this message. It would not do, however, for Jesus to re-create the community-of-God during his lifetime. His love had to become complete by fulfilling the law—that is, the claim of God and of human beings—even to death. The revealed community-of-love had to be broken up one more time   150 by its founder's own action, though not before Jesus had tied them tightly together with a close bond at the very last hour. This happened in the Last Supper. Jesus says: just as I break this bread, so my body will be broken tomorrow, and as all of you eat and are filled from *one* loaf, so too will all of you be saved and united in me alone. The Lord of the disciple-community grants his disciples community with him and thus with each other. With considerable plausibility this event has been considered the point where the church was founded (Kattenbusch). Jesus has now openly expressed his will for the church-community to exist; yet theologically the moment of the church's birth is to be sought in another event.

Serving the law leads Jesus to the cross, truly leads him into the most profound solitude that the curse of the law brings upon human beings. When Jesus is arrested all the disciples forsake him, and on the cross Jesus is quite alone. The disciple-community seems to be broken up. This has a meaning that is theologically significant and is not simply to be dismissed as the weakness or disloyalty of the disciples. It is an event with an objective meaning; it had to happen in this way, "so that everything would be fulfilled," one would like to add. In the death of Jesus on the cross God's judgment and wrath are carried out on all the self-centeredness of humanity, which had distorted the meaning of the law. This distortion brought the Son of God to the cross. With this the burden becomes unbearably heavy. Each individual is Adam; everyone is entirely responsible. Here each person stands

151   alone before God. Here all hope is gone; the disciple-community existed
only as long as one knew that Jesus was alive. But, in going to the cross, in
submitting to the law, in taking the curse of the law upon himself on our
behalf, Jesus himself had apparently accepted that the world was right. The
old 'community-of-God' seemed to have won. Because he was made sin for
us, and because he was accursed by the law for us, Jesus died in solitude.
Therefore the disciples, for whom the present had no future, had to be
alone too. To us, for whom Easter also lies in the past, the death of Christ is
conceivable only in the light of the victory of love over law, of life over death.
The absolutely contemporary character of the death of Jesus is no longer
available to us. This results for us in *the paradoxical reality of a community-of-
the-cross*, which contains within itself the contradiction of simultaneously
representing utmost solitude and closest community. *And this is the specifically Christian church-community.* But a community-of-the-cross exists only
through the Easter message. In the resurrection of Jesus Christ his death is
revealed as the death of death itself, and with this the boundary of history
marked by death is abolished, the human body becomes the resurrection-
152   body, and the humanity-of-Adam has become the church of Christ. To be
sure, the church could be created only in an empirical form by the Holy
Spirit. In the resurrection it is 'created' only insofar as it has now run the
course of its dialectical history. It is realized, but not actualized. In the resurrection the heart of God has broken through sin and death; it has really
conquered God's new humanity and subjected it to God's rule.

Admittedly, the existing empirical community cannot be the actualized
church, since Christ has not yet ascended. The time between the resurrection and the ascension and the time after Pentecost are different insofar as
in the first case the disciple-community lives in Christ as its Lord and life-
principle, whereas in the second case Christ lives in the community. Formerly the disciple-community 'represented' Christ; now it possesses him as
revelation, as Spirit. *Thus the day of the founding of the actualized church remains
Pentecost.* Since human community was formed only when it became a community of will and spirit, and since human spirit is operative only in sociality, *the church originates with the outpouring of the Holy Spirit, and so too the Holy
Spirit is the spirit of the church-community of Christ. But if the Spirit is operative only
within the church-community, then the genesis of the latter cannot be deduced from
the spirits of individuals.* In the perspective of systematic sociology, the problem of the church therefore cannot consist in the question of the empirical
association of people and their psychological motivation. It can consist only
in *exhibiting the essential structure of the social entity*, its volitional acts, and its
objective form in connection with the concept of spirit—consistent with the
definition of sociology given above.

Now the relationship of Christ to the church can be stated by saying that in essence Jesus Christ was no more the founder of the Christian religious community than the founder of a religion. The credit for both of these belongs to the earliest church, i.e., to the apostles. This is why the question   153 whether Jesus founded a church is so ambiguous. He brought, established, and proclaimed the reality of the new humanity. The circle of disciples around him was not the church; its history prefigured the inner dialectic of the church. It is not a new religion recruiting followers—this is the picture of a later time. Rather, God established the reality of the church, of humanity pardoned in Jesus Christ—not religion, but revelation, *not religious community, but church*. This is what the reality of Jesus Christ means.

And yet there is a necessary connection between revelation and religion as well as between religious community and the church. Nowadays this is often overlooked. And yet only because of this connection can Paul call Jesus the foundation and the cornerstone of the building of the church. As pioneer and model, Jesus also is founder of a religious community, though not of the Christian church (for it indeed exists only after Pentecost—Matt. 16:18 and the scene of the Last Supper express this). And, after the resurrection, Christ himself restores both forms of community that had been broken: with Peter through Christ's appearance to him as presumably the first to whom this was granted (1 Cor. 15:5), perhaps with an express conferral of office (John 21:15ff.); and after that with the Twelve through an appearance in their midst (1 Cor. 15:5; John 20:19). Christ is thus the sole foundation upon which the building of the church rests, the reality from which the historical 'collective life' originated.

The relationship of Jesus Christ to the Christian church is thus to be understood in a dual sense. (1) *The church is already completed in Christ, time is suspended.* (2) *The church is to be built within time upon Christ as the firm foundation. Christ is the historical principle of the church.* Time belongs to   154 him, the vertical direction, as it were. These statements correspond to the well-known New Testament view concerning the Realm of God as present and still to come, but they are not identical with it; for the church is not the same as the Realm of God. The church is not the Realm of God any more than the Christian, who is iustus-peccator [*justified-sinner*], is actually already completed, even though in reality the Christian is just that. The Realm of God is a strictly eschatological concept, which from God's point of view is present in the church at every moment, but which for us remains an object of hope, while the church is an actually present object of faith. The church is identical with the realm of Christ, but the realm of Christ is the Realm of God that has been realized in history since the coming of Christ.

What is the *principle*, then, upon which the *efficacy of Christ* rests with regard to the new social basic conditions? The crucified and risen Christ is recognized by the church-community as God's incarnate love for us—as God's will to renew the covenant, to establish God's rule, and thus to create community. Two things are still opposed to this, *time* and the *will to do evil*. The second is self-evident; the first means that what has happened cannot be undone. This is the gravity of time that became a burden for us

155 since sin and death appeared. If human beings are to have community with God, then both of these must somehow be removed: their sin must be forgiven, and what has been done must be judged undone by God's sovereign decree. Now human sin cannot be viewed by the true God 'as if it did not exist'; it must truly be 'undone', that is, it must be wiped out. This occurs not by reversing time, but through divine punishment and re-creating the will to do good. God does not 'overlook' sin; that would mean not taking human beings seriously as personal beings in their very culpability; and that would mean no re-creation of the person, and therefore no re-creation of community. But God does take human beings seriously in their culpability, and therefore only punishment and the overcoming of sin can remedy the matter. Both of these have to take place within concrete time, and in Jesus Christ that occurs in a way that is valid for all time. He takes the punishment upon himself, accomplishes forgiveness of sin, and, to use Seeberg's expression, stands as surety for the renewal of human beings. *Christ's action as vicarious representative* can thus be understood from the situation itself. It is simultaneously 'within concrete time' and the 'for all times'. Vicarious representative action for sin does take place. Here the one requires the other, for 'punishment' obviously does not mean taking the consequences of sin upon oneself, but considering these consequences as 'punishment'. The punitive character of the suffering of Jesus has frequently been denied. But Luther placed all the emphasis especially on this very idea. To take the consequences of sin upon oneself is conceivable in the framework of ethical behavior in civic life. But what characterizes the Christian notion of vicarious representative action is that it is vicariously representative strictly with respect to sin and punishment. Though innocent, Jesus takes the sin

156 of others upon himself, and by dying as a criminal he is accursed, for he bears the sins of the world and is punished for them. However, vicarious representative love triumphs on the criminal's cross, obedience to God triumphs over sin, and thereby sin is actually punished and overcome. So much for a brief sketch of Christ's vicarious representative action. It contains profound implications for social philosophy.

Is this Christian view of vicarious representative action for sin ethically tenable? As ethical persons we clearly wish, after all, to accept responsibility ourselves before God for our good and evil deeds. How can we lay our fault upon another person and ourselves go free? It is true, the doctrine of vicarious representative action includes more than our ethical posture, but we *ought* to let our sin be taken from us, for we are not able to carry it by ourselves; we *ought not* reject this gift of God. It is God's love that offers it to us, and only for the sake of this love ought we abandon our ethical position of responsibility for ourselves—a position that counts for nothing before God—thereby demonstrating precisely the necessity for vicarious representative action. The idea of vicarious representative action is therefore possible only so long as it is based on an offer by God; this means it is in force only in Christ and Christ's church-community. *It is not an ethical possibility or standard, but solely the reality of the divine love for the church-community; it is not an ethical, but a theological concept.*[26] Through the Christian principle of vicarious representative action the new humanity is made whole and sustained. This principle gives Christian basic-relations their substantive uniqueness. We will discuss later the extent to which this principle not only unites the new humanity with Christ, but also links its members to each other in community. It is certain, however, that human community comes into being where community with God is a reality.   157

Thus the church is established in and through Christ in the three basic sociological relationships known to us: his death isolates the *individuals*— all of them bear their own culpability and have their own conscience; in the light of the resurrection the community of the cross is justified and sanctified in Christ as *one*. The new humanity is seen synoptically in *one* point, in Christ. And since the love of God, in Christ's vicarious representative action, restores the community between God and human beings, so the *community of human beings with each other has also become a reality in love once again.*

2. The Holy Spirit and the Church of Jesus Christ: The Actualization of the Essential Church

In and through Christ the church is established in reality. It is not as if Christ could be abstracted from the church; rather, it is none other than

---

26. There is, however, also an ethical concept of vicarious representative action; it signifies the voluntary assumption of an evil in another person's stead. It does not remove the self-responsibility of the other person, and remains as an act of human heroic love (for one's country, friend, etc.) even within the bounds of the highest ethical obligation. In acknowledging it we do not put our ethical person as a whole at stake, but only as much as we owe (body, honor, money) to the person who acted vicariously on our behalf; we acknowledge Christ, however, as vicarious representative for our person as a whole, and thus owe everything to him.

Christ who 'is' the church. Christ does not represent it; only what is not present can be represented. In God's eyes, however, the church is present in Christ. Christ did not merely make the church possible, but rather realized it for eternity. If this is so, then the significance of Christ must be made the focal point in the temporal actualization of the church. This is accomplished by the Spirit-impelled word of the crucified and risen Lord of the church. The Spirit can work only through this word. If there were an unmediated work of the Spirit, then the idea of the church would be individualis-

158 tically dissolved from the outset. But in the word the most profound social nexus is established from the beginning. The word is social in character, not only in its origin but also in its aim. Tying the Spirit to the word means that the Spirit aims at a plurality of hearers and establishes a visible sign by which the actualization is to take place.

The word, however, is qualified by being the very word of Christ; it is effectively brought to the heart of the hearers by the Spirit. Christ himself is in the word; the Christ in whom the church-community is already completed seeks to win the heart by his Spirit in order to incorporate it into the actualized community of Christ. But in the word of Christ the actualized church-community is also present, as every word of Christ comes out of that community and exists only in it. If one asks how the actualized church-community could have been present at the time of the first sermons, before individuals who were moved joined together to form the church, then one forgets what has been said earlier, that the Spirit is solely the Spirit of the church, of the church-community, and therefore, that there were no individuals moved by the Spirit before the church-community existed. Community with God exists only through Christ, but Christ is present only in his church-community, and therefore *community with God exists only in the church*. Every individualistic concept of the church breaks down because of this fact. The individual and the church have the following mutually conditioned relationship: the Holy Spirit is at work only in the church as in

159 the community of saints; thus every person who is really moved by the Spirit has to be within the church-community already; but, on the other hand, no one is in the church-community who has not already been moved by the Spirit. It follows that *in moving the elect who are part of the church-community established in Christ, the Holy Spirit simultaneously leads them into the actualized church-community*. Faith is based on entry into the church-community, just as entry into the church-community is based on faith.

160 The church does not come into being by people coming together (genetic sociology), rather its *existence is sustained* by the Spirit who is a reality within the church-community; therefore, it cannot be derived from individual wills, since an individual will can at most be an expression of belonging to

the church. Thus the individual is possible only as a member of the church-community, and this is not merely a preparation for higher individual life, but *personal* life is possible only *within* the church-community. A person who is not in the church has no real living-community with Christ; but a person who is in Christ, is also in the church-community, that is, in both the completed and the actualized church. A person is in Christ, however, through the word of the church-community. Therefore, in the word that comes to the individual both the already completed community of saints and the community of saints developing in time are present; for Christ and the Holy Spirit are at work in this word; and both are inseparably linked—the Holy Spirit has no other content than the fact of Christ. Christ is the criterion and the aim of the work of the Holy Spirit, and to this extent Christ himself also participates in building the church in time, although only through the work of the Holy Spirit. 161

**

This being-for-each-other must now be actualized through acts of love. *Three great, positive possibilities of acting for each other* in the community of saints present themselves: *self-renouncing, active work for the neighbor; intercessory prayer; and, finally, the mutual forgiveness of sins* in God's name. All of these involve giving up the self 'for' my neighbor's benefit, with the readiness to do and bear everything in the neighbor's place, indeed, if necessary, to sacrifice myself, standing as a *substitute* for my neighbor. Even if a purely vicarious action is rarely actualized, it is intended in every genuine act of love. 184

**

The unity of spirit of the church-community is a fundamental synthesis willed by God; it is not a relation that must be produced, but one that is already established (iustitia passiva! [*passive righteousness*]), and that remains hidden from our eyes. Neither unanimity, uniformity, nor congeniality makes it possible, nor is it to be confused with unity of mood. Rather, it is a reality precisely where the seemingly sharpest outward antitheses prevail, where each person really leads an individual life; and it is perhaps missing just where it seems to prevail most. It is thrown into much sharper relief where wills clash than where they agree. When one person clashes with another, it might very well lead them to remember the One who is over them both, and in whom both of them are one. Precisely where Jew and Greek clash, out of their completely different psychological dispositions, their intuitive and intellectual perceptions, there unity is established through God's will; "here, there is neither Jew nor Greek, neither slave nor 192

free, neither man nor woman: for you are all one in Christ Jesus" (Gal.
3:28). Christ has created, out of two, a single new person in himself, and
has made peace (Eph. 2:15); but this continues to be a peace that passes
all understanding. For the contrasts remain, they even become more acute;
in the community all are led to carry their individual viewpoints to the
limit, to be really serious about it, in keeping with the basic sociological
laws of social vitality. But—to put it paradoxically—the more powerfully
the dissimilarity manifests itself in the struggle, the stronger the objective
193   unity. The decisive passages in the New Testament do not say: *one* theology
and *one* rite, *one* opinion on all matters public and private, and *one* kind of
conduct. Instead they say: *one* body and *one* Spirit, *one* Lord, *one* faith, *one*
baptism, *one* God and father of us all (Eph. 4:4ff.; 1 Cor. 12:13; Rom. 12:5);
various gifts—*one* Spirit, various offices—*one* Lord, various powers—*one*
God (1 Cor. 12:4ff.). The point is not "unanimity in spirit," but the "unity
of the Spirit," as Luther puts it in his exposition of Eph. 4:3; this means
the objective principle sovereignly establishes unity, unites the plurality
of persons into a single collective person without obliterating either their
singularity or the community of persons. *Rather, unity of spirit, community
of spirit, and plurality of spirit are intrinsically linked to each other through their
subject matter.*

**

198   The unity of the Christian church is *not based on human unanimity of spirit,*
but on *divine unity of Spirit,* and the two are *not* identical from the outset. In
199   discussing the sociological community-type[27] we found its ultimate unity to
be its existence as a collective person. This insight must be applied to the
Christian religious community as well as to the concept of the church. In
the first case the presentation would proceed from below upwards, whereas
in the case of the concept of the church it moves from above downwards.
The personal unity of the church is 'Christ existing as church-community'; Paul
could also speak of Christ himself being the church.

       Being in Christ means being in the church. The unity of the church as a
structure *is* established 'before' any knowing and willing of the members;
it is not ideal, but real. It is a reality as truly as the church is the church of
Christ, and as truly as the body of Christ never becomes fully manifest in
history. In Christ all are one, differences no longer exist; there is not even a

---

27. [*"Community-type" refers to Tönnies's typology of* Gemeinschaft *(community) and* Gesellschaft *(society); in the former, the community is willed as an end in itself, whereas a society is willed
as a means to achieving an end. Bonhoeffer finds both sociological characteristics in the church.*]

plurality any more. They are all *one*, "one loaf," to use Luther's phrase. Only all members together can possess Christ entirely, and yet every person possesses him entirely too. This unity is based on the fact that Christ is "the one beyond every other" (Barth). It must be believed, and will always remain   200
invisible to our eyes. This unity does not exist because the members of the body have the same intentions; rather, if they have the same intentions at all, they have them only as members of the body of Christ; for obviously they remain members, even when they sin (cf. the indicative sense of 1 Cor. 6:15). But there is no divine will for human beings that would not be realized at least to some small extent in them. In this way the objective unity already existing in Christ is realized in the persons, and only in this realization is it this objective unity.

**

Thus we have, on the one hand, the ever-changing, imperfect, sinful,   215
objective human spirit; on the other hand we have the Holy Spirit who bears this human spirit, and is eternally one and perfect, and we have 'Christ   216
existing as church-community'. The objective spirit is subject to the historical ambiguity of all profane communities, of all so-called ideal associations with all their vanity, eccentricity, and mendacity. But this objective spirit claims and is certain that it is nevertheless Christ's church, that in spite of everything it stands within a church that is built and borne by the Holy Spirit. It is a certainty that is in danger of foundering again and again precisely because of this similarity to other 'religious communities'. Here we have on the one hand the purely historical collective person of the church, and on the other the person of Christ as the presence of God within the church-community; on one side the human 'religious community', and on the other the church-community of the Spirit. And insofar as the former, in spite of all appearances to the contrary and fully aware of its situation, *believes* it is identical with the latter, it believes in the church, the community of saints. . . . Thus this identity cannot be historically verifiable. It is 'invisible' and will be visible only in the eschaton;[28] and yet it already has its actual beginning in the present. The objective spirit is bearer and instrument of the spirit of the church of Christ; it has certain visible forms that the Holy Spirit produced and implanted into it. The Holy Spirit thus stands behind the objective spirit as the guarantor of the efficacy of these forms; these forms are preaching and the celebration of the sacraments. But the

---

28. [*The redemption and consummation of all things at the end of history in the kingdom of God.*]

objective spirit does not bear these forms as one would carry a sack on one's back; rather it is itself sanctified through the load, *it carries it in its heart.* This is of course true only insofar as the Holy Spirit does the carrying within it, for the objective spirit is not the Holy Spirit. But the objective spirit is, according to our earlier definition of the community of love, *both instrument and end in itself.* It is both the object and the means of the Holy Spirit's work, in an interrelated fashion that was described above. This then clearly shows that the objective spirit and the Holy Spirit cannot be equated.

**

226   *c)* Sociological forms and functions of the empirical church

(1) Assembling for worship
A Christian church-community, whether a publicly visible congregation or a house-church, is held together by its *assembling around the word.* The word constitutes the unity between essential and empirical church, between Holy Spirit and objective spirit. The concrete function of the empirical church, therefore, is *worship that consists of preaching and celebrating the sacraments.* Preaching is an 'office' of the church-community, so there must also be an *assembly* since both concepts imply one another. This was axiomatic from earliest Christianity up to the time of Pietism and Protestant Orthodoxy.

227   Only when an individualistic outlook began to transform this *obvious neces-sity* into a *psychological* one did it ask about the meaning of the assembly in terms of its usefulness and necessity for the individual. This question reveals a fundamental misunderstanding of the concept of the church-community. It is therefore also completely useless to attempt to respond to it by listing a whole host of internal or external advantages, or moral obligations, which might lead the individual into the church; to do so would mean relinquish-ing from the very outset the right to have one's own basic premises. [. . .] preaching is a divinely ordained activity *of the church for the church.* Since I belong to the church-community, I come to the assembly; this is the simple rationale of those who are assembled. This act is not based on utilitarian considerations, or a sense of duty, but is 'organic' and obvious behavior. [. . .] A Christian who stays away from the assembly is a contradiction in terms. The church-community, united by one word, hears this word again and again while assembled; conversely, *the word that created the church-community again and again calls it together* into concrete assembly. For it is the word *preached* according to the will of God and of the church-community that is the means through which this will is actualized.

**

To summarize: *the assembly embodies God's will to use the social connections*   230
between human beings to extend God's rule. The objective spirit of the church-com-
munity actualizes this will of God by establishing regular worship. Assembling for
worship belongs to the essence of the church-community. This is the objective side.
Subjectively, individuals continue to be attached to the assembly because
they *accept that God wills to speak in the empirical church, and because they are*
aware that they belong to the church-community that bears the office of preaching,
and is also the recipient of the preaching. There is an organic link between the
assembly and the life of individuals. It originates from the *gratitude* of the
latter toward the mother who gave them their life; it is further based on
their love for her, coupled with the *trust* that she will time and again bestow
her gifts upon them; and finally it springs from the certain hope that in the
assembly they will again and again receive concrete and compelling assurance of being members of God's church-community, which means being
embraced by God's grace.

**

To summarize, the word is the sociological principle by which the entire   246
church is built up. It is the word by which the church is built up, both in
numbers and in its faith. Christ is the foundation upon which, and according to which, the building (οἰκοδομή) of the church is raised (1 Corinthians
3; Eph. 2:20). And thus it grows into a "holy temple of God" (Eph. 2:21),
and "with a growth that is from God" (Col. 2:19), "until all of us come to
maturity, to the measure of the full stature of Christ" (Eph. 4:13), and in all   247
this growing "into him who is the head, into Christ." The entire building
begins and ends with Christ, and its unifying center is the word. Whereas
baptism signifies the will of the church-community in its most comprehensive form to spread God's rule, which for us implies the fact of a *church-*
of-the-people, the church addressed by preaching consists of those who are
personally faced with the decision whether to accept or reject God's gift,
and is thus both a *church-of-the-people and a voluntary church*. In the Lord's
Supper the church-community manifests itself purely as a *voluntary church*,
as a *community confessing its faith*, and is summoned and recognized by God
as such. It is not a manifestation of the pure sanctorum communio, however; rather it is the smallest of the three concentric, sociologically distinct
circles, and is both the source from which all effectiveness of the church-
community springs, and the focal point into which all its life flows. This

duality is what constitutes its vitality, which is the vitality of the church, in that it is simultaneously the aim and the instrument of God's work.

**

280   But then what does it mean 'to believe in the church'? We do not believe in an invisible church, nor in the Realm of God within the church as coetus electorum [*company of the elect*]. Instead we believe that God has made the concrete, empirical church in which the word is preached and the sacraments are celebrated to be God's own church-community. We believe that it is the body of Christ, Christ's presence in the world, and that according to the promise God's Spirit is at work in it. We have faith that God is also at work in the others. We do not believe in the call of individuals, but rather in that of the church-community. We believe in the church as the church of God, as the community of saints, those who are sanctified by God. We believe, however, that this takes place always within the historical framework of the empirical church. Thus we believe the means of grace to be effective within the empirical church and hence have faith in the holy church-community created by these means of grace. We believe in the church as *una* [*one*], since it is 'Christ existing as church-community', and *Christ is the one Lord* over those who are all one in him; as *sancta* [*holy*], since the Holy Spirit is at work in it; as *catholica* [*catholic*], since as *God's church* its call is to the entire world, and wherever in the world God's word is preached, there is the church. We believe in the church not as an ideal that is unattainable or yet to be fulfilled, but as a present reality. Christian thinking, in contrast to all idealist theories of community, considers Christian community to be God's
281   church-community at every moment in history. And yet within its historical development it never knows a state of fulfillment. It will remain impure as long as there is history, and yet in this concrete form it is nevertheless God's church-community.

4. JESUS CHRIST AND THE ESSENCE OF CHRISTIANITY

DBWE 10:342–359

Beginning in February 1928, Bonhoeffer spent a year as vicar to a German congregation in Barcelona.[1] There he undertook his first sustained church work, preaching regularly and providing pastoral care to the community. He also delivered three lectures to the congregation on the topic "Crisis and Hope in the Contemporary Religious Situation."

In the second lecture, printed below, Bonhoeffer is eager to demonstrate Christ's decisive relevance for his modern audience. This requires engaging with a number of modern intellectual trends—life of Jesus research, historical criticism of the New Testament, comparative history of religions—that threaten to marginalize Christ or restrict his absolute claim. Against this threat, he argues that the central message of the Synoptic Gospels—that Jesus is the Christ—requires of the contemporary reader absolute acceptance or rejection. There is no place for the lukewarm reception of Jesus as a teacher or moral sage.

A central theme of this lecture is what Bonhoeffer calls "the Christian idea of God," the transcendent God who makes a divine path to humanity via the cross, in the process condemning attempts to reach God through the human paths of religion, morality, and the church. Echoing Barth's thinking, Bonhoeffer concludes that "the Christian message is basically amoral and irreligious, paradoxical as that may sound." This, of course, raises the question about the relationship of ethics to this Christian idea of God, a topic to which Bonhoeffer returns in the next lecture.

---

1. [*For historical background, biographical information, and a summary of texts from the Barcelona period (1928–1929), see* DBWE *10:4–13, editor's introduction, and* DB-ER, *97–123.*]

342   The question before us today is whether in our own day Christ still stands in the place where decisions are made concerning the most profound matters we are facing, namely, concerning our own lives and the life of our people. We want to examine whether the spirit of Christ can still speak to us concerning the ultimate, final, decisive matters. We all know that, for all practical purposes, Christ has been eliminated from our lives. Although we still build his temple, we live in our own houses. Christ, instead of being the center of our lives, has become a thing of the church, or of the religiosity of a group of people. To the nineteenth- and twentieth-century mind, religion plays the part of the so-called parlor into which one doesn't mind withdrawing for a couple of hours, but from which one then immediately returns to one's place of work. However, one thing is clear, namely, that we understand Christ only if we commit to him in an abrupt either-or. He was not nailed to the cross as an ornamentation or decoration for our lives. If we want to have *him*, we must recognize that he makes crucial claims on our entire lives. We understand him not if we make room for him in merely one province of our spiritual life, but only if our life takes its orientation from him alone or, otherwise, if we speak a straightforward no. Of course, there are those who are not concerned with taking seriously the claims Christ makes on us in his question, Do you want to commit completely, or not? They should rather not get mixed up with Christianity at all; this is better for Christianity, since such people no longer have anything in common with Christ. The religion of Christ is not the tidbit after the bread; it is the bread itself, or it is nothing. Those who would call themselves Christians should understand and acknowledge at least that much.

343   Various attempts have been made to eliminate Christ from the contemporary life of the human spirit. And indeed, what is seductive about these attempts is that they seem finally to put Christ into the appropriate and worthy position. Those undertaking such attempts explain Christ according to aesthetic categories as a religious genius. They declare him to be a great ethicist or admire his path to the cross as a heroic sacrifice for the sake of his idea. The only thing these attempts do not do is take him seriously. That is, they do not draw the center of their own lives into contact with Christ's claim to speak and indeed to be *the* revelation of God. They preserve a certain distance between themselves and Christ's words, thereby thwarting any serious encounter. I can live with or without Jesus as a religious genius, as an ethicist, as master[2]—just as I can certainly also live without Plato or

---

2. ["Translating *Herr* in this sentence as 'master' does not at all mean—as in some Christian discourse—an equivalence with 'Lord' in the sense of '*the* revelation of God'

Kant; all this has merely relative significance. But if there is something in Christ that makes claims upon my entire life, from top to bottom, and does so with the full seriousness of the realization that it is God who is speaking here, and if it is only in Christ that God's word once became a present reality, then Christ possesses for me not only merely relative but also absolutely urgent significance. Although I am still free to say yes or no, it can no longer be an ultimately indifferent matter to me. To understand Christ means to understand this claim; taking Christ seriously means taking seriously his absolute claim on human decision.

Our concern now is to make the seriousness of this matter clear and to remove Christ from the process of secularization into which he has been drawn since the Enlightenment. Finally, we will also show that in our own age the questions to which Christ provides the answers are as acutely relevant as ever, and that the spirit of Christ is quite justified in raising its claims.

Hence our first, and main, question concerns the essence of the Christian message, the essence of Christianity.

People are utterly at sea not only in lay circles but in professional theological circles as well. From the pulpits and the lecterns, we hear things described and preached as "essentially Christian" that could just as easily find their spiritual author in Plato, Buddha, or Goethe. Moreover, the far-reaching history-of-religions research[3] of the past few decades has pushed Christianity so completely into the culture of Hellenistic religious syncretism that we have gradually lost sight of what is unique in Christianity to begin with, a uniqueness to which Christianity does, after all, owe its victory over the Mithras cult and the mystery religions.

344

The central idea of the Hellenistic cult during the period when Christianity emerged is the idea of redemption. We hear, for example, about a world redeemer who will be born of a virgin, about a primal being who descends into the world, whose scattered parts are the souls of people who will one day come together again, whereupon the primal human being will once more be resurrected with all its members. We hear about the god Osiris, who dies and whose bones the women seek and bring together and the god once again is resurrected, analogous to what is still the contempo-

---

who makes an 'absolute claim on human decision.' As the context shows, the meaning in this sentence has the sense of guide, teacher, leader, etc.," *DBWE* 10:343, n. 3.]

3. ["The History of Religions School (*Religionsgeschichtlicheschule*), a group of German biblical scholars who flourished in the late nineteenth and early twentieth centuries, used data from the comparative study of ancient Near Eastern and Hellenistic religions to interpret the Bible and Christian origins," *DBWE* 10:344, n. 4.]

rary custom in the Greek church, where, during the night before Easter, women seek Jesus until they break out in cries of joy at morning: He is risen! Similar elements are found in the cults of Antaeus, Attis, and Dionysus. The myths of the dying and resurrected gods are nature myths symbolizing the sleep of winter and the reawakening of spring. We also hear about sacramental meals similar to the Christian Eucharist where, through physical connection with the god, adherents seek to deify themselves. Such similarities extend even into details. Just as today the bishop still blesses the people with three raised and two folded fingers, so also in distant antiquity did the priest of the god Sabazios bless the adherents of that god.

We see that Christianity is embedded in the religious forms of its age. This also applies to the portrayal of the life of Jesus of Nazareth. As portrayed by the first three Gospels of our New Testament, his life has become so overgrown with legendary features that scholarship is able to peer though the foliage in only a few passages. Tradition all too hastily clothed and draped Jesus in the conventional costume of a saint and miracle worker. Ancient fairy-tale motifs, in part from India and the Orient, and miracle stories of the sort also told about the more popular Roman emperors, all contributed to the myth of Jesus of Nazareth such that today little of the actual humanity of this man can be ascertained with any certainty.

345

The most concrete result yielded by one and a half centuries of New Testament source criticism is the familiar assertion: Vita Jesu scribi non potest [*it is not possible to write the life of Jesus*].[4]

The main reason for this situation is that our New Testament originated in a church-community that worshiped Jesus not as a historical personality but as the *kyrios*, the Lord (the Greek translates the Hebrew "Yahweh"), and thus as God himself. Any psychologizing or historicizing interest is thus quite naturally absent. Its interest is rather purely to the point, immediate, and aims at the center of the phenomenon of Jesus of Nazareth, over against which all historical elements become unimportant. Even in the Synoptics, that is, the first three Gospels, which seem to express some historical interest, the main focus is invariably on portraying Jesus as the Son of God and doing so through Jesus's deeds and words. The historical arrangement is wholly unreliable.

This whole situation has prompted one group of scholars to draw a false historical conclusion, namely, that the entire figure of Jesus is to be under-

---

4. [". . . [S]ee the beginning of Albert Schweitzer's concluding observations in his *Quest of the Historical Jesus*, 478: 'Those who are fond of talking about negative theology can find their account here. There is nothing more negative than the result of the critical study of Jesus,'" *DBWE* 10:345, n. 7.]

stood as a mythological character, as a product of the church-community analogous, for example, to Mithras. This suggestion has proven to be utterly erroneous. Nonetheless, we have reason enough to view our sources quite critically in terms of their historical assertions. At the same time, however, we must get beyond this shortcoming if we are to discover the essence of Christianity and grasp the undeniable uniqueness of the Christian message despite Christianity's seemingly utter congruency with the religions of its own time. A brief general observation can help us get under way.

Two possible modes of historical observation are possible, and here I am understanding specifically "historical" investigation to involve an understanding and interpretation of history. The first mode was influenced by idealist philosophy. Here one interprets history according to a system. One possesses the method through which one can interpret history and has access to the idea and thus apparently also to history. For such observation, history itself can offer nothing essentially new; everything fits into the system one already possesses. That is, history can now no longer possess absolute significance for me; history itself is relativized through the idea.   346 Put concretely, this means that in understanding historical circumstances one cannot transcend the standards of evaluation already at one's disposal from the very outset, even if those standards cannot hope to do justice to a particular set of historical circumstances. One does not want to learn anything new from history; history is not allowed to make any urgent claims on human beings.

The other mode of historical observation is completely different. It is interested in history only to the extent that the latter possesses absolute significance. That is, one approaches history with no preconceived ideas, categories, or tables of values according to which one will judge; one allows history itself to speak, and one listens as it does so. One does not have access beforehand to what history can say to us, but rather allows history to present its claims to us. One even allows one's own preconceived notions to be shattered if necessary, since history is more than the idea. The only thing that concerns us is what in history still has the power to speak to us down through the millennia, to make claims on us to which we must respond responsibly and with our entire existence rather than just with our ideology. Only here does time become transparent. We experience contemporaneity with historical events only where we perceive the claims of history, that is, where we accept or reject those claims and allow ourselves to be touched by them in our most profound existence. Here, however, the path is clear.

Either we already have access to what a Jesus of Nazareth might have to say, that is, we are already familiar in principle with the psychological laws and probabilities and can speak confidently, as those who basically already know everything in advance, about Jesus's psychology; then we can give free rein to our imagination in the way that Jesus novels have naively done even up to the present. Moreover, because we already know from our own philosophy about the best possible morality, and the highest, most appropriate idea of God, we can simply insinuate this information into Jesus's own words.

Or we allow the New Testament truly to speak, and for once we are only listeners, hearing the claim this book presents in its entire power, and thus at the center of the matter we genuinely try to come to terms with history. That is the path we will take. There is absolutely no value in reading the New Testament according to twentieth-century concepts; one must read it rather as it was intended. In so doing, however, we do indeed encounter a great deal that runs contrary to modern psychology and philosophy.

The first thing we encounter throughout the entire New Testament is a surprising lack of interest in anything concerning the psychology of Jesus; the same goes for chronological considerations. The primary focus is on the unsettling experience the church-community had in the figure of Jesus of Nazareth, who called himself the Christ, that is, the Messiah, God's anointed, that is, God's revelation in the world. It is about these concerns that we want to hear, since even Jesus himself is only important as the essence of Christianity.

About midway through the three Synoptic Gospels, we read that Jesus asked his disciples what the people thought of him. They responded that some were saying he was the resurrected Elijah, or John the Baptist, others that he was one of the prophets. "He said to them, 'But who do you say that I am?' Simon Peter answered, 'You are the Christ, the Son of the living God.' And Jesus answered him, 'Blessed are you, Simon son of Jonah! For flesh and blood has not revealed this to you, but my Father in heaven.' . . . Then he sternly ordered the disciples not to tell anyone that he was the Christ" [*Matt. 16:15–20*].

This is the great, overwhelming, decisive moment in Jesus's life. He, the son of a carpenter, hears others call him the Son of God, the Christ, and he conceals this secret in the most profound silence. He knows God has sent him into the world with enormous authority. He is the bringer of God's kingdom into the world. "But if it is by the Spirit of God that I cast out demons, then the kingdom of God has come to you" [*Matt. 12:28*]. Or as he says in the one rather strange image, "I watched Satan fall from heaven like a flash of lightning" (Luke 10:18), that is, the kingdom of God is here. To the question "when is the kingdom coming?" he answers, "the kingdom of God is not coming with things that can be observed; nor will they say, 'Look, here it is!' or 'There it is!' For, in fact, the kingdom of God is among you" (the translation "within you" is wrong), "the blind receive their

347

sight, the lame walk, the lepers are cleansed, the deaf hear, the dead are raised, and the poor have good news brought to them" [*Luke 17:20–21; Matt. 11:5*]. Such is Jesus's cry of joy regarding the new age. He acts with the full authority of God's Spirit. His coming confronts the world with a decision: either with him and for God, or against him and against God. "Whoever is not with me is against me, and whoever does not gather with me scatters" (Matt. 12:30). Because he bears God's revelation, because he is the Christ, it is with regard to him and his word that a person's life is decided. "Do not think that I have come to bring peace to the earth; I have not come to bring peace, but a sword. For I have come to set a man against his father, and a daughter against her mother. . . . Whoever loves father or mother more than me is not worthy of me; and whoever loves son or daughter more than me is not worthy of me" (Matt. 10:34ff.). Or even more harshly in another passage: "Whoever comes to me and does not hate father and mother, wife and children, brothers and sisters, yes, and even life itself, cannot be my disciple" (Luke 14:26). Jesus is demanding a direct, uncompromising decision, a decision in favor of God's will, leading to participation in God's kingdom. To a man grieving at the death of his father, Jesus says, "Let the dead bury their own dead; but as for you, go and proclaim the kingdom of God" [*Luke 9:60*]. Or, "No one who puts a hand to the plow and looks back is fit for the kingdom of God" [*Luke 9:62*]. God's lordship requires everything or nothing: "The kingdom of heaven is like treasure hidden in a field, which someone found and hid; then in his joy he goes and sells all that he has and buys that field. Again, the kingdom of heaven is like a merchant in search of fine pearls; on finding one pearl of great value, he went and sold all that he had and bought it" [*Matt. 13:44–46*]. Before God's will, there is no consideration of human matters: "If your right eye causes you to sin, tear it out and throw it away; it is better for you to lose one of your members than for your whole body to be thrown into hell. And if your right hand causes you to sin, cut it off and throw it away; it is better for you to lose one of your members than for your whole body to go into hell" (Matt. 5:29–30). "Enter through the narrow gate; for the gate is wide and the road is easy that leads to destruction, and there are many who take it. For the gate is narrow and the road is hard that leads to life, and there are few who find it" (Matt. 7:13).

348

Jesus is able to confront human beings with this alternative of "all or nothing" only because he knows he is acting with God's authority; "and blessed is anyone who takes no offense at me" [*Matt. 11:6*]. At the same time, however, anything involving his own person as an individual personality, for example, with whatever fascinating or repulsive characteristics may attach to that personality, is infinitely insignificant to Jesus compared to the main issue, which is the decision for God's will. Luke recounts how, "while he was saying this, a woman in the crowd raised her voice and said to him, 'Blessed is the womb that bore you and the breasts that nursed you!' But he said, 'Blessed rather are those who hear the word of God and obey it!'" [*Luke 11:27–28*] This statement constitutes an unequivocal renunciation of any cult attaching to Jesus's individual, personal human appearance. Those who venerate Jesus as a genius or as a fascinating personality do not understand him; they only understand him who hear his message and accept him as the one sent by God.

349

Jesus's consciousness of his messianic authority prompts his family to think him crazy. They go to bring him home: "Then his mother and his brothers came; and standing outside, they sent to him and called him. A crowd was sitting around him; and they said to him 'Your mother and your brothers and sisters are outside, asking for you.' And he replied, 'Who are my mother and my brothers?' And looking at those who sat around him, he said, 'Here are my mother and my brothers! Whoever does the will of God is my brother and sister and mother'" (Mark 3:31–35). Jesus consistently turns attention away from his own person and back to the only important and urgent issue, the decision for God's dominion. "I came to bring fire to the earth, and how I wish it were already kindled!" [*Luke 12:49*]

In all these episodes, we thus see Jesus up on the icy heights of that unrelenting demand on human beings. Who will dare to follow him? Who will enter his discipleship? It is no accident that Ibsen's *Brand*, in which the demand for all or nothing tears a family apart, takes place high up in the icy Nordic regions. This either-or is unrelentingly cold. Nor is it inappropriate that Dostoyevsky has the Grand Inquisitor ask Jesus:

> But is it only to the elect and for their sake that you descended straight down from heaven? Let me assert that human beings are weaker and baser than you thought. Can they really successfully do all the things you have directed them to do? By thinking so highly of them, you in fact acted like someone who felt no compassion for them at all and as a result constantly demanded too much of them; and it was you who did this, you who loved them more than you loved yourself. If you had thought less of them, you would have demanded less of them. . . . Your great prophet says that in his visions he has seen all those who took part in the resurrection, and that there were twelve thousand from each tribe—but if there were no more than that, then they were not human beings at all, but already gods. They bore your cross, lived ten years in the hungry, barren wilderness, living on locusts and roots—certainly, you can now point to them with pride, these children of freedom, of free love, of free and noble sacrifice in your name. But do not forget that their number was only a few thousand, and that they were gods. But what happens to the others? What did

350

the remaining ones, the weak ones, do to you by not enduring what the strong were able to endure? Is it the fault of the weak soul that it is not strong enough to endure such terrible gifts?

Everywhere we encounter the same trembling apprehension before the terrible severity of Jesus's demand. He turns to the moral heroes and pays no attention to the weak; he leads the way to the Overman.[5]

Closer examination, however, reveals a surprising picture. He who was seemingly so unapproachable, who came with his razor-sharp either-or, now appears not among the ascetics or moral heroes or Pharisees, but rather among two groups of people hitherto living completely unnoticed beneath the surface, people who seemed least to fulfill his severe demands. Jesus turns his attention to children and to the morally and socially least of these, those viewed as less worthy. This turn is something totally unprecedented and new in world history, and in the person of Jesus it seems to constitute a break. Plato opened his school for those who love wisdom, for the philosophers, for those who strive to live an ethical life. Buddha sought his following among the ascetics, among those who had turned their backs on the world. Jesus goes to the children and holds them up as examples to those who are already decidedly moral. When Jesus enters Jerusalem, apparently so many children already know him that they surge toward him and sing hosanna to him in the temple—quite to the consternation of   351 the moral party, the Pharisees. The apocryphal, or extrabiblical, Gospels recount many fantastic stories about how Jesus played with the children in the streets. When mothers bring their children to have Jesus bless them, those who consider themselves to be the real, genuine disciples of Jesus run in and want to drive the women out. It was then that Jesus said, "Let the little children come to me" [*See Matt. 19:14*].

Once when Jesus is out with his disciples and they are arguing over the rewards they will receive for living in his discipleship, Jesus "called a child, whom he put among them, and said, 'Truly I tell you, unless you change and become like children, you will never enter the kingdom of heaven'" (Matt. 18:2–3), or "if any of you put a stumbling block before one of these little ones who believe in me, it would be better for you if a great millstone were

---

5. ["With this phrase, 'the way to the Overman,' and later 'the transvaluation of all values' (see esp. *DBWE* 10:366–367 [*Reader* 80–81]) Bonhoeffer uses key concepts of Nietzsche's anti-Christian later writings, especially from *The Antichrist* and *The Will to Power*. . . . Nonetheless, 'Jesus's unprecedented new understanding of God,' which Bonhoeffer develops in the following discussion, contains a thorough critique of Nietzsche's concept . . . ," *DBWE* 10:350, n. 22.]

hung around your neck and you were thrown into the sea" (Mark 9:42). For Jesus the child is not merely a transitional stage on the way to adulthood, something to be overcome; quite the contrary, he or she is something utterly unique before which the adult should have the utmost respect. For indeed, God is closer to children than to adults. In this sense, Jesus becomes the discoverer of the child. He sees the children and wants to belong to them; who would block his path? God belongs to children, the good news belongs to children, and joy in the kingdom of heaven belongs to children. "Woe to anyone who puts a stumbling block before one of these little ones" [*Matt. 18:6*]. This notion is so utterly alien to the sensibility of antiquity that only one other might seem even more alien, namely, that Jesus, this man of the ruthless either-or, goes not only to children but also to sinners. He traffics with the socially despised, the outcasts, the tax collectors, the deceivers, and the prostitutes. People see this preacher of purity and holiness eating at midday among these people—a horrible sight for a Jewish rabbi—going into their homes, talking with them on the street, defending adulterers before the entire community. They are horrified when they hear him speak out against those who are in fact moral: "Truly I tell you, the tax collectors and the prostitutes are going into the kingdom of God ahead of you" (Matt. 21:31).

352

In one scene, a prostitute comes to Jesus while he is eating, anoints him with ointment, and, overcome by his presence, sinks down on her knees and breaks out in tears. The tears wet his feet, and the woman, in her distress, dries his feet with her hair. To the Pharisees, who take offense at this display, Jesus says: Leave her alone; she has been forgiven much, for she has loved much.

Jesus tells a parable about two brothers. One takes his father's inheritance and squanders it on dissolute living and prostitutes; the other stays at home with the father. When the first remorsefully returns home, his father greets him, the sinner, the lost son, with more love than the son who remained at home ever experienced. Jesus also tells about a Pharisee who prays in the temple and offers all his earnings to God, and about a tax collector who has nothing to bring to God but a broken heart and the words, "God, be merciful to me, a sinner." Jesus concludes with the words: "This man went down to his home justified rather than the other." All traditional values seem to topple, to be revalued. The equation "ethics is religion" seems to teeter when God's emissary really does commit himself to the villains instead of to the righteous. Jesus's own behavior appears profoundly contradictory.

The answer, or rather the paradox, is found in Jesus's unprecedented idea of God. God is utterly superior to the world, utterly transcends it, that is, is removed from the world, is totally different;[6] God is wholly unlike human beings and human nature and is eternally inaccessible to human thought and will. This God wants only one thing from people, namely, that they be nothing before him, and demands nothing from people but that they make absolutely no claims. God wants human beings to be inwardly completely poor, completely unknowing, God wants an empty space in them into which he can move. God wants only the outstretched hand of the beggar so that he can fill it, God wants those who have nothing; God does not want the righteous or those who already know, the saints, but rather the unrighteous, the foolish, the sinners. Every knowledge, every moral claim before God, violates his claim for exclusive honor, encroaches upon his honor and majesty. God is the absolute sovereign and is utterly superior to human beings even with regard to any ultimate human holiness. And from the perspective of human initiative, this chasm remains unbridgeable. Human knowledge of God remains precisely that: human, limited, relative, anthropomorphic knowledge. The human desire to believe remains precisely that: human desire accompanied by ultimately human goals and motives. The human religious path to God leads to the idol of our own hearts, which we have created in our own image. It is not knowledge or morality or religion that leads us to God—even religion is merely a piece of our own bodily nature, as Luther once put it—there is absolutely no path leading from human beings to God, for such a path is ultimately based on human capabilities. The tower of Babel is the arrogance that infringes upon God's honor. If human beings and God are to come together, there is but one way, namely, the way from God to human beings. Here all human claims are at an end; God alone has the honor. As the sovereign, God bestows his grace on whom he will. Who dares grumble if that grace be denied to him? God is the potter, we are the clay, as Paul puts it [*see Rom. 9:21*].

353

God comes to those who make no claims. In Paul's words, "God chose what is foolish in the world to shame the wise; God chose what is weak in the world to shame the strong; God chose what is low and despised in the world, things that are not, to reduce to nothing things that are, so that no flesh might boast in the presence of God" [*1 Cor. 1:27–29*] When people merely listen, merely receive, that is, when they seem to be farthest from God in irreligion and immorality, then God is closest to them. Religion and morality contain the germ of hubris, the quintessential Greek concept of hostility toward the divine, the germ of pride, of arrogance. People think

---

6. ["An echo of the '*ganz andere*' [*totally other*] of Barth's *Epistle to the Romans*," *DBWE* 10:352, n. 33.]

they have discovered deep within themselves something that does after all resemble the divine, or even is divine, something elevating us to the level of the divine, something giving us the right to make claims. In this sense, religion and morality can become the most dangerous enemy of God's coming to human beings, the most dangerous enemy of the Christian message of good news. Thus the Christian message is basically amoral and irreligious, paradoxical as that may sound.

354

With that we have articulated a basic criticism of the most grandiose of all human attempts to advance toward the divine—by way of the church. Christianity conceals within itself a germ hostile to the church. It is far too easy for us to base our claims to God on our own Christian religiosity and our church commitment, and in so doing utterly to misunderstand and distort the Christian idea. And yet Christianity needs the church; that is the paradox we will be able to elucidate and understand only in the next session. Here we encounter the enormous responsibility placed upon the church.

Ethics and religion and church all go in this direction: from the human to God. Christ, however, speaks only and exclusively of the line from God to human beings, not of some human path to God, but only of God's own path to humans. Hence it is also fundamentally wrong to seek a new morality in Christianity. In actual practice, Christ offered hardly any ethical prescriptions not already attested among his contemporary Jewish rabbis or even in pagan literature. The essence of Christianity is found in its message about the sovereign God to whom alone, above the entire world, all honor is due; it is a message about the eternally other, the God removed from the world who from the primal ground of his being has loving compassion for those who render honor to him alone, the God who traverses the path to human beings in order to find there vessels of that honor precisely where human beings are nothing, where they fall silent, where they give space to God alone.

Here the light of eternity falls upon that which is eternally disregarded, the eternally insignificant, the weak, ignoble, unknown, the least of these, the oppressed and despised; here that light radiates out over the houses of the prostitutes and tax collectors—one need only recall Dostoyevsky's Raskolnikov[7]—here that light pours out from eternity upon the working, toiling, sinning masses. The message of grace travels over the dull sultriness of the big cities but remains standing before the houses of those who spiritually speaking are satisfied, knowing, and possessing. It pronounces upon the death of people and nations its eternal: I have loved you from eter-

---

7. ["Dostoyevsky, *Crime and Punishment*; which also appeared under the title *Raskolnikov*," *DBWE* 10:354, n. 37.]

nity; stay with me, and you will live. Christianity preaches the infinite worth of that which is seemingly worthless and the infinite worthlessness of that   355 which is seemingly so valued. What is weak shall become strong through God, and what dies shall live.

Against this understanding of Christianity, something in us rises up in protest, what I would call the Greek spirit, the most severe enemy of Christianity ever: humanism. It is the spirit that we as children of the nineteenth and twentieth centuries have absorbed, as it were, along with our mother's milk. After the Renaissance and the Enlightenment, it reached its high point during the classical period of German literature and philosophy. Born of cultural confidence, it believes in the divine in every human being, in the unlimited potential of the human spirit in the general sense, and in a progressive history moving toward God. The crown of human culture, however, is morality and religion. The moral-religious person (a characteristic combination) is godlike. A divine soul dwells within each human being, and the presence of sin in the world results merely from the subjugation of the soul to the body, a body in which it is trapped as if in a prison.

Such notions are diametrically opposed to Christianity.[8] In the first place, the concept of human beings here is a completely different one. It is not the body that is bad but the will, the spirit; that is, precisely the human soul is bad and is the seat of evil. The assertion of the infinite value of the soul is un-Christian. The New Testament passages that speak of the soul can usually be translated with the term "life." The concept of the soul is Greek; the Jew understands human beings to be a unity of body and spirit that was created by and has fallen away from God. All else derives from this understanding. Nothing in human beings makes them similar to God; but this assertion again levels criticism at the idea of culture, an idea that is, by the way, specifically Greek and not at all oriental or Semitic. Christianity is neither congenial to culture nor does it have faith in progress. It has peered too deeply into the two deepest realities of life. The trembling fear of death and guilt has seized Christianity too powerfully. The seriousness of having to die and of having to bear guilt—this universal human fate is too frightening to allow any hope in solutions deriving from human initiative. Christians see a terrible rift running through the world, a rift that is utterly irreparable through recourse to any human initiative; and they see this rift—thus the tragedy of their lives—still or even for the first time in its full

---

8. ["In this statement Bonhoeffer is clearly distancing himself from Harnack's understanding of the 'infinite value of the human soul' (cf. Harnack, *What Is Christianity*, 63–70)," *DBWE* 10:355, n. 38.]

scope precisely at the heights of human initiative, that is, in culture itself. Greek sensibility understands nothing of such things; from its very inception, gentle fate blessed it with an undivided joy of life. The naive Greek faith in immortality can be seen in this connection. The divine soul must be eternal. By contrast, Christianity knows nothing of such faith in immortality; in its place, however, it does indeed entertain hope in a resurrection of the dead. Although human beings die in body and soul, the command of the sovereign God calls the dead back to life, to a genuinely new, genuinely pure, holy life. We are led again and again back into the depths of the Christian understanding of God. Wherever the Greek spirit is regnant, the Christian idea of God is not understood.

The religious consequences of the Greek spirit ultimately lead to mysticism. Mysticism and the good news, however, mutually and radically exclude each other. Mysticism is the religious attempt to attain, in various forms, unity with the deity on one's own initiative and based on one's own divine potential. Such unity can be intellectual, voluntaristic, or emotional, but it is in any case unchristian because it overlooks the humanly unbridgeable gulf between God and human beings, a gulf that remains as that between the creator and the creature even when God does indeed incline toward human beings. Humanism and mysticism, the seemingly most beautiful blossoms put forth by the Christian religion, extolled today as the highest ideals of the human spirit, indeed often as the crown itself of the Christian idea—it is precisely the Christian idea itself that must reject them as an apotheosis of the creature and as such as a challenge to the honor belonging to God alone. The deity of humanism, of the idea of humanity, and of mysticism is the idol of human wishes; only the idea of God presented by Christianity orients those human wishes to itself rather than the reverse.

By turning against ethics and religion and church as human knowledge of God, against humanism and mysticism with their cultural confidence and idolization of creatures, we seem to have robbed humanity of its highest possession. Only in the next session will we be able to show how Christianity gives all this its perfectly limited, relative due once more. The first thing we must do, however, is radically to turn away from all this. What is Christianity's counteroffer? Merely another religion? A new cultural idea? Has it merely pointed out a path to God not yet taken? No, the Christian idea is the path of God to human beings, and its visible manifestation is the cross. At this point, we generally shake our heads and turn away from Christianity. It was Paul, we point out, who first placed the cross into the center of the Christian message; Jesus said nothing of such things. And yet the correct understanding of Christ's cross is nothing more than the most severe intensification of Jesus's own idea of God, the historically visible form, as it were, adopted by that idea. God comes to people who have nothing but space for God, and the language of Christianity calls this void, this emptiness in human beings: "faith."[9] In Jesus of Nazareth, the bearer of God's revelation, God inclines toward the sinner. Jesus seeks the company of sinners, follows them with limitless love; Jesus wants to be where human beings are no longer anything. The meaning of Jesus's life is the documentation of this divine will toward the sinner, toward the unworthy. God's love is wherever Jesus is. This documentation, however, acquires its true seriousness only when Jesus or God's love not only is present where human beings are mired in sin and misery, but when Jesus also takes upon himself that which stands above every person's life, namely, death; that is, when Jesus, who is God's love, genuinely dies. Only thus can human beings be assured that God's love will accompany and lead them through death. Jesus's death on the cross of the criminal, however, shows that divine love extends even to the death of the criminal, and when Jesus dies on the cross with the cry, "My God, my God, why have you forsaken me?" [*Matt. 27:46; Ps. 22:1*] it shows once more that God's eternal love does not abandon us even when we despair and feel forsaken by God. Jesus genuinely dies despairing in his own work and in God, and yet precisely that situation constitutes the crown of his message; God loves us so much that with us, for us, and as a documentation of that love, God accepts and experiences death itself. And only because Jesus in the humiliation of the cross proves both his own love and God's love does resurrection follow death. Death cannot keep back love; love is stronger than death. The meaning of Good Friday and of Easter Sunday is that God's path to human beings leads back to God. Thus Jesus's idea of God is summed up in Paul's interpretation of the cross; thus the cross becomes the center and the paradoxical emblem of the Christian message. A king who dies on the cross must be the king of a rather strange kingdom. Only those who understand the profound paradox of the cross can also understand the whole meaning of Jesus's assertion: my kingdom is not from this world. Remaining faithful to the idea of God that led him to the cross meant declining the royal crown offered to him and renouncing the idea of the "Imperium Romanum" [*Roman Empire*] that tempted him on that path.

This understanding of Christ's cross also answers another urgent question. What are we to make of other religions? Are they nothing compared to Christianity? The answer is that it is not the Christian religion itself that,

---

9. ["... Here Bonhoeffer's critique of religion, in particular of Christianity, echoes Barth's treatment in *Romans* that was further expounded in *Church Dogmatics* 1/2:280–361," *DBWE* 10:357, n. 39.]

357

358   as a religion, is something divine. It is itself merely one human path toward God, just as is the Buddhist and the other religions, albeit, of course, of a different sort.

Christ is not the bringer of a new religion, but the bringer of God. Hence as the impossible path from human beings to God, the Christian religion stands alongside other religions. Christians can never boast of their own Christian religiosity, for it, too, remains humanly all-too-human. Christians do, however, live from God's grace, grace that comes to us and to every person who opens up to it and comes to understand it in Christ's cross. Thus Christ's gift is not the Christian religion but God's grace and love, which culminate in the cross.

And now we must address the question: What does the cross say to *us, today*? Can it replace the ideals of humanism? The cross and the twentieth century is the problem. Here we shift from scholarly concerns to personal concerns. Like the Roman imperial age, our own age thirsts for something ultimate, for substance that transcends all that is customary and banal; it thirsts for redemption. This situation is attested by the youth movement[10] and by phenomena such as sectarianism, mysticism, anthroposophy, the so-called occult sciences, as well as—we hope—by the unquenchable desire of our age for sensation and entertainment. It is a thirst that only becomes more burning with every drink. And now we ask: Is not the expression concerning the transitoriness of all human wishes and concerning the enormous dying in the world written on the brow of our wrecked age? Do not all of us who have a world war behind us, who live in an age of horrific economic competition, an age in which all values and ideals are in decline—do not all of us bear an enormous guilt whose weight threatens to burden us down to the ground? And does the cross have nothing to say to us in this situation, the cross that speaks about the compassionate, revivifying love of God toward those who die and those burdened by guilt? Does looking at the cross of Jesus Christ not open up our gaze far beyond our own age to that time when God will make everything new again? And one more thing: Anthroposophy and mysticism and sectarianism all make claims on people before they get to God that not everyone can fulfill (humanism did this as well). Christianity is completely different in this sense. It requires neither

---

10. ["The youth movement (*Jugendbewegung*) was an idealistic countercultural movement widely influential among the post–World War I German youth of Bonhoeffer's generation. Especially strong among the bourgeois, it emphasized nature and values considered authentic as opposed to the upper-middle-class lifestyle . . . Bonhoeffer critically observes that the youth of the German colony in Barcelona were untouched by this important cultural phase . . . ," *DBWE* 10:63, n. 24.]

training nor any specialized aptitude for a person to understand the depths
of life and of the deity. It requires merely that we acknowledge the exclusive
honor due the eternal God and acknowledge our own nothingness before
God. It speaks of God's grace toward the sins of the big cities, about God's   359
love where misery and guilt accumulate in frightening proportions, where
calloused hands perhaps are clenched fists, in defiance of fate. You, human
being, no matter who you are, you are God's child, you are included in
God's love, out of the pure, incomprehensible grace of God; accept this
word, believe in it, trust in his rule rather than in yourself or in your own
party, rather than in your own work or your own religion. God does as he
wills. Turn your misery into God's blessed presence, and from within your
guilt and distress hear the voice of the eternal, living God.

It is said that before the battle that ultimately brought him victory and
established his rule, the Emperor Constantine saw the sign of the cross
emblazoned across the heavens with the words ἐν τούτῳ νικᾷς . . . [*in this
sign you will be victorious*]. Spiritual battles of unusual proportions are taking
place among our people; the birth of modernity is accompanied by severe
labor pains; our age senses this, but the moment of decision is nearing.
Will we conquer what is oppressing us, our fate, or will we be defeated?
Will the twentieth century be the hour of death for Europe and Germany?
Let us point to one thing here, to the sign of the cross. The God of the
world will incline toward us, we who are dust before God, if we but accord
honor to God alone, if we but entrust ourselves to God alone. God will
cause grace and compassion to radiate over the dark guilt of our century
and the human race; God will enter into our time, live with us, for us, even
unto death, taking the path to human beings all the way to the cross.

German people, that is your God, the God who formed you and will
abide with you. In your struggles with fate, keep your eyes on the cross, the
most wonderful emblem of your God, and be assured that only in this sign
will you be victorious!

5. Basic Questions
of a Christian Ethic

DBWE 10:359–378

As Clifford Green notes in the introduction to DBWE *10, "Bonhoeffer's third lecture . . . contains some characteristic ideas that will continue to be important in the* Ethics, *his magnum opus, some views that will change through the next decade, and some that will mercifully disappear forever."[1] Among the characteristic ideas is the rejection of ethical principles, which are a way to "control my own relationship with God," in favor of a life in "immediate relationship with God." The latter, Bonhoeffer argues, is compatible with the paradoxical, amoral character of Christianity introduced in the previous lecture; the commandments of Jesus do not deliver moral principles but rather place the believer in immediate relationship to God where the human will can be guided by God's will. Among the ideas that "mercifully disappear forever" are Bonhoeffer's appeal to the people or nation (Volk) as an order of creation, and the "conventionally Lutheran"[2] dismissal of the nonviolent Sermon on the Mount, both of which support Bonhoeffer's justification of war. In the years following this lecture, Bonhoeffer deepened his appreciation of the Sermon on the Mount (see especially* Discipleship) *and spoke out against those who relied on orders of creation to justify war.[3]*

359   In speaking today about basic questions of a Christian ethic, we do not
intend to embark on the essentially hopeless attempt to present universally
valid Christian norms and commandments applicable to contemporary
360   ethical questions. We intend instead merely to examine and to participate
in the peculiar movement of ethical problems in today's world from the per-

---

1. [DBWE *10:10.*]
2. [DB-ER, *119–120.*]
3. [DBWE *12:258–262* (Reader *128–134*).]

spective of basic Christian ideas. The deepest reason why we confine our-selves in this manner is that, as we will see in greater depth later, there are not and cannot be Christian norms and principles of a moral nature. Only in the actual execution of a given action do the concepts of "good" and "bad" apply, that is, only in the given present moment; hence any attempt to explicate principles is like trying to draw a bird in flight. But more on that later.

Ethics is a matter of blood and a matter of history. It did not simply descend to earth from heaven. Rather, it is a child of the earth, and for that reason its face changes with history as well as with the renewal of blood, with the transition between generations. There is a German ethic as well as a French ethic and an American ethic. None is more or less ethical than the other, for all remain bound to history and all are [. . .][4] decisively influ-enced today by the terrible experience of the world war and by how that war is viewed from various perspectives. The only common feature is that this experience has stirred up the depths of the people's soul and that now things are everywhere emerging that have hitherto gone unnoticed and have remained concealed in the depths of the sea. In Germany the experience of war was joined by the experience of revolution, and the one absolutely unmistakable result seems to be that these historical events have prompted a hitherto unprecedented revolution in morals. If I see it correctly, we can distinguish four groups of people in working Germany today, each of which has arrived at a different ethical ideology through recent historical develop-ments. The first are those whose years of development and maturation lie before the beginning of the war; then those whom sooner or later the war itself brought to maturity; then the generation of youth associated with the revolution, those whose awakening and development took place between 1918 and, say, 1923; and finally, let us not forget those to whom the future belongs, those who know war and revolution only from hearsay and who are now eighteen to twenty years old. Hence the rapid sequence of events spanning fewer than twenty years has produced four spiritual or intellectual generations, and if we are to understand the unprecedented confusion with regard to the ethical problems in their broadest scope within contemporary Germany, we must constantly keep in mind that not two, but four different generations are now struggling with one another.[5]

361

---

4. ["Illegible," *DBWE* 10:360, n. 3.]

5. ["The generational problem as a specifically German problem following World War I still informs the presentation in March 1933 (*DBWE* 12:268–282 [*Reader* 359–369])," *DBWE* 10:361, n. 4.]

The significance of the revolutionary year 1918 only marginally derives from the political turn in Germany's history. The enormous intellectual revolution that erupted and in which we still find ourselves has had incomparably greater consequences. It would be difficult to find a period in history that has experienced as radical a change in, say, literature as has the period between 1910 and approximately 1925. All that seemed solid has become soft, all that seemed certain has become uncertain, all that seemed self-evident has become questionable—politically, literarily, philosophically, ethically. This onslaught began and was carried and enthusiastically received by young people. Despite the unmistakable fact that unprincipled circles exploited and debased the excitement and lack of clarity of these spirits, one can reasonably say that the deepest foundation of this intellectual movement was a genuine and sincere idealism. The central idea emerging again and again from all this literature is that of truth. The intent is to mount an assault on a culture that in the broader sense has become inwardly untrue, and in so doing to break the bonds that fetter truth. This is what one hears everywhere. Unless one insists on remaining utterly skeptical, this intent does guarantee the profoundly ethical character of the movement.

Consider the so-called belles lettres as but one example. Without a shadow of a doubt, never before in all of world history have so many and such crudely obscene things been written or been brought to the stage as they have today. Equally certain is that a great many authors as well as readers and spectators seek nothing more in such material than to satisfy their own derailed imagination. And yet it would be unfair for us to present this as our final judgment. Rather, it is a matter of the aforementioned need to confront the various aspects of life honestly, truthfully, even if such things offend public morals. An almost naive idealism permeates this literary genre; at the same time, though, we cannot deny the presence of an ethical concern within the overall undertaking, even if we believe it to be moving in the wrong direction.[6]

The same seems to apply to the youth problem. The freedom of youth in so many aspects of life, a freedom the prewar generation naturally finds almost incomprehensible, is based on the desire of youth to avoid imposing unsuitable fetters on its life merely because the previous generation may have borne such fetters. And what seems to overstep the mark can often

362

6. ["The period Bonhoeffer is criticizing here (1910–1925) coincides with the period known as 'expressionism' in German literature, which included authors such as Trakl, Lasker-Schüler, Benn, and others, whom Bonhoeffer avoided reading his entire life," *DBWE* 10:362, n. 5.]

be attributed simply to the previously mentioned naive idealism. I am not even remotely suggesting, however, that everything in Germany today looks wonderful and full of hope. Quite the contrary. This movement has stirred up so much filth along the way that we can now hardly see through the murky waters.

That the contemporary ethical will also assumes such forms today is profoundly disturbing, and this should be taken seriously, since, truth be told, we are indeed still far from finding solutions to the problems that confront us. But the situation is this, that there is a will toward new ethical formation and fullness of life, and the only thing lacking is the correct point of departure. Our task, no more and no less, should be the attempt to show this point of departure.

We said earlier that there is a German, an American, and a French ethic, since ethics is a matter of blood and history. But what about the idea of a so-called Christian ethic? Are these two words not perhaps intrinsically utterly incompatible, "Christian" and "ethic"? Does such a combination not secularize the idea of what is Christian? Does the so-called Christian ethic not thereby become merely one alongside others, one of many, perhaps a bit better or even a bit worse, but in any case now drawn wholly into historical relativity? If so, then alongside the German ethic there is also a Christian ethic, without either being in a position to claim superiority.

Hence talking about a Christian ethic while at the same time maintaining the exclusive claim of such an ethic will apparently be an extremely awkward undertaking.

During the previous lecture, we encountered an assertion that was perhaps not yet entirely clear, namely, that Christianity is basically amoral, that Christianity and ethics represent two entities that at first are not entirely compatible and in fact are quite disparate.[7] And why? Because Christianity speaks of the exclusive path from God to human beings from within God's own compassionate love toward the unholy, the sinful, while ethics speaks of the path from human beings to God, about the encounter between the holy God and the holy human being; in other words, because the Christian message speaks of grace while ethics speaks of righteousness. 363

Because there are innumerable human paths to God, there are also innumerable ethics. But there is but one path from God to human beings, and that is the path of love in Christ, the path of the cross, as we saw during the last session.[8]

---

7. [See *DBWE* 10:354 (*Reader* 68).]
8. [See *DBWE* 10:356 (*Reader* 70).]

The question of Christianity is not the question of good and evil among people but the question whether God wishes to be gracious or not. The Christian message stands beyond good and evil,[9] and this is how it must be; for if God's grace is made dependent on human beings according to the categories of good and evil, this would constitute a human claim on God. This, however, would challenge the power and honor due exclusively to God.

One particularly profound feature of the old story of the fall is that it was caused by eating from the tree of the knowledge of good and evil. The primal—let us say, childlike—community between human beings and God stands beyond this knowledge of good and evil; it knows only one thing: God's limitless love for human beings.

Hence the discovery of the world beyond good and evil is by no means to be attributed to the enemy of Christianity Friedrich Nietzsche, whose polemic against the self-righteousness of Christianity derived from this perspective. It belongs rather to the original, albeit concealed material of the Christian message.

If our line of argument is correct to this point, then the conclusion seems quite clear. Christianity and ethics have absolutely nothing to do with each other. There is no Christian ethic. From the idea of Christianity, there is absolutely no transition to the idea of ethics. And yet this line of reasoning clearly leads us off track. We simply must raise the question: Why, then, are all the Gospels and the entire New Testament nonetheless full of obviously ethical regulations? What is the Sermon on the Mount doing in the New Testament?

The question is as obvious as it is serious. What is the meaning of the so-called New Testament ethic?

364   Since the third and fourth centuries, numerous movements have arisen presenting the proclamation of a new ethic as the center of Christianity; the new commandment, of course, was the commandment of love.[10] Such a view, though doubtless extremely shallow, was possible and even tenable into the nineteenth century. Since then, however, history-of-religions research and literary scholarship have thoroughly examined the rabbinic literature both contemporary with and prior to the time of Jesus as well as the contemporaneous philosophical-ethical tractates of the philosophical

---

9. ["Cf. Nietzsche, *Beyond Good and Evil*," *DBWE* 10:363, n. 8.]

10. ["Bonhoeffer is probably referring to the Novatians (third century) and the Donatists (fourth century) in the ancient church. The commandment of love as a new commandment, however, better fits the Marcionites (second century), the subject of the last great work of Bonhoeffer's teacher Adolf von Harnack; see Harnack, *Marcion*, esp. 'The Redeemer God as the Good God,' 81–92," *DBWE* 10:364, n. 10.]

schools in the West. The results clearly show that such statements about the New Testament are demonstrably false. Rather than being something specifically or uniquely Christian, the commandment of love was already widely acknowledged and familiar at the time of Jesus.

The first thing we should notice is that the Synoptic Gospels very rarely mention it. We are all familiar with the passage in which Jesus is asked about the highest commandment and offers the twofold response, "'You shall love the Lord your God with all your heart, and with all your soul, and with all your mind.' . . . And a second is like it: 'You shall love your neighbor as yourself'" [*Matt. 22:37–39*]. We also recall Jesus's words concerning love of one's enemies: "Love your enemies, bless those who curse you, do good to those who hate you and pray for those who persecute you, so that you may be children of your Father in heaven; for he makes his sun rise on the evil and on the good, and sends rain on the righteous and on the unrighteous. For if you love those who love you, what reward do you have? Do not even the tax collectors do the same?" [*Matt. 5:44–46*]. If the proclamation of this particular commandment really had been the focal point of Jesus's whole ministry, he would have commenced at precisely this point ever anew. But he did not. This same conclusion emerges with unequivocal clarity from a comparison of the words of Jesus with those of Jewish rabbis and pagan philosophers, which often resemble one another even in their wording. When asked what the highest commandment is, Rabbi Hillel responded: "Love your neighbor as yourself. That is the highest commandment." Another advised: "What you would not want to happen to yourself, do not to others." The Roman philosopher Seneca urged us "not to tire of working for the common good, of helping individuals, and of providing help even to our enemies." To the objection, "But anger gives us a release! Requiting pain refreshes us!" he responds, "No; it is honorable in the case of good deeds to repay good with good, but not injustice with injustice. It is despicable to allow oneself to be conquered in the first instance and despicable to conquer in the second."[11]

But what is now left of a Christian ethic? Does the Sermon on the Mount really have nothing new to say to us? It has nothing "new" in the sense of new demands, but it does have something completely different to offer. The significance of all of Jesus's ethical commandments is rather to say to people: You stand before the face of God, God's grace rules over you; but you are at the disposal of someone else in the world. You must act and behave

365

---

11. ["Here Bonhoeffer is drawing on work he did during his university years, esp. his seminar paper on *1 Clement*: concerning Hillel, see *DBWE* 9:245, n. 207 . . . ," *DBWE* 10:365, n. 13.]

such that in each of your actions you are mindful of also acting before God, mindful that God has a certain will and wants to see that will done. Each particular moment will reveal the nature of that will. You must merely be perfectly clear that your own will must in every instance be accommodated to the divine will; your will must be surrendered if the divine will is to be realized. Hence to the extent that acting before God requires utter renunciation of personal demands and claims from us, Christian ethical acts can be characterized as love. This assertion is not a new principle, however, but derives rather from the status of human beings before God. There are no ethical principles enabling Christians, as it were, to make themselves moral. Instead, one has only the decisive moment at hand, that is, every moment that is of potential ethical value.[12] Never, however, can yesterday decisively influence my moral actions today. I must rather always establish anew my immediate relationship with God's will. I will do something again today not because it seemed the right thing to do yesterday, but because today, too, God's will has pointed me in that direction.

This ongoing relationship to God's will is the great moral renewal Jesus brought about, the dismissal of principles, of fundamental rules—in biblical terms, the law. And precisely this dismissal is a consequence of the Christian idea of God. For if there were indeed a universally valid moral law, following it would involve taking the path from human beings to God. If I have principles, I feel I am secured *sub specie aeternitatis* [*under the aspect of eternity*]. In that case, I would control my own relationship with God, as it were, and there could be ethical action without any immediate relationship with God. But the most important aspect is that I would then become a slave to my principles and would be surrendering the most precious human possession, my freedom. When Jesus places people immediately under God, new and afresh at each moment, he restores to humanity the immense gift that it had lost, freedom.

366

Christian ethical action is action out of freedom, out of the freedom of those who have nothing in themselves and everything in their God, those who ever anew have their actions confirmed and reinforced by eternity. The New Testament speaks of this freedom in great words. "Now the Lord is the Spirit, and where the Spirit of the Lord is, there is freedom" [*2 Cor. 3:17*]. John says that "if you continue in my word, you are truly my disciples; and you will know the truth, and the truth will make you free. . . . So if the Son makes you free, you will be free indeed" [*John 8:31b-32, 36*] Or, "The

12. ["Cf. this idea in *Sanctorum Communio, DBWE* 1:48–49 (*Reader* 23–24)," *DBWE* 10:365, n. 14.]

creation itself will be set free from its bondage to decay and will obtain the freedom of the glory of the children of God" [*Rom. 8:20–21*]. Or, "For freedom Christ has set us free. Stand firm, therefore, and do not submit again to a yoke of slavery" [*Gal. 5:1*]. We could cite many more examples. Christ is the bringer of the freedom to become free from the world, free for eternity. There is now no other law for Christians except the law of freedom, as the New Testament puts it paradoxically [*cf. James 1:25, 2:12*], not a universally valid law imposed by others or even by themselves. Those who surrender their freedom also surrender their status as Christians. Christians stand in freedom, without any backing, before both God and the world; they alone bear the entire responsibility for how they will deal with this gift of freedom. Through precisely this freedom, however, Christians become creative in their ethical actions. Acting according to principles is unproductive and merely reflects or copies the law. Acting in freedom is creative. Christians draw the forms of their ethical activity out of eternity itself, as it were, put these forms with sovereignty in the world, as deed, as their own creations born of the freedom of God's children. Christians create their own standards for good and evil; only Christians themselves provide the justification for their acts, just as they alone bear responsibility for them. Christians create new tables, new decalogues, as Nietzsche said of the Overman. Indeed, Nietzsche's Overman is not, as he imagined, the opposite of the Christian; without realizing it, Nietzsche imbued the Overman with many of the fea- 367 tures of the free Christian as described and conceived by both Paul and Luther. Traditional morals—even if propagated for Christians—or public opinion can never provide the standards for the action of Christians.

Christians act according to how God's will seems to direct them, without looking sideways at others, that is, without considering what is usually called morals. No one but Christians and God, however, can know whether they are indeed acting rightly or wrongly. Ethical decisions lead us into the most profound solitude, the solitude in which a person stands before the living God. Here no one can help us, no one can bear part of the responsibility; here God imposes a burden on us that we must bear alone. Only in the realization that we have been addressed by God, that God is making a claim on us, does our self awaken. Only through God's call do I become this "self," isolated from all other people, called to account by God, confronted, alone, by eternity. And precisely because I am face-to-face with God in this solitude, I alone can know what is right or wrong for me personally.

There are no acts that are bad in and of themselves; even murder can be sanctified. There is only faithfulness to or deviation from God's will. There is no law with a specific content, but only the law of freedom, that is, bearing responsibility alone before God and oneself.

The law has been overcome once and for all. It follows from the Christian idea of God that there can be no more law. It is from this same perspective that we must thus understand the ethical commandments and apparent laws we find in the New Testament itself.

It is the most serious misunderstanding to turn the commandments of the Sermon on the Mount once again into a law by applying them literally to the present. Not only is such transference meaningless because impracticable, it also goes against the spirit of Christ, who brought freedom from the law. The whole life of someone like Count Tolstoy, and many others beside him, was based on this misunderstanding. The New Testament contains no ethical prescription that we are supposed to adopt literally or even that we could so adopt. The letter kills, but the Spirit gives life, as Paul put it in a familiar passage [*2 Cor 3:6*], meaning that the Spirit is found only in the execution of actions, in the present; a fixed Spirit is no Spirit at all. Hence ethics is found only in the execution of a deed, not in the letter, that is, in the law. The Spirit that is indeed at work in our own ethical actions, however, is to be the Holy Spirit. The Holy Spirit is found only in the present, in ethical decision, not in fixed moral regulations or in an ethical principle. Hence Jesus's new commandments can never be taken as new ethical principles; they are to be understood in their spirit, not in their letter. Nor is this view merely an excuse to avoid an otherwise uncomfortable situation; the idea of freedom and the concept of God that Jesus articulated demand it. The familiar radical edge that Jesus's demands have acquired derives from the radical renunciation of one's own person and one's own will that is required of Christians in ethical decision before God. But not every one of Jesus's behavioral rules is valid for us; merely imitating them would be slavish and unfree.

From all these considerations it follows that one absolutely cannot speak about specific ethical problems from the Christian perspective. There is absolutely no possibility for establishing universally valid principles, since each individual moment lived before God can confront us with completely unexpected decisions. Hence for our own age, too, we can only repeat that we must put ourselves under God's will when making ethical decisions and consider our actions *sub specie aeternitatis* [*under the aspect of eternity*]; then regardless of how things go, they will go correctly.

From day to day and from hour to hour, however, we are confronted by utterly new situations in which we are supposed to make decisions and in which we repeatedly have the surprising and terrifying experience that God's will as a matter of fact does not reveal itself to us as clearly as we might have hoped. Because God's will seems to contradict itself, because two of God's orders seem to conflict, we find ourselves in a position of hav-

ing to choose not between good and evil but between evil and evil.[13] It is
here that we encounter the real, most difficult problems of ethics. And in   369
the following discussion what we have just said should make it clear that
we will not be able to present any universally valid decisions that might be
designated as uniquely Christian; to do so would merely be to present new
principles, bringing us into conflict with the law of freedom. All we can
do is examine the concrete situation of decision and point out one of the
possibilities for decision that emerges there. The decision demanded in
reality, however, must be made in freedom in the concrete situation by the
individual involved.

There is one set of problems that is never settled, since it suffers from
the internal contradictions of two divine orders. The first general question
involves the relationship between historical development and the divine
commandment of love. Here the problem of national expansion, growth,
war, and the struggle of economic competition unfolds before us. The second question involves the relation between love and truth, love and righteousness, both of whose origin we seek in God; this question in its own
turn involves the questions of social forms and of the administration of
justice. And finally the question that is more burning than any other today:
the problem "nature and spirit," whose common origin again is God; or,
more precisely, the problem of sexuality.[14]

The difficulty in solving these problems is that of finding a hierarchy in
the divine orders. With what right do I put the commandment of love above
that of truth, or vice versa? We again find a point of departure in the Christian idea of God, that is, by making our decision in immediate relationship
with God's will, rather than isolated from God. In every instance the idea
of the cross, as the example of God's love actualized even unto death, determines our actions, since it places divine love above all other characteristics
of God. Now, the possibility always exists that the commandment of love   370
itself might seem self-contradictory; here we encounter that particular problem that has been discussed again and again, the problem of war. During
the war and after the war, we heard, and we are still hearing, that the entire
weakness and wretchedness of Christianity, its churches and followers, was

---

13. [". . . After 1932, when the concept of the 'divine order of creation' moved one-
sidedly toward a nationalistic discussion of the separateness and differences between
peoples, Bonhoeffer moved away from the concept. See *DBWE* 11:351–353; see also Martin Rüter and Ilse Tödt in the editors' afterword to *Creation and Fall* (*DBWE* 3:148–149) .
. .," *DBWE* 10:368–369, n. 25.]

14. [". . . On 'nature and spirit,' see Green, *Bonhoeffer*, 197–199, 325–326, and note 98,"
DBWE 10:369 n. 27.]

revealed in the inability to prevent the war; even more, it is said that if Christians really wanted to be true Christians, they would resolutely have refused to serve in the war. Just as various Christian sects indeed paid for their Christian position by going to prison, so also would it be the duty of those who seriously call themselves Christians to accept the most horrible punishments rather than go to war. For it is clearly written: You shall not kill; you shall not requite evil with evil; rather if anyone strikes you on the right cheek, turn the other also; and if anyone wants to sue you and take your coat, give your cloak as well; and if anyone forces you to go one mile, go also the second mile [*Matt. 5:39–41*]. You have heard that it was said to those of ancient times, You shall not murder; and whoever murders shall be liable to judgment. But I say to you that if you are angry with a brother, you will be liable to judgment [*Matt. 5:21–22*]. You have heard that it was said that you should love your neighbor and hate your enemy. But I say to you, Love your enemies and pray for those who persecute you, so that you may be children of your Father in heaven [*Matt. 5:43–45*]. For what will it profit them if they gain the whole world but forfeit their souls [*Matt. 16:26*]? Thus do we find it clearly and unequivocally stated in the New Testament, and no amount of quibbling will help: You shall not resist against evil; you shall not kill.

And now one dares to justify war somehow from the Christian perspective? Now millions of Christian men go to war, and not just because they are compelled, but presenting it as God's will? They hold services of worship in the field and dare drag God and the holy name of Jesus Christ into this horrific murder? War is nothing but murder. War is a crime. No Christian can go to war. This case for this seems entirely clear and convincing, yet it suffers at the central issue: it is not concrete and as a result does not look into the depths of Christian decision. It invokes the commandment not to kill and believes that commandment to be the solution.

Here, however, we are overlooking the decisive dilemma that precisely when my own people are attacked, the commandment of love does extend at least as far as defending them as it does to the commandment not to
371 kill one's enemy. It would be an utter perversion of one's ethical sensibility to believe that my first duty is to love my enemy and precisely in so doing to surrender my neighbor to destruction, in the most concrete sense. It is simply not possible to love or, as the case may be, to protect both my enemy and my people. I am confronted by the concrete situation of surrendering to destruction either my brother or my enemy. I am put in this dilemma at the very moment when war is declared against me, that is, when I either go to war or do not go to war. If out of conviction I do not go, then I am leaving my people in the lurch in their hour of distress, and am doing so by citing Christ, who said to me love your neighbor as yourself, which doubt-

less means love your neighbor more than your fearful conscience, love your neighbor first and foremost; what then follows is a secondary question.

Indeed, is not my enemy just as much my neighbor as is my biological brother? Is not the great deed of Christianity precisely that it leveled these distinctions, through the powerful notion of universal brotherhood? Although this is doubtless the case, these questions derive from a consideration of principles rather than from the concrete situation. If ever I find myself in the distressing situation of having to decide whether to expose my biological brother, my biological mother, to the hand of the attacker, or to raise my own hand against the enemy, then the moment itself will doubtless tell me which of these two is and must be my neighbor, including before the eyes of God. God gave me my mother, my people. For what I have, I thank my people; what I am, I am through my people, and so what I have should also belong to my people; that is in the divine order of things, for God created the peoples. If for a single dangerous moment I do not act, then I am doing nothing other than surrendering my neighbors.

And now one more thing. Christians who go to war will not hate their enemy, since they cannot hate in any case. In battle they will still pray for their enemies and for their souls when they deliver their bodies to death and will still bless those enemies when they themselves, the Christians, are 372 mortally wounded by them. For those enemies are in the same distress as are the Christians themselves; the enemies, too, are defending their mothers, their children, their people.

The situation seems clear to me. In such cases, I no longer have the choice between good and evil; regardless of which decision I make, that decision will soil me with the world and its laws. I will take up arms with the terrible knowledge of doing something horrible, and yet knowing I can do no other. I will defend my brother, my mother, my people, and yet I know that I can do so only by spilling blood; but love for my people will sanctify murder, will sanctify war. As a Christian, I will suffer from the entire dreadfulness of war. My soul will bear the entire burden of responsibility in its full gravity. I will try to love my enemies against whom I am sworn to the death, as only Christians can love their brothers. And yet I will have to do to those enemies what my love and gratitude toward my own people commands me to do, the people into whom God bore me. And finally I will recognize that Christian decisions are made only within the ongoing relationship with God, within a constantly renewed surrender of oneself to the divine will. I can rest assured that even if the world does violence to my conscience, I can make only one decision, namely, the one to which God leads me in the sacred hour of encounter between my will and God's will, in the hour in which God conquers my will.

If we examine once more the argumentation of the other party, we find the decisive point is that they make the New Testament commandments into new laws and in so doing enslave themselves to those laws, whereas they should be making decisions in freedom. They judge according to the letter rather than according to the spirit of Christ. They act according to principles rather than from the concrete situation of crisis with which God confronts me. Sparks, however, are not created in empty space; sparks are created when hard stones strike against each other. The sparks of the Holy Spirit flash not in ideas and principles but in the necessary decision of the moment.

373   Admittedly, this discussion does not yet exhaust the problem of war. One might also ask whether war can be justified from the Christian ethical perspective when one starts the war oneself. This question, however, leads back to a broader problem, to the question of the relation between history and God, people and God, growth and God. Peoples are like individuals. At first they are immature and need guidance. Then they grow into the blossom of youth, mature into adults, and die. This situation is neither good nor bad in and of itself, yet profound questions are concealed here. For growth involves expansion; an increase in strength involves pushing aside other individuals. In that respect the life of an individual person is no different than that of a people. Every people, however, has within itself a call from God to create its history, to enter into the struggle that is the life of nations. This call must be heeded amid the growth and development so that it takes place before the face of God. God calls a people to diversity, to struggle, to victory. Strength also comes from God, and power, and victory, for God creates youth in the individual as well as in nations, and God loves youth, for God himself is eternally young and strong and victorious. And fear and weakness will be conquered by courage and strength. Now, should a people experiencing God's call in its own life, in its own youth, and in its own strength, should not such a people also be allowed to follow that call even if it disregards the lives of other peoples? God is the Lord of history; and if a people bends in humility to this holy will guiding history, then with God in its youth and strength it can overcome the weak and disheartened. Then God will be with it. The determination as to when this moment has arrived for a people can and may only be made by human beings who are conscious of the grave responsibility for what they do, surrendering their own selfish will to the divine will that guides world history.

     The same applies to the individual. If our own intellectual growth, our own intellectual youth, our own power leads us beyond others, that is, if

374   through God's actions with us we find ourselves inwardly prompted to separate from a friend, there is no room for sentimentality. God wants us cou-

rageously to resolve to go beyond the other even if by moving beyond the other person we hurt that person. For God wills strength of life, not anxiety. And it is God who will find a way of amply healing the wounds he inflicts through us, that we inflict for his sake. This is the Christian criticism of the assertion—an assertion so often understood in the manner of the petit bourgeois—concerning faithfulness and gratitude and love. Live from God and you will live strongly, and even if you do not notice it, you will live from love.

History and love, two entities born of God and yet apparently not always reconcilable in this world, only reach their synthesis in eternity. The history of our life—and our life ought to have a history if it is to be something other than a divine life—often takes us down paths seemingly at odds with love; but if we remain on this path with God, we will also always remain on the path of love.

The problem of history, however, conceals yet another question of great importance today, namely, how one is to judge contemporary economic life ethically. Perhaps some of us are already familiar with Friedrich Naumann's *Briefe über Religion* [*Letters on Religion*] in which he speaks almost despairingly about this problem, suggesting that Christian ethics leaves us completely in the lurch here. Such might be the case, however, only if one understands Christian ethics as individual commandments and laws, something inapplicable in this case. If by contrast we understand Christian ethics to be rooted in responsibility before God, such an ethic will never fail us. Put briefly, the situation is the following. We find ourselves today in an economic and business climate in which smaller parties must be ruined by the larger ones, and in which we ourselves, if we are to participate in economic life, are compelled to be part of all this. Can a Christian responsibly be a businessperson in this sense? We often hear of a double morality, one for personal life and one for business. But this assertion is obviously impossible because we have but *one* conscience, which we must obey in all situations. The question is merely whether with this *one* conscience we can also be business people. The first consideration is that the way things are, our economic and business life is indispensable to our people; moreover, Christians are obliged to do what they can for the welfare of their neighbors, that is, to become engaged wherever there is something to be done. The question is 375 merely whether they are serving some broader purpose with their business lives. If so, then here, too, one is choosing not between *good* and *evil*; rather, what is recognized as the good, right decision also leads us to engage in harsh actions strongly resembling evil ones. Precisely here, too, we end up in distressing situations that require the ever-renewed relationship with the divine will. In such cases Christians will find ways to help, if such help is possible, even when ruining someone else in business. And if they can no longer help, they will go silent in reverential, humble astonishment before God's strange ways with humanity and pray: Give us all this day our daily bread [*Matt. 6:11*].

We are living in a strange world, and yet we do want to be Christians. Fleeing that world does not help; the only thing that helps is entering this complicated reality fully conscious and fully trusting that, as long as we abide with God, he will also guide us through this world. And the more deeply we look into this odd life of the world, the more deeply we understand that it is apparently only through evil that good is realized, the more we are astonished at how the divine orders of the world permeate and contradict one another—then all the more deeply will our souls sigh: rescue us from evil, do not bring us into temptation, your kingdom come [*Matt. 6:13, 10*].

It is easier to address the problem of truth and love. It confronts us with the questions of life in society, the questions of conventional lies and white lies. I believe too much moral indignation has arisen and still arises about the so-called conventional lies. In direct address and other forms of social intercourse, the so-called conventional lie does not really constitute a lie as long as the person uses the socially established form, a form that will not cause misunderstanding among those to whom it is directed about the actual opinion of the person using it. No one will assume that the familiar forms of address mean something different, and thus there are, it seems to me, really no ethical objections for Christians in normal social intercourse. The case of the white lie has also been amply discussed, and it does indeed offer an extraordinarily peculiar example of how love and truth can come into conflict. As long as the white lie serves purely personal interests, it is, as a lie, simply unethical. But if a serious conflict with the commandment of love arises—something that does, however, happen more rarely than one might believe—then truth must genuinely be violated by love. This situation is indeed wholly peculiar and directs us again to a time to come, when all these interrelationships may be clearer to us. In any case, the apparent conflict seems to obtain more in our own incapacity to articulate truth in a loving fashion and thus does not seem to be an absolute conflict.

376

By far the most turbulent and difficult problem today is the sexual question. The generally increasing value given to the physical—for example, in sports—has also prompted us to concede new rights to the body. Nature originates in God no less than does spirit, perhaps even more immediately. This realization, doubtless a genuinely Christian one, begins to sink in, and leads to the charge to grant to nature what it demands, if indeed it is divine. The seriousness of this question cannot be over-estimated, for here perhaps we find Germany's entire future at stake. Our first duty is to examine things without prudery. Those unable to do so will never attain a healthy understanding of the question. God created us as man and woman [*Gen. 1:27*] and wants us to be completely man and woman. God sanctified our maleness and femaleness, sanctified those emerging as men and women; our body is the temple of God the Holy Spirit [*1 Cor. 3:16*]. God calls the genders each to its own specific role in God's service; we live our lives as men and women before God, who is the God of purity and of holiness. Each of us, however, must decide alone with God, who made us, what it means to be pure. Being pure means allowing God to radiate through us, through our physical and spiritual lives, in eternal purity. But this radiance emerges only where I conduct my life as a man or as a woman before God's eyes. There nature and spirit will mate in the beauty and harmony of a well-created being, neither against nature nor against spirit, rather both being ordered and permeated by God's spirit.

It is in this sense that we should present these problems to our youth. Real enlightenment comes about when, through the mysteries of nature and spirit, a child begins to sense something of God's eternal mysteries and revelations, when it senses that these questions touch on questions of eternity and that its own body, in all its strange and wonderful qualities, points to the eternal miracle and eternal holiness and purity of the Creator. Then each individual will be able to attain and find his or her own answer to the question, "Are we permitted to do this or that?" and, "What should we do now?"

Let us break off here and summarize. Ethics is a matter of earth and blood, but also of God, who made them both; it is from this duality that the crisis arises. The ethical can be found only within the bonds of history, in 377 concrete situations, in the moment of the divine call, of being addressed, of the demands made by concrete crisis and the concrete circumstances of decision, of a demand I must answer, to which I am accountable. The ethical does not exist as a principle in a vacuum; good and evil exist not as universal ideas but as qualities of a will that makes decisions. Good and evil exist only as something effected in freedom, while a principle binds us to the law. Bound to the concrete situation by God and with God, Christians act with the authority of those who have become free. They are subject to no other court than their own and God's. Precisely through this freedom from the law, from principles, however, Christians must enter into the complicated reality of the world. They cannot decide a priori what to do but rather will know only when they have actually entered into the situation of crisis itself and are conscious of being addressed by God. They remain bound to the earth if they are intent on attaining a relationship with God; they must partake of the entire anxiety before the world's laws, must experience paradoxically that the world offers them the choice not between good and evil, but between evil and evil, and that nonetheless even evil can provide a path to God. They must experience the crass contradiction between how they want to act and how they must act; they must mature through this crisis, must mature better, by not turning loose of God's hand, in the words: Your will be done [*Matt. 6:10*]. It is only through the depths of the earth, only through the storms of a human conscience, that the window to eternity opens itself up to us.

An ancient and profound legend tells us about the giant Antaeus,[15] who was stronger than all the men of the world. No one could defeat him until during one battle his adversary lifted him up off the ground, whereupon the giant lost the power that had flowed into him only from his contact with the earth. Those who would abandon the earth, who would flee the crisis of the present, will lose all the power still sustaining them by means of eternal, mysterious powers. The earth remains our mother just as God remains our father, and only those who remain true to the mother are placed by her into the father's arms. Earth and its distress—that is the Christian's Song of Songs.

All the examples that we have examined show that we must place ourselves in the concrete situation and from there direct our gaze toward eternity. Within the contradictory nature of each situation, we must then struggle ever anew to reach our decision from within God's will and let that decision be whatever it may be. In the final analysis, however, ethics will not become merely one more path from human beings to God. Like everything else done by human beings whom Christ has liberated from the world, ethics remains merely a sacrifice, a demonstration of our weak will, that emerges from our own gratitude for what God has done through us, a sacrifice, an offering, a demonstration that God can accept as easily as reject. Human deeds originate in the recognition of God's grace toward humanity and toward each person; those deeds hope in God's grace, which releases us from the crisis of our age. In this way the kingdom of grace establishes itself above the kingdom of the ethical. The crisis and anxiety of conscience must come to an end, the incomprehensible contradictions of the divine orders in the world must become clear if the kingdom of grace is to replace the kingdom of the world, if the kingdom of God is to replace

378

---

15. ["Son of Poseidon and of Gaia. One of Bonhoeffer's favorite motifs; see *DBWE* 10:531 and a passage in his prison fiction (*DBWE* 7:68) . . . The Antaeus metaphor also represents a popularized philosophical modification of Nietzsche, *Thus Spoke Zarathustra* (prologue, pt. 3) . . .," *DBWE* 10:377, n. 44.]

the kingdom of human beings. Only those who have tasted the entire seriousness and the entire depth and crisis of the kingdom of the world, the kingdom of the ethical, yearn beyond this, and have but one wish: May our world pass away and your kingdom come.

6. ACT AND BEING

DBWE 2:136–161

After finishing his Barcelona vicariate in early 1929, Bonhoeffer returned to Berlin and began working on the postdoctoral dissertation necessary for teaching in the German university system.[1] The result was Act and Being, *completed in February 1930 and published the following year. Like* Sanctorum Communio *before it,* Act and Being *is a wide-ranging and technical academic text.*

Bonhoeffer attempts in Act and Being *to articulate basic theological concepts having to do with God and revelation, human knowledge of God and self in faith, and human existence. Of these, the concept of revelation is most important, since Bonhoeffer thinks all the others depend on it. Other theologians have failed to articulate a satisfactory concept of revelation, argues Bonhoeffer, by depending too much on notions of either* act *or* being. *Treating revelation as an act of God has the benefit of communicating the free and transcendent character of revelation but fails to communicate the constancy of God's relationship to humans in revelation. This also makes it difficult to think theologically about the continuity of the Christian's life of faith. Treating revelation in terms of being encounters the opposite problem; God's revelation, as well as the Christian life of faith that depends on it, can be thought about in continuity, but the radical otherness and novelty of revelation and the Christian life of faith is lost. Bonhoeffer builds on* Sanctorum Communio *to offer his own understanding of revelation as the person of Christ existing in the church-community. This solves the "problem of act and being," thinks Bonhoeffer, since such a concept of revelation unites the characteristics of act and being—the person of Christ as church-community encounters believers as something new and transcendent but also exists in historical continuity. On the basis of this understanding of revelation, Bonhoeffer develops theology's other basic concepts to reflect the unity of act and being.*

---

1. [*For historical background, biographical information, and a summary of texts from this period (Berlin, 1929–1930), see* DBWE *10:13–17, editor's introduction, and* DB-ER, *125–145.*]

Bonhoeffer divides Act and Being *into three main parts. In Part A, he develops the problem of act and being against the background of modern philosophy, with Immanuel Kant and Martin Heidegger playing especially important roles. In Part B, he first shows how other theologies have failed to solve that problem before offering his own alternative. Part B is noteworthy for its engagement with Karl Barth, whom Bonhoeffer presents as an act-theologian. In developing his own person-theology as an alternative, Bonhoeffer in important ways tempers the actualism of his earlier thinking. Part C, excerpted here in full, is the concrete application of the preceding argument to issues of human existence. Especially important in this section is Bonhoeffer's articulation of sin in terms of person, that is, as something that corrupts both the act and being of human existence. Against the theology and Luther interpretation of his own teacher Karl Holl, Bonhoeffer argues that such an understanding of sin rules out treating the conscience as a privileged locus for revelation. Instead, we encounter God in the person of Christ existing as the church-community.*

C. The Problem of Act and Being in the Concrete Teaching Concerning Human Beings 'In Adam' and 'In Christ'

136

1. Being in Adam

a) Definition of 'Being' in Adam

Sola fide credendum est nos esse peccatores [*By faith alone we know that we are sinners*].[2] 'Being in Adam' is a more pointed ontological, and a more biblically based (1 Cor. 15:22; cf. 15:45; Rom. 5:12–14), designation for *esse peccator* [*being a sinner*]. Were it really a human possibility for persons themselves to know that they are sinners apart from revelation, neither 'being in Adam' nor 'being in Christ' would be existential designations of their being. For it would mean that human beings could place themselves into the truth, that they could somehow withdraw to a deeper being of their own, apart from their being sinners, their 'not being in the truth.' Being in Adam would, consequently, have to be regarded as a potentiality of a more profound 'possibility of being in the truth.' It would rest on a being untouched by sin. In theological terms, it would mean that the sinner remains creature, that being-'there' as creature lies at the foundation of 'how' one ontically is as sinner. If one disputes that being a sinner involves all of the being of human beings, then the danger of semi-Pelagianism, the ontological teaching of

137

---

2. Luther, *Lectures on Romans, LW* 25:215. [*See also Bonhoeffer's comment on Luther's* Lectures on Romans *in* DBWE *9:300. In relation to knowledge of sin, see* DBWE *12:229–230.*]

causae secundae [*secondary causes*],[3] is unavoidable. Seen in this light, the
words of Luther cited above become intelligible: we can never comprehend
our existence as a whole, because it is entirely founded on God's word—and
God's word demands faith. Only to faith, in revelation, do we have access
to the knowledge that we are sinners in the wholeness of our being, since it
is only then, by God's word, that the wholeness of our being can be placed
into the truth.

This is knowledge from revelation, which can never be had apart from
it, that is, precisely, in Adam. For 'in Adam' means to be in untruth, in
culpable perversion of the will, that is, of human essence. It means to be
turned inward into one's self, *cor curvum in se* [*the heart turned in upon itself*].[4]
Human beings have torn themselves loose from community with God and,
therefore, also from that with other human beings, and now they stand
alone, that is, in untruth. Because human beings are alone, the world is
'their' world, and other human beings have sunk into the world of things
(cf. Heidegger's 'being-with'). God has become a religious object, and
human beings themselves have become their own creator and lord, belonging to themselves. It is only to be expected that they should now begin and
end with themselves in their knowing, for they are only and utterly 'with
themselves' in the falsehood of naked self-glory.

Ontologically this means that sin is the violation of Dasein[5] (created
being) by its concrete being-how-it-is. It means that in face of the concept
of sin, this ontological distinction between human existence and the form
in which one actually exists becomes meaningless, because the I is its own
master now and has itself taken possession of its Dasein. Furthermore,
this knowledge is not possible within the state of sin, because here Dasein
is still in the power of how-it-is as sinner; rather, it is knowledge that has
to be deduced from revelation, in which creatureliness and sin are separated in a manner yet to be described. Therefore, the ontological designation of human beings as being sinners, as existing in sin 'in reference
to' God, remains correct. Every attempt to utilize the idea of creature in
a fundamentally ontological fashion, when speaking of the human being
'in Adam,' leads directly to the Catholicism of the *analogia entis* [*analogy*

138

---

3. [". . . causes which in relation to the first mover are of a second order. Scholastic
thought uses the term to depict the work of the creature as distinct from that of the creator . . . ," *DBWE* 2:74, n. 83.]

4. [*This phrase, which repeats in* Act and Being, *alludes to Luther's characterization of sin in*
Lectures on Romans, *LW* 25:291.]

5. [*Bonhoeffer borrows from Martin Heidegger the term* Dasein *to refer to human existence. See*
DBWE 2:35, n. 4.]

of being]⁶ to a pure metaphysics of being. As long as it will not allow revelation to drive it into the historical church of Christ, the thinking and philosophizing of human beings in sin is self-glorifying, even when it seeks to be self-critical or to become 'critical philosophy.' All knowledge, including particularly γνῶθι σεαυτόν [*know thyself*],⁷ seeks to establish the ultimate self-justification of human beings. Under the heavy burden of being both creator and bearer of a world, and in the cold silence of their eternal solitude, they begin to be afraid of themselves and to shudder. Then they arise and declare themselves their own final judges and proceed to their own indictment—couched in the language of conscience. But the response of the indicted human being is repentance (*contritio activa!*) [*active repentance*].⁸   **139**
The conscience and repentance of human beings in Adam are their final grasp at themselves, the confirmation and justification of their self-glorifying solitude. Human beings make themselves the defendant, they appeal to their better selves. But the cries of conscience only dull the mute loneliness of a desolate 'with-itself'; they ring without echo in the world that the self rules and explains. Human beings in Adam are pushed to the limits of their solitude but, misunderstanding their situation, "they seek themselves in themselves" (Luther),⁹ hoping that in being repentant they may yet save their sinful existence.¹⁰ As sinners they keep their sins with them, for they see them through their conscience, which holds them captive in themselves and only bids them to look at sin over and again. But "sin grows and gets bigger also through too much looking and thinking on it, aided by   **140**
the foolishness of our conscience, which is ashamed before God and sorely punishes itself."¹¹ For this reason, such conscience is of the devil, who leaves human beings to themselves in untruth; for this reason this conscience must be mortified when Christ comes to human beings. Conscience can torment and drive to despair; but it cannot of itself kill human beings—it cannot because it is their final grasp at themselves. Human beings are unable to will their own death, even in conscience.¹² Here is their limit: **141**
human beings cling to themselves, and thus their knowledge of themselves

---

6. [*The analogy of being is a doctrine usually associated with Catholic theology that posits a likeness between God and creation because both are related (in different ways) to being. The doctrine is generally taken to suggest the possibility of natural theology, the knowledge of God apart from special revelation.*]

7. [*See also* DBWE *10:533.*]

8. [*See below (*DBWE *2:141 [Reader 96]). See also* DBWE *9:335ff.*]

9. Luther, "A Sermon on Preparing to Die," *LW* 42:106.

10. Luther, "The Sacrament of Penance," *LW* 35:16.

11. Luther, "A Sermon on Preparing to Die," *LW* 42:102, 104.

12. Luther, "The Bondage of the Will," *LW* 33:106.

is imprisoned in untruth.[13] To be placed into truth before God means to be dead or to live; neither of these can human beings give themselves. They are conferred on them only by the encounter with Christ in *contritio passiva* [*passive repentance*] and faith. Only when Christ has broken through the solitude of human beings will they know themselves placed into truth. It matters not whether, in the offense that the cross causes the sinner, human beings die forever and remain in solitude, or whether they die in order to live with Christ in the truth (for die they must, as Christ died). In both cases, true knowledge of themselves is given here only through Christ. If "thinking that knows itself to be lord of its world" previously corresponded to the situation of solitude, it is now recognized in its true nature as guilt toward Christ. That is to say, it is recognized really only in the moment when Christ breaks through the solitude. When conscience is said to be an immediate relation to God, Christ and the church are excluded, because God's having bound the divine self to the mediating word is circumvented.[14]

142   Even temptation, which leads to death, is the work of Christ, for human beings die of the law only because Christ died through the law or—this applies to the time before Christ—was to die through it. The temptation that comes through the death of Christ as the end is the most severe temptation of the law, of the *deus in sua majestate* [*God in God's majesty*].[15] In principle it is impossible to draw the distinction between real temptation by Christ and temptation as the final grasp for oneself, a distinction analogous to the relation between faith and credulity. Wherever the I is truly at the end, where it truly reaches out of itself, and where this reaching is no final 'seeking the self in oneself', there Christ is at work. However, certainty about this is never won by reflecting on the act—psychologically we remain opaque to ourselves—but only in each case in pure regard to Christ and Christ's action for us. Hence Luther's countlessly repeated admonition not to look upon one's own repentance, one's own faith, but precisely upon the Lord Christ. For, in order to find Christ, as long as I still reflect on myself, Christ is not present. If Christ is truly present, I see only Christ. Conscience can be termed the voice of God only insofar as conscience is the place where Christ, in real temptation, kills human beings in order to give

---

13. Luther, "The Bondage of the Will," *LW* 33:121–122.

14. It is no coincidence that Holl both defines Luther's religion as a religion of conscience and admits to the possibility of finding God without Christ in the first commandment. Holl, *Luther*, 70.

15. Luther uses this term essentially to speak of God's not being bound by the word of grace. It is not intended to imply an impossibility of encountering the *deus in sua majestate* in Christ.

them life or not.[16] It is crucial that self-understanding is possible only where   143
the living Christ approaches us, only in beholding him. αὐτοὶ ἐν ἑαυτοῖ   144
ἑαυτοὺς μετροῦντες καὶ συγκρίνοντες ἑαυτοὺς ἑαυτοῖς οὐ συνιᾶσιν [*But*
when they measure themselves by one another, and they compare themselves with one
another, they do not show good sense] (2 Cor. 10:12).

But because the attempt to understand oneself from oneself remains in
sin, the designation of human existence in Adam as the being-of-a-sinner is
correct at the formal ontological level and sufficient. To being-in-sin, there
corresponds an act of sin—the act of misconstruing the self that takes place
when Dasein is violated by its being-how-it-is as one who falsely claims to
possess full power over the self. How act and being are related 'in Adam'
remains to be seen.

b) 'Adam' as I and as Humanity

Sin is the inversion of the human will (of human essence) into itself.
Will has no reality save as free and conscious, and thus sin must be understood as act. Every decision made in a self-seeking sense is to be judged as
a sinful act. The seriousness of this definition of sin lies in the fact that it
does not seem otherwise possible to maintain the guilt-character of sin; the
experiential base for this definition is the verdict of conscience, according
to which one is responsible only for decisions of the self against God taken
willfully. One may well then differentiate between sin and guilt, as between
being and act. But to understand sin *qua* guilt as the being of human beings
appears untruthful in light of the experience of one's own conscience and
seems to minimize the gravity of the concept of guilt. Sin, therefore, is act.
Underlying this view is a concept of conscience as the unmediated voice of   145
God in human beings. But this argument breaks down before the different interpretation of the experience of conscience that was given above.
The attempt of conscience to limit sin to the act must be understood as
a human attempt at self-deliverance. The knowledge of what sin is comes
solely through the mediation of the Word of God in Christ; and that knowledge overrules the dissenting conscience. *Sola fide credendum est nos esse pec-*
catores [*by faith alone we know that we are sinners*].

If sin were no more than a free act of the particular moment, a retreat
to sinless being would in principle be possible, revelation in Christ having
become redundant. The death of Christ reveals that the whole human must
die to the law, because the totality of the old human is in sin. The continu-

---

16. [*At this point Bonhoeffer includes a long footnote on contemporary discussions of con-*
science.]

ity of the human being in Adam is judged by the death of Christ. Thus it is necessary to understand sin in some way as being.

There are two possibilities for understanding sin as having the form of the being of entities.

1. We may historicize, psychologize, and naturalize the doctrine of original sin. Somehow sin clings to human nature as humanly generated. *Non posse non peccare* [*not able not to sin*] holds true for this tarnished nature.[17] The concept of nature is intended to warrant the continuity and existentiality of sin.

2. Sin may be understood as a pretemporal deed that gave rise to sin in the present (a view proposed lately by Julius Müller). All speculative dualisms, as well as the metaphysical theory of satanic revolt, subscribe to this view. In undialectical fashion, something ontologically prior—something in the sense of entity with all the implacability of the 'there is'—is being placed here ahead of the act of sinning. Yet sin as entity cannot touch me existentially. It is transcended within me; I remain its lord even when it overpowers me. Sin understood as entity is the exoneration of human beings. A mode of being must be ascribed to sin which, on the one hand, expresses the fully inexcusable and contingent character of sin that breaks forth anew in the act and which, on the other hand, makes it possible to understand sin as the master into whose hands human beings are utterly delivered. The New Testament itself provides the concept of being that is sought: Adam as I and as the being-of-the person-of-humanity.

In the judgment brought upon me by the death of Christ, I see myself dying in my entirety, for I myself, as a whole, am guilty as the actor of my life, the decisions of which turned out to be self-seeking ever and again. I made false decisions and, therefore, Christ is my death; and because I alone sought to be the master, I am alone in my death as well. But the death of Christ kills my entire being human, as humanity in me, for I am I and humanity in one. In my fall from God, humanity fell. Thus, before the cross, the debt of the I grows to monstrous size; it is itself Adam, itself the first to have done, and to do again and again, that incomprehensible deed—sin as act. But in this act, for which I hold myself utterly responsible on every occasion, I find myself already in the humanity of Adam. I see humanity in me necessarily committing this, my own free deed. As human being, the I is banished into this old humanity, which fell on my account. The I 'is' not

---

17. [. . . "[T]he phrase Augustine coined in his debate with Pelagius about the meaning of sin for the free will ("A Treatise on Nature and Grace," chap. 57, in *Saint Augustine: Anti-Pelagian Works*, 140)," *DBWE* 2:145, n. 29.]

as an individual, but always in humanity. And just because the deed of the individual is at the same time that of humanity, human beings must hold themselves individually responsible for the whole guilt of humankind. The interrelation of individual and humanity is not to be thought of in terms of causality—otherwise the mode of being of the entity would once again come into play; rather, it is a knowledge given the individual in God's judgment—given in such a way that it cannot be used, in detachment from that judgment and in theoretical abstraction, for purposes of exoneration. On the contrary, because everyone, as human being, stands within the humanity of Adam, no one can withdraw from the sinful act to a sinless being; no, the whole of one's being a person is in sin. Thus, in Adam act is as constitutive for being as being is for act; both act and being enter into judgment as guilty. The structure of Adam's humanity should not be conceived in terms of theories of psychological-historical interpretation; no, I myself am Adam—am I and humanity in one. In me humanity falls. As I am Adam, so is every individual; but in all individuals the one person of humanity, Adam, is active. This expresses both the contingency of the deed and the continuity of the being of sin. Because sin is envisaged through the concept of 'Adam', in the mode of being of 'person', the contingency of conduct is preserved, as is the continuity of the person of humanity, which attests itself in action—the person that I also am.

This perspective agrees with Luther's view of sin, which wishes to define it equally as original sin and as one's own act and guilt: sin as egocentricity, as the seeking of one's own person after itself. The being of sin is being-a-person. In the knowledge of my being-a-sinner as an individual, I see that my Dasein is in the power of the form in which I actually exist; I cannot know it in its creaturely being. In the knowledge of my being a sinner as humanity, I see my sinful Dasein as the basis of the form in which I actually exist, yet never as an exoneration—never, that is to say, as if from the position of a neutral observer who looks at an entity. On the contrary, I see this only in the judgment in which I must die as 'Adam'.

c) Everydayness, Knowledge of Conscience, and Temptation

The *everydayness* of human beings in Adam is guilt. It is the decision for solitude which, because it has already been taken, is being taken all the time. It is a *coercive* seeking after pleasure in the creature and, for that reason, always in flight from that the right knowledge of which sets pleasure within its proper limits: from death and the self. But the flight is hopeless,[18]

147

---

18. Luther, *Lectures on Romans, LW* 25:401.

for human beings are to be revealed before the tribunal of Christ, if not today, then certainly in death (2 Cor. 5:10). Because this is so, the wilder the flight and the less human beings are conscious of that hopelessness, the more desperate is everydayness in Adam. Superficiality masks solitude; it is oriented toward life, but its ground and end is death in guilt.

148   *Conscience,* in which desperation and solitude become-conscious-of-themselves, seeks thereby to overcome them. Solitude is not grasped in its authentic sense. There arises merely a general consciousness of being-left-alone, and this is what conscience is to eliminate by restoring human beings once again to themselves. In conscience, the powers of this world, law and death, fall upon human beings and make them anxious; here, anxiety in the face of oneself erupts from life, because it neither knows the future nor holds it in its power. Yet there is in this anxiety an inability to break free of oneself, a final perseverance of the I in itself. In conscience death steps within the horizon of the I, but only as an entity, as an event that conscience can conquer. Human beings think themselves immortal and remain alone.

Temptation, in which Christ assails human beings through the law, discloses that this solitude has the character of guilt. All that has gone before becomes deadly serious here. Here human beings are detained from their ultimate flight, which conscience makes possible for them, and are forced to recognize that their guilt and death are the ground and end of their flight. Moment by moment their guilt brings death near. Death is no longer an entity to be conquered. Rather, the moment guilt and the curse of death are recognized, human beings see that they are already in death. They are dead before they die and they die every moment anew.[19] Their knowledge
149   and volition come from death, for they do not come from the life of God. This perennial dying is accompanied by anxiety and uneasiness. Guilt, death, and the world press in upon human beings and make the world too 'narrow'[20] ('narrowness,' 'anxiety,' and 'uneasy,' have a common root).[21] Here, human beings are no longer alone; everything now speaks to them, becomes their accuser, and yet they nonetheless remain alone and without defense. In this temptation human beings die of Christ; they die of the law that is of the spirit. In the death of the sinner, however, predestination takes its course: for one, eternal death, for another, eternal life. Temptation itself is part of being human in Adam and must lead to death. It brings

---

19. [*At this point Bonhoeffer includes a long footnote contrasting Heidegger's concept of death with what Bonhoeffer considers the Christian one.*]

20. Luther, "A Sermon on Preparing to Die," *LW* 42:99–100.

21. [*Bonhoeffer is making an etymological observation regarding* Enge *(narrowness),* Angst *(anxiety), and* bange *(uneasy).*]

with it ever anew the horrors of eternal death. In it sin, guilt, and the law obscure the cross and resurrection and seek to be accepted as definitive. Whether Christ will give himself to the tempted one in grace and faith ever and again remains in the balance, for which reason temptation must never be regarded as a dialectical point of transition toward faith.[22] Temptation is, indeed, the real end of sinners, their death. That life should come from death is God's free gift to God's community, free also for those who 'are' in the community—that is to say, find themselves believing. God can let human beings die of the knowledge of their sin and can lead them through this death into community. For then God turns one's eyes away from oneself, and gives them God's own orientation (the pure intentionality of the *actus directus* [*direct act*]) towards Christ, the crucified and risen one who is   150
the overcoming of the temptation to death.

2. Being in Christ

a) The Definition of 'Being' in Christ

"Seek yourself only in Christ and not in yourself, and you will find yourself in him eternally."[23] Here, the person *in se conversus* [*turned in upon itself*][24] is delivered from the attempt to remain alone—to understand itself out of itself—and is turned outwards towards Christ. The person now lives in the contemplation of Christ.[25] This is the gift of faith, that one no longer looks upon oneself, but solely upon the salvation that has come to one from without. One finds oneself in Christ, because already one is in Christ, in that one seeks oneself there in Christ. If in Adam Dasein was violated by the form in which it actually exists—through the encapsulation of human beings in themselves—then the solution to this problem comes as humanity reorients its gaze towards Christ. Dasein becomes free, not as if it could stand over against its being-how-it-is as autonomous being, but in the sense of escaping from the power of the I into the power of Christ, where alone it recognizes itself in original freedom as God's creature.

Only in Christ do human beings know themselves as God's creatures; in   151
Adam they were creator and creature all at once. In order to know itself as a creature of God, the old human being has to have died and the new one arisen, whose essence it is to live in disregard of self and wholly in contemplation of Christ. As those living in Christ, the new human beings know

---

22. Holl is inclined toward this view; see his *Luther*, 67 ff., and elsewhere.
23. Luther, "A Sermon on Preparing to Die," *LW* 42:106.
24. Luther, *Lectures on Galatians, LW* 26:166.
25. Luther, *Lectures on Galatians, LW* 26:167.

themselves in identity with the old human beings that have passed through death—as God's creatures. That sinners too are still creatures is something that can be expressed only by a believer; as long as this is an insight of sinners, it stays an idea in untruth.

It well may be objected that the ontological definition of being human as being-the-sinner and being-in-Christ needs to be undergirded by a general ontology of being-a-creature. That would take us into Catholicism. Being-a-creature is only 'in faith'; it is the Dasein of the one who believes, which cannot be divorced from how-one-is in faith. Being-a-creature is not something in the manner of 'there is'; being-a-creature is in the agitation of being in faith. Ontologically this means that God is at once the creature's ground of being and lord; transcendentally it means that Dasein is 'amidst' and 'in reference to' transcendence. There is no ontological specification of that which is created that is independent of God being reconciler and redeemer, and human beings being sinners and forgiven. In the Christian doctrine of being, all metaphysical ideas of eternity and time, being and becoming, living and dying, essence and appearance must be measured against the concepts of the being of sin and the being of grace or else must be developed anew in light of them. For only on this basis was it also possible to define the being of sin, grace, and revelation as a being that was described as the unity of act and being, as personal being. In the idea of the creature, however, the personal-being of God and revelation manifests itself as creative-being and lordly-being over my human personal being. And the second of these is the more encompassing of the two latter designations.

152

Even though I am able through faith alone to know myself as God's creature, I know, nonetheless, that I have been created by God in my entirety, as an I and as humanity, and that I have been placed into nature and history. I know, therefore, that these factors, too, have to do with creatureliness. The faith of the creature, however, refuses to call the 'world' that has become its own—which has been defined in the form in which it actually exists by sin and death and has been violated in its Dasein—the creation of God. Nevertheless, God remains lord even of this world. In view of the hope offered in the resurrection of the historical Christ and in the life I live with him—a hope to which has been promised a new heaven and a new earth—faith must believe that the world is God's creation, despite its falling away. It follows that an ontology that conforms to the so-called 'pure creative being' ends up transforming itself into a definition of being apart from the revelation in Christ, since it is only in Christ that authentic faith in creation arises.

If one desired to discover the ontological boundaries of the being-of-the-creature, the being assumed in being-the-sinner and being-justified, it is to be found in the structure of its being-there—as it is violated in sin and liberated in grace—as well as in the structure of its being-how-it-is as 'directed-towards-being'. The 'there' of human beings is not to be defined independently of the 'how.' No metaphysical deductions or distinctions (*existentia, essentia, ens* [*existence, essence, a being*]), and no ontological structures of existence can reach up to the 'there' as created. Creaturely-being is what Dasein is called by means of and for God in faith—that is to say, being touched by revelation. This very general definition indicates already that in the concept of the creature, too, the 'there' and 'how' belong indissolubly together.

Creaturely Dasein is 'there' only in being directed towards revelation; conversely, being-directed is an ontological definition of the 'there'—which is to say, 'there' and 'how' are grounded solely in revelation, inseparable from one another. Here alone is the understanding of the 'there' and 'how' protected against interference from extraneous categories.

Likewise, it is only in revelation itself that being-a-creature can be defined in terms of being-a-person, insofar as it is the person whose existence has been encountered, judged, or created anew by Christ. Thus, all ontological definitions remain bound to the revelation in Christ; they are appropriate only in the concretions of being-the-sinner and being justified. This does not do away with the idea of the creature; it is preserved and expressed, rather, in the concretion of "what Dasein is called by means of and for God." Nor is the possibility of reflecting theologically on such 'creaturely' categories as individuality, being in history, in nature, being and becoming, and so forth, eliminated. But this can be done only on the presupposition of existence touched by revelation.

153

The objection that categories of a general metaphysical kind also have been employed in these proceedings overlooks the necessity of a certain formal 'preunderstanding,' on the basis of which alone questions—even if wrong ones—can be raised, whose answer is then surrendered by revelation, together with a fundamental correction of the question.

And so, the idea of creation is unable to provide a basis for the ontological definition of the human being in Christ. The human being only 'is' in Adam or in Christ, in unfaith or in faith, in Adamic humanity and in Christ's community; God only 'is' as the creator, reconciler, and redeemer, and that being as such is personal being. The world of entity is transcended and qualified by this personal being. That world 'is for' human beings in Adam their own, violated, 'interpreted' world under the curse of death; and it 'is for' human beings in Christ the world set free from the I and, yet, given anew by God into their dominion, in the hope for the new creation (Rom. 8:19ff.). It is ultimately the world utterly for God, who remains its Lord. There is no more general definition of its being.

Being in Christ, as being directed towards Christ, sets Dasein free.
Human beings are 'there' for and by means of Christ; they believe as long as
they look upon Christ. In the depiction of faith in terms of pure intentionality, one must avoid every attempt, on the one hand, to freeze the temporality of faith by exhibiting it—which is what the theology of consciousness
had done and which, in my view, is repeated again by H. M. Müller. And,
154   on the other hand, one must avoid every attempt to incorporate into the
act of faith itself the reflection that meets with faith merely as 'credulity'.
This is the danger in Barth. Faith and 'credulity' lie together in the same
act. Every act of faith is credulous insofar as it is an event embedded in the
psyche and accessible to reflection; it is 'faith' in its intentionality towards
Christ, which is grounded in being in the community of Christ. A faith
that grows doubtful of itself because it considers itself unworthy, stands in
temptation. Faith itself knows that it is Christ who justifies and not faith
as *opus* [*work*]; it requires no reflection to find this out, particularly since
reflection declares something quite different, as it brings faith into temptation. The theological right with which Barth reproached Schleiermacher
for his "grand confusion" of religion and grace[26] is compromised when one
allows reflection to enter into the act of faith itself, thereby casting doubt
on Christ right along with faith. This is the penalty paid for the inadequate
distinction between theological knowing and that of faith. Doubt is cast
when one forgets that Christ is apprehended in believing faith; it is in such
forgetfulness that all the ominous terms such as enthusiasm, experience,
piety, feeling, and conversion of the will recur by necessity. It must be stated
clearly that in the community of Christ faith takes form in religion and
that, consequently, religion is called faith—that seen in light of Christ I may
and must calmly confess, "I believe," only to add, of course, with a view to
myself, "help my unbelief." For reflection, all praying, all searching for God
in God's Word, all clinging to promise, every entreaty in the name of God's
grace, all hope with reference to the cross is 'religion', 'credulity'. But in the
community of Christ, even though it is always the work of human beings,
it is faith, given and willed by God, faith in which God may truly be found.
Were faith to inquire about its own sufficiency, it would have fallen already
155   from intentionality into temptation. Rather, faith only assures itself of its
contents by laying hold of them, relating them to itself, and in so doing,
abiding in an undisturbed contemplation of Christ that can be destroyed

26. Barth, *Die christliche Dogmatik im Entwurf* [*Christian Dogmatics in Outline*], 1: *Die Lehre vom Worte Gottes: Prolegomena zur christlichen Dogmatik* [*The Doctrine of the Word of God: Prolegomena to Christian Dogmatics*] (Munich: Chr. Kaiser, 1927), 301ff.

only by self-reflection. Being-in-Christ is being directed towards Christ, and that is possible only through 'being already in the community of Christ' (in the sense presented above).[27] And so, the transcendental and ontological points of departure again find themselves brought together.

If this, as it were, is only a formal definition, then being in Christ, as historical, is also defined by past and future (see above, pages 110f.[28]). Here the concrete manner of being pertaining to being directed towards Christ, and pertaining to being in the community, clearly emerges for the first time.

b) The Definition of Being in Christ through the Past: The Conscience

"Whoever is without conscience is Christ or the evil Spirit" (*Theologia deutsch*) [*German theology*].[29] The historical human being has conscience, not only in Adam as a protection against God's assault, but also in the church of Christ. Conscience is only where sin is. But since the human being in Christ is no longer governed by sin, conscience is something defined by the past in Adam. Human beings have conscience by and in themselves; it does not belong to the things 'to come'. It is the reflection on one's self beyond which human beings in Adam cannot advance. Conscience primarily is not God's but the human being's own voice. If being-in-Christ means being oriented towards Christ, reflection on the self is obviously not part of that being. Here lies the problem of Christian conscience.

A distinction has to be made between two forms of conscience that pertain to the human being in Christ.

1. Conscience interposes itself between Christ (the community of faith) and me, and either obscures my view of Christ or shows Christ to me as my judge on the cross, thereby pointing relentlessly to my sin. The spiritual law has arisen against me. I hear only my accuser, see myself rejected; death and hell grasp for me. Truly, this is temptation[30] and rebellion against Christ, since it is disregard for the grace offered in Christ. In this temptation even those in Christ's community stand in real danger of losing Christ if this very one does not come forward to kill their conscience, declare Christ's self anew to human beings, and give them back their faith. In faith, however,

156

---

27. [DBWE *2:117.*]

28. [*This refers to* DBWE *2:110.*]

29. ["An ascetic-mystical tract, the first writing of which is dated circa 1430 and attributed to Johannes de Francfordia, professor of theology at Heidelberg. Cf. Willo Uhl: 'Whoever now is without conscience is Christ or the evil Spirit' (*Der Franckforter*, 45)," *DBWE* 2:155, n. 45.]

30. Cf. Luther's entire "A Sermon on Preparing to Die," *LW* 42:99–115.

human beings find themselves once again already in the community of faith. They know that through faith, for those who stand in the community of faith, temptation through sin and death is overcome. The belief that such temptation is required in order to come to faith turns evil into a necessary stage on the way to the good, as in Hegel's dialectics. This temptation belongs entirely to the righteousness of the flesh, and this conscience is itself defection from Christ.

2. The other form of conscience, that of reflection on the self, is included within the intention towards Christ. It is the 'look of sin' within faith. Those who seek themselves in Christ see themselves always in sin; but now this sin can no longer distort their contemplation of Christ (it is, after all, the basis on which I, ἐν σαρκί [*in the flesh*], can look upon Christ and him alone). I see my sin within the forgiveness through Christ. "You may, therefore, safely look upon your sin without your conscience (!), as sins are no longer sins there; they are overcome and swallowed up in Christ . . . If you believe that, they can do you no harm."[31] Repentance, too, is now no longer the last grasp for oneself, but rather repentance within the belief in forgiveness[32] (*contritio passiva* [*passive repentance*]). This is the meaning of daily penance and repentance. It is not the loss of oneself to the self; rather, it is finding oneself in Christ. True, even the reflection of repentance presupposes life ἐν σαρκί [*in the flesh*], the sin of falling away from the intention towards Christ. If there were no sin, repentance could have become thanksgiving. This final barrier put up by sin against the pure contemplation of Christ is conquered by the faith, which sees its sin only within the context of Christ's forgiveness, within the community. This faith is called penitence. Reflection as such can no longer break the intentionality towards Christ. And yet, intentionality is caught again and again in struggle, as it is not yet in the pure form of 'being defined by the future alone'. (See below.)

157

The self-reflection of sinful human beings in face of Christ and in Christ is the death of human beings ἐν σαρκί [*in the flesh*], just as the self-reflection of human beings in Adam was the death of spiritual human beings. Because Christ died, and because we, too, died that death with Christ in baptism (Romans 6), death is concealed in faith; for that reason the faithful must daily die that death. The strength to die is not given by asceticism or focusing on the self—that is a work of natural human beings who cannot desire cross and death; rather, they die solely in faith. They do not give themselves death but, in faith, see themselves given into death by Christ.

31. Luther, "A Sermon on Preparing to Die," *LW* 42:105.
32. Cf. Luther, "The Sacrament of Penance," *LW* 35:9ff.

They see themselves in the daily death throes of σάρξ [*the flesh*], drawn into the agony of the old human being; believing, they see Christ fighting with death in them. They believe in Christ's victory and, yet, are subject in body and soul to the power of death. The death of the old human is guilt, the future's recompense to the past for having snatched the new human from its clutches. Those over whom the future of Christ has triumphed in faith must daily die the death of that past anew with open eyes. The more forcefully death assails human beings, the mightier the power of the past over them. Thus being in Christ—which when defined by the past is the reflection, taking place in faith, of repenting and dying—is taken up and determined by the future; and this future is holiness and life.

c) The Definition of Being in Christ by Means of the Future: The Child

Future means: the definition of being by something outside 'yet to come'. There is a genuine future only through Christ and the reality, created anew by Christ, of the neighbor and creation. Estranged from Christ, the world is enclosed in the I, which is to say, already the past. In it life is reflection. What is 'yet to come' demands immediate acceptance or rejection, and reflection signifies refusal, as the one absolutely yet to come, Christ demands faith directed towards Christ without reflection.[33]

Here, the second stage of reflection is also superseded—not only self-reflection outside of Christ, but also the reflection of the 'Christian' conscience. As long as there is sin, there is also Christian conscience. In the pure orientation towards Christ there is no sin, and consequently there is no reflection of repentance in faith. In their definition by the future, human beings are wholly detached from themselves into contemplation of Christ. Of course, this is no mystical self-dissolving contemplation; no, I behold Christ as 'my Lord and my God'. But that is no longer a reflection upon the I. Rather, it expresses the personality in relation, which, even in the position of intentionality, remains a personality in relation.

Classical Protestant dogmatics spoke of *fides directa* [*direct faith*] to describe the act of faith which, even though completed within a person's consciousness, could not be reflected in it. The act of faith rests on the objectivity of the event of revelation in Word and sacrament. Clinging to Christ need not become self-conscious; rather, it is wholly taken up by completion of the act itself. Human beings are in Christ, and as there is no sin and death in Christ, human beings do not see their sin or death, nor do they see themselves or their own faith. They see only Christ and their Lord

158

---

33. ["See *DBWE* 2:99–100, 111, and 131–132," *DBWE* 2:157, n. 51.]

and God. To see Christ in Word and sacrament means to see, all in one act,

159   the resurrected Crucified One in the neighbor and creation. Here alone does that future reveal itself which in faith determines the present. In the definition of being in Christ by means of the future, the dialectic of act and being recurs. In faith the future is present; but inasmuch as faith suspends itself before the future (knowing itself to be its mode of being, but not as productive), the human being 'is' in the future of Christ—that is, never in being without act, and never in act without being.

To-let-oneself-be-defined by means of the future is the eschatological possibility of the child. The child (full of anxiety and bliss) sees itself in the power of what 'future things' will bring, and for that reason alone, it can live in the present. However, they who are mature, who desire to be defined by the present, fall subject to the past, to themselves, death and guilt. It is only out of the future that the present can be lived.

Here the child becomes a theological problem. *Actus directus* [*direct act*] or *reflexus* [*reflexive*], infant baptism or religiosity? *Actus directus*, as an act directed solely by and on Christ, and infant baptism, as the paradoxical occurrence of revelation without the reflexive answer of consciousness, as brought together in classical Protestant dogmatics, are the eschatological prelude under which life is placed. Both can be understood only in con-

160   nection with the last things. Baptism is the call to the human being into childhood, a call that can be understood only eschatologically. The meaning of infant baptism is something about which only the community of its members can speak. The child is near to what is of the future—the eschata [*last things*]. This too is conceivable only to the faith that suspends itself before revelation. Faith is able to fix upon baptism as the unbreakable Word of God, the eschatological foundation of its life.

Because baptism lies temporally in the past and is, nonetheless, an eschatological occurrence, the whole of my past life acquires seriousness and temporal continuity. It lies between eternity and eternity, founded by means of and 'in reference to' God's Word. And so, my past and that of the Christian community in general is founded, defined, and 'directed' by means of the future that is called forth from it by the Spirit.

Our discussion of the *actus directus*—as something that can never be captured in reflection (I cannot capture the act in myself, not to mention in someone else)—and of infant baptism—as of faith that excludes itself—allows a perspective to open up in which not all roads appear blocked to the

161   eschatology of apocatastasis.[34] And yet, this very talk of apocatastasis may

---

34. ["the doctrine of the 'recapitulation of all,' the salvation of all," *DBWE* 2:160, n. 60.]

never be more than the sigh of theology whenever it has to speak of faith and unfaith, election and rejection.

In pure orientation towards Christ, there-being and how-being are restored to their right status. The 'there' is delivered from the violation wrought by the 'how', while conversely the 'how' finds itself anew in the 'there' appointed by God. The echoless cries from solitude into the solitude of self, the protest against violation of any sort, have unexpectedly received a reply and gradually melt into the quiet, prayerful conversation of the child with the father in the Word of Jesus Christ. In the contemplation of Christ, the tormented knowledge of the I's tornness finds 'joyful conscience', confidence, and courage. The servant becomes free. The one who became an adult in exile and misery becomes a child at home. Home is the community of Christ, always 'future', present 'in faith' because we are children of the future—always act, because it is being; always being, because it is act.

This is the new creation of the new human being of the future, which here is an event already occurring in faith, and there perfected for view. It is the new creation of those who no longer look back upon themselves, but only away from themselves to God's revelation, to Christ. It is the new creation of those born from out of the world's confines into the wideness of heaven, becoming what they were or never were, a creature of God, a child.

7. Inaugural Lecture: The Anthropological Question in Contemporary Philosophy and Theology

DBWE 10:389–408

The following is Bonhoeffer's inaugural lecture, delivered in Berlin after fulfilling the qualifications to become a university lecturer. The lecture, closely related to his recently completed Act and Being,[1] *focuses on theological anthropology through the question, "What does it mean to be a human being?" Bonhoeffer organizes the lecture according to what he identifies as two contemporary approaches to answering that anthropological question, one based on the notion of the human "boundary" and the other on the notion of the human "possibility," which correspond to the postdoctoral dissertation's language of "act" and "being." After presenting philosophical and then theological representatives of both approaches, Bonhoeffer returns to his concern with finding their theological unity, which he argues emerges only out of the self-understanding of one who exists in Christ.*

389   The question as to what it means to be a human being is kept current by two factors. First, by human works themselves; and second, by the experience of limits—physical limits, intellectual limits, and the limits of the human will. Wherever the human being begins to be astonished at his own capabilities and his own works, and wherever reality ruthlessly demonstrates human limits, the ancient biblical questions emerge: "What are human beings, Lord, that you are mindful of them? . . . You have made them a little lower

---

1. [*Especially* DBWE *2:59–103. For more on the inaugural lecture in relationship to* Act and Being, *see DeJonge,* Bonhoeffer's Theological Formation, *58–68.*]

than God" (Ps. 8), and the other, "What are human beings, that you . . . haunt them every morning, test them every moment?" (Job 7:17). Stated historically, this means that the question about the human being is necessarily raised anew and more urgently, on the one hand, by a century of engineers who built a new world on the foundations of the old and, on the other hand, by a lost war. Two great possibilities present themselves. The human being tries to understand himself either from the perspective of his *works* or from that of his *limits*. Understanding emerges only from a still *point of unity*. A person tries to find such a point either in his works or in his limits, that is, where his essence seems to be suspended from temporal change, where it seems graspable in the condition of rest, of objectification. The unity of a human being means first that the person's existence is genuinely addressed, and second that his existence can be conceived in continuity. These are the formal definitions within which the question of the human being must be posed and answered. Human works and limits are the places from which self-understanding is sought; they are deeply grounded in the idea of the human quest for self-understanding. This question differs fundamentally from all other questions since the one who poses the question is himself a human being; that is, one cannot simply ask about the human being in such a way that he appears as an object. Rather, the person who is thereby made into an object is already no longer the same as the person who himself is now engaged in the act of posing the question. The questioning person does not simply enter into the person about which the question is asked. The I is unable to capture itself. It views itself as something transcendent to itself. In the question about himself, the individual encounters the boundary of transcendence. Here he finds himself transcended within himself. In this situation, the person who questions must decide between two possibilities, a decision that logic cannot compel. Either the person acknowledges that here he encounters an insuperable boundary, namely, that the I being searched for can never become an object of reflection but rather has its essence in relation to the questioning self, that is, to transcendence; the essence of the human being then rests no longer in itself, but rather in the ever-renewed act of relating to transcendence. The other possibility is to draw the transcendent, questioning I itself into the question, to gain control of one's own I such that one then views the act of the I coming-to-itself as the central occurrence of all intellectual processes.

 The characteristic feature of the first decision about the question is that the person can be understood only from his boundaries or limits; the characteristic feature of the second is that the person is fundamentally accessible and transparent to himself and understands himself through himself; he finds within himself the point of unity from which his own

390

essence reveals itself. The I becomes an object to itself by thinking its I. Here conceptualization of one's own I, as the process of conceptualization out of unity, becomes the primal position of all philosophy. Hence philosophy means posing the question about the human being and providing the answer in one and the same act. The person understands himself because he philosophizes. Philosophy is the human work κατ' ἐξοχήν [*par excellence*]. The individual understands himself out of his most characteristic activity.

391

Work or activity, however, is the concretization of a possibility. If the person understands himself on the basis of his work, then he understands himself out of his possibilities. Even a way of thinking that endeavors to distinguish fundamentally between the actualized and the nonactualized possibility, as for example Judaic thought, does not thereby move out of the category of possibility. The essence of the person is his possibilities, which means that the person remains within himself, grasping his essence immanently. A human being is a self-subsisting world, needing no others (only itself) in order to come into his own essence. By contrast, the self-understanding that emerges from the first decision is always reaching beyond itself. The essence of the human being resides not in immanent quiescent possibilities but in the ever-active relating to his own boundaries or limits. The person is in his essence act-movement[2] precisely because he comes to his essence at any given time only through limitation. In the first instance, we have the person of the infinite, inalienable wealth of possibilities; in the second, the person who loses himself at his limits in order to find himself, who protests against every insistence on something inalienable.

We see how the idea of this question about the human being directly generates two differing understandings of the essence of the human, depending on whether the question concerning the person becomes the point of limitation or the systematic point of departure of all philosophy. We saw further that the question about the human being touches directly on the problem of transcendence; everything depends on whether the I misappropriates transcendence and draws it into itself or instead acknowledges this limit. Hence whenever we inquire about how the human being is understood in any philosophy or theology, the question of transcendence must be raised as the decisive question.

---

2. ["As he wrote in *Act and Being*, for Bonhoeffer 'act' is a technical term encompassing both 'pure intentionality' (*DBWE* 2:28) or relationality (*Beziehung*) and also 'occurrence' from time to time (*DBWE* 2:29 and 113). In short, 'act' has dimensions of intentionality-relationality and eventful temporality. Act-movement (*Aktbewegung*), which highlights movement (*Bewegung*), thus emphasizes the ongoing event of act, which always begins anew," *DBWE* 10:391, n. 11.]

If as theologians we turn to hear what contemporary philosophy has to   392
say about the human, we find first of all that the question about the human
being is one of the most passionately posed questions in contemporary
philosophy. Today one sees old ideologies collapse and must fear that the
human being is being buried along with them. One sees a new intellectual
and cultural reality emerging in which the human being is assaulted by
powers and demons and yet is intent on not surrendering. One finds oneself
imprisoned and yet wants to be free. One feels the ground pulled out from
under one's feet and yet does not want to fall. Here the person must preserve
himself in the most passionate search for himself, in positing himself anew,
in finding himself in the question about himself, the question about what
could ground his existence anew. We can only outline these attempts here.

First attempt: the person reaches for himself into the deepest unrevealed
strata of his being, strata that are untouched by change and persist in eternal rest and order. Beyond himself and beyond the reality of the world, he
grasps for the cosmos of pure values, which are captured and reflected by
the beholding soul. This is Scheler's initial point of departure. His phe-
nomenological epistemological theory, the legitimacy of which I will not
discuss here, enables him, on the basis of a material a priori, juxtaposed
to Kant's formal a priori, to construct a world of the being of values transcending consciousness. God is in this world. The human being is able to
behold God not in the intellectual process but in his feeling of values, a
feeling whose purest form is love. Only in love is there true recognition of
values. In love the person swings aloft to a vision of the eternal and highest value of the Holy One, of God. Here the person grasps the All within
himself and can even grasp God in passionate beholding. This is the "totality of life," namely, that it discloses and encloses within itself the totality of
values. With riveting pathos, Scheler unfolds the motionless, unchangeable, shining heaven of values above the world of subjectivity and relativity
that has been constructed and distorted by thinking, a world restricted to
consciousness; and into that world he places the human being as the spirit
who seizes control of God in the reflection of love. The human being is   393
understood from his possibilities. He bears within himself the possibility of
drawing the transcendent into himself, through his beholding. And that is
his essence. Here everything is conceived statically, the world of values as
well as the possibility of beholding them. The manner of being of both is
that of something existing, that is, of something given, objective. This is why
Catholicism has been able to celebrate triumphs here; the person is secured
as a human being because he holds within himself the possibility of coming
to God, because he bears within himself from creation onward potential
points of contact with God. Hence *the question about* the human cannot as

such be a real problem here. One inquires about the human as concerning a thing, some existing entity. In Scheler's early literary period, we find not even the slightest trace of the notion that the person, as the one who must first inquire about himself and who in and for himself obviously does not yet possess the answer, finds himself in a truly questionable situation, one characterized essentially by precisely this question concerning himself. But something else has already begun to emerge. Over against the realm of values is juxtaposed a realm of being of the world, of evil. Scheler still believes that the latter is unable to harm the former. But an enormous upheaval is coming. It is shocking to see how Scheler's system collapses under the overwhelming impression of the demonic world of human desires. The rigidity of Scheler's conceptual edifice proved to be too brittle to offer resistance to this suddenly erupting reality. It collapses completely. And Scheler's understanding of the person ends in his final literary period with the resigned recognition that the human being is the being in whom the world of the desires gains control of the world of values. Here the human has helplessly fallen prey to demonic powers. The divine human being becomes the plaything of a world emptied of all meaning.

How did this happen? Scheler tried to understand the human being as an entity whose sphere of being was conceived beyond its existence as *ens creatum* [*created entity*] in a created world, that is, as an entity basically untouched by the fact that it must first inquire regarding itself, an entity that "is" in the form of a timelessly existing being. As such an entity, however, the human being could no longer recognize himself the moment he found himself violated in the very ground of his essence by the powers of his own creatureliness, by the powers of society running diametrically opposite to that presumed original being. Scheler separated the *essentia* [*essence*] from the *existentia* [*existence*]. He was well able to conceive the continuity, but not the existentiality, of human being. Hence the magnificent edifice of Schelerian metaphysics had to collapse at the first storm. The human being misunderstood himself. If one wanted to get beyond this misunderstanding, the path had been indicated. The concept of existence had to become constitutive for understanding the human. The person exists, that is, he is in time and in the world as the one who must inquire about himself at any given time. The person thus does not know in general who he is, but rather it is part of his essence to inquire about himself. The being of human beings—that is, their Dasein[3]—does not have the same manner of being as

394

---

3. ["A key term in Heidegger, the German word *Dasein* has been adopted into philosophical English; for Bonhoeffer's understanding of the term, including his critique

an extant being or thing, of something present-at-hand, something accessible; being is found instead only in self-understanding, that is, in the intellectual act of reflection.

Such was the point of departure of Martin Heidegger. Dasein, however, can understand itself not floating freely in space but rather only in being bound to a historical situation of existing in the world. For Dasein, too, it is decisive not that the *understanding of being* is, but that the understanding of being *is*. Dasein thus always finds itself already determined in some way; hence it obviously does not posit itself. Rather it always already *is* as that which it understands itself. This being in the concrete situation, however, is the decision, one always already made, of a potentiality-for-being, that is, the concept of possibility comes into sight. The being of existence is construed as being in possibility and dissipates. In Heidegger's words: "Dasein is primarily being-possible. Dasein is in every case what it can be, and in the way in which it is its possibility." Dasein finds itself in the world in "being with others," in "being fallen into captivity to the anonymous," in day-in, day-out sameness, to use Heidegger's own expressions. Dasein is in a world it cares for. Dasein is care. It recognizes itself as having been thrown into this world of care, as "something having been thrown" into the world, that is, it cannot dispose over itself; it always finds itself only in the situation for which it has already decided. In its captivity to the world, to the anonymous, to talk, however, Dasein disintegrates; it does not come to its own wholeness, something that is, after all, essential for it. Because it is historical, Dasein is subject to death. The totality of Dasein is oriented toward death; it is "being toward death." If Dasein wants to come to its wholeness, then precisely because self-understanding is part of its essence it must understand itself from the perspective of death, that is, it may not accept death as an existing event when it comes, but rather must in every instance go to it ahead of time, incorporate it into its own self-understanding, and thus in the "decision unto death" bring itself to wholeness. Instead of grasping Dasein in its authenticity as being toward death, Dasein falls captive to its own inauthenticity in the world. This being in inauthenticity and nonwholeness is revealed as guilt where Dasein is summoned to its authenticity and out of that captivity—in the call of conscience. But it is Dasein itself that summons in conscience, "anxious in its thrown state" about its potentiality-for-being. Dasein summons itself back to itself; it has lost itself to the world, it is in a foreign country, the world's uncanniness makes it anxious, that is its guilt

395

---

of Heidegger, see his usage in the following sentences and the numerous references in *DBWE* 2," *DBWE* 10:394, n. 20.]

or its nullity, as Heidegger conceives the concept of guilt. In the summons of conscience Dasein takes its guilt upon itself and comes to wholeness by entering into resoluteness to death and in that way finding itself. Dasein seizes its most authentic possibility, its most authentic existence, by coming to itself and in this way understanding itself.

Hence for Heidegger, the wholeness of Dasein means Dasein's being-for-itself. Dasein bears its unity within itself. This is the necessary consequence of understanding Dasein as being-possible and nothing else. The possibilities of Dasein include the possibility of coming to unity. Hence the person understands himself from the perspective of his possibilities. Nonetheless an essential distinction obtains compared with Scheler's construction. Scheler conceives the possibilities of the human being statically, hence in continuity but not in existentiality. Heidegger succeeds in combining the two. The human being exists within time, and only within time are the possibilities actualized; indeed, whenever the human being reflects on them, he already finds himself in a chosen possibility. Every moment is a decision for the possibility of authenticity or inauthenticity. This protects Heidegger's understanding of the human being against the eruption of the world powers that destroyed Scheler's construction. Ultimately Heidegger's human being does not bear any divine features, and is not, as spirit, lord of the world, but instead is to be the human being existing in the world who is threatened precisely by that world, who is exposed to the forces of death, exposed to day-in, day-out sameness, exposed to the anonymous, who falls captive to the world through his own existential possibilities, who ever anew must ask about and seek himself. This is why Heidegger's human being lacks the otherworldly pathos and the luster of Scheler's human being. This person is introduced as the worried, anxious human being of resignation, of daily life; this person has been accused of being petit-bourgeois, but that is not all; the element of pathos resides only a bit deeper in Heidegger's understanding of the human than in Scheler's and is colored differently. Where the person is summoned by conscience, he is able to extract himself from his captivity to the world, albeit not in such a way that he might escape the forces of temporality without responsibility, but such that he takes his guilt, the nullity of his life upon himself and orients himself toward the most unconquerable of all forces—death. He draws death into his life and lives a being toward death. Up to this point, Heidegger seems to remain faithful to his will genuinely to grasp existence, but by knowingly taking upon himself these realities even unto the reality of death, he overcomes them in their character as boundaries and so attains not the end but rather the completion, the wholeness of Dasein. The person gains command of the world by elevating himself into a tragically isolated individual. The person

396

remains alone, understanding himself from himself; being in the world has no meaning for one's authentic self-understanding. Ultimately the person himself answers the question about the human being. The world of demonic forces has been overcome and dominated in the spirit. Captivity in this world is merely the transition to the spirit's finding itself. And precisely by grasping his own existence completely in this world, the human being ultimately is able to do violence to the world. We sense that we are getting extremely close to Hegel, and yet, on the other hand, it comes as no surprise that Heidegger refers to the Kant of the first edition of the *Critique of Pure Reason*. Although Heidegger does indeed acknowledge the human being's self-questioning as the fundamental problem, ultimately here, too, the question becomes the answer; the human being basically knows about himself; the question has no ultimate seriousness.

397

Only one step remains, and the whole picture seems to change completely. It is part of human nature that the human being must inquire about himself, that he remains absolutely questionable to himself, albeit not such that he might entice an answer to this question from even deeper strata of his own being; instead, he remains in the questionableness of his existence. Paul Tillich, whose thought begins at this point, views the human being as a finite being characterized by not coming to his own essence through himself, since there is absolutely no secure, unified point from which self-understanding might be possible. The human being is not able to elevate himself to lord over the world because all that is human is basically called into question by the ground of all being, all that is finite by the infinite. Hence the person comes to his essence only where, standing at his boundary, he experiences the inbreaking of the infinite. Here he understands himself in "living through the boundary situation," in "being threatened in the unconditional sense," that is, in acknowledging the responsibility attaching to every moment, the irresponsibility of daily life. He understands himself because the preeminent characteristic of the boundary situation is that, where the human being stands radically under the No, the Yes to the human being is perceived. Not in the form of a Christian proclamation—here all religious content also falls under the No, "even Christ or God"—but rather the Yes in its absoluteness. The absolute *boundary* is the inbreaking of the absolute itself; the absolute No *is* the absolute Yes. The human being understands himself on the basis of his boundary. This is apparently a fundamental contrast to the person who understands himself on the basis of his possibilities: the person who completes himself from within himself is juxtaposed to the one who at the boundary protests against all human self-positing and securing. The human being at the boundary is the human being of fundamental protest.

398

Before we examine this contrast more closely, however, we must follow the most recent philosophy one step further. Starting from the recognition that as long as the person encounters the world as a thinking being he will interpret the world according to himself and do violence to it, Eberhard Grisebach manages to fix the boundary of the human being in a fashion other than by thinking, namely, address the concrete You as the boundary of the human being. In reality, existence is only in an encounter with a You. Here is the real boundary, not the boundary that is thought nor the boundary that enters into reflection, here is "presence." Human existence is only in the present, where it bears the claim of the other person, does not do violence to the other person, but rather enters into a διαλέγεσθαι [*discuss, speak with another*] with that person. Hence the person genuinely understands himself only in concretely bearing the claim at the concrete boundary that [is erected before him and that allows the person being encountered always to be himself][4] disrupts a person in every act of self-absolutization. Here we seem to have the most incisive articulation of the recognition that the person can understand himself only on the basis of his boundaries that is, in relation to transcendence, in contrast to all human self-understanding from the perspective of immanent possibilities. What is really new in Grisebach's position is that he cannot conceive the human being apart from the concrete other person. This position clearly expresses the will to overcome every sort of individualism, that is, any restricting of the I only within itself. Grisebach manages to do this, however, only by abso-

399 lutizing the You in the place of the I and attributing to it a status belonging only to God. Hence the I posits the other as absolute, acknowledges that other as its concrete, absolute boundary only to have its own absolute essence ultimately returned to it through that absolute You. After all, since I myself posit the claim of the You as absolute, I could just as easily relativize it, and thus with my own possibilities I remain the master of the other person as well. Although Grisebach's intentions are certainly worthy of serious attention, he cannot carry them out by these means. Here, however, we find ourselves in the very midst of the critique of what philosophy can even call the boundary of the human being.

We must raise one significant objection against the attempt to understand the human being on the basis of his limits rather than from that of his possibilities. The boundary by which the human being limits him-

---

4. ["This terse and seemingly opaque statement that was omitted from the actual lecture recapitulates fundamental ideas about persons, encounter, boundary, and reality that Bonhoeffer had worked out in his theological anthropology in *Sanctorum Communio*; cf. *DBWE* 1:44–57, esp. 45–46, 49–52 (*Reader* 21–29, esp. 21–22, 24–26)," *DBWE* 10:398, n. 39.]

self remains a self-drawn boundary, that is, a boundary the human person essentially has already crossed, a boundary that person must already have stood beyond in the first place in order to draw it. The boundary is thus the absolute possibility that turns against itself. By limiting my own possibilities in thought—and I really cannot limit them in any other way in philosophy—I demonstrate through the very possibility of limitation the infinity of my possibilities, from which I can no longer go back. Here, however, these attempts to understand the person on the basis of his boundaries or limits joins the ranks of those they objected to in the first place, namely, the attempts to understand the human being on the basis of his possibilities. The human being essentially has no boundaries within himself; he is infinite within himself. To that extent, idealism is correct. The question is merely how this fact is to be understood. In philosophy, the question about the human being is ultimately always posed such that the human being himself finds the answer, because that answer is already contained in the question. The human being remains within himself, either as the one with eyes that behold the eternal values, or as the tragically isolated individual, or as the individual at the boundary with the rigid gesture of protest. The human being understands himself on the basis of his possibilities in self-reflection, meaning further that he understands himself only in connection with his works.

Although theology accepts these results of philosophical inquiry, it interprets them in its own fashion as the thinking of the *cor curvum in se* [*the heart turned in upon itself*].[5] The I does indeed remain self-enclosed; this, however, is not to its credit but is its guilt. This self-imprisoned thought is the true expression of self-questioning human beings in *status corruptionis* [*state of corruption, i.e., after the fall*]. In a clearly related fashion and yet with an essential difference, as we will yet see, theology is unable to conceive the human being except in relation to his boundary, which here is called God. If the question about the human being is to be posed seriously, it can be so only where the human being is before God. Whenever this question is posed elsewhere, it is never really posed seriously. That is, the human being is torn completely out of himself, drawn as a whole person before God, and here the question about the human being becomes serious precisely because it no longer includes its own answer. Instead, God gives the human being the answer completely freely and completely anew, since it is now God who has placed the human before God himself and instructs the human being

400

---

5. ["... one of Luther's favorite expressions, here taken from his lectures on Romans (*LW* 25:291); cf. *DBWE* 2:41, n. 11 and n. 20 et passim)," *DBWE* 10:399, n. 41.]

to question in this way. That is, the human being experiences his foundation not through himself, but through God. Whomever God summons is in essence a human being. The point of unity from which the human being understands himself thus resides with God. To this extent, contemporary theology is agreed since its latest reorientation toward Luther. The great points of contention reside only in the interpretation of these statements. The two approaches we encountered in philosophy now recur in theology.

First, the human being understands himself from his self-reflection on his possibilities. If the human being is to understand himself only in connection with the transcendent, in this case God, then God somehow must attest himself in that human being; otherwise there is no relation to God. The place where God attests himself must be the place from which the human being understands himself and at the same time the place where his unity is founded. This place, however, is obviously conscience. Here the human being knows himself to be summoned, called to accountability, judged, and justified. Here is God's gateway into the person; here we find the immediate connection with God. The human being is a person of conscience who understands himself out of the reflection on his own conscience in which God encounters him. We mention the name of Karl Holl[6] here merely as one particularly impressive representative of the overwhelming majority of contemporary theologians. Holl characterized Luther's religion as "religion

401   of conscience." For now I will merely point out that this position included a peculiarly meager estimation of Christology in Luther. The human being finds God within himself in some fashion; he has God in self-reflection. Because the human being is able to hear and have God within his conscience, he is able to understand himself from within his conscience as his most authentic possibility of being human.

At precisely this point, however, Holl encountered the most spirited opposition from the so-called dialectical theology. The question in which the human being reflects on himself always remains a question; he cannot find answers from within himself since there is no point within him at which God might gain space. Indeed, the essence of human being is to be *incapax infiniti* [*incapable of infinity*],[7] that is, it is impossible for the finite human essence to unite directly with the infinite, and this precludes the possibility that the human being might absolutize himself at even a single point within

---

6. ["Cf. *DBWE* 2:141–143 (*Reader* 96–97)," *DBWE* 10:400, n. 44.]

7. ["This is an allusion to a formulation that had caused controversy within Protestantism. Lutherans had described the phrase '*finitum non est capax infiniti*' (the finite is not capable of bearing the infinite) as the *extra calvinisticum*; for further discussion, see *DBWE* 2:84, n. 7," *DBWE* 10:401, n. 46.]

his essence. He remains totally unsecured because he remains completely within himself. Even thought, ethical consciousness of responsibility, and religiosity remain hopeless attempts to anchor the I within the absolute. All these belong to the φρόνημα σαρκός [*fleshly way of thinking*] in all this the human being is misappropriating God's honor insofar as he does not want to remain unsecured or want to secure himself at least through his own self-understanding. He declares himself good, he declares himself bad, but whether good or bad, both declarations are merely attempts at least to be secured; but he does not recognize one thing, namely, his own guilt before God in his good and his evil, guilt consisting precisely in wanting to self-posit and self-secure himself once and for all. That is, he does not want to be broken apart and healed, judged, and pardoned ever anew by God alone; he does not want to be justified by grace. The human being wants to justify himself; that is his guilt, since he could do so only if he had God in his power. But God remains eternally beyond, eternally distant, even and precisely where God comes close to human beings, in revelation. Barth says that "those to whom God is revealed are the very ones to whom God cannot become revealed" (*Dogmatik* [*Dogmatics*], 1:287).[8] If the human being is to get an answer to the question about the human, to the question he not only   402
raises but is himself, then he must be torn completely out of his inversion into himself and be directed to that which is absolutely exterior to his own existence. Only from beyond himself can he perceive the answer as God's answer. The human being is established by God's constantly renewed deed, which God can either do or not do *quia sic vult* [*because God wants it thus*]. Never, however, does God's word of justification enter into the person such that the latter now merely has to adduce it; rather, God must in every case speak it ever anew, it must come to the person from the outside. The human being understands himself ever anew out of the word of God that comes from without, out of his absolute boundary that is called God. Whereas Barth amplifies these ideas from the perspective of the Kantian idea of the person who exists only in relation to transcendence, Bultmann tries to make Heidegger fruitful for theology. The human being does not dispose over himself, for he exists within history, not in the manner of objective things, but rather his being is potentiality-for-being, that is, being-determined by sin or by God. Here the idea of the human being at the boundary

---

8. ["Bonhoeffer means Barth, *Die christliche Dogmatik im Entwurf* [*Christian Dogmatics in Outline*], and quotes the 1927 edition that he owned; cf. Barth, *Gesamtausgabe*, 2:383. Cf. also *Act and Being*, where Bonhoeffer cites the same passage (*DBWE* 2:99)," *DBWE* 10:401, n. 48.]

seems to be united with that of the human being of infinite possibilities. Friedrich Gogarten went beyond these ideas of Barth and Bultmann. Gogarten maintains that Barth's point of departure is speculative, that Barth ultimately views the human being not in the existential situation but somehow in the absolute sphere. Human existence is not grasped until it is conceived as being addressed by the historical You posited by God. The neighbor takes God's place. Just as with Grisebach, with whom Gogarten initially concurred, the neighbor is posited absolutely here in order to set historical reality against all speculative flight. History is the encounter between I and You; there is no I without You. Gogarten's corrective to Barth here reveals that Barth's thinking, too, is individualistic, that is, the human being remains alone with himself. Gogarten sees, however, that the theology of revelation excludes individualistic thinking. By granting God's absolute claim to the neighbor, however, Gogarten slides from the theology of revelation into an inner-worldly ethic; this, in turn, means that the I and the You can bring each other mutually to their essence. Thus they understand themselves in such a way that one is there for the other, in order to enable the other to understand himself; this however excludes revelation.

403   The human being perceives the claim of the neighbor as the absolute only if God's absolute claim in Christ has encountered him and given him the answer to the question about himself. Thus, according to Gogarten, human self-understanding is still possible quite independently of revelation; that is, the question about the human being can be answered immanently. Hence Gogarten's boundary, too, is not the real boundary of revelation.

As long as the human being can posit a self-imposed boundary by thinking, that boundary is characterized by the possibility of being transcended; that is, even the person who intends to understand himself on the basis of his boundaries ultimately understands himself on the basis of his own possibilities. By contrast, we maintain that *the concept of possibility has no place in theology and thus no place in theological anthropology*.[9] The following arguments support this.

I. The person who understands himself from the perspective of his possibilities understands himself from within his own self-reflection. In revelation, however, the human being is torn out of this reflection and receives the answer to his question only from and before God. The question about the human being is derived from the question about God. Here we find the fun-

---

9. ["Cf. *DBWE* 1:126–130 (*Reader* 36–38). Cf. graduation thesis 4, criticizing the use of the concept of 'potentiality' (*Potentialität*) in theology; *DBWE* 9:440," *DBWE* 10:403, n. 54.]

damental difference between philosophical and theological anthropology.

II. The concept of possibility rationalizes reality. It determines every reality according to the manner of a logically existing thing. That is, it fixes it, makes it universally accessible. In this way, it is possible to place the point of unity of self-understanding into one's own ego through rationalization. For theological anthropology, this means that the human being is conceived with certain possibilities in relation to God, to which he can withdraw at any given time. That human being is *capax* or *incapax infiniti* [*capable or incapable of infinity*], that the being of the human is potentiality-for-being, these are conditions that fix a person's being a priori and independently of the reality of revelation, and thereby yield revelation itself to human interpretation.

III. The concept of possibility is inadequate because the human being is either understood from revelation or not, because one cannot speak at all about a possibility of, or capacity for, revelation independent of the reality of revelation, since otherwise it would not be absolutely external. Hence it is precisely because of the emphasis on revelation coming from beyond existence that one has to reject every fixed *finitum incapax* [*incapable of the infinite*].

IV. The concept of possibility includes semi-Pelagianism.[10] If sin and faith are among the possibilities of human beings, then the complete incomprehensibility, inexcusability, and infinity of the fall is rationalized into a comprehensible actualization of immanent possibilities. Here sin loses the weight of infinity, the result being that the forgiveness and the wiping out of sins can be understood only as the actualization—albeit from God—of human possibilities that are no more infinitely significant than sin itself. That is, from this perspective one cannot comprehensibly explain how sin and grace mean eternal judgment and eternal life.

V. The concept of possibility does indeed allow an understanding of the human being in continuity. The human being is perpetually his own possibility. If, however, this possibility is fixed in the form-of-being of some extant thing, then it does not affect the human being's existence, which cannot be conceived in the form-of-being of an extant thing but transcends such a form. The true continuity of the human being must be grounded at the center of that person's existence.

VI. The critique of the concept of the boundary occurs simultaneously with the concept of possibility. We have already shown that this concept itself falls prey to the concept of possibility. Clearly, however, theology must also speak of a boundary between God and human. Three things, however,

404

---

10. ["For further discussion, see *DBWE* 2:136–137 (*Reader* 93–94)," *DBWE* 10:404, n. 56.]

should be kept in mind. *First,* that this boundary constitutes not a formal boundary between two manners-of-being in the form of some extant thing but rather a boundary between persons. *Second,* that the content of this boundary is determined by the concepts of sin and holiness. *Third,* that the theme of theology is the crossing of this boundary by God, namely, forgiveness of sins and sanctification. What follows, however, is that the theological concept of boundary is determined not through the rational stasis of the concept of possibility but rather through the dynamic reality of God.

405

Even though this position excludes the concept of possibility from theology, we can add positively that it is not in self-reflection that the human being understands himself but in the act-of-relating to God, that is, only where the person genuinely stands before God. Not where the person finds the possibilities within himself by virtue of which he can then stand before God. Here we must distinguish between *actus directus* and *actus reflexus* [*direct act and reflective act*].[11] True self-understanding is found only in the *actus directus;* in the *actus reflexus* immediacy has already been disrupted, and thus there can no longer be any self-understanding. Since theology takes place only within the *actus reflexus,* it cannot itself constitute the true self-understanding of the human being—as philosophy claims for itself— but can only trace it. In such tracing, all depends on not rationalizing reality again through the category of possibility.

The human being understands himself only by his act-of-relating to God, which only God can establish. The human being sees his own unity grounded in God's word directed toward him, a word whose content is judgment and grace. Here the human being recognizes that his own essence is neither to be *capax* nor *incapax infiniti* [*capable nor incapable of infinity*], that his essence is not his own possibilities but rather is determined by the statements, "You are under sin," or "You are under grace."

Now, how does the essence of the human appear in sin and in grace? In recognizing sin, a recognition that occurs within God's revelation, the human being knows himself to be under God's judgment and finds himself as part of a humanity that has fallen away from God, fallen away because he wanted to be like God; now he stands under God's judgment. He finds himself condemned both as an individual and as a human being per se. Every person represents fallen humanity, and when each person fell from his common vocation as a human being, humanity fell as well. Each and

---

11. ["Bonhoeffer adopted this distinction from Franz Delitzsch and already employed it as the 'central idea,' according to Hans-Richard Reuter, in *Act and Being;* see *DBWE* 2:28, n. 17, and 158–161," *DBWE* 10:405, n. 59.]

every person is Adam, who brought sin into the world, and the entirety of humanity stands under the aeon of Adam. The human being is no longer alone, because he stands in the humanity of Adam in which each person is Adam. Within this humanity, however, that person remains lonely. The spirit of sin has torn him away from the spirit of God and from his neighbor. Now the human spirit circles perpetually around itself. Now this spirit is master of the world, but only of the world its ego interprets and thinks up, master in its own, self-restricted, violated world. He sees his fellow human beings as things and sees God as the one who satisfies his religious needs; and now he seeks to posit himself eternally in this world; he does not want to die; he wants to justify himself and live eternally. But during this search, which leads him through philosophy and through religion, the human being begins to sense his enormous solitude. He becomes anxious in the face of this dominion over a dead world; in his anxiety he breaks the terrible silence of his solitude and breaks away from himself, stands over against himself in order to replace the missing other, and accuses himself. That is conscience. But since he is simultaneously accuser, accused, and judge, this summons of conscience proves to be merely the last grasp of the ego for itself, for its own possibilities. And its summons dies away in the silent, dominated world of the ego.

This is the world in which the human being finds himself and into which God enters, brings him before his judgment, and condemns him. This takes place in the cross of Christ. In his death, however, the old, violated, interpreted world of the ego dies along with the ego, and the new aeon, the aeon of Christ, dawns in his resurrection and his life. The humanity of Adam is overcome by the humanity of Christ, albeit not such that the former is completely extirpated, but such that it is fundamentally robbed of its power. Just as the world of Adam violated Christ, so too does it violate the new humanity of Christ. But just as Christ deprived it of its power in his own death, so too is it deprived of power over human beings in the new humanity of Christ, over human beings in Christ. The human being who has been initiated into the death and resurrection of Christ through God's word, that is, the Christian, now understands his present being as determined from two sides. First and decisively through his future, which is Christ alone, but then also through his past, which is Adam and which must ever and again be given over to the death of Christ. The person in Christ is one who is tempted,[12] to the extent that Adam's humanity remains in effect. The law, the flesh, and the world all stand against that person, grasping, creating

406

---

12. ["Cf. *DBWE* 2:155–156 (*Reader* 105–106)," *DBWE* 10:406, 63.]

407

fear, obscuring the view of Christ, and driving conscience so that the devil himself speaks in it. The person in Christ has not been removed from the world. That person is the person of normal daily work, of labor, of vocation

[*page missing, see n. 13*][13]

mystery of the church-community that Christ is in it and only through it seizes the human being; Christ exists among us as church-community, as church in the hiddenness of historicity. The church is the hidden Christ among us. Hence the human being is never alone; instead he exists only through the church-community that brings Christ, a community incorporating the human being, drawing that person into its life. The person in Christ is the person in the church-community; wherever that person is, there is the church-community. But because that person as an individual is simultaneously wholly a member of the church-community, only here is the continuity of that person's existence in Christ guaranteed.

Hence the human being can understand himself no longer from within himself but rather from within the Christ who exists as church-community, from within his word that supports the church-community and without which that church-community does not exist. But because this word affects his existence and as the word of the church-community simultaneously founds the continuity of that person's being, the human being can understand himself only in direct relation to that word. People of the children of God, "children of mercy" (Luther): that is the self-understanding of the person in Christ, tempted here and repeatedly brought down, torn out of the *actus directus* [*direct act*], ultimately completely surrendered in the relaxed disposition of a child toward its father.

I have been able to examine only briefly the distinctiveness of the question about the human being; my attempt to provide guidelines for a genuine theological anthropology had to limit itself to an outline. To the extent that this attempt represents a piece of genuine theological thought, it escapes the charge that it too derives from reflection and does not offer any genuine self-understanding, if this is acknowledged without qualification, and only if this theological undertaking is itself incorporated into the reality of the church in which Christ is present. Ultimately, only as the thinking of

---

13. ["Page 20 of the typescript has been lost. After the discussion of the human being in sin, 'in Adam' (*DBWE* 2:136–148 [*Reader* 93–100]), and now in grace, 'in Christ' (*DBWE* 2:150–161 [*Reader* 101–109]), the lost page probably discussed how this 'being in Christ' takes place in a continuing and contingent fashion within the church and finds its locus of recognition in the church (*DBWE* 2:108–109)," *DBWE* 10:407, n. 65.]

the church does theological thought remain the only form of thought that does not rationalize reality through the category of possibility. Therefore, every individual theological problem not only points back to the reality of 408 the church of Christ, but theological thought in its entirety also recognizes itself as something that belongs solely to the church.

8. LECTURE ON "WAR"

DBWE 10:411–418

Bonhoeffer spent the American academic year 1930–1931 as a postdoctoral student at Union Theological Seminary, in New York.[1] North America provided Bonhoeffer with a number of novel experiences, many of which stimulated his life and thought in the years to come. He was not impressed with most American churches, where he experienced an "almost frivolous attitude."[2] But Bonhoeffer found a bright spot in the otherwise depressing theological and ecclesial landscape: Abyssinian Baptist Church in Harlem. He later recalled that here, as in other black churches, "the Gospel of Jesus Christ, the savior of the sinner, is really preached and received with great welcome and visible emotion."[3] During his time in America, Bonhoeffer invested heavily in developing relationships with friends from a variety of national and ecclesial backgrounds.[4] It seems that these friendships encouraged his budding internationalism and ecumenism, which are on display in the brief lecture printed below. In the address, which he probably delivered several times, Bonhoeffer speaks as a German intent to make his American audience sympathetic to specifically German hardships, but he ends with a call to take "seriously the great idea of the unity of Christianity, above all personal and national desires."[5]

411   It is indeed a strange feeling for me just coming over here from Germany now to stand for an american christian young people group trying to talk about this event of the recent history, which had seperated our peoples for

---

1. [*For historical background, biographical information, and a summary of texts from Bonhoeffer's first stay in America (1930–1931), see* DBWE *10:17–43, editor's introduction, and* DB-ER, *147–169.*]
2. [DBWE *10:261.*]
3. [DBWE *15:458.*]
4. [DBWE *10:25–34, editor's introduction.*]
5. [*Bonhoeffer wrote this and the next two selections in English. They are reproduced as he wrote them, errors included.*]

many years. But I think, that only an open and franc discussion just of these questions, can help us for the deeper understanding of each other and for a more successful common work in the future. For I stand before you here in the church not only as a Christian, but as a German, who loves his home the best of all, who rejoices with his people and who suffers, when he sees his people suffering, who confesses gratefully, that he received from his people all that he has and is. So I bring you today a double message; the message of Germany and of the Christianity in Germany. I hope you will hear this message with a christian heart, with the readiness of the christian soul to understand and to love, whereever and whomever it might be. The 11. of November 1918[6] brought to Germany the end of a frightful unparalleled time, a time, which we pray if God wills, will never return. For four years german men and lads stood for their home with an unheard of tenacity and intrepidity with the imperturbable consciousness of their duty, with an inexorable selfdiscipline and with a glowing love for their fatherland and with the believe in its future. For weeks and months these people suffered privations of every kind, they persevered in hunger and thirst in pain and affliction, in craving after the home, after mothers and wifes and brothers and children. In the country did not cease the stream of tears, of old and young people. Every day the message came to more than 1000 familys, that the husband, the father, the brother had died in a foreign country. Hardly any family was spared. I tell you from my personal experience, two brothers of mine stood on the front. The older one 18 years old was wounded, the younger one 17 years old was killed. 3 first cousins of mine were also killed, boys of 18 to 20 years old. Although I was then a small boy, I never can forget those most gloomy days of the war. Death stood for the door of almost every house and called for entrance. Once came the message about the death of many thousands seventeen and eighteen years old boys killed in a few hours.[7] Germany was made a house of mourning. The break down could not be delayed longer. Famine and enervation were to powerful and

---

6. ["The decisive historical date in Germany was November 9, 1918, the symbolic date of Kaiser Wilhelm II's abdication and the end of the *Kaiserreich* (cf. Erdmann, *Die Zeit der Weltkriege*, 141–143 and 181; see also *DB-ER*, 30). Here Bonhoeffer prefers the date November 11, 1918, because this day was celebrated as Armistice Day, a holiday in the United States," *DBWE* 10:412, n. 2.]

7. ["Bonhoeffer is referring to the Battle of Langemarck in September 1914 in which 'young regimental soldiers,' including many high school and university students, poorly trained, poorly equipped, and poorly led, were senselessly slaughtered in an assault through the mud on regular British troops in fixed positions. Propaganda turned this tragedy into a heroic deed," *DBWE* 10:412, n. 6.]

413   destructive. In the treaty of Versailles Germany was compelled to sign that
        she and her allies bore the sole guilt of the war and that she was responsible
        for all reparations.[8] I think you release me from talking about our feeling
        in Germany in the first days after this end. The recollection of this time is
        gloomy and sad. Very seldom you will hear today in Germany anybody talk-
        ing about those days. We will not reopen an old and painful wound. But
        however we felt, the war and its dreadful killing and dying and suffering
        was finished. Our minds were still too confused and bewildered, we could
        not yet conceive and quietly consider the meaning of all these events of the
        last years and months. As a matter of fact, we had neither time nor rest for
        a quiet and objectiv consideration. While Germany still was trembling and
        quailing under the last shots of the canons a fatal revolution was prepared
        in the country, which threatened to overthrow the last foundations of our
        external and internal life. Germany was broken down economically and
        inwardly. The same 11. November 1918 which brought to us the end of the
        war, was the beginning of a new epoch of suffering and grief.[9] The first
        years after the war showed to us the corruption in our public life, in our
        social and economic order. Very hardly you can imagine the poverty of our
        people and its consequences in those days. England had cut off Germany
        from any import of food. This hunger blockade was against all international
        law, since only ships carrying arms could be attached and sunk. The conse-
        quences of the blockade were frightful. I myself was in these years a school-
        boy and I can assure you, that not only I had in those days to learn, what
414   hunger means. I should wish, that you would have to eate this food for only
        one day, that we had for 3 or 4 years and I think, you would get a glimpse
        of the privations, which Germany had to endure. Put yourself in the situa-
        tion of the german mothers, whose husbands were standing or were killed

---

    8. ["Bonhoeffer wrote down article 231 of the Versailles Treaty (of June 28, 1919) in
English on p. 3 of his notebook: 'The Allied and Associated Governments affirm and
Germany accepts the responsibility of Germany and her allies for causing all the loss
and the damage to which the Allied and Associated Governments and their nations have
been subjected as a consequence of the war imposed upon them by the aggression of Germany and her allies.' This article became one of the important psychological arguments
used by opponents of the Weimar Republic, including and especially in National Socialist
propaganda. Cf. Erdmann, *Die Zeit der Weltkriege*, 208–210, 328, and 337. For Bonhoeffer's
immediate impressions of the effects of the Versailles Treaty, see his letter of May 20, 1919
(*DBWE* 9:29)," *DBWE* 10:413, n. 7.]

    9. ["Bonhoeffer's negative assessment of the effects of the 1918 November revolution
here derives especially from his experience of the economic crisis that developed during
the postwar years. It is worth noting that Bonhoeffer avoided the widespread legend of
the 'stab in the back,' which alleged that the military defeat was brought about only by
the revolution (cf. Erdmann, *Die Zeit der Weltkriege*, 219)," *DBWE* 10:413, n. 8.]

in the war and who had to provide for growing hungry children. Countless tears are flowen in these last years of the war and the first years of the peace by desperated mothers and hungry children. As a matter of fact, instead of good meal were many percent saw dust in our bread, and the fixed portion for every day was 5 or 6 slices of that kind of bread. You could not get butter at all. Instead of sugar we had sacharin tabletts. The substitute for meat, fish, vegetables, even for coffee, jam and toast—were turnips for breakfast, lunch and supper. Germany really was starved out. Thousand and thousand of old and young people, of little children died simply, because there was not enough to eate. Fatale epidemics ran through the country. The "Grippe" [*flu*] of 1918 demanded more than hundred thousand victims. People were physically to enervated and could not resist. When the wintertime came, we had not enough coal for heating our rooms. We had not cloth for our clothes, it is not exeggerated, that many people had to buy in these days suits made more by paper than by real cloth. On the street you could see the undernourished and poorly dressed people, the pale and sickly children. The number of the suicides increased in a terrifying way. I remember very well, I had on the way to my school to pass by a bridge and in the winters from 1917–1919 almost every morning when I came to this bridge I saw a group of people standing on the river and everybody, who passed by, knew, what had happened. These impressions were hard for young boys.

I will stopp picturing these frightful months and years; but before I go on, I will not forget to tell you, that the Quaker congregations of the States were the first, who after the war in an admirable work supported the german children. Many thousand children were saved from starvation. Germany remembers in deep thankfullness this work of love of the Quaker society. Hearing all that, you can get no more than a glimpse of the reality. Such were the conditions in Germany in the end of the war, really unparelled months and years. But there was one wound, which was much more painfull than all these privations and needs, that was the art. 231 of the treaty of Versailles. I will tell you francly, that this is the wound, which still is open and bleeds in Germany. I will try to explain to you briefly, what our attitude toward this question was and is. When the war broke out, the German people did not consider very much the question of guilt. We thought it to be our duty to stand for our country and we believed of course in our essential guiltlessness. You cannot expect in such a moment of excitement an objective and detached valuation of the present conditions. The war has its own psychology. The german soldiers stood in the war in the confident faith in the righteousness of their country. But already during the war you could hear in Germany some skeptical voices: who can tell, who is wrong and who is right? We all fight for our country and believe in it, Germans no less than

415

French. Now 12 years after the war the whole question has been thoroughly searched historically. I personally see many faults in our policy before the war, I am not going to defend my country in every point. But a study of the diplomatic documents of Belgium of the years before the war for instance shows irrefutably, that other countrys had committed the same or greater faults than Germany, I mean especially Russia and France. In 1914 everybody in Europe expected more a war caused by Russia and France, than by Germany. It can be proved historically, that the art. 231 of the treaty of Versailles is an injustice against our country and we have a right to protest.[10] That fact is recognised by the largest parts of educated people in Europe and in America. When I think of the guilt of Germany, I mean something deeper, than some political faults. But now I am going to speak from a Christian point of view. Christian people in Germany, who took the course and the end of the war seriously, could not help seeing here a judgment of God upon this fallen world and especially upon our people. Before the war we lived too far from God, we believed too much in our own power, in our allmightiness and righteousness. We attempted to be a strong and good people, but we were to proud of our endeavours, we felt too much satisfaction with our scientific economic and social progress and we identified this progress with the coming of the Kingdom of God; we felt too happy and complacent in this world, our souls were too much at home in this world.

416   Then the great disillusionment came. We saw the impotence and weakness of humanity, we were suddenly awaked from our dream, we felt the wrath of God upon us, and we recognised our guiltiness before God. But let me go on to a further point.

Everyone who knows the conditions in Germany today, 12 years after the war, knows, that inspite of some changes in their external aspect social conditions are almost as unhappy as 10 or 12 years ago. The debts of the war press us not only in regard to our financial standard but likewise in regard to our whole behaviour, we see the hopelessness of our work; it is impossible for us to provide social and economic conditions for our children in the future, in which we can trust for security. I must know, that my grandchildren still will have to pay reparations and war debts.[11]

---

10. ["On page 2 of his notebook, Bonhoeffer enumerated examples of Allied 'atrocity propaganda,' and both here and on page 25 listed the opinions of persons who had come out against the 'sole guilt' thesis. The question of guilt for the outbreak of World War I was discussed from the first day of World War I onward and is occasionally debated even today . . . ," *DBWE* 10:415, n. 15.]

11. [*Bonhoeffer alludes to the Young Plan,* "[t]he plan for regulating German reparation payments presented in 1930 by an international commission of experts under Owen D.

The Germans are a suffering people today, but thei will not despair. Thei will work for building up a new and better home, thei will work for peace in their country, thei will work for peace in the world. When I came over here, I was astonished on beeing asked again and again, what German people think about a future war. I tell you the truth, German people do not speak at all about that, they dont even think of it. You almost never would hear in Germany talk about war and much less about a future war. We know, what a war means for a people. I have been accustomed once in every year since my boyhood to wander on foot through our country, and so I happen to know many classes of German people rather well. Many evening I have sat with the familys of paysants around the big stove talking about the next genera- tion and their chances. But always when the talk happened to touch the war, I observed, how deep the wound was, which the past war had caused in every one. The german paysants like the paysants of every country want above all peace. They want to work peacefully in their fields, they fear any disturbance. But it is not different among other classes in Germany. In the workers class for instance started the german peace movement, and the interest for an international trade makes those people naturally pacifistic. It was in Germany, that the thought arose, that the worker in France and in Germany are closer to one another, then the various classes within each country separately belong to one another. You will find large worker organ- isations with a particularly pacifistic programme, especially also the chris- tian organisations of workers work in this very direction. The bourgeois in Germany had to bear the hardest burden after the war, but nevertheless I can assure you, that by far the most of them would abominate a war more 417 then anything else. You might be interested in hearing something about the attitude of the youth toward war and peace. The youthmovement,[12] which started immediately after the war, was in its tendencies entirely pacifistic. In deep religious feeling we recognised every people as brothers, as children of God. We wanted to forget all hard and bitter feeling after the war. We had anew discovered an genuine and true love for our homecountry and that helped us to get a great and deep love for other people, for the whole

---

Young. It was vehemently rejected in church circles; see *DB-ER*, 125 and Meier, *Kirch- enkampf*, 1:7. The Young Plan revised the earlier unworkable Dawes Plan, reducing the amount significantly but requiring Germany to pay $26.35 billion over some fifty-eight years. In 1995, after reunification, the German government resumed interest payments," *DBWE* 10:283, n. 10.]

12. ["The youth movement (*Jugendbewegung*) was an idealistic countercultural move- ment widely influential among the post–World War I German youth of Bonhoeffer's generation. Especially strong among the bourgeois, it emphasized nature and values con- sidered authentic as opposed to the upper-middle-class lifestyle . . . ," *DBWE* 10:63, n. 24.]

mankind. You see, there are many various motives working for peace, but whatever motive it might be, there is one great aim and one great work; the peacemovement in Germany is an enormous power.[13]

Returning to the Christian point of view, it seems to me one of the greatest tasks for our church, to strengthen the work of peace in every country and in the whole world. It must never more happen, that a christian people fights against a christian people, brother against brother, since both have one Father. Our churches have already begun this international work.[14] But more important than that is, it seems to me, that every christian man and woman, takes seriously the great idea of the unity of Christianity, above all personal and national desires, of the one christian people in the whole world, of the brotherhood of mankind, of the charity, about which Paul says: 1 Cor. 13:4. Let us consider, that the last judgement comes for everyone, in America and Germany; and God will judge us according to our faith and love. How can the man, who hates his brother, expect grace by God.

This is my message for you: hear the voice of your german brothers and sisters, take their stretched out hand. We know, it is not enough only to talk and to feel the necessity of peace, we must work seriously. There is so much meanness, selfishness, slander, hatred, prejudice among the nations. But we must overcome it. Today as never before nations of Europe—except Germany—are preparing for war. This makes our work very urgent. We must no longer waste time. Let us work together for an everlasting peace. And the peace of God, which passeth all understanding shall keep your hearts and minds through Christ Jesus [*Phil. 4:7*].

418

---

13. ["This positive description does not, however, correspond to the actual situation of the peace movement in the Weimar Republic; see Holl and Wette, *Pazifismus in der Weimarer Republik*, as well as the excursus in Röhm, *Sterben für den Frieden*, 41–72, esp. 68," *DBWE* 10:417, n.19.]

14. ["Bonhoeffer is presumably thinking in particular of the World Alliance for Promoting International Friendship through the Churches, founded in 1914, whose youth secretary he would become a year later, and of the International Fellowship of Reconciliation, also founded in 1914 by Friedrich Siegmund-Schultze and the British Quaker Henry Hodgkin," *DBWE* 10:417, n. 20.]

9. CONCERNING THE
CHRISTIAN IDEA OF GOD

DBWE 10:451–461

*Bonhoeffer was dismayed by the state of American theology,[1] writing that Union Semi-
nary had "forgotten what Christian theology in its very essence stands for."[2] He had
drunk deeply from the Barthian spring and was convinced that theology needed to
distinguish itself from philosophy, ethics, or any other field of inquiry by starting from
God's revelation. Because this understanding of the theological task had not yet made
inroads in America, the theological scene there must have appeared to him as stuck in
a pre-Barthian era of liberal theology. Bonhoeffer's judgment that American theology
lacked critical self-understanding was closely related to his verdict regarding the fri-
volity of American churches: Union Seminary and the American church scene in general were preoccupied with organizational, political, and ethical projects[3] because they
had set aside their essential task—preaching the gospel based on God's revelation. In
the next two selections, Bonhoeffer articulates the theological self-understanding that
he judged absent from the American scene. In the paper below, written for Eugene
Lyman's Union course on "The Philosophy of the Christian Religion" and later published in the Journal of Religion,[4] Bonhoeffer defines theology in opposition to other
disciplines as reflection on the reality of revelation, before characteristically elaborat-
ing the personal character of that reality.*

In the present article I do not pretend to present the Christian idea of God   451
in its entirety. I am trying to give no more than the framework within which
this idea should be thought. The fact that I am concerned only with the

---

1. [DBWE *10:22–23, editor's introduction. This selection reproduces Bonhoeffer's English,
errors included.*]

2. [DBWE *10:310.*]

3. [DBWE *10:309.*]

4. [DBWE *10:451, n. 1.*]

Christian idea of God and not some general speculation, that is to say, the fact that the theme is essentially dogmatical, has led me to select the following topics for discussion: First, the reality of God with regard to the problem of the theory of knowledge; second, God and history; third, the paradoxical God in the doctrine of justification. The connection between these three parts and the progress from the first to the last one will be seen in the course of the treatment.

452

I. GOD AND THE PROBLEM OF KNOWLEDGE

If this inquiry were purely philosophical we should never be permitted to start with the reality of God; and as long as theology does not see its essential difference from all philosophical thinking, it does not begin with a statement concerning God's reality but tries rather to build a support for such a statement. Indeed, this is the main fault with theology, which in our day no longer knows its particular province and its limits. It is not only a methodological fault but, likewise, a misunderstanding of the Christian idea of God from the very beginning. Philosophical thinking attempts to be free from premises (if that is possible at all); Christian thinking has to be conscious of its particular premise, that is, of the premise of the reality of God, before and beyond all thinking. In the protection of this presupposition, theological thinking convicts philosophical thinking of being bound also to a presupposition, namely, that thinking in itself can give truth. But philosophical truth always remains truth which is given only within the category of possibility. Philosophical thinking never can extend beyond this category—it can never be a thinking in reality. It can form a conception of reality, but conceived reality is not reality any longer. The reason for this is that thinking is in itself a closed circle, with the ego as the center. The last "reality" for all consequent[5] philosophical reflection must be an ego, which is removed from all conceivability, a "nicht-gegenständliches Ich" [*non-objective I*]. Thinking does violence to reality, pulling it into the circle of the ego, taking away from it its original "objectivity." Thinking always means system and the system excludes the reality. Therefore, it has to call itself the ultimate reality, and in this system the thinking ego rules.

453

It follows that not only the other man but also God is subordinated to the ego. That is the strict consequence of the idealistic and, as far as I see, of all

---

5. ["That is, consistent, systematic, thoroughgoing, as in the German *konsequent*," *DBWE* 10:452, n. 8.]

exact philosophical thought which tries to be autonomous. This fact of the captivity of human thinking in itself, that is to say, of its inevitable autocracy and self-glorification as it is found in philosophy, can be interpreted theologically as the corruption of the mind, which is caused by the first fall. Man "before" the fall must be thought of as being able to think of "reality," that means to think of God and of the other man as realities. Man "in" and "after" the fall refers everything to himself, puts himself in the center of the world, does violence to reality, makes himself God, and God and the other man his creatures. He never can get reality back because his thinking is no longer "in reality"; it remains in the category of possibility. But there is no bridge between possibility and reality. Possibility might be conceived of and even proved, reality must be given before and beyond all thinking. Reality is consequently beyond my own self, transcendent—but, again, not logically transcendent, but really transcendent. Reality limits my boundlessness from outside, and this outside is no more intellectually conceivable but only believable. This remains to be explained below.

Theology, then, starts with the statement of the reality of God and that   454
is its particular right. But that at once gives rise to the question, how can theology state the reality of God without thinking it? And, if it thinks it, how can it be avoided that God should again be pulled into the circle of thought? That is the central and most difficult problem of a genuine theological epistemology, which springs from the Christian idea of God.

The basis of all theology is the fact of faith. Only in the act of faith as a direct act[6] God is recognized as the reality which is beyond and outside of our thinking, of our whole existence. Theology, then, is the attempt to set forth what is already possessed in the act of faith. Theological thinking is not a construction a priori, but a posteriori as Karl Barth has maintained.[7] Therefore, it has to be conscious of its limitations. As thinking per se [*in itself*], it is not excepted from the pretension and boundlessness of all thinking. But the property of theological thinking is that it knows of its own insufficiency and its limitations. So it must be its highest concern to guard these limitations and to leave room for the reality of God, which can never be conceived by theological thinking. That means that there is no one theo-

---

6. ["... The concept of *actus directus* [*direct act*] (in contrast with *actus reflexus* [*reflective act*]) derives from early Protestant thinking and was suggested to Bonhoeffer by Delitzsch, *System of Biblical Psychology* ... ," *DBWE* 10:454, n. 20. *See* DBWE *2:28, 158–160 (Reader 107–108), and* DBWE *12:221.*]

7. ["Cf. the adoption of this notion from Barth, *Epistle to the Romans*, 206, in *DBWE* 2:45, 81, et passim," *DBWE* 10:454, n. 22.]

logical sentence which could presume to speak "truth" unless it refers to the reality of God and the impossibility of embracing this reality in theological sentences. Every theoretical sentence generalizes. But God does not permit of generalization. Because he is reality, he is absolutely free of all theoretical generalization. Even a sentence like "God is love" [*1 John 4:8*] is, in the last analysis, not the truth about God, because it is not a matter of course that by such a sentence I could calculate that God is love. On the contrary, God is wrath as well as love and this we also should know. Therefore, every statement concerning God's essence must contain both of these contradictory aspects in order to give room to the reality of God.

455

This reality, which is said to be transcendent to all thinking, is now to be defined more exactly as "personality."[8] The transcendence of God does not mean anything else than that God is personality, provided there is an adequate understanding of the concept of personality. Idealism defines personality as the subjective realization of objective spirit—that is, of absolute spirit. Each personality is constituted by the same spirit, which is, in the last analysis, reason. Each personality is personality as far as it participates in reason. Thus each one knows the other. Personality is no secret and, therefore, another personality is no real limit for me because, in the last analysis, I have at my disposal the spirit of reason, as does also the other person.

For Christian thought, personality is the last limit of thinking and the ultimate reality. Only personality can limit me, because the other personality has its own demands and claims, its own law and will, which are different from me and which I cannot overcome as such. Personality is free and does not enter the general laws of my thinking. God as the absolutely free personality is, therefore, absolutely transcendent. Consequently, I cannot talk about him in general terms; he is always free and beyond these terms. The only task of my theological thinking must be to make room for the transcendent personality of God in every sentence. Only when he himself avows a human word, whenever and wherever he pleases, is my word "about" God to be accepted as truth—that means, only then is my word God's own word. But the question is, Where does God speak? Where can I find his inaccessible reality which is so entirely hidden from my thinking? How do I know about his being the absolutely transcendent personality? The answer

456

---

8. ["... By using 'personality' instead of his normal 'person,' Bonhoeffer adapts to the early twentieth-century usage of American English. For Bonhoeffer's use in *Sanctorum Communio* of 'person' in theological anthropology and also for God, see *DBWE* 1:44–57 (Reader 21–29), 79," *DBWE* 10:455, n. 28. *For an argument that "person" is a central concept in Bonhoeffer's thinking, see DeJonge,* Bonhoeffer's Theological Formation.]

is given and must be given by God himself, in his own word in Jesus Christ, for no one can answer this question except God himself, in his self-revelation in history, since none can speak the truth except God.

II. GOD AND HISTORY

The problem that thus sets itself to us is complicated. We see that there is no other way to talk about God than that God himself speaks his word in his self-revelation. This self-revelation is executed in history.

No man can reveal God because God is absolutely free personality. Every human attempt to discover God, to unveil his secret reality, is hopeless because of God's being personality. All such attempts remain in the sphere of the idea. Personality as reality is beyond idea. So that even the self-revelation of personality cannot be executed in the sphere of idea. The idea is in the realm of generality. Personality exists in "once-ness" because of its freedom. The only place where "once-ness" might occur is history. Therefore, revelation of personality—that is to say, the self-revelation of God—must take place in history if at all. That happened according to the testimony of the Bible and the present Christian church in the revelation of God in Christ. God spoke his word in history, yet not only as a doctrine but as the personal revelation of himself. Thus, Christ becomes not the teacher of mankind, the example of religious and moral life for all time, but the personal revelation, the personal presence of God in the world. It is important to point out emphatically that it is not Jesus who reveals God to us (that view is the consequence of all theology which is not in the strict sense theology of revelation, and leads to a very confused Christology), but it is God who reveals himself in absolute self-revelation to man. Since God 457 is accessible only in his self-revelation, man can find God only in Christ. That does not exclude God's being elsewhere too, but he cannot and should not be grasped and understood except in Christ. God entered history and no human attempt can grasp him beyond this history. This is the great stumbling-block for all general religious thinking. God revealed himself in "once-ness" from the years from one to thirty in Palestine in Jesus.

The main difference between a so-called revelation in the sphere of idea and a revelation in "once-ness" is that man always will be able to learn a new idea and to fit it into his system of ideas; but a revelation in "once-ness" in a historical fact, in a historical personality, is always anew a challenge to man. He cannot overcome it by pulling it into the system which he already had before. That is the reason why God reveals himself in history: only so is the freedom of his personality guarded. The revelation in history means revelation in hiddenness; revelation in ideas (principles, values, etc.) means revelation in openness.

We are going to speak below concerning the content of this revelation. Christianity gives us a new conception of history. The idealistic philosophy conceives of history as of the realization of ideas, values, etc. History becomes "symbol," transparent to the eternal spirit. The essence of single historical facts is that they mean something general, but not that they really are something. The earnestness of ontological consideration is weakened through reinterpretation in axiological judgments. Jesus becomes here the symbol of God's love, his cross means forgiveness, and in the very moment that we know what all that means we could, theoretically, forget the facts forever. The fact being only the transient bearer of eternal values and ideas— that is to say, Jesus being only the transient bearer of the general new truth taught by him according to the will of God. In short, idealistic philosophy does not take seriously the ontological category in history. Which means that it does not take history seriously. This is true, not only as far as an interpretation of the Christian revelation is concerned, but likewise everywhere; and it becomes very conspicuous in the interpretation of the other man, of the neighbor, that is, of present history.

We cannot pursue this point further here. The fact is that Christianity brings a new interpretation of history. History in its essence does not enter our system of ideas and values. On the contrary, it sets for us our limitations. History in its essence is to be interpreted ontologically. The true attitude of man toward history is not interpretative, but that of refusing or acknowledging, that is to say, deciding. History is the place of decision, nothing else. Decision in its most inward sense is possible only as a decision for or against God. This decision is executed in facing Christ. Within the world of ideas there is no such thing as decision because I always bear already within myself the possibilities of understanding these ideas. They fit into my system but they do not touch and challenge my whole existence. Thus, they cannot lead me into the situation of personal decision.

III. The Paradoxical God of the Doctrine of Justification

Here the Christian "idea" of God comes to its sharpest issue. The question becomes one of applying this most objective "idea" of God to man—which is absolutely necessary if the whole treatment is not to remain merely in the metaphysical realm. If God alone can speak truth and I with all my thinking remain within my own limitations, not being able to reach God, how can I

know anything at all about God? Moreover, there must be some knowledge   459
of God, if Christianity has a message to bring to the world.

The pathway to this knowledge is action. I can know God only if I can effect an act—an act which makes me transcend the limits of myself, which carries me out of the circle of my self-hood in order to acknowledge the transcendent God. While it is obvious that I myself cannot effect such an act, there is, nevertheless, such an act, which is executed by God himself, and which is called "faith." In my faith God reveals himself through Christ in me. In his self-revelation in Jesus Christ he gives himself to be known. In my faith no one speaks other than God, because, if so, it would not be the truth. The word of God spoken to me in the act of my faith in Christ is God in his revelation as the Holy Spirit. Faith is nothing but the act of receiving this word of God. God remains always and entirely subject, and even the answer of man can never be more than "I believe, help thou mine unbelief" [*Mark 9:24*].

It is just here that the personalities of God and of man come in contact with each other. Here God himself transcends his transcendence, giving himself to man as Holy Spirit. Yet, being personality, he remains in absolute transcendence; the immanence of God means that man hears God's own word, which is spoken in absolute self-revelation, always anew.

It is not unessential to note that we have been able to conceive of the idea of faith only from the rigorous conception of the self-revelation of God, and this without having touched the matter of the content of this revelation. The formal idea of self-revelation has as its counterpart the idea of faith, whatever content the self-revelation may possess. Faith is primarily directed toward the authority of God, not to the content of his word, whether it be understandable or ununderstandable. It is the authority that gives weight to   460
the content, not the reverse. In the Christian message, the particular proportion between authority and content is expressed by saying that the latter is not only an appendix of the former, but that the content itself is the message of the sole authority of God. Therefore, when we come to interpret the content of the self-revelation of God, we will see that this content is only the explication of the fact of the absolute self-revelation and authority of God.

God entered history in Jesus, and so entirely that he can be recognized in his hiddenness only by faith. God gives an amazing proof of his sole authority in the cross of Christ. In the very same moment when Christ dies upon the cross, the whole world dies in its sinfulness and is condemned. That is the extreme judgment of God upon the world. God himself dies and reveals himself in the death of a man, who is condemned as a sinner. It is precisely this, which is the foolishness of the Christian idea of God, which has been witnessed to by all genuine Christian thinking from Paul, Augustine, Luther, to Kierkegaard and Barth. God is where death and sin are, not where righteousness is. Further, it is to be said that the absolute knowledge of the sinfulness of the world or of the single individual person is a judgment of faith. Without faith no one can know what sin is. He will inevitably confuse sin with moral imperfection, which constitutes a grave misunderstanding.

But the cross would not be the revelation of God were it not followed by the resurrection of Christ. With Christ's death and resurrection the old world of righteousness is dead. He who is in Christ is a new creature. The resurrection of Christ as well as the resurrection of man was and is conceivable only by faith. God remains in His hiddenness. In Christ all men are respectively condemned or resuscitated and it is the work of God, the Holy Spirit, to apply this general condition in which all men are, to the single person. The act of application is the act of faith—that is to say, of this faith, which believes that God's word in Christ is valid for itself; or, in other words, the act of justification.

461 Here the paradoxical essence of God becomes visible to the faith of the Christian believer. Justification is pure self-revelation, pure way of God to man. No religion, no ethics, no metaphysical knowledge may serve man to approach God. They are all under the judgment of God, they are works of man. Only the acknowledgment that God's word alone helps and that every other attempt is and remains sinful, only this acknowledgment receives God. And this acknowledgment must be given by God, as the Holy Spirit, as faith. That is the foolishness of the revelation of God and its paradoxical character—that just there, where the power of man has lapsed entirely, where man knows his own weakness, sinfulness, and consequently the judgment of God upon him, that just there God is already working in grace, that just and exactly there and only there is forgiveness, justification, resuscitation. There, where man himself no longer sees, God sees, and God alone works, in judgment and in grace. There, at the very limits of man, stands God, and when man can do nothing more, then God does all. The justification of the sinner—this is the self-proof of the sole authority of God. And in this justification man becomes a new personality by faith, and he recognizes here—what he never before could understand or believe—God as his creator. In the act of justification God reveals himself as Holy Trinity.

10. The Theology of Crisis and Its Attitude toward Philosophy and Science

DBWE 10:462–476

Bonhoeffer presented the following paper in a seminar on Philosophy of Religion at Union on the topic "The Bearing of Recent Cosmological Theories on Theology."[1] In it, Bonhoeffer introduces Barth's thought to his American audience, suppressing his own critiques elaborated elsewhere and occasionally presenting his own thoughts as Barth's. Because the Barthian grounding of theology in revelation distinguishes it from philosophical and scientific pursuits of knowledge, the thrust of Bonhoeffer's presentation undermines the very presupposition of the seminar. Recent cosmological theories have no bearing on theology, he argues, since theology takes its cues from revelation rather than any scientific discovery or theory about the natural world.

It is a difference of method, whether at the occasion of examining a man one asks him for things, which he probably will know or whether one tries to find the limits of his knowledge by asking him questions, which he very likely cannot answer quite as well; the more modern and for the examined man by far more pleasant education principle at least is the first way of asking. However Barth today is supposed to be the victim of the other type of examination, and [. . .][2] it is not merely his fault if the result of this examination is not going to be as satisfactory as it could have been. Barth has never prepared himself for an examination in science or in philosophy, but he always has prepared himself for a quite different and distinct field, 462

---

1. [DBWE *10:20, editor's introduction. This selection reproduces Bonhoeffer's English, errors included.*]

2. ["Illegible. Possibly 'thus,'" *DBWE* 10:462, n. 2.]

namely for christian theology; that is to say, Barth has been thinking all
the time exclusively and intensively of the λόγος θεοῦ [*word of God*] and he
found—perhaps strangely enough for our allinclusive and extensive kind
of thinking—in this object manifold and most important problems, that
he felt not very much attracted by the variety of countless other problems,
before he would have thought through the richness of his proper field, of
theology in its strict sense. Now theology does not answer every question in
the whole world; but since it tries to answer at least one question, namely
that question about God, it contains a certain attitude toward all other questions. That is to be admitted, although it will have to be shown that the
essential possibility of this attitude as well as its concrete character is a problem of exceeding difficulty.

463   In order not to confuse your impressions, I will give you in this paper
mainly the position of the founder and most original thinker of the theology of crisis, of Karl Barth.[3] The differences between him and Fr. Gogarten
and Emil Brunner will be better explained in whatever brief ways the discussion will point.

Since Barth never has published any comprehensive treatment of our
problem, we will have to use some single utterances of his and try to show
the lines of connection with his whole thought, which sometimes Barth
himself did not draw. Coming after half a year of consideration of the problem of the relation between cosmology, philosophy and theology, to a man
like K. Barth I confess that I do not see any other possible way for you to
get into real contact with his thought than by forgetting at least for this
one hour everything you have learned before concerning this problem. We
have in Barth's theology not one of the countless variations of the solution
of this problem from the Scholastics over Kant to Bergson or Dewey, but
here we stand at an entirely different and new point of departure of the
whole problem. We stand in the tradition of Paul, Luther, Kierkegaard, in
the tradition of genuine christian thinking. We do injustice to Karl Barth if
we take him as a philosopher, he is not and does not claim to be, he is just
a christian theologian. This at least has to be clear, what we intend to be,
christian theologians or philosophers. To be unclear in this point means,
that we in any case are not christian theologians. For the christian theologian must know the proper and steadfast premise of his whole thinking,
which the philosopher does not recognize: the premise of the revelation

---

3. ["The expression 'theology of crisis' more accurately describes the theological situation in the German-speaking realm evoked by Barth's commentary on Romans than the
otherwise frequently used expression—one Bonhoeffer also adopts—'dialectical theology,'" *DBWE* 10:463, n. 6.]

of God in Christ or on the objective side: the faith in this revelation.[4] Two
questions arise: 1.) What is the meaning of this premise according to Karl   464
Barth? 2.) What makes such a premise necessary? *Firstly.* The meaning of
the proper presupposition of christian theology is, that God entered history
in Jesus Christ, made himself known to the world in this revelation. The
word or the will of God, God himself was made flesh. But the revelation
of God in Christ was a revelation of his judgement as well as of his grace.
Christ's cross is the judgement of God upon the world. Christ's resurrection
is his grace. That is to say, the revelation of God in Christ is not a revelation
of a new morality, of new ethical values, a revelation of a new imperativ, but
a revelation of real reacting of God for mankind in history, a revelation of
a new indicativ; It is not a new "you ought," but "you are." In other words
the revelation of God is executed not in the area of ideas, but in the area of
reality. The importance of this difference is to be explained later. The *fact*
that God himself comes into the world convicts the world of impossibility
to come to God by itself; the fact, that God's way in the world leads to the
cross, that Christ must die condemned as a sinner on the cross, convicts
the world that this impossibility to come to God is its condemnation, its sin
and its guilt. The fact of Christ's resurrection proves to the world that only
God is right and powerfull, that the last word is his, that by an act of his will
alone the world can be renewed. Finally the fact that the holy Spirit still
comes to man and moves man's hearts with the message of Christ's death
and resurrection convicts the world that God is still God and the world still
the world, that God's word in Christ is God's word for ever. In short, the fact
of God's coming into the world in Christ makes the world see, that here in
the life of Jesus of Nazareth God is acting with mankind in an eternal way,
that in this life the decision upon the world fells, and that in this decision
God does everything, man nothing.

Yet it is exactly the fact, that God really entered history, which makes him
invisible for human eyes. If the revelation was a revelation of new ideas, new
moral imperatives, then it would be a revelation, which everybody could
recognize as such by virtue of his own ideal or ethical presuppositions; for
then it would have its place in the world of general truth, which is selfevident
to the human mind by its generality. This is the conception of revelation in
other religions and in our modern liberal thought. The objects of revelation
are ideas, which are supposed to be congenial to our deepest essence, to the   465
good in man. The christian idea of revelation is the strict opposite of this

---

4. ["By 'objective side' Bonhoeffer means that 'the revelation of God in Christ' is the
'object' of the 'whole thinking' of the Christian theologian," *DBWE* 10:463, n. 10.]

view; it is revelation [. . .]⁵ not in ideas, but in historical facts, not in imperatives but in indicatives, not in generality, but in once-ness; it is revelation because it is not congenial to our own deepest essence, but entirely beyond our whole existence. For would it otherwise have had to be revealed, if it has been before potentially in us? The fact of God's encarnation in Christ, the fact of Christ's suffering and death, the fact of his resurrection are the revelation of God. But of course who would be willing to see in these facts God's word? Who would not be offended by the foolishness of such a claim? God revealed in the poor life of a suffering man, God revealed on the cross, God revealed in the depth of history, in sin and death, is this a message worth hearing by a wise man, who really would be able to invent a nobler and prouder God. Karl Barth finds the Bible full of the testimony of the awkwardness and foolishness of God's revelation. "Blessed is he, whosoever shall not be offended in me" [*Matt. 11:6*], Jesus says; and Paul: "the cross to them is foolishness; . . . it pleased God by the foolishness of preaching to save them that believe . . . we preach Christ crucified, unto the Jews a stumbling block and unto the Greeks foolishness . . . the foolishness of God is wiser than men; and the weakness of God is stronger than men. God hast chosen the foolish things of the world . . . that no flesh should glory in his presence" [*1 Cor. 1:18, 21, 23, 25, 27, 29*]. All that means that God's revelation in Christ is revelation in concealment, secrecy, all other socalled revelation is revelation in openness. But who then, can see the revelation in concealment? Nobody but to whom God himself reveals this most secret mystery of his revelation in weekness, nobody but to whom God gives the faith, which is not offended, but which sees God's judgment and grace in the midst of human weakness, sin and death, where otherwise man can see only godlessness, faith which sees God coming most closely to man, where a man hanging on the cross dies in despair with the loud cry: my God, my God, why hast thou forsaken me [*Mark 15:34; Ps. 22:1*]? And the centurion, which stood over against him saw that he so cried out and gave up the ghost, said: truly this man was the Son of God.⁶ This is the real world of biblical faith, which sees God's work not on the top but in the depth of mankind; and because faith sees God in Christ it sees God, the same God of Christ, in man's own life, in man's own sin, weakness and death as judgment and as grace. It is God's own work to let men see into these secrets of his revelation; as Christ says to Peter after his confession: flesh and blood hath not revealed it unto thee, but my

466

---

5. ["Illegible. Though not written here, elsewhere Bonhoeffer uses the formulation 'in hiddenness'; see below on 'concealment' and 'secrecy,'" *DBWE* 10:456, n. 13.]

6. ["Mark 15:39; concerning the status of Mark 15:34 and 39, cf. *DBWE* 10:357 (*Reader* 71), *DBWE* 8:479 (*Reader* 803), and *DBWE* 7:165," *DBWE* 10:466, n. 20.]

Father which is in heaven [*Matt. 16:19*]. So everything points back to God's own decree, to his free predestination. He comes where he wants to come, and he renounces whoever he pleases. For he is unconditioned and free.

This is the way Barth tries to make living the world of biblical thinking. He sees everything in the Bible referring to God's sole truth, right, freedom, judgment, grace. This precisely is the logic of the Bible, God's coming which destroys all human attempts to come, which condemns all morality and religion, by means of which man tries to make superfluous God's revelation. God's sole truth and word, which has to be spoken anew again and again, God coming not to the most seriously moral and pious group of Pharisees and Scribes but to those who were entangled in public sin. "Verily I say unto you, that the publicans and the harlots go into the kingdom of God before you" [*Matt. 21:31*]. Here all human order and ranking is subverted, for God's new order has been established, which is contrary and beyond all human understanding. It convicts man of his godlessness in his bad and his good deeds. God's coming in Christ is the proof of God himself, that man cannot come to God; that is to say: God's coming in Christ must be the judgment upon mankind, in other words it shows to man his limitations, which are lieing exactly there, where God's work begins. Therefore God's work with man does not begin as a continuation and perfection of his highest, although as every decent man will admit imperfect enterprises, as religion and morality, but on the contrary it begins as the irrefragable limitation of man, it begins at man's limits that is to say in sin and death. This act of limiting man is God's judgement and grace *in one*; for the limited man is the judged man and at the same time the limited man giving all righteousness and glory to God is so justified by God's work and grace alone. The acknowledgment of one's limits before God is faith, not as a possible act of man, but only as an act of God, who sets and shows these limits to man. This is the message of justification by grace or by faith alone.   467

But the revelation of God in the justification by faith and grace implies that man's continuity always is continuity in sin, that he by himself can never get outside of the circle of sin, for otherwise grace would not be grace, and justification would not be necessary. Revelation in Christ, justification, means breaking through the circle of sin. Thus God's first word is the radical breaking of all continuity with man in his radical judgement upon man as sinner, and his act of grace is the creation of a new man, with whom God remains in continuity. Since only the revelation in Christ claims to constitute the real outside of man it implies that it is the only criterion of any revelation. Since this claim puts itself essentially beyond all proof, it demands to be taken as a presupposition of thinking or to be refused at all. It is perhaps too obvious to mention, that as a consequence of this notion of

revelation the question of grounds for belief in God is superfluous because
it involves a contradiction. For what better ground does one need and is
possible than God's word itself. Any theology that is ashamed of this petitio
principii [*question begging*] cannot escape being ashamed of Him who gives
it whatever meaning it posesses.

Herewith I think we have the chief presuppositions, which are indispen-
sible for an understanding of Barth's attitude toward all other problems.
The category which Barth tries to introduce into theology in its strict sense
and which is so refractory to all general thinking and especially religious
thinking is the category of the word of God, of the revelation straight from
above,[7] from *outside* of man, according to the justification of the sinner by
grace. Theology is the scientific[8] consideration of this category. But exactly
here the difficulty comes in. Scientific consideration is based upon general formal presuppositions of thinking. Since these presuppositions cannot be taken from the object of theological thinking—just because it never
becomes actually object but always remains subject—and since on the other
hand they must be taken from this subject=object, if they should be at all
adequate, the deepest contradiction in the task of theology becomes obvious. It is in the last analysis the great antithesis of the word of God and the
word of man, of grace and religion, of a pure christian category and general
religious category, of reality and interpretation. In every theological statement we cannot but use certain general forms of thinking. Theology has
those forms in common with philosophy. Thus our next problem will be to
consider the relation between theology and philosophy with regard to the
use of forms of general philosophical thinking in theology. Let us take the
following example: Theological thinking, which is based upon the general
notion of substance and accidence (and it seems to me that our western
thinking at least will never be able to overcome completely this basic presupposition for the one reason if for no other namely the grammatical constructions of our languages)—this type of thinking, I say, will conceive for
instance of sin as substance in man or as accidens. Both in their pure form

468

7. ["Concerning this familiar formulation of revelation 'vertically, from above,' cf.
Barth, *Epistle to the Romans*, 30, 102, et passim," *DBWE* 10:467, n. 27.]

8. ["Here Bonhoeffer is almost certainly thinking of the German *wissenschaftlich*,
which could also be translated as 'academic' or 'scholarly.' Bonhoeffer is aware that
Barth defines dogmatics as the theological discipline concerned with the 'scientific self-
examination' of the church concerning its language about God (*Church Dogmatics* 1/1:3),
and he points out that theology defines 'science' according to its own distinctive subject
matter, while sharing certain 'general forms of thinking' with other disciplines and 'sciences,'" *DBWE* 10:467, n. 28.]

seemed inadequate for the notion of sin to orthodox dogmatics. The consequence is either to express the real fact of sin in rather contradictory terms of the type of substantial thinking as it was done after the famous struggle with Flacius Illyricus by orthodox protestants, or to look for different presuppositional forms of thinking for example for a dynamic-voluntaristic thinking, if that can be considered a genuine form of thinking at all. The history of theology was to a large extent a permanent seeking for more adequate forms of thinking in order to express the facts of the revelation. Two great christian churches have settled in a long history of exceedingly keen and serious thinking their forms of thinking definitely; both of them are based upon the scheme of substance and accidence, the greek church more in the platonic, the roman church more in the aristotelian interpretation. (Quite recently it seems that a movement in Benedictine order tries to modify this old form of thinking; specially in the modern catholic theories of the sacrifice in the Holy Communion this becomes obvious.)

Luther recognized the insufficiency of the scholastic form of thinking for an interpretation of the facts of revelation. He sees in the notion of substance a great danger of making revelation static and depriving it of its actual liveliness. Luther sees this static character attributed to grace in the catholic Church which gives grace into the disposal of man. Thus the whole misinterpretation of the doctrine of justification in the catholic church is deeply connected with the basic presuppositional form of thinking.   469

Luther himself has not developed his own philosophical terminology. Without doubt his forms of thought are essentially dynamical voluntaristic[9] herewith accepting a tradition which came from Paul over Augustine and the Mystics to him. But very often he himself falls back into the substantial form of thinking (for instance in the Christology) and it has to be confessed that Protestantism as yet lacks its proper philosophical terminology. Orthodox Protestantism took up the old substantial form of thinking and it was Kant, who showed its impossibility and substituted for it a transcendental philosophy.[10] The theological language of 19th century until our present day has been based not so much upon Kants as upon the idealistic philosophy, even where the respective theologie was not conscious of the fact. Ritschl, in whose theology I was brought up in Berlin, could not succeed in his attempt to free theology from wrong metaphysical premises, because he

---

9. ["By 'voluntaristic' Bonhoeffer means an emphasis on the will; cf. *DBWE* 1:19, 35, 48 (*Reader* 23–24), 296," *DBWE* 10:469, n. 33.]

10. ["Cf. in this regard the section in *Act and Being* on the transcendental approach (*DBWE* 2:33–59)," *DBWE* 10:469, n. 36.]

had not thought through the christian category of revelation, as it becomes obvious in his christology, doctrine of sin and of justification.

470   There is finally a realistic philosophy, which could offer its service to theology. Now Karl Barth is faced with this situation, when he looks for a philosophical terminology for his theology. He is well aware of the fact though, that in accepting a certain philosophical terminology theology is insolubly connected with a whole philosophy. In his Römerbrief [*Letter to the Romans*] and his later writings Barth uses the philosophical terminology of Kant and the Neokantians in Marburg and he is conscious of this fact. Like everything in Barth's thought this also is in closest connection with the doctrine of justification by faith and by grace alone and we will have to explain that. Three questions are to be answered: 1.) what is for Barth the task of philosophy in general? 2.) what kind of philosophy is adequate to the christian idea of justification by faith. 3.) what is true philosophy from a theological point of view.

    1.) The task of philosophy has always been an interpretation of the general principles of the universe according to some principles which have been considered as true. Philosophical interpretation claims to be true, even if it is skeptical. More accurately: the predicate "true" can essentially be referred only to the *interpretation*, and *all* philosophy *is* interpretation, whether it be idealistic or realistic. The statement: there is a table is by no means selfinterpretiv for philosophical thinking: What does "there," what does "is," what does "table" mean? All that is matter of interpretation. Idealism recognizes that, as well as critical Realism and even Behaviorism, as I understand it, only "naiv Realism" tries to ignore the complexity of the problem and can hardly be considered a philosophical position. But even critical realism still has to prove its logical consistency over against the superior logical right of idealism. As long as philosophy has to do with the sheer question of truth and not with some arbitrary statements, logical consistency is an essential predication of every relevant philosophy. Barth's

471 theology was from the very beginning connected with an energetic attack against Idealism. Here the ego is found as not only the interpreting but even a creative ego; it creates its world itself. The ego stands in the centre of the world, which is created, ruled, overpowered by the ego. The identification of the ego with the ground of everything which has been called God is inevitable. There are no limits for the ego, its power and its claim is boundless, it is its own standard. Here all transcendence is pulled into the circle of the creative ego (which of course must not be confused with the empirical ego). Man knows himself immediately by the act of the coming of the ego to itself and knows through himself essentially everything, even God. God is in man, God is man himself. Barth and his friends discovered in this phi-

losophy the most radical, most honest and most consistent expression of the philosophical enterprise as such. Although realism claims to leave room for transcendent reality, it still owes us the proof, which of course it never will be able to bring, that its definition of reality is not its own interpretation of it; As long as realism fail here, it must admit that reality has to be referred to the interpreting ego, which constitutes reality and which, even although it denies it remains the center of reality. The ego knows reality, it knows itself, it is essentially autonomous. At the basis of all thinking lies the necessity of a system. Thinking is essentially systematic thinking, because it rests upon itself, it is the last ground and criterion of itself. System means interpretation of the whole through the one, which is its ground and its center, the thinking ego. Idealism saw and affirmed that as the proof for the freedom, autonomy, the deity of man. Realism tries to escape this consequence and fails. There is only one philosophy, which recognizes this fact and states it as the definite and essential limit of man; this is according to Barth and his friends the essence of Kantian philosophy. (It be shortly noted, that Barth and his friends here do not care so much for a complete presentation of the manifold sides of Kant's philosophy, but that they try to point out, what seems to them the most important trend in Kant's thought) Kant did not want to be called an idealist nor a dogmatist, he considers both of them as equally untenable, his philosophy is critical philosophy or transcendental philosophy; "transcendental" means for Kant (as it has been shown clearly by Knittermeyer and others) not involving transcendence, but referring to transcendence. Thinking is an act which never involves transcendence, but refers to it. The transcendence itself does not enter thinking. The ego never knows itself in coming to itself, but it always remains transcendent to itself,   472 because it never is static-objective, but always acting. Likewise thinking does not reach the transcendence of the object, but it always is directed to it, because transcendence never can be "object." This is the deep meaning of the "Ding an sich" [*thing in itself*] and the transcendental apperception for Kant. Thinking is limited and put into the midst between two transcendences, to which it refers, but which always remain transcendent. In the very moment when the Idealists pushed away the "Ding an sich" Kant's critical philosophy was destroyed. The philosophy of the pure act turned to be a new ontology; a fact, which Hegel clearly recognized. Kant had tried to limit human thinking, in order to establish it anew. But Hegel saw that limits only can be set from beyond these limits. That means applied to Kant, that his attempt to limit reason by reason presupposes that reason must have already passed beyond the limits before it sets them. So Kant's critical philosophy presents itself as the attempt of man to set himself the limits in order to avoid the boundlessness of his claim, but the fact is that thinking never can limit itself; in limiting itself it establishes itself. Thinking as such is boundless, it pulls transcendent all reality into its circle. The last consequence of this knowledge has been drawn by E. Grisebach (and from another side by M. Heidegger.) Grisebachs question is the question of reality. He sees that thinking as essentially systematic thinking does violence to reality in pulling it into the circle of the egocentricity. Systematic thinking remains far from reality. Reality only is given in the concrete situation of the ethical meeting of man with man; Thus thinking has to remove itself in order to give room to reality. Grisebach's philosophy is the ultimate possible critic[11] of thinking toward itself, but even here thinking remains dominant and constitutive of the world of reality. For the limits of thinking is a thought limit. This is the inevitable circle of all philosophy. Here at the limits, where philosophy tries to remove itself and cannot but establish itself where philosophy comes to its own crisis we are ready for our second question, namely what philosophical terminology could be adequate for a theology of revelation, of the justification by faith, for the theology of Barth.

473

Barth sees in the essential boundlessness of thinking, in its claim a closed system, in its egocentricity a philosophical affirmation of the theological insight of the Reformers, which they expressed in terms of cor curvum in se [*the heart turned in on itself*], corruptio mentis [*corruption of the mind*]. Man in statu corruptionis [*in the state of corruption*][12] is indeed alone, he is his own creator and Lord, he is indeed the center of his world of sin. He made himself God, and God his creature. The fact that the basic question of philosophy necessarily leads into this situation proves the deepest godlessness of man, even in his profoundest philosophical ideas of God. Man remains with himself, in his thinking not less than in his ethical and religious attempt. The world of man is the world of egocentricity, of godlessness. The fact that philosophy essentially gives its sanction to this situation in making man inevitably the God of his world, even if it denies it, shows the impossibility for philosophy to interpret the situation right as well as it shows philosophy as the most dangerous grasp after God, in order to be like God is and thus to justify man by his own power—in godlessness. We ask: Can then man do anything in order to overcome this fatale situation? Kant still believed, critical philosophy could make room for faith by means of limiting reason by reason. But he failed. Barth sees there is no way out. Man must die in his sin

---

11. ["Bonhoeffer uses the English 'critic' like the German *Kritik*, which means 'critique,'" *DBWE* 10:472, n. 50.]

12. [*These Latin phrases all refer to* "the condition of human beings after the fall. Bonhoeffer cites these expressions extensively in *Act and Being* according to Luther's commentary on Romans (*DBWE* 2:40–41)," *DBWE* 10:473, n. 53.]

inspite of philosophy, must remain alone in his overpowered and misinterpreted world. But now the christian message comes: entirely from outside of the world of sin God himself came in Jesus Christ, he breaks as the holy Ghost into the circle of man, not as a new idea, a new value by virtue of which man could save himself, but in concreteness as judgment and forgiveness of sin, as the promise of eschatological salvation. God makes himself known to man who is sinner in his whole existence. The whole existence of man in his egocentric world has to be shaken (erschüttert) before man can see God as really outside of himself.

Therefore there is no spectator-knowledge of God, but only man in the act of despair of himself can know God by faith. Idealistic and realistic philosophy fail to give the term for describing these facts. And yet Barth discovers in both of them elements which could be used by theology. Idealism sees God as eternal subject, realism sees reality as transcendent object. Barth can express his idea of the transcendent God in terms of God's essential subjectivity, and his idea of God's coming to man in history in terms of God's most objective reality. But he knows that both these terms are essentially inadequate since they derive from a godless philosophy. Barth's own writings are based upon a Kantian terminology. Here he finds expressed   474 the critic of thinking upon thinking, here he sees man considered not in his full possession of transcendence but in the eternal act of referring to transcendence, man not in boundlessness, but in limitation. Although Barth knows that even this philosophy remains in boundlessness he sees here the attempt of philosophy to criticize itself basically and takes from here the terminology in order to express the eternal crisis of man, which is brought upon him by God in Christ and which is beyond all philosophical grasp. Barth sees that there is no christian philosophy nor philosophical terminology at all. So he can say, it does not make very much difference what philosophy a theologian has, but everything depends upon how strongly he keeps his eyes on the category of the word of God, on the fact of revelation, of justification by faith.

Now our third question can be answered: what ought to be according to Barth and his friends the task of philosophy. Barth himself has not answered this question sufficiently, but his friends have thought a great deal about this problem: philosophy remains profane science, there *is* no christian philosophy. But philosophy has to be critical philosophy, not systematic. But since even critical philosophy is bound to be systematic (as we have seen before), philosophy must work in sight of this fate, it must try to think truth with regard to the real existence of man and it must see that it is itself an expression of the real existence of man and that it by its own power not only cannot save man, but that it cannot even be the crisis of man. By doing so it gives as far as it can room to God's revelation, which indeed makes room for itself by itself. The deepest antinomy seems to me to be the antinomy between pure act and reflection as the old dogmaticians said: actus directus and reflexus.[13] God is known only in pure act of referring to God, theology and philosophy are executed in reflection, which God does not enter. Philosophy essentially remains in reflection, man knows himself and God only in reflection, theology at least knows of an act of God, which tears man out of this reflection into an actus directus toward God. Here man knows himself and God not by looking into himself, but by looking to the word of God, which tells him that he is sinner and justified, which he never before could understand. So as Luther said pecca fortiter sed crede fortius [*sin boldly but believe more boldly*] Barth could say reflecte fortiter, sed crede fortius [*reflect boldly but believe more boldly*].

475   Concerning science not very much has to be added. As far as science is a discovery of happening facts, theology is not touched (because theology is concerned only with an certain interpretation of facts.) If science itself gives its own interpretation of the world, than it belongs to philosophy and is subjected to the critic of theology. The attempt of cosmology, that is of a genetical interpretation of the world on the basis of natural science, can never reach beyond the limits of human thinking. Cosmology may come to the assumption of a last ground of the world and may call that "God," all we can say in the name of christian theology is that this God is not the God of revelation and not the creator. Two reasons are to be given: firstly I know God as creator not without the revelation in Christ. For God's being the creator means being the judge and the saviour too; and I know all that only in Christ. Secondly: creation means creation by absolute freedom, creation out of nothing. So the relationship of God to the world is completely free, it has been set and is always set anew "creatio continua" [*continuing creation*] by God. Thus God is not the first cause, the ultimate ground of the world, but its free Lord and creator as such he is not to be discovered by any cosmology, but he reveals himself in sovereign freedom wherever and whenever he wants. The world is fallen away from God; therefore it is the world of sin and evil and death. No human attempt can unify "what has been broken asunder, no thinking, no moral acting, no religion." Only an act of God himself can do, what no man can do. God has unified the broken and contradictory world. In Christ death and evil and sin are overcome by an act of God visible for faith; and at the end of everything God will show his power over death

---

13. [*See earlier, n. 6 in "Concerning the Christian Idea of God* (Reader 137).*"*]

and sin to everybody. He will solve this problem of death and evil and sin by an act of his power.

Our thinking in terms of a Theodicee[14] tries to justify God in the world. But for christian thinking God justifies the world and that has been done in Christ. Thus only through Christ we see the creator and the preserver and the Lord *of* the world *and in* the world; and only through Christ we see the world in God's hands. Far from Christ we live in our own overpowered and egocentric world, which is not the world of God.

Here at the end we stand again where we stood in the beginning; and that cannot be otherwise; for *everything* is included in God's revelation in Christ, in the justification of the sinner by faith and grace alone. And must not the solution of *everything* be there, where *God himself* is?

In the following discussion we shall not be able to do justice to Barth, if we do not refer every thought to its theological premise of the justification by faith.

476

---

14. [*Theodicy, derived from two Greek words meaning "God" and "justice," is the attempt to justify God's goodness in the face of sin and evil.*]

PART 2
University Lectures

11. THE HISTORY OF TWENTIETH-CENTURY SYSTEMATIC THEOLOGY

DBWE 11:224–244

Upon his return from America in 1931, Bonhoeffer began teaching at the Friedrich Wilhelm University in Berlin.[1] He was by all accounts a popular instructor in a popular department. "Bonhoeffer's entry into teaching came at a time of substantial expansion of interest in theology, and it is estimated that more than a thousand students were enrolled in the university's theology department. Bonhoeffer had no difficulty attracting students; word seems to have spread that, in addition to offering intellectual rigor, he represented a refreshing and challenging new voice in the political and theological context of the times. In his critique of traditional theology and the new nationalism, he pressed the kind of foundational questions that students felt necessary."[2]

The next four selections are from Bonhoeffer's lecture courses at the university. The excerpt below comes from the end of his lectures on the history of recent systematic theology (as reconstructed from student notes). Bonhoeffer spends the first two-thirds of the lectures surveying late-nineteenth- and early-twentieth-century theological discussions surrounding the concept of religion, the essence of Christianity, and issues of ethics and culture. The "turning point" of the lecture course, and indeed of recent theology, is the theology of Karl Barth, which redirects theology away from the concerns of religion, culture, history, and ethics, and toward the "hearing of the Word of God." Bonhoeffer endorses Barth's turn toward revelation but, as in Act and Being, criticizes Barth's understanding of revelation in terms of "act" as inconsistent with the New Testament, Luther, and the reality of Christ's presence in the church.

---

1. [*For historical background, biographical information, and a summary of texts from Bonhoeffer's time as a lecturer (1931–1933), see* DBWE *11:17–23 and* DB-ER, *207–221.*]

2. [DBWE *11:17, editor's introduction.*]

224   *§10 The turning point*

In all three areas (the problems of knowledge, history, and ethics), there was the issue of balance with culture. In all three there is the same structure; culture should not be confronted with a claim that is unsustainable.

225   In the first decade there were more and more thinkers whose attempts to fit things together broke apart. It began with the tragic philosophies of Dilthey, Troeltsch, Simmel; there was no sense of anything beyond the historical. Resistance to metaphysics is characteristic, most of all in Max Weber's case. Incredible objectivity, that is all theology can learn from him. Max Scheler: the realm of values and the realm of being fall apart so thoroughly that nothing remains for the realm of being but a system of bestial humanity (*Man's Place in Nature*).[3]

The attempt at objectivity is also part of the development at the turn of the century, but without revolutionary power. Ethos of restrained objectivity that classifies things but also has an inkling that the autonomous culture is breaking down. Still seen as a unity in the 1890s, the culture itself began to show cracks. But it was more exploding than breaking down, each area standing out against the other. Countless separate units emerged side by side. In the process, the church received its last gift of grace from the culture: its independence. For Dibelius, the church is definitely a gift from the culture; it values its connection to the culture like every other area. The church's program is no different from the programs of the turn of the century. It would be completely wrong to assert that the church's specific

226   nature was being given expression today,[4] that the church leadership represented a church perhaps parallel to Barthian theology! The church today does not see itself as fundamentally different from what it was thirty years ago; there has been no turning point here.

During the world war the process had to go through its catastrophe, through the crisis of culture itself. To see the power of fate amid the ruins could mean the turning point; being uprooted from the world of harmonious finitude into God's transcendence could be the turning point. But here[5] we are talking about another turning point. Critical theology is not

---

3. ["For the refutation of Scheler's view, see Bonhoeffer's inaugural lecture, 'The Anthropological Question in Contemporary Philosophy and Theology,' *DBWE* 10:389–408 (*Reader* 110–127). See also the discussion of Scheler in *Act and Being* (*DBWE* 2:64–67)," *DBWE* 11:225, n. 251.]

4. ["I.e., after the state church had been dissolved. The Weimar Constitution of 1919 established the principle of separation of church and state. In the prior arrangement, the Protestant *Landeskirchen* held the established status of state churches, with close official recognition and administrative privilege," *DBWE* 11:226, n. 254.]

5. ["I.e., in dialectical theology," *DBWE* 11:226, n. 255.]

to be explained by the breakdown of war; that is the most foolish impertinence and ignorance! We refuse to give in to the amateurish spirit that turns up its nose, we protest!

Even before the war there were flickering signs of the turning point, and during the war: Overbeck, Kutter, Blumhardt. The war only completed the bankruptcy of the culture. Barth too was among those for whom the experience of the war was decisive. Hopefully this will be true of every theologian. However, Barth's message does not come from that experience, nor from the cultural problems, but rather from a new reading of the Bible, a new way of seeing humankind from God's perspective, from the most positive and the most negative, from God's own word spoken in God's revelation. With the cross as starting point, he fundamentally surmounts the question of the relation of religion and culture, which is still at the basis of Tillich's work, for example. The issue is that of God and humankind; culture merely takes its place on the side of humankind and of religion. To the extent that Barth no longer wants to confuse religion with God, this indicates that the turning point has been reached; it is not psychosis resulting from war but rather listening to God's word.   227

Barth comes not from the trenches but rather from the pulpit of a Swiss village church. This means everything for his understanding. The struggle here is no less decisive than that of the war; it is a fight between God and the devil; the pulpit is the strangest place in the world. Barth's theology comes from preaching; this is his only concern. But what does it mean to preach rightly? It means to speak the very word of God. Where does this terrible "as if" come from? But it should come to the speaking of God. I am to speak, yet it is not I, but God—I have to confess that I am not capable of it. Thus I can do nothing but speak about God, in the knowledge that it is God who must speak; I can only wait and pray for this.

Talking about God is a different thing from speaking from God. These are two different spheres. Our preaching may be boring, or may not be; what happens in church is what has to happen there; otherwise nothing happens in church. It is God who must speak on Sundays at ten o'clock if anything is to happen at all, no matter whether the sermon is stupid or wise.   228
My words are like the spokes of a wheel; the hole in the middle stays empty. Where God comes, human beings know that terrifying things happen. It is so easy for our words to cover up God's word. Troeltsch and others saw that, but it didn't disturb them: there was no other way in their view, only speech about God is possible.

We can also speak of "humankind" in another sense, as for instance Tillich did. New life in nature, community, rediscovery of transcendence, etc. But there are very different ways of speaking of transcendence. A great deal of mischief has been done with this word as found in Barth. What does he mean by it? It is about the humiliation of the human being who is supposed to speak the word of God but only talks about God. Human beings do not have God at their disposal. But the word is bound to the past act of God (of Christ). For Tillich and the youth movement, transcendence means broadening one's perspectives; for Barth, standing in the decision, the God who is to come in contrast to the God who is there. God is not far away and not near, but rather is the One who is to come.

So this turning point is not a general historical event but rather something eminently taking place in theology. There is really a desire again to "speak rightly of God."

229

§11 God

Barth would protest that this is not the way to introduce a theology. He would say that, for him, this is only a marginal comment with the aim of speaking only of God. Nevertheless, we do not misunderstand Barth if we spell the word "God" in a new way, if we remove it from edifying speech, because it is not at all self-evident. One acts as if one is sure of all that and goes on to peripheral matters. But one can never assume a God of mercy and judgment; one can only reach out toward such a God! Whoever talks in that way is not speaking of God, as much as he may say he is. If God stands behind someone, that person now has other concerns. But God is not only the One who did come but also the One who comes again and again, and is only wholly the First through also being the Last. Who knows that God is merciful, if he or she does not know it now! Who knows that God judges, if not the person whose sin has just been forgiven today! God's truth is never general truth but rather always new truth.

The meaning of this for human religious life: There can be no point in human life when we can speak of God as our possession. Barth opposes religion in the name of God. (Line: from OT—Luther—Kierkegaard.) A struggle against religion that exists to cater to humankind. There is no such thing as spiritual recovery by religion, but only becoming ill through God. Religion is always in danger of thinking it has God, knows about God, even humbly and modestly. Religion then becomes one area among others, possibly as the basis, but still only one among others. With this as the starting point, the central issue becomes that of religion and culture. God is then

230 not allowed to speak in God's own voice. That God also judges religion, and passes over pious actions, is an attack on the whole person. The issue of God is ever and again one that is open for human beings. The space that is open to God remains open to the end of time. The future is still to be awaited. Humankind is still oriented to God and to the word of God.

These are all conclusions to be drawn from the freedom of God. They say the decisive word: God remains Lord. This is the epitome of an act ex nihilo out of nothing, a predestination and rejection that can no longer be accounted for: eternal beginning, not something that continues. God is always the One who is to come; that is God's transcendence. One can only have God by expecting God. Instead of beginning with religion, theology should begin by speaking from the word of God.

It appears that this idea of God arose from philosophical speculation. This God cannot be arrived at by any kind of thinking; this would be another way of accounting for God. God must be the One who says, "I am the absolute beginning." We know about God only when God is the One who speaks. This is not a concept of revelation postulated after the fact; only from the revelation itself do we know God as the absolute beginning of self-revelation in Jesus Christ, in a generally understandable way. This word is really God's as such, wholly free, but at the same time shrouded in the garment of history, in humanity. God is indeed something entirely different from humankind, but when God speaks, the speech is veiled; my hearing is shrouded by religion. Faith is not something supernatural but rather takes place in the forms of the physical, but it is only faith to the extent that God judges and has mercy upon it. To the question of why, there is only this answer: Look upon and listen to the Word, Christ, preaching. We would know nothing about God if God did not come in this way. That God comes in such a way is the mystery of God. Every attempt to account for this would mean that God is not absolutely free after all. There can no longer be any general accounting given by religion, unless we are trying to go back behind God. We should begin with God's own beginning set for us.   231 Nobody knows that in advance; we must each receive it as told to us; God's word is the absolute *petitio principii* [*begging the question*]. *Deus dixit* [*God has spoken*][6]—to accept this is the beginning of all genuine theological thinking, to allow space for the freedom of the living God.

§12 The Word of God and Theology[7]
Theology may not, at any price, be confused with the philosophy of religion or with the doctrine of faith. In the philosophy of religion, reasons must be given for that which theology takes as its object, because this means

---

6. [". . . *Deus dixit* is the formula through which Barth explores revelation in his dogmatics," *DBWE* 11:231, n. 277.]

7. [*This is the title of a collection of Barth's essays, translated into English as* The Word of God and Word of Man.]

giving evidence for the truth. But the object of theology may only be the *logos theou* [*word of God*], the act of God, which is its own reason for being. Human beings cannot go back behind this beginning. Theology no longer has to ground its truth outside itself in another discipline, but must proceed from its own basis, its own presuppositions. Is theology a positive science, which accepts its object like biology? To a certain degree this is true. But the objects of study for the other branches of knowledge can be accounted for by general considerations that precede them, and mathematical axioms could be false. In theology, however, truth itself is the object; it has no foundation in general knowledge; it begins with a proof of God established by

232   the word of God, which is its own proof, but this is a real proof for the truth, a *petitio principii* [*begging the question*] that cannot be abolished. It begins with an act of recognition. The only possibilities are rejection or acknowledgment, and neither can be accounted for. So also in theology, in the beginning is faith. This does not mean that a theologian must be a believer; we cannot distinguish between converted and unconverted theologians. The *logos theou* [*word of God*] demands to be believed; only where one still believes at all does theology make any sense.

Theology: as a doctrine of faith? "God and faith belong together" (Luther). So theology is to be traced in the consciousness of a believer? (E. Schaeder, *Das Geistproblem* [*The Spiritual Problem*], 1920). The subject that speaks in the word of God is always God, but this is not to be turned into thinking of God as an object. We can believe the word of God, but only in such a way as to leave God fully as subject. It is not possible to go backward from faith to God. The doctrine of faith always makes God an object.

There is another immanent critique to be directed at the theology of consciousness of faith. I am always looking for something that I already know beforehand. Isn't this examination of consciousness a deceptive maneuver, putting on an act in the marketplace of knowledge? When philosophy sees through this performance, there is bound to be laughter. It is better to admit openly that we are defenseless (contrary to Schaeder and

233   also Althaus[8]). Only when our essential weakness is ruthlessly uncovered are we pointing to the power of the word of God, like the boy David against the Goliaths of the other academic disciplines.

Only when God as subject consents to become the object of theology can any theology be done. God is entirely free to decide whether to be known and to be sought by us. Thus no philosophy of religion can be the start-

8. [*Bonhoeffer is referring to Paul Althaus's doctrine of "original revelation." For more, see* DBWE *11:232, n. 287.*]

ing point; true theology begins with *veni creator spiritus* [*come creator spirit*] (Anselm, Kierkegaard). To know is to acknowledge, to think is to reflect.[9] Seeking and finding God means being sought and found by God. Theology begins with the *petitio principia* [*begging the question*].

How does theology account for this unique state of affairs? The only appropriate form of speech for theology is dialectical speech. The word of God exists only in shrouded form, appears to have become an object like Jesus Christ, the Holy Scriptures, and preaching. The historicity of God's word is its objectivity. The divinity of God's word is its nonobjectivity. From God's viewpoint, of course, the word is one; from ours, we always see it in this double character. I speak of God's revelation, though I ought to say that this is not revelation; I say Jesus and must say Christ, and vice versa, etc. Dialectics aims to defend the freedom of God and the mystery of predestination. We may speak of God never along one line only but always and only in thesis and antithesis. But even this invention of dialectics is not a way of capturing God after all. Genuine dialectics places thesis and antithesis over against each other, but the truth remains somewhere beyond, in the unintuitable middle. God is still free and above even dialectics.

Is Barth's theology one among the many that come and go? Barth does not insist that God be defined by his theology; on the contrary, he insists much more that God is free of such definition. Barth makes use of the philosophical language of neo-Kantianism; he knows that all terminology acts as a lens. The concept is never the thing itself. Thus he is not a neo-Kantian but a theologian. So for him it is essential to speak adequately of nonobjectivity. P. Natorp: *Praktische Philosophie* [*Practical Philosophy*], 1925, related to Barth in his use of terminology, and to some extent in content. The nonobjective is the absolute origin and culmination. Thus God is Not-God, since God as a concept has often already become an object once again. Atheism from religion appears to be the end of neo-Kantianism. Perhaps Barth, in his *Epistle to the Romans*, did not always see the danger of this proximity. But he begins with the concrete revelation; where Natorp and Tillich say Not-God, he has to say Jesus Christ.

234

The object of theology is the word of God as it appears indirectly in the form of Christian speech in the church. The task of theology is the effort to speak rightly of God. Thus theology is completely the servant of the church. *Habitus practicus* [*habit gained through practice*]—most decidedly

---

9. ["*Nachdenken,* here translated as 'reflect,' is to 'think after' what has been given in revelation. It suggests the image of a mirror that only reflects an object after it has been put before the mirror," *DBWE* 11:233, n. 289.]

235   the enemy of all apologetics. Theology begins in the middle, without introduction. Brunner's thinking is characterized more and more by the will
to explain himself: eristic.[10] According to Gogarten and Bultmann, Barth
has his philosophy and has contaminated his theology, not having a clear
foundation in philosophy; terminology must be clarified beforehand. Of
necessity Barth rejects this; he knows about his philosophy, but this is his
way of being a human being, and as such he hears God's word. The quality
of theology cannot depend on good philosophical terminology, which is a
piece of pietistic perfectionism in the conception of academic work. Thus
philosophy is only a technical aid. The mark of good theology is that it provokes good philosophers until their blood boils (cf. Luther's disputation).[11]

§13 Preaching

What should we preach? This question has no clear answer, for if it did, it
would be in our hands again. It is not the statement of something as being
true but rather refers to something which is becoming true, has already
become true. It is the proclamation of the spoken, and ever to be spoken
236   anew, word in Christ. The way to God for human beings has been diverted
once and for all by God's way toward humankind; here is no Christian way
to God either. But our faith can always also be regarded as religion. This
is how the word of God is veiled in that which is human. We can be free of
this ambiguity only in the act of believing. God's way is judgment and mercy
together as one. The word means quintessentially falling, it is impossible to
pull oneself back. In the depth of his being he nevertheless discovers the
divine spark. Against it comes, through the cross, the radical No of God,
the word telling the person, you don't have any possibility to reach God. As
human beings, we must not make a work out of having heard this, or out
of humility; this is the most dangerous form of arrogance to which church
Christians are subject. Nietzsche saw through this; his critique of glorying
in one's servitude is often really a Christian critique.[12]

---

10. [*Brunner used "eristic" to refer to the apologetic and polemical tasks of theology. For more, see* DBWE *11:235, n. 297.*]

11. ["Martin Luther, 'Disputation concerning Man,' *LW* 34:137–144. In forty theses, Luther debates the philosophical (theses 1–19) as opposed to the theological definition of the human being (theses 20–40)," *DBWE* 11:235, n. 300.]

12. [". . . In his 1929 lecture in Barcelona, 'Basic Questions of a Christian Ethic,' Bonhoeffer takes up the critique of Nietzsche and states that the 'Overman' is not, as he imagined, the opposite of the Christian; without realizing it, Nietzsche imbued the Overman with many of the features of the free Christian" (*DBWE* 10:366–367 [*Reader* 80–81]) . . . ," *DBWE* 11:236, n. 305.]

When a human being says Yes to the radical No, God's righteousness is   237
restored. God has taken back God's rights and has received *satisfactio* [*satisfaction*].[13] Thus human beings receive their righteousness from God alone
and are open to God; there are no issues remaining between them and
God. In this relationship of obedience, God affirms human beings. People
do not become worthy of mercy through total denial of themselves. Since
Christ, the Yes is no longer grounded in the No, but the No is grounded in
the Yes. We hear the Yes only in the No, but only because the Yes is there do
we hear the No.

This is the essential difference from Tillich. It is at the boundaries of
our existence that according to Tillich, we experience the radical No; if we
accept this boundary situation we find ourselves affirmed. In recognizing
that we are sinners, in essence we already have the recognition of mercy.
This identification (Holl) must be broken; it means preemption, by our own
power, of God's act of grace. God is completely free, even above and beyond
the recognition of sin.

When the No turns to a Yes, that is of course an act of God in complete
freedom and is not based on the No. It is God who must overcome God's
own No and become angry at God's own anger (Luther);[14] this is the reason
for the cross. Christology is by nature bound up with the doctrine of justi-   238
fication. In Christ, God gets serious with human beings about our dependence on *iustitia aliena* [*alien or external righteousness*]. The human being still
remains totally *peccator* [*sinner*], and righteousness of the human being is
quintessentially imputed.[15] Even faith is not a divinely determined human
capacity but rather the expression of the most profound human passivity;
it is to be understood not as a psychic phenomenon but rather as the determination of human beings in their existence, which by itself is *mere passive*
[*purely suffering*]. Here religious states and experiences are no longer taken
into consideration; it is still *iustitia aliena* [*alien or external righteousness*], even
with regard to our Christianity.

If justification is understood as receiving a share in a divine power, a
Catholic tendency is introduced; it cannot be thought of together with
psychological justification (Holl, R. Seeberg). Here again we encounter a   239

---

13. ["Technical term central to Anselm's doctrine of atonement (*Cur Deus Homo*, in
1098) according to which God's anger and justice is atoned for, or satisfied, by the gracious offering of the God-man in the sacrifice of the cross," *DBWE* 11:237, n. 307.]

14. [". . . God's wrath as the 'alien work' of God is understood in juxtaposition to
God's love as God's proper work . . . ," *DBWE* 11:238, n. 310.]

15. ["'Imputed' righteousness is not a quality that is possessed or something a person
achieves, but is a juridical judgment passed upon him or her," *DBWE* 11:238, n. 313.]

iustitia interna [*inner righteousness*]. Human beings exist only in being face-to-face with the crucified one. Where judgment is seen as having begun, even in part, I no longer see myself as the absolute *peccator* [*sinner*]. Then Christ, through what he has done for me, has made himself superfluous; this is why, for Holl, the doctrines of justification and Christology are no longer the main focus.

Both these things are given fundamental significance by Barth. Preaching can be preaching only when it is preaching of Christ and his righteousness. Christ is completely present in history, but this then is qualified prehistory; its qualification as such remains invisible. A historian sees only the Jewish rabbi, but he is seen as something more at the point where history is revealed as prehistory, that is at the same time a God event. Jesus on the cross is the *kyrios* [*Lord*]; in him the church-community sees the sentence of death and of judgment meted out to all flesh. Through the resurrection, God's righteousness in Christ becomes our righteousness. The Holy Spirit is not a dynamic principle through which this act of Christ is appropriated. For then the cross is made superfluous. The Holy Spirit allows human beings to believe and to hear that the righteousness of humankind lies entirely in Christ.

All that we say must remain Advent speech. Like the OT, the NT also has the character of promise; Christ alone is the world of Christmas. The human attitude is to be captivated by the future. This future is in every case Christ himself, as the absolute One who is outside us. The gospel has an essentially eschatological character.

240   Between the first and the second edition, Barth made essential changes in his eschatology:[16] in the 1st ed., the visible coming of God into this world; in the second edition: only coming from time to time.

The problem of ethics, of obedience

A human being remains totally *peccator* [*sinner*]; the works of the justified are never holy. The kingdom of God is not for us to build. Only when God says that God is pleased with this work, then it is a good work. The conscience is not the judge of what is good. To do well means to act at God's

241   good pleasure. In faith we are called to obedience, but in obeying we are always in need of forgiveness. Obedience is thus our sacrifice to God, and God remains fully free to accept it or reject it.

---

16. [*Bonhoeffer is likely referring to the revision of* Romans, *not* Die Christliche Dogmatik. *See* DBWE *11:240, n. 321.*]

Naumann: Human beings first serve themselves as human beings, and then beyond that are Christians. Barth: the human being is first of all a human being, and not a Christian at all. But because he experiences forgiveness of sins, that is what makes him a Christian. Does this mean morality is threatened? Yes, it must be, to the extent that it is a morality that does not think it needs to put itself at the mercy of God. God says of godless persons whatever God wills. But those who know that they are dependent on the Christ who is to come bow in obedience, as if pointing out their own weakness in the faith, so that in their weakness Christ may give his power its full sway.

§14 Where do we stand?[17]

The clichés about Barth have been consciously avoided. This is a theology that seeks to understand completely the *sola fide* [*through faith alone*] and therefore speaks from the viewpoint of predestination, and therefore dialectically. There are questions to be asked of this approach. In all of recent literature no one is seriously the equal of Barth.

(1) To understand the *sola fide* [*through faith alone*] requires the concept of God's radical freedom. Barth's term "from time to time" (does justice to this concept). Only this is an adequate way to speak of grace. By nature God is understood as act, without predicates of being, because otherwise we would be conceiving of God as an object. On the other hand, the Lutheran: It is God's freedom and honor to have completely bound himself to the word. Not freedom from, but rather freedom for.

242

Everyone in the church-community may forgive the sins of another. It is God who has promised that I may speak for God to others; from that the church-community lives in freely given continuity, which is the very presence of Christ, but not directly as an object, rather only through faith. According to this concept of the church, the church is not only the community of sinners and pardoned persons who hear the word, but rather the presence of Christ himself.[18] Preaching and sacrament are not only promises but rather partake themselves, with their word, in the world of Christmas, on the authority of the church-community and not depending on the need of the individual preacher. The church-community is the world of Christmas. The most important change for Christology: helpless waver-

---

17. [*See* Act and Being, *especially Part B* (DBWE *2:81–135*), *for Bonhoeffer's extended discussion of the following themes.*]

18. [*The theme of "Christ existing as church-community" is central to Bonhoeffer's thinking. See especially* DBWE *1:121,* DBWE *2:112, and* DBWE *9:440.*]

ing between old substantive concepts and new dynamic concepts. Neither alone is adequate.

The pure interpretation of the act does not do justice to New Testament thinking and that of Luther. (Here) again the confessional issue becomes clear. A situation of which today's Lutherans must be ashamed; they stand for a theology that no longer perceives the boundary between itself and Catholicism. Barth saw and recovered the Reformed boundary with Catholicism.

243

(2) Clarification of the relation between philosophy and theology. We recognize the difference in their object. Is theology to be integrated into the system of fields of knowledge, and if so, where? As a positive academic discipline, should it be subordinate to philosophy, or should it again become the primary discipline? Should it be detached from universities and be taught in church academies?

The relation between church and state plays a role here.

(3) The problem of ethics. Barth's conception of it as demonstration excludes any concrete teaching and any teaching of ethics based on principles. How is Christian ethics as an academic discipline possible? How shall I preach the law? The statement of forgiveness is the foundation of the Ten Commandments. The dogmatic statement retains its primary importance. Preaching of the gospel and of the law are not coordinated. To preach Christ concretely means also that one always preaches within a concrete situation. What is the scholarly basis on which ethics is to be constructed? Where is the principle of concretion of the general call to obedience?

244

Our messages from the church have so little power because they sit in the middle, between general principles and concrete situations. The trouble with the church is also the trouble with theological faculties, but this trouble is so little noticed.

Luther was able to write *On the Bondage of the Will* and his piece on usury at the same time. Why can't we do that anymore?

Who will show us Luther!

12. THE NATURE OF THE CHURCH

DBWE 11:269–332

The first section of Bonhoeffer's lectures on the church,[1] which he delivered in the summer semester of 1932, approaches from a number of angles the theme of the church's place, arguing that the church's place in the world is the "place of God himself" and that the church's place in theological reflection is as both its presupposition and its object. The second section treats the church as the form of God's revelation, drawing extensively on material developed in Sanctorum Communio, *such as the contrast between community in Adam and in Christ, and the nature of Christ's presence in the church as vicarious representative action. The lectures conclude with a discussion of the church's relation to the state that prefigures the various occasional papers Bonhoeffer would produce on that issue at the beginning of the Church Struggle in 1933.*

In view of this impending struggle, it is crucial to note a fundamental theological affirmation that dates back to Bonhoeffer's doctoral dissertation: the church is created by God's self-revelation in Jesus Christ; it is a social reality of revelation. There is no institutional fundamentalism in Bonhoeffer's ecclesiology. Not everything that calls itself "church" is church. Reciting creeds, consecrating bishops, preaching Luther's doctrine of justification, and so on do not guarantee that an organization is church. Holding the actual church accountable to the meaning of the revelation in Christ applied not only to pro-Nazi parties like the German Christians; Bonhoeffer also applied it those he called pseudo-Lutherans, for example, in his critique of "cheap grace" in Discipleship *and his critique of the church in general in* Ethics.[2]

---

1. [*These lectures are reconstructed from a student's notes. Because a second student's notes often clarify some confusions in the first, extensive portions of those are included as footnotes in* DBWE 11. *For reasons of space, however, those footnotes are not reproduced here. The interested reader is referred to* DBWE 11.]
2. [*See* DBWE 4:43–56 (Reader 459–469) on "Costly Grace" and DBWE 6:138–142, *concluding with* "The church confesses itself guilty of violating all of the Ten Commandments."]

---

3. ["*Stellvertretung*, a central concept in Bonhoeffer's Christology and ethics, is translated throughout *DBWE* as 'vicarious representative action' (cf. *DBWE* 1:120, n. 17). The basic idea is one who stands in the place of and acts for the sake of others, whether collectively or individually. God's becoming human in Jesus Christ is the paradigmatic instance of *Stellvertretung*," *DBWE* 11:270, n. 3.]

4. ["This is the standard *DBWE* translation of *Gemeinde*. It is Bonhoeffer's preferred word to describe the church as a theological entity, and it emphasizes its communal character. *Christus als Gemeinde existierend*, Christ existing as church-community, is the axiom of Bonhoeffer's ecclesiology. For discussion of *Gemeinde* and related terms in Bonhoeffer's ecclesiology, see *DBWE* 1:14–17. Contexts where *Gemeinde* simply means congregation are usually obvious," *DBWE* 11:270, n. 4.]

Bonhoeffer: The Nature of the Church
Summer Semester 1932—Berlin—Wednesday and Saturday
9–10:00 a.m.

April 20, 1932

Introduction

Do we need the church? This is the question asked by lukewarm, skeptical individuals from the historical tradition of liberalism, from the history-of-religion,[6] or from the bourgeoisie. Others who have been inspired by mysticism: the same question. Another group from the church spectrum: the church is necessary; great *official authority* of the church, *the ideology of leadership*, community is necessary (emphatically so). Models of the Anglo-Saxon nature of the church, the ecumenical forms! (In the Anglo-Saxon model: church action is encouraged! Misuse of the word, of speech.)[7] Among us in

272

---

5. [*"Christlichkeit"* (literally 'Christianness'), *DBWE* 11:271, n. 6.]

6. [*The "history of religions school"* was "a scholarly movement that promoted the scientific study of religion, using a comparative historical method. It arose primarily in nineteenth-century German biblical studies and examined especially the way cultural factors conditioned texts and ideas," *DBWE* 11:187, n. 52.]

7. ["Within the context of his ecumenical activities, Bonhoeffer often criticized the practical church activism of Anglo-Saxon participants, who did not appear willing or able to ground their work theologically and ecclesiastically (*DBWE* 11:356–357, 369–370, and 385)," *DBWE* 11:272, n. 10.]

Germany, the general direction of Dibelius's conception: the most powerful
intrusion of Anglo-Saxon influence into Germany. [. . .] Cultural encounters between Anglo-Saxons and Germany.

The demand for the ideology of leadership through the youth movement
and National Socialism. The leader in the church, who dares to give orders.
We need strong direction in the church; that is why we need the ideology
of leadership in the church. *Community* is necessary: the youth movement is
behind this; in the postwar years community was the basis of all life. Theological working communities. Outside the church, one found fulfillment
of the meaning of life in the community. Religious community is a special
group. Because of this one needs church.

273   This demand for an ideology of leadership and community in the church
arises out of the *secular* realm. Authority, community in the state. A "Führer"[8] is not named in the Bible; there are apostles, etc. In the Reformation
there is the preacher and the teacher, insofar as he serves properly, not
insofar as he leads properly. Transposed now into the ecclesiastical realm
having moved first out of the secular realm.

There has always been a "call for the church." Today the source of the
call openly in the secular realm. Community arising from romantic life-
forms, erotic. The concept of community in communism and in National
Socialism. Church demand for community in secular form. Yearning arises
out of events in the secular sphere. Here the church is the means for other
purposes! Community, authority, a Führer are demanded directly. Church
is only secondary.

Skepticism: "We need the church"? Doubt about the word "need." Is the
need decisive, where God is simply there as Lord, where he wants us, where
we are here for him? *"Do I need God?"* is senseless. We are bound to him.
The word and revelation of God even in the church, where he so speaks to
human beings. "I need" for my own purposes always! But not in this case.
Question about the usefulness of the church is senseless. God has spoken
and has revealed himself to us in the church. "The Church of Christ" as the
revelation of God! We believe this because we believe in Christ. *What is the
church as the revelation of God!?* That is our question! "Do I need a Christian
God?" This is a question one cannot ask because then "God" is not. *"One
does not need the church!"* [. . .] particularly not as church with its human ser-

---

8. ["We have retained the German word here because it was already a loaded term in
Germany, even before the National Socialists came to power. The 'ideology of the Führer' was attractive to German youth throughout the 1920s. See Bonhoeffer's early reflections on this in *DBWE* 12:266–268, 268–282 (*Reader* 359–369)," *DBWE* 11:273, n. 18.]

vants, its errors. In this context, the deep need of the church is visible. [. . .]   274
The church doesn't bind us anymore. [. . .] The church is the *place where God speaks, where God is!!!*

April 23, 1932

One cannot bypass God. "Do I need?" is a question that simply may not be asked in theology. He God is simply here! No postulates of thought! Theology is related to the God-given realities given to us that are not bound to us.

What is the church as the revelation of God? What is the claim of the church!? The Catholic concept of church seems not to include thoughts of claims on the church (the church is a being!).[9] Barth: seemingly speaks only of claims and sees therein the essential nature of the church. (The church is an *actus* [*act*].)[10] One must speak of the being and act of the church together.

Disposition   275
I. Locating the church as the place of God in the world! Locality has both being and claim at the same time. *God* is, as far as we can think of God, *in one place*. In the church, in the word, as "God for us." "God without a place" is an expression of modern religiosity (stemming from mysticism—Angelus Silesius—and from rationalism).

II *The Form of the Church*: (a) Adam and Christ; (b) The present Christ in the church as the body of Christ; (c) the acting congregation, the acting Christ; (d) worldliness of the church; (e) Christianity of the church; (f) boundaries of the church! (can be seen through the concept of the world and predestination and the kingdom of God).[11]

---

9. [". . . Cf. *DBWE* 2:104–105. On Bonhoeffer's critical discussion of the Catholic concept of church, see *DBWE* 1:125 (*Reader* 36), 256–257, 260–261, and 187–188. For the literature cited by Bonhoeffer in his critique of Catholicism, see *DBWE* 1:125–126, n. 11," *DBWE* 11:274, n. 29.]

10. [". . . During the 1920s, Barth developed his concept of church within the determination of the relationship between God and the human being, which was characterized by a newly promulgated claim of God to the individual human being (see, for example, Barth, *Die christliche Dogmatik*, 295). Cf. also Bonhoeffer's discussion with the 'actualism' of the early Barth and his attempt to overcome the opposition between act and being in his 1930 dissertation (*DBWE* 2:82–87). For Barth the church is not 'being,' e.g., qua institution, but rather 'event,' as an act of God speaking and the believer responding to God's word. This event character is Barth's 'actualism.' See Hunsinger, *How to Read Karl Barth*," *DBWE* 11:274, n. 30.]

11. [*At this point in* DBWE, *there is a bibliography of mainly German literature, which has been omitted from this* Reader. *See* DBWE *11:275–276.*]

276   I. The Place of the Church

(a) in the World
Today's theology is the theology of understanding, not of the solution. That
is decisive. Here also that is, in the doctrine of the church the question of
understanding. [. . .] Churches and castles towered over the Middle Ages;
today note New York (Trinity Church!).[12]

1. Our church is without a place
The desire of our church to be everywhere results in its being nowhere.
That which is tangible becomes unassailable! The church is never and
nowhere itself anymore. Existence without a place is the existence of Cain,
of the refugee. Therefore despised! Misfortune: The church did not wish
to isolate itself, wanted to fit in. Only since then has the church remained
277   behind. The attitude of the world toward the church is determined essentially by the fact that the church has no place. The sects that are tied to a
place are often to be taken much more seriously. Because the church has
become without a place, the church has only favored and no longer *actual*
places.

April 27, 1932

2. The church has only favored places in the world
The church is hated because it accidentally prefers certain places [. . .]
although it doesn't know that it is placeless. Favored places are still available where traditional ties still exist. The *bourgeoisie* is the favored place of
the church, until it finds its own place again. Anxious conservatism and
place-bound conservatism; our church does not belong to the first sort of
conservatism. The transformation of our church by *bourgeois standards.*[13]
(Tillich: *The Religious Situation*). Ecclesiastical action concerns itself mostly
only with the *petite bourgeoisie*; it cannot incorporate intellectuals, capitalists,
and workers. (The needs of the *petite bourgeoisie* are those mostly mentioned;
the needs of the enemies of the church are missing.) The horizon shrinks!
        The church has lost its *real* place and has become acculturated. Dibelius:
278   the church has become independent and occupies its own place. But this

---

12. ["Trinity Church Wall Street, at the southern tip of Manhattan, stands in the
shadow of countless skyscrapers," *DBWE* 11:276, n. 50.]
13. ["The criticism of the bourgeois transformation of the church can be found in
Bonhoeffer's 1927 dissertation; see esp. *DBWE* 1:271–274," *DBWE* 11:277, n. 58.]

place since 1918, is *not* its *own place!*[14] Autonomous culture has been shaken off. Now that the church has supposedly become autonomous, it has made itself harmonious with culture, and it seeks new cultural forms; therefore it has become the slave of culture. Church—place of today is privileged place! (built into the contemporary culture); the church is without a place.

(3) What is the proper place of the church?
This cannot be stated concretely. It is the place of the present Christ in the world. It is God's own will that chooses his place. That is the *place of God himself*; therefore it can never be a place assumed by a human being. It must be qualified through God's gracious presence. God must reveal himself to it. The place that could be the proper place as such cannot be the locus of the church. The church cannot appeal to the particular place. The church is really and truly without a place! No human being can dispose over this; even the church cannot.

The place of God in the world is not the same as the place of the church. How can the church make the historical place a real place? It must be conscious of the fact that it can never create the place itself. The church cannot do this, but *it should know that God can do this deed.* The church is aware of   279
its own lack of a particular place, therefore that there is no favored place for it before God chooses the place for it. The church's characteristic place is there where it waits *for God to give it its characteristic place* (namely to be the place of God himself). God has no place; the church must know this. It is then that it has escaped from the human odyssey of being without a place. *There where no human place can establish the church, there is the* place *of the church*; namely, there where God is alone with his congregation! Yet the church is always in the midst of culture. The same "Yes" and the same "No" of all human places, the absolute center of the church! There where God allows the church to find its own place, is the place of the church! Then the church will be loved or hated only because of its own cause (the gospel). The church's proper place is the *"critical center of the world."* From that point there are no longer any favored places. The *crisis is God himself*, not the pastor; the church is the critical center. Where one is completely without a place, where one is on the periphery, there is the critical center of the world (*Galilee* in the Roman Empire or *Wittenberg*).

---

14. ["In the August 11, 1919, Weimar Republic constitution, the concept of a state church was, on the one hand, rejected; on the other, however, Articles 137 and 138 gave the churches extensive rights and the status of public legal corporations (see H. Hildebrandt, *Die deutsche Verfassungen*, 102)," *DBWE* 11:278, n. 63.]

April 30 1932—no lecture held.

280   May 4, 1932

(b) The Place of the Church in Christendom

On what has the hatred for the church been founded? It is not hatred against the Christian people. *The church on the periphery*: where the life of the individual stands at its high points or turning points (baptism, confirmation, marriage, death), there are the high points of the ecclesiastical activities of Christianity. There is the church. *Nature* and celebration belong together, so one thinks; the church is merely the bond. *Ecclesiastical celebration of nature!* The church is the exception from the everyday. Celebration is (1) only, to *interrupt* everyday activities, and yet always with an eye to the everyday; celebration as the boundary of the everyday. (2) In the midst of celebration everyday thoughts are to be suppressed. The church should *distract*, deepen, and ennoble. A worship service is an ecclesiastical celebration. And yet under the rule of the everyday the church still stands. The church feels comfortable as the *place of celebration*. A cinema: doesn't a cinema serve this purpose better (than the church)? The sphere of profanity. *Profanity can be celebrated better in a cinema.*

The contemporary church is only "celebratory" Christianity. The Christianity of everyday life is not in the church. The church is on *the periphery of life*, not in the center! The church would like to step into the center. But it is abandoned on Sundays. Therefore, *hate* for the church exists [. . .] church's place on the periphery! From lack of criticism,[15] the church speaks about central matters from the periphery.

What is *the proper place of the church in Christianity*, the church of Christ? God's reality must not be seen as a kind of exception, also *not as a holiday in an ethical or religious sense!* Therefore, the celebratory character of the church. God is not an aspect of reality! The *entire reality, including the everyday*, must be seen! Even the Christian religion can have the character of an exception, but God cannot. One does not celebrate with thoughts alone of God. God penetrates the entire everyday reality and must be felt in everything! *The* absolute exception is the church as the word of God for all of Christianity. Where the word breaks in, there is the church, is *the center of Christianity*; there the church as *a whole* is Christianity, insofar as it hears God's word over *all* reality. *The church is the church-community, is there where the word is believed and obeyed; there is the center!* The church is the center of the

---

15. ["This must mean 'self-criticism,'" *DBWE* 11:281, n. 83.]

world and is the church-community of God. It is not true that the church-community can refer to itself as the center (Rome!), rather insofar as it points to God, who occupies the center.

Christianity is not removed from the world. It is in the everydayness of the world. Therefore, the word must stand in the sphere of the everyday. The church is not an "exceptional light" outside the profane realm, not a separation of church and the world.

(c) The Place of the Church in Dogmatic Theology   282
Theology is a function of the church.[16] How is a scholarly understanding of the church about its nature possible?[17] *Augustine*: "church" writings; with him the problem of the church is solved for the Catholic Church. It was first treated again in 1489 by Cardinal Torquemada in his *Summa de ecclesia*. For one thousand years, one did not see this problem. Only the primacy of the pope is problematic; beginning with Hus and Wycliffe we have ecclesiological literature again. In the era of the Reformation the article "De ecclesia" [*On the Church*] was worked out by Bellarmine. *Scholasticism* needed no treatise about it: it was naturally a self-evident presupposition. There would be no theology if the Catholic Church did not exist. In scholastic dogmatics *the concept of the church stands outside the problematic brackets!* 283
[...] Articles are mere pieces of theology. Augustine thought of the church as the presupposition of all articles of dogmatics.

May 7, 1932[18]

The church in the world cannot declare favored places as its own proper place. People consider the place of celebrations as the place of the church; it is, however, the most easily expendable for any person. The right place for the church is available only for those who are in the church. [...] The state cannot give the church its proper place.

---

16. ["See *DBWE* 11:284, n. 107, and 285, n. 117. The formulation oriented toward Barth, 'theology as function of the church,' can already be found in Bonhoeffer in his 1929–1930 postdoctoral dissertation. Cf. *DBWE* 2:130," *DBWE* 11:282, n. 93.]

17. ["In reply to the question Bonhoeffer at first gave a historical survey . . . ," *DBWE* 11:282, n. 94.]

18. ["The following section at the beginning of the new lecture hour presents a postscript to '(b) The Place of the Church in Christendom' and interrupts the train of thought within the paragraph '(c) The Place of the Church in Dogmatic Theology,'" *DBWE* 11:283, n. 103.]

The essential problem: why does Catholic *Scholasticism* leave a lacuna where an article "de ecclesia" should be included? Historical explanation! But similarly a substantive explanation is necessary. The significance of the church is made clear where the church is the presupposition of all theology. An isolated theology cannot build a private opinion about God, Christ, and the Holy Spirit, because previously the genuine testimony (has occurred) inside the church; therefore one cannot put the church inside the brackets. But this does not leave a lacuna there! It is a sign of uncertainty when one finally again refers to "Articulus de ecclesia" [*article of faith about the church*].

284   The church is the presupposition. Treatment of the concept of the church becomes more and more isolated. Protestant theology became more independent and could when necessary be understood even without the church. *Schleiermacher* brings back the connection between the church and theology (as Barth does today in a different way). In him,[19] there is a new valuation of the church. [. . .] The central thought is the "church." [. . .] His "church" is the voluntary union of pious Christians. Thereby the church is traced back to the piety of the individual. The church is not the ultimate presupposition. Individual religiosity is the presupposition of everything.[20]

Ritschl: Ideas about the congregation! He too doesn't see the church as presupposition of everything.[21] Insight into the Catholic, Scholastic theol-
285   ogy, therefore, is missing here as well. For the Scholastics, to speak of God is to no longer have God at one's disposal. Theological expression is not isolated but rather stands within the church.

We Protestants approach Catholic dogma with the wrong premise: we look at it as an isolated factor. Its emphasis is the daily witness of God in the church. The Catholics carry dogma lightly. We have lost this knowledge. Theology must emerge from the *isolation* from *what happens in the church*; otherwise theology is a lost outpost. Until today *Protestant theology has been in isolation*, so it has become a heavy, earnest matter. Catholic theology by contrast is a "cheerful matter."

Barth experienced the burden of dogmatic theology. He seeks relief from this burden, therefore sets something before the brackets as the presupposition. Theology is related to the *"preaching" church!* Theology is the church's function. Church as legally constituted, organized church is not the premise for theology. Thus understood, it is not the ultimate presuppo-

---

19. ["The reference is to Schleiermacher," *DBWE* 11:284, n. 108.]

20. ["On Bonhoeffer's dispute with Schleiermacher, see *DBWE* 1:158–161 (*Reader* 50–51), esp. Bonhoeffer's note 18 on p. 159...," *DBWE* 11:284, n. 109.]

21. ["Already in *Sanctorum Communio*, Bonhoeffer had criticized Ritschl's individualism in his doctrine of sin. See *DBWE* 1:113–114 (*Reader* 33)," *DBWE* 11:284, n. 112.]

sition. Barth seeks the power *that constitutes the Church*, i.e., *predestination.* So finally predestination is the presupposition that stands before the brackets of theology! Predestination exists; it appears daily in the proclamation; therefore, one can speak daily about God and the Holy Spirit. *A theological statement stands in connection with the daily event of predestination!* There is exoncration! The cramp of theology is dissolved here. Barth doesn't execute these ideas; rather he merely opens a way for them. Theology should nevertheless express the burden and in every sentence point to the fact that predestination stands behind everything. Now Barth burdens everything once more *with the reservation of predestination* (dialectical procedure)! The   286
concept of predestination gained through the concept of the church is the presupposition, yet the burden remains. Dogmatic theology treats the church as an element of doctrine but is nevertheless also in the entirety of its statements conditional on the church!! That is the difficult problem. The church is *presupposition for and object of dogmatics at the same time.* Two possibilities:[22] (1) What is meant here by "object" and presupposition must be explained. *Dialectics!* This tense relationship must be expressed thus: where one speaks of the spirit and of God as "object," one must always say that this is also a presupposition! One cannot speak simultaneously about object and presupposition. From this arises the difficulty of the dialectical language.

May 11, 1932

The Catholic sacramental church stands before all theology. Barth: the concept of predestination gained through the church stands before all theology. The *problem* for the Protestant situation: *church is presupposition and at the same time object of theology.*

Two possibilities:

1. *Dialectical theology:* in every doctrinal element of dogmatics one must point out the ultimate presupposition of that doctrinal element (e.g., [. . .] church is Protestant; [. . .] not church as an objective thing).

Critique: 287

(a) Does a scholarly possibility of a reference exist? No. Does the presupposition remain a complete presupposition? A reference is always only possible to an object. There is no possibility for a scholarly reference from the object to the presupposition.

---

22. ["The second possibility will be developed only after the new explication of the first possibility at the beginning of the next hour," *DBWE* 11:286, n. 121.]

(b) The necessity of such a reference from the object to the presupposition must be doubted. This is an impossible and unnecessary attempt on the part of dialectical theology!! Its value lies in the posing of the problem!

2nd attempt: The church as presupposition, as the place of revelation. Theology is not metaphysics when it serves the church concretely in the sermon. *The empirically concrete church* is presupposed by theology. [. . .] Although, according to Barth, predestination is the ultimate presupposition.

Critique: The presupposition of theology can only be the empirical church. The presupposition and boundary of theology is the empirical church. Theology is the boundary of the word of forgiveness and grace. *The first presupposition is predestination, which is the boundary of the church*; from this (emerges a) *theology* of the empirical church, which *is limited* by *the empirical church*. Is this a Catholic concept of church?? No. For there church is eschatological [. . .][23] Here the church is already realized for us; Bonhoeffer is speaking of Protestant theology; it [i.e., the church] has eschatological boundaries. Theology must allow the church itself to assign its place.

288

The Concept of the Church in the Theological System

Where in dogmatics should we talk about the church? [. . .] Picture of dogmatics. [. . .] Theology as monad. The method of theology must be descriptive, not deductive. *Synthetic* theological method: proceeding from the cause; Georg Calixtus brings the *analytical* method (*finis* [*goal*] → *subiectum* [*one who is affected*] → *media* [*means or medium*] (church), coming from the future).

The starting point in theology begins with contemporary knowledge. God's giving himself in revelation. Dogmatics must *begin with the church as the place of revelation.*

Protestant theology however proceeds from the individual. The concept of church as presupposition points to the fact that the *community* is *primum* [*first*] (church as church-community). The significance of the concept of church for theological prolegomena! The basic error of our Protestant theology heretofore has been the individualization. Luther wanted to preserve the original church-community of Christ (not only teaching activity; that is secondary). For Luther disentanglement from the church is burdensome; pain because of the lost theological community. [. . .] Thus a Lutheranism developed that had broken away from the communal idea of the church!

289

---

23. ["In his dissertation, Bonhoeffer accused Catholicism of a religious misunderstanding of the church, since the church was mistaken for the kingdom of God and the historicity of humankind and of the church was 'objectified and deified' (*DBWE* 1:125 [*Reader* 36])," *DBWE* 11:287, n. 130.]

May 25, 1932

Isolation of theology from the church-community! Even individual points of theological doctrine become isolated (e.g., justification). The knowledge of God in the church-community becomes the knowledge of God by the individual; *Troeltsch: the individual is the subject of knowledge of God.* He finds this in the religious a priori.[24] Dialectical theology: there is no systematic knowledge of God a priori, but rather always and ever knowledge as God speaks to the individual (*revelation* means: God brings knowledge, not an a priori)! The character of revelation of that which is to be known. That which should be known is subjectivized in Barth, no communication with the other, who can only know of God ever and again.

The starting point for Barth and Troeltsch is still the same: *the individual's* knowledge of God! Yet, knowledge of God has as its primary subject the *church-community* (Luther).[25] The church knows, my testimony is unbur-   290
dened. The objective statement, which takes place within the realm of the church-community. [. . .] I am unburdened as a member of the church-community. The church-community knows the truth (of the knowledge of God); it is no longer a matter of my personal faith. The church-community believes always, because God has given himself to it. The church-community does not protect my testimony; it judges my testimony; therefore my theology is unburdened. The congregation, which has authority, is a function above me. The church-community is the subject of knowledge! Therefore I too can be objective. The challenge of a nonexistential knowledge. The *foundation is the knowledge of the church-community! Ecclesial epistemology*, not a transcendental philosophy. The church as presupposition of all theology.

The question about the place of the church must first be redirected toward the other issue: the place of dogmatic theology in the church. The empirical church is the presupposition for theology. However, the church also remains the object of dogmatic theology. As such, it is to be treated as the first topic of dogmatics. The recognition of the church (church-

---

24. ["For Bonhoeffer's argument with Troeltsch's understanding of a religious a priori, see *DBWE* 11:187–189, 196–197," *DBWE* 11:289, n. 146.]

25. ["Bonhoeffer here and elsewhere in his lectures (*DBWE* 11:319–321 [*Reader* 201–202]) refers to Luther's 1519 sermon on 'The Sacrament of the Holy and True Body of Christ,' *LW* 35:45–67. There Luther had developed the idea that Christians are a part of the church as the body of Christ. Here he emphasizes that the individual, precisely in his temptation, was dependent on his incorporation into the body of Christ through the Lord's Supper, to gather strength and support of the body of Christ; see *LW* 35:53–55," *DBWE* 11:290, n. 148.]

community) as presupposition of theology means overcoming false Protestant subjectivism, not only for theological prolegomena but also for every individual point of doctrine. It's a matter of the discovery of a new ecclesial way of thinking and knowledge (ecclesial epistemology).

In all that has been said about the place of the church, the peculiar difficulty is to identify this place. The reason for this is that the church has empirical places favored places; however, as an empirical church of God, the church can only have the place that God chooses for it and to that extent as the place of God in the world is itself the presupposition of all possible places (in the world, in Christianity, and in dogmatic theology).

291   Part II: The Form of the Church

(A) Adam-Christ
(B) The Church and Christ
(C) The Acting Church-Community
(D) The Worldliness of the Church
(E) The Christianity of the Church

Preliminary Comment about "Form"
Form means unity, multiplicity within the finite boundary. Form is never only finite; form is infinite because it transcends the sum of all boundaries. Synthetic forms are inauthentic (e.g., synthetic precious stones). The human will tries to create wholeness for a certain *goal*. Beauty for example is a goal. Communities can be similar to genuine ones; they become inauthentic when they are created for a purpose. Genuine forms, these are the forms that precede all the human deeds and desires and are existentially related solely to God, forms as reconciliation, redemption, or creation.[26]

We see and think in forms (a priori conceptual perception in forms)! How broadly do we think in genuine and inauthentic forms (question of philosophy, also question of theology)? The primal state of thinking is thinking in forms. The inauthentic forms of our thinking are in opposition
292   to the genuine forms. Those force the genuine forms back into their primal state and do not grasp them as form in the being of God.

---

26. ["In the background of this paragraph are ideas about a typology of social forms that was worked out in *Sanctorum Communio*; see *DBWE* 1:86–94," *DBWE* 11:291, n. 157.]

May 28, 1932

The form-unity established by God is genuine form, and indeed this can be in the form of creation, redemption, or forgiveness. Our thinking is fulfilled in the form of human logos. Our thinking is blind to the forms of revelation.

The church as the form of revelation of God should be portrayed. But: With our thinking we will always portray only the inauthentic form of the church!

The church as a genuine form is *unity*, basically the unity of God! The form reveals itself under the presupposition of unity. Differentiation: the church over against a religious community (arisen from individual converging wills!) is necessary. The church is the *primary unity*. Those who do not start with unity confuse the church with a religious community. Unity is not the ideal of a world church; it is not "unity of the church" (Roman, ecumenical, Anglicanism). Only faith in the unity of God in Christ is possible. "Wholeness" is to be understood not as the state of not being broken, but rather as the wholeness of the revelations of God. The church is not just any *form of revelation* of God, but rather the *entire* form of revelation of God. The *believed form of the church* is the genuine form. It can only be believed; it is *never visible*.

(A) Adam and Christ[27]   293

The church is the newly created humanity through Christ, the new people, the second humanity. It is a collective form! On the ground of the humanity-in-Adam! There is only *humanity-in-Adam and the church!* The first already overcome by the second, yet they are always struggling against each other. "Humanity" is not a biological concept, rather derived from revelation. It encompasses the entire history of the world; not until the end of the world can there be something entirely new. Everything is *a struggle between humanity-in-Adam and the church!* Faith and unbelief is the issue of humanity as old and new.

The relationship between these collective forms: Adam is the rebel against the Creator, destroyer of the community of God. He sees the other

27. ["On the following, see *DBWE* 1:107–118 (*Reader* 31–34)," *DBWE* 11:293, n. 164.]

human being as object of his own desire, not as one given to him for community, as the creature of God.

(1) The human being has thrown off the reign of God! His own *master*! (2) The community of God is torn asunder! The human being wants to be *alone*!

Paradise is torn asunder; therefore a kingdom arises where the human being is his own master and is alone; this is the world of Adam. The human being cannot come out of the isolation; his voice remains without an echo. Adam is a human being; he is simultaneously *individual* and *species*.[28] The category of individual means that the human being stands over against God entirely as individual. There the human is wholly species. Where the highest deed of the individual is done, it is also a deed of the entire species. *Sin is sin of the individual and of humanity* at the same time. Therefore, *all humanity falls together in Adam*. In Adam all humanity sins. Addressed by God, the human being is simultaneously wholly individual and wholly the human species. Where this is understood, Adam's sin is understood.

Who is Adam? *The one who committed the first sin.* Actually there is no difference: every sin is the first sin, a tearing asunder of community with God. Also *every* sin that follows is the first sin. *Every human then is Adam!* We are guilty of the sins of humanity. Adam is "one" human; he is all of humanity in one. Adam is the person who personifies the whole.[29] Every individual human must recognize himself as humanity's Adam and allow himself to be judged. ". . . is entirely my burden." *Not the community of sinners*; everyone is an individual as sinner, everyone is Adam alone. In the humanity-in-Adam, all forms of community are formed, even *the religious community*. Here humanity-in-Adam is not overcome. Form of Adam! Every individual is this whole Adam. With every new human being Adam starts anew. The new humanity is created on the *cross of Christ*. The cross is the *dividing line between*

294

295

---

28. ["In *Sanctorum Communio* and *Act and Being*, Bonhoeffer had worked out the idea of *Kollektivperson*, 'collective person,' a figure who represents and personifies a certain mode of existence of both individuals and communities—in the cases of Adam and Christ, representatives of the old sinful humanity and of the new humanity inaugurated by Christ. Foreign as such vocabulary is to an individualistic and atomistic anthropology, Bonhoeffer holds that it does justice to the biblical narrative as well as giving a realistic description of human affairs," *DBWE* 11:293, n. 170.]

29. ["Bonhoeffer's use of the term *Gesamtperson*, literally 'person of the whole,' recalls the fifteenth-century English morality play *Everyman*, in which the title character is understood as the representative human being. *Gesamtperson* and *Kollektivperson* (see ed. note 28 above) are interchangeable and are key terms in the argument of *Sanctorum Communio*, on which these lectures draw heavily; see, for example *DBWE* 1:77–79," *DBWE* 11:294, n. 174.]

old and new humanity. There humanity-in-Adam is overcome! Insofar as the human being recognizes sin and the "no" of the cross, he is set straight.

In the resurrection of Christ, the Yes of God is spoken to the human being. The cross and resurrection of the human Jesus and of the Christ: Christ is fully human, individual and species in one. Golgotha is at the same time the act of the individual and the species. The new, whole humanity is set in Christ. Christ as new humanity, as church; the church is with Christ on the cross and resurrected with him. *Only one* is Christ; only one has broken through the humanity-in-Adam! New humanity,

June 1, 1932

since Christ's merit belongs to humanity itself. The new humanity knows itself to be holy, just, because God knows it as holy, just. The humanity of Christ understands itself only through Christ! He is the Lord! Not Adam! The Christian too is Adam, but overcome through Christ. The church has its own foundation and object in Christ. Christ is the unifying principle of the church. The church as the unity set in Christ is the true form of revelation!

B. Church and Christ   296

(1) Christ's Vicarious Representative Action as the Founding of the Church
    One stands for all; Christ is the vicarious representative of humanity. Adam stands not in the place of the other but rather in his own. Christ stands in the place of humanity!

(a) Ethical Concept of Vicarious Representative Action
[. . .] For example, soldiers in a war, the friend in Schiller's ballad "Die Bürgschaft" [*The Hostage*]. Possessions, body, and honor are goods that the one gives away for the other. The sphere of existence and the ethically independent person is here. I can allow myself to be given goods with the feeling that I am worthy of them. The other person cannot ever stand in my place before the ethical command. He must then always degrade me. That person cannot stand where there is suffering and judgment. The other can never take "punishment" as such upon himself for me without degrading me, but only the consequence of the punishment. Punishment can only be taken on vicariously when one also accepts the evil of the other person. First of all, it is a negation of my person as an ethical being when the other person takes my responsibility. Second, it is an illusion that another person can step in as   297
vicarious representative in the place of my ethical personality. The sacrifice

of goods must be accepted, for the sake of the ethical side of the person. *In cases where the sphere of the person is not involved, a vicarious representative sacrifice can be made*; not, however, where the sphere of the person is touched. The ethical is built upon humanity-in-Adam. The attempt to have a community is illusory—only Adam torn asunder is there.

(b) Christ's Vicarious Representative Action
This is not an ethical concept of vicarious representation. *Vicarious personal sacrifice*, not a vicarious sacrifice of goods! *His suffering is a vicarious representative act for the new humanity.*
  Four Steps:
  1. *Incarnation*: God becomes human. In order to destroy humans, God becomes human. Here the human being is judged in his ethical self-responsibility. Action on his person, which with others of the whole humanity is taken up by Christ.
  2. *Christ enters the community of Israel: he fulfills the law as vicarious representative.* Israel should live from the law in community. Transgression produces isolation of the individual. Justified wrath of the law; Christ takes this upon himself and fulfills it. Not as individual but as new humanity, he is the vicarious representative actor for the church. He is the one who acts as the new humanity.
  3. *Christ dies on the cross* and takes the wrath of God upon himself to the end. His sacrifice is *vicarious representative personal sacrifice!* In Christ the human being must suffer the death of his ethical conscience. Vicarious representative action is this; it is the negation of ethical independence. In the ethical sphere this was impossible. [. . .] As true punishment for true sin! Christ steps into the place where the human being was a sinner. He becomes "the greatest robber and sinner" (Luther). With this our independent standing before God is made impossible. We are judged in him and with him on the cross. Christ is risen!

June 4, 1932

The breakthrough of humanity-in-Adam by Christ! Independent stance before God is impossible for us all. We are judged with Christ on the cross. Christ did the will of God in that he suffers his will. Doing the will of God, of the good is only to be suffered! *Vicarious representative "suffering" of the will of God!* "Suffering" is deepened here. Suffering does not only mean death and poverty. Being strong in God can also only be endured against all fleshly lust. Our suffering is both negated and overcome in Christ's suffering. The vicarious representative action of Christ is also the vicarious representation of suffering for humankind. Yet all suffer in Christ. There the humanity-in-Adam in the church is affected: the disunity is overcome where one suffers on its behalf. "If one member is honored, all rejoice together with it!"   299

4. *Christ is risen.* Humanity is justified in Christ. The righteousness of a human being is judged on the cross. Righteousness can never be done. Christ does, suffers righteousness. The dead body becomes the resurrected body, so too the *corpus Adae* [*body of Adam*][30] becomes *the corpus Christi* [*body of Christ*]. The resurrection community is the church!

Vicarious representative action thus means that (1) Jesus did what no other could do; he is the *Lord.* (2) He did it in such a way that the whole new humanity acts and suffers with him. Thus is Christ the *brother*! In the ethical sphere there is not the Lord and the brother (isolation and lack of brotherhood). Christ is Lord of the church-community. *Community under the lordship of Christ* and at the same time characterized by *brotherhood.* (3) *Christ existing as church-community.*[31] These are the three fundamental conditions for the church. Paradoxical state of contradiction. Yet these three orders are not possible without one another. Church-community as subject, being-with-one-another is the church-community in Christ; Christ as the church-community is the most intimate in-one-another!

(2) Jesus Christ and the Founding of the Church

Problem: *Jesus Christ and the founding of the church* (to point 2); One can raise the objection: the church is the religious community founded by Christ; it was founded already before the cross and resurrection. Therefore, the church is not to be understood from the point of view of the cross and resurrection.

Cf. Matt. 16:18; 18:17: Jesus wanted a messianic community, at first all Israel. Later he wanted a representative, the remnant of Israel, which inherits the kingdom. This follows out of the messianic self-consciousness of Jesus. The messianic community. Yet first it must be broken up and must be under the promise of unification in the new Lord's Supper (meaning of the act of the Lord's Supper) [. . .]; Good Friday: the messianic community is really broken apart. There is no community beneath the cross, only individuals, as Jesus dies. The community is torn apart. Humanity-in-Adam is victorious; every person bears alone the guilt of the entire world.   300

---

30. ["Here in the sense of humanity-in-Adam," *DBWE* 11:299, n. 213.]

31. [". . . Bonhoeffer here quotes the ecclesiological axiom of *Sanctorum Communio*, 'Christus als Gemeinde existierend'; cf. *DBWE* 1:121 and throughout," *DBWE* 11:299, n. 216.]

Under the cross Adam triumphs! Every single person is guilty of this. Here Adam understands himself as the one he is. The cross is the end of God for the community and is the end of the community itself. The *resurrection now means*: from the broken *corpus Adam* [*body of Adam*] emerges the *corpus Christi* [*body of Christ*]. The church-community is indeed a broken church-community but a church-community in which the cross is seen from the perspective of Easter. The church-community gathers around the center. The light of the resurrection cannot be seen without the cross. *Paradoxical form of a church-community of the cross!* The church-community is founded precisely through God's act (through the cross). Under the cross alone there is no church-community. Even here in the community of the resurrection it is not yet church. The community of the resurrection still lives with Christ until the day of the Ascension. After that Christ lives in the church-community. The church is decisively determined through the vicarious suffering and action of Christ.

301   June 15, 1932

As Christ is crucified, the community collapses, but through the resurrection, the church becomes the church-community it could not be during his lifetime. Jesus did not wish to found the church during his lifetime, but the church is newly created as the community of the resurrection.

Christ is not the founder of a new religion and religious community. He is the Redeemer, *the foundation* of the church, *not the founder.* The religious community that Jesus Christ founded is not our contemporary church! Death and resurrection now constitute the church after the outpouring of the Spirit. The apostles (especially Paul) are the founders. As such a one, who he is, Christ is the new humanity. Christ is simultaneously the foundation and beginner and fulfiller of the church. In his historicity and divinity, Christ is the beginner and the fulfiller of the church.

(3) Fundamental Structure of the Church in and through Christ

(a) Structure of Unity: Christ Existing as Church-Community
The church-community is Christ; *Christ is the church-community.* How is the church structured through the vicarious representative action of Christ? The form of revelation as person or the word of God is Christ and Spirit; as work it is the creation. The church itself is the present Christ! The presence of God on earth is Christ; the presence of Christ on earth is the church. [. . .] *Person is the church, is the form of the presence of the Second Person of the Trinity.* The church-community is Christ; Christ stands where the church-

community stands before God. It has conceded its existence to him as the vicarious representative! 1 Cor. 12:12; 6:15; 1:13: *To be in Christ is to be in the church.* (Cf. Kattenbusch in the Harnack Festschrift, 1921; Traugott Schmitt, σῶμα [*body*]; Bousset, co-community; Deißmann, Zu Jesus Christus.)

1 Cor. 1:30; 3:16; 6:15; 2 Cor. 6:16; 13:5; Col. 2:17; 3:16; Gal. 3:28; Eph. 1:23; 4:24; 5:30; Rom. 6:13; 13:14;

For Paul the church-community in the sense of the idea of identity is the body of Christ (body is not to be separated from the person! It represents the person). Christ as the head is first of all a second idea; first church-community as body and person of Christ only afterward: Christ is the Lord, is head. Originally, where the body is, there is the person of Christ! Christ existing as church-community is not visible, rather only to be believed.

To put on the new Adam is to put on Christ, to put on the new church-community! *Christ also stands over against the church-community.* In the Catholic conception there is no one standing over against the church. Different identification; it may not be absolutely set in our tradition. For Christ has ascended, eschatological! [. . .] The law (Gal. 4:8;[32] 1 Thess. 4 and 5; Phil. 3:20; 1 Cor. 15:23!)! Christ is there the Lord of the church-community.

(b) The Structure of Lordship[33] in the Church: Christ as the Lord of the Church-Community

Christ is our Lord, because he justifies. He is the one who has been exalted (Ascension!). He stands before God as the intercessor for the church-community! The church-community not seen without Christ by God! Christ in the front of the church-community. The Father must act with the church-community through the Son. *Intercessio Christi* [*intercession of Christ*]! Christ as Lord is the perpetual intercessor! Through him we have God's grace! The church-community is oriented toward its Lord! Judgment and righteousness only through Christ. The church-community can never be sure of itself. (Catholicism has daily offering in the Mass, but it rests in the hand of the priest; that subordinates the idea of the Lord to the idea of identity. [. . .] unified structure of the church-community; [. . .] Christ as the brother.)

---

32. ["This must be Eph. 4:8," *DBWE* 11:302, n. 239.]

33. ["In *Sanctorum Communio* Bonhoeffer argues that the church, understood from revelation, has a unique sociological structure, combining aspects of community (*Gemeinschaft*), society (*Gesellschaft*), and authority or rule (*Herrschaft*). He then interprets theologically each of these terms taken from the systematic sociology of his time, thus transforming their normal meaning. Hence, Christ's lordship (*Herrschaft*) leads to the statement that 'God's love, in ruling, serves' (*DBWE* 1:63; see also 60 [*Reader* 29–30])," *DBWE* 11:303, n. 241.]

302

303

(c) Community Structure: Christ Is the Brother

He is this to the individual, never to the church-community. Christ *stands there as vicarious representative where my brother should stand.* He, my brother, cannot really be my brother. He does not transcend the sphere of goods; he never enters the sphere of the person. He cannot see my person (he sees me as "It" not as "You"). Christ is there where the brother should stand! For

304   *Christ is my brother; our brother is Christ.* The other as human being will never truly become physically a Christ; the brother is *never* Christ; (it is) not (to be understood) as an absolute! Matt. 25: I was hungry.

June 18, 1932

I *The church of today is the presence of Christ on earth.*

II (a) This presence is to be understood as follows, that the church-community is Christ. The bodily characteristic of the church-community.

   (b) *Christ as Lord* of the church-community; (c) *Christ is the brother.* Catholicism remains at II (a) [. . .] A priest remains Lord as Christ! The word "You belong to me because I belong to you" makes the other a brother. God pronounces the identical statement! Vicarious representative action makes Christ our brother. The brotherhood established through Christ is built upon the law of vicarious representative action!

   The character of the church as a unity! Community character is equally original. It is not possible to have one thought without the other: "Brother" is never absolute, always Lord at the same time. *An absolute judgment about identity is never* possible; that would lead to Catholicism. I can never stand before God for myself; [. . .] *iustitia aliena* [*alien righteousness*]; through vicarious representative action *imputativa iustitia* [*imputed righteousness*] [. . .] Four directions of structure: identity, community, individual.[34]

305   Summary

Guiding principle: "The church is grounded in and through Christ, who as vicarious representative actor is simultaneously individual and humankind." The vicarious representative action of Christ means the deed by which he puts himself in our place where we must stand before God. Vicarious representative action in the ethical sense is the sacrifice of goods; in the deed of Christ it is the sacrifice of a person. As the vicarious representative

---

34. ["In the following summary Bonhoeffer includes four concepts: 'authority,' 'unity,' 'community,' and 'individuality' through which the structure of the church-community is characterized," *DBWE* 11:304, n. 257.]

actor, Christ acts as the new humanity, and the new church is grounded in him. The church is not the foundation of Jesus Christ during his lifetime; rather it is founded in the reality of his vicarious representative action as God-human; the following characteristics of the form of the church emerge from the concept of vicarious representative action: (1) Christ is himself the church-community; (2) Christ is the Lord of the church-community; (3) Christ is the brother in the church-community.

Thereby the church-community is structurally determined by concepts of authority, unity, community, individuality. Every one of these concepts is to be interpreted solely through the concept of vicarious representative action. The reality and the law of vicariousness are constitutive for the church of Christ!

(C) The Acting Church-Community

I. The Holy Spirit and Christ
The Holy Spirit *actualized*[35] that which has been realized through Christ.[36] The church was actually there with the resurrection: it is actualized on Pentecost: the occurrence of judgment and grace! Through the spirit we know the I and You and We of God (that is already included in Christ!). The deed of the Spirit is proclamation and the appropriation of the deed of Christ!   306
The Spirit is the proclaiming Spirit; therefore the Spirit is word. Only the Holy Spirit assures us of the presence of Christ.

The church realized as Christ is actualized through the Spirit! The church may not be individualized through the fact that the Spirit drives the individuals and therefore the church-community together! The concept of *individualism* is still enriched in Schleiermacher! The church is not the community of individual pious people.[37] The church regarded in that way is something secondary, not the form of divine revelation. Primarily it would then be the piety of individuals. In that case one would then also have to appeal for a willing of churchliness.

The main thing would be the knowledge of Christ whereby one is necessarily led into the church. This leads to the socialistic phrase: the church is

---

35. [". . . Bonhoeffer in *Sanctorum Communio* (*DBWE* 1) argues that the church is an ontological reality in Christ that is socially and historically actualized by the Holy Spirit," *DBWE* 11:305, n. 259.]

36. ["For the difference between 'realization' and 'actualization,' see *DBWE* 1:143–144 (*Reader* 40–41)," *DBWE* 11:305, n. 261.]

37. ["For Bonhoeffer's criticism of Schleiermacher's understanding of the church, see *DBWE* 11:284 (*Reader* 180 n. 20), n. 109, and 292, n. 162," *DBWE* 11:306, n. 265.]

a *private matter*!³⁸ Schleiermacher forged the weapons for this! Psychological and historical view of the leadership of the church! Church, however, is *the church that is already actually established in Christ*!! The church is there through the act of God, and has not been made by human beings! Actualizing and acting congregation! Church is not something derived, not something secondary! It is there where it is seen as religious community.

307   II. Church and Religious Community
Church is not to be understood *as a religious community*! Church is a reality of faith. An ideal of experience, rather than of reality, that is religious community.

June 22, 1932

Religious community is always something secondary, even when the concept of community is derived from the concept of religion, for religion must be there first. Three attempts to derive community from religion: (1) purely conceptual derivation; (2) psychological derivation; (3) derivation through philosophy of history.

Regarding (1)³⁹ *Max Scheler*: hierarchy of values with a priori intrinsic laws. The higher the value the less divisible it is. The Holy is the highest. The concept of the religious community should be derived from *the value of the Holy*! The entire value of the Holy becomes the basis of the community. But this is based on the concept of possibility. Each one enjoys the value alone; this is the only possible community. This attempt is *thoroughly individualistic* and purely *formalistic*, since there is no distinction made from the diabolical. The same thing is possible in the diabolical.

308   *Heinrich Scholz*: The concrete form of religion is proof [. . .]! The religion of revelation is an example of this. Religion belongs first of all to the things that the human spirit ponders. Religion, second, is a religion of revelation. There is the necessity of *education* in religion; this is possible only through community!

---

38. [". . . At the beginning of the Weimar Republic, the view of religion as a private matter, the separation of church and state, as well the secular school were the church policy principles not only of the Independent Social Democratic Party but also of the Social Democratic Party and other groups," *DBWE* 11:306, n. 266.]

39. ["The following passage corresponds extensively to statements in *Sanctorum Communio*. See *DBWE* 1:127–130 (*Reader* 37–38)," *DBWE* 11:307, n. 273.]

Critique: Neither a general value of the holy nor the concept of the religion of revelation contains religious community. Religious community cannot be derived from religion conceptually.

Regarding (2) psychological: religious community arises through the human drive to communicate, evangelize, etc., to human beings. Yet that is nonetheless not a specific religious community. This need to communicate is a sign of every community. Piety is also possible individualistically. Mutual communication is not a basis for a religious community, for this has a purpose while the former is merely being sociable.[40] The goal or purpose that is external to a society is in a community constitutive—the goal of being together is an end in itself. Every purpose of a community is intrinsic to itself.

Regarding (3) religion is a highest achievement of human culture! Religious community here is understood as the crown of cultural community. Derived from the concept of culture! (Lohmeyer: concept of religious community!) 309

Against this: the concept of church-community cannot be derived from the concept of religion. Religious community is individualistic. Religious community is atomistic. Religious community is the *form of community of* humanity-in-Adam; it is a final attempt on the part of humankind to save itself from being alone, saving itself selfishly.

There are proposals for improving a new community life in the church: the youth movement, the ecumenical movement, and others. But church can only be believed, this is possible only through faith in Christ. For the most part, this church of faith is not seen; rather only the religious community is seen! The church *cannot be experienced*. Walking in faith, not in seeing. The church proclaims in every word, [. . .] grounded in baptism. Without wishing to or willing to, the human being is incorporated into the church. This cannot be understood from the standpoint of the concept of religious community. *The understanding of the difference between church and religious community is decided with baptism.* The word of God alone constitutes the church; this can only be believed. Baptism is only a form of the word of God. The church is experienced there where it becomes clear that only the one Lord makes all human beings equal. Genuine community of human beings in the church and the community of the Lord's Supper. As paradoxical unity, which God has established, that encompasses militarists, pacifists, and the like! Thus no religious community is the church. With religious experiences, we remain in humanity-in-Adam!

---

40. ["Uncertain reading," *DBWE* 11:308, n. 284.]

310   III. Proclamation and the Church
      (1) The Word
      The church is constituted through the word of God in Christ's redemp-
      tive act. The word, and nothing else, is constitutive! The church is always
      already there. What comes from Christ comes out of the church and is
      directed toward the church. Because there is the word, there is the church;
      because there is the church, there is the word. The word exists *only* in the
      church! "Outside the church there is no salvation;"[41] that is Protestant! The
      church is always already included when we talk about the word. The holy
      community speaks to the church-community in the word. The Protestant
      concept of the congregation is built upon the church because it is built
      upon the word.

                                                                  June 25, 1932

      The church is constituted by the word of Christ. The concept of the *church-
      community* is included in the concept of the *word*. Christ is the new humanity
      itself. In the center stands the church-community. The word comes out of
      the church-community; *church as word and as church-community.* The word of
      justification is the word from the church-community for the church-com-
      munity. "Word and congregation belong together." Church-community is
      there where the word is proclaimed, and it is absolutely *visible church-commu-*
311   *nity.* In contrast to this, faith is invisible. The faith of the church-community
      is invisible; yet as church-community it is visible.

      (2) The Assembly[42]
      Where the word is, there must also be the *assembly* around this word. *The*
      word of God is primarily in the assembly for worship! To keep the word is to
      adhere to the assembly! For the Christian this is self-evident. The Spirit is
      received within the church-community. The Catholic Church preserves the
      assembly. Reformation: did not preach freedom of the individual far away
      from the assembly. Luther is not to be understood individualistically. The
      experience of the church is something for pious individuals.

      ───────────────

      41. ["Bonhoeffer takes the well-known phrase by Cyprian of Carthage, 'Salus extra
      ecclesiam non est' (Outside the church there is no salvation). In 1936, Bonhoeffer para-
      phrased this statement during the heated debates in the Confessing Church about legal-
      ization: 'Whoever knowingly separates himself from the Confessing Church in Germany
      separates himself from salvation.' See *DBWE* 14:675 (*Reader* 448)," *DBWE* 11:310, n. 294.]
      42. ["Cf. for the following *DBWE* 1:226–231 (*Reader* 54–55)," *DBWE* 11:311, n. 299.]

I belong to Christ, to the assembly. Where the word is, there am I primarily. I belong in the assembly. I cannot ask: "What do I get out of this?" (as: "What do I get from my mother?"). I belong to her! Why was this so in early Christianity? Why is this no longer so today? In ancient days something happened in the assembly: God's revelation was present there. I hear God's word entirely and really: one can barely think this now. Then one would say: from there I take my existence; there God gives it to me again and again. Reasons for the change: "Our pride?" Or is the gospel no longer proclaimed rightly? Or has "God" taken away his promise? The illness of the church-community: is it unto death?

(3) The Office of Preacher[43]   312

The word is given to the church-community through God: the word from the cross is proclaimed through the sermon. Who should preach? Who may preach? The unbeliever? The sermon is the office of the church-community of Christ. Even the unbeliever can preach and proclaim the word. The charisma of the office is the charisma of the church-community. Proclamation must occur rightly. Who can do this? He who has learned these things and studied them. People who have studied the word are pastors. The church-community remains the bearer of the sermon. The preacher has received the commission to carry out the office from the church-community. Priesthood of all believers.

The office is never the permanent property of the pastor. The pastor has the *promise* of the office. This promise does not become invalid even when the pastor himself does not have faith. The promise depends on the correct preaching of the pastor, not on faith. The word is there (even when I cannot believe it)! Therefore I preach. [. . .] He should speak the word correctly. Then he has the promise. Preaching leads away from one's own faith. The recognition of faith must be distinguished from the recognition of preaching: The message on the basis of the commission.

(4) The Confession of Faith

The assembly and the office of preacher belong to the church-community. It must confirm that it lives through the word alone. It does this in the confession of faith. There is no worship without confession of faith. The church-community must confess or deny. We cannot remain neutral. One   313
can leave the confession of faith [. . .] be—this is the constitution of the

---

43. ["On the following passage, cf. *DBWE* 1:231–236," *DBWE* 11:312, n. 307.]

church-community. The confession of faith is the only genuine constitution, in the confession the church-community separates itself from the world. The confession of faith must be *completely true*. It is the answer to the true word of God. Confession of faith concerns immediate presence. [. . .] "I recognize your *truth* and I confess it!" The confession must contain what the truth proclaims. *Against the Apostles' Creed Bonhoeffer* offers the objection: questions of liberalism (and Harnack) are still open; that is not a finished matter. Confession of faith concerns our true stance before God! Confession is not uncertain; it is one's confession to truth. It should be universal confession of all of Christianity. Yet we do have a different confession.

June 29, 1932

Truthfulness of the confession: The *word* itself must be true! Not just what it means! "Descended into hell," "born of a virgin." *The clarity of the word* must be for the sake of the church-community. Often the creedal confession is a deterring element! The word must be true and clear, also in consideration for those who do not yet believe. No general truth should be laid down in a confession of faith. Specific recognition of truth in the confessio [*confession*] must be retained in the confession. Heim and Schmitz want discussion

314 about this! "κύριος Χριστός" [*Christ the Lord*] they recommend for all! Everyone, however, means something else by these words. Among us this means: "by grace alone!" The Protestant confession must [. . .] this side of . . .

We can no longer confess our faith as the first Christians did! Now only as Protestants or Catholics. *The Apostles' Creed is not adequate for the Protestant Confessio.* The ordination of the pastor on the basis of the Apostles' Creed is not tenable!! The new liturgy puts other possibilities beside the Apostles' Creed.[44] This does not remove the offense. The question of the confession is not yet resolved! Confessionalism and confession are different: confessionalism uses confession as a means of propaganda against the godless. Confession of faith belongs in the Christian assembly of the faithful. Nowhere else is confession of faith sustainable (for example, confession is not sustainable in the "confessional hours").[45] *The first confession of*

315 *the Christian church-community before the world is the deed!* (Confession belongs

---

44. ["The Prussian general synod decided in 1925 to begin preliminary work for the publication of a new liturgy . . . ," *DBWE* 11:314, n. 327.]

45. ["The so-called confessional hours newly taken up at the time were supposed to be a preparation for the struggle with the opponents of the Christian faith," *DBWE* 11:314, n. 328.]

as *arcanum* [*arcane or concealed*] within the worship service.)[46] Then after the deed the church-community needs the verbal confession of faith. The confession is not to be screamed loudly in a propagandistic manner; it must be preserved as the sacred possession of the church-community. The deed alone is our confession before the world.

In summary: That of which we have spoken is an uninterrupted series: word, assembly, office of preacher, confession of faith. Always a *vertical line*! From God to human beings and from human beings to God. The church-community as a unity: "I (as the "I" of the assembly) believe"! *Unified* structure and structure of *identity* (with Christ) and structure of *lordship* (of Christ) at the same time. The church-community[47] is itself the Lord; he [. . .] confesses the congregation. Then there is the *horizontal line* of the church-community *as the structure of community.* The Spirit actualizes the church-community only where there is correct preaching. The gospel is correctly proclaimed in the Protestant church (not true for the Catholic Church); the rightness of the proclamation is characteristic of the confession. How can the *"recte docere"* [*right teaching*] of the pastor be *secured*?

(5) Theology
That is the *task of theology*! Theology must come to the aid of the pastor. No Protestant sermon, no Protestant confession of faith without theology. Theology is absolutely necessary. The church's first duty after liturgy is theology. A correct sermon doesn't come from living, correct religiosity alone! Arrogance toward theology is unjustified.

(6) Dogma
Dogma is the formed shape of theology, is not personal confession of faith. No theologian creates dogma; only the *entire church* as theologically responsible creates dogma.

316

(7) The Council
The "council" alone creates dogma, as an aid to preaching and the confession!

---

46. ["Bonhoeffer is referring to the early church's 'arcane discipline' (*disciplina arcani*) which understood certain 'hidden' aspects of the church's liturgical life that expressed mysteries of faith revealed in Christ. In the early church between the second and fifth centuries, baptism and the celebration of Holy Communion were kept strictly hidden . . . ," *DBWE* 11:315, n. 331.]

47. ["This should be 'Christ,'" *DBWE* 11:315, n. 332.]

The church-community alone can protest against the council. The concept of "heresy" is a component of the concept of "council"! Today there are "ecumenical assemblies," but they have no heresies. Today there are no longer any true councils! Because our theology for the past two hundred years is disorganized and because [. . .] the crisis affects the church momentarily as the preaching church! Alongside the sermon and the assembly, theology and council appear with dogma!

(8) Summary
The church of the word is as such the church-community! Assembly, the office of preacher, and confession create a necessary connection and are necessarily established in the church as proclamation of the word of Christ. Not a single one of these three can be understood apart from the word. Every attempt at an individualistic rationale must fail! The *correct* proclamation of the word requires *theology* as the first extra-ecclesial function next to the church, the assembly of the church (council), which makes decisions about theology (heresy), and the *dogma* created by the council. This trinity is intended to serve the first trinity. The first shall rule and should allow itself to be served!

317

July 2 (1932)

IV. The Priesthood of All Believers
Luther's concept has been individualized today. It is false to make a right of the individual out of this and thereby conclude that the priest, the assembly (private religiosity) as well as the church and priesthood, or the worship service, are superfluous. That is contrary to Luther's thinking!! Individual confession of sin is not superfluous; it is necessary. A priest stands for everyone before God. The decisive function of the priest must belong *to all*; therefore the office can belong to only one. Everyone needs the other as priest. Everyone is dependent on the other! Through this the members of the church-community are closely bound to one another. [. . .] Permanent proclamation. [. . .] *communio sanctorum* [*communion of saints*]. The congregation is primarily community.[48] The horizontal line! Christ is the brother

318

---

48. ["Here Bonhoeffer emphasizes the communal character of the congregation as an end in itself. In *Sanctorum Communio* (*DBWE* 1), he argues that the church also had other sociological characteristics: like a society (*Gesellschaft*), it has a purpose, namely, mission, and like an association under authority (*Herrschaftsverband*), it is under the lordship of Christ," *DBWE* 11:318, n. 351.]

as human being, who stands in the church-community of Christ. The body is a multiplicity of members.

[. . .] The relationship of the horizontal line to the vertical line. The Christian basis for individualization. Originally, not every single person can have God alone; that is individualizing; rather, originally there is a church-community of brother with brother, without a detour through God. I have Christ in my brother; in Christ I am directed toward my brother. No individualizing of the church!

Actualization occurs through the proclaiming Spirit. Proclamation is the constitutive element for pastoral care as it is for the church. Proclamation also occurs in the solitude of the liturgical dialogue between brother and brother. Christ is in the center where the brother speaks. (That is the central event for the Christian church-community.) That is *love!* This love is not a deed that the human being does from his own power. God alone tears the human being out of hell, through his deed upon the cross. The love of God on the cross of Golgotha. *The love of God in Golgotha* steps between brother and brother, poured into hearts by the Holy Spirit. There is only one love of God, which the human being receives through faith. Love can be received only through faith in the love of God. *Love is faithful behavior toward the other!* Faith is the believing relationship to God! *Faith and love* structure the church along the horizontal line. *Unity of faith! Community of love!*

Concept of the *community of love*: not the activated side of the concept of the church. Love of the one to the other brother is *the reception of the love of God.* Action in love is always passive: reception from God.

(1) The structural being-with-each-other[49] of members!
(2) The structural being-for-each-other[50] of the members[51]
The church-community is the overcoming of loneliness, not as togetherness! Where one member is, there is the entire body of Christ. The church-community has *one* life; it is impossible to think of its members as separated. Where the church-community is, there Christ is always also; (Ps. 139, pres-

---

49. ["Cf. *DBWE* 1:178...," *DBWE* 11:319, n. 358.]

50. ["Cf. *DBWE* 1:178. Here appropriated from his first book is found the recurrent key concept of 'being-free-for' the other, which remains formative in Bonhoeffer's thinking through to *Letters and Papers from Prison*," *DBWE* 11:319, n. 359.]

51. ["The second header here was mentioned by Bonhoeffer in conjunction with the first; however, it introduces the section below that begins on *DBWE* 11:322 (*Reader* 203)," *DBWE* 11:319, n. 360.]

ence of Christ!):[52] as forgiving or judging. The structure is therefore that of being-with-one-another. Not primarily the reality of consciousness.[53] The church-community leads *one* life. The need of the other must be such that I feel it as mine. (Luther's sermon on the sacraments, 1519, W. A. II 750ff.;

320   sermon on the Holy Body and dying; sermon on baptism; *Tesseradecas consolatoria pro laborantibus* [*Fourteen Consolations for Those Who Labor and Are Heavy Laden*], W. A. VI, 130ff.).

You must allow your heart to feel the infirmity that your brothers experience as if it were your own! The strength of the other is my strength. My temptation is borne by the faithful church-community. My dying is not alone. Christ and the church-community suffer and die with us. W. A. vol. 17 p. 100 (book 10, vol. 3 p. 308).

321   July 6, 1932

I and You are not fused together! The "I" before God is not abolished. The individual is perceived as standing within the church-community as soon as he is perceived as individual before God! Structural existence of the church-community there where the individual is!! [. . .] Without always knowing about the suffering of the other. In this case the church-community is Christ himself. The merits of the brothers, the merit of Christ, are also my merits. No one has himself alone; the individual lives the church-community. Close to the Catholic teaching of "*thesaurus sanctorum*" [*treasury of the saints*].[54] But the human being can never do more than he is obliged

322   to do. The treasure is the merit of Christ in the church-community. Christ allows the one to enjoy the deed of the other. We cannot do the intercession of the other, we cannot achieve abstinence for the other, but Christ makes this action of the other great for me! The Catholic doctrine is objectification and rationalization: The deed of the other is in and of itself effective.

---

52. ["Bonhoeffer understands the omnipresence of God described in Ps. 139 as that of Christ," *DBWE* 11:319, n. 361.]

53. ["Bonhoeffer is saying that it is not primarily a question of being conscious (of the situation of the other); cf. *DBWE* 1:181 . . . ," *DBWE* 11:319, n. 362.]

54. ["The doctrine of the *thesaurus ecclesiae* (treasury of the church) or the *thesaurus meritorum* (treasury of merits) unfolded as part of the theory of penance during the Middle Ages. According to this, the church has been entrusted with a treasure of a 'surplus of satisfactions,' through the surplus merits of Christ and the saints; on the basis of these the pope or even the bishops could grant the faithful indulgence after fulfilling certain conditions," *DBWE* 11:321, n. 376.]

(2) The structural being-for-each-other of the members
The being-for-each-other of the church-community is established in the being-with-each-other of the church-community: (a) The readiness to give up anything or to make any sacrifice for one's neighbor! (b) Intercession! (c) Forgiveness of sins.

Regarding (a) the sacrifice refers first to the goods of life, to all the everyday things. The one who owns goods steps into the place of the one who owns nothing; the people of honor step into the place of those who have no honor. One's own life, one's honor is a good, which the good person receives in order to serve the weak! One has honor for the common good (1 Cor. 12:7). One paradoxical, strange possibility consists in the following: sacrifice of community with God for the sake of one's brothers, voluntary bearing of wrath (Exod. 32:32!)! Such a thing is hardly mentioned in the Bible (Rom. 9!). Only these two passages concern themselves with this possibility. The paradox of love for God is shown here! Paul loves the community with God more than the community with human beings. He fulfills the last commandment in place of the cursed[55] beloved people. This is not a moment of weakness of Paul but rather the final fulfillment of the commandment of Christ. The imitation of Christ is almost tried here. This leads   323
as a biblically inspired act almost to insanity. This must be fulfilled over and over again; it is not a foregone conclusion! [. . .] It is like a possibility at the margin of human existence, close to blasphemy![56] The promise of the resurrection is valid here also.

Regarding (b) Intercession. The church-community leads *one* life. My prayer belongs to the church-community; the church-community prays in the prayer of the individual. (Chomjakoff: "Einheit der Kirche" [*Unity of the Church*], *Östliches Christentum* [*Eastern Christianity* anthology] by Hans Ehrenberg). The power of intercession! If there is still any doubt about this, then behind it stands a self-righteousness of the human being (he doesn't want to be given anything). I really stand in the place of the other. Not particularly a gift of empathy (empathy for the other one's suffering), rather vicarious acting by one for the other.

---

55. ["This may be a misreading (it contradicts Rom. 11:1ff., where Paul states that God has not rejected his people), but it is impossible to determine what Bonhoeffer would have said here . . . ," *DBWE* 11:322, n. 384.]

56. ["Bonhoeffer had already introduced this passage in his postdoctoral dissertation, *Act and Being* (see *DBWE* 2:160, n. 31, and *DB-ER*, 176; cf. *DBWE* 12:37, n. 5)," *DBWE* 11:323, n. 387.]

July 9, 1932

Intercession is vicarious representative action. [. . .] Not primarily a gift of empathy; otherwise there is no prayer for the other. Intercession is not limited psychologically. The boundaries are where the boundaries of the church-community are. There is the possibility of incorporation! For the one who is hated by God, there is no prayer, for the devil. But one may believe the love of God against God's own word. Here there is not something that can be psychologically experienced. The intercession is grounded in the recognition that the church-community carries the guilt of the individual, that each person is guilty of Christ's death. In this way, each person can become Christ for the other, even when he does not know him. Compare the reference to the "sins of the unknown sailor" in prayer spoken in worship service: "One guilt, that is my guilt." In this way the brotherhood of vicarious representation for all happens. There only intercessory prayer is possible. The individual finds the gift of the church-community through intercession. It is based only in the congregation. [. . .] Vicarious endurance for the other. Thus the individual is led into the church-community more and more through intercession.

324

Regarding (c) it is a marvel of the church-community that one person cannot only sacrifice himself, but rather also that one person has the *authority to forgive sins* through Christ. In the Old Testament this is still impossible: Ps. 49! The law and the gift of the community became the possession of Christ! The congregation acts as *Christus praesens* [*Christ present*], what Jesus once did. The form of Christ multiplied a thousandfold. Either this is the worst kind of profanity. Or else it is the coming of the living God himself. It is a miracle of God that the human being is redeemed by the other. The daily bloodless repetition of the sacrifice! This one deed is ever and again actualized through the church-community. The Catholic interpretation: this attempt reaches back behind the revelation of God in Christ! [. . .] Speculation. Matt. 18:18. John 20:23: What you have loosed on earth, shall also be loosed in heaven. How is this to be understood?? Luther: as members of the church-community, we are all Peter. This word has been spoken to us all. God has put his entire power into the church-community. In the church-community the divide between the kingdom of God and the kingdom of the world is consummated.

325

It is not we who carry the word with our faith; rather, the church-community carries the word and carries us as well. The first and second word is given to us: from the gospel and office follows: preaching of reconciliation is the first word. The second point, the proclamation of the wrath of God is unbearable for us; [. . .] the binding transcends the power of responsibility. In both promises lies God's word: in fact our responsibility rests on both words. The love and wrath of God is also God's will and stands under the heavy weight of responsibility. The forgiveness of sins within the church-community is only possible through the preaching of the gospel. The preaching of the gospel becomes judgment when it is not believed. This is spoken not only in the assembly but also in the confession of sin, where the congregation confesses itself as sinful and pronounces forgiveness.

There is confession of sin only in connection with the sacrament! The proclamation of the word in the sermon is not to be understood by itself; in the sacrament something new enters in: here the pastor is bound. The promise of God stands over the sacraments. Here the pastor is free from his own word. There is not less certainty in the sermon; the sermon is borne by the sacrament. He, the pastor, may administer the sacrament.   326

A church without sacrament loses the sermon and the confession of sin! In confession of sin concretion occurs. Here the word of God is spoken; here is the occurrence of the Last Judgment. Here punishment and absolution take place! Whoever goes to confession, performs not an act of personal trust but rather a *confession of truth*; only, however, where the other is seen as a brother. In the confession of sin, we cannot avoid speaking simply out loud! The act of confession of sin was until now like a loud scream for everyone, the birth of a new world. Here, however, is now the answer of God through the brother, which ends all torture. Because the word of God's truth takes place through the brother, therefore authorization. The word of God follows the untrue word of human beings. Personal confession of sin is not the possibility of κάθαρσις [*cleansing*], but rather a self-positioning toward the truth! This is different from the psychoanalytic hour. "The doctor is the father confessor today!" Confession of sin is misunderstood. The self-expression in one's own interest is only a degree of talking about oneself that people of all time have done. This has nothing to do with confession of sin. The purpose of the confession of sin is for the one who confesses to receive God's truth. It is the occurrence of God's truth! That is the center of the church-community. There is no longer a church-community where there is no confession of sin. Luther fights against compulsory confession in   327 order to remove the routine observance of confession of sin.[57]

---

57. ["Cf. *DBWE* 1:165–192," *DBWE* 11:327, n. 412.]

July 20 (1932)

Hearing confession belongs to the pastoral office. Hearing confession is a commission of the church-community; it exists only among brothers. To take the sins of the brother upon oneself because one knows that Christ bears one's sins. The constant flooding back of sinful deeds upon Christ. Confession of sin is founded on the reality of the vicarious representative action of Christ. Even private confession has been frequently eliminated after the Reformation! Thereby a living fountain for the church-community has died off (Löhe: *Three Books Concerning the Church*). The reason for this lies solely in the process of increasing individualism in Protestantism. The church, however, is the present Christ. One does not believe this any longer. We must once more learn to see and believe properly in the church-community and the church. We do not believe that the truth is spoken in the church. We must learn again what confession of sin is.

Isn't this abstract? Is there not priestly action and beside it the vicarious representative action of the brother? "Christ is the *donum* [*gift*] and the *exemplum* [*example*]!"[58] This is also true for Christians in the church-community. It must be a gift for the brother, a priestly act of absolute validity. But the human being also stands before the brother as a human example. The concept of the tradition, of history, plays a role here: One must "come clean" to the brother. One must accept advice from the other! From this follows a twofold picture of the pastoral care of the Protestant church: (1) ministerial pastoral care based on vicarious representative action; (2) counseling pastoral care! Both are near each other here!

(D) and (E) Worldliness and Christianity of the Church

[. . .] Our church is here. It is not an ideal; otherwise we would still be in Advent. Christ is present in his church today. That is no ideal but rather reality. The worldliness of the church is real, not only illusion. The church is wholly world! Furthermore, where the church has become homeless, this must be so. The church has become quite worldly for our benefit. It denies itself everything except Christ's word. The church existing in the world knows that it must renounce everything else.

---

58. ["... The formula of 'Christ as gift and example' was used frequently by Luther ...," *DBWE* 11:328, n. 419.]

The church is in the world: it does not wish to give a picture of the church-community of saints; renunciation of the ideal of purity. As such, as something becomes worldly, it is not pure from the beginning onward; even the early Christian church-community is not pure. (To believe this would be a confusion with a religious experience as ideal)! There are perfectionistic sects up to today ("communities"). Everywhere this is an attempt to usurp the kingdom of God; it should be exposed. One wishes to see the kingdom in the saintliness of human beings. As the church that has become worldly, it may not let itself succumb to this temptation because it knows that it faces justification and the Last Judgment. It cannot uproot the weeds. The church cannot be pure before God and the world. Everyone baptized belongs to the church. *Renunciation of purity*, a return to solidarity with the sinful world! The church as a wholly worldly church; courageous confession to worldliness; in this way the church is free from the world! The church no longer shrinks from the sanctuaries of the world. It is then free among the "pariahs" and the "aristocracy." Its place is not only among the poor; it will not disdain the wealthy, the pious, or the aristocrats. Both groups are "world." The church will be unbeholden to both sides. The faith has conquered the world for the pariah and the rich. Renunciation of purity alone makes the church free!

329

But also the boundaries of worldliness must be taken seriously; the church must concern itself about purity! *The wish to be pure* [. . .] must be in the world at the same time: discipline, purity of doctrine, and [. . .] the individual [. . .] pastors may not be moralists, clericalists, demagogues. No politics in the worship service, no outward celebration. The church will reject letting oneself go, deliberate worldliness. The Protestants [. . .] not vain bondage. The church will wish to be most sharply conscious of its purity.

330

There is a justification for *excommunication* as the last step, in cases where the church-community itself is at risk. But there are also concrete limits to this act. Today it is to be decided according to each particular case. [. . .] Also, the sphere in which excommunication is pronounced remains open. (1) The church may execute the ban only for the sake of the church-community. (2) The ban can be pronounced only "in order to save a soul"; "Sancta" is the predicate of the believed church. As the impure we are *sancta ecclesia* [*the holy church*] concretely today.

July 23, 1932

Realization occurs in the world as visible church! Therefore, it is the *una ecclesia* [*one church*], the believed church. There is a disunity, not only in form but in the truth as well! The church will not want to reach an illusory unity.

Sincere, bona fide faith is not to be confused with the truth of the content of faith (ecumenical danger: the question of heresy is no longer noted). Heresy of doctrine is to be combated sharply! The church must deny itself the act of portraying the unity of truth. Division is to be carried as cross; believing that God has called it as *una sancta* [*the one holy*].

The *visible unity* of the church is demanded for the sake of the church and the world. *Catholic*: this is a predicate of the church that concerns its worldliness. Even the Protestant church raises the complete *claim* to be the catholic church, *not in* the sense of a *world power*, but rather *in the proclamation of the worldwide word of Christ*! As a whole it remains invisible, yet it is visible within given boundaries. The church exists *in regno cruces* [*in the kingdom of the cross*]. (Against this the Catholic Church says: *in regno gloriae* [*in the kingdom of glory*].) To take worldliness seriously on the basis of taking the divinity of the church seriously is the Christianity of the church.

331

(F) The Boundaries of the Church

The church as the revelation of God in the world is a whole. But there are boundaries, because the church is in the world where people do not know of God's revelation in the church. Here, from within, one can speak of the boundaries. The boundaries of the church are given in the concept of *predestination* or the *kingdom of god*, respectively, and of the *state*. The first one is the boundary toward the new world; the other is the boundary toward the old world. The church is built on the *doctrine of the cross of Christ* (Reformed churches build on *predestination*). The knowledge of God in Christ is the only revelation. The church-community that believes in this is the church! There is a danger when one seeks another word behind the one word of God! But the church must be able to proclaim this one word with authority. The concept of predestination may not desire to say more than what is said in the cross.

The church is not the *kingdom of God*; it does not even know those who belong to the kingdom. It may not even know this for the sake of its worldliness. It knows about the will of God, that God has mercy for all. God alone must give faith. The church must see the cross and also the brothers in need. It remains a mystery. It is mysterious that God wishes to help all and yet gives only these human beings faith. We are left only with astonished sighing and hoping for the church as we bow beneath the mystery of God. It knows: there is salvation in no other! But it also knows: God is greater. He wants to help all human beings. That is why there is mission. But it uses the Lord's word against the Lord. It hopes that God can do great mysterious things with the other. Prayer about this is necessary; this touches on the mystery of God himself, which will one day be revealed, but now the

church lets the mystery remain! The word of Christ and the promise (grace and judgment) given to it,[59] that is the *boundary* of the church! It knows that God is free and that God can withdraw his word from the church! The church must bear the mystery when God says No upon it. The church awaits   332
the visible revelation, the new world of God. It knows of the fulfillment. It knows that one day it will be in the visible sacrament of God, in the new creation. Then the subjugation of the world will have occurred. [. . .] God is the master and the servant in his church-community [. . .] in the new world.

Finally, boundaries in the *state*. God's word has power also over the state. Through this the state is set as a critical warning for the church, that God has not given the judging sword of power to the church. Its sword is the word and prayer. Thereby it serves the state. When it is threatened by the state, it fights against the state. It will not try to govern the state. The goal is the proclamation of the lordship of Christ over the whole world in faith and in the word. The church and the state are side by side. The church may not become the state; the state is recognized as an autonomous worldly power. [. . .] A call to a completely responsible, true action, each according to its own office. Obedience to the state exists only when the state does not threaten the word. The battle about the boundary must then be fought out![60] The decision will be difficult in the development of our future state:[61] The office of the state is neither Christian nor godless; the office must be carried out in a responsible and objective way. The existence as church depends on whether its criticism can come from listening to the gospel alone. Criticism of the state is demanded where it threatens the word. The church can come through difficulties only when it sees to it that it stands or falls with the word of *Christus praesens* [*Christ present*] as its Lord alone.

End July 23, 1932

---

59. ["The church," *DBWE* 11:331, n. 450.]

60. ["That is, the battle must be fought when the state threatens the church's free preaching of the word," *DBWE* 11:332, n. 453.]

61. ["Bonhoeffer made this assessment about the future relationship of state and church three days after the dismissal of the Prussian government by Reich Chancellor von Papen and one week before the decisive Reichstag elections of July 31, 1932, in which the National Socialist party won 37.2 percent of the vote, making it the strongest faction in the Reichstag," *DBWE* 11:332 n. 454.]

13. CREATION AND FALL

DBWE 3:21–39, 60–67, 74–130

In 1933, Bonhoeffer published Creation and Fall: A Theological Exposition of Genesis 1–3, *which was based on a lecture course delivered in Berlin during the winter semester 1932–1933. Its significance is in part its character as a "theological exposition." The historical-critical approach to the Bible as well as the results of modern sciences had led many biblical scholars in Germany to treat the first chapters of Genesis as primitive myths irrelevant for a modern world. Barth's commentary on Romans introduced a new form of interpretation that "in principle accepted the findings of historical and literary criticism but sought to move* beyond *them to grapple with the question, What is the word of God as it addresses itself to us today in this scripture?"*[1] *Such theological exegesis, as introduced by Barth and appropriated by Bonhoeffer, provided a way to read the Bible theologically without resisting the results of modern scholarship.*[2]

Creation and Fall *is a milestone in Bonhoeffer's intellectual journey as the beginning of a more sustained and serious engagement with the Bible. He returns here to many of the themes from his earlier works—sociality, isolation, limits, sin—but he develops them in dialogue with the Bible rather than academic philosophy and theology, and he abandons much of the technical jargon in favor of a direct, existential style. Bonhoeffer had by this point been vacillating for several years between a career in the academy and a career in the church. In* Creation and Fall, *he displays both sets of skills, delivering a sophisticated, philosophical, and theological interpretation of the Bible in an engaging homiletic style.*

1. [DBWE *3:7, editor's introduction.*]
2. [*For more on Bonhoeffer's understanding of the exegetical task, see* DBWE *14:413–433* (Reader 416–431).]

INTRODUCTION

21

The church of Christ witnesses to the end of all things. It lives from the end, it thinks from the end, it acts from the end, it proclaims its message from the end. "Do not remember the former things or consider the things of old. I am about to do a new thing" (Is. 43:18–19). The new is the real end of the old; the new, however, is Christ. Christ is the end of the old. Not the continuation, not the goal, the completion in line with the old, but the end and therefore the new. The church speaks within the old world about the new world. And because it is surer of the new world than of anything else, it sees the old world only in the light of the new world.

The church cannot please the old world because the church speaks of the end of the world as though this has already happened, as though the world has already been judged. The old world is not happy to let itself be declared dead. The church has never been surprised at this. It also is not surprised that again and again there appear within it people who think as the old world does. Who after all does not still at times think like this? What must certainly arouse the church to real indignation, however, is that these children of the world that has passed away wish to claim the church, the new, as belonging to them. They want the new, and they know only the old. And in that way they deny Christ, the Lord.

22

Only the church, which knows of the end, knows also of the beginning. It alone knows that between the beginning and now there lies the same breach as between now and the end, that the beginning and now are related in the same way as life is to death, as the new is to the old. The church therefore sees the beginning only in dying, from the viewpoint of the end. It views the creation from Christ; or better, in the fallen, old world it believes in the world of the new creation, the new world of the beginning and the end, because it believes in Christ and in nothing else.

The church does all this because it is founded upon the witness of Holy Scripture. The church of Holy Scripture—and there is no other 'church'—lives from the end. Therefore it reads the whole of Holy Scripture as the book of the end, of the new, of Christ. Where Holy Scripture, upon which the church of Christ stands, speaks of creation, of the beginning, what else can it say other than that it is only from Christ that we can know what the beginning is? The Bible is after all nothing other than the book of the church. It *is* this in its very essence, or it is nothing. It therefore needs to be read and proclaimed wholly from the viewpoint of the end. In the church, therefore, the story of creation must be read in a way that begins with Christ and only then moves on toward him as its goal; indeed one can read it as a book that moves toward Christ only when one knows that Christ is the beginning, the new, the end of our whole world.

Theological exposition takes the Bible as the book of the church and interprets it as such. This is its presupposition and this presupposition constitutes its method; its method is a continual returning from the text (as determined by all the methods of philological and historical research) to this presupposition. That is the objectivity in the method of theological exposition. And on this objectivity alone does it base its claim to have the nature of a science.

When Genesis says "Yahweh," it 'means', from a historical or psychological point of view, nothing but Yahweh; theologically, i.e., from the viewpoint of the church, however, it is speaking of God. For in the whole of Holy Scripture God is the one and only God; with this belief the church and theological science stand or fall.

CHAP. 1, VV. 1–2

THE BEGINNING

In the beginning God created heaven and earth, and the earth was formless and empty; and it was dark upon the deep. And the spirit of God hovered over the water.

The place where the Bible begins is one where our own most impassioned waves of thinking break, are thrown back upon themselves, and lose their strength in spray and foam. The first word of the Bible has hardly for a moment surfaced before us, before the waves frantically rush in upon it again and cover it with wreaths of foam. That the Bible should speak of the beginning provokes the world, provokes us. For we cannot speak of the beginning. Where the beginning begins, there our thinking stops; there it comes to an end. Yet the desire to ask after the beginning is the innermost passion of our thinking; it is what in the end imparts reality to every genuine question we ask. We know that we continually have to ask about the beginning—and yet that we can never ask about it. Why not? Because the beginning is the infinite, and because we can conceive of the infinite only as what is endless and so as what has no beginning. Because the beginning is freedom, and we can never conceive of freedom except in terms of necessity and thus as one thing among others but never as the one thing that utterly precedes all other things.

We may ask why it is that we always think from the beginning and with reference to it and yet can never conceive it, never indeed ask after the beginning to find out about it. The question why, however, only gives expression to a series of questions that could be pushed back endlessly, yet would not reach the beginning. Thinking can never answer its own last question why, because an answer to this would produce yet another why? The question 'why' is really only an expression, an expression κατ᾽ ἐξοχήν [*par excellence*], of thinking that lacks a beginning. Our thinking, that is, the thinking of those who have to turn to Christ to know about God, the thinking of fallen humankind, lacks a beginning because it is a circle. We think in a circle. But we also feel and will in a circle. We exist in a circle. It is possible to say that in that case the beginning is everywhere. But against that stands the equally valid statement that for that very reason there is no beginning at all. The decisive point, however, is that thinking takes this circle to be the infinite, the beginning itself, and is thereby caught in a circulus vitiosus [*vicious circle*]. For where thinking looks to itself as the beginning, it posits itself as an object, as an entity over against itself, and so again and again withdraws behind this object—or rather, finds itself in every instance before the object it is positing. It is therefore impossible for thinking to make this final pronouncement about the beginning. Thinking pounds itself to pieces on the beginning. Because thinking wants to reach back to the beginning and yet never can want it, all thinking pounds itself to pieces, shatters against itself, breaks up into fragments, dissolves, in view of the beginning that it wants and cannot want.

The Hegelian question how we are to make a beginning in philosophy can therefore be answered only by the bold and violent action of enthroning reason in the place of God. That is why critical philosophy is but a systematic despair of its own beginning, indeed of any beginning. Critical philosophy may proudly renounce what it lacks the power to attain, or else lapse into a resignation that leads to its complete destruction; either alternative stems from the same human hatred of the unknown beginning.

Humankind no longer lives in the beginning; instead it has lost the beginning. Now it finds itself in the middle, knowing neither the end nor the beginning, and yet knowing that it is in the middle. It knows therefore that it comes from the beginning and must move on toward the end. It sees its life as determined by these two factors, concerning which it knows only that it does not know them. The animals know nothing about the beginning and the end; they therefore know no hatred and no pride. Humankind knows itself to be totally deprived of its own self-determination, because it comes from the beginning and is moving toward the end without knowing what that means. This makes it hate the beginning and rise up in pride against it.

There can therefore be nothing more disturbing or agitating for human beings than to hear someone speak of the beginning as though it were not the totally ineffable, inexpressibly dark beyond of our own blind existence. People will fall upon such a person; they will call such a person the chief of liars, or else indeed the savior, and they will kill that person when they hear what he says.

Who can speak of the beginning? There are two possibilities. The speaker may be the one who has been a liar from the beginning, the evil one, for whom the beginning is the lie and the lie is the beginning, whom human beings believe because the evil one deceives them with lies. And as one who lies, the evil one will say: I am the beginning, and you, O humankind, are the beginning. You were with me from the beginning. I have made you what you are, and with me your end is done away.[3] I am the Beginning and the End, the Alpha and the Omega;[4] worship me. I am the truth out of which comes the lie; for I am the lie that first gives birth to the truth. You are the beginning and you are the end, for you are in me. Believe me, the liar from the beginning: lie, and you will be in the beginning and will be lord of the truth. Discover your beginning yourself. So speaks the evil one, as the liar from the beginning. It is either *the evil one* who speaks or that other who speaks, the one who has been the truth from the beginning, and the way and the life, the one who was in the beginning, the very God, Christ, the Holy Spirit. No one can speak of the beginning but the one who was in the beginning.

Thus the Bible begins with the free confirmation, attestation, and revelation of God by God: In the beginning God created. . . . But this rock hardly surfaces for a moment in the sea, before the sea, roused to a furious storm by the sight of the one who is immovable, covers it again. What does it mean that in the beginning God is? Which God? Your God, whom you make for yourself out of your own need because you need an idol, because you do not wish to live without the beginning, without the end, because being in the middle causes you anxiety? In the beginning, God—that is just your lie, which is not better but even more cowardly than the lie of the evil one. How do you, an unknown stranger, you, the writer of this sentence, know about the beginning? Have you seen it, were you there in the beginning? Does your God not say to you, "Where were you when I laid the foundations of the earth? Tell me, if you are so clever!" (Job 38:4).

29

---

3. [*The German word translated by "do away" is Aufheben,* ". . . a key term in Hegel. The Hegelian meaning of this term is a dialectical one: it means 'negating' or 'overcoming,' and yet at the same time 'preserving' or 'sustaining' in a higher unity (cf. *DBWE* 2:31, n. 20). Thus the German sentence could also be interpreted to mean 'and your end has been raised up to [be with] me,'" *DBWE* 3:28–29, n. 12.]

4. ["Revelation 1:8. Alpha and Omega are the first and last letters of the Greek alphabet," *DBWE* 3:29, n. 13.]

So what sort of statement are these first words of Scripture? An illusion produced by the fainthearted imagination of a person who is unable to live in the middle with pride or with resignation? And are we not all that person—we who out of the faintheartedness of our own lives, with their lack of a beginning and an end, cry out to a god who is but our own ego?[5] How can we meet this reproach? It is after all true that one who speaks of the beginning speaks of one's own anxiety within life's circle. This is true even of the person who wrote the Bible. Or rather it is not that person who speaks; it is God, the absolute beginning or primal reality, who had being before our life and thinking, with all its anxiety. God alone tells us that God is in the beginning; God testifies of God by no other means than through this word, which as the word of a book, the word of a pious human being, is wholly a word that comes from the middle and not from the beginning. In the beginning God created. . . . This word, spoken and heard as a human word, is the form of a servant in which from the beginning God encounters us and in which alone God wills to be found. It is neither something profound nor something frivolous but God's truth, to the extent that *God* speaks it.

In the beginning—God. That is true if by this word God comes alive for us here in the middle, not as a distant, eternal being in repose but as the Creator. We can *know* about the beginning in the true sense only by hearing of the beginning while we ourselves are in the middle, between the beginning and the end; otherwise it would not be the beginning in the absolute sense which is also our *beginning*. Here in the middle, between the beginning we have lost and the end we have lost, we know of God as the beginning only—as God the Creator.

In the beginning God *created* heaven and earth. Not that first God was and then God created, but that in the beginning God created. This beginning is the beginning in the anxiety-causing middle and at the same time beyond the anxiety-causing middle in which we have our being. We do not know of this beginning by stepping out of the middle and becoming a beginning ourselves. Because we could accomplish that only by means of a lie, we would then certainly not be in the beginning but only in the middle that is disguised by a lie. This needs to be kept clearly in mind in everything that follows. It is only in the middle that we come to learn about the beginning.

The twofold question arises: Is this beginning God's own beginning, or is it God's beginning with the world? But the very fact that this question is asked shows that we no longer know what the beginning means. When the

5. [*According to Bonhoeffer, Hegel's idealism and, in less direct ways, all modern philosophy end in the identification of the self and God. See* DBWE 2, Part A.]

beginning can be spoken about only by those who are in the middle and worry about the beginning and the end, those who tug at their own chains, those who—to anticipate for a moment something that comes later—know only in their sin about having been created by God,[6] then it can no longer be asked whether this beginning is God's own beginning or God's beginning with the world. This is because for us God as the beginning is no other than the one who in the beginning created the world and created us, and because we can know nothing at all of *this* God except as the Creator of our world. Luther was once asked what God was doing before the creation of the world. His answer was that God was cutting sticks to cane people who ask such idle questions.[7] In this way Luther was not just cutting the questioner short; he was also saying that where we do not recognize God as the merciful Creator, we can know God only as the wrathful judge—that is, only standing in relation to the middle, between the beginning and the end. There is no possible question that could go back behind this God who created in the beginning. Thus it is also impossible to ask why the world was created, what God's plan for the world was, or whether the creation was necessary. These questions are exposed as godless questions and finally disposed of by the statement: In the beginning God created heaven and earth. The statement declares not that in the beginning God had this or that idea about the purpose of the world, ideas that we must now try to discover, but that in the beginning God *created*. No question can go back behind the creating God, because one cannot go back behind the beginning.

From this it follows that the beginning is not to be thought of in temporal terms. We can always go back behind a temporal beginning. But the beginning is distinguished by something utterly unique—unique not in the sense of a number that one can count back to, but in a qualitative sense, that is, in the sense that it simply cannot be repeated, that it is completely free. One could conceive of a continual repetition of free acts;[8] such a concept would be basically mistaken only because freedom does not allow itself to be repeated. Otherwise freedom would have freedom as its own precondi-

---

6. ["See the exposition of Gen. 2:8–17 below, e.g., *DBWE* 3:90–92 (*Reader* 235–237)," *DBWE* 3:31, n. 20.]

7. [". . . Bonhoeffer is referring to the passage in Luther's *Table Talk* where Luther is recalling Augustine, who wrote in his *Confessions* (11/12:253) that God 'was preparing hell for those who pry too deep'. Luther's actual words were: '. . . Once, when he was asked, [Augustine] said, "God was making hell for those who are inquisitive"' (*LW* 54:377)," *DBWE* 3:31, n. 21.]

8. ["Cf. *DBWE* 3:46–47, concerning *creatio continua*," *DBWE* 3:32, n. 22.]

tion, that is, freedom would be unfree, and no longer the beginning κατ' ἐξοχήν [*par excellence*].

This quite unrepeatable, unique, free event in the beginning, which must in no way be confused with the number 4800[9] or any such date, is the creation. In the beginning God created heaven and earth. In other words the Creator—in freedom!—creates the creature. The connection between them is conditioned by nothing except freedom, which means that it is unconditioned. This rules out every application of causal categories for an understanding of the creation. The relation between Creator and creature can never be interpreted in terms of cause and effect, because between the   33 Creator and the creature there stands no law of thought or law of effect or anything else. Between Creator and creature there is simply *nothing*. For freedom is exercised in, and on the basis of, this nothing. No kind of necessity that could, or indeed had to, ensue in creation can therefore be demonstrated to exist in God. There is simply nothing that provides the ground for creation. Creation comes out of this nothing.

Now human beings could certainly once again attempt to move away from the middle that causes them anxiety and become a beginning themselves. They could endeavor to think of this nothing as something that in turn gives birth to creation. But where one speaks of *creation*—that is, theologically—there nothingness has a wholly different meaning from where it appears as the endless end in thinking that lacks a beginning. Nothingness, nonbeing, arises in our philosophical thinking at the point where the beginning cannot be conceived. Thus it is in the end never anything but the ground for being. Nothingness as the ground for being is understood as a creative nothingness. One then has to ask what lies back beyond this nothingness, yet without coming up against the beginning. Nothingness, as humankind in the middle conceives it without knowing about the beginning, is the ultimate attempt at explanation. It is the point through which   34 that which is has passed in coming to be. We call it a filled, charged, self-glorifying nothingness.

The nothingness that lies between the freedom of God and creation is by contrast not an attempted explanation for the creation of that which has being. It is thus not a substance out of which, paradoxically, the world then arose, the point through which what has being had to pass. It is not a something at all, not even a negative something. It is the particular word that alone is able to define and express the relation between God's freedom and God's creation.

---

9. ["This is a calculation based on the figures given in the Bible, e.g., in Genesis 5 (the genealogy from Adam to Noah) . . . ," *DBWE* 3:32, n. 24.]

This nothingness is therefore not a primal possibility or a ground of God; it 'is' absolutely 'nothing'. It happens instead in God's action itself, and it happens always as what has already been negated, as the nothing that is no longer happening but has always already happened. We call it the obedient nothing, the nothing that waits on God, the nothing whose glory and whose existence are neither in itself nor in its nothingness but only in God's action. Thus God needed no link between God and the creation; even the nothing constitutes no such 'between'. On the contrary God affirms the nothing only to the extent that God has already overcome it. This is what people of a bygone time tried to express with their somewhat clumsy description of the nothing as the nihil negativum [*negative nothing*] (as distinct from the nihil privativum [*privative nothing*],[10] which was understood as primal being). The nothing poses no reason for anxiety to the first creation. Instead, it is itself an eternal song of praise to the Creator who created the world out of nothing.

The world exists in the midst of nothing, which means in the beginning. This means nothing else than that it exists wholly by God's freedom. What has been created belongs to the free Creator. It means also, however, that the God of creation, of the utter beginning, is the God of the resurrection. The world exists from the beginning in the sign of the resurrection of Christ from the dead. Indeed it is because we know of the resurrection that we know of God's creation in the beginning, of God's creating out of nothing. The dead Jesus Christ of Good Friday and the resurrected κύριος [*Lord*] of Easter Sunday—that is creation out of nothing, creation from the beginning. The fact that Christ was dead did not provide the possibility of his resurrection but its impossibility; it was nothing itself, it was the nihil negativum. There is absolutely no transition, no continuum between the dead Christ and the resurrected Christ, but the freedom of God that in the beginning created God's work out of nothing. Were it possible to intensify the nihil negativum even more, we would have to say here, in connection with the resurrection, that with the death of Christ on the Cross the nihil negativum broke its way into God's own being.—O great desolation! God, yes God, is dead.[11]—Yet the one who is the beginning lives, destroys the

35

---

10. [*According to Kant, a "negative nothing" is nothing because it contradicts itself, e.g., a rectangle with two sides. A "privative nothing" is nothing by virtue of the absence of something, e.g., a shadow. See Kant,* Critique of Pure Reason, *382–383.*]

11. ["In his *Lectures on the Philosophy of Religion* Hegel discusses the idea of the death of God as meaning that there is suffering, pain, and negation in God. He quotes the words of the Lutheran hymn, 'God, yes God, is dead' (*Gott selbst ist tod*) . . . See Tödt (ed.), *Bonhoeffers Hegel-Seminar*, 99–100. . . . ," *DBWE* 3:35, n. 35.]

nothing, and in his resurrection creates the new creation. By his resurrection we know about the creation. For had he not risen again, the Creator 36 would be dead and would not be attested. On the other hand we know from the act of creation about God's power to rise up again, because God remains Lord over nonbeing.

In the beginning—that is, out of freedom, out of nothing—God created heaven and earth. That is the comfort with which the Bible addresses us who are in the middle and who feel anxiety before the spurious nothingness, before the beginning without a beginning and the end without an end. It is the gospel, it is Christ, it is the resurrected one, who is being spoken of here. That God is in the beginning and will be in the end, that God exists in freedom over the world and that God makes this known to us—that is compassion, grace, forgiveness, and comfort.

"And the earth was formless and empty; and it was dark upon the deep; and the spirit of God hovered over the waters."

The beginning has been made. But attention still remains fixed on that event, on the free God. That it is true, that it has been done, that heaven and earth are there, that the miracle has come to pass, deserves all wonder. Not the created work, no, but the Creator wills to be glorified. The earth is formless and empty; but the Creator is the Lord, the one who brings about the wholly new, the strange, inconceivable work of God's dominion and love. "The earth was formless and empty." It was nevertheless our earth which came forth from God's hand and now lies ready for God, subject to God in devout worship. God is praised first by the earth that was formless and empty. God does not need us human beings to be glorified, but brings about divine worship out of the world which is without speech, which, mute and formless, rests, slumbering, in God's will.

"And it was dark upon the deep, and the spirit of God hovered over the waters. . . ." What can be said about the work considering the act, and what can be said about the creature considering the Creator, except that it is dark and that it is in the deep? That the creature is God's work, that is its honor; and that it lies dark before God, that is the glory of God's majesty as Creator. It lies in the abyss beneath God. Just as we look down, dizzy, from a high mountain into the depths, and the darkness of the depths lies 37 beneath us, so the earth is at God's feet—distant, strange, dark, deep, but God's work.[12]

---

12. ["Bonhoeffer takes v. 1 (in the Luther Bible: 'In the beginning God created heaven and earth. And . . .') to be not a heading or superscription for the acts of creation depicted from v. 3 on ('And God spoke . . .') but the start of creation itself . . . Bonhoeffer's

The dark deep—that is the first sound of the power of darkness, of the passion of Jesus Christ. The darkness, the tehōm, the tihāmat, the Babylonian "primeval sea," contains within itself—precisely in its depth—power and force. This power and force still serve to honor the Creator now, but once torn away from the origin, from the beginning, they become tumult and rebellion. In the night, in the abyss, there exists only what is formless. Thus the formless, empty, dark deep, which is not able to take on form by itself, the agglomeration of formlessness, the torpid unconscious, the unformed, is both the expression of utter subjection and the unsuspected force of the formless, as it waits impatiently to be bound into form.

38
It is a moment in God in which the unformed mass and its Creator exist over against each other. It is a moment of which it is said that the spirit of God hovered over the waters; it is a moment in which God is thinking, planning, and bringing forth form. It cannot be said that the relation of Creator and creature is in any way affected, that God here espouses what God has created in order to make it fruitful, or that God becomes one with it. The cosmogonic idea of the world-egg over which the divine being broods is at any rate not intended here. God remains utterly Creator *over* the deep, *above* the waters.

But this God who is the Creator now begins again. The creation of that which is formless, empty, and dark is distinguished from the creation of form by a moment in God that is described here as the hovering of the spirit over the waters. God reflects upon the divine work. The unbinding or release of formless force and the simultaneous binding of it into form, so that what merely exists begins to exist in a particular way,[13] is a moment of hesitation in God. The divine praise that God prepares out of the rude
39
darkness of the unformed is to be completed through its being given form. The creation still rests entirely in God's hand, in God's power; it has no being of its own. Yet the praise of the Creator is completed only when the creature receives its own being from God and praises God's being by its own being. In the creation of form the Creator denies the Creator's own self, in that this grants form to what is created and grants to it its own being or existence before the Creator; in that the existence of what is created serves the Creator, however, the Creator chooses to be glorified. Thereby the Creator

interpretation corresponds to the reflections of Augustine in the twelfth and thirteenth books of his *Confessions* (see 12/29:294–295 and 13/33:330) about the *informitas* (formlessness) of what was created out of nothing *primo* (at first), the *materia* (matter, material, stuff) that waited to be given form," *DBWE* 3:37, n. 39.]

13. ["Cf. Bonhoeffer's discussion of 'Definition of "Being" in Adam' in *DBWE* 2:136–150 (*Reader* 93–101)," *DBWE* 3:38, n. 44.]

enormously increases the power of the creation, by giving to creation its own being as that which has form. In this form creation exists over against God in a new way, and in existing over against God it wholly belongs to God.

** **

CHAP. 1, VV. 26–27   60

THE IMAGE OF GOD ON EARTH

Then God said: Let us make humankind in our image, according to our likeness; and let it have dominion over the fish in the sea and over the birds in the sky and over the cattle and over all wild animals and over all reptiles that creep about upon the earth. And God created human beings in God's own image—God created them in the image of God, created them as man and woman.

God loves God's work, loves it in that it has its own existence; for the creature honors the Creator. God still does not recognize God's self in the work, however; God beholds that work but not God's own self. To behold oneself means, so to speak, to recognize one's own face in a mirror, to see oneself in an image of oneself. But how could that possibly take place? God, after all, remains without qualification the Creator before whose feet the work lies; how then will God be able to find God in this work? The work does not resemble the Creator, it is not the Creator's image; instead it is the form that the Creator's command takes. What is decisive is that at the very moment when the Creator has brought it forth, the work is already torn away from, and alien to, the Creator; it is no longer the Creator. Even in its living nature the work is dead, because it is created, conditioned—because, though it arises out of freedom, it itself is not free but conditioned. Only   61
that which is itself free would not be dead, would not, as a creature, be alien or torn away. Only in that which is itself free could the free Creator behold the Creator. But how can what is created be free? What is created is determined, bound by law, conditioned, not free. If the Creator wishes to create the Creator's own image, then the Creator must create it free. And only such an image, in its freedom, would fully praise God, would fully proclaim God's glory as Creator.

At this point the narrative is about us; it is about the creation of humankind. The Bible expresses the essential difference between this work and all God's previous creative activity by the way in which it introduces this work. The Hebrew plural here indicates the significance and sublimity of the Creator's action. It is also to be noted, however, that God does not simply call humankind forth out of nonbeing, as God called forth everything else;

instead we are taken up into God's own planning, as it were, and thereby become aware that something new, something that has not yet been, something altogether original, is about to happen.

And God said: Let us make humankind in our image, after our likeness. Humankind is to go forth from God as the last work, as the new work,

62 as the image of God in God's work. There is no transition from somewhere else here; here there is new creation. This has nothing whatsoever to do with Darwin. Quite apart from that issue humankind remains in an unqualified way God's new, free work. We in no way wish to deny humankind's connection with the animal world—on the contrary. Our concern, our whole concern, nevertheless, is that we not lose sight of the peculiar relation between humankind and God above and beyond this. The attempt—with the origin and nature of humankind in mind—to take a gigantic leap back into the world of the lost beginning, to seek to know for ourselves what humankind was like in its original state[14] and to identify our own ideal of humanity with what God actually created is hopeless. It fails to recognize that it is only from Christ that we can know about the original nature of humankind. The attempt to do that without recognizing this, as hopeless as it is understandable, has again and again delivered up the church to arbitrary speculation at this dangerous point. Only in the middle, as those who live from Christ, do we know about the beginning.

To say that in humankind God creates God's own image on earth means that humankind is like the Creator in that it is free. To be sure, it is free only through God's creation, through the word of God; it is free for the worship of the Creator. For in the language of the Bible freedom is not something that people have for themselves but something they have for others. No one is free 'in herself' or 'in himself'—free as it were in a vacuum or free in the same way that a person may be musical, intelligent, or blind in herself or

63 in himself. Freedom is not a quality a human being has; it is not an ability, a capacity, an attribute of being that may be deeply hidden in a person but can somehow be uncovered. Anyone who scrutinizes human beings in order to find freedom finds nothing of it. Why? Because freedom is not a quality that can be uncovered; it is not a possession, something to hand, an object; nor is it a form of something to hand; instead it is a relation and nothing else. To be more precise, freedom is a relation between two persons. Being free means 'being-free-for-the-other', because I am bound to the other. Only by being in relation with the other am I free.

---

14. ["Cf. *DBWE* 1:58–62, n. 1," DBWE 3:62, n. 10.]

No one can think of freedom as a substance or as something individual-istic. Freedom is just not something I have at my command like an attribute of my own; it is simply something that comes to happen, that takes place, that happens to me through the other. We can ask how we know this and whether it is not once again just speculation about the beginning that is part of the fall-out of being in the middle. The answer is that it is the mes-sage of the gospel itself that God's freedom has bound itself to us, that God's free grace becomes real with us alone, that God wills not to be free for God's self but for humankind. Because God in Christ is free for human-kind, because God does not keep God's freedom to God's self, we can think of freedom only as a 'being free for. . . .'[15] For us in the middle who exist through Christ and who know what it means to be human through Christ's resurrection, the fact that God is free means nothing else than that we are free for God. The freedom of the Creator demonstrates itself by allowing us to be free, free for the Creator. That, however, means nothing else than that the Creator's image is created on earth. The paradox of created free-dom remains undiminished. Indeed it needs to be expressed as sharply as possible. Created *freedom* then means—and it is this that goes beyond all God's previous acts and is unique κατ' ἐξοχήν [*par excellence*]—that God's self enters into God's creation.

Now not only does God command and God's word comes to pass; now God enters into creation and so creates freedom. Humankind differs from the other creatures in that God is in humankind as the very image of God in which the free Creator looks upon the Creator's own self. This is what the older dogmatic theologians meant when they spoke of the indwelling of the Trinity in Adam. In the free creature the Holy Spirit worships the Creator; uncreated freedom glorifies itself in view of created freedom. The creature loves the Creator, because the Creator loves the creature. Created *freedom* is freedom in the Holy Spirit, but as *created* freedom it is *human-kind's* own freedom. How does this created existence of a free humankind express itself? In what way does the freedom of the Creator differ from the freedom of that which is created? How is the creature free? The creature is free in that one creature exists in relation to another creature, in that one human being is free for another human being. And God created them man and woman. The human being is not alone. Human beings exist in dual-ity, and it is in this *dependence on the other that their creatureliness consists.* The creatureliness of human beings is no more a quality or something at hand

64

---

15. [*Bonhoeffer often contrasts two understandings of freedom—freedom from and freedom for. See, for examples,* DBWE *2:82 and* DBWE *11:242 (Reader 169).*]

or an existing entity than human freedom is. It can be defined in simply no other way than in terms of the existence of human beings over-against-one-another, with-one-another, and in-dependence-upon-one-another.

65   The "image that is like God" is therefore no analogia entis [*analogy of being*][16] in which human beings, in their existence in-and-of-themselves, in their being, could be said to be like God's being. There can be no such analogy between God and humankind. This is so in the first place because God—who alone has self-sufficient being in aseity, yet at the same time is there for God's creature, binding God's freedom to humankind and so giving God's self to humankind—must be thought of as one who is not alone, inasmuch as God is the one who in Christ attests to God's 'being for humankind'.[17] The likeness, the analogia, of humankind to God is not analogia entis but *analogia relationis* [*analogy of relation*]. What this means, however, is, firstly, that the relatio [*relation*] too is not a human potential or possibility or a structure of human existence; instead it is a given relation, a relation in which human beings are set, a justitia passiva [*passive righteousness*]! And it is in this relation in which they are set that freedom is given. From this it follows, secondly, that this analogia must not be understood as though humankind somehow had this likeness in its possession or at its disposal. Instead the analogia or likeness must be understood very strictly in the sense that what is like derives its likeness *only* from the prototype, so that it always points us only to the prototype itself and is 'like' it only in pointing to it in this way. Analogia relationis is therefore the relation which

66   God has established, and it is analogia only in this relation which God has established. The relation of creature with creature is a relation established by God, because it consists of freedom and freedom comes from God.

Humankind in the duality of man and woman, that is, in its likeness to God, is created within the world of the fixed and of the living. And whereas the freedom of human beings over against one another consisted in being free *for* one another, humankind's freedom over against the rest of the created world is to be free *from* it. That means that humankind is its lord; humankind has command over it, rules it. And that constitutes the other side of humankind's created likeness to God. Humankind is to rule—though it is to rule over God's creation and to rule as having been commissioned and empowered to rule by God.

---

16. ["... In *Act and Being* Bonhoeffer had taken issue with the 'ontology of the *analogia entis*' of the Catholic Erich Przywara; see *DBWE* 2:27, 73–76, 138. (*Reader* 94–95). . . ," *DBWE* 3:64, n. 20.]

17. ["Cf. *DBWE* 2:90–91. 'Aseity' means having one's origin in oneself, underived being," *DBWE* 3:65, n. 21.]

Being free from created things is not the same as, say, the ideal of the spirit's being free from nature. On the contrary this freedom to rule includes being bound to the creatures who are ruled. The ground and the animals over which I am lord constitute the world in which I live, without which I cease to be. It is my world, my earth, over which I rule. I am not free from it in any sense of my essential being, my spirit, having no need of nature, as though nature were something alien to the spirit. On the contrary, in my whole being, in my creatureliness, I belong wholly to this world; it bears me, nurtures me, holds me. But my freedom from it consists in the fact that this world, to which I am bound like a master to his servant, like the peasant to his bit of ground, has been made subject to me, that over the earth which is and remains my earth I am to *rule*, and the more I master it, the more it is *my* earth. What so peculiarly binds human beings to, and sets them over against, the other creatures is the authority conferred on humankind by nothing else than God's word.

This is said to us who, being in the middle, no longer know anything about all this and to whom it is all a pious myth or a lost world. We too think that we rule, but the same applies here as on Walpurgis Night: we think we are the one making the move, whereas instead we are being moved. We do not rule; instead we are ruled. The thing, the world, rules humankind; humankind is a prisoner, a slave, of the world, and its dominion is an illusion. Technology is the power with which the earth seizes hold of humankind and masters it. And because we no longer rule, we lose the ground so that the earth no longer remains *our* earth, and we become estranged from the earth. The reason why we fail to rule, however, is because we do not know the world as God's creation and do not accept the dominion we have as God-given but seize hold of it for ourselves. There is no 'being-free-from' without a 'being-free-for'. There is no dominion without serving God; in losing the one humankind necessarily loses the other. Without God, without their brothers and sisters, human beings lose the earth. Already in sentimentally shying away from exercising dominion over the earth, however, human beings have forever lost God and their brothers and sisters. God, the brother and sister, and the earth belong together. For those who have once lost the earth, however, for us human beings in the middle, there is no way back to the earth except via God and our brothers and sisters. From the inception humankind's way to the earth has been possible only as God's way to humankind. Only where God and the brother, the sister, come to them can human beings find their way back to the earth. Human freedom for God and the other person and human freedom from the creature in dominion over it constitute the first human beings' likeness to God.

67

**

74

CHAP. 2, V. 7

THE HUMAN BEING OF EARTH AND SPIRIT

Then Yahweh God fashioned humankind out of dust from the ground, and blew into its nose the breath of life; so the human being became a living being.

Here we are directed to the earth in a distinct and exclusive way that is quite different from before. What is of primary interest here is not at all the cosmos but our earth and humankind. Here God also receives a very specific proper name, Yahweh (on the meaning of which there is no agreement). This is God's real name; that is, it is the name of *this* God, the God who is being spoken of here. *Elohim* in Genesis 1 is not a proper name but a generic term and so means roughly 'deity'. One could suppose that such a proper name is evidence of a very primitive idea of God and shows that we have no right at all to be speaking here of the same God whose power chap.

75   1 has set forth. And yet just at this point one must reply that anthropomorphism in thinking of God, or blatant mythology, is no more irrelevant or unsuitable as an expression for God's being than is the abstract use of the generic term 'deity'. On the contrary, clear anthropomorphism much more plainly expresses the fact that we cannot think of 'God as such' whether in one way or another. The abstract concept of God, precisely because it seeks not to be anthropomorphic, is in actual fact much more so than is childlike anthropomorphism. And we need a proper name for God so that we can think of God in the right way. Indeed the proper name is God as such. We have God in no other way than in God's name. This is true today as well. Jesus Christ—that is the name of God, at once utterly anthropomorphic and utterly to the point.

God fashioned humankind out of dust from the ground and blew into its nostrils the breath of life. Here again everything takes place in a very down-to-earth way. The way of speaking is extremely childlike and, for the person who wishes truly to comprehend or to 'know' something, very offensive. How can one talk of God in the same way as one talks about a person who fashions a vessel out of earth and clay? The anthropomorphisms become more and more insupportable: God models or molds with clay, and the human being is fashioned like a vessel out of an earthen clod. Surely no one can gain any knowledge about the origin of humankind from this! To be sure, as an account of what happened this story is at first sight of just as little consequence, and just as full of meaning, as many another myth of cre-

76   ation. And yet in being distinguished as the word of God it is quite simply *the source* of knowledge about the origin of humankind. And now it will also

become evident that this account belongs closely with the previous account and forms a unity with it.

To say that Yahweh fashions humankind with Yahweh's own hands expresses two complementary things. On the one hand, it expresses the physical nearness of the Creator to the creature—expresses that it is really the Creator who makes me, the human being, with the Creator's own hands; it expresses the trouble the Creator takes, the Creator's thinking about me, the Creator's intention with me and nearness to me. On the other hand, it expresses also the omnipotence, the utter supremacy, with which the Creator fashions and creates me and in terms of which I am the Creator's creature; it expresses the fatherliness with which the Creator creates me and in the context of which I worship the Creator. That is the true God to whom the whole Bible bears witness.

The human being whom God has created in God's image—that is, in freedom—is the human being who is taken from earth. Even Darwin and Feuerbach could not use stronger language than is used here. Humankind is derived from a piece of earth. Its bond with the earth belongs to its essential being. The 'earth is its mother'; it comes out of her womb. To be sure, the ground from which humankind is taken is not the cursed but the blessed ground. It is God's earth out of which humankind is taken. From it human beings have their *bodies*. The body belongs to a person's essence. The body is not the prison, the shell, the exterior, of a human being; instead   77 a human being is a human body. A human being does not 'have' a body or 'have' a soul; instead a human being 'is' body and soul. The human being in the beginning really is the body, is one—just as Christ is wholly his body and the church is the body of Christ. People who reject their bodies reject their existence before God the Creator. What is to be taken seriously about human existence is its bond with mother earth, its being as body. Human beings have their existence as existence on earth. They do not come from above; they have not by some cruel fate been driven into the earthly world and been enslaved in it. Instead, the word of God the almighty one summoned humankind out of the earth in which it was sleeping, in which it was dead and indeed a mere piece of earth, but a piece of earth called by God to have human existence. "Wake up, you who are sleeping, rise up from the dead, and Christ will give you light" (Eph. 5:14).[18]

---

18. ["... Bonhoeffer used this text in Ephesians as a basis for his baptismal address in October 1932 (*DBWE* 11:473–475) ... Cf. also *DBWE* 2:148–149, n. 15," *DBWE* 3:77, n. 14.]

78   This is also what Michelangelo thought. The Adam who rests on the newly created earth is so closely and intimately bound up with the ground on which Adam lies that Adam is, even in this still-dreaming state, a most singular and wonderful piece of earth—but even so still a piece of earth. Indeed it is precisely in this state of nestling so closely to the blessed ground of the created earth that the whole glory of the first human being becomes visible. And in this resting on the earth, in this deep sleep of creation, the human being now experiences life through being physically touched by the finger of God. It is the same hand that has made the human being that now, as though reaching from afar, tenderly touches and awakens the human being to life. God's hand no longer holds the human being in its grasp; instead it has set the human being free, and the creative power of that hand turns into the yearning love of the Creator toward the creature. The hand of God in this picture in the Sistine Chapel discloses a greater knowledge about the creation than does much profound speculation.

And God blew into the human being's nostrils the breath of life; so the human person became a living being. Here body and life merge completely. God breathes the spirit of God into the body of the human being. And this spirit is life; it brings the human being to life. Other life is created through God's word, but in the case of human life God gives of God's own life, of God's own spirit. Human beings do not live as human beings apart from God's spirit. To live *as a human being* means to live as a body in the spirit. Flight from the body is as much flight from being human as is flight from the spirit. The body is the form in which the spirit exists, as the spirit is the form in which the body exists. All this is said only about humankind, for only in the case of human beings do we know about body and spirit. The

79   human body differs from all non-human bodies in that it is the form in which the spirit of God exists on earth, just as it is altogether identical with all other life in being earth-like. The human body really does live only by God's spirit; that is what constitutes its essential being.[19] God as such is glorified in the body, that is, in the body that has the specific being of a human body. That is why where the original body in its created being has been destroyed, God enters it anew in Jesus Christ, and then, where this body too is broken, enters the forms of the sacrament of the body and blood. The body and blood of the Lord's Supper are the new realities of creation promised to fallen Adam. Because Adam is created as body, Adam is also

---

19. ["In German nouns such as *Geist*, whether meaning 'Spirit' or 'spirit,' are spelled with an initial capital letter. In these paragraphs Bonhoeffer seems to slide from the idea of God's spirit to that of the human spirit and back," *DBWE* 3:79, n. 19.]

redeemed as body and God comes to Adam as body, in Jesus Christ and in
the sacrament.

Humankind created in this way is humankind as the image of God. It
is the image of God not in spite of but precisely in its bodily nature. For
in their bodily nature human beings are related to the earth and to other
bodies; they are there for others and are dependent upon others. In their
bodily existence human beings find their brothers and sisters and find the
earth. As such creatures human beings of earth and spirit are 'like' God,
their Creator.

CHAP. 2, VV. 8–17   80

THE CENTER OF THE EARTH

*And Yahweh God planted a garden in Eden towards the east and put in it the
human being God had made. And Yahweh God made grow out of the earth all
kinds of trees that were delightful to see and good to eat and the tree of life in the
center of the garden and the tree of the knowledge of good and evil. And a river
flowed out of Eden to water the garden, and from there divided into four main
rivers. The first is named Pishon; it flows around the whole land of Havilah,
and there one finds gold. And the gold of the land is precious; and one finds
bdellium resin and shoham stone there. The second river is named Gihon; it
flows around the whole land of the Moors. The third river is named Hiddekel;
it flows on this side of Assyria. The fourth river is the Phrates. And Yahweh
God took the human being and put the human being in the garden of Eden to
till it and keep it. And Yahweh God commanded the human being, saying: You
shall eat from every kind of tree in the garden, but from the tree of the knowledge
of good and evil you shall not eat; for on the day you eat from it you shall die.*

How can one speak of the first earth, earth in its youth, except in the lan- 81
guage of fantasy? God prepares an exceedingly magnificent garden for the
human being created with God's own hands. What else would a person
from the desert think of here but a land with magnificent rivers and trees
full of fruit? Precious stones, rare odors, gorgeous colors surround the first
human being. The fruitful land in the distant east, between the Euphrates
and the Tigris, of which so many wonderful things were being told—perhaps that was the place, the garden of the first human being.

Who can speak of these things except in pictures? Pictures after all are
not lies; rather they indicate things and enable the underlying meaning to
shine through. To be sure, pictures do vary; the pictures of a child differ
from those of an adult, and those of a person from the desert differ from

those of a person from the city. One way or another, however, they remain true, to the extent that human speech and even speech about abstract ideas can remain true at all—that is, to the extent that God dwells in them.

In complete consistency with the framework of the picture, the story is told how the human being was put into this garden to live in it, and how in the center of the garden stood two trees: one the tree of life and the other the tree of the knowledge of good and evil. The destiny of humankind is now to be decided in relation to these two trees. We remain wholly in the world of pictures, in the world of the magical, with spells that are effected through forbidden contacts with sacred objects. We hear about trees of miraculous power, about enchanted animals, about fiery angel figures, the servants of a God who walks in this, God's enchanted garden. We hear about this God's mysterious deeds, about the creation of the woman from the man's rib—and in the midst of this world is the human being, the intelligent creature, who knows the surrounding world, who freely gives names to it, and before whom the whole animal kingdom appears in order to receive their names. The human being is naked and not ashamed, speaks with, and has to do with, God as though they belonged to each another, talks with the beasts in the fields and lives sumptuously and with delight in the enchanted garden—and then reaches out for the fruit of an enchanted tree and in that moment is displaced from paradise. This is a myth, a childlike, fanciful picture of the dim and distant past—so says the world. This is God's word; this is an event at the beginning of history, before history, beyond history, and yet in history; this is a decision that affects the world; *we ourselves* are the ones who are affected, are intended, are addressed, accused, condemned, expelled; *God, yes God*, is the one who blesses and curses; it is *our* primeval history, truly our own, every individual person's beginning, destiny, guilt, and end—so says the church of Christ.

Why contend for the one assertion at the expense of the other? Why not see that all our speaking of God, of our beginning and end, and of our guilt *never* communicates these things themselves but always only pictures of them? Why not see that in both instances, with these ancient magical images as well as with our technical, abstract images, God must reach out to us, and that God must teach us if we are to become wise?

The exposition of what follows must therefore seek to translate the old picture language of the magical world into the new picture language of the technical world. This must always be done, however, on the basis of the presupposition that, whether in the one language or the other, *we* are the ones intended to be addressed. We must be open and prepared to be addressed by what was said at that time about human beings in that magical picture of the world. To be sure, we differ from the people who thought in terms of that worldview in that Christ has appeared, whereas they were waiting; but we are *the same* as they were in that—whether in hope or in fulfillment—we can live only through Christ as people who have been lost and, whether in hope or in fulfillment, have been graciously pardoned.

In the center of the garden stand two trees with particular names that connect them to human existence in a peculiar way: the tree of life and the tree of the knowledge of good and evil. To the latter is attached the prohibition against eating of its fruit and the threat of death. *Life, knowledge, death*—these three things are spoken of here as connected with one another, and it is important to understand this connection. Historical research seems to show that the stories of the tree of life and of the tree of knowledge originally came from different sources. But that is all very uncertain. Our concern is the text as it presents itself to the church of Christ today.

We begin with the tree of life. It follows from the context that humankind was not expressly forbidden to eat from this tree. Indeed this tree first gains its particular significance only after humankind has fallen prey to death by eating from the tree of knowledge. Before that, life is not something problematic or to be sought after or snatched at; instead it is just there, as a given life, indeed life before God.

For that reason the tree of life is in this passage mentioned with such little ceremony. *It was at the center*; that is all that is said about it. The life that comes from God is at the center; that is to say, God, who gives life, is at the center. At the center of the world that has been put at Adam's disposal and over which Adam has been given dominion is not Adam himself but the tree of divine life. Adam's life comes from the center which is not Adam but God; it revolves around this center constantly, without ever trying to take possession of this center of existence. It is characteristic of humankind that human life constantly revolves around its own center, but that it never takes possession of it. And this life that stems from the center, which God alone possesses, remains unassailed as long as humankind does not let itself be pushed off the track from another side. Adam is not, in temptation, to touch the tree of life, to seize hold of the divine tree at the center. There is no need at all to forbid Adam—who would in no way understand the prohibition—to do this. Adam has life.

Adam has life, however, in a particular way. In the first place, *Adam* really possesses it and is not merely possessed by it. In the second place, Adam has life in the unity of unbroken obedience to the Creator—has life just because Adam lives from the center of life, and is oriented toward the center of life, without placing Adam's own life at the center. The distinctive characteristic of Adam's life is utterly unbroken and unified obedience, that is, Adam's innocence and ignorance of disobedience.

84

The life that God gave to humankind is not simply part of the makeup, a qualitas [*quality, property, or attribute*], of humankind; instead it is something given to humankind only in terms of its whole human existence. Human beings have life from God and *before* God. They receive it; they receive it, however, not as animals but as human beings. They possess it in their obedience, in their innocence, in their ignorance; that is, they possess it in their freedom. The life that human beings have happens in an obedience that issues from freedom. So while it cannot occur to Adam directly to lay hands on the tree of life, because Adam already has life, the tree of life can nevertheless come indirectly under danger from elsewhere. It can be endangered by the freedom in the unbroken unity of obedience in which Adam has life. This means that it can be endangered by the tree of the knowledge of good and evil. *In what way?*

The tree of the knowledge of good and evil, just like the tree of life, stands at the center of the garden. But as soon as this tree is pointed out, a special word of God is immediately attached—the prohibition against eating from it and the threat of death as soon as human beings transgress this commandment.

85   How is Adam to grasp what death is, what good and evil are, indeed even what a prohibition is, living as Adam does in unbroken obedience to the Creator? Can any of this mean anything else than empty words to Adam? Certainly Adam cannot know what death is, what good and evil are; but Adam understands that in these words God confronts Adam and points out Adam's limit. It is we who ask: How can Adam, who does not know about good or evil, who is innocent and ignorant, understand the word of God that addresses Adam as a prohibition? The prohibition contained two complementary aspects. On the one hand it indicated that Adam was human, was free (free 'for' and 'from')—it is Adam, the human being, who is addressed concerning Adam's own human existence, and Adam understands this. On the other hand it indicates to this human being who is addressed as a free person their limit or boundedness, that is, the human being's creatureliness. The prohibition addresses Adam concerning Adam's freedom and creatureliness and binds Adam to this existence, the existence that belongs to Adam's own being. The prohibition means nothing other than this: Adam, you are who you are because of me, your Creator; so now be what you are. You are a free creature, so now be that. You are free, so be free; you are a creature, so be a creature. And this "—so be . . ." is not a second thing besides the first but something always given already in and along with the first and guaranteed by the first. It is about being human—about the human existence that Adam receives from God at any given time—that Adam is addressed.

This singular interrelatedness, which is basically only the interrelated-   86
ness of freedom and creatureliness, is expressed here in the picture language of the Bible in that the tree of knowledge, the forbidden tree that
denotes the human being's boundary, stands at the center. *The human being's
limit is at the center of human existence,* not on the margin; the limit or constraint that people look for on the margin of humankind is the limit of the
human condition, the limit of human technology, the limit of what is possible for humanity. The boundary that is at the center is the limit of human
reality, of human *existence as such.* Knowledge of the limit or constraint on
the margin is always accompanied by the possibility of failing to know any
internal limit. Knowledge of the boundary at the center means knowing
that the whole of existence, human existence in every possible way that it
may comport itself, has its limit.

There where the boundary—the tree of knowledge—stands, there
stands also the tree of life, that is, the very God who gives life. *God is at once
the boundary and the center of our existence.* Adam knows that. But Adam knows
it in such a way that this knowing is only an expression of Adam's existence
from the center—Adam's being oriented toward the center; it is an expression of Adam's creatureliness and freedom. Adam's knowing is embedded
in Adam's freedom for God, in unbroken obedience to God; it is *knowledge
arising from the freedom of the creature, knowledge in life, knowledge in ignorance.*   87
Thus Adam cannot know evil, cannot conceive it, and cannot know or conceive death either. But Adam knows the limit of human beings because
Adam knows God. Adam does not know the boundary as something that
can be transgressed; otherwise Adam would know about evil. Adam knows
it as the given grace that belongs to his creatureliness and freedom. Adam
also knows, therefore, that life is possible only because of the limit; Adam
lives from this boundary that is at the center. Thus Adam understands this
prohibition and the threat of death only as a renewed gift, as the grace of
God. The limit is grace because it is the basis of creatureliness and freedom;
the boundary is the center. Grace is that which holds humankind over the
abyss of nonbeing, nonliving, not-being-created, and Adam can think of all
this nothingness only in terms of the given grace of God.

Thus not a word in the story up to this point hints at the possibility of
understanding the prohibition differently, say as a temptation. The *prohibition* in paradise is the *grace* of the Creator toward the creature. God tempts
no one. Only the Creator knows what the tree of the knowledge of *good* and
evil is up to this point; Adam does not yet know it. As one who lives in the
unity of obedience Adam does not comprehend that which is two-sided;
as one who lives in the unity of the knowledge of God as the center and
the boundary of human life Adam cannot conceive of the breaking apart

of that knowledge into good and evil. Adam knows neither what good nor what evil is and lives in the strictest sense *beyond good and evil*;[20] that is,

88 Adam lives out of the life that comes from God, before whom a life lived in good, just like a life lived in evil, would mean an unthinkable falling away.

Good and evil, tob and ra,[21] thus have a much wider meaning here than good and evil in our terminology. The words tob and ra speak of an ultimate split in the world of humankind in general that goes back behind even the moral split, so that tob means also something like "pleasurable" and ra "painful" (Hans Schmidt). Tob and ra are concepts that express what is in every respect the deepest divide in human life. The essential point about them is that they appear as a pair, that in being split apart they belong inseparably together. There is no tob, nothing that is pleasurable/good/beautiful, without its being always already immersed in ra, in that which is painful/evil/base/false. And what is painful/evil—in this wide sense—does not occur without a glimmer of desire for pleasure, which is what makes pain so completely pain. That which is good, in the sense of tob, is for us always only something that has been torn from evil, that has passed through evil, that has been conceived, carried, and borne by evil. The luster of the pleasurable/good is its origin in evil, in its overcoming of evil, to be

89 sure, but in the same way that a child overcomes the mother's womb, that is, in such a way that the good is enhanced by the greatness of the evil from which it has torn itself. To us Ignatius is 'greater' than Francis, Augustine is greater than Monica, Hagen is greater than Siegfried.[22]

In the same way, however, 'evil' is enhanced by the 'good' from which it comes; pain is enhanced by the pleasure out of whose depths alone it has become possible. No real evil wholly lacks the luster of the good. We have no utter evil, nothing that is utterly painful, in human beings. Where there is utter evil with no good to enhance it, where baseness itself takes form,

---

20. ["*Beyond Good and Evil* is the title of a work that Friedrich Nietzsche wrote in 1885–1886 . . . ," *DBWE* 3:87, n. 22.]

21. ["*Tob* and *ra* are Hebrew words, each having a range of meanings. *Tob* means 'good, pleasing, pleasant, delightful, delicious, happy, glad, joyful,' while *ra* means 'bad, evil, disagreeable, displeasing, unpleasant, harmful.' (See *The New Brown-Driver-Briggs-Gesenius Hebrew and English Lexicon*.) Hence *tob* can be translated by the German *lustvoll*, which means either 'pleasurable' or 'joyful,' and *ra* by *leidvoll*, which means either 'painful, suffering' or 'sorrowful,'" *DBWE* 3:88, n. 23.]

22. ["The steeliness of will of Ignatius of Loyola (1491–1556) contrasts with the gentleness of Francis of Assisi (c. 1181–1226). Augustine tells us about his pious mother Monica especially in the ninth book of his *Confessions*. Hagen is the murderer of Siegfried in the *Nibelungenlied* [*Songs of the Nibelungs*], a Middle High German epic poem," *DBWE* 3:89, n. 28.]

there human beings have lost their humanity and we call them sick; where that which is utterly painful has managed to lay hold of human beings, so that pleasure has been wholly destroyed in pain, there the sickness of mind called melancholia has overwhelmed human beings and they are no longer human. Healthy human beings in pain are borne up and nourished by what brings pleasure; in their experience of pleasure they are churned up by what is painful, in good by evil, in evil by good. They suffer from an inner split.

This describes *us*; it is we who have eaten from the tree of knowledge, not Adam. But we must go on and enquire further in order to understand the import of what the Bible says about the tree of knowledge: ". . . as soon as you eat from it you must die." The tree of knowledge is the *tree of death*. It stands immediately next to the tree of life, and *the tree of life is endangered only by this tree of death*. Both trees are still untouched and untouchable; both constitute the boundary and the center. Whoever grasps at life must die; "those who want to save their life will lose it" [*Matt. 16:25*]. Only those who have lost it, however, will grasp at it. And those who have attained the knowledge of good and evil, who live as people who are split apart within themselves, have lost their life.

Why have they lost life? We have said that what is pleasurable/good is immersed in what is painful/evil, and vice versa. But just what is painful in pleasure? It is that in all pleasure a person desires eternity, but knows that pleasure is transient and will end. That is not a knowing that comes from a prior knowledge now applied to every pleasurable event; it is something that the depth of pleasure itself discloses to us if we listen to it: a thirst, a craving, for eternity, precisely because pleasure is not eternal but instead has fallen prey to death. On the other hand we ask: What pleasure is there in pain? It is that in the depth of pain a person feels pleasure in transience, pleasure in the obliteration of apparently endless pain, pleasure in death.

What is the evil in good? It is that the good dies. What is the good in evil? It is that the evil dies. What is the state of being divided or torn apart into tob and ra in the world and in humankind? It is the pain and the pleasure with which a human being dies. A human being who knows about tob and ra knows immediately about death. Knowing about tob and ra itself constitutes death. Humankind dies from knowing good and evil. Humankind is dead in its own good and in its own evil. Death in terms of transience is not the death that comes from God. What does it mean to be dead? It does not mean the abolition of one's being a creature. Instead it means no longer being able to live before God, and yet having to live before God. It means standing before God as an outlaw, as one who is lost and damned, but not as one who no longer exists. It means receiving life from God no longer as

90

grace coming from the center and the boundary of one's own existence but as a commandment that stands in one's way and with a flaming sword denies one any way of retreat.

Being dead in this sense means to have life not as a gift but as a *commandment*. But from this commandment no one can escape, not even by choosing oneself to die, for to be dead is itself to be subject to the commandment to live. *To be dead means to-have-to-live.* That irks our natural way of thinking. Being dead is not deliverance, salvation, or the final possibility of fleeing; instead flight into death is flight into the most terrible bondage to life. The *inescapable nature of life as a commandment*—to know that is *to know death*.

The *commandment to live* demands from me something that I am not in a position to fulfill. It obliges me to live out of myself, out of my own resources, and I am unable to do that. Just this, however, is the commandment that burdens those who know about *tob* and *ra*. They are obliged to live out of their own resources, and they do so, yet are unable to do it. *They do so* by living out of their own inner split, by living with their own good that comes out of evil and by their own evil that comes out of good, by deriving the strength of pain from pleasure and the strength of pleasure from pain. Humankind lives in a circle; it *lives* out of its own resources; it is alone. Yet *it cannot live*, because in fact it does not live but in this life is dead, because it *must* live, that is, it *must* accomplish life out of its own resources and just that is its death (as the basis at once of its knowledge and of its existence!). Humankind whom God's commandment confronts with a demand is thrown back upon itself and now has to live in this way. Humankind now lives only out of its own resources, by its knowledge of good and evil, and thus is dead.

After all this, it is now at last quite clear that the tree of life comes to be in danger only where the tree of death has had its effect. It is clear why the prohibition was attached to the tree of death but not to the tree of life—or, to put it the other way around, why the tree to which the prohibition was attached has to be the tree of death. There is still one thing that remains quite unclear, however: how this deed that opened up world that has been torn apart into tob and ra is known only in death. And Adam knows nothing of this world. To Adam it remains hidden in the tempting fruit of the tree of knowledge. What Adam knows is that the secret of humankind's limit, of the life of the human being, is in God's keeping.

At this point, however, we need to remind ourselves again that this is not a tale about some primeval human being that hardly affects us. If it were only a tale like that, our main task would be to give rein to our imagination so that it would transport us to this fairyland beyond tob and ra. Every such game of imagination would altogether discount our actual situation; indeed it is possible only in the split-apart world in which human beings suppose that they could somehow still escape from themselves. What is important to understand, however, is that this story claims us not as listeners with the gift of imagination but as human beings who, no matter how much they stretch their imaginations and all their other mental or spiritual powers, are simply unable to transport themselves to this paradise 'beyond good and evil', 'beyond pleasure and pain'; instead, with all their powers of thinking, they remain tied to this torn-apart world, to antithesis, to contradiction. This is so because our thinking too is only the expression of our being, of our existence, which is grounded in contradiction. Because we do not exist in a state of unity, our thinking is torn apart as well.

Instead of sanctioning this impossibility of transporting ourselves to that fairyland beyond, however, and instead of being allowed to judge what the Bible calls good by our idea of what is good and on that basis to criticize what the Bible says here about what is beyond good and evil, we are confronted by this Adam who disturbs us and criticizes us. This is so just because Adam is a human being like us and Adam's history is our history, with the one decisive difference, to be sure, that for us history begins where for Adam it ends. Our history is history through Christ, whereas Adam's history is history through the serpent. But precisely as those who live and have their history through Christ alone we are enabled to know about the beginning not by means of our own imagination but only from the new center, from Christ. We have this knowledge as those who by faith have been set free from the knowledge of good and evil, from death, and who by faith 93 alone are able to make Adam's image their own.

CHAP. 2, VV. 18–25 94

THE POWER OF THE OTHER

And Yahweh God said: It is not good that the human being should be alone; I will make a helper who is a suitable partner. So out of the ground Yahweh God formed all the beasts of the field and all the birds of heaven and brought them to the human being to see what they would be called; and whatever the human being called the living creatures, so they were named. The human being gave names to all cattle and all the birds of heaven and all the beasts of the field; but God found no helper who was a partner suitable for the human being. So Yahweh God let a deep sleep fall upon the human being, and when sleep had come, God took a rib and filled out its place with flesh. Then Yahweh God formed into a woman the rib he had taken from the human being and brought her to the human being. Then the human being said: "This at last is bone of my

95 *bones and flesh of my flesh. She shall be called woman, because she was taken*
out of man." That is why a man will leave father and mother and cleave to his
woman, and they will be one flesh. And they were both naked, the man and his
woman, and they were not ashamed.

At this point the text all at once, with no apparent relation to what has gone
before, tells us how woman came to be. No doubt in terms of narrative
technique it is a mistake that the woman has not heard God's prohibition,
for no intrinsic significance of any kind is attached to this circumstance.
Yet the story does have its own special significance in just this place. Let us
keep in mind that the tree of life was mentioned first, not yet as something
which was desired, or to which any prohibition was attached, but as the *tree*
around whose fruit everything in the end revolves. We saw how it was first placed
in danger by the tree of knowledge; now more and more links are added
to the chain, increasing the danger, and making it ever more threatening.
After the tree of knowledge comes the creation of the woman, and, finally, it
is the serpent that leads to the act of grasping at the tree of knowledge and
of life. The incomprehensibility of this deed makes the author of the story,
with exceptional profundity, look at, and take up, everything conceivable
in connection with this deed in order to make it more comprehensible—or,
more exactly, to make clear its incomprehensibility. It is clear that for the
author the creation of the woman belongs already to the prehistory of the
fall.[23]

96 "It is not good that the human being should be alone; I will make a
helper who is a suitable partner."

The first person is alone. Christ also was alone; we also are alone. But
everyone is alone in his or her own way. Adam is alone in anticipation of
the other person, of community. Christ is alone because he alone loves
the other person, because Christ is the way by which the human race has
returned to its Creator. We are alone because we have pushed other people
away from us, because we have hated them. Adam was alone in hope, Christ
was alone in the fullness of deity, we are alone in evil, in hopelessness.

God creates a suitable partner, a helpmate, for Adam. It is not good that
Adam should be alone. To what end does the human being who lives in

---

23. [*Bonhoeffer implies that marriage should not be taken as an order of creation. Order of cre-*
ation was a misused concept in Bonhoeffer's time. ". . . Whereas Martin Luther had maintained
that marriage or the family (like the state) is a natural order of creation that confronts us
with ethical obligations, some German Protestants used the concept to justify nationalist and even National Socialist ideas about the demands of the nation or even the race.
See the section 'Ethics Based on Orders of Creation,' *DBWE* 3:148ff," *DBWE* 3:95, n. 5.]

God's keeping need a helper who is a partner? The answer becomes clear only if we continue to reflect on the story in its context. Elsewhere in the Bible God alone is a partner, a help to human beings. So when the text here speaks of the woman *in this way*, it must mean something quite unusual. That also becomes evident from what the story depicts. God first of all forms animals out of the ground from which God has taken humankind. According to the Bible human beings and animals have the same kind of body! Perhaps the human being would find a helper who is a suitable partner among these brothers and sisters—for that is what they are, the animals who have the same origin as humankind does. The peculiar feature here is that evidently it is precisely the human being who must know whether or not this could provide a helper who is a suitable partner. Whether one of the creatures that are led before the human being would be a helper and partner depends on whether the human being would call it such. There sits wise Adam, at once calling all the animals by name and letting them pass by—the fraternal world of animals that has been taken from the same ground as has the human being. It was Adam's first occasion of pain that these brothers and sisters whom Adam loved did not fulfill the human being's own expectation. They remained a strange world to Adam; indeed they remain, for all their nature as siblings, creatures subjected to, named by, and ruled over by, Adam. The human person remains alone. As far as I know, nowhere else in the history of religions have animals been spoken of in terms of such a significant relation. At the point where God wishes to create for the human being, in the form of another creature, the help that God is as God—this is where the animals are first created and named and set in their place.

97

Yet Adam is still alone. What has come out of the ground remains alien to humankind. Now the strange thing happens that Adam must fall into a deep sleep. What the human being is unable to achieve or find while awake God does for the sleeping human being. Thus Adam essentially does not know how it happens. But Adam knows that God has made use of the human, has taken a piece of the sleeping human body, and has formed the other person from it. And it is with a true cry of joy that Adam recognizes the woman: "This at last is bone of my bones and flesh of my flesh. She shall be called woman, because she was taken out of man."

Thus Adam understands the uniqueness of this creature that God has shaped with the contribution Adam has made, out of human flesh, but Adam sees what Adam has done for the other wholly in the light of God's gift. That Eve is derived from Adam is a cause not for pride, but for particular gratitude, with Adam. Adam does not infer from it any claim for himself; instead Adam knows that he is bound in a wholly new way to this

Eve who is derived from him. This bond is best described in the expression: he now belongs to her, because she belongs to him. They are now no longer without each other; they are one and yet two. And the two becoming one is the real mystery that God has initiated by what God did to sleeping Adam. They have from their origin been one, and only in becoming one do they return to their origin. But this becoming one never means the merging of 98   the two or the abolition of their creatureliness as individuals. It actualizes to the highest possible degree their belonging to each other, which is based precisely on their being different from each other.

In what way then is Eve a "helper who is a partner" to Adam? In terms of the whole context this can only mean that the woman becomes the helper who is a partner of the man in bearing the limit imposed upon him. What does this mean? Adam was alone. In the prohibition Adam was addressed— as we have seen—as a human being, in his human freedom and creatureliness.[24] Adam had these gifts, because Adam received them in unbroken obedience—and received them in daily converse with the Creator. Adam knew of humankind's boundedness, but only in the positive sense that to Adam the idea of transgressing against the boundary was unthinkable. Adam lived his life, to be sure, within this boundary, but Adam could still not really love this life in its boundedness. Instead, between love and hate, Adam lived as one who received the divine gift with pure faith and sight. The Creator knows that this free life as a creature can be borne within its limit only if it is loved, and out of unfathomable mercy the Creator creates the helper who is a partner suitable for a human being. The helper who is a partner had to be at once the embodiment of Adam's limit and the object of Adam's love. Indeed love for the woman was now to be the human being's very life (in the deepest sense of the word).

Limit and *life* constitute the inviolable, inaccessible center of paradise 99   around which Adam's life circles. This center *takes on form* and by the hand of God the Creator becomes Adam's helper who is a partner. Knowing the other person as God's creature, simply as the other, as the other who stands beside me and constitutes a limit for me, and at the same time knowing that the other person is derived from me, from my life, and so loving the other and being loved by the other because the other is a piece of me—all that is for Adam the bodily representation of the limit that should make Adam's limit easier for Adam to bear. In other words, love for a person helps one to bear the limit. The other person is the limit that God sets for me, the limit that I love and that I will not transgress because of my love. This means

---

24. ["See above, *DBWE* 3:85 (*Reader* 232)," *DBWE* 3:98, n. 13.]

nothing other than that both people, while remaining *two* as creatures of God, become *one* body, that is, belong to one another in love. By the creation of the other person freedom and creatureliness are bound together in love. That is why the other person is once again grace to the first person, just as the prohibition against eating from the tree of knowledge was grace.[25] In this common bearing of the limit by the first two persons in community, the character of this community as the church is authenticated.[26]

This means, however, that one thing is quite certain, namely that at the point where love for the other is obliterated, a human being can only hate the limit. A person then desires only, in an unbounded way, to possess the other or to destroy the other. For now the human being insists on that human being's own contribution to, and claim upon, the other, insists that the other is derived from oneself; what the human being until now accepted humbly at this point becomes a cause for pride and rebellion. That is our world. The grace of the other person's being our helper who is a partner because he or she helps us to bear our limit, that is, helps us to live before God—and we can live before God only in community with our helper—this grace becomes a curse. The other becomes the one who makes our hatred of God ever more passionate, the one because of whom we can no longer live before God, and who again and again becomes a judgment against us. As a result marriage and community inevitably receive a new and different meaning. The power of the other which helps me to live before God now becomes the power of the other because of which I must die before God. The power   100 of life becomes the power of destruction, the power of community becomes the power of isolation, the power of love becomes the power of hate.

"That is why a man will leave father and mother and cleave to his woman, and they will be one flesh." One could say that at this point the storyteller plainly stumbles. How can Adam, who knows nothing of father and mother, say such a thing? One could also call this saying "the storyteller's own practical application" or put forward similar ways of looking at it. Deep down, however, we recognize a basic fact that until now has been kept more in the background and that now unintentionally, as it were, breaks out into the open. The Adam who speaks like this is we ourselves, we who have fathers and mothers, we who know the uniqueness of belonging to one another in the love of man and woman but for whom this knowledge has been wholly spoiled and destroyed by our guilt. This statement is not a justification for running away from the worldly order, that is, from the ties one has

---

25. ["See above, *DBWE* 3:87 (*Reader* 233)," *DBWE* 3:99, n. 15.]
26. ["See below, *DBWE* 3:100–101 (*Reader* 241–243) . . . ," *DBWE* 3:99, n. 16.]

with one's father and mother; instead it is the only possible way in which to describe the depth and seriousness of belonging to one another. This ultimate belonging to one another is, however, unquestionably associated with human sexuality. Quite plainly sexuality expresses the two complementary sides of the matter: that of being an individual and that of being one with the other. Sexuality is nothing but the ultimate possible realization of belonging to each other. It has here as yet no life of its own detached from this, its purpose.

The community of husband and wife is a community of love that is accepted as given by God and that glorifies and worships God as the Creator. It is therefore the church in its original form. And because it is the church, it is a community bound with an eternal bond. Such statements for us do not mean the glorification of marriage as we know it; instead they point out that at any rate for us the bond between husband and wife does not partake of this unambiguous reality, and that the most questionable of all the church's official functions may be precisely its role in officiating at marriage. Sexuality has torn the community of love completely to pieces, so that it has turned into an obsessive desire that affirms itself and denies the other as God's creature. This community which is based upon the claim that the one makes by reason of one's share in the other—of one's rib in the other, of the other's being derived from oneself—plainly fails to glorify the Creator in such a way that the Creator may again do the work of creation with the unknowing, sleeping human beings, Adam and Eve. Instead of such a community glorifying the Creator there is a reaching out to grasp the strength and glory of the Creator for oneself—a raising to unconscious awareness of one's own ego, a begetting and giving birth by one's own power, in an awake but delirious state. Nevertheless this profound destruction of the original human condition does not abrogate one thing: that in its deepest sense the community of husband and wife is destined to be the church (Eph. 5:30–32).

"And they were both naked, the man and his woman, and they were not ashamed."

Shame arises only out of the knowledge of humankind's dividedness, of the world's dividedness in general, and thus also of one's own dividedness. Shame expresses the fact that we no longer accept the other as God's gift but instead are consumed with an obsessive desire for the other; it also expresses the knowledge that goes along with this that the other person too is no longer content to belong to me but desires to get something from me. Shame is a cover in which I hide myself from the other because of my own

evil and the other person's evil, that is, because of the dividedness that has
come between us. Where one person accepts the other as the helper who
is a partner given by God, where one is content with understanding-one-
self-as-derived-from and destined-for-the-other, in belonging-to-the-other,
there human beings are not ashamed. In the unity of unbroken obedience
one human being stands naked before another, uncovered, revealed in
body and in soul, and is not ashamed. Shame arises only in a split-apart
world. Knowledge, death, sexuality—the relation between these three pri-   102
mal words of life is what is at issue here and in what follows.

CHAP. 3, VV. 1–3   103

THE PIOUS QUESTION

And the serpent was more cunning than all the animals in the field that Yah-
weh God had made, and it said to the woman: Did God really say, You shall
not eat from every kind of tree in the garden? And the woman said to the ser-
pent: We do eat from the fruit of the trees in the garden; but of the fruit of the
tree in the center of the garden God has said, Do not eat from it, and do not
even touch it, lest you die.

The prohibition against eating from the tree of knowledge, the creation of
Eve, and the serpent are to be understood as all links in one chain, linked
together for a common assault upon the tree of life. All come from God the
Creator, and yet now, strangely, they form a common front with humankind
against the Creator. The prohibition that Adam has heard and obeyed as
grace becomes the law that provokes wrath in human beings and in God;   104
the woman who was created to be a man's helper who is a suitable partner
and to give him the strength to bear his boundary leads him astray; the serpent, one of God's creatures, even becomes an instrument of evil.

How does this come about? To this question the Bible gives no answer,
or at any rate no unequivocal or direct answer, but only a peculiarly indirect one. Simply to blame the devil as God's enemy for bringing all this
about would be to vulgarize and distort the biblical account completely.
This is just what the Bible, for very definite reasons, does not say. Likewise
to blame the freedom of human beings to do good or evil as something
that human beings use only in the wrong way would be to misinterpret the
context completely. The characteristic and essential thing about the biblical narrative by contrast is precisely that the whole course of events takes

place in the world God has created and that no diaboli ex machina [*devils from the machine*]²⁷ are set in motion to make this incomprehensible event understandable or to dramatize it.

The *twilight* in which what has been created and what is evil appear here cannot in any way be made an unmixed light without destroying something that is decisive. The ambiguity of the serpent, of Eve, and of the tree of knowledge as creatures of God's grace and yet as the place where the voice of evil is heard must be preserved as such; it must on no account be crudely simplified and its two aspects be torn apart to make it unambiguous. For precisely this twilight, this ambiguity, in which the creation here stands constitutes the only possible way for human beings in the middle to speak about this event—and the Yahwist too was a human being in the middle. Only in this way is it possible to maintain two complementary concerns: truly to lay all the guilt on human beings and at the same time to express how inconceivable, inexplicable, and inexcusable that guilt is.

105   The Bible does not seek to impart information about the origin of evil but to witness to its character as guilt and as the unending burden that humankind bears. To pose the question about the origin of evil as something separate from this is far from the mind of the biblical author. Yet when the question is posed in the way that the biblical author poses it, the answer cannot be unequivocal or direct. It will always contain two sides: that I as a creature of God have done what is completely opposed to God and is evil, and that just for that very reason this constitutes guilt and indeed inexcusable guilt. It will therefore never be possible simply to blame the devil who has led one astray; instead this same devil will always be precisely in the place where I, as God's creature in God's world, ought to have been living and did not wish to live. It is, of course, just as impossible to accuse creation of being imperfect and to blame it for my evil. The guilt is mine alone: I have committed evil in the midst of the original state of creation. The complete incomprehensibility of this act is expressed in Genesis 3 by the fact that an evil force does not suddenly and manifestly break its way into creation from somewhere or other; instead this evil is completely veiled in the world of creation, and it takes place in creation through humankind. If an account of the fall of Lucifer had preceded this, as Catholic theology and as Luther too would have it, then Adam, as the first human being to fall

27. [". . . This is an expression of Bonhoeffer's formulated by analogy with *deus ex machina* ('the god from the machine'). The latter term refers to the figure in the theater of classical antiquity who appeared suddenly with the aid of a mechanical contrivance and solved problems by means of a 'supernatural' miracle," *DBWE* 3:104, n. 4.]

victim to this Lucifer, would in principle be exonerated. But it is precisely
in accord with the completely down-to-earth nature of the biblical account
that what prepares the way for the fall and the fall itself take place in the
midst of what has been created, and in this way the fall's complete inexcusability is expressed as plainly as possible.

"The serpent was more cunning than all the animals in the field." The
text does not state simply that the serpent is the devil. The serpent is a
creature of God, but it is more cunning than all the others. Nowhere in the   106
entire story is the devil introduced in bodily form. And yet evil takes place;
it takes place through humankind, through the serpent, through the tree.
At first it is only God's word itself that is taken up again. The serpent asks:
Did God really say, You shall not eat from every kind of tree in the garden?
It does not dispute this word, but opens the eyes of the human being to a
depth of which the human being has until now been unaware, a depth from
which one would be in a position to establish or to dispute whether a word
is God's word or not. The serpent itself at first only poses the possibility that
perhaps the human being has in this regard misheard, as God could not
possibly have meant it in that way. God, the good Creator, would surely not
impose something like that on God's own creature; that would surely be to
limit God's love.

The decisive point is that through this question the idea is suggested
to the human being of going behind the word of God and now providing it with a human basis—a human understanding of the essential nature
of God. Should the word contradict this understanding, then the human
being has clearly misheard. After all, it could only serve God's cause if one
put an end to such false words of God, such a mistakenly heard command,
in good time.

The question is thus one that is put by a forked tongue, for it plainly
wants to be thought of as coming from God's side. For the sake of the true
God, so it appears, it wants to cause the given word of God to fall. In this
way the serpent purports somehow to know about the depths of the true
God beyond this given word of God—about the true God who is so badly
misrepresented in this human word. The serpent claims to know more
about God than the human being who depends on God's word alone. The
serpent knows of a more exalted God, a nobler God, who has no need to
make such a prohibition. It wants to be somehow itself the dark root from
which the visible tree of God then first stems. And from this strongly held
position the serpent now fights against the word of God. It knows that it has
power only where it purports to come from God and to represent God's
cause. Only as the pious serpent is it evil. In posing its question it derives its
existence from the power of God alone, and it is able to be evil only where it

107 is pious. So now it purports to be the power that stands behind God's word and from which God then draws God's own power.

The question that the serpent posed was a perfectly pious one. But with the first pious question in the world, evil appears on the scene. Where evil shows itself in its godlessness, it is altogether powerless; at that point it is just a bogeyman, something we have no need to be afraid of. Indeed evil does not concentrate its power at that point at all; instead it there most often diverts attention away from the other place where it really wishes to break through. And in this latter place it is veiled in the garb of piety. The wolf in sheep's clothing, Satan in the form of an angel of light—that is the figure that is in keeping with evil. Did God really say . . . ?—that is the utterly godless question.[28] Did God really say that God is love, that God wishes to forgive us our sins, that we need only believe God, that we need no works, that Christ died and was raised for our sakes, that we will have eternal life in the kingdom of God, that we are no longer alone but upheld by God's grace, that one day all grieving and wailing shall come to an end? Did God really say: You shall not steal, you shall not commit adultery, you shall not bear false witness. . . . ? Did God really say this to me? Or does it perhaps not apply to me in particular? Did God really claim to be a God of wrath toward those who do not keep God's commandments? Did God really demand the sacrifice of Christ—the God whom I know better, the God whom I know to be the infinitely good, all-loving Father? This is the question that appears so innocuous but through which evil wins its power in us and through which we become disobedient to God. Were the question to come to us with its godlessness unveiled and laid bare, we would be able to resist it. But Christians are not open to attack in that way; one must actually approach them with God, one must show them a better, a prouder, God than they seem to have, if they are to fall.

What is the real evil in this question? It is not that a question as such is 108 asked. It is that this question already contains the wrong answer. It is that with this question the basic attitude of the creature toward the Creator comes under attack. It requires humankind to sit in judgment on God's word instead of simply listening to it and doing it. And this is achieved by proposing that, on the basis of an idea, a principle, or some prior knowl-

---

28. ["Bonhoeffer uses this text to great effect in his address on 'The Church and the Peoples of the World,' which he delivered at the crucial Life and Work ecumenical conference at Fanø, Denmark, in September 1934 (*DBWE* 13:307–310 [*Reader* 393–397]). It was at this conference that the ecumenical movement aligned itself with the Confessing Church in Germany, even if only for the moment," *DBWE* 3:107, n. 11.]

edge about God, humankind should now pass judgment on the concrete word of God. But where human beings use a principle, an idea of God, as a weapon to fight against the concrete word of God, there they are from the outset already in the right; at that point they have become God's master, they have left the path of obedience, they have withdrawn from being addressed by God. In other words, in this question what is possible is played off against reality, and what is possible undermines what is reality. In the relation of human beings to God, however, there are no possibilities: there is only reality.[29] There is no "let me first . . . " [*Luke 9:61*]; there is only the commandment and obedience.   109

For the first human being, who lives entirely within this reality, being addressed with regard to what might be possible—namely, to disobey the word of God—is equivalent to being addressed with regard to freedom, the freedom in which that human being belongs wholly to God. The first human being can be addressed in this way only when this possibility of disobeying God is veiled in the reality of 'being for God'. It is only because the question is asked in a such way that Adam understands it as a new possibility of 'being for God' that it can lead him to 'being against God'. The possibility of Adam's *own* 'wanting to be for God', as Adam's own discovery, is the primal evil in the pious question of the serpent.

It is not a piece of stupidity but the very pinnacle of the serpent's cunning that the serpent so crudely exaggerates when it asks the question: "Did God really say—'You shall not eat from every kind of tree in the garden'?" In this way the serpent has Eve on its side from the outset and compels her to acknowledge . . . No, God naturally did not say that. And already this reaction, in which Eve is made to qualify something with regard to a word of God—even though it has been misconstrued to her—must throw her into the greatest confusion. Indeed it must make her aware, for the first time, of the fascination of passing judgment on the word of God. By means of what is obviously false the serpent will now also bring about the downfall of what is right. May we be on our guard against such cunning exaggerations of God's commandment. Evil is certainly at work in them.

The serpent's question, then, proves to be *the* satanic question κατ᾽   110
ἐξοχήν (*par excellence*), *the* question that robs God of God's honor and seeks to lead human beings astray from the word of God. Against this question, which under the appearance of being pious attacks God as the ultimate

---

29. [*The rejection of possibility or potentiality in favor of reality is central to Bonhoeffer's theology. For examples,* DBWE *1:126–130 (Reader 36–38),* DBWE *9:440,* DBWE *11:403.*]

presupposition of all existence, human beings can defend themselves in no other way than with an ὕπαγε σατανᾶ [*Begone, Satan*] [*Matt. 4:10*].

Eve's answer remains on the level of ignorance. She does not know about evil; she does not recognize it. Therefore all she is able to do is to repeat the given commandment and state it correctly. And that is a great deal: she holds fast to the commandment. But in doing this she allows herself to become involved in this clever conversation. It has somehow struck a spark within her. The old order still remains intact, however. Humankind cannot go behind God's word. The tree of knowledge and the tree of life remain untouched.

111

Chap. 3, vv. 4–5

Sicut Deus [Like God]

And the serpent said to the woman: You will not die at all. Instead God knows that on the day you eat from it your eyes will be opened, and you will be like God and know what good and evil is.

The first part of the conversation is over. But Eve's answer does not forbid the serpent from trying again. So the conversation continues—the first conversation *about* God, the first religious, theological conversation. It is not common worship, a common calling upon God, but a speaking about God, about God in a way that passes over, and reaches beyond, God. Inasmuch

112 as Eve has let herself become involved in this conversation, the serpent can now risk the real attack. It speaks about God, speaks indeed with the attitude of having a deep knowledge of the secrets of God; that is, it speaks in a pious way. This mask of piety, however, is now taken off in an open attack. *Did* God really say. . . ? Yes, God *did* say. . . . But *why* did God say it. . . ? That is how the conversation proceeds. God said it out of envy. . . . God is not a good but an evil, cruel God; be clever, be cleverer than your God and take what God begrudges you. . . . God did say it, yes indeed, you are right, Eve, but God lied; God's word is a lie . . . for you will not die at all. . . . That is the ultimate possible rebellion, that the lie portrays the truth as a lie. That is the abyss that underlies the lie—that it lives because it poses as the truth and condemns the truth as a lie. "You will not die at all. Instead God knows that on the day you eat from it your eyes will be opened, and you will be like God and know what good and evil is."

It had been the very Creator who had said that this tree would impart knowledge; the only difference is that the Creator had decreed death for this deed, whereas the serpent links it with the promise of being sicut deus.

And to anticipate something that is to be spelled out only later: for humankind to become sicut deus as the serpent promises can mean nothing but what the Creator calls death. It is true that humankind becomes sicut deus through the fall; but human beings who are sicut deus human beings can no longer live—they are in a state of death. That means that the serpent, in all its attempt to pretend that God's truth is a lie, can never escape this truth. On the contrary, even in its lie the serpent *must* grant that this truth is valid; the serpent too speaks of the death of humankind, but only in another form. But more on this later.[30]

We stand here at the last point to which the biblical author brings humankind, before the abyss comes and the inconceivable, infinite chasm opens up. The chain of events—a chain that starts with God's prohibition, continues with the creation of the woman and goes on to the serpent's question, events that link up together in the struggle against the tree of life— here reaches its end. In what does this final step toward the inconceivable consist? For at this point we need to state once more[31] that it can in no way lead to what is conceivable but strictly and only toward the inconceivable. This very step has to leave the inconceivable wholly inconceivable and unpardonable.   113

"You will not die at all." "You shall die." These two statements mark the cleavage that now splits the world apart for Adam. Statement stands against statement. This goes beyond his power of comprehension; for how is he to know what a lie is? Truth against truth—God's truth against the serpent's truth. God's truth tied to the prohibition, the serpent's truth tied to the promise, God's truth pointing to my limit, the serpent's truth pointing to my unlimitedness—both of them truth, that is, both originating with God, God against God. And this second god is likewise the god of the promise to humankind to be sicut deus. God against humankind sicut deus; God and humankind in the imago dei versus God and humankind sicut deus. Imago dei—humankind in the image of God in being for God and the neighbor, in its original creatureliness and limitedness; sicut deus—humankind like God in knowing out of its own self about good and evil, in having no limit and acting out of its own resources, in its aseity [*underived being*], in its being alone. Imago dei—bound to the word of the Creator and deriving life from the Creator; sicut deus—bound to the depths of its own knowledge of God, of good and evil. Imago dei—the creature living in the unity of obedience; sicut deus—the creator-human-being who lives on the basis of the divide

---

30. ["See *DBWE* 3:135," *DBWE* 3:112, n. 4.]
31. ["Cf. above, *DBWE* 3:95 (*Reader* 238)," *DBWE* 3:112, n. 5.]

between good and evil. Imago dei, sicut deus, agnus dei [*image of God, like God, Lamb of God*]—the human being who is God incarnate, who was sacrificed for humankind sicut deus, in true divinity slaying its false divinity and restoring the imago dei.

How can Adam understand the serpent's sicut-deus-promise? At any rate not as the diabolical promise of death and of rebellion against the Creator. As one who is altogether ignorant of the possibility of evil he can understand the promise in no other way than as the possibility of being more pious, more obedient, than he is in his imago-dei-structure. Sicut deus—for Adam that can only be a new possibility within the given possibility of being a creature in the imago dei. It can only mean a new, deeper kind of creaturely being. *That* is how he is bound to understand the serpent.

114   To be sure, Adam sees that the new, deeper kind of creatureliness must be won at the cost of transgressing the commandment. And this very fact must focus his attention. Adam is in fact *between* God and God, or better, between God and a false god, in a situation in which the false god portrays itself as the true God. But what else does the false god represent to Adam but the primordial possibility for creaturely being? What else can the false god do but merely point out Adam's dependence upon the Creator and usher Adam anew into it? What can this promise—that being sicut deus will be a deeper kind of being for God—accomplish other than to enable Adam to hold fast to the given reality of the Creator and the Creator's word all the more firmly? What can the false god be to him other than the final and the most profound pointer to the only true word of God, to God the Creator? What is the false god to Adam other than the ultimate grace with which God binds humankind to God? What else is the pious conversation of Eve with the snake but the final sealing of the right that the Creator alone has over humankind? How then can Eve's answer be anything else but praise for the incomparable, incomprehensible grace of the Creator, praise that now breaks out from the *ultimate* depth of her creatureliness and her freedom for God and the neighbor

115   CHAP. 3, V. 6

THE FALL

And the woman saw that it would be good to eat from the tree and that it was beautiful to look at, and that it was an enjoyable tree to be desired because it would make one wise, and she took of its fruit and ate and also gave of it to her husband, and he ate.

Instead of any reply, instead of any further theological discussion with the serpent, what now follows is—the deed. We ask, what has happened? In the first place what has happened is that the center has been intruded upon, the boundary has been transgressed. Now humankind stands in the middle, with no limit. Standing in the middle means living from its own resources and no longer from the center. Having no limit means being alone. To be in the center and to be alone means to be sicut deus. Humankind is now sicut deus. It now lives out of its own resources, creates its own life, is its own creator; it no longer needs the Creator, it has itself become creator, inasmuch as it creates its own life. Thereby its creatureliness is eliminated, destroyed. Adam is no longer a creature. Adam has torn himself away from his creatureliness. Adam *is* sicut deus, and this "is" is meant with complete seriousness—not that Adam feels this, but that Adam is this. Losing *the limit* Adam has lost *creatureliness*. Adam as limitless or boundless can no longer be addressed with regard to Adam's creatureliness.

This faces us with a fact that is central: creatureliness and the fall are not   116
related to each other as if the fall were a creaturely act that could not abolish creatureliness but at most merely modify it or make it less good. On the contrary, the fall *really* makes the creature—humankind in the imago dei— into a creator sicut deus. In the first place, then, the right to address humankind sicut deus with regard to creatureliness no longer exists. Moreover it is no longer possible to recognize such human beings in their creatureliness, just because of their being sicut deus. From now on no human assertion can be made about human beings that fails to bear in mind, and to take into specific account, their being sicut deus. The reason for this is that such an assertion would have to come from beyond humankind; but humankind in its unlimitedness allows no such beyond out of which anything could be stated about it. Humankind's being sicut deus after all *includes* precisely its not wanting to be a creature. God alone can address humankind in a different way; that is, God alone can address humankind with regard to its creatureliness that can never be abrogated. And God does that in Jesus Christ, in the cross, in the church. Only as the truth that is spoken by God, and that we believe in for God's sake despite all our knowledge of reality, does God speak of the creatureliness of humankind.

In what does humankind's being sicut deus consist? It consists in its own attempt to be for God, to have access to a new way of 'being-for-God', that is, in a special way of being pious. Indeed this piety was supposed to consist in humankind's going back behind the given word of God to procure its own knowledge of God. This possibility of a knowledge of God that comes from beyond the given word of God is humankind's being sicut deus; for from where can it gain this knowledge if not from the springs of its own life and being? Thus for their knowledge of God human beings renounce the word

117 of God that approaches them again and again out of the inviolable center and boundary of life; they renounce the life that comes from this word and grab it for themselves. They themselves stand in the center. This is disobedience in the semblance of obedience, the desire to rule in the semblance of service, the will to be creator in the semblance of being a creature, being dead in the semblance of life.

How have things come to such a state? We shall answer this question biblically, in the following way. First, we shall once again indicate the chain of events that is now in retrospect to be understood as leading up to the deed. Second, we shall point to the infinite chasm that lies between the end of this chain of events and the deed itself. And, third, we shall correct the question itself by extricating the theological question from the speculative one and answering it.

1. It is in principle never wrong to recall the chain of events that have preceded an evil deed. Everything depends, however, on never making the chain of events itself responsible for the deed, extending it no further than the point where the chasm opens, where it becomes completely incomprehensible how the evil could have been done. Only by way of showing this incomprehensibility may the deed be retrospectively related to the chain of events preceding it. At the beginning of this particular chain of events stands the prohibition that is laid upon Adam. It points out to Adam his creatureliness and his freedom, which can be understood only as a freedom for God. Thus this very prohibition could only have made the grace of the Creator all the more apparent to Adam. But being addressed in this way with regard to his creatureliness and his freedom made the distance between the Creator and the creature all the more evident and so also had to emphasize the creature's distinct existence.

Adam's awareness of his own distinct being is then enormously intensified by the creation of woman from Adam's rib. The boundary within which

118 Adam lives has now taken on bodily form. To be sure, Adam loves this form of limit that the other, different person now constitutes; Adam also knows a piece of himself to be in it, however, so that the boundary in this bodily form alerts Adam to what Adam can rightfully claim as his own and so, in turn, to his own being.

Humankind's limit has drawn nearer, but for that reason has become all the more sharply defined. But this very revelation of the limit in bodily form, in the love he has for the other person, would have brought Adam an ever deeper knowledge of the grace of the Creator. With the creation of woman, humankind's limit has advanced into the midst of the created world. This, to be sure, did not increase the danger of transgressing against the limit; on the contrary it lessened it, for Adam would now be obliged to worship God as his only Creator all the more fervently. Nevertheless it is clear that if between the creature and the Creator the boundary were to be transgressed, then this would coincide with the transgression of the boundary within creation. Every transgression of the boundary would at the same time injure the creatureliness of the other person. Violating the tree of life would at the same time violate the other person. But how can one speak of danger at the point where an unbroken unity of obedience would make impossible any idea that the given limit could be transgressed and where the limit was known only as grace?

To this must now be added a final point. It was pointed out to the human beings that their obedience and the object of that obedience were two very different things, and that they would be under no necessity at all to let their obedience be determined by this particular object; their obedience to God would not have to consist in refraining from eating the fruit. This means that they are now made particularly aware of their freedom in unbroken obedience as something *in addition to* their creatureliness; indeed their freedom is set over against their creatureliness as a second, different entity. Yet their freedom is made out to belong to their creatureliness, so that to exercise it would be nothing other than service, the service they owe God. At this point the human beings have an ultimately clear knowledge of themselves as they stand before God. We ask, once more: Why does the created world at this point not break out in rejoicing, thanks, and praise to the Creator of a kind that never ends and never wants to end? Why does this not mean new power for a new obedience?

Eve falls first. She falls as the weaker one, as the one who is partly taken 119 from the man. But there is no excuse for her fall; she is fully her own person. Yet the culmination of the story is Adam's fall. Only when Adam falls does Eve fall wholly, for the two are after all one. Adam falls because of Eve, and Eve falls because of Adam; the two are one. They are two and yet one also in their guilt. They fall together as one, yet each carries the whole burden of guilt alone. God created humankind as man and woman—and humankind fell away from God as man and as woman.

How could it happen that Adam did not regard Eve's deed as a last sign pointing to the one who created him? He was not even able to understand what Eve had done. He was still only able to understand it as another infinite reinforcement of the serpent's word that pointed out to him his creatureliness and freedom for God. "And he ate."

2. There are three things to establish. *First,* that the act was something inconceivable and hence inexcusable. Nothing in the nature of humankind

or of creation or of the serpent can be uncovered as a basis on which to explain this event. No theory of posse peccare [*able to sin*] or of non posse peccare [*not able to sin*]³² is able to comprehend the fact that the deed was done. Every attempt to make it understandable merely takes the form of an accusation that the creature hurls against the Creator. *Second*, however, from a human point of view this deed is final; it cannot be abrogated. Otherwise Adam would be able to absolve himself from his guilt. Then his guilt would not be guilt, and Christ would have died in vain. *Third*, this deed by human beings whom God created as male and female is a deed done by humanity; no human being can absolve himself or herself from it. The guiltiness of the deed becomes immeasurable inasmuch as no one commits the deed in isolation, but each bears guilt for what the other has done. Adam falls through Eve, and Eve through Adam. This does not mean, however, that the other person thereby relieves me of my burden; instead I am infinitely burdened with the guilt of the other.

120

Because the fall of humankind is both inconceivable and finally inexcusable in God's creation, the word *disobedience* fails to describe the situation adequately. It is rebellion, the creature's stepping outside of the creature's only possible attitude, the creature's becoming creator, the destruction of creatureliness, a defection, a falling away from being safely held as a creature. As such a defection it is a *continual* fall, a *dropping* into a bottomless abyss, a state of being let go, a process of moving further and further away, falling deeper and deeper. And in all this it is not merely a *moral lapse* but the destruction of creation by the creature. The extent of the fall is such that it affects the whole created world. From now on that world has been robbed of its creatureliness and drops blindly into infinite space, like a meteor that has torn itself away from the core to which it once belonged. It is of this fallen-falling world that we must now speak.

3. The question why there is evil is not a theological question, for it presupposes that it is possible to go back behind the existence that is laid upon us as sinners. If we could answer the question why, then *we* would not be sinners. We could blame something else. So the 'question why' can never be answered except by the statement 'that' which burdens humankind so completely.

---

32. ["... The differentiation between *posse peccare* [*able to sin*] or *posse non peccare* [*able not to sin*] (as applying before the fall), *non posse non peccare* [*not able not to sin*] (after the fall), and *non posse peccare* [*not able to sin*] (the eschatological prospect) was developed by Augustine in his dispute with Pelagius. Cf. Adolf von Harnack, *History of Dogma*, on Augustine (4:175–180). See also *DBWE* 2:145–146 (*Reader* 98–99)," *DBWE* 3:119, n. 9.]

The theological question is not a question about the origin of evil but one about the actual overcoming of evil on the cross; it seeks the real forgiveness of guilt and the reconciliation of the fallen world.

CHAP. 3, V. 7   121

THE NEW THING

Then the eyes of them both were opened, and they became aware that they were naked; and they sewed fig leaves together and made themselves an apron.

"The end of God's ways is bodily existence."[33] The text does not say: Then they came to know and recognized what good and evil are; instead it says: Then their *eyes* were opened and they saw that they were naked. Are we really to understand from this that after all the whole story is about the question of the origin of love between man and woman? That eating from the tree of knowledge was the great, proud, liberating act of humankind through which it won for itself the right to love and create life? Was the knowledge of good and evil essentially the new knowledge of the child who has become an adult? Was Adam's only mistake in the end that he did not   122 rush immediately from the tree of knowledge to the tree of life to eat its fruit as well?

What is correct in all this is that what is essentially at issue here is the problem of sexuality. The knowledge of good and evil is for Adam, who lives in unity, an impossible knowledge of duality, of the whole as torn apart. This duality is comprehensively expressed in the terms tob and ra, or in our language pleasurable-good and painful-evil. And precisely the fact that pleasurable and good are so closely related deprives the moralistic interpretation of any weight. In this split, fallen world the pleasurable has in the end as much seriousness about it as the 'good', inasmuch as both alike have fallen out of their original unity. Both exist only in duality and find no way back to unity.

This breaking apart into tob and ra expresses itself first of all in Adam's relation to Eve. Eve, the other person, was the limit given to Adam in bodily form. He acknowledged this limit in love, that is, in the undivided unity of giving himself; he loved it precisely in its nature as a limit for him, that is, in Eve's being human and yet 'being another human being'. Now he has transgressed the boundary and come to know that he has a limit. Now he no longer accepts the limit as God the Creator's grace; instead he hates it as

---

33. [*A well-known saying of the eighteenth-century German theologian F. C. Oetinger.*]

God begrudging him something as Creator. And in the same act of transgressing the boundary he has transgressed the limit that the other person represented to him in bodily form. Now he no longer sees the limit that the other person constitutes as grace but as God's wrath, God's hatred, God's begrudging. This means that the human being no longer regards the other person with love. Instead one person sees the other in terms of their being over against each other; each sees the other as divided from himself or herself. The limit is no longer grace that holds the human being in the unity of creaturely, free love; instead the limit is now the mark of dividedness. Man and woman are divided from each other.

123 This means two things. First it means that the man claims his share of the woman's body or, more generally, that one person claims a right to the other, claims to be entitled to possess the other, and thereby denies and destroys the creaturely nature of the other person. This obsessive desire of one human being for another finds its primordial expression in sexuality. The sexuality of the human being who transgresses his or her boundary is a refusal to recognize any limit at all; it is a boundless obsessive desire to be without any limits. Sexuality is a *passionate hatred* of any limit. It is extreme lack of respect for things-as-they-are; it is self-will, an obsessive but powerless will for unity in a divided world. It is obsessive because it knows of a common *human being* from the beginning; it is powerless because in losing his or her limit a human being has finally lost the other person. Sexuality seeks to destroy the other person as a creature, robs the other person of his or her creatureliness, lays violent hands on the other person as one's limit, and hates grace. By destroying the other person one seeks to preserve and reproduce one's own life. Human beings create by destroying; in sexuality the human race preserves itself while it destroys. Unbridled sexuality is therefore destruction κατ᾽ ἐξοχήν [*par excellence*]; it is a mad acceleration of the fall, of the downward drop. It is affirming oneself to the point of self-destruction. Obsessive desire and hate, tob and ra—these are the fruits of the tree of knowledge.

124 From this dividedness, however, there now follows a second thing, humankind's covering itself up. Human beings with no limit, in their hatred and in their obsessive desire, do not show themselves in their nakedness. Nakedness is the essence of unity, of not being torn apart, of being for the other, of respect for what is given, of acknowledging the rights of the other as my limit and as a creature. Nakedness is the essence of being oblivious of the possibility of robbing others of their rights. Nakedness is revelation; nakedness believes in grace. Nakedness does not know it is naked, just as the eye does not see itself or know about itself. Nakedness is innocence.

Covering oneself up is the essence of a world split into tob and ra; hence in the world of tob and ra even revelation must veil itself. It is therefore a most profoundly contradictory state of affairs that human beings who are rid of all limits are, after all, compelled to point out their limit without wanting to do so, inasmuch as they cover themselves up and feel shame. In their shame human beings acknowledge their limit. This is the peculiar dialectical nature of a world that is torn apart, that human beings live in it without a limit, and so as one, yet always with hatred against the limit, and so as divided, and are ashamed in their nakedness. The shame of human beings is an unwilling pointer to revelation, to the limit, to the other, to God. For that reason the persistence of shame in the fallen world constitutes the only—even though an extremely contradictory—possibility of a sign pointing to original nakedness and the sanctity of this nakedness. This is not because shame in itself is something good—that is the moralistic, puritanical, and totally unbiblical interpretation—but because it is compelled to give unwilling witness to the fallen state of the ashamed.

That church dogmatics has sometimes seen the essence of original sin in sexuality is not as absurd as Protestants have often declared on the basis   125
of a moralistic naturalism. Knowing about tob and ra is not to begin with an abstract knowledge of ethical principles; on the contrary it starts out as sexuality, that is, as a perversion of the relation of one human being to another. And as the essence of sexuality consists of creating in the midst of destroying, so the dark secret of the nature of humankind, essentially conditioned by original sin, is preserved from generation to generation in the course of continuing procreation. The protest that appeals to the natural character of sexuality is unaware of the highly ambivalent character of every so-called 'natural' aspect of our world. The way in which sexuality is sanctified is by being restrained by shame, that is, by being veiled, and by the calling of the community of marriage, which is under this restraint, to be   126
in church. The deepest reason for this is that human beings have lost their creaturely nature; this has been corrupted by their being sicut deus. The whole created world is now covered in a veil; it is silent and lacking explanation, opaque and enigmatic. The world of human beings who are sicut deus is ashamed along with them and hides itself from their view.

CHAP. 3, VV. 8–13   127

THE FLIGHT

And they heard the steps of Yahweh God, who was walking in the garden, for the day had turned cool. And Adam hid himself with his woman from the face of Yahweh God beneath the trees in the garden. And Yahweh God called Adam and said to him: Where are you? And he said: I heard the sound of your steps in the garden, and I was afraid, for I am naked, and so I hid myself. And God said: Who told you that you are naked? You have not eaten from the tree from which I commanded you—You shall not eat from it—have you? So Adam said: The woman whom you made my companion gave to me from the tree, and I ate. Then Yahweh God said to the woman: Why did you do this? The woman said: The serpent beguiled me; that is why I ate.

Adam, as one who knows *tob* and *ra* and has fallen from unity into divided-ness, can no longer stand before the Creator. Adam has transgressed the boundary, and now he hates his limit. Indeed Adam denies the limit, as one who is sicut deus—limitless, boundless. But just as Adam, in shame, against Adam's own will, has to acknowledge the other person, so against Adam's own will Adam admits to the Creator that Adam is fleeing from his Creator, hiding from God. Adam does not boldly confront God; instead when Adam hears God's voice, Adam hides. What a strange delusion of Adam's, both then and today, to suppose that one could hide from God—as though the world were opaque to God to the same extent that it appears veiled, hidden, and opaque to us after we have fallen out with it!

128

Humankind, which has fallen away from God in a precipitous plunge, now still flees from God. For humankind the fall is not enough; its flight cannot be fast enough. This flight, Adam's hiding away from God, we call conscience.[33] Before the fall there was no conscience. Only since human-kind has become divided from the Creator are human beings divided within themselves. Indeed it is the function of conscience to make human beings flee from God and so admit against their own will that God is in the right; yet, conscience also lets human beings, in fleeing from God, feel secure in their hiding place. Thus humankind, instead of realizing that it really is in flight, is deluded by conscience into believing that its flight is a triumphal procession and that all the world is in flight before it. Conscience chases humankind away from God into its secure hiding place. Here, far away from God, humankind itself plays the role of being judge and in this way seeks to evade God's judgment. Humankind now lives truly out of the resources of its own good and evil, its own innermost dividedness from itself.[34] Con-science means feeling shame before God; at the same time one conceals

---

33. [*For other discussions of conscience, see* DBWE *2:136–161*, (*Reader* 93–109), *and* DBWE 6 passim.]

34. ["See above, *DBWE* 3:87–89 (*Reader* 233–235)," *DBWE* 3:128, n. 4.]

one's own wickedness in shame, humankind in shame justifies itself—and
yet, on the other hand, at the same time there is in shame an unintentional
recognition of the other person. Conscience is not the voice of God within
sinful human beings; instead it is precisely their defense against this voice.
Yet precisely as a defense against this voice, conscience still points to it, in
spite of all that human beings know and want.

Adam, where are you . . . ? This word of the Creator calls the fleeing
Adam away from his conscience to stand before his Creator. Humankind
is not permitted to remain alone in its sin; God speaks to Adam and halts
him in his flight. Come out of your hiding place, out of your self-reproach,
out of your cover-up, out of your secrecy, out of your self-torment, out of   129
your vain remorse. Confess who you are, do not lose yourself in religious
despair, be yourself. Adam, where are you? Stand before your Creator. This
challenge goes directly against the conscience. The conscience says: Adam,
you are naked, hide yourself from the Creator; you dare not stand before
God. God says: Adam, stand before me. God slays the conscience. Adam in
fleeing must realize that he cannot escape from his Creator. We have all had
the dream in which we want to flee from something horrible and yet cannot
flee from it. That dream is one that repeatedly rises up out of the subconscious as knowledge of this, the true situation of fallen humankind. The
same thing is now expressed in Adam's answer: I am naked, and so I hid
myself. Adam tries to excuse himself with something that accuses him. He
tries to flee further and yet knows that he has already been apprehended. I
am sinful, I cannot stand before you. As though one could use sin itself as
an excuse—the inconceivable folly of humankind! Just because you are a
sinner, stand before me and do not flee.

Adam, however, still fails to stand; instead he answers: The woman whom
you made my companion gave to me from the tree, and I ate. He confesses
his sin, but in the very act of confessing it he seeks to flee again. You gave
me the woman, not I; I am not guilty, you are guilty. The ambiguous twilight of creation and sin is turned to account. The woman was after all your
creature; it is your own work that brought about my fall. Why did you bring
forth an imperfect creation? What can I do about it? So instead of standing before God, Adam falls back on the trick learned from the serpent of
correcting what is in God's mind, of appealing from God the Creator to a
better god, a different god.[35] That is, Adam tries once again to escape. The

---

35. ["According to the heretical teaching of Marcion, who was excommunicated by
Rome in 144 c.e., the God to whom the New Testament witnesses could not be the same
as the Creator of the world about whom the Old Testament speaks. Bonhoeffer's teacher

130   woman takes to flight with him, pointing, as she does so, to the serpent—
which means that she actually points to the serpent's Creator. Adam has
not come to stand before God; he has not confessed. He has appealed to
his conscience, to his knowledge of good and evil, and on the basis of this
knowledge accused his Creator. He has not recognized the grace of the
Creator that shows itself precisely in that God calls Adam and does not let
him flee. Instead Adam sees this grace only as hate, as wrath, a wrath that
inflames his own hate, his rebellion, his desire to get away from God. Adam
keeps on falling. The fall drops with increasing speed for an immeasurable
distance.

Adolf von Harnack (1851–1930) in his 1921 book *Marcion* advanced the point of view that
one could not learn what is Christian from the Old Testament (138) . . . ," *DBWE* 3:129,
n. 7.]

14. Lectures on Christology

DBWE 12:299–360

As Bonhoeffer told the students that packed his lecture hall during the tumultuous German summer of 1933, the task of Christology is to examine "who Christ is." This deceptively simple statement charted the course through his "Lectures on Christology."[1] *Drawing on key concepts developed earlier in his theology, Bonhoeffer answers the question of "who Christ is" by claiming that Christ is person and Christ is present. This sets the boundaries of christological inquiry; proper christological reflection starts from the present person of Christ. Much of Bonhoeffer's work in the lectures is negative or critical, showing how christological thinking has failed to observe these limits. In the introduction, he shows how questions of "how Christ is," which treat Christ as an object to be understood rather than a person to be encountered, and questions of "what Christ does," which direct attention away from Christ's person toward his work, crowd out proper reflection on "who Christ is." In Part 2, he shows how the history of Christology has often thought not from Christ but toward Christ, as when metaphysical Christologies have argued toward Christ from abstract conceptions of divinity and humanity, or when historical Christologies have argued toward Christ from the historical Jesus. Christology must begin and end with "who Christ is," the person of Christ present to us in word, sacrament, and church-community. The acknowledged centrality of Christology in Bonhoeffer's thinking makes these lectures worthy of careful and repeated study.*

---

1. [*These lectures have been reconstructed on the basis of student notes since only two pages of Bonhoeffer's own lecture notes have survived. See* DBWE *12:299, n. 1.*]

Introduction
I. The Development of the Christological Question
Mystagogical silence is prattle. The silence of the church is silence before the Word. In proclaiming Christ, the church falls on its knees in silence before the inexpressible, the ἄρρητον [*inexpressible*]. To speak of Christ is to be silent, and to be silent about Christ is to speak. That is obedient affirmation of God's revelation, which takes place through the Word. The
301 church's speech through silence is the right way to proclaim Christ. σιωπῇ προσκυνείσθω τὸ ἄρρητον [*Let the inexpressible be honored with silence.*] (Cyril).

To pray is to keep silent and at the same time to cry out, before God in both cases, in the light of God's Word. Christology, as the doctrine about

---

2. ["'Form' is the translation of *Gestalt* here. It refers to an integrated structure and pattern that comprises a whole and is more than the sum of its parts. Bonhoeffer refers to the *Gestalt* of Christ extensively in *Ethics*. See especially the section 'Ethics as Formation,' in *DBWE* 6:76–102," *DBWE* 12:300, n. 3.]

Christ, is a rather peculiar area of scholarship, to the extent that Christ is the very Word of God. Christology is doctrine, speaking, the word about the Word of God. Christ is the Logos of God. Christology is logology. It is knowledge par excellence. From outside, Christology becomes the center of knowledge. The Logos we are talking about here is a person. This human person is the transcendent.

This means two things: first, that wherever the idea of the Logos is considered to be its ultimate reality, there can be no true understanding of the central character of Christology; second, that Christology, with its claim to be the center of the sphere of knowledge, stands alone. It cannot point to anything other than the transcendence of its object. The fact that the Logos became flesh, a human being, is the prerequisite, not the proof. It has to be so, because the transcendent is always only the prerequisite for our thinking, never the proof. For as an object providing proof it would no longer be the transcendent.

Only scholarship that knows itself to be within the realm of the Christian church could agree here that Christology is the center of the realm of scholarship itself. That means that Christology is the invisible, unrecognized, hidden center of scholarship, of the *universitas litterarum* [*universe of scholarship*].

All scholarly questions can be reduced to two fundamental questions: First, what is the cause of X? Second, what is the meaning of X? The first question covers the realm of the natural sciences; the second, that of the arts and humanities. The object X is grasped by natural science by being understood in its causal relationship with other objects. The object X is grasped by the arts and humanities by being understood in its relationship of meaning with other known objects. In both cases it is necessary to understand a classification of relationships; how does this object X fit into the classification that I already have at hand?

How is it possible to classify an object? This is important for the question of Christology. The object is defined, recognized, and understood by means of its possibilities, by means of its "how," by the immanent logos of human beings. The final prerequisite is determined by the human logos. But what if the final prerequisite is subject to doubt? What happens if it is claimed that the human logos is dead, condemned, superseded? What answer does the human logos give, after having been told that it is the final prerequisite? The logos repeats its old question, that of how this demand can be met within history. Thus the logos stays with the question of "how." The logos sees that its autonomy is being threatened from outside. It meets the demand made upon it by negating itself. That is the last thing it has the power to do. It is what Hegel did in his philosophy. Thus what the logos does

302

under attack from the other Logos represents not philistine self-defense but rather a great insight into its power of self-negation, for self-negation signifies the self-affirmation of the logos. So it appears that the attack on the final prerequisite has failed, for the logos has assimilated the counter Logos into itself.

But what happens if the counter Logos suddenly presents its demand in a wholly new form, so that it is no longer an idea or a word that is turned against the autonomy of the human logos, but rather the counter Logos appears, somewhere and at some time in history, as a human being, and as a human being sets itself up as judge over the human logos and says, "I am the truth" [*John 14:6*], I am the death of the human logos, I am the life of God's Logos, I am the Alpha and the Omega [*Rev. 1:8*]? Human beings are those who must die and must fall, with their logos, into my hands. Here it is no longer possible to fit the Word made flesh into the logos classification system. Here all that remains is the question: Who are you?

This is the question asked by horrified, dethroned human reason, and also the question of faith: Who are you? Are you God's very self? This is the question with which Christology alone is concerned. Every possibility of classification must fall short, because the existence of this Logos means the end of my logos. He *is* the Logos. He *is* the counter Word. We are now talking about "Being"! The question of "who" is the question about transcendence. The question of "how" is the question about immanence. But because the One who is questioned is the Son himself, the immanent question of "how" can never comprehend him. Not "how" is it possible for you

303   to exist?—that is the godless question, the serpent's question—but rather, "who" are you? The question of "who" expresses the otherness of the other. At the same time the "who question" interrogates the very existence of the one asking it. With the "who question," the person asking is queried about the limits of his or her own being. If the person asking must hear, in reply, that his or her own logos has reached its limits, then the questioner has encountered the boundaries of his or her own existence. To sum up: the question of one's existence is the question of transcendence.

In our everyday speech, the question, "Who are you?" does exist. But it can always be dissolved into the "how question." Tell me *how* you exist, tell me *how* you think, and I'll tell you who you are.

The "who question" is the quintessential religious question. It is the question that asks about the other person, the other being, the other authority. It is the question about love for one's neighbor. The question of transcendence, of existence, is the question about the neighbor; it is the question about being a person. That we are always asking the "how" question shows how we are chained to our own authority. It is the *cor curvum in se* [*the heart turned in on itself*] (Luther). When we ask, *Who* are you, we are speaking the language of the obedient Adam, but we are *thinking* the "how" of the fallen Adam.

But can *we* then really ask the question, who? Can we, when we ask *who*, really mean anything other than *how*? No, we cannot. The mystery of *who* remains hidden from us. The ultimate question for critical thinking is that it *must* ask *who* but it *can* not. That means that one can legitimately ask *who* only after the self-revelation of the other to whom one puts the question has already taken place, after the immanent logos has already been superseded. That is, the question of *who* can only be asked on condition that the answer has already been given. And this in turn means that the christological question can only be asked, as a scholarly question, within the sphere of the church, and the prerequisite for it is the fact that Christ's claim to be the Word of God is a just claim. There is only one possibility for me to be truly searching for God—that I already know who God is. There is no such thing as blindly setting out to search for God. I can only search for what has already been found. "You would not seek me if you had not already found me" (Pascal).

With that the place where our work must begin is clearly indicated. In   304
the church, where Christ has revealed himself as the Word of God, the human logos asks the question: Who are you, Jesus Christ? Logos of God! The answer is given. The church receives it every day anew. It is up to the human logos to understand the question as it is given, and to reflect upon and analyze it as it exists. But it remains always the question, "Who."

Two questions are prohibited:

(1) Whether the answer that is given is the right answer. This question has no right to be asked, because there can be no authority for our human logos to cast doubt on the truth of this Logos. Jesus's own witness to himself, then and now, stands on its own and substantiates itself. The "that" in "that God was revealed in Christ" cannot be theologically questioned.

(2) The second prohibited question is how the "that" of the revelation can be *conceived*. This question leads in the direction of trying again to get behind Christ's claim, and to ground it on our own. In doing so, our own logos is presuming on the role of the Father of Jesus Christ himself, when all we actually know is the fact of God's revelation.

Having *excluded* these two questions, what we have is the question of *who*, the question of *being*, of the essence and nature of Christ. So the christological question is in its essence an ontological question. Its purpose is to bring out the ontological structure of the *who*, without getting caught in either the Scylla of the "how question" or the Charybdis of the "that question." The early church foundered on the "how question," modern theology since the Enlightenment on the "that question." Luther, Paul, and the New Testament stayed on track through the middle.

To go back to the question with which we began: in what way is the christological question the central question of all knowledge? Insofar as it alone poses the question of existence as an ontological question about the being of Jesus Christ; insofar as the ontological question asked here is the question about the being of the person Jesus Christ; insofar as the ontological question asked here is the question of the being of Christ's person as clearly being the revealed Logos of God. Only on the basis of having been judged by this Logos can the old logos learn anew to comprehend the relative rights to which it is entitled. Only from the question of transcendence does the human logos receive the rights peculiar to it, its necessity and also

305 its limits. In this way, Christology as logology becomes that which makes all knowledge possible.

But this is only the formal side of the matter; the side that deals with content is more important. Let us ask again what happens if the claim of the counter Logos is questioned. The human logos kills the Logos of God, the Word become human, which it has just questioned. Because the human logos does not want to die itself, the Logos of God, which is death to the human logos, must die instead. The Word become human must be hung on the cross by the human logos. Then the person who was causing the worry has been killed, and along with that person, the question.

But what happens when this counter Word, though it has been killed, raises itself from the dead as the living, eternal, ultimate, conquering Word of God, when it rises up to meet its murderers and rushes at them again, appearing as the Resurrected One who has overcome death? Here the question, "Who are you?" becomes most poignant. Here it stands, alive forever, over and around and within humankind. The human being can still fight against the Word become human and kill him, but against the Resurrected One the human being has no power. We ourselves are now the ones who stand convicted. Now our question has been turned around. The question we have put to the person of Christ, "Who are you?" comes back at us: who are you, that you ask this question? Do you live in the truth, so you can ask it? Who are you, you who can only ask about me because you have been justified and received grace through me? Only when this question has been heard has the christological question been definitively formulated.

For the human being, the question of existence is the question of transcendence. Transcendence is the boundary of the being that has been given to me. The question that asks about my existence, and calls it into question, is also the question of transcendence, because it is with reference to transcendence that my own being is called into question; in theological terms, because it is only with reference to God that human beings know who they are. If the "who question" is the only question I ask that goes beyond my own being, then this is the only question that asks about transcendence and existence. The "who question" cannot be answered by human beings themselves. Even existence cannot provide the answer, because the existence of a human being cannot go beyond its own limits but remains entirely within its own frame of reference and mirrors itself to itself.

Human beings destroy the Who standing over against them. Who are you? people ask Jesus. Silence is his reply. Human beings cannot wait for the answer. They kill him. The logos cannot bear the presence of the counter Logos, because it knows that one of them must die. So the human logos kills the Jesus Christ Logos who has appeared before it and challenged it, 306 and goes on living with the unanswered question of existence and transcendence. But the counter Logos, which has risen from the dead, can no longer be killed by human beings. They either are not aware of him at all, or they are aware of him as one who asks them, Who are you? Since Christ is the Son, the question asked of Christ, Who are you? has been answered.

But what does all this mean in concrete terms? Human beings today still cannot get around the figure of Jesus Christ. They have to deal with him. Take Socrates and Goethe, for example. It may be that our education depends on the confrontation with these two. But on our confrontation with Jesus depend life and death, salvation and damnation. From an outside point of view, this is not understandable. It is from the church that we learn that the sentence on which everything else depends is this: "There is salvation in no one else" [*Acts 4:12*]. The encounter with Jesus has a different cause than does the encounter with Socrates and Goethe. One can get past the person of Goethe, because he is dead. The encounter with Jesus Christ is different. The attempts to face up to this encounter and at the same time avoid it are thousandfold.

For example, in the world of the proletariat Christ may appear to be as finished off as the church and bourgeois society as a whole. There seems to be no occasion for giving Jesus a qualified place. The church is the stultifying institution that sanctions the capitalist system. But this is not the case. The proletariat actually disassociates Jesus from his church and its religion. When the proletariat says that Jesus is a good human being, it means more than the bourgeoisie means when it says that Jesus is God. Jesus is present in factory halls as a worker among workers, in politics as the perfect idealist, in the life of the proletariat as a good human being. He stands beside members of the proletariat as a fighter in their ranks against the capitalist enemy.[3]

Dostoyevsky portrays the idiot as a Christ figure. The idiot does not isolate himself, but he is awkward and gives offense. He associates not with the powerful but rather with children, who like him. He is mocked, and he is loved. He is the fool, and he is the wise one. He is the one who bears all things and forgives all things. He is the revolutionary, and also the one who goes along with everything. He is the one who, through no intent of his own, calls attention to himself by his very existence, so that the question pops up again and again, Who are you? Are you an idiot, or Jesus Christ himself?

One could also read Gerhart Hauptmann's novel about Emanuel Quint. Or think of Grosz and his distortion of Christ. Here in the end we also have the question, Who are you really? So Jesus Christ passes through our time, through different stations and occupations in life, always being asked anew, Who are you? and yet always, when some person is aware of having confronted this question, being killed anew. These are all attempts to be finished with Christ. Even theologians do the same. Everywhere the Son of Man is betrayed with the kiss of Judas. Wanting to be finished with Christ means that now and then we kill him, crucify him, commit shameful acts against him, kneel before him with the scornful and say, "Greetings, Rabbi! [*Matt. 26:49, 27:29*]."

There are only two possibilities when a human being confronts Jesus: the human being must either die or kill Jesus. Thus the question, Who are you? remains ambiguous. It can also be the question of those who realize, as soon as they ask the question, that they themselves are meant by it, and instead of hearing the answer, hear the question in return: Who then are you? Only then is it the question of those judged by Jesus. The "who question" can only be asked of Jesus by those who know that it is being asked of them. But then it is not the human beings who are finished with Jesus, but rather Jesus who is finished with them. Strictly speaking, the "who question" can be asked only within the context of faith, and there it will receive its answer. As long as the christological question is one asked by our logos, it always remains within the ambiguity of the "how question." But as soon as it stands within the act of faith, it becomes a form of knowledge, which has the possibility of posing the "who question."

There are two contrasting types of authority in the world: the authority deriving from office, and the authority inherent in the person. When these

---

3. ["... See 'Church and Proletariat' in *Sanctorum Communio, DBWE* 1:271–274," *DBWE* 12:306, n. 15.]

two authorities confront each other, then the question posed to the authority of the person is "What" are you? The "what" means, what office do you hold? The question of the individual person to the person in authority is where do you as an individual get your authority? The answer is from myself, since I recognize your authority over me. Both questions about authority are derived from the "how question." All people are holders of some office, of some community, of themselves. Even prophets are only bearers of the word; they are not the word itself.   308

What happens, then, when someone appears who claims not only to bring the divine office and Word but actually to be that very office and Word? That is, not only to have authority but to be authority itself? Here a new existence breaks into our existence. Here the highest authority in the world, that of the prophet, is superseded. This is no longer the saint, the reformer, the prophet, but rather the Son himself. Here we no longer ask, What are you, where do you come from? Here the question asked is that of the very revelation of God.

II. The Person and Work of Christ

Christology is not soteriology. How are the two related? In his *Loci* of 1521, Melanchthon says: "Hoc est Christum cognoscere, beneficia eius cognoscere, non, quod isti (the Scholastics) docent, eius naturas, modos incarnationis contueri" [*For by them (sin, law, grace) is Christ properly known, if indeed this is to know Christ, to wit, to know his benefits and not as they (Scholastic theologians) teach, to perceive his natures and the mode of his incarnation*]. This refers the christological question back to the soteriological question and settles it there. "Who" Christ is, is known solely on the basis of his works. In consequence, Christology as such would be considered superfluous. This has been an epoch-making view and was fully developed by Schleiermacher and Ritschl. For systematics the question is do the works interpret the person or the person the works?

Luther says that everything depends on whether someone is a good person. If the person is good, then the works will be good, even if it appears to be otherwise. If the works are good, this does not allow for any conclusion to be drawn about the person. Works can appear to be good and still be the work of the devil. The devil can appear as an angel of light.

Any other view of the human person leads to justification of the person through works. Luther's thinking is that it is the person through whom the works are to be interpreted. However, it is also true that we do not really recognize the person; only God does so. "The Lord knows those who are his" [*2 Tim. 2:19*]. There is no access to the works except through the person.   309
However, our access to the person is barred by God's mysterious predestina-

tion. The attempt to grasp the person through his works cannot succeed, because the character of works remains ambiguous. There is no access to the human person, other than the person's decision to reveal himself. I cannot get to another person unless that person reveals himself to me. This self-revelation of one person to another, however, in reality takes place in the church of Jesus Christ, in the event of the forgiveness of sins, when one presents oneself to another as a sinner, confesses oneself to be a sinner, and receives from the other forgiveness for one's sin.

These thoughts are applicable to Christology. Only when I know who has done any particular work do I understand these works. Everything depends on knowing whether Jesus Christ was the idealistic founder of a religion or the very Son of God. This is no less than a matter of life or death for a human being. If Jesus was only the idealistic founder of a religion, I can be uplifted by his work and feel the urge to follow his example, but my sins are not forgiven me. In that case God is still angry with me, and my life is forfeit to death. In that case the works of Jesus would lead me to utter despair over myself.

But if the works of Christ are God's own works, then I am not called to do exactly as God does, to emulate God; instead, I am affected by these works as one who could in no way perform them myself. At the same time, through this discovery, through these works, through this Jesus Christ, I have found the God of mercy. My sin is forgiven me, and I am no longer in the realm of death, but rather in that of life. Thus it depends on the person of Christ, whether his works perish in the old world of death or last eternally in a new world of life.

But how is the person of Christ to be recognized, other than through his works? This objection contains the deepest error of all. Even the works of Christ are not unambiguous. They are open to the most varied interpretations. Christ's works permit the interpretation that he is a hero, that his cross represents the consummate act of a courageous man who is true to his convictions. There is no point in the works of Jesus to which one can unambiguously refer and say that here Jesus can truly be recognized, unambiguously and without doubt, as the Son of God on the basis of his works. This is the issue, that the Son entered into the flesh, that he wants to do his work within the ambiguity of history, incognito. This incognito is the basis for the

310 two reasons why it is impossible to recognize the person of Jesus through his work; first, because it is never possible, in human terms, to draw conclusions about a person from his works, and second, because Jesus is God, and direct conclusions about God on the basis of history are never possible either.

But if this way to knowledge is closed to me, then there is only one other way by which I can try to approach Jesus. This can happen only in relation to that place where his person reveals himself to me as he really is. Only through Christ's own revelation do I have opened to me his person and his works.

In this way, the christological question is shown to have theological priority over the soteriological question. I must first know who it is who does something before I can know what it is that the person has done. Nevertheless, it would be wrong to conclude that person and works should be considered separately. We are talking here only about the connection between the knowledge of works and the knowledge of the person, not about the real connection between person and works. The separation is only necessary for reasons of theological method. For the theological question, by nature, can only be asked of Christ in his whole being. It is the Christ of history, the whole Christ, whom we ask and who answers. But Christology asks not about what Christ has done but rather who Christ is. To put it in the abstract: The personal ontological structure of the whole, historical Christ is the subject matter of Christology.

Part 1. The Present Christ—The *pro-me* [*for me*]
As the Crucified and Risen One, Jesus is at the same time the Christ who is present now. This is the first statement: that Christ is the Christ who is present in history. He is to be understood as present in time and space. *Nunc et hic* [*now and here*], the two flow together in the concept of the church. Christ in his person is indeed present in the church as person. Thus the presence of Christ is there in the church. Only because Christ is the Christ who is present are we still able to inquire of him. Only because proclamation and the sacraments are carried out in the church can we inquire about Christ.

This has been subject to two serious misinterpretations. The presence of Christ was understood, on the one hand, as the influence that emanates from him, extending into the church-community—thus not Christ himself, but the effective influence he has had in history. This is a dynamic understanding of Christ—he is seen as an energy in history that is not lost but goes on communicating itself. The presence of Christ can be seen here as belonging to the category of cause and effect. Or, on the other hand, the   311
attempt is made to reach across history to keep bringing the image of Christ into view; the image is either that of the Enlightenment and rationalism, or that of the inner life of Jesus, as sketched by Wilhelm Herrmann. One sees the image face-to-face. (Often these two observations go hand in hand, as they do for Schleiermacher.) Ritschl subscribes to the former; Herrmann, his student, to the latter.

Here lies an error common to Christology of this kind; in both these interpretations, Christ is seen only in terms of his influence in history.

Christ is essentially power here, δύναμις [*power*], but not person. Christ is understood in terms of his works, not in terms of his person. This power can be conceived in different ways, be it as historical power or as the image of Jesus as the ideal human being shining forth anew, that is, as ideational power. Here the historical power corresponds more to the temporal character of Jesus's presence, while the image corresponds to its spatial character.

If the Christ who is present is seen in this way, Christology misses its point, because it represents Christ as power but not as person. This is also the case when efforts are made to speak of the personality of Jesus. *Personality*, in this context, means the opposite of what is meant by *person*. For personality is the fullness and harmony of the values that are summed up in the phenomenon of Jesus Christ. Personality is by nature an apersonal concept. Personality is realized in the concepts of power and value, that is, it is realized within history. The person, however, is beyond power and value, beyond influence and image. In asking about personality, one asks "how" and "what"; in asking about person, one asks "who." If Jesus, in his essence, is a power, then his being is no more than his works and his person no more than what he has done. Then conclusions about his person can only be drawn from his works. The ultimate ground for rejecting this view of Christ's presence is that such an interpretation does not take into account the resurrection of Christ. It would see Jesus Christ only as dead and gone, the way we might think about Goethe or Socrates. Only where the risen Christ is understood as the ground and the prerequisite for Christology is it possible to grasp his presence as person. The person of Jesus Christ is, in fact, its own work.

312

Luther tried to make the concept of Christ's presence understandable in terms of the concept of his ascension. By virtue of sitting at God's right hand, Christ is able to be present to us. "When he was on earth, he was far away from us here. Now that he is far from earth, he is near to us."[4] Christ's ascension means that, with Christ's distancing, his presence everywhere becomes possible. Because human thought is afraid of the resurrection, theology pushes it aside, as Ritschl and Herrmann do, or thinks of it symbolically, like Schleiermacher. Paul says, "If Christ has not been raised, your faith is futile and you are still in your sins" [*1 Cor. 15:17*]. To be present means to be in the same place at the same time (presence). We are talking about Christ's ability to be simultaneously present to us all. Even as the Risen One, Jesus remains the human Jesus. Only because he is human can he be present to us. But that he is eternally with us here, eternally with us in the now—that

---

4. [*"Cf. Luther, 'Sermon on Ascension Day'* (WA *12:562, 25–26*)," DBWE *12:312, n. 29.*]

is his presence as God. Only because Jesus is God can he be present to us.

The presence of Jesus Christ compels the statement that Jesus is wholly human, as well as the other statement that Jesus is wholly God—otherwise he would not be present. Thus, from the presence of Christ arises the two-fold certainty that he is both human being and God. Therefore it is impossible to ask how the human Jesus can be simultaneously with each of us—as if this Jesus could exist in isolation! It is just as impossible to ask how God can enter into time—as if such an isolated God could exist! The only question that makes sense is: who is present, who is with us here and now? The answer is: the human-God Jesus. I cannot know who the human Christ is if I do not simultaneously think of the God-Christ and vice versa. God in his timeless eternity is *not* God. Jesus Christ in his humanity, limited in time, is *not* Jesus Christ. Instead, in the human being Jesus Christ, God is God. Only in Jesus Christ is God present.

The starting point for Christology has to be the God-human. Time and space determine not only the humanity of Christ but also his divinity. The God-human who is present in time and space is veiled in the ὁμοίωμα σαρκός [*likeness of flesh*] (Rom. 8:3).[5] The presence of Christ is a veiled presence. But it is not God veiled in the human being; instead, the whole God-human is hidden, and it is the principle of hiddenness that is the ὁμοίωμα σαρκός.

This means the problem has shifted: it is not the relation of God and human in Jesus Christ, but rather the relation of the God-human, as already given, to the ὁμοίωμα σαρκός. The God-human is present in the form of the σάρξ [*flesh*], the form that is a stumbling block [*1 Cor. 1:23*]. The hidden form in which Christ is *present* is, for us, the church's proclamation. Jesus Christ as the already existing God-human is present to the church alone in the scandalous form of its preaching. The Christ who is proclaimed is the real Christ. It is not the hiddenness of God that is the stumbling block but rather the hiddenness of the God-human. A careful distinction must surely be made between the humanity of Christ and the humiliation of Christ. Jesus Christ is human both as the Humiliated One and as the Exalted One. Jesus Christ is a stumbling block only as the Humiliated One. The doctrine of the stumbling block has its place not in the doctrine of God's taking

313

314

---

5. [*Romans 8.3 reads "likeness of sinful flesh" which is summarized here and elsewhere in short-hand as (ὁμοίωμα σαρκός) "likeness of flesh." In Paul, σαρξ (flesh) often refers to sinfulness, as here, not to human bodiliness. Bonhoeffer distinguishes sharply between incarnation (God becoming human) and humiliation (Christ taking on human sinfulness). God is not hidden by taking on human form, i.e. God's divinity is not compromised by incarnation; but Jesus Christ is hidden and humiliated, i.e. is a "scandal" and a "stumbling block," by taking on human sinfulness in the cross. The following paragraph elaborates this argument.*]

human form but rather in the doctrine of the God-human's humiliation. Here, in the humiliation of the God-human, is where the ὁμοίωμα σαρκός belongs. For us, this means that the presence of the God-human as the Resurrected One, that is, the Exalted One, is at the same time the presence of the humiliated Christ.

As *presence* in the threefold form of Word, sacrament, and church-community, the basic question of the presence of Christ is not answered. The question is not, how can the human Jesus, or the God Jesus, be simultaneously here? The question must be, by virtue of what personal ontological structure is Christ present to the church? If one answers, by virtue of his God-humanity, that is correct but still needs explication. It is the *"pro-me"* [*for me*] structure. The being of Christ's person is essentially relatedness to me. His being-Christ is his being-for-me. This *pro-me* is not to be understood as an effect that issues from Christ or as a form that he assumes incidentally, but is to be understood as the being of his very person. The very core of his person is *pro-me*. This is not a historical, factual, or ontic statement, but rather an ontological one: that is, I can never think of Jesus Christ in his being-in-himself, but only in his relatedness to me. This in turn means that I can think of Christ only in existential relationship to him and, at the same time, only within the church-community. Christ is not in-himself and also in the church-community, but the Christ who is the only Christ is the one present in the church-community *pro-me*. This *pro-me* should not be forgotten; according to Luther, "Because it is one thing if God is present, and another if he is present for you." It is not only useless to meditate on a Christ-in-himself but godless, precisely because Christ is not there in-himself, but rather is there for you. From this perspective one can comprehend Melanchthon's aversion to Christology.

All theology and all Christology condemn themselves if they do not say right from the beginning that God and Christ can only be Christ *pro-me*. Where this *pro-me* has been assumed, there the specific work begins. But here theology has deserted its God. It has either carried on with Scholastic substance and condemned being-there-for-you to simply being-there, or else it looks only at Christ's actions, his effects. And yet what is decisive about the *pro-me* structure is that, with it, both the being and the works of Christ are maintained. Being-there-for-*you* comes together with being-*there*-for you. The presence of Christ as the *pro-me* is his real being-for-me.

The *pro-me* structure means three things for the relation of Christ to the new humanity:

(1) Jesus Christ, as the one who is *pro-me*, is the beginning, the head, the firstborn within a large family. So the *pro-me* structure refers first of all to the historical Jesus.

(2) He is there for his brothers and sisters in that he stands in their stead. Christ stands for his new humanity before God, that is, he takes their place and stands in their stead before God. If this is so, then he *is* the new humanity. There where the new humanity should stand, he himself stands, by virtue of his *pro-me* structure. That means he *is* the church-community. He is no longer acting *for* it, on its behalf, but rather *as* it, in his going to the cross, dying, and taking the sins of the church-community upon himself. Thus in him the new humanity is crucified and dies.

(3) Because Christ acts as the new humanity, he is in it, because it is in him, because in him God both judges the new humanity and pardons it.

The God-human Jesus Christ is the one who, in his *pro-me* structure, is present in his person to the church as Word, sacrament, and church-community.

I. The Form of Christ
1. Christ as Word

(1) That Christ is the Word means that he is the truth. Truth is only in the Word and through the Word. Spirit is, to begin with, Word and not power, action, or feeling. "In the beginning was the Word. . . . All things came into being through him" [*John 1:1, 3*]. Only as Word is the Spirit power and action. "The word of God is . . . sharper than any two-edged sword, piercing until it divides" [*Heb. 4:12*], it destroys. The Word of God carries within it the lightning that destroys and the rain that makes alive. As Word of God, it is the truth, which destroys and creates. God, of course, has the freedom to walk in ways unknown to us, and the freedom to choose other ways of self-revelation. But God wanted to reveal himself in the Word. God cannot speak to human beings otherwise than through this Word. God has bound himself. And God's Word never changes—that is not God's way.

316

(2) That Christ is the Word, and not a stone, means that Christ is there for the sake of humankind. Because the human being has a logos, therefore God encounters the human being in the Logos. Therefore the human being is the Homo sapiens. The truth of the human logos therefore originates in the Word, because the Word alone communicates clear and unambiguous meaning. Clarity and lack of ambiguity are of the essence of the Word. The Word interprets itself according to its nature. This clarity and consonance is the reason why it is universally valid. By entering into this human logos, Jesus Christ was humbled. Here it must be said that the Logos of God is not to be identified with, or analyzed by, the human logos.

(3) Christ as the Word of God is distinguished and separated from the human logos in that he is the Word in the form of the living Word to humankind, whereas the human word is word in the form of an idea. These

are the structures that the word as such can have: a word spoken to us, or an idea. But the two are mutually exclusive. Our human thinking still knows only the form of the word as idea. The word in this form can include the idea of openness to all. The idea is there. A human being can accept it in full freedom, can make it his own. If it is applied to Christ, it would mean that the "idea of God" that is embodied in Christ is directly accessible by any person at any time. The person needs only take possession of it.

The complete opposite is true, however, of the word that is not an idea, but rather a word spoken to us. The word as idea remains essentially within itself, but the word in the form of address is only possible as word between two persons, as speaking and response, responsibility. It is not timeless but rather takes place within history. Thus it is not generally accessible to anyone at any time but rather happens there where it is spoken to someone by another. This word is wholly subject to the freedom of the one who speaks. By nature it is a one-time event, a new event every time. By its character as word spoken by one to another, it desires community. By its character as truth, it seeks this community only by bringing the other person into the truth. Truth here is something that takes place between two persons, not something eternally at rest within itself. Truth happens only in community between two persons.

Christ as Word of God in the sense of word spoken to us does not mean Christ as timeless truth, but rather as truth breaking into a concrete moment, as God's speaking to us. Thus Christ is not timelessly and universally accessible as an idea; instead, he is heard as Word only there where he allows himself to be heard. That means it is entirely within his freedom to reveal himself to me or to hide himself from me. Christ is revealed only when and where it pleases the Father in heaven. Christ as the Word expresses both the contingent character of his revelation and his commitment to humankind. Christ is by nature, as God's Word spoken to me, *pro-me.*

(4) This prerequisite determines what the content will be. Christ is not a new concept of God or a new moral teaching. Christ is, instead, God's Word personally addressed to the human being, calling him to responsibility. That is the meaning of the statement that Christ is commandment and forgiveness. The important thing is not whether this is an old or a new commandment, or whether we have ever heard about it before or not; the important thing is where forgiveness really takes place. It is because here forgiveness really takes place that Christ is, in his person, the Word of God.

(5) The relationship of the Word to the person of Christ can be thought of in different ways. Christ can be thought of as the bearer of the idea, and Christ can be thought of as prophet. That would mean that God speaks through Christ. Christ *speaks* the Word instead of *being* the Word. The

important thing here is not his personality but his mission. To see Christ in this way contradicts the New Testament, for there Christ says of himself, "I am the way, and the truth, and the life" [*John 14:6*]. This is what happened—the quintessential, unique possibility of God's revelation was in him who, in his person, is the Word.

(6) This Christ who is the Word in person is present in the word of the church or as the word of the church. His presence is, by nature, his existence as preaching. His presence is not power or the objective spirit of the church-community out of which it preaches, but rather his presence is preaching. If this were not so, the sermon would not have the exclusive status that the Reformation gives it. The sermon is the poverty and the riches of our church. The sermon is the form of the present Christ to whom we are committed, whom we are to follow. If Christ is not wholly present in the sermon, the church breaks down. The human word and God's Word are not simply mutually exclusive; instead, God's Word, Jesus Christ, as the Word of God that has taken human form, is the Word of God that has humbled itself by entering into the human word. That is why Luther says, "This is the human being to whom you should point and say, this is God!" We say, this is the human word to which you should point and say, this is God! The two statements mean the same thing. For I cannot point to the human being unless I am pointing to this Jesus. Christ is in the church as the spoken Word in the form of both sermon and sacrament. Two statements with the same meaning stand side by side. I could not preach if I did not know that I am speaking *God's Word*, and I could not preach if it were *I* who is supposed to be speaking God's Word.

2. Christ as Sacrament

Here there are two things to be said. First: Christ is wholly Word, and the sacrament is wholly Word. Second: The sacrament is different from the Word in that it has its own right to exist in the church as sacrament.

(1) The sacrament is Word of God, for it proclaims the gospel, not as a wordless action, but as action that is made holy and given its meaning by the Word. The promise of "forgiveness of sins" makes the sacrament what it is. Whoever believes in the Word in the sacrament has received the sacrament wholly.

(2) The Word in the sacrament is the Word in bodily form. The sacrament does not represent the "Word," for only that which is not present can be represented. The sacrament is the form of the Word that, because God speaks it, becomes sacrament. The bodily form of the sacrament exists only through the Word, but only as Word, as Word in bodily form. The sacrament, in the form of nature, engages human beings in their nature.

318

The fallen creation is no longer the creation of the first Word. The "I" is no longer that which God called "I." The *people* is no longer *people*; *history* is no longer *history*; *church* is no longer *church*. With that the continuity between Word and creature has been lost. That is why the natural world is no longer a transparent world. That is why the whole creation is no longer sacrament. Sacrament exists only where God, in the midst of the world of creatures, names an element, speaks to it, and hallows it with the particular word God has for it by giving it its name. Through God's speaking to it, this element becomes what it is. This is what happens in the Lord's Supper; God hallows the elements of bread and wine by speaking the divine word. But the name of God's Word is Jesus Christ. It is through Jesus Christ that the sacrament is hallowed and given its meaning. By his Word, God has bound himself to the sacrament, that is, Jesus Christ is one who is bound by the sacrament. The God-human Jesus Christ is wholly present in the sacrament. As God spoke at the creation, "'Let there be light'; and there was light" [*Gen. 1:3*], so the Word addressed to the sacrament becomes reality.

(3) As Jesus Christ, the sacrament is essentially Word. The church's answer to the understanding of Christ as *doctrina* [*doctrine or teaching*], as generalized truth, is to maintain that Christ is sacrament, which means that in his essence, he is not *doctrina*. This refutes the error that Christ is only an idea and does not exist in both history and nature.

But not everything in nature or everything in bodily form is destined to become sacrament. Christ's presence is limited to preaching and sacrament. Why do we have precisely these sacraments? The Protestant church answers, because they are actions instituted by Jesus Christ. This should not be understood in the sense of historicism. Actions instituted by Jesus Christ should not mean anything but that, as Christ exalted and present, he gave them to his church-community. The number of sacraments in which Christ is present, and what is his will, still need no other grounds than their institution by the exalted Lord, thus purely positivist grounds. However, they are not symbols, but Word of God. They do not *mean* something—they *are* something.

(4) The sacrament is not the hiddenness of a bodiless Word of God in a body, so that the sacrament would constitute a second becoming-human of God. Instead, the Word of God made flesh, the God who has become human, the God-human, is present now in the sacrament in the form of the stumbling block. The sacrament is not the becoming-human of Christ but rather the ultimate humiliation of the God-human. This is analogous to what was said earlier, that Christology is primarily asking, not about the possible union of divinity with humanity, but rather about the hiddenness of the God-human who is present in his humiliated state. God is revealed in the flesh but hidden in the stumbling block. Consequently, the question of

Christ's presence in the sacrament can be analyzed not as the question of the humanity and divinity of Christ but rather as the presence of the God-human in humiliated form, as the stumbling block.

(5) A maze of problems has arisen in Protestant theology because the wrong questions were asked. On one hand, the question was about the possibility of the presence of Christ's humanness in the sacrament; on the other, it was about the relation between Christ's being-there and Christ's being-*pro-me*. In the words of institution of the Lord's Supper, Christ himself expressed that he wants to be present to his church as a human being. According to Luther, there is nothing more to say about it. This was the recognition that Christ as human being must be there if his works are to do us any good. Everything depends on the concurrency and presence of the human being Jesus Christ in his church. Thus for Luther the entire gospel depended on Christ's words of institution.

This was contested by saying that Christ was he who had ascended to heaven. The Reformed churches said this. Luther at first unleashed his scorn for it: God must not be imagined as confined by space, like a bird in a cage. The Reformed say that Christ remains only as Logos-person outside the sacrament of the body of Christ. Christ in his bodily form is not the Logos. He remains *extra*, outside it.

Luther answered the Reformed question in the form of his doctrine of ubiquity. He said that it is the body of Christ that, as the body of the God-human and in its communication with the divine nature itself, has taken on divine characteristics. The body of Christ is not bound by its bodily nature but is present everywhere simultaneously as the *genus majestaticum* [*the kind related to majesty*]. The resurrected body of Christ is everywhere. Luther speaks of three different ways of being in a place:

(a) Something can be in a place *localiter, circumscriptive* [*spatially, circum-* 321 *scribed*].

(b) Something can be in a place *diffinitive* [*without limitation*]. This, he said, is the way angels and demons are present.

(c) Something can be in a place *repletive* [*all-embracing*], that is, there where something is everywhere and yet not measurable in any place.

This is the way in which Christ is present. He is everywhere, and yet we cannot get hold of him. He is not in the bread like straw in a sack; instead, this *in* must be thought of in a theological, spiritual way. He is there, but he is only there where he reveals himself through his Word. Luther says: "It is merely for the sake of revelation. He is everywhere. But you will not catch him unless he offers himself to you and he himself gives the bread meaning for you through his Word. You will not eat of him, unless he wants to reveal himself to you." Christ is even in the rustling leaves, as Luther says, but his presence is not obvious; he is not there for *you*, not *pro-me*, so you cannot grope for him in the rustling leaves.

What do these statements mean for Christology? Here Christology truly becomes eucharistic Christology, that is, Christology derived from the Lord's Supper.

To the "how" question of Christ's presence, Luther has two different answers: (a) the doctrine of ubiquity in the sense of substance; (b) but Christ is only there when he wants to be there for you. This is the doctrine of ubivolipresence. Both doctrines are impossible metaphysical hypostatizations. In each of them, one element of the reality has been isolated and made into a system. Neither the one statement nor the other does justice to the facts of the matter, which must include the being-there-for-*you* and the being-*there*-for-you of Christ. The doctrine of ubiquity teaches an existence of Christ outside revelation. In this way, revelation becomes an incidental state of an existing substance. The ubivolipresence teaches the presence

322 of Christ not as a characterization of his person but rather as a promise, derived from Jesus's words, of his will to be present. Both fail to understand Christ's presence as Christ's way of being. Neither the doctrine of ubiquity nor the doctrine of ubivolipresence can express the presence of the God-human person as the exalted and humiliated Christ. They are theologically inadequate to do so. Both doctrines are necessary consequences of the "how" question in Lutheran territory, that is, of the Reformed question within Lutheran theology. This conceptual *aporia* [*impasse*] is nevertheless better, more honest and objective, than the rationalist simplification in Schleiermacher's theology, in which the content is measured and conformed to the form of the "how" question.

(6) Who is the Christ who is present in the sacrament? This is the way the question must be put. The God-human, the Exalted One! Jesus exists in such a way that he is the one who is present in the sacrament *existentialiter* [*existentially*]. His being the sacrament is not a particular desire he expresses nor a characteristic, but rather he exists by nature as sacrament in the church, and this because he is the Humiliated One. His being sacrament is his being humiliated in the present. It is not an incidental aspect of his God-human substance, but rather his existence is a humiliated existence.

What is the distinction between the Christ who is present *in* and *as* sacrament and the Christ who is present *in* and *as* Word? None. It is the one forgiving and judging Christ who is Word and remains so in both cases. In the sacrament Christ is present to us in the sphere of our body's tangible nature. Here he is by our side as a creature, in our midst as a brother among brothers and sisters. As sacrament he is the restored creation of our spirit-bodily existence; he is the new creature, and in such a way that he is the human being humiliated in bread and wine. Because he is the new creature in the bread and wine, therefore bread and wine are the new creation. Bread and wine are, by nature and *realiter* [*really*], the new food for the person who receives them in faith. As newly restored creation, they are no longer anything in and for themselves, but rather for that person. This being-for-the-person is their being newly created. Christ is present in the sacrament simultaneously as creator of all nature and as creature. As Creator, he is present as *our* Creator, who, through this new creation, makes us ourselves into new creatures. The question, "how" can this be? must be turned into the question, "who" is this who does so? And the answer is the historical, crucified, resurrected, heaven-ascended Jesus of Nazareth, the God-human, but here revealed as brother and Lord, creature and creation.

323

3. Christ as Church-Community

As Word and sacrament, Christ is present as church-community. The presence of Christ as Word and sacrament is related to Christ as church-community, just as reality is related to form. Christ is the church-community by virtue of his being-*pro-me*. He takes action as the new humanity. The church-community, between his ascension and his second coming, is the form he takes. What does it mean that Word and sacrament are the church-community?

Word exists as the word of God's church-community, that is, it exists in time and space. It is not just the poor words of human doctrine, but the mighty Word of the Creator. By speaking, it creates the form of the church-community. Church-community is Word of God, insofar as Word of God is God's revelation. Only because the church-community is itself Word of God can it understand the Word of God alone. Revelation can be understood only because it has been revealed. Word is in the church-community insofar as the church-community is that which receives the Word.

The sacrament, too, is in the church-community and is present as church-community. It does have, beyond the Word, a bodily form. This form in which it becomes bodily present is the body of Christ himself, and as such it is at the same time the form of the church-community. It is not a mere *image*; the church-community *is* the body of Christ. It is so in reality. The concept of the body as applied to the church-community is not a functional concept referring to the members but is instead a concept of the way in which the Christ exists who is present, exalted, and humiliated.

Insofar as the church-community is the church-community, it no longer sins. But it remains in the world of the old Adam, and as such it still lives in the aeon of sin. Christ's being as the church-community is, like his being as Word, a being in the form of the stumbling block.

324 II. The Place of Christ

If we ask about the place of Christ, we are asking about the "where-structure" within the "who-structure" of the Christ. Where this structure can be demonstrated, it provides the theological proof that Christ's incidental appearance in space and time is his manner of existing as a person, as the risen Lord. Where does he stand? For me, he stands in my place, where I should be standing. He stands there because I cannot, that is, he stands at the boundary of my existence and nevertheless in my place. This is an expression of the fact that I am separated, by a boundary that I cannot cross, from the self that I ought to be. This boundary lies between my old self and my new self, that is, in the center between myself and me. As the limit, Christ is at the same time the center that I have regained. As boundary, the boundary can only be seen from its other side, outside the limit. Thus it is important that we human beings, in recognizing that our limit is in Christ, at the same time see that in this limit we have found our new center. It is the nature of Christ's person to be in the center. The One who is in the center is the same One who is present in the church as Word and sacrament. If we bring the question of "where" back into the question of "who," the answer is given: Christ, as the one who is being-there *pro-me*, is the mediator. That is Christ's nature and way of existing.

Being in the center means a threefold being-there:

(1) being-there for humankind,
(2) being-there for history,
(3) being-there for nature.

This is the Christ *pro-me* translated into the "where structure." Christ's status as mediator must be proven in that he can be seen as the center of human existence, of history, and of nature.

1. Christ as the Center of Our Existence

The center of our existence is not the center of our personality. This is not a psychological statement, but rather an ontological-theological one, because it refers not to our personality but rather to the persons we are before God. Christ is not the center that we can see is here but rather the center according to our faith. In the fallen world, however, the center is at the same time a boundary. Human beings stand between law and fulfillment. We have the law but not the possibility of fulfilling the law. Christ as the center means

325 that he is the fulfillment of the law. Thus he is both the limit of human life and the court in which humankind is judged. But Christ is not only the end of our existence—its limit—but also the beginning of the new existence, and that means the center. That Christ is the center of our existence says that he is the judgment and the justification.

2. Christ as the Center of History

Any attempt to substantiate philosophically the idea that Christ is at the center of all religions, or that he is the limit or the end of all religion, must be rejected. Even here, we are not dealing with preexisting historical space. This means that all questions about Jesus as absolute are not the right questions, for these questions are comparing Christ with all other relative phenomena. This would mean that the proof would remain always connected to a relative question. The question about absoluteness is the liberal, distorted question.

Christ is at the center of history by being both its boundary and the center, that is, history lives between promise and fulfillment. History carries a promise for us, that of becoming God's people, and also the promise of the Messiah. This has become a living promise everywhere. History lives toward the fulfillment of this promise alone; this means history is essentially messianic history. The meaning of history is nothing other than the coming of the Messiah. But it is subject to this promise as an individual is subject to the law, that is, it cannot fulfill the promise by itself. History wants to glorify itself in the Messiah. History is struggling toward the impossible fulfillment of a degenerate promise. History knows about its messianic destiny but is defeated by it. There is only one place where the idea makes any headway, against the current of the messianic promise, that the Messiah cannot be the preexisting center in the midst of history's space but is and must be the hidden center of history put there by God. Thus Israel stands alone among nations with its prophetic hope. Thus Israel becomes the place where God fulfills this promise.

That Christ is the Messiah cannot be proven; he can only be proclaimed. This statement means that in Christ the messianic expectation of history is crushed as well as fulfilled. It is crushed because its fulfillment is hidden. It is fulfilled because the Messiah has truly come. The meaning of history is swallowed up in an event that takes place in the deepest desolation of human life, on the cross. History finds its meaning in the humiliation of Christ. Here, every other claim that history might make is finished, condemned, destroyed. History, with all its promises, has reached its boundary here. By its nature it has come to an end. But with that the boundary is simultaneously once again the center. In this way also, Christ is here seen to be the limit and the center of history's being. In the place where history should also stand, Christ stands before God. Thus he is also the mediator of history.

The church should be understood as the center of history. The church is the center of a history that is made by the state. The church must be understood to be the center, the hidden center, of the state. The church, as

326

the Christ who is present, gives proof of its being in the center not by being visibly at the center of the state, not by being a state church. Not through its visible position within the realm of the state does the church prove what its place is in the state, but only in that the church judges and justifies the state, assuming that it is the nature of the state, through actions that create law and order, to bring the goals of its people nearer to fulfillment. Thus in every state, behind the idea of creating order, the messianic idea lies hidden.

The church, as the center of the state, also constitutes the limit of the state, because the church recognizes and must preach that the entire promise, from a human point of view, was broken on the cross of Christ. The church thereupon becomes the fulfillment of the state's history, because in the cross it is the fulfillment of both the law and the state. The church proclaims, in the cross, both the affirmation of law and order and its ultimate breaking and abolition by God's entering into history and having to die within history.

As a result, there has been a new relation between state and church since the historical event of the cross. The state has existed in its truest sense only since there has been a church. The true origin of the state is only found together with the church, on the cross, insofar as the cross fulfills and affirms law and order and at the same time breaks through it. As a result, the cross of Christ is doubly present to us, in the forms of both the church and the state. Christ himself is present to us, takes shape, only in this twofold form, but is only present to us if we live by his cross. This is why Luther can say that the state is the "kingdom of God on the left hand." As long as Christ was on earth, he alone was the kingdom of God. Since he was crucified, it is as if his form is broken into the right hand and the left hand of God. He can now be recognized only in twofold form, as church and state. Christ as the center of history is the mediator between the state and God in the form of the church. But Christ as the center of history is just as much the mediator between the church and God, for he is also the center of the church, insofar as the church is the center of history.

3. Christ as the Center of Nature

Christ is the new creation. As the new creation, Christ makes all other creatures into the old creation. Nature is subject to the curse of God upon Adam's field, whereas it was nature's original role to be and to proclaim God's Word. But as the fallen creation it is now dumb, in servitude, not free, a creature in subjection, a guilty creature that has lost its freedom, a creature awaiting a new freedom with eager longing. Thus nature is between servitude and liberation, between servitude and redemption. Nature will receive its freedom not through reconciliation but through redemption. What are natural catastrophes if not nature's dim desire to free itself, to make itself into a new creation?

In the sacraments of the church, the old creation is set free from its servitude and obtains its new freedom. Christ cannot be proved to be the redeeming creation within nature; he can only be preached as such. The enslaved creation is, however, only redeemed into hope. In this enslaved creation a sign is set up in which the elements of the old creation become the elements of the new creation. To what extent? To the extent that they are set free from their dumb condition, from their interpretation by humankind. These elements themselves speak and say what they are. Only in the sacrament is Christ the center of nature, as the mediator between nature and God.

In summary we can say that to call Christ the center of human existence, of history, and of nature—these are never abstract matters and are never to be distinguished from one another. It is a fact that human existence is both history and nature. Christ as the center means that Christ, as the mediator for the creation in its servitude, is the fulfillment of this law, the liberation from this servitude for the whole human being. Christ is all this only because he is the one who stands in my place, in my behalf before God, *pro-me*. Christ as the mediator is precisely the end of the old, fallen world and the beginning of the new world of God.

Part 2. The Historical Christ 328
I. Access to the Historical Christ

The Christ who is present today is the historical Christ. He is the Jesus of history. If this were not so, then we would have to say with Paul that our faith would be in vain, for then the substance of our church would be taken away.

The distinction that liberal theology tries to make between the Jesus of the Synoptic Gospels and the Christ of Paul is dogmatically and historically impossible. Why? The preaching of the church would be an illusion if this distinction between Jesus and Christ were possible. But the distinction is also historically impossible. Liberal theology up to 1900 can be described as an indirect, unintended, and therefore even more emphatic confirmation of precisely this dogmatically necessary statement. Liberal theology is itself undermined by its own conclusions. It has nullified itself; thus it makes way for the statement with which we began, that Jesus and Christ are the same. For liberal theology stands and falls, first of all, by its distinction between Jesus and Christ. It considers Christ to be the Jesus who is enthusiastically idolized by the church-community. Jesus is not Christ in his own being, in his own person, but rather in his effect upon others. The judgment of

Jesus's church-community about Jesus Christ must be kept strictly separate from Jesus's actual being, says liberal theology.

Scholarly research was supposed to discover and bring forth this historical Jesus. But that was not the result it obtained. It did not prove possible to write a historically credible biography of Jesus. Then the research on Jesus's life came to a conclusion with Albert Schweitzer's dictum that the search for the historical Jesus is an impossibility. And Wrede recognized that a historical Jesus in the sense of a biography of Jesus is unimaginable, since even the Synoptic Gospel writers depended on the faith of their church-communities as their source.

This ending of liberal theology with Wrede has a twofold significance:

a. on the negative side, the actual undermining of its own presupposition, namely, that Jesus is someone other than the Christ;

329   b. on the positive side, that from now on the New Testament can only be correctly interpreted historically if its own presupposition is taken seriously, namely, that Jesus is the *Kyrios*, the Lord.

So there are the two ways out: remaining on the historical level, to see this *Kyrios*-Christ-cult and the other view of Jesus alongside each other, or to make the transition from the historical level to dogmatic studies. The result of the historical research is that Jesus cannot be separated from Christ. So it does not work to distinguish between the cult of Jesus and the religion of Christ. That result was all the more surprising because faith and research appeared to be opposed to each other. So, after pursuing liberal theology to its final outcome, one finds history and dogmatics allied once again. History has worked out anew the dogmatic assumptions of the New Testament: that the Christ who is present to us, the Christ whom we proclaim, is the historical Christ.

Martin Kähler, in his book *The So-Called Historical Jesus and the Historic Biblical Christ*, proposes both theses, that the biographical research on Jesus was a wrong track to pursue, and that the Christ whom we preach is the historical Christ. This means that dogmatics says the same thing that historical theology subsequently recognized. Thus the cardinal assertion that Jesus is the Christ is confirmed by history against its own will.

But to what degree does this dogmatic assertion depend on historical confirmation? What would happen if historical criticism at some later stage made such a dogmatic assertion impossible? What would become of our faith? Two things are to be said here. On the one hand, dogmatics does need the certainty of Jesus Christ's historical existence, that is, that Christ present and the historical Christ are identical. On the other hand, however, the question must be asked, How can dogmatics be certain of this historical truth? Can history ever sustain dogmatic assertion? If it were not so, how should we ever be able to find an access to the historical figure of Jesus Christ? Thus we need either history that is *historia sacra* [*sacred history*][6]— but this is not a good option, either theologically or empirically—or there must be an access to history from outside history. To put it another way, how can I be absolutely certain of the historical fact of Jesus Christ? Answer: an essential aspect of historical research is that it no longer considers any individual fact as an absolute. Never does everything depend on one fact alone. Every individual fact preserves an element of chance. Its absolute validity cannot be proven. If Jesus never lived, the church and our faith are damned; we would be far away from God.

330

Let us ask again: How can I be absolutely certain of the historical fact of Jesus Christ? Evidently this is too much to ask of the historical method. Our answer is

a. Historical research cannot absolutely deny a fact, any more than it can affirm one. Thus the existence of Jesus Christ cannot be absolutely denied, though one can indeed question it and say it is *probably* not so. The historical truth of Jesus Christ can therefore neither be denied nor affirmed with absolute certainty.

b. Absolute certainty about a historical fact is *in itself* not to be had; it remains a paradox. Only for the church is it essential, constitutive. What does that mean? It means that the historical fact is not in the *preterite*, but rather the present tense; that precisely that which happens by chance is the absolute, that precisely the past is that which is present; that the historical is that which is simultaneously here and now. When we can bear this contradiction, then the historical becomes an absolute. But the assertion that the historical is simultaneously present is made historically possible only through faith in the miracle that God accomplished in Jesus's resurrection.

There is no historical [*historisch*] access to the person of Jesus that can oblige us to believe. Access through the historical [*geschichtlich*] Jesus is only possible through the Risen One, through the Word by which Christ resurrected bears witness to himself. It is not so, as Wilhelm Herrmann says, that our conscience in its distress encounters Jesus in our inner life, and that through this encounter we become convinced that Jesus existed in history. Instead, it is the Risen One who himself creates faith and makes possible

---

6. ["... The Latin term refers to a particular stream of historical events understood by those within the community of faith to be the history of salvation. Secular historians interpreting the same events would not deem these events to be qualitatively different in this way, i.e., 'sacred,' and would not use the term or recognize this distinctive narrative set within a broader history," *DBWE* 12:329, n. 76.]

our access to the historicity of Jesus. After that, it is irrelevant whether history says Christ existed or not. Through faith, history is recognized by eternity, not by itself or from within itself.

Here we must keep in mind that the witness to Jesus as the Resurrected One is none other than that which is handed down to us in the Bible. Thus, as persons of faith, we remain sober and objective. We have to read this book of books with all our human resources, and even as we do so, we remain in the profane world. This is very difficult ground on which we stand. For it is difficult to preach about words that history cannot prove were actually spoken by Jesus. On the other hand, verbal inspiration means to deny the Christ who alone is present as the Risen One. Inspiration from the literal words is a poor surrogate for the resurrection. It eternalizes the historical, instead of recognizing the historical as coming from God's eternity and God's resurrection. Only if we are prepared to make our peace with this veiling of the truth within history do we know that the historical-critical method is, for us, a belief in [sentence incomplete].[7] But through the Bible in its fragility, God comes to meet us as the Risen One. Thus as long as we live on earth, we must go ahead and use historical criticism, inadequate though it is. For us, the historicity of Jesus has both aspects, that of history and that of faith. The two are linked together by our saying that this is the way the historical Jesus humbled himself, and that the historically incomprehensible Jesus is as Christ the object of faith.

The understanding of the risen Lord as a historical figure is the object of the following observation. Ancient history actually, the early church assumed Christ to be a historical figure and did not speak of Christ present, the Risen One, because it took this for granted. For us, this assumption has gradually shrunk, almost to the vanishing point. That is why we have to begin with Christ present.

II. Critical Christology or Negative Christology

This is the part of Christology that seeks to make the incomprehensibility of the person of Jesus Christ comprehensible. That which is incomprehensible is not to be turned into something comprehensible; rather, that which can be comprehended should serve to let stand that which we cannot comprehend. And in critical Christology, the goal of our effort to comprehend is the incomprehensible. It is critical because it tests every assertion about

---

7. [*According to another student's notes,* ". . . 'Faith knows that it will find Christ in this humble condition, and having found [him], faith will then be strengthened by the humble circumstances' . . . ," *DBWE* 12:331, n. 79.]

Christ against this limitation. The conclusions of critical Christology are therefore of a negative nature. This is why we say that we are speaking here of "negative Christology." Afterward, in the last section, we will develop a positive Christology.

332

Approaches to a positive Christology have always been launched by individual theologians. The decisions of the councils, however, expressed only the conclusions of critical Christology. The progress made between one council and the next was always due to the appearance of men who worked on positive Christology. The official church makes critical Christology its business—setting limits, issuing negative statements—because in the church, the proclamation of the living Christ is always taking place alongside the decisions of councils.

For us the concept of heresy no longer exists, because there is no longer a doctrinal authority vested in councils. Our ecumenical councils of today[8] are anything but councils, because the word heresy has been struck from our vocabulary. And yet the concept of heresy is a necessary, nonnegotiable factor for the confessing church. Doctrine must always be set over against false doctrine; otherwise one does not know what doctrine means. However, care must be taken that the concept of heresy be one that is used by the church out of love, not out of lack of love. For if I do not speak the truth to my brethren, I am considering them as heathens; if I do speak the truth to them, I am doing it out of love.

1. The Docetic Heresy

This is the attempt to make the incarnation of Christ so comprehensible that Jesus Christ is understood as only the appearance of the godhead in history. Christ's humanness is only the garment, the wrapping, the means by which God speaks to humankind, but is not of the essence of God's nature. "Jesus the human being as God's stained-glass window" is a shorthand formula for expressing the docetic heresy. This heresy is as old as Christianity and is still alive today.

333

This heresy gets its strength from two motives.

The first is an abstract idea of God, a doctrine of God that prefers to leave the human element to one side. The godhead is already known before its revelation, the truth is already known as an absolute idea; therefore its meaning is independent of all human nature. The origin of this thinking

---

8. ["Bonhoeffer meant the councils of the ecumenical movement (cf. his appeal to 'the one Great Ecumenical Council of the Holy Church of Christ,' *DBWE* 13:309 [*Reader* 397])," *DBWE* 12:332, n. 81.]

lies in the antithesis between idea and appearance. The docetic heresy is the typical heresy of Greek thinking, which can be generally designated as pagan thinking and which historically is the opposite of Jewish thinking. The latter had no place for docetism, because it lacked the presupposition regarding idea versus appearance.

The second motive is a certain way of thinking about redemption. The early church put it this way: human nature must be redeemed by Christ, meaning the individual human being who, in his or her individuality, has fallen. Or, as Schelling said, individuality is sin. It is the destiny of human beings to return, from captivity to individuality, to their true nature. This human nature is now common to all people. By nature they are all one. Thus redemption can be nothing other than the liberation of human beings to their true nature, in which the unity and naturalness of the entire human race is reestablished. "O human, become your essence!" says Angelus Silesius. Here he is saying the same thing that was said by the early church and later by the idealists.

When the Bible speaks of Christ's becoming human for our redemption, the becoming human is to be understood as nothing other than the prerequisite for redemption, as God's taking on the nature and essence of humanity, but not as God's becoming a human being in the sense of individuality. Because God takes on only the essence of humankind, human beings are redeemed and restored to their original essence. The question then is how can God become fully human by taking on only the general nature and essence of humankind, and not the individuality that is ours? For the early church, what was decisive was that God could not become an individual human person, because then God could not redeem humanity, and the human being would fall back into sin. The crucial thing is that God takes on human nature.

This is the starting point for the teaching of Apollinaris of Laodicea, one of the ablest and most influential dogmaticians of the early church. He taught that the God-Logos had taken on the whole nature of humankind, with flesh and soul, but had not taken on the νοῦς [*mind*] of a human being, that which governed the human being as a personality. Thus God's appearance in human nature is becoming human, but with the elimination of the individuality that is characteristic of human nature.

This refined variety of docetism was immediately detected by the church at that time and was condemned as a heretical doctrine. For then Christ would not be fully human; the becoming human of Christ would be altogether annulled and with it redemption itself. It had to be acknowledged that, in truly becoming human, Christ had taken on not only the σάρξ [*flesh*] and ψυχή [*soul*], but also the νοῦς [*mind*] of a human being. Thus the problem was posed as to how Jesus the human being could be understood as an individual person with νοῦς, yet the unity of Jesus Christ's person could be affirmed.

So the following progression becomes essential. The νοῦς is recognized as being necessary. But in the church's orthodox thinking, one suffered from the thought that this meant being human in the sense of fallen human individuality. So one shifted the problem. One now taught that it was impossible to accept that this Jesus in human form could have only one hypostasis, only one way of being. The human hypostasis of Jesus would be existing enhypostatically in the divine hypostasis. So Jesus's manner of existing was God's manner of existing. If Jesus as a human being had a hypostasis of his own, the result would be that Jesus and Christ could not be held together.

In this doctrine of "en-hypostasia," it is important for us to see that in this final rearguard action by early church dogmatics against docetism, docetism in a refined form had nevertheless crept into the early church dogmatics itself, even into orthodox dogma itself. For what is the doctrine of en-hypostasia if not an ultimately concealed form of docetism?

Where docetism goes astray is in its concept of redemption, in which a distinction is made between human nature and a human being's actual, personal way of being. It can be demonstrated that in every abstract doctrine of God and in every concept of redemption, there is at bottom the same presupposition, namely, the opposition between idea and appearance. The appearance of the human being is his individuality, and the idea of the human being is his human nature. The appearance is that which is incidental, and the idea is the substance. Jesus as a human being is incidental, as opposed to the substance that is God. Thus there is a philosophical presupposition in docetism. If one does not rid oneself of this presupposition—about idea and appearance—one will never be free of docetism in some form.

The earliest form of docetism is represented by the gnostics, specifically Basilides and Valentinus. Basilides taught that there is no way to reconcile the idea of Christ with the human being Jesus. The unity between them was only ephemeral and was dissolved at the crucifixion. At the crucifixion, Jesus ascended to heaven and triumphed over the devil. Jesus was a real human being. Only quite incidentally was he the basis for the aeon Christ.[9]

---

9. ["'Aeon' is 'spiritual being.' The reference to 'aeon' in Gnosticism is to the various emanations of God. Two of these are Jesus and Sophia, who constitute the *pleroma*, or regions of light. In gnostic teaching of the Jesus aeon, Jesus is not truly, fully human," *DBWE* 12:335–336, n. 96.]

335

336   Valentinus and his pupil Apelles taught that Jesus's body came from heaven and was not a body born of a human being. Jesus only passed through Mary. Saturninus of Antioch, however, said that Jesus was an imaginary figure. He was never born. What all three have in common is their indifference to Jesus. What is important is the idea and its development. It does not matter who he was or whether he even existed.

The early church stood against this, because it knew what the docetists of every age have forgotten, namely, that Christ was not an idea but rather an event. It is not the idea of a Redeemer that must be proclaimed, but rather Christ who must be understood as having become human. Only he can redeem real human beings. Everything depends on Jesus's existence in history. The intention was then to bring the history of Jesus into harmony with the idea of God. This is where the reductions[10] came in. The ultimate reduction was the doctrine of the "en-hypostasia." This was the insurmountable remnant of orthodox dogmatics, with the docetic presupposition. In the theological formulation, the becoming human remains conceived, in the final analysis, as incidental compared to the substance. Yet docetism was condemned as faulty.

Docetism has openly emerged again in recent Protestant theology, though in a different form. There is a new interest in the historical Jesus. There one must see the speculative concept of history. In this way of thinking, history is the carrier of certain religious ideas—it is the appearance of an idea that is above and beyond history. One of these values is, for example, the idea of the religious personality, the personality with a strong and unclouded "God-consciousness" (cf. Schleiermacher). Christ is the representative of this idea, he who embodied it in history.

Why is this docetism? Because, once again, it is not the real human being, but rather an image of the human being obtained from a particular concept of history, which is then applied to Jesus. One starts with a particular religious idea that one already has and applies it to this historical Jesus. Thus it is decisive that Jesus as a historical person is reduced to the embodiment of a religious idea. Here his becoming-human once again becomes the means to an end.

337   In Ritschl's Christology this appears very clearly. He says that Christ can only be described as God through a value judgment by his church-community. The church-community addresses him as God, and only through this judgment by the church-community does Christ become God. Ritschl

---

10. ["That is, of the historical Jesus," *DBWE* 12:336, n. 97.]

distinguishes between the being-judgment and the value judgment, that is, the church-community has a scale of values with which it comes to the historical figure of Christ and attributes these values to him. Such values, which Christ embodies, are named by Ritschl as mercy, faithfulness, lordship over the world. Jesus as a human being is the appearance of these values.

From this point on, all liberal theology must be understood in the context of a docetic Christology. Liberal theology only wanted to see, in Jesus, the embodiment of a certain doctrine. Thus the humanity of Jesus is basically not taken seriously, even though liberal theology has so much to say about Jesus as a human being. The idea of Jesus's humanity bypasses here the reality of Jesus as a human being, confuses the ideal of his humanity with its reality, in short, makes his humanity into a symbol.

The most brilliant exposition of docetism is found where the concept of idea versus appearance has been brought to perfection, in the work of Hegel. Here, the appearance is *necessarily* the taking shape of the idea. For Hegel, the becoming human is not illusion but rather *essential* appearance, the *necessary* appearance of God in history.[11] God appears by necessity. That is the nature of God. God is only God by appearing in history. It is precisely this *necessity* of the incarnation, God's becoming human, that is dangerous. It makes a principle out of something that cannot and should not be a necessity.

That God becomes a human being is, of course, that which is in principle incomprehensible; otherwise it is not a real human being about which we are speaking but rather the idea of one. God's becoming a human being is not a necessity that follows from God's self. Such a thesis, once again, misses the whole human being as a historical reality. God's becoming a human being is that which is impossible, incomprehensible, God's coming into history in a way that cannot be deduced from God. God and humanity cannot be drawn together in this relationship as a necessity.

The work of Biedermann, a Hegelian, announces the dissolution of christological dogma. Jesus of Nazareth is a replaceable figure. Christ only represents a principle. Although Biedermann denies it, this makes Jesus's humanity, his historical reality, incidental to the divine substance. With this, docetism in a pure cultural form makes its appearance in the Protestant camp.

338

---

11. ["... For Bonhoeffer's critique of Hegel, see also I. Tödt, *Dietrich Bonhoeffers Hegel-Seminar*, 11," *DBWE* 12:337, n. 101.]

The church must reject every form of docetism. Along with it, we must refuse every form of Greek idealistic thinking to the extent that it works with the distinction between idea and appearance. For with this distinction such idealism abolishes the first premise of all theology, that God, out of mercy freely given, truly became a human being, rather than becoming, out of necessity, the realization of some human principle. The rupture in every kind of docetism is its closeness to rationalism.

2. The Ebionite Heresy

The Ebionite heresy does not derive from a heathen philosophy, for which the dogma of becoming-human is foolishness. It sees in the cross of Christ the stumbling block, the slander, the dishonoring of God. Its root is in Israelite thinking, the critique of the exalting of a man to divine status. Its starting point is a strictly monotheistic belief in God. For the Ebionites, it is blasphemy to place anyone else at the same level as the *one* God. Nor is it acceptable to think of Jesus as a form in which God appeared. Israelite thinking does not countenance any metamorphosis of God as heathen-Greek-docetic thinking does. There is no possibility of giving up the monotheistic God, but rather Jesus is God's creature, thus a real human being. This is the advantage of the Ebionite heresy over docetism; its God is the God of the Bible. God is not a God of metamorphosis. But the relationship of God to this human being cannot be recognized in any way as an identity of being. The Ebionite heresy rejects the supernatural birth, on the one hand, and the preexistence of Christ, on the other, and thus rejects his divinity altogether.

Christ's significance comes through his baptism. It is here that he is accepted as the Son of God who does the will of the Father. Jesus is not one with God in substance but rather receives his status as God's Son. A development takes place in him. He *is* not God but rather becomes God, and becomes more and more so as the Spirit takes possession of him. Christ becomes God through the Holy Spirit. This becoming-God is made visible for Jewish Christians, for Ebionite heretics, in that Jesus fulfills the law through his obedience unto death. Christ is designated sometimes as God, sometimes as the prophet of truth. Jesus Christ is a human being who has been raised to divine rank. The leitmotif of Israelite thinking is the preservation of the distance between Creator and creature. The leitmotif of heathen thinking is the disregard of the Creator and creature. There, where the human being is considered a servant and a creature, and where metamorphosis is excluded from the beginning, you have Ebionite thinking. The Israelite idea of Jesus—Jesus is the human being elevated to Messiah—and the Greek idea of Jesus—Jesus was half divine—are very similar.

Yet the heathen thinking is of docetic origin, while the Israelite thinking is Ebionite.[12]

The Monarchists were concerned with preserving the unity of God. This is what interested Paul of Samosata. He gives short shrift to the divinity of the created man Jesus Christ and sees Jesus's divinity in nothing other than his willingness to bind himself to the Father. He thinks of the Spirit as an impersonal power at work in Jesus. Jesus's baptism is his calling to be the Son of God. There is a development here. Paul's teachings were condemned as heretical by the church because they diminish the divinity of Jesus.

Liberal theology likes to refer to Paul of Samosata as a forerunner. There are indeed analogies, but the reference is not justified, for liberal theology is not by nature Ebionitic but rather docetic. It recognizes the human being precisely as being of infinite value. This faith in the value of the human being is the characteristic point. This assertion also tends toward the cult of heroism and of genius.

What we have in Ebionitism is the all-obedient servant whose glory is to glorify God. Ebionitism, despite its superficially great similarity to docetic liberalism, is thus substantially superior to it, because it keeps the real human being in concrete terms, Jesus the human being, in view. Our entire salvation begins with Jesus the servant. Ebionitism keeps the real human being and the Creator God in view. The crucial thing is this: that the Ebionites do not find the way from the *real* Creator God to the *real* servant. The church must reject Ebionite thinking as heresy, because it undoes Christ's work of salvation by seeing Christ as a true human being but not *simultaneously* as true God.

340

In summary, it must be said that the concept of God's becoming human is negatively determined in such a way that its theological interpretation must reject any diminishment of full humanness or full divinity. God as human being, and human being as God, must be held together in our thinking at the risk of sacrificing the rationality of such an assertion. The positive statement on the becoming human must tread a middle path between the docetic and the Ebionite heresies. Between the two "how" questions of docetic and Ebionite theology, we must keep our eyes on the "who" question.

3. The Monophysite and the Nestorian Heresies

How must we conceive of the Person of God, if Christ really became a human being? Here we have arrived at the issue of the divinity of Christ.

---

12. [*What follows traces the Ebionite heresy and its convergence with docetism in the history of dogma.* See DBWE *12:339, n. 105.*]

Within the doctrine of the God-humanness of Christ, the Monophysite and Nestorian heresies developed.

(a) According to the Monophysites: the meaning of the person Jesus for salvation history requires that the events of salvation history be fulfilled in human nature. It is crucial that human nature, our nature, be entirely accepted by God. The key word is the ἕνωσις φυσική [*according to the oneness of nature*]. Christ is not an individual person; instead, he put on human nature like a garment. He did suffer and thirst and weep as we do, but he did so because he *wanted* to, not because it was his *nature*. For the devout believers of the early church, everything depended on the establishment of this unity between the human and the divine natures. For if God's nature had not been revealed within our human nature, how then could our nature have been made divine, been redeemed and healed!

(b) For the Nestorians: the facts of the matter according to the *Bible* are different. Here we read that Jesus was an individual person, with all the weaknesses of a human being as such, a human being who did not claim to be omniscient. Here the issue is apparently Christ's humanness. This humanness is to be understood in the fullest, realistic sense as a τέλειος ἄνθρωπος [*perfect human being*]. It is important here, however, that two distinct natures be present in Christ, and not a unity of substance, for the latter would be an offense against the Creator. We have here a ἕνωσις σχέτικη, that is, a unity of attitude, a uniting of the human will with God's, thus the distance between God and human being and there is no transformation. In contrast to the Monophysite view, the element of salvation history is set aside entirely. For how should human nature there become a new creation, if one cannot believe that the two natures were united in Christ!

341

The struggle over the doctrine of the two natures became a passionate one. For the Nestorians it was a deeply serious matter.[13] The Monophysites taught the mystery of the unity of divine and human nature; the Nestorians made a plain distinction between them, emphasizing the rationality of two entities over against the mystery of their unity. With the former, the mystery of the deification of the human; with the latter, the ethos of the servant's will gradually raising itself toward God, yielding itself to the will of God. In the one, the brighter glow of passion, the greater fervor, the more tenacious insistence; in the other, greater clarity and sobriety of thinking. On one hand, the priestly figure, like an Athanasius (who was not yet one of them); on the other hand, the laity, the ascetics who took an Arian line.

---

13. [*Another student's* ". . . notes are clearer, distinguishing between the 'greater seriousness about salvation history' of the Monophysites and the 'greater biblical seriousness' of the Nestorians," *DBWE* 12:341, n. 111.]

Inevitably it came to conflict and radicalization. On the Monophysite side, the moment of decision arrived when Eutyches of Constantinople confessed: my God is not of the same nature as we; he has no σῶμα ἀνθρώπου [*no human body*], but rather ἀνθρώπινον [*something similar to a human body*]. Christ is not an individual person; rather, he is human in essence. This radical assertion serves to defend and to settle the question of μία φύσις [*one nature*]. The Nestorians took the debate to new heights of indignation and rejection with the assertion that Mary should no longer be called the birthgiver of God.[14]

These are the two boundaries between which the real assertion about the mystery of Christ takes place. Monophysitism had to be rejected as heresy because it allowed the human nature of Christ to be swallowed up in the divine nature. Furthermore, it led to speculation about the nature of God and of the human being, through which the identity of God with the human[15] is ultimately expressed. Nestorianism had to be rejected because   342 it allowed the humanity and divinity to be so torn apart that the unity of Christ's person could no longer be conceived, so that one could no longer speak of God's becoming human.

In opposition to both these fronts, the classical formulation of the doctrine of Christ as God-human was established in the Chalcedonian formula of 451. It is said: ἕνα καὶ τὸν αὐτὸν Χριστόν . . . ἐν δύο φύσεσιν [*one and the same Christ . . . in two natures*]. That is to say:

a. ἀσυγχύτως (without confusion)

b. ἀτρέπτως (without change)

c. ἀδιαιρέτως (without distinction, contradicting the Nestorians)

d. ἀχωρίστως (without separation)

The concern here is the fully divine and the fully human nature. There is only *one* Christ. But he has two natures.

What is being said with the Chalcedonian formula is this: *that all options for thinking of all this together and in juxtaposition are represented as impossible and forbidden options.* Then there is no longer any positive assertion that can be made about what happens in Jesus Christ. In him we are to think of all possibilities about God and human being at once. Thus the matter itself is left as a mystery, for we cannot enter into it within the parameters of positive thinking. We can only enter in faith. All forms of thought are outside the realm of possibility. This means that from the Council of Chalcedon onward, it is no longer permissible to talk about the human and divine

---

14. [*This refers to the controversy over calling Mary "theotokos," which means "bearer of God" or, less literally, "mother of God."*]

15. ["That is, in Christ," *DBWE* 12:341, n. 115.]

natures of Jesus Christ as about things or facts. Thus one cannot think of a concept of God and draw a line there. To draw such a line is not permitted.

343   These negative formulations started a movement in theological thought. For theology had to abide within these conceptual tensions. That simply made things hard for the struggling theologians.

In its peculiar form, Chalcedon cancels itself out. The Chalcedonian formula itself reveals the limitations of its own concepts. It works with the concepts regarding the natures and demonstrates that these concepts are inappropriate and heretical forms. It brings the concept of substance that underlies this thinking to its high point and immediately goes beyond it, by saying that from now on assertions about the substance of Jesus Christ will no longer be permitted. If here a continuation of Chalcedon is conceivable, it is no longer a continuation of the thinking about relationships between natures, but rather something else, which we will take up later.[16] The Chalcedonian formula is an objective, living assertion about Christ that goes beyond all conceptual forms. Everything is encompassed in its very clear yet paradoxical agility.

The Chalcedonian formula was followed by a far-reaching development; people wanted to go beyond it. The orthodox and Protestant formulations said that Christ is one person in two natures (for example, this was already Tertullian's view). This was considered valid from then on. Thus was Chalcedon to be interpreted, with the soteriological leitmotif, on the one hand, and the biblical leitmotif, on the other. The representation of Christ's nature must also include the understanding that this God is completely human. Then how can it be true that Jesus is omnipotent, present, and yet only a human being? This question must be answered in such a way as neither to question the divinity of Christ nor to eliminate his humanness. Here the conceptual scheme of two natures in one person became crucial.

(c) The doctrine of the *unio hypostatica* [*unity of the person*]. The presupposition for this doctrine is that the integrity of both natures must be preserved: the divine nature in its fundamental and unchangeable essence, and the human nature in its finitude and changeability. These two assertions are first made in isolation from each other—precisely that which was forbidden by Chalcedon—and in such a way that the human nature, right from the start, no longer retained its completely human character.

344   The first assertion is thus the one that has both natures joining together in a *unitio* [*union*]. It is characterized by the divine nature's defining of the

---

16. ["This means the doctrine of the two states of Christ: that of humiliation and that of exaltation, which Bonhoeffer accepted as positive; cf. *DBWE* 12:314 and 355–360 (*Reader* 308–313)," *DBWE* 12:343, n. 121.]

human nature. The divine nature is active and suffuses the human nature, which is passive, as fire does to iron. The result of the union is the *unio personalis* [*unity of the person*], that is, the henceforth indissoluble bond between the two natures. That means that the λόγος [*Logos*] no longer exists otherwise than in the σάρξ [*flesh*]. God is no longer other than the one who has become human. God is bound up in the human being. The result of this indissoluble bond between Logos and flesh is the *unio naturalis* [*unity of natures*], the union of divinity and humanity. The *communio naturarum* [*communion of natures*] is expressed in the *propositiones personales* [*statements about the persons*]. That is to say, the concrete existence of one nature is expressed by the concrete existence of the other nature. We may say that God is the human being, but not that divinity is humanity. The two natures remain separate. But the concrete existence of God and that of the human being must be expressed by each other.[17]

What is crucial, however, is that the union of the two natures develops a *communicatio idiomatum* [*communication of properties*], that is, a sharing of the individual attributes of the two natures. This is conceived in the following terms:

(1) *The genus idiomaticum* [*the kind that refers to the properties (of the natures)*]. This says that whatever is true of the one nature or the other can be said to be true of the person as a whole. Thus, Jesus Christ was born or Jesus was born. Jesus suffers or Christ suffers. Jesus Christ suffers.

(2) *The genus apostelesmaticum* [*the kind that refers to the activities (of the person)*]. Whatever can be asserted about the person of Jesus Christ can be said of each of the two natures of Jesus Christ: Jesus Christ cleanses us from sin, or the blood of Jesus Christ cleanses us. We now can also speak of the relationship of the two natures to each other, as if divinity and humanity had an immediate relationship with each other. For Luther the crucial term is

(3) *The genus majestaticum* [*the kind that refers to the majesty (of God)*]. This 345 asserts that the attributes of the divine nature can and must be expressed by the human nature. Jesus is all-powerful; Jesus is ever-present. It is based on the "*est*" [*is*][18] in the doctrine of the Eucharist. The *genus majestaticum* is at the core of Lutheran theology. But conflicts arise here with the asser-

---

17. ["Incorrectly noted? Cf. an undated note by Bonhoeffer: 'The concrete existence of each nature can be predicated by the concrete existence of the other: "the human being (Jesus Christ) is God"; God is the human being (in Jesus Christ), but not "divinity is humanity"' (Meyer and Bethge (eds.), *Nachlaß Dietrich Bonhoeffer*, A 54,13)," *DBWE* 12:344, n. 128.]

18. [*This refers to the "is" in the Eucharist's "words of institution," where Christ says, "This is my body . . . This is my blood . . ." Luther's view of the sacrament emphasized this "is."*]

tions in the Bible. This is precisely where we come very close to the danger of Monophysitism, that is, the transformation of the human nature into the divine nature.

The Formula of Concord says in its article "Concerning the Person of Christ": "Since both natures are personally united (that is, united in one person) we believe, teach, and confess that this union is not a connection or association of the sort that neither nature shares things with the other personally (that is, because of the personal union), as if two boards were glued together, with neither giving the other anything or receiving anything from the other. Instead, here is the most complete communion, which God truly has with this human being; out of this personal union and out of the most complete and most indescribable communion that results from it flows everything human that can be ascribed to and believed about God and everything divine that can be ascribed to and believed about the human Christ. The ancient teachers of the church have explained this union and communion of the natures using similes of a glowing iron and of the union of body and soul in the human being."[19]

Reformed theologians raise three objections against Lutherans:

(1) That the person of Christ as portrayed here is not the figure of the Redeemer of whom the New Testament speaks.

(2) That Lutheran thinking has envisioned a change in God. This is not possible, because God's essence as such can never be that of human beings. The essence of each remains separate from the other, but the two natures become one.

(3) That Lutheran Christology is no longer speaking of the real humanity of Jesus.

346

Reformed thinkers assert, in opposition, that the λόγος [*Logos*] does not enter into the σάρξ [*flesh*] in such a way that it no longer exists outside the σάρξ. The λόγος remains in its Trinitarian relationship and thus apart from the flesh. There is, then, no indissoluble bond with the σάρξ. Consequently, there is a development in the human nature. There is no *genus majestaticum*, that is, no deification of human nature, because the sentence begins: *finitum incapax infiniti* [*the finite cannot bear the infinite*].[20] The two natures are

---

19. ["See the Formula of Concord, Epitome VIII, 5 (*Book of Concord*, 510)," *DBWE* 12:345, n. 135.]

20. [". . . Bonhoeffer's discussion reflects a major difference and point of conflict in the Reformation debate between Lutherans and Calvinists. The former argued that 'the finite can take on the infinite,' the latter that 'the finite cannot take on the infinite,'" *DBWE* 12:346, n. 138.]

not united in any other way than indirectly through the person, that is, what can be said about one of the two natures can be said of the person.

But what does Reformed theology make of the New Testament assertions that Jesus Christ had the authority to say, "This is my body" [*Matt. 26:26*]? This is where the concept of ἀλλοίωσις [*change*] comes in. This is all to be understood in its symbolic expression.[21] Luther was vehemently opposed to this idea, because it does not allow the Word to stand as Word. The Reformed say that the Logos is everywhere, but in a particular place as God-human. In Reformed Christology, the emphasis is on preserving clearly what belongs to God and what to humanity. The emphasis is on the pure humanity of Christ. Lutherans reply that in Reformed thinking, the two natures relate to each other like two boards glued together. But if true unity is lacking, redemption is called into question. Finitum capax infiniti non per se sed per infinitum [*the finite cannot by itself bear the infinite, but it can through the infinite*]. The criterion by which this is decided must be the Bible. The abstract separation of the two natures here is, like their abstract unity, unbiblical.

Luther spoke of the divinity and humanity of Jesus as if they were one nature. He felt it was important to see Christ's humanity as divinity. This is the origin of the doctrine of *genus majestaticum*, which teaches that Christ's human nature is suffused by the divine and receives the attributes of the divine nature. Luther does not keep Jesus separate from Christ; at least, he often does not do so. Because the danger was sensed here that one might find oneself talking of a deified human being, this doctrine of the *genus majestaticum* was complemented by the doctrine of the two states of Christ. This Jesus Christ had submitted to two different states, the *status exinanitionis* [*state of humiliation*] and the *status exaltationis* [*state of exaltation*]. This doctrine of the two states makes it possible to speak of the historical Jesus and the Redeemer Christ Jesus together as one. According to orthodox Lutheranism, the subject of the *exinanitio*, the one who is humiliated, is the one who has already become human, not the one in the process of becoming human. The one who has become human freely accepts and enters into his humiliation. Christ's nature, endowed with divine properties, humbles itself. The humiliation of Christ is an attribute only of the one who has become human, not of the Logos itself. Humiliation means that as long as he lived on earth, Jesus did not exercise his divine attributes in his human nature. Here the question is how this nonexercise of divine attributes is to be understood. Do we really have here a renunciation, an emptying of the divine attributes, in the humiliation, or is it a veiling of the divine pow-

347

---

21. [*That is, Zwingli understood the "is" in "this is my body" symbolically.*]

ers in Jesus, making them invisible? Thus the doctrine of the two states of Christ led to the argument between the *kenotic* and the *cryptic* thinkers. Those who took the former view were called the kenotics. They say that Jesus really renounced his divine attributes; the cryptics said that these were only veiled.[22]

The cryptics insisted on the identity of the one who became human, who exists in eternity, with the God-human as the one who is humiliated. The Exalted and the Humiliated One must be the same; else all would be lost. The one who must suffer would be, simultaneously, the one who would not have had to suffer. The objection is, if that were so, then Christ did not really suffer, did not really die; it would only have been an illusion that he really died. Cryptic Christology would then be a docetic Christology. It is far more a matter of a real κένωσις [*an emptying*], as in Philippians 2. Christ really died. One can speak not of a κένωσις κτίσεως [*veiling of power*], but rather of a κένωσις χρήσεως [*emptying of power*]. Christ is said to have been continually suppressing in himself the exercise of his divine attributes. If that is so, one said elsewhere, then the reality of the renunciation is lost. Then this, again, would only be an illusion.

Cryptics and kenotics eventually agreed on an unpretentious formulation: The humiliated Christ made use of his godly attributes when he wanted to and did not use them when he did not want to. The issue of the κτίσις [*possession*] of the divine attributes was put aside. In either case, one sees a glimmer of the divine attributes (but this can cause harm to the concept of faith). Here the entire christological problem is shifted to a different level. It is now concerned with the one God-human, but in two different states (this is important to the kenotics), with the identity of the God-human and yet in two different forms of being God-human, one veiled, one visible.

The doctrine of kenosis was taken up again in the nineteenth century, revived by Thomasius and Geß. Kenosis had the same appeal for them (uniting Christ with the Logos image) as for the Lutherans. They shifted it by applying it to the Logos rather than the God-human. The Logos, humbling itself, becomes a human being. What does this turnaround signify? A simplification of the understanding of Christ. For the modern kenotics, the renunciation of the divine attributes takes place in the beyond, in a metaphysical act of the Logos. The historical picture of Jesus Christ is thus freed from the inner violence of needing to repress them.

---

22. [*Bonhoeffer is referring to a seventeenth-century intra-Lutheran debate between the cryptics based in the theology faculty at Tübingen, who argued that in the state of humiliation Christ hid his divine properties, and the kenotics based in the theology faculty at Gießen, who argued that Christ emptied himself of those properties. See Pelikan,* From Luther to Kierkegaard, *57–58.*]

But this raises the question of what kind of renunciation it was. Thomasius says that God has both relative and immanent attributes. The immanent attributes are those that belong to God's absolute nature. The relative attributes concern God's relationship to the world. These include God's being all-powerful, ever-present, and all-knowing. God's immanent attributes are holiness, love, truth. For Christ it is only valid to say that he bore God's immanent attributes, not the relative ones. Thus Jesus Christ as a human being was not all-powerful, ever-present, all-knowing, but he did possess the truth, the love, and holiness of God.

349

Geß is not happy with this; he goes further. He says that in Christ God renounces his entire divine nature, that in Christ God entirely gives up being God, and only through the gradual self-awareness of Jesus returns to self-understanding as God. Biedermann called this the consummate kenosis of the mind, of which nobody could make any sense.

None of these attempts succeeded. First of all, they diminish the divinity of Jesus by having only a part of him become human through God becoming human. But everything depends on the whole of God, the Omnipotent and Glorious One, being the one who becomes human and who comes to meet us in Jesus. This is one of the first statements in theology—that wherever God is, God is wholly there. Second, they do not make the humanity of Jesus understandable. They fill it out with some divine characteristics, making it the form of a demigod living on earth. The kenosis doctrine tries to play down the divine nature. The divine and human natures are attuned to each other in such a way as to make them fit each other. A concept of the divine and a concept of the human are worked out and put together in such a way that they cannot get away from each other. They must match without the slightest unevenness. If the smallest detail is not right, the whole point is missed.

This whole attempt misses the point, in its very conception, for the following reasons:

(a) If we compare the results it obtains with the Chalcedonian formula, we see that the attempt has again been made to evade the contradictory, mutually exclusive opposites, and to try and even them out. These theologians thought they could define *in abstracto* [*in the abstract*] the divine and human natures in such a way that they had to fit into each other. This would simplify the problem. The recognition of the real Jesus Christ was turned into a construction.

(b) The doctrine of kenosis is, for Lutheran dogmatics, a necessary complement to the *genus majestaticum,* with which the kenotic theologians juxtapose a *genus tapeinoticum* [*the kind that refers to lowliness*]. This amounts straightaway to a rejection of the doctrine of the two natures altogether,

350

since it goes beyond the negative definitions at which the Chalcedonian formula had arrived. Here we have a construction of the affirmation of Christ, and not the unvarnished assertion of the "who." Here the question is the "how." The Chalcedonian formula is an answer to the "how" question, but it is an answer in which the "how" question has already been surmounted. In the Chalcedonian formulation, the doctrine of the two natures has itself been surmounted. We must carry on in this Chalcedonian sense. This can only happen when we have overcome our way of thinking about the divinity and humanity of Christ as objects that are before us, when our thinking does not begin with the two natures in isolation, but rather with the fact that Jesus Christ is God. The *is* may not be interpreted any further. It has been established by God and is therefore the premise for all our thinking and not subject to any further constructions.

Since the Chalcedonian formula, we can no longer say, how shall we think about the difference of the two natures and the unity of the person? but rather: who is this human being who is said to be God?

4. The Modalist and the Subordinationist Heresies
Here we are dealing with assertions about the person of Jesus Christ as that of the God who became human in his sonship to God, in his *homoousia*. If we could not speak of the *homoousia*, none of what we have said up to now would make any sense.

The concept of the ὁμοουσία has gone through various transformations. Here ὁμοουσία means not similarity of substance but rather identity of substance.[23] Why is it necessary to assert this? Because this is the only way to maintain the biblical witness to the revelation of God in Jesus Christ, because this is the only way we can speak of revelation. Revelation presupposes that the God revealed to us is identical with God himself; otherwise we would have not a revelation of God but only an appearance or an idea. So, to say that Christ became a human being compels us to say that Christ is identical with God in substance. Any attempt to depart from this toward a ὁμοιούσιος [*similar in substance*] goes straight in the direction of the Arian ἀνόμοιος [*unlike*].[24]

351

The subordinationists were concerned with preserving the unity and monarchy of God. These would be destroyed if a second God had to be accepted. Therefore Jesus had to be thought of as ἀνόμοιος, dissimilar to

---

23. [*The Council of Nicaea (325 C.E.) relied on the concept of* ὁμοουσία *(homoousia, meaning same substance or same essence) to claim that the Son of God was the same substance as the Father.*]

24. ["Refers to Arius's assertion that the Logos was in every way unlike the *ousia* of the Father," *DBWE* 12:351, n. 162.]

God, or at most as ὁμοιούσιος, like God. This seems to be the only way to preserve the unity of God, though certainly a unity at the expense of revelation, since we can only speak of revelation when we are talking about a human being of the same substance as God. Then this would not be a revelation in the decision about my life that is being made. It is an either-or question: the unity of God or revelation.

This puts before us the profound error of any subordinationist Christology. For this is precisely not the way to preserve the unity of God; rather, it breaches it. If Christ is understood as a human being who is exalted to the rank of God, who in his substance is not God but human and nevertheless is revered as God, if there is a demigod standing between God and humankind, this demigod totally contests the unity of God. It opens the door wide to polytheism. Modern Arianism has revered Christ as a genius or a hero and thereby breaches the content of the revelation.

A clear attempt to think of the unity of Christ and revelation together is what we have in modalism.

The modalists. For the modalists, Christ is the πρόσωπον [*face*] of God, that is, the form in which God appears. The question for us is, does this take the concept of revelation seriously? The concepts of revelation and monotheism represent a challenge each to the other. As God's revelation, Christ is either identical in substance to the Father, or revelation gets thrown out along with monotheism. Both are wrong, Christ as πρόσωπον and as the adoptionist theory. The particularity of Christ's person is that he is God's revelation; it is identity of substance between the Son and the Father. Two natures—one person; two states—one God-human; two divine persons— Father and Son, and yet one God.

5. What Has Been Gained from Critical Christology

We should distinguish between the following boundaries drawn against the false Jesus Christ. On the one hand, limits against false theological content; on the other, against inappropriate ways of thinking.

Those characterized as false theological content are those that attempt to assert something about Jesus Christ with unambiguous directness. Whoever, for the sake of Jesus's full humanity, sees Christ's divinity only as an ultimate, virtuoso human achievement is condemned as an Ebionite. Whoever speaks of the unity of Jesus Christ's person without speaking of its being God-human is rejected as a Monophysite or a Nestorian. The point of critical theology is to indicate the limits of every assertion as they are found in the actual reality of Jesus Christ.

What we have here is a particular way of thinking within which theological thinking takes place. All the thinking of the early church was based on

352

the fundamental concept of nature. Liberal theologians say that it was the introduction of the concept of nature that has corrupted all of dogmatics. But it must be said in opposition that nothing is further from being a product of Greek thinking than the Chalcedonian formula. In the early church οὐσία is not to be thought of as the antithesis of nature and ethos. οὐσία really means here the essence of God, what God is all about, the entirety of God. The error of the *ousia* concept lies not in the twisting of the moral understanding into a physical understanding but rather in that it speaks of the nature of God and human nature in the theoretical manner of an onlooker, as if these were two material things, normally distinguished from each other, which only come together in Jesus Christ. But the relation between God and human being should be understood never as the relation between two things but only as that between two persons. Nothing can be known about either God or human being, until God has become a human being in Jesus Christ.

The advantage of the *ousia* concept, over against the dynamic understanding of the Logos (as in Paul of Samosata), rests in the fact that the nature concept understands salvation straightaway as universal. Consequently, the reality of salvation can be spoken of differently from the way it is conceived if nature itself is seen as deified. The dynamic view also assumes two separate natures. It *constructs* the God-human, rather than letting the fact of the God-human stand as the presupposition. And letting this stand is precisely the result that Christology achieves in the Chalcedonian formula! The forms of thinking shaped by materiality are rejected. Critical theology does not admit them, in that it points to the fact itself. Only at this point do we begin to know who God is.

353

What has been gained from critical theology can be summed up in three thoughts:

(1) It has gone beyond the one unambiguous positive assertion about Jesus Christ; instead it has opened this assertion into two that stand over against each other (in the Chalcedonian formula).

(2) It has overcome material thinking in Christology; this has been overcome in an immanent sense, in that material thinking has come up against its own limitations. Material thinking reaches its limit at the point where it has to acknowledge that the opposite, contradictory assertion is just as necessary as its own assertion. When this limitation is acknowledged, then there is space for that which is actually, factually true.

(3) It has gone beyond the "how" question. This has been overcome in an immanent sense, since the "how" question subverts itself. The result of critical theology is the recognition that this "how" of relationship is impossible to think through.

How can we now construct a positive Christology on the foundation of this critical Christology?

III. Positive Christology
1. The One Who Became Human
Who is this God? He is the God who became human as we became human. He is completely human. Nothing human is foreign to him. The human being that I am is what Jesus Christ was also. We say of this human being, Jesus Christ, that he is God. This does not mean that we already knew before-hand who God is. It also does not mean that the assertion that this human being is God adds something onto his being human. God and human are not thought of together through a single concept of nature. The assertion that this human being is God means something else altogether. This per-son's being God is not something added onto the being human of Jesus Christ. It is not a continuum, into which Jesus Christ just manages to extend himself, but rather this assertion that this person is God *is the vertical Word from above* that neither takes anything away from nor adds anything to Jesus Christ, but rather qualifies this entire human being as God. *It is God's judg-ment about this human being!* It is God's Word, which takes this human being Jesus Christ and qualifies him as God. But the essential difference between him and all other human beings is that the Word of God that comes from above is at the same time right here in Jesus Christ himself. Because Jesus is himself God's judgment about him; he points both to himself and to God. 354

This does away conclusively with the attempt to unite two isolated exist-ing realities. We believe that Jesus the human being is God, and that he is so as *the* human being, not in spite of his humanity or beyond his humanity. It is Jesus Christ the human being who ignites faith. Jesus Christ is God, not in a divine nature, but rather God in our faith alone, thus no longer in a way that we can touch and describe. If we are to describe Jesus as God, we would not speak of his being all-powerful or all-knowing; we would speak of his birth in a manger and of his cross. There is no "divine nature" as all-powerful and ever-present.

We have the reports of Jesus's birth and of his baptism side by side. In the birth narrative, the focus is on Jesus himself; in the baptism story, the focus is on the Holy Spirit coming from God. The difficulty in thinking of both these stories together, of birth and baptism, is in the doctrine of the two natures. If we leave that out, then we are speaking in the one instance of the Word of God being in Christ, and in the other of the coming down of the Word of God spoken over Christ. The child in the manger is God. The naming of Jesus as God's son at his baptism is the confirmation of the earlier event. If we speak of the human being Jesus Christ as we speak of

God, we should not speak of him as representing an idea of God, that is, in his attributes as all-knowing and all-powerful, but rather speak of his weakness and manger.

We should speak not of God becoming human but of the God who became human, for the former is a "how" question, to be found in the old doctrine of the virgin birth. The biblical witness is uncertain with regard to the virgin birth. If the biblical witness really gave this as a fact, the dogmatic lack of clarity about it would have nothing to say. The doctrine of the virgin birth is supposed to express how God becomes human. But does it not result in the decisive point being missed, that Jesus became like us? This question remains open, because the Bible leaves it open.

God who became human is the God of glory; God glorifies himself in the human. This is the ultimate mystery of the Trinity. From "now unto eternity" [*Ps. 41:13*], God regards himself as the God who became human. God's self-glorification in the human is thus the glorification of the human, which shall have eternal life with God the Three in One. Therefore, it is not right to see God's becoming human as judgment upon humankind. God remains human even after the judgment. God's becoming human is God's message about the glorification of God, who honors himself by being in human form.

God's becoming human means first of all simply the revelation of the Creator through the creature. It is wrong to derive God's becoming human from an idea, such as the idea of the Trinity. When we speak of God's becoming human as glorifying God, we are not talking about a speculative idea of God. Every idea of God on which the doctrine of God's becoming human could be speculatively based is impossible, because the relationship of the Creator to the creature is conceived as a necessity.

Why does that sound so improbable and strange to us? Because God's becoming human in Jesus Christ does not visibly glorify God; because God who became human is the Crucified One.

2. The Humiliated and Exalted One
To speak of Jesus's being humiliated is not to put any limit on his divinity. It is a question put to Jesus as a human being, about his way of existing as a human being. To be humiliated does not mean to be *more* human and *less* God, and to be exalted does not mean to be *more* God and *less* human. Both in being humiliated and in being exalted, Jesus remains wholly human and wholly God. The assertion that he is God must be made in the same way in his being humiliated as in his being exalted. In his death, Jesus does not reveal any of his divine attributes. To the contrary, he is a dying human being, despairing of God. And of this one we say, this is God. God is not

concealed in Christ as a human being but rather is revealed as God-human. But this God-human is veiled in his existence as the Humiliated One. In Christ's being humiliated, we are talking about neither divinity nor humanity, but rather the ὁμοίωμα σαρκός [*likeness of flesh*]. For this is cast off when he is exalted, but his humanity remains.

The question now is who is the God-human who is humiliated? The doctrine of God who became human and the humiliation of Christ must be kept radically separate. Taking on the humiliated way of life is an act of the God-human. It is not to be separated in time from the act of having become human, but rather the God-human of history is always, already, the God-human who is humiliated, from the manger to the cross.

How is Jesus's particular way of existing as the Humiliated One expressed? In that he has taken on sinful flesh. The conditions for his humiliation are set by the curse, the fall of Adam. In being humiliated, Christ, the God-human, enters of his own free will into the world of sin and death. He enters there in such a way as to conceal himself there, so that he is no longer recognizable visibly as the God-human. He comes among us humans not in μορφὴ θεοῦ [*form of God*] but rather incognito, as a beggar among beggars, an outcast among outcasts; he comes among sinners as the one without sin, but also as a sinner among sinners. This is the central problem for all Christology.

The doctrine that Jesus was without sin is not just one word, one doctrine among others, but rather the central point that decides everything. The question is this: Did Jesus, as the God-human who is humiliated, enter wholly into human sin? Was he a human being like us, with our sinfulness? If he was not, then did he really become human at all? Can he help us human beings at all? And if he was as we are, in the same peril in which we are, how can he help us escape that peril?

What we need to understand is what is meant by the ὁμοίωμα σαρκός [*likeness of flesh*]. This is the true image of the human σάρξ [*flesh*]. His σάρξ is our σάρξ. What is essential about our σάρξ is our vulnerability to temptation, our self-will. Christ took on all the mortifying aspects of being human; otherwise he could not help us in our σάρξ. Then how was he different from us? The first answer is, not at all. He is a human like us and is tempted as we are, even more than we are. In his σάρξ too there was a law, which was opposed to the will of God. It was a constant struggle for him. He also did things that appeared to be sins. He gave a hard answer to his mother in the temple; he evaded his opponents' questions; he called for resistance against the ruling castes of the pious and of people. In people's eyes, he must have looked like a sinner. So he entered in, to the extent of being unrecognizable.

357

But what is all-important is that *he* was the One who entered therein, who did this and that, which the onlookers in his life could only reckon as transgressions. And because this *One* is Christ, these assertions must be seen in another light. It is the true human σάρξ that he bears; that is why the σάρξ is stripped of its rights. He is afraid like us; he is tempted as we are and thus is under the same condemnation as we are. But because *this One* is subject to the same condemnation as we, therefore we are saved. As *the One* who he is, Jesus was afraid like us. On this basis, of *the One* who he is, we must dare to make and to endure all the most scandalous assertions about this God-human who has been humiliated.

For our sake God made him to be sin. Christ is the very *peccator pessimus* [*worst sinner*]. Luther even said that Christ was a robber, murderer, and adulterer like ourselves, because he carries our sins. But *he* is at the same time the One who is without sin, the Holy One, the Eternal, the Lord, the Son of the Father.

We cannot speak of balancing these two assertions against each other, as if it were yet possible to tear Jesus, in his humiliated state, from the ὁμοίωμα σαρκός. He lets the law have its way and takes from it and upon himself sin and the power of sin. He is in the ὁμοίωμα σαρκος, yet without sin, tempted as we are in the ὁμοίωμα σαρκός, yet without sin. The statement about his being without sin goes astray if it is focused on the deeds of Jesus that have been reported to us. These actions took place within the ὁμοίωμα σαρκός. We can and should see in them the ambiguity of good and evil. If someone prefers to remain incognito, it is an offense to say, "But I saw you right away." Therefore we should not base his being without sin on his actions. The statement about Jesus being without sin in his actions is not a judgment within a moral system but rather a recognition, through the eyes of faith, of the One who does these things, the One who is without sin for all eternity.

358 The statement about Jesus being without sin is not a moral pronouncement but rather an insight of faith.

The God-human who is humiliated is the stumbling block to the pious human being and to the human being, period. What is scandalous is the lack of historical clarity of this God-human. The most incomprehensible thing for the pious is this human being's claim to be not only a believer in God but the Son of God. Hence the authority with which Jesus says, "But I say to you" [*Matt. 5:22*], and, "Your sins are forgiven" [*Matt. 9:2*]. If Jesus's human nature had been deified, people would have accepted this claim. If he had done signs and wonders on demand, people would have believed him. But when it comes down to cases, he withdraws. That creates a stumbling block. But everything depends on the fact that he did so. If he had replied to the question, are you the Christ? by doing a miracle, then the statement that he became a human being like us would no longer be true, since at the decisive moment an exception would have been made. That is why Christ's incognito had to become even more impenetrable, the more urgently people asked whether he were the Christ.

This means that the form of the stumbling block is the form that makes possible all our faith in Christ. That is, Christ in the form of stumbling block is in the form of *Christus pro nobis* [*Christ for us*]. Because Jesus wants to be our freedom, he must first become a stumbling block for us before he can be our salvation. Only by being humiliated can Christ become *pro nobis*. If he had documented himself by performing miracles, we would indeed believe, but then Christ would not be our salvation, because that would not be faith in God become human but only recognition of a supposedly supernatural event. But that is not faith. Faith exists when I yield myself to God, to the extent that I will wager my life on God's Word, even and especially there where it goes against all visible appearances. Only when I give up having visible confirmation do I believe in God. The only guarantee that faith can bear is the Word of God itself.

Christus pro nobis is the Christ who reconciles me with God, and that is only possible through this stumbling block and through faith. The stumbling block, which we accept, is that our faith is continually tested. But this teaches us to pay attention to the Word. Faith comes through temptation.

From this point, how are we to understand that Jesus performed miracles? Didn't that jeopardize his incognito? Liberalism replies that miracles are ghost stories of their time. We reply that the miracles of Jesus do not jeopardize his incognito. The ancient religious world was full of miracles. That is to say, the realm of miracles is not identical with God's realm. The realm of miracles is only superior to that of humankind. The category to which miracles belong is not that of God but rather that of magic. When Jesus performed miracles, he was preserving his incognito in a world of magic. Doing miracles did not serve to authenticate him either; to the contrary, people thought his power was demonic.

359

The believing community, however, saw in him that the kingdom was near. That still did not lift his incognito for those who did not believe. The unbeliever speaks of magic and means the world in its ambiguity. The believer speaks of the kingdom of God. Our age, which does not believe in magic, is inclined to consider miracles as an unambiguous, visible manifestation of the divine. The miraculous itself is still ambiguous and needs interpretation. It can be interpreted through faith or through lack of faith. The unbeliever does not see God in the miraculous; only the believer does so. Faith that cleaves to the incognito sees, in these miracles, something of the glory of God. "We have seen his glory" [*John 1:14*]. Only *in faith* is there seeing.

The Humiliated One is *pro nobis* only as the Exalted One. Only in seeing him as the Risen One, the Exalted One, do we know this incognito God-human. We have the One who was born as a baby as the Ever-Present One, the One laden with sin as the One without sin. So the converse must also be true: we can have the Exalted One only as the Crucified One. The resurrection of Christ does not get us around the stumbling block. Even the Risen One remains the stumbling block for us. If it were not so, he would not be for us. Jesus's resurrection does not jeopardize the incognito. We only believe in the resurrection of Jesus if we do not take away Jesus Christ as the stumbling block. Only the disciples see the Son of God. They see with the eyes of blind faith, because as believers who see nothing they become, as such, those who see, in their belief in God's glory.

Between the humiliation and the exaltation of Christ lies the historical fact of the empty grave. This is one of the most decisive elements in Christology. What does the story of the empty grave mean before the report of the resurrection? If the grave is really empty, then it is the visible authentication of the resurrection. If it is not empty, then Christ was not resurrected. It seems as though our "resurrection faith" is bound up with the story of the empty grave. If the grave were not empty, we would not have our faith.

360

This is the final stumbling block, which we have to accept as believers in Christ. Either way, there is a stumbling block. The impossible possibility that the grave was empty is the stumbling block of faith. The affirmation of the empty grave is also a stumbling block. Who is going to prove to us that the disciples did not find Jesus's body? Here once again we cannot get around the stumbling block. To the very end, even through the empty grave, Jesus remains incognito, in the form of a stumbling block. Jesus does not emerge from his incognito, not even as the Risen One. He will not lay it aside until he comes again, for the Last Judgment. Then he will come visibly as the Eternal, the God who became human, in divine power and glory.

With the humiliated Christ, his church must also be humiliated. It cannot seek any visible authentication of its nature, as long as Christ has renounced doing so for himself. Nor may it, as a humiliated church, look upon itself with vain self-satisfaction, as though being humiliated were the visible proof that Christ is with it. There is no law here, and the humiliation of Christ is not a principle for the church to follow but rather a fact. Even the church can be high, and it can be lowly, if only both conditions occur for the sake of Christ. It is not good for the church to hasten to proclaim its lowliness. But it is not good either for the church to hasten to proclaim its greatness and power; it is only good for the church to seek forgiveness for its sins.

Even the church, as the presence of Jesus Christ—God who became human, was humiliated, resurrected, and exalted—must receive the will of God every day anew from Christ. For the church, too, Christ becomes, every day anew, an offense to its own desires and hopes. The church must stumble every day anew over the sentence, "You will all become deserters because of me" [*Matt. 26:31*] and it must hold on to the promise, "Blessed is anyone who takes no offense at me" [*Matt. 11:6*].

PART 3
Ecumenical and Pastoral Writings

15. Report on a Conference
of the World Alliance

DBWE 11:165–169

Bonhoeffer's theological education, international experience, and growing proficiency in English prepared him well for the international ecumenical work he pursued upon returning from the United States. His efforts focused on the World Alliance for Promoting International Friendship among the Churches, an organization which he served as Germany's youth secretary.[1] The selection below is Bonhoeffer's report on the World Alliance's 1931 conference in Cambridge, England.[2]

As Bonhoeffer relates in the opening lines, this conference met against the background of a "world crisis." With this phrase, Bonhoeffer likely had in mind a number of issues, including the economic devastation facing North America and Europe following the New York stock-market crash of October 1929, as well as the recent Japanese invasion of China. Foremost, however, is clearly the rearmament of the European nations, which he took as a violation of the 1920 League of Nations covenant as well as the 1919 Versailles Treaty.[3]

The publication of this report in a theological journal (Theologischer Blätter) *was appropriate since many of "those who view[ed] the World Alliance with disinterest or resentment" were theologians. Paul Althaus and Emanuel Hirsch, whose theologies tied Christianity with nationalism, had recently published in the same journal a statement suspicious of ecumenical organizations.[4] Such statements were incompatible with Bonhoeffer's deepening sense that Christianity could not be reconciled with "Germanism."[5] Bonhoeffer had his own frustrations with the ecumenical movement,*

---

1. [DBWE *11:9–11, editors' introduction. For more on Bonhoeffer's ecumenical work in 1931–1932, see* DB-ER, *238–255.*]

2. [*For more on this conference specifically, see* DB-ER, *189–202.*]

3. [DBWE *11:165–166, nn. 3–9.*]

4. [DBWE *11:35, n. 6.*]

5. [DBWE *11:159.*]

*though, chief among them the superficiality of its theology and the vacuity of its resolu-
tions, as discussed in the report below.*

165   The International Conference of the World Alliance for Promoting
International Friendship through the Churches
in Cambridge (September 1–5, 1931)

Those who view the World Alliance with disinterest or resentment should
take the opportunity either to confirm their judgment based on the results
of the Cambridge meeting or to revise it. The forthcoming disarmament
conference in Geneva[6] and the world crisis, whose problems are not insigni-
ficantly related to it, dictated the theme of the conference for the assembled
166 representatives of the churches. In the disarmament question, which was
the banner under which the conference took place, the important thing
for the churches was not primarily the political debate among the nations
that were particularly affected by it, but rather the question whether the
nations that are presently rearming will be resolved to stand by their given
word (in Article 8 of the League of Nations covenant and in the Preamble
of Part V of the Versailles treaty) or whether, by breaking their word, the
first attempt toward a moral order in international relations among nations
shall hopelessly collapse. At the very edge of the abyss of yet another complete moral chaos in the lives of the nations, the churches are standing firm
and summon all to truthfulness and faithfulness, to respect and honor the
foresworn promise. The honor of the rearming nations and the justice of
this cause are at stake. The English and the Americans expressed this at the
conference with unparalleled clarity. Even the French presentation on the
167 disarmament question was in agreement with this thinking and, furthermore, was characterized by an extension of the concept of *securité* [*security*]
as a fundamental international principle, as opposed to their previously
narrower version. This included a clear recognition of the justice of the
German position, which means that an attempt was made to engage with
deep sincerity on the level of unconditional equality of rights that serve the
common cause. In this way, the conference was able to issue the proclamation unanimously to the churches of the world that, in its conviction, war
as a means of settling international disputes contradicts the spirit ("mind
and method"!) of Christ and his church. Further, the conference called for
(1) a substantial reduction in armaments of every form down to the lowest

---

6. [*This 1932 conference would fail. Bonhoeffer alludes to this at* DBWE *12:258* (Reader *353*).]

level; (2) reasonable and just relations between the armed peoples; and (3) security for all peoples against potential attacks. This message is to be advocated publicly by the churches, and the regional governments should place their full support along these lines.

It will not be possible to avoid the criticism coming from the most diverse sides that too much or too little has been said here or, on the other hand, that once again something has been merely *said*. We don't wish to minimize this criticism but would simply explain some things. The "too much" rests particularly in the theological formulations, which have been determined essentially by Anglo-Saxon theology and grasp the problematic of something like war only in the realization of an already well-established ideal, that is, conceiving the matter as a problem of action rather than as a problem of its essential nature. This is what so often gives the international church resolutions a full-bodied ring and yet to our ear a tone that is devoid of real content. The "too little" certainly lies in what was said. At the conclusion of the plenary meeting, a man from India vehemently called upon the assembly to say something more, something conclusive, that is, about what the church's actual position would be, were it to find itself again in a catastrophe. This was simply the expression of the justified and yet repeatedly disappointed hope that the church would finally, finally speak out very concretely for once. It is precisely at such conferences that "Christian principles"—the applied art—become most dangerous to authentic Christianity. Nonetheless, such principles must be articulated as long as one simply doesn't know what more to do, in which case it would certainly be good to admit that openly. Most circles in our countries will simply overlook the fact that the churches have once again drafted a resolution. As long as the churches do not know how to do otherwise . . .

It is not a significant counterargument that people in England and   168
America still believe in resolutions more than we do. And yet it will not do here to try to force more than is given us at this point. It is of more decisive importance for the meaning and progress of the work of the World Alliance that the churches give the message of the World Alliance the fullest resonance in their countries and that they provide for a hearing in the congregations as well as in the broadest public arena. Thus, in England on the day after the conference ended, the president of the English group, the Lord Bishop of Ripon, Bishop Dr. Ammundsen (Hadersleben), Prof. D. Dr. Martin Dibelius (Heidelberg), and others in various large churches spoke in their worship services about the message of the World Alliance. In the evening, there was also a worship service in three languages broadcast by radio, in which the retired president of the German Supreme Court, D. Dr.

Walter Simons, delivered the message and the bishop of Ripon in his sermon summoned the congregation to the work of Christian peace.

It is worth noting that the international youth conference affiliated with the World Alliance was unable to decide to issue a resolution. The sense was too strong that they needed first to learn to see the new circumstances in a fresh way and not immediately enter into the matter with grand pronouncements. The major conference had other things to consider here, and we must be grateful that it brought about such a resolution, which without doubt signifies a stronger step forward than all that had been conveyed previously. Nowhere has the critique against the entire enterprise, from the most different viewpoints, been louder than in the circle of the youth conference. Incidentally, here again there has been a very pronounced intellectual grouping of the Continental and particularly the German-French (and Danish) on the one side and the Anglo-American on the other. The young French saw many essential matters very much as we did, particularly theological matters. In these young circles, there was much thought, with great honesty, about the enormous barriers that stand in the way of total openness in our relations. Not only here, however, but essentially in the lack of a major, fundamentally theological understanding of our work (for which the hitherto almost universally accepted Anglo-Saxon foundation simply does not suffice), we saw a mutual need and a common obligation. In order to carry on the ecumenical work among young people, perceived as an urgent necessity, three international youth secretary offices have been established, for which England, France, and Germany each provide one secretary.[7] For all the criticism, however, it remained evident that the work of the World Alliance is progressing slowly but surely. The urgency of its work today must fire the heart and soul of every person, but at this point we do not yet know how we could pursue it better and faster.

169

Despite its extremely cautious wording, the recently drafted resolution from the twentieth international YMCA (CVJM)[8] convention in Cleveland, U.S.A., opposing the idea of Germany's exclusive guilt for the war, is characteristic of a strong shift in American thinking right now—though the churches didn't initiate it—especially if it is compared to the similar message of the Federal Council of Churches of Christ in America in November 1930.

---

7. [*Bonhoeffer was appointed Germany's youth secretary.*]

8. ["CVJM (Christlicher Verein Junger Männer) is the German branch of the Young Men's Christian Association," *DBWE* 11:169, n. 17.]

The resolution, furthermore, is clearly of very great significance for the entire work of the YMCA and will facilitate education toward Christian thinking with a broadened human vision. And yet only with difficulty will it avoid the accusation that serious Americans leveled at the Federal Council declaration at the time: once again it is ten years too late. When will the time come that Christianity speaks the right word at the right hour?

Berlin-Grunewald   Dietrich Bonhoeffer

16. Draft for a Catechism: As You Believe, So You Receive

DBWE 11:258–267

In the summer of 1931, Bonhoeffer wrote the following catechism with his close friend Franz Hildebrandt, who had suggested the project. The title is borrowed from Luther, who used similar phrases to emphasize that God's promises are fulfilled for those who believe.[1] This sets the tone for the catechism itself, which Bonhoeffer and Hildebrandt present as an attempt "to formulate what the Lutheran faith is saying today." The basis of the catechism is not, as is traditional, the Apostles' Creed, but rather a statement of faith from one of Luther's catechetical sermons. The two friends likely first discussed this statement several years before, when Hildebrandt had discovered it during his dissertation research. Bonhoeffer carried a copy of it in his prayer book for the rest of his life. After establishing the foundation of Christian knowledge on the gospel known in faith, the catechism proceeds in a Trinitarian fashion, asking and answering questions in turn about the Father, Son, and Holy Spirit. The catechism is noteworthy for including modern questions (e.g., "Doesn't the creation story contradict science?") and questions about war, peace, and ecumenism. It ends by reiterating one of Bonhoeffer's favorite Luther quotations: "This is the Christian faith: to know what you must do and what has been given to you."[2]

---

1. [DBWE *11:258, n. 2.*]
2. [*Introductory material drawn from* DB-ER, *186–189.*]

As You Believe, So You Receive[3]   258
Attempt at a Lutheran Catechism
by
Dietrich Bonhoeffer and Franz Hildebrandt

Preface

This catechism is for students in a confirmation class and yet is intended
not only for them. It serves their distinctive concerns, as it attempts to for-   259
mulate what the Lutheran faith is saying today. Questions and answers are
posed for carefully focused reading. Additional material and interpretations remain reserved for the lesson time.

What is the gospel?

This is the message of God's salvation that has appeared to us in Jesus
Christ and has been conveyed to us through his Spirit. This is the message
of the kingdom of God that is contested in the world and intended for
God's righteous. This is the message of God's will, which speaks today and
decides over life and death.

Who is *Evangelisch*?[4]

Whoever rejoices in God's grace, professes the name of Christ, and invokes
the Holy Spirit. Whoever is ready for God's rule, does not fear outside power,
and knows that all will be fulfilled ultimately. Whoever hears God's word
preached, loves his church-community, and lives from forgiveness.

The Protestant faith confesses that God has given himself fully and completely to us, with all that God is and has (Luther), in these words:

"I believe in God, that he is my creator, in Jesus Christ, that he is my Lord,
in the Holy Spirit, that he is my sanctifier. God has created me and given
me life, soul, body, and all goods; Christ has brought me into his lordship

---

3. ["... The German title, 'Glaubst du, so hast du,' translates literally, 'If you believe,
you will have it,'" *DBWE* 11:258, n. 1. "This title picks up a formulation from Luther,
which Franz Hildebrandt had previously cited in his dissertation; see Hildebrandt, *EST,*
27. With this he wanted to emphasize in the discussion concerning the Lord's Supper
that for Luther there is no true perception of reality apart from faith, i.e., in this context
faith is a way of perceiving ...," *DBWE* 11:258, n. 2.]

4. ["We have chosen to use the German word *Evangelisch* here because of its nuances
for this Lutheran catechism. Throughout most of *DBWE*, it is usually translated as 'Protestant,' referring to the Protestant Church of Germany, which encompasses Lutheran,
Reformed, and United traditions. Yet the meaning in this case is clearly those who follow the gospel as taught by the Lutheran Reformation (the German word for 'gospel' is
Evangelium) ...," *DBWE* 11:259, n. 5. *The German word "evangelisch" should not be confused
with the American "evangelical."*]

260 through his body; and the Holy Spirit sanctifies me through his Word and the sacraments, which are in the church, and will sanctify us wholly on the last day. [. . .] This is the Christian faith: to know what you must do and what has been given to you" (Luther, *WA* 30/1:94; *LW* 51:169).

Of the true God

Where does my knowledge of God come from?

From your baptism, because before you even asked, God had spoken to you. From your church, for as you sought God, you were already part of the church-community. From the Bible, for your church lives from the power of its preaching.

Why is God present in this way?

God alone is the Lord. God can speak of himself wherever he wishes. It is, however, in God's loving-kindness that he encounters us in earthly form, and that we can know where he is to be found. That is the revelation in Christ and in his church.

Is this the only God?

In every other case, you pray to the god of your wishes. There is only one God who comes to you himself, so that you can no longer elude him. His word alone calls the whole world into life, and you as well as his own.

On faith

How can I be certain of this?

Through faith alone, which has grasped the good news with both hands. No other way is given to us, for if we were able to see God, we would be in eternal life. Therefore, it is faith that dares to put our trust in God.

Where do we find the proof for this?

A god who could be proved by us would be an idol. The Lord in whom we trust binds us so firmly to himself that we become free of superstition and the desire for proof through miracles. The one to whom God has given the gift of faith in turn presents faith back to God, no matter what happens to that person.

261 Is God really concerned about me?

Whoever acts all too piously in contrast is thinking not of what is divine but rather of what is human. Because that is the glory of God, that God comes down to us in Christ in order that we might be raised in the Spirit to God. He is the trinitarian God.

Since God belongs to us and we to God, we proclaim faith in the Father: I believe in God, who is my creator.

May we call God our Father?

This is the only name that discloses the mystery of God to us. God cannot forget what God has created. How should we forget that we are his children!

Doesn't the creation story contradict science?

To engage in scientific research and to have faith are two different things. Science has its own full and distinctive authority. Every child knows that the earth did not come about simply in six days. Yet not everyone knows that God creates the world through his Spirit and human beings according to God's own image.

Why don't we see this image in anyone?

It sounds really strange to us. The demonic spirits of the world, such as money, power, desires, rob us of God's light, so that we have to die. God's orders have been destroyed. Through our disbelief, we have abused our freedom, using it against God, and this has made us slaves to our false idols.

How can a righteous God allow so much injustice?

The catastrophes of nature and of humankind render our wisdom silent. Where God's gracious will is concealed entirely from us, our will certainly cannot judge God. Nonetheless, we know that to those who love God all things work out for the best.

What, then, am I to pursue in the world?

You should do what your occupation has given you to do. God has called each of us to a particular work in a particular time. This is God's law. And we owe God our obedience, until God summons us.

Is there no unrighteousness in our occupation?

Admittedly, everyone today who earns his living is taking bread from another. Work becomes a curse whenever our power over things reverses itself into the power of things over us. Whoever knows this becomes humble 262 and asks that God make him joyful once more in his work.

How may a Christian own property?

Certainly, he would often be happier without it. He knows the power and deceptiveness of money, but at the same time he wants to care for the other person. So he should possess all that he has as though he did not have these things.

Is the instinct for self-preservation in fact a sin?

Nature and the unnatural are completely interwoven in it. As Christians, we believe that our body belongs to God. But wherever the drives of hunger and sex break away from their origins, they blindly go astray.

Are there no rules for our physical life?

Deliberately to destroy one's health is to harm one's soul and God's possession. To fulfill the communion between body and soul, God has given us marriage. Whoever has been given eyes open to the miracle of each birth will shy away from laying hands on another's life and will ask God to forgive him when he sins by being arrogant and falling away from God.

But doesn't one have to destroy life in war?

For that very reason the church knows nothing of the sanctity of war. For in war, the struggle for existence is fought with dehumanized means. The church that prays the Lord's Prayer calls to God only for the cause of peace.

But isn't that unpatriotic?

God has arranged it so that all races of humanity of the earth come from *one* blood (Acts 17:26). Therefore, a defiant ethnic pride in flesh and blood is a sin against the Holy Spirit. Zeal that only blindly asserts itself is brought under control by the state. God has established the state for the service of God, so that we might serve God as Christians.

How then should the Christian behave politically?

As much as the Christian would like to remain distant from political struggle, nonetheless, even here the commandment of love urges the Christian to stand up for his neighbor. His faith and love must know whether the dictates of the state may lead him against his conscience. In every such decision, he experiences the irreconcilable conflict between the peace of Christ and the hate of the world.

263

Have Christians no other solution?

We recognize that we are wrong in thought and deed. For this reason, the whole world restlessly hopes for the appearance of the Savior and the justice of God. We pray to God that we be not judged but rather that God would make us truly ready for his work.

That God enters into our life and we into God's, we proclaim our faith in the Son: I believe in Jesus Christ, that He is my Lord.

Did Jesus actually live?

Whoever knows the Bible and the Gentile testimonies about Jesus sees the proof of his life through its variety and contradictions. The Jews themselves have never contested that. The statements such as in Matt. 11:19; 21:31; Mark 10:18; 15:34; Luke 14:26, and images as in Matt. 15:21ff.; Mark 10:13ff.; 14:32ff.; Luke 7:36ff.; 15:1ff. could not have been invented. All attempts to dismiss his church by denying Jesus fail before the experience of his inescapable presence.

How does Jesus of Nazareth help me today?

To know about Jesus does not yet mean to believe in him. Merely considering him to be true is, of course, lifeless. Faith depends not on lifeless letters but rather on the living Lord who stands commandingly before us, above all doubt about the Bible and its stories.

Why is actually Jesus the Lord?

He is the answer to every human question. He is the salvation in all the sufferings of the world. He is the victory over all our sins. In him, you have God himself in his power and the human being in complete powerlessness.

How can a human being be God?

In no other way than that God miraculously humiliates himself in order   264
to share everything with us. The human Jesus, born of his mother, Mary, through temptation and suffering until death on the cross, is the miracle and word of God. He himself says this, and on this authority he acts. "This is the person to whom you should point and say: Here is God" (Luther).

Why do so few acknowledge this?

Even if Jesus were today still performing miracles, we would remain unconverted. We want a prouder God than the one who became our brother in the manger and on the cross. This God, however, willingly became veiled in sin and death for our sake, so that solely by faith we might see that which remains incomprehensible to the rest of the world.

Why did Jesus have to go to the cross?

This remains God's secret. We can say only this about it: What takes place here is not human heroism. Here is God's own action. The Holy One enters into a world alienated from God in order to bring the sinners home. He has to suffer being forsaken by God and death just as we do. It is his very own sacrifice for us that judges and overcomes our sins and opens for us the door to our Father's house.

Has evil thereby really been driven from the world?

Christ is risen. He has taken away Satan's power. Yet nobody sees that, and there is still a battle in the world between Christ and the Antichrist. Only within his church-community does he appear as the conqueror, as the head to its members. He makes the church to be his body and through it to reveal his life.

Does the church, then, act according to the will of Christ?

The church knows today more than ever how little it obeys the Ser-   265
mon on the Mount. Yet the greater the discord in the world becomes, the more Christ wants to have proclaimed the peace of God that reigns in his kingdom. The church still continues daily in prayer for the return of its divine Lord, and he lays his hand upon it, until he leads the church to its fulfillment.

That God exalts us and we him, we proclaim by our faith in the Holy Spirit: I believe in the Holy Spirit, who is my sanctifier.

Who is the Holy Spirit?

The Holy Spirit is no spirit of this world but rather the Spirit of God and Christ, who is present in the church. Without this Spirit, we would know nothing of Christ, just as we would know nothing of God without Christ. In the Spirit divinity perfects itself on earth, since "were you to have no church, then you would not be God" (Luther).

Is God to be found only in the Christian church?

The spirit of hope has spoken in every people and in every age. Yet the Holy Spirit is the Spirit of fulfillment, by which every other spirit is judged. Where apart from Christ humanity's religion is determined by fear or delusion, the Holy Spirit leads Christianity to grace and truth.

Why, then, are there so many churches?

We really should be *one* church. Due to our inexplicable disunion, we insist on a new community of all Christians. To have such a new community is never possible for us as human beings other than in expectation and in a faith that is faithful to God's church.

Where is the true church?

The true church is where preaching stands and falls with the pure gospel of a gracious God over against all human self-righteousness. It is where the sacraments depend on the word of Christ without any element of magic. It is where the community of the Spirit exists in service and not in domination.

266   Do I need the church?

Were you to know what the church is and why it needs you, you would not ask such a question, but rather you would rejoice. The good news would leave you no peace as long as you could have it. You would seek the community where one exists for the other in prayer, tells him all and forgives him all, and the promise that here one may become "a Christ to the other person" (Luther).

Will one become a different person through the church?

Here, God awakens you out of sleep into sober awareness, out of narrowness into breadth, out of servitude into freedom. Here, you surrender yourself daily and become in your discipleship of Christ lord of all things. This is faith and the new life. But as long as the church is in the world, no one can decide whom God has chosen for eternity.

Who is chosen?

At the beginning and the end of every life there stands the mystery of the divine Spirit, who pardons and repudiates whomever he chooses and allows every question and every law to fall silent. In the midst of history stands the cross of Christ who died for us all. To him we flee and pray that he might make us certain of his grace until all the world gives God alone the glory.

What do we know of eternal life?

Whether we want it or not—as truly as God lives—our life has come under God's judgment and has been sustained by God's hand. Not flesh and blood, but rather spirit, soul, and body are to rise up from the dead. We know not when the hour will come, but the church looks forward with all creation to a new earth and a new heaven.

This is the Christian faith: to know what you must do and what has been given to you.

Confirmation

267

You should thank God that your church has the gospel. You should ask God that your faith remain loyal to God. You should vow to God that you dare to live your life according to God's word.

The Lord's Supper

You have the first Lord's Supper, which Christ himself gives you. You have in this holy Lord's Supper the daily bread of the church-community and consolation for all sadness. You have the eternal Lord's Supper in the blessedness of the kingdom of the Father.

17. THE RIGHT TO SELF-ASSERTION

DBWE 11:246–257

After returning from the ecumenical conference in Cambridge, Bonhoeffer undertook a new assignment as a chaplain at Berlin's Technical College. Of this role, which Bonhoeffer filled in 1931–1932, his close friend and biographer, Eberhard Bethge, offers this blunt assessment: "Bonhoeffer's work as student chaplain was unfruitful."[1] The College lacked a strong tradition of chaplaincy, and Bonhoeffer had difficulty attracting students to his devotions and talks.

The following talk delivered at the College shows that in his chaplaincy as much as in his ecumenical work Bonhoeffer was forced to deal with National Socialist ideology. The Nazi rhetoric of expansionism, which traded on the purported right of the nation to assert itself, provides Bonhoeffer with the opportunity to expound on a foundational issue in his ethics: the question of self-assertion and self-denial.[2] He argues that true freedom comes through the denial of the self for others, a denial open to us through the self-sacrifice of Christ. Characteristically, Bonhoeffer discusses self-denial as applying not only to individuals but to communities as well. Thus the critique of National Socialism: as the individual lays down his life for his brother, so the nation might deny itself that others might live.

This talk is noteworthy for more than Bonhoeffer's resistance to Nazi ideology, however. Its opening passage demonstrates how heavily the economic depression weighed on Germans; at the time of this address in February 1932, more than 30 percent of the German workforce was unemployed.[3] It also provides a glimpse into Bonhoeffer's fascination with—and romanticizing of—India. He had at several points made serious plans to visit India, even securing a personal invitation from Mahatma Gandhi, only to have his plans fall through.

---

1. [DB-ER, *223. For more on the chaplaincy, see* DBWE *11:480–482 and* DB-ER, *222–226.*]
2. [DBWE *11:246, n. 2. For his later reflections, see* DBWE *6:239–245.*]
3. [DBWE *11:247, n. 4.*]

No working person today can escape the observation that he is replaceable, 246
that, indeed, behind him stand many who are only waiting, either to convince him of his dispensability during his very lifetime, or are just as eagerly
ready to assure him of an immediate honor in his memory in the newspaper
when things get serious. We are infinitely unimportant not only in terms of
the overall picture of working humanity, but even from the particular place
where we happen to find ourselves: It is extremely unimportant, whether I
am studying or not; names are trivial and boring. Numbers say more and
are more appropriate. And what city dweller does not know this impression 247
of empty, futile importance at 7:30 in the morning, in the streets, on the
trains, as thousands hurry to their work, to their livelihood, a condemned,
patient, replaceable mass. It conveys something endlessly desolate and boring, yet exciting and outrageous at the same time. And we belong in the
midst of the superfluous ones, and even our own situation has at the same
time something very boring and very shocking for us. Partly out of bore-
dom, partly out of indignation, we then decide in some way to put an end
to the feeling of our being superfluous, be it through fired-up work performance, be it by getting married and bringing new beings into superfluous
human existence and making them dependent on us, be it by forgetting
our own pointlessness and now simply allowing ourselves to take it easy
and enjoy ourselves in a vegetative existence. These are, indeed, three very
different behavior patterns, but no one likes to be superfluous and one
becomes inventive in making excuses.

Every day you read new statistics in the newspapers that have only one purpose, namely, to show that there are too many people out there. Between 35
and 50 percent of all the pupils at the secondary schools, around 50 percent
of university students, and 60 percent of the students at the technical col-
leges will not find a position. In the job market[4] basically everything hinges
on one question: Who buys people? People become like goods, which are
devalued by the massive scale. There are too many examples of this kind.
This devalues the individual and the species. One can deceive oneself about
this state of affairs and dream, if one happens not to be personally affected,
but one cannot deny the situation. In any case, this situation offers a major
opportunity, namely, to submerge, easily and always excusably, to fit into
an environment where one feels comfortable and where one actually also 248
probably belongs. And the weak person and the frivolous person will not

---

4. ["In February 1932, unemployment reached its highest point, with 6,128,000 persons unemployed, over 30 percent of the German workforce. This was a recurring issue
for Bonhoeffer in 1932. See the German editor's afterword *DBWE* 11:477, and the editors'
introduction, *DBWE* 11:2," *DBWE* 11:247, n. 4.]

let this opportunity pass by. To all others, this state of affairs poses the one question of life: How do you come to do something that a thousand others could and would want to do just as well and even better? How do you come to earn money, where two thousand others have nothing? What right have you to enjoy status and honor, where thousands like you live from the bread of charity? What right do you have to assert yourself in the struggle for human existence, in full awareness that you are thereby ruining, destroying, and leaving the lives of others prey to meaninglessness? Stand up for your rights! Or surrender them! We are here today to discuss this problem.

We also know, however, that today the question of the right to self-assertion is not only posed to the individual with particular urgency but rather that it signifies the question of existence of almost all large communities. The trade professions are waging a desperate battle for their right to exist; the fragmentation of society into classes has driven these groups into increasingly sharp confrontations against one another. The bourgeoisie[5] is threatened in the most dangerous way and is fighting to preserve the bourgeois spirit and its rights. The proletariat believes that it will be able to shape its own rights only on the ruins of the middle class. However, even the basic forms of human communal life are questioned and called upon to preserve their rights. Marriage and family are experiencing a violent crisis. Has the institution of marriage, as it has been conducted for hundreds of years, a right to make a stand against the attempts at dissolution? Or has it not proved sufficiently that it leads to human catastrophes, that it has become an outdated, lifeless form? And the same questions would then be leveled at the institution of the family. The new form of the childless marriage and, for instance, the ever stronger removal of children from the family and pulling them into school and clubs makes this question clear. Or let us consider the struggle for existence of two institutions, once looked upon as most powerful cultural factors: the university and the church. The university is supposed to become the vocational school, and the church of the people[6] the private religious association. What right does the university have to assert itself? What right does the church have to fight for

249

---

5. ["The terms 'bourgeoisie' and 'proletariat' convey the broader cultural and political nuance of Bonhoeffer's reference here to the concerns of the propertied and the working classes," *DBWE* 11:248, n. 5.]

6. [*The phrase "church of the people" translates* Volkskirche, *which* ". . . refers to the majority churches—the German Evangelical Church and the Roman Catholic Church, to which the great majority of German citizens belonged—in contrast to the much smaller and diverse minority churches; the term is still used in this sense today . . . ,'" *DBWE* 11:249, n. 7.]

its existence in defiance of all attacks and slander as being an outdated, ever reactionary, obsolete institution? It is rare in history to see that without exception all the previous orders of human life are being questioned, dragged into an existential struggle so that they are confronted with the alternative of justifying their right to exist or else surrendering it. And now we cannot stop here, for even the greatest and highest forms of human social life, the nations themselves, are not untouched; they are particularly addressed by the question: What right to existence do you have? Do you have any right as an old nation to face the striving young nation, to deny its rise? Do you have a right, as a young, strong nation, to take over the old one with violence, to push it out? Do you have any right to extend your boundaries, if your fellow citizens are suffocating in these narrow confines? Do you have a right to destroy the thriving culture of the neighboring land for the sake of your own? You, people, preserve your right or give it up. [. . .][7] It is possible here to dismiss all this and say: These are all questions not of rights but simply of historical development, of the division of power, of might. This possibility exists, but it is not a moral possibility, and it has never been a German possibility so far. We want to note this as well.

250

Our purpose this evening is to trace all these questions back to one question and thereby answer it. The right to self-assertion is the single question, whose multifaceted contemporary meaning we have only illustrated up to this point.

Humanity has given essentially two answers to this fundamental question of all life. One emerged in the distant, fertile, sunny, form- and idea-rich world of India, in which the body is easily provided with good things and thus the soul is left free for surrender and self-deepening. The world in which the active, productive hand of work need only open itself in order richly to receive its fruits engenders a great tranquillity in the heart, and the soul breathes the life that surrounds it in its abundance, penetrating the experience of life in the midst of this great abundance, uniting itself with it, probing and pondering its rhythm and its depths, which are basically the depths of the soul itself, and the expanses of the Indian soul are the expanses of all living things. In this way the submerging soul recognizes itself again in all that lives, as if in thousands of mirrors; out of every form of nature it hears the quiet answer: *tat tvam asi* [*you are that*], this is you, you yourself. And the eternal awe of the sanctity of all life comes over the soul. It

---

7. ["Here there are four illegible letters with periods, probably an abbreviation for 'And that is today,'" *DBWE* 11:250, n. 12.]

aches if nature suffers from violence; it is torn apart when living things are injured. You should not kill, for life is the soul, and life is you yourself; you should not do violence to any living thing; you should resist and reject anything in you that stimulates you to get your way with violence; you should

251   tame the thirst of your passions, your hatred and your love, if they drag you to assert yourself and hurt other life. Learn to suffer, learn to go by, learn to die, all this is better than to assert oneself and to violate and live. Only in this way will your soul, which indeed is the soul of the Universe, be uninjured and holy. Through love and suffering, we enter the Universe and overcome it.

In order to understand this idea, it is necessary for us to be clear that at the beginning there is the sentence: *tat tvam asi.* Everything is you. You are alone. You are also responsible solely to yourself, live for you yourself and your soul, for you are the whole. It is the powerful act of Gandhi to extend this teaching of life, which is directed toward the individual, now toward a people in a national question and now, too, to place the community under the commandment: You should not destroy any life; suffering is better than living with violence. If it then happens that at a gathering, thousands of Gandhi's followers, who are to be dispersed by the government police, attempt to carry out their will without force in passive resistance till the white machine guns are pointed at them, and hundreds are mowed down there,[8] then this is the great expression and solution that the question of the right to self-assertion still finds today in India.

The other big solution is that of European-American civilization, the solution of wars and factories; already, the first look at Western history teaches us that this has been a history of wars. The history of India is to this day a history of suffering. And that war in European history had a very different intellectual structure and significance than, for instance, war between two wild tribes, could, in my opinion, be proved by the writing of history. It is, so to say, the forerunner of the machine in its intellectual meaning. But this means, of course, that it[9] was truly to be overcome in the

252   era[10] of the machine. But be that as it may, the machine and the war are the

---

8. ["The reference is to the Jallianwallah Bagh massacre in the Punjab city of Amritsar on April 13, 1919, in which a contingent of British soldiers killed and wounded over 1,500 unarmed men, women, and children attending a protest rally that Gandhi had initiated but was prevented from attending," *DBWE* 11:251, n. 17.]

9. ["I.e., war," *DBWE* 11:251, n. 21.]

10. ["Uncertain reading," *DBWE* 11:251, n. 22.]

two forms of the Western solution to our problem.[11] And we must seek to grasp its intellectual meaning, in order to understand the problem.

One might now think that this is the quintessential animalistic, instinctive solution, whereas the Indian solution is the essentially humane one. But this is superficial. In both cases the human being steps outside the connection to nature and is something utterly different from an animal. The animal lives only through adapting itself to the laws of nature; the human being stands facing nature, ruling and conquering it. In the Oriental world this happens when the human being is able to suffer for the soul's sake; in the West, the human being is able to master nature, fight against it, force it to his service. This position of human mastery over nature is the fundamental theme of European-American history. The human being in India, too, is deeper and stronger than nature, because he understands it and, knowing it, suffers for it and from it. But the human being is deeper and stronger than nature, because he is its enemy and conqueror. The human being has this as an innate priority over all that lives. For that reason, a European also cannot love nature without taking note of its demonic powers, which threaten him, and in the deep delight that the fear of nature and the struggle against it gives him, the human being loves it. The human path to nature is a broken one. It[12] refuses him everything; for that reason he must extract it from it against its will; for the sake of this struggle he loves it. The individual human being receives everything from nature and loves it for that; his life is not a struggle against it but rather a receiving from it.

The European must struggle against nature to receive the right to life, but not only against nature, but also against other human beings. His life means in the most essential sense "killing." This has never been so horrifyingly clear as in the last decade and a half.[13] And yet we all stand in this life; we have all apparently already decided to affirm this fate, whether consciously or not. In any case, the decision has been made, and now the task is to understand what we have thereby done.

Not only the attitude toward nature is something else for the European but also the attitude toward history and toward other human beings; and only from this starting point can we completely understand the European-American resolution of the question. Right to self-assertion is right to life. 253

---

11. ["Cf. *DBWE* 6:120–122. At this point in the *Ethics*, Bonhoeffer reflects upon the inherently unstable interrelation of nationalism, technology, and mass movements," *DBWE* 11:252, n. 23.]

12. ["I.e., nature," *DBWE* 11:252, n. 26.]

13. ["Bonhoeffer is referring here to the First World War and the events in Russia during and after the Russian Revolution," *DBWE* 11:252, n. 27.]

Life, however, is not primarily something that we give ourselves but something that is given to us, something that we suffer. Through our birth, our life is determined primarily passively. And it is now a characteristic of mature European thought to acknowledge this passive event as a bond. Life means being bound through history and that means to other human beings. I grow up in a world that I do not give myself but which determines me and to which I acknowledge my bond. Thus life means being connected backward and forward, to have claims made on me from outside, from the other human beings in my surroundings; it means to be responsible. Here we have in principle the possibility of the great individualists to curse this being bound through birth and life as horrible destiny, as Jeremiah cursed the day of his birth and as Nietzsche's Zarathustra did in a similar fashion. This means tearing oneself out of history and society, and for that reason it ultimately means nothing other than the proclamation of the right to the great human possibility, which testifies most deeply to the human being's freedom from nature, superiority over the animal, the right to a free death, the right to suicide. Here the individual becomes outraged against his destiny and defies it to the end. The human being is free over nature and history if he is free unto death. The right to self-assertion becomes here the right to a free death. That is one possibility. And it is the unmistakable truth that the human being only becomes human, first truly asserts himself, when he is free unto death. But this truth will also be heard and absorbed there where the human being seizes his historical bonds in responsibility, where he understands himself not as master over his own life, but where he understands his life as responsibility toward his fellow human beings. He lives here not alone but fundamentally through and for the others with whom he is associated in responsibility.[14] Only out of responsibility does life take its right to self-assertion, not because it belongs to me, but rather because it belongs to society, to others, to the fellow human being. Here the possibility of free death is dismissed on principle, but the deeper truth that it contains is taken up in the much more unfathomable depth of a different thought, and out of these hidden dark depths that life of responsibility wells up: the human being is free only in death; right to self-assertion means right to death, freedom unto death, now, however, not to the free death of self-destruction, but rather to the freedom to sacrifice.[15] This is

254

---

14. ["This concept will become a central feature of Bonhoeffer's ethical theology, e.g., in his *Ethics* (*DBWE* 6:259 [*Reader* 638])," *DBWE* 11:253, n. 31.]

15. ["Cf. Bonhoeffer's poem many years later: 'Stations on the Way to Freedom,' written as a gift for Eberhard Bethge from Tegel prison in the context of the events of July 20, 1944 (*DBWE* 8:512–514)," *DBWE* 254, n. 33.]

the consummation of the thought of life as responsibility, as being bound to history and society, that this life has right only through sacrifice. There is right to life only through the ability to die for the other, in responsibility. Living means killing. For that reason, however, life itself must be open to death, now, however, not for the glorification of personality but as sacrifice for a brother. Only where the individual is able to understand and assess his life from the perspective of death does he win the answer to the question of his right to life, of the right to self-assertion.[16]

But already through saying this, we expand our view. We are not only individuals, but we are also placed within life-communities. It is precisely here that our burning interest lies today. Our marriage, our church, Germany are called before the forum of responsibility. And now what counts is to see these communities in the light of that which gives an individual's life the right to self-assertion—in the light of responsibility for the other and of the ability to die. And what we say in the following holds true for each community that acts responsibly, whether it be a community of blood, of work, of a factory, or of a commune. Every community, even the great community of the people, lives not only for itself but for the others, lives in responsibility for the brother, for the people to whom one is bound in brotherhood. There is absolutely no isolated life for the people. It is bound through its birth onward to the community and through its life to the peoples in brotherhood. Admittedly, even for the people, there is that demonic possibility to tear itself out of the historical context, the attempt of absolute being-alone and being-for-itself, the denial of responsibility, which in turn draws its strength from the possibility of the free death of the entire people. And the danger of this action hangs above the community as it does above the individual life. This means that a people has a right, there where life is unbearable for it, to curse its birth and to bring itself to an end with an honorable death, but in turn here, too, this thought must be taken up and led into the depths of the responsible life.[17] It is true that a people only lives, which means it may destroy life, if it is free unto death; only in the light, only out of the power of death does the community live. But when a people

255

---

16. ["Bonhoeffer returns extensively in the second version of the section on 'History and Good' in his *Ethics* to the interconnection of freedom and responsibility within an analysis of the 'structure of responsible action' and as 'mutually corresponding concepts. . . . Responsibility presupposes freedom . . . just as freedom can exist only in the exercise of responsibility. Responsibility is human freedom that exists only by being bound to God and neighbor' (*DBWE* 6:283 [*Reader* 655])," *DBWE* 11:254, n. 35.]

17. ["Cf. *DBWE* 6:246–257 and *DBWE* 6:257–298 (*Reader* 637–666)," *DBWE* 11:255, n. 39.]

responsibly affirms its bond to history, its bond to its brothers, to other people in brotherhood that may at the same time be its deadly enemy, then it no longer has the freedom to a free death, but rather lives solely from the freedom for sacrificial death for its brothers. It may live only because it is ready to die for the brother. War and machine as a means to the self-assertion of the community demand sacrifice of individuals, but they have their sole right from the readiness of the community for sacrificial death for others, even for the enemy brother; never may they become a means for egoism and self-idolization, and where they lower themselves to this, it is time to protest. War originates from the era when the European thought that only by killing the other could one create living space for oneself. The machine directs this fight primarily not against the human being but against nature. That is the reason why its means are more ruthless. That is why it leads to catastrophe, where the machine is placed in the deliberate service of destroying human life. The machine has made war impossible, not just according to its idea of subjugating nature to human beings and thus letting them live, but also according to its [i.e., the machine's] reality. But this only incidentally.

Peoples, too, can and should sacrifice themselves. And in this way the view broadens and encompasses the entire earth, humanity. And now today our Western thought is universal; the concept of humankind is a Western concept. It governs our entire thinking. But we reach it in no other way but by the historical path through the individual and the community; here, however, as a historical final concept, it has its inextricable meaning. The life and sacrifice of the individual is for the brother, for the community that embraces him; the life and sacrifice of the community is for other peoples in brotherhood, for the brotherly community that embraces it, and so it grows into the understanding that life, responsibility, and sacrifice finally belong to the unity of the human race, to a human being as such who alone can live through the sacrifice. Humankind lives through the sacrifice that the individuals and the communities bring to it. But why should we hold back the last question, which is indeed unavoidable? Does humanity itself no longer need the sacrifice, the openness toward death, because humanity is what finally, unconditionally, only demands sacrifices but does not sacrifice itself? Does it have its right simply through itself, through its very existence? Or must even it fight against this, through the readiness unto death?

And now today: Why should we not simply at this decisive point take the step forward that has become necessary through what has just been said? Even humanity, even the human being as such, who is nothing as a human being, hence even humanity, according to our thinking, is responsible for its right to life, and it exercises this responsibility only where it sees that it too only lives from being able to die, from death, from sacrifice. It lives from the sacrifice that it now brings simultaneously to itself and to the brothers in the one who has made them all brothers and in whose spirit and life they are all one. The end of human beings, of humanity, is the readiness for this deed, for sacrifice for the fellow human being, and that is offered to the Spirit, who lives out of himself and creates life.

And now, here in the background of this Western conception, Christianity emerges on the horizon and in it the figure of Jesus of Nazareth, the Son of Man, who is called the Son of God, the Christ. He fulfills the sacrifice of humanity, out of which alone humanity can live, and now, since the act of Golgotha, humanity lives entirely out of that act, which the Son of Man offered for the brothers to the Father. He also really lived, but his faithful see his life in the shadow or in the light of the act of Golgotha, his death for the brothers. Because he was free to die, therefore he could live, because he died as sacrifice for the brotherhood of the world, therefore his life was plainly life in service to the most holy brotherhood. For that reason the Gospels proclaim that all should take up their cross and follow him; his death   257
sanctifies his life, his death and our death sanctify our life, and only when we become free to sacrifice for the holiest brotherhood of humanity, for whom the prophet from Nazareth, the Christ, died, only so do we become free for life.

18. Thy Kingdom Come! The Prayer of the Church-Community for God's Kingdom on Earth

DBWE 12:285–297

In this late 1932 lecture from a devotional retreat of the Protestant Continuing Education tion Institute for Women,[1] Bonhoeffer argues that praying "thy kingdom come" means praying that God's kingdom comes on earth. It is an escapist misunderstanding, on the one hand, to pray for an otherworldly kingdom; such a prayer forgets that God's kingdom is on earth. It is equally mistaken, on the other hand, for the church or the individual Christian to take on the responsibility for ushering in the kingdom; such "pious secularism" forgets that God's kingdom is God's. Both otherworldliness and "the utopia of this-worldly secularism" reveal that we have stopped believing in the kingdom as God's kingdom on earth.

The lecture also includes a discussion of church and state, since the two are divinely ordained to anticipate the coming kingdom. The earth to which God's kingdom comes is in its present state a cursed or sinful earth. On this cursed earth, the church is to preach the coming kingdom while the state preserves the world for the kingdom by maintaining order. Lest either the church or the state claim the place of the kingdom itself, Bonhoeffer emphasizes that their mandates are provisional, limited to this state of sin. When the kingdom comes in fullness to create a new earth, church and state pass away.

Thus Bonhoeffer offers a vision of the kingdom while targeting a range of opponents. Drawing on his early love of Nietzsche and anticipating his prison critique of religion, Bonhoeffer envisions a this-worldly, social kingdom that resists escape into individu-

---

1. [DBWE *12:285, n. 1.*]

alistic interiority or otherworldliness.[2] *With his emphasis on the divine character of the kingdom and the sinful state of the earth and its present institutions, he chastens program-oriented, progress-minded liberal Christianity (familiar especially from his time in New York*[3]*) as well as the millennial pretenses of the growing Nazi movement.*[4]

We are otherworldly or we are secularists, but in either case this means that we no longer believe in God's kingdom. We are hostile to the Earth, because we want to be better than it, or we are hostile to God, because God robs us of the Earth, our mother. We flee the power of the Earth, or we hold hard and fast to it. Either way we are not the wanderers who love the Earth that bears them, and who only truly love it because it is on it that they travel toward that foreign land that they love above all; otherwise they would not be wandering at all. Only wanderers of this kind, who love the Earth and God as one, can believe in God's kingdom.

We have been otherworldly ever since we discovered the devious trick of being religious, indeed "Christian," at the expense of the Earth. Otherworldliness affords a splendid environment in which to live. When life begins to be difficult and oppressive, one leaps boldly into the air and soars, relieved and worry free, in the so-called eternal realm. One leapfrogs over the present, scorns the Earth; one is better than it; indeed, next to the temporal defeats, one has eternal victories that are so easily achieved. Otherworldliness also makes it easy to preach and speak words of comfort. An otherworldly church can be sure that it will in no time at all attract all the weaklings, all those who are only too glad to be deceived and deluded, all the dreamers, all disloyal children of the Earth. When the explosions start, who among us is not so human that he won't quickly mount the chariot that descends from the sky with the promise of taking us to a better world on the other side? What church would be so merciless, so inhuman that it wouldn't deal compassionately with this weakness of suffering human beings—thereby saving their souls for the kingdom of heaven? The human being is weak and cannot bear having the Earth so near, the Earth that supports him. He cannot stand it because the Earth is stronger than him, and because he wishes to be better than the evil Earth. So he wrests himself from it and refuses to take it seriously. And who can blame him—unless it be the have-nots, in their envy? The human being is weak and this weakling is susceptible to the religion of otherworldliness—should we deny him, should the weak individual remain without aid? Is that the spirit of Jesus

285

286

2. [*E.g.,* DBWE *8:364* (Reader *778*).]
3. [DBWE *12:236–243*.]
4. [*See* DBWE *12:278* (Reader *366*).]

Christ? No, the weak human being should receive help and receives it from Christ. But Christ does not want these weaknesses; rather Christ makes the human being strong. Christ does not lead him into the otherworldliness of religious escapism. Rather, Christ returns him to the Earth as its true son.

287　　　"Do not be otherworldly, be strong!"

Or we are children of the world. Those who feel that what has been said up to now does not apply to them at all should give heed to whether what now follows does not strike painfully home. We have succumbed to secularism, and here I mean the pious, Christian secularism. Not godlessness or cultural Bolshevism[5] at all, but the *Christian* renunciation of God as the Lord of the Earth. Here we can see that we are bound to the Earth. We have to deal with it. There is no escape. Power confronts power. World confronts church; worldliness confronts religion. How could it be otherwise than that religion and church are forced into this struggle, this controversy? Moreover, faith is compelled to harden into religious convention and morality, and the church into an organization of action for religious-moral reconstruction. Thus faith arms itself because the powers of the Earth compel it to do so. After all, we are to represent God's cause. We need to build ourselves a strong fortress within which we can dwell safe and secure with God. We build the kingdom. We can also live quite well with such cheerful secularism. The human being—including the religious person—enjoys a good fight and putting his strength to the test. Who would begrudge him this good gift of nature—unless it be the have-nots in their envy? This pious secularism also makes it possible to preach and say nice things. The church may be certain, if only it makes a somewhat more spirited effort, that it will soon have all the brave, determined, well-meaning, all the all-true sons of the Earth on its side in this happy war.[6] Which upright human being would not gladly represent God's cause in this wicked world and do so as the ancient Egyptians are said to have done? They carried the images of their gods against their enemies—in order to hide behind them. But in this case

---

5. ["Originally a term for the new proletarian, revolutionary art in the Soviet Union; here generally derogatory with respect to modern art and literature in the period after the First World War. German nationalists, especially the Nazis, used 'godless or cultural Bolshevism' to fan the flames of anti-Communism; it was also a code word in the propaganda of that era for the 'worldwide Jewish conspiracy.' In his arguments throughout this period, Bonhoeffer often took the slogans of his opponents and critiqued them," *DBWE* 12:287, n. 8.]

6. ["This is a wordplay on the dictum of the 'fresh, happy war,' which Heinrich Leo wished for in the 1850s, in order to be rid 'of the European mess of peoples' . . . ," *DBWE* 12:287, n. 11.]

the human being wants to hide not just from the enemy, from the world, but from God, from that God who destroys the mask created for him on earth, who does not wish for human beings to assume his role on earth in loud, boastful strength—just as the strong acquire the weak. On the contrary, God manages his own cause and, by free grace, accepts humans or not. God intends to be Lord on Earth and regards all exuberant human zeal on his behalf to be a real disservice. Our Christian secularism lies precisely in our readiness to earn God his right in the world, only to escape from him, and in our love of the Earth for its own sake and for the sake of this struggle. But we do not thereby elude God. We are brought back under God's dominion.

Become weak in the world and let God be the Lord!

Now, however, otherworldliness and secularism are simply two sides of the same coin—*namely, the lack of belief in God's kingdom.* He who would flee from the world, seeking in the kingdom a place removed from his troubles, does not believe. Nor does the one who presumes that he must establish a worldly kingdom. Whoever evades the Earth finds not God but only another world, his own better, lovelier, more peaceful world. He finds a world beyond, to be sure, but never God's world, which is dawning in this world. Whoever evades Earth in order to find God finds only himself. Whoever evades God in order to find the Earth does not find the Earth as God's Earth; he finds the jolly scene of a war between good and evil, pious and impious, which he kindles himself—in short, he finds himself. He who loves God, loves God as the Lord of the Earth as it is; he who loves the Earth, loves it as God's Earth. He who loves God's kingdom loves it entirely as *God's* kingdom, and he loves it wholly as *God's kingdom on Earth.* And this because the king of the kingdom is the creator and preserver of the Earth, who has blessed the Earth and taken us from earth.

But—this blessed Earth has been cursed by God. We live on cursed ground that yields thorns and thistles; but—Christ has entered into this cursed Earth; the flesh Christ bore was taken from this ground. On this ground the tree of the curse stood, and this second "but" establishes the kingdom of Christ as God's kingdom on this cursed ground. This is why the kingdom of Christ is a kingdom that has been lowered into the cursed ground from above. It is there, but like a hidden treasure in the cursed field. We pass over it unaware, and this not-seeing becomes a judgment on us. You saw only the field, saw its thistles and thorns, maybe even its seeds and grain, but you did not find the hidden treasure in the cursed ground. Indeed, this is the true curse that is a burden upon the ground of the Earth; not that it yields thistles and thorns, but rather that it hides God's countenance, so that even the deepest furrows in the Earth do not unveil for us the hidden God.

If we are to pray for the coming of the kingdom, we can pray for it only as those wholly on the Earth. Praying for the kingdom cannot be done by the one who tears himself away from his own misery and that of others, who lives unattached and solely in the pious hours of his "own salvation." The church may have hours in which it can sustain even that, but we cannot. The hour in which the church prays for the kingdom today forces the church, for better or worse, to identify completely with the fellowship of the children of the Earth and world. It binds the church by oaths of fealty to the Earth, to misery, to hunger, to death. It renders the church completely in solidarity with that which is evil and with the guilt of their brothers. The hour in which we pray today for God's kingdom is the hour of the most profound solidarity with the world, an hour of clenched teeth and trembling fists. It is not a time for solitary whispering, "Oh, that I might be saved." Rather, it is a time for mutual silence and screaming, that this world which has forced us into distress together might pass away and Your kingdom come to us. It is the eternal right of Prometheus to love the Earth, the "Earth, which is the mother of us all" (Sir. 40:1); this allows him to draw near the kingdom of God in a way that the coward fleeing to other worlds cannot.

No one can pray for the kingdom who imagines himself in bold utopias, in dreams and hopes of the kingdom, who lives his ideologies, who knows thousands of programs and prescriptions with which to heal the world. We should look at ourselves very carefully when we catch ourselves thinking such thoughts, and in doing so we will be in for a surprise. None of us knows what we basically want, so let us pose a very simple question: How do you really imagine your kingdom of God on Earth? How do you really want the people to be? Should they be more moral, more pious; should they be more homogeneous? Should they be less passionate; should they no longer be ill and hungry, no longer subject to death? Should there no longer be the smart and the stupid, the strong and the weak, the poor and the rich? It is truly amazing that as soon as we honestly pose this question and attempt to answer it, we are no longer able to provide even one. We want the one all right, and then again, for good reasons, we do not want it either. With a little honesty and some serious thought, it is simply not possible to come up with any kind of utopia for a kingdom of God on Earth. The possibility of thinking in universal terms, of seeing the big picture, fails us. All our longing to transform the cursed field into a blessed one, to regain it, fails because it is God who cursed the ground, and it is God alone who can retract this word and bless the Earth again. We must awaken from the state of intoxication with which the poison of the cursed ground has drugged us and become sober. The Earth wants us to take it seriously. It will not let us escape, not into the salvation of otherworldly piety nor into the utopia

290

of this-worldly secularism. Instead, it comes right out and shows us how it is enslaved in finiteness. Its enslavement is our enslavement; with it we, too, are subjected.

Death, loneliness, and desire—these are the three powers that enslave the Earth. Better, they are the one force, the adversary, the evil one, who will not surrender the rights he has gained over the fallen creature. Yet it is the force of the curse that came from the mouth of the Creator. And for this reason we cannot get beyond our death, our loneliness, and our desire with our utopias—they all belong inextricably to the cursed Earth. But in fact we are not supposed to get beyond them at all. Rather, the kingdom comes *to us* in our death, in our loneliness, in our desire. It comes where the church perseveres in solidarity with the world and expects the kingdom from God alone.

"Thy kingdom come"—this is not the prayer of the pious soul of the individual who wants to flee the world, nor is it the prayer of the utopian and fanatic, the stubborn world reformer. Rather, this is the prayer only of the church-community of children of the Earth, who do not set themselves apart, who have no special proposals for reforming the world to offer, who are no better than the world, but who persevere together in the midst of the world, in its depths, in the daily life and subjugation of the world. They persevere because they are, in their own curious way, true to this existence, and they steadfastly fix their gaze on that most unique place in the world where they witness, in amazement, the overcoming of the curse, the most profound yes of God to the world. Here, in the midst of the dying, torn, 291 and thirsting world, something becomes evident to those who can believe, believe in the resurrection of Jesus Christ. Here the absolute miracle has occurred. Here the law of death is shattered; here the kingdom of God itself comes to us, in our world; here is God's declaration to the world, God's blessing, which annuls the curse. This is the event that alone kindles the prayer for the kingdom. It is in this very event that the old Earth is affirmed and God is hailed as lord of the Earth; and it is again this event that over-comes, breaks through, and destroys the cursed Earth and promises the new Earth. God's kingdom is the *kingdom of resurrection* on Earth.

We resist this kingdom with our hypocritical lack of faith. We place limits on God by declaring with false humility that God cannot come to us because God is too great and God's kingdom is not meant for this Earth, that God and God's kingdom are in the eternal hereafter. But what humility could presume to define the limits of God's action—the limits of the one who died and rose again? This humility is nothing other than the poorly concealed pride of those who think they know what God's kingdom is and who then, in equally poorly concealed zeal, wish to perform the miracle themselves. They themselves wish to create the kingdom of God, and they see the coming of the kingdom in the strengthening of the church, in the Christianizing of culture and politics and upbringing, and in a renewal of Christian moral convention. In this way they thus fall once again under the curse of the Earth in which the treasure of the kingdom of God is *hidden*. Who wish to deceive themselves so completely that they do not see that it is God alone who effects this breakthrough, this miracle, this kingdom of resurrection.

It is not what *God* could do and what *we* could do that forms the basis of our prayer for the coming of the kingdom, but what God *does* for us and what God will do for us again and again. It is God's kingdom for the Earth, on the Earth under the curse; it is overcoming the law of death, loneliness, and desire in the world; and it is wholly God's kingdom, God's actions, God's word, God's resurrection. It is truly the miracle, God's miracle, of breaking through death to life, and it is the miracle that supports our faith and our prayer for the kingdom. Why should we be ashamed that we have a God who performs miracles, who creates life and conquers death? We ourselves are a god who cannot perform miracles. If God is truly God—then God is God, then God's kingdom is miraculous, the epitome of miracles. Why are we so anxious, so cautious, so cowardly? God will shame us all when one day he lets us see things that are a thousand times more miraculous than anything seen until now. We will feel shame before the miraculous God. Thus we look upon God's miraculous acts and say: Your kingdom come to us. The petition for the kingdom is not the begging of the anxious soul for its salvation. It is not Christian trimming to be used by the world's reformers. It is the plea of suffering and struggling communities in the world, on behalf of the human race, asking that God's glory be manifest in it. Not I and God, but we and God, we ask today. Not that God dwell in my soul, but that God should create the kingdom in our midst; that is our prayer today. How does God's kingdom come to us? No differently than God comes, in overcoming the law of death, in the resurrection, in miracles, and at the same time in the affirmation of the Earth, in entering into its order, its communities, its history. The two belong completely together. For only where the Earth is fully affirmed can its curse be seriously broken through and destroyed; and only the fact that the Earth's curse is broken through allows the Earth to be taken truly seriously. In other words God directs the Earth in such a manner that God breaks through the law of death. Thus God is always the one who binds himself to the Earth and the one who overcomes its curse. The Earth to which God is bound is the Earth that God preserves, the fallen, lost, cursed Earth. God binds himself to Earth as God's own work. But where God is, there is God's kingdom.

292

God always comes with the kingdom. God's kingdom must follow the same path as God. The kingdom comes with God to the Earth, and it is among us in no other way than a dual form: as the kingdom on Earth for all, the ultimate kingdom of resurrection, of miracles, breaking through, negating, overcoming, destroying all human works, which are subjected to the curse of death; and at the same time the kingdom of order, which affirms and preserves the Earth with its laws, communities, and its history. *Miracle* and *order* are the two forms in which God's kingdom on Earth presents itself and in which it is scattered. The miracle as the breaking through of all order, and the order as the preservation in preparation for the miracle. But also the miracle completely veiled in the world of orders, and order maintained by virtue of its limitation by the miracle. The form in which the *kingdom of God* is attested as miracle we call—the *church*; the form in which the kingdom of God is attested as order we call—the *state*.   293

The kingdom of God exists in our world exclusively in the duality of church and state. Both are necessarily linked to each other. Every attempt to control the other ignores this relationship of God's kingdom on Earth. Every prayer for the coming of the kingdom to us that does not have in mind both church and state is either otherworldliness or secularism. It is, in any case, a lack of faith in the kingdom of God.

The kingdom of God takes form *in the church*, insofar as the church gives witness to the miracle of God. The ministry of the church is to witness to Christ's resurrection from the dead, to the end of the law of death of this world under the curse, and to the power of God in the new creation.

The kingdom of God takes form *in the state* insofar as the state recognizes and maintains the order of preservation of life and insofar as it accepts responsibility for preserving this world from collapse and for exercising its authority here against the destruction of life. Not the creation of new life, but preservation of existing life is its ministry.

Thus the power of *death*, of which we spoke, is destroyed in the church through the authoritative witness to the miracle of the resurrection; it is restrained in the state through the order of the preservation of life. With its entire authority, with which it alone is responsible for the order of life, the state points to the church's witness to the breaking up of the law of death in the world of resurrection. And the church, with its witness to the resurrection, points to the preserving, ordering action of the state in the preserved world of the curse. Thus they both bear witness to the kingdom of God, which is entirely God's kingdom and wholly a kingdom for us.

The kingdom of God takes form in the *church*, insofar as here the loneliness of human beings is overcome through the miracle of confession and forgiveness. This is because in the church, in the communion of saints created by the resurrection, one person can and should bear the guilt of the other, and for this reason the last shackle of loneliness—hatred—is shattered and the community is established and created anew. It is through confession, a miracle that defies explanation, that all previously existing community is shown to have been illusory, is annulled, destroyed, and broken through, and that here and now the new community of the resurrection world is created.

The kingdom of God takes form in the *state,* insofar as here the orders of existing communities are maintained with authority and responsibility. So that humanity does not collapse through the will of the individual who wants to go his own way, the state pledges to preserve the order of the community, marriage, family, and nation in the world of the curse. The state does not create new communities, but it maintains the existing ones; that is its office.

In the church the power of *loneliness* is destroyed in the act of confession; in the state it is restrained through preservation of communal order. And in turn the state, in its limited range of action, points to the final miracle of God in the resurrection, just as the church, in its authoritative witness to God's breaking through to the world, points to the preservation of order in the world under the curse.

The kingdom of God takes form in the *church* insofar as the power of *desire* is transfigured through the witnessing of God's miracle. Human desire, which is turned in on itself, is judged, destroyed, nullified in the proclamation of the cross and the resurrection of Jesus Christ. On the body of Christ on the cross our desire is judged. Yet, at the same time, transfigured and created anew in the resurrection world, where it becomes the desire of one person for another, for God and the brother, for love, peace, happiness, blessedness.

The kingdom of God takes form in the *state* insofar as here human desire is restrained with authority and responsibility, is kept within the order, to the extent that each is protected and preserved from the desire of the other. However, desire is not destroyed, only restrained, so that it may prove its value and bear fruit in the service of the community of the fallen world. Here, too, is love—although always immersed in the possibility of hate; here, too, is joy—but never without the bitter awareness of its transitory nature;—and salvation—but always at the edge of despair.

The power of desire is *overcome* and *transfigured* in the church, *restrained* and ordered in the state. Here, too, the limited range of state action points to the authoritative testimony of the church, just as the church points to the order of the state, which fulfills its office in this cursed world.

The church limits the state, just as the state limits the church. And both

294

must remain aware of this mutual limitation and support this tense juxta-position, which should never be a coalescence. Only thus do both *together*, and never one alone, point to the kingdom of God, which is here attested in such a splendid twofold form.

This consideration does not remain theoretical, however, but becomes truly serious at the point where between church and state we speak of a *people*. Because the people are called to the kingdom of God, they have a place in both state and church. As a result, the people, indeed we ourselves, now become the setting in which their encounter takes place. We ourselves become those who are called, on the one hand, to take seriously the limits and, on the other, where the limits truly collide and produce sparks, to per-ceive the living heart of God's kingdom itself. When we pray: Thy kingdom come! we are then praying for the church, that it might bear witness to the miracle of the resurrection, and for the state, with its authority, that it may defend the orders of the preserved world of the curse. That the church has its office solely in relation to miracle and that the state has its office solely in relation to order, and that between church and state the people of God, Christendom, live in obedience—that is the prayer for God's kingdom on Earth, for the kingdom of Christ.

Christ's kingdom is God's kingdom, but God's kingdom in the form ordained for us; not as a visible, powerful empire, as the "new" kingdom of the world, but as the kingdom of the other world that has entered completely into the discord and contradiction of this world. At the same time it appears as the powerless, defenseless gospel of the resurrection, of miracle, and as the state that possesses authority and power that preserves order. Only in the true relation and delimitation of the two is Christ's kingdom reality.

This may sound somber, but then it should, and only thus does it call us to obedience. Obedience toward God in the church and in the state. The kingdom of God is found not in some other world beyond but in our midst. It seeks our obedience despite contradictory appearances, and then it con-stantly seeks, through our obedience, the miracle, like lightning allowed to flash from the perfect, blessed new world of the final promise. On Earth, God seeks to be honored by us in the other, and nowhere else. God plants his kingdom in the cursed ground. We must open our eyes, become sober, obey God here. Come, you that are blessed by my father, inherit the king-dom! This the Lord says to none other than those to whom he said: I was hungry and you gave me food, I was thirsty and you gave me drink. Just as you did it to one of the least of these who are members of my family, you did it to me.

Because God's kingdom is to exist eternally, God will create a new Heaven and a new Earth. But truly a new *Earth*. It will then be God's kingdom on Earth, on the new Earth of the promise, on the old Earth of the creation. This is the promise: that one day we shall behold the world of the resurrection, which we here comprehend in the words of the church and to which the state points. We shall not remain divided, but God will be all in all. Christ will lay his kingdom at God's feet, and the kingdom of the consummation will be at hand. The kingdom where there will be no more tears, no more sorrow, no more crying, no more death. It is the kingdom of life, of community, of transfiguration. And there will no longer be church or state; rather, they will return their offices to the One from whom they originally received them, and God alone will be the Lord as the Creator, the crucified and resurrected One, and the Spirit that reigns in his holy community.

Thy kingdom come. Thus we pray also for that ultimate kingdom in the certainty that his kingdom has already dawned among us. It comes even without our prayer—says Luther, but in this prayer we ask that it may also come among us, that we not be left outside.

The Old Testament tells the strange story of Jacob, who has fled his homeland, from the land God promised, and has lived abroad for many years in a state of enmity with his brother. Then, one day, he can no longer stand it; he wants to return home to the promised land, the land of God's promise; he wants to return to his brother. He is on his way; it is the last night before he is to enter once again into the promised land. Only a narrow river still separates him from it. As he prepares to cross it, he is stopped. Someone wrestles with him in the dark, someone he does not recognize. It seems Jacob is not to reenter his homeland; he is to be pinned down and to die at the gate to the promised land. But incredible powers come upon Jacob, and he fights back against his attacker and takes hold of him and does not let him go until he hears his attacker say: "Let me go, dawn is breaking." With his last ounce of strength, Jacob refuses to let his attacker go: "I will not let you go unless you bless me." It seems to him then as if the end had come, so hard his attacker struggles against him. Yet at that moment, he is blessed, and the attacker disappears. Then the sun rises upon Jacob, and limping from one hip, he enters into the promised land. The way is clear; the dark door to the promised land had been blown open. The curse had been transformed into a blessing. And now the sun rises upon him. That for all of us the way into the promised land passes through the night, that we too only enter it as those strangely marked with scars from the struggle with God, the struggle for God's kingdom and grace; that we enter into the land of God and of our brother as limping warriors—this we Christians share with Jacob. And we know, too, that the sun is destined for us as well. This allows us to bear with patience the time of wandering and waiting and believing that has been imposed on us. But this we know more than Jacob, that it is not we who must go, but rather that God comes to us. Our consolation today, on the eve of All Souls' Day,[7] is that Advent and Christmas follow. That is why we pray: Thy kingdom come to us as well.

7. ["November 20, 1932," *DBWE* 12:297, n. 31.]

19. CHRIST AND PEACE

DBWE 12:258–262

In this short meditation delivered to a student organization at the end of 1932, Bonhoeffer challenges the facile reconciliation of love of God with military hostility toward the neighbor. While Bonhoeffer's assertion that obedience to God might imply peaceful intentions toward neighboring nations seems supported by a straightforward interpretation of the greatest commandment (Matt. 22:37–39), a number of factors would have prevented many of his contemporaries from seeing things this way. Many Germans, drawing on Paul's appeal to Christians to subject themselves to governing authorities (Rom. 13:1), had restricted the range of the Sermon on the Mount's application to interactions among citizens rather than interactions among nations and governments. Challenging such thinking therefore requires Bonhoeffer to assert here that the center of the New Testament is the Sermon on the Mount—a provocative claim in an environment informed by Luther's privileging of Romans as the heart of the gospel.

A second challenge facing Bonhoeffer's argument was the idea of the nation as a God-ordained order of creation, an idea often invoked to restrict neighbor status to citizens of one's own nation in direct contrast to Bonhoeffer's application of neighbor love to the Christian brother "on this side or on the other side" of national divides. Bonhoeffer argues in this address, and later in Discipleship, *that his audience should set aside patterns of thinking, including certain understandings of subjection to authority and orders of creation, that stand in the way of simple obedience to God's command, a command that might include peaceful intention toward neighboring nations. Phrases like 'cheap grace,' and ideas like the centrality of the Sermon on the Mount, the unity of faith and discipleship, and simple obedience to the command of Christ, show that by late 1932 key ideas of the book* Discipleship *had already formed in Bonhoeffer's mind.*

"You shall love the Lord your God with all your heart, and with all your soul,   258
and with all your mind." This is the greatest and first commandment. And
the second is like it: "You shall love your neighbor as yourself."

Once again, the human authorities who sought to build peace upon a political foundation find themselves shipwrecked.[1] It would be good to reflect on
this, and not to be too amazed, for *worldly authorities* are set up by human   259
beings and thus do not constitute absolute authority.

There is only one *authority* who has spoken definitively on this question,
and that is *Jesus Christ.*

It is true that Christ has not given us specific rules for our conduct in
every possible complex political, economic, or other situation that may arise
in human life. However, this does not mean that the gospel of Jesus Christ
does not give a clear answer to the problems that confront us. To the simple
reader of the Sermon on the Mount, what it says is unmistakable.

Let us begin at the very center of the New Testament, so that we can
subject these questions to the first and greatest commandment and to
the preaching of our Lord. Let us not pull one single word about worldly
authority out of the whole context of the New Testament,[2] thereby failing to
recognize that Christ proclaimed the reign of God, which the entire world,
including its governance, meets with hostility.

Let me first discuss a few points that can easily be occasions for misunderstanding.

(1) It was not Christ's concern to change the conditions he found in this
world in order to bring about security, peace, and quiet. Much less should
we think that *we* can do away with outward sins and the horrors of war
through political treaties. As long as the world is free of God, there will be
wars.

Christ was much more concerned that we should love God, that we
become disciples of Jesus, as we are called to do through the promise of the
Beatitudes, and that we thus become witnesses for peace.

This *discipleship of Christ* arises from and is based entirely on simple *faith*,
and inversely, faith is only true in discipleship.[3] So these words are addressed
to the faithful, but the world is judged by Christ's witness to peace. Faith,

---

1. [*Bonhoeffer likely has in mind the recent breakdown of talks at the Geneva Disarmament
Conference. See* DBWE *12:41.*]

2. [*Bonhoeffer likely refers to Rom. 13:1, which enjoins subjection to governing authorities.*]

3. ["These ideas hint at those developed later in *Discipleship*; cf. *DBWE* 4:63–64,"
DBWE 12:259, n. 8.]

however, must be simple; otherwise it will bring about reflection rather than obedience; the left hand will know what the right hand is doing, and this is not discipleship, which knows nothing of good or evil. Moreover, only such discipleship encompasses the right attitude toward those who have given their lives in war.

260   So there are no possibilities at the human level to organize or to build peace. Indeed, human attempts to do so by political means can become domination of self-glorifying human beings and thus be sinful. There is no *guaranteed* peace. A Christian can only dare to make peace through faith. So there is no direct way to make all people brothers and sisters; the way to one's enemy is only through prayer to the Lord of all peoples.

    (2) Conversely, the relationship between *law and gospel* is often misunderstood. Here the gospel is understood as the message of forgiveness of sin that doesn't address the citizen or indeed deal with any aspect of the earthly life of human beings. The human being is told that he is a sinner but is not called to lay aside his sin and sinful connections. If we do not walk the path of obedience, if we sin in confidence that grace exists, how shall we take seriously the grace of the forgiveness of sins, or even take prayer itself seriously, and believe in God with pure hearts? At that point we are asking for cheap grace. We are forgetting, in the justification of the sinner through the cross of Christ, the cry of the Lord, who never justifies sin.

    The commandment "You shall not kill" [*Exod. 20:13*], the word that says, "Love your enemies" [*Matt. 5:44*], is given to us simply to be obeyed. For Christians, any military service, except in the ambulance corps, and any preparation for war, is forbidden. The belief that sees freedom from the law as meaning you can do anything you like outside the law is a human belief and defies God. Simple obedience knows nothing of good and evil but lives in discipleship to Christ and does its good works as a matter of course.

    (3) The commandment to love is addressed to us Christians first of all in the sense that we *ourselves* have peace with every other person, as Christ did when he preached peace to his congregation, using the example of making peace with one's brother or with one's neighbor, or the example of the Good Samaritan. If we do not have this personal peace, we cannot preach peace to the nations. And most people who are annoyed by hearing about peace among nations already question the love for one's personal enemies.

    So when we speak of matters of peace, we must always keep in mind that relations between two nations are deeply analogous with relations between two individual persons.

    The things that stand in the way of peace are in both cases thirst for power, pride, the drive to seek fame and honor, as well as arrogance and feelings of inferiority, fear of other people, and the struggle for living space[4] and for bread. What is sinful for an individual person, however, can never 261 be a virtue for a *nation*.

That which is proclaimed as gospel to the church, to the church-community, and to individual Christians is spoken as judgment on the world. But if a nation will not listen to this commandment, Christians from within that nation are called to be witnesses to it.

But let us take care that we, who are miserable sinners, preach peace out of love, and not out of zeal to bring about security, to pursue a political end.

(4) Peace with whom? True peace can only be in God and come from God. This peace is a gift given to us with Christ, that is, peace is inseparably bound up with the gospel. So peace can never consist in reconciling the gospel with religious worldviews. Jesus said: "I have not come to bring peace, but a sword" [*Matt. 10:34*]. Forgiveness of sins is granted to sinners who repent, who have lost their way, and we should love them, not judge them. The commandment serves as judgment for the defiant sinner. But there is no reconciliation with sin, any more than with a false doctrine. In the struggle between the gospel and these earthly powers, the Christian becomes separated from father and mother.

The Christian's struggle is therefore a struggle for the cause. In the conflict with the enemy of the gospel, the Christian's *weapons*, however, are faith and love, which are purified in suffering. How much more so than in quarrels that are only about earthly possessions.[5]

What does this greatest and highest commandment tell us? It calls upon us to love and makes the love of our neighbor a *parable* for our love of God. We do not *truly* love God unless we love our neighbor as ourselves. Our love for our neighbor is not *pure* if we do not love God in and with him. Love is self-seeking if it does not seek God and God's commandments. In the pure love with which God first loved us is the peace that Christ gives (John 14:27), which is promised in the Beatitudes [*Matt. 5:3-11*]. Pure love, however, would rather see a defenseless brother be killed than to see his soul, or 262 our own, stained with blood. Pure love, in obedience to the fifth commandment,[6] gives up its life for a brother, whether he is on this side or on the

---

4. [*The need for "living space"* (Lebensraum) *was one of the justifications offered by the Third Reich for its expansion.*]

5. ["It is unclear in the manuscript as to whether this last word is 'possessions' or 'virtue,'" *DBWE* 12:261, n. 14.]

6. ["According to the numbering in the Lutheran Catechism: 'You shall not kill!,'" *DBWE* 12:262, n. 16.]

other side. Pure love quite simply cannot lift up a sword against a Christian, because that would mean to lift it against Christ.

When we confront these individual questions, the thought that always comes is that following Christ means very simply, Go and do likewise—do as the Lord himself did. The question of whether God actually commanded *us* to do these things is the serpent's question.[7] What we learn from the commandment is what Christ would have done in this or that concrete situation.

And let us be glad: "Little children, you are from God, and have conquered them; for the one who is in you is greater than the one who is in the world" (1 John 4:4).

---

7. [*Bonhoeffer alludes to the serpent's question, "Did God really say . . . ?," in Gen. 3:1. For his commentary on this question, see* DBWE *3:103–110* (*Reader* 243–248).]

PART 4
Theology and the Third Reich

20. The Führer and the Individual in the Younger Generation

DBWE 12:268–282

Bonhoeffer originally presented the following as his contribution to a series of radio addresses on the theme "the younger generation."[1] Although the topic of the Führer[2] (leader) had been decided before Hitler's rise to power, Bonhoeffer delivered the address on February 1, 1933, two days after Hitler ascended to the chancellorship. He begins by suggesting a division of the young generation into three subgenerations, a schema that seems to reflect his own family experience, before turning to the central issue: authority. He draws a contrast between leadership, where authority originates from above and rests in God-ordained offices, and the leader, where authority originates from the people below and rests in the person of the leader. Bonhoeffer finds the latter model of authority dangerous and unstable, liable to slide from leader into misleader. Unfortunately, the crises of the war and postwar era have left the younger generation without proper leadership, hungry for a leader.

Bonhoeffer was distressed that this radio address was cut short just as he reached its theological heart, which he had reserved for the conclusion. To remedy this, he had the address printed in several newspapers. Contrary to what has been widely reported in the Bonhoeffer literature, there is no evidence to suggest that the conclusion of the address was censored for political reasons; it seems Bonhoeffer simply went over his allotted time.[3]

---

1. [DBWE *12:268, n. 1.*]

2. ["We have retained the German word here because it was already a loaded term in Germany, even before the National Socialists came to power . . . ," *DBWE* 11:273, n. 18.]

3. [DBWE *12:91.*]

268   If today we take up a question from among the problems of the younger generation, we can only do so if we ourselves are sure of having overcome the unpleasant self-reflection with which this sort of subject has been dealt with countless times, if we do not take a sensationalist approach . . . and do not

269   take ourselves too seriously—but rather take this on as an attempt at critical self-reflection in the service of a greater good. Three brothers, of whom the eldest was born in 1900, the second in 1905, and the third in 1910, who are therefore thirty-three, twenty-eight, and twenty-three years old, embody the difference today between three generations. They all, however, belong to that which we like to call the "young generation"—the eldest, who reached maturity during the war, the second under the impression of the years after the collapse, and the third in a still-untitled epoch, let us say since 1926. The rush of historical events has accelerated the speed of the change in generations by nearly a factor of 10. A period of three to five years separates the generations today. We must speak of a generational change when the ranks of young people of the same age invoke one reason for their general intellectual position, thereby setting themselves apart from the older generation as an independent group shaped by a particular experience—and where, on the other hand, those who are older are already engaged in the strange process of clarifying their own range of experience and intellectual position. The greatest difficulties in the current debate with and within the younger generation have their roots in this same inner disunity. The *first*: people who have experienced death, who have, so to speak, stepped daily out of death into life, who have come to know life as action and profit, and who thus have a very special range in their thinking and desires. They are characterized, on the one hand, by an almost injurious hardness toward their own lives and acts and those of others and, on the other, by a strong affirmation of life and responsibility toward others' lives. This generation of youth who experienced war exists as a closed group vis-à-vis their younger brothers. Whether conscious or not, their entire stance is the expression of an unachievable superiority over the others; there is almost an expression of mockery on the faces of these youth marked by life and death, a mockery of those who are completely inexperienced, who live without really knowing

270   what it means. There is an invisible but impenetrable barrier between those who fought in the war and those who are only a little younger, who reached maturity during the period of collapse. This is felt even more greatly among the younger ones than among the older. For the first postwar generation there is nothing more impressive than the fact that among them live these men who have escaped from the world of death. There is something frightening, worrying, terrifying in this knowledge. And the strange silence that lay over this world in the first postwar years, replaced only some years later

by a no longer very original talkativeness, strengthens the awareness of the unapproachability of this world for all the others.

It was under pressure from this generation of war veterans that the younger generation grew up. They have two main characteristics: On the one hand, they have been given the knowledge that their older brothers acquired firsthand, and thus they have been made aware of life in its entirety, with all its uncertainty and dubiousness. On the other, this problem differs from the question facing the older ones in that the latter experienced it themselves in the middle of a situation of responsibility, that is, one they continually had to overcome in their lives. The problem for the younger ones was not bound to responsibility and was therefore radical, and at the same time they had to push to create a situation of responsibility in which this problem could be experienced. Thus the younger ones, due to this contrast with the older ones, were led to be actively constructive, and less to responsibly accept and tolerate the given, to freely create their own way of life out of their radical critique.

With the end of the era of the youth movement—in the largest sense of the term—that is, at the moment that this second group of youth accepted the responsibility of professional life, today's youngest generation arose. Without being aware of it, they know that life cannot be constructed out of the radical problematic. It does not therefore become unproblematic, as is often said, because the inheritance from their older brothers is too much a part of them, but the focus of their problems has shifted; indeed one could say that the problem has split. The ultimate questions of life are answered with silence—in deliberate opposition to the talkativeness of the preceding generation—a silent alliance with the reality in sport, travel, does not permit curiosity and sensation for the problem to arise for itself, without our being able to say that this silence is a deathly silence. On the other hand, the problem of life turns from a general question to a concrete one with respect to the time for political action. And to this point it must be said that the youngest generation's sense of reality has and is becoming a metaphysic of reality. Reality is not taken as that which it is; there is no reflection on what it can and cannot be; rather, reality is taken as what it should be; it is naively held   271 to be open to any development and construction; in it the elements of God's kingdom on earth are seen in the process of coming into being. Where this metaphysic of reality is bound to an awareness of the concrete political difficulties, there arises a political-chiliastic way of thinking like that which generally characterizes the youngest generation.

It is now understandable that, on the intellectual battlefield where these three young generations find themselves together with the older generation, that is, where these four generations struggle against one another, the situation is as unclear as it appears today. However, for an understanding of the decisive contemporary cultural-political and other questions, it is necessary to keep in mind these divisions brought about by the historical developments, for which no one is to blame.

Nonetheless a few generalizations may be made about the younger generation as a whole. They reached maturity during a period of history during which the previously well-established Western world came apart at the seams—war, postwar period, crisis. Thus the inner task facing them could only consist of the attempt to avoid being pulled into a complete collapse and instead to find the foothold that would allow them a continued existence. Three impressions shaped their move toward this foothold: first, in the collapse they experienced the triumph of objects over humans, of machines over their creators. Technology, which was intended to master nature, had been turned against defenseless humans and thus robbed of its essential meaning! Second, the impotence of the entire existing political, intellectual, and religious ideology seemed to have been proven, and third, the millions who fell in the Great War, the revolutionizing masses of the postwar period, and the million-strong army of unemployed during the crisis must have given the younger generation a convincing impression of the meaninglessness and complete isolation of the individual and of the blunt power of the masses. The masses and lifeless objects appeared to have emerged from this collapse as victors. In neither, however, was the younger generation able to find the foothold that could help sustain their lives in this chaos. A sense of the individual and the sense of true community seemed to have been completely destroyed. An individualistically formed autonomous personality and an idea separated from the reality of the [. . .][4] life went bankrupt. It was out of this crisis that an impassioned call arose for new authority, new ties, for community. The common concern of the younger generation as a whole vis-à-vis the older generation can be seen in the opposition to an unreal individualism and the attempt at a new, meaningful common life. The extent to which an unreal individualism is being contrasted here with an equally unreal collectivism will be examined later. A quite simple fact of experience led initially to this opposition, namely, that at the turn of the century and later the educated classes were unable to deal with the important problems of life, both public and private. The lost war made this latent crisis obvious. Germany came apart at the seams. And the younger generation found itself more or less abandoned and having to fend for itself. The problem of the meaning of the defeat in

272

---

4. ["One word illegible," *DBWE* 12:271, n. 9.]

intellectual historical terms was taken up and discussed, with the conclusion that the answer was to be found by overcoming the lack of community among Germans, and that the defeat had to lead to a new sense of community, to new bonds, new authority. Fairly and unfairly, this was suggested to the older generation. These concepts naturally underwent a superficial schematization: individualism, liberalism, personality became terms of denigration for something generally misunderstood that people did under other names. These, however, are natural processes and not to be taken too seriously. Hidden behind these words was a serious desire, intended to lead people from the individual to the collective, from lack of attachment to interdependence, from a lack of authority to new authority. This new authority, however, could only be imagined in terms of a new human being, one not disconnected from the reality of life, based on a new idea of life   273
overcoming the isolation of individuals. The ideal of the leader was thus outlined. Authority in the form of the leader—it was in this demand that the younger generation liberated itself from the burden forced upon it.

With the postwar youth movement, the idea of the leader in its new form spread throughout Germany for the first time. This was the movement's first creative act, one through which these youth also prompted their elder brothers to act; the younger ones became the creative force for the elder ones. Naturally, there have always been leaders. Where there is community   274
there is leadership. However, here we are interested only in the particular form that the idea of the leader took in the young generation, and here is a first characteristic: previously, leadership had found its expression in teachers, statesmen, fathers, that is, in the given social structure and offices, but now the leader has become a completely autonomous form. The leader has become totally divorced from an office; he is essentially and only leader. What does this mean? While leadership was previously based on bonds, it is now based on choice. This is understandable, as the bonds from which any previous leader could arise have become obsolete. Thus the problem of leadership, one of the oldest problems of community altogether, became concentrated in the problem of the *leader*. For both parties[5] leadership remains something neutral, neutered—or to be more specific, objective; the ideology of the leader relates to the person of both parties. Leadership arises through superiority in something objective, through office, knowledge, ability; with the leader, it is essentially a dominance of the person. For both it is a question of power relations, for leadership superiority in something objective, for a leader in the dominance of his person. Thus it is

---

5. ["The leader and the follower," *DBWE* 12:274, n. 18.]

quite clear that there can be a more rational basis for leadership than for the ideology of the leader. It is inherent to the ideology of the leader that it cannot be rationally based. That is both its strength and its limitation. For leadership it is essentially a question of "what," and for the ideology of the leader a question of "who"; the object of leadership is those who are being led, the view is from above to below; the object of the ideology of the leader is the leader himself, the view is from below to above. Thus a sociologically interesting new phenomenon has been introduced into the structure of authority. The leader as autonomous form has its own particular sociological place. We will conclude our thoughts here by systematically defining the sociological place of the leader—in the modern understanding of the term. First, in the historical developments of the last decades, the concept of leader has undergone an essential transformation, and this we need to examine.

The leader in the sense used in the youth movement arose from a small group; he was not one of those in charge, but a person elected by the group. It was the good, the inwardly noble, who were to be raised up by the group and entrusted by them. The group is the cradle of the leader. It gives the leader everything, including authority. It is the person of the leader onto which all authority, honor, and glory of the group are transferred. Leadership is not an office independent of the person. The group expects that a leader who emerges from the group will embody the group's ideals. This task, in itself impossible, is made easier for the leader in that the group that produced the leader regards that person in the light of their ideals. They are looking not at his reality but at his purpose. It is essential for the image of the leader that the group does not see the face of the past but only regards him from behind; as the figure of the one who strides forward, the leader's humanity is veiled in his form of leader. In the youth movement, however, this leader was meant to be essentially human; it was on the leader's ideal humanity that these youth sought their foothold and a fulfillment for their collapsing personal lives. The leader was meant to be the friend whom one worshipped, loved, for whom one was willing to sacrifice everything. The leader was meant to be that which they had failed to find in their fathers or teachers. These are the two major factors that must be considered in any discussion of the concept of leader: the individual and the father, that is, the given, existing office here. The symptomatic problem of the youth movement was the father-and-son problem. It was here that an explosion was repeatedly sparked off. The father was replaced by the leader, the authority of the father denied in favor of the authority of the leader; the leader was placed above the father; the father would only be an authority when he himself became a leader of youth. Thus the individual is freed from his ties to the existing order and becomes free to choose, completely free; the leader then becomes—in a very particular way in the youth movement—the leader of his own heretofore undiscovered, better self. In the election of the leader, the individual is liberated to himself. In the leader, the one who is led sees his own ideal human self. In the youth movement the group and the leader are essentially a mere extension of one's own self; for all the searching for community and authority, it is essentially a matter of the individual's own soul, which then plunges into the supposed You, only to find itself in every mirror. The sociological category of the individual, with its unbridgeable eternal individuality, as well as the sociological category of the father, that is, the given order, was swallowed up in the first form of the idea of leader in a broad, extended new individualism. Thus the terms "responsibility" and "order" were subsumed in a free, self-legislating individual. In the youth movement—one can say today—it was always only a matter of a new, *individual* soul; the leader of the youth movement was the leader for a spiritual-human fulfillment of the individual. It was because of this definition that the fate of the leader was repeatedly a tragic one. One wanted to see the entire ideal humanity of the leader; one didn't want merely to be permitted to see him as the progressive one. Here, however, where the leader was to be leader in the totally human sense and where he himself understood his task as only personal and not objective, it was unavoidable that both the led and the leader saw through the illusion of such an unlimited ideology of leader. The secret of the leader's authority was unveiled and destroyed, and it was in naked humanity that leader and led separated. Authority collapsed, and with it loyalty and obedience. All that was left was a romantic memory.

The youth movement of the war and the postwar generation was replaced by that of the third—today's youngest generation—at the same time that their supporters had to enter professional life. These young people, originally instilled with a greater sense of reality than their elder siblings and more certain of their direction, saw the hopelessness and meaninglessness of their own futures and those of their fellows most particularly in the political crisis. Thus the aim of these new youth was initially much more concrete and clearly defined than that of their elders; and to a much greater extent the lack of authority in political thought and action was seen as the ultimate cause of all that was bad. The call for political authority, however, in view of the apparently complete failure of previously existing order and conditions, had to become the call for a great person, for a political leader, and in this call—this is the most significant and specific factor—the differences in generation among the youth suddenly disappeared; indeed, the "father-and-son problem," which was the central focus of the youth move-

277

ment, was completely overshadowed; emphasis was placed no longer on the differences but on common obligation. The form of political leader lost its familiarity; friendship was replaced by comradeship, dedication replaced by obedience. The individualistic remnants of the youth movement have been overcome. That is to say, a strange transfer has occurred. The individual sees his duty in unconditional obedience to the leader. The individual is totally dissolved; he becomes a tool in the hands of the leader; the individual is not responsible; it is the leader who is responsible. In his faith in the leader, the individual surrenders ultimate responsibility to the leader, just as for Catholics their faith in their church includes belief in the justness of its commandments and its guarantee for my obedience. In this submission, this disconnection of the individual, individualism is truly overcome, but it reappears in the form of the transfer to the new. That which the individual must surrender is transferred from all individuals onto the form of one person who is the leader. The individual is renounced in favor of the leader. The leader is that which no one else may be, an individual, personality. The relation of the led to their leader is that of the transfer of their own rights onto the leader. As such, it is a form of collectivism that turns into an individualism of the nth degree. For this reason the true sense of community, which is based on the responsibility of individuals to hold one another responsible, does not find its fulfillment here. However, let us continue with the description of this concept of leader. The leader is placed at an enormous distance from the led but—and this is the decisive point—the leader is only such as the one elected by those he leads. Having come from them, the leader receives authority only from his retinue, from below, from the people. The spirit of the people—it is imagined—brings the leader out

278 from its metaphysical depths and raises him to great heights. This leader, arising from the collective power of the people, now appears in the light as the one awaited by the people, the longed-for fulfillment of the meaning and power of the life of the Volk. Thus the originally prosaic idea of political authority is transformed into the political-messianic idea of leader that we see today. All the religious thinking of its supporters flows into it as well. Where the spirit of the people is a divine-metaphysical factor, the leader who embodies this spirit has a religious function in the true sense of the term, becoming the messiah, and thus his appearance heralds the dawn of the fulfillment of ultimate hope, and with the kingdom that he brings in his wake, the eternal kingdom comes closer. While the religious attitude of the group toward their leader in the youth movement could be related to the pietistic ideal of community, the political-messianic idea of leader is closer to the ideal of a universal kingdom of God on earth, which was the goal of

enthusiasm and the French Revolution and has been repeatedly taken up ever since.

But it is exactly this idea that is decisively rejected in the young generation. For all the unanimity in their call for political authority, there are the deepest of divisions as to the exact nature of this authority. This is the fundamental question: Authority of the leader or authority of the office? And this brings us to the most burning question of the day. The leader has authority from below, from the led; the office has authority from above; the authority of the leader depends on the leader's person; the authority of the office is beyond personality; authority from below is self-justification of the people; authority of the office is recognition of given limits; authority from below is authority lent; authority of office is original authority. The key word of the authority of the leader is the Reich [*empire, kingdom*]; the key word of the authority of office is the state. For the problem of the individual this means the following: In the authority of the office, the individual experiences his self will over against the existing ties, his ordered place in the world, his inability to determine his destiny, and at the same time his responsibility in the very place where he finds himself. Authority of office means limitations on the individual in his individual freedom, restrictions, calling attention to the other, to reality. Authority of the leader means for the individual: the free choice of obedience, radical surrender of his right as individual, and nonetheless measureless, limitless freedom of the individual according to the law of transfer. Admittedly, however, neither the limited nor the unlimited individual is as such the individual in his indestructible unity and responsibility, and neither obedience toward the father nor submission to the leader can establish the community in which You and I are truly related to each other. Neither the office nor the leader is, as such, the ultimate given condition.

Nonetheless, the following must initially be said concerning this conflict: the concept of "authority" contains, from its origin, the idea of authorship. Authority is more original than those for whom it is authority. I can therefore only recognize authority as the authority set over me. The authority that I allow others to have over me is basically only my own authority. It is for this reason that the one is true and limited authority, and the other is lent and in danger of becoming excessive. It is for this reason that I am under the control of the one authority, and from the other I can free myself only by myself, and I gain worth from myself. There is a decisive difference between the authority of the father, the teacher, the judge, the statesman, on the one hand, and the authority of the leader, on the other. The former have authority from their office and only through it; the leader has authority only by virtue of his person. The authority of the former can be infringed, violated, but it continues to exist; the authority of the leader is constantly at risk; it is in the hand of his followers. I can choose the leader, but I cannot choose a father and a teacher; I submit to the authority of the leader; I am subordinate to the authority of the father and the teacher. Father, teacher, statesman are essentially not leaders but rather administrators of their office. Those who expect something else do not see the reality, are dreamers. With their idea of leadership, they are certainly dependent on a historical necessity as well as on a necessity arising from a certain youthful sense of life, and there remains only the final fundamental question of the place that the "leader"—in the most portentous sense of the term—takes in the construction of authority and the place from where the individual comes to that authority. People and especially youth will feel the need to give a leader authority over them as long as they do not feel themselves to be mature, strong, responsible enough to themselves fulfill the demands placed in this authority. The leader will have to be responsibly aware of this clear restriction of authority. If the leader understands his function differently from that thus established, if the leader does not repeatedly provide the led with clear details on the *limited nature* of the task and on their own responsibility, if the leader tries to become the idol the led are looking for—something the led always hope from their leader—then the image of the leader shifts to one of a misleader, then the leader is acting improperly both toward the led as well as toward himself. The true leader must always be able to disappoint. This, especially, is part of the leader's responsibility and objectivity. The leader must lead the led from the authority of the leader's person to a recognition of the true authority of order and office. The leader must lead the led into responsibility toward the social structures of life, toward father, teacher, judge, state. The leader must radically reject the temptation to become an idol, that is, the ultimate authority of the led. In all soberness, the leader must confine himself to the task at hand. The leader serves the order of the state, the community, and the service of the leader can be of incomparable value; indeed it can be essential. This, however, only as long as the leader keeps strictly to the task. The leader temporarily takes decision-making powers from the individual but must always remember that this state is a *temporary* necessity and must always remind the led of this. The leader should accept this self-deprivation of rights, self-incapacitation in order to lead the individuals back to their responsibility. To the responsibility of human beings belongs, however, the responsibility vis-à-vis the others, vis-à-vis existing orders, of adapting, ordering oneself, accepting limits. It is thus the case that the leader accepts in their stead that responsibility toward the order and offices of life that the followers are not capable of, and fulfills it for them. While the led believe and hope that their leader is the epitome of an autonomous human being, the masterful human being who is totally free, the leader must be aware that because of the followers, the leader is the most bound, the one most burdened with the responsibility for the orders of life, the epitome of a servant. It is quite obvious that here neither the idea of the individual nor the idea of the community is given due justice, that instead both here are in a historically and psychologically necessary but penultimate stage of development. The leader serves the office. However, this service in office is itself only a penultimate matter. In the authority of office, the individual experiences his bonds, his limits, but also his responsibility. However, here too, the human being is not seen for what he is. It *can* be the case that the individual is in the right vis-à-vis the office, since it is not the ultimate authority. From where can the individual take this right vis-à-vis the office? Nowhere else than there where he sees that the office is the penultimate authority with respect to an ultimate unutterable authority, with respect to the authority of God. And from this authority the individual truly knows himself to be an individual. It is to God that the individual is responsible. And this individuality of standing before God, this submission to the ultimate authority, is destroyed when the authority of a leader or an office is seen as the ultimate authority. The irrefutable indication of this inevitability of individuality for the human being is this: that he must die alone, that he must bear his own body, his suffering and guilt as an individual. Only before God does the human being become what he is, an individual, free, and at the same time bound in responsibility. And each individual knows that he is placed among other individuals, that he is bound to them, that he exists in community. Community of individuals, not a melting together of I and You, the strictest distinction and therefore the strictest responsibility for each other and only for this reason, where the human being becomes an individual before God, community, the community of suffering, of guilt, of death, and of life. There is currently a terrible danger that, in the crying out for authority, for a leader or office, we forget that the human being is an individual before the ultimate authority, and that everyone who misappropriates this breaks an eternal law and takes on superhuman responsibility, which in the end will crush him. The eternal law of individuality before God is terribly vengeful when offended and perverted. Thus the leader points to the office; leader and office, however, to the ultimate authority itself, before which Reich and state are penultimate authorities. Leader and office that turn themselves into gods mock God and the solitary individual before him who is becoming the individual, and must collapse. Only the leader who is in the service of the penultimate and ultimate authority merits loyalty.

282

21. THE CHURCH
AND THE JEWISH QUESTION

DBWE 12:361–370

The historical context of the remaining selections in this section of the Reader *was the Church Struggle, which involved three interwoven dimensions.[1] The first dimension was the struggle between the German Christian movement, a pro-Nazi faction of the church, and the opposing Confessing Church, in which Bonhoeffer was active. The second dimension was the struggle between the Confessing Church and the Nazi state over spheres of influence. And the third was within the Confessing Church itself between those who more willing to compromise with the German Christians and those, including Bonhoeffer, who were not.*

Bonhoeffer wrote the next three selections in the aftermath of "the Aryan paragraph," a law used to exclude Jews from various organizations and professions. Its first formulation was the Law for the Restoration of the Professional Civil Service of April 7, 1933.[2] As Bonhoeffer argues in "The Church and the Jewish Question," such legislation raises two questions for the church, "How does the church judge this action by the state, and what is the church called upon to do about it?" and "What are the consequences for the church's position toward the baptized Jews in its congregations?"

In response to the question about the church's relation to the state, Bonhoeffer reiterates his view[3] that the state is divinely mandated to maintain order. It does not fall to the church to challenge how the state maintains order. Rather, the church challenges the state only if the state ceases to function as a state, that is, if it fails to maintain order. In such a case, the church should take direct political action against the state. Given this framework, the interpretive question is whether the German state's treatment of the Jews falls within a state's right to maintain order as it sees fit,

---

1. [*Hockenos,* Church Divided, *15.*]
2. [*United States Holocaust Memorial Museum, "Antisemitic Legislation, 1933–1939."*]
3. [*See, for example,* DBWE *12:293–296 (Reader 347–350).*]

or constitutes a failure to maintain order and therefore undermines the state as state. Bonhoeffer leaves the interpretation to a church council.

In response to the second question about the church's position toward Christians of Jewish descent, Bonhoeffer argues that the church maintains the right to set the condition of membership, and that condition is not race but baptism. Thus the church should welcome baptized Jews as full members.

This controversial essay has been variously interpreted.[4] Detractors often see in Bonhoeffer's position elements of traditional theological anti-Judaism. Defenders often argue that such elements are superseded in his later thinking, and they point to his legitimation of church action against the state as radical in its historical context. Interpretation of the essay is complicated by the fact (indicated in editorial footnotes below) that important passages are of uncertain origin. For the complex manuscript and publishing history of this text, see DBWE 12:261, n. 1.

Luther, 1546: "We would still show them the Christian doctrine and ask   361 them to convert and accept the Lord whom they should by rights have honored before we did. . . . When they repent, leave their usury, and accept Christ, we would gladly regard them as our brothers."

Luther, 1523: "If the apostles, who also were Jews, had dealt with us Gentiles as we Gentiles deal with the Jews, there would never have been a Christian among the Gentiles. Since they dealt with us Gentiles in such brotherly fashion, we in our turn ought to treat the Jews in a brotherly manner in order that we might convert some of them. For even we ourselves are not yet all very far along, not to speak of having arrived. . . . But when we are trying only to drive them by force . . . how can we expect to work any good among them? Again, when we forbid them to labor and do business and have any   362 human fellowship with us, thereby driving them into usury, how is that supposed to make them better?"[5]

The fact, unique in history, that the Jew is subjected to special laws by the state, solely on the basis of his race and regardless of the religion to which he adheres, presents theologians with two new problems, which must be dealt with separately. How does the church judge this action by the state, and what is the church called upon to do about it? What are the consequences for the church's position toward the baptized Jews in its

---

4. [*For a summary of the scholarship on Bonhoeffer and the Jews, see Haynes,* Bonhoeffer Legacy, *19–41.*]

5. [*The quotations from Luther at the beginning and end of the essay may have been inserted by the editor of* Der Vormarsch, *where this essay was published. They are not in the three drafts written by Bonhoeffer. See* DBWE *12:361, n. 1.*]

congregations? Both these questions can only be answered on the basis of a right concept of the church.

I.

There is no doubt that the church of the Reformation is not encouraged to get involved directly in specific political actions of the state. The church has neither to praise nor to censure the laws of the state. Instead, it has to affirm the state as God's order of preservation[6] in this godless world. It should recognize and understand the state's creation of order—whether good or bad from a humanitarian perspective—as grounded in God's desire for preservation in the midst of the world's chaotic godlessness. This judgment by the church on what the state does stands quite apart from any moralizing and is to be distinguished from every sort of humanitarianism, because of the radical separation between the place of the gospel and the place of the law. The actions of the state remain free from interference by the church. This is not a schoolmaster-like or peevish objection on the part of the church. History is made not by the church but rather by the state. But it is certainly only the church, which bears witness to God's entering into history, that knows what history is and therefore what the state is. And precisely out of this knowledge the church alone bears witness to God's *breaking into* history through Christ and lets the state go on making history. Without doubt one of the historical problems that must be dealt with by our state is the Jewish question, and without doubt the state is entitled to strike new paths in doing so. It remains for the humanitarian associations and individual Christian men who see themselves called to do so, to make the state aware of the moral aspect of the measures it takes in this regard, that is, should the occasion arise, to accuse the state of offenses against morality. Every strong state needs such associations and such individual personages and will foster them with a certain amount of reserved encouragement. Insight into the finer art of statecraft will tell the state how to make use of this advice in a relative sense. In the same way, however, a church that is regarded essentially as a cultural function of the state will interfere in the work of the state with advice of this kind, and all the more wherever the state incorporates

363

---

6. ["Bonhoeffer here uses 'order of preservation' in explicit contrast to 'order of creation' . . . For an extensive discussion of the use of 'orders of creation' at this time, see Ericksen, *Theologians under Hitler*, 98–104. See also the editor's introduction to *DBWE* 3:11–12 for Bonhoeffer's explicit choice of 'orders of preservation' as the alternative," *DBWE* 12:362, n. 6.]

the church more substantially, that is, by relegating essentially moral and educational duties to it.

But the true church of Christ, which lives by the gospel alone and knows the nature of state actions, will never interfere in the functioning of the state in this way, by criticizing its history-making actions from the standpoint of any sort of, say, humanitarian ideal. The church knows about the essential necessity for the use of force in this world, and it knows about the "moral" injustice that is necessarily involved in the use of force in certain concrete state actions. The church cannot primarily take *direct* political action, since it does not presume to know how things should go historically. Even on the Jewish question today, the church cannot contradict the state *directly* and demand that it take any particular different course of action. But that does not mean that the church stands aside, indifferent to what political action is taken. Instead, it can and must, precisely because it does not moralize about individual cases, keep asking the government whether its actions can be justified as *legitimate state* actions, that is, actions that create law and order, not lack of rights and disorder. It will be called upon to put this question as strongly as possible wherever the state seems endangered precisely in its *character as the state*, that is, in its function of creating law and order by force. The church will have to put this question with the utmost clarity today in the matter of the Jewish question. This does not mean interfering in the state's responsibility for its actions; on the contrary, it is thrusting the entire burden of responsibility upon the state itself for the actions proper to it. Thus the church spares the state any moralizing reproach, referring it instead to the function ordained to it by the One who sustains the world. As long as the state acts in such a way as to create law and order—even if it means new laws and a new order—the church of the Creator, Reconciler, and Redeemer cannot oppose it through direct political action. Of course it cannot prevent individual Christians, who know that they are called to do so in certain cases, from accusing the state of "inhumanity"; but as church it will only ask whether or not the state is creating law and order. In doing so the church will, of course, see the state as limited in two ways. Either *too little* law and order or *too much* law and order compels the church to speak. There is too little law and order wherever a group of people is deprived of its rights; although in concrete cases it will always be extraordinarily difficult to distinguish actual deprivation of rights from a formally permitted minimum of rights. Even under serfdom a minimum of law and order was preserved, and yet if serfdom were reintroduced now it would represent deprivation of rights. It is remarkable that Christian churches tolerated serfdom for eighteen hundred years, and

364

365

only in an era when the Christian substance of the church could at least be called into question were new rights created, with the help of the churches (but not significantly or even solely due to their help). Nevertheless, for the church today, a step backward in this direction would be the expression of a lawless state. From this we may conclude that the concept of rights is subject to historical transformations, which has the effect of affirming the state's proper right to make history. It is not the church but rather the state that makes and changes laws. At the other extreme from too little law and order, there can be too much law and order. This would mean the state developing its use of force to such a degree as to rob the Christian faith of its right to proclaim its message. (This does not apply to restriction of free conscience—that would be the humanitarian version, which is an illusion, since every state in its life impinges on the so-called free conscience.) This would be a grotesque situation, since it is from the Christian proclamation and faith that the state receives its own rights, so that it would be dethroning itself. The church must repudiate such an encroachment by the state authorities, precisely because it knows better about the state and the limits of its actions. A state that threatens the proclamation of the Christian message negates itself. There are thus three possibilities for action that the church can take vis-à-vis the state: *first* (as we have said), questioning the state as to the legitimate state character of its actions, that is, making the state responsible for what it does. *Second* is service to the victims of the state's actions. The church has an unconditional obligation toward the victims of any societal order, even if they do not belong to the Christian community. "Let us work for the good of all" [*Gal. 6:10*]. These are both ways in which the church, in its freedom, conducts itself in the interest of a free state. In times when the laws are changing, the church may under no circumstances neglect either of these duties. The *third* possibility is not just to bind up the wounds of the victims beneath the wheel but to seize the wheel itself. Such an action would be direct political action on the part of the church. This is only possible and called for if the church sees the state to be failing in its function of creating law and order, that is, if the church perceives that the state, without any scruples, has created either too much or too little law and order. It must see in either eventuality a threat to the existence of the state and thus to its own existence as well. There would be too little if any one group of citizens is deprived of its rights. There would be too much in the case of an attack, coming from the state, on the nature of the church and its proclamation, such as the obligatory exclusion of baptized Jews from our Christian congregations or a ban on missions to the Jews. In such a case, the church would find itself in *statu confessionis*,[7] and the state would find itself in the act of self-negation. A state that incorporates a church that it has violated has lost its most loyal servant. But even this third kind of action by a church, which in a given case leads it into conflict with the existing state, is only the paradoxical expression of its ultimate recognition of the state, for the church itself is aware that it is here called upon to protect the state from itself and to preserve it. For the church today, the Jewish question poses the first two possibilities as challenges of the hour, which it has a duty to meet. The necessity for immediate political action by the church must, however, be decided by an "evangelical council" as and when the occasion arises and hence cannot be casuistically construed beforehand.[8]

The measures of the state against Judaism, however, have for the church 367 a very particular context. The church of Christ has never lost sight of the thought that the "chosen people," which hung the Redeemer of the world on the cross, must endure the curse of its action in long-drawn-out suffering. "The Jews are the most miserable people on earth. They are plagued everywhere, and scattered about all countries, having no certain resting place" (Luther, *Table Talk*). But the history of suffering of this people that God loved and punished will end in the final homecoming of the people Israel to its God. And this homecoming will take place in Israel's conversion to Christ. "When the hour comes when this people, humbled and repentant, lets go of the sins of its fathers, to which it has been clinging with terrible obstinacy to this day, and begs for the blood of the Crucified One to come down to reconcile them, the world will be astonished at the wonders God has wrought! has wrought for this people! And the scoffing Philistines will be just so much filth in the street and dry straw on the rooftops. Then God will gather this people together out of all nations and bring it back to Canaan. O Israel, who is your equal? Blessed is the people whose God is the *Lord*!" (Menken, 1795). The conversion of Israel is to be the end of its people's sufferings. From this perspective, the Christian church trembles at the sight of the people Israel's history, as God's own free, terrible way with God's own people. We know that no state in the world can deal with this enigmatic people, because God has not yet finished with it. Every new attempt to "solve" the "Jewish question" comes to grief because of the mean-

---

7. [*For more on* "statu confessionis," *see the next selection and the introduction to it.*]

8. ["The paragraph that follows appeared only in the published version. It is not in any of Bonhoeffer's three drafts of the essay," *DBWE* 12:367, n. 15.]

ing of this people for salvation history, and yet such attempts have to be made again and again. The church's knowledge of the curse that weighs upon this people takes it far beyond any sort of cheap moralizing. Instead, it knows itself as the church that is unfaithful to its Lord over and over again, and that it shares in the humiliation that it sees in this outcast people, and full of hope it views those Israelites who have already come home, who have come to faith in the one true God in Christ, and it knows it has a bond with them as brothers and sisters. That brings us to the second question.

368

II.

The church cannot allow the state to prescribe for it the way it treats its members. A baptized Jew is a member of our church. For the church, the Jewish question is therefore different from what it is for the state.

From the point of view of Christ's church, Judaism is never a racial concept but rather a religious one. Rather than the biologically dubious entity of the Jewish race, it means the "people Israel." It is God's law that constitutes the "people" Israel; thus one can *become* a Jew by accepting the law. But in the racial sense one cannot become a Jew. At the time of the great Jewish missions to the Gentile world, there were various steps toward becoming a Jew (Schürer III 1909, pages 150ff.). In the same way, being a Jewish Christian is a religious and not a racial concept. The Jewish Christian mission also extended to Gentile regions (see Paul's opponents in the Letter to the Galatians). There were Gentile Jewish Christians and Jewish Gentile Christians.

From the point of view of Christ's church, therefore, Jewish Christians are not people of the Jewish race who have been baptized Christians, but rather *Jewish Christians* in the church's sense are those who see their belonging to the people of God, to the church of Christ, as *determined* by their observance of a divine law. Gentile Christians, on the other hand, see no other prerequisite for their belonging to the people of God, to the church of Christ, than being called to it by God, through God's Word in Christ.

This alone was the difference in understanding with regard to the appearance of Christ, to the gospel, which led to the first division in Christ's church into Gentile Christianity and Jewish Christianity (council of the apostles). This division was understood by some as an unendurable heresy and by others as a schism that could be endured.

An analogous occurrence today would be a case in which a church group within the church of the Reformation made church membership dependent on observance of a divine law, for example, racial uniformity among the members of a congregation. By making this requirement, the people concerned would become a type of Jewish Christian, regardless of whether 369 they actually belong to the Jewish race or not. Let us then suppose that these Jewish Christians of the modern type *withdraw* from the Gentile Christian congregation and establish their own church-community bound by laws. It would, however, be ecclesiastically impossible for persons in this congregation who are racially Jewish then to be excluded, on the grounds that they spoil the claim to be Jewish Christian through the law. For that would mean claiming that a Gentile Christian congregation is Jewish Christian, a claim that the congregation would rightfully have to refuse.

To exclude persons who are racially Jewish from our ethnically German church would mean to make it into a church of the Jewish Christian type. Such exclusion is therefore not possible in the church.

Only the presence of congregations of foreign origin already in Germany, that is, French, English, and so on, allows us to conclude that there would be no ecclesiastical obstacle to Christians of Jewish origin coming together voluntarily to form their own congregation (as happened with the Jewish Christian Alliance in London in 1925). But in no case may a Gentile Christian congregation whose members are of German descent be compelled to exclude Gentile Christian Jews who are already members in it, quite apart from the difficulty of proving that these Jews are not Germans (cf. Stöcker's thesis that Jews become Germans through baptism). Such compulsory exclusion would always mean a genuine church schism, even if it is done as a purely corporate organizational measure, because it would make racial uniformity a church law to be fulfilled as a requirement for fellowship in the church. The church-community *doing the excluding* would thus be constituting itself as a *Jewish Christian* community.

The question here is not at all about whether our church members of 370 German descent can support fellowship in the church with Jews. In reality, it is the duty of Christian proclamation to say: here, where Jew and German together stand under God's Word, is church; here it will be proven whether or not the church is still church. If someone feels unable to continue in church fellowship with Christians of Jewish origin, nothing can prevent him from leaving this church fellowship. But it must be made clear to him, with ultimate seriousness, that he is turning his back on the place where the church of Christ stands, and that with that he himself is bringing about the Jewish Christian idea of a religion of law, that is, he is lapsing into a modern type of Jewish Christianity. It still remains an open question whether or not such a division can be seen as an endurable schism. Furthermore, one must be extraordinarily unobservant not to notice that any behavior other than the just-mentioned one on the part of our church toward baptized Jews would meet with far-reaching lack of understanding among our church people.

(Manuscript completed on April 15, 1933)

"There is no other rule or test for who is a member of the people of God or the church of Christ . . . than this: where there is a little band of those who accept the word of this Lord, teach it purely and confess it against those who persecute it, and for that reason suffer what is their due."

Luther on Psalm 110, v. 3

22. THE JEWISH-CHRISTIAN QUESTION AS *STATUS CONFESSIONIS*

DBWE 12:371–373

In the following piece, Bonhoeffer responds to a July 13, 1933, news item, "Main Outlines of the Constitution," which implied that the recently signed German Evangelical Church constitution would extend the Aryan paragraph's exclusion of Jews to the sphere of church leadership. (The constitution did not in fact adopt the Aryan paragraph but relied on quotas to exclude Jewish students from theological study, thus working toward a future exclusion of Jews from church leadership.[1]) Bonhoeffer argues that such exclusion of ethnically Jewish Christians would undermine the church's very nature. For this reason, the adoption of such a policy would put the church in status confessionis, in a state of confessional protest where "the truth of the gospel and Christian freedom are at stake."[2] The question whether the Aryan paragraph constituted a status confessionis for the German Evangelical Church (colloquially referred to as the Reich Church) was a central issue at the beginning of the Church Struggle.[3]

In the just published "Outlines" of the new church constitution it is implied   371
that this law guarantees the exclusion of non-German baptized Christians
from positions of ecclesiastical leadership. This clause impels us to draw
attention again to the question that is of fundamental significance for the
Church in view of the pending decision of all the Synods.

The Aryan paragraph in the form contained in the first program of the   372
'German Christians,'[4] is a "*status confessionis*" for the Church. Nothing is

---

1. [*See* DBWE *12:371, n. 3.*]
2. [*Formula of Concord, Epitome, Article X/6*, Book of Concord, *516. See* DBWE *12:366, n. 14.*]
3. [DBWE *12:371, n. 2.*]
4. ["*In 1932, the German Christian Faith Movement published its ten-point guidelines. Those principles illustrate how German Christians extrapolated an anti-Jewish platform from their view of*

more dangerous than for us to allow ourselves to be hoodwinked by statements as to its relative harmlessness. The constantly repeated effort to befog the questions relative to it is intended to keep us from seeing clearly the fact by the very substance of which the Church is endangered, and thus wrest out of our hands the decision for which we are responsible to the Church alone. Do not let us be deceived by all sorts of material considerations about the significance or insignificance of the matter, and lose sight of its spiritual substance, which demands a spiritual decision.

The exclusion of the Jewish Christians from our communion of worship would mean:

The excluding Church is erecting a racial law as a prerequisite of Christian communion.[5] But in doing so, it loses Christ himself, who is the goal of even this human, purely temporal law. The Christian Church cannot deny to any Christian brother the Christian communion which he seeks. A Church which excludes the Jewish Christians puts itself under the Law; it is then a Church of Jewish Christian type.

A Christian Church cannot exclude from its communion a member on whom the sacrament of baptism has been bestowed, without degrading baptism to a purely formal rite to which the Christian communion that administers it is indifferent. It is precisely in baptism that God calls man into this concrete Church and into its communion.

The question whether an Aryan paragraph is endurable by the church boards is to be distinguished from the first question. But here, too, a certain laziness and indifference must not be allowed to cloud the issue. Pastors are not state officials. Hence, official regulations cannot be applied to them under any circumstances. Concerning admission to the ministry, as to other church positions, only ecclesiastical viewpoints are decisive, i.e., right doctrine, Christian conduct, and spiritual endowments alone qualify for the ministry. It is therefore an ecclesiastical impossibility to exclude, as a matter of principle, Jewish Christian members from any offices of the Church. It is a different matter if, from case to case, consideration is shown for the weakness of others, so that, for instance, a preponderantly 'German Christian'

373

---

race as God's revelation. . . . In May 1933, near the peak of their period of ascendancy, the German Christians issued revised guidelines," Bergen, Twisted Cross, 23–24.]

5. ["This statement had already appeared in the essay 'The Church and the Jewish Question' (*DBWE* 12:368–369 [*Reader* 376–377]), and reappears verbatim in the Bethel confession (*DBWE* 12:419–420) and in the theses on 'The Aryan Paragraph in the Church' (*DBWE* 12:425–426 [*Reader* 383–384])," *DBWE* 12:372, n. 5.]

parish will not have a Jewish Christian assigned to it as sole pastor.[6] But even here the possibility remains open of doing just that—for ecclesiastical reasons, on principle. And from this principle, relatively unimportant as it may seem, hangs the very substance of the Church itself. With exclusion of the Jewish Christians from the communion of worship, he who realizes the nature of the Church must feel himself to be excluded also. How can he who holds a church office administer that office if he knows that there are in the communion brethren of fewer rights to whom such office is not open because of their race? Will he not then best safeguard his Christianity and his churchliness by preferring to be where the most despised brethren are, and no longer sit at the head of the table, "among those who are first" [*Matt. 20:16*]?

On a church whose substance, whose essential nature has been violated, the blessing of God can no longer rest—despite the honest and best intentions of individual members. May we here make a clear decision, responsible only to the Church of Christ!

---

6. [*Many church leaders, even in the Confessing Church, supported allowing individual congregations to decide whether they wanted a Jewish Christian pastor. See* DBWE *12:373, n. 7, and* DBWE *12:430, n. 16.*]

23. The Aryan Paragraph
in the Church

DBWE 12:425–432

The late summer of 1933 was a tumultuous time in German church politics. The Aryan paragraph that passed earlier in the year had excluded Jews and other non-Aryans from civil service positions. This exclusion did not apply to the church since church leaders were not civil servants. But members of the German Christian movement were pushing for versions of the Aryan paragraph or similarly antisemitic legislation at both the Reich and regional church levels. While the Reich Church had not adopted the Aryan paragraph, as Bonhoeffer had feared it would, in August the Brandenburg provincial synod did extend the exclusion to the church and submitted a corresponding resolution to the Prussian General Synod.[1] Moreover, these efforts targeted not just non-Aryan clergy but non-Aryan congregants as well. German Christians in Mecklenburg as well as the prominent theologian Emanuel Hirsch were calling for segregating Jewish Christians into their own congregations.[2] It was in this foreboding context that Bonhoeffer composed the following discussion theses in preparation for the Old Prussian General Synod of September 5–6, 1933.[3] In them, he reasserts the claim that a racial precondition for church membership undermines the nature of the church, for which the only membership "criterion is the Word of God and faith."

---

1. [DBWE *12:425, n. 4.*]
2. [DBWE *12:421–422, n. 92.*]
3. [*See* DBWE *12:425, n. 1.*]

1. Radical version of the Aryan Paragraph: 425

Non-Aryans are not members of the German Reich Church and are to be excluded through the establishment of their own Jewish Christian congregations.

2. Second version of the Aryan Paragraph:

The law governing state officials is to be applied to church officials; thus employment of Jewish Christians as pastors should be discontinued, and none should be accepted for new employment.

3. Third version of the Aryan Paragraph:

Although the Reich Church constitution has not adopted the Aryan paragraph, it has made clear by its silence that it recognizes the regulations affecting students, which are designed to exclude Jewish Christians from theological study, as binding on the church. Thus it accepts the future exclusion of Jewish Christians from the ministry of the church.[4]

Re: version 1. The exclusion of Jewish Christians from the church-community destroys the substance of Christ's church, because

first: it reverses the work of Paul, who assumed that through the cross of   426
Christ the dividing wall between Jews and Gentiles had been broken down, that Christ has "made both groups into one" (Eph. 2), that here (in Christ's church) there should be neither Jew nor Gentile . . . but rather all should be one.

second:[5] if the church excludes the Jewish Christians, it is setting up a law with which one must comply in order to be a member of the church-community, namely, the racial law. It means that Jews can be asked at the door, before they can enter Christ's church in Germany, "Are you Aryan?" Only when they have complied with this law can I go to church with them, pray, listen, and celebrate the Lord's Supper together with them. But by putting up this racial law at the door to the church-community, the church is doing exactly what the Jewish Christian church was doing until Paul came, and in defiance of him; it was requiring people to become Jews in order to join the church-community. A church today that excludes Jewish Christians has itself become a Jewish Christian church and has fallen away from the gospel, back to the law.

---

4. [*It is not clear which of the several regulations affecting students Bonhoeffer has in mind. For more, see* DBWE *12:425–426, n. 5.*]

5. ["The following statement is almost the same as in *DBWE* 12:368–369, 372 (*Reader* 376–377, 380), and 420–421," *DBWE* 12:426, n. 7.]

The German Christians say:

The church is not allowed to undo or to disregard God's orders, and race is one of them, so the church must be racially constituted.

We answer:

The given order of race is misjudged just as little as that of gender, status in society, etc. . . . In the church, a Jew is still a Jew, a Gentile a Gentile, a man a man, a capitalist a capitalist, etc., etc. But God calls and gathers them all together into one people, the people of God, the church, and they all belong to it in the same way, one with another. The church is not a community of people who are all the same but precisely one of people foreign to one another who are called by God's Word. The people of God is an order

427 over and above all other orders. "Who is my mother, and who are my brothers? . . . whoever does the will of my Father in heaven is my brother and sister and mother" [*Matt. 12:48, 50*]. Race and blood are one order among those who enter into the church, but it must never become a criterion for belonging to the church; the only criterion is the Word of God and faith.

The German Christians say:

We don't want to take away from Jewish Christians the right to be Christians, but they should organize their own churches.[6] It is only a matter of the outward form of the church.

We answer:

(1) The issue of belonging to the Christian community is never an outward, organizational matter, but is of the very substance of the church. Church is the congregation that is called together by the Word. Membership in a congregation is a question not of organization but of the essence of the church.

(2) To make such a basic distinction between Christianity and the church, or between Christ and the church, is wrong. There is no such thing as the idea of the church, on one hand, and its outward appearance, on the other, but rather the empirically experienced church is the church of Christ itself. Thus to exclude people forcibly from the church-community at the empirical level means excluding them from Christ's church itself. That part of the church that excludes another is, of course, the one that is truly shut out—that is the particular danger of the German Christians' undertaking.

---

6. [*See* DBWE *12:420–421, n. 92.*]

(3) When the church's organizers exclude anyone, they are interfering with the authority of the sacraments. Here in our church, Jewish Christians have been accepted, by the will of God, through the sacrament of baptism. Through baptism they are joined together with our church, and our church with them, by indissoluble ties. If the church that has baptized Jewish Christians now throws them out, it makes baptism into a ceremony, which implies no obligation on its part.

The German Christians say:

We are not so much concerned with these thousand Jewish Christians as with the millions of our fellow citizens who are estranged from God. For their sake, these others might in certain cases have to be sacrificed.

We answer: 428

We too are concerned for those outside the church, but the church does not sacrifice a single one of its members. It may even be that the church, for the sake of a thousand believing Jewish Christians that it is not allowed to sacrifice, might fail to win over those millions. But what good would it do to gain millions of people at the price of the truth and of love for even a single one? This could represent not gain but only loss, for the church would no longer be the church.

The German Christians say:

The German church people can no longer endure communion with Jews, who have done them so much harm politically.

We answer:

This is the very point where it must be made crystal clear: here is where we are tested as to whether we know what the church is. Here, where the Jewish Christian whom I don't like is sitting next to me among the faithful, this is precisely where the church is. If that is not understood, then those who think they cannot bear it should themselves go and form their own church, but never, ever, can they be allowed to exclude someone else. The continuity of the church is in the church where the Jewish Christians remain.

In summary:

The church is the congregation of those who are called, where the gospel is rightly taught, and the sacraments are rightly administered,[7] and it

---

7. ["See the Augsburg Confession VII, *Book of Concord*, 42," *DBWE* 12:428, n. 11.]

does not establish any law for membership therein. The Aryan paragraph is therefore a false doctrine for the church and destroys its substance. Therefore, there is only one way to serve the truth in a church that implements the Aryan paragraph in this radical form, and that is to withdraw. This is the ultimate act of solidarity with my church. I can never serve my church in any other way than by adhering to the whole truth and all its consequences.

Re: version 2. Removal of Jewish Christians from the pastorate contradicts the nature of the ministry. Luther taught that through baptism all Christians are made priests, they all have the same rights, and each has the right

429   and the duty to obey and to teach the word of God. The office of the ministry is conferred by the Christian community on a Christian who has already been consecrated a priest through baptism, and demands right teaching, Christian living, and spiritual gifts of the pastor. The pastor takes up this office as the call of Christ, and only an offense against one of these requirements can be grounds for the congregation to revoke this ministry.

If Jewish Christians are barred in principle from the pastorate, they become church members with *lesser rights*. To cite the biblical admonition, "Women should be silent in the churches" [*1 Cor. 14:34*], does not lead to any conclusion with regard to Jewish Christians as such. Either we consider this admonition as legally binding, in which case it still does not say anything about Jewish Christians' keeping silent in the churches, or we do not consider it legally binding, that is, women also are allowed to speak in the churches, in which case there is no possibility of forbidding Jewish Christians to speak as a matter of principle. As soon as Jewish Christians are excluded, moreover, the meaning of the ministry itself is destroyed, since it is subjected to the whim of the congregation. Ordination itself is then revoked and made invalid; the *ordinatio* is placed, in a disorderly way, at the mercy of the congregation.

The German Christians say:
For the sake of the patriotic sentiments of German church people, a leader in the church must be Aryan.

We answer:
Church people must learn to pay attention not to the person of the pastor but rather to the pastor's proclamation. "What does it matter? Just this, that Christ is proclaimed in every way . . ." [*Phil. 1:18*]. If Paul, a Jew, had not proclaimed Christ to the heathen world, without worrying about any patriotic sentiment, there would never have been a German church.

This demand for the gospel to be preached by Aryans is a typical demand   430
of those who are weak in the faith, so they want to set up legal restrictions
in matters where, in truth, only faith and the Word of God has a say. This
demand from the weaker members of the congregation might possibly be
considered in exceptional individual cases, for pastoral reasons, to avoid
giving serious offense. But in each such case the most earnest thought
should be given to whether, for the sake of what church is about, the congregation should be asked to tolerate an offense to its sensibilities. It is totally
impossible, however, to allow the demands of the weak in the faith to rule
the church, because that means turning the freedom of the gospel into its
opposite, a law.

The German Christians say:
    The laws that apply to state officials must also apply to church officials;
otherwise the church is placed in opposition to the will of the state.

We answer:
    This is precisely where the completely political character of all the Ger-
man Christians' arguments about the Aryan paragraph is revealed. Seen in
connection with current political events, they can appear only as the church
emulating whatever the state does. However, the true service and loyalty
that the church must render to the state consists never in blindly emulating
its methods but only in the freedom of its own preaching and in displaying
the form and character that properly belong to it as the church.

In summary:
    The German Christians' demands destroy the substance of the minis-
try by making certain members of the Christian community into members
with lesser rights, second-class Christians. The rest, those not affected by
this demand, who remain privileged members, should prefer to stand by
those with lesser rights rather than to benefit from a privileged status in the
church. They must see their own true service, which they can still perform
for their church, in resigning from this *office of pastor as a privilege,* which is   431
what it has now become.

Re: version 3. If regulation of the right to university study makes it impossible for Jewish Christians to become pastors, the church, for its part, must
open new doors to the ministry for Jewish Christians and thereby protest,
through its proclamation, against such measures that attack the substance
of the ministry. If the church does not do so, it is guilty of responsibility for
the entire Aryan paragraph.

The German Christians say:

The Aryan paragraph is an *adiaphoron*,[8] which doesn't affect the confession of the church.

We answer:

1. All that we have said above is evidence that the church and the ministry have been attacked in their substance, that is, the confession has been attacked.

2. Even if this were not the case, the following judgment on the part of the confessional writings would be true. "Thus, Paul submits and gives in to the weak in matters of food or days (Rom. 14:6). But he does not want to submit to false apostles, who wanted to impose such things upon consciences as necessary even in matters that were in themselves free and indifferent. Col. 2:16: 'Do not let anyone make matters of food or drink or the observation of festivals a matter of conscience for you.' And when in such a case Peter and Barnabas did give in to a certain degree, Paul criticized them publicly, as those 'who were not acting consistently with the truth of the gospel' (Gal. 2:14).

"For in such a case it is no longer a matter of external matters of indifference, which in their nature and essence are and remain in and of themselves free, which accordingly are not subject to either a command or a prohibition regarding their use or discontinuance. Instead, here it is above all a matter of the chief article of our Christian faith, as the Apostle testifies, 'so that the truth of the gospel might always remain' (Gal. 2:5). Such coercion and command *obscure and pervert the truth of the gospel, because either these opponents will publicly demand such indifferent things as a confirmation of false teaching, superstition, and idolatry for the purpose of suppressing pure teaching and Christian freedom* or they will misuse them and as a result falsely reinstate them. . . .

"Thus, submission and compromise in external things *where Christian agreement in doctrine has not already been achieved strengthens idolaters in their idolatry.*"[9]

432

---

8. ["The Greek *adiaphoron* means a 'matter of indifference.' For the meaning of an *adiaphoron* in a confessional situation, see the quotation from the Formula of Concord that follows in the text. See also *DBWE* 12:366, n. 14, regarding Bonhoeffer's contrast between the *status confessionis* and the *adiaphora*," *DBWE* 12:431, n. 18.]

9. ["Cited from Article X of the Formula of Concord, paragraphs 13–14 and 16, in *Book of Concord*, 637–638 . . . ," *DBWE* 12:432, n. 19.]

24. What Should a Student of Theology Do Today?

DBWE 12:432–435

Worn down by repeated disappointment in the Church Struggle and doubting himself in the role he was playing in it, Bonhoeffer made the difficult decision to leave the German scene to pastor two German churches in London.[1] In the text below, he says good-bye to his theology students in Berlin, encouraging them to pursue theology passionately in the service of the church and on the basis of "the true Bible" and "the true Luther."

One should, above all, only study theology out of the sincere opinion   432
that one cannot choose any other course of study. Far less harm is done if many who might have become good pastors or teachers of religion instead become good lawyers or physicians than if a single person pursues theology who should not have done so. A large new generation of theological students is always a very ambiguous phenomenon.

One should not think that, as someone who truly had to study theology, one is superior to other students. For theological students will find in the course of their studies that the reasons that persuaded them that it must be theology or nothing will gradually fall away, and by the time they reach the end of a proper theological course they will have entirely different reasons for pursuing a career in theology—if indeed they are still convinced that they must do so—from those they had in the beginning.

One should not think it necessary to wait for particular experiences of "being called" to the ministry. A student who is simply gripped by the subject matter of theology and cannot turn away from it can consider that a calling.

---

1. [DB-ER, *286, 299. For more on Bonhoeffer's time in London (1933–1935), see* DB-ER, *325–417, and the editor's introduction to* DBWE *13.]*

But certainly, it must be what theology is really about that enthralls the student—a real readiness to think about God, the Word, and the will of God, a "delight in the law of the Lord" and readiness to meditate on it "day and night" [*Ps. 1:2*]; a real willingness to work seriously, to study, and to think. It is not the experience of a call but the determination to do sober, earnest, and responsible theological work that is the gateway to the study of theology.

One may bring to theological studies one's own passions, one's philosophical, ethical, pedagogical, patriotic, or social zeal. These belong to the student as a whole person, and one must truly enter into theology with one's whole self. The person who is not driven to theological study at least in part by these very passions will certainly be a poor theologian. But theological students must then learn and know that the driving force in their lives and thinking, as theologians, can only come from the passion of Jesus Christ, our crucified Lord. The study of theology cannot be conquered by the overflowing vitality of one's own passion; rather, the real study of *theologia sacra* [*sacred theology*] begins when, in the midst of questioning and seeking, human beings encounter the cross; when they recognize the endpoint of all their own passions in the suffering of God at the hands of humankind, and realize that their entire vitality stands under judgment. This is the great turnaround, which for the course of study means the turn toward theological objectivity. Theological study no longer means revealing the passions of one's ego; it is no longer a monologue, no longer religious self-fulfillment. Rather, it is about responsible study and listening, becoming attentive to the Word of God, which has been revealed right here in this world; it is toning down one's self in the face of what is far and away the most important matter.

A young theological student should have the will to become a theologian in this sense, openly and honestly, or else waste no more time in pursuing the course. The real task of the theologian should not be a cause for shame, once the student discovers it; there should be no attempt to dress it up in all sorts of irrelevancies. Why should it be theological students and graduates who find it relevant and necessary, from their first semester until they reach the highest offices in the church, to talk disparagingly about theological studies? How can it be a good sign in them that they avoid the company of honest theologians from Paul to Augustine, from Thomas to Luther, and claim to have no need of what was immeasurably important to these teachers? How can such a facile setting aside of issues that were important to wiser and more serious people be evidence of anything but poorly concealed ignorance? How can such a student avoid being asked in astonishment: Do you really think you belong here, studying theology? Shouldn't you perhaps think of some more enticing, visible, imposing, in any case quite different place to be? Since when is a person especially qualified for a theological career who cares so little about theology as to talk as everyone else does about it? And ultimately, since when does it make someone a good Christian to presume to talk about things that he or she is far from understanding?

A young theological student should know that to pursue theology is to serve the true church of Christ, which is unwavering in confessing its Lord, and should live with this responsibility. It is detestable to see theological students fail to take this seriously and feel better about being seen as worldly than as dedicated to theology. With such an attitude, far from winning others over, one only invites their boundless and justified contempt and risks making the whole theological community a laughingstock once again, along with oneself. A theological student who likes to stand out, who likes to be made the center of attention at the expense of colleagues, in the end will achieve only the opposite. Moreover, those who like to display their worldliness will find that it actually plays dirty tricks on them. So it is really not clear at all how keeping all one's worldliness should be the decisive criterion for a good theological career.

One should prepare oneself, through the study of theology, to discern the spirits in Christ's church. One should learn from the Holy Scriptures and the confessions of the Reformation what is the pure and true teaching of the gospel of Jesus Christ, and which are human teachings, human laws, false doctrines, and idolatry. One should learn, through these studies, not to turn black into white, but to call truth truth, and false doctrine false doctrine. One should think this through carefully, modestly, objectively, lovingly but also with boldness and complete determination, and in the same spirit bear witness to it. Whoever fails to do this must answer for it, to the Lord of the church that we serve! One should know where the wellspring of the church's life is found, and how it can become clogged and poisoned. One must learn to recognize where and when the church of Christ reaches its hour of decision, when it is time for confession—the *status confessionis*.[2]

And if the church that one serves is in *status confessionis*, he is called upon to recognize that the gospel is being turned into a false doctrine; he must see with his trained vision that new and strange meanings are being concealed behind the old words—and he must say so out loud, openly, right where he is. As a student of theology, no one can and should do otherwise than keep inquiring after the true gospel, ever more attentively and objectively, in ever more truth and love.   435

---

2. [*See editorial introduction,* Reader *379.*]

In such times one should in no way become emotional in one's thinking and action but remain completely sober. Especially at this point, one should not seek to play a role but rather read and study one's Bible as never before.

One should know, in such times, that under no circumstances are tactical considerations the way to serve one's church or the aims of theology; only the purest, most refined truth will do. Even with the best will in the world, tactical solutions only cloud and obscure the situation. The student of theology is the last one who should be thinking tactically and instead should carry on working with purely theological objectivity, in service to God.

One should, in such times, err on the side of being too quiet rather than too loud. For the false confidence of a loud voice has nothing to do with the assurance of repentance and the gospel.

Finally, one should know as a true theologian that, even where our knowledge of the gospel of Jesus Christ in its truth and purity keeps us away from false doctrines, we stand beside our brethren who have wandered and been misled, sharing their guilt, interceding and praying for them, knowing that our own life depends, not on our better knowledge or being on the right side, but on forgiveness.

One should, in such times of confusion, go back to the very beginning, to our wellsprings, to the true Bible, to the true Luther. One should keep on, ever more undaunted and joyfully, becoming a theologian ἀληθεύοντες ἐν ἀγάπῃ [*speaking the truth in love, Eph. 4:15*].

25. Fanø Theses Paper and Address: The Church and the Peoples of the World

DBWE 13:304–310

In the summer of 1934, Bonhoeffer delivered an address at an ecumenical confer-ence on the Danish island of Fanø. A transcription of that talk as well as the theses Bonhoeffer wrote in preparation for it are printed below. He opens the theses by posing to the World Alliance the question that for him was decisive: Is the Alliance an orga-nization or a church? For Bonhoeffer, an organization works to realize defined goals while a church preaches God's word and obeys God's commandments. This distinc-tion between a church and a humanitarian organization was central to Bonhoeffer's ecclesiology; it found sociological expression in Sanctorum Communio, *informed his evaluation of American churches and theological movements, and guided his reflection on the task of the church in the German Church Struggle. On the issue of war and peace specifically, Bonhoeffer here urges the ecumenical movement to under-stand itself as church and therefore as occupying a third space beyond nationalist warmongering, on the one hand, and internationalist peace activism, on the other. In this space, the church does not work toward human ends, be they peaceful or hostile, but simply responds to God's command.*

Theses Paper   304

Summary

1. The destiny of the Alliance is determined by the following: whether it regards itself as a Church or as a society with a definite purpose. The World Alliance is a Church as long as its fundamental principles lie in obediently listening to and preaching the Word of God. It is a society, if its essential object is to realise aims and conditions of whatever kind they

305　may be. It is only as a Church that the World Alliance can preach the Word of Christ in full authority to the Churches and nations. As a society it stands without authority with innumerable other societies of the same kind.

2. The work of the World Alliance means work of the Churches for peace amongst the nations. Its aim is the end of war and the victory over war.

3. The enemy of work for peace is war. War must be understood
   a) as a conscious action of the human will, for which it is fully responsible;
   b) as the work of the evil powers of this world, enemies of God, similar to diseases, catastrophes, etc;
   c) as the revelation of a world which has fallen under the law of death.

4. Corresponding to this, the justification of war takes the following three forms:
   a) War—according to the conscious will of its leaders—works for the maintenance of the State and future peace, this is its moral justification;
   b) War is an irresistible event, over which no man has any power (so-called realism or, rather, naturalism);
   c) War reveals an heroic world of sacrifice.

5. Secular pacifism answers:
   a) the pacific welfare of humanity will not be brought about by means of war. War cannot be justified morally on that basis;
   b) a rational organisation must be created which will hold back the powers leading to war;
   c) war must be suppressed so as to reveal the world as a good world.

6. These two arguments are of equal value and are equally unchristian. They are not Christ-inspired but inspired by a desired or non-desired picture of the world.

7. The Christian Church answers:
   a) The human will must be confronted with the commandment: Thou shalt not kill. God does not exempt us from obeying His commandments. Man by his transgressions will be guilty before God. The God of the Sermon on the Mount will judge him. To the objection: The State must be maintained: the Church answers: Thou shalt not kill. To the objection: War creates peace: the Church answers: This is not true, war creates destruction. To the objection: The nation must
306　defend itself: the Church answers: Have you dared to entrust God, in full faith, with your protection in obedience to His commandment? To the objection: Love for my neighbour compels me: the Church answers: The one who loves God keeps His commandments. To the question: What shall I do then? the Church answers: Believe in God

and be obedient. But to the secular pacifism the Church answers: The motives of our actions are not the welfare of humanity, but obedience to God's commandments. Even if war meant the good of humanity, God's commandment would remain steadfast.

b) The powers of evil will not be broken by means of organisations, but by prayer and fasting (Mark 9:29). Any other attitude under-estimates these powers and regards them as naturalistic or materialistic. The spirits of hell will be banished only by Christ Himself. Neither fatalism, nor organisation, but prayer! Man, feeling responsible for peace, although subject to evil powers, is being led to recognise that help and the solution will be brought about by God alone. Prayer is stronger than organisation. It is easy to hide the burden of evil and struggle by organisation. (Not against enemies of blood and flesh . . . (Eph. 6:12.)

c) War revealing as it does a world under the law of death shows also that the abolition of war would only be the suppression of a horrible symptom, but would not cut the root of the evil itself. It is not pacifism that is the victory which overcomes the world (1 John 5:4) but faith, which expects everything from God and hopes in the coming of Christ and His Kingdom. Only then will the cause of evil—that is to say, the Devil and the demons—be overcome.

Address   307

"I will hear what God the LORD will speak: for he will speak peace unto his people, and to his saints" (Psalm 85:9). Between the twin crags of nationalism and internationalism ecumenical Christendom calls upon her Lord and asks his guidance. Nationalism and internationalism have to do with political necessities and possibilities. The ecumenical Church, however, does not concern itself with these things, but with the commandments of God, and regardless of consequences it transmits these commandments to the world.

Our task as theologians, accordingly, consists only in accepting this commandment as a binding one, not as a question open to discussion. Peace on earth is not a problem, but a commandment given at Christ's coming. There are two ways of reacting to this command from God: the unconditional, blind obedience of action, or the hypocritical question of the Serpent: "Yea, hath God said . . . ?"[1] This question is the mortal enemy of obedience, and therefore the mortal enemy of all real peace. "Hath God not said . . . ? Has

---

1. ["Gen. 3:1; cf. also the interpretation in *Creation and Fall, DBWE* 3:103–110 (*Reader* 243–248)," *DBWE* 13:307, n. 5.]

God not understood human nature well enough to know that wars must occur in this world, like laws of nature? Must God not have meant that we should talk about peace, to be sure, but that it is not to be literally translated into action? Must God not really have said that we should work for peace, of course, but also make ready tanks and poison gas for security?" And then perhaps the most serious question: "Did God say you should not protect your own people? Did God say you should leave your own a prey to the enemy?"

308

No, God did not say all that. What He has said is that there shall be peace among men—that we shall obey Him without further question, that is what He means. He who questions the commandment of God before obeying has already denied Him.

There shall be peace because of the Church of Christ, for the sake of which the world exists. And this Church of Christ lives at one and the same time in all peoples, yet beyond all boundaries, whether national, political, social, or racial. And the brothers who make up this Church are bound together, through the commandment of the one Lord Christ, whose Word they hear, more inseparably than men are bound by all the ties of common history, of blood, of class and of language. All these ties, which are part of our world, are valid ties, not indifferent; but in the presence of Christ they are not ultimate bonds. For the members of the ecumenical Church, in so far as they hold to Christ, His word, His commandment of peace is more holy, more inviolable than the most revered words and works of the natural world. For they know that whoso is not able to hate father and mother for His sake is not worthy of Him, and lies if he calls himself after Christ's name. These brothers in Christ obey His word; they do not doubt or question, but keep His commandment of peace. They are not ashamed, in defiance of the world, even to speak of eternal peace. They cannot take up arms against Christ himself—yet this is what they do if they take up arms against one another! Even in anguish and distress of conscience there is for them no escape from the commandment of Christ that there shall be peace.

How does peace come about? Through a system of political treaties? Through the investment of international capital in different countries? Through the big banks, through money? Or through universal peaceful rearmament in order to guarantee peace? Through none of these, for the single reason that in all of them peace is confused with safety. There is

309

no way to peace along the way of safety. For peace must be dared. It is the great venture. It can never be made safe. Peace is the opposite of security. To demand guarantees is to mistrust, and this mistrust in turn brings forth war. To look for guarantees is to want to protect oneself. Peace means to give oneself altogether to the law of God, wanting no security, but in faith and obedience laying the destiny of the nations in the hand of Almighty God, not trying to direct it for selfish purposes. Battles are won, not with weapons, but with God. They are won where the way leads to the cross. Which of us can say he knows what it might mean for the world if one nation should meet the aggressor, not with weapons in hand, but praying, defenseless, and for that very reason protected by "a bulwark never failing"?[2]

Once again, how will peace come? Who will call us to peace so that the world will hear, will have to hear? so that all peoples may rejoice? The individual Christian cannot do it. When all around are silent, he can indeed raise his voice and bear witness, but the powers of this world stride over him without a word. The individual church, too, can witness and suffer—oh, if it only would!—but it also is suffocated by the power of hate. Only the one great Ecumenical Council of the Holy Church of Christ over all the world can speak out so that the world, though it gnash its teeth, will have to hear, so that the peoples will rejoice because the Church of Christ in the name of Christ has taken the weapons from the hands of their sons, forbidden war, and proclaimed the peace of Christ against the raging world.

Why do we fear the fury of the world powers? Why don't we take the power from them and give it back to Christ? We can still do it today. The Ecumenical Council is in session; it can send out to all believers this radical call to peace. The nations are waiting for it in the East and in the West. Must we be put to shame by non-Christian peoples in the East? Shall we desert the individuals who are risking their lives for this message? The hour is late. The world is choked with weapons, and dreadful is the distrust which looks out of all men's eyes. The trumpets of war may blow tomorrow. For what are we waiting? Do we want to become involved in this guilt as never before?

"What use to me are crown, land, folk and fame?   310
They cannot cheer my breast.
War's in the land, alas, and on my name
I pray no guilt may rest."

M. Claudius[3]

We want to give the world a whole word, not a half word—a courageous word, a Christian word. We want to pray that this word may be given us, today. Who knows if we shall see each other again another year?

---

2. ["Allusion to Martin Luther's hymn 'A Mighty Fortress Is Our God.'. . . See also Bonhoeffer's sermon of February 26, 1933 (*DBWE* 12:461–467)," *DBWE* 13:309, n. 9.]

3. ["Bonhoeffer has rephrased the first line of this last verse of Matthias Claudius's 'Kriegslied' (War song) from *Wandsbecker Boten*. Cf. Henkys, *Gefängnisgedichte*, 15. Claudius's line reads: 'What use to me are crown, land, gold, and fame?' Bonhoeffer has replaced 'gold' with 'folk,'" *DBWE* 13:310, n. 10.]

26. THE CONFESSING CHURCH
AND THE ECUMENICAL MOVEMENT

DBWE 14:393–412

The impetus for the following essay, published in August 1935, was a series of letters exchanged between Bonhoeffer and Canon Leonard Hodgson, the general secretary of the World Conference on Faith and Order Continuation Committee.[1] When Hodgson invited Bonhoeffer to participate in a meeting of this committee, Bonhoeffer asked whether representatives of the Reich Church would also be in attendance, in which case he, as a representative of the Confessing Church, would not attend. Hodgson replied that representatives of both the Confessing Church and the Reich Church were invited, since the ecumenical movement could not discriminate against any church claiming to follow Christ. The epistolary exchange, therefore, fell into the now famil-iar pattern: to the "Confessing Christians the ecumenical world seemed irritating and unserious theologically, while the humanist and liberal ecumenists viewed the Confessing Church as theologically carried away and hysterical."[2] This essay was Bonhoeffer's attempt to bring this argument up for public discussion at what he con-sidered a decisive moment for both the ecumenical movement and the Confessing Church. In it, he pushes the ecumenical movement, as he had at Fanø, toward a theological understanding of itself as church. Here he emphasizes that such a self-understanding entails the willingness to declare certain churches, such as the Reich Church, to be false churches.[3]

393   From the very beginning, the struggle of the Confessing Church has been accompanied with considerable concern by the Christian churches outside Germany. This is something that has been frequently noted and assessed

---

1. [*For this background, see* DBWE *14:393–394 n. 1.*]
2. [DB-ER, *482.*]
3. [*For more on this essay, see* DB-ER *482–486.*]

with suspicion in both political and church quarters. It is understandable   394
that for politicians this was a rather odd surprise and might well occasion
false interpretations, since never before has the Protestant ecumenical
movement been so much in evidence on the occasion of a church dispute
as in the past two years, and never before has the position taken by ecumenical Christendom concerning a question of faith been as unequivocal
and unanimous as here. The German Church Struggle is the second great
stage in the history of the ecumenical movement and will be decisive for its
future. By contrast, it was less understandable that our own church largely
appeared so ill prepared and undiscerning in its encounter with this event
that it was almost ashamed of the voices of our foreign brothers, perceiving their presence as something embarrassing instead of rejoicing in their
witness and in our own fellowship with them. The fright and confusion
prompted in church circles by the proscription of the political concept of   395
internationalism had blinded them to something completely new that was
just emerging, namely, the Protestant ecumenical movement. That no distinction was made here between the political and the ecclesiastical spheres
merely proves the unprecedented absence of independent thinking on the
part of the church. The fact, to which both the New Testament and the
confessional writings attest to the fullest, namely, that the church of Christ
transcends rather than stops at national and racial boundaries,[4] has been
much too easily forgotten and disowned under the onslaught of recent
nationalism. And even when one was unable to object theoretically on this
point, one never stopped emphasizing that any dialogue with foreign Christians about so-called internal German church matters naturally could not
be countenanced, and that certainly any judgment or, heaven forbid, public
statement concerning these matters from outsiders was both impossible and
reprehensible. Voices from various quarters tried to convince ecumenical
organizations that such behavior would only cause damage. Ecumenical
relationships were assessed largely from the viewpoint of church political
strategy. Doing so, however, constituted a sin against the seriousness of
the ecumenicity of the Protestant church. It is merely an expression of the
genuine power of the concept of an ecumenical movement that despite all
reticence, all internal resistance, indeed, all honorable and dishonorable   396
attempts to disinterest the ecumenical movement, that movement has none-

---

4. ["For the New Testament, cf. Gal. 3:28 (among the baptized, 'there is no longer
Jew or Greek'); for the confessional writings, cf. the preface to the Augsburg Confession
(1530) with its advocacy of a general, free Christian council (*Book of Concord*, 34)," *DBWE*
14:395, n. 4.]

theless participated in the struggle and sufferings of German Protestantism by making its voice repeatedly heard, for example, when as president of the Universal Christian Council for Life and Work the bishop of Chichester wrote to the Reich bishop imploring the latter to be mindful of his office as protector of Protestant Christianity in Germany, when in his Ascension 1934 message he drew the attention of all Christian churches to the seriousness of the church situation in Germany and invited them to a council meeting, and when finally at the noteworthy conference in Fanø in August 1934 the Universal Council articulated its clear and brotherly resolution concerning the German church dispute and, at the same time elected the president of the confessing synod, Dr. Koch, to the Universal Council.[5] It was in those days that many prominent church leaders first came face-to-face with the reality of the ecumenical movement.

In this entire matter the spokespersons of the ecumenical movement have taken as their point of departure two insights: (1) the struggle of the Confessing Church involves the proclamation of the gospel in the larger sense; (2) the Confessing Church is carrying on and suffering this struggle on behalf of all Christendom, particularly for Western Christendom. This insight necessarily shaped a twofold position. First: the natural internal and external concern for this struggle—a concern incapable of being thwarted by any persuasions to the contrary—as a common concern. Countless foreign churches have prayed for the pastors of the Confessing Church, numerous ministerial conferences have sent messages to the Confessing Church assuring the latter of their heartfelt concern, and young students in theological seminaries include the Confessing Church and its struggle in their daily prayers. Second: such concern and participation can endure only within the strict church posture of brotherly help and a common focus on the gospel and the right to proclaim it in all the world unhindered and undaunted.

On the one hand, because church responsibility rather than an arbitrary decision prompted this involvement, all attempts to gain an advantage in the arena of church politics by confusing and obscuring the issues were doomed to failure from the outset. On the other hand, and for the same reason, spokespersons for the ecumenical movement were able to maintain the disciplined spiritual orientation of their own task and follow their chosen path without wavering.

397

---

5. ["See *DB-ER*, 381–383. In the essay, Bonhoeffer does not mention that alongside President Karl Koch, he himself had been co-opted as an advisory member of this Universal Council," *DBWE* 14:396, n. 8.]

The ecumenical movement and the Confessing Church have encountered each another. At the birth of the Confessing Church, the ecumenical movement both acted as intercessor and took a committed position as godparent. That is a fact, albeit one that is extremely unusual and for some quite repugnant: extremely unusual because it is precisely in Confessing Church circles that one would from the outset have expected the least understanding for ecumenical work, and because it is precisely in ecumenical circles that one would from the outset have expected the least interest in the theological problem of the Confessing Church repugnant; because it annoys German nationalists to have to view the situation of their own church from the outside and allow it to be seen from the outside, since no one wants to show their sores to a stranger. This fact, however, is not only unusual and repugnant; it is also a decidedly and enormously promising fact, since it is in precisely this encounter that the ecumenical movement and the Confessing Church mutually pose the question of existence to each other. The ecumenical movement must justify itself before the Confessing Church, and the Confessing Church must justify itself before the ecumenical movement. The ecumenical movement is forced into serious internal movement and crisis by the Confessing Church, just as the Confessing Church is forced into serious internal movement and crisis by the ecumenical movement. This question for each must now be examined.

I.   398

The Confessing Church constitutes a genuine question for the ecumenical movement insofar as it confronts the latter in its totality with the question of the confession of faith.[6] The Confessing Church is the church that in its totality seeks to be a church determined exclusively by its confession of faith. It is fundamentally impossible to enter into dialogue with this church without immediately raising the confessional question. Because the Confessing Church has learned in the Church Struggle that, from the proclamation of the gospel itself to the issue of church taxes, it is the confession and the confession alone that must determine the church; because there is no confession-free or neutral space within the Confessing Church, it immediately confronts every dialogue partner with the confessional question. There is no access to the Confessing Church apart from the confessional

---

6. ["Bonhoeffer had already addressed the question 'What is confession?' in Zingst at the beginning of May, before the preachers' seminary moved to Finkenwalde at the end of June 1935; cf. *DBWE* 14:325–328 and *DB-ER*, 444–445," *DBWE* 14:398, n. 11.]

question. There is no possibility for common tactical activity beyond the confessional question. Here the Confessing Church seals itself off hermetically from any political, social, humanitarian intrusion. The confession fills its entire space.

There is only a yes or a no to this confession as articulated *in a binding fashion* in the Barmen and Dahlem synodal resolutions.[7] Hence here, too, neutrality is impossible; here, too, any concurrence on this or that point beyond the confessional question is excluded. The Confessing Church must rather insist that it is taken seriously in every responsible church dispute only insofar as this, its claim, is recognized and acknowledged. It must also insist that in every dialogue with it, the element of church solidarity comes to expression insofar as its dialogue partner not enter into simultaneous dialogue with the Confessing Church and with the churches of false doctrine rejected by the Confessing Church; indeed, insofar as its ecumenical dialogue partners definitively break off discussion, the Confessing Church itself, in its own responsibility as a church, declares such discussions to be broken off.

399

This is an unprecedented claim. But only in this way can the Confessing Church enter into the ecumenical discussion. And one must recognize this if one is to understand it and interpret its language correctly. If the Confessing Church were to relent regarding this claim, the Church Struggle in Germany would already be decided *against* it and with that the struggle for Christianity as well. Because the ecumenical movement has indeed entered into dialogue with the Confessing Church, it has consciously or unconsciously heard this claim, and the Confessing Church can gratefully take this presupposition as its point of departure. At the same time, however, the ecumenical movement has backed itself into a serious internal crisis, since the characteristic claim of the Confessing Church remains in effect in the very sphere of the ecumenical movement as well. The questions of the Confessing Church, which the ecumenical movement has agreed to hear, now stand there unanswered for all to see and can no longer be made retroactive.

1. Is the ecumenical movement in its visible form church? Or conversely: Has the real ecumenicity of the church as attested in the New Testament come to visible and appropriate expression in ecumenical organizations? The younger theological generation now engaged in ecumenical work is

---

7. [*Bonhoeffer refers to the Barmen Declaration of May 1934 and the Dahlem Declaration of October 1934. For more, see* DBWE *14:398, n. 12.*]

raising this question today with great emphasis everywhere. And the import of this question is immediately clear. It is the question of the authority by which the ecumenical movement itself speaks and acts. By what authority do you do that? is the usual question.[8] This question of authority is decisive, and our failure to answer it profoundly damages our work. If the ecumenical movement does indeed claim to be the church of Christ, then it is just as unchanging as the church of Christ in the larger sense; in that case, its work possesses ultimate seriousness and ultimate authority, and what we find fulfilled is either the old hope of Protestant Christianity in its beginnings for the one, true church of Christ among all the nations of the earth or the titanic and anti-Christian human attempt to make visible what God would rather conceal from our eyes. In that case, the unity of this ecumenical church is either obedience to the promise of Jesus Christ that there be   400 one flock and one shepherd, or it is the reign of false peace and false unity constructed on the lie of the devil in the guise of an angel. It is between these two alternatives, alternatives between which every church stands, that the ecumenical movement itself now stands.

It is certainly understandable that people tried to avoid answering this question for so long; it is also certainly more pious to admit one's own ignorance, when one really does know nothing concerning such things, than to make a false statement. At this time, however, this question has been raised anew by the Confessing Church and now demands clarification. It can no longer be left unanswered in *docta ignorantia* [*learned ignorance*]. It is now threatening every word and every deed of the ecumenical movement; precisely this is the first service that the Confessing Church performs for the ecumenical movement.

It is obvious that the possibility certainly exists that one not understand the ecumenical movement in its present visible form as church; it might, after all, be an association of Christians, all of whom are rooted in their own churches, an association that now either comes together for the sake of common tactical-practical action or for nonbinding dialogue with other Christians. In that case, they leave open the question of the result and the theological possibility of such practical action and such dialogue, entrusting that issue entirely to the actual implementation of these activities. That is, one should simply go ahead and begin, and leave it to God to make of it what God will. Such action may have only a confessionally neutral charac-

---

8. ["On speaking ecumenically 'with full authority,' see Bonhoeffer's lecture 'On the Theological Foundation of the Work of the World Alliance,' *DBWE* 11:356–369," *DBWE* 14:399, n. 13.]

ter, such dialogue only informational, discursive character, and is never to issue a judgment or certainly any decision regarding this or that doctrine or, certainly, this or that church.

The internal progress achieved by ecumenical work during recent years derives from having broken through the purely tactical-practical front from the perspective of the theological problem, and for this we owe special thanks to the Geneva Research Department and to participants such as Dr. Oldham. In this respect, ecumenical work stands largely under the auspices of theological discussion. While the fruit this work has yielded during the past few years is not to be underestimated, let us not forget that the construction of the ecumenical concept as characterized by the notion of "theological discussion" *in the first place* takes as its point of departure very specific theological presuppositions that by no means enjoy universal acceptance and, *second,* is not yet capable of doing justice to the present crisis in the ecumenical movement.

First: Such theological discussion is to be conducted between "Christian persons"—so we are told. Where, however, are we to derive the criterion for what a Christian person is or, for that matter, for what an unchristian person is? Are not judgment and sentence—things one tries to avoid in the case of doctrinal decisions in the church—being pronounced here in a much more dangerous place, namely, in the judgment of individuals and their Christian orientation? And does the Bible not prohibit precisely such judgment while demanding it in decisions of doctrine and heretical teaching in the church? Has not excessive caution turned into enormous carelessness here? Do we not see here the unavoidable law under which ecumenical work stands, namely, to examine and discern hearts, and might it not be a more humble undertaking to engage such distinctions instead on points of church doctrine rather than descending judgmentally into the hidden and ambiguous depths of the human personality? There can be absolutely no serious dialogue without mutual clarity about the disposition and authority from which each party speaks to the other. If, however, as the more responsible parties in ecumenical circles would have it, one wishes to emphasize the nonbinding nature of such dialogue even more strongly by acknowledging as determinative not this notion of the Christian person but rather solely our mutual interest and the capacity for contributing something to the debate, then doing so basically grants to non-Christians the same rights as Christians in questions concerning the church of Christ, and then it becomes questionable to what extent the name of the ecumenical movement is now being used legitimately at all and to what extent we are even dealing now with something that is still of relevance to the church.

401

Second: There is a very great danger, one that—as anyone acquainted   402
with the matter knows—has already become acute, that precisely this inherently necessary theological dialogue will be used to veil the real issue. Theological dialogue then becomes a nasty game by concealing the fact that, in
truth, it is a matter not of nonbinding theologizing but rather of responsible, legitimate church decisions. The question of the Confessing Church
has already taken us past the inherently necessary stage of theological dialogue. The Confessing Church is aware of the dangerous ambiguity of any
theological dialogue and is pressing for an unequivocal church decision.
That is the real situation.

The question of the authority of the ecumenical movement drives all
such constructions to their most extreme consequences and undermines
them from within. Either one acknowledges the necessity of discerning
the spirits as a presupposition of ecumenical work, in which case one must
then speak about the character of such discernment and take seriously its
practical implementation, or one rejects such discernment as a false and
impermissible presupposition, in which case the concept of the ecumenical
movement in the sense of the New Testament and the Reformation confessions is dissolved from the outset. The group against which this particular
part of the dispute directs itself finds its representatives in a large portion
of the German, English, and American theologians within the ecumenical movement and enjoys considerable acceptance in active ecumenical
circles.

This group's strongest argument is the prediction that ecumenical work
will collapse at the very moment one seriously raises the question of its
ecclesiastical character, that is, where any sort of judicial functions or doctrinal decisions have to be exercised. This tells us that ecumenical work has
hitherto been conducted by deliberately avoiding the confessional ques-   403
tion; at the same time, however, it tells us that only thus can it be conducted
further. The first assertion is as correct as the second is impermissible and
presumptuous. During the past few years, and especially since August 1931[9]
and largely at the initiative of the Geneva Research Department, it is precisely the more fundamental theological questions that have repeatedly
been raised at virtually every ecumenical conference, and it is clear that the

---

9. ["At the annual conference of the World Alliance for Promoting International
Friendship through the Churches in Cambridge on September 1–5, 1931, which was preceded by a youth conference (August 29–31), three honorary youth secretaries—one of
whom was Bonhoeffer—were appointed; they quite resolutely pressed for more attention
to be given to theological questions; cf. *DB-ER*, 189–190, 199–202," *DBWE* 14:403 n. 25.]

internal development of ecumenical work itself is pressing for this clarification; both the words and the deeds of the ecumenical movement have been undermined. The entry of the Confessing Church, however, now makes it impossible to stop this development. Other rescue attempts are useless. There is only one way for ecumenical work to be rescued, namely, that it courageously take up this question as it has been posed and obediently leave the rest to the Lord of the church. Who can say that the ecumenical movement will not emerge more strongly and more authoritatively from the struggle prompted precisely by this disruptive challenge? And even if it must pass through a difficult break in the process, is God's commandment and promise not strong enough to guide the church through such a break, and is this commandment not more sure than are the false peace and illusory unity, which will inevitably collapse one day? Historical speculation ends at God's commandment.

And the ecumenical movement has not withdrawn. At the conference in Fanø, albeit with some hesitation and personal scruples, it did indeed issue a genuinely ecclesiastical statement, and that also means a judicial statement, insofar as it condemned very specific points in the doctrine and actions of the German Christian regime and adopted a position in favor of the Confessing Church. This statement emerged quite simply from the necessity of the moment in responsible obedience to God's commandment. With the conference in Fanø, the ecumenical movement entered a new epoch, coming face-to-face with its church commission with respect to a very specific issue, and this is its enduring significance.

404   The question has thus been raised and still awaits an answer, not today or tomorrow, but it awaits it nonetheless: Is the ecumenical movement church or not?

2. How can the ecumenical movement be church and on what does it base this claim? That is the next question that the Confessing Church raises for the ecumenical movement. The church can exist only as a confessing church, that is, as a church that confesses to its Lord and against its Lord's enemies. A confessionless or confession-free church is not church but rather merely rapturous enthusiasm that makes itself lord over the Bible and the word of God. A confession is the church's response, as formulated and spoken in its own words, to the word of God in the Holy Scriptures. The true unity of the church, however, includes unity in confession. How can the ecumenical movement be church in this sense?

It seems that confessional unity alone, as found for example in world Lutheranism, opens up this possibility. But how then is one to assess from such a perspective one's position toward the Church of England or, certainly, toward Eastern Orthodoxy? How can churches standing on such different confessional foundations be *one* church and issue common, authoritative statements?

The only possibly valid construction in ecumenical circles that will help address this problem is the following:

According to Scripture, there is one, holy, ecumenical church; each existing church represents one particular form and figure of that one church. Just as from the root and trunk of the tree many branches grow, and just as all these together are what first constitutes the entire tree, just as the body with all its appendages constitutes a whole body, so also is the community of churches in the world that which first constitutes the one, true, ecumenical church. The point of ecumenical work is then to illustrate the wealth and harmony of Christendom. None can claim exclusive validity; each brings a specific gift and performs a specific service on behalf of the whole; only in unity does truth reside.

The attraction of this notion throughout the entire Christian world, a notion nourished from the most varied spiritual and intellectual sources, is surprising. In one manner of speaking, this very notion represents the dogma of the ecumenical movement, and opposing it is difficult.

And yet it is precisely this construction that the Confessing Church must   405 destroy, for it veils the seriousness of the ecumenical problem and of the church itself in the broader sense.

As true and biblical as the assertion may well be that truth exists only in unity, the assertion is equally true and biblical that unity is possible only in the truth. Where one church solely seeks unity with another, without consideration of or beyond the truth claim, truth itself is being denied and there the church has abandoned itself. Truth itself has the inherent power to distinguish and separate; otherwise it is dissolved. Wherever truth opposes truth, however, one no longer has harmony and an organism. There one can no longer barricade oneself behind the universal inadequacy of human knowledge. There one stands at the threshold of anathema.[10] The romantic-aesthetic-liberal understanding of the ecumenical movement does not take the question of truth seriously and therefore offers no possibility for making the ecumenical movement intelligible as church.

---

10. ["Cf. Gal. 1:8 and 1 Cor. 16:22. Later in Roman Catholic Church law this was the formula used to declare excommunication," *DBWE* 14:405, n. 31.]

The question of truth, however, is nothing more than the question of the confession in the positive and delimited sense, that is, of the *confitemur* [*we confess*] and the *damnamus* [*we reject*].[11] It would behoove the Christian churches of the West not to overlook the Confessing Church's experience that a church without a confession is a defenseless and forsaken church, and that a church with the proper confession possesses the only weapon that will not shatter.

These considerations push the ecumenical movement into an ultimate crisis, one that threatens to shatter it. For how can unity be possible when ultimate truth claims are being made on every side? Given the experience of conferences up to this point, some of which have already been anything but simple, it is understandable that people are disinclined to take this step, that is, disinclined to allow themselves to be pushed into such a hopeless situation. Such dialogue, we are told, would break off virtually before it had even begun.

The first response is to point out emphatically that there is indeed a situation in which any dialogue between churches is to be viewed as already having been broken off. At the present moment, the Confessing Church is perhaps more familiar with this situation than is any other church in the world. The dialogue between the German Christian Church and the Confessing Church has been broken off once and for all. That is an undeniable fact. Nor is it a judgment concerning Christian or unchristian persons, but rather one concerning the spirit of a church that has been recognized and condemned as an antichristian spirit. It is a self-evident consequence that such dialogue, once broken off, cannot be reopened in a different setting, for example, in that of an ecumenical conference. The ecumenical movement must understand—and it did so in Fanø—that representatives of the Confessing Church and of the German Christians cannot be dialogue partners at an ecumenical conference. One of the great moments at the conference was when Bishop Ammundsen, immediately following the final speech of the German Christian regime, raised his voice as bishop on behalf of the absent representatives of the Confessing Church. The issue here is not persons but churches, a matter of Christ and the Antichrist; there is no neutral ground here. The ecumenical movement would transgress against its own mission, as well as against the Confessing Church, if it sought to evade a clear decision here.

---

11. ["... Both expressions represent characteristic structural elements in any current confession; cf. the Athanasian Creed (ca. 500), the Augsburg Confession (1530), and the Barmen Theological Declaration (1934)," *DBWE* 14:405, n. 32.]

406

Only pure doctrinarism could conclude here that such a position also makes it impossible to sit together, for example, with representatives of Anglicanism or of a semi-Pelagian[12] free-church theology. Such talk does not understand the meaning of a living confession, viewing confession instead as a dead system to be applied schematically as a standard to other churches. The Confessing Church is not confessing *in abstracto* [*in the abstract*]; it is not confessing against the Anglicans or the free churches, at the moment it is not even confessing against Rome, not to speak of Lutherans today confessing against the Reformed. Rather, it is confessing *in concretissimo* [*utterly concretely*] against the German Christian Church and against the new pagan idolization of creatures. As far as the Confessing Church is concerned, the Antichrist is sitting not in Rome or even in Geneva but in the Reich Church government in Berlin. It is against the Antichrist that the Confessing Church confesses, and it does so because it is from there rather than from Rome or Geneva or London that the very life of the Christian church in Germany is threatened and because it is there that the will to destruction is at work. It is here that the songs of the Psalter against the godless and the prayers petitioning God to conduct war against God's enemies come alive. Our only weapon is and remains our living confession.

407

A living confession does not mean pitting one dogmatic thesis against another; it refers rather to a confession in which the issue really is life and death. A naturally formulated, clear, theologically grounded, true confession. Here, however, theology is not itself the combative party but rather stands entirely in the service of the actively confessing and struggling church.

It is clear that, despite all theological analogies, the ecumenical situation is fundamentally different from this one. The Confessing Church does not approach confessionally different churches as its mortal enemies who are intent on its demise; rather, it enters into such contact bearing its own share of the guilt for the inner turmoil of Christendom, enters into that guilt, and, amid all false theologies it may encounter along the way, acknowledges first of all its own guilt and the inadequate power of its own proclamation. It acknowledges God's incomprehensible ways with the church. It is terrified by the serious nature of any church schism and by the burden such would impose on subsequent generations. It hears here the summons and

---

12. ["'Half-Pelagian.' The monk Pelagius contested Augustine's doctrines of original sin and grace, maintaining instead the free decision each person makes for good or evil; 'semi-Pelagianism' deviates from Pelagius insofar as it does admit original sin," *DBWE* 14:406, n. 35.]

admonition to accept responsibility and penitence. Given this situation, it will experience the entire distress of its own decision anew, and its own confession here will first of all be a *confession of sin*.

II.

Here things are reversed, and the Confessing Church stands there no longer, not even primarily, as the church that questions and demands but rather as the church that the ecumenical movement itself questions and indeed calls into question. And the surprising thing is that the very question the ecumenical movement receives from the Confessing Church is now reversed and posed to the Confessing Church itself. The weapon directed against the ecumenical movement has now been turned against the Confessing Church itself. How can the confession: Christ alone, grace alone, Scripture alone, how can the confession of justification from faith alone become true other than insofar as the confession of the Confessing Church itself be first of all a confession of sin, a confession that this entire church, along with all its theology and its ritual and its institutions, lives solely from the grace of God and from Jesus Christ and is in need of justification? The confession of the Confessing Church becomes serious only *in actu* [*in the act*], in this case meaning in a confession of sin, in penitence. Does the Confessing Church know that the confession of the fathers and the confession against the enemies of Jesus Christ attain credibility and authority only where a confession against oneself comes first, where the *damnamus* [*we reject*] is directed first of all against one's own front? Will the Confessing Church enter into the ecumenical community in concurrence with this presupposition?

The ecumenical movement poses these questions to the Confessing Church *first* through its very existence. The simple fact that Christian churches from throughout the world—with the exception of the Roman Catholic Church—have come together to enter into dialogue and to reach agreements on various issues stands, whether the Confessing Church says yes or no to it. It is a fact that a divided Christendom is coming together in a unanimous confession of its own distress and in unanimous prayer for the promised unity of the church of Jesus Christ; indeed, that common worship services, common sermons, even common celebrations of the Eucharist are being shared, and ecumenical Christendom is still or once again a possibility, and all these things are happening in the name of Jesus Christ and with a prayer for the support of the Holy Spirit. In view of this fact, is countering it with a pathetic "impossible!" really the first and only appropriate response? Does one really have the right to summon the anathema

over all such activity from the very outset? Is not this witness of all Christian churches at the very least something that must prompt a moment's pause and reflection? We must openly and unequivocally acknowledge that the concrete existence of the ecumenical movement does not in and of itself represent a proof of its truth and Christian legitimacy. But if it cannot represent a proof, can it not at least be an indication of the promise that God wants to bestow on this activity? Can there be any genuinely sincere prayer for the unity of the church if from the very outset some are to be excluded? Since the church is indeed concerned with truth, should not precisely the church be summoned, first of all, to take heed here for the sake of that very truth? Should not precisely a church in the narrow confines of Germany, a church that has such difficulty extending its gaze beyond its own borders, become more attentive here out of necessity? Should not even a church that is in a struggle for its own existence gratefully and heed-   409
fully take note of the prayers and community of the whole of Christendom? It remains that none of these considerations can ever represent a proof, though they are certainly an indication of God's promise and as such are to be taken and examined seriously. Admittedly, though, examined only through the confessional question, through the evidence of Scripture. It would be unwise for the Confessing Church to act as if its task were to call the ecumenical movement into being in the first place. A more appropriate, humble posture would be to recognize that something exists here quite apart from the Confessing Church itself, quite independently of its yes or no, something the Confessing Church now encounters as it moves along its own path, something that questions and summons it. It is in penitence that the Confessing Church must meet the ecumenical movement. Only a truly bad theology would forbid the Confessing Church from taking these things extremely seriously.

But this is not all that can be said. The very place from which ecumenical work becomes an ultimate commitment must be found in the foundation of the Confessing Church as church. There must be not only a concrete necessity but a theological one as well.

Second: It is understandable that the ecumenical movement itself emphatically insists on precisely this question of innermost necessity, since ultimately this determines whether the will of the Confessing Church to engage in the ecumenical movement will be an accidental one, possibly even merely a utilitarian one, or a necessary and for that reason an enduring one. Hence the question that the ecumenical movement hands back to the Confessing Church becomes even more pointed: If the Confessing Church isolates itself behind its confessional claims such that its own confession leaves no room for the ecumenical idea itself, the question arises in all seriousness as to whether in the Confessing Church itself the church of Christ is still to be found. Whenever a confessional claim becomes so absolute that it declares all dialogue with every confessionally different church a priori [*from the outset*] as broken off, whenever in blind zealousness it manages to see in other churches only its own missionary field, whenever the willingness to listen is already branded as a betrayal of the gospel, whenever orthodoxy remains totally isolated in unrestricted self-glorification, and finally whenever only the Western belief in progress is perceived in the ongoing protest of the ecumenical movement against injustice and violence—then the moment has come when one must seriously ask whether human dominion has taken the place of the dominion of Jesus Christ over his own church, whether human statutes have not taken the place of God's grace, and whether the Antichrist has not taken the place of the Christ. Yet when—and here the circle of questions closes—precisely such a church questions the ecumenical movement itself regarding the latter's own Christian orientation, the ecumenical movement has every right to perceive here merely the insane claim to dominion of a church engaged in self-idolatry, and the movement must certainly beware of lending an ear to such a voice.

The question of the church has been handed back to the Confessing Church itself. The Confessing Church must state where the boundaries of its own confessional claim are to be found.

The Confessing Church responds first by concretely entering ecumenical work, insofar as it participates in prayer and worship and in theological and practical work. It does so because it is called to do so and because it takes this call seriously. It leaves it to God to make of it what God will and in the meantime waits by working.

The Confessing Church takes the call of the ecumenical movement seriously because it feels a connection with that movement's members through the sacrament of holy baptism. It realizes that the total number of baptized persons does not yet constitute the church. It realizes that despite this one baptism the church is nonetheless at odds with itself, and the Confessing Church has not forgotten its own origins. At the same time, however, it does recognize in baptism the grace and promise of the one church that the Holy Spirit alone can assemble through its word. If the Reformation churches were to recognize the baptism of, for example, the Roman Catholic Church, they would be doing so not to ameliorate the seriousness of the church schism—since that schism would instead be made even more incisive, insofar as, despite the one baptism, those churches would still have to engage in mutual excommunication—but rather to raise the claim to be nothing other than the purified Catholic Church themselves, the heir of the Church of Rome, and to implement their own claim to catholicity.

At the same time, however, this places the grace of God *above* the doctrine of the church, albeit not such that the church schism thereby becomes less serious and perhaps even capable of retraction, but rather such that precisely thereby it is perceived even more painfully. By coming together on the basis of their baptism, the Reformation churches of the ecumenical movement are consciously laying claim to the heritage of the original Catholic Church, simultaneously now raising the question concerning the right and legitimacy of that claim, that is, concerning the scriptural purity of these churches.

The Confessing Church is the church that lives not from its purity but from its impurity—the church of sinners, the church of penitence and grace, the church capable of living only through Christ, only through grace, only through faith. As such a church, as one engaged in daily penitence, it is a church that confesses its own guilt in the discord of Christendom and that at every moment remains wholly dependent on the gift of God's grace. It thus exists only as a church that listens; it is open to hear those others who might call it to penitence. Hence its knowledge of the gospel as the sole grace of God through Jesus Christ, our brother and Lord, also contains the necessity and possibility of listening and of the ecumenical movement. Because this church lives not in and of itself but rather from the perspective of an external orientation, it has always existed—in every word it speaks—from the perspective of the ecumenical movement. That is the most inherently pressing consideration for it to engage in ecumenical work.

The Confessing Church is finally taking seriously the knowledge of the gospel, which God bestowed through the Holy Scriptures in the confessions of the fathers and bestows anew today. It has seen that this truth alone is its weapon in the struggle for life and death. It cannot desist even the smallest bit from this truth; at the same time, however, it understands that with precisely this truth it is called not to rule but to serve and to listen, and it will provide this service in full within the ecumenical movement.

The Confessing Church participates in the ecumenical work *as church*. Its word seeks to be heard as the word of church precisely because the Confessing Church itself seeks to witness not to its own word but to the binding word of God. It seeks to speak as church itself to other churches. It thereby forces a decision through its word.

The Confessing Church will always grant to the ecumenical movement the right to brotherly help, brotherly admonition, and brotherly objection, and by so doing will attest that the unity of Christendom and the love for Jesus Christ transcend all boundaries. *It will never be ashamed of the voices of its* 412 *brothers* and will instead gratefully grant and try to provide them a hearing.

The question has been raised. The future of the ecumenical movement and of the Confessing Church depends on it being addressed. Nor may this issue be watered down. No one can know into which crises this issue may lead both the ecumenical movement and the Confessing Church. What remains as a positive "program"? Nothing other than that this question not go unaddressed. Because it bears within itself the genuine power of the church, we entrust ourselves to it.

Whether the hope for the Ecumenical Council of Protestant Christendom will be fulfilled, whether such a council will not only witness the truth and unity of the church of Christ authoritatively but also be able to witness against the enemies of Christianity throughout the world, whether it will pronounce judgment on war, racial hatred, and social exploitation, whether through such true ecumenical unity among all Protestant churches in all nations war itself might one day become impossible,[13] whether the witness of such a council will fall on receptive ears—that depends on our own obedience to the question now posed to us and on how God chooses to use our obedience. It is not an ideal that has been set up but a commandment and a promise—it is not high-handed implementation of one's own goals that is required but obedience. The question has been posed.

---

13. ["Cf. the remarks in Bonhoeffer's lecture 'The Church and the Peoples of the World' on Ps. 85:9 in Fanø on August 28, 1934 (*DBWE* 13:309 [*Reader* 396–397]) . . . ," *DBWE* 14:412, n. 45.]

27. CONTEMPORIZING
NEW TESTAMENT TEXTS

DBWE 14:413–433

In 1936, Bonhoeffer expressed the desire to write a book on hermeneutics, but he abandoned this plan when the project that became Ethics *seemed more pressing.[1] This decision left the following 1935 lecture as Bonhoeffer's most sustained treatment of biblical hermeneutics. Its background was the German Christians' demand for a biblical message that was relevant to contemporary needs, which amounted to a demand that the church conform its message to the National Socialist agenda.[2] As Bonhoeffer develops below, this German Christian understanding of contemporizing insists that the biblical message justify itself to the standard of the present. He contrasts this with proper contemporizing, which submits the concerns of the present to the standard of the biblical message. Here contemporizing does not constitute a distinct method, but is rather included in the task of interpretation: exegesis of the Scriptures as a witness to the word of God.*

This lecture is remarkable for its continuity with Bonhoeffer's earliest and latest writings. Bonhoeffer argues below that the German Christian understanding of contemporizing entails a style of exegesis that applies German national identity as a standard for separating the time-bound elements of the Bible from those eternally valid elements that merit application in the present. This analysis recalls the young Bonhoeffer's critiques of his teachers' historical-critical method, where, for example, Harnack applied his cultured sensibility to distinguish the divine, eternal kernel from the human, temporal husk of the gospel.[3] The biblical message admits of no such division, Bonhoeffer argues in the essay below, since the whole Bible is the witness to God's

---

1. [DB-ER, *567–568.*]

2. [DBWE *14:413, n. 5.*]

3. [*For criticism of historical-critical exegesis, see* DBWE *9:285–300* (Reader *4–14). For discussion of Harnack specifically, see* DBWE *11:199–206.*]

word. This argument anticipates the Letters and Papers from Prison, *where Bonhoeffer resists Rudolf Bultmann's treatment of the New Testament as "a mythological dressing up of a universal truth" in favor of a nonreligious mode of interpreting the entire Bible, myths and all.*[4]

413   The question of contemporizing the New Testament message is basically capable of a dual exposition. Either one understands it to mean that the biblical message must justify itself to the present and thus demonstrate that it can be contemporized or that the present must justify itself to the biblical message and that thus the message must be made contemporary. Wherever the question of contemporization is posed today with that particular familiar, unnerving urgency, indeed posed as the central question of theology itself, it is always assumed it will serve the first goal mentioned above. The New Testament is to justify itself to the present.

It was in this form that the question first became acute during the era of the emancipation of autonomous reason, that is, in the era of rationalism,
414   and it is in this form that the question has shaped theology all the way to the theology of the German Christians. To the extent that rationalism was nothing other than the emergence of the previously latent claim of human beings to shape their own lives autonomously from the forces of the given world, this question does indeed represent a question that has already been raised in the human claim to autonomy itself. That means that autonomous human beings who would also confess to be Christians will demand the justification of the Christian message before the forum of their own autonomy. If this succeeds, then they call themselves *Christians*; if it does not succeed, they call themselves *pagans*. It makes not the slightest difference whether the forum before which the biblical message is to justify itself is called "reason" in the eighteenth century, "culture" in the nineteenth century, or *"Volkstum"*[5] in the twentieth century or in the year 1933, along with everything that entails, it is *exactly the same question*: Can Christianity become contemporary for us as we simply—thank God!—are now? It is exactly *the same urgent need* felt by all who would claim the Christian name for whatever reason—either reasons commensurate with the faculty of reason itself, cultural reasons, or political reasons—to justify Christianity to the present; *it is precisely the same presupposition*, namely, that the Archimedean point, that fixed, unquestionable point of departure, has already been determined

    4. [DBWE *8:430* (Reader *795*).]
    5. ["*Volkstum* means a national and cultural tradition; in the context of the Nazi era, this was understood as ethnically defined, i.e., 'Aryan,'" *DBWE* 14:414, n. 7.]

(either in reason, in culture, or in *Volkstum*) and that the shifting, *questionable*, unfixed element is precisely the Christian message itself; and it is *precisely the same methodology*, namely, that one undertake such contemporizing so that the biblical message must pass through the sieve of one's own knowledge . . .—whatever does not pass through is disdained and thrown away, so that one trims and prunes the Christian message until it fits the fixed framework, until the eagle can no longer rise and escape into its true element and instead is put on display with clipped wings as a special exhibit among the other domesticated pets. Just as a farmer who needs a field horse passes by the fiery stallion and buys the feeble, tamed horse instead, so 415 also does one purchase a useable Christianity, tamed . . .—and it is only a question of honesty before one quickly loses all interest in this construction and turns away from it. *This contemporizing* of the Christian message leads directly to paganism, which means first that the only difference between German Christians and so-called neopagans is *honesty*. Second, however, it means that even the call for contemporizing the Christian message that the German Christians raised—doubtlessly to some extent with great passion and subjective commitment—during their beginnings *may not* as such be taken seriously either ecclesiastically or theologically; that call was at best merely the cry of terror of those for whom the break between Christianity and world is visible, who are aware of how completely the world has formed them, who recognize that they are finished with Christianity but are not strong enough to declare either a clear "yes" or an equally clear "no," and who instead cowardly seek to pull Christianity itself into their own apostasy to the world. The clearest proof of this is that no one here had the courage to raise anew the question of the actual *substance* of the Christian message and instead merely cried out for *contemporizing*, thereby—differently than in liberal theology! Naumann![6]—*avoiding the issue entirely!* Wherever the 416 question of contemporizing *is taken as the theme of theology*, however, we can be sure that the substance has already been betrayed and sold away. We must be quite careful not to allow the struggle itself to impose false questions and false themes on us. The danger is very real. I need only recall

---

6. ["Friedrich Naumann was the cofounder and principal architect of the 'Christian Social Movement' in Germany, which tried to reach the proletariat, which was rather distant from the church, by adopting socioethical elements of the Christian message in an affirmation of the proletariat's struggle for emancipation. For a long time, Naumann considered the ideological foundation of this program to consist of a liberal, nonsoteriological understanding of Jesus. Ultimately, however, it became clear to him that one could not so easily derive a sociopolitical program from the New Testament Jesus," *DBWE* 14:415–416, n. 20.]

the theological literature of the past two years—precisely from our own side!—(Althaus *Deutsche Stunde der Kirche* [*The German Hour of the Church*], Heim, even Schlatter *neue deutsche Art in der Kirche*! [*The New German Kind in the Church*]) to make this clear. The question of *contemporization* too easily acquires a false accent! and displaces the question of *substance*. What sense does it make to speak about contemporizing when we are not even of one mind yet concerning the substance?

What happens is that those who are thirsty will drink water from whatever vessel is available, be it ever so difficult. But it is better to have to draw pure water laboriously than to drink murky water from a glass. Those who are thirsty have always found *living* water in the Bible itself and in a *substantively* biblical sermon, even when such was quite out of sync with the times— and it betrays a dangerous decadence of faith whenever the question of contemporizing the message becomes excessively loud as a methodological question. For those who are genuinely concerned with the substance, to wit, with the salvation of their soul, the German Luther Bible, *Luther's translation of the Holy Scriptures into German*, still best fulfills the demand for contemporizing and *translating the gospel into German*. It is here that one finds contemporized Christianity, German Christianity.

For the time being, however, that is enough negation and delimitation. The positive meaning of the question of contemporization can now move into the correct light. The meaning is not a justification of Christianity to the present but a *justification of the present to the Christian message*. Here contemporizing means that the present is put before the forum of the Christian message; in other words, one asks the question of the *substance*, of the "What?" of the Christian message, whereas the false concept of contemporization asked about the "What?" of the present. True contemporization is found in the question of substance. One puts one's confidence in the *substance itself*, trusting that wherever it genuinely comes to expression, it is indeed—in and of itself—the most contemporary element; there is then no longer any need for any special act of contemporizing; that contemporizing takes place in the substance itself. To be sure—only because it is *this particular* substance, the substance with which the New Testament is concerned, because the substance here is Christ and Christ's word. Wherever Christ is expressed in the word of the New Testament, one has contemporization. Not where the present registers its own claims before Christ but rather where the present itself stands before the claims of Christ—*there one has the present*. *For*: The concept of the present is not a temporal determination; instead it is determined through the word of Christ as the word of God. The present is not some temporal feeling, temporal interpretation, or zeitgeist; instead, the present is solely the Holy Spirit. Wherever God is present in the divine word, there one has the present; there God posits the present. The *subject of the present* is the Holy Spirit, not we ourselves, and that is also why the subject of *contemporization* is the Holy Spirit itself. The *concretissimum* [*utter concretion*] *of the Christian message* and textual exposition is not a human act of contemporizing but rather always God, the Holy Spirit. Because the "substance" of the New Testament is that Christ speaks to us through Christ's Holy Spirit, and because this takes place not outside of or alongside but only and exclusively *through the word* of Scripture itself, one can say that *an orientation to that substance*, that is, the scriptural orientation of proclamation itself, is what constitutes contemporizing—"an orientation to substance"—both as a methodology—we will address this soon—and as obedience and trust in the substance of the Holy Spirit. For the salient element in this substance is precisely the Holy Spirit itself, and It is the present God and Christ.

It is here that the *concept of the present* first comes to full expression *linguistically* as well. That something is "present" or situated "toward" with respect to us—waits there before us—does after all imply that *the present is determined externally* rather than internally, cannot be determined by us, is determined instead by that which approaches us externally, by that which approaches, by the future. The present is determined primarily not by the past but by the *future*, and this future is Christ, is the Holy Spirit. "Contemporization" thus means an orientation toward this *future*, to this *outside*— and it is a disastrous mix-up between present and past to believe that one can define the present as something that resides *within itself* and *bears its own criterion within itself*. The criterion of the authentic present resides outside that present itself, resides in the future, in Scripture and in the word of Christ attested there. And thus an orientation toward substance will consist in allowing that external element, that element before us, that "future element" that comes toward us to come to expression as the present—the alien gospel, not the familiar gospel, will be the present or contemporary gospel. Point of contact with the scandalum [*scandal*]!

2. Contemporizing as Methodology

Once we have recognized that proper contemporizing means getting to the substance and allowing that substance to come to expression, the corresponding methodology would accordingly stipulate that a contemporizing proclamation *must* essentially *be exegesis*, exegesis of the only word that has at its disposal the power of contemporizing, namely, an exegesis of Scripture.

To the extent that we are able to engage it methodologically at all, the act of contemporizing consists in the strict and exclusive reference to the word of Scripture. Hence the movement is not from the word of Scripture to the present but rather from the present to the word of Scripture, where it then abides! Hence seemingly away from the present in order to move away from the false present to the authentic present.[7]

419

Those who find this incomprehensible have not yet grasped the presupposition that the present can be found only where Christ and the Holy Spirit speak. This turn back to Scripture corresponds exactly to the turn undertaken by Christian faith and Christian hope, namely, back to the cross of Christ. In both cases, it is the historicity of God's revelation that comes to expression here.

"Exegesis" is not an unequivocal concept; it must be clearly delimited from other, untheological methodologies of contemporization.

The presupposition for any contemporizing in an untheological understanding is apparently that there is something in the past that is *not only past* but extends beyond the past. Indeed, this element that extends beyond the past is basically (essentially, in and of itself) *not something that is past*, not something temporal, but rather supertemporal. Within history, we are told, there is something *eternal*, in the accidental something necessary, in the individual-unique a universal meaning. This meaning, this eternal element can be a teaching; it can be an ethical norm; it can be a universally human feeling; it can be a myth. Contemporization involves finding this eternal element, this meaning, this essence, which is just as valid today as earlier. In our own case, it means *finding* the eternal teaching or the universal ethical norm or the myth contained by Holy Scripture, and it then also means applying this universal element to the present, to the individual "today."

How is it possible to find the eternal in the temporal? Only insofar as interpreters themselves have access a priori to the eternal standards they find in Scripture. Because like can only be recognized by like, interpreters of the Holy Scriptures are able to recognize and disclose within Scripture the universal ideas and standards already inhering within themselves. That is, the *principle of contemporizing resides* within me, in the interpreter. In the strict, logical sense, I am the *subject of contemporizing*, and only that which is already

420

---

7. ["See Bonhoeffer's description of the role of Scripture in *Life Together* (*DBWE* 5:62), where the emphasis is placed not on finding Scripture relevant to our world but rather that we find ourselves placed in the midst of the Scripture's world . . . ," *DBWE* 14:419, n. 34.]

present within me as a principle of contemporizing can be evoked in a contemporary fashion. Here scriptural exposition means referring Scripture to the eternal truths with which I am already familiar—either as an intellectual truth, as an ethical principle, as a universal human insight, or as a myth. In other words, truth is already fixed before I even begin my exegesis of Scripture.

We recognize in this particular method of contemporizing that first, false understanding of contemporization mentioned at the beginning. Scripture is brought before the forum of the present and must justify itself before that forum; it must yield knowledge, norms, universal truths already given in the present. Whatever resists this procedure is left in the past as something temporally bound, something that cannot be evoked or interpreted in a contemporary fashion, something that is not eternal, divine.

Here interpreters claim the ability to distinguish between the word of God and the word of human beings in the Holy Scriptures. They themselves know where the word of God is and where the word of human beings is. For example: Paul's theology is the word of a human being, whereas the so-called religion of Jesus is divine. The doctrines of sin and justification are temporally bound and past, whereas the struggle for the good and the pure is eternal. Or: the ethical teaching of Jesus is eternal, whereas the miracle stories are temporally bound. Or: the fighter Jesus and his death are expressions of the eternal struggle of light against darkness, whereas the suffering, defenseless Jesus does not concern us. Or: the doctrine of grace is eternal—whereas the commandments of the Sermon on the Mount are no longer valid for us!

This method hands us the key to interpreting Scripture. Just as in a secular text we can distinguish the authentic words of an author from the inauthentic addenda, so too in the Bible we can distinguish the word of God from the word of human beings and extract it. The criterion to be applied to the word of God resides in us, either in our reason, in our conscience, or in our *völkisch*[8] or other experiences. The criterion for the word of God resides outside that word itself, in us—*the norm of contemporizing resides within us; the Bible is the material to which this norm is applied.*

This sentence must now be exactly reversed so that our own concept of exegesis and contemporization may become clear—the norm for the word of God in Scripture is the word of God itself, and our own circumstances, reason, conscience, and *völkisch* experience are the material to which this

421

---

8. [*Meaning "populist," "nationalist," and often "racist."*]

norm is to be applied. To be sure, we, too, say that the word of God and the word of human beings are bound together in the Holy Scriptures, but they are bound such that God himself states where his word is and that he speaks that word *within the word of human beings.* The human word does not cease being temporally bound and transient by becoming God's word; instead, it is precisely as such a historic, temporal word that it is indeed the word of God. The distinction between the eternal and the temporal, the accidental and the necessary . . . in the Bible is fundamentally false. The temporal word of Scripture itself—for example, Jesus's own admission that he does not know the hour at which the reign of God will commence, or the question: Why do you call me good? are God's word precisely as a wholly temporally bound statement. God alone says where his word is—and that means again that God alone evokes his word in a contemporary fashion, and the Holy Spirit is the principle of that contemporization. As far as the methodology of contemporizing exegesis is concerned, this means that it does not approach Scripture as a book in which universal truths, universal ethical norms, or myths might be discovered; for such exegesis, Holy Scripture is rather as a whole *the witness* of God in Christ, and in every passage the point is to make the character of this word as a witness audible. There are basically no preferred passages in this sense unless one understands such to involve the degree of clarity exhibited by a given witness. *Contemporizing comes about not through the selection of certain texts but by making the whole of Holy Scripture audible as a witness to the word of God.* The only *method* of contemporization is thus the substantive textual exposition of the Holy Scriptures as the witness of Christ, and such exegesis has the promise of Christ's presence.

420

Two questions: (1) Must I, as the preacher, not follow the exposition itself with concrete application, must I not speak this word to the congregation authoritatively in an unequivocally concrete fashion, and must not the accent of eternity itself be on this concretion, and does this form of contemporizing not considerably transcend the exposition itself?

The text itself is not the universal point of departure to which I might then give the congregation a concrete example upon which the accent of eternity would then fall. The *concretissimum* of the sermon is not the *application I provide* but the Holy Spirit itself speaking through the text of the Bible. Even the clearest scopus, the most clearly audible appeal to the congregation remain unconcrete as long as it is not the Holy Spirit itself that is creating this *concretissimum*, this contemporaneity, this present. As far as the accent of eternity is concerned, one must say that the accent of eternity has already fallen, namely, on Christ and on Christ's cross, and here it stays, and in every sermon this accent of eternity falls again only on Christ and on

Christ's cross and on nothing else. Wherever an accent of eternity is sought apart from Christ, one falls prey to Enthusiasm.[9]

(2) Does the concrete situation of the congregation itself not demand a form of contemporization going beyond mere exegesis? One must make the so-called concrete situation of the congregation comprehensible to the congregation as the universal situation of human beings before God, of human beings in their pride, in their unbelief, in their insensitivity to others, in their question. The answer is Christ as he comes to us through his word, always simultaneously as the judging, commanding, and forgiving one. Not this or that concretion which I might speak to the so-called concrete situation, but Christ alone as the Lord, Judge, and Savior is the word addressing the concrete situation. That I happen to sit beneath the pulpit as a man or a woman, as a National Socialist or a reactionary or a Jew, coming from this or that particular experience, in and of itself gives me absolutely no rights or claims concerning the word; instead, I as a man or as a National Socialist am one who has become a sinner and nonbeliever before God, a person who is asking about God, that is my true concrete situation as revealed and resolved for me by the sermon. Wherever Christ himself speaks in the exegesis of the text as witness, it is there that those who previously took themselves seriously as a man or as a National Socialist or as a Jew become those who now take themselves seriously only as sinners and as those who are called and pardoned. Precisely by *not taking seriously in any ultimate sense* the so-called concrete situation of the congregation, one is able to see the true situation of human beings before God. God queries us not about whether we are a man or a woman or a National Socialist but rather about our faith in God and in God's forgiving love and about our obedience to God's word as attested in the Bible.

Oddly, the opinion persists that something must be added to textual exegesis—something transcending it, something more concrete—what can be more concrete today than an exegesis of certain chapters of Revelation or of the prophets or of the Sermon on the Mount or of the story of the good Samaritan? Is not the exegesis of the text itself everything, to the extent it genuinely takes this particular text as a witness to the living Christ? Is that not precisely the surprising thing about our own age, namely, that we can take almost any text, and by giving it a clear and substantive exegesis have already also contemporized it?! (The opinion has gradually emerged that

---

9. [*In a Lutheran theological context, enthusiasts are those who seek the Holy Spirit apart from Christ, or truth apart from the external word and sacrament. E.g., Smalcald Articles, III, viii, 9–10, in* Book of Concord, 323.]

a Confessing sermon must always contain some concrete polemic against Rosenberg[10] etc., as if that were the form of contemporizing—nothing against this view—but a good sermon does not need that at all, certainly not today! The polemic resides in the textual exegesis itself!)

424   3. Contemporizing the New Testament Message

The New Testament is the *witness* of the promise of the Old Testament as fulfilled in Christ. It is not a book containing eternal truths, teachings, norms, or myths, but the sole *witness* of the God-human Jesus Christ. As a whole and in all its parts, it is nothing other than this witness of Christ, Christ's life, death, and resurrection. This Christ is attested not as the eternal in the temporal, as the meaning within the accidental, as the essence within the nonessential! but as the absolutely unique one, the incarnate one, the one who died, was raised, and it is *this* uniqueness of Christ in history that fills the entire New Testament. Here there is no distinction between *doctrinal texts* (in the epistles and in Jesus's discourses) and the *historic* texts. Both are equally *witnesses to the unique Christ*; hence it is not that a doctrinal text might be expressing a universal truth about Christ, whereas a miracle story, for example, is recounting something accidental or singular—instead, both equally attest the uniqueness and complete historicity of Jesus Christ. In the miracle story, just as in the parable or in the commandments of the Sermon on the Mount, the one proclaimed is *Christ alone*, not this or that truth or teaching concerning Christ or Christ's deed, but rather Christ. Christ, and Christ alone, and Christ "*completely*"! *The common character of the New Testament witness* is that it is Christ who performs this miracle, speaks the parable, issues the commandment, and that through such a miracle, parable, commandment, or teaching Christ is always aiming at one and the same thing, *namely, to bind human beings to himself* as the absolutely unique, historic one. Similarly, however, a Pauline doctrinal text is not essentially a dogmatic statement—though it is that as well—but a unique witness to the unique Christ. Although one may say that in the Gospels the miracle of Christ's incarnation and human existence is more perceivable, and in the Epistles the miracle of the cross and the resurrection more perceivable, it is never such that in the Gospels, too, the entire crucified and resurrected

425

---

10. ["Hitler had appointed Alfred Rosenberg to oversee the general spiritual and ideological training of the NSDAP. His book, *The Myth of the Twentieth Century*, was widely distributed," *DBWE* 14:423, n. 52.]

Christ, and in the Epistles the entire incarnate human being Christ is not also attested in all its uniqueness.

Although it may seem that doctrinal texts are easier to contemporize than are historic ones, here, too, one falls prey to the false assumption that the Bible contains something akin to a doctrine that is valid for all time, whereas the historic events it recounts are merely temporally bound. The New Testament is a *witness in* both doctrine *and* history. The New Testament is not something *itself* but witnesses to something else; it has no inherent value but value only as a witness to Christ. It does not rest within itself but points beyond itself; its sentences and words are not true and eternal and valid in and for themselves but only to the extent that they witness to Christ—that is, only to the extent that they allow Christ alone to be true. The entire New Testament, in all its parts, is intended to be interpreted as a witness—not as a wisdom book, as a book of teaching, as a book of eternal truth, but as a book of unique witness to a unique fact. It is the "joyful cry": *This Jesus is Christ!* "You are to point to and speak about this human being: that is God." (Luther!)

One does not correctly interpret a Pauline doctrinal text if one transmits it as a piece of genuine theology, as *pura doctrina* [*pure doctrine*]; instead one must make this theology comprehensible as the witness to the living Christ. Difficult—because easy universal truths—misunderstanding as if that were Christ—theology as witness!

One interprets a miracle story correctly neither by referring it back to a universal truth—wedding in Cana: "Jesus deserts no one"—nor by directing our attention basically to the miracle itself and then adducing corresponding examples from the present; the miracle narrative is to be proclaimed   426
instead as a witness to Christ as the one who can break the power of demons, as the Lord over the demons—which Christ became as the Crucified. That precisely these miracle stories are beginning to speak especially in such a demonized age as our own makes it easier to preach them today. That these demons do not step aside or perish on their own, that is, that they must be *driven out*, that Christ is the Lord who alone can drive out demons and that Christ has also promised us the power to perform such miracles if we but have faith, that we can become master of such demons not through hatred and violence but only through fasting and prayer and faith—all this offers an extremely contemporary exposition of these miracle stories.

The parable is the most highly powerful witness to Christ. One must guard against misunderstanding the parables in two different ways: *first*, as if the *content* of the parables actually illustrated universal truths—not a universal truth but "the kingdom of God is like . . ." [*Matt. 13:31–47*] is clearer to us: "Christ is like . . ." Christ is the content goal of every parable.

Second: as if *the form of the parable* were a psychologically based rhetorical form that Jesus uses for the sake of popularization, or let us say: contemporizing his own thoughts, as if this were being presented to us as a model suggesting that we, too, ought to preach in parables. According to Jesus's own words (Mark 4:11ff.), the parable is not a psychologically based, exemplary rhetorical form but the form of *his own* discourse as grounded in the cause of God's kingdom itself and as already attested in the Psalter . . . , through which Christ carries out the separation of spirits into believers and those who are stubborn. The luminosity and clarity and unequivocal nature of the parable now prevent human beings from avoiding a decision for or against Christ. In this way, it is precisely the luminosity of the parable that judges them—"that they may indeed look, but not perceive . . ." [*Mark 4:12*] thus does that which is most clear become that which is most obscure, the revealed day become the hidden night, thus does that which all can understand become precisely the most profound mystery of election, of disciples—as attested by Psalm 78—cf. Matt. 13:35. Hence Christ is not only the goal of the parable but also the one who forces a decision and then as judge carries out the separation. In this sense, especially, the parables are to be preached not as the immutable metaphors of eternal truths but as a witness to Christ, who both bestows and denies, who reveals and conceals through the same word, as the Crucified who through his clear word separates the spirits, through whose word the mystery of the eternal election and rejection is fulfilled.

Ultimately, however, the commandments and parenesis [*exhortation, moral instruction*] of the New Testament are also to be understood strictly as a *witness* to Christ as the crucified and resurrected Lord. Not as eternal norms and laws but as commandments of a Lord, in which the commandment is only understood correctly where the Lord is recognized. A commandment without a Lord is nothing, and the basis, the content, and the goal—that is, the fulfillment of the commandment is always the Lord, specifically as the crucified. Hence the commandments of the Sermon on the Mount or a Pauline parenesis must be understood as a witness to the Lord, the crucified and resurrected, not with any intention of minimizing the commandment itself in the process, which remains as it is, but it is a witness, proclamation of Christ, and that means it is now grace. The question should be: To what extent is this commandment fulfilled in Christ, to what extent does Christ authoritatively speak this commandment? Only those who hear and heed the commandment perceive in it the witness of Christ. Hence the commandments of the New Testament are not the principles of a Christian ethics but rather the unique witness of the present and commanding Christ, and it is as such that they are to be interpreted.

Contemporizing New Testament texts thus means, first of all, interpreting them as a witness to Christ as the crucified, resurrected Lord who calls to discipleship, and to do so with the assurance that Christ is the subject of this contemporization. This witness is to be understood as the strictly one- 428
time witness to a one-time event. Only where the New Testament retains this character of singularity can it be understood seriously as a witness to Christ. The possibility of contemporizing depends on this one-time character—that is, on the rejection of any possibility of disclosing and distinguishing between something eternal and something temporally bound, between the word of God and the word of human beings—for contemporizing means that Christ alone speaks through the Holy Spirit as the historical person attested through Scripture—that Christ steps *toward* us—not on finding some universal truth confirmed in the New Testament. Contemporizing depends on interpreting the New Testament as the unique witness to the historical and living Christ.

One final problem in this context: Because Scripture as a whole and in all its parts is to be understood as a witness to Christ, and because difficulties do apparently arise in the concrete demonstration of this assertion—the question arises whether it is permissible to employ *allegorical exegesis*[11] for obscure scriptural passages. In this regard, one can point out the following: (1) The proof of the nature of Scripture as testimony derives neither from a literal nor from an allegorical interpretation, but from God alone, who confesses his witness in his own time. Hence it is impossible to justify the allegorical interpretation in this way. (2) The right of the allegorical interpretation consists in acknowledging the possibility that God does not allow his word to be exhausted in its grammatical, logical, unequivocal meaning, but rather that this word has even other perspectives and can serve better understanding. Luther emphatically insisted on the *unequivocal meaning of Scripture* over against the *four- or sevenfold* meaning of Scripture—unanimity, truth . . .—he himself *allegorized* in his own lecture on the Psalms! But certainly no right to reject the other possibility—why should the word not *also* have symbolic 429
or allegorical meaning? The decisive element and only criterion is whether something other than Christ is disclosed here—hence the issue is (1) the What! the *content* of the allegorical and symbolic and typological exposition;

---

11. ["Historically, the church has understood that Scripture can be interpreted on multiple levels. Classically formulated, it resulted in a 'fourfold' approach, employing the literal, the allegorical, the moral, and the anagogical in recognition of the various ways that Scripture could be both interpreted and applied to the Christian life. An allegorical interpretation of Scripture would involve a symbolic interpretation," *DBWE* 14:428, n. 78.]

(2) that only to the *word of Scripture* itself can this power to witness allegori-
cally, symbolically, etc. to Christ, this transparency, be attributed. *Within the
parameters of these two restrictions, it seems to me that one must grant to allegorical
etc. interpretation a measure of freedom,* and indeed the New Testament itself
engaged in such interpretation within these parameters. How might we then
consider it impossible? The allegorical exegesis retains a nice bit of freedom
of church exegesis of Scripture not as a false means of proof but as praise for
the fullness of the scriptural witness to Christ.

(b) our witness: The boundaries have been established within which one
can legitimately speak about contemporization. Within these boundaries,
however, the preacher does retain some not-inconsiderable freedom: *The
first freedom* is that of translation, the translation of the original text into
German. The Luther Bible provides us with witness to Christ in German.
For any doctrine of verbal inspiration, a translation already represents a
remove, since only the original text itself is inspired. For us, translation
represents both freedom and commitment. The *language* is left to the freedom of the church-community, that is, to service to the church-community.
430   *Translation* is the first, necessary, legitimate form of contemporization. The
problem of an appropriate theological and church language is inordinately
important and as yet still wholly undiscussed.[12] This much must be said:
The demands of *contemporary* language, of the language of the *people* represent merely a formal point of contact for comprehension—but by no means
is one to allow free rein to the inherent laws of language, the demonic
powers—bring the *condescension*[13] of the *word* to expression only through
language, but not to be used as *captatio benevolentiae* [*courting the favor (of the
listener or reader)*]. Language remains strictly in *service* precisely because it
functions as a means for mediating the word. *The second freedom* is that
of *choosing the text to be preached.* Even though every textual sermon must
preach Christ, and just as in each instance it must be the entire Christ that
is actually preached, *nonetheless the choice of text is open*—(relatively speaking!—this is not the place to address the pericope problem![14]). How does

---

12. ["... Bonhoeffer subsequently dealt with the issue of 'correct theological and
church language' in his lectures on homiletics (see esp. pp. 503–506," *DBWE* 14:430, n.
86.]

13. ["'Condescension' analogous to the incarnation of Jesus Christ," *DBWE* 14:430,
n. 87.]

14. ["Question of the binding character of ecclesiastical pericope series indicating
the previously determined, fixed sermon texts for the individual Sundays of the church

one appropriately use this freedom? Am I to ask: What does the congregation want to hear today? What are its questions? What happened during the past week? Although these questions are certainly legitimate and necessary ones for the pastor to ask, they still require a precondition. The precondition is that the pastor knows that in truth a congregation is not asking about this or that topic that may currently occupy the foreground, but instead is always asking, in the back of its mind and whether it knows it or not, about the *entire Christ*, and that only the proclamation of the entire Christ will be able to address those questions. This means that I will have to raise those particular questions not with respect to which specific truth is to be spoken to the congregation in this or that instance but rather with respect to *the entirety of the witness to Christ*. The freedom to choose a text thus serves the entirety of the witness to Christ. Wherever this entirety is threatened, it is there that I must preach. Whether such a threat to the entirety derives from inadequacies in my own previous sermon or in certain circumstances in this particular congregation is a different question.—Possibility of error!— But wherever Christ is preached rather than this or that particular truth, such errors are balanced out. The freedom of contemporization serves the 431 entirety of the Christ witness.

Before mentioning in conclusion *the third and what I consider the decisive freedom* in connection with a contemporizing of the New Testament message, I would first like to address a quite concrete issue by indicating three points at which the totality of the Christ proclamation is threatened today and in so doing make a concrete contribution to contemporizing New Testament texts. I would like to illustrate this with regard to three central points of the New Testament message:

1. *Grace and Discipleship*
2. *Church and World.* (church discipline—false teaching!)
3. The Good Samaritan.

Concluding Section of the Lecture (student notes)

1. Grace: in the Protestant tradition—living from grace alone. Proclaim this because attested to in Scripture. Untrue, if principle of grace.

As soon as proclamation of grace blocks the way to Christ, it is apostasy and lies.

Here, however, Christ attested only where at the same time the one who calls to discipleship is recognized and witnessed.

---

year," *DBWE* 14:430, n. 91. *"Pericope Series" refers to lectionaries, such as the Revised Common Lectionary, used in many denominations.*]

Otherwise costly grace of the gospel (Matt. 13) instead of cheap grace.[15]

Is *costly* grace for us simultaneously a call to discipleship? New Testament proclaims costly grace?

When Luther proclaimed grace, he had already struggled for twenty years to live according to the law. There for the first time he had taken seriously the call away from orders. Out of the monastery not because it would be good on the outside. Not canonization of some *iustitia civilis* [*civil justice*]. Renunciation of *any* canonization of human life.

Luther's understanding of vocational life meant as criticism. Because he knew Christ only as the one who calls to discipleship, could call grace.

432   What truth is as result is a lie as presupposition, what is obedience as result is disobedience as presupposition.

Understand the path of discipleship, however, as the infinitely consoling path with its conclusion.[16]

Are we really proclaiming costly grace? or grace as a cheap commodity? Here we in alliance with antinomianism,[17] which Paul is against!

2. Consequence of the Lutheran doctrine of grace is that the church is to live in the world, within its institutions. Romans 13. Here Luther confirms in his own age Constantine's alliance with the church.[18] Result: minimal ethics was victorious. He, however, wanted full ethics for everyone, not just for monasteries.

Existence of the Christian the existence of the citizen. Hence now the essence of church invisible. This fundamentally misunderstands the New Testament message. Innerworldliness now no longer possibility but rather has become principle. Hence today witnesses to otherworldliness. Hence precisely today New Testament witness to the city on the hill. Church-community that dares to live its *own* life in simple obedience to outside the world.

---

15. ["Cf. allusion to Matt. 13:44–46 in the introductory chapter, 'Costly Grace,' in *Discipleship* (*DBWE* 4:43–44 [*Reader* 459–461])," *DBWE* 14:431, n. 96.]

16. ["Concerning 'conclusion' and 'presupposition,' see *DBWE* 4:49–51 (*Reader* 464–466)," *DBWE* 14:432, n. 98.]

17. ["Doctrine declaring that the claim God's law makes on the life of a Christian is obsolete," *DBWE* 14:432, n. 99. ". . . On Bonhoeffer's own repudiation of antinomianism, cf. '"Personal" and "Objective" Ethics,' *DBWE* 16:547, n. 40," *DBWE* 16:593, n. 69.]

18. ["During the fourth century, the religious and ecclesiastical politics of Emperor Constantine the Great prepared the way for the Christian church to be recognized as the sole privileged state church. The state and the church were organized together in such a way that both acknowledged the emperor as their common, divinely ordained head, something that happened more unequivocally and to a greater extent in east Rome than in the western part of the empire," *DBWE* 14:432, n. 100.]

Leave *everything* in order to receive back a hundredfold *here*.

Church-community that sets itself apart. Elimination of false teaching. Perhaps even distance oneself from the courts.[19] Community that also hears Revelation.

Witnessing to the state of being sojourners in the world! Renounce the false *principle* of innerworldliness. Innerworldliness is a comfort but not a principle or program.

[433 in margin]

Friendship between church and world not the normal but rather the abnormal: Christ and the first community. The church-community *must* suffer, without astonishment. The cross stands *visibly* over the church-community.

This witness as the word of the *entire* Christ. Contemporizing: proclamation of the entire Christ.

3. Ministry of the church to those who suffer violence, injustice. Old Testament still demands justice from the state. New Testament no longer does so. Without asking about justice or injustice, the church accepts the suffering, *all* who have been abandoned, all parties and classes. "Speak out for those who cannot speak" [*Prov. 31:8*]. Perhaps here the decision of whether we are still a church.

Contemporizing as making credible.

Freedom (decisive!) to make credible. The real offense of the world, no longer found in comprehensibility, in the cross, but in credibility!!

Because the church and the pastor speak differently than they behave. Because the existence of the pastor no longer differs from that of the citizen.

Existence of the one who proclaims is a mediating element.

Contemporizing: as much as we can, make credible.

Ask ourselves whether through our own lives we have not already robbed our scriptural word of credibility.

---

19. ["Cf. *DB-ER*, 444–445: Bonhoeffer was 'more skeptical' of the lawsuits in which the Confessing Church sued in public courts to retain their withdrawn or contested rights; cf. *DBWE* 4:105 (*Reader* 493): The disciples 'do not sue for their rights,'" *DBWE* 14:432, n. 103.]

28. On the Question
of Church Communion

DBWE 14:656–678

Bonhoeffer claimed in "The Confessing Church and the Ecumenical Movement" that the Reich Church was a false or heretical church. In the following essay, first presented in 1936 as a lecture to seminarians and subsequently published in Evangelische Theologie,[1] *Bonhoeffer further develops this claim in conversation with the Lutheran confessional tradition's reflection on the nature of the church. Drawing on Luther's motif of the alien and proper work of God, Bonhoeffer argues that the church's proper work is to preach the gospel, to proclaim that Christ is present in word, church, and sacraments. This proclamation, not the question about the scope of the church, is to be the church's focus. There are times, however, when questions about the scope of the church arise from outside the church. At such times, the church must, in an alien work that supports its proper work, address the question of its own boundaries. Since the church draws its own boundaries in response to outside challenges, the church does not do so in principle or in perpetuity but in acts of decision. It is such a decision about boundaries that occurs when the church issues a confession. Because Bonhoeffer interprets the Confessing Synods at Barmen and Dahlem to have confessed in this sense, those synods have drawn a definitive boundary between the Confessing Church as the true church and the Reich Church as apostate. From this follows Bonhoeffer's provocative conclusion: since there is no salvation outside the church, "Whoever knowingly separates himself from the Confessing Church in Germany separates himself from salvation."*

---

1. [DBWE *14:656, n. 1.*]

I.

The Reformation separated the question of what the church is from the question of who belongs to the church. This was a decisive step. Roman Catholicism and pre-Reformation thinkers[2] believed that the question of the essence of the church could be answered by defining its scope. The Reformation, and especially the Lutheran understanding, first determined what the church itself is, leaving open the question concerning the boundaries of the church. Their primary concern was not the discovery of the divine mystery, who does or does not belong to the church, or the question of election and rejection, nor was their first step to judge and assess human beings, but rather above all it was God's own revelation and salvific deed, namely, the present Christ, Christ's word, and Christ's sacrament that was to be beheld and worshipped. Rather than examining theoretical statements concerning those who are saved or lost, rather than assessing and judging that some belong to the church while others do not, they focused on the cry of joy of those who have received a great, surprising gift: Here is the gospel! Here are the pure sacraments! Here is the church! Come hither!

Just what this meant for the relationship with other churches, for the boundaries of the church, was a wholly second question. The essence of the church is determined not by those who belong to it but by the word and sacrament of Jesus Christ; wherever this word and these sacraments are efficaciously present, they will assemble a church-community according to the promise. Their firm faith, based on the promise, was that there will always be those who belong to the church as long as the word and sacrament are rightly administered. Just who does indeed belong to the church, only the Lord, who calls and gathers them, knows. That was enough.

It was not a primary concern to identify these members by name, to count them, and to distinguish them from those who did not belong to the church or who merely pretended to belong, since the latter are already judged in any case. Moreover, the Last Judgment will also bring all such things to light. Of what concern is it for faith to know all these things today, to delimit and separate out some and not others? Is it not enough for faith that it is permitted to know of God's gracious, salvific deed? Of what concern is it for faith to expose hypocrites and heretics? Why would faith seek to disclose prematurely the terrible mystery of rejection before its own joy at eternal life with Christ has helped it overcome its own fear and pain

657

658

---

2. ["In the 1932 lecture 'The Nature of the Church' (*DBWE* 11:282 [*Reader* 179]), Bonhoeffer mentioned John Wycliff and Jan Hus," *DBWE* 14:656, n. 3.]

concerning God's final judgment? For faith already knows the terrors concealed in this allegedly harmless concept of the "scope of the church." And it thanks God daily that it may remain blind to such things, that it is permitted to abide yet in intercession, that it is permitted to hold to the church of salvation together with the believing church-community in the full joy bequeathed by its knowledge of salvation. Faith offers thanks to God that it has once again received the pure, honest gift of the word and the sacrament, and that it knows where the church of God is. Why, when it is already so completely taken by this joy, should it ask about where the church is not to be found?

Hence both early Christianity and the Reformation are doing nothing other than calling out repeatedly and cheerfully: Here is the church!, the true church of Jesus Christ! This call is both humble and grateful. Not self-praise, but praise of God. Once one has truly heard and believed, why would it occur to that person to ask whether perhaps the church might also be found elsewhere? Who would be interested in such questions besides precisely those do not want to hear and believe here? If we were to hear and believe that an inestimable gold mine had been found that would provide enough gold for all people for all time, we would certainly be less interested in the question of whether perhaps gold might not also be found somewhere else. Perhaps it might indeed be found elsewhere, but perhaps not—in either case, what would I care, given that there is already enough here? Would we not be more inclined to bring the good news to all those who labor so intensively trying to find other gold mines, to call out to them to come with us, to abandon all those laborious attempts and simply to come and draw from this source which offers enough for everyone? Would we not doubt the seriousness of their search if they were not to heed that call and come, if they were to insist that they wanted to find their own gold? In such cases, obstinacy is stronger than the wish to find gold. With great consternation, we would have to abandon them, for who can say that they may ultimately go away empty-handed despite all their searching? We ourselves would have to go where this great offering has been made.

Such was the Reformation message concerning the church. Here is the true church. Might it also be found elsewhere? That is not the question. It is here that God has granted it to us as a gift. Do you really want to stand off to the side and stubbornly search to see whether God might not grant you this gift elsewhere? Perhaps—but that may also well not be the case. Do you really want to wager here? Those who wager have basically already lost, for they have neither heard nor believed that the true church is already here. Otherwise they would no longer gamble at such a time. If they have genuinely not heard, then they similarly do not know what the true church really is and thus also do not know what it is they are seeking and will accordingly never find it. But then the search itself has become an end in itself and is thus no longer a genuine search at all.

Hence always starting from the recognized truth concerning what and where the church is, the church itself now calls out into the world: Come hither, here is the church! Hence it refuses to enter into any discussion concerning where else the church might be. Compared to the certitude that the church is genuinely here, everything else is merely incertitude, nonchurch. Of course nonchurch! Otherwise those others would also be precisely here where the church is. Because they are not here, however, nor even want to come here, they must be the nonchurch. But what point is there in saying this in the first place? Nothing other than to call out now with even more assurance and with even greater rejoicing: God has given us the gift of the true church again. Here is the church!

Hence the true church can never determine *from its own perspective* those who do not belong to it, and its claim to be the church can never mean that some separation of the righteous from the unrighteous is now to take place. Instead, this claim "Here is the church!" is itself precisely the salvific cry that goes out to all the world. It is itself the gospel. It is in this and no other way that it is to be proclaimed. Admittedly, those unable to hear it as gospel will hear it as *law*. And understood as law, it will now bear all the harshness inhering in the question concerning the *scope of the church*. Those who hear the church's salvific call as law already understand themselves to be subject to that law; they resist and invariably recognize themselves as those to whom this call does not apply. It is here that the question arises concerning the scope of the church, concerning the boundaries, concerning how to distinguish between the elect and the rejected. Where this salvific call is not perceived, the church's claim turns into judgment, into a separation of those who belong to the church and those who do not. Whereas this distinction is repeatedly suspended through the proclamation of the gospel, which offers and promises the salvation of the church to everyone, in a legalistic understanding of the church it becomes rigid. The question of the scope of the church will significantly determine its essence. This legal understanding, however, is in any case alien to the essence of the church. It is not its goal and commission to comprehend the gospel in numerical terms. The Old Testament prohibition against census taking serves as a warning here. It is enough to know that salvation is here and that God will always create 660 his church-community. Knowledge of the actual scope of the church-community is reserved for God alone.

Our findings thus far are then that *the question of the scope of the church, that is, of its boundaries, derives from a legal understanding of the Protestant concept of the church*. Hence this question will never be raised from within the essence of the church itself but only as an alien query made by those with a legal understanding of the church's claim. It will always be posed to the church from the outside, and only if the church itself understands this situation can and indeed must it then address the question.

The question of the scope of the church is the question of church communion. Who belongs to the church? Who no longer belongs to it? That is the question. The church reflects on its own boundaries. Why? Because its call to salvation is not being heard and believed; instead, it encounters limits. The church finds that some people fail to heed its call. Hence instead of creating limits itself, it instead comes up against limits that have been imposed from the outside. Now the church experiences its call as the law that judges the world, as a boundary that cannot be crossed. And now the church must render an account for itself concerning this situation.

It is not the church that sets boundaries excluding people. It is the world that arbitrarily sets these boundaries to exclude itself from the church by not hearing and not believing. Hence the church itself cannot determine a priori [*from the outset*] where its boundaries will run; instead, it can only note and confirm where the boundaries are that are imposed on it from the outside. It is not the church that decides how unbelief will delimit itself over against the church. *The church does not determine its own boundaries and scope.* Hence the determination of its boundaries will always be different. Because no theoretical knowledge is available for determining that scope, that is, because such knowledge must always be acquired anew, there are also no theoretical norms according to which membership in the church might be determined. If such existed, then the church would already have misunderstood itself legally as in Catholicism, Orthodoxy, and Pietism. This view introduces an element of living decision into the Reformation's understanding of the boundaries of the church. Just where the boundaries of the church are to be found is thus always determined only in the encounter between the church and unbelief and is thus an act of *decision* on the part of the church; if the church already knew the answer to this question, it would already have separated itself from the world and would have betrayed the commission of its own call to salvation. Its most characteristic decision must be to recognize and to confirm as such any boundary that the world sets for it. It must itself decide whether and where its call encounters ultimate limits. Hence the question of church communion can only be answered concretely in the authoritative decision of the church itself. What is absolutely objective here is the character of this decision. That is, were the church to set boundaries beforehand and in so doing carry out this separation on its own initiative, it would be acting subjectively and arbitrarily. The

661

seemingly objective nature of any theoretical knowledge of the boundaries of the church instead actually subverts the true objectivity that is fulfilled in the decision.

By the same token, the church has not been left entirely without norms according to which it might make decisions on its own. A consideration of these norms, however, does demonstrate to us the very impossibility of accepting them as legally unequivocal criteria for making those decisions. Over the continuing course of such decisions, the church has learned to understand *baptism* as one way of defining its own boundaries.[3] Yet even this definition of scope immediately causes enormous difficulties. On the one hand, it is not broad enough (whence so quickly the notion of the "desired baptism," "baptism of blood," and so on[4]). On the other hand, it is not narrow enough, since even those who have already been baptized include false teachers and inactive members who cannot belong to the church. In any event, baptism is recognized as the one sacrament common to all Christian churches that may not be repeated should a person transfer to a different Christian church. As such, it is the bond uniting all Christian churches and thus cannot itself be constitutive for church communion. Although the true church can never abandon its assertion that all baptized persons do indeed belong to it, it must at the same time also allow that some of those do not in fact stand within its communion. Hence the church acknowledges on the one hand a relative external boundary accompanying baptism and at the same time also an internal boundary encompassing only one part of those baptized.

662

The church has learned to define this internal boundary through the concept of doctrine and confession. The church's confession of faith is constitutive for the church-community. But which confession of faith? The early church symbols?[5] The unification formula of Lausanne?[6] What rights remain then for the doctrines that distinguish the different individual churches?

---

3. ["See *DBWE* 14:325–328 (1935: 'What Is Confession?') . . . ," *DBWE* 14:661, n. 13.]

4. ["If someone desired baptism but was unable to receive it for reasons beyond that person's control, one could, as it were, count the 'desire' itself as the deed. In the case of martyrs who were still catechumens, martyrdom itself—'blood baptism'—substituted for normal baptism," *DBWE* 14:661, n. 14.]

5. ["Luther's 'three symbols' or confessions of faith were the Apostles' Creed, the Nicene Creed, and the Athanasian Creed (*Book of Concord*, 21–25) . . . ," *DBWE* 14:662, n. 17.]

6. ["Following the first World Conference for Faith and Order in Lausanne in August 1927, churches participating in the ecumenical movement agreed that they 'accept our Lord Jesus Christ as God and Saviour'; see Hodgson's letter to Bonhoeffer of July 26, 1935 (*DBWE* 14:76–80)," *DBWE* 14:662, n. 18.]

The Lutheran confessional writings believed that the Lutheran and the Roman churches shared a common confessional basis. Even though in the Smalcald Articles Luther included the doctrines of God, of the Trinity, and Christology in this common foundation, these articles still did not provide a sufficient basis for unification because of disagreement regarding the doctrine of justification. Unification would be possible if this disagreement could be settled. Similarly, in the relationship with the Reformed Church it was the doctrine of the Eucharist that sundered church communion.[7] Did the authors of these confessional writings not realize that disagreement regarding these particular articles must necessarily cause total disagreement regarding every article? That a false doctrine of justification necessarily resulted in a false Christology, a false doctrine of the Trinity, a false doctrine of God? In a reverse fashion, a genuine consensus regarding Christology, for example, would also bring about genuine consensus regarding the doctrine of justification and as such also reestablish the church-community.

Our question now is *What does it mean if this conclusion is nonetheless not drawn, if on the one hand one subscribes to the notion of a common confessional basis while, on the other, church communion itself collapses because of disagreement regarding a particular article of faith?*

663

It means *first* that the assertion raised earlier concerning those baptized in other churches is now expanded to include the believers of other churches as well. They have the correct confession of faith; they have merely fallen away from it. In truth the One Confession is indeed there, even though the other church has severely misunderstood it. This confirmation of the confession upholds the Protestant call to salvation: There is only One Confession; here is the true confession; come hither! The focus is not at all on any delimitation as such, that is, in the manner of a law. Instead, although the boundary set by the other churches is indeed taken seriously, but only in order to make the call to salvation all the more unequivocal: In truth you belong to us, here is the true confession!

It means, *second*, that church communion is always something qualitatively whole. It cannot be attained through an enumeration of all the common points that seemingly outweigh the differences; as long as a single point of disagreement remains, consensus is impossible. It is total unity that is bestowed. This unity is the a priori of church communion. It cannot be established through comparison; it must be a bestowed unity. By the

---

7. ["Between 1525 and 1529, Reformation theologians argued about the correct understanding of the Eucharist," *DBWE* 14:662, n. 20.]

same token, however, it is on the basis of this unity that all potential differences, which necessarily emerge and which the Lutheran confessional writings have indeed largely taken into account, are sustainable. Because of the present unity, they no longer constitute schismatic antitheses. Whether this unity is present, however, is another question. It is indeed expressed through the full consensus evident in these confessional writings, and yet this willingness—not to allow theological differences to become schismatic antitheses in the creation of the confession itself but instead to reach a unifying formulation of that confession, that is, the reality of reaching consensus regarding the confessional formulation itself—already constitutes an act of decision by the church that can never be logically or even theologically coerced. That is to say, the confessional unity of a church is an act of decision by the church as a decision of faith, not a theological formulation.

Third, it means that the determination of the point at which disagreement does become a schismatic antithesis is itself an act of decision on the part of the church. Why did the Reformation not develop the doctrine of God into a schismatic antithesis? The decision emerges when the church perceives the intrusion of an enemy at a specific point and then accordingly resists the enemy at precisely that point. The outcome of a war is decided by a limited battle. Just where this battle is actually fought depends on where the enemy stands. Here a decision must be made. Hence one particular place will not *always* represent the locus of decision. It may well be that a situation that is dangerous today no longer influences the overall disposition of the war tomorrow. The same article that leads to a schism in the church today may very well not be schismatic in that sense at all tomorrow. As a matter of fact, precisely this follows from the Reformation having freely chosen to tie its own opposition to Rome to a single article and to let all other antitheses alone. Only where the church itself legally fixes its own boundaries from the outset and in so doing also voluntarily abandons its commission to issue the call to salvation does this antithesis become hardened and tied to a single point. This situation in its own turn leads then to the ultimate.

Fourth, it means that a clear distinction emerges between the task of dogmatics and that of the confession of faith. The confession is not a compilation of dogmatic statements from which all subsequent conclusions are drawn. Otherwise the Augsburg Confession and the Smalcald Articles would be the worst of all possible confessions insofar as the isolation of the doctrine of justification involves an obvious lack of dogmatic rigor. Moreover any disagreement regarding any single doctrinal point would of necessity also become schismatic. In that sense, every individual theological school would have to become its own church. That such is in fact not the case,

664

however, indeed this mere fact as such proves that the question of church communion must be answered by a church decision rather than by theology alone. Believers group themselves around confessions, not around theologies. One must carefully guard against mistaking the one for the other here. Although theology does indeed supply the entire army with weapons that can be engaged anywhere and at any time, the external battle is engaged with the confession, not with theology. Otherwise one succumbs to orthodoxy and becomes legalistic, as if one knew ahead of time where the boundaries of the church were to be found and thus also robbed the church of the freedom of decision. The confession is the church's decision concerning its own boundaries on the basis of theological considerations. It is not a presentation of the entirety of doctrine but rather the decision that the church makes based on the entirety of doctrine to take up the battle at a specific place. In the confession, theology is implemented in a contemporary situation through a decision the church itself makes. The limitations distinguishing the confession from the entirety of doctrine always includes the church's assertion of confessional unity with those who disagree, a unity to which ideally the latter are to be recalled; it also confirms that the church itself does not draw up these boundaries but merely acknowledges the boundaries imposed on it from the outside; and finally it also includes the possibility that the church can continue to proclaim the unrestricted call of salvation.

665   What we find, then, is that the current confession is also unsuitable for definitively determining the scope of the church. One cannot in principle fix the boundary between antitheses that are schismatic within schools of thought and those that are schismatic within the church. Hence the various facts of baptism, of the common confessional material inhering in the symbols, or the various articles of disagreement—all these considerations can only provide the material on the basis of which the church chooses to decide one way rather than another in any given situation concerning the scope of the church. The boundary itself, however, is not something over which the church itself has any power but rather is itself to be confirmed in the decision. The ultimately open character of this decision alone is what makes it possible for antitheses that are schismatic for the church to become antitheses within schools of thought and vice versa.

Because the boundary of the church is drawn from the outside, it can be as varied as is the hostility toward the gospel. It makes a difference, for example, if it is the world, or an anti-Christian church, or "another" church that constitutes that boundary. Only theological doctrinarism can deny these differences. The Reformation unequivocally acknowledged these differences; one need only consider the different Lutheran positions over against the Roman Church, on the one hand, and the Greek

Orthodox Church, on the other. On the other hand, theology cannot determine unequivocally the distinction between an anti-Christian church and "another" church; this determination, too, is a matter of church decision. It may well be that theologically the same heresies can be discerned in both instances and that nonetheless one church may be anti-Christian and the other merely "another" church. In that case, one must break with the former while yet continuing dialogue with the latter, all the while maintaining hope in reestablishing communion. Here we see that apart from false teaching, yet another factor is present that influences the decision. This becomes quite evident wherever a church declares that it does indeed acknowledge the confession and has no intentions of spreading false teaching and then, having allayed suspicion, engages all the more resolutely in a battle against the true church. Here true teaching becomes false teaching the moment it is used in the battle against the true church. To remain with this metaphor for a moment: in such cases, officers desert with their weapons and go over to the enemy camp along with their soldiers. Although they have the same   666
weapons as the army they have betrayed, they now use them against those who were once their friends.

It is a decisive difference whether this false teaching stands over against the true church with openly declared hostile intentions or whether it merely stands there without any such intentions. In the first instance, the true and false churches face each other, each intending to be the death of the other. Here it is a struggle of life and death. Here there can be no talk of communion. Here the true church recognizes the Antichrist. In the second instance, the true church realizes that there are erring churches that are by no means hostile to the true church in that sense, churches that themselves also bear the mystery of the disunion in the church and with which the true church thus stands together in a shared confession of guilt. Here one can seek unity once again by focusing on the common confession. This is somewhat the situation in ecumenical work. Here we learn that church communion, too, can assume various forms commensurate with the boundaries of the church: from the full communion based on word and sacrament as expressed in creedal consensus, to a communion that is sought on the basis of the common possession of faith. Rejecting and denying such community *a limine* [*in principle*] is as false as is equating it with full church communion. On the one hand, it is a fact of the church, on the other, an emergency situation, a transition that must lead either to full communion or to separation. Yet because the church cannot a priori determine where such communion or definitive separation in fact obtains, it must take any given situation seriously and leave it to God to make of it what he will, and await the hour of decision.

If indeed it has become clear that the question of church communion can be answered only by the church's own decision, then one must also point out that this decision must indeed be made. It should accompany the struggle of the church every step of the way. Although the decision itself will always remain the "alien work" of the church, it must nonetheless be done, else the church's real work can no longer be done. Ultimately this decision concerning its own boundary is an act of compassion on the part of the church both toward its members and toward outsiders. It is the final, "alien" possibility of allowing the call of salvation to be heard.

667   II.

The Confessing Synod in Barmen rejected the key points of the doctrine of the German Christians as false teaching. This rejection means that this false teaching has no place in the church of Jesus Christ. The Confessing Synod in Dahlem assumed responsibility by declaring that through word and deed the Reich Church government has separated itself from the Christian church. Rather than excluding someone from the church, this synod instead merely confirmed an action that had already taken place. At the same time, it formed its own church administration and made the claim that it represented the true church of Jesus Christ in Germany. Thereafter the Confessing Church accepted the responsibility and commission of being the one, true church of Jesus Christ in Germany. That is a fact of church history.

What does this mean? What has really been said here? Today everything in the Confessing Church revolves around this question. It cannot possibly be answered by the futile attempt—one which in any event can never yield certitude—to ask the opinions of those who were actually responsible for this synodal resolution. If we genuinely take the synod's statement seriously, then we must acknowledge that our Lord God is responsible for it. In that case, however, the statement must be taken just as it is and the task is then to inquire concerning God's will inhering within it. Once the synod declared that the Reich Church government had separated itself from the church of Jesus Christ, we must assume that, despite human frailty and differences of opinion, the word of the Lord has been clearly spoken to the church and is audible even amid all the various human moods, anxieties, and even audacity that may have accompanied that resolution, and we must further ask what this statement really means. Whoever does not share this assumption will not be speaking about Barmen and Dahlem as Christian

668   synods and will not share the presuppositions of the Confessing Church. Things have gotten truly bad now insofar as in broad circles of the Con-

fessing Church—and more among pastors even than among laypersons—people are making willful, irresponsible statements. Although indeed we cannot retract what happened in Barmen and Dahlem, it is not because they merely represent historical facts of our church to which we owe pious obedience but because we cannot retract God's own word.

The question is thus: In speaking through Barmen and Dahlem, what has God said concerning the church and its path? The Reich Church government has separated itself from the Christian church. The Confessing Church is the true church of Jesus Christ in Germany. What does this mean? It doubtless means that a definitive boundary has been recognized and confirmed between the Reich Church government and the true church of Christ. The Reich Church government is heretical. But does this also mean that those holding the office of ministry who continue to obey this rejected church government are subject to the same judgment? Has every German Christian pastor separated himself from the church of Jesus? Furthermore: Must we also view as separated from the Christian church the German Christians among our own congregational members or even every congregation that accepts its German Christian pastor without opposition? Can the pastor of a Confessing Church address German Christian members of the congregation as his own parishioners? Can he perform his official duties for members of the Confessing Church and for German Christians without distinction? For the Confessing Church pastor, where are the boundaries of his congregations to be found? Is there here a fundamental difference between church administration and the congregation itself? And furthermore: What about the so-called neutrals?[8] Finally: Do those who take the side of the German Christians in shared ecclesiastical and administrative work bear responsibility for the German Christians' sin that is destroying the church? Does the judgment of Dahlem also apply to the church committees? Does this apply to all those who obey these committees? In summary: Must the schism that has emerged between the Reich Church government and the church itself now logically extend to all the persons mentioned above? This question must be answered. The congregation must know to whom it should listen and where it should not. The pastor must know how he is to execute his office properly. Today, however, pastors and congregations largely do not know what to do because no one has told them.

669

---

8. ["Those who were yet undecided with respect to the Confessing Church claimed to be 'neutral,' see *DBWE* 14:674–675 (*Reader* 448), point 4, in this essay. Regarding the role of the 'neutrals' in the Church Struggle, see Barnett, *For the Soul of the People*, 66–71," *DBWE* 14:668:, n. 29.]

The simplest thing would doubtless be either to accept all the consequences just mentioned or to abide with Dahlem and not draw any conclusions at all. Given all that has been said up to this point, however, both
choices would be inappropriate for the church. Drawing conclusions will
not help because God's word requires obedience, not conclusions. Not
drawing any conclusions, however, can constitute conscious disobedience
to the word. Hence one must examine every individual question and come
to a decision step-by-step. For example, a certain measure of clarification
has already been reached regarding German Christians holding the office
of ministry. In congregations with only such clergy, the Confessing Church
itself has seen to it that vicars or pastors ensure that the proper proclamation and proper office are being maintained. It has established emergency
ministries and in so doing asserted that the German Christian ministers
have forfeited their offices. Nothing similar has happened with regard to
the neutrals. The position over against congregations is also quite different.
Precisely through the establishment of emergency ministries, of course, the
Confessing Church's complete claim regarding those congregations has
been articulated. What remains wholly unclear is the position toward the
committees and toward members of the Confessing Church who belong to
them, toward pastors who are obeying those committees. This lack of clarity
is pernicious. Before drawing any conclusions here, however, let us examine
the situation from the other side.

Even though, on the one hand, an ongoing process of separation and
schism is under way, on the other, the Lutheran and the Reformed churches
are quite significantly coming ever closer together. Since Barmen, Lutheran
and Reformed members have been speaking together in synodal declarations. What were formerly schismatic creedal antitheses now no longer
make it impossible to conduct Confessing synods, albeit without a common
Eucharist. This situation is first of all merely one fact among others to be
noted. Although opposition from confessional quarters is, of course, still
670   an issue, the fact itself remains, and it is for God alone to do with it what
he will.

The confession offers no means for contesting this reality that the recognition of a "Confessing Church with equal rights"[9] has already decisively left
the Augsburg Confession behind. The Confessing synod cannot stand up to

9. ["Cf. the preamble to the German Evangelical Church constitution of July 11, 1933:
'The German Evangelical Church is a federation of Confessional Churches that grew
out of the Reformation and that enjoy equal rights' (text in Huber and Huber, *Staat und
Kirche*, 4:861)," *DBWE* 14:670, n. 33.]

the letter of the Lutheran confessional writings. The question is then how we are to explain that, despite ongoing instruction to the contrary, these Confessing synods nonetheless came about and that Lutheran theologians consciously participated in them? The only thing one can do is acknowledge that the Confessing synod exists; and given the fact that these synods do indeed exist, one must either reject them *a limine* from the perspective of the Augsburg Confession or accept them with astonishment and humility and leave it to God to make of them what he will.

In any event, the present situation itself is certainly significant and instructive enough with regard to the question of church communion. On the one hand, the rigorous application of the doctrinal concept is leading to a church schism; on the other, the doctrinal concept is being obviously neglected, and a church communion is already emerging that believes it can ignore significant, previously schismatic doctrinal antitheses. If one were to apply the doctrinal concept against, for example, the Reformed as rigorously as has already been the case against the German Christians, it might be theoretically conceivable that different understandings of the Eucharist or of Christology might well ignite those older, schismatic antitheses. Analogously, neglect of such rigorous application might well create a common foundation for the German Christians. At least this is how the situation must appear to those who are confessionally orthodox. What is the basis for this absurd possibility? Is a dirty game being played with church communion here?   671

A further complication emerges here. The Confessing Church has encountered the ecumenical movement, and this encounter has hitherto yielded two characteristic results. In the presence of representatives of the Confessing Church in Fanø in 1934, the ecumenical movement declared that the "principles and methods" of the German Christian church government were incompatible with the essence of the church of Christ. By electing a representative of the Confessing Church to the ecumenical council, it sought the cooperation of that church and received assurance of such cooperation in return. Until now, however, the Confessing Church has yet to send official representatives to an ecumenical conference. The reason must be the presence of representatives of the Reich Church, with whom the Confessing Church can no longer carry on dialogue of any sort, even on neutral ground. Hence even though dialogue with other, erring "churches" might still be possible, it is no longer possible between the Reich Church and the Confessing Church. Even though it would doubtless be easy to demonstrate that the false teachings of the German Christians are present in many other churches as well, the Confessing Church sees a qualitative distinction here.

Both the Orthodox as well as those who are basically nonconfessional[10] must find all this equally incomprehensible and contradictory. The Orthodox cannot comprehend how one can manipulate confessional statements in these various ways. They cannot comprehend the openness shown by the Lutherans of the Confessing Church toward the Reformed or toward the ecumenical movement. By contrast, the nonconfessional denominations, including a large number of pastors influenced by Pietism and by liberal theology, cannot comprehend the rigid application of the doctrinal concept against the German Christians.

672   The Confessing Church securely traverses its path between the Scylla of orthodoxy and the Charybdis of the nonconfessional churches.[11] It bears the burden of responsibility for being the true church of Jesus. It calls out: Here is the church! Come hither! In issuing this call, it encounters both friends and foes. Where it encounters foes, it confirms rigorously and without compromise the boundaries those foes have drawn for it. Where it encounters friends, it seeks a common ground for dialogue in the hope of establishing communion. Although it is through the confession that the church can recognize whether it is standing before friend or foe, the confession is nonetheless not the ultimate, unequivocal norm. The church itself must decide where its foe stands. Such decision is necessary because in one case it may involve the Eucharist, in another the doctrine of justification, and in another the doctrine of the church itself. And by making this decision, the church is also confessing. Orthodoxy confuses theological systems with the confession. The nonconfessional denominations confuse the confession of the church with the witness of piety. Although it would be considerably easier if the Confessing Church could think linearly here, by trying to be at once both open and restricted it would be unfaithful to its commission of issuing the call to salvation.

Although it has thus become clear enough that the church can make decisions concerning its own boundaries only on a case-by-case basis, we still need to consider briefly some of the concrete questions raised earlier.

1. That the German Christian in the office of ministry has separated himself from the church is a realization that merely needed synodal confirmation. Only when it is declared unequivocally that he has actually

---

10. ["I.e., denominations that don't rely on the traditional confessions such as the Augsburg Confession," *DBWE* 14:671, n. 37.]

11. ["The names of the two sea monsters in Homer's *Odyssey* (chap. 12) refer metaphorically to the straits whose navigation is perilous for ships. Bonhoeffer uses this distinction in other contexts as well, for example, his Christology lectures (*DBWE* 12:304 [*Reader* 256])," *DBWE* 14:672, n. 38.]

forfeited his office is there the possibility in Lutheran doctrine of establishing emergency pastoral ministries, which otherwise would constitute an impermissible intrusion into an alien office, a procedure against which Luther could not issue a strong enough warning. Hand in hand with these measures, however, one must also advise congregations that for the sake of God's word and for the sake of their own souls, it is best to avoid all official contact with a false teacher and indeed better to live and die without either sermon or sacrament than to stand by such a false teacher.

2. Here one must distinguish between the person holding office and parishioners, between deceivers and deceived. It is not possible to declare that the exclusion of someone holding the office automatically includes the exclusion of the congregation as well. The Lutheran confessional writings declared not the individual Catholic but rather the pope, that is, the church government, to be the Antichrist. The Dahlem Synod made a similar declaration. The church government has become heretical. This declaration by no means, however, abandons all claim to the congregations involved. Instead, precisely these congregations must be helped to find proper clergy. We might also add that the congregation itself is called to judge concerning false teaching. If it fails to do so, if despite warnings and admonitions it persists with its false teachers, then after a certain period of patience one must confirm that here, too, a boundary has been drawn, and must view church communion as being suspended, and must do so with all the consequences extending from a refusal to perform official acts and so on. This is the final act of compassion that the church shows to the congregation, the final call to communion, the "alien work" through which the call to salvation is issued. It is also, however, an obligation that the church has to the office of ministry, which otherwise would itself daily incur guilt by squandering the sacrament.

3. The Confessing Church can also no longer put off making an unequivocal decision regarding the church committees. The statement of the Synod of Oeynhausen is not enough. There is no cogent explanation for how the church administration of the committees differs from the Reich Church government. It is doubtless a greater threat to the true church administration than is the Reich Church government itself. Although the Confessing Synod has indeed declared that this church administration cannot be recognized, it has not yet issued an unequivocal prohibition against participating in it. The result is confusion. Once one has recognized such boundaries, one must also draw the practical conclusions. Just as any members of the Confessing Church exclude themselves from the church of Jesus by joining the Reich Church government, so also—according to the principal resolutions of the Oeynhausen Synod—do those who participate in the

673

674

administrative work of the church committees. From these considerations, however, there necessarily follows a prohibition against precisely such participation. The same applies to those holding the office of ministry who submit to the committees. Nor is it acceptable to impose on candidates that which one does not also apply to pastors. The longer the church administration delays the decision placed before it, the more it confuses congregations, the more merciless it acts toward pastors, and the less it is able to issue its own commission.

4. The neutrals pose a special problem. In the first place, there aren't really any; they simply belong to the other side. Subjectively, however, they claim to be neutral. An unequivocal position toward them is impossible because their own position is equivocal, because the boundary they have drawn up over against the true church is not clear. Jesus Christ pronounced two judgments on such neutrals: Whoever is not with me is against me (Matthew 12:30), and: Whoever is not against us is for us (Mark 9:40). The neutrals cannot claim the second assertion alone for themselves, nor can the church adduce the first assertion alone against them. But one must never cease pointing out that the neutrals persist in precisely the questionable status characterized by these two assertions. If, of course, neutrality itself is elevated to the status of a principle, then it certainly becomes possible to pronounce the first assertion alone against them, since in that case they have assumed an unequivocal position outside the church and have drawn a clear boundary against the claim of the true church.

It cannot be the purpose of these brief remarks to anticipate the decision of the church. It must, however, be their purpose to remind the church administration that it must indeed make this decision. By doing so step-by-step, it will be performing that alien work that makes it possible to carry out its true work. The suspension of communion is the final offer of communion.

675

III.

Extra ecclesiam nulla salus [*Outside the church there is no salvation*].[12] The question of church communion is the question of the community of salvation. The boundaries of the church are the boundaries of salvation. Whoever knowingly separates himself from the Confessing Church in Germany separates himself from salvation. This is the insight that has always forced itself on the true church. This is its humble confession. Those who separate the

---

12. [*A phrase from Bishop Cyprian of Carthage (third century).*]

question of the Confessing Church from the question of their own salvation have not comprehended that the struggle of the Confessing Church is the struggle for their salvation.

Is that not the Roman heresy concerning the church? Insofar as Catholic doctrine cannot conceive of salvation without the church nor the church without salvation, it is correct. But insofar as the assertion that salvation is to be found only in the church means something other to it than the call 676 to the visible church, that is, insofar as this assertion is understood not as an existential statement of faith of the true church but as a theoretical truth concerning those who are saved and lost, insofar as it represents something other than the offer of grace and salvation, it is reprehensible, since in that case it has turned a statement of faith into a speculative assertion. Strictly speaking, *extra ecclesiam nulla salus* is a statement of faith. Faith is tied to God's salvific revelation, from the perspective of which it perceives absolutely no other salvation than salvation in the visible church. From this perspective, faith is in fact not free to seek God's salvation anywhere other than where the promise is given in the first place. Because salvation beyond the church is fundamentally inconceivable for faith, such a notion can also never constitute a doctrinal point. It is in the promise alone that salvation is recognized. In its own turn, however, the promise includes the proclamation of the pure gospel.

What would happen, however, if the pure gospel were proclaimed in a single congregation of the Roman Church or of the Reich Church? Is the true church not to be found there as well? There is no pure proclamation of the gospel independent of the church as a whole. Indeed, even if someone were to proclaim the gospel as purely as did the apostle Paul and yet were obedient to the pope or to the Reich Church government, that person would be a false teacher deceiving the congregation.

What if, however, the piety and Christian strength of some people in that other church are being severely tested? What about good Christians on the other side? Is it not uncompassionate and indeed un-Christian to pronounce judgment on them as well? Is one not being unbearably pharisaic toward them by claiming to be the only church? Here one is accused of being mean-spirited and judgmental. An element of indignation against the church's claim inheres within this question and is moreover quite at home in the Confessing Church itself. It is precisely this indignation that is currently undermining the church at the present. The response must begin with the counterquestion: 1. Why are these Christians with the German Christians instead of with the true assembly of believers? Why do they not come to where the call of the true church is issued? Why? Because it 677 is not important enough to them which church they belong to? Because they have enough of their own piety and sanctity? Is that what it means to be a good Christian? 2. How do they even know who is a good Christian and who is not? Am I to judge the Christian conviction of others? Is it not a much more unbearable judgmental attitude that thinks it can look into another person's heart? Is this alleged Christian love that claims it would exclude no one from salvation not in fact the most unprecedented hubris and most profound misanthropy insofar as it anticipates God's hidden judgments concerning the souls of individuals? 3. Who is it that actually calls the church? The Holy Spirit through word and sacrament? Or is it I myself, with my judgment concerning good or bad Christians? It is a frightful blasphemy that rests in the question of these loving Christians, that they want to establish, assemble, and delimit God's church themselves, thereby destroying and denying the true church of the word.

One cannot repeat often enough that the church is not performing any sort of compassionate act by denying its own boundaries. The true church will always come up against boundaries. By acknowledging these boundaries, it is performing the work of love toward human beings insofar as it gives priority to the truth. *Extra ecclesiam nulla salus.* If this statement is certain, then the other, which finds its analogy in the doctrine of God, must be added as well. Although God is indeed omnipresent, God does not intend that we perceive God just anywhere. Just because God is present does not mean that God can also be recognized; there is a difference between the two. As assuredly as the God we are able to recognize is alone our God, and as assuredly as the God we are unable to recognize can never be our God, just as assuredly must this distinction remain precisely as a statement of faith, which abides with the revealed God and therein extols the singularity and miraculous nature of revelation itself. Hence one can now also say that the church can be recognized only where God's promise abides, namely, in the visible church. There alone is the church our church. But faith, which has become confident of its salvation in the visible church alone, praises the miraculous nature of this salvation precisely by daring to speak as well
678   about an existence of the church beyond the revealed church of salvation. Never, however, can it do this in order to suspend sole salvation through the visible church, nor ever for the sake of this or that pious individual who may be standing off to the side, and certainly never in order to usurp for itself the power to judge and recognize where this "church beyond" might be. Although that church remains unrecognizable, the church of salvation does believe in it for the sake of praising even more highly the majesty of revelation. Woe to those who take this ultimate possibility of faith offered by the church as lived within faith itself, namely, *Extra ecclesiam nulla salus,* and turn it into a subterfuge for their own pious speculation about who is saved

and who is lost. This is not our commission. Instead we are better served by fleeing from the temptation of such questions to God's revealed salvation in the true church.

The question of the boundaries of the church can easily turn into a temptation for faith. This question, however, should serve faith solely for the sake of greater certitude. The perpetual task of the church should be to make this clear and to decide concerning its own boundaries in such a way that the church-community thereby becomes ever more assured of its own salvation.

PART 5
Christian Life and Community

29. *DISCIPLESHIP*

DBWE 4:37–83, 100–110, 137–146,
161–169, 181–182, 201–204

*In 1935, the Confessing Church established its own seminaries to circumvent the
German Christian–controlled official path for theological education and ordination.
Bonhoeffer returned from London to direct one such seminary located first in Zingst
and then in Finkenwalde. The state-supported church viewed these seminaries as
illegal, and the students who chose to be educated in them faced danger, surveillance,
and uncertain vocational futures. Bonhoeffer directed Finkenwalde until September
1937, when it was closed by the German secret police, the Gestapo. This forced the
Confessing Church's theological education "underground"; Bonhoeffer used circular
letters and brief meetings to educate his students, most of whom were apprentices
under Confessing Church pastors.[1] Between 1935 and the beginning of World War
II, then, Bonhoeffer poured his time and energy into providing education, pastoral
care, and mentoring for his seminarians.*

*The task of teaching seminarians while living with them in intentional commu-
nity solidified Bonhoeffer's thinking about the Christian life. The theological classics
for which he is perhaps best known,* Discipleship *(titled* The Cost of Discipleship
in previous translations) and Life Together, *grew out of the lecture courses and
seminars, and practices of community life, from this period.*

Discipleship, *as Bonhoeffer put it in a letter to Karl Barth, is an "interpretation
of the Sermon on the Mount and the Pauline doctrine of justification and sanctification."[2] The "Pauline doctrine of justification and sanctification" had been central to
his thinking from his student years, when he learned from the great Luther scholar
Karl Holl that the "by grace alone" of Pauline-Lutheran thought was the one article*

---

1. [DBWE *15:4–6, editor's introduction.*]
2. [DBWE *14:253.*]

by which the church stands and falls.[3] *In the intervening years, he came to see that the contemporary church's understanding of that article had degenerated into a "cheap grace" that excused Christians from obedience. Bonhoeffer contrasts cheap grace with discipleship, which is characterized by both reception of God's grace in faith and obedience to God's command. He develops this vision of discipleship through an exposition of Jesus' Sermon on the Mount recorded in Matthew 5–7. As Bonhoeffer wrote to Reinhold Niebuhr in a 1934 letter, he had become convinced that it was "high time to bring the focus back to the Sermon on the Mount . . . but in a way different from the Reformation understanding."*[4] *When Discipleship was published in 1937, it revealed how the Sermon had become central to Bonhoeffer's thinking during the previous six years.*

Bonhoeffer arranged Discipleship in two parts, Part One on the Sermon on the Mount and Part Two on the Pauline letters. He argued that the call to discipleship heard in the Sermon on the Mount is still heard today: in the preaching of the gospel the resurrected Christ is present and "speaks to us exactly as he spoke to . . . the first disciples. . . ."

37   PREFACE

In times of church renewal holy scripture naturally becomes richer in content for us. Behind the daily catchwords and battle cries needed in the Church Struggle, a more intense, questioning search arises for the one who is our sole concern, for Jesus himself. What did Jesus want to say to us? What does he want from us today? How does he help us to be faithful Christians today? It is not ultimately important to us what this or that church leader wants. Rather, we want to know what Jesus wants. When we go to hear a sermon, his own word is what we want to hear. This matters to us not only for our own sakes, but also for all those who have become estranged from the church and its message. It is also our opinion that if Jesus himself and Jesus alone with his word were among us in our preaching, then quite a different set of people would hear the word and quite a different set of people would again turn away from it. It is not as if our church's preaching were no longer God's word, but there are so many dissonant sounds, so many human, harsh laws, and so many false hopes and consolations, which still obscure the pure word of Jesus and make a genuine decision more difficult. We surely intend our preaching to be preaching Christ alone. But it is not solely the fault of

---

3. [DB-ER, *68.*]
4. [DBWE *13:183–184.*]

others if they find our preaching harsh and difficult because it is burdened with formulations and concepts foreign to them. It is simply not true that every word critical of our preaching today can be taken as a rejection of Christ or as anti-Christianity. Today there are a great number of people who come to our preaching, want to hear it, and then repeatedly have to admit sadly that we have made it too difficult for them to get to know Jesus. Do we really want to deny being in community with these people? They believe that it is not the word of Jesus itself that they wish to evade, but that too much of what comes between them and Jesus is merely human, institutional, or doctrinaire. Who among us would not instantly know all 38 the answers which could be given to these people and with which we could easily evade responsibility for them? But would an answer not also demand that we ask whether we ourselves get in the way of Jesus' word by depending perhaps too much on certain formulations, or on a type of sermon intended for its own time, place, and social structure? Or by preaching too "dogmatically" and not enough "for use in life"?[5] Or by preferring to repeat certain ideas from scripture over and over and thus too heedlessly passing over other important passages? Or by preaching our own opinions and convictions too much and Jesus Christ himself too little? Nothing would contradict our own intention more deeply and would be more ruinous for our proclamation than if we burdened with difficult human rules those who are weary and heavy laden, whom Jesus calls unto himself. That would drive them away from him again. How that would mock the love of Jesus Christ in front of Christians and heathen! But since general questions and self-accusations do not help here, let us be led back to scripture, to the word and call of Jesus Christ himself. Away from the poverty and narrowness of our own convictions and questions, here is where we seek the breadth and riches which are bestowed on us in Jesus.

We desire to speak of the call to follow Jesus. In doing so, are we burdening people with a new, heavier yoke? Should even harder, more inexorable rules be added to all the human rules under which their souls and bodies groan? Should our admonition to follow Jesus only prick their uneasy and wounded consciences with an even sharper sting? For this latest of innumerable times in church history, should we make impossible, tormenting, eccentric demands, obedience to which would be the pious luxury of the few? Would such demands have to be rejected by people who work and worry about their daily bread, their jobs, and their families, as the most god-

5. ["See letter to Rüdiger Schleicher, April 8, 1936 (*DBWE* 14:166–170)," *DBWE* 4:38, n. 1.]

less tempting of God? Should the church be trying to erect a spiritual reign of terror over people by threatening earthly and eternal punishment on its own authority and commanding everything a person must believe and do

39 to be saved? Should the church's word bring new tyranny and violent abuse to human souls? It may be that some people yearn for such servitude. But could the church ever serve such a longing?

When holy scripture speaks of following Jesus, it proclaims that people are free from all human rules, from everything which pressures, burdens, or causes worry and torment of conscience. In following Jesus, people are released from the hard yoke of their own laws to be under the gentle yoke of Jesus Christ. Does this disparage the seriousness of Jesus' commandments? No. Instead, only where Jesus' entire commandment and the call to unlimited discipleship remain intact are persons fully free to enter into Jesus' community. Those who follow Jesus' commandment entirely, who let Jesus' yoke rest on them without resistance, will find the burdens they must bear to be light. In the gentle pressure of this yoke they will receive the strength to walk the right path without becoming weary.[6] Jesus' commandment is harsh, inhumanly harsh for someone who resists it. Jesus' commandment is gentle and not difficult for someone who willingly accepts it. "His commandments are not burdensome" (1 John 5:3). Jesus' commandment has nothing to do with forced spiritual cures. Jesus demands nothing from us without giving us the strength to comply. Jesus' commandment never wishes to destroy life, but rather to preserve, strengthen, and heal life.

But the question still troubles us: What could the call to follow Jesus mean today for the worker, the businessman, the farmer, or the soldier? Could it bring an intolerable dilemma into the existence of persons working in the world who are Christian? Is Christianity, defined as following Jesus, a possibility for too small a number of people? Does it imply a rejection of the great masses of people and contempt for the weak and poor?

40 Does it thereby deny the great mercy of Jesus Christ, who came to the sinners and tax collectors, the poor and weak, the misguided and despairing? What should we say to that? Is it a few, or many, who belong with Jesus? Jesus died on the cross alone, abandoned by his disciples. It was not two of his faithful followers who hung beside him, but two murderers. But they all stood beneath the cross: enemies and the faithful, doubters and the fearful,

---

6. ["On the image of *yoke*, see Bonhoeffer's sermon on Matt. 11:28–30, London, September 1934 (*DBWE* 13:371–375): 'A burden which would simply press a person to the ground becomes bearable through a yoke'; a person can bear it 'under the yoke of Jesus, hitched together with him . . . ,'" *DBWE* 4:39, n. 3.]

the scornful and the converted, and all of them and their sin were included in this hour in Jesus' prayer for forgiveness. God's merciful love lives in the midst of its foes. It is the same Jesus Christ who by grace calls us to follow him and whose grace saves the thief on the cross in his last hour.

Where will the call to discipleship lead those who follow it? What decisions and painful separations will it entail? We must take this question to him who alone knows the answer. Only Jesus Christ, who bids us follow him, knows where the path will lead. But we know that it will be a path full of mercy beyond measure. Discipleship is joy.

Today it seems so difficult to walk with certainty the narrow path of the church's decision[7] and yet to remain wide open to Christ's love for all people, and in God's patience, mercy, and loving-kindness (Titus 3:4) for the weak and godless. Still, both must remain together, or else we will follow merely human paths. May God grant us joy in all seriousness of discipleship, affirmation of the sinners in all rejection of sin, and the overpowering and winning word of the gospel in all defense against our enemies. "Come to me, all who are weary and heavy laden, and I will give you rest. Take my yoke upon you, and learn from me; for I am gentle and humble in heart, and you will find rest for your souls. For my yoke is easy, and my burden is light" (Matt. 11:28–30).

PART ONE   41

CHAPTER ONE   43

COSTLY GRACE

Cheap grace is the mortal enemy of our church. Our struggle today is for costly grace.

Cheap grace means grace as bargain-basement goods, cut-rate forgiveness, cut-rate comfort, cut-rate sacrament; grace as the church's inexhaust-

---

7. ["The 'church's decision' refers specifically to the Confessing Church and its decision to resist incorporation into the Reich Church. The direction the Confessing Church took was decided in May 1934 at the Barmen Synod and October 1934 at the Second Confessional Synod in Dahlem. Those supporting the Dahlem decisions, known as 'Dahlemites,' rejected any intervention of the state (i.e., the Nazi regime) into the order of the church. Bonhoeffer belonged to that minority. They were viewed in other church circles in 1937 as unnecessarily stubborn. On Bonhoeffer's evaluation of the 'church's decision,' see his April 1933 lecture 'The Church and the Jewish Question' (*DBWE* 12:361–371 [*Reader* 371–378]); and his April 22, 1936, lecture on church union (*DBWE* 14:656–678). His reference to the 'narrow path' derives from Matt. 7:14," *DBWE* 4:40, n. 7.]

ible pantry, from which it is doled out by careless hands without hesitation or limit. It is grace without a price, without costs. It is said that the essence of grace is that the bill for it is paid in advance for all time. Everything can be had for free, courtesy of that paid bill. The price paid is infinitely great and, therefore, the possibilities of taking advantage of and wasting grace are also infinitely great. What would grace be, if it were not cheap grace?

Cheap grace means grace as doctrine, as principle, as system. It means forgiveness of sins as a general truth; it means God's love as merely a Christian idea of God. Those who affirm it have already had their sins forgiven. The church that teaches this doctrine of grace thereby confers such grace upon itself. The world finds in this church a cheap cover-up for its sins, for which it shows no remorse and from which it has even less desire to be set free. Cheap grace is, thus, denial of God's living word, denial of the incarnation of the word of God.

Cheap grace means justification of sin but not of the sinner. Because grace alone does everything, everything can stay in its old ways. "Our action is in vain." The world remains world and we remain sinners "even in the best of lives." Thus, the Christian should live the same way the world does. In all things the Christian should go along with the world and not venture (like sixteenth-century enthusiasts) to live a different life under grace from that under sin! The Christian better not rage against grace or defile that glorious cheap grace by proclaiming anew a servitude to the letter of the Bible in an attempt to live an obedient life under the commandments of Jesus Christ! The world is justified by grace, therefore—because this grace is so serious! because this irreplaceable grace should not be opposed—the Christian should live just like the rest of the world! Of course, a Christian would like to do something exceptional! Undoubtedly, it must be the most difficult renunciation not to do so and to live like the world. But the Christian has to do it, has to practice such self-denial so that there is no difference between Christian life and worldly life. The Christian has to let grace truly be grace enough so that the world does not lose faith in this cheap grace. In being worldly, however, in this necessary renunciation required for the sake of the world—no, for the sake of grace!—the Christian can be comforted and secure (*securus*)[8] in possession of that grace which takes care of everything by itself. So the Christian need not follow Christ, since the Christian is comforted by grace! That is cheap grace as justification of

44

---

8. [". . . In 1935 Bonhoeffer illustrated 'false security' (*securitas* in contrast to *certitudo* or certainty) using King David: he 'sinned on the basis of the promise; he sinned on the basis of grace' (*DBWE* 14:885–886)," *DBWE* 4:44, n. 4.]

sin, but not justification of the contrite sinner who turns away from sin and repents. It is not forgiveness of sin which separates those who sinned from sin. Cheap grace is that grace which we bestow on ourselves.

Cheap grace is preaching forgiveness without repentance; it is baptism without the discipline of community; it is the Lord's Supper without confession of sin; it is absolution without personal confession. Cheap grace is grace without discipleship, grace without the cross, grace without the living, incarnate Jesus Christ.

Costly grace is the hidden treasure in the field, for the sake of which people go and sell with joy everything they have. It is the costly pearl, for whose price the merchant sells all that he has; it is Christ's sovereignty, for the sake of which you tear out an eye if it causes you to stumble. It is the call of Jesus Christ which causes a disciple to leave his nets and follow him. 45

Costly grace is the gospel which must be sought again and again, the gift which has to be asked for, the door at which one has to knock.

It is costly, because it calls to discipleship; it is grace, because it calls us to follow *Jesus Christ*. It is costly, because it costs people their lives; it is grace, because it thereby makes them live. It is costly, because it condemns sin; it is grace, because it justifies the sinner. Above all, grace is costly, because it was costly to God, because it costs God the life of God's Son—"you were bought with a price" [*1 Cor. 6:20, 7:23*]—and because nothing can be cheap to us which is costly to God. Above all, it is grace because the life of God's Son was not too costly for God to give in order to make us live. God did, indeed, give him up for us. Costly grace is the incarnation of God.

Costly grace is grace as God's holy treasure which must be protected from the world and which must not be thrown to the dogs. Thus, it is grace as living word, word of God, which God speaks as God pleases. It comes to us as a gracious call to follow Jesus; it comes as a forgiving word to the fearful spirit and the broken heart. Grace is costly, because it forces people under the yoke of following Jesus Christ; it is grace when Jesus says, "My yoke is easy, and my burden is light" [*Matt. 11:30*].

Twice the call went out to Peter: Follow me! It was Jesus' first and last word to his disciple (Mark 1:17; John 21:22). His whole life lies between these two calls. The first time, in response to Jesus' call, Peter left his nets, his vocation, at the Sea of Galilee and followed him on his word. The last time, the Resurrected One finds him at his old vocation, again at the Sea of Galilee, and again he calls: Follow me! Between the two lies a whole life of discipleship following Christ. At its center stands Peter's confession of Jesus as the Christ of God. The same message is proclaimed to Peter three times: at the beginning, at the end, and in Caesarea Philippi, namely, that Christ is his Lord and God. It is the same grace of Christ which summons 46 him—Follow me! This same grace also reveals itself to him in his confessing the Son of God.

Grace visited Peter three times along his life's path. It was the one grace, but proclaimed differently three times. Thus, it was Christ's own grace, and surely not grace which the disciple conferred on himself. It was the same grace of Christ which won Peter over to leave everything to follow him, which brought about Peter's confession which had to seem like blasphemy to all the world, and which called the unfaithful Peter into the ultimate community of martyrdom and, in doing so, forgave him all his sins. In Peter's life, grace and discipleship belong inseparably together. He received costly grace.

The expansion of Christianity and the increasing secularization of the church caused the awareness of costly grace to be gradually lost. The world was Christianized; grace became common property of a Christian world. It could be had cheaply. But the Roman Church did keep a remnant of that original awareness. It was decisive that monasticism did not separate from the church and that the church had the good sense to tolerate monasticism. Here, on the boundary of the church, was the place where the awareness that grace is costly and that grace includes discipleship was preserved.[9] People left everything they had for the sake of Christ and tried to follow

47 Jesus' strict commandments through daily exercise. Monastic life thus became a living protest against the secularization of Christianity, against the cheapening of grace. But because the church tolerated this protest and did not permit it to build up to a final explosion, the church relativized it. It even gained from the protest a justification for its own secular life. For now monastic life became the extraordinary achievement of individuals, to which the majority of church members need not be obligated. The fateful limiting of the validity of Jesus' commandments to a certain group of especially qualified people led to differentiating between highest achievement and lowest performance in Christian obedience. This made it possible, when the secularization of the church was attacked any further, to point to the possibility of the monastic way within the church, alongside which another possibility, that of an easier way, was also justified. Thus, calling attention to the original Christian understanding of costly grace

---

9. ["See Bonhoeffer's letter to his brother Karl-Friedrich, January 14, 1935, in which he writes: 'The restoration of the church must surely depend on a new kind of monasticism, which has nothing in common with the old but a life of uncompromising discipleship, following Christ according to the Sermon on the Mount' (*DBWE* 13:285) . . . ," *DBWE* 4:46, n. 16.]

as it was retained in the Roman Church through monasticism enabled the church paradoxically to give final legitimacy to its own secularization. But the decisive mistake of monasticism was not that it followed the grace-laden path of strict discipleship, even with all of monasticism's misunderstandings of the contents of the will of Jesus. Rather, the mistake was that monasticism essentially distanced itself from what is Christian by permitting its way to become the extraordinary achievement of a few, thereby claiming a special meritoriousness for itself.

During the Reformation, God reawakened the gospel of pure, costly grace through God's servant Martin Luther by leading him through the monastery. Luther was a monk. He had left everything and wanted to follow Christ in complete obedience. He renounced the world and turned to Christian works. He learned obedience to Christ and his church, because he knew that only those who are obedient can believe. Luther invested his whole life in his call to the monastery. It was God who caused Luther to fail on that path. God showed him through scripture that discipleship is not the meritorious achievement of individuals, but a divine commandment to all Christians. The humble work of discipleship had become in monasticism the meritorious work of the holy ones. The self-denial of the disciple is   48
revealed here as the final spiritual self-affirmation of the especially pious. This meant that the world had broken into the middle of monastic life and was at work again in a most dangerous way. Luther saw the monk's escape from the world as really a subtle love for the world. In this shattering of his last possibility to achieve a pious life, grace seized Luther. In the collapse of the monastic world, he saw God's saving hand reaching out in Christ. He seized it in the faith that "our deeds are in vain, even in the best life." It was a costly grace, which gave itself to him. It shattered his whole existence. Once again, he had to leave his nets and follow. The first time, when he entered the monastery, he left everything behind except himself, his pious self. This time even that was taken from him. He followed, not by his own merit, but by God's grace. He was not told, yes, you have sinned, but now all that is forgiven. Continue on where you were and comfort yourself with forgiveness! Luther had to leave the monastery and reenter the world, not because the world itself was good and holy, but because even the monastery was nothing else but world.[10]

---

10. ["In his 1936 draft of a catechism for a confirmation lesson plan, Bonhoeffer wrote: 'The world is everything that seeks to draw my heart away from God' (*DBWE* 14:794)," *DBWE* 4:48, n. 23.]

Luther's path out of the monastery back to the world meant the sharpest attack that had been launched on the world since early Christianity. The rejection which the monk had given the world was child's play compared to the rejection that the world endured through his returning to it. This time the attack was a frontal assault. Following Jesus now had to be lived out in the midst of the world. What had been practiced in the special, easier circumstances of monastic life as a special accomplishment now had become what was necessary and commanded for every Christian in the world. Complete obedience to Jesus' commandments had to be carried out in the daily world of work. This deepened the conflict between the life of Christians and the life of the world in an unforeseeable way. The Christian had closed in on the world. It was hand-to-hand combat.

Luther's deed cannot be misunderstood more grievously than by thinking that through discovering the gospel of pure grace, Luther proclaimed a dispensation from obeying Jesus' commandments in the world. The Reformation's main discovery would then be the sanctification and justification of the world by grace's forgiving power. For Luther, on the contrary, a Christian's secular vocation is justified only in that one's protest against the world is thereby most sharply expressed. A Christian's secular vocation receives new recognition from the gospel only to the extent that it is carried on while following Jesus. Luther's reason for leaving the monastery was not justification of the sin, but justification of the sinner. Costly grace was given as a gift to Luther. It was grace, because it was water onto thirsty land, comfort for anxiety, liberation from the servitude of a self-chosen path, forgiveness of all sins. The grace was costly, because it did not excuse one from works. Instead, it endlessly sharpened the call to discipleship. But just wherein it was costly, that was wherein it was grace. And where it was grace, that was where it was costly. That was the secret of the Reformation gospel, the secret of the justification of the sinner.

Nonetheless, what emerged victorious from Reformation history was not Luther's recognition of pure, costly grace, but the alert religious instinct of human beings for the place where grace could be had the cheapest. Only a small, hardly noticeable distortion of the emphasis was needed, and that most dangerous and ruinous deed was done. Luther had taught that, even in their most pious ways and deeds, persons cannot stand before God, because they are basically always seeking themselves. Faced with this predicament, he seized the grace of free and unconditional forgiveness of all sins in faith. Luther knew that this grace had cost him one life and daily continued to cost him, for he was not excused by grace from discipleship, but instead was all the more thrust into it. Whenever Luther spoke of grace, he always meant to include his own life, which was only really placed into

49

full obedience to Christ through grace. He could not speak of grace any
other way than this. Luther said that grace alone did it, and his followers   50
repeat it literally, with the one difference that very soon they left out and
did not consider and did not mention what Luther always included as a matter of course: discipleship. Yes, he no longer even needed to say it, because
he always spoke as one whom grace had led into a most difficult following of
Jesus. The followers' own teaching ["by grace alone"] was, therefore, unassailable, judged by Luther's teaching, but their teaching meant the end and
the destruction of the Reformation as the revelation of God's costly grace
on earth. The justification of the sinner in the world became the justification of sin and the world. Without discipleship, costly grace would become
cheap grace.

When Luther said that our deeds are in vain, even in the best of lives,
and that, therefore, nothing is valid before God "except grace and favor to
forgive sins," he said it as someone who knew himself called to follow Jesus,
called to leave everything he had up until this moment, and in the same
moment called anew to do it again. His acknowledgment of grace was for
him the final radical break with the sin of his life but never its justification.
Grasping at forgiveness was the final radical rejection of self-willed life; the
acknowledgment of grace itself his first really serious call to discipleship.
It was a "conclusion" for him, although a divine conclusion, not a human
one. His descendants made this conclusion into a principled presupposition on which to base their calculations. That was the whole trouble. If
grace is the "result" given by Christ himself to Christian life, then this life is
not for one moment excused from discipleship. But if grace is a principled
presupposition of my Christian life, then in advance I have justification of
whatever sins I commit in my life in the world. I can now sin on the basis
of this grace; the world is in principle justified by grace. I can thus remain
as before in my bourgeois-secular existence. Everything remains as before,
and I can be sure that God's grace takes care of me. The whole world has
become "Christian" under this grace, but Christianity has become the world
under this grace as never before. The conflict between a Christian and a
bourgeois-secular vocation is resolved. Christian life consists of my living
in the world and like the world, my not being any different from it, my not   51
being permitted to be different from it—for the sake of grace!—but my
going occasionally from the sphere of the world to the sphere of the church,
in order to be reassured there of the forgiveness of my sins. I am liberated
from following Jesus—by cheap grace, which has to be the bitterest enemy
of discipleship, which has to hate and despise true discipleship. Grace
as presupposition is grace at its cheapest; grace as a conclusion is costly
grace. It is appalling to see what is at stake in the way in which a gospel

truth is expressed and used. It is the same word of the justification by grace alone, and yet false use of the same statement can lead to the complete destruction of its essence.

When Faust says at the end of his life of seeking knowledge, "I see that we can know nothing," then that is a conclusion, a result. It is something entirely different than when a student repeats this statement in the first semester to justify his laziness (Kierkegaard). Used as a conclusion, the sentence is true; as a presupposition, it is self-deception. That means that knowledge cannot be separated from the existence in which it was acquired. Only those who in following Christ leave everything they have can stand and say that they are justified solely by grace. They recognize the call to discipleship itself as grace and grace as that call. But those who want to use this grace to excuse themselves from discipleship are deceiving themselves.

But doesn't Luther himself come dangerously close to this complete distortion in understanding grace? What does it mean for Luther to say: "Pecca fortiter, sed fortius fide et gaude in Christo"—"Sin boldly, but believe and rejoice in Christ even more boldly!" So you are only a sinner and can never get out of sin; whether you are a monk or a secular person, whether you want to be pious or evil, you will not flee the bonds of the world, you will sin. So, then, sin boldly, and on the basis of grace already given! Is this blatant proclamation of cheap grace carte blanche for sin, and rejection of discipleship? Is it a blasphemous invitation to sin deliberately while relying on grace? Is there a more diabolical abuse of grace than sinning while relying on the gift of God's grace? Isn't the Catholic catechism right in recognizing this as sin against the Holy Spirit?

To understand this, everything depends on how the difference between result and presupposition is applied. If Luther's statement is used as a presupposition for a theology of grace, then it proclaims cheap grace. But Luther's statement is to be understood correctly not as a beginning, but exclusively as an end, a conclusion, a last stone, as the very last word. Understood as a presupposition, pecca fortiter becomes an ethical principle. If grace is a principle, then pecca fortiter as a principle would correspond to it. That is justification of sin. It turns Luther's statement into its opposite. "Sin boldly"—that could be for Luther only the very last bit of pastoral advice, of consolation for those who along the path of discipleship have come to know that they cannot become sin-free, who out of fear of sin despair of God's grace. For them, "sin boldly" is not something like a fundamental affirmation of their disobedient lives. Rather, it is the gospel of God's grace, in the presence of which we are sinners always and at every place. This gospel seeks us and justifies us exactly as sinners. Admit your sin boldly; do not try to flee from it, but "believe much more boldly." You are a sinner, so just be a sinner. Do not want to be anything else than what you are. Become a sinner again every day and be bold in doing so. But to whom could such a thing be said except to those who from their hearts daily reject sin, who every day reject everything that hinders them from following Jesus and who are still unconsoled about their daily unfaithfulness and sin? Who else could hear it without danger for their faith than those who are called anew by such consolation to follow Christ? In this way, Luther's statement, understood as a conclusion, becomes that costly grace which alone is grace.   53

Grace as a principle, pecca fortiter as a principle, cheap grace—all these are finally only a new law, which neither helps nor liberates. Grace as a living word, pecca fortiter as comfort in a time of despair and a call to discipleship, costly grace alone is pure grace, which really forgives sins and liberates the sinner.

Like ravens we have gathered around the carcass of cheap grace. From it we have imbibed the poison which has killed the following of Jesus among us. The doctrine of pure grace experienced an unprecedented deification. The pure doctrine of grace became its own God, grace itself. Luther's teachings are quoted everywhere, but twisted from their truth into self-delusion. They say if only our church is in possession of a doctrine of justification, then it is surely a justified church! They say Luther's true legacy should be recognizable in making grace as cheap as possible. Being Lutheran should mean that discipleship is left to the legalists, the Reformed, or the enthusiasts, all for the sake of grace. They say that the world is justified and Christians in discipleship are made out to be heretics. A people became Christian, became Lutheran, but at the cost of discipleship, at an all-too-cheap price. Cheap grace had won.

But do we also know that this cheap grace has been utterly unmerciful against us? Is the price that we are paying today with the collapse of the organized churches anything else but an inevitable consequence of grace acquired too cheaply?[11] We gave away preaching and sacraments cheaply; we performed baptisms and confirmations; we absolved an entire people, unquestioned and unconditionally; out of human love we handed over what was holy to the scornful and unbelievers. We poured out rivers of grace without end, but the call to rigorously follow Christ was seldom heard. What   54 happened to the insights of the ancient church, which in the baptismal

---

11. ["On the situation of the Protestant church, see Bonhoeffer's 1936 essay on church union. There he states categorically that 'The essence of the church is determined not by those who belong to it but by the word and sacrament of Jesus Christ; wherever this word and these sacraments are efficaciously present, they will assemble a church-community according to the promise' (*DBWE* 14:657 [*Reader* 433])," *DBWE* 4:53, n. 35.]

teaching watched so carefully over the boundary between the church and the world, over costly grace?[12] What happened to Luther's warnings against a proclamation of the gospel which made people secure in their godless lives? When was the world ever Christianized more dreadfully and wickedly than here? What do the three thousand Saxons whose bodies Charlemagne killed compare with the millions of souls being killed today?[13] The biblical wisdom that the sins of the fathers are visited on the children unto the third and fourth generation has become true in us [*Exod. 20:5*]. Cheap grace was very unmerciful to our Protestant church.

Cheap grace surely has also been unmerciful with most of us personally. It did not open the way to Christ for us, but rather closed it. It did not call us into discipleship, but hardened us in disobedience. Moreover, was it not unmerciful and cruel when we were accosted by the message of cheap grace just where we had once heard the call to follow Jesus as Christ's call of grace, where we perhaps had once dared to take the first steps of discipleship in the discipline of obedience to the commandments? Could we hear this message in any other way than that it tried to block our way with the call to a highly worldly sobriety which suffocated our joy in discipleship by pointing out that it was all merely the path we chose ourselves, that it was an exertion of strength, effort, and discipline which was unnecessary, even very dangerous? For, after all, everything was already prepared and fulfilled by grace! The glowing wick was mercilessly extinguished. It was unmerciful to
55   speak to such people since they, confused by such a cheap offer, were forced to leave the path to which Christ called them clutching instead at cheap grace. Cheap grace would permanently prevent them, from recognizing costly grace. It could not happen any other way but that possessing cheap grace would mislead weaklings to suddenly feel strong,[14] yet in reality, they had lost their power for obedience and discipleship. The word of cheap grace has ruined more Christians than any commandment about works.

---

12. ["In Finkenwalde, Bonhoeffer discussed at length catechizing in the early church (including 'the discipline of the secret') in light of the church's behavior in his time . . . (*DBWE* 14:551–556)," *DBWE* 4:54, n. 36.]

13. ["In 782 c.e., Charlemagne had thousands of people from the Saxon tribe executed. The National Socialist propaganda machine used this historical fact against the church . . . ," *DBWE* 4:54, n. 37.]

14. ["On Bonhoeffer's reference to 'weak' and 'strong' people, see Romans 14. In the confrontation with German Christians in the new auditorium of Berlin University on June 22, 1933, Bonhoeffer described the 'weak' as those aggressive ones who wanted to prohibit all that was Jewish from the German church (*DB-ER*, 287; cf. *DBWE* 12:127–128)," *DBWE* 4:55, n. 40.]

In everything that follows, we want to speak up on behalf of those who are tempted to despair, for whom the word of grace has become frightfully empty. For integrity's sake someone has to speak up for those among us who confess that cheap grace has made them give up following Christ, and that ceasing to follow Christ has made them lose the knowledge of costly grace. Because we cannot deny that we no longer stand in true discipleship to Christ, while being members of a true-believing church with a pure doctrine of grace, but no longer members of a church which follows Christ, we therefore simply have to try to understand grace and discipleship again in correct relationship to each other. We can no longer avoid this. Our church's predicament is proving more and more clearly to be a question of how we are to live as Christians today.

Blessed are they who already stand at the end of the path on which we wish to embark and perceive with amazement what really seems inconceivable: that grace is costly, precisely because it is pure grace, because it is God's grace in Jesus Christ.[15] Blessed are they who by simply following Jesus Christ are overcome by this grace, so that with humble spirit they may praise the grace of Christ which alone is effective. Blessed are they who, in the knowledge of such grace, can live in the world without losing themselves in it. In following Christ their heavenly home has become so certain that they   56
are truly free for life in this world. Blessed are they for whom following Jesus Christ means nothing other than living from grace and for whom grace means following Christ. Blessed are they who in this sense have become Christians, for whom the word of grace has been merciful.

CHAPTER 2   57

THE CALL TO DISCIPLESHIP

"As Jesus was walking along, he saw Levi son of Alphaeus sitting at the tax booth, and he said to him, 'Follow me.' And he got up and followed him" (Mark 2:14).

The call goes out, and without any further ado the obedient deed of the one called follows. The disciple's answer is not a spoken confession of faith in Jesus. Instead, it is the obedient deed. How is this direct relation

---

15. ["In the year 1937 alone, twenty-seven former Finkenwalde seminarians were imprisoned for shorter or longer periods for disobeying wanton government prohibitions, according to Bonhoeffer's annual report on 1937 (*DBWE* 15:20) . . . ," *DBWE* 4:54, n. 41.]

between call and obedience possible? It is quite offensive to natural reason. Reason is impelled to reject the abruptness of the response. It seeks something to mediate it; it seeks an explanation. No matter what, some sort of mediation has to be found, psychological or historical. Some have asked the foolish question whether the tax collector had known Jesus previously and therefore was prepared to follow his call. But the text is stubbornly silent on this point; in it, everything depends on call and deed directly facing each other. The text is not interested in psychological explanations for the faithful decisions of a person. Why not? Because there is only one good reason for the proximity of call and deed: *Jesus Christ himself.* It is he who calls. That is why the tax collector follows. This encounter gives witness to Jesus' unconditional, immediate, and inexplicable authority. Nothing precedes it, and nothing follows except the obedience of the called. Because Jesus is the Christ, he has authority to call and to demand obedience to his word. Jesus calls to discipleship, not as a teacher and a role model, but as the Christ, the Son of God. Thus, in this short text Jesus Christ and his claim on people are proclaimed, and nothing else. No praise falls on the disciple or on his espoused Christianity. Attention should not fall to him, but only to the one who calls, to his authority. Not even a path to faith, to discipleship, is aimed at; there is no other path to faith than obedience to Jesus' call.

What is said about the content of discipleship? Follow me, walk behind me! That is all. Going after him is something without specific content. It is truly not a program for one's life which would be sensible to implement. It is neither a goal nor an ideal to be sought. It is not even a matter for which, according to human inclination, it would be worth investing anything at all, much less oneself. And what happens? Those called leave everything they have, not in order to do something valuable. Instead, they do it simply for the sake of the call itself, because otherwise they could not walk behind Jesus. Nothing of importance is attached to this action in itself. It remains something completely insignificant, unworthy of notice. The bridges are torn down, and the followers simply move ahead. They are called away and are supposed to "step out" of their previous existence, they are supposed to "exist" in the strict sense of the word. Former things are left behind; they are completely given up. The disciple is thrown out of the relative security of life into complete insecurity (which in truth is absolute security and protection in community with Jesus); out of the foreseeable and calculable realm (which in truth is unreliable) into the completely unforeseeable, coincidental realm (which in truth is the only necessary and reliable one); out of the realm of limited possibilities (which in truth is that of unlimited possibilities) into the realm of unlimited possibilities (which in truth is the

only liberating reality).[16] Yet that is not a general law; it is, rather, the exact
opposite of all legalism. Again, it is nothing other than being bound to   59
Jesus Christ alone. This means completely breaking through anything pre-
programmed, idealistic, or legalistic. No further content is possible because
Jesus is the only content. There is no other content besides Jesus. He himself
is it.

So the call to discipleship is a commitment solely to the person of Jesus
Christ, a breaking through of all legalisms by the grace of him who calls. It
is a gracious call, a gracious commandment. It is beyond enmity between
law and gospel. Christ calls; the disciple follows. That is grace and commandment in one. "I walk joyfully, for I seek your commands" (Ps. 119:45).

Discipleship is commitment to Christ. Because Christ exists, he must
be followed. An idea about Christ, a doctrinal system, a general religious
recognition of grace or forgiveness of sins does not require discipleship.
In truth, it even excludes discipleship; it is inimical to it. One enters into a
relationship with an idea by way of knowledge, enthusiasm, perhaps even
by carrying it out, but never by personal obedient discipleship. Christianity
without the living Jesus Christ remains necessarily a Christianity without
discipleship; and a Christianity without discipleship is always a Christianity
without Jesus Christ. It is an idea, a myth. A Christianity in which there is
only God the Father, but not Christ as a living Son actually cancels discipleship. In that case there will be trust in God, but not discipleship. God's Son
became human, he is the *mediator*—that is why discipleship is the right relation to him. Discipleship is bound to the mediator, and wherever discipleship is rightly spoken of, there the mediator, Jesus Christ, the Son of God,
is intended. Only the mediator, the God-human, can call to discipleship.

Discipleship without Jesus Christ is choosing one's own path. It could
be an ideal path or a martyr's path, but it is without the promise. Jesus will
reject it.

"Then they went on to another village. As they were going along the   60
road, someone said to him, 'I will follow you wherever you go.' And Jesus
said to him, 'Foxes have holes, and birds of the air have nests; but the Son
of Man has nowhere to lay his head.' To another he said, 'Follow me.' But he

---

16. ["Bonhoeffer is using the pair of philosophical concepts, 'possibility/reality' or
'potentiality/actuality'. . . . For Bonhoeffer the concept of reality takes precedence over
that of possibility in theological statements. As early as 1927, for example, his fourth
proposition in defense of his doctoral dissertation states: "The introduction of the concept of potentiality in the *Christian* concept of God means a limitation of divine omnipotence" (*DBWE* 9:440. See also *DBWE* 1:143 (*Reader* 40–41), n. 40 . . . ," *DBWE* 4:58, n. 4.]

said, 'Lord, first let me go and bury my father.' But Jesus said to him, 'Let the dead bury their own dead; but as for you, go and proclaim the kingdom of God.' Another said, 'I will follow you, Lord; but let me first say farewell to those at my home.' Jesus said to him, 'No one who puts a hand to the plow and looks back is fit for the kingdom of God'" (Luke 9:57–62).

The *first* disciple took the initiative to follow Jesus. He was not called, and Jesus' answer shows the enthusiastic man that he does not know what he is doing. He cannot know at all. That is the meaning of the answer which shows the disciple the reality of life with Jesus. The answer is spoken by the one who is going to the cross, whose whole life is described in the Apostles' Creed with the one word "suffered." None can want that by their own choice. None can call themselves, says Jesus; and his word receives no reply. The gap between the free offer of discipleship and real discipleship remains wide open.

When Jesus himself calls, however, he overcomes the widest gap. The *second* disciple wants to bury his father before he follows Jesus. The law obliges him. He knows what he wants to do and has to do. First he has to fulfill the law; then he will follow. Here a clear command of the law stands between the one called and Jesus. Jesus' call forcefully challenges this gap. Under no circumstances is anything permitted to come between Jesus and the one called, even that which is greatest and holiest, even the law. Just at that point, for the sake of Jesus, the law which tries to get in the way has to be broken through, because it no longer had any right to interpose itself between Jesus and the one called. So Jesus here opposes the law and bids the man follow him. Only Christ speaks that way. He has the last word. The other person cannot contradict. This call, this grace, is irresistible.

61   The *third* one called, like the first, understands discipleship as an offer made only by him, as his own self-chosen program for life. But in contrast to the first, he thinks he is justified in setting his own conditions. Doing so entangles him in a complete contradiction. He wants to join Jesus, but at the same time he himself puts something in the way between himself and Jesus: "Let me first." He wants to follow, but he wants to set his own conditions for following. Discipleship is a possibility for him, whose implementation requires fulfilling conditions and prerequisites.[17] This makes discipleship something humanly reasonable and comprehensible. First one does the one

17. ["In *Creation and Fall*, Bonhoeffer uses the same expression, 'Let me first . . . ,' to characterize a potential disciple's fleeing into a mere possibility of following Jesus. He writes, 'In other words, in this question what is possible is played off against reality, and

thing, and then the other. Everything has its own rights and its own time. The disciple makes himself available, but retains the right to set his own conditions. It is obvious that, at that moment, discipleship stops being discipleship. It becomes a human program,[18] which I can organize according to my own judgment and can justify rationally and ethically. This third one wants to follow Christ, but already in the very act of declaring his willingness to do so, he no longer wants to follow him. He eliminates discipleship by his offer, because discipleship does not tolerate any conditions that could come between Jesus and obedience. Hence, this third one gets caught in a contradiction, not only with Jesus, but with himself. He does not want what Jesus wants; he does not even want what he himself wants. He likewise does not want what he thinks he wants. He judges himself; he causes his own downfall, all by his request, "Let me first." Jesus' answer graphically attests to this person's inner conflict, which rules out discipleship. "No one who puts a hand to the plow and looks back is fit for the kingdom of God" [*Luke 9:61-62*].

Following Christ means taking certain steps. The first step, which responds to the call, separates the followers from their previous existence. A call to discipleship thus immediately creates a new situation. Staying in the old situation and following Christ mutually exclude each other. At first, that was quite visibly the case. The tax collector had to leave his booth and Peter his nets to follow Jesus. According to our understanding, even back then things could have been quite different. Jesus could have given the tax collector new knowledge of God and left him in his old situation. If Jesus had not been God's Son become human, then that would have been possible. But because Jesus is the Christ, it has to be made clear from the beginning that his word is not a doctrine. Instead, it creates existence anew. The point was to really walk with Jesus. It was made clear to those he called that they only had one possibility of believing in Jesus, that of leaving everything and going with the incarnate Son of God.

The first step puts the follower into the situation of being able to believe. If people do not follow, they remain behind, then they do not learn to believe. Those called must get out of their situations, in which they cannot believe, into a situation in which faith can begin. This step has no intrinsic worth of its own; it is justified only by the community with Jesus Christ that

62

---

what is possible undermines what is reality. In the relation of human beings to God, however, there are no possibilities: there is only reality' (*DBWE* 3:108–109 [*Reader* 246–247])," *DBWE* 4:61, 11.]

18. ["In a 1932 sermon Bonhoeffer contrasts 2 Chron. 20:12: 'We do not know what to do, but our eyes are on you' with 'Christian programmatic speech' in which 'prayers become programs and petitions become orders' (*DBWE* 11:435)," *DBWE* 4:61, n. 12.]

is attained. As long as Levi sits in the tax collector's booth and Peter at his nets, they would do their work honestly and loyally, they would have old or new knowledge about God. But if they want to learn to believe in God, they have to follow the Son of God incarnate and walk with him.

Things used to be different. Then they could live quietly in the country, unnoticed in their work, keep the law, and wait for the Messiah. But now he was there; now his call came. Now faith no longer meant keeping quiet and waiting, but going in discipleship with him. Now his call to discipleship dissolved all ties for the sake of the unique commitment to Jesus Christ. Now all bridges had to be burned and the step taken to enter into endless insecurity, in order to know what Jesus demands and what Jesus gives. Levi at his taxes could have had Jesus as a helper for all kinds of needs, but he would not have recognized him as the one Lord, into whose hand he should entrust his whole life. He would not have learned to have faith. The situa-
63   tion has to be initiated which will enable faith in Jesus, the incarnate God. This is the impossible situation, in which everything is based on only one thing, the word of Jesus. Peter has to get out of the boat into the waves, in order to experience his own powerlessness and the almighty power of his Lord. If he had not gotten out, he would not have learned to believe. His situation on the tempestuous sea is completely impossible and, ethically, simply irresponsible, but it has to happen for him to believe. The road to faith passes through obedience to Christ's call. The step is required; other- wise Jesus' call dissipates into nothing. Any intended discipleship without this step to which Jesus calls becomes deceptive enthusiasts' illusion.

There is a great danger in telling the difference between a situation where faith is possible and where it is not. It is clear that there is nothing in the situation as such to indicate which kind it is. Only the call of Jesus Christ qualifies it as a situation where faith is possible. Second, a situation where faith is possible is never made by humans. Discipleship is not a human offer. The call alone creates the situation. Third, the value of the situation is never in itself. The call alone justifies it. Finally and most of all, the situation which enables faith can itself happen only in faith.

The concept of a situation in which faith is possible is only a description of the reality contained in the following two statements, both of which are equally true: *only the believers obey,* and *only the obedient believe.*

It is really unfaithfulness to the Bible to have the first statement without the second. Only the believer obeys—we think we can understand that. Of course, obedience follows faith, the way good fruit comes from a good tree, we say. First there is faith, then obedience. If this meant only that faith alone justifies us and not deeds of obedience, then it is a firm and necessary precondition for everything else. But if it meant a chronological sequence, that faith would have to come first, to be later followed by obedience, then faith and obedience are torn apart, and the very practical question remains open: when does obedience start? Obedience remains separated from faith. Because we are justified by faith, faith and obedience have to be distinguished. But their division must never destroy their unity, which lies in the reality that faith exists only in obedience, is never without obedience. Faith is only faith in deeds of obedience.

64

Because talk about obedience as a consequence of faith is unseemly, due to the indissoluble unity between faith and obedience, the statement "only the believers obey" has to be paired with the other one, "only the obedient believe." In the first, faith is the precondition of obedience; in the second, obedience is the precondition of faith. In exactly the same way that obedience is called a consequence of faith, it is also called a prerequisite of faith.

Only the obedient believe. A concrete commandment has to be obeyed, in order to come to believe. A first step of obedience has to be taken, so that faith does not become pious self-deception, cheap grace. The first step is crucial. It is qualitatively different from all others that follow. The first step of obedience has to lead Peter away from his nets and out of the boat; it has to lead the young man away from his wealth. Faith is possible only in this new state of existence created by obedience.

This first step should, to begin with, be viewed as an external deed which exchanges one mode of existence for another. Anyone can take that step. People are free to do that. It is a deed within the *iustitia civilis* [*civil righteousness*],[19] within which people are free. Peter cannot convert himself, but he can leave his nets. In the Gospels that first step consists of a deed which affects all of one's life. The Roman Church required such a step only for the exceptional alternative of monasticism. For the other faithful it was enough to be willing to subject themselves unconditionally to the church and its commands. In the Lutheran confessions the importance of a first step is recognized in a significant way: after they thoroughly removed the danger of a synergistic misunderstanding,[20] space could be kept and had to be kept for that first external deed required to enable faith—the step, in this case, to

65

---

19. ["'Civil righteousness' (in contrast to spiritual righteousness). The term is often used in Lutheran confessional writings for outward discipline that people can accomplish with their natural powers—reason and free will—while *iustitia spiritualis* ('spiritual righteousness') is only granted by the Holy Spirit. See 'Apology of the Augsburg Confession' (*Book of Concord*, 234–235, art. 18, par. 9, et passim)," *DBWE* 4:64, n. 19.]

20. ["The reformers rejected as a misunderstanding the notion that human 'co-working' (σύν—ἔργον) for grace to happen could count as a human merit and could contribute to salvation. Cf. *DBWE* 14:441," *DBWE* 4:64, n. 20.]

the church, where the word of salvation is preached. This step can be taken in full freedom. Come to the church! You can do that on the strength of your human freedom. You can leave your house on Sunday and go to hear the preaching. If you do not do it, then you willfully exclude yourself from the place where faith is possible. In this the Lutheran confessions show that they know there is a situation which enables faith and one in which faith is not possible. To be sure, this knowledge is very hidden here, almost as if they were ashamed of it, but it is present as one and the same knowledge of the significance of the first step as an external deed.

Once this knowledge is ascertained, then something else must be acknowledged, namely, that this first step as an external deed is and remains a dead work of the law, which can by itself never lead to Christ. As an external deed, the new existence just remains the old existence. At best, a new law of life, a new lifestyle, is reached, which has nothing to do with the new life in Christ. The alcoholic who gives up alcohol or the rich man who gives away his money are truly freed from alcohol and money, but not from themselves. They remain as their old selves, maybe even more so than before. Subject to the demand for works, they remain in the death of their old lives. The works do have to be done, but by themselves they do not lead out of death, disobedience, and godlessness. If we ourselves understand our first step as a precondition for grace, for faith, then we are judged by our works and completely cut off from grace. Everything we call convictions or good intentions is included in those external deeds, everything which the Roman Church calls facere quod in se est [*to do what is in oneself, i.e., to act according to one's own abilities*]. If we take the first step with the intention of putting ourselves into the situation of being able to believe, then even this ability to believe is itself nothing but works. It is but a new possibility for living within our old existence and thereby a complete misunderstanding. We remain in unbelief.

66   But the external works have to take place; we have to get into the situation of being able to believe. We have to take the step. What does that mean? It means that we take this step in the right way only when we do not look to the necessity of our works, but solely with a view to the word of Jesus Christ, which calls us to take the step. Peter knows that he cannot climb out of the boat by his own power. His first step would already be his downfall, so he calls, "Command me to come to you on the water." Christ answers, "Come" [*Matt. 14:28–29*]. Christ has to have called; the step can be taken only at his word. This call is his grace, which calls us out of death into the new life of obedience. But now that Christ has called, Peter has to get out of the boat to come to Christ. So it is, indeed, the case that the first step of

obedience is itself an act of faith in Christ's word. But it would completely misrepresent the essence of faith to conclude that that step is no longer necessary, because in that step there had already been faith. To the contrary, we must venture to state that the step of obedience must be done first, before there can be faith. The disobedient cannot have faith.

You complain that you cannot believe? No one should be surprised that they cannot come to believe so long as, in deliberate disobedience, they flee or reject some aspect of Jesus' commandment. You do not want to subject some sinful passion, an enmity, a hope, your life plans, or your reason to Jesus' commandment? Do not be surprised that you do not receive the Holy Spirit, that you cannot pray, that your prayer for faith remains empty! Instead, go and be reconciled with your sister or brother; let go of the sin which keeps you captive; and you will be able to believe again! If you reject God's commanding word, you will not receive God's gracious word. How would you expect to find community while you intentionally withdraw from it at some point? The disobedient cannot believe; only the obedient believe.

Here the gracious call of Jesus Christ to discipleship becomes a strict law: Do this! Stop that! Come out of the boat to Jesus! Jesus says to anyone who uses their faith or lack of faith to excuse their acts of disobedience to his call: First obey, do the external works, let go of what binds you, give up what is separating you from God's will! Do not say, I do not have the faith for that. You will not have it so long as you remain disobedient, so long as you will not take that first step. Do not say, I have faith, so I do not have to take the first step. You do not have faith, because and so long as you will not take that first step. Instead, you have hardened yourself in disbelief under the appearance of humble faith. It is an evil excuse to point from inadequate obedience to inadequate faith, and from inadequate faith to inadequate obedience. It is the disobedience of the "faithful" if they confess their unbelief where their obedience is required and if they play games with that confession (Mark 9:24). You believe—so take the first step! It leads to Jesus Christ. You do not believe—take the same step; it is commanded of you! The question of your belief or unbelief is not yours to ask. The works of obedience are required and must be done immediately. The situation is given in which faith becomes possible and really exists.

Actually, it is not *the works* which create faith. Instead, you are given a situation in which you can have faith. The point is to get into such a situation, so that faith is true faith and not self-deception. Because the only goal is to have true faith in Jesus Christ, because faith alone is and remains the goal ("out of faith into faith," Rom. 1:17), this is an indispensable situation. Anyone who protests too quickly and in too Protestant a manner should be asked whether or not they are defending cheap grace. In fact the two statements, if they remain juxtaposed, will not offend true faith, but if each is taken alone it would cause serious offense. Only the believers obey—that is said to the obedient person inside the believer. Only the obedient person believes; this is what is said to the believer in his obedience. If the first statement remains alone, the believer is prey to cheap grace, that is, damnation. If the second statement remains alone, the believers are prey to their works, that is, damnation.

At this point let us now take a look at Christian pastoral care.[21] It is particularly important for pastors giving care to speak from knowledge of both of these statements. They need to know that sorrow over a lack of faith repeatedly comes from disobedience, which may be intentional or even no longer noticed, and that such sorrow all too often corresponds to the comfort of cheap grace. But the disobedience remains unbroken, and words of grace become a consolation which the disobedient grant to themselves and a forgiveness of sins they accord themselves. But for such people, the Christian message becomes empty; they no longer hear it. Even though they forgive

68 themselves a thousand times over, they are incapable of believing in true forgiveness, because in truth, it has not been granted them. Unbelief feeds on cheap grace, because it clings to disobedience. This is a common situation in today's pastoral care. What then happens is that people get so stubborn in their disobedience through their self-granted forgiveness that they claim they can no longer discern what is good and what is God's command. They claim it is ambiguous and permits various interpretations. At first they know clearly that they were disobedient, but their knowledge is gradually dimmed until they become unapproachable. Then the disobedient have entangled themselves so badly that they simply are no longer *able* to hear the word. Then they can no longer have faith. Something like the following conversation will take place between the obstinate disbeliever and the pastor: "I can believe no longer."—"Listen to the Word, it is being proclaimed to you!"—"I hear it, but it doesn't say anything to me. It seems empty to me; it is beyond me."—"You don't want to hear."—"Yes, I do." With that, they reach the point where most pastoral conversations break off, because the pastors do not know what is going on. They only know the one statement: only the believer obeys. With this statement, they are no longer able to help the obstinate unbeliever, who does not and cannot have this kind of faith. Pastors think they are standing here before an ultimate puzzle, that God

21. ["According to his students' notes, this section corresponds largely to Bonhoeffer's lectures on pastoral care from 1935 to 1939 (*DBWE* 14:564–575)," *DBWE* 4:67, n. 26.]

gives faith to some and denies it to others. With this one statement, they surrender their efforts. The obstinate persons remain alone and continue to bewail their predicament. But this is the turning point in the conversation. The change is a complete one. There is no longer any sense in arguing; the questions and worries of the other person are no longer taken so seriously. Instead the person hiding behind them is taken all the more seriously. The pastor breaks through the walls such a person has built with the statement, "Only the obedient have faith." So the conversation is interrupted, and the pastor's next sentence is, "You are disobedient; you refuse to obey Christ; you desire to keep a piece of autonomy for yourself. You cannot hear Christ, because you are disobedient; you cannot believe in grace, because you do not want to obey. You have hardened some corner of your heart against Christ's call. Your trouble is your sin." At this point Christ reappears on the scene; he attacks the devil in the other person, who until then had been hiding behind cheap grace. At that point everything depends on the pastor having both statements ready: only the obedient believe, and only the believer obeys. In the name of Jesus, the pastor must call the other to obedience, to a deed, to a first step. Leave what binds you and follow him! 69 At that moment everything depends on that step. The position taken by the disobedient person must be broken through, for in it Christ can no longer be heard. Fugitives must leave the hiding places they built for themselves. Only when they get out of them can they again see, hear, and believe freely. Indeed, as far as Christ is concerned, doing the deed itself gains nothing; it remains a dead work. But in spite of that, Peter has to step out onto the rolling sea, so that he can believe.

In short, the situation is that people have poisoned themselves with cheap grace by the statement that only the believer obeys. They remain disobedient and console themselves with a forgiveness that they grant themselves, and in doing so, they close themselves off from the word of God. The fortress walls around them cannot be broken through, so long as all they hear is the statement they are hiding behind being repeated. A change has to come about by calling people to obedience: only the obedient have faith!

Will people thus be led down the fatal path of belief in their own works? No, they will learn instead that their faith is not faith; they will be liberated from their entanglement with themselves. They have to get out in the fresh air of a decision. In that way Jesus' call to faith and discipleship is made audible anew.

This brings us already to the middle of the story of the rich young man.

"Then someone came to him and said, 'Teacher, what good deed must I do to have eternal life?' And he said to him, 'Why do you ask me about what is good? There is only one who is good. If you wish to enter into life, keep the commandments.' He said to him, 'Which ones?' And Jesus said, 'You shall not murder; You shall not commit adultery; You shall not steal; You shall not bear false witness; Honor your father and mother; also, You shall love your neighbor as yourself.' The young man said to him, 'I have kept all these, what do I still lack?' Jesus said to him, 'If you wish to be perfect, go, sell your possessions, and give the money to the poor, and you will have treasure in heaven; then come, follow me.' When the young man heard this word, he went away grieving, for he had many possessions" (Matt. 19:16–22).

The young man's question about eternal life is the question of salvation. It is the only really serious question there is. But it is not easy to ask it in the right way. This is made evident by the way the young man, who obviously intends to ask this question, actually asks a quite different one. He even avoids the real question. He addresses his question to the "good master." He wants to hear the opinion, advice, the judgment of the good master, the great teacher, on the matter. In doing so he reveals two points: First, the question is really important to him, and Jesus should have a meaningful answer to offer. Second, however, he is expecting from the good master and great teacher a significant response, but not a divine order with unconditional authority. For the young man, the question of eternal life is one which he desires to speak of and discuss with a "good master." But right away Jesus' answer trips him up. "Why do you ask me about what is good? No one is good except the one God." The question had already betrayed what was in his heart. He wanted to talk about eternal life with a good rabbi, but what he got to hear was that with his question he was in truth not standing before a good master, but before none other than God. He will not get an answer from the Son of God that would do anything else but clearly refer him to the commandment of the one God. He will not get an answer of a "good master," who would add his own opinion to the revealed will of God. Jesus directs attention away from himself to the God who alone is good, and in doing so proves himself to be the fully obedient Son of God. But if the questioner is standing directly before God, then he is exposed as one who was fleeing from God's revealed commandment, which he himself already knew. The young man knew the commandments. But his situation is that he is not satisfied with them; he wants to move beyond them. His question is unmasked as a question of a self-invented and self-chosen piety. Why is the revealed commandment not enough for the young man? Why does he act as if he did not already know the answer to his question? Why does he want to accuse God of leaving him in ignorance in this most decisive question of life? So the young man is already caught and brought to judgment. He is called back from the nonbinding question of salvation to simple obedience to the revealed commandments.

He tries a second attempt to flee. The young man answers with a sec- 71
ond question: "Which ones?" Satan himself is hiding in that question. This
was the only possible way out for someone who felt himself trapped. Of
course the young man knew the commandments, but who should know
which commandment is meant just for him, just for right then, out of the
full number of commandments? The revelation of the commandment is
ambiguous and unclear, says the young man. He is not looking at the commandments. He is instead looking at himself again, his problems, his conflicts. He retreats from God's clear commandment back to the interesting,
indisputably human situation of "ethical conflict." It is not wrong that he
knows about such a conflict, but it is wrong that the conflict is played off
against God's commandments. The commandments are actually given in
order to bring ethical conflicts to an end. Ethical conflict is the primordial
ethical phenomenon for human beings after the fall. It is the human revolt
against God. The serpent in paradise put this conflict into the heart of the
first human. "Did God say?"[22] People are torn away from the clear commandment and from simple childlike obedience by ethical doubt, by assert-
ing that the commandment still needs interpretation and explanation. "Did
God say?" People are made to decide by the power of their own knowledge
of good and evil, by the power of their conscience to know what is good.
The commandment is ambiguous; God intends for people to interpret it
and decide about it freely.

Even thinking this way is already a refusal to obey the commandment.
Double-minded thinking has replaced the simple act. The person of free
conscience boasts of being superior to the child of obedience. To invoke
ethical conflict is to terminate obedience. It is a retreat from God's reality
to human possibility, from faith to doubt. So the unexpected now happens.
The same question with which the young man tried to hide his disobedience now unmasks him for who he is, namely, a person in sin. Jesus' answer
does this. God's revealed commandments are named. By naming them,
Jesus confirms anew that they are, indeed, God's commandments. The
young man is once again caught. He hoped to evade once more and reenter
into a nonbinding conversation about eternal questions. He hoped Jesus 72
would offer him a solution to his ethical conflict. But Jesus lays hold, not
of the question, but of the person himself. The only answer to the predicament of ethical conflict is God's commandment itself, which is the demand
to stop discussing and start obeying. Only the devil has a solution to offer

22. [*Gen. 3:2. See also* DBWE *3:112–114* (Reader *248–250*), DBWE *13:307–308* (Reader *395–396*).]

to ethical conflicts. It is this: keep asking questions, so that you are free from having to obey. Jesus takes aim at the young man himself instead of his problem. The young man took his ethical conflict deadly seriously, but Jesus does not take it seriously at all. He is serious about only one thing, that the young man finally hears and obeys God's command. When ethical conflict is taken so seriously that it tortures and subjugates people because it hinders their doing the liberating act of obedience, then it is revealed in its full godlessness as complete disobedience in all its insincerity. Only the obedient deed is to be taken seriously. It ends and destroys the conflict and frees us to become children of God. That is the divine diagnosis the young man receives.

The young man is subjected to the truth of God's word twice. He can no longer avoid God's commandment. Yes, the commandment is clear and has to be obeyed. But it is not enough! "I have kept all these from my youth, what do I still lack?" [*Matt. 19:20*]. With this answer the young man will still be just as convinced of the sincerity of his concern as he was previously. That is precisely what makes him defiant against Jesus. He knows the commandment; he has kept it, but he thinks that it could not be the whole will of God. Something else has to be added, something extraordinary, unique. He desires to do that. God's revealed commandment is incomplete, the young man says in his final flight away from the true commandment, in his last attempt to retain his autonomy and to decide good and evil on his own. He affirms the commandment, and launches a frontal attack against it at the same time. "I have kept all these, what do I still lack?" Mark adds at this point: "Jesus, looking at him, loved him" (Mark 10:21). Jesus recognizes how hopelessly the young man has closed himself off from God's living word, how his whole being is raging against the living commandment, against simple obedience. He wants to help the young man; he loved him. That is why he gave him one final answer: "If you wish to be perfect, go, sell your possessions, and give the money to the poor, and you will have treasure in heaven; then come, follow me!" [*Matt. 19:21*].

73   Three points should be noted in these words to the young man: *First,* it is now Jesus himself who is commanding. Jesus had just referred the young man away from the good master to God who alone is good. Now Jesus claims authority to say to him the last word and commandment. The young man has to recognize that the Son of God himself is standing before him. Jesus' reality as the Son of God was hidden from the young man when Jesus pointed away from himself toward the Father. Yet this pointing away from himself united him completely with his Father. It is this unity which now enables Jesus to speak his Father's commandment. That must have become unmistakably clear to the young man when he heard Jesus' call to follow

him. This call is the sum of all commandments the young man is called to live in community with Christ. Christ is the fulfillment of the commandments. This is the Christ who is standing before him and calling him. He cannot flee any longer into the untruth of ethical conflict. The commandment is clear: follow me.

The *second* point is this: Even this call to discipleship needs clarification so it will not be misunderstood. Jesus has to make it impossible for the young man to misunderstand following him as an ethical adventure, an unusual, interesting, but potentially revocable path and lifestyle. Discipleship would also be misunderstood if the young man were to view it as a final conclusion of his previous deeds and questions, as a summary of what went before, as a supplement, completion, or perfection of his past. In order to eliminate all ambiguity, a situation has to be created in which the person cannot retreat, in other words, an irrevocable situation. At the same time it must be clear that it is not just a complement to life before the call. Jesus' challenging the young man to voluntary poverty creates the situation that is called for. This is the existential, pastoral side of the matter. It is intended to help the young man finally to understand and to obey in the right way. It arises from Jesus' love for the young man. It is only the intermediate link between the young man's previous life and discipleship. But notice that it is not identical with discipleship itself. It is not even the first step of discipleship. Rather, it is the obedience within which discipleship can then become real. *First* the young man must go and sell everything and give to the poor, and *then* come and follow Jesus. The goal is following Jesus, and the way in this case is voluntary poverty.

The *third* point is that Jesus accepts the young man's question about what he is still lacking: "If you want to be perfect . . ." That really could give the impression that Jesus is talking about adding something on to the young man's previous life. It really is an addition, but one whose content abolishes everything of one's past. The young man has not been perfect so far, for he has wrongly understood and obeyed the commandment. Now he can rightly understand and obey in discipleship, but even then only because Jesus Christ has called him to it. By accepting the young man's question, Jesus has wrested it from him. The young man asked about his path to eternal life. Jesus answered: I am calling you, that is all.

The young man seeks an answer to his question. The answer is: Jesus Christ. The young man wanted to hear the word of a good master, but now he has to recognize that this Word is actually the man himself whom he is questioning. The young man is standing before Jesus, the Son of God. The full encounter is present. The only choices are yes or no, obedience or disobedience. The young man's answer is no. He went away sadly; he was

74

disappointed and had lost his hope, but he still could not abandon his past. He had a lot of property. The call to discipleship here has no other content than Jesus Christ himself, being bound to him, community with him. But the existence of a disciple does not consist in enthusiastic respect for a good master. Instead, it is obedience toward the Son of God.

This story of the rich young man has a direct correspondence with the story framing the parable of the Good Samaritan. "Just then a scribe stood up to test Jesus. 'Teacher,' he said, 'what must I do to inherit eternal life?' He said to him, 'What is written in the law? What do you read there?' He answered, 'You shall love the Lord your God with all your heart, and with all your soul, and with all your strength, and with all your mind; and your neighbor as yourself.' And he said to him, 'You have given the right answer; do this, and you will live.' But wanting to justify himself, he asked Jesus, 'And who is my neighbor?'" (Luke 10:25–29).

75

The scribe's question is the same as the young man's. Only here it is clear from the outset that the question is intended as a temptation. The tempter's solution is already set. It is intended to dead-end in the aporia [*perplexity*] of ethical conflict. Jesus' answer fully resembles his answer to the young man. The questioner basically knows the answer to his question. But by asking it, even though he already knows the answer, he is shirking obedience to God's commandment. The only thing left for him is the advice: do what you know; then you will live.

This takes his first position away from him. There follows, again like the young man's, the scribe's flight into ethical conflict: "Who is my neighbor?" Since then, this question of the tempting scribe has been asked countless times in good faith and ignorance. It has the good reputation of being a serious and reasonable question from an inquiring person. But people doing so have not carefully read the context. The whole story of the Good Samaritan is Jesus' singular rejection and destruction of this question as satanic. It is a question without end, without answer. It springs from "those who are depraved in mind and bereft of the truth," who are "conceited, understanding nothing, and have a morbid craving for controversy and for disputes about words." From them flow "envy, dissension, slander, base suspicions, and wrangling" (1 Tim. 6:4f.). It is a question from the pompous, "who are always being instructed and can never arrive at a knowledge of the truth," who are "holding to the outward form of godliness but denying its power" (2 Tim. 3:5ff.).[23] They are unqualified to have faith. They ask ques-

---

23. ["... On the Timothy passages in *Discipleship*, see 'The Servant in the House of God,' in the Bible study on the Letters to Timothy, October 20, 1936 (*DBWE* 14:939–953)," *DBWE* 4:75, n. 38.]

tions like this because their "consciences are seared with a hot iron" (1 Tim. 4:2), because they do not want to obey God's word. Who is my neighbor? Is there an answer to this, whether it is my biological brother, my compatriot, my brother in the church, or my enemy? Could we not assert or deny the one just as rightly as any other? Is the end of this question not division and disobedience? Yes, this question is rebellion against God's commandment itself. I want to be obedient, but God will not tell me how I can be so. God's commandment is ambiguous; it leaves me in perpetual conflict. The question What should I do? was the first betrayal. The answer is: do the com- 76 mandment that you know. You should not ask; you should act. The question Who is my neighbor? is the final question of despair or hubris, in which disobedience justifies itself. The answer is: You yourself are the neighbor. Go and be obedient in acts of love. Being a neighbor is not a qualification of someone else; it is their claim on me, nothing else. At every moment, in every situation I am the one required to act, to be obedient. There is literally no time left to ask about someone else's qualification. I must act and must obey; I must be a neighbor to the other person. If you anxiously ask again whether or not I should know and consider ahead of time how to act, there is only the advice that I cannot know or think about it except by already acting, by already knowing myself to be challenged to act. I can only learn what obedience is by obeying, not by asking questions. I can recognize truth only by obeying. Jesus' call to the simplicity of obedience pulls us out of the dichotomy of conscience and sin. The rich young man was called by Jesus into the grace of discipleship, but the tempting scribe is shoved back to the commandment.

CHAPTER THREE   77

SIMPLE OBEDIENCE

When Jesus demanded voluntary poverty of the rich young man, the young man knew that his only choices were obedience or disobedience. When Levi was called from tax collecting and Peter from his nets, there was no doubt that Jesus was serious about those calls. They were supposed to leave everything and follow him. When Peter was called to step out onto the stormy sea, he had to get up and risk taking the step. Only one thing was demanded in each of these cases. That was their entrusting themselves to the word of Jesus Christ, believing it to be a stronger foundation than all the securities of the world. The forces that wanted to get between the word of Jesus and obedience were just as great back then as they are today. Reason objected; Conscience, responsibility, piety, even the law and the principle of Scripture

intervened to inhibit this most extreme, this lawless "enthusiasm."[24] Jesus'
call broke through all of this and mandated obedience. It was God's own
word. Simple obedience was required.

78   If Jesus Christ were to speak this way to one of us today through the
Holy Scripture, then we would probably argue thus: Jesus is making a specific commandment; that's true. But when Jesus commands, then I should
know that he never demands legalistic obedience. Instead, he has only one
expectation of me, namely, that I believe. My faith, however, is not tied to
poverty or wealth or some such thing. On the contrary, in faith I can be
both—rich and poor. The main concern is not whether or not I have any
worldly goods, but that I should possess goods as if I did not possess them,
and inwardly I should be free of them. I should not set my heart on my
possessions. Thus, Jesus says, "Sell your possessions!" But what he intends
is that it is not important if you actually do this literally, outwardly. You are
free to keep your possessions, but have them as if you did not have them. Do
not set your heart on your possessions. Our obedience to Jesus' word would
then consist in our rejecting simple obedience as legalistic obedience, in
order to be obedient "in faith." This is the difference between us and the
rich young man. In his sadness, he is not able to calm himself by saying to
himself, "In spite of Jesus' word, I want to remain rich, but I will become
inwardly free from my riches and comfort my inadequacy with the forgiveness of sins and be in communion with Jesus by faith." Instead, he went
away sadly and, in rejecting obedience, lost his chance to have faith. The
young man was sincere in going away. He parted from Jesus, and this sincerity surely had more promise than a false communion with Jesus based on
disobedience. Apparently Jesus thought that the young man was unable to
free himself inwardly from his wealth. Probably the young man, as a serious
and ambitious person, had tried to do it himself a thousand times. The fact
that at the decisive moment he was unable to obey the word of Jesus shows
that he failed. The young man was sincere in parting from Jesus. By the way
we argue, we distance ourselves fundamentally from a biblical hearer of
Jesus' word. If Jesus said: leave everything else behind and follow me, leave

79   your profession, your family, your people, and your father's house, then the
biblical hearer knew that the only answer to this call is simple obedience,
because the promise of community with Jesus is given to this obedience.

---

24. ["Here Bonhoeffer objects to the way that simple obedience was labeled a 'heresy'
against the Reformation, an accusation that some Lutherans liked to make; for example,
see Althaus, *Der Geist der lutherischen Ethik im Augsburgischen Bekenntnis*, 45: 'Even among
us today, what the reformers called enthusiasm is a powerful element' in the form of
'Christian-pacifist and other irrational opinions,'" DBWE 4:77, n. 2." *DBWE* 4:77, n. 2.]

But we would say: Jesus' call is to be taken "absolutely seriously," but true obedience to it consists of my staying in my profession and in my family and serving him there, in true inner freedom. Thus, Jesus would call: come out!—but we would understand that he actually meant: stay in!—of course, as one who has inwardly come out. Or Jesus would say, do not worry; but we would understand: of course we should worry and work for our families and ourselves. Anything else would be irresponsible. But inwardly we should be free of such worry. Jesus would say: if anyone strikes you on the right cheek, turn the other also. But we would understand: it is precisely in fighting, in striking back, that genuine fraternal love grows large. Jesus would say: strive first for the kingdom of God. We would understand: of course, we should first strive for all sorts of other things. How else should we survive? What he really meant was that final inner willingness to invest everything for the kingdom of God. Everywhere it is the same—the deliberate avoidance of simple, literal obedience.

How is such a reversal possible? What has happened that the word of Jesus has to endure this game? That it is so vulnerable to the scorn of the world? Anywhere else in the world where commands are given, the situation is clear. A father says to his child: go to bed! The child knows exactly what to do. But a child drilled in pseudotheology would have to argue thus: Father says go to bed. He means you are tired; he does not want me to be tired. But I can also overcome my tiredness by going to play. So, although father says go to bed, what he really means is go play. With this kind of argumentation, a child with its father or a citizen with the authorities would run into an unmistakable response, namely, punishment. The situation is supposed to be different only with respect to Jesus' command. In that case simple obedience is supposed to be wrong, or even to constitute disobedience. How is this possible? 80

It is possible, because there is actually something quite right at the basis of this wrong argumentation. Jesus' command to the rich young man or his call into a situation that enables faith really has only the one goal of calling a person to faith in him, calling into his community. Nothing finally depends on any human deed at all; instead, everything depends on faith in Jesus as the Son of God and the mediator. Nothing finally depends on poverty or riches, marriage or the single state, having or leaving a profession. Rather, everything depends on faith. To this extent, we really are right that it is possible to believe in Christ while we have wealth and possess the goods of this world, so that we have them as if we did not have them. But this is a last possible form of Christian existence, a possibility of living in the world, only in light of the serious expectation that Christ would return in the immediate future. It is not the first and simplest possibility. A paradoxical understanding of the commandments has a Christian right to it, but it must never lead to the annulment of a simple understanding of the commandments. Rather, it is justified and possible only for those who have already taken simple obedience seriously at some point in their lives, and so already stand in community with Jesus, in discipleship, in expectation of the end. Understanding Jesus' call paradoxically is the infinitely more difficult possibility. In human terms it is an impossible possibility, and because it is, it is always in extreme danger of being turned over into its opposite and made into a comfortable excuse for fleeing from concrete obedience. Anyone who does not know that it would be the infinitely easier way to understand Jesus' commandment simply and obey it literally—for example, to actually give away one's possessions at Jesus' command instead of keeping them—has no right to a paradoxical understanding of Jesus' word. It is therefore necessary always to include a literal understanding of Jesus' commandment in every paradoxical interpretation.

Jesus' concrete call and simple obedience have their own irrevocable meaning. Jesus calls us into a concrete situation in which we can believe in him. That is why he calls in such a concrete way and wants to be so understood, because he knows that people will become free for faith only in concrete obedience.

Wherever simple obedience is fundamentally eliminated, there again the costly grace of Jesus' call has become the cheap grace of self-justification. But this too constructs a false law, which deafens people to the concrete call of Christ. This false law is the law of the world, matched by an opposing law of grace. The world here is not that world which has been won over by Christ and is daily to be won over anew in his community. Rather, it is the world which has become a rigid, inescapable law of principles. But in that case grace is also no longer the gift of the living God, rescuing us from the world for obedience to Christ. Rather, it becomes a general divine law, a divine principle, whose only use is its application to special cases. The principle of struggle against the "legalism" of simple obedience itself erects the most dangerous law of all, the law of the world and the law of grace. The struggle based on principle against legalism is itself the most legalistic attitude. It is overcome only by genuine obedience to Jesus' gracious call to follow him. The law is fulfilled and done away with by Jesus himself for those who follow.

Fundamentally eliminating simple obedience introduces a principle of scripture foreign to the Gospel. According to it, in order to understand scripture, one first must have a key to interpreting it. But that key would not be the living Christ himself in judgment and grace, and using the key would not be according to the will of the living Holy Spirit alone. Rather, the key to scripture would be a general doctrine of grace, and we ourselves would decide its use. The problem of following Christ shows itself here to be a hermeneutical problem. But it should be clear to a Gospel-oriented hermeneutic that we cannot simply identify ourselves directly with those called by Jesus. Instead, those who are called in scripture themselves belong to the word of God and thus to the proclamation of the word. In preaching we hear not only Jesus' answer to a disciple's question, which could also be our own question. Rather, question and answer together must be proclaimed as the word of scripture. Simple obedience would be misunderstood hermeneutically if we were to act and follow as if we were contemporaries of the biblical disciples. But the Christ proclaimed to us in scripture is, through every word he says, the one whose gift of faith is granted only to the obedient, faith to the obedient alone. We cannot and may not go behind the word of scripture to the actual events. Instead, we are called to follow Christ by the entire word of scripture, simply because we do not intend to wish to violate scripture by legalistically applying a principle to it, even that of a doctrine of faith.

This shows that a paradoxical understanding of Jesus' commandments must include a simple understanding, precisely because we do not intend to set up a law, but to proclaim Christ. That nearly takes care of the suspicion that simple obedience might mean some sort of meritorious human achievement, a facere quod in se est [*to do what is in oneself*], and a precondition one would have to fulfill for faith. Obedience to Jesus' call is never an autonomous human deed. Thus, not even something like actually giving away one's wealth is the obedience required. It could be that such a step would not be obedience to Jesus at all, but instead, a free choice of one's own lifestyle. It could be a Christian ideal, a Franciscan ideal of poverty. It could be that by giving away wealth, people affirm themselves and an ideal, and not Jesus' command. It could be that they do not become free from themselves, but even more trapped in themselves. The step into the situation is not something people offer Jesus; it is always Jesus' gracious offer to people. It is legitimate only when it is done that way, but then it is no longer a free human possibility.

"Then Jesus said to his disciples, 'Truly I tell you, it will be hard for a rich person to enter the kingdom of heaven. Again I tell you, it is easier for a camel to go through the eye of a needle than for someone who is rich to enter the kingdom of God.' When the disciples heard this, they were greatly astounded and said, 'Then who can be saved?' But Jesus looked at them and said, 'For mortals it is impossible, for God all things are possible'" (Matt. 19:23–26). It can be inferred from the perplexity of the disciples about Jesus' word and from their question—"Who, then, can be saved?"—that they believe that the case of the rich young man is not an individual case, but the most general case possible. They do not ask, "Which rich person?" Instead, they ask the general question, "Who, then, can be saved?" This is because everyone, even the disciples, forms part of those rich people, for whom it is so difficult to enter heaven. Jesus' answer confirms this interpretation of his words by his disciples. Being saved by discipleship is not a human possibility, but for God all things are possible.

**

100

CHAPTER SIX

THE SERMON ON THE MOUNT

Matthew 5: On the "Extraordinary" of Christian Life

The Beatitudes [Matt. 5:3-11]

Jesus on the mountain, the crowd, the disciples. *The crowd sees*: There is Jesus with his disciples, who have joined him. The disciples—not so long before, they themselves were fully part of the crowd. They were just like all the others. Then Jesus' call came. So they left everything behind and followed him. Since then they have belonged to Jesus—completely. Now they go with him, live with him, follow him wherever he leads them. Something has happened to them which has not happened to the others. This is an extremely unsettling and offensive fact, which is visibly evident to the crowd. *The disciples see*: this is the people from whom they have come, the lost sheep of the house of Israel. It is the chosen community of God. It is the people as church. When the disciples were called by Jesus from out of the people, they did the most obvious and natural thing lost sheep of the house of Israel could do: they followed the voice of the good shepherd, because they knew his voice. They belong to this people, indeed, especially because of the path on which they were led. They will live among this people, they will go into it and preach

101	Jesus' call and the splendor of discipleship. But how will it all end? *Jesus sees*: his disciples are over there. They have visibly left the people to join him. He has called each individual one. They have given up everything in response to his call. Now they are living in renunciation and want; they are the poorest of the poor, the most tempted of the tempted, the hungriest of the hungry. They have only him. Yes, and with him they have nothing in the world, nothing at all, but everything, everything with God. So far, he has found only a small community, but it is a great community he is looking for, when he looks at the people. Disciples and the people belong together. The disciples will be his messengers; they will find listeners and believers here and there. Nevertheless, there will be enmity between the disciples and the people until the end. Everyone's rage at God and God's word will fall on his disciples, and they will be rejected with him. The cross comes into view. Christ, the disciples, the people—one can already see the whole history of the suffering of Jesus and his community.

Therefore, "Blessed!" Jesus is speaking to the disciples (cf. Luke 6:20ff.). He is speaking to those who are already under the power of his call. That call has made them poor, tempted, and hungry. He calls them blessed, not because of their want or renunciation. Neither want nor renunciation are in themselves any reason to be called blessed. The only adequate reason is the call and the promise, for whose sake those following him live in want and renunciation. The observation that some of the Beatitudes speak of want and others of the disciples' intentional renunciation or special virtues has no special meaning. Objective want and personal renunciation have   102 their joint basis in Christ's call and promise. Neither of them has any value or claim in itself.

Jesus calls his disciples blessed. The people hear it and are dismayed at witnessing what happens. That which belongs to the whole people of Israel, according to God's promise, is now being awarded to the small community of disciples chosen by Jesus: "Theirs is the kingdom of heaven." But the disciples and the people are one in that they are all the community called by God. Jesus' blessing should lead to decisions and salvation for *all* of them. All are called to be what they truly are. The disciples are blessed because of Jesus' call that they followed. The entire people of God is blessed because of the promise which pertains to them. But will God's people, in faith in Jesus Christ and his word, now in fact seize the promise or will they, in unfaith, depart from Christ and his community? That remains the issue.

"Blessed are the poor in spirit, for theirs is the kingdom of heaven." The disciples are needy in every way. They are simply "poor" (Luke 6:20). They have no security, no property to call their own, no piece of earth they could call their home, no earthly community to which they might fully belong.   103 But they also have neither spiritual power of their own, nor experience or knowledge they can refer to and which could comfort them. For his sake they have lost all that. When they followed him, they lost themselves and everything else which could have made them rich. Now they are so poor, so inexperienced, so foolish that they cannot hope for anything except him who called them. Jesus also knows those others, the representatives and preachers of the national religion, those powerful, respected people, who stand firmly on the earth inseparably rooted in the national way of life, the spirit of the times, the popular piety. But Jesus does not speak to them; he speaks only to his disciples when he says, blessed—for theirs is the kingdom of heaven. The kingdom of heaven will come to those who live thoroughly in *renunciation and want* for Jesus' sake. In the depths of their poverty, they inherit the kingdom of heaven. They have their treasure well hidden, they have it at the cross. The kingdom of heaven is promised them in visible majesty, and it is already given them in the complete poverty of the cross.

Here Jesus' blessing is totally different from its caricature in the form of a political-social program. The Antichrist also declares the poor to be blessed, but he does it not for the sake of the cross, in which all poverty is embraced and blessed. Rather, he does it with political-social ideology precisely in order to fend off the cross. He may call this ideology Christian, but in doing so he becomes Christ's enemy.

"Blessed are those who mourn, for they will be comforted." Every additional Beatitude deepens the breach between the disciples and the people. The disciples' call becomes more and more visible. Those who mourn are those who are prepared to renounce and live without everything the world calls *happiness and peace*. They are those who cannot be brought into accord with the world, who cannot conform to the world. They mourn over the world, its guilt, its fate, and its happiness. The world celebrates, and they stand apart. The world shrieks "Enjoy life," and they grieve. They see that the ship, on which there are festive cheers and celebrating, is already leaking. While the world imagines progress, strength, and a grand future, the disciples know about the end, judgment, and the arrival of the kingdom of heaven, for which the world is not at all ready. That is why the disciples are rejected as strangers in the world, bothersome guests, disturbers of the peace. Why must Jesus' community of faith stay closed out from so many celebrations of the people among whom they live? Does the community of faith perhaps no longer understand its fellow human beings? Has it perhaps succumbed to hating and despising people? No one understands people better than Jesus' community. No one loves people more than Jesus' disciples—that is why they stand apart, why they mourn. It is meaningful and lovely that Luther translates the Greek word for what is blessed with "to bear suffering." The important part is the bearing. The community of disciples does not shake off suffering, as if they had nothing to do with it. Instead, they bear it. In doing so, they give witness to their connection with the people around them. At the same time, this indicates that they do not arbitrarily seek suffering, that they do not withdraw into willful contempt for the world. Instead, they bear what is laid upon them, and what happens to them in discipleship for the sake of Jesus Christ. Finally, disciples will not be weakened by suffering, worn down, and embittered, until they are broken. Instead, they bear suffering by the power of him who supports them.

104

The disciples bear the suffering laid on them only by the power of him who
bears all suffering on the cross. As bearers of suffering, they stand in communion with the Crucified. They stand as strangers in the power of him
who was so alien to the world that it crucified him. This is their comfort,
or rather, he is their comfort, their comforter (cf. Luke 2:25). This alien 105
community is comforted by the cross. It is comforted in that it is thrust out
to the place where the comforter of Israel is waiting. Thus it finds its true
home with the crucified Lord, here and in eternity.

"Blessed are the meek, for they will inherit the earth." No rights they
might claim protect this community of strangers in the world. Nor do they
claim any such rights, for they are the meek, who *renounce all rights of their
own* for the sake of Jesus Christ. When they are berated, they are quiet.
When violence is done to them, they endure it. When they are cast out,
they yield. They do not sue for their rights; they do not make a scene when
injustice is done them. They do not want rights of their own. They want to
leave all justice to God; non cupidi vindictae [*not desirous of vengeance*] is
the interpretation of the early church. What is right for their Lord should
be right for them. Only that. In every word, in every gesture, it is revealed
that they do not belong on this earth. Let them have heaven, the world says
sympathetically, that is where they belong. But Jesus says, they will inherit
the earth. The earth belongs to these who are without rights and power.
Those who now possess the earth with violence and injustice will lose it,
and those who renounced it here, who were meek unto the cross, will rule
over the new earth. We should not think here of God's punishing justice in
this world (Calvin). Rather, when the realm of heaven will descend, then
the form of the earth will be renewed, and it will be the earth of the community of Jesus. God does not abandon the earth. God created it. God sent
God's Son to earth. God built a community on earth. Thus, the beginning
is already made in this world's time. A sign is given. Already here the powerless are given a piece of the earth; they have the church, their community,
their property, their brothers and sisters—in the midst of persecution even 106
unto the cross. But Golgotha, too, is a piece of the earth. From Golgotha,
where the meekest died, the earth will be made new. When the realm of
God comes, then the meek will inherit the earth.

"Blessed are those who hunger and thirst for righteousness, for they
will be filled." Disciples live with not only renouncing their own rights, but
even *renouncing their own righteousness*. They get no credit themselves for
what they do and sacrifice. The only righteousness they can have is in hun-
gering and thirsting for it. They will have neither their own righteousness
nor God's righteousness on earth. At all times they look forward to God's
future righteousness, but they cannot bring it about by themselves. Those

who follow Jesus will be hungry and thirsty along the way. They are filled with longing for forgiveness of all sins and for complete renewal; they long for the renewal of the earth and for God's perfect justice. But the curse upon the world still conceals God's justice, the sin of the world still falls on it. The one they are following must die accursed on the cross. His last cry is his desperate longing for justice; "My God, my God, why have you forsaken me?" [*Matt. 27:46; Ps. 22:1*]. But a disciple is not above the master. They follow him. They are blessed in doing so, for they have been promised that they will be filled. They shall receive righteousness, not only by hearing, but righteousness will physically feed their bodies' hunger. They will eat the bread of true life at the future heavenly Supper with their Lord. They are blessed because of this future bread, since they already have it in the present. He who is the bread of life is among them even in all their hunger. This is the blessedness of sinners.

"Blessed are the merciful, for they will receive mercy." These people without possessions, these strangers, these powerless, these sinners, these followers of Jesus live with him now also in the *renunciation of their own dignity*, for they are merciful. As if their own need and lack were not enough, they share in other people's need, debasement, and guilt. They have an irresistible love for the lowly, the sick, for those who are in misery, for those who are demeaned and abused, for those who suffer injustice and are rejected, for everyone in pain and anxiety. They seek out all those who have fallen into sin and guilt. No need is too great, no sin is too dreadful for mercy to reach. The merciful give their own honor to those who have fallen into shame and take that shame unto themselves. They may be found in the company of tax collectors and sinners and willingly bear the shame of their fellowship. Disciples give away anyone's greatest possession, their own dignity and honor, and show mercy. They know only *one* dignity and honor, the mercy of their Lord, which is their only source of life. He was not ashamed of his disciples. He became a brother to the people; he bore their shame all the way to death on the cross. This is the mercy of Jesus, from which those who follow him wish to live, the mercy of the crucified one. This mercy lets them all forget their own honor and dignity and seek only the company of sinners. If shame now falls on them, they still are blessed. For they shall receive mercy. Some day God will bend down low to them and take on their sin and shame. God will give them God's own honor and take away their dishonor. It will be God's honor to bear the shame of the sinners and to clothe them with God's honor. Blessed are the merciful, for they have the merciful one as their Lord.

"Blessed are the pure in heart, for they will see God." Who is pure in heart? Only those who have completely given their hearts to Jesus, so that he alone rules in them. Only those who do not stain their hearts with their own evil, but also not with their own good. A pure heart is the simple heart of a child, who does not know about good and evil, the heart of Adam before the fall, the heart in which the will of Jesus rules instead of one's own conscience. Those who *renounce their own good and evil*, their own heart, who are contrite and depend solely on Jesus, have purity of heart through the word of Jesus. Purity of heart here stands in contrast to all external purity, which includes even purity of a well-meaning state of mind. A pure heart is pure of good and evil; it belongs entirely and undivided to Christ; it looks only to him, who goes on ahead. Those alone will see God who in this life   108 have looked only to Jesus Christ, the Son of God. Their hearts are free of defiling images; they are not pulled back and forth by the various wishes and intentions of their own. Their hearts are fully absorbed in seeing God. They will see God whose hearts mirror the image of Jesus Christ.

"Blessed are the peacemakers, for they will be called children of God." Jesus' followers are called to peace. When Jesus called them, they found their peace. Jesus is their peace. Now they are not only to have peace, but they are to make peace. To do this they *renounce violence and strife*. Those things never help the cause of Christ. Christ's kingdom is a realm of peace, and those in Christ's community greet each other with a greeting of peace. Jesus' disciples maintain peace by choosing to suffer instead of causing others to suffer. They preserve community when others destroy it. They renounce self-assertion and are silent in the face of hatred and injustice. That is how they overcome evil with good. That is how they are makers of divine peace in a world of hatred and war. But their peace will never be greater than when they encounter evil people in peace and are willing to suffer from them. Peacemakers will bear the cross with their Lord, for peace was made at the cross. Because they are drawn into Christ's work of peace and called to the work of the Son of God, they themselves will be called children of God.

"Blessed are those who are persecuted for righteousness' sake, for theirs is the kingdom of heaven." This does not refer to God's righteousness, but   109 to suffering for the sake of a righteous cause, suffering because of the righteous judgment and action of Jesus' disciples. In judgment and action those who follow Jesus will be different from the world in renouncing property, happiness, rights, righteousness, honor, and violence. They will be offensive to the world. That is why the disciples will be persecuted for righteousness' sake. Not recognition, but rejection, will be their reward from the world for their word and deed. It is important that Jesus calls his disciples blessed, not only when they directly confess his name, but also when they suffer for a just cause. They are given the same promise as the poor. As those who are persecuted, they are equal to the poor.

Here at the end of the Beatitudes the question arises as to where in this world such a faith-community actually finds a place. It has become clear that there is only one place for them, namely, the place where the poorest, the most tempted, the meekest of all may be found, at the cross on Golgotha. The faith-community of the blessed is the community of the Crucified. With him they lost everything, and with him they found everything. Now the word comes down from the cross: blessed, blessed. Now Jesus is speaking only to those who can understand it, to the disciples. That is why he uses a direct form of address: "Blessed are you when people revile you and persecute you and utter all kinds of evil against you falsely on my account. Rejoice and be glad, for your reward is great in heaven, for in the same way they persecuted the prophets who were before you." "On my account"—the disciples are reviled, but it actually hurts Jesus. Everything falls on him, for they are reviled on his account. He bears the guilt. The reviling word, the deadly persecution, and the evil slander seal the blessedness of the disciples in their communion with Jesus. Things cannot go any other way than that the world unleashes its fury in word, violence, and defamation at those meek strangers. The voice of these poor and meek is too threatening, too loud. Their suffering is too patient and quiet. In their poverty and suffering, this group of Jesus' followers gives too strong a witness to the injustice of the world. That is fatal. While Jesus calls, "blessed, blessed," the world shrieks, "Away, away with them!" Yes, away! But where will they go? Into the kingdom of heaven. Rejoice and be glad, for your reward is great in heaven. The poor will stand there in the joyous assembly. God's hand will wipe away the tears of estrangement from the eyes of the weeping.

110

God feeds the hungry with the Lord's own Supper. Wounded and martyred bodies shall be transformed, and instead of the clothing of sin and penitence, they will wear the white robe of eternal righteousness. From that eternal joy there comes a call to the community of disciples here under the cross, the call of Jesus, "blessed, blessed."

**

137 **The Enemy—the "Extraordinary"**

"You have heard that it was said, 'You shall love your neighbor and hate your enemy.' But I say to you, Love your enemies; bless those who curse you, do good to those who hate you, and pray for those who abuse and persecute you, so that you may be children of your Father in heaven; for he makes his sun rise on the evil and on the good, and sends rain on the righteous and on the unrighteous. For if you love those who love you, what reward do you have? Do not even the tax collectors do the same? And if you greet only your brothers and sisters, what more are you doing than others? Do not even the Gentiles do the same? Be perfect, therefore, as your heavenly Father is perfect" (Matt. 5:43–48).

This is the point in the Sermon on the Mount where we encounter for the first time the word which summarizes everything in it: love. Immediately it is put into the clear-cut context of love for our enemies. Loving one's kindred is a commandment that could be misunderstood. Loving enemies makes unmistakably clear what Jesus intends.

"Enemy" was no empty concept for the disciples. They knew it well. They met enemies daily. There were those who cursed them as destroyers of the faith and lawbreakers; there were those who hated them because they had left everything for Jesus' sake and did not highly value anything but communion with him; there were those who insulted and scorned them for their weakness and humility; there were those who persecuted them, who feared a growing revolutionary danger in the group of disciples and were intent on destroying them. One kind of enemy were the representatives of a people's piety, who could not tolerate Jesus' claim to exclusive and complete loyalty.[25] They were armed with power and respect. Another enemy, which would be apparent to every Jew, was the political enemy in Rome. The Jews experienced powerful oppression from that enemy. In addition to these two inimical groups, there was all the personal enmity which anyone encounters who does not participate in the norms of the majority: daily defamation, humiliation, and threats.

To be sure, nowhere in the Old Testament is there a statement which commands us to hate our enemies. On the contrary, we find the commandment to love our enemies (Exod. 23:4f.; Prov. 25:21f.; Gen. 45:1ff.; 1 Sam. 24:7; 2 Kings 6:22; and elsewhere). But Jesus is speaking here, not of natural enmity, but of the enmity of God's people against the world. Israel's wars were the only "holy" wars the world has ever known. They were God's wars against the world of idols. Jesus does not condemn that enmity, otherwise he would have to condemn God's entire history with God's own people. Instead, Jesus affirms the Old Covenant. His only concern is to overcome enemies, to achieve victory for God's community. But in this command, once again he released his community of disciples from the political form of the people of Israel. As a result, there will be no more wars of faith. God promised that we would gain victory over our enemies precisely by loving them.

138

---

25. ["In the Barmen Theological Declaration of 1934 Christ was confessed as the only Lord in all areas of life—'solus [*alone*] Christus'—a refutation of the German Christians' allegiance to the people and its traditional way of life," *DBWE* 4:138, n. 132.]

Loving one's enemies is not only an unbearable offense to the natural person. It demands more than the strength a natural person can muster, and it offends the natural concept of good and evil. But even more important, loving one's enemies appears to people living according to the law to be a sin against God's law itself. Separation from enemies and condemning them is what the law demands. But Jesus takes God's law into his hands and interprets it. To overcome enemies by loving them—that is God's will which is contained in the law.

In the New Testament, the enemy is always the one who hates me. Jesus does not even consider the possibility that there could be someone whom the disciple hates. Enemies should receive what sisters and brothers receive, namely, love from Jesus' followers. The actions of the disciples should not be determined by the human actions they encounter, but by Jesus acting in them. The only source of the disciples' action is the will of Jesus.

Jesus speaks of enemies, that is, of those who will remain our enemies, unmoved by our love; those who do not forgive us anything when we forgive them everything; those who hate us when we love them; those who insult us all the more, the more we serve them. "In return for my love they accuse me, even while I make prayer for them" (Ps. 109:4). But love must not ask if it is being returned. Instead, it seeks those who need it. But who needs love more than they who live in hate without any love? Who, therefore, is more worthy of my love than my foe? Where is love praised more splendidly than amidst love's enemies?

This love knows no difference among diverse kinds of enemies, except that the more animosity the enemy has, the more my love is required. No matter whether it is a political or religious enemy, they can all expect only undivided love from Jesus' followers. This love recognizes no inner conflict within myself, even between my being a private person and my being an officeholder. In both cases I can be only one who follows Jesus, or I am no follower of Jesus at all. I am asked, how does this love act? Jesus says: bless them, do good to them, pray for them without condition, without regard for who they are.

"Love your enemies." While the previous command spoke only of defenseless suffering from evil, Jesus here goes much further. We should not only bear evil and the evil person passively, not only refuse to answer a blow with a blow, but in sincere love we should be fond of our enemies. Unhypocritically and purely we are to serve and help our enemies in all things. No offering which a lover would bring to a beloved can be too great and too valuable for our enemies. If, because of love for our kindred, we are obliged to offer our goods, our honor, and our life, then in the same way we are obliged to offer them for our enemies. Does this, then, make us participants in the evildoing of our enemies? No, for how should that love which is born not of weakness but of strength, which comes not from fear but from the truth, become guilty of the hatred of another? And to whom must such love be given, if not to those whose hearts are suffocating in hate?

"Bless those who curse you." If our enemies curse us because they cannot bear our presence, then we should lift our hands to bless them: "You, our enemies, be blessed by God; your curse cannot harm us, but may your poverty be filled by the riches of God, by the blessing of God, against whom you rail in vain. We shall willingly bear your curse, if only God's blessing comes over you."

"Do good to those who hate you." Words and thoughts are not enough. Doing good involves all the things of daily life. "If your enemies are hungry, feed them; if they are thirsty, give them something to drink" (Rom. 12:20). In the same way that brothers and sisters stand by each other in times of need, bind up each other's wounds, ease each other's pain, love of the enemy should do good to the enemy. Where in the world is there greater need, where are deeper wounds and pain than those of our enemies? Where is doing good more necessary and more blessed than for our enemies? "It is more blessed to give than to receive" [*Acts 20:35*].

"Pray for those who abuse and persecute you." That is the most extreme. In prayer we go to our enemies, to stand at their side. We are with them, near them, for them before God. Jesus does not promise us that the enemy we love, we bless, to whom we do good, will not abuse and persecute us. They will do so. But even in doing so, they cannot harm and conquer us if we take this last step to them in intercessory prayer. Now we are taking up their neediness and poverty, their being guilty and lost, and interceding for them before God. We are doing for them in vicarious representative action what they cannot do for themselves. Every insult from our enemy will only bind us closer to God and to our enemy. Every persecution can only serve to bring the enemy closer to reconciliation with God, to make love more unconquerable. 141

How does love become unconquerable? By never asking what the enemy is doing to it, and only asking what Jesus has done. Loving one's enemies leads disciples to the way of the cross and into communion with the crucified one. But the more the disciples are certain to have been forced onto this path, the greater the certainty that their love remains unconquered, that love overcomes the hatred of the enemy; for it is not their own love. It is solely the love of Jesus Christ, who went to the cross for his enemies and prayed on the cross for them. Faced with the way of the cross of Jesus Christ, however, the disciples themselves recognize that they were among the enemies of Jesus who have been conquered by his love. This love makes the disciples able to see, so that they can recognize an enemy as a sister or brother and behave toward that person as they would toward a sister or brother. Why? Because they live only from the love of him who behaved toward them as toward brothers and sisters, who accepted them when they were his enemies and brought them into communion with him as his neighbors. That is how love makes disciples able to see, so that they can see the enemies included in God's love, that they can see the enemies under the cross of Jesus Christ. God did not ask me about good and evil, because before God even my good was godless. God's love seeks the enemy who needs it, whom God considers to be worthy of it. In the enemy, God magnifies divine love. Disciples know that. They have participated in that love through Jesus. For God lets the sun shine and the rain fall on the righteous and the unrighteous. It is not only the earth's sun and earthly rain which descend on good and evil, but it is also the "sun of righteousness" [*Mal. 4:2*] Jesus Christ himself, and the rain of God's word, which reveal the grace of his Father in heaven toward sinners. Undivided, perfect love is the act of the Father; it is also the act of the children of their Father in heaven, just as it was the deed of God's only begotten Son.

142

"The prayers of neighborly love and of nonrevenge will be especially important in the struggle fought by God toward which we are moving, and in which to some extent we have already been engaged for years. On one side, hatred is fighting, and on the other, love. Every Christian soul must seriously prepare for this. The time is coming in which everyone who confesses the *living* God will become, *for the sake of that confession*, not only an object of hatred and fury. Indeed, already we are nearly that far along now. The time is coming when Christians, for the sake of their confession, will be excluded from 'human society,' as it is called, hounded from place to place, subjected to physical attack, abused, and under some circumstances even killed. *The time of a widespread persecution of Christians is coming*, and that is actually the real meaning of all the movements and struggles of our time. Those opponents intent upon destroying the Christian church and Christian faith cannot live together with us, because they see in all of our words and all of our actions that their own words and deeds are condemned, even if ours are not directed against them. And they are not wrong in seeing this and feeling that we are indifferent to their condemnation of us. They have to admit that their condemnation is completely powerless and negligible. They sense that we do not relate to them at all, as would be quite all right with them, on the basis of mutual blaming and quarreling. And how are we supposed to fight this fight? The time is approaching when we—no longer as isolated individuals, but *together* as congregations, as the church—shall lift our hands in prayer. The time is coming when we—as crowds of people, even if they are relatively small crowds among the many thousands-times-thousands of people who have fallen away—will loudly confess and praise the crucified and resurrected Lord, and his coming again. And what prayer, what confession, what song of praise is this? It is a prayer *of most intimate love for those who are lost*, who stand around us and glare at us with eyes rolling with hatred, some of whom have already even conspired to kill us. It is a prayer for peace for these distraught and shaken, disturbed and destroyed souls, a prayer for the same love and peace that we ourselves enjoy. It is a prayer which will penetrate deeply into their souls and will tug at their hearts with a much stronger grip than they can manage to tug at our hearts, despite their strongest efforts to hate. Yes, the church which is truly waiting for its Lord, which really grasps the signs of the time of final separation, such a church must fling itself into *this prayer of love*, using all the powers of its soul and the total powers of its holy life" (A. F. C. Vilmar, 1880).[26]

What is undivided love? Love which does not show special favor to those who return our love with their own. In loving those who love us, our kindred, our people, our friends, yes, even our Christian community, we are no different than the Gentiles and the tax collectors. That kind of love is self-evident, regular, natural, but not distinctly Christian. Yes, in this case it really is "the same" thing that non-Christians and Christians do. Loving those who belong to me through blood,[27] history, or friendship is the same for non-Christians and Christians. Jesus does not have a lot to say about that kind of love. People know all by themselves what it is. He does not need to light its flame, to emphasize it or exalt it. Natural circumstances alone force it to be recognized, for non-Christians and for Christians. Jesus does not need to say that people should love their sisters and brothers, their people, their friends. That goes without saying. But by simply acknowledging that and not wasting any further words on it, and, in contrast to all that, commanding only love for enemies, he shows what he means by love and what they are to think about the other sort of love.

How are disciples different from nonbelievers? What does "being Christian" consist of? At this point the word appears toward which the whole fifth

---

26. [*This unusually long quotation, from an 1850 essay on "Hate and Love" by A. F. C. Vilmar, was inserted by Bonhoeffer after he received the galley proofs. Written just after the 1848 revolutions, Vilmar's observations obviously struck Bonhoeffer as pertinent to the situation of the Confessing Church in the Third Reich.*]

27. ["When National Socialist ideology spoke of 'blood,' it was understood to speak of race far more than the common use of 'blood' as a metaphor for relationship," *DBWE* 4:143, n. 152.]

144 chapter is pointed, in which everything already said is summarized: what is Christian is what is *"peculiar,"* περισσόν, the extraordinary, irregular, not self-evident. This is the "better righteousness" which "outdoes" that of the Pharisees, towers over them, that which is more, beyond all else. What is natural is τὸ αὐτὸ (one and the same) for non-Christians and Christians. What is distinctly Christian begins with the περισσόν, and that is what finally places what is natural in the proper light. When this specialness, this extraordinariness, is absent, then what is Christian is absent. What is Christian does not take place in naturally given circumstances, but in stepping beyond them. The περισσόν never dissolves into τὸ αὐτό. It is the great mistake of a false Protestant ethic to assume that loving Christ can be the same as loving one's native country, or friendship or profession, that the better righteousness and justitia civilis [*civil righteousness*] are the same. Jesus does not talk that way. What is Christian depends on the "extraordinary." That is why Christians cannot conform to the world, because their concern is the περισσόν.

What does the περισσόν, the extraordinary, consist of? It is the existence of those blessed in the Beatitudes, the life of the disciples. It is the shining light, the city on the hill. It is the way of self-denial, perfect love, perfect purity, perfect truthfulness, perfect nonviolence. Here is undivided love for one's enemies, loving those who love no one and whom no one loves. It is love for one's religious, political, or personal enemy. In all of this it is the way which found its fulfillment in the cross of Jesus Christ. What is the περισσόν? It is the love of Jesus Christ himself, who goes to the cross in suffering and obedience. It is the cross. What is unique in Christianity is the cross, which allows Christians to step beyond the world in order to receive

145 victory over the world. The passio [*passion, suffering*] in the love of the crucified one—that is the "extraordinary" mark of Christian existence.

The extraordinary is doubtless that which is visible, which magnifies the Father in heaven. It cannot remain hidden. The people have to see it. The community of Jesus' disciples, the community of better righteousness, is the visible community, that took the step beyond the orders of the world. It has left everything behind to gain the cross of Christ.

What are you *doing* that is special? The extraordinary—and that is what is most offensive—is a *deed* the disciples do. It has to be done—like the better righteousness—and done visibly! Not in ethical rigor, not in the eccentricity of Christian ways of life, but in the simplicity of Christian obedience to the will of Jesus. This deed will prove to be what is "special" by leading Christians to the passio of Christ. Such action itself is continuous suffering. In this action Christ is his disciples' passio. If it is not that, then *this* is not the deed which Jesus intends.

The περισσόν is, thus, the fulfillment of the law, the keeping of the commandments. In Christ the Crucified and his community, the "extraordinary" occurs.

Here are those who are perfect, perfect in undivided love, just as their Father in heaven is. It was the undivided, perfect love of the Father which gave the divine Son up to die on the cross for us. Likewise, the passio of the communion with this cross is the perfection of the followers of Jesus. The perfect are none other than those who, in the Beatitudes, are called blessed.

Matthew 6: On the Hidden Nature of the Christian Life   146

**

The Simplicity of a Carefree Life   161

"Do not store up for yourselves treasures on earth, where moth and rust consume and where thieves break in and steal; but store up for yourselves treasures in heaven, where neither moth nor rust consumes and where thieves do not break in and steal. For where your treasure is, there your heart will be also. The eye is the lamp of the body. So, if your eye is healthy, your whole body will be full of light; but if your eye is unhealthy, your whole body will be full of darkness. If then the light in you is darkness, how great is the darkness! No one can serve two masters; for a slave will either hate the one and love the other, or be devoted to the one and despise the other. You cannot serve God and wealth" (Matt. 6:19–24).

The life of those who follow proves to be on the right course when nothing comes between them and Christ, not the law, not their own piety, and not the world. The disciples always see only Christ. They do not see Christ *and* the law, Christ *and* piety, Christ *and* the world. They do not even begin to reflect that; they just follow Christ in everything. So their vision is simple. Its sole focus is on the light which comes from Christ. There is no darkness or ambiguity in their eyes. Just as the eye must remain simple, clear, and pure, so that the body may remain in the light, just as the foot and the hand have no other source of light except the eye, just as the foot stumbles and the hand gropes when the eye is clouded, just as the whole body is in darkness when the eye is blinded, so disciples are in the light only as long as they look simply to Christ and not to this or that. The disciples' hearts must simply be focused on Christ alone. If the eye sees something other than what is real, then the whole body is deceived. If the heart clings to the appearances of the world, to the creatures instead of the creator, then the disciple is lost.

162 It is the goods of the world which try to turn away the hearts of Jesus' disciples. What is it that attracts the heart of a disciple? That is the question. Is it attracted by the goods of the world, or even by Christ *and* the goods of the world? Or does it stand by Christ alone? The light for the body is the eye, and the light for a disciple is the heart. If the eye is dimmed, how dark the whole body must be. If the heart is darkened, how dark it must be in the disciple. The heart becomes dark when it clings to the goods of the world. Then Jesus' call, be it as urgent as can be, nevertheless bounces off; it finds no entry in the person, because the heart is closed. It belongs to another. Just as no light can enter the body if the eye is evil, so the word of Jesus cannot enter the disciple if the heart is shut. The word is choked off, just as the seed among thorns is choked by the "cares, riches, and pleasures of this life" (Luke 8:14).

The simplicity of the eye and the heart is like the hiddenness in which nothing except Christ's word and call is known and complete communion with Christ is all there is. How should disciples deal simply with the goods of the earth?

Jesus does not forbid them to use the goods. Jesus was human. He ate and drank just as his disciples did. In doing so, he purified the use of the goods of the earth. Disciples should gratefully use the goods required for their bodies' daily need and nutrition—goods which are consumed in sustaining life. "We're wandering Pilgrims day by endless days, / ill-clothed and poor yet freed in fearless ways. / We need not gather, hoard, nor trade, / lest our paths to God overburdened fade. / Who so craves with greed's lethal eyes, / cannot along life's journey with us have ties. / Few goods at hand, we live at peace, / with God our lot our needs decrease." Goods are given to us to be used, but not to be stored away. Just as Israel in the desert received manna daily from God and did not have to worry about food and drink, and just as the manna which was stored from one day for another rotted, so should Jesus' disciples receive their share daily from God. But if they store it up as lasting treasure, they will spoil both the gift and themselves. The heart clings to collected treasure. Stored-up possessions get between

163 me and God. Where my treasure is, there is my trust, my security, my comfort, my God. Treasure means idolatry.

But where is the boundary between the goods I am supposed to use and the treasure I am not supposed to have? If we turn the statement around and say, What your heart clings to is your treasure, then we have the answer. It can be a very modest treasure; it is not a question of size. Everything depends on the heart, on you. If I continue to ask how can I recognize what my heart clings to, again there is a clear and simple answer: everything which keeps you from loving God above all things, everything which gets between you and your obedience to Jesus is the treasure to which your heart clings.

Because the human heart needs a treasure to cling to, it is Jesus' will that it should have a treasure, but not on earth where it decays. Instead, the treasure is in heaven, where it is preserved. The "treasures" in heaven of which Jesus is speaking are apparently not the One Treasure, Jesus himself, but treasures really collected by his followers. A great promise is expressed in this, that disciples will acquire heavenly treasures by following Jesus, treasures which will not decay, which wait for them, with which they shall be united. What other treasures could they be except that extraordinariness, that hiddenness of life as a disciple? What treasures could they be except the fruits of Christ's suffering, which the life of a disciple will bear?

If disciples have completely entrusted their hearts to God, then it is clear to them that they *cannot* serve two masters. They simply cannot. It is impossible in discipleship. It would be tempting to demonstrate one's Christian cleverness and experience by showing that one did know how to serve both masters, mammon [*wealth*] and God, by giving each their limited due. Why shouldn't we, who are God's children, also be joyous children of this world, 164 who enjoy God's good gifts and receive their treasures as God's blessings? God and world, God and earthly goods are against each other, because the world and its goods reach for our hearts. Only when they have won our hearts are they really what they are. Without our hearts, earthly goods and the world mean nothing. They live off our hearts. In that way they are against God. We can give our hearts in complete love only to one object, we can cling only to one master. Whatever opposes this love falls into hatred. According to Jesus' word, there can be only love or hate toward God. If we do not love God, then we hate God. There is no in-between. That is the way God is, and that is what makes God be God, that we can only love or hate God. Only one or the other option is possible. Either you love God or you love the goods of the world. If you love the world, you hate God; if you love God, you hate the world. It does not matter at all whether you intend to do it or whether you know what you are doing. Of course, you will not intend to do so, and you will probably not know what you are doing. It is much more likely that you do not *intend* what you do; you just *intend* to serve both masters. You intend to love God and goods, so you will always view it as an untruth that you hate God. You love God, you think. But by loving God and also the goods of the world, our love for God is actually hate; our eye no longer views things simply, and our heart is no longer in communion with Jesus. Whether it is your intention or not, it cannot be otherwise. You cannot serve two masters, you who are following Jesus.

"Therefore I tell you, do not worry about your life, what you will eat or what you will drink, or about your body, what you will wear. Is not life more than food, and the body more than clothing? Look at the birds of the air; they neither sow nor reap nor gather into barns, and yet your heavenly Father feeds them. Are you not of more value than they? And can any of you by worrying add a single hour to your span of life? And why do you worry about clothing? Consider the lilies of the field, how they grow; they neither toil nor spin, yet I tell you, even Solomon in all his glory was not clothed like one of these. But if God so clothes the grass of the field, which is alive today and tomorrow is thrown into the oven, will he not much more clothe you—you of little faith? Therefore do not worry, saying, 'What will we eat?' or 'What will we drink?' or 'What will we wear?' For it is the Gentiles who strive for all these things; and indeed your heavenly Father knows that you need all these things. But strive first for the kingdom of God and righteousness, and all these things will be given to you as well. So do not worry about tomorrow, for tomorrow will bring worries of its own. Today's trouble is enough for today" (Matt. 6:25–34).

165

Do not worry! Earthly goods deceive the human heart into believing that they give it security and freedom from worry. But in truth, they are what cause anxiety. The heart which clings to goods receives with them the choking burden of worry. Worry collects treasures, and treasures produce more worries. We desire to secure our lives with earthly goods; we want our worrying to make us worry-free, but the truth is the opposite. The chains which bind us to earthly goods, the clutches which hold the goods tight, are themselves worries.

Abuse of earthly goods consists of using them as a security for the next day. Worry is always directed toward tomorrow. But the goods are intended only for today in the strictest sense. It is our securing things for tomorrow which makes us so insecure today. It is enough that each day should have its own troubles. Only those who put tomorrow completely into God's hand and receive fully today what they need for their lives are really secure. Receiving daily liberates me from tomorrow. The thought of tomorrow gives me endless worries. "Do not worry about tomorrow"—that is either cruel ridicule of the poor and suffering, whom Jesus is addressing, of all those who—in human perspective—will starve tomorrow if they do not worry today; it is either an intolerable law that people will reject and detest *or* it is the unique gospel proclamation of the freedom of God's children, who have a Father in heaven, who has given them the gift of his dear Son. Will he not with him also give us everything else?

"Do not worry about tomorrow"—we should not understand that to be human wisdom or a law. The only way to understand it is as the gospel of

Jesus Christ. Only those disciples who have recognized Jesus can receive from this word an affirmation of the love of the Father of Jesus Christ and liberation from all things. It is not worrying which makes disciples worry-free; it is faith in Jesus Christ. Now they know: we *cannot* worry (v. 27). The next day, the next hour is completely out of our hands' reach. It is meaningless to behave as if we could worry. We can change nothing about the conditions of the world. Only God can change the conditions, for example, a body's height, for God rules the world. Because we cannot worry, because we are so powerless, we *should* not worry. Worrying means taking God's rule onto ourselves. 166

Disciples know not only that they may not and cannot worry, but also that they need not worry. It is not worry, it is not even work which produces daily bread, but God the Father. The birds and the lilies do not work and spin, but they are fed and clothed; they receive their daily share without worry. They need the goods of the world only for daily life. They do not collect them. By not collecting they praise the creator, not by their industry, their work, their worry, but by receiving daily and simply the gifts God gives. That is how birds and lilies become examples for disciples. Jesus dissolves the connection between work and food, which is conceived in terms of cause and effect apart from God. He does not value daily bread as the reward for work. Instead, he speaks of the carefree simplicity of those who follow the ways of Jesus and receive everything from God.

"Now no animal works for its living, but each has its own task to perform, after which it seeks and finds its food. The little birds fly about and warble, make nests, and hatch their young. That is their task. But they do not gain their living from it. Oxen plow, horses carry their riders and have a share in battle; sheep furnish wool, milk, cheese, and so on. That is their task. But they do not gain their living from it. It is the earth which produces grass and nourishes them through God's blessing. . . . Similarly, man must necessarily work and busy himself at something. At the same time, however, he must know that it is something other than his labor which furnishes him sustenance; it is the divine blessing. Because God gives him nothing unless he works, it may seem as if it is his labor which sustains him; just as the little birds neither sow nor reap, but they would certainly die of hunger if they did not fly about to seek their food. The fact that they find food, however, is not due to their own labor, but to God's goodness. For who placed their food there where they can find it? . . . For where God has not laid up a supply no one will find anything, even though they all work themselves to death searching" (Luther). But if the creator sustains birds and lilies, won't the 167 Father also feed his children, who daily ask him to do so? Shouldn't God give them what they need for their daily lives, God, to whom all the goods of the earth belong and who can distribute them according to God's own pleasure? "God give me every day as much as I need to live. He gives it to the birds on the roof, how should he not give it to me?" (Claudius).

Worry is the concern of nonbelievers, who rely on their strength and work, but not on God. Nonbelievers are worriers, because they do not know that the Father knows what their needs are. So they intend to get for themselves what they do not expect from God. But disciples are to "strive first for the kingdom of God and his righteousness, and all these things will be given to you as well" [*Matt. 6:33*]. This makes clear that concern for food and clothing is not yet concern for the kingdom of God, as we would like to understand it. We would like to consider performing our work for our families and ourselves, our worrying for food and a place to live and sleep, to be the same thing as striving for the kingdom of God, as if striving for the kingdom took place only in the context of those concerns. The kingdom of God and God's righteousness are something entirely different from the gifts of the world that are to come to us. It is nothing other than the righteousness about which Matthew 5 and 6 have spoken, the righteousness of the cross of Christ and discipleship under the cross. Communion with Jesus and obedience to his commandment come *first*; then everything else follows. There is no blending of the two; one follows the other. Striving for the righteousness of Christ stands *ahead of* the cares of our lives for food and clothing, or for job and family. This is the most exacting summary of everything which has been said before. This word of Jesus, like the commandment not to worry, is either an unbearable burden, an impossible destruction of human existence for the poor and suffering—or it is the gospel itself, which can make us completely free and completely joyous. Jesus is not speaking of what people should do but cannot do. Rather, he is speaking of what God has granted us and continues to promise us. If Christ has been given to us, if we are called to follow him, then everything, everything indeed is given us with him. Everything else shall be given to us. Those who in following Jesus look only to his righteousness are in the care and protection of Jesus Christ and his Father. Nothing can harm those who are thus in communion with the Father; they cannot doubt that the Father will feed his children and will not let them starve. God will help them at the right time. God knows what we need.

Jesus' disciples, even after having followed him for a long time, will be able to answer the question, "Were you ever in need?" with "Lord, never!" How could they suffer need who in hunger and nakedness, persecution and danger are confident of their community with Jesus Christ?

Matthew 7: The Community of Disciples Is Set Apart   169

**

The Conclusion   181

"'Everyone then who hears these words of mine and acts on them will be like a wise man who built his house on rock. The rain fell, the floods came, and the winds blew and beat on that house, but it did not fall, because it had been founded on rock. And everyone who hears these words of mine and does not act on them will be like a foolish man who built his house on sand. The rain fell, and the floods came, and the winds blew and beat against that house, and it fell—and great was its fall!'

"Now when Jesus had finished saying these things, the crowds were astonished at his teaching, for he taught them as one having authority, and not as their scribes" (Matt. 7:24–29).

We have heard the Sermon on the Mount; perhaps we have understood it. But who has heard it correctly? Jesus answers this question last. Jesus does not permit his listeners to simply walk away, making whatever they like of his discourse, extracting what seems to them to be useful in their lives, testing how this teaching compares to "reality." Jesus does not deliver his word up to his listeners, so that it is misused in their rummaging hands. Instead, he gives it to them in a way that it alone retains power over them. From the human point of view there are countless possibilities of understanding and interpreting the Sermon on the Mount. Jesus knows only one possibility: simply go and obey. Do not interpret or apply, but do it and obey. That is the only way Jesus' word is really heard. But again, doing something is not to be understood as an ideal possibility; instead, we are   182
simply to begin acting.

This word, which I accept as valid for myself; this word, which arises from "I have known you," which immediately draws me into acting, into obedience, is the rock on which I can build a house. This word of Jesus coming from eternity can only be answered by simply doing it. Jesus has spoken; the word is his; our part is to obey. The word of Jesus keeps its honor, its strength, and power among us only by our acting on it. Then a storm can sweep over the house, but it cannot tear apart the unity with Jesus created by his word.

The only thing which exists besides action is inaction. There is no such thing as intending to act and not doing it. Those who treat the word of Jesus any other way except by acting on it assert that Jesus is wrong; they say no to the Sermon on the Mount; they do not do his word. All our questions, complications, and interpretations are inaction. The rich young man and the scribe in Luke 10 are examples. I can insist on my faith and my fundamental recognition of this word as much as I want; Jesus calls it inaction. The word that I do not want to do is no rock for me on which I can build a house. I have no unity with Jesus. He has never known me. Hence, when the storm comes, I will lose the word quickly and I will learn that in truth I never really had faith. I did not have the word of Christ. Instead, I had a word I wrested away from him and made my own by reflecting on it, but not doing it. Then my house falls down with a great fall, because it does not rest on the word of Christ.

"And the crowds were astonished . . ." What had happened? The Son of God had spoken. He took the judgment of the world into his hands. And his disciples stood beside him.

**

199   Part Two: The Church of Jesus Christ and Discipleship
                               Chapter Eight

Preliminary Questions

To his first disciples Jesus was bodily present, speaking his word directly to them. But this Jesus died and is risen. How, then, does his call to discipleship reach us today? Jesus no longer walks past me in bodily form and calls, "Follow me," as he did to Levi, the tax collector [*Mark 2:14*]. Even if I would be truly willing to listen, to leave everything behind, and to follow, what justification do I have for doing so? What for the first disciples was so entirely unambiguous is for me a decision that is highly problematic and fraught with uncertainty. What gives me the right, for example, to hear Jesus' call of the tax collector as being addressed to me? Did Jesus not say quite different things to others on other occasions? What about the paralytic to whom he extended forgiveness and healing? And what about Lazarus whom he raised from the dead? Did he love them any less than his disciples? And yet he did not call them to leave their profession and follow him, but left them at home with their families and their jobs. Who am I to recommend myself to do something unusual and extraordinary? Who is to judge whether I or others are not simply acting out of our own authority and religious enthusiasm? But that would definitely mean something other than discipleship!

There is something wrong with all of these questions. Every time we ask them, we place ourselves outside the living presence of the Christ. All of these questions refuse to take seriously that Jesus Christ is not dead but

alive and still speaking to us today through the testimony of scripture. He is
present with us today, in bodily form and with his word. If we want to hear   202
his call to discipleship, we need to hear it where Christ himself is present.
It is within the church that Jesus Christ calls through his word and sacrament. The preaching and sacrament of the church is the place where Jesus
Christ is present. To hear Jesus' call to discipleship, one needs no personal
revelation. Listen to the preaching and receive the sacrament! Listen to the
gospel of the crucified and risen Lord! Here he is, the whole Christ, the
very same who encountered the disciples. Indeed, here he is already present
as the glorified, the victorious, the living Christ. No one but Christ himself
can call us to discipleship. Discipleship in essence never consists in a decision for this or that specific action; it is always a decision for or against Jesus
Christ. And this is exactly why the situation was not any less ambiguous
for the disciple or the tax collector who was called by him than it is for us
today. The obedience of those who were first called constituted discipleship
precisely in that they recognized Christ in the one who was calling them.
For them, as for us, it is the hidden Christ who calls. The call as such is
ambiguous. What counts is not the call as such, but the one who calls. But
Christ can only be recognized in faith. That was true in the same way for
the first disciples as it is for us. They saw the rabbi and the miracle worker,
and believed in Christ. We hear the word and believe in Christ.

But did those first disciples not have an advantage over us in that, once
they had recognized Christ, they received his unambiguous command from
his very own lips and were told what to do? And are we not left to our own
devices precisely at this crucial point of Christian obedience? Does not the
same Christ speak differently to us than he spoke to them? If this were
true, then we would indeed be in a hopeless situation. But it is far from
true. Christ speaks to us exactly as he spoke to them. For the first disciples
of Jesus it was also not as if they first recognized him as the Christ, and
then received his command. Rather, it was only through his word and his
command that they recognized him. They trusted in his word and his command, and thereby recognized him as the Christ. There was no other way   203
for the disciples to know Christ than through his clear word. Conversely,
therefore, to recognize Jesus truly as the Christ necessarily included a recognition of his will. To recognize the person of Jesus Christ did not undermine the disciples' certainty about what to do, but on the contrary created
that certainty. Indeed, there is no other way to recognize Christ. If Christ
is the living Lord of my life, then I am addressed by his word whenever I
encounter him; indeed, I do not really know him except through his clear
word and command. There are those who object that this is precisely our
dilemma: we would like to know Christ and have faith in him, and yet we are

unable to recognize his will. This objection, however, springs from a vague and mistaken knowledge of Christ. To know Christ means to recognize him in his word as Lord and savior of my life. But that includes an understanding of his clear word spoken to me.

Suppose we say finally that, whereas the command the disciples received was unambiguous, we have to decide for ourselves which of his words is addressed to us. In that case, we have once again misunderstood not only the situation of the disciples, but also our own. Jesus' command always has a single purpose: it demands faith from an undivided heart, and love of God and neighbor with all our heart and soul. This is the only aspect in which the command was unambiguous. Any attempt to carry out the command of Jesus, without also understanding it in this way, would again mean that we misinterpret and disobey Jesus' word. However, this does not mean that we would have no way of knowing the concrete command.[28] On the contrary, we hear it clearly in every word of proclamation in which we hear Christ, but we hear it knowing that it can only be fulfilled through faith in Jesus Christ. The gift Jesus gave to his disciples is thus fully available to us too. In fact, it is even more readily available to us now that Jesus has ascended, by our knowledge of his transfiguration, and by the Holy Spirit that has been sent.

All this makes it abundantly clear that we cannot play off the narrative of the calling of the disciples against other parts of the gospel account. It is never a question of our having or taking on the same identity as the disciples or other people in the New Testament. The only issue of importance is that Jesus Christ and his call are the same, then and now. His word remains one and the same, whether it was spoken during his earthly life or today, whether it was addressed to the disciples or to the paralytic. Then and now, it is the gracious call to enter his kingdom and to submit to his rule. The question whether I ought to compare myself with the disciple or with the paralytic poses a dangerous and false alternative. I need not compare myself with either of them. Instead, all I have to do is to listen and do Christ's word and will as I receive them in both of these biblical accounts. Scripture does not present us with a collection of Christian types to be imitated according to our own choice. Rather, in every passage it proclaims to us the one Jesus Christ. It is him alone whom I ought to hear. He is one and the same everywhere.

---

28. ["Regarding Bonhoeffer's efforts to come to terms with this epistemological problem, see *DBWE* 11:357–370. Also see *DBWE* 6:388–408 (*Reader* 685–698)," *DBWE* 4:203, n. 6.]

Thus, when we ask the question of where we can hear Jesus' call to discipleship today, there is no other answer than this: listen to the word that is preached, and receive the sacrament. In both of these listen to Christ himself. Then you will hear his call!

30. *LIFE TOGETHER*

DBWE 5:25–92

The seminary at Finkenwalde provided Bonhoeffer with the opportunity for reflection on and practical experimentation with Christian community. He established for the community a daily routine bookended by a long worship service and meditation session in the morning and another long service at night. In between, the seminary director and his students did academic work, except when good weather made outdoor recreation irresistible.[1] *Bonhoeffer described this period spent together in community as the fullest of his life, both professionally and personally.*[2]

When Finkenwalde was closed by the Gestapo in 1937, Bonhoeffer wanted to record and disseminate the community's experiences. The result was Life Together, *which appeared in 1939 and became Bonhoeffer's most widely read book in his lifetime.*[3] *No doubt some of this interest was due to the widely circulating rumors of monkish, legalistic, and otherwise un-Lutheran practices under way at Finkenwalde. In the opening section of* Life Together, *he deals with these objections head-on, portraying communal life and its practices as consequences of that most Lutheran of doctrines, justification by grace through faith. As he developed the doctrine in his earlier writings, any justification that is not mediated through sociality does not genuinely come from outside ourselves* (extra nos), *and thus degenerates into self-justification. Seen from this view,* Life Together *is about the dynamics of justification as mediated by the Christian community.*

---

1. [DB-ER, *428–429.*]
2. [DB-ER, *419.*]
3. [DB-ER, *469.*]

PREFACE   25

The subject matter I am presenting here is such that any further development can take place only through a common effort. We are not dealing with a concern of some private circles but with a mission entrusted to the church. Because of this, we are not searching for more or less haphazard individual solutions to a problem. This is, rather, a responsibility to be undertaken by the church as a whole. There is a hesitation evident in the way this task has been handled. Only recently has it been understood at all. But this hesitation must give way to the willingness of the church to assist in the work. The variety of new ecclesial forms of community makes it necessary to enlist the vigilant cooperation of every responsible party. The following remarks are intended to provide only one individual contribution toward answering the extensive questions that have been raised thereby. As much as possible, may these comments help to clarify this experience and put it into practice.

COMMUNITY   27

"How very good and pleasant it is when kindred live together in unity!" (Ps. 133:1). In what follows we will take a look at several directions and principles that the Holy Scriptures give us for life together under the Word.

The Christian cannot simply take for granted the privilege of living among other Christians. Jesus Christ lived in the midst of his enemies. In the end all his disciples abandoned him. On the cross he was all alone, surrounded by criminals and the jeering crowds. He had come for the express purpose of bringing peace to the enemies of God. So Christians, too, belong not in the seclusion of a cloistered life but in the midst of enemies. There they find their mission, their work. "To rule is to be in the midst of your enemies. And whoever will not suffer this does not want to be part of the rule of Christ; such a person wants to be among friends and sit among the roses and lilies, not with the bad people but the religious people. O you blasphemers and betrayers of Christ! If Christ had done what you are doing,   28 who would ever have been saved?" (Luther).

"Though I scattered them among the nations, yet in far countries they shall remember me" (Zech. 10:9). According to God's will, the Christian church is a scattered people, scattered like seed "to all the kingdoms of the earth" (Deut. 28:25). That is the curse and its promise. God's people must live in distant lands among the unbelievers, but they will be the seed of the kingdom of God in all the world.

"I will . . . gather them in. For I have redeemed them, . . . and they shall . . . return" (Zech. 10:8–9). When will that happen? It has happened in Jesus Christ, who died "to gather into one the dispersed children of God" (John 11:52), and ultimately it will take place visibly at the end of time when the angels of God will gather God's elect from the four winds, from one end of heaven to the other (Matt. 24:31). Until then, God's people remain scattered, held together in Jesus Christ alone, having become one because they remember *him* in the distant lands, spread out among the unbelievers.

Thus in the period between the death of Christ and the day of judgment, when Christians are allowed to live here in visible community with other Christians, we have merely a gracious anticipation of the end time. It is by God's grace that a congregation is permitted to gather visibly around God's word and sacrament in this world. Not all Christians partake of this grace. The imprisoned, the sick, the lonely who live in the diaspora, the proclaimers of the gospel in heathen lands stand alone. They know that visible community is grace. They pray with the psalmist: "I went with the throng, and led them in procession to the house of God, with glad shouts and songs of thanksgiving, a multitude keeping festival" (Ps. 42:5). But they remain alone in distant lands, a scattered seed according to God's will. Yet what is denied them as a visible experience they grasp more ardently in faith. Hence "in the Spirit on the Lord's Day" (Rev. 1:10) the exiled disciple of the Lord, John the author of the Apocalypse, celebrates the worship of heaven with its congregations in the loneliness of the Island of Patmos. He

29 sees the seven lampstands that are the congregations, the seven stars that are the angels of the congregations, and in the midst and above it all, the Son of Man, Jesus Christ, in his great glory as the risen one. He strengthens and comforts John by his word. That is the heavenly community in which the exile participates on the day of his Lord's resurrection.

The physical presence of other Christians is a source of incomparable joy and strength to the believer. With great yearning the imprisoned apostle Paul calls his "beloved son in the faith" [*1 Tim. 1:2*], Timothy, to come to him in prison in the last days of his life. He wants to see him again and have him near. Paul has not forgotten the tears Timothy shed during their final parting (2 Tim. 1:4). Thinking of the congregation in Thessalonica, Paul prays "night and day . . . most earnestly that we may see you face to face" (1 Thess. 3:10). The aged John knows his joy in his own people will only be complete when he can come to them and speak to them face to face instead of using paper and ink (2 John 12). The believer need not feel any shame when yearning for the physical presence of other Christians, as if one were still living too much in the flesh. A human being is created as a body; the Son of God appeared on earth in the body for our sake and was raised in the body. In the sacrament the believer receives the Lord Christ in the body, and the resurrection of the dead will bring about the perfected community of God's spiritual-physical creatures. Therefore, the believer praises the Creator, the Reconciler and the Redeemer, God the Father, Son and Holy Spirit, for the bodily presence of the other Christian. The prisoner, the sick person, the Christian living in the diaspora recognizes in the nearness of a fellow Christian a physical sign of the gracious presence of the triune God. In their loneliness, both the visitor and the one visited recognize in each other the Christ who is present in the body. They receive and meet each other as one meets the Lord, in reverence, humility, and joy. They receive each other's blessings as the blessing of the Lord Jesus Christ. But if there is so much happiness and joy even in a single encounter of one Christian with another, what inexhaustible riches must invariably open up for those who by God's will are privileged to live in daily community life with other Christians! Of course, what is an inexpressible blessing from God for the lonely individual is easily disregarded and trampled under foot by those   30 who receive the gift every day. It is easily forgotten that the community of Christians is a gift of grace from the kingdom of God, a gift that can be taken from us any day—that the time still separating us from the most profound loneliness may be brief indeed. Therefore, let those who until now have had the privilege of living a Christian life together with other Christians praise God's grace from the bottom of their hearts. Let them thank God on their knees and realize: it is grace, nothing but grace, that we are still permitted to live in the community of Christians today.

The measure with which God gives the gift of visible community is varied. Christians who live dispersed from one another are comforted by a brief visit of another Christian, a prayer together, and another Christian's blessing. Indeed, they are strengthened by letters written by the hands of other Christians. Paul's greetings in his letters written in his own hand were no doubt tokens of such community. Others are given the gift on Sundays of the community of the worship service. Still others have the privilege of living a Christian life in the community of their families. Before their ordination young seminarians receive the gift of a common life with their brothers for a certain length of time. Among serious Christians in congregations today there is a growing desire to meet together with other Christians during the midday break from work for life together under the Word. Life together is again being understood by Christians today as the grace   31 that it is, as the extraordinary aspect, the "roses and lilies" of the Christian life (Luther).

Christian community means community through Jesus Christ and in Jesus Christ. There is no Christian community that is more than this, and none that is less than this. Whether it be a brief, single encounter or the daily community of many years, Christian community is solely this. We belong to one another only through and in Jesus Christ.

What does that mean? It means, *first*, that a Christian needs others for the sake of Jesus Christ. It means, *second*, that a Christian comes to others only through Jesus Christ. It means, *third*, that from eternity we have been chosen in Jesus Christ, accepted in time, and united for eternity.

First, Christians are persons who no longer seek their salvation, their deliverance, their justification in themselves, but in Jesus Christ alone. They know that God's Word in Jesus Christ pronounces them guilty, even when they feel nothing of their own guilt, and that God's Word in Jesus Christ pronounces them free and righteous, even when they feel nothing of their own righteousness. Christians no longer live by their own resources, by accusing themselves and justifying themselves, but by God's accusation and God's justification. They live entirely by God's Word pronounced on them, in faithful submission to God's judgment, whether it declares them guilty or righteous. The death and life of Christians are not situated in a self-contained isolation. Rather, Christians encounter both death and life only in the Word that comes to them from the outside, in God's Word to them. The Reformers expressed it by calling our righteousness an "alien righteousness," a righteousness that comes from outside of us (*extra nos*). They meant by this expression that Christians are dependent on the Word of God spoken to them. They are directed outward to the Word coming to them.

32 Christians live entirely by the truth of God's Word in Jesus Christ. If they are asked "where is your salvation, your blessedness, your righteousness?," they can never point to themselves. Instead, they point to the Word of God in Jesus Christ that grants them salvation, blessedness, and righteousness. They watch for this Word wherever they can. Because they daily hunger and thirst for righteousness, they long for the redeeming Word again and again. It can only come from the outside. In themselves they are destitute and dead. Help must come from the outside; and it has come and comes daily and anew in the Word of Jesus Christ, bringing us redemption, righteousness, innocence, and blessedness. But God put this Word into the mouth of human beings so that it may be passed on to others. When people are deeply affected by the Word, they tell it to other people. God has willed that we should seek and find God's living Word in the testimony of other Christians, in the mouths of human beings. Therefore, Christians need other Christians who speak God's Word to them. They need them again and again when they become uncertain and disheartened because, living by their own resources, they cannot help themselves without cheating themselves out of the truth. They need other Christians as bearers and proclaim-

ers of the divine word of salvation. They need them solely for the sake of Jesus Christ. The Christ in one's own heart is weaker than the Christ in the word of another Christian. The heart in one's heart is uncertain; the Word is sure. At the same time, this also clarifies that the goal of all Christian community is to encounter one another as bringers of the message of salvation. As such, God allows Christians to come together and grants them community. Their community is based only on Jesus Christ and this "alien righteousness." Therefore, we may now say that the community of Christians springs solely from the biblical and reformation message of the justification of human beings through grace alone. The longing of Christians for one another is based solely on this message.

Second, a Christian comes to others only through Jesus Christ. Among human beings there is strife. "He is our peace" (Eph. 2:14), says Paul of Jesus Christ. In him, broken and divided humanity has become one. Without Christ there is discord between God and humanity and between one human being and another. Christ has become the mediator who has made peace with God and peace among human beings. Without Christ we would not know God; we could neither call on God nor come to God. Moreover, without Christ we would not know other Christians around us; nor could we approach them. The way to them is blocked by one's own ego. Christ opened up the way to God and to one another. Now Christians can live with each other in peace; they can love and serve one another; they can become one. But they can continue to do so only through Jesus Christ. Only in Jesus Christ are we one; only through him are we bound together. He remains the one and only mediator throughout eternity.

Third, when God's Son took on flesh, he truly and bodily, out of pure grace, took on our being, our nature, ourselves. This was the eternal decree of the triune God. Now we are in him. Wherever he is, he bears our flesh, he bears us. And, where he is, there we are too—in the incarnation, on the cross, and in his resurrection. We belong to him because we are in him. That is why the Scriptures call us the body of Christ. But if we have been elected and accepted with the whole church in Jesus Christ before we could know it or want it, then we also belong to Christ in eternity with one another. We who live here in community with Christ will one day be with Christ in eternal community. Those who look at other Christians should know that they will be eternally united with them in Jesus Christ. Christian community means community through and in Jesus Christ. Everything the Scriptures provide in the way of directions and rules for Christians' life together rests on this presupposition.

"Now concerning love of the brothers and sisters, you do not need to have anyone write to you, for you yourselves have been taught by God to

33

love one another. . . . But we urge you, beloved, to do so more and more" (1 Thess. 4:9f.). It is God's own undertaking to teach such love. All that human beings can add is to remember this divine instruction and the exhortation to excel in it more and more. When God had mercy on us, when God revealed Jesus Christ to us as our brother, when God won our hearts by God's own love, our instruction in Christian love began at the same time. When God was merciful to us, we learned to be merciful with one another. When we received forgiveness instead of judgment, we too were made ready to forgive each other. What God did to us, we then owed to others. The more we received, the more we were able to give; and the more meager our love for one another, the less we were living by God's mercy and love. Thus God taught us to encounter one another as God has encountered us in Christ. "Welcome one another, therefore, just as Christ has welcomed you, for the glory of God" (Rom. 15:7).

In this way the one whom God has placed in common life with other Christians learns what it means to have brothers and sisters. "Brothers and sisters . . . in the Lord," Paul calls his congregation (Phil. 1:14). One is a brother or sister to another only through Jesus Christ. I am a brother or sister to another person through what Jesus Christ has done for me and to me; others have become brothers and sisters to me through what Jesus Christ has done for them and to them. The fact that we are brothers and sisters only through Jesus Christ is of immeasurable significance. Therefore, the other who comes face-to-face with me earnestly and devoutly seeking community is not the brother or sister with whom I am to relate in the community. My brother or sister is instead that other person who has been redeemed by Christ, absolved from sin, and called to faith and eternal life. What persons are in themselves as Christians, in their inwardness and piety, cannot constitute the basis of our community, which is determined by what those persons are in terms of Christ. Our community consists solely in what Christ has done to both of us. That not only is true at the beginning, as if in the course of time something else were to be added to our community, but also remains so for all the future and into all eternity. I have community with others and will continue to have it only through Jesus Christ. The more genuine and the deeper our community becomes, the more everything else between us will recede, and the more clearly and purely will Jesus Christ and his work become the one and only thing that is alive between us. We have one another only through Christ, but through Christ we really do *have* one another. We have one another completely and for all eternity.

This dismisses at the outset every unhappy desire for something more. Those who want more than what Christ has established between us do not want Christian community. They are looking for some extraordinary experiences of community that were denied them elsewhere. Such people are bringing confused and tainted desires into the Christian community. Precisely at this point Christian community is most often threatened from the very outset by the greatest danger, the danger of internal poisoning, the danger of confusing Christian community with some wishful image of pious community, the danger of blending the devout heart's natural desire for community with the spiritual reality of Christian community. It is essential for Christian community that two things become clear right from the beginning. *First, Christian community is not an ideal, but a divine reality; second, Christian community is a spiritual and not an emotional reality.* 35

On innumerable occasions a whole Christian community has been shattered because it has lived on the basis of a wishful image. Certainly serious Christians who are put in a community for the first time will often bring with them a very definite image of what Christian communal life should be, and they will be anxious to realize it. But God's grace quickly frustrates all such dreams. A great disillusionment with others, with Christians in general, and, if we are fortunate, with ourselves, is bound to overwhelm us as surely as God desires to lead us to an understanding of genuine Christian community. By sheer grace God will not permit us to live in a dream world even for a few weeks and to abandon ourselves to those blissful experiences and exalted moods that sweep over us like a wave of rapture. For God is not a God of emotionalism, but the God of truth. Only that community which enters into the experience of this great disillusionment with all its unpleasant and evil appearances begins to be what it should be in God's sight, begins to grasp in faith the promise that is given to it. The sooner this moment of disillusionment comes over the individual and the community, the better for both. However, a community that cannot bear and cannot 36 survive such disillusionment, clinging instead to its idealized image, when that should be done away with, loses at the same time the promise of a durable Christian community. Sooner or later it is bound to collapse. Every human idealized image that is brought into the Christian community is a hindrance to genuine community and must be broken up so that genuine community can survive. Those who love their dream of a Christian community more than the Christian community itself become destroyers of that Christian community even though their personal intentions may be ever so honest, earnest, and sacrificial.

God hates this wishful dreaming because it makes the dreamer proud and pretentious. Those who dream of this idealized community demand that it be fulfilled by God, by others, and by themselves. They enter the community of Christians with their demands, set up their own law, and judge one another and even God accordingly. They stand adamant, a living reproach to all others in the circle of the community. They act as if they have to create the Christian community, as if their visionary ideal binds the people together. Whatever does not go their way, they call a failure. When their idealized image is shattered, they see the community breaking into pieces. So they first become accusers of other Christians in the community, then accusers of God, and finally the desperate accusers of themselves. Because God already has laid the only foundation of our community, because God has united us in one body with other Christians in Jesus Christ long before we entered into common life with them, we enter into that life together with other Christians, not as those who make demands, but as those who thankfully receive. We thank God for what God has done for us. We thank God for giving us other Christians who live by God's call, forgiveness, and promise. We do not complain about what God does not give us; rather we are thankful for what God does give us daily. And is not what has been given us enough: other believers who will go on living with us through sin and need under the blessing of God's grace? Is the gift of God any less immeasurably great than this on any given day, even on the most difficult and distressing days of a Christian community? Even when sin and misunderstanding burden the common life, is not the one who sins still a person with whom I too stand under the word of Christ? Will not another Christian's sin be an occasion for me ever anew to give thanks that both of us may live in the forgiving love of God in Jesus Christ? Therefore, will not the very moment of great disillusionment with my brother or sister be

37 incomparably wholesome for me because it so thoroughly teaches me that both of us can never live by our own words and deeds, but only by that one Word and deed that really binds us together, the forgiveness of sins in Jesus Christ? The bright day of Christian community dawns wherever the early morning mists of dreamy visions are lifting.

Thankfulness works in the Christian community as it usually does in the Christian life. Only those who give thanks for little things receive the great things as well. We prevent God from giving us the great spiritual gifts prepared for us because we do not give thanks for daily gifts. We think that we should not be satisfied with the small measure of spiritual knowledge, experience, and love that has been given to us, and that we must be constantly seeking the great gifts. Then we complain that we lack the deep certainty, the strong faith, and the rich experiences that God has given to other Christians, and we consider these complaints to be pious. We pray for the big things and forget to give thanks for the small (and yet really not so small!) gifts we receive daily. How can God entrust great things to those who will not gratefully receive the little things from God's hand? If we do not give thanks daily for the Christian community in which we have been placed, even when there are no great experiences, no noticeable riches, but much weakness, difficulty, and little faith—and if, on the contrary, we only keep complaining to God that everything is so miserable and so insignificant and does not at all live up to our expectations—then we hinder God from letting our community grow according to the measure and riches that are there for us all in Jesus Christ. That also applies in a special way to the complaints often heard from pastors and zealous parishioners about their congregations. Pastors should not complain about their congregation, certainly never to other people, but also not to God. Congregations have not been entrusted to them in order that they should become accusers of their congregations before God and their fellow human beings. When pastors lose faith in a Christian community in which they have been placed and begin to make accusations against it, they had better examine themselves first to see whether the underlying problem is not their own idealized image, which should be shattered by God. And if they find that to be true, let them thank God for leading them into this predicament. But if they find that it is not true, let them nevertheless guard against ever becoming an accuser of those whom God has gathered together. Instead, let them accuse themselves of their unbelief, let them ask for an understanding of their own failure and their particular sin, and pray that they may not wrong other Christians. Let such pastors, recognizing their own guilt, make intercession for those charged to their care. Let them do what they have been instructed to do and thank God.

Like the Christian's sanctification, Christian community is a gift of God to which we have no claim. Only God knows the real condition of either our community or our sanctification. What may appear weak and insignificant to us may be great and glorious to God. Just as Christians should not be constantly feeling the pulse of their spiritual life, so too the Christian community has not been given to us by God for us to be continually taking its temperature. The more thankfully we daily receive what is given to us, the more assuredly and consistently will community increase and grow from day to day as God pleases.

Christian community is not an ideal we have to realize, but rather a reality created by God in Christ in which we may participate. The more clearly we learn to recognize that the ground and strength and promise of all our community is in Jesus Christ alone, the more calmly we will learn to think about our community and pray and hope for it.

Because Christian community is founded solely on Jesus Christ, it is a spiritual and not an emotional reality. In this respect it differs absolutely from all other communities. The Scriptures call pneumatic or "spiritual" what is created only by the Holy Spirit, who puts Jesus Christ into our hearts as lord and savior. The scriptures call "emotional" what comes from the natural urges, strengths, and abilities of the human soul.

39		The basis of all pneumatic, or spiritual, reality is the clear, manifest Word of God in Jesus Christ. At the foundation of all emotional reality are the dark, impenetrable urges and desires of the human soul. The basis of spiritual community is truth; the basis of emotional community is desire. The essence of spiritual community is light. For "God is light and in God there is no darkness at all" (1 John 1:5); and "if we walk in the light as he himself is in the light, we have fellowship with one another" (1 John 1:7). The essence of emotional community is darkness, "for it is from within, from the human heart, that evil intentions come" (Mark 7:21). It is the deep night that spreads over the sources of all human activity, over even all noble and devout impulses. Spiritual community is the community of those who are called by Christ; emotional community is the community of pious souls. The

40	bright love of Christian service, *agape*, lives in the spiritual community; the dark love of pious-impious urges, *eros*, burns in the emotional community. In the former, there is ordered, Christian service; in the latter, disordered desire for pleasure. In the former, there is humble submission of Christians one to another; in the latter, humble yet haughty subjection of other Christians to one's own desires.[4] In the spiritual community the Word of God alone rules; in the emotional community the individual who is equipped with exceptional powers, experience, and magical, suggestive abilities rules along with the Word. In the one, God's Word alone is binding; in the other, besides the Word, human beings bind others to themselves. In the one, all power, honor, and rule are surrendered to the Holy Spirit; in the other, power and personal spheres of influence are sought and cultivated. So far as these are devout people, they certainly seek this power with the intention of serving the highest and the best. But in reality they end up dethroning the Holy Spirit and banishing it to the realm of unreal remoteness; only what is emotional remains real here. Thus, in the spiritual community the Spirit rules; in the emotional community, psychological techniques and methods. In the former, unsophisticated, nonpsychological, unmethodical, helping love is offered to one another; in the latter, psychological analysis and design. In the former, service to one another is simple and humble; in the latter, it is to strangers treated in a searching, calculating fashion.

---

4. ["See *DBWE* 1:166ff. for Bonhoeffer's earlier development of the contrast of *agape* with *eros* in order to clarify his concept of Christian community and to avoid confusing these two kinds of love . . . ," *DWBE* 5:40, n. 18.]

Perhaps the contrast between spiritual and emotional reality can be made most clear in the following observation. Within the spiritual community there is never, in any way whatsoever, an "immediate" relationship of one to another.[5] However, in the emotional community there exists a profound, elemental emotional desire for community, for immediate contact with other human souls, just as in the flesh there is a yearning for immediate union with other flesh. This desire of the human soul seeks the complete intimate fusion of I and You, whether this occurs in the union of love or—what from this emotional perspective is after all the same thing—in forcing the other into one's own sphere of power and influence. Here is where emotional, strong persons enjoy life to the full, securing for themselves the admiration, the love, or the fear of the weak. Here human bonds, suggestive influences, and dependencies are everything. Moreover, everything that is originally and solely characteristic of the community mediated through Christ reappears in the nonmediated community of souls in a distorted form. 41

There is, likewise, such a thing as "emotional" conversion. It has all the appearances of genuine conversion and occurs wherever the superior power of one person is consciously or unconsciously misused to shake to the roots and draw into its spell an individual or a whole community. Here one soul has had an immediate effect on another. The result is that the weak individual has been overcome by the strong; the resistance of the weaker individual has broken down under the influence of the other person. One has been overpowered by something, but not won over. This becomes apparent the moment a commitment is demanded, a commitment that must be made independently of the person to whom one is bound or possibly in opposition to this person. Here is where those emotional converts fail. They thus show that their conversion was brought about not by the Holy Spirit, but by a human being. It is, therefore, not enduring. 42

There is, likewise, a "merely emotional" love of neighbor. Such love is capable of making the most unheard-of sacrifices. Often it far surpasses the genuine love of Christ in fervent devotion and visible results. It speaks the Christian language with overwhelming and stirring eloquence. But it is what the apostle Paul is speaking of when he says: "If I give all I possess to the poor, and surrender my body to the flames" (1 Cor. 13:3)—in other words, if I combine the utmost deeds of love with the utmost of devotion—"but do not have love (that is, the love of Christ), I would be nothing" (1

---

5. [*Bonhoeffer's rejection of immediacy goes hand in hand with his understanding of Christ as the mediator. See Green,* Bonhoeffer, *220ff.*]

Cor. 13:2).[6] Emotional love loves the other for the sake of itself; spiritual
love loves the other for the sake of Christ. That is why emotional love seeks
direct contact with other persons. It loves them, not as free persons, but
as those whom it binds to itself. It wants to do everything it can to win and
conquer; it puts pressure on the other person. It desires to be irresistible,
to dominate. Emotional love does not think much of truth. It makes the
truth relative, since nothing, not even the truth, must come between it and
the person loved. Emotional love desires other persons, their company. It
wants them to return its love, but it does not serve them. On the contrary, it
continues to desire even when it seems to be serving.

43   Two factors, which are really one and the same thing, reveal the difference between spiritual and emotional love. Emotional love cannot tolerate
the dissolution of a community that has become false, even for the sake of
genuine community. And such emotional love cannot love an enemy, that
is to say, one who seriously and stubbornly resists it. Both spring from the
same source: emotional love is by its very nature desire, desire for emotional
community. As long as it can possibly satisfy this desire, it will not give it
up, even for the sake of truth, even for the sake of genuine love for others.
But emotional love is at an end when it can no longer expect its desire to
be fulfilled, namely, in the face of an enemy. There it turns into hatred,
contempt, and slander.

Spiritual love, however, begins right at this point. This is why emotional
love turns into personal hatred when it encounters genuine spiritual love
that does not desire but serves. Emotional love makes itself an end in itself.
It turns itself into an achievement, an idol it worships, to which it must
subject everything. It cares for, cultivates, and loves itself and nothing else
in the world. Spiritual love, however, comes from Jesus Christ; it serves him
alone. It knows that it has no direct access to other persons. Christ stands
between me and others. I do not know in advance what love of others means
on the basis of the general idea of love that grows out of my emotional
desires. All this may instead be hatred and the worst kind of selfishness in
the eyes of Christ. Only Christ in his Word tells me what love is. Contrary to
all my own opinions and convictions, Jesus Christ will tell me what love for
my brothers and sisters really looks like. Therefore, spiritual love is bound
to the word of Jesus Christ alone. Where Christ tells me to maintain community for the sake of love, I desire to maintain it. Where the truth of Christ

---

6. ["... During his ministry as pastor of two German-speaking parishes in and around
London in 1934, Bonhoeffer preached four sermons on 1 Cor. 13 (*DBWE* 13:375–396) ...,"
DBWE 5:42, n. 21.]

orders me to dissolve a community for the sake of love, I will dissolve it, despite all the protests of my emotional love. Because spiritual love does not desire but rather serves, it loves an enemy as a brother or sister. It originates neither in the brother or sister nor in the enemy, but in Christ and his word. Emotional love can never comprehend spiritual love, for spiritual love is from above. It is something completely strange, new, and incomprehensible to all earthly love.

Because Christ stands between me and an other, I must not long for unmediated community with that person. As only Christ was able to speak to me in such a way that I was helped, so others too can only be helped by Christ alone. However, this means that I must release others from all my attempts to control, coerce, and dominate them with my love. In their freedom from me, other persons want to be loved for who they are, as those for whom Christ became a human being, died, and rose again, as those for whom Christ won the forgiveness of sins and prepared eternal life. Because Christ has long since acted decisively for other Christians, before I could begin to act, I must allow them the freedom to be Christ's. They should encounter me only as the persons that they already are for Christ. This is the meaning of the claim that we can encounter others only through the mediation of Christ. Emotional love constructs its own image of other persons, about what they are and what they should become. It takes the life of the other person into its own hands. Spiritual love recognizes the true image of the other person as seen from the perspective of Jesus Christ. It is the image Jesus Christ has formed and wants to form in all people.

Therefore, spiritual love will prove successful insofar as it commends the other to Christ in all that it says and does. It will not seek to agitate another by exerting all too personal, direct influence or by crudely interfering in one's life. It will not take pleasure in pious, emotional fervor and excitement. Rather, it will encounter the other with the clear word of God and be prepared to leave the other alone with this word for a long time. It will be willing to release others again so that Christ may deal with them. It will respect the boundary of the other, which is placed between us by Christ, and it will find full community with the other in the Christ who alone binds us together. This spiritual love will thus speak to Christ about the other Christian more than to the other Christian about Christ. It knows that the most direct way to others is always through prayer to Christ and that love of the other is completely tied to the truth found in Christ. It is out of this love that John the disciple speaks: "I have no greater joy than this, to hear that my children are walking in the truth" (3 John 4).

Emotional love lives by uncontrolled and uncontrollable dark desires; spiritual love lives in the clear light of service ordered by the *truth*. Emo-

44

tional love results in human enslavement, bondage, rigidity; spiritual love creates the *freedom* of Christians under the Word. Emotional love breeds artificial hothouse flowers; spiritual love creates the *fruits* that grow healthily under God's open sky, according to God's good pleasure in the rain and storm and sunshine.

45   The existence of any Christian communal life essentially depends on whether or not it succeeds at the right time in promoting the ability to distinguish between a human ideal and God's reality, between spiritual and emotional community. The life and death of a Christian community is decided by its ability to reach sober clarity on these points as soon as possible. In other words, a life together under the Word will stay healthy only when it does not form itself into a movement, an order, a society, a *collegium pietatis* [*school or association of piety*],[7] but instead understands itself as being part of the one, holy, universal, Christian church,[8] sharing through its deeds and suffering in the hardships and struggles and promise of the whole church. Every principle of selection, and every division connected with it that is not necessitated quite objectively by common work, local conditions, or family connections is of the greatest danger to a Christian community. Self-centeredness always insinuates itself in any process of intellectual or spiritual selectivity, destroying the spiritual power of the community and robbing the community of its effectiveness for the church, thus driving it into sectarianism. The exclusion of the weak and insignificant, the seemingly useless people, from everyday Christian life in com-

46   munity may actually mean the exclusion of Christ; for in the poor sister or brother, Christ is knocking at the door.[9] We must, therefore, be very careful on this point.

The undiscerning observer may think that this mixture of ideal and real, emotional and spiritual, would be most obvious where there are a number of layers in the structure of a community, as in marriage, the family, friendship—where the emotional element as such already assumes a central

---

7. [*Schools of piety, groups within churches that met for Bible study and devotion, were a feature of Lutheran Pietism.*]

8. ["The four classical marks of the church (one, holy, catholic, and apostolic) were incorporated into the Nicean-Constantinopolitan Symbol of Faith at the Council of Constantinople in 381 . . . ," *DWBE* 5:45, n. 25.]

9. ["Bonhoeffer's statement here should be seen in the context of Nazism's deliberate attempt to exclude, even exterminate, the weak, insignificant, 'seemingly useless people.' Christ's identification with the 'least' of people is at the heart of Bonhoeffer's Christology . . . ," *DBWE* 5:46, n. 26. *See* DBWE *12:356 as well as Bonhoeffer's Advent 1928 sermon,* DBWE *10:542–546.*]

importance in the community's coming into being at all, and where the spiritual is only something added to humanity's physical-emotional nature. According to this view, it is only in these multifaceted communities that there is a danger of confusing and mixing the two spheres, whereas such a danger could hardly arise in a community of a purely spiritual nature. Such ideas, however, are a grand delusion. On the basis of all our experience—and as can be easily seen from the very nature of things—the truth is just the opposite. A marriage, a family, a friendship knows exactly the limitations of its community-building power. Such relationships know very well, if they are sound, where the emotional element ends and the spiritual begins. They are aware of the difference between physical-emotional and spiritual community. On the other hand, whenever a community of a purely spiritual nature comes together, the danger is uncannily near that everything pertaining to emotion will be brought into and intermixed with this community. Purely spiritual life in community is not only dangerous but also not normal. Whenever physical-familial community, the community formed among those engaged in serious work, or everyday life with all its demands on working people is not introduced into the spiritual commu-   47
nity, extraordinary vigilance and clear thinking are called for. That is why it is precisely on short retreats that, as experience has shown, emotion spreads most easily. Nothing is easier than to stimulate the euphoria of community in a few days of life together; and nothing is more fatal to the healthy, sober, everyday life in community of Christians.

There is probably no Christian to whom God has not given the uplifting and blissful *experience* of genuine Christian community at least once in her or his life. But in this world such experiences remain nothing but a gracious extra beyond the daily bread of Christian community life. We have no claim to such experiences, and we do not live with other Christians for the sake of gaining such experiences. It is not the experience of Christian community, but firm and certain faith within Christian community that holds us together. We hold fast in faith to God's greatest gift, that God has acted for us all and wants to act for us all. This makes us joyful and happy, but it also makes us ready to forgo all such experiences if at times God does not grant them. We are bound together by faith, not by experience.

"How very good and pleasant it is when kindred live together in unity" [*Ps. 133:1*]. This is the Scripture's praise of life together under the Word. But now we can correctly interpret the words "in unity" and say "when kindred live together through Christ." For Jesus Christ alone is our unity. "He is our peace" [*Eph. 2:14*]. We have access to one another, joy in one another, community with one another through Christ alone.

THE DAY TOGETHER

To you our morning song of praise,
To you our evening prayer we raise;
In lowly song your glory we adore
O God, now, forever and forevermore.
(Luther, following Ambrose)

"Let the Word of Christ dwell in you richly" (Col. 3:16). The Old Testament day begins on one evening and ends with the sundown of the next evening. That is the time of expectation. The day of the New Testament church begins at sunrise in the early morning and ends with the dawning light of the next morning. That is the time of fulfillment, the resurrection of the Lord. At night Christ was born, a light in the darkness; noonday turned to night when Christ suffered and died on the cross. But early on Easter morning Christ emerged victorious from the grave. "Ere yet the dawn has filled the skies / Behold my Savior Christ arise, / He chases from us sin and night, / And brings us joy and life and light. Halleluia." So sang the church 49 of the Reformation. Christ is the "Sun of righteousness," who has risen upon the expectant congregation (Mal. 4:2), and they who love him will be like the sun when it rises in its strength (Judg. 5:31). The early morning belongs to the church of the risen Christ. At the break of light it remembers the morning on which death, the devil, and sin were brought low in defeat, and new life and salvation were given to human beings.

What do we, who today no longer have any fear or awe of the darkness or night, know about the great joy that our forebears and the early Christians felt every morning at the return of the light? If we were to learn again something of the praise and adoration that is due the triune God early in the morning, then we would also begin to sense something of the joy that comes when night is past and those who dwell with one another come together early in the morning to praise their God and hear the Word and pray together. We would learn again of God the Father and Creator who has preserved our life through the dark night and awakened us to a new day; God the Son and Savior of the World, who vanquished death and hell for us, and dwells in our midst as Victor; God the Holy Spirit who pours the bright light of God's Word into our hearts early in the morning, driving away all darkness and sin and teaching us to pray the right way. Morning does not belong to the individual; it belongs to all the church of the triune God, to the community of Christians living together, to the community of 50 brothers. The ancient hymns that call the community of faith to praise God together in the early morning are inexhaustible. That is why the Bohemian Brethren sing in this manner at the break of day: "The day does now dark night dispel; / Dear Christians, wake and rouse you well. / Your praises to the Lord sing true; / And pondering the image of God in you, / Proclaim the Lord's wonders ever anew. / Once more the daylight shines abroad, / O brethren, let us praise the Lord, / Whose grace and mercy thus have kept / The nightly watch while we have slept. / We beg your care this new born day, / For us, poor pilgrims on our way, / O by us stand to help and guide, / That evil on us ne'er betide. / For this there comes the light of day, / O brethren, let us thanksgiving say, / To gentle God who guarded us this darkened night, / Whose grace stood watch o'er us in every plight. / We offer up ourselves to you, / May our wants, words, and deeds be true. / In union with your heart will you us lead. / In you will our work be graced indeed."

Life together under the Word begins at an early hour of the day with a worship service together. A community living together gathers for praise and thanks, Scripture reading, and prayer. The profound silence of morning is first broken by the prayer and song of the community of faith. After the silence of the night and early morning, hymns and the Word of God will be heard all the more clearly. Along these lines the Holy Scriptures tell us that the first thought and the first word of the day belong to God: "O Lord, in the morning you hear my voice; in the morning I plead my case to you, and watch" (Ps. 5:4 [3]). "In the morning my prayer comes before you" (Ps. 88:14 [13]). "My heart is steadfast, O God, my heart is steadfast; I will sing and make melody. Awake, my soul! Awake, O harp and lyre! I will awake the dawn" (Ps. 57:8f. [7f.]). At the break of dawn the believer thirsts and yearns for God: "I rise before dawn and cry for help. I put my hope in your words" (Ps. 119:147). "O God, you are my God, I seek you, my soul thirsts for you; my flesh faints for you, as in a dry and weary land where there is no water" (Ps. 63:2 [1]). The Wisdom of Solomon would have it "known that one must rise before the sun to give you thanks, and must pray to you at the dawning of the light" (16:28), and Jesus Ben Sirach says especially of the teacher of the law that "he sets his heart to rise early to seek the Lord who made him, and to petition the Most High" (39:6 [5]). The Holy Scriptures also speak of the morning hours as the time of God's special help. It is said of the city of God: "God will help it when the morning dawns" (Ps. 46:6 [5]), and again, that God's blessings "are new every morning" (Lam. 3:23).

For Christians the beginning of the day should not be burdened and haunted by the various kinds of concerns they face during the working day. The Lord stands above the new day, for God has made it. All the darkness and confusion of the night with its dreams gives way to the clear light of Jesus Christ and his awakening Word. All restlessness, all impurity, all worry and anxiety flee before him. Therefore, in the early morning hours of the day may our many thoughts and our many idle words be silent, and may the first thought and the first word belong to the one to whom our whole life belongs. "Sleeper, awake! Rise from the dead, and Christ will shine on you" (Eph. 5:14).

With remarkable frequency the Holy Scriptures remind us of various men of God who got up early to seek God and carry out God's commands, as for example, Abraham, Jacob, Moses, and Joshua (cf. Gen. 19:27, 22:3; Exod. 8:16 [20], 9:13, 24:4; Josh. 3:1, 6:12, etc.). The Gospel, which never speaks a superfluous word, reports about Jesus himself: "In the morning, while it was still very dark, he got up and went out to a deserted place, and there he prayed" (Mark 1:35). Some people get up early because of uneasiness and worry; the Scriptures call that pointless, saying, "It is in vain that you rise up early . . . eating your bread with tears" (Ps. 127:2). But there is such a thing as rising early for the love of God. That was the practice of the men of the Holy Scriptures.

Scripture reading, song, and prayer should be part of daily morning *worship together.* Daily morning worship will take as many different forms as there are communities. That is the way it is bound to be. When a community living together includes children, it needs a different sort of daily worship than a community of seminarians.[10] It is by no means healthy when one becomes like the other, when, for example, a brotherhood of seminarians is content with a form of family daily worship for children. However, *the word of Scripture, the hymns of the church, and the prayer of the community* should form a part of every daily worship that they share together. I will now speak here of the individual parts of such daily worship together.

"Speak to one another with psalms" (Eph. 5:19). "Teach and admonish one another . . . and . . . sing psalms" (Col. 3:16). From ancient times in the church a special significance has been attached to the *praying of Psalms* together. In many churches to this day the Psalter is used at the beginning of every service of daily worship together. The practice has been lost to a large extent, and we must now recover the meaning of praying the Psalms. The Psalter occupies a unique place in all the Holy Scriptures. It is God's Word, and with few exceptions it is at the same time the prayer of human beings. How are we to understand this? How can God's Word be at the same

53

---

10. ["This is clearly a reference to the difference between the practice of the seminarians at Finkenwalde and that of other Christian communities to whom Bonhoeffer also addresses this book," *DBWE* 5:52, n. 15.]

time prayer to God?[11] This question is followed by an observation made by all who begin to pray the Psalms. First, they try to repeat the Psalms personally as their own prayer. But soon they come across passages that they feel they cannot pray as their own personal prayers. We remember, for example, the psalms of innocence, the psalms of vengeance, and also, in part, the psalms of suffering. Nevertheless, these prayers are words of the Holy Scriptures that believing Christians cannot simply dismiss as obsolete and antiquated, as a "preliminary stage of religion."[12] Thus they do not   54 desire to gain control over the word of Scripture, and yet they realize that they cannot pray these words. They can read and hear them as the prayer of another person, wonder about them, be offended by them, but they can neither pray them themselves nor expunge them from the Holy Scriptures. The practical thing to say here would be that people in this situation should first stick to the psalms they can understand and pray, and that in reading the other psalms they should quite simply learn to overlook what is incomprehensible and difficult in the Holy Scriptures, returning again and again to what is simple and understandable. However, this difficulty actually indicates the point at which we may get our first glimpse of the secret of the Psalter. The psalms that will not cross our lips as prayers, those that make us falter and offend us, make us suspect that here someone else is praying, not we—that the one who is here affirming his innocence, who is calling for God's judgment, who has come to such infinite depths of suffering, is none other than Jesus Christ himself. It is he who is praying here, and not only here, but in the whole Psalter. The New Testament and the church have always recognized and testified to this truth. The *human* Jesus Christ to whom no affliction, no illness, no suffering is unknown, and who yet was the wholly innocent and righteous one, is praying in the Psalter through the mouth of his congregation. The Psalter is the prayer book of Jesus Christ in the truest sense of the word. He prayed the Psalter, and now it has become   55 his prayer for all time. Can we now comprehend how the Psalter is capable of being simultaneously prayer to God and yet God's own Word, precisely because the praying Christ encounters us here? Jesus Christ prays the Psalter in his congregation. His congregation prays too, and even the individual prays. But they pray only insofar as Christ prays within them; they pray

---

11. ["This is a question that Bonhoeffer addresses in two significant works, *Prayerbook of the Bible: An Introduction to the Psalms, DBWE* 5:141ff., and his Finkenwalde lecture of July 31, 1935, 'Christ in the Psalms,'" *DBWE* 14:386–393, *DBWE* 5:53, n. 18.]

12. ["See Bonhoeffer's treatment of the troubling aspects of the psalms of vengeance in *The Prayerbook of the Bible, DBWE* 5:174–176 . . . ," *DBWE* 5:53–54, n. 19.]

here not in their own name, but in the name of Jesus Christ. They pray not from the natural desires of their own hearts, but rather out of the humanity assumed by Christ. They pray on the basis of the prayer of the human Jesus Christ. Their prayer will be met with the promise of being heard only when they pray on this basis. Because Christ prays the prayer of the Psalms with the individual and with the church before the heavenly throne of God, or rather, because those who pray the Psalms are joining in the prayer of Jesus Christ, their prayer reaches the ears of God. Christ has become their intercessor.

The Psalter is the vicarious prayer of Christ for his congregation.[13] Now that Christ is with the Father, the new humanity of Christ—the body of Christ—on earth continues to pray his prayer to the end of time. This prayer belongs not to the individual member, but to the whole body of Christ. All the things of which the Psalter speaks, which individuals can never fully comprehend and call their own, live only in the body of Christ as a whole. That is why the prayer of the Psalms belongs in the community in a special way. Even if a verse or a psalm is not my own prayer, it is nevertheless the prayer of another member of the community; and it is quite certainly the prayer of the truly human Jesus Christ and his body on earth.

In the Psalter we learn to pray on the basis of Christ's prayer. The Psalter is the great school of prayer. *First*, we learn here what prayer means: it means praying on the basis of the Word of God, on the basis of promises. Christian prayer takes its stand on the solid ground of the revealed Word and has nothing to do with vague, self-seeking desires. We pray on the basis of the prayer of the truly human Jesus Christ. This is what the Scripture means when it says that the Holy Spirit prays in us and for us, that Christ prays for us, that we can pray to God in the right way only in the name of Jesus Christ.

56   *Second*, we learn from the prayer of the Psalms what we should pray. As certain as it is that the prayer of the Psalms ranges far beyond the experiences of the individual, nevertheless, the individual prays in faith the whole prayer of Christ, the prayer of one who was truly human and who alone possesses the full range of experiences expressed in these prayers. Can we, then, pray the psalms of vengeance? Insofar as we are sinners and associate evil thoughts with the prayer of vengeance, we must not do so. But insofar as Christ is in us, we, too, as members of Jesus Christ, can pray these psalms

---

13. ["Bonhoeffer's usage here dates to his doctoral dissertation, where he speaks of Jesus as *Stellvertreter* (a term that can mean 'vicarious representative,' 'substitute,' or 'deputy'), one who acts on behalf of and for others, especially representing humanity before God. See, e.g., *DBWE* 1:145ff. (*Reader* 42–44, 48–49)," *DBWE* 5:55, n. 20.]

through and from the heart of Jesus Christ, who took all the vengeance of God on himself, who was afflicted in place of us by the vengeance of God, who was in this way stricken by the wrath of God and in no other way could forgive his enemies, and who himself suffered this wrath so that his enemies might go free.[14] Can we, with the psalmist, call ourselves innocent, devout, and righteous? We cannot do so insofar as we are ourselves. We cannot do it as the prayer of our own perverse heart. But we can and should do it as a prayer from the heart of Jesus Christ that was sinless and pure, from the innocence of Christ in which he has given us a share by faith. Insofar as "Christ's blood and righteousness" have become "our robe of honor and adornment," we can and we should pray the psalms of innocence as Christ's prayer for us and gift to us. These psalms, too, belong to us through Christ. And how should we pray those prayers of unspeakable misery and suffering, since we have hardly begun to sense even remotely something of what is meant here? We can and we should pray the psalms of suffering, not to become completely caught up in something our heart does not know from its own experience, nor to make our own complaints, but because all this suffering was genuine and real in Jesus Christ, because the human being Jesus Christ suffered sickness, pain, shame, and death, and because in his suffering and dying all flesh suffered and died. What happened to us on the cross of Christ, the death of our old self, and what actually does happen and should happen to us since our baptism in the dying of our flesh, is what gives us the right to pray these prayers. Through the cross of Jesus these psalms have been granted to his body on earth as prayers that issue from his heart. We cannot elaborate on this theme here. Our concern has been only to suggest the depth and breadth of the Psalter as the prayer of Christ. In this regard, we can only grow into the Psalter gradually.

Third, the prayer of the Psalms teaches us to pray as a community. The body of Christ is praying, and I as an individual recognize that my prayer is only a tiny fraction of the whole prayer of the church. I learn to join the body of Christ in its prayer. That lifts me above my personal concerns and allows me to pray selflessly. Many of the Psalms were very probably prayed antiphonally by the Old Testament congregation. The so-called parallelism of the verses (*parallelismus membrorum*),[15] that remarkable repetition of the same idea in different words in the second line of the verse, is not merely a literary form. It also has meaning for the church and theology. It

---

14. ["See Bonhoeffer's 'Sermon on Psalm 58' *DBWE* 14:963–970 . . ." *DBWE* 5:56, n. 22.]

15. [*See* DBWE *5:161.*]

would be worthwhile sometime to pursue this question very thoroughly. One might read, as a particularly clear example, Psalm 5. Repeatedly there are two voices, bringing the same prayer request to God in different words. Is that not meant to be an indication that the one who prays never prays alone? There must always be a second person, another, a member of the church, the body of Christ, indeed Jesus Christ himself, praying with the Christian in order that the prayer of the individual may be true prayer. In the repetition of the same subject, which is heightened in Psalm 119 to such a degree that it seems it does not want to end and becomes so simple that it is virtually impervious to our exegetical analysis, is there not the suggestion that every word of prayer must penetrate to a depth of the heart which can be reached only by unceasing repetition? And in the end not even in that way! Is that not an indication that prayer is not a matter of a unique pouring out of the human heart in need or joy, but an unbroken, indeed continuous, process of learning, appropriating and impressing God's will in Jesus Christ on the mind?[16] Oetinger, in his exegesis of the Psalms, brought out a profound truth when he arranged the whole Psalter according to the seven petitions of the Lord's Prayer. What he meant was that the long and extensive book of Psalms was concerned with nothing more or less than the brief petitions of the Lord's Prayer. In all our praying there remains only the prayer of Jesus Christ, which has the promise of fulfillment and frees us from the vain repetitions of the heathen. The more deeply we grow into the Psalms and the more often we ourselves have prayed them, the more simple and rewarding will our praying become.

58

The prayer of the Psalms, concluded with a hymn by the house church, is followed by a *Scripture reading.* "Give attention to the public reading of scripture" (1 Tim. 4:13). Here, too, we will have to overcome some harmful prejudices before we achieve the right way of reading the Scripture together. Almost all of us have grown up with the idea that the Scripture reading is solely a matter of hearing the Word of God for today. That is why for many the Scripture reading consists only of a few brief selected verses that are to form the central idea of the day. There can be no doubt that the daily Bible passages published by the Moravian Brethren, for example, are a real blessing to all who have ever used them.[17] Many people have realized

---

16. ["On the connection between the deliberate repetitiveness of the verses of the Psalms and the manner in which prayer is an impression on our hearts of God's word and will, see especially Bonhoeffer's 'Meditation on Psalm 119' (*DBWE* 15:496–526) . . . ," *DBWE* 5:58, n. 25.]

17. ["The 'Daily Texts' . . . are small meditation books with a short Bible text from the Old Testament and a selected passage from the New Testament for every day of the year,

that to their great amazement and have been grateful for the daily Bible   59
readings particularly during the time of the church struggle.[18] But equally
there can be little doubt that brief passages cannot and must not take the
place of reading the Scripture as a whole. The verse for the day is not yet the
Holy Scriptures that will remain throughout all time until the Day of Judgment. The Holy Scriptures are more than selected Bible passages. It is also
more than "Bread for Today."[19] It is God's revealed Word for all peoples, for   60
all times. The Holy Scriptures do not consist of individual sayings, but are
a whole and can be used most effectively as such. The Scriptures are God's
revealed Word as a whole. The full witness to Jesus Christ the Lord can be
clearly heard only in its immeasurable inner relationships, in the connection of Old and New Testaments, of promise and fulfillment, sacrifice and
law, Law and Gospel, cross and resurrection, faith and obedience, having
and hoping. That is why daily worship together must include a longer Old
and New Testament lesson besides the prayer of the Psalms. A community of
Christians living together surely should be able to read and listen to a chapter of the Old Testament and at least half a chapter of the New Testament
every morning and evening.[20] When the practice is first tried, however,
such a community will discover that even this modest measure represents a
maximum demand for most people and will meet with resistance. It will be
objected that it is impossible really to take in and retain such an abundance
of ideas and interconnections, that it even shows disrespect for God's Word
to read more than one can seriously digest. In the face of these objections,
we will easily content ourselves again with reading only verses. In truth,
however, a serious failing lies hidden beneath this attitude. If it is really
true that it is hard for us, as adult Christians, to comprehend a chapter of
the Old Testament in its context, then that can only fill us with profound
shame. What kind of testimony is that to our knowledge of the Scriptures
and all our previous reading of them? If we were familiar with the substance
of what we read, we could follow the reading of a chapter without difficulty,

---

as well as a verse from a hymn or a short prayer text . . . ," *DBWE* 5:58–59, n. 28. *First published in 1730, the English version of Moravian Daily Texts is published by the Moravian Church
in North America, Bethlehem, Pennsylvania.*]

18. ["The 'Church Struggle' refers to the conflicts within the German churches and
the collective resistance of churches, and of individuals, to the policies of the National
Socialist Party under Hitler . . . ," *DBWE* 5:59, n. 29.]

19. ["This is an allusion to the title of a well-known tear-off calendar of that period,
'Brot für den Tag' (Bread for the day)," *DBWE* 5:59, n. 30.]

20. ["This appears to be an indication of the actual expectations Bonhoeffer had for
the Finkenwalde community," *DWBE* 5:60, n. 31.]

especially if we have an open Bible in our hands and are reading it at the same time. However, since that is not the case, we must admit that the Holy Scriptures are still largely unknown to us. Can this sin of our own ignorance of God's Word have any other consequence than that we should earnestly and faithfully recover lost ground and catch up on what we have missed? And should not the seminarians be the very first to get to work here? Let us not argue that it is not the purpose of daily worship together to get to know the contents of Scripture, that this is too profane a purpose, something that must be achieved apart from daily worship. This argument is based on a completely wrong understanding of what a daily worship service is. God's

61   Word is to be heard by all in their own way and according to the measure of their understanding. A child hears and learns the biblical story for the first time during daily worship. Mature Christians keep on learning it and learn it better and better; and as they read and hear it on their own, they will never finish this learning.

Not only immature Christians, but also mature Christians will complain that the Scripture reading is often too long for them and that there is much they do not grasp. In response to this complaint it must be said that indeed for the mature Christian every Scripture reading will be "too long," even the shortest one. What does that mean? The Scripture is a complex unity, and every word, every sentence, contains such a diversity of relationships to the whole that it is impossible always to keep track of the whole when listening to an individual portion of it. Therefore, it appears that the whole of Scripture as well as every passage in it far surpasses our understanding. It can only be a good thing when we are daily reminded of this fact, which again refers us to Jesus Christ himself "in whom are *hidden* all the treasures of wisdom and knowledge" (Col. 2:3). So one may perhaps say that every Scripture reading always has to be somewhat "too long" if it is not to be aphoristic worldly wisdom, but God's Word of revelation in Jesus Christ.

Because the Scripture is a corpus, a living whole, the so-called *lectio continua,*[21] or consecutive reading, will above all be worth considering for the Scripture reading of the house church. Historical books, the Prophets, Gospels, Epistles, and Revelation are read and heard as God's Word in their context. They put the listening congregation in the midst of the wonderful revelatory world of the people of Israel with their prophets, judges, kings, and priests, with their wars, festivals, sacrifices, and sufferings. The commu-

---

21. ["For a long time in the ancient church the biblical books were read consecutively in the sequence of their canonical ordering, especially in the monasteries . . . ," *DBWE* 5:61, n. 34.]

nity of believers is drawn into the Christmas story, the baptism, the miracles and discourses, the suffering, dying, and rising of Jesus Christ. It participates in the events that once occurred on this earth for the salvation of the whole world. In so doing, it receives salvation in Jesus Christ here and in all these events. For those who want to hear, reading the biblical books in a sequential order forces them to go, and to allow themselves to be found, where God has acted once and for all for the salvation of human beings. The historical books of the Holy Scriptures come alive for us in a whole new way precisely when they are read during worship services. We receive a part of that which once took place for our salvation. Forgetting and losing ourselves, we too pass through the Red Sea, through the desert, across the Jordan into the promised land. With Israel we fall into doubt and unbelief and through punishment and repentance experience again God's help and faithfulness. All this is not mere reverie, but holy, divine reality. We are uprooted from our own existence and are taken back to the holy history of God on earth. There God has dealt with us, and there God still deals with us today, with our needs and our sins, by means of the divine wrath and grace. What is important is not that God is a spectator and participant in our life today, but that we are attentive listeners and participants in God's action in the sacred story, the story of Christ on earth. God is with us today only as long as we are there. A complete reversal occurs here. It is not that God's help and presence must still be proved in our life; rather God's presence and help have been demonstrated for us in the life of Jesus Christ. It is in fact more important for us to know what God did to Israel, in God's son Jesus Christ, than to discover what God intends for us today. The fact that Jesus Christ died is more important than the fact that I will die. And the fact that Jesus Christ was raised from the dead is the sole ground of my hope that I, too, will be raised on the day of judgment. Our salvation is "from outside ourselves" (*extra nos*). I find salvation not in my life story, but only in the story of Jesus Christ. Only those who allow themselves to be found in Jesus Christ—in the incarnation, cross, and resurrection—are with God and God with them.

From this perspective the whole reading of the Holy Scriptures in worship services becomes every day more meaningful and more beneficial. What we call our life, our troubles, and our guilt is by no means the whole of reality; our life, our need, our guilt, and our deliverance are there in the Scriptures. Because it pleased God to act for us there, it is only there that we will be helped. Only in the Holy Scriptures do we get to know our own story. The God of Abraham, Isaac, and Jacob is the God and Father of Jesus Christ and our God.

We must once again get to know the Scriptures as the reformers and our forebears knew them. We must not shy away from the work and the time required for this task. We must become acquainted with the Scriptures first and foremost for the sake of our salvation. But, besides this, there are enough weighty reasons to make this challenge absolutely urgent for us. For example, how are we ever to gain certainty and confidence in our personal deeds and church activity if we do not stand on solid biblical ground? It is not our heart that determines our course, but God's Word. But who in this day has any proper awareness of the need for evidence from Scripture? How often do we hear innumerable arguments "from life" and "from experience" to justify the most crucial decisions? Yet the evidence of Scripture is excluded even though it would perhaps point in exactly the opposite direction. It is not surprising, of course, that those who attempt to discredit the evidence of Scripture are the people who themselves do not seriously read, know, or make a thorough study of the Scriptures. But those who are not willing to learn how to deal with the Scriptures for themselves are not Protestant Christians.

Perhaps we should ask a further question: How are we supposed to help rightly other Christians who are experiencing troubles and temptation if not with God's own Word? All our own words quickly fail. However, those who "like the master of a household who brings out of his treasure what is new and what is old" (Matt. 13:52)—who can speak out of the abundance of God's Word the wealth of instructions, admonitions, and comforting words from the Scriptures—will be able to drive out demons and help one another through God's Word. We will stop here. "From childhood you have known the sacred writings that are able to instruct you for salvation" (2 Tim. 3:15).

How should we read the Holy Scriptures? In a community living together it is best that its various members assume the task of consecutive reading by taking turns. When this is done, the community will see that it is not easy to read the Scriptures aloud for others. The reading will better suit the subject matter the more plain and simple it is, the more focused it is on the subject matter, the more humble one's attitude. Often the difference between an experienced Christian and a beginner comes out clearly when Scripture is read aloud. It may be taken as a rule for the correct reading of Scripture that the readers should never identify themselves with the person who is speaking in the Bible. It is not I who am angry, but God; it is not I giving comfort, but God; it is not I admonishing, but God admonishing in the Scriptures. Of course, I will be able to express the fact that it is God who is angry, God who is giving comfort and admonishing, by speaking not in a detached, monotonous voice, but only with heartfelt involvement, as one who knows that I myself am being addressed. However, it will make all the difference between a right and a wrong way of reading Scripture if I do not confuse myself with, but rather quite simply serve, God. Otherwise I become rhetorical, over-emotional, sentimental, or coercive; that is to say, I divert the reader's attention to myself instead of the Word—this is the sin of Scripture reading. If we could illustrate this with an example from everyday life, the situation of the one who is reading the Scripture would probably come closest to that in which I read to another person a letter from a friend. I would not read the letter as though I had written it myself. The distance between us would be clearly noticeable as it was read. And yet I would also not be able to read my friend's letter as if it were of no concern to me. On the contrary, because of our close relationship, I would read it with personal interest. Proper reading of Scripture is not a technical exercise that can be learned; it is something that grows or diminishes according to my own spiritual condition. The ponderous, laborious reading of the Bible by many a Christian who has become seasoned through experience often far surpasses a minister's reading, no matter how perfect the latter in form. In a community of Christians living together, one person may also give counsel and help to another in this matter.

The short devotional Bible texts do not need to be lost but can supplement the continuous reading of the Scriptures. They may find their place as weekly or as daily Bible verses at the beginning of daily worship or at some other time.   65

Singing together joins the praying of the Psalms and the reading of the Scriptures. In this, the voice of the church is heard in praise, thanksgiving, and intercession.

"O sing to the Lord a new song" [*Ps. 98:1*], the Psalter calls out to us again and again. It is the Christ hymn, new every morning, that a community living together begins to sing in the early morning, the new song that is sung by the whole community of faith in God on earth and in heaven. We are called to join in the singing of it. It is God who has prepared one great song of praise throughout eternity, and those who enter God's community join in this song. It is the song that "the morning stars sang together and all the children of God shouted for joy" (Job 38:7). It is the victory song of the children of Israel after passing through the Red Sea, the Magnificat of Mary after the Annunciation, the song of Paul and Silas when they praised God in the darkness of prison, the song of the singers on the sea of glass after their deliverance, the "song of Moses, the servant of God, and the song of the Lamb" (Rev. 15:3). It is the new song of the heavenly community. Every day in the morning the community of faith on earth joins in this song and in the evening it closes the day with this hymn. The triune God and the works of God are being extolled here. This song has a different sound on earth than it does in heaven. On earth, it is the song of those who believe;

in heaven, the song of those who see. On earth, it is a song expressed in inadequate human words; in heaven they are the "things that are not to be told, that no mortal is permitted to repeat" (2 Cor. 12:4), the "new song that no one could learn, except the 144,000" (Rev. 14:3), the song to which the "harps of *God*" are played (Rev. 15:2). What do we know of that new song and the harps of God? Our new song is an earthly song, a song of pilgrims and sojourners on whom the Word of God has dawned to light their way. Our earthly song is bound to God's Word of revelation in Jesus Christ. It is the simple song of the children of this earth who have been called to be God's children, not ecstatic, not enraptured, but soberly, gratefully, devoutly focused on God's revealed Word.

66

"Sing and make music in your heart to the Lord" (Eph. 5:19). The new song is sung first in the heart. It cannot be sung at all in any other way. The heart sings because it is filled with Christ. That is why all singing in the congregation is a spiritual thing. Devotion to the Word, incorporation into the community, great humility, and much discipline—these are the prerequisites of all singing together. Wherever the heart does not join in the singing, there is only the dreadful muddle of human self-praise. Wherever the singing is not to the Lord, it is singing to the honor of the self or the music, and the new song becomes a song to idols.

"Speak to one another with psalms, hymns and spiritual songs" (Eph. 5:19). Our song on earth is speech. It is the sung Word. Why do Christians sing when they are together? The reason is, quite simply, that in singing together it is possible for them to speak and pray the same Word at the same time—in other words, for the sake of uniting in the Word. All daily worship, all human concentration should be focused on the Word in the hymn. The fact that we do not speak it in unison, but sing it, only expresses the fact that our spoken words are inadequate to express what we want to say, that the object of our singing reaches far beyond all human words. Nevertheless, we do not mumble unintelligible words; rather we sing words of praise to God, words of thanksgiving, confession, and prayer. Thus the music is completely the servant of the Word. It elucidates the Word in its incomprehensibility.

67

Because it is completely bound to the Word, the singing of the congregation in its worship service, especially the singing of the house church, is essentially singing in unison. Here words and music combine in a unique way. The freely soaring tone of unison singing finds its sole and essential inner support in the words that are sung. It does not need, therefore, the musical support of other parts. The Bohemian Brethren sang: "With one voice let us sing today, in unison and from the bottom of our heart." "So that together you may with one voice glorify the God and Father of our Lord Jesus Christ" (Rom. 15:6). The essence of all congregational singing on this earth is the purity of unison singing—untouched by the unrelated motives of musical excess—the clarity unclouded by the dark desire to lend musicality an autonomy of its own apart from the words; it is the simplicity and unpretentiousness, the humanness and warmth, of this style of singing. Of course, this truth is only gradually and by patient practice disclosed to our oversophisticated ears. Whether or not a community achieves proper unison singing is a question of its spiritual discernment. This is singing from the heart, singing to the Lord, singing the Word; this is singing in unity.

There are several elements hostile to unison singing, which in the community ought to be very rigorously weeded out. There is no place in the worship service where vanity and bad taste can so assert themselves as in the singing. First, there is the improvised second part that one encounters almost everywhere people are supposed to sing together. It attempts to give the necessary background, the missing richness to the free-floating unison sound and in the process kills both the words and the sound. There are the bass or the alto voices that must call everybody's attention to their astonishing range and therefore sing every hymn an octave lower. There is the solo voice that drowns out everything else, bellowing and quavering at the top of its lungs, reveling in the glory of its own fine organ. There are the less dangerous foes of congregational singing, the "unmusical" who cannot sing, of whom there are far fewer than we are led to believe. Finally, there are often those who will not join in the singing because they are particularly moody or nursing hurt feelings; and thus they disturb the community.

As difficult as it is, unison singing is much less a musical than a spiritual matter. Only where everybody in the community is prepared to assume an attitude of devotion and discipline can unison singing give us the joy that is its alone, even if it exhibits many musical shortcomings.

Primarily the Reformation chorales, as well as the hymns of the Bohemian Brethren and pieces from the historic church, are worth considering for practice in unison singing. Starting here, the community will form an opinion on its own as to which hymns in our hymnbook lend themselves to unison singing and which do not. Any doctrinaire attitude, which we encounter so often in this area, is a bad thing. The decision on this issue can only be made on the merits of each case, and here too we should not become iconoclastic. A community of Christians living together will therefore try hard to master as rich a store of hymns as possible that can be sung without music and from memory. It will achieve this goal if in addition to a freely chosen hymn it inserts in every daily worship service several set verses that can be sung between the readings.

Singing, however, should be practiced not just in the daily worship services, but at regular times during the day or week. The more we sing, the

68

more joy we will derive from it. But, above all, the more concentration and discipline and joy we put into our singing, the richer will be the blessing that will come to the whole life of the community from singing together.

It is the voice of the church that is heard in singing together. It is not I who sing, but the church. However, as a member of the church, I may share in its song. Thus all true singing together must serve to widen our spiritual horizon. It must enable us to recognize our small community as a member of the great Christian church on earth and must help us willingly and joyfully to take our place in the song of the church with our singing, be it feeble or good.

God's Word, the voice of the church, and our prayer belong together. So we must now speak of prayer together. "If two of you agree about anything you ask for, it will be done for you by my Father in heaven" (Matt. 18:19). There is no part of daily worship together that causes us such serious difficulties and trouble as does common prayer, for here we ourselves are supposed to speak. We have heard God's Word and we have had the privilege of joining in the song of the church, but now we are to pray to God as a community, and this prayer must really be *our* word, *our* prayer—for this day, for our work, for our community, for the particular needs and sins that commonly oppress us, for the persons who are committed to our care. Or should we really not pray for ourselves at all? Should the desire for prayer together with our own lips and in our own words be a forbidden thing? No matter what objections there may be to prayer together, it simply could not be any other way. Christians may and should pray together to God in their own words when they desire to live together under the Word of God. They have requests, gratitude, and intercessions to bring in common to God, and they should do so joyfully and confidently. All our fear of one another, all our inhibitions about praying freely in our own words in the presence of others, can diminish where the common prayer of the community is brought before God by one of its members with dignity and simplicity. Likewise, however, all our observations and criticisms should cease whenever weak words of prayer are offered in the name of Jesus Christ. It is in fact the most normal thing in our common Christian life to pray together. As good and useful as our scruples may be about keeping our prayer pure and biblical, they must nevertheless not stifle the free prayer itself that is so necessary, for it has been endowed with great promise by Jesus Christ.

The extemporaneous prayer at the close of daily worship normally will be said by the head of the house. But in any case it is best that it always be said by the same person. That places an unexpected responsibility on this person, but in order to safeguard the prayer from the wrong kind of scrutiny and from false subjectivity, one person should pray for all the community for an extended period of time.

The first condition that makes it possible for individuals to pray for the community is the intercession of all the others for such persons and for their praying. How could one person pray the prayer of the community without being held up and supported in prayer by the community itself? At precisely this point every word of criticism must be transformed into more faithful intercession and mutual help. How easily a community can split apart if this is not done!

Extemporaneous prayer in daily worship together should be the prayer of the community and not that of the individual who is praying. It is this individual's task to pray for the community. Thus such a person will have to share the daily life of the community and must know the cares and needs, the joys and thanksgivings, the requests and hopes of the others. The community's work and everything that it involves must not be unknown to the individual who prays for the community. One prays as a believer among other Christians. It will require self-examination and watchfulness if individuals are not to confuse their own hearts with the heart of the community, if a person really is to be guided solely by the task of praying for the community. For this reason it will be good if the persons who have been assigned this task are constantly given the benefit of counsel and help from others in the community, if they receive suggestions and requests to remember this or that need, work, or even a particular person in the prayer. Thus the prayer will become more and more the common prayer of all.

Even extemporaneous prayer will be determined by a certain internal order. It is not the chaotic outburst of a human heart, but the prayer of an internally ordered community. Thus certain prayer requests will recur daily, even if they may perhaps recur in different ways. At first there may be some monotony in the daily repetition of the same petitions that are entrusted to us as a community, but later freedom from an all too individualistic form of prayer will surely be found. If it is possible to add to the number of daily recurring petitions, a weekly order might be tried, as has been proposed on occasion. If that is not possible in the common prayers, it is certainly a help in one's personal times of prayer. Relating the prayer to one of the Scripture readings also will prove helpful for liberating spontaneous prayer from the arbitrariness of subjectivity. This gives support and substance to the prayer.

From time to time a problem will arise where the person given the job of offering prayer for the community feels inwardly unable to offer prayer and would prefer to turn over the task to someone else for the day. However, that is not advisable. Otherwise, the community's prayers will be too easily controlled by moods that have nothing to do with life in the spirit. The persons assigned to pray for the community should learn what it means to have a duty to perform in the congregation even at a time when they would like to avoid this task because they are weighed down by inner emptiness and weariness or by personal guilt. The other members of the community should support them in their weakness, in their inability to pray. Perhaps then the words of Paul will come true: "We do not know how to pray as we ought, but that very Spirit intercedes with sighs too deep for words" (Rom. 8:26). It is of great importance that the community understands, supports, and prays the prayer of these individuals as its own.

71 The use of set prayers can be a help even for a small community living together under certain circumstances, but often it becomes only an evasion of real prayer. By using ecclesial forms and the church's wealth of thought, we can easily deceive ourselves about our own prayer life. The prayers then become beautiful and profound, but not genuine. As helpful as the church's tradition of prayer is for learning how to pray, nevertheless it cannot take the place of the prayer that I owe to my God today. Here the poorest stammering can be better than the best-phrased prayer. It goes without saying that the state of affairs in public worship services is different from the daily worship of the community living together.

Often in Christian everyday-life communities there will be a desire for special communities of prayer over and above the prayers in the daily worship together. Here there can probably be no set rule except one—the meetings of such groups should be held only where there is a common desire for them and where it is certain that there will be common participation in a particular prayer service. Any individual undertakings of this kind can easily plant the seed of corruption in the community. It is precisely in this area that it must prove true that the strong support the weak, and the weak not rule over the strong.[22] The New Testament teaches us that a free community of prayer is the most obvious and natural thing and may be viewed without suspicion. But where mistrust and anxiety exist, one must bear with the other in patience. Let nothing be done by force, but everything be done in freedom and love.

---

22. ["This is an allusion to Rom. 14:1–15 and 1 Cor. 8:1–13. In the background lurk the arguments over the Aryan Clause and the continued resistance of the Confessing Church to the proposed laws that appeared to legalize discrimination against baptized members of Jewish ancestry. Eberhard Bethge reports that Bonhoeffer used Romans 14 in his stinging rejection of proposals that the churches effect a compromise on the issue of expelling the Jewish Christians from their ranks, perhaps even to the extent of setting up separate congregations based on racial conformity or nonconformity. See *DB-ER*, 287–288," *DBWE* 5:71, n. 51.]

We have considered thus far the daily morning worship of Christian everyday-life communities. God's Word, the hymns of the church, and the prayers of the community of faith stand at the beginning of the day. Only when the community has been provided and strengthened with the bread of eternal life does it gather together to receive from God earthly bread for this bodily life. Giving thanks and asking God's blessing, the Christian house church takes its daily bread from the hand of the Lord. Ever since 72 Jesus Christ sat at table with his disciples, the community at the table of Christ's congregation has been blessed by his presence. "When he was at the table with them, he took bread, blessed and broke it, and gave it to them. Then their eyes were opened, and they recognized him" (Luke 24:30–31a). The Scriptures speak of three kinds of community at the table that Jesus keeps with his own: the daily breaking of bread together at meals, the breaking of bread together at the Lord's Supper, and the final breaking of bread together in the reign of God. But in all three, the one thing that counts is that "their eyes were opened and they recognized him." What does it mean to recognize Jesus Christ by way of these gifts? It means, *first*, to recognize Christ as the giver of all gifts, as the Lord and Creator—with the Father and the Holy Spirit—of this our world. Therefore, the community at the table prays "and let *your* gifts to us be blessed," and thus declares its faith in the eternal deity of Jesus Christ. *Second*, the congregation recognizes that all earthly gifts are given to it only for the sake of Christ, as this whole world is preserved only for the sake of Jesus Christ—for the sake of Christ's Word and its proclamation. Christ is the true bread of life, not only the giver but the gift itself, for whose sake all earthly gifts exist. God patiently preserves us with God's own good gifts only because the Word of Jesus Christ is still to go forth and encounter faith, because our faith is not yet perfected. That is why the Christian congregation breaking bread together at the table prays in Luther's words, "O Lord God, dear heavenly Father, bless us and these your gifts which we receive from your bountiful goodness, through *Jesus Christ our Lord.* Amen"—and thus declares its faith in Jesus Christ as the divine mediator and savior. *Third*, the community of Jesus believes that its Lord desires to be present wherever it asks him to be present. That is why it prays: "Come, Lord Jesus, be our guest," thus confessing the gracious omni- 73 presence of Jesus Christ. Every breaking of bread together fills Christians with gratitude for the present Lord and God, Jesus Christ. It is not as if they were seeking any unhealthy spiritualization of material gifts; rather, in their wholehearted joy in the good gifts of this physical life, Christians recognize their Lord as the true giver of all good gifts. And beyond this, they recognize their Lord as the true gift, the true bread of life itself, and finally as the one who calls them to the joyful banquet in the reign of God. So in a special way, the daily breaking of bread together binds Christians to their Lord and to one another. At the table they recognize their Lord as the one who breaks bread for them. The eyes of their faith are opened.

The breaking of bread together has a festive quality. In the midst of the working day given to us again and again, it is a reminder that God rested after God's work, and that the Sabbath is the meaning and the goal of the week with its toil. Our life is not only a great deal of trouble and hard work; it is also refreshment and joy in God's goodness. We labor, but God nourishes and sustains us. That is a reason to celebrate. People should not eat the bread of anxious toil (Ps. 127:2). Rather "eat your bread with enjoyment" (Eccles. 9:7), "so I commend enjoyment, for there is nothing better for people under the sun than to eat, and drink, and enjoy themselves" (Eccles. 8:15). But of course, "apart from him, who can eat or who can have enjoyment?" (Eccles. 2:25). It is said of the seventy elders of Israel who climbed Mount Sinai with Moses and Aaron that "they beheld God, and they ate and drank" (Exod. 24:11). God will not tolerate the unfestive, joyless manner in which we eat our bread with sighs of groaning, with pompous, self-important busyness, or even with shame. Through the daily meal God is calling us to rejoice, to celebrate in the midst of our working day.

Christian community at the table also signifies obligation. It is *our* daily bread that we eat, not my own. We share our bread. Thus we are firmly bound to one another not only in the Spirit, but with our whole physical being. The *one* bread that is given to our community unites us in a firm covenant. Now no one must hunger as long as the other has bread, and whoever shatters this community of our bodily life also shatters the community of the Spirit. Both are inextricably linked together. "Share your bread with the hungry" (Is. 58:7). "Do not despise the hungry" (Sirach 4:2), for the Lord meets us in the hungry (Matt. 25:37). "If a brother or sister is naked and lacks daily food, and one of you says to them, 'Go in peace; keep warm and eat your fill,' and yet you do not supply their bodily needs, what is the good of that?" (James 2:15f.). As long as we eat our bread together, we will have enough even with the smallest amount. Hunger begins only when people desire to keep their own bread for themselves. That is a strange divine law. Could not the story of the miraculous feeding of the 5,000 with two fish and five loaves of bread also have this meaning, along with many others?

The breaking of bread together teaches Christians that here they still eat the perishable bread of the earthly pilgrimage. But if they share this bread with one another, they will also one day receive together imperishable bread in the Father's house. "Blessed is the one who will eat bread in the reign of God" (Luke 14:15).

After the first morning hour, the Christian's day until evening belongs to *work*. "People go out to their work and to their labor until the evening" (Ps. 104:23). In most cases a community of Christians living together will separate for the duration of the working hours. Praying and working are two different things. Prayer should not be hindered by work, but neither should work be hindered by prayer. Just as it was God's will that human beings should work six days and rest and celebrate before the face of God on the seventh, so it is also God's will that every day should be marked for the Christian both by prayer and work. Prayer also requires its own time. 75 But the longest part of the day belongs to work. The inseparable unity of both will only become clear when work and prayer each receives its own undivided due. Without the burden and labor of the day, prayer is not prayer; and without prayer, work is not work. Only the Christian knows that. Thus it is precisely in the clear distinction between them that their oneness becomes apparent.

Work puts human beings in the world of things. It requires achievement from them. Christians step out of the world of personal encounter into the world of impersonal things, the "It"; and this new encounter frees them for objectivity, for the world of the It is only an instrument in the hand of God for the purification of Christians from all self-absorption and selfishness. The work of the world can only be accomplished where people forget themselves, where they lose themselves in a cause, reality, the task, the It. Christians learn at work to allow the task to set the bounds for them. Thus, for them, work becomes a remedy for the lethargy and laziness of the flesh. The demands of the flesh die in the world of things. But that can only happen where Christians break through the It to the "You" of God,[23] who commands the work and the deed and makes them serve to liberate Christians from themselves. In this process work does not cease to be work; but the severity and rigor of labor is sought all the more by those who know what good it does them. The continuing conflict with the It remains. But at the same time the breakthrough has been made. The unity of prayer and work, the unity of the day, is found because finding the You of God behind the It of the day's work is what Paul means by his admonition to "pray without ceas- 76 ing" (1 Thess. 5:17). The prayer of the Christian reaches, therefore, beyond the time allocated to it and extends into the midst of the work. It surrounds the whole day, and in so doing, it does not hinder the work; it promotes

---

23. [*For Bonhoeffer's understanding of God as person rather than an object, see* DBWE 2, *especially 103–116.*]

work, affirms work, gives work great significance and joyfulness. Thus every word, every deed, every piece of work of the Christian becomes a prayer, not in the unreal sense of being constantly distracted from the task that must be done, but in a real breakthrough from the hard It to the gracious You. "And whatever you do, in word or deed, do everything in the name of the Lord Jesus" (Col. 3:17).

The whole day now acquires an order and a discipline gained by winning this unity of the day. This order and discipline must be sought and found in the morning prayer. It will stand the test at work. Prayer offered in early morning is decisive for the day. The wasted time we are ashamed of, the temptations we succumb to, the weakness and discouragement in our work, the disorder and lack of discipline in our thinking and in our dealings with other people—all these very frequently have their cause in our neglect of morning prayer. The ordering and scheduling of our time will become more secure when it comes from prayer. The temptations of the working day will be overcome by this breakthrough to God. The decisions that are demanded by our work will become simpler and easier when they are made not in fear of other people, but solely before the face of God. "Whatever you do, do it from your hearts, as done for the Lord and not done for human beings" (Col. 3:23). Even routine mechanical work will be performed more patiently when it comes from the knowledge of God and God's command. Our strength and energy for work increase when we have asked God to give us the strength we need for our daily work.

77   Where it is possible, the midday hour becomes for a community of Christians living together a brief rest on their journey through the day. Half of the day is past. The congregation thanks God and asks for protection until evening. It receives its daily bread and prays in the words of a Reformation hymn: "Feed your children, God most holy, / Comfort sinners poor and lowly." It is God who must feed us. We cannot and dare not take it for ourselves because we poor sinners have not merited it. Thus the meal God serves us becomes a consolation for the afflicted, for it is proof of the grace and faithfulness with which God preserves and guides God's children. It is true that the Scripture says that "anyone unwilling to work should not eat" (2 Thess. 3:10) and thus makes the receiving of bread strictly dependent on working for it. But the Scriptures do not say anything about any claim that working persons have on God for their bread. It is true that work is commanded, but the bread is God's free and gracious gift. We cannot simply take it for granted that our own work provides us with bread; rather this is God's order of grace. The day belongs to God alone. Hence in the middle of the day, the Christian community of faith gathers and lets God invite

them to the table. The midday hour is one of the seven prayer hours of the church and of the singer of the Psalms.[24] At the height of the day the church invokes the triune God in praise of God's wonders and in prayer for help and speedy redemption. At midday the heavens were darkened above the cross of Jesus. The work of atonement was approaching its completion. Where a community of Christians living together is able to be together at this hour for a brief daily worship time of song and prayer, it will not do so in vain.

The day's work comes to an end. When the day has been hard and toilsome, the Christian will understand what Paul Gerhardt meant when he sang: "Head, hands and feet so tired, / Are glad the day's expired, / That work comes to an end; / My heart is fill'd with gladness / That God from all earth's sadness, / And from sin's toil relief will send." One day is long enough to keep one's faith; the next day will have its own worries.

The community of Christians living together gathers together again. The evening breaking of bread together and the final daily worship service bring them together. With the disciples in Emmaus they ask: "Lord, stay with us, because it is almost evening and the day is now nearly over." It is a good thing if the daily evening worship can really be held at the end of the day, thus becoming the last word before the night's rest. When night falls, the true light of God's Word shines brighter for the community of faith. The prayer of the Psalms, a Scripture reading, a hymn, and a prayer together close the day as they opened it. We still need to say a few words on the subject of evening prayer. This is the special place for intercession together. After the day's work has been completed, we ask for God's blessing, peace, and preservation for the whole of Christianity, for our congregation, for pastors in their ministries, for the poor, the wretched and lonely, for the sick and dying, for our neighbors, for our family at home, and for our community. When could we ever have a deeper awareness of God's power and working than in the hour when we lay aside our own work and entrust ourselves to God's faithful hands? When are we more prepared to pray for blessing, peace, and preservation than the time when our activity is at an end? When we grow tired, God works. "The Guardian of Israel neither slumbers nor sleeps" [Ps. 121:4]. Our request for the forgiveness of every wrong we have done to God and to one another, for God's forgiveness and that of our brothers, and for the willingness gladly to forgive any wrong

78

79

---

24. [*Bonhoeffer refers to the "Hour of Sext," the noon hour of prayer according to the liturgical practice of many Christian traditions.*]

done to us, belongs then, too, especially in the evening prayers of a community of Christians living together. It is an old custom of the monasteries that by set practice in the daily evening worship the abbot asks his brothers to forgive him for all the sins of omission and wrongdoings committed against them. After the brothers assure him of their forgiveness, they likewise ask the abbot to forgive them for their sins of omission and wrongdoings and receive his forgiveness. "Do not let the sun go down on your anger" (Eph. 4:26). It is a decisive rule of every Christian community that every division that the day has caused must be healed in the evening. It is perilous for the Christian to go to bed with an unreconciled heart. Therefore, it is a good idea especially to include the request for mutual forgiveness in every evening's prayers, so that reconciliation can be achieved and renewal of the community established. Finally, in all the old evening prayers, it is striking how frequently we encounter their plea for preservation during the night from the devil, from terror and from an evil, sudden death. The ancients were keenly aware of human helplessness while sleeping, the kinship of sleep with death, and the devil's cunning in causing our downfall when we are defenseless. That is why they prayed for the assistance of the holy angels and their golden weapons, for the presence of the heavenly hosts at the time when Satan would gain power over us. Most remarkable and profound is the ancient church's request that, when our eyes are closed in sleep, God may nevertheless keep our hearts alert to God. It is a prayer that God may dwell with us and in us, even when we feel and know nothing, that God may keep our hearts pure and holy in spite of all the worries and temptations of the night, that God may prepare our hearts to hear the call at any time and, like
80 the boy Samuel, answer even in the night, "Speak, Lord, for your servant is listening" (1 Sam. 3:10). Even while sleeping we are in the hands of God or in the power of the evil one. Even while we sleep, God can perform miracles upon us or the evil one can cause devastation in us. So we pray in the evening: "Though our eyes in sleep will close, / May our hearts in you repose, / Protect us, God, with your right arm, / And shield our souls from sin's cruel harm" (Luther). But the word of the Psalter stands over the morning and the evening: "Yours is the day, yours also the night" (Ps. 74:16).

The Day Alone

81 "The praise of silence befits you, O God, in Zion" (Ps. 65:2 [1]). Many persons seek community because they are afraid of loneliness. Because they can no longer endure being alone, such people are driven to seek the company of others. Christians, too, who cannot cope on their own, and who in

their own lives have had some bad experiences, hope to experience help with this in the company of other people. More often than not, they are disappointed. They then blame the community for what is really their own fault. The Christian community is not a spiritual sanatorium. Those who take refuge in community while fleeing from themselves are misusing it to   82
indulge in empty talk and distraction, no matter how spiritual this idle talk and distraction may appear. In reality they are not seeking community at all, but only a thrill that will allow them to forget their isolation for a short time. It is precisely such misuse of community that creates the deadly isolation of human beings. Such attempts to find healing result in the undermining of speech and all genuine experience and, finally, resignation and spiritual death.

Whoever cannot be alone should beware of community. Such people will only do harm to themselves and to the community. Alone you stood before God when God called you. Alone you had to obey God's voice. Alone you had to take up your cross, struggle, and pray and alone you will die and give an account to God. You cannot avoid yourself, for it is precisely God who has singled you out. If you do not want to be alone, you are rejecting Christ's call to you, and you can have no part in the community of those who are called. "The confrontation with death and its demands comes to us all; no one can die for another. All must fight their own battle with death by themselves, alone. I will not be with you then, nor you with me" (Luther).

But the reverse is also true. *Whoever cannot stand being in community should beware of being alone.* You are called into the community of faith; the call was not meant for you alone. You carry your cross, you struggle, and you pray in the community of faith, the community of those who are called. You are not alone even when you die, and on the day of judgment you will be only one member of the great community of faith of Jesus Christ. If you neglect   83
the community of other Christians, you reject the call of Jesus Christ, and thus your being alone can only become harmful for you. "If I die, then I am not alone in death; if I suffer, they (the community of faith) suffer with me" (Luther).

We recognize, then, that only as we stand within the community can we be alone, and only those who are alone can live in the community.[25] Both belong together. Only in the community do we learn to be properly alone; and only in being alone do we learn to live properly in the community. It is

---

25. ["The reader should note the similar dialectical relationship between belief and obedience as stated in *DBWE* 4:77–84 (*Reader* 485–490), which also is from the Finkenwalde period," *DBWE* 5:83, n. 5. *This "dialectical" thinking first appears in* Sanctorum Communio *and programmatically so in* Act and Being.]

not as if the one preceded the other; rather both begin at the same time, namely, with the call of Jesus Christ.

Each taken by itself has profound pitfalls and perils. Those who want community without solitude plunge into the void of words and feelings, and those who seek solitude without community perish in the bottomless pit of vanity, self-infatuation, and despair.

Whoever cannot be alone should beware of community. Whoever cannot stand being in community should beware of being alone.

The day together of Christians who live in community is accompanied by each individual's day alone. That is the way it must be. The day together will be unfruitful without the day alone, both for the community and for the individual.

The mark of solitude is silence, just as speech is the mark of community. Silence and speech have the same inner connection and distinction as do being alone and community. One does not exist without the other. Genuine speech comes out of silence, and genuine silence comes out of speech.

Silence does not mean being incapable of speech, just as speech does not mean idle talk. Being incapable of speech does not create solitude, and idle talk does not create community. "Silence is the excess, the inebriation, the sacrifice of speech. But being incapable of speech is not holy; it is like a thing that has only been mutilated, not sacrificed. Zachary was incapable of speech, rather than being silent. If he had accepted the revelation, he may perhaps have come out of the temple not incapable of speaking, but silent" (Ernest Hello). That speaking which reestablishes and binds the community together is accompanied by silence. "There is a time . . . to keep silence and a time to speak" (Eccles. 3:7). Just as there are certain times in a Christian's day for speaking the Word, particularly the time of daily worship and prayer together, so the day also needs certain times of silence under the Word and silence that comes out of the Word. These will mainly be the times before and after hearing the Word. The Word comes not to the noise-makers but to those who are silent. The stillness of the temple is the sign of God's holy presence in the Word.

There is an indifferent or even negative attitude toward silence which sees in it a disparagement of God's revelation in the Word. Silence is misunderstood as a solemn gesture, as a mystical desire to get beyond the Word. Silence is no longer seen in its essential relationship to the Word, as the simple act of the individual who falls silent under the Word of God. We are silent before hearing the Word because our thoughts are already focused on the Word, as children are quiet when they enter their father's room. We are silent after hearing the Word because the Word is still speaking and living and dwelling within us. We are silent early in the morning because God

should have the first word, and we are silent before going to bed because   85
the last word also belongs to God. We remain silent solely for the sake
of the Word, not thereby to dishonor the Word but rather to honor and
receive it properly. In the end, silence means nothing other than waiting
for God's Word and coming from God's Word with a blessing. But everybody knows this is something that needs to be learned in these days when
idle talk has gained the upper hand. Real silence, real stillness, really holding one's tongue, comes only as the sober consequence of spiritual silence.

This silence before the Word, however, will have an impact on the whole
day. If we have learned to be silent before the Word, we will also learn to
manage our silence and our speech during the day. Silence can be forbidden, self-satisfied, haughty, or insulting. From this it follows that silence in
itself can never be the issue. The silence of the Christian is listening silence,
humble stillness that may be broken at any time for the sake of humility. It is
silence in conjunction with the Word. This is what Thomas à Kempis meant
when he said: "No one speaks more confidently than the one who gladly
remains silent." There is a wonderful power in being silent—the power of
clarification, purification, and focus on what is essential. This is true even
when considered from a purely profane point of view. But silence before the
Word leads to proper hearing and thus also to proper speaking of God's
Word at the right time. Much that is unnecessary remains unsaid. But what
is essential and helpful can be said in a few words.

When a community lives close together in a confined space and outwardly cannot give the individual the necessary quiet, then regular times of
silence are absolutely essential. After a period of silence, we encounter others in a different and fresh way. Many a community living together will only
be able to ensure the individual's right to be alone by adopting a set daily
discipline, and thereby will keep the community itself from harm.   86

We will not discuss here all the wonderful fruits that can come to Christians in solitude and silence. It is all too easy to go dangerously astray in
this matter. We could also probably cite many a dubious experience that
can grow out of silence. Silence can be a dreadful wasteland with all its
isolated stretches and terrors. It can also be a paradise of self-deception.
One is not better than the other. Be that as it may, let none expect from
silence anything but a simple encounter with the Word of God for the sake
of which Christians have entered into silence. This encounter, however, is
given to them as a gift. Their silence will be richly rewarded if they do not
set any conditions on how they expect this encounter to take place or what
they hope to get from it, but simply accept it as it comes.

There are three things for which the Christian needs a regular time
alone during the day: *meditation on the Scripture, prayer,* and *intercession.* All

three should find a place in the *daily period of meditation*.[26] There is no reason to be concerned about the use of this word "meditation." In this case we are making our own an old word of the church and the Reformation.

One might ask why a special time is needed for this, since we already have everything we need in daily worship together. In the following we will arrive at the answer to this question.

The period of meditation is useful for personal consideration of Scripture, personal prayer, and personal intercession. It serves no other purpose. Spiritual experiments have no place here. But there must be time for these three things, because it is precisely God who requires them of us. Even if for a long time meditation were to mean nothing but that we are performing a service we owe to God, this would be reason enough to do it.

This time for meditation does not allow us to sink into the void and bottomless pit of aloneness, rather it allows us to be alone with the Word. In so doing it gives us solid ground on which to stand and clear guidance for the steps we have to take.

87   Whereas in our daily worship together we read long, continuous texts, in our personal meditation on Scripture we stick to a brief selected text that will possibly remain unchanged for an entire week. If in our communal reading of the Scriptures we are led more into the whole length and breadth of the Holy Scriptures, here we are guided into the unfathomable depths of a particular sentence and word. Both are equally necessary, "that you may have the power to comprehend, with all the saints, what is the breadth and length and height and depth" (Eph. 3:18).

In our meditation we read the text given to us on the strength of the promise that it has something quite personal to say to us for this day and for our standing as Christians—it is not only God's Word for the community of faith, but also God's Word for me personally. We expose ourselves to the particular sentence and word until we personally are affected by it. When we do that, we are doing nothing but what the simplest, most unlearned Christian does every day. We are reading the Word of God as God's Word for us. Therefore, we do not ask what this text has to say to other people. For those of us who are preachers that means we will not ask how we would preach or teach on this text, but what it has to say to us personally. It is true that to do this we must first have understood the content of the text. But in this situation we are neither doing an exegesis of the text, nor preparing a sermon or conducting a Bible study of any kind; we are rather waiting

---

26. ["See Bonhoeffer's 'Guide to Scriptural Meditation', *DBWE* 14:931–936," *DBWE* 5:86, n. 11.]

for God's Word to us. We are not waiting in vain; on the contrary, we are waiting on the basis of a clear promise. Often we are so burdened and overwhelmed with other thoughts, images, and concerns that it may take a long time before God's Word has cleared all that away and gets through to us. But it will surely come, just as surely as none other than God has come to human beings and wants to come again. For that very reason we will begin our meditation with the prayer that God may send the Holy Spirit to us through the Word, and reveal God's Word to us, and enlighten our minds.

It is not necessary for us to get through the entire text in one period of meditation. Often we will have to stick to a single sentence or even to one word because we have been gripped and challenged by it and can no longer evade it. Are not the words "father," "love," "mercy," "cross," "sanctification," or "resurrection" often enough to fill amply the brief time set aside for our meditation?

It is not necessary for us to be anxious about putting our thoughts and 88 prayers into words as we meditate. Silent thinking and praying, which comes only from our listening, can often be more beneficial.

It is not necessary for us to find new ideas in our meditation. Often that only distracts us and satisfies our vanity. It is perfectly sufficient if the Word enters in and dwells within us as we read and understand it. As Mary "pondered . . . in her heart" [*Luke 2:19*] what the shepherds told her, as a person's words often stick in our mind for a long time—as they dwell and work within us, preoccupy us, disturb us, or make us happy without our being able to do anything about it—so as we meditate, God's Word desires to enter in and stay with us. It desires to move us, to work in us, and to make such an impression on us that the whole day long we will not get away from it. Then it will do its work in us, often without our being aware of it.

Above all, it is not necessary for us to have any unexpected, extraordinary experiences while meditating. That can happen, but if it does not, this is not a sign that the period of meditation has been unprofitable. Not only at the beginning, but time and again a great inner dryness and lack of concern will make itself felt in us, a listlessness, even an inability to meditate. We must not get stuck in such experiences. Above all, we must not allow them to dissuade us from observing our period of meditation with great patience and fidelity. That is why it is not good for us to take too seriously the many bad experiences we have with ourselves during the time of meditation. It is here that our old vanity and the wrongful demands we make on God could sneak into our lives in a pious, roundabout way, as if it were our right to have nothing but edifying and blissful experiences, and as if the discovery of our inner poverty were beneath our dignity. But we will not make any headway with such an attitude. Impatience and self-reproach only foster our complacency and entangle us ever more deeply in the net of introspection. But there is no more time to observe ourselves in meditation than there is in the Christian life as a whole. We should pay attention to the Word alone and leave it to the Word to deal effectively with everything. For may it not be the case that it is none other than God who sends us these hours of emptiness and dryness, so that we might once again expect everything from God's Word? "Seek God, not happiness"—that is the fundamental rule of all meditation. If you seek God alone, you will gain happiness—that is the

89   promise of all meditation.

The consideration of Scripture leads into prayer. We have already said that the most promising way to pray is to allow oneself to be guided by the words of the Bible, to pray on the basis of the words of Scripture. In this way we will not fall prey to our own emptiness. Prayer means nothing else but the readiness to appropriate the Word, and what is more, to let it speak to me in my personal situation, in my particular tasks, decisions, sins, and temptations. What can never enter the prayer of the community may here silently be made known to God. On the basis of the words of Scripture we pray that God may throw light on our day, preserve us from sin, and enable us to grow in holiness, and that we may be faithful in our work and have the strength to do it. And we may be certain that our prayer will be heard because it issues from God's Word and promise. Because God's Word has found its fulfillment in Jesus Christ, all the prayers we pray on the basis of this Word are certainly fulfilled and answered in Jesus Christ.

A special difficulty in the time of meditation is that it is so easy for our thoughts to wander and go their own way, toward other persons or to some events in our life. As much as this may sadden and shame us, we must not become despondent and anxious, or even conclude that meditation is really not something for us. If we find ourselves in this situation, it is often a help not frantically to restrain our thoughts, but quite calmly to draw into our prayer those people and events toward which our thoughts keep turning, and thus patiently to return to the starting point of the meditation.

Just as we tie our personal prayers to the words of the Bible, we do the same with our intercessions. It is not possible to remember in the intercessory prayers of daily worship together all the persons who are entrusted to

90   our care, or at any rate to do it in the way that is required of us. All Christians have their own circle of those who have requested them to intercede on their behalf, or people for whom for various reasons they know they have been called upon to pray. First of all, this circle will include those with whom they must live every day. With this we have advanced to the point at which we hear the heartbeat of all Christian life together. A Christian community either lives by the intercessory prayers of its members for one

another, or the community will be destroyed. I can no longer condemn or hate other Christians for whom I pray, no matter how much trouble they cause me. In intercessory prayer the face that may have been strange and intolerable to me is transformed into the face of one for whom Christ died, the face of a pardoned sinner. That is a blessed discovery for the Christian who is beginning to offer intercessory prayer for others. As far as we are concerned, there is no dislike, no personal tension, no disunity or strife, that cannot be overcome by intercessory prayer. Intercessory prayer is the purifying bath into which the individual and the community must enter every day. We may struggle hard with one another in intercessory prayer, but that struggle has the promise of achieving its goal.

How does that happen? Offering intercessory prayer means nothing other than Christians bringing one another into the presence of God, seeing each other under the cross of Jesus as poor human beings and sinners in need of grace. Then, everything about other people that repels me falls away. Then I see them in all their need, hardship, and distress. Their need and their sin become so heavy and oppressive to me that I feel as if they were my own, and I can do nothing else but bid: Lord, you yourself, you alone, deal with them according to your firmness and your goodness. Offering intercessory prayer means granting other Christians the same right we have received, namely, the right to stand before Christ and to share in Christ's mercy.

Thus it is clear that intercessory prayer is also a daily service Christians owe to God and one another.[27] Those who deny their neighbors prayers of intercession deny them a service Christians are called to perform. Furthermore, it is clear that intercessory prayer is not something general and vague, but something very concrete. It is interested in specific persons and specific difficulties and therefore specific requests. The more concrete my intercessory prayer becomes, the more promising it is. 91

Finally, we can no longer close our eyes to the realization that the ministry of intercession demands time of every Christian, but most of all of the pastor on whom the needs of the whole community of faith rest. Intercessory prayer alone would occupy the entire time of daily meditation if it were done properly. All this proves that intercessory prayer is a gift of God's grace for every Christian community and for every Christian. Because God has made us such an immeasurably great offer here, we should accept it joy-

---

27. ["On Bonhoeffer's 'theology of intercession,' see especially *DBWE* 1:186–189, and the section on intercession from his lectures, 'The Nature of the Church' (*DBWE* 11:323–324 [*Reader* 203–204]) . . . ," *DBWE* 5:91, n. 18.]

fully. The very time we give to intercession will turn out to be a daily source of new joy in God and in the Christian congregation.

Because consideration of the Scriptures, prayer, and intercession involve a service that is our duty, and because the grace of God can be found in this service, we should train ourselves to set a regular time during the day for them, just as we do for every other service we perform. That is not "legalism," but discipline and faithfulness. For most people, the early morning will prove to be the best time. We have a right to this time, even prior to the claims of other people, and we may demand it as a completely undisturbed quiet time despite all external pressures. For the pastor, it is an indispensable duty on which the whole practice of ministry will depend. Who can really be faithful in great things, if they have not learned to be faithful in the things of daily life?

Every day brings the Christian many hours of being alone in an unchristian environment. These are times of *testing*. This is the proving ground of a genuine time of meditation and genuine Christian community. Has the community served to make individuals free, strong, and mature, or has it made them insecure and dependent? Has it taken them by the hand for a while so that they would learn again to walk by themselves, or has it made them anxious and unsure? This is one of the toughest and most serious questions that can be put to any form of everyday Christian life in community. Moreover, we will see at this point whether Christians' time of meditation has led them into an unreal world from which they awaken with a fright when they step out into the workaday world, or whether it has led them into the real world of God from which they enter into the day's activities strengthened and purified. Has it transported them for a few short moments into a spiritual ecstasy that vanishes when everyday life returns, or has it planted the Word of God so soberly and so deeply in their heart that it holds and strengthens them all day long, leading them to active love, to obedience, to good works? Only the day can decide. Is the invisible presence of the Christian community a reality and a help to the individual? Do the intercessory prayers of the others carry me through the day? Is the Word of God close to me as a comfort and a strength? Or do I misuse my solitude against the community, against the Word and prayer? Individuals must be aware that even their hours of being alone reverberate through the community. In their solitude they can shatter and tarnish the community or they can strengthen and sanctify it. Every act of self-discipline by a Christian is also a service to the community. Conversely, there is no sin in thought, word, or deed, no matter how personal or secret, that does not harm the whole community. When the cause of an illness gets into one's body, whether or not anyone knows where it comes from, or in what member it has lodged, the body is made ill. This is the appropriate metaphor for the Christian community. Every member serves the whole body, contributing either to its health or to its ruin, for we *are* members of one body not only when we want to be, but in our whole existence. This is not a theory, but a spiritual reality that is often experienced in the Christian community with shocking clarity, sometimes destructively and sometimes beneficially.

Those who return to the community of Christians who live together, after a successful day, bring with them the blessing of their solitude, but they themselves receive anew the blessing of the community. Blessed are those who are alone in the strength of the community. Blessed are those who preserve community in the strength of solitude. But the strength of solitude and the strength of community is the strength of the Word of God alone, which is meant for the individual in the community.

31. *PRAYERBOOK OF THE BIBLE*

DBWE 5:155–160

Bonhoeffer begins Prayerbook of the Bible *with the disciples' realization—"Lord, teach us to pray!"—that we cannot pray. As Bonhoeffer had argued from the beginning of his theological career, our sinful state guarantees that our words do not reach God but rather turn back on ourselves. How then can we pray? Though our words fail to reach God, God's words have reached us. Thus we pray by praying God's own words. And within the Bible, the book of Psalms is unique in containing only prayers. To pray with God's own words means especially to pray the Psalms. Further, because for Bonhoeffer the Word of God is not primarily the words in the Bible but rather the person of Christ who binds himself to those words, we pray the Psalms with Christ, who prays them for us. Through participation in the church-community, which itself participates in Christ, we are able to pray by praying the Psalms with Christ.*

Here as elsewhere,[1] then, Bonhoeffer reads the Old Testament or Hebrew Bible christologically. From the contemporary vantage point, this kind of interpretation is ambivalent. On the one hand, such christological reading of the Psalms, which maintains that the Psalmist "David prayed not only out of the personal raptures of his heart, but from the Christ dwelling in him," strikes us now as dated exegesis and perhaps even pernicious anti-Judaism. On the other hand, this christological interpretation allowed Bonhoeffer to maintain a vital role for the Hebrew Scriptures in a church context where they had largely been dismissed as entirely superseded by the New Testament, and were especially at risk from the German Christians and the National Socialists.

---

1. [*Regarding Bonhoeffer's christological interpretation of the Psalms, see* DBWE *5:53–58* (Reader *532–536*), *"Sermon on Psalm 58" (*DBWE *14:963–970), "Christ in the Psalms" (*DBWE *14:386–393), and* DBWE *15:496–526. For Bonhoeffer's christological interpretation of Genesis, see* DBWE *3. See also* Kuske, Old Testament as the Book of Christ.]

INTRODUCTION 155

"Lord, teach us to pray!" [*Luke 11:1*]. So spoke the disciples to Jesus. In doing so, they were acknowledging that they were not able to pray on their own; they had to learn. "To learn to pray" sounds contradictory to us. Either the heart is so overflowing that it begins to pray by itself, we say, or it will never learn to pray. But this is a dangerous error, which is certainly very widespread among Christians today, to imagine that it is natural for the heart to pray. We then confuse wishing, hoping, sighing, lamenting, rejoicing—all of which the heart can certainly do on its own—with praying. But in doing so we confuse earth and heaven, human beings and God. Praying certainly does not mean simply pouring out one's heart. It means, rather, finding the way to and speaking with God, whether the heart is full or empty. No one can do that on one's own. For that one needs Jesus Christ.

The disciples want to pray, but they do not know how they should do it. It can become a great torment to want to speak with God and not to be able to do it—having to be speechless before God, sensing that every cry remains enclosed within one's own self, that heart and mouth speak a perverse language which God does not want to hear. In such need we seek people who can help us, who know something about praying. If someone who can pray would just take us along in prayer, if we could pray along with that person's prayer, then we would be helped! Certainly, experienced Christians can help us here a great deal, but even they can do it only through the one who alone must help them, and to whom they direct us if they are true 156 teachers in prayer, namely through Jesus Christ. If Christ takes us along in the prayer which Christ prays, if we are allowed to pray this prayer with Christ, on whose way to God we too are led and by whom we are taught to pray, then we are freed from the torment of being without prayer. Yet that is what Jesus Christ wants; he wants to pray with us. We pray along with Christ's prayer and therefore may be certain and glad that God hears us. When our will, our whole heart, enters into the prayer of Christ, then we are truly praying. We can pray only in Jesus Christ, with whom we shall also be heard.

Therefore we must learn to pray. The child learns to speak because the parent speaks to the child. The child learns the language of the parent. So we learn to speak to God because God has spoken and speaks to us. In the language of the Father in heaven God's children learn to speak with God. Repeating God's own words, we begin to pray to God. We ought to speak to God, and God wishes to hear us, not in the false and confused language of our heart but in the clear and pure language that God has spoken to us in Jesus Christ.

God's speech in Jesus Christ meets us in the Holy Scriptures. If we want to pray with assurance and joy, then the word of Holy Scripture must be the firm foundation of our prayer. Here we know that Jesus Christ, the Word of God, teaches us to pray. The words that come from God will be the steps on which we find our way to God.

Now there is in the Holy Scriptures one book that differs from all other books of the Bible in that it contains only prayers. That book is the Psalms. At first it is something very astonishing that there is a prayerbook in the Bible. The Holy Scriptures are, to be sure, God's Word to us. But prayers are human words. How then do they come to be in the Bible? Let us make no mistake: the Bible is God's Word, even in the Psalms. Then are the prayers to God really God's own Word? That seems difficult for us to understand. We grasp it only when we consider that we can learn true prayer only from Jesus Christ, and that it is, therefore, the word of the Son of God, who lives with us human beings, to God the Father who lives in eternity. Jesus Christ has brought before God every need, every joy, every thanksgiving, and every hope of humankind. In Jesus' mouth the human word becomes God's Word. When we pray along with the prayer of Christ, God's Word becomes again a human word. Thus all prayers of the Bible are such prayers, which we pray together with Jesus Christ, prayers in which Christ includes us, and through which Christ brings us before the face of God. Otherwise there are no true prayers, for only in and with Jesus Christ can we truly pray.

If we want to read and to pray the prayers of the Bible, and especially the Psalms, we must not, therefore, first ask what they have to do with us, but what they have to do with Jesus Christ. We must ask how we can understand the Psalms as God's Word, and only then can we pray them with Jesus Christ. Thus it does not matter whether the Psalms express exactly what we feel in our heart at the moment we pray. Perhaps it is precisely the case that we must pray against our own heart in order to pray rightly. It is not just that for which we ourselves want to pray that is important, but that for which God wants us to pray. If we were dependent on ourselves alone, we would probably often pray only the fourth petition of the Lord's Prayer.[3] But God wants it otherwise. Not the poverty of our heart, but the richness of God's word, ought to determine our prayer.

---

3. [*I.e., give us this day our daily bread.*]

Thus if the Bible contains a prayerbook, we learn from this that not only the word which God has to say to us belongs to the Word of God, but also the word which God wants to hear from us, because it is the word of God's dear Son. It is a great grace that God tells us how we can speak with, and have community with, God. We can do so because we pray in the name of Jesus Christ. The Psalms have been given to us precisely so that we can learn to pray them in the name of Jesus Christ.

At the request of the disciples, Jesus gave them the Lord's Prayer. In it every prayer is contained. Whatever enters into the petitions of the Lord's Prayer is prayed aright; whatever has no place in it, is no prayer at all. All the prayers of the Holy Scriptures are summed up in the Lord's Prayer and are taken up into its immeasurable breadth. They are, therefore, not made superfluous by the Lord's Prayer, but are rather the inexhaustible riches of the Lord's Prayer, just as the Lord's Prayer is their crown and unity. Luther says of the Psalter: "It runs through the Lord's Prayer and the Lord's Prayer runs through it, so that it is possible to understand one on the basis of the other and to bring them into joyful harmony." The Lord's Prayer thus becomes the touchstone for whether we pray in the name of Jesus Christ or in our own name. It makes good sense, then, that the Psalter is very often bound together with the New Testament. It is the prayer of the church of Jesus Christ. It belongs to the Lord's Prayer.

158

Those Who Pray the Psalms

Of the 150 psalms, 73 are attributed to King David, 12 to the choirmaster Asaph appointed by David, 12 to the levitical family of the children of Korah working under David, 2 to King Solomon, and one to each of the master musicians, Heman and Ethan, probably working under David and Solomon. So it is understandable that the name of David has been connected with the Psalter in special ways.

It is reported that after his secret anointing as king, David was called to play the harp for King Saul, who was abandoned by God and plagued with an evil spirit. "And whenever the evil spirit from God came upon Saul, David took the lyre and played it with his hand, and so Saul would be relieved and feel better, and the evil spirit would depart from him" (1 Sam. 16:23). That may have been the beginning of David's composition of the psalms. In the power of the spirit of God, which had come upon him with his anointing as king, he drove away the evil spirit through his song. No psalm from the time before the anointing has been handed down to us. David first prayed the songs, which were later taken up into the canon of Holy Scripture, after he was called to be the messianic king—from whose lineage the promised king, Jesus Christ, was to come.

According to the witness of the Bible, David, as the anointed king of the chosen people of God, is a prototype of Jesus Christ. What befalls David occurs for the sake of the one who is in him and who is to proceed from him, namely Jesus Christ. David did not remain unaware of this, but "being therefore a prophet, and knowing that God had sworn with an oath to him that he would set one of his descendants upon his throne, he foresaw and spoke of the resurrection of the Christ" (Acts 2:30f.). David was a witness to Christ in his kingly office, in his life, and in his words. And the New Testament says even more. In the Psalms of David it is precisely the promised Christ who already speaks (Heb. 2:12; 10:5) or, as is sometimes said, the Holy Spirit (Heb. 3:7). The same words that David spoke, therefore, the future Messiah spoke in him. Christ prayed along with the prayers of David or, more accurately, it is none other than Christ who prayed them in Christ's own forerunner, David.

This short observation about the New Testament sheds significant light on the entire Psalter. It refers the Psalter to Christ. How that is to be understood in detail is something we still have to consider. It is important for us that even David prayed not only out of the personal raptures of his heart, but from the Christ dwelling in him. To be sure, the one who prays these psalms, David, remains himself; but Christ dwells in him and with him. The last words of the old man David express the same thing in a hidden way: "The oracle of David, son of Jesse, the oracle of the man whom God exalted, the anointed of the God of Jacob, the dear psalmist of Israel: 'The Spirit of the Lord speaks through me, his word is upon my tongue.'" Then follows a final prophecy of the coming king of righteousness, Jesus Christ (2 Sam. 23:2ff.).

With this we are led once again to the realization that we had affirmed earlier. Certainly not all the Psalms are from David, and there is no word of the New Testament that places the entire Psalter in the mouth of Christ. Nevertheless, the hints already stated must be sufficiently important to us to apply to the entire Psalter what is decisively linked to the name of David. Jesus himself says of the Psalms in general that they announced his death and resurrection and the preaching of the gospel (Luke 24:44ff.).

How is it possible that a human being and Jesus Christ pray the Psalter simultaneously? It is the incarnate Son of God, who has borne all human weakness in his own flesh, who here pours out the heart of all humanity before God, and who stands in our place and prays for us. He has known torment and pain, guilt and death more deeply than we have. Therefore it is the prayer of the human nature assumed by Christ that comes before God here. It is really our prayer. But since the Son of God knows us better than we know ourselves, and was truly human for our sake, it is also really the Son's prayer. It can become our prayer only because it was his prayer.

Who prays the Psalter? David (Solomon, Asaph, etc.) prays. Christ prays. We pray. We who pray are, first of all, the whole community of faith in which alone the entire richness of the Psalter can be prayed. But those who pray are also, finally, all individuals insofar as they have a part in Christ and in their congregation and share in the praying of their prayer. David, Christ, the congregation, I myself—wherever we consider all these things with one another, we become aware of the wonderful path that God follows in order to teach us to pray.

32. PROTESTANTISM
WITHOUT REFORMATION

DBWE 15:438–462

A March 1939 conversation with ecumenical colleagues in London led to an invita-
tion for Bonhoeffer to teach at Union Seminary while also working with European
refugees through the New York office of the Federal Council of Churches. Frustrated
with the church situation in Germany and eager to avoid military conscription, Bon-
hoeffer chose the path of emigration taken by many European intellectuals. But once
in New York, he was haunted by the sense that he had betrayed his seminary students,
choosing his own safety while abandoning them to their uncertainty. To the dismay of
those who had arranged for his escape from Germany, he returned. His self-imposed
exile was thus short-lived; he arrived in New York on June 2, 1939, and left for Ger-
many on July 8.[1]

During and immediately after this brief, second stay in America, Bonhoeffer
produced the following essay. When the young Bonhoeffer first visited America in
1930–1931, he was preoccupied with what German theology had to offer American
Christianity. There is still much of that attitude in "Protestantism without Reforma-
tion," but Bonhoeffer's goal is now mutual edification, a dialogue. He asks, "What is
God doing to and with his church in America? What is he doing through this church
to us and, through us, to it?" With this more open-minded approach, Bonhoeffer is
able to offer a more sympathetic, historically narrated account of the American eva-
sion of theology. Its history as a nation of refugees fleeing religious persecution and
division stands behind America's reticence to work for confessionally grounded church
unity. Americans are happy to be generically "Protestant" rather than, say, Lutheran
or Reformed, and they are happy to be a collection of denominations rather than
the one true church. Bonhoeffer contrasts all of this with the German church, which

---

1. [DBWE *15:8–13. For more on Bonhoeffer's second trip to America, see* DB-ER, *648–662.*]

begins with the Reformation assumption of church unity grounded in confession.
These contrasts enable the ecumenical dialogue: "The denominations in America
confront the German churches with the question of the multiplicity of churches . . .
Conversely, the church of Jesus Christ in Germany poses the question of the unity of
the church on earth to the American denominations."

There are two obstacles to the proper assessment of a foreign church, and   438
they repeatedly hinder the genuine encounter with it:

First: The observer has the tendency to attribute the strangeness of
another church to the peculiarities of its geographical, national, and social
location, that is, to understand it in terms of its historical, political, and
sociological context. The great revivalist and sanctification movements[2] and
Puritanism are thus "typically Anglo-Saxon," the "social gospel"[3] is thus
"typically American," and conversely, the Reformation is "typically Continental or German." Such an observation is as common as it is ultimately boring and false. It has become common since there is a greater interest in the
historical peculiarities of Christianity than in its truth; it is boring because it
leads to a dead and convenient schematization. It is false because it dissolves
from the outset the mutual obligation that churches have for each other's
proclamation and doctrine. For why should a Christian in Germany be concerned with something typically American, and why should a Christian in
America be interested in the typical Continental Reformation? At most it
may be possible to take a certain aesthetic joy in the variety of appearances
and forms of Christianity; it is also possible to welcome the other church   439
as a complement to one's own church. But in this way it is impossible to
come to a genuine encounter or to have an exchange that leads to commitment. As long as we are interested in American peculiarities, we are
merely operating in the realm of detached observations. It is a different
question what God does to and with his church, in and with America, how

---

2. ["The roots of the sanctification movements can be traced back to the Reformation. In the United States, it was called the Holiness movement and grew out of the so-
called Second Great Awakening during the nineteenth century. It emphasizes the role of
grace and the Holy Spirit in the sanctification of the faith and witness of the individual
Christian. Because Bonhoeffer here speaks of these movements in the plural, referring
to developments both in Europe and in North America, *Heiligungsbewegung* has been
translated here as 'sanctification movement,'" *DBWE* 15:438, n. 2.]

3. ["This essentially North American movement within Protestantism was crucially
shaped by Walter Rauschenbusch. Cf. *DBWE* 10:317–318 and Bonhoeffer's memorandum
on the 'Social Gospel' in the fall of 1932 based on a draft by Paul Lehmann (*DBWE*
12:236–243)," *DBWE* 15:438, n. 3.]

God reveals himself to the church and whether and how we may recognize God in that church. With that, the question of God's word, of God's will, and of God's action is raised between us. It is the same word, the same commandment, the same promise, the same office, the same church-community of Jesus Christ that is at stake, both in America and among us. And only the quest for this does justice to the matter. Indeed, the Reformation is not to be understood as a typically German event; it does not work this way. The same is true with respect to the forms and events of foreign churches. They cannot be explained objectively on the basis of the characteristics of other peoples. There is something more, and that is the issue here.

Second: The observer of a foreign church is all too easily content with the current picture of that church's situation. One can easily forget how important it is to take the history of that foreign church seriously. God speaks differently to his church in different times. God spoke to the church in Germany during the Reformation in a different manner, that is, more urgently, clearly, and publicly than in any other subsequent period. Just as the German church cannot be understood apart from the Reformation, so likewise American Christianity remains concealed from those who do not know the beginning of the Congregationalists in New England, the Baptists in Rhode Island, or the revival movement led by Jonathan Edwards. American Christianity is also and especially what happened in those days, but it bears as little resemblance to American Christianity today as our church at the turn of the century did to the church of the Reformation.

What is God doing to and with his church in America? What is he doing through this church to us and, through us, to it? The following observations seek to contribute an answer to this question.

I. The Unity of the Church and the Denominations

Americans have been less able than any other people on earth to realize the visible unity of God's church on earth. Americans have been more able than any other people on earth to envision the variety of Christian forms of knowledge and community. Statistics show that there are more than two hundred different denominations (church-communities), with approximately fifty of them having more than fifty thousand members. Apparently, on one street in Minneapolis there are four different Lutheran churches with different affiliations. American Christendom has no central organization, no common confession, no common ritual practices, no common church history, no common ethical, social, or political principles. North and south (the question of slavery) but also the migration from east to west (the "boundary = frontier") signify changes and separations of the denominations. In addition there is the segregation of the races (color-line) between Negroes and whites, which repeats itself even within the churches; finally, the denominational forms have also been determined by social differences. The "Federal Council of the Churches of Christ in America"[4] is an association of twenty-nine denominations for common public action. It does not, however, represent *the* church of Jesus Christ in America but is representative of the *churches*.

Even the term "church" is often viewed with suspicion. The characteristic term is "denomination." For many American Christians, church is associated with too much clericalism, autocracy, confessional conceit, intolerance, persecution of heretics, a desire for worldly power and political favors. To be sure, Episcopalians, Lutherans, and Presbyterians are consciously churches, but in the eyes of the others, they are merely denominations. The remaining communities have more a denominational than an ecclesial self-understanding.

The concept of denomination is not entirely clear. It is not a theological concept. It says more about historical, political, and social conditions. 441 The denomination is a free association of Christians on the basis of certain shared Christian experiences as well as historical, political, and social ones. From the outset it allows for the possibility of other such associations. There is a certain humble hesitation in the denominations' self-understanding not to claim the name of the church of Jesus Christ for themselves, because that name seems too big and too dangerous to them. The church is beyond the denominations. In this respect, the concept of the invisible church is bound to come to mind. Denominations are the visible member bodies of the invisible church.

The deeper sources of denominational self-understanding in the history of the church need to be indicated. *First*, the origins of the Presbyterian-Congregationalist denominational formation in England were determined by the message of the exclusive reign of God on earth. All human claims must bow before the sovereign reign of God. Thus the denomination in America is the negative stamp of the onset of God's reign. *Second*, one must also see how the concept of tolerance of Congregationalist-Baptist Enthusiasm,[5] influenced especially by Roger Williams in Maryland,[6] was respon-

---

4. ["... In the 1930s, the Federal Council of Churches actually had thirty-three member churches," *DBWE* 15:440, n. 6.]

5. ["Here and throughout this essay, 'Enthusiasm' refers specifically to the so-called left wing of the Reformation—the movement within the Reformation that split early from Luther's followers. See also Bonhoeffer's comment on the distinction between the two groups, *DBWE* 15:302," *DBWE* 15:441, n. 7.]

6. ["Williams was in Rhode Island, not Maryland," *DBWE* 15:441, n. 8.]

sible. Here the reign of God is equated with the individual's freedom to
follow only the inner voice and inner light. This paves the way for the formation of denominations without confession. *Third*, the denominational
self-understanding implies a certain relation to the state. An American
denomination is not a state church, but it is also not a free church in the
sense of the English free church, which is a conscious counterpart to the
state church. The American denomination is independent from the state
and yet understands itself—in spite of its own internal limitations—as a
piece of God's free church on earth. Nowhere does the denominational
self-understanding come as close to the self-understanding of the church as
in the denomination's relation to the state.

The denomination is not primarily determined by a confession. Most
denominations do not have a firmly articulated confession. The *Lutheran
and Episcopalian churches*, however, demand in their ordination formulas a
binding pledge to their respective confessions. The *Presbyterians* are satisfied—strangely enough—with the commitment to the Scriptures. The *Congregationalist* ordination formula is entirely free; it requires only a confession
of one's personal commitment to the Lord Christ in personal experience,
442   in the certainty of the call to ministry and in belief. But even in cases where
there are confessional obligations, these are limited to a certain degree
since most denominations mutually recognize the administration of the
sacraments, of the ministry, and ordination. This is true for Presbyterians,
Methodists, Congregationalists, Reformed, United Lutherans, Northern
Baptists, evangelicals.[7] Only the Episcopalians, the Missouri Lutherans,
and the Southern Baptists have resisted such recognition to this day. The
doctrinal differences are often more significant within denominations (e.g.,
Baptists, Presbyterians) than among the different denominations. Denominations are not churches based on a confession, and where an individual
denomination makes such a claim, it is limited denominationally by the
others. Today the relationship of the denominations with one another is less
than ever a struggle about the truth of proclamation and doctrine.

This situation might suggest that American Christendom offers preconditions that are especially advantageous for a proper understanding of the
unity of the church of Jesus Christ. Where churches are not divided by the
struggle about the truth, the unity of the church should already be won.
But the real picture is exactly the opposite. Precisely here, where the ques-

7. ["The German *Evangelische* usually means Protestant; here, however, since Bonhoeffer is referring to a number of different U.S. Protestant churches, he probably means
'evangelical' in the U.S. sense," *DBWE* 15:442, n. 10.]

tion of truth does not become the criterion either for community or for
church schisms, there is greater fragmentation than anywhere else. Hence,
precisely where the struggle for a true confession is not decisive, the unity
of the church is further away than where the confession alone unites and
divides the churches. Why is this so? In order to answer this question, we
must turn our attention to a deeper distinction.

The churches of the Reformation start from the assumption of the unity of
the church of Christ. There can be only one church on earth. And this one
church is alone the true church constituted by Jesus Christ. Church schism
means church apostasy, unfaithfulness against the true church of Christ.
The division of the church that came about in the Reformation can only be
understood as a struggle for the true unity of the church. For this reason,
the churches of the Reformation understand themselves as the One Church
on earth, not as splinter groups of individual Christians driven from the
one church by personal conscience, nor are they individual manifestations
of the one church. The Reformation was about the one, universal, holy   443
church of Jesus Christ on earth.

The denominations in America are faced from the start with an unimaginable variety of Christian communities. None of them can dare to make
the claim to be the one church. It is part of Christian humility not to make
such a claim, given this astonishing picture of fragmentation. American
Christendom has experienced the consequences of church schism, but not
the act of the schism itself. For that reason they are no longer themselves
engaged in the struggle for the one church; rather, they stand astonished
before the results of that struggle and can merely accept with great humility what they find and heal the wounds. For American Christendom, the
unity of the church of Jesus Christ is not so much something that is given
originally by God and already exists as it is something that is demanded and
should be. Church is less origin than it is goal. The unity of the church here
thus belongs in the realm of sanctification.[8]

Here it should be pointed out—although this comment does not suffice—that since Occam *nominalism* has been rooted in Anglo-Saxon thinking. This means that the existing particular has priority before the whole
in the sense that the particular and empirically given is the real, while the
whole is merely a notion, a name. The particular stands at the beginning,

---

8. ["On Bonhoeffer's understanding of the unity of the church that is constituted
(realized) in Christ, see *DBWE* 1:192–198, *DBWE* 1:198–204 (*Reader* 52–53) and his 1932
lecture 'The Nature of the Church,' *DBWE* 11:269–332, esp. 305–307 (*Reader* 171–209,
esp. 192–194)," *DBWE* 15:443, n. 11.]

unity at the end. Conversely, the German-Continental philosophical tradition is determined by *realism and idealism*, for which the whole is the original reality, and the particular is merely that which has fallen away from the unity. But these conceptual formulas cannot be taken as sufficient explanations for the different ways of thinking about the unity of the church, because they themselves are based on philosophical-methodological demands derived from theological insights. Nominalism and the philosophy of realism cannot be understood without the background of theology, and therefore they cannot provide a fundamental interpretation of the theological question.

Only the truth revealed in Holy Scripture can and must decide between the existing differences. Churches must allow themselves to be questioned by one another on the basis of Holy Scripture. *The denominations in America confront the German churches with the question of the multiplicity of churches*: What is the significance of church fragmentation? Is only a church that is based on confession a true church, and, therefore, are American denominations not churches because for the most part they are not based on a confession? Is only the church that has a specific confession church, over against which the other confessional churches are false churches? Does one church on earth become the measure by which all others can and must be measured, for their justification or condemnation? Does multiplicity of churches imply only apostasy; do we have here only the harsh contrast between true and false? Is the unity of the church given only through the confession, or to what degree can actual common action be the foundation for fellowship between churches?[9]

Conversely, the church of Jesus Christ in Germany poses the question of the unity of the church on earth to the American denominations: May one simply accept the multiplicity of the churches as a given and therefore God-intended fact? Can there be a unity of the church other than in the unity of faith and confession in the one Lord? Isn't all the unity in action and organization merely a self-deception that covers up the true divisions in faith? Isn't the indifference or resignation toward the question of truth a guilt that has as its consequence the disintegration of the churches through organizational, ritual, and political contradictions? Why is it that the fragmentation of the churches is greatest precisely where the confessional question is relativized?

444

---

9. ["On these questions, see Bonhoeffer's essay 'On the Question of Church Communion,' June 1936, *DBWE* 14:656–678, esp. 656–666 (*Reader* 433–451, esp. 433–442)," *DBWE* 15:444, n. 13.]

Is not the unity of the church first and foremost origin and only afterward goal?[10]

From over there[11] they say to us: you overestimate reason, theology, dogma; these are only one among many expressions of the church and not even the most important ones. We reply: it is a matter not of reason but of the truth of the word of God with which we wish to live and die. It is a matter of salvation. The unity of the church is surely based not on human thinking nor on human "life and work" (Life and Work!),[12] but solely on the life and work of Jesus Christ in which we participate in faith. Unity in thought is not superior to unity in work, but unity in faith, namely, confession, breaks through both and thus creates the precondition for common thought and action.

This conversation cannot take place here. But this much can be said: 445

First: The unity of the church is both origin and goal, both fulfillment and promise; it belongs to both faith and sanctification. Where the unity of the church as origin is forgotten, human organizations that seek unity take the place of the unity in Jesus Christ; the spirit of the times, which aims toward harmonization, takes the place of the Holy Spirit, which unites only in truth; and the life and work of Jesus Christ is pushed out by human "life and work." Conversely, where the unity of the church as goal is forgotten, the living contradictions become lifeless; the work of the Holy Spirit, which seeks to bring about the fulfillment of the unity of the church, is no longer taken seriously; and the divine unity of the church is replaced with a separatist pharisaic claim. But where unity is understood as origin and goal alike, the life and work of Christendom, which seeks and finds the unity of the fragmented church, grows from the foundation of the life and work of Jesus Christ, in whom all unity of the church is fulfilled.

Second: The claim to be the church of Jesus Christ has nothing to do with pharisaic conceit; rather, it is an understanding that humbles because it moves toward penance. Church is the church of sinners and not of the righteous. There may be more self-righteousness in the claim to be church than in the claim itself. It may conceal a false humility that desires something better and more pious than the church that God has elected from among sinners. Denominational self-understanding does not protect from

---

10. ["On the method and content of a theological conversation between different churches, see Bonhoeffer's August 1935 essay, 'The Confessing Church and the Ecumenical Movement,' *DBWE* 14:393–412 (*Reader* 398–414)," *DBWE* 15:444, n. 14.]

11. ["I.e., across the Atlantic," *DBWE* 15:444, n. 15.]

12. ["This is an allusion to the ecumenical organization 'Life and Work,' which was established at the 1925 world church conference in Stockholm," *DBWE* 15:444, n. 16.]

spiritual arrogance. Conversely, ecclesiastical self-understanding must let itself be summoned, again and again, to penance and humility. It remains a fact that the New Testament gives legitimacy to the concept of church, not to the one of denomination.

Third: The unity of the church as promise, as future, as the fruit of sanctification, is a work of the Holy Spirit. This unity cannot be forced, either through theological discussion or through common action. But we know that God may bring the churches together, through both the path of common understanding and the path of common action. Often, common understanding is granted only through common action, and common action from common understanding. There are no methods that lead to the unity of the church. Only total obedience to the Holy Spirit will lead us to common understanding, confession, action, and suffering.

Fourth: The particular problem for an understanding between the churches of the Reformation and the American denominations is that

446 they cannot simply encounter one another on the level of the confessional question. The reason for this is that the confession is not the constitutive moment for the denomination, whereas, conversely, it is the only relevant ecumenical element for the Reformation churches.[13] In the denominations, church ritual, liturgy, the life of the congregation, and the church constitution occupy the same place that confession has for us. This encounter is fruitful for this very reason, however, because it calls into question the entire existence as church or, respectively, as denomination. If we ask American denominations first and foremost about their confession, the question is as unessential as the question of constitution and the relation to the state is for the churches of the Reformation. And yet to ask essential questions of the other church opens up unknown riches for one's own church. For the one side, it opens up the full richness of various forms of worship and liturgy, active congregational life, rich experiences of the meaning of the church constitutions; for the other, it reveals the urgency of the question of truth, the riches of Christian knowledge that are in the church's confession—and what is most important—in this encounter both are brought to humility and the expectation of salvation not from their own form but from the grace of God alone. It is a difficult task for American denomina-

---

13. ["See here Bonhoeffer's 1935 essay, 'The Confessing Church and the Ecumenical Movement,' *DBWE* 14:393–412, esp. 402 (*Reader* 398–414, esp. 405), where he questions the authority of the ecumenical movement precisely because of the overriding authority (for the churches of Reformation) of the Scriptures and confessions," *DBWE* 15:446, n. 18.]

tions to understand properly the struggle for a confessional church;[14] and it is no less difficult for the churches of the Reformation to understand the path of American denominations. Precisely because a common level of understanding seems to be missing in this encounter, it becomes easier to envision the only level on which Christians can encounter one another, the Holy Scripture.

II. The Refuge of Christians

The distinctiveness of the history of the church of Jesus Christ in America, in comparison with all other churches on earth, lies in the fact that America was from the very beginning a place of refuge for the persecuted Christians of the European continent. Since the seventeenth century, America has been the asylum for the victims of religious intolerance, for those who desired to live and serve God in freedom. To be sure, America is consciously a "Protestant" country. Americans have been captivated from the beginning   447 by the notion of a special providence that reserved the discovery of America until the emergence of Protestantism. America is thus the only country in which the concept of "Protestantism" gained church-historical significance and reality, for America wants to be not the country of the Lutheran or the Reformed church but precisely the country of "Protestantism" in its full denominational breadth. Perhaps it is true to say that the Lutherans of America conform the least to American Protestantism. The notion of America as the place of refuge for persecuted "Protestants" is what constitutes the church-historical uniqueness and, indeed, even today the continuing church-historical self-understanding of American Christendom.

A large sector of the American denominations began with voluntary or involuntary flight and the entire complex of problems this poses for Christians. Throughout the history of the church, endurance and flight in times of persecution have been the two Christian possibilities, since the days of the apostles. Endurance to the point of last resistance may be commanded; flight may be permitted or perhaps even commanded. The flight of a Christian in times of persecution is not apostasy and disgrace as such, for God does not call every person into martyrdom. Not flight but denial is sin, although there may be a situation where flight is the same as denial or, conversely, where flight itself may be a part of martyrdom.[15] Protestant refugees who traveled

---

14. ["This can certainly be seen as a more specific reference to the German Church Struggle," *DBWE* 15:446, n. 19.]

15. ["Cf. *DBWE* 4:193–195," *DBWE* 15:447, n. 20.]

to the unknown America came not to a paradise but to a place of hard work. They tackled the struggle of colonizing a country in order to be able to live their faith in freedom without a fight. This sheds some light on the plight of the Christian refugee. He has claimed the right to avoid ultimate suffering in order to serve God in quietness and peace. But now, in the place of refuge, the continuation of the fight has no right to exist. Here are gathered Protestants of all confessions who have already renounced the ultimate fight about confession. There is no room for strife in asylum. Confessional stridency and intolerance must cease for the one who has left intolerant conditions. By virtue of using the right of flight, the Christian refugee has forfeited the right to fight. This, at least, is how the American Christian understands it. Certainly, there has been strife among American churches and even instances of severe persecution, especially in the beginning. But in American Christendom the deep abhorrence that always meets every kind of confessional discrimination can essentially be explained by the Christian right of the refugee, by the American character of political asylum.

448   For the first generation of refugees, the path to America was a decision of faith for their entire life. For them, the renunciation of the confessional battle was a Christian possibility they had fought for. Here, however, a danger exists for the coming generations who are born into a situation without struggle and for whom a life decision is no longer at stake. Sooner or later they will misunderstand their situation. What for the fathers was a right of their Christian faith, which they acquired at the risk of their lives, will be regarded by the sons as a general Christian rule. The confessional battle for the sake of which the fathers fled has become for the sons something that in itself is not Christian. The absence of a struggle will be the normal and ideal condition for them. The peace in which the descendants of the refugees grow up has been not fought for but inherited.

Hence, the notion of *tolerance* becomes the fundamental notion of everything Christian for American Christendom. All intolerance is un-Christian as such. Understanding and empathy are aroused not by a confessional struggle as such but rather for the victims of such a struggle. This must remain unsatisfactory for the victims themselves, since they are not so much concerned for their personal plight as they are for the truth of their cause. For the Christian refugee, the renunciation of the fight to the end for the truth remains a most troubling and lifelong issue. Only the deep sincerity and unlimited scope of compassion and the right to asylum in his country of refuge can be convincing in Christian terms. His yearning to decide for the truth against its distortion remains unfulfilled and must remain so. It is ultimately the faithfulness toward one's own church history that is expressed in this strange relativization of the question of truth in the thinking and action of American Christendom.

III. Freedom

America calls itself the land of freedom. Today this means the right of the individual to think, speak, and act independently. In this framework, religious freedom is a self-evident possession for the American. The church's proclamation, organization, and congregational life can flourish in complete independence and without interference. The praise of freedom can be heard everywhere from the pulpit, coupled with the sharpest condemnation of any attempt to curtail such freedom anywhere. Here freedom entails the possibility—as a possibility for the church offered by the world—for unhindered effectiveness.

But as long as the freedom of the church is essentially understood as this possibility, the concept of church freedom remains unrecognized. *The freedom of the church is not where it has possibilities, but only where the gospel is truly effective in its own power to create space for itself on earth, even and especially when there are no such possibilities for the church.*[16] The essential freedom of the church is not a gift of the world to the church but the freedom of the word of God to make itself heard. The freedom of the church is not the unlimited fullness of possibilities. Rather, freedom is only there where a "must" compels it, if need be against all possibilities. The praise of freedom as the possibility that the world offers the church for its existence might stem precisely from a bond with the world, entered into by the church, which has thereby given up the genuine freedom of God's word.[17] It may happen that a church that praises its freedom as a possibility offered by the world succumbs to the world to a particular degree, that is, a church that is free in this way may be secularized faster than a church that does not possess freedom as a possibility. The American praise of freedom is more a tribute to the world, the state, and society than it is a statement concerning the church. Such freedom may be a sign that in truth the world belongs to God. But whether the world belongs to God in reality depends not on freedom as a possibility but on freedom as a reality, as urgency, as factual event.[18] Freedom as an

---

16. ["On the power of the gospel *to create its own* 'space' on earth, cf. *DBWE* 4:225–230 and 236–237," *DBWE* 15:449, n. 21.]

17. ["Again, this appears to be a direct reference to the controversy about the legalization of Confessing Church pastors by the church authorities," *DBWE* 15:449, n. 23.]

18. ["On Bonhoeffer's consistent polemic against the category of 'possibility' in theology, see the thesis in his 1930 inaugural lecture, 'The Anthropological Question in

institutional possession is not an essential predicate of the church. Freedom may be a gracious gift to the church given by God's providence, but it may also be a great temptation to which the church succumbs when it sacrifices its essential freedom to an institutional freedom. Only the actual proclamation of the word of God determines whether the American churches are essentially free. Only where this word can be concretely proclaimed in the midst of historical reality as judgment, commandment, gracious salvation of the sinner, and deliverance from all human ordinances is there freedom of the church. But where the gratitude for institutional freedom must be paid for through the sacrifice of the freedom of proclamation, there the church is in chains, even if it believes itself to be free.

450   IV. Church and State

Nowhere does the principle of separation of church and state have such a general, almost dogmatic, significance as in American Christendom, and arguably, nowhere is the participation of the churches in political, social, economic, and cultural affairs as lively and influential as in the country that does not have a state church. This seems to be a contradiction; the only explanation for this is to be found in the uniqueness of the American separation of church and state.[19]

Church and state were not always separated in America. In the seventeenth century, in New England the Congregationalists were a state church, likewise the Anglicans in Virginia and the Catholics in Maryland. However, these were instances of civil bodies controlled by the church more than of churches controlled by a state. *The state church privileges gradually ceased only after the foundation of the federal government following the American Revolution,* for the union is on principle religionless. Questions of religion are left to the individual states. The first major interstate unions of the denominations have their beginnings in these years. In 1784 the *Methodists* established the Episcopal-Methodist Church, in 1788 the *Presbyterians* established the General Assembly, and in 1789 the *Anglicans* united, but—to this day—without electing an archbishop. The political movement toward

---

Contemporary Philosophy and Theology': '*The concept of possibility has no place in theology and thus no place in theological anthropology*' (*DBWE* 10:403 [*Reader* 122]). Cf. the fourth thesis of his doctoral promotional theses from 1927, *DBWE* 9:440. See also Feil, *Theology of Dietrich Bonhoeffer,* 30–32," *DBWE* 15:449, n. 24.]

19. ["This is a reference to the First Amendment of the U.S. Constitution: 'Congress shall make no law respecting an establishment of religion, or prohibiting the free exercise thereof," *DBWE* 15:450, n. 25.]

union corresponds to these church unions. The complete separation of church and state was achieved and generally accepted by the nineteenth century. Not only the union but also the states are religionless. There are no public statistics on religion, religion is not taught in public schools, and in hiring for civil service positions there are no questions about confession. All of this originally was done in agreement with the denominations, for in this way competitive proselytization in state institutions, particularly in the schools, is obstructed. Also, denominational influence determines the lives of Christians to such an extent that there is no need for federal aid. Above all, however, one fact manifests itself in the state's separation from religion, and that is of fundamental importance to American Christendom, namely, that the churches mark the boundaries of the state. From this perspective, the state's religionlessness is not so much a triumph of secular powers over Christianity as it is rather the victory of the churches over any unlimited claims of the state.[20]

Here we find the key for understanding the original meaning of the American separation of church and state as well as that of the American constitution.[21] Even though they are nearly contemporaneous and are not connected politically, there is a profound difference between the American and the French revolutions. *American democracy is founded not on humanitarian principles or human right, but on the kingdom of God and the limitation of all earthly powers.* It is significant when eminent American historians can say that the American federal constitution was written by men who knew about original sin. Those who hold human power, as well as the populace itself, are put in their place because of the wickedness of the human heart and for the sake of the exclusive sovereignty of God. This notion, which stems from *Puritanism,* is connected to another consideration that stems from

451

---

20. ["Bonhoeffer's use of the words 'religionless' and 'religionlessness' in this section of his essay is striking, since the phrase 'religionless Christianity' in his prison letters (cf. *DBWE* 8:361–367, 371–374 [*Reader* 777–782], and his 'Outline for a Book,' *DBWE* 8:499–504 [(*Reader* 811–815)]) has been one of the most provocative and variously interpreted aspects of his thought. It is an unusual word in German, and clearly Bonhoeffer does not merely mean secularism (since he uses that word elsewhere) but is describing something about the nature of the church-state relationship. His description here of a 'victory of the churches over any unlimited claims of the state' suggests that *Religionslosigkeit* may not mean the absence of religion or religiosity, but rather implies a true independence of church and state from each other," *DBWE* 15:450–451, n. 26.]

21. ["Regarding the passage that follows, cf. the section in *Ethics* titled 'Heritage and Decay,' *DBWE* 6:124–27. The wording of the section in *Ethics* is clearly drawn from this earlier essay; several sentences are almost verbatim. See esp. *DBWE* 6:126, n. 102," *DBWE* 15:451, n. 27.]

spiritualism,[22] namely, that the kingdom of God on earth can be built not by the state but solely by the church-community of Jesus Christ. Hence, the church has clear priority before the state. The church proclaims the principles of social and political order, while the state merely lends the technical means to achieve these. These original and essentially different rationales for democracy offered by Puritanism and spiritualism soon become almost imperceptibly intertwined; for American Christendom it is the latter, however, that becomes more influential than the former. "Christians nowadays think in terms of Christian principles (the sphere of the church) and of technical policies whereby they can be put into practice (the sphere of the state)" (W. A. Brown).

452

The fundamental difference between this church-state relation and that of the churches of the Reformation is obvious. *The American separation of church and state is not based on the doctrine of two offices or the two kingdoms* that were ordered by God to remain until the end of the world, each serving in a fundamentally different way. The dignity of the state, nowhere else more strongly emphasized than in the teaching of the Reformation, fades into the background in American thinking. The juxtaposition of state and church becomes a subordinate relationship wherein the state becomes merely the executive of the church. *State* is essentially a technical organization and administrative apparatus. But the dignity of the state to wield the divine power of the sword "to avenge the evil ones, to reward the good"[23] seems to have been lost. American thinking is governed by the Enthusiast doctrine of the state as being destined in this earthly life to be integrated into the church, but it is at the same time a teaching that places American democracy on firm Christian ground. This should make us think about why on the European continent it has never been possible to base a democracy on Christian principles, about why on our continent democracy and Christianity are always seen somewhat in opposition to each other, while in America democracy can be glorified as the epitome of a Christian form of

---

22. ["This is a reference to the 'spiritualists' of the Reformation period. Considered part of the radical, or left, wing of the Reformation, they included figures such as Thomas Müntzer and Kaspar Schwenckfeld von Ossig. As the name implies, the spiritualists were skeptical of external institutions and authority, even that of Scripture, focusing instead on the importance of inner spirituality and the work of the Holy Spirit. See Spitz, *Renaissance and Reformation Movements,* 404–408," *DBWE* 15:451, n. 28.]

23. ["Cf. Luther's functional classification of the 'temporal authority and the sword it bears' in 'Temporal Authority: To What Extent It Should Be Obeyed' (1523), as it is a divine ordinance (*ordinatio*) 'to punish the wicked and to praise the righteous' (*LW* 45, 86)," *DBWE* 15:452, n. 33.]

government. In answering this question, one must recall that the European continent ruled out this possibility when it persecuted and expelled the spiritualists. But the country that offered hospitality to the Enthusiasts has been shaped fruitfully by them, even in its political thinking.

It lies in the uniqueness of the relation of church and state in America that, despite the fundamental separation of the two institutions, there is still cause for conflict. The *church* claims the right for itself to address and act on almost any topic in public life, since only in this way can the kingdom of God be built. In the process, the distinction between the offices is not recognized, on principle. The life of the state and public life in general are subsumed under the judgment of the church without distinction; hence, there can be no significant public decision in which the church would not raise its voice and issue pronouncements. Therefore, the sermons coming from American pulpits deal usually with thematic discussions of certain public events or conditions. A glance at the New York church bulletins is evidence enough.[24] But it would be a false verdict if we were to appraise this type of sermon merely as a manifestation of secularization. It is that indeed, but behind this stands the old spiritualist claim to build the kingdom of God, publicly and visibly. *The European-continental* secularization of the church stems from the—misinterpreted—Reformation distinction of the two kingdoms; *the American secularization* stems precisely from the lack of the distinction of the kingdoms and the offices of state and church, as well as from the Enthusiast claim that the church is the agent of the universal formation of the world. This is a significant difference. While the churches of the Reformation need a new examination and correction of the doctrine of the two kingdoms,[25] the American denominations must learn the necessity of this distinction today if they are to escape complete secularization.

Our knowledge of the American church situation can teach us the following lesson: *a church that is independent of the state is no more protected from secularization than a state church.* Whether the church is connected to the world or independent of it, the threat of infringement in the church remains the same. There is no form of church as such that preserves it fundamentally from secularization.

The following list of decisions in matters public and political, as recorded in a report by the *General Council of the Presbyterians*, is representative of

453

---

24. ["Bonhoeffer provides a few examples in his report on his academic year at Union Theological Seminary in New York in 1930–1931; see *DBWE* 10:312," *DBWE* 15:453, n. 34.]

25. ["This was one of the tasks Bonhoeffer saw himself faced with in writing *Ethics* (*DBWE* 6), which he began in 1940," *DBWE* 15:453, n. 35.]

the state of affairs in America. It should also be noted that we are dealing not with a spiritualist denomination but with the Presbyterians, who hold a Reformed position regarding state and church. The starting point of the report is the refutation of the state's right to curtail religious freedom. The government agreement with Uruguay in this matter is seen positively.Moreover, it includes steps for the colonization of American Negroes in Africa, the demand for a new marriage and divorce law, as well as laws for vaccinations and the right of women to vote. It takes a stand against gambling, lotteries, horse racing, and the practice of lynching. The government is asked to recognize Liberia as an independent republic; better race relations, old-age pensions, and unemployment aid, and simplification of civil legal proceedings are all demanded. The church conferences also deal in general with the International Court of Justice, disarmament, naturalization laws, etc. This corresponds to a Congregationalist statement: "We have stood resolutely for the separation of state and church but with equal insistence have we stood for the continuous impact of the church upon the state" (cited in W. A. Brown). Brown summarizes the position of American denominations toward the state in three points: 1. all proclaim the separation between state and church as a prerequisite; 2. all recognize state authority as instituted by God; 3. all claim the self-evident right to speak to social, political, and economic questions insofar as these entail general ethical issues.

At the moment there are two questions of special importance that are strong sources of conflict between state and church in America. First, the question of schooling, second, the question of peace.

The question of schooling: The absence of religion in the public schools is a matter of serious concern today for the denominations. What the churches once endorsed as the limitation of the state's power[26] now begins to be an instrument against the denominations. Today, the more the pedagogical tasks of the schools expand, the more the denominations find it necessary to have their input. It is possible today in a public school to speak out deliberately against the church, while it is impossible to speak in the public schools in the name of the church. Hence, there is a growing movement within American Christianity against the absence of religion in the schools. Curiously, among the Protestants, only the Lutherans opposed from the beginning the absence of religion in the schools and thus maintained their own confessional schools. This is all the more noteworthy since it was the American Lutherans in particular who never adopted a spiritualist understanding of the state and church relationship and who decided, unlike the

454

---

26. ["Cf. diary entry for July 4, 1939, *DBWE* 15:236," *DBWE* 15:454, n. 40.]

large denominations, to refrain from any kind of interference in the realm of the state. They alone kept the schools under the authority of the church, and to this day they support their own schools, even if that means paying twice as much.[27]

The peace question in America primarily concerns the issue of whether Christians and the clergy of various denominations should serve in the military.[28] Today there are three conditions in the United States under which a person can be released from military service: first, by virtue of being a member of a church that refuses military service on the grounds of Christian convictions (Quakers and others); second, by virtue of being a member of a church (for example, the Protestant Episcopalians since 1936, Methodist Episcopalians since 1932, Northern Baptist since 1934, Unitarians since 1936) that affirms the right of a "conscientious objector" (one who refuses to fight in a war on the grounds of conscience); third, for personal convictions of conscience. The decision in each individual case depends on whether the personal hearing clearly establishes that the decisive motive for objection is genuinely a religious or a conscientious one. The struggle concerning this question has been particularly fierce during the last ten years.

A question of somewhat lesser significance concerns *the display of the American flag in churches*, a practice that began during the war[29] but is widespread today. Public opinion polls have shown it is more the desire of lay-people than pastors to continue with the practice. In any case, it is a surprising custom in the land of church-state separation.

The strongest influence of the church on the state comes in America not through the congregation or the pulpit but *through the considerable power of the free Christian associations that are not denominationally connected.* It is impossible to understand the picture of American Christendom apart from this decisive link that connects congregation and public life. These are private associations that have been established by individual Christians with some kind

455

---

27. ["I.e., they would be paying state taxes to support public schools and private donations and tuition to support their own confessional school," *DBWE* 15:454, n. 41.]

28. ["As World War II loomed, this issue was hotly debated in U.S. church circles; Bonhoeffer would have heard a great deal on this topic during his brief stay in New York. It was also a theme elsewhere in his writing; see, for example, *DBWE* 6:407 (*Reader* 689) and *DBWE* 10:27, n. 130," *DBWE* 15:455, n. 42.]

29. ["The widespread practice of displaying a U.S. flag in church sanctuaries dates back to the Civil War, when it was adopted by some churches in the Union states as a symbol of their support; it became more widespread during the First World War (this is what Bonhoeffer is referring to here) and even more so during the Second, when President Franklin Roosevelt asked churches to fly the flag," *DBWE* 15:455, n. 43.]

of specific purpose for the work of the kingdom of God in America. Great
financial sacrifices are made for these organizations, and there is no comparison between their extent and influence and that of similar European
associations. There are associations for evangelization, for social purposes,
the YMCA (Young Men's Christian Association), YWCA (Young Women's
Christian Association), temperance and abstinence associations, groups for
keeping the Sabbath holy, for prison reform, for the fight against vice, for
unemployment aid, for the improvement of race relations, especially for the

456 promotion of the living conditions of Negroes; there is also an overwhelming number of peace movements, and many others. The legal enactment
of Prohibition in the Eighteenth Amendment was largely achieved by the
relentless work of the Methodist-sponsored Women's Christian Temperance
Union and the Anti-Saloon League, which were supported by all denominations except the Lutherans and the Episcopalians.[30] With regard to this,
however, American Christendom has had a unique and probably a very con-
sequential experience. It had to realize that the imposition of Christian
principles on the life of the state led to a catastrophic collapse. The Prohibition legislation caused an unprecedented upsurge in crime in the large
cities. A "Christian" law had brought disaster for the state and had to be
rescinded—with the consent of the churches. This reality gave American
Christians food for thought, as it should also cause us to reflect.[31]

V. The Negro Church[32]

For American Christendom *the racial issue* has been a real problem from
the beginning. Today almost every tenth American is a Negro. The young,
forward-looking generation of Negroes are turning away from the faith of
their elders because they view its strong eschatological orientation as an

---

30. ["After around 1900, several states legally prohibited the production, transport,
and sale of alcoholic beverages; in 1919–1920, with the passage of the Eighteenth Amendment to the U.S. Constitution, Prohibition was in force throughout the United States. In
1933, however, the Twenty-first Amendment rescinded Prohibition, and control of alcohol consumption was then left up to the individual states," *DBWE* 15:456, n. 45.]

31. ["Cf. *DBWE* 6:355, esp. n. 11," *DBWE* 15:456, n. 46.]

32. ["The situation of the 'church of the outcasts of America' and their social discrimination was a burning issue for Bonhoeffer already in 1930–1931 (see *DBWE* 10:314, and
DB-ER, 150–151, 154–155). In fact, the situation and church life of African Americans
in the United States became a primary focus for Bonhoeffer during his 1930–1931 stay
at Union Theological Seminary. See the editor's introduction to *DBWE* 10:28–33, esp. n.
146. See also Young, *No Difference in the Fare*, for a contemporary evaluation of how this
affected Bonhoeffer's theology," *DBWE* 15:456, n. 47.]

obstacle to the progress of their race and rights. This is one of the dangerous signs of the church's guilt in past centuries and a grave problem for the
future. The fact that today the "black Christ" of a young Negro poet[33] is
pitted against the "white Christ" reveals a destructive rift within the church
of Jesus Christ. It cannot be overlooked that many white Christians through   457
influential organizations do whatever they can to improve the relations
between the races and that discerning Negroes recognize the serious difficulties. But today the general picture of the church in the United States is
still one of racial fragmentation. Blacks and whites come separately to word
and sacrament. They have no common worship.

Historically, this stems from the following development: when the first
larger transports of Negroes—who had been stolen from Africa as slaves—
arrived in America, the slave masters were generally opposed to the chris-
tianization of the slaves. They justified slavery by citing the slaves' paganism.
Baptism, however, would have called into question the legitimacy of slavery
and brought undesirable privileges and rights to the Negroes. The slave
masters agreed that the gospel could be preached among the slaves only
after the bishop of London wrote a fateful letter to calm things down. In it
he reassured the white masters that nothing whatsoever had to change in
the outward conditions of the slaves who were baptized, since baptism signi-
fied the deliverance from sin and evil lust, and not so much a release from
slavery or any other such external fetters. After all, it brought with it the
advantage of having more control over the slaves than would leaving them
to their pagan rituals. So it happened that Negroes became Christians and
were allowed to attend the worship services of the white people while sitting
in the balconies; they were also allowed to partake of communion—as the
last guests. Any further participation in the life of a congregation was ruled
out; all the offices of the congregation and ordination remained the privilege of the whites. Under these conditions, the common worship service
became for Negroes more and more a farce. Once all attempts had failed
to be recognized as equal members in the church of Jesus Christ, Negroes
made an effort to organize themselves in their own congregations. This was
both a forced and a free decision on the part of the Negroes. A number of
incidents, particularly during the time of the Civil War, which also brought
the abolition of slavery, led to the independent organization of the Negro

---

33. ["*The Black Christ and Other Poems* is the title of a collection of poetry (1929) by the
black poet Countee Cullen (cf. *DBWE* 10:315, esp. n. 31). See also Bonhoeffer's reading
notes on 'Negro Literature,' *DBWE* 10:421–422, and the editor's introduction to *DBWE*
10:30–31," *DBWE* 15:456, n. 48.]

church. Since then, the large denominations are split; here we have a telling example of the formation of denominations in the United States. The strongest contribution of the Negroes for American Christendom lies in their spiritual songs ("Negro spirituals"), in which they sing with moving expression about the distress and liberation of the people of Israel ("Go down, Moses . . ."), the misery and distress of the human heart ("Nobody knows the trouble I have seen . . .") and love for the Redeemer and yearning for the kingdom of heaven ("Swing low, sweet chariot . . .").[34] Every white American knows, loves, and sings these songs. It is difficult to understand how famous Negro singers can sing these songs in the overcrowded concert halls of white people and receive resounding applause, while at the same time the same men and women find no acceptance in the communities of the whites because of social discrimination. We should furthermore point out that nowhere else is revivalist preaching still so alive and widespread as it is for Negroes; here the gospel of Jesus Christ, the Savior of sinners, is truly preached and received with great welcome and visible emotion. The issue of the Negro is one of the most decisive future tasks for the white churches.

458

VI. Theology

Given everything that has been said up to this point, it should not come as a surprise that we are discussing theology last. This is not to imply that American theology as such is insignificant. It merely reflects the fact that American denominations must be understood primarily in terms of their church services, their practical work in the congregation, and their public engagement rather than their theologies. The same is true for almost all Anglo-Saxon churches, and this poses a great difficulty for us. No one can do justice to these churches as long as they are judged by their theology. The order and tradition pertaining to the worship services, offices, and congregations carry such weight here that even a bad theology cannot do too much damage. But it is not only this—viewed from the perspective of intellectual history—conservative background that explains this peculiar situation; rather here we find a virtually irreconcilable contrast between the churches of the Reformation and the "Protestantism" without Reformation. We will return to this at the conclusion.

---

34. [". . . On Bonhoeffer's deep appreciation for Negro spirituals, see also *DBWE* 10:269 and 315 as well as *DBWE* 10:30–31," *DBWE* 15:458, n. 50.]

At the beginning of this year, the journal *Christian Century* published a series of essays on the topic: "How my mind has changed in the last decade." *Men of the church and teachers of theology* are asked to give a brief *autobiographi-* 459 *cal and theological report on their own development in the last ten years* for the Christian public. A *common* thread in all these essays—with the exception of the fundamentalists, who deliberately declare that nothing essential could have changed in their thinking since they espouse the same teaching then and now—is the admission of a decisive theological turn in the last ten years. *Common* is also the direction in which the turn is seen: it is a return to revelation from secularism in its many forms as modernity, humanitarianism, and naturalism. While ten years ago there was a predominant interest in the "social gospel," today there is an awakening of a greater interest in dogmatics, a fact that is especially noticeable in one of the most prestigious theological institutions of the country, namely, at Union Theological Seminary in New York. German theology, inasmuch as it is translated into English—mainly the works of Barth, Brunner, Heim, and a somewhat undifferentiated Tillich as well—has left deep impressions. Kierkegaard is being introduced to wider circles through new translations. There is also—with an almost stronger effect—the new English theology with its strong emphasis on the necessity of a natural theology. *Common* is also the explanation for this shift, namely, the collapse of the old social orders in America and other countries and the ensuing critique of a liberal, optimistic faith in progress, which until now dominated theology. Prompted by this new insight is now the *common* speech, more than ever, of sin and God's judgment, as is evident in the current world crisis. Finally, *common* is also the deliberate rejection of Barth's critique of natural theology. Within these boundaries there are all kinds of nuances of theological thinking; this is possible given the combination of a new search for a Christian theology of revelation with the tradition of American thinking.

The essays of the following authors are especially worthwhile reading: *W. L. Sperry* (professor of practical theology at Harvard), whose views may be summarized in these words: "American life has been until most recently, optimistic, once-born . . . our once-born America is changing before our eyes"; *H. N. Wieman* (professor for philosophy of religion in Chicago), an advocate of "theistic naturalism," whose definition of sin is a strange mix- 460 ture of Reformation insight and the naturalistic anthropology of James and Whitehead: "Therefore, he, who makes ideas supreme over his life, no matter how lofty and no matter how perfectly he may live up to them, is sinning." Similarly remarkable is the following sentence about grace: "The grace of God is the good which God puts into each concrete situation over and above all that man can do or plan or even imagine"; by contrast, the text becomes completely obscure in treating the living Christ as the "working of a process of history which used that human personality" (of Jesus), or as "the growth of a community" that breaks through all natural human communities; similarly weak is the definition of the church as "a new way of living." On the other hand, there is a notable remark concerning the otherness of God: "God alone is concrete in his working . . . man must work abstractly"; and based on this a special appreciation of the apostle Paul. The failure in Christology is characteristic of all current American theology (with the exception of fundamentalism). *Reinhold Niebuhr* (professor at Union Theological Seminary), one of the most important and creative theologians in America today, whose main work one should know in order to appreciate the theological landscape (*Moral Man and Immoral Society, An Interpretation of Christian Ethics, Beyond Tragedy*), is the sharpest critic of current American Protestantism and the contemporary social order. For years now he has left a deep impression by strongly emphasizing the cross as the center and the end of history, tied to a strong and active political theology. He sees the right way between neo-orthodoxy, for which Jesus Christ becomes the basis for human despair, and a true liberalism, for which Christ is the Lord, the norm, the ideal, and the revelation of our essential being. Both are equally necessary. But even here a doctrine on the person and the work of salvation of Jesus Christ is missing. *W. M. Horton* (professor at Oberlin College) wants to work out a synthesis among Augustine, Calvin, Barth, Wieman, and the "social gospel." *E. S. Ames* (former professor and pastor in Chicago) refuses as the only liberal to recognize a change in his thinking through recent developments and defiantly gives his article the title "Confirmed Liberalism." According to him, new theology is and remains an atavism, because it is unscientific. "God is life as you live it" (!). "Worship as praise and adulation does not fit with my idea of either God or man. It tends to separate them, to exalt one too much and to debase the other too much." It is hardly comprehensible how someone can be a pastor for decades with such a teaching! On the other hand, however, he is stating with frank openness what others, past and present, may be thinking.

With few exceptions, current American theology presents a fairly uniform picture, at least for someone who comes from the churches of the Reformation. This brings us to the last point.

God did not grant a Reformation to American Christendom. He gave strong revivalist preachers, men of the church, and theologians, but no reformation of the church of Jesus Christ from the word of God. Those churches of the Reformation that came to America either stand in deliberate seclusion and distance from general church life or have fallen victim to Protestantism without Reformation. There are Americans who announce with certainty and pride that they build on principles that are pre-Reformation and radical Reformation and see in this their essential nature. It cannot be denied that the dangers for American Christendom today are seen clearly by some of the leading theologians. Reinhold and Richard Niebuhr, Pauck, Miller, and several others among the younger theologians speak largely in the spirit of the Reformation. But these are exceptions. American theology and the churches as a whole have never really understood what "critique" by God's word means in its entirety. That God's "critique" is also meant for religion, for the churches' Christianity, even the sanctification of Christians, all that is ultimately not understood.[35] One sign of this is the general insistence on natural theology. Christendom in American theology is essentially still religion and ethics. Hence, the person and work of Jesus Christ recedes into the background for theology and remains ultimately not understood, because the sole foundation for God's radical judgment and radical grace is at this point not recognized. The decisive task today is the conversation between the Protestantism without Reformation and the churches of the Reformation.

462

---

35. ["On Bonhoeffer's earlier critique—drawing on Karl Barth—of 'religion' and the cultural-Protestant synthesis of religion and ethics, see especially his lecture 'Jesus Christ and the Essence of Christianity,' delivered to the Barcelona congregation in December 1928 (*DBWE* 10:303–359 [*Reader* 57–73]). See also his New York seminar paper from 1930–1931 'The Theology of Crisis and Its Attitude toward Philosophy and Science' (*DBWE* 10:462–476 [*Reader* 143–155]); and Feil, *Theology of Dietrich Bonhoeffer*, 67–74," *DBWE* 15:462, n. 67.]

PART 6
Christian Ethics and Public Life

33. CHRIST, REALITY, AND GOOD. CHRIST, CHURCH, AND WORLD

DBWE 6:47–75

With France's surrender to Germany in June 1940, it was clear that German military defeat was not imminent. Bonhoeffer came to terms with this reality and soon at the invitation of his brother-in-law Hans von Dohnanyi, joined the resistance movement that was actively conspiring to overthrow Hitler and set the foundations for a new government.[1] The surveillance and censorship to which all citizens were subject under the German military dictatorship was even more oppressive in Bonhoeffer's case; his participation in the conspiracy required utmost secrecy,[2] and his previous clashes with the National Socialist regime had made him a marked man.[3] His life became one of subterfuge.

At the same time, Bonhoeffer began working on what he hoped would become his magnum opus. This work, left unfinished with Bonhoeffer's execution in 1945, was published in 1949 by Bethge as a collection of essay fragments under the title Ethics. *Two concerns animate* Ethics: *"first, the desire to contribute to the reconstruction of life in Germany and the West in the peace that would follow the war; and second, the precondition for this, his involvement in the resistance movement conspiracy that was working to overthrow Hitler and National Socialism."[4] What follows in this section of the Reader is a selection of essays from* Ethics *as well as thematically related papers from that period.*

---

1. [DBWE *16:2, editor's introduction. For more, see* DB-ER, *681ff.*]

2. [DBWE *16:8, editor's introduction.*]

3. [*His previous run-ins included the loss of authorization to teach at the university (1936), the dissolution of Finkenwalde seminary (1937), a prohibition against staying in Berlin (1938), the dissolution of underground theological education (1940), and a prohibition on public speaking in Germany (1940). He would also be prohibited from writing for publication in 1941. See* DBWE *6:420, editors' afterword.*]

4. [DBWE *6:1, editors' introduction.*]

The essay below is one of three in Ethics *that reads like a possible beginning to the book; in all three cases, Bonhoeffer begins by posing a stark contrast between his vision of ethics and what has traditionally gone by that name.*[5] *As Bonhoeffer puts it in this essay, Christian ethics must "pivot" away from traditional questions about being good and doing good, which presuppose the self and the world as ultimate realities, toward the question of God's will, which recognizes ultimate reality to be God as revealed in Christ. In the opening pages of this and the other two introductory-style essays, Bonhoeffer characteristically subverts readers' expectations to offer a fresh entrée into what might otherwise be a stale topic.*

Those who wish even to focus on the problem of a Christian ethic are faced   47
with an outrageous demand—from the outset they must give up, as inappropriate to this topic, the very two questions that led them to deal with the ethical problem: "How can I be good?" and "How can I do something good?" Instead they must ask the wholly other, completely different question: what is the will of God? This demand is radical precisely because it presupposes a decision about ultimate reality, that is, a decision of faith. When the ethical problem presents itself essentially as the question of my own being good and doing good, the decision has already been made that the   48
self and the world are the ultimate realities. All ethical reflection then has the goal that I be good, and that the world—by my action—becomes good. If it turns out, however, that these realities, myself and the world, are themselves embedded in a wholly other ultimate reality, namely, the reality of God the Creator, Reconciler, and Redeemer, then the ethical problem takes on a whole new aspect. Of ultimate importance, then, is not that I become good, or that the condition of the world be improved by my efforts, but that the reality of God show itself everywhere to be the ultimate reality. Where God is known by faith to be the ultimate reality, the source of my ethical concern will be that God be known as the good, even at the risk that I and the world are revealed as not good, but as bad through and through. All things appear as in a distorted mirror if they are not seen and recognized in God. All that is—so to speak—given, all laws and norms, are abstractions, as long as God is not known in faith to be the ultimate reality. That God alone is the ultimate reality, is, however, not an idea meant to sublimate the actual world, nor is it the religious perfecting of a profane worldview. It is rather a faithful Yes to God's self-witness, God's revelation. If God is merely a religious concept, there is no reason why there should not be, behind this apparent "ultimate" reality, a still more ultimate reality: the twilight or the

---

5. [*The others are* DBWE *6:299–338 and* DBWE *6:363–387 (Reader 667–684).*]

death of the gods. Only insofar as the ultimate reality is revelation, that is, the self-witness of the living God, is its claim to ultimacy fulfilled. But then the decision about the whole of life depends on our relation to God's revelation. Awareness of it is not only a step-by-step progress in the discovery of deeper and more inward realities, but this awareness is the turning point, the pivot, of all perception of reality as such. The ultimate, or final, reality discloses itself to be at the same time the first reality, God as the first and last, the Alpha and Omega. Without God, all seeing and perceiving of things and laws become abstraction, a separation from both origin and goal. All questions of our own goodness, as well as of the goodness of the world, are impossible unless we have first posed the question of the goodness of God. For what meaning would the goodness of human beings and the world have without God? Since God, however, as ultimate reality is no other than the self-announcing, self-witnessing, self-revealing God in Jesus Christ, the question of good can only find its answer in Christ.

The source of a Christian ethic is not the reality of one's own self, not the reality of the world, nor is it the reality of norms and values. It is the reality of God that is revealed in Jesus Christ. This is the demand, before all others, that must honestly be made of anyone who wishes to be concerned with the problem of a Christian ethic. It places us before the ultimate and decisive question: With what reality will we reckon in our life? With the reality of God's revelatory word or with the so-called realities of life? With divine grace or with earthly inadequacies? With the resurrection or with death? This question itself, which none can answer by their own choice without answering it falsely, already presupposes a given answer: that God, however we decide, has already spoken the revelatory word and that we, even in our false reality, can live no other way than from the true reality of the word of God. The question about ultimate reality already places us in such an embrace by its answer that there is no way we can escape from it. This answer carries us into the reality of God's revelation in Jesus Christ from which it comes.

The *subject matter of a Christian ethic is God's reality revealed in Christ becoming real among God's creatures,* just as the subject matter of doctrinal theology is the truth of God's reality revealed in Christ. The place that in all other ethics is marked by the antithesis between ought and is, idea and realization, motive and work, is occupied in Christian ethics by the relation between reality and becoming real, between past and present, between history

---

6. ["On the 'becoming real' of 'reality,' see *Sanctorum Communio* about 'actualizing . . . the reality,' (*DBWE* 1:144 [*Reader* 41]) . . . ," *DBWE* 6:50, n. 14.]

and event (faith) or, to replace the many concepts with the simple name of the thing itself, the relation between Jesus Christ and the Holy Spirit.[6] The question of the good becomes the question of participating in God's reality revealed in Christ. Good is no longer an evaluation of what exists, for instance my essence, my moral orientation, my actions, or of a state of affairs in the world. It is no longer a predicate that one can apply to something that exists of itself. Good is the real itself, that is, not the abstractly real that is separated from the reality of God, but the real that has its reality only in God. Good is never without this reality. It is no general formula. And this reality is never without the good. The will to be good exists only as desire for the reality that is real in God. A desire to be good for its own sake, as some sort of personal goal or life vocation, falls prey to an ironic unreality; honest striving for good turns into the ambitious striving of the paragon of virtue. Good as such is no independent theme for life. To take it as such would be the craziest Don Quixotry.[7] Only by participating in reality do we also share in the good.

51

There is an old argument about whether only the will, the act of the mind, the person, can be good, or whether achievement, work, consequence, or condition can be called good as well—and if so, which comes first and which is more important. This argument, which has also seeped into theology, leading there as elsewhere to serious aberrations, proceeds from a basically perverse way of putting the question. It tears apart what is originally and essentially one, namely, the good and the real, the person and the work. The objection that Jesus, too, had this distinction between person and work in mind, when he spoke about the good tree that brings forth good fruits, distorts this saying of Jesus into its exact opposite. Its meaning is not that first the person is good and then the work, but that *only the two together*, only both as united in one, are to be understood as good or bad.[8]

The same is true of the distinction that the American philosopher of religion Reinhold Niebuhr has made with the concepts moral man and immoral society. The split between individual and society that is expressed here is just as abstract as that between person and work. What is inseparable is here torn apart, and each part, which by itself is dead, is examined separately. The result is the complete ethical aporia that today goes by the

---

7. ["See *DBWE* 6:80, on Cervantes's novel *Don Quixote*, First Part, chap. 8. The titular hero, like a knight errant from a chivalry romance, rides to defend the good. In his imaginary distortion of reality, he fights with lance and sword against windmill blades, two herds of sheep, and several skins of red wine, among other things," *DBWE* 6:51, n. 16.]

8. ["See . . . *DBWE* 12:308ff. (*Reader* 269ff.)," *DBWE* 6:51, n. 18.]

52 name "social ethics." Of course, if good is seen as an existing entity's conformity to what ought to be, then the more massive resistance that society
sets against what ought to be must lead to an ethical preference for the
individual over society. (And conversely, precisely this result should warn
us to detect in this concept of the ethical its sociological origin in the age
of individualism.) The question of good must not be narrowed to investi-
gating the relation of actions to their motives, or to their consequences,
measuring them by a ready-made ethical standard. An ethic of disposition
or intention is just as superficial as an ethic of consequences. For what right
do we have to stay with inner motivation as the ultimate phenomenon of
ethics, ignoring that "good" intentions can grow out of very dark backgrounds in human consciousness and subconsciousness, and that often
the worst things happen as a result of "good intentions"? As the question
of the motives of action finally disappears in the tangled web of the past, so
the question of its consequences gets lost in the mists of the future. There
are no clear boundaries on either side. Nothing justifies us in stopping at
any arbitrary point we choose in order to make a definitive judgment. In
practice, we ever and again stop to make such an arbitrary determination,
whether along the lines of an ethic of motives or an ethic of consequences.
Whatever we do will depend on the different needs of the changing times.

53 Neither has any fundamental advantage over the other, because in both
cases the question of good is posed abstractly, severed from reality. Good
is not the agreement of some way of existence that I describe as reality with
some standard placed at our disposal by nature or grace. Rather, good
is reality, reality itself seen and recognized in God. Human beings, with
their motives and their works, with their fellow humans, with the creation
that surrounds them, in other words, reality as a whole held in the hands
of God—that is what is embraced by the question of good. The divine
"behold, it was very good" [*Gen. 1:31*] meant the whole of creation. The
good desires the whole, not only of motives but also of works; it desires
whole persons along with the human companions with whom they are
given to live. What could it mean anyway that only a part be named good,
motives for instance, while works are bad, or vice versa? *Human beings are
indivisible wholes, not only as individuals in both their person and work, but also
as members of the human and created community* to which they belong. It is this
indivisible whole, that is, this reality grounded and recognized in God,
that the question of good has in view. "Creation" is the name of this indivisible whole according to its origin. According to its goal it is called the
kingdom of God. Both are equally far from us and yet near to us, because
God's creation and God's kingdom are present to us only in God's self-
revelation in Jesus Christ.

To participate in the indivisible whole of God's reality is the meaning of the Christian question about the good. To avoid misunderstanding, we need at this point a further clarification of what is meant here by reality.

There is a way of grounding ethics in a concept of reality that is completely different from the Christian way, namely, the positivist-empiricist approach. It attempts to remove the concept of norms from ethics completely, and sees in them only the idealizing of actual ways of behavior that are useful in life; good is seen as basically nothing but that which serves reality usefully and purposefully.[9] It follows that there is no generally valid good, but only an endlessly manifold good that is determined to be such by whatever "reality" there happens to be. The advantage of this perspective over the idealistic view[10] lies in its undoubtedly greater "closeness to reality."   54 Good here does not consist of an impossible "realization," i.e., making real something that is unreal; it is not a realization of ethical ideas. Rather, reality itself teaches what is good. The question is only whether reality as understood here is capable of meeting this demand. It thereby becomes clear that the concept of reality underlying this positivistic ethic is the vulgar concept of that which can be empirically established, which involves denying any foundation of this reality in the ultimate reality, that is, in God. This vulgar understanding of reality is therefore unsuited to become the origin of the good, because it requires nothing less than complete surrender to what is at hand, given, accidental, and driven by temporary goals in any given time. It is unsuited because it does not recognize ultimate reality and so surrenders and destroys the unity of the good.

Christian ethics speaks otherwise of the reality that is the origin of the good. It means thereby the reality of God as the ultimate reality beyond and in all that exists. It means also the reality of the existing world that is real only through the reality of God. The reality of God is not just another idea. Christian faith perceives this in the fact that the reality of God has revealed itself and witnessed to itself in the middle of the real world. *In Jesus Christ the reality of God has entered into the reality of this world.* The place where the questions about the reality of God and about the reality of the world are answered at the same time is characterized solely by the name: Jesus Christ.

---

9. ["See Bonhoeffer's report on his study in New York in 1930–1931 where he describes William James, John Dewey, and others as 'these radically empirical thinkers,' and comments that 'the truth as the absolute norm of all thinking is limited by that which shows itself "in the long run as useful"' (*DBWE* 10:310–311)," *DBWE* 6:53, n. 26.]

10. ["This refers to the philosophy of German idealism around the turn from the eighteenth to the nineteenth century, especially the philosophy of Hegel," *DBWE* 6:54, n. 27.]

God and the world are enclosed in this name. In Christ all things exist (Col. 1:17). From now on we cannot speak rightly of either God or the world without speaking of Jesus Christ. All concepts of reality that ignore Jesus Christ are abstractions. All thinking about the good that plays off what ought to be against what is, or what is against what ought to be, is overcome where the good has become reality, namely, in Jesus Christ. Jesus Christ cannot be identified either with an ideal, a norm, or with what exists. The enmity of the ideal toward what exists, the fanatical imposition of an idea on an existing entity that resists it, can be as far from the good as the surrender of the ought to the expedient. The ought as well as the expedient receive in Christ a completely new meaning. The irreconcilable opposition of ought and is finds reconciliation in Christ, that is, in ultimate reality. To participate in this reality is the true meaning of the question concerning the good.

In Christ we are invited to participate in the reality of God and the reality of the world at the same time, the one not without the other. The reality of God is disclosed only as it places me completely into the reality of the world. But I find the reality of the world always already borne, accepted, and reconciled in the reality of God. That is the mystery of the revelation of God in the human being Jesus Christ. The Christian ethic asks, then, how this reality of God and of the world that is given in Christ becomes real in our world. It is not as if "our world" were something outside this God-world reality that is in Christ, as if it did not already belong to the world borne, accepted, and reconciled in Christ; it is not, therefore, as if some "principle" must first be applied to our circumstances and our time. Rather, the question is how the reality in Christ—which has long embraced us and our world within itself—works here and now or, in other words, how life is to be lived in it. What matters is *participating in the reality of God and the world in Jesus Christ today*, and doing so in such a way that I never experience the reality of God without the reality of the world, nor the reality of the world without the reality of God.

As we travel further along this road, a large part of traditional Christian ethical thought stands like a Colossus obstructing our way. Since the beginnings of Christian ethics after New Testament times, the dominant basic conception, consciously or unconsciously determining all ethical thought, has been that two realms bump against each other: one divine, holy, supernatural, and Christian; the other worldly, profane, natural, and unchristian. This view reached its first peak in the High Middle Ages, and its second in the pseudo-Reformation thought of the post-Reformation period. Reality as a whole splits into two parts, and the concern of ethics becomes the right relation of both parts to each other. In the high scholastic period the natural realm was subordinated to the realm of grace. In pseudo-Lutheranism the autonomy of the orders of this world is proclaimed against the law of Christ. Among the Enthusiasts the church-community of the elect sets out to struggle against the enmity of the world in order to build the kingdom of God on earth. In all of this the concern of Christ becomes a partial, provincial affair within the whole of reality. One reckons with realities outside the reality of Christ. It follows that there is separate access to these realities, apart from Christ. However important one may take reality in Christ to be, it always remains a partial reality alongside others. 57

This division of the whole of reality into sacred and profane, or Christian and worldly, sectors creates the possibility of existence in only one of these sectors: for instance, a spiritual existence that takes no part in worldly existence, and a worldly existence that can make good its claim to autonomy over against the sacred sector. The monk and the cultural Protestant of the nineteenth century represent these two possibilities.[11] The whole of medieval history turned around the theme of the rule of the spiritual realm over the worldly, the regnum gratiae [*kingdom of grace*] over the regnum naturae [*kingdom of nature*], whereas the modern age is characterized by an ever-progressing independence of the worldly over against the spiritual. As long as Christ and the world are conceived as two realms bumping against and repelling each other, we are left with only the following options. Giving up on reality as a whole, either we place ourselves in one of the two realms, wanting Christ without the world or the world without Christ—and in both cases we deceive ourselves. Or we try to stand in the two realms at the same time, thereby becoming people in eternal conflict, shaped by the post-Reformation era, who ever and again present ourselves as the *only* form of Christian existence that is in accord with reality.[12] 58

As hard as it may now seem to break the spell of this conceptual framework of realms, it is just as certain that this perspective deeply contradicts both biblical and Reformation thought, therefore bypassing reality. There are not two realities, but *only one reality*, and that is God's reality revealed in Christ in the reality of the world. Partaking in Christ, we stand at the

---

11. ["On a misguided sort of monasticism, see *DBWE* 4:47f. (*Reader* 462–463); and Feil, *Theology of Dietrich Bonhoeffer*, 128f. The term 'cultural Protestantism,' *Kulturprotestantismus*, refers to a reigning tendency in broad sections of German Protestantism, since the nineteenth century, toward adapting the biblical and Christian traditions to modern cultural conditions . . . ," *DBWE* 6:57, n. 40.]

12. ["Bonhoeffer found such 'conflict thinking' in Friedrich Naumann, among others; see *DBWE* 6:237–238, n. 74. On Bonhoeffer's theological rejection of this thinking, see *DBWE* 4:70–72 (*Reader* 480–482), and his 1939–1940 meditation on Ps. 119:19, *DBWE* 15:524," *DBWE* 6:58, n. 42.]

same time in the reality of God and in the reality of the world. The reality of Christ embraces the reality of the world in itself. The world has no reality of its own independent of God's revelation in Christ. It is a denial of God's revelation in Jesus Christ to wish to be "Christian" without being "worldly," or to wish to be worldly without seeing and recognizing the world in Christ. Hence there are not two realms, but only *the one realm of the Christ-reality*, in which the reality of God and the reality of the world are united. Because this is so, the theme of two realms, which has dominated the history of the church again and again, is foreign to the New Testament. The New Testament is concerned only with the realization of the Christ-reality in the contemporary world that it already embraces, owns, and inhabits. There are not two competing realms standing side by side and battling over the borderline, as if this question of boundaries was always the decisive one. Rather, the whole reality of the world has already been drawn into and is held together in Christ. History moves only from this center and toward this center.[13]

Thinking in terms of two realms understands the paired concepts worldly-Christian, natural-supernatural, profane-sacred, rational-revelational, as ultimate static opposites that designate certain given entities that are mutually exclusive. This thinking fails to recognize the original unity of these opposites in the Christ-reality and, as an afterthought, replaces this with a forced unity provided by a sacred or profane system that overarches them. Thus the static opposition is maintained. Things work out quite differently when the reality of God and the reality of the world are recognized in Christ. In that way, the world, the natural, the profane, and reason are seen as included in God from the beginning. All this does not exist "in and for itself." It has its reality nowhere else than in the reality of God in Christ. It belongs to the real concept of the worldly that it is at all times seen in the movement of the world's both having been accepted and becoming accepted by God in Christ. Just as the reality of God has entered the reality of the world in Christ, what is Christian cannot be had otherwise than in what is worldly, the "supernatural" only in the natural, the holy only in the profane, the revelational only in the rational. The unity of the reality of God and the reality of the world established in Christ (repeats itself, or, more exactly) realizes itself again and again in human beings. Still, that

59

---

13. ["See especially the 1933 Christology lectures, where Christ is described as the center of human existence, history, and nature *DBWE* 12:324–327 (*Reader* 282–285); and Feil, *Theology of Dietrich Bonhoeffer*, 72–76. See also Green, *Bonhoeffer*, 220–233," *DBWE* 6:58, n. 44.]

which is Christian is not identical with the worldly, the natural with the supernatural, the revelational with the rational. Rather, the unity that exists between them is given only in the Christ-reality, and that means only as accepted by faith in this ultimate reality. This unity is preserved by the fact that the worldly and the Christian, etc., mutually prohibit every static independence of the one over against the other, that they behave toward each other polemically, and precisely therein witness to their common reality, their unity in the Christ-reality. As Luther polemically led the worldly into battle against the sacralizing trend of the Roman Church, so this worldliness must be polemically contradicted by the Christian, by the "sacred,"   60 in the very moment when it is in danger of making itself independent, as happened soon after the Reformation, reaching its high point in cultural Protestantism. The issue in both cases is precisely the same, namely referring to the reality of God and the reality of the world in Jesus Christ. In the name of a better Christianity Luther used the worldly to protest against a type of Christianity that was making itself independent by separating itself from the reality in Christ. Similarly, Christianity must be used polemically today against the worldly in the name of a better worldliness; this polemical use of Christianity must not end up again in a static and self-serving sacred realm. Only in this sense of a polemical unity may Luther's doctrine of the two kingdoms be used. That was probably its original meaning.

Realm thinking as static thinking is, theologically speaking, legalistic thinking. This is easy to show. Where the worldly establishes itself as an autonomous sector, this denies the fact of the world's *being accepted* in Christ, the grounding of the reality of the world in revelational reality, and thereby the validity of the gospel for the whole world. The world is not perceived as reconciled by God in Christ but as a domain that is still completely subject to the demands of Christianity, or, in turn, as a sector that opposes its own law against the law of Christ. Where, on the other side, what is Christian comes on the scene as an autonomous sector, the world is denied the community that God has formed with it in Christ. A Christian law that condemns the law of the world is established here, and is led, unreconciled, into battle against the world that God has reconciled to himself. As every legalism flows into lawlessness, every nomism into antinomianism, every   61 perfectionism into libertinism, so here as well. A world existing on its own, withdrawn from the law of Christ, falls prey to the severing of all bonds and to arbitrariness. A Christianity that withdraws from the world falls prey to unnaturalness, irrationality, triumphalism, and arbitrariness.

Since ethical thinking in terms of realms is overcome by faith in the revelation of ultimate reality in Jesus Christ, it follows that there is no real Christian existence outside the reality of the world and no real worldliness outside the reality of Jesus Christ. For the Christian there is no-where to retreat from the world, neither externally nor into the inner life. Every attempt to evade the world will have to be paid for sooner or later with a sinful surrender to the world.[14] (It is a fact of experience that where the gross sins of sexuality are conquered, sins will flourish that are just as gross but less derided by the world, such as greed or avarice.) In the eyes of a worldly observer, there is usually something tragicomic about the cultivation of a

62 Christian inwardness undisturbed by the world; for the sharp-eyed world recognizes itself most clearly at the very place where Christian inwardness, deceiving itself, dreams it is furthest away from the world. Whoever confesses the reality of Jesus Christ as the revelation of God confesses in the same breath the reality of God and the reality of the world, for they find God and the world reconciled in Christ. Just for this reason the Christian is no longer the person of eternal conflict. As reality is *one* in Christ, so the person who belongs to this Christ-reality is also a whole. Worldliness does not separate one from Christ, and being Christian does not separate one from the world. Belonging completely to Christ, one stands at the same time completely in the world.

Proceeding from the Christ-reality and wishing to leave thinking in realms behind, we still face, however, an important question: Are there really no ultimate static oppositions, no realms that are definitively separated from each other? Is not the church of Jesus Christ such a realm that is divided from the realm of the world? And finally, is not the kingdom of the devil such a realm, which will never enter into the kingdom of Christ?

Without doubt there are statements about the church in the New Testament that use spatial analogies; one thinks of the church described as a temple, a building, a house, and also as a body. It is clear from this that where the church is to be described as the visible church-community of God on earth, spatial images cannot be avoided. In fact, the church occupies a certain space in the world that is determined by its worship, its order, and its congregational life,[15] and this very fact is the point of departure for thinking in terms of realms in general. It would be very dangerous to overlook this, to deny the visibility of the church, and thus to devalue it into a purely

63 spiritual entity. Then the fact of the revelation of God in the world would

---

14. ["See *DBWE* 4:245 on Luther's protest against 'the secularization of Christianity within the monastic life.' See also *DBWE* 4:78 (*Reader* 486) on the evasive concept of 'inner' freedom from worldly goods . . . ," *DBWE* 6:61, n. 50.]

15. See *Discipleship*. ["See *DBWE* 4:225–248 and (in the exposition of the Sermon on the Mount) 110–114. Both carry the heading 'The Visible Church-Community,'" *DBWE* 6:62, n. 55.]

be deprived of its power and Christ would be spiritualized. It is intrinsic to God's revelation in Jesus Christ that it occupied space in the world. It would, however, be fundamentally wrong simply to explain this space empirically. When God in Jesus Christ claims space in the world—even space in a stable because "there was no other place in the inn" [*Luke 2:7*]—God embraces the whole reality of the world in this narrow space and reveals its ultimate foundation. So also the church of Jesus Christ is the place—that is, the space—in the world where the reign of Jesus Christ over the whole world is to be demonstrated and proclaimed. This space of the church does not, therefore, exist just for itself, but its existence is already always something that reaches far beyond it. This is because it is not the space of a cult that would have to fight for its own existence in the world. Rather, the space of the church is the place where witness is given to the foundation of all reality in Jesus Christ. The church is the place where it is proclaimed and taken seriously that God has reconciled the world to himself in Christ, that God so loved the world that God gave his Son for it. The space of the church is not there in order to fight with the world for a piece of its territory, but precisely to testify to the world that it is still the world, namely, the world that is loved and reconciled by God. It is not true that the church intends to or must spread its space out over the space of the world. It desires no more space than it needs to serve the world with its witness to Jesus Christ and to the world's reconciliation to God through Jesus Christ. The church can only defend its own space by fighting, not for space, but for the salvation of the world. Otherwise the church becomes a "religious society"[16] that fights in its own interest and thus has ceased to be the church of God in the world. So the first task given to those who belong to the church of God is not to be something for themselves, for example, by creating a religious organization or leading a pious life, but to be witnesses of Jesus Christ to the world. For this the Holy Spirit equips those to whom the Spirit comes. Of course, it is presupposed that such a witness to the world can only happen in the right way when it comes out of sanctified life in God's church-community.[17]

64

---

16. ["See Bonhoeffer's remarks in *Sanctorum Communio* on 'the empirical phenomenon "church" qua . . . religious society' (*DBWE* 1:126 [*Reader* 36–37]). Bonhoeffer found groups that are content with the satisfaction of human religious needs to be inadequate in not taking account of God's commission concerning the whole of humanity," *DBWE* 6:64, n. 60.]

17. ["See *DBWE* 4:253–280. See also *DBWE* 6:407–408 (*Reader* 697–698), at the end of the last *Ethics* manuscript. A 'sanctified life' is not free of faults and sin but is determined by the forgiveness of sins and by the will to bear witness to the one who sanctifies it by stamping it in a special way," *DBWE* 6:64, n. 61.]

Nevertheless, true sanctified life in the church-community of God is distinguished from any pious imitation by the fact that it leads the believer at the same time into witness to the world. Where that witness has become silent it is a sign of inner decay in the church-community, just as failure to bear fruit is a sign that a tree is dying.

When one therefore wants to speak of the space of the church, one must be aware that this space has already been broken through, abolished, and overcome in every moment by the witness of the church to Jesus Christ. Thus all false thinking in terms of realms is ruled out as endangering the understanding of the church.

So far we have spoken of the world always in the sense of its being reconciled in Christ to God, and of reality always as accepted by God, existing in God, as reconciled reality. From this perspective, thinking in realms must be rejected. This still leaves open the question whether the "world," insofar as it is understood as the "evil" world fallen under the power of the devil—that is, whether sinful reality—must be understood as a realm erected against the church, that is, against the kingdom of Christ. Is not

65 the final static opposition, which justifies thinking in terms of realms, the opposition between the kingdom of Christ and the kingdom of the devil? However much this question seems at first glance to demand an affirmative answer, on closer examination it is not self-evident. Christ and Christ's adversary the devil are mutually exclusive opponents, but in such a way that even the devil, unwillingly, must serve Christ, and, willing evil, must ever again do good, so that the kingdom of the devil is always only under the feet of Christ. Even if we understand by the kingdom of the devil the world that "lies in the evil one" [*1 John 5:19*]—that is, the world that has fallen under the power of the devil—here again is the limitation of thinking in terms of realms. For it is just the "evil world" that is reconciled in Christ to God and has its ultimate and true reality not in the devil but, again, in Christ. The world is not divided between Christ and the devil; it is completely the world of Christ, whether it recognizes this or not. As this reality in Christ it is to be addressed, and thus the false reality that it imagines itself to have, in itself or in the devil, is to be destroyed. The dark, evil world may not be surrendered to the devil, but must be claimed for the one who won it by coming in the flesh, by the death and resurrection of Christ. Christ gives up nothing that has been won, but holds it fast in his hands. Because of Christ

66 it will not do to partition the world into a demonized and a Christian world. Every static distinction between one domain as belonging to the devil and another as belonging to Christ denies the reality that God has reconciled the whole world with himself in Christ.

The central message of the New Testament is that in Christ God has loved the world and reconciled it with himself. This message presupposes that the world needs reconciliation with God, but cannot achieve it by itself. Acceptance of the world is a miracle of divine mercy. Therefore the church-community's relation to the world is completely determined by God's relation to the world. There is a love of the world that is enmity toward God (James 4:4; 1 John 2:15), because it arises from the essence of the world in itself and not from God's love for the world. The world "in itself," as it understands itself and as it defends itself against—yes, even repudiates—the reality of God's love in Jesus Christ that is valid for it, is subject to God's judgment upon all enmity to Christ. This world is engaged in a life-and-death struggle with the church-community. Still, it is the task and the essence of the church-community to proclaim precisely to this world its reconciliation with God, and to disclose to it the reality of the love of God, against which the world so blindly rages. Thus, even the lost and condemned world is being drawn ceaselessly into the event of Christ.

It is hard to give up an image that we have customarily used to integrate our thoughts and concepts. Yet we must get beyond this two-realms image. The question is now whether we can replace it with another image that is just as simple and plausible.

Above all we must turn our eyes to the image of Jesus Christ's own body—the one who became human, was crucified, and is risen. In the body of Jesus Christ, God is united with humankind, all humanity is accepted by God, and the world is reconciled to God. In the body of Jesus Christ, God took on the sin of all the world and bore it. There is no part of the world, no matter how lost, no matter how godless, that has not been accepted by God in Jesus Christ and reconciled to God. Whoever perceives the body of Jesus Christ in faith can no longer speak of the world as if it were lost, as if it were separated from God; they can no longer separate themselves in clerical pride from the world. The world belongs to Christ, and only in Christ is the world what it is. It needs, therefore, nothing less than Christ himself. Everything would be spoiled if we were to reserve Christ for the church while granting the world only some law, Christian though it may be. Christ has died for the world, and Christ is Christ only in the midst of the world. It is nothing but unbelief to give the world—for well-intended pedagogical reasons to be sure, which nonetheless leave an aftertaste of clericalism—less than Christ. It means not taking seriously the incarnation, the crucifixion, and the bodily resurrection. It means denying the body of Christ.

When the New Testament transfers the concept of the body of Christ to the church-community, this is in no way an expression that the church-community is first and foremost set apart from the world. On the contrary, in line with New Testament statements about God becoming flesh in Christ, it expresses just this—that in the body of Christ all humanity is accepted, included, and borne, and that the church-community of believers is to make this known to the world by word and life. This means not being separated from the world, but calling the world into the community of the body of Christ to which the world in truth already belongs. This witness is strange to the world, and in giving this witness the church-community experiences itself as strange to the world. Yet such strangeness is a consequence that ever and again follows from the communion that the body of Christ has with the world. The church-community is separated from the world only by this: it believes in the reality of being accepted by God—a reality that belongs to the whole world—and in affirming this as valid for itself it witnesses that it is valid for the entire world.

The body of Jesus Christ, especially as it is presented to us on the cross, makes visible to faith both the world in its sin and in its being loved by God, 68   and the church-community as the company of those who recognize their sin and gratefully submit to the love of God.

This belonging together of God and world that is grounded in Christ does not allow static spatial boundaries, nor does it remove the difference between church-community and world. This leads to the question of how to think about this difference without falling back into spatial images. Here we must ask the Bible itself for advice, and it has its answer ready.

Like all of creation, the world has been created through Christ and toward Christ and has its existence only in Christ (John 1:10; Col. 1:16). To speak of the world without speaking of Christ is pure abstraction. The world stands in relationship to Christ whether the world knows it or not. This relation of the world to Christ becomes concrete in certain *mandates of God* in the world. The scripture names four such mandates: *work, marriage, government, and church*. We speak of divine mandates rather than divine orders, because thereby their character as divinely imposed tasks, as opposed to determinate forms of being, becomes clearer.[18] In the world God wills work, marriage, government, and church, and God wills all these, each in its own way, through Christ, toward Christ, and in Christ. God has 69   placed human beings under all these mandates, not only each individual under one or the other, but all people under all four. There can be no

---

18. ["This polemic against 'orders of creation' was already found in *Creation and Fall* in Bonhoeffer's idea of 'orders of preservation' (*DBWE* 3:140), which was later dropped and is here superseded by his doctrine of mandates," *DBWE* 6:69, n. 76.]

retreat, therefore, from a "worldly" into a "spiritual" "realm." The practice of the Christian life can be learned only under these four mandates of God. It will not do to depreciate the first three mandates as "worldly," over against the last. It is a matter of "*divine*" mandates in the midst of the world, whether they concern work, marriage, government, or church. These mandates are divine, however, only because of their original and final relation to Christ. Detached from this relation, "in themselves," they are not divine, just as the world "in itself" is not divine. Work "in itself" is not divine, but work for the sake of Jesus Christ, for the sake of a divine task and goal, is divine. Only because God, for Christ's sake, has commanded human beings to work and has placed a promise on it, is work divine. The reason for the divine character of work cannot be seen in its general usefulness, its value, but can only be found when looking to the origin, the existence, and the goal of work given in Jesus Christ. So it is also with the other mandates. Only as God's mandates are they divine, not in their actual givenness in this or that concrete form. Not because there *is* work, marriage, government, or church is it *commanded* by God, but because it is *commanded* by God, therefore it *is*. Only insofar as its being is subjected—consciously or unconsciously—to the divine task is it a divine mandate. In the concrete case, persistent, arbitrary violation of this task through concrete forms of work, marriage, government, and church extinguishes the divine mandate. Still, what concretely exists receives a relative justification through the divine mandate. The existing marriage, government, etc., always has a relative advantage over what does not yet exist. Specific faults do not give the right to abolish or destroy what exists. They rather prompt a return to a true ordering under the divine mandate, and a restoration of true responsibility for the divine task. Such true responsibility consists in aligning the concrete form of the divine mandates with their origin, existence, and goal in Jesus Christ.

70

We encounter the mandate of work in the Bible already with the first human being. Adam was placed in the garden of Eden "to till it and keep it" (Gen. 2:15). After the fall, work remains a mandate of divine discipline and grace (Gen. 3:17–19). By the sweat of his brow Adam wrests nourishment from the field, and soon the range of human work embraces everything from agriculture through economic activity to science and art (Gen. 4:17ff.). The work founded in paradise calls for cocreative human deeds. Through them a world of things and values is created that is destined for the glory and service of Jesus Christ. It is not creation out of nothing, like God's creating, but it is the creation of new things on the basis of God's initial creation. No one can withdraw from this mandate. For in the work that humans do according to divine commission, a reflection of the heav-

enly world emerges that reminds those who know Jesus Christ of that world.
Cain's first creation was a city, the earthly reflection of the eternal city of
71   God. Then followed the invention of violins and flutes, which give us on
earth a foretaste of heavenly music. Then comes the extraction and pro-
cessing of metallic treasures dug out of the earth, partly to decorate the
earthly house like the heavenly city that shines with gold and precious
stones, and partly to make swords of avenging justice. Through the divine
mandate of work, a world should emerge that—knowingly or unknowingly
—expects Christ, is directed toward Christ, is open for Christ, and serves
and glorifies Christ. That the descendants of Cain should fulfill this mandate casts a deep shadow over all human work.

Like the mandate of work, so the mandate of marriage is encountered in
the Bible with the first human beings. In marriage human beings become
one before God, as Christ becomes one with the church. "This is a great
mystery" (Eph. 5:31f.). God blesses such becoming one with fruitfulness,
with the procreation of new life. By participating in creating, human beings
enter into the will of the Creator. Through marriage human beings are
procreated for the glory and service of Jesus Christ and the enlarging of
Christ's kingdom. This means that marriage is the place where children not
only are born but also are educated into obedience to Jesus Christ. As their
procreators and educators, parents are commissioned by God to be representatives of God for the children. Just as in work new values are created,
so in marriage new persons are created to serve Jesus Christ. But because
the first son of the first human beings, Cain, was born far from paradise
and became the murderer of his brother, here, too, a dark shadow falls over
marriage and family in this our world.

72   The divine mandate of government[19] already presupposes the mandates
of work and marriage. In the world that it rules, government finds already
existing these two mandates through which God the Creator exercises creative power and upon which government must rely. Government itself cannot produce life or values. It is not creative. Government maintains what is
created in the order that was given to the creation by God's commission.
Government protects what is created by establishing justice in acknowledgment of the divine mandates and by enforcing this justice with the power of

---

19. ["On 'government,' *Obrigkeit,* as a New Testament theological concept, see the
beginning of 'State and Church,' where Bonhoeffer wrote that while 'state' includes
rulers and ruled, 'in the concept of government only those who govern are meant. . . . It
can only be understood from above' (*DBWE* 16:503–504 [*Reader* 700]) . . . ," *DBWE* 6:72,
n. 87.]

the sword.[20] Thus, marriage is not made by government, but is affirmed by government. The great spheres of work are not themselves undertaken by government, but they are subject to its supervision and within certain limits—later to be described—to governmental direction. Government should never seek to become the agent of these areas of work, for this would seriously endanger their divine mandate along with its own. By establishing justice, and by the power of the sword, government preserves the world for the reality of Jesus Christ. Everyone owes obedience to this government—according to the will of Christ.

In contrast to the three mandates named above, the divine mandate of the church is the commission of allowing the reality of Jesus Christ to   73 become real in proclamation, church order, and Christian life—in short, its concern is the eternal salvation of the whole world. The mandate of the church embraces all people as they live within all the other mandates. Since a person is at the same time worker, spouse, and citizen, since one mandate overlaps with the others, and since all the mandates need to be fulfilled at the same time, so the church mandate reaches into all the other mandates. Similarly, the Christian is at the same time worker, spouse, and citizen. Every division into separate realms is forbidden here. Human beings as whole persons stand before the whole earthly and eternal reality that God in Jesus Christ has prepared for them. Only in full response to the whole of this offer and this claim can the human person fulfill this reality. This is the witness the church has to give to the world, that all the other mandates are not there to divide people and tear them apart but to deal with them as whole people before God the Creator, Reconciler, and Redeemer—that reality in all its manifold aspects is ultimately *one* in God who became human, Jesus Christ. The divine mandates in the world are not there to wear people down through endless conflicts. Rather, they aim at the whole human being who stands in reality before God. The human person is not the place where the divine mandates show that they cannot be united. Rather, nowhere else but in the human person, in concrete human life and action, is the unity created of that which "in itself," that is, theoretically, cannot be unified. This happens, to be sure, in no other way than when people allow themselves to be placed through Jesus Christ before the completed reality of God's becoming human, the reality of the world that was reconciled to God in the manger, the cross, and the resurrection of

---

20. ["On 'sword' see above, *DBWE* 6:71 (*Reader* 610), the exposition of Gen. 4:22ff. See also *Discipleship* on Matt. 5:38, which speaks of justice 'under the protection of divine retribution' (*DBWE* 4:132) . . . ," *DBWE* 6:72, n. 89.]

Jesus Christ. Thus the doctrine of divine mandates—which in the form of a doctrine of "estates" threatens to lead to a dangerous partition between human beings and reality—serves to place human beings before the *one* and whole reality as we find it revealed in Jesus Christ. So here again everything finally flows into the reality of the body of Jesus Christ, in whom God and human being became one.

74

We said at the beginning that the question of the will of God must take the place of the question about one's own being good and doing good. But the will of God is nothing other than the realization of the Christ-reality among us and in our world. The will of God is therefore not an idea that demands to be realized; it is itself already reality in the self-revelation of God in Jesus Christ. The will of God is neither an idea nor is it simply identical with what exists, so that subjection to things as they are could fulfill it; it is rather a reality that wills to become real ever anew in what exists and against what exists. The will of God has already been fulfilled by God, in reconciling the world to himself in Christ. To disregard the reality of this fulfillment and to set a fulfillment of one's own in its place would be the most dangerous relapse into abstract thinking. Since the appearance of Christ, ethics can be concerned with only one thing: to partake in the reality of the fulfilled will of God.[21] But to partake in this is possible only because of the fact that even I myself am already included in the fulfillment of the will of God in Christ, which means that I have been reconciled to God. The question of the will of God is not asking about something hidden or unfulfilled, but about what has been revealed and fulfilled. It remains, however, a genuine question insofar as I myself, together with the world around me, am placed into this question by the answer given by the revelation and fulfillment.

The will of God, as it was revealed and fulfilled in Jesus Christ, embraces the whole of reality. There is access to this wholeness, without being torn apart by manifold influences, only through faith in Jesus Christ, "in whom the whole fullness of deity dwells bodily" (Col. 2:9; 1:19), "through whom everything is reconciled, whether on earth or in heaven" (Col. 1:20), whose body, that is, the church-community, is the fullness of the One who fills all in all (Eph. 1:23).[22] Faith in this Jesus Christ is the single source of all good.

75

---

21. ["This idea is continued and sharpened in the prison letters where Bonhoeffer speaks of sharing the sufferings of God at the hands of a godless world (see *DBWE* 8:480–482, 485–487 [*Reader* 805–806])," *DBWE* 6:74, n. 96.]

22. ["See the use of this verse and Col. 2:9 in *Discipleship* (*DBWE* 4:220)," *DBWE* 6:75, n. 98.]

34. ULTIMATE AND PENULTIMATE THINGS

DBWE 6:146–170

In the following Ethics *essay, Bonhoeffer offers this diagnosis of modern Western culture. Disregard for the ultimate, namely the word of God as recognized in the justification of the sinner by grace through faith, leads to disregard for the penultimate, the human life that is justified by grace. This disregard for the penultimate leads in turn to greater disregard for the ultimate. The cure, he argues, is correctly relating the ultimate and penultimate. "[T]he task is to strengthen the penultimate through a stronger proclamation of the ultimate and to protect the ultimate by preserving the penultimate." Here Bonhoeffer uses the language of ultimate and penultimate toward an end pursued in a number of* Ethics *essays (including "Natural Life," the next selection): the valuing of the created but sinful world, not in itself but in its orientation toward Christ.*

Also characteristic in this essay is the way Bonhoeffer develops his own position in contrast to two false (or, more precisely, partially true) alternatives.[1] In this case, those alternatives are "radicalism," which unduly emphasizes the ultimate, and "compromise," which excessively accentuates the penultimate. As examples, we can imagine a form of Christian radicalism where Christ stands in utter judgment of the world as it exists and a form of Christian compromise where Christ simply underwrites the status quo. When posed with such oppositions, Bonhoeffer inevitably characterizes them as false alternatives, since the opposing elements have been reconciled in Christ. In this case, Christ has resolved the relationship of the ultimate and penultimate; Christ loves the fallen world in a way that ushers it toward its consummation.

---

1. [*For analyses of this feature of Bonhoeffer's argumentation, see DeJonge, "Between Fundamentalism and Secularism," and DeJonge,* Bonhoeffer's Theological Formation, *129–146.*]

146   The origin and essence of all Christian life are consummated in the one event that the Reformation has called the justification of the sinner by grace alone. It is not what a person is per se, but what a person is in this event, that gives us insight into the Christian life. Here the length and breadth of human life are concentrated in one moment, one point; the whole of life is embraced in this event. What happens here? Something ultimate[2] that cannot be grasped by anything we are, or do, or suffer. The dark tunnel of human life, which was barred within and without and was disappearing ever more deeply into an abyss from which there is no exit, is powerfully torn open; the word of God bursts in. In this saving light, people recognize God and their neighbors for the first time. The labyrinth of their previous lives collapses. They become free for God and for one another. They realize that there is a God who loves and accepts them, that alongside them stand others whom God loves equally, and that there is a future with the triune God and God's church-community. Each believes, loves, hopes. The past

147   and future of the whole of life flow together in God's presence. The whole of the past is embraced by the word "forgiveness"; the whole of the future is preserved in the faithfulness of God. Past sin has been sunk in the depths of God's love in Jesus Christ and overcome; the future will be, without sin, a life born of God (1 John 3:9).[3] This life knows itself stretched and sustained from one eternal foundation to another, from its election before the time of the world toward eternal salvation to come. This life knows itself as a member of a church and of a creation that sings the praises of the triune God. All this happens when Christ comes to each person. In Christ all this is truth and reality. Precisely because it is not a dream, the life of a person who has encountered Christ's presence is no longer lost, but has become justified, by grace alone.

However, not only by grace alone, but also by faith alone. So scripture and the Reformation teach. Not love or hope, but only faith justifies a life. It is faith alone that sets life on a new foundation, and only on this new foundation can I live justified before God. This foundation is the living, dying, and rising of the Lord Jesus Christ. Without this foundation a life before God is unjustified; it is surrendered to death and damnation. The justification of my life before God is to live because of and toward the living, dying, and rising of Jesus Christ. Faith means to find, hold to, and cast my anchor on this foundation and so to be held by it. Faith means to base

---

2. ["... As the following text shows, Bonhoeffer uses 'ultimate' in two senses, qualitative (i.e., most important) and temporal (i.e., last, final)," *DBWE* 6:146, n. 2.]

3. ["... On this idea cf. *DBWE* 4:263 and 206, n. 10," *DBWE* 6:147, n. 4.]

life on a foundation outside myself,[4] on an eternal and holy foundation, on
Christ. Faith means to be captivated by the gaze of Jesus Christ; one sees
nothing but him. Faith means to be torn out of imprisonment in one's own
ego,[5] liberated by Jesus Christ. Faith is letting something happen, and only
therein is it an activity. Yet both words together cannot adequately express
its mystery. Faith alone is certainty; everything outside of faith is subject to
doubt. Jesus Christ alone is the certainty of faith. I believe the Lord Jesus
Christ who tells me that my life is justified. So there is no way toward the
justification of my life other than faith alone.

148

But faith is never alone. As surely as it is the genuine presence of Christ,
so surely love and hope are with it. Faith would be a false, illusory, hypocritical self-invention, which never justifies, were it not accompanied by love and
hope. It would be a rote-learned repetition of articles of faith, a dead faith,
if the works of repentance and love did not accompany it. Faith and evil
intentions cannot exist together even for an instant. Everything is given to
me in the event of justification, but only faith justifies. All that Christ is and
has is made mine in the encounter with Christ, but my life is justified only
by that which belongs to Christ and never by what became mine. So heaven
is torn open above us humans, and the joyful message of God's salvation in
Jesus Christ rings out from heaven to earth as a cry of joy. I believe, and in
believing I receive Christ, I have everything. I live before God.

He never knew before what life is. He did not understand himself. He
could only try to understand himself and to justify his life by his own poten-
tialities or his own works. So he justified himself before himself and before
a God of his own imagination. The possibilities and works of the living
God had to seem inaccessible to him, and a life rooted in those possibilities
and works inconceivable. Life on another foundation, drawing on another
strength and another help, remained alien to him. He found this life when
he was justified by Christ in Christ's own way. He lost his life to Christ, and
now Christ became his life. "It is no longer I who live, but it is Christ who
lives in me" (Gal. 2:20). Christian life is life-in-Christ.

149

We said at the beginning that the event of justification of a sinner is
something ultimate. That was meant in a strict sense. God's mercy to a sinner must and can be heard only as God's final word, or it will not be heard
at all. The ultimacy of this word has a double sense. Through its content it

4. ["See the phrase 'from outside' (*extra nos,* 'outside of us') in Bonhoeffer's *Habilitationsschrift, Act and Being* (*DWBE* 2:126) . . . ," *DBWE* 6:147, n. 6.]

5. ["Imprisonment in one's own ego is a central theme in Bonhoeffer's anthropology and soteriology; see, e.g., *DBWE* 2:136–142 (*Reader* 92–97); *DBWE* 3:142; and *DBWE*
4:282," *DBWE* 6:148, n. 8.]

is a *qualitatively* ultimate word. There is no word of God that goes beyond God's grace. There is nothing greater than a life that is justified before God. Because it involves a complete break with everything penultimate, with all that has gone before; because it is never the natural or necessary end of a way already pursued but rather the complete condemnation and devaluation of that way; because it is God's own free word that can never be forced from God by anything whatsoever; therefore it is the irreversibly ultimate word, the ultimate reality. It excludes every method of reaching it by one's own way. There is no Lutheran or Pauline method for attaining the ultimate word. Neither the way of Paul, glorying in the law and the ensuing enmity to Christ, nor the way of Luther, broken by the law in the monastery and in despair, was justified by the ultimate word. On the contrary, both ways were ultimately condemned. It was the sinner Paul and the sinner Luther, not their sin, who were justified by God's grace for the sake of Christ. The ultimate word was at the same time the judgment on the penultimate ways and things. From the beginning, the qualitatively ultimate word of God forbids us from looking at the way of Paul or the way of Luther as if we had to go that way again. There are ways that are condemned. Strictly speaking, we should not repeat Luther's way any more than the way of the woman caught in adultery, the thief on the cross, Peter's denial, or Paul's zealous persecution of Christ. The qualitatively ultimate word excludes every method once and for all. It is the word of forgiveness, and only in forgiving does it justify. It is therefore neither reasonable nor right to preach to a Christian congregation today—as too often happens—that everyone must first become like Mary Magdalene, like poor Lazarus, or like the thief on the cross—that one must first become like these biblical "marginal figures" before one can hear the ultimate word of God. The more one tries to emphasize the ultimate character of the word of God in this way, the more one undermines it in reality. The content of the Christian message is not that we should become like one of these biblical figures, but that we should be like Christ himself. No method leads to this end, only faith. Otherwise the gospel would lose its price, its value. Costly grace would become cheap.[6]

The justifying word of God is also, however, the *temporally* ultimate word. Something penultimate always precedes it, some action, suffering, movement, intention, defeat, recovery, pleading, hoping—in short, quite literally a span of time at whose end it stands. The only thing that can be justified is something that has already come under indictment in time. Justification

150

151

6. ["See Bonhoeffer's 'Christ and Peace' from the winter of 1932 (*DBWE* 12:258–262 [*Reader* 459–491]); and esp. *DBWE* 4:43–45 (*Reader* 353)," *DBWE* 6:150, n. 19.]

presupposes that the creature became guilty. Not all time is a time of grace; but now—precisely now and finally now—is the "day of salvation" (2 Cor. 6:2). The time of grace is the final time in the sense that one can never reckon with a further, future word beyond the word of God that confronts me now. There is a time of God's permission, waiting, and preparation; and there is an ultimate time that judges and breaks off the penultimate. In order to hear the ultimate word, Luther had to go through the monastery; Paul had to go through his piety toward the law; even the thief "had to" go through conviction and the cross. They had to travel a road, to walk the full length of the way through penultimate things; they had to sink to their knees under the burden of these things. And yet the ultimate word was not a crowning but a complete break with the penultimate. Before the ultimate word Luther and Paul stood no differently than the thief on the cross. We must travel a road, even though there is no road to this goal, and we must travel this road to the end, that is, to the place where God puts an end to it. The penultimate remains in existence, even though it is completely superseded by the ultimate and is no longer in force.

The word of God's justifying grace never leaves its place as the ultimate word. It never simply presents itself as an achieved outcome that could now just as well be placed at the beginning as at the end. The way from the penultimate to the ultimate cannot be abandoned. The word remains irreversibly the ultimate; otherwise it would be degraded to something calculable, a commodity, and would be robbed of its essential divinity. Grace would become cheap; it would not be a gift.

Since God's justification by grace and by faith alone remains in every respect the ultimate word, now we must also speak of penultimate things not as if they had some value of their own, but so as to make clear their relation to the ultimate. For the sake of the ultimate we must speak of the penultimate. This we must now explain.

The question may be raised here, without answering it yet, whether one can live by the ultimate alone, whether faith, so to speak, can be extended 152 through time, or whether it becomes real in life only as the ultimate, the last moment of a time span or of many time spans. We are not speaking here of the memory of past faith or of repeating articles of faith, but of the living faith that justifies a life. We are asking whether this faith can or should be realized daily and hourly, or whether here also one must walk the long way through the penultimate for the sake of the ultimate. *We are asking, in other words, about the penultimate in the life of a Christian*—whether it is a pious self-deception to deny it, or whether it is a sin to think like this. Thereby we also ask whether the word, the gospel, can be extended in time, whether it can be expressed in the same way every time, or whether here, too, the ultimate differs from the penultimate. To make this quite clear: why, precisely in completely serious situations—for instance, when facing someone grieving deeply over a death—do I often decide on a "penultimate" response, such as a kind of helpless solidarity in the face of so terrible an event, expressed through silence, instead of speaking the words of biblical comfort familiar to me, which are at my disposal? Why is it that I do so even when dealing with Christians? Why is my mouth often closed when it should give voice to the ultimate, and why do I opt for a thoroughly penultimate human solidarity? Do I mistrust the power of the ultimate word? Is it human fear? Or is such a response objectively justified, because knowing the word and having it at one's disposal—in other words controlling the situation spiritually—gives only the appearance of ultimacy, but is in reality something totally penultimate? Isn't it occasionally, perhaps, a more genuine reference to the ultimate—which God will speak in God's own time (to be sure, likewise only through a human mouth)—to remain consciously in the penultimate? Won't the penultimate now and again be appropriate precisely for the sake of the ultimate, and mustn't this be done with a good conscience instead of a burdened one? This question embraces not just a single case but basically the entire range of Christian common life, especially the broad area of Christian pastoral care. What was said about the particular case holds for countless other situations in the daily common life of Christians, just as it does for the Christian preacher's dealings with the congregation.

The relationship between the penultimate and the ultimate in Christian life can be resolved in two extreme ways, one "radical" and the other as compromise, noting right away that compromise is also an extreme solution.[7]

The radical solution sees only the ultimate, and in it sees only a complete break with the penultimate. Ultimate and penultimate stand in mutually exclusive opposition. Christ is the destroyer and enemy of everything penultimate, and everything penultimate is the enemy of Christ. Christ is the sign that the world is ripe to be consigned to the fire. Here there are no distinctions; all must come to judgment. In the judgment there is only one division: to be for or against Christ. "Whoever is not with me is against me" [*Matt. 12:30*]. Everything penultimate in human behavior is sin and denial. Faced with the coming end there is for Christians only the ultimate word and ultimate behavior. What will happen to the world as a result is no lon-

---

7. ["See *DBWE* 6:57 (*Reader* 601), on 'the monk and the cultural-Protestant,'" *DBWE* 6:153, n. 31.]

ger important; the Christian has no responsibility for that. The world must burn in any case. Let the whole order of the world break down under the word of Christ; here it is a matter of all or nothing. The ultimate word of God, which is a word of grace, becomes here the icy hardness of the law that crushes and despises all resistance (cf. the figure of Ibsen's Brand).

The other solution is compromise. Here the ultimate word is divorced in principle from all that is penultimate. The penultimate retains its inherent rights, but it is not threatened or endangered by the ultimate. The world still stands; the end has not yet come. Penultimate things must still be done in responsibility for this world that God created. We must still reckon with human beings as they are. (Dostoyevsky's Grand Inquisitor.) The ultimate stays completely beyond daily life and in the end serves only as the eternal justification of all that exists, as a metaphysical cleansing of the indictment that burdens all existence. The free word of grace becomes a law of grace reigning over all that is penultimate, justifying and preserving it.[8]

Both solutions are extreme in the same respect, and likewise both contain truths and falsehoods. They are extreme because they make the penultimate and the ultimate mutually exclusive, sometimes by destroying the penultimate through the ultimate, other times by banishing the ultimate from the domain of the penultimate. In the one case the ultimate cannot come to terms with the penultimate; in the other the penultimate cannot come to terms with the ultimate. Both wrongly absolutize ideas that are necessary and right in themselves. The radical solution approaches things from the end of all things, from God the judge and redeemer; the compromise solution approaches things from the creator and preserver. One absolutizes the end, the other absolutizes what exists. Thus creation and redemption, time and eternity, fall into an insoluble conflict; the very unity of God is itself dissolved, and faith in God is shattered.

To advocates of the radical solution it must be said that Christ is not radical in their sense; to followers of the compromise solution it must likewise be said that Christ does not make compromises. Accordingly, Christian life is a matter neither of radicalism nor of compromise. The fight over which of the two views is more serious is pointless when confronted with Jesus Christ, in whom alone there is real seriousness, for this exposes how unserious both solutions are. Neither the idea of a pure Christianity as such nor the idea of the human being as such is serious, but only God's reality and human

---

8. ["See Bonhoeffer's statement: 'Grace as principle, pecca fortiter [*sin boldly*] as a principle, cheap grace—all these are finally only a new law, which neither helps nor liberates' (*DBWE* 4:53 [*Reader* 467])," *DBWE* 6:154, n. 37.]

reality as they have become one in Jesus Christ. What is serious is not some kind of Christianity, but Jesus Christ himself. In Jesus Christ God's reality and human reality take the place of radicalism and compromise. There is no Christianity as such; if there were, it would destroy the world. There is no human being as such; if there were, God would be excluded. Both are ideas. There is only the God-man Jesus Christ who is real, through whom the world will be preserved until it is ripe for its end.

Radicalism always arises from a conscious or unconscious hatred of what exists. Christian radicalism, whether it would flee the world or improve it, comes from the hatred of creation. The radical cannot forgive God for having created what is. It is Ivan Karamazov, the one totally at odds with the created world, who creates the figure of a radical Jesus in the legend of the Grand Inquisitor. When evil becomes powerful in the world, it simultaneously injects the Christian with the poison of radicalism. Reconciliation with the world as it is, which is given to the Christian by Christ, is then called betrayal and denial of Christ. In its place come bitterness, suspicion, and contempt for human beings and the world. Love that believes all things, bears all things, and hopes all things, love that loves the world in its very wickedness with the love of God (John 3:16), becomes—by limiting love to the closed circle of the pious—a pharisaical refusal of love for the wicked. The open church of Jesus Christ, which serves the world to the end, becomes a kind of supposed ur-Christian ideal church-community[9] that in turn mistakenly confuses the realization of a Christian idea with the reality of the living Jesus Christ. Thus a world that has become evil succeeds in making Christians evil also. The identical sickness dismisses the world and radicalizes Christians. In both cases it is hatred toward the world, whether it is the hate of the godless or of the pious. On both sides it is refusal to believe in God's creation. One cannot drive out any devils with Beelzebub.

Compromise always arises from hatred of the ultimate. The Christian spirit of compromise comes from this animosity against the justification of the sinner by grace alone. The world, and life in it, must be protected from this invasion into its domain. One must manage the world only by worldly means. The ultimate is to have no say in the formation of life in the world. Even to ask about the ultimate, to try to establish the authority of God's word for life in the world, is regarded as radicalism, as a lack of love toward the given orders of the world and toward those who are dependent on them.

---

9. ["See *Sanctorum Communio:* 'Every misunderstanding of this idea of earliest Christianity has always led to a sectarian ideal of holiness' (*DBWE* 1:138, n. 29; see also 141 on 'perfectionist sectarianism')," *DBWE* 6:156, n. 43.]

Freedom from the world, which is Christ's gift to Christians, and renunciation of the world (1 John 2:17) are accused of being unnatural and opposed
to creation, an estrangement from, or even hostility toward, the world and
humanity. Instead, accommodation to the point of resignation, or to a trite
worldly wisdom, is passed off as genuine Christian openness to the world
and love.

> Radicalism hates time. Compromise hates eternity.
> Radicalism hates patience. Compromise hates decision.
> Radicalism hates wisdom. Compromise hates simplicity.
> Radicalism hates measure. Compromise hates the immeasurable.
> Radicalism hates the real. Compromise hates the word.

To contrast radicalism and compromise like this makes clear enough   157
that both attitudes are equally opposed to Christ; for the concepts that are
here set up against each another are one in Jesus Christ. The question about
the Christian life, therefore, will be answered neither by radicalism nor by
compromise; Jesus Christ himself decides and answers it. The relationship
between the ultimate and the penultimate is resolved only in Christ.

In Jesus Christ we believe in the God who became human, was crucified,
and is risen. In the becoming human we recognize God's love toward God's
creation, in the crucifixion God's judgment on all flesh, and in the resurrection God's purpose for a new world. Nothing could be more perverse
than to tear these three apart, because the whole is contained in each of
them. Just as it is improper to pit against one another a theology of the
incarnation, a theology of the cross, or a theology of the resurrection, by
falsely absolutizing one of them, such a procedure is false as well in any
consideration of Christian life. A Christian ethic built only on the incarnation would lead easily to the compromise solution; an ethic built only on
the crucifixion or only on the resurrection of Jesus Christ would fall into
radicalism and enthusiasm. The conflict is resolved only in their unity.

Jesus Christ the human being—that means that God enters into created reality, that we may be and should be human beings before God.
The destruction of humanness is sin, and as such it hinders God's work
of redeeming humanity. Still, Jesus Christ's being human does not mean
simply the confirmation of the existing world and of human existence. Jesus
was human "without sin" (Heb. 4:15); that is the decisive thing. But Jesus
lived among us in deepest poverty, was unmarried, and died as a criminal. Jesus' being human embodies therefore a double judgment on human
beings—the absolute condemnation of sin and the relative condemnation
of existing human orders. Included in this condemnation, however, is that

158   Jesus is really human and wants us to be human beings. Jesus lets human reality exist as penultimate, neither making it self-sufficient nor destroying it—a penultimate that will be taken seriously and not seriously in its own way, a penultimate that has become the cover of the ultimate.

    Jesus Christ the crucified—that means that God speaks final judgment on the fallen creation. The rejection of the whole human race without exception is included in the rejection of God on the cross of Jesus Christ. Jesus' cross is the death sentence on the world. Here human beings cannot boast of their being human, nor the world of its divine orders. Here human glory has come to its final end in the image of the beaten, bleeding, spat-upon face of the crucified. Yet the crucifixion of Jesus does not mean simply the annihilation of creation. Human beings will live on under this death-sign of the cross, living on toward judgment when they despise it, but living on toward salvation when they accept it. The ultimate has become real in the cross—as judgment on all that is penultimate, but at the same time as grace for the penultimate that bows to the judgment of the ultimate.

    Jesus Christ the resurrected—that means that God, in love and omnipotence, makes an end of death and calls a new creation into life. God gives new life. "The old has gone." "See, I am making all things new" [*2 Cor. 5:17; Rev. 21:5*]. The resurrection has already broken into the midst of the old world as the ultimate sign of its end and its future, and at the same time as living reality. Jesus has risen as human; so he has given human beings the gift of resurrection. Thus human beings remain human, but in a new resurrected way that is completely unlike the old. To be sure, those who are already risen with Christ will remain, until they reach the frontier of death, in the world of the penultimate to which Jesus came and in which the cross stands. Even the resurrection does not abolish the penultimate as long as the earth remains; but eternal life, the new life, breaks ever more powerfully into earthly life and creates space for itself within it.[10]

    The unity and differentiation of incarnation, cross, and resurrection should be clear. Christian life is life with Jesus Christ who became human, 159   was crucified, and is risen, and whose word as a whole encounters us in the message of the justification of the sinner by grace. Christian life means being human in the power of Christ's becoming human, being judged and pardoned in the power of the cross, living a new life in the power of the resurrection. No one of these is without the others.

    Concerning the relationship to the penultimate, it can be concluded that Christian life neither destroys nor sanctions the penultimate. In Christ

---

10. ["See *DBWE* 4:232," *DBWE* 6:158, n. 55.]

the reality of God encounters the reality of the world and allows us to take part in this real encounter.[11] It is an encounter beyond all radicalism and all compromise. Christian life is participation in Christ's encounter with the world.

Since it has become clear that the ultimate holds open a certain space for the penultimate, we can now focus more precisely on this penultimate.

What is this penultimate? It is all that precedes the ultimate—the justification of the sinner by grace alone—and that is addressed as penultimate after finding the ultimate.[12] At the same time it is everything that follows the ultimate, in order again to precede it. There is no penultimate as such, as if something or other could justify itself as being in itself penultimate; but the penultimate becomes what it is only through the ultimate, that is, in the moment when it has already lost its own self-sufficiency. The penultimate does not determine the ultimate; the ultimate determines the penultimate. The penultimate is not a condition in itself; it is a judgment by the ultimate on what has gone before. It is therefore never something present, but always something already past. Concretely, from the perspective of the justification of the sinner through grace two things are addressed as penultimate: *being human and being good.* It would be false, and a violation of the ultimate, for example, to call being human a precondition for justification by grace. Instead, only from the perspective of the ultimate can we recognize what being human is, and therefore how being human is based on and determined by being justified. Still, it is the case that being human precedes being justified, and seen from the perspective of the ultimate must precede it. The penultimate therefore does not negate the freedom of the ultimate; instead, the freedom of the ultimate empowers the penultimate. So, for example, being human may—with all necessary reservations—be addressed as penultimate to justification by grace. Only the human being can be justified, simply because only the one who is justified becomes a "human being."

From this follows now something of decisive importance, that the penultimate must be preserved for the sake of the ultimate. Arbitrary destruction of the penultimate seriously harms the ultimate. When, for example, a human life is deprived of the conditions that are part of being human, the justification of such a life by grace and faith is at least seriously hindered, if not made impossible. Concretely stated, slaves who have been so

160

---

11. ["See *DBWE* 6:55 (*Reader* 600), on participating '*in the reality of God and the world in Jesus Christ today,*'" *DBWE* 6:159, n. 58.]

12. ["See *DBWE* 4:44f. (*Reader* 461) on finding costly grace like treasure in a field, or a precious pearl (Matt. 13:44f.)," *DBWE* 6:159, n. 59.]

deprived of control over their time that they can no longer hear the proclamation of God's word cannot be led by that word of God to a justifying faith. Given this fact, in addition to proclaiming the ultimate word of God—the justification of the sinner by grace alone—it is necessary to care for the penultimate in order that the ultimate not be hindered by the penultimate's destruction. Those who proclaim the word yet do not do everything possible so that this word may be heard are not true to the word's claim for free passage, for a smooth road. The way for the word must be prepared. The word itself demands it.

161 What concerns us in all that has been said about penultimate things is this: preparing the way for the word.[13] "Prepare the way of the Lord, make his paths straight! Every valley shall be filled, and every mountain and hill shall be made low, and the crooked shall be made straight and the rough ways made smooth. And all flesh shall see the Savior of God" (Luke 3:4–6). Of course, when Christ comes he will make his own way. Christ is "the one who breaks all bonds" (Mic. 2:13). He "breaks the doors of bronze, and shatters the bars of iron" (Ps. 107:16). He "brings down the powerful from their thrones, and lifts up the lowly" (Luke 1:52). His entry is a parade of victory over his enemies. In order, however, that the force of his coming does not strike down humanity in anger, but rather meets them waiting in humility, the call goes out before his entry to prepare the way. And this preparation is not only an inward process, but a visible, creative activity on the greatest scale. "Every valley shall be lifted up" [*Luke 3:5; Is. 40:4*]. What has been pushed into the depths of human misery, what is lowly and humiliated, will be raised. There is a depth of human bondage, of human poverty, and of human ignorance that hinders the gracious coming of Christ. "Every mountain and hill shall be made low." If Christ is to come, all that is proud and high must bow. There is a degree of power, of wealth, and of knowledge

162 that is a hindrance to Christ and the grace of Christ. "The crooked shall be made straight." The way of Christ is straight. There is a degree of distortion and self-entrapment in lying, in guilt, in one's own occupation, one's own work (Ps. 9:17 [16]), and in self-love that makes the coming of grace especially difficult. So the way must be made straight on which Christ is to come to humanity. "The rough ways shall be made smooth." Defiance, obstinacy, and rejection may have so hardened a person that Christ can only destroy the obstinate in anger; Christ can no longer come into that person in grace.

---

13. ["See Bonhoeffer's letter of November 27, 1940: 'Today a possible title for my book occurred to me: "Preparing the Way and Entering In", corresponding to the division of the book (into penultimate and ultimate things)' (*DBWE* 16:92)," *DBWE* 6:161, n. 64.]

The gates are bolted against the gracious coming of Christ, and no door is opened when Christ knocks.

Christ comes, to be sure, clearing the way for this coming, whether one is ready for it or not. No one can hinder Christ's coming, but we can oppose that coming in grace. There are conditions of the heart, of life, and in the world that especially hinder the receiving of grace, that is, which make it infinitely difficult to believe. We say hinder and make difficult, not make impossible. We know too that even the way that has been smoothed, even the removal of hindrances, cannot compel the coming of grace. The gracious coming of Christ must still "break the doors of bronze and shatter the bars of iron" [*Ps. 107:16; Is. 45:2*]. Grace must finally clear and smooth its own way; it alone must again and again make the impossible possible. But all this does not release us from preparing the way for the coming of grace, from doing away with whatever hinders and makes it more difficult. The condition in which grace meets us is not irrelevant, even though it is always only by grace that grace comes to us. We can make it hard for ourselves and others to come to faith. It is hard for those thrust into extreme disgrace, desolation, poverty, and helplessness to believe in God's justice and goodness. It becomes hard for those whose lives have fallen into disorder and a lack of discipline to hear the commandments of God in faith. It is hard for the well-fed and the powerful to comprehend God's judgment and God's grace. It is hard for those who are disappointed by a false faith and who have lost self-control to find the simplicity of surrendering their hearts to Jesus Christ. This is not to excuse or discourage those to whom this applies. Instead, they must learn all the more that in Jesus Christ God comes down into the very depths of the human fall, of guilt, and of need, that the justice and grace of God is especially close to the very people who are deprived of rights, humiliated, and exploited, that the help and strength of Jesus Christ are offered to the undisciplined, and that the truth will lead the erring and despairing onto firm ground again.

163

None of this excludes the task of preparing the way. It is, instead, a commission of immeasurable responsibility given to all who know about the coming of Jesus Christ. The hungry person needs bread, the homeless person needs shelter, the one deprived of rights needs justice, the lonely person needs community, the undisciplined one needs order, and the slave needs freedom. It would be blasphemy against God and our neighbor to leave the hungry unfed while saying that God is closest to those in deepest need. We break bread with the hungry and share our home with them for the sake of Christ's love, which belongs to the hungry as much as it does to us. If the hungry do not come to faith, the guilt falls on those who denied them bread. To bring bread to the hungry is preparing the way for the coming of grace.

What happens here is something penultimate. To give the hungry bread is not yet to proclaim to them the grace of God and justification, and to have received bread does not yet mean to stand in faith. But for the one who does something penultimate for the sake of the ultimate, this penultimate thing is related to the ultimate. It is a *pen*-ultimate, before the last. The entry of grace is the ultimate. But we must speak of preparing the way, of the penultimate—for the sake of those who have failed with their radicalism that denied penultimate things, and are now in danger themselves of being pushed back behind penultimate things, as well as for the sake of those who remained stuck in penultimate things, who have made themselves comfortable with

164   them, and who now must be claimed for the ultimate. In the end, however, perhaps we speak of penultimate things primarily for the sake of those who have never achieved these penultimate things, whom no one has helped to gain them, for whom no one has prepared the way, and who now must be helped so that the word of God, the ultimate, grace, can come to them.

Of course, all this would have been misunderstood if one were to say that first the slave must have been freed, those without rights must have had their rights restored, and the hungry must have been given bread—in short, that first the world must have been put in order—before they could become Christians. Against this stand the witness of the New Testament and the history of the church. Perhaps it was in those very times in which the world seemed to be relatively in order that estrangement from faith was especially deep and alarming. Preparing the way for Christ cannot be simply a matter of creating certain desired and conducive conditions, such as creating a program of social reform.[14] Preparing the way is indeed a matter of concrete intervention in the visible world, as concrete and visible as hunger and nourishment. Nevertheless, everything depends on this action being a spiritual reality, since what is finally at stake is not the reform of worldly conditions but the coming of Christ. Only a spiritual preparation of the way will be followed by the gracious coming of the Lord. This means that visible deeds, which must be done to make people ready to receive Jesus Christ, must be deeds of humility before the coming Lord, which means deeds of repentance. Preparation of the way means repentance (Matt. 3:1ff.). But

165   repentance means concrete changing of one's ways. Repentance demands deeds. So preparing the way indeed has quite definite conditions in view that are to be produced. In attempting to speak concretely about these con-

---

14. ["Social reform programs in the American Social Gospel Movement (see *DBWE* 12:236–243), as well as in German cultural Protestantism, were associated with high religious expectations," *DBWE* 6:164, n. 84.]

ditions toward which preparing the way is directed, we come to the two formulations, *being human* and *being good.*

Only the entrance of the Lord will bring fulfillment to being-human and being-good. But a light from the coming Lord already falls on being human and being good, as is required for proper readiness and expectation. We can only know from the Lord, who is coming and has come, what being human and being good are. Because Christ comes, therefore we should be human and be good. Christ comes, not into hell, but "to what is his own" (John 1:11). He comes to his creation that, despite the fall, remains his creation. Christ comes not to devils but to human beings, certainly to sinful, lost, and damned humans, but still to human beings. Because Christ comes to them, because Christ redeems them from sin and from the power of the devil, sinful human beings are still human, the fallen creation remains creation. From a Christian perspective the fallen world becomes understandable as the world preserved and maintained by God for the coming of Christ, a world in which we *as human beings* can and should live a *"good"* life in given orders.[15] But where human beings become things, commodities, or machines—where the orders are arbitrarily destroyed and the distinction is no longer made between "good" and "evil"—a special hindrance is placed in the way of receiving Christ that goes beyond the world's general   166
sinfulness and forlornness. There the world destroys itself; it is in serious danger of becoming demonic. It makes a difference before God whether, in the midst of a fallen, lost world, people preserve or violate the order of marriage, whether they practice justice or despotism. Of course, those who preserve marriage and those who protect justice are still sinners, but it makes a difference whether the penultimate is respected and taken seriously. Part of preparing the way is to respect the penultimate and to enforce it, because of the ultimate that is approaching.

It is characteristic of divine revelation through the word that I must go where it is preached if I am to hear this word. "Faith comes from the sermon" (Rom. 10:17). Thus, in order that the word may come to me, my last act of preparing the way, the last deed in the penultimate, is that I go where it has pleased God to give that word. In preserving the given orders, going to church is as far as one can go in the context of what the penultimate commands. The fathers could still so speak.[16] It was presupposed that everyone

---

15. ["On the theme of 'given orders,' see *DBWE* 6:68–69 (*Reader* 608–609), 358–359, 372–73, and 389–390 (*Reader* 686–687), where Bonhoeffer discusses mandates and offices," *DBWE* 6:165, n. 91.]

16. [". . . 'Fathers' here means Lutheran theologians of the Reformation," *DBWE* 6:166, n. 94.]

possessed what was needed to respond to this demand—the external possibility, the physical ability, and enough inner concentration and ability to think. But when it becomes evident that one day these presuppositions no longer apply, that the call to hear the word proclaimed can no longer be followed for entirely external reasons, then taking care of the penultimate shifts to another place. Then our first concern must be to make it outwardly possible for people to hear and follow the call to where the word is proclaimed. That may mean that people must become human again before they can be addressed in this way. Preparing the way for the coming Lord is not taken seriously when this task is not dealt with. Compassion for people and responsibility before Jesus Christ, who desires to come to all people, compel us to this activity.

In all of this it cannot be said too strongly that only the coming Lord can
167 prepare the way, that Christ will lead people to an entirely new way of being human and being good, that the end of all preparing the way for Christ must be the recognition that we ourselves can never prepare the way, and that therefore the demand that we prepare the way leads us to repentance in every respect. "Lord Jesus, in your mercy and kindness, prepare your poor one at this holy time—it must be done by you." Right here is the difference between preparing the way for Christ and all self-made ways to Christ. As we said at the beginning, there is in fact no "method," no way of reaching the ultimate. Preparing the way, in contrast to all methods, starts from the clear recognition that Christ himself must travel the way. It is Christ's way to us that must be prepared, not our way to Christ; and Christ's way can only be prepared in full awareness that it is precisely Christ who must prepare it. Method is the path from the penultimate to the ultimate. Preparing the way is the path from the ultimate to the penultimate. We are made preparers of Christ's way because, and really *only* because, Christ comes of Christ's own will, strength, and love; because Christ wills to overcome all obstacles, and can, even the greatest; and because Christ alone prepares the way of Christ's coming. For such a Lord, do we not want to be, are we not obliged to be, preparers of the way? How should we not let the One who comes make us preparers of the way, in earnest expectation? Because we await Christ, because we know that Christ will come, therefore and only therefore do we prepare the way.

Christ alone creates faith. Nevertheless, there are situations that make it either harder or easier to have faith.[17] There are degrees of hardening

17. Cf. *Discipleship,* chap. 1. ["The listing 'faith, situation of' in the index that Bonhoeffer personally made for *Discipleship* refers to passages in the chapter 'The Call to Discipleship' (*DBWE* 4:61–64 and 66–69 [*Reader* 476–480]) . . . ," *DBWE* 6:167, n. 97.]

and obduracy. Only Christ brings us the ultimate, the justification of our 168
lives before God; still, or rather therefore, we are not deprived of, or spared
from, living in the penultimate. The penultimate will be swallowed up by
the ultimate, yet it retains its necessity and its right as long as the earth
endures.

Christian life is the dawn of the ultimate in me, the life of Jesus Christ
in me. But it is also always life in the penultimate, waiting for the ultimate.
The seriousness of Christian life lies only in the ultimate; but the penultimate also has its seriousness, which consists, to be sure, precisely in never
confusing the penultimate with the ultimate and never making light of the
penultimate over against the ultimate, so that the ultimate—and the penultimate—retain their seriousness. Once again it becomes clear that every
radical Christianity and every compromise Christianity is impossible in view
of the reality of Jesus Christ and Christ's coming into the world.

The spiritual situation of Western Christianity with regard to our problem is characterized by the fact that since the ultimate has been increasingly questioned over the past two hundred years, the penultimate, which in 169
the West was closely connected with it, is threatened and is moving toward
dissolution. The breakup of the penultimate, in turn, leads to strengthened
disregard for, and devaluation of, the ultimate. The ultimate and the penultimate are closely bound to one another. From this perspective the task
is to strengthen the penultimate through a stronger proclamation of the
ultimate and to protect the ultimate by preserving the penultimate. Alternatively, in Western Christianity today there is a broad sector of people who
certainly hold to penultimate things and are determined to go on holding
to them, without clearly recognizing or decisively affirming the connection
of those things with the ultimate, even though they are in no way hostile
toward this ultimate. At this point, the loss of this ultimate will sooner or
later lead to the collapse of the penultimate, if we do not succeed in claiming these penultimate things once again for the ultimate. Whatever in the
fallen world is found to be human and good belongs on the side of Jesus
Christ.[18] We truncate the gospel when we proclaim that only the broken
and the evil are near to Jesus Christ and when, proclaiming the love of the
father for the prodigal, we belittle the father's love for the son who stayed
at home. Certainly the human and the good of which we speak are not the
humanness and the goodness of Jesus Christ. It cannot stand in the judgment, and yet Jesus loved the young man who had kept the commandments

---

18. ["Bonhoeffer develops this point in the manuscript "Church and World I." See
DBWE 6, esp. pages 341–342 and 346–347," *DBWE* 6:169, n. 104.]

(Mark 10:21).[19] The human and the good should not be made into self-sufficient values, but they may and should be claimed for Jesus Christ, especially where, as an unconscious remnant, they represent a previous bond to the ultimate. It may often seem more serious to address such people 170   simply as non-Christians and to urge them to confess their unbelief. But it would be more Christian to claim as Christians precisely such persons who no longer dare to call themselves Christians, and to help them with much patience to move toward confessing Christ. The next two chapters should be understood in this *perspective*.

---

19. [*See* DBWE *4:72* (*Reader* 481–482).]

35. Natural Life

DBWE 6:171–178

When the National Socialist programs of forced sterilization and "euthanasia" came to light, Bonhoeffer sensed that contemporary Protestant ethical reflection lacked the conceptual framework for an appropriate response.[1] Specifically, he saw that Protestant ethics lacked a developed notion of "the natural" to oppose these "unnatural" Nazi programs. In "Natural Life," presented in part below, Bonhoeffer navigates a middle space between recent wholesale Protestant rejections of the natural on the one side and traditional Catholic reliance on non-christological construals of it on the other to develop a distinctively Protestant notion of the natural as "that which, after the fall, is directed toward the coming of Jesus Christ." This understanding of the natural allows Bonhoeffer to elaborate, in the portion of this essay not reprinted here, the series of natural rights violated by the Nazi ethos in general and these programs in particular.[2]

The concept of the natural has fallen into disrepute in Protestant ethics.[3] 171
For some theologians it was completely lost in the darkness of general sinfulness, whereas for others it took on the brightness of the primal creation.
Both were grave misuses that led to the complete elimination of the category 172
of the natural from Protestant thought; it was left to Catholic ethics.[4] This
meant, however, a heavy substantive loss for Protestant thought, because

---

1. [DBWE *6:422, editors' afterword.*]

2. [*For an interpretation of this essay, see DeJonge, "Respecting Rights and Fulfilling Duties."*]

3. ["For Bonhoeffer's earlier uses of the concept of the natural see, for example, *DBWE* 4:143 (*Reader* 502) and *DBWE* 3:126f. (*Reader* 257). These usages are different from that in *Ethics*; the usage in *Creation and Fall* is very similar to the first view rejected here. For usage that anticipates *Ethics*, see Green, *Bonhoeffer*, 197ff., on the human being as spirit and nature, and 217ff., on the correlation of sacrament and nature in the 1933 Christology lectures," *DBWE* 6:171, n. 2.]

4. ["In the Catholic tradition of moral theology, which Bonhoeffer takes up especially in this manuscript, the doctrine of natural law and the interrelation of nature and grace

one was left to confront questions of natural life more or less without any orientation. The significance of the natural for the gospel was obscured, and the Protestant church lost the ability to give clear guidance on the burning questions of natural life. Thereby it left numerous people without answers or help in vital decisions, and fell more and more into a static proclamation of divine grace. Confronted by the light of grace, everything human and natural sank into the night of sin, so one no longer dared pay attention to the relative differences within the human and the natural, for fear that grace would lose its character as grace. In dealing with the concept of the natural, it became most clear that this kind of Protestant thought no longer recognized the right relation of the ultimate to the penultimate. The results of this loss were grievous and far-reaching. If there were no longer any relative differences within a fallen creation, then the way was clear for any kind of arbitrariness and disorder, and natural life, with its concrete

173   decisions and orders, could no longer be considered responsible to God. The only antithesis to the natural was no longer the unnatural, but the word of God. God's word condemned the natural and unnatural alike. That meant complete dissolution in the sphere of natural life.

Thus, the concept of the natural must be recovered from the gospel itself. We speak of the natural as distinct from the created, in order to include the fact of the fall into sin. We speak of the natural as distinct from the sinful in order to include the created. The natural is that which, after the fall, is directed toward the coming of Jesus Christ. The unnatural is that which, after the fall, closes itself off from the coming of Jesus Christ. To be sure, the difference between that which is directed toward the coming of Christ and that which closes itself off from Christ is relative. The natural does not compel the coming of Christ, nor does the unnatural make it impossible; in both cases the real coming is an act of grace. Only through the coming of Christ is the natural confirmed in its character as penultimate and the unnatural definitively exposed as the destruction of the penultimate. So, even in the presence of Christ, there remains a difference between the natural and the unnatural that cannot be erased without serious damage.

The concept of the natural (derived from the Latin nasci, natura) in distinction from the creaturely (derived from creare, creatura) contains a moment of independence, of self-development, that is indeed appropriate to the natural. Through the fall, "creation" became "nature." The unme-

preserved the relevance of the natural . . . The dominant pattern in Catholicism could suggest that nature is prior to the perfecting grace that is added to it," *DBWE* 6:172, n. 4.]

diated relation to God of the true creation becomes the relative freedom of natural life. Within this freedom there is a difference between its right use and its misuse, and this is the difference between the natural and the unnatural; there is therefore a relative openness and a relative closedness for Christ. It is critical, however, that this relative freedom not be confused with an absolute freedom for God and for our neighbor, a freedom that is created and given only by God's word itself. Nevertheless, this relative freedom also remains important for those who in Christ have been granted freedom for God and for their neighbor.

174

Natural life may not be understood simply as a preliminary stage toward life with Christ; instead, it receives its confirmation only through Christ. Christ has entered into natural life. Only by Christ's becoming human does natural life become the penultimate that is directed toward the ultimate. Only through Christ's becoming human do we have the right to call people to natural life and to live it ourselves.

How is the natural recognized? The natural is that form of life preserved by God for the fallen world that is directed toward justification, salvation, and renewal through Christ. The natural therefore is determined both formally and according to its content. Formally, the natural is determined by the preserving will of God and by its orientation toward Christ. Its formal side, then, can only be recognized by looking at Jesus Christ. As to content, the natural is determined by the form of preserved life itself as it embraces the whole human race. With respect to content, human "reason" is the organ for recognizing the natural. Reason is not a divine principle of cognition and order in human beings, superior to the natural. Rather, it is the part of this preserved form of life that is able to make us conscious, i.e., to "take in" as a unity, the whole and the universal in reality. Reason itself is therefore completely embedded in the natural. It is the conscious perception of the natural in its givenness. The natural and reason relate to one another as do the form of being and the form of consciousness of preserved life. The suitability of reason for grasping the natural is based neither on the spontaneity of a reason that supposedly creates the natural in the first place, nor on the divinity of a reason that supposedly was able to discern the natural, but on the fact of the fall into sin, into which reason was drawn as much as the rest of the world. To be sure, reason does not cease to be reason, but it is now fallen reason, which perceives only what is given in the fallen world and, indeed, exclusively according to its content.

175

Reason perceives the universal in what is given, in the particular; so the natural that is given, as reason perceives it, is also something universal. It embraces the whole of human nature. Reason recognizes the natural as the given, as what is universally established, independently of being able to prove it empirically.[5]

A decisive consequence follows from this. The natural can never be a construct of some part or some authority in the fallen world. Neither the individual nor any community or institution in the preserved world can set and decide what is natural. It has already been set and decided, and in such a way that the individual, the communities, and the institutions receive their respective share in it. What is natural cannot be determined by an arbitrary construct; instead, every arbitrary construct of this kind, whether by an individual, a community, or an institution, will inevitably be shattered 176   and will destroy itself against the natural that already exists. Injury and violation of the natural avenge themselves on the violator.

The reason for this is that the natural is also the true protection of preserved life. Thus, the recognition of the natural by "reason" corresponds to the affirmation of the natural through the "basic will" of preserved life. Furthermore, it is not as if this "basic will" were a divine remnant in human beings, uninjured by the fall into sin, and thus able to affirm the divine order. Instead, this basic will is just as embedded within and immersed in the fall and the preserved world as is reason. Therefore it concerns itself exclusively with the content of the natural and affirms it because there it seeks and finds the protection of life. The natural guards life against the unnatural. In the end, it is life itself that tends toward the natural and ever again turns against the unnatural and breaks it down. Here lies the ultimate basis of health and healing, both of body and soul. Life, whether of the individual or of the community, is its own doctor. It fends off the unnatural as life-destroying. Only when life itself is no longer capable of this necessary defense are the destructive powers of the unnatural victorious.

Destruction of the natural means destruction of life. Knowledge and the will to life fall into disorder and confusion. They direct themselves toward false objects. The unnatural is the enemy of life.

The relative freedom of preserved life sufficiently explains why violations of the natural happen at all. When this relative freedom is misused a given entity in the fallen world sets itself up as absolute, declares itself to be the 177   source of the natural, and thereby corrodes natural life. In the struggle

---

5. What is said here differs from Catholic theory in that for us (1) the full scope of reason is understood as entangled in the fall, whereas in Catholic theology reason has retained an essential integrity; (2) related to the first point, according to Catholic doctrine reason is able to grasp as well the formal determination of the natural. All this differs from the Enlightenment in basing the natural in that which is objectively given and not in the subjective spontaneity of reason.

that follows between the unnatural and the natural, the unnatural may for a while prevail by force, because the unnatural is something that requires organization, while the natural cannot be organized but is simply there. So, for example, one can organize the undermining of respect for parents,[6] whereas respect for parents is simply practiced and in its essence cannot be organized. Because of this the unnatural can temporarily overpower the natural. In the long run every organization breaks down, while the natural persists and prevails by its own strength, since life itself is on the side of the natural. Before that outcome, of course, there may be great shocks and revolutions in the external aspects of life. But insofar as life continues, the natural will reassert itself.

In this context, there is good reason for the optimism about human history that persists within the limits of the fallen world. It should have become clear enough that this optimism has nothing to do with the idea of a gradual overcoming of sin.[7] It is a thoroughly immanent optimism, grounded in the natural, that is meant here. Of course, the destruction of the natural in every respect is, according to Holy Scripture, among the signs of the approaching end of the world (Luke 21:16). At this point immanent optimism has its limits; indeed, scriptural prophecy drives this optimism from the role of a historical principle and pacifier once and for all. It remains a not unjustified, but a purely immanent—and therefore never certain—hope.

With these presuppositions we may now turn to a presentation of the natural, in its orientation toward the coming of Christ, as the form of life preserved by God after the fall.

6. ["During the Third Reich, the National Socialist youth organization, Hitler Youth (1926–1945), used children to spy on their parents ideologically and to report their behavior . . . ," *DBWE* 6:177, n. 21.]

7. [". . . See Bonhoeffer's 1932 essay on the American social gospel: 'Optimism, the ideology of progress, does not take seriously the command of God (Luke 17:10). It is modern enthusiasm. It fails to recognize human limits; it disregards the fundamental difference between the kingdom of the world and the kingdom of God' (*DBWE* 12:241)," *DBWE* 6:177, n. 22.]

36. History and Good [2]

DBWE 6:257–298

The following excerpt comes from the second of two incomplete Ethics *drafts, both titled "History and Good." In these essays, Bonhoeffer attempts to develop a Christian ethic that is above all concrete, in other words, in tune with reality. For Bonhoeffer, any account of reality is an account of Christ, since Christ is reality. Thus an ethic is concrete when it accords with Christ.*

Bonhoeffer uses this criterion of Christ-reality to rid ethics of several persistent abstractions. That Christ has entered history as humanity's vicarious representative means that reality is historical and social. This in turn means ethics must drop the tendencies of thinking about the good in the abstract rather than in relation to lived historical existence, and thinking about the ethical actor as an isolated individual rather than a person in community. That Christ reconciles himself to the world means the sphere of ethical action is the world which is fallen yet preserved toward Christ. It is abstract, therefore, for ethics to fall into simple affirmation of the status quo, which forgets that the world is fallen, or simple rebellion, which forgets that the world is reconciled to Christ. In these and other ways, Bonhoeffer distances his ethics from abstract principles or programs, grounding it in the reality of social and historical existence in a sinful world reconciled to Christ.

The ethical framework Bonhoeffer presents here incorporates a number of his long-held ideas. The central concept of vicarious representative action, for example, he developed christologically and anthropologically already in Sanctorum Communio.[1] *And the definition of reality in terms of the Christ who reconciles oppositions is a consistent deep structure of his thinking. But there is a new urgency and gravity to these themes in the context of his participation in the conspiracy to overthrow Hitler. This is especially so when Bonhoeffer argues that, in extraordinary circumstances, responsibility requires taking on guilt by venturing free acts that cannot be justified by any moral law.*

---

1. [DBWE *1:120, 146f., 155f.* (Reader *48–49*), *182ff., 187f. For more, see* DBWE *6:257, nn. 38 and 41.*]

The Structure of Responsible Life   257

The structure of responsible life is determined in a twofold manner, namely, by life's bond to human beings and to God, and by the freedom of one's own life. It is this bond of life to human beings and to God that constitutes the freedom of our own life.[2] Without this bond and without this freedom there can be no responsibility. Only the life that, within this bond, has become selfless has the freedom of my very own life and action. The *bond* has the form of *vicarious representative action* and *accordance with reality*. *Freedom* exhibits itself in *my accountability* for my living and acting, and in the *venture* of concrete decision. This, then, is the framework[3] within which we have to consider the structure of responsible life.

Responsibility is based on vicarious representative action. This is most evident in those relationships in which a person is literally required to act on behalf of others, for example, as a father, as a statesman, or as the instructor of an apprentice. A father acts on behalf of his children by work-   258
ing, providing, intervening, struggling, and suffering for them. In so doing, he really stands in their place. He is not an isolated individual, but incorporates the selves of several people in his own self. Every attempt to live as if he were alone is a denial of the fact that he is actually responsible. He cannot escape the responsibility, which is his because he is a father. This reality refutes the fictitious notion that the isolated individual is the agent of all ethical behavior. It is not the isolated individual but the responsible person who is the proper agent to be considered in ethical reflection. The extent of the responsibility makes no difference in this regard, that is, whether it is borne only for a single human being, for a community, or for entire groups of communities. Nobody can altogether escape responsibility, which means vicarious representative action. Even those who are alone live as vicarious representatives. Indeed, they do so in an especially significant sense, since their lives are lived in a vicarious representative way for human beings as such, for humanity as a whole.[4] For the idea of having responsibility for myself is naturally meaningful only insofar as it denotes

---

2. ["... In this regard see *DBWE* 6:267 (*Reader* 643), regarding 'system.' See also *DBWE* 3:64 (*Reader* 223–224) on created freedom," *DBWE* 6:257, n. 37.]

3. ["The summary on *DBWE* 6:288 (*Reader* 658–659) lists the concepts 'vicarious representative action,' 'accordance with reality,' 'taking on guilt,' and 'freedom,'" *DBWE* 6:257, n. 40.]

4. ["See *DBWE* 1:120, 146f. (*Reader* 43–44), 178, 191," *DBWE* 6:258, n. 44.]

the responsibility that I exercise toward myself as a human being, that is, because I am human. Responsibility for myself is in fact responsibility for human beings as such, that is, for humanity. The fact that Jesus lived without the particular responsibility of a marriage, a family, and a vocation does not at all remove him from the domain of responsibility. Instead, it shows all the more clearly his responsibility and his vicarious representative action for all human beings. With this we already touch on the foundation that undergirds everything that has been said thus far. Jesus—the life, our life—the Son of God who became human, lived as our vicarious representative. Through him, therefore, all human life is in its essence vicarious representation. Jesus was not the individual who sought to achieve some personal perfection, but only lived as the one who in himself has taken on and bears the selves of all human beings. His entire living, acting, and suffering was vicarious representative action. All that human beings were supposed to live, do, and suffer was fulfilled in him. In this real vicarious representative action, in which his human existence consists, he is the

259   responsible human being par excellence. Since he is life, all of life through him is destined to be vicarious representative action. Even if a life resists this intrinsic character, it nevertheless remains vicariously representative, be it with regard to life or with regard to death, just as a father remains a father for good or for ill.

Vicarious representative action and therefore responsibility is possible only in completely devoting one's own life to another person. Only those who are selfless live responsibly, which means that only selfless people truly *live*. Human beings live responsibly where the divine Yes and the divine No become one within them. The selflessness in responsibility is so complete that here it is apt to cite Goethe's statement that the person who acts is without conscience.

The vicariously responsible life is in danger of being corrupted in two different ways, namely, by absolutizing either my own self or the other person. In the first case, the relation of responsibility leads to violation and tyranny. This case ignores the fact that only the selfless person is able to act responsibly. In the second case, the welfare of the other person for whom I am responsible is made absolute while ignoring all other responsibilities. This leads to an arbitrariness in my action, which makes a mockery of my responsibility before God, who in Jesus Christ is the God of all people. The origin, essence, and goal of responsible life is denied in both cases, and responsibility has become a self-made, abstract idol.

As vicariously representative life and action, responsibility is essentially a relation from one human being to another. Christ became human, and thus bore vicarious representative responsibility for all human beings.

There is also a responsibility for things, conditions, and values, but only by strictly keeping in mind that the origin, essence, and goal of all things, conditions, and values is determined by Christ (John 1:4), the God who   260 became human. It is through Christ that the world of things and values is given back its orientation toward human beings, as was originally intended in their creation.[5] The frequent talk about responsibility toward a cause is legitimate only within these limits. Outside these limits it serves in a dangerous fashion the inversion of all life through the dominance of things over people. There is a kind of dedication to the cause of the true, the good, the right, and the beautiful that would be desecrated by questioning their usefulness, although that dedication makes it self-evident that the highest values have to serve human beings. However, there also exists an idolization of all these values, which no longer has anything to do with responsibility but springs from an obsession that destroys human beings by sacrificing them to the idol. "Responsibility for a cause" must therefore be understood not as the usefulness of that cause for human beings, thereby abusing its very nature, but as the intrinsic orientation of that cause toward human beings. This, then, totally excludes the kind of myopic pragmatism[6] that turns the goddess into a milk cow, in Schiller's words, by shortsightedly and directly making something valuable in itself subservient to what is useful for human beings. However, the world of things receives its full freedom and depth only where it is seen as oriented toward the world of persons in its origin, essence, and goal. For all of creation, as Paul says, waits with longing for the revelation of the glory of the children of God; indeed, creation itself will be freed from the bondage of its transience (which also consists of its false self-deification) to participate in the glorious freedom of the children of God (Rom. 8:19, 21).

The attention of responsible people is directed to concrete neighbors   261 in their concrete reality. Their behavior is not fixed in advance once and for all by a principle, but develops together with the given situation. They do not have at their disposal an absolutely valid principle that they have to enforce fanatically against any resistance from reality. Instead, they seek to understand and do what is necessary or "commanded" in a given situation. For those who act responsibly, the given situation is not merely treated as

---

5. ["Bonhoeffer had made this point in his Christology lectures when treating Christ as the mediator of God and nature (*DBWE* 12:327 [*Reader* 284–285])," *DBWE* 6:260, n. 51.]

6. ["... This is the way issues such as justice were understood during the Third Reich; see the National Socialist slogan, '*Recht ist, was dem Volke nützt,*' 'Justice is what is useful for the people,'" *DBWE* 6:260, n. 52.]

the raw material on which they want to impose and imprint their idea or program, but instead it is included in their action as the formation of the act itself. The goal is not to realize an "absolute good." Instead, the self-denial of those who act responsibly includes choosing something relatively better over something relatively worse, and recognizing that the "absolute good" may be exactly the worst. Responsible people are not called to impose a foreign law on reality. On the contrary, their action is in the true sense "*in accord with reality.*"

However, this concept of accordance with reality requires further clarification. It would be a complete and dangerous misunderstanding to view it as that "servile attitude toward the facts" of which Nietzsche speaks that always retreats from wherever the pressure is greater, that justifies success on principle, and that in any given situation chooses the expedient as being in accord with reality. "Accordance with reality" in this sense would be the opposite of responsibility, namely, irresponsibility. However, just as a servile attitude toward the status quo fails to meet the true standard of accordance with reality, so too does a protest based on principle, or a principled rebellion against the status quo, in the name of some ideal higher reality. Both extremes fall equally wide of the heart of the matter. In any action that is truly in accord with reality, acknowledgment of the status quo and protest against the status quo are inextricably connected. The reason for this is that *reality* is first and last not something impersonal, but *the Real One*, namely, the God who became human. Everything that actually exists receives from *the* Real One, whose name is Jesus Christ, both its ultimate foundation and its ultimate negation, its justification and its ultimate contradiction, its ultimate Yes and its ultimate No. Trying to understand reality without the Real One means living in an abstraction, which those who live responsibly must always avoid; it means living detached from reality and vacillating endlessly between the extremes of a servile attitude toward the status quo and rebellion against it. God became human, taking on human being in bodily form, thus reconciling humanity's world with God.

The affirmation of human beings and their reality was based on God's taking on humanity, not vice versa. God did not take on humanity because human beings and human reality were worthy of divine affirmation. Instead, it is because human beings and human reality deserved the divine No that God took on humanity and affirmed it; God became human in the body, thus bearing and suffering, as God, the curse of the divine No upon human nature. Because of what God has done, because of the Real One, because of Jesus Christ, reality now receives its Yes and its No, its legitimacy and its limitation. Affirmation and protest now unite in the concrete action of those who have come to know the Real One. Neither affirmation nor contradiction now comes from an unreal world, nor from a programmatic understanding of the expedient or the ideal. Instead, they come from the reality of the world's reconciliation with God as it has taken place in Christ. In Jesus Christ, the Real One, all reality is taken on and summed up; Christ is its origin, essence, and goal. That is why it is only in and from Christ that it is possible to act in a way that is in accord with reality. The origin of action that is in accord with reality is neither the pseudo-Lutheran Christ whose only purpose is to sanction the status quo, nor the radical Christ of religious enthusiasts who is supposed to bless every revolution; it is rather the God who became human, Jesus Christ, who took on humanity and who has loved, judged, and reconciled humanity, and with it the world.

This, then, leads us to the statement that action in accordance with Christ is action in accord with reality. This statement is not an ideal demand but an assertion that springs from knowledge of reality itself. Jesus Christ does not encounter reality as someone who is foreign to it. Instead, it is he who alone bore and experienced in his own body the essence of the real, and who spoke out of knowledge of the real like no other human being on earth. He alone did not lapse into any ideology but is *the* Real One as such, who in himself has borne and fulfilled the essence of history, and in whom the inner law of history itself is embodied.[7] As the Real One he is the origin, essence, and goal of all reality. That is why he himself is the lord and the law of the real. The sayings of Jesus Christ are therefore the interpretation of his existence, and thus the interpretation of that reality in which history finds its fulfillment. They are the divine commandment for responsible   264
action in history insofar as they are the reality of history that has been fulfilled in Christ, that is, insofar as they are the responsibility for human beings that has been fulfilled in Christ alone. Therefore they are valid not within an abstract ethic—indeed, there they are completely incomprehensible and lead to insoluble conflicts. Rather, they are valid within the reality of history, because this is their source. Any attempt to disconnect them from this origin distorts them into a weak ideology. Only when rooted in their origin do they possess the power to gain control of reality.

Action in accordance with Christ is in accord with reality because it allows the world to be world and reckons with the world as world, while at the same time never forgetting that the world is loved, judged, and reconciled in Jesus Christ by God. This does not involve a confrontation between a "worldly principle" and a "Christian principle." Indeed, any such attempt

7. ["See the section of the Christology lectures on Christ as the center of history (*DBWE* 12:325–327 [*Reader* 282–284])," *DBWE* 6:263, n. 62.]

to make Christ and the world commensurate, if only through the conceptual construct of a principle, and thus to enable Christian action in the world based on that principle, leads in two directions. On the one hand, it leads to different forms of secularism or the teaching about "autonomous spheres of life"; or, on the other hand, it leads to religious enthusiasm. What results in both cases is the destruction of the world reconciled in Christ with God. This approach leads to those eternal conflicts that are the basic elements of all tragedy, thereby in fact destroying the unity of Christian life and action, which is not tragic at all. Wherever a worldly and a Christian principle are set over against each other, there the ultimate reality is the law—or rather, a number of mutually irreconcilable laws. The

265 essence of Greek tragedy is that human beings are destroyed by the clash of incompatible laws. Creon and Antigone, Jason and Medea, Agamemnon and Clytemnestra, are all subject to the claim of two eternal laws that cannot be reconciled in one and the same life; one pays for obedience toward one law with guilt for breaking the other.[8] The meaning of all genuine tragedies is not that one person is proven right over against another, but that both become guilty toward life itself, that life's intrinsic structure is transgression against the laws of the gods. Western thought, especially since the Renaissance, is so decisively shaped by this deepest insight of antiquity that only very rarely has it been noticed that the Christian message has actually overcome this insight. In the early church and the Middle Ages, tragedies do not exist. But even the most recent Protestant ethics still portrays the intractable conflict of the Christian in the world, colored by a dark pathos. In its claim to depict ultimate realities, there is certainly no doubt that Protestant ethics is still firmly under the spell of antiquity without being aware of that fact. It is not Luther but Aeschylus, Sophocles, and Euripides who have given human life this tragic aspect. Luther's seriousness is completely different from the seriousness of those classical tragedians. What must ultimately be taken seriously in the view of the Bible and in Luther's view is not the conflict between the gods as expressed in their laws, but the unity of God and the reconciliation of the world with God in Jesus Christ; not the inevitability of becoming guilty, but the plain and simple life that flows from reconciliation; not fate, but the gospel as the ultimate reality of

266 life; not the cruel triumph of the gods over the perishing human being, but

---

8. ["Bonhoeffer refers here to three particularly important Greek tragedies, *Agamemnon* by Aeschylus, *Antigone* by Sophocles, and *Medea* by Euripides . . . In Bonhoeffer's interpretation, Antigone also follows a law, namely, that of the sacred bonds of kinship," *DBWE* 6:265, n. 67.]

the election of human beings as children of God in the midst of the world reconciled by grace.

However, just as it is a regression from the Christian reality back to that of antiquity to posit a worldly principle and a Christian principle as two opposing ultimate realities, so it is likewise wrong to understand the Christian and the worldly as a unity in principle. The reconciliation of God and world accomplished in Christ consists solely and exclusively in the person of Jesus Christ; it exists in him as the God who acts in vicarious representative responsibility, who became human out of love for humanity. Originating from him alone, human action occurs that is not crushed by conflicts of principle, but springs instead from the already accomplished reconciliation of the world with God. This is an action that soberly and simply does what accords with reality, an action done in vicarious representative responsibility. What is "Christian" and what is "worldly" are now no longer defined from the outset. Instead, both are understood in their respective uniqueness and their unity only within the concrete responsibility of action that is based on the unity of the reconciliation accomplished in Jesus Christ.

We have stated that action that is in accord with reality allows the world to remain the world. But after all that has been said, this fact can no longer mean an isolation of the world in principle or a declaration of its autonomy. Instead, it must itself directly follow the foundation of all reality in Jesus Christ. The world remains the world *because* it is the world that in Christ is loved, judged, and reconciled. No one is commissioned to leap over[9] the world and turn it into the kingdom of God. However, this does not lend legitimacy to the kind of pious indolence that only preserves its own virtue and abandons the evil world to its fate. Instead, human beings are placed in a position of concrete and thus limited, i.e., created, responsibility that recognizes the world as loved, judged, and reconciled by God, and acts accordingly within it. The "world" is thus the *domain of concrete responsibility* that is given to us in and through Jesus Christ. It is not some kind of general concept from which one could deduce a corresponding system. Those who encounter the world in a way that accords with reality do not perceive the world as containing a self-sufficient principle—whether it be good, evil, or a mixture of both—and then act accordingly. Instead, they live and act in limited responsibility, and in so doing allow for the world's nature and character to be revealed to them ever anew.

267

---

9. ["See exactly this language in Bonhoeffer's 1932 address 'Thy Kingdom Come' (*DBWE* 12:286 [*Reader* 341–342])," *DBWE* 6:267, n. 73.]

Action in accord with reality is *limited by our creatureliness*. We do not create the conditions for our action but find ourselves already placed within them. In our action we are bound by certain limitations from both the past and the future that cannot be leaped over. Our responsibility is not infinite but limited. Nevertheless, within these limits it includes the whole of reality. It is not merely concerned with good intention, but also with the good outcome of action; not only with motive, but also with content. It seeks to

268 understand the entire given reality in its origin, essence, and goal, seeing it under the divine Yes and No. The objective is not the application of some kind of limitless general principle. Thus, in the given situation it is necessary to observe, weigh, evaluate, and decide, and to do all that with limited human understanding. We must have courage to look into the immediate future; we must seriously consider the consequences of our actions; and we must attempt seriously to examine our own motives and our own hearts. It cannot be our task to revolutionize the way the world operates, but at the given place to consider reality and do what is necessary. In so doing we must also ask what is possible, since we cannot always take the final step right away, and responsible action does not want to be blind. All of this must be so because God in Christ became *human*, because God said Yes to humanity, and because we as human beings are permitted and called to live and act before God and the neighbor within the confines of our limited human judgment and knowledge. However, because it was *God* who became human, responsible action, although conscious of the human character of its decision, can never prematurely judge its own origin, essence, and goal, but must completely surrender such judgment to God. Whereas all action based on ideology is already justified by its own principle, responsible action renounces any knowledge about its ultimate justification. The deed that is done after responsibly weighing all personal and factual circumstances, in light of God becoming *human* and *God* becoming human, is completely surrendered to God the moment it is carried out. Ultimate ignorance of one's own goodness or evil, together with dependence upon grace, is an essential characteristic of responsible historical action. Those who act on the basis of ideology consider themselves justified by their idea. Those who

269 act responsibly place their action into the hands of God and live by God's grace and judgment.

Another limitation of responsible life and action is that other people who are encountered must be regarded as responsible as well. What distinguishes responsibility from violation is this very fact of recognizing other people as responsible persons, indeed making them aware of their own responsibility. The responsibility of a father or a statesman finds its limit in the responsibility of the child or the citizen. Indeed, the responsibility of the father or the statesman consists precisely in raising to a conscious level the responsibility of those entrusted to their care, in strengthening their responsibility. There can never be an absolute responsibility that does not find its essential limit in the responsibility of the other person.

By recognizing that responsible action is limited both by surrendering our action to God's grace and judgment, and by the responsibility of the neighbor, it simultaneously becomes apparent that precisely these limits qualify the action as responsible in the first place. For God and neighbor, as we encounter them in Jesus Christ, are not only the limits of responsible action, as we have already recognized,[10] but they are also its origin. Irresponsible action is defined by its disregard for these limits of God and neighbor. Responsible action, on the other hand, gains its unity, and ultimately also its certainty, from this very limitation by God and neighbor. It is not its own lord and master, nor is it unbounded or frivolous. Instead, it is creaturely and humble. This is precisely why it can be sustained by an ultimate joy and confidence, knowing that in its origin, essence, and goal it is sheltered in Christ.

Thus far we have come to understand that responsibility is always a mutual relation between persons, derived from the responsibility of Jesus Christ for human beings, so that the origin, essence, and goal of all reality is the Real One, who is God in Jesus Christ. Based on this foundation, we now can and must also speak about the relationship of the responsible person to the world of things. This relationship we call *appropriate to the subject matter*. This implies a dual thesis.

First, in dealing with things in a way that is appropriate to the subject matter, it is imperative to keep in view that in their origin, essence, and goal they are related to God and human beings. This kind of relationship does not impair but cleanses objectivity; it does not stifle but instead purifies and intensifies the ardor of dedication to a cause. The more purely one serves a cause, free from secondary personal agendas, the more it regains its original relation to God and human beings, and the more it frees us from ourselves. The cause to which the ultimate personal sacrifice is made must, in this very act, serve human beings. For example, wherever there is an attempt—based on demagogic, pedagogic, or moralistic reasons—to make

270

---

10. ["Cf. *DBWE* 6:254, and the section on the concept of responsibility, which Bonhoeffer inserted at that point on *DBWE* 6:254–257," *DBWE* 6:269, n. 86.]

an academic discipline useful for human beings in a mistakenly direct way, damage is done not only to people but also to that particular field itself.[11] But where people, in whatever field of inquiry, are exclusively and unreservedly committed to knowing the truth and selflessly renounce all their own aspirations, there they find themselves; and the cause that they served selflessly must in the end serve them. Thus, appropriate action must never overlook how the subject matter is related to the person. At issue is the restoration of the original relationship of subject matter and person based on the responsibility derived from Jesus Christ. True, we know this relationship only in a thoroughly distorted form. Either the subject matter claims an independent status in opposition to the person or the person in opposition to the subject matter, or both stand unrelated side by side.

Second, in every subject matter, whether it be an existing natural entity or a creation of the human spirit, whether a material entity or a mental one, there is an intrinsic law that is grounded in its origin. As an "object" or subject matter in this sense, we thus define any given thing in which there is an intrinsic law, again regardless of whether it is a more impersonal or a more personal entity. The axioms of mathematics and logic are as much a part of this as the state and family, a factory, or a corporation. The task in each case is to discover the respective intrinsic law by which the entity subsists. The more the object is tied to human existence, the more difficult it is to discern its intrinsic law. The laws of logical thought are easier to define than, for example, the law of a state. In the same way is it easier to discover the law of a corporation than those of entities such as the family or the nation, which have evolved gradually. To be in accord with reality, responsible action has to discern and comply with these laws. At first, the law appears to be a formal technique to be mastered. However, the closer the particular entity in question is related to human existence, the more it becomes obvious that the intrinsic law cannot be exhausted by a formal technique, but instead challenges any purely technical approach. The best example in this regard is the problem of developing a technique or craft of political governance, whereas the technique for manufacturing radios is relatively unproblematic. Admittedly, political governance also has its technical side; there is a technique to administration and diplomacy. In

272

---

11. ["Wilhelm von Humboldt, on whose initiative the University of Berlin was founded, had promoted freedom of academic inquiry. In the Third Reich this spirit was replaced by an ideological use of the academic disciplines for the National Socialist regime. See *DBWE* 6:260 (*Reader* 639), Bonhoeffer's phrase 'myopic pragmatism,'" *DBWE* 6:271, n. 92.]

the widest sense this would include not only positive legal regulations and treaties, but also those rules that have not been legally codified, as well as historically sanctioned forms of national and international political coexistence, and finally even generally accepted moral principles of political life. No statesman can disregard one of these laws without having to pay a price. Reckless disrespect and violation of these laws is a misperception of reality, which sooner or later must exact its revenge. Appropriate action will operate within the confines of these laws. It will do so not merely out of hypocrisy, but recognizing that they constitute an essential component of any order. It will utilize such forms, recognizing that they embody the wisdom distilled from the experience of many generations.[12] However, it is precisely at this point that appropriate action is inevitably forced to recognize that these laws of statecraft do not exhaust the content of the intrinsic law of the state, and indeed that the law of the state ultimately extends beyond any legal definition, precisely because the state is inextricably linked to human existence. And it is only at this point that responsible action reaches its most profound expression.

There are occasions when, in the course of historical life, the strict observance of the explicit law of a state, a corporation, a family, but also of a scientific discovery, entails a clash with the basic necessities of human 273 life. In such cases, appropriate responsible action departs from the domain governed by laws and principles, from the normal and regular, and instead is confronted with the extraordinary situation of ultimate necessities that are beyond any possible regulation by law. In his political theory Machiavelli coined the term necessità for such a situation. For politics this means that the craft of political governance becomes political necessity. There can be no doubt that such necessities actually exist. To deny them would mean ceasing to act in accord with reality. It is equally certain, however, that these necessities, as primordial facts of life itself, cannot be captured by any law and can never become laws themselves. They appeal directly to the free responsibility of the one who acts, a responsibility not bound by any law. They create an extraordinary situation, and are in essence borderline cases. They no longer permit human reasoning to come up with a variety of exit strategies, but pose the question of the ultima ratio [*final argument*

---

12. Appropriate action is certainly not necessarily dependent on specialized training, as has been assumed in Germany for far too long. In England it is precisely the amateurs rather than the specialists who, on wide-ranging issues, are consulted on appropriate action. A healthy balance between specialists and amateurs will, in sociological terms, most likely result in appropriate action.

or last resort]. In politics this ultima ratio is war, but it can also be deception or breaking a treaty for the sake of one's own life necessities. In economic life it means the destruction of people's livelihoods for the sake of business necessities. The ultima ratio lies beyond the laws of reason; it is irrational action. It would now be a complete and total misunderstanding if the ultima ratio itself were again turned into a rational law, if the borderline case were made the norm, the necessità a technique. Baldwin was right in saying that there is only one evil greater than force, namely, force as a principle, a law, a norm.

274   He did not intend by this to deny that the necessity for the use of force as ultima ratio can occur as the extraordinary, as the borderline case; otherwise he would be a dreamer and not a statesman. However, under no circumstances did he want to see the extraordinary, the borderline case, be mistaken as the norm, the law. In other words, for him the borderline case could never justify substituting chaos for the relative order that is ensured by an appropriate observance of the law.

Extraordinary necessity appeals to the freedom of those who act responsibly. In this case there is no law behind which they could take cover. Therefore there is also no law that, in the face of such necessity, could force them to make this rather than that particular decision. Instead, in such a situation, one must completely let go of any law, knowing that here one must decide as a free venture. This must also include the open acknowledgment that here the law is being broken, violated; that the commandment is broken out of dire necessity, thereby affirming the legitimacy of the law in the very act of violating it. In thus giving up the appeal to any law, indeed only so, is there finally a surrender of one's own decision and action to the divine guidance of history. The question, never to be answered theoretically, remains whether in historical action the ultimate is the eternal law or free responsibility that is contrary to all law but before God. Here great nations stand on opposite sides of a final, irreconcilable divide. Acknowledging the law as the ultimate authority defines the greatness of English statesmen—Gladstone, for example, comes to mind here. Standing in free responsibility before God, on the other hand, defines the greatness of German statesmen—here I am thinking of Bismarck. Neither side can claim here to be more in the right than the other. The ultimate question remains open and must be kept open. For in either case one becomes guilty, and is able to live only by divine grace and forgiveness. Those bound by the law as

275   well as those acting in free responsibility must hear and accept the indictment by the other side. Neither can be the judge of the other. Judgment remains with God.

From the discussion thus far, it follows that the structure of responsible action involves both *willingness to become guilty*[13] and *freedom*.

By turning our focus back to the origin of all responsibility, we come to understand what willingness to become guilty means. Jesus' concern is not the proclamation and realization of new ethical ideals, and thus also not his own goodness (Matt. 19:17!), but solely love for real human beings. This is why he is able to enter into the community of human beings' guilt, willing to be burdened with their guilt. Jesus does not want to be considered the only perfect one at the expense of human beings, nor, as the only guiltless one, to look down on a humanity perishing under its guilt. He does not want some idea of a new human being to triumph over the wreckage of a humanity defeated by its guilt. He does not want to acquit himself of the guilt by which human beings die. A love that would abandon human beings to their guilt would not be a love for real human beings. As one who acts responsibly within the historical existence of human beings, Jesus becomes guilty. It is his love alone, mind you, that leads him to become guilty. Out of his selfless love, out of his sinlessness, Jesus enters into human guilt, taking it upon himself. In him, sinlessness and bearing guilt are inextricably linked. As the sinless one, Jesus takes the guilt of his brothers and sisters upon himself, and in carrying the burden of this guilt he proves himself as the sinless one. Now in this sinless-guilty Jesus Christ all vicarious representative responsible action has its origin. Precisely because and when it is responsible, because and when it is exclusively concerned about the other human being, because and when it springs from the selfless love for the real human brother or sister—it cannot seek to withdraw from the community of human guilt. Because Jesus took the guilt of all human beings upon himself, everyone who acts responsibly becomes guilty. Those who, in acting responsibly, seek to avoid becoming guilty divorce themselves from the ultimate reality of human existence; but in so doing they also divorce themselves from the redeeming mystery of the sinless bearing of guilt by Jesus Christ, and have no part in the divine justification that attends this event. They place their personal innocence above their responsibility for other human beings and are blind to the fact that precisely in so doing they become even more egregiously guilty. They are also blind to the fact that

276

---

13. ["*Schuldübernahme* involves an active *taking on* of guilt—in the course of, and incidental to, responsible action—and, depending on the context, can mean both becoming guilty oneself and taking on the guilt of others," *DBWE* 6:275, n. 106.]

genuine guiltlessness is demonstrated precisely by entering into community with the guilt of other human beings for their sake. Because of Jesus Christ, the essence of responsible action intrinsically involves the sinless, those who act out of selfless love, becoming guilty.

Against all this one can raise an objection of indisputable gravity. It springs from the lofty authority of conscience,[14] which refuses to sacrifice its integrity to any other good, which refuses to become guilty for the sake of another human being. Here, responsibility for the neighbor has its limit in the inviolable voice of conscience. A responsibility that would force a person to act against conscience would thereby condemn itself. What is correct and what is false in this line of argument?

It is correct that it can never be advisable to act against one's own conscience. All Christian ethics agrees on this point. But what does this mean? Conscience is the call of human existence for unity with itself, voiced from a deep wellspring beyond one's own will and reason. It manifests itself as the indictment of lost unity and as the warning against losing one's self. Its primary focus is not a specific act, but a specific way of being. It protests against activity that threatens this being in unity with one's own self.

277   According to this formal definition, conscience remains an authority the defiance of which is extremely inadvisable; disregarding the call of one's conscience, rather than leading to a meaningful surrender of oneself, must result in the destruction of one's own being, a disintegration of human existence. Acting against one's conscience is similar to suicidal action against one's own life, and it is no accident that both frequently go together. Responsible action that would violate one's conscience, defined in this formal sense, would indeed be reprehensible.

However, this does not yet fully answer the question. If the call of one's conscience comes from the threatened unity with one's own self, then we must now also investigate the content of that unity. It is, first of all, one's own ego in its demand to be "like God"—*sicut deus*—in knowing good and evil.[15] In the natural human being, the call of conscience is the attempt of the ego who knows good and evil to justify itself to God, to others, and to itself, and to be able to sustain this self-justification. The ego, which fails to

---

14. ["Regarding conscience see also *DBWE* 2:138f. (*Reader* 94–95); and *DBWE* 3:128–130 (*Reader* 258–260) et passim," *DBWE* 6:276, n. 110.]

15. ["Gen. 3:5. See also Bonhoeffer's commentary on that verse and on the tree of the knowledge of good and evil in *Creation and Fall* (*DBWE* 3:111ff. and 80ff. [*Reader* 229ff.])," *DBWE* 6:277, n. 116.]

find any grounding in its contingent[16] individuality, traces itself back to a general law of the good and seeks unity with itself by conforming to this law. The call of conscience has its origin and goal in the *autonomy* of one's own ego. The task in following this call is to re-create this autonomy, whose origin is "in Adam" beyond our own desires and knowledge, each time.[17] So in conscience human beings remain bound to a self-discovered law. Although it can manifest itself concretely in different forms, it remains an inviolable law lest one lose one's own self.

The great change takes place, as we now come to understand, the moment the unity of human existence no longer consists in its own autonomy, but, by the miracle of faith, is found in Jesus Christ, beyond one's own ego and its law. This relocation of the center of unity in fact has its formal analogy in the secular domain. When the N.S. [*National Socialist*] says, "my conscience is A.H. [*Adolf Hitler*]," then this is also the attempt to ground the unity of the ego beyond one's own self. The consequence is the surrender of the self's autonomy in favor of an unconditional heteronomy. This, in turn, is possible only if the other human being, in whom I seek the unity of my life, takes on the role of my redeemer. This would be the closest secular parallel to Christian truth and thus its most pronounced antithesis.

Where Christ, true God and true human being, has become the unifying center of my existence, conscience in the formal sense still remains the call, coming from my true self, into unity with myself. However, this unity can now no longer be realized by returning to my autonomy that lives out of the law,[18] but instead in community with Jesus Christ. The natural conscience, even the most scrupulous, is now exposed as the most godless self-justification. It is overcome by the conscience that has been set free in Jesus Christ, calling me to unity with myself in Jesus Christ. Jesus Christ has become my conscience. This means that from now on I can only find unity with myself by surrendering my ego to God and others. The origin

278

---

16. ["Bonhoeffer employed the philosophical term 'contingent,' as in 'contingency of revelation' (from the Latin *contingens*, 'not necessary,' not graspable by any law or rule), in his *Habilitationsschrift*, or postdoctoral dissertation, *Act and Being* (see *DBWE* 2:82)," *DBWE* 6:277, n. 117.]

17. ["See *Act and Being*: 'The conscience . . . of human beings in Adam [is] . . . the confirmation and justification of their self-glorifying solitude' (*DBWE* 2:139 [*Reader* 95]). Regarding 'autonomy,' see *DBWE* 6:252–253," *DBWE* 6:277, n. 118.]

18. ["By 'law' Bonhoeffer does not mean only or primarily religious law such as the Decalogue, but law as an 'abstract ethical principle'; see *DBWE* 6:279 (*Reader* 652), the discussion of Kant's 'grotesque' principle of truthfulness," *DBWE* 6:278, n. 122.]

and goal of my conscience is not a law but the living God and the living human being as I encounter them in Jesus Christ. For the sake of God and human beings Jesus Christ became a breaker of the law: he broke the law of the Sabbath in order to sanctify it, out of love for God and human beings;

279   he left his parents in order to be in his Father's house, and thus to purify the obedience owed to one's parents; he ate with sinners and outcasts, and, out of love for humanity, he ended up being forsaken by God in his final hour. As the one who loved without sin, he became guilty, seeking to stand within the community of human guilt. He rejected the devil's accusation that sought to distract him from this path.[19] So Jesus Christ is the one who sets the conscience free for the service of God and neighbor, who sets the conscience free even and especially where a person enters into the community of human guilt. The conscience that has been set free from the law will not shy away from entering into another's guilt for that person's sake. Rather, precisely in so doing it will prove its purity. Unlike the conscience bound to the law, the freed conscience is not fearful. Instead, it is wide open to the neighbor and the neighbor's concrete distress. The freed conscience aligns itself with the responsibility, which has been established in Christ, to bear guilt for the sake of the neighbor. In contrast to the essential sinlessness of Jesus Christ, human action is never sinless but always contaminated by original sin, which is part of human nature. Nevertheless, as responsible action, in contrast to any self-righteous action justified by a principle, it does participate indirectly in the action of Jesus Christ. Responsible action is thus characterized by something like a relative sinlessness, which is demonstrated precisely by the responsible taking on of another's guilt.

Treating truthfulness as a principle leads Kant to the grotesque conclusion that if asked by a murderer whether my friend, whom he was pursuing, had sought refuge in my house, I would have to answer honestly in

280   the affirmative. Here the self-righteousness of conscience has escalated into blasphemous recklessness and become an impediment to responsible action. Since responsibility is the entire response, in accord with reality, to the claim of God and my neighbor, then this scenario glaringly illuminates the merely partial response[20] of a conscience bound by principles. I come into conflict with my responsibility that is grounded in reality when I refuse to become guilty of violating the principle of truthfulness for the sake of my

---

19. ["... See also *DBWE* 4:84f.," *DBWE* 6:279, n. 126.]

20. ["See *DBWE* 6:254, the reference to 'partial answers,'" *DBWE* 6:280, n. 131.]

friend, refusing in this case to lie[21] energetically for the sake of my friend—
and any attempt to deny that we are indeed dealing with lying here is once
again the work of a legalistic and self-righteous conscience—refusing, in
other words, to take on and bear guilt out of love for my neighbor. Here, as
well, a conscience bound to Christ alone will most clearly exhibit its innocence precisely in responsibly accepting culpability.

It is astounding how close Goethe comes to these thoughts from a purely
profane knowledge of reality. To quote the dialogue in which Pylades urges
Iphigenia to act responsibly in violation of her inner law:

PYLADES. Too strict demands betoken secret pride. . . .
IPHIGENIA. The spotless heart alone has pure enjoyment.
PYLADES. You have remained untainted in this temple;[22]
   life teaches us, and you will learn it too,
   to be less rigorous with ourselves and others.
   This human breed is formed in such astounding fashion,
   so variously linked up and interwoven,
   that keeping pure and disentangled
   within ourselves or with regard to others
   is far beyond a human being's grasp.
   Nor are we meant to judge ourselves:
   our first duty is to walk and watch our path,
   for we can seldom rightly judge what we have done,
   and still less judge what we are doing. . . .
   It seems you have not known the pain of loss
   if to avoid such great calamity
   you will not even pay the price of speaking falsely.
IPHIGENIA. Oh, if only I had a man's heart in me
   which, when it harbors some bold resolution,
   closes itself to all dissuading voices!

281

---

21. ["Concerning 'lying,' see *DBWE* 6:77 . . . See also his exegesis of Matt. 5:33–37 in
DBWE 4:128–131. During his imprisonment in Tegel, Bonhoeffer emphasized his reservations against truthfulness as a 'principle'. . . in the letter of the second Sunday of Advent
(December 5, 1943), *DBWE* 8:212–216, and in the essay fragment 'What Does It Mean to
Tell the Truth?' (*DBWE* 16:601–608 [*Reader* 749–756]). A person who, during interroga-
tions by the National Socialist regime, could not 'lie energetically' posed a deadly threat
to co-conspirators," *DBWE* 6:280, n. 132.]

22. The introduction of the characteristic concept of "enjoyment" is also notable in
this context.

No matter how much the conscience freed in Jesus Christ and responsibility might agree with each other, there nevertheless remains an irremovable tension between them.

In two ways conscience still limits taking on and bearing guilt, which a particular responsible action necessarily entails.

First, the conscience freed in Jesus Christ still essentially remains the call to unity with myself. Acceptance of responsibility must not destroy this unity. Surrendering the self in selfless service must never be confused with destroying and annihilating the self, which would then also no longer be able to take on responsibility. The measure of guilt incurred in connection with a particular responsible action has its concrete limit in one's unity with oneself, in one's ability to bear the weight. There are responsibilities that I am not able to bear without being broken by them, whether it be a declaration of war, the breach of a political treaty, a revolution, or merely the dismissal[23] of a single father of a family who thus finds himself unemployed, or, lastly, just giving advice in a personal life decision. It is true that the ability to bear the weight of making responsible decisions can and should grow. It is also true that each time I fail to meet a responsibility, I have also already made a decision for which I am responsible. Nevertheless, in the concrete situation the call of the conscience to unity with oneself in Jesus Christ remains inescapable. This explains the infinite variety of responsible decisions.

Second, even the conscience freed in Jesus Christ confronts responsible action with the law that, when obeyed, keeps one in unity with oneself as grounded in Jesus Christ, whereas disregarding it can lead only to irresponsibility. This is the law to love God and neighbor as spelled out in the Decalogue, in the Sermon on the Mount, and in the apostolic parenesis [*exhortation*]. In its content, the law of the natural conscience corresponds remarkably closely with the conscience set free in Jesus Christ. This correct observation is due to the fact that conscience has indeed to do with preserving life itself and therefore contains basic traits of the law of life, even if it is distorted in detail and fundamentally perverted. Even in its liberated form, conscience still has the function it had in its natural state, namely, to warn us not to violate the law of life. However, Jesus Christ rather than the law is now the ultimate. Wherever conscience and concrete responsibility clash, we must therefore freely decide in favor of Jesus Christ. This does not entail an eternal conflict, but rather means gaining the ultimate unity; for the

282

---

23. ["... Under the National Socialist regime, members of persecuted groups were dismissed from civil service," *DBWE* 6:281, n. 134.]

ground, essence, and goal of concrete responsibility is, of course, the very same Jesus Christ who is lord of the conscience. So responsibility is bound by conscience, but conscience is set free by responsibility. It has now become evident that these two statements are saying the same thing: those who act responsibly become guilty without sin; and only those whose conscience is free can bear responsibility.

Those who in acting responsibly take on guilt—which is inescapable for any responsible person—place this guilt on themselves, not on someone else; they stand up for it and take responsibility for it. They do so not out of a sacrilegious and reckless belief in their own power, but in the knowledge of being forced into this freedom and of their dependence on grace in its exercise. Those who act out of free responsibility are justified before others by dire necessity;[24] before themselves they are acquitted by their conscience, but before God they hope only for grace.[25]

The analysis of the structure of responsible action thus requires us to deal finally with *freedom.*

Responsibility and freedom are mutually corresponding concepts. Responsibility presupposes freedom substantively—not chronologically—just as freedom can exist only in the exercise of responsibility. Responsibility is human freedom that exists only by being bound to God and neighbor.

Those who are responsible act in their own freedom, without the support of people, conditions, or principles, but nevertheless considering all existing circumstances related to people, general conditions, or principles. That nothing comes to their defense or exoneration, other than their own action and person, is proof of their freedom. They themselves have to observe, judge, weigh, decide, and act on their own. They themselves have to examine the motives, the prospects, the value, and meaning of their action. But neither purity of motive, nor favorable conditions, nor the meaningfulness of an intended action can become a rule for their action behind which they can hide, appealing to its authority, and by which they can be exonerated and acquitted.[26] For in such a case, of course, they would no longer be

283

---

24. ["See *DBWE* 6:272–273 (*Reader* 646–648), regarding 'the basic necessities of human life,'" *DBWE* 6:282, n. 137.]

25. ["Although disguised by translation in the plural, in this sentence and in the last sentence of the previous paragraph, Bonhoeffer writes *der Mann*, 'the man,' rather than his normal *der Mensch*, 'the human being.' Given the pertinence of these sentences to his personal involvement in the conspiracy against Hitler, this usage suggests an autobiographical interpretation of these sentences," *DBWE* 6:283, n. 138.]

26. This also eliminates the spurious question of determinism or indeterminism—whether the essence of decisions of the human spirit is to be falsely subsumed under the law of cause and effect.

284   truly free. Those who act responsibly do so while bound to God and neighbor as they encounter me in Jesus Christ, the only bond that is liberating, totally liberating. Responsible action takes place in the sphere of relativity, completely shrouded in the twilight that the historical situation casts upon good and evil. It takes place in the midst of the countless perspectives from which every phenomenon is seen. Responsible action must decide not simply between right and wrong, good and evil, but between right and right, wrong and wrong. "Right collides with right," as Aeschylus stated. This very fact defines responsible action as a free venture, not justified by any law; rather, those who act responsibly relinquish any effectual self-justification; indeed, in so doing they relinquish an ultimately dependable knowledge of good and evil. As responsible action, the good takes place without knowing,[27] by surrendering to God the deed that has become necessary and is nevertheless (or because of it!) free, surrendering it to God, who looks upon the heart, weighs the deeds, and guides history.

Thus a profound mystery of history as such is disclosed to us. Precisely those who act in the freedom of their very own responsibility see their activity as flowing into God's guidance. Free action recognizes itself ultimately as being God's action, decision as God's guidance, the venture as divine necessity. In freely surrendering the knowledge of our own goodness, the

285   good of God occurs. Only in this ultimate perspective can we speak about good in historical action. We will have to come back to this point later in our discussion.

Before that, however, we must explore a decisive question that is essential to clarifying the issue at hand, namely, what is the relation between free responsibility and obedience? At first it would appear that everything we have said about free responsibility would actually find its application only where someone "holds a responsible position" in life, as we say—that is, where a person needs to make independent decisions of some significant magnitude. But how does responsibility play any role in the steady routine of daily work of a day laborer, a factory worker, a lowly office worker or a military recruit, an apprentice, or a pupil. The situation is admittedly somewhat different for an independent farmer, a business owner, a politician or statesman, a military commander, an instructor of an apprentice, a teacher, or a judge. But how many technical details and prescribed routines finally do govern their lives, and how few truly free decisions do they actually make? It would therefore seem as if everything we have said about

---

27. ["See *Discipleship*, where Bonhoeffer writes that 'the goodness of discipleship takes place without awareness' (*DBWE* 4:151) . . . ," *DBWE* 6:284, n. 143.]

responsibility applied in the end only to a very small group of people, and
to them only in a few moments of their lives, and as if for the great majority
of people we consequently would have to speak about obedience and duty,
rather than responsibility. This would mean one kind of ethic for the great,
the strong, and the rulers, and another kind for the little people, the weak,
and the subordinates. Responsibility on the one side, obedience on the
other, freedom here and servitude there. In our modern social order, especially in Germany, the existence of the individual is doubtless prescribed,
regulated, and therefore also secured to such an extent that only a few
are granted the opportunity to breathe the free air sweeping the wide-
open spaces of major decisions, and to become acquainted with the danger   286
of acting responsibly on their very own. The compulsory structuring of
life into a specific apprenticeship, education, and vocation has made our
lives relatively safe from ethical dangers. People who are embedded in this
process since childhood are ethically emasculated; they have been robbed
of their creative ethical power, which consists in freedom. This reveals
an aberration that is deeply rooted in the nature of our modern social
order and that can be challenged only by clearly lifting up the fundamental concept of responsibility. Given the situation as it stands, the bulk of
experiential resources relating to the problem of responsibility will have to
be sought among the great political leaders, the captains of industry, and
military commanders, because the few others who venture to act in free
responsibility amid the pressures of daily life are crushed by the machinery
of all-pervasive rules and regulations.

It would nevertheless be a mistake to consider the question only from
this perspective. For in fact there is not a single life that cannot come to
know the situation of responsibility, indeed in its most distinctive form,
namely, in the encounter with other human beings. Thus, even where
free responsibility is more or less excluded from one's vocational and public life, one's relation to other human beings, from the family to one's
coworker, will always demand responsibility;[28] and the exercise of genuine
responsibility in this arena provides the only sound possibility to expand
the sphere of responsibility once again into one's vocational and public
life. Wherever human beings encounter one another, including the world
of work, genuine responsibility arises, and no rules and regulations are
able to invalidate these relationships of responsibility. This is true not only

---

28. ["From his earliest work Bonhoeffer had defined the human person in terms of
ethical encounter with an other, e.g., *DBWE* 1:48–52 (*Reader* 23–26)," *DBWE* 6:286, n.
151.]

for the relationship between spouses, parents and children, and between friends, but also for instructors and their apprentices, teachers and their pupils, judges and defendants.

And we can even go one step further. Responsibility exists not only 287 *alongside* relationships based on obedience, but also *within* this arena. Apprentices, whose duty it is to obey their instructors, are at the same time freely responsible for their work, their achievement, and thus also for their instructors. The same is true for pupils, for students, but also for employees in any company, and soldiers in war. Obedience and responsibility are interwoven, so that responsibility does not merely begin where obedience ends, but obedience is rendered in responsibility. There will always be relationships based on obedience and dependence.[29] The only thing that is important, though, is that they not eliminate responsibilities, as is already the case today to a large extent. It is more difficult for those who are socially dependent to be aware of their responsibility than it is for those who are socially free. However, by no means does a relationship of dependence as such preclude free responsibility. Master and servant can and ought to be freely responsible for one another while maintaining their relationship based on obedience.

The relationship between God and human beings that has been realized in Jesus Christ is the ultimate reason why this is the case. Jesus stands before God as the obedient one and as the free one. As the obedient one, he does the will of the Father by blindly following the law he has been commanded. As the free one, he affirms God's will out of his very own insight, with open eyes and a joyful heart; it is as if he re-creates it anew out of himself. Obedience without freedom is slavery, freedom without obedience is arbitrariness. Obedience binds freedom, freedom ennobles obedience. Obedience binds the creature to the Creator, freedom places the creature, made in God's image, face-to-face with the Creator. Obedience makes clear to human beings that they have to be *told* what is good and what the Lord requires of them (Mic. 6:6), freedom lets them create the good themselves. Obedience knows what is good and does it. Freedom dares to act and leaves 288 the judgment about good and evil up to God. Obedience follows blindly,

---

29. ["... See *DBWE* 6:390–393 (*Reader* 687–689), regarding 'above and below.' It is important to note that relationships of obedience are not blind submission to authority but involve mutual responsibilities; the parties ought to be 'freely responsible for one another,' as Bonhoeffer states at the end of the paragraph," *DBWE* 6:287, n. 153.]

freedom has open eyes. Obedience acts without asking questions, freedom asks about the meaning. Obedience has tied hands, freedom is creative. In rendering obedience, human beings observe God's Decalogue, in exercising freedom, they create new decalogues (Luther).

In responsibility both obedience and freedom become real. Responsibility has this inner tension. Any attempt to make one independent of the other would be the end of responsibility. Responsible action is bound and yet creative. Making obedience independent would lead to Kant's ethic of duty, making freedom independent to a romantic ethic of genius. The person bound by duty as well as the genius have their justification within themselves. Responsible human beings, who stand between obligation and freedom and who, while bound, must nevertheless dare to act freely, find justification neither by their bond nor by their freedom, but only in the One who has placed them in this—humanly impossible—situation and who requires them to act. Responsible human beings surrender themselves and their action to God.

We have sought to grasp the *structure of responsible life* with the concepts of vicarious representative action, accordance with reality, taking on guilt, and freedom. The desire to become even more concrete now leads us to the question whether it is possible to determine more precisely the *place* at which the responsible life is realized. Does responsibility place me into an unlimited field of activity, or does it tie me firmly to the limits given with my concrete daily tasks? For what am I genuinely responsible, and for what am I not? Does it make sense to consider myself responsible for everything that happens in the world, or can I watch the great world events as an uninvolved observer, as long as my own minute domain is in order? Should I let myself be worn down while eagerly but powerlessly confronting all the injustice and all the misery in the world, or may I, in self-satisfied security, let the evil world run its course, so long as I myself cannot do anything to change it and have done my part? What is the place and what are the limits of my responsibility?

289

The Place of Responsibility

In this section we will draw on the concept of *vocation*, which in the history of ethics has gained an almost unique significance. However, in so doing we must be clear from the outset about the following: (1) what we have in mind here is not the secularized concept of vocation as "a definite field of activity" (Max Weber); (2) nor do we think of the kind of pseudo-Lutheranism that views vocation merely as the justification and sanctification of the worldly orders as such;[30] (3) even Luther's own concept of vocation[31] is not simply identical with that of the New Testament; with great boldness, he fills the New Testament concept of vocation (1 Cor. 7:20) with a richness that, although justified in substance just like his translation of Rom. 3:28, stretches the actual Greek usage. We will therefore start with the biblical evidence. (4) The two concepts of vocation and responsibility have such a uniquely fortuitous correspondence that it seems especially appropriate to employ them here, even though in our usage neither term is identical with that of the New Testament.

In encounter with Jesus Christ, a person experiences God's call, and in it the calling to a life in community with Jesus Christ. Human beings experience the divine grace that claims them. It is not human beings who seek out grace in its place, for God lives in unapproachable light (1 Tim. 6:16). Instead, grace seeks out and finds human beings in their place—the Word became flesh (John 1:14)—and claims them precisely there. It is a place that in every case and in every respect is burdened with sin and guilt, be it a royal throne, the home of a respected citizen, or a shanty of misery. It is a place of this world. This visitation by grace took place in Jesus Christ becoming human, and still occurs in the word about Jesus Christ that the Holy Spirit brings. The call reaches us as Gentile or Jew, slave or free, man or woman, married or unmarried. Right where they happen to be, human beings ought to hear the call and allow themselves to be claimed by it. It is not as if this would imply a justification of slavery, marriage, or singleness as such.[32] Instead, those who are called may belong to God in one state or the other. Only by the call of grace heard in Jesus Christ, by which I am claimed, may I live justified before God as slave or free, married or single. From Christ's perspective this life is now my vocation; from my own perspective it is my responsibility.

---

30. ["See *Discipleship* regarding Luther's successors (or 'descendants') on the conflict between 'a Christian and a bourgeois-secular vocation'; for the latter the 'Christian life consists of my living in the world and like the world' (*DBWE* 4:50 [*Reader* 465]). Bonhoeffer's own subject index of *Discipleship* references this page under 'vocation,'" *DBWE* 6:289, n. 162.]

31. ["... See *Discipleship*, on 'The Call to Discipleship' (*DBWE* 4:57–76 [*Reader* 469–485] et passim) ...," *DBWE* 6:289, n. 163.]

32. ["... See *Discipleship* regarding not adding a 'religious anchor' for slavery (*DBWE* 4:238), as well as the statement that 'Jesus does not make either marriage or celibacy into a required program' (*DBWE* 4:127)," *DBWE* 6:290, n. 168.]

This rules out two disastrous misunderstandings, that of cultural Protestantism[33] and that of monasticism. People do not fulfill the responsibility laid on them by faithfully performing their earthly vocational obligations as citizens, workers, and parents, but by hearing the call of Jesus Christ that, 291 although it leads them also into earthly obligations, is never synonymous with these, but instead always transcends them as a reality standing before and behind them. Vocation in the New Testament sense is never a sanctioning of the worldly orders as such. Its Yes always includes at the same time the sharpest No, the sharpest protest against the world. Luther's return from the monastery into the world, into a "vocation," is, in the genuine spirit of the New Testament, the fiercest attack that has been launched and the hardest blow that has been struck against the world since the time of earliest Christianity.[34] Now a stand against the world is taken *within* the world. Vocation is the place at which one responds to the call of Christ and thus lives responsibly. The task given to me by my vocation is thus limited; but my responsibility to the call of Jesus Christ knows no bounds.

The misunderstanding of medieval monasticism lies not in the recognition that the call of Jesus Christ enlists human beings in the struggle against the world.[35] Instead, it lies in the attempt to find a place that is not the world and from which one could therefore respond more appropriately. This futile attempt to escape from the world takes seriously neither God's No, which applies to the whole world including the monastery, nor, on the other hand, God's Yes, in which God reconciles the world with himself. The monastic enterprise thus takes God's call, even its No to the world, less seriously than the worldly vocation as understood by Luther (although certainly not by pseudo-Lutheranism). It is certainly in line with Luther that the response to the call of Jesus Christ might in a concrete case consist in leaving a particular earthly vocation in which it is no longer possible to live responsibly. It is only pseudo-Lutheranism, with its faith in the sanctity of vocational obligations and earthly orders as such, that cannot conceive this thought. Against this distortion of the New Testament understanding of vocation, the protest of the monastery remains justified. Luther's sole purpose in returning to the world was to be fully responsible to the call

---

33. ["By 'cultural Protestantism,' *Kulturprotestantismus,* Bonhoeffer means a Protestantism that is domesticated and virtually indistinguishable from the culture of its society," *DBWE* 6:290, n. 169.]

34. ["This sentence corresponds, in part word for word, to sentences in *Discipleship* (*DBWE* 4:48 [*Reader* 463–464] and 244f.)," *DBWE* 6:291, n. 171.]

35. ["See *Discipleship* on monasticism and on Luther (*DBWE* 4:47ff. [*Reader* 462ff.])," *DBWE* 6:291, n. 172.]

292 of Christ. In light of this call, the monastic solution remains wrong in two respects. First, it confines the ultimately responsible life to the space within the walls of the monastery. Second, it regards as only a false compromise the life in which the Yes and the No to living in this world—both of which are included in the call of Jesus Christ—are to be united in concrete responsibility to this call. Against this misunderstanding, Luther interpreted the meaning of human responsibility as limited yet at the same time grounded in the unlimited; he coupled the fulfillment of one's earthly vocation in responsibility before the call of Jesus Christ with the free and joyful conscience that stems from being in community with Jesus Christ. Thus the good and free conscience does not come from fulfilling one's earthly vocational obligations as such. On that level, the unresolved conflict between multiple obligations will always remain an open wound for the conscience, and one can never manage more than a compromise with a semiclear conscience. In concrete deeds, conscience can be free only by fulfilling one's concrete vocation in responsibility to the call of Jesus Christ, that is, only from knowledge of Jesus Christ's becoming human. Only the call of Christ, which is responsibly followed in one's vocation, overcomes the compromise and the resultant uncertainty of the conscience.

The question of the place and the limit of responsibility has led us to the concept of vocation. However, this answer is valid only where vocation is understood simultaneously in all its dimensions. The call of Jesus Christ is the call to belong to Christ completely; it is Christ's address and claim at the place at which this call encounters me; vocation comprises work with things and issues as well as personal relations;[36] it requires "a definite 293 field of activity," though never as a value in itself but only in responsibility to Jesus Christ. By being related to Jesus Christ, the "definite field of activity" is set free from any isolation. The boundary of vocation has been broken open not only vertically, that is, through Christ, but also horizontally, with regard to the extent of responsibility. Let us say I am a medical doctor, for example. In dealing with a concrete case I serve not only my patient, but also the body of scientific knowledge, and thus science and knowledge of truth in general. Although in practice I render this service in my concrete situation—for example, at a patient's bedside—I nevertheless remain aware of my responsibility toward the whole, and only thus fulfill my vocation. In so doing, it may come to the point that in a particular case I

36. ["See the text '"Personal" and "Objective" Ethics' (*DBWE* 16:540–551), which critically discusses a thesis by Dilschneider; see also *DBWE* 6:333. . . ," *DBWE* 6:292, n. 175.]

must recognize and fulfill my concrete responsibility as a physician no longer only at a patient's bedside, but, for example, in taking a public stance against a measure that poses a threat to medical science, or human life, or science in general.[37] Vocation is responsibility, and responsibility is the whole response of the whole person to reality as a whole. This is precisely why a myopic self-limitation to one's vocational obligations in the narrowest sense is out of the question; such a limitation would be irresponsibility. The nature of free responsibility rules out any legal regulation of when and to what extent human vocation and responsibility entail breaking out of the "definite field of activity." This can happen only after seriously considering one's immediate vocational obligations, the dangers of encroaching on the responsibilities of others, and finally the total picture of the issue at hand. It will then be my free responsibility in response to the call of Jesus Christ that leads me in one direction or the other. Responsibility in a vocation follows the call of Christ alone.

There is a wrong and right limitation of responsibility, as well as a wrong 294 and right expansion of it; there is an enthusiastic transgression of all boundaries, as well as a legalistic erecting of boundaries. From the outside, it is difficult or impossible to determine whether in a concrete case an action is responsible or whether it is born from enthusiasm or legalism. Nevertheless, there are criteria for self-examination, even though they cannot provide complete certainty about one's own self. The following are such criteria: neither the limitation nor the expansion of my field of responsibility must be based on principles, but rather on the concrete call of Jesus alone; if, according to my character traits, I know that I tend to be a reformer, a know-it-all, a fanatic, one who does not heed any limits, there I run the risk of expanding my responsibility arbitrarily, and confusing my natural desire with the call of Jesus; if I know myself to be cautious, anxious, insecure, and legalistic, there I must be careful not to equate the call of Jesus Christ with my limiting responsibility to a narrow domain; and finally, I am never set free to act in genuine responsibility by looking at myself, but only by attending to Christ's call.

---

37. ["Threats of this kind were posed by the race-based eugenics programs of the National Socialist regime, such as forced sterilizations and murders that were termed 'euthanasia.' In choosing the example of the medical doctor here in this manuscript, Bonhoeffer was certainly also conscious of his own father, the psychiatrist Karl Bonhoeffer. Through public declarations, the elder Bonhoeffer attempted to limit the number of sterilizations. See Uwe Gerrens, *Medizinisches Ethos und theologische Ethik,*" *DBWE* 6:293, n. 177.]

Unknowingly, Nietzsche speaks in the spirit of the New Testament when he chides the legalistic and narrow-minded misunderstanding of the commandment to love our neighbor with the following words: "You crowd around your neighbor and have fine words for it. But I say unto you: your love of the neighbor is your bad love of yourselves. You flee to your neighbor from yourselves and would like to make a virtue out of that: but I see through your 'selflessness.' . . . Do I advise love of those nearest to you? Sooner I should even advise you to flee from those nearest you and to love those farthest away." Behind the neighbor, whom the call of Jesus commends to us, also stands, according to Jesus, the one who is farthest from us, namely, Jesus Christ himself, who is indeed God. Whoever does not know this "far-

295   thest" behind the "nearest," and at the same time this "farthest" as this "nearest," does not serve the neighbor but themselves, and shuns the free and open air of responsibility to hide in the more comfortable narrowness of fulfilling a duty. Even the commandment to love the neighbor therefore does not mean a legalistic restriction of my responsibility to the neighbor whom I encounter while sharing the same place, citizenship, profession, or family. The neighbor can be met precisely in the one who is farthest away, and vice versa. In a terrible miscarriage of justice in the United States in 1931, nine young black men accused of raping a white girl of dubious reputation were sentenced to death even though their guilt could not be proven. This triggered a storm of outrage that found expression in open letters from the most respected European public figures. A Christian, disturbed by these events, asked a leading church official in Germany to consider raising his voice also in protest against this case. For his refusal to do so, the official cited the "Lutheran" understanding of vocation, that is, the limitation of the extent of his responsibility. But in fact it was protest from all around the world that eventually led to the revision of the verdict. Does the call of Jesus Christ itself lead us here to understand Nietzsche's statement: "My brothers, love of the neighbor I do not recommend to you: I recommend to you love of the farthest"? We say this without making a judgment in this particular case. We say it in order to keep the boundary open.

296   The Bible is loud and clear in its instruction to do whatever is right in front of us (Eccles. 9:10), to be faithful in the smallest things (Luke 16:10; 19:17), to fulfill our domestic duties before assuming larger ones (1 Tim. 3:5), and to be cautious about interfering with another person's responsibility or office (1 Pet. 4:15). Nevertheless, all of these exhortations remain bound to the call of Jesus Christ, and so they are not legalistic restrictions against exercising free responsibility toward this call. In the German Church Struggle there have been many cases of pastors refusing to assume the public responsibility of speaking out on the affliction of their

colleagues and those suffering persecution of all kinds, precisely because their own congregations had not yet been affected. They did so not out of cowardice or unwillingness to act, but solely because they considered this an illegitimate transgression of their assigned vocation to protect their own congregation in its concrete travails and trials. If at a later point their own congregation was also affected, then this led frequently to a responsible action carried out with authority and the greatest freedom. This too we say, not to render a premature judgment, but in order to guard the commandment to love the neighbor against any false limitation, and thus to preserve the freedom that the gospel gives to the concept of vocation.

But now is it not the case that the law of God as revealed in the Decalogue, and the divine mandates of marriage, work, and government, establish an inviolable boundary for any responsible action in one's vocation? Would any transgressing of this boundary not amount to insubordination against the revealed will of God? Here the recurring problem of law and freedom presents itself with ultimate urgency. It now threatens to introduce a contradiction into the will of God itself. Certainly no responsible activity is possible that does not consider with ultimate seriousness the boundary that God established in the law. Nevertheless, precisely as responsible action it will not separate this law from its giver. Only as the Redeemer in Jesus Christ will it be able to recognize the God by whose law the world is held in order; it will recognize Jesus Christ as the ultimate reality to whom it is responsible, and precisely through Christ it will be freed from the law for the responsible deed. For the sake of God and neighbor, which means for Christ's sake, one may be freed from keeping the Sabbath holy, honoring one's parents, indeed from the entire divine law. It is a freedom that transgresses this law, but only in order to affirm it anew. The suspension of the law must only serve its true fulfillment. In war, for example, there is killing, lying, and seizing of property solely in order to reinstate the validity of life, truth, and property. Breaking the law must be *recognized* in all its gravity—"blessed are you if you know what you are doing; however, if you do not know what you are doing you are cursed and a transgressor of the law" (Luke 5:39 in hʳ).[38] Whether an action springs from responsibility or

297

---

38. ["The quoted text 'blessed are you . . .' is a translation of part of a textual variant to Luke 6:5 cited in the critical apparatus of the Nestle edition of the Greek New Testament. The top line of this Nestle page contains the reference '5:39—6:9' (Bonhoeffer cited 5:39 from this reference instead of the correct verse within it); in Bonhoeffer's 1929 Nestle, 'hʳ' refers to a 'noteworthy rejected reading' as designated in the appendix of the small 1895 edition of Westcott and Hort, *The New Testament in the Original Greek*," *DBWE* 6:297, n. 189.]

cynicism can become evident only in whether the objective guilt one incurs by breaking the law is recognized and borne, and whether by the very act of breaking it the law is truly sanctified. The will of God is thus sanctified in the deed that arises out of freedom. Precisely because we are dealing with a deed that arises from freedom, the one who acts is not torn apart by destructive conflict, but instead can with confidence and inner integrity do the unspeakable, namely, in the very act of breaking the law to sanctify it.

298   Love and Responsibility[39]

---

39. [*The manuscript ends with the title "Love and Responsibility."*]

37. The "Ethical" and the "Christian" as a Topic

DWBE 6:363–387

The first half of this Ethics *essay offers what Bonhoeffer calls "a general phenomenology of the ethical." The ethical phenomenon is, he writes, "'the experience of the ought,' the conscious fundamental decision between what is good in principle and what is evil in principle, the orientation toward the highest norm, [and] the ethical conflict and its resolution." The ethical phenomenon arises in the boundary events of life, when what the "ethical" is ceases to be self-evident and becomes a topic of reflection.*

The "ethical" contrasts with the "Christian," he argues, in that the latter rests not on principles and norms revealed in the conscience's experience of the ought but in God's command. And God's command differs from the ethical imperative because it supplies not only prohibitions and obligations, but also permission. God commands freedom. Thus while God's command does indeed concern the boundary situations of life (though Bonhoeffer prefers the biblical term "law" to the philosophical term "ethical"), it concerns much more: the fullness of life. Under God's command, the boundary of life emerges from the center.[1]

With its contrast between ethics traditionally conceived and ethics in a Christian context, this essay reads like another attempted beginning for the book now known as Ethics.[2] *But this particular essay also displays a freshness that may have resulted from Bonhoeffer's 1942 visit with Barth in Basel, a visit that afforded Bonhoeffer access to Barth's soon-to-be-published treatment of "The Command of God, some aspects of which he drew upon in this manuscript."[3]*

---

1. [*The notion of a boundary that is also the center recurs frequently in Bonhoeffer's thinking. See, for examples,* DBWE *12:324* (Reader *282),* DBWE *3:80–93* (Reader *229–237), and* DBWE *8:366–367* (Reader *779–780).*]

2. [*The other two are* DBWE *6:47–75* (Reader *595–612) and* DBWE *6:299–338.*]

3. [DBWE *6:415, editors' afterword. See Barth,* Church Dogmatics *2/2, 509–781.*]

363   A Christian ethic will have to begin with the question of whether and to what extent the "ethical" and the "Christian" can be treated as a topic at all. This is not at all as self-evident as one might assume, given the confidence with which this has repeatedly been done and continues to be done. Indeed, one has not really entered the arena of Christian ethics at all unless one has understood how dubious it is to make the "ethical" and the "Christian" into a topic of separate reflection, of discussion, or even of a scholarly exposition.

364   There is a certain way of treating the "ethical" as a topic that a Christian ethic must rule out from the start. Friedrich Theodor Vischer has his literary character "Someone Too"[4] make the statement: "Morality is always self-evident." Within certain limits this quiet, ironic gesture, which rejects any attempt to let the ethical become an independent topic of discussion, shows perhaps more insight into the nature of the "ethical" than quite a few textbooks of Christian ethics. This does not merely entail rejecting the overly loud and obtrusive word—whether spoken or written—but the corresponding internal process as well. "Someone Too" remarks: "The higher is of course always self-evident! The basis, the preconditions, must be worked out." The big decision, the momentous situation, "the upper floor" (Vischer)—without a lot of words that is clear, self-evident, simple. However, what is difficult, problematic, and demands the highest attention is "the lower floor" of "dissonant obstructions," of disorders and accidents; "I cannot calculate them or organize them, they bounce all over the place and are completely unpredictable . . . since there is no plan for what is planless,

365 no system for what is unsystematic," sighs "Someone Too." In other words, it is the arena of everyday life that presents the fundamental difficulties, and which one has to have first experienced in order to sense how insufficient, inappropriate, and unsuitable it is to address it with general moral principles. Whether to help someone who is in trouble or whether to confront someone who is cruel to animals is not a problem for "Auch Einer," "it is self-evident." However, it is something else to cope with the small issues of daily life, with "sniffles," for example, or with the "fickleness," "the tendentiousness of the object," in short, with the countless cases in which what is great and governed by principle is "frustrated" by what is peripheral, trifling, contrary, and irritating.

    The "ethical" as a topic has its particular time and its particular place. This is so because human beings are living and mortal creatures in a finite

---

4. ["The name of this character, '*Auch Einer*,' is as unusual in German as it is in English. The German suggests a person who is ignored or treated slightingly but who insists on being taken seriously, saying, in effect, 'I am someone too,'" *DBWE* 6:364, n. 4.]

and fragile world. They are not essentially and exclusively students of ethics. It is part of the great naïveté or, more accurately, folly of ethicists to overlook this fact willfully, and to start from the fictional assumption that human beings at every moment of their lives have to make an ultimate, infinite choice; as if every moment of life would require a conscious decision between good and evil; as if every human action were labeled with a sign, written by divine police in bold letters, saying "Permitted" or "Prohibited"; as if human beings incessantly had to do something decisive, fulfill a higher purpose, meet an ultimate duty. This attitude is a misjudgment of historical human existence in which everything has its time (Ecclesiastes 3)—eating, drinking, sleeping, as well as conscious decision making and acting, working and resting, serving a purpose and just being without purpose, meeting obligations and following inclinations, striving and playing, abstaining and rejoicing. It is the presumptuous misjudgment of this creaturely existence that must drive a person either into the most mendacious hypocrisy or into madness. Indeed, it turns the ethicist into a dangerous pest and tyrant, into a fool or a tragicomical figure.

366

The so-called ethical phenomenon, that is, "the experience of the ought," the conscious fundamental decision between what is good in principle and what is evil in principle, the orientation of life toward a highest norm, the ethical conflict and its resolution—this certainly has its necessary place and time within human existence. And why should it not be allowed and necessary to take it up as a topic within these limits? However, precisely these proper limits of space and time are of crucial importance, if one is to prevent that unhealthy takeover of life by the ethical, that abnormal fanaticizing, that total moralizing of life, which leads to a constantly interrupting stream of judging or exhorting comments, to interfering, and to an unsolicited meddling with the activities of concrete life that are not governed by fundamental principles. In the sense just described, the "ethical phenomenon" is misunderstood in its essence if one understands the unconditional quality of the experience of the ought as an exclusive claim on the totality of life. This claim would injure and destroy the creaturely integrity of life. The limitation of the ethical phenomenon to its place and time does not imply its rejection but, on the contrary, its validation. One does not use canons to shoot sparrows.

The ethical phenomenon is a boundary event,[5] both in its content and as an experience. According to both its content and the experience, the

367

---

5. ["See *DBWE* 6:273–274 (*Reader* 647–648), on 'borderline cases' in contrast to the normal state of affairs," *DBWE* 6:366, n. 14.]

"ought" only belongs where something *is not*, either because it *cannot* be or because it is not *willed*. The fact that I live within the community of a family, of a marriage, within an order of work and of property, is primarily a freely accepted bond, in which the "ethical phenomenon," the ought, is dormant and not apparent in its objective and subjective sides.[6] Only where the community disintegrates or where the order is endangered does the ought raise its voice, only to recede and fall silent again, once the order has been restored. However, it falls silent only in its acute form as concrete demand and accusation. But given the experience, born of the concrete disintegration of community, that any community is in a real sense always disintegrating, from now on the ought accompanies human life as an awareness of its own boundary, that is, as self-restraint, as resignation, or as "humility" in the mundane sense of the word; this is the secular analogy of the doctrine of original sin. However, in its acute as in its permanent form, the ought merely defines a boundary situation, both with regard to its content and as an experience. It always means an inner dissolution of the ought if the boundary concept is turned into a pedagogical tool or method. The ought is always an "ultimate" word. Wherever it is taken up as a topic, its character as qualitatively "ultimate" must always be preserved. Depending on the circumstances, it may very well be the case that this qualitatively "ultimate" character is best preserved by not making it a topic for discussion since "it is self-evident." Wherever the ought, as something self-evident, is turned into a topic for discussion, it will all too easily lose its character as ultimate and become something penultimate, a method.[7]

368   There are undoubtedly situations and times in which what is moral is not self-evident, be it because it is not done or because its content has become questionable. During such periods the ethical becomes a topic for discussion. This results, on the one hand, in a refreshing simplification of the problems of life, in a return to basics, in a necessity to make clear personal decisions and take a stand. Under such circumstances, the discussion will be determined more strongly than usual by dispositions, value judgments, convictions, declamations, and outbursts of natural indignation and unqualified admiration. What happens is a general reduction to what is fundamental and therefore simple. Interest in the actual multifaceted and

---

6. ["The objective side refers to an ethical imperative, 'You ought,' the subjective to ethical obligation, 'I ought,'" *DBWE* 6:367, n. 16.]

7. ["Regarding method, see *DBWE* 6:149–150 and 167 (*Reader* 615–616, 628). The distinction between the ultimate and the penultimate was spelled out *DBWE* 6:149–153 (*Reader* 615–619), and is presupposed here," *DBWE* 6:367, n. 18.]

complex processes of life recedes strongly behind fundamental principles. Sociologically, this means casting aside an upper class with its mainly intellectual, relativistic, and individualistic point of view, and the framing of the topic that this group dictates. The topic of public discussion has become understandable by all so that everyone can participate. A decent disposition suffices to form community over against intellectual and material corruptibility. However, no matter how purifying, renewing, and necessary for the human community such times may be in which the ethical becomes a topic for discussion, nevertheless they can always be regarded only as necessary emergency situations—precisely because of the nature of *this* topic. If extended beyond their necessary duration, they become disastrous in many ways: the ethical ceases to be understood as the "ultimate" word. It is replaced by a flat-footed moralizing and a homespun pedagogical approach to all of life. This leads to a dull monotony and uniformity in all questions of life, to a trivial reduction of all cultural functions to a primitive level, and to a forced leveling of mind and society. Consequently it is not only the richness of life that suffers a significant loss, but also the nature of the ethical itself. Times when the ethical became, and needed to become, a topic for discussion must be followed by times when what is moral is once again self-evident; when one does not merely operate at the boundaries but in the center and richness of daily life. This is true for the life of the individual no less than for the human community. Viewed sociologically, the persistent effort to hold on to the ethical as a topic beyond its appropriate time springs from the frustrated desire for continued prestige by those who have excellent attitudes but who are ineffectual in life. During times of social transformation, when the ethical was a topic for debate, history offered them the chance to prove themselves not only by their character but by their achievements; but they missed it. Now "that morality is again self-evident" and no longer a topic for discussion, they see their opportunities in life dwindling and so persist in ethical debate, thereby excluding themselves definitively from the process of life. What has been spelled out here about human society has its exact analogy in individual life. Desperately clutching to the ethical topic, in the form of the moralization of life, results from fear of the richness of daily life and from awareness of being ineffectual in life; it is retreating to a position on the sidelines of real life from which one can now only look at life itself with arrogance and envy at the same time. Thus it should have become clear that what has been lost here is not only life, but also the essence of the ethical, precisely because it was wrongly made into a topic of ongoing debate.

369

Now, after all this, what is an "ethic," since by definition it treats the ethical as a topic for debate? And what is an "ethicist"? First of all, it is easier to say what an ethic and an ethicist definitely cannot be. An ethic cannot be a book in which is written out how everything in the world really ought to be, but unfortunately is not. Likewise, an ethicist cannot be a person who always knows better than others what is to be done and how it is to be done. An ethic cannot be a reference manual that guarantees flawless moral behavior, and an ethicist cannot be the competent appraiser and judge of every human action. An ethic cannot be a chemist's laboratory for producing the ethical and Christian person, and the ethicist cannot be the embodiment and the ideal type of a fundamentally moral life.

370

Ethics and ethicists do not constantly meddle in life, but rather draw attention to the disturbance and disruption that all of life experiences from its boundary through the ought. Ethics and the ethicist do not intend to describe being good as such, that is, as an end in itself. Instead, precisely because they speak strictly from the perspective of the "ethical," from the ought that is experienced at the boundary, they intend to make room for the ethical and thus help people *learn to live with others*.[8]

To learn to live with others within the boundaries of the ought means not standing outside the processes of life as a spectator, critic, or judge. Living with others means not being motivated by the ought but by the richness of life's impulses, by what is natural and has grown, by what is freely affirmed and willed. It does not mean humorless hostility against the art of living, against any weakness and disorder. Living with others does not consist of the suspicious, watchful measuring of what is by what ought to be, nor in the anxious subordination of everything natural to the requirements of duty, of everything free to what is necessary, of everything concrete to the general, of everything without purpose to a purpose—so that finally, in a grotesque transgression of the boundary of the "ethical," the concluding paragraph of one Christian ethic has to be called "Morally Permitted Relaxation" (Wilhelm Herrmann)! Living with others means living within the boundaries of the ought—though not motivated at all by the ought—in the midst of the abundance of the concrete tasks and processes of life with their infinite variety of motives. Setting aside for now many of the problems that have already been raised, we will initially stay with our guiding question about how the ethical is determined by time and place,[9] and add a few qualifications to what has already been said.

371

---

8. ["See the major's speech on the theme of living with others in Bonhoeffer, *DBWE* 7:167–170 (*Reader* 758–760)," *DBWE* 6:370, n. 27.]

9. ["See *DBWE* 6:365 (*Reader* 668–669)," *DBWE* 6:371, n. 29.]

Timeless and placeless ethical discourse lacks the concrete *authorization* that any genuine ethical discourse requires. It is the youthful, presumptuous, usurping declamation of ethical principles that, in spite of the subjective seriousness with which it is presented, contradicts the essence of genuine ethical discourse—in a way that is perhaps difficult to define but is nevertheless clearly perceptible. Although one often cannot challenge the correctness of the abstractions, generalizations, and theories, they nevertheless lack the specific weight of ethical statements. The words are correct, but they have no weight. In the end they will be perceived not as helpful but as chaotic. Due to some dim but irresistible notion of the way things are, it is simply not possible, out of order, not appropriate to the situation at hand, if, within the circle of those who are experienced and advanced in years, the young person declaims ethical generalities. Young people will again and again find themselves in a situation that is so irritating, astounding, and incomprehensible to them that their word falls on deaf ears, while the word of an older person is heard and has weight even though its content is no different at all. It will be a sign of maturity or immaturity whether this experience leads them to understand that what is at stake here is not the stubborn self-satisfaction of old age, or the anxious effort to keep youth in their place, but the preservation or violation of an essential ethical law. Ethical discourse needs authorization, which youth are simply not able to bestow upon themselves, even if they speak out of the purest pathos of their ethical conviction. Ethical discourse does not merely depend on the correct content of what is said, but also on the speaker being authorized to say it. Its validity depends not only on what is said, but also on who says it.

Now what is this authorization, on whom is it bestowed, and who bestows it?   372

This authorization, without which no ethical discourse is possible, necessarily involves a concrete limitation of ethical discourse. It is not possible to speak ethically in a vacuum, that is, in the abstract, but only within a concrete bond of mutual relationship. Thus ethical discourse is not a system of statements that are true as such, and which would be at the disposal of everyone, at every time, and everywhere. Instead it is intrinsically bound to persons, times, and places. This specific determination does not diminish the import of ethical discourse, but is the very source of its authorization and weight, whereas the ethical is weakened to the point of powerlessness when it is left unspecific and generally applicable.

No one can give themselves authorization for ethical discourse. Rather, it is granted to and bestowed on people, not primarily because of their subjective achievements and distinctions, but because of their objective position in the world. Thus it is the old person and not the young, the parent and

not the child, the master and not the servant, the teacher and not the student, the judge and not the defendant, the governing authority and not the subject, the preacher and not the parishioner, to whom the authorization for ethical discourse is granted. This is an expression of the *orientation from above to below*, which is an intrinsic and essential quality of the ethical, even though it is so highly offensive to the modern mind. Without this objective
373   order of above and below, and without the courage to be "above"—which modern people have so completely lost—ethical discourse degenerates into generalities and vacuous talk, and forfeits its character as ethical.

The ethical is thus not a principle that levels, invalidates, and shatters all human order. Instead, it inherently involves a certain order of human community and entails certain sociological relationships of authority.[10] Only in their context does the ethical manifest itself and receive the concrete authorization that is essential to it.

These assertions stand in stark contrast to the understanding of the ethical as a generally valid rational principle that entails the negation of everything concrete and specific to time and place, of all relationships based on order and authority, and instead proclaims the equality of all human beings, based on innate universal human reason. The real goal of this new conception of the ethical was overcoming a fossilized form of society, characterized by hostility between the privileged and the nonprivileged, in favor of a universal fraternity of all people. As one must recognize and as the history of the last 150 years has made abundantly clear, not only has this goal not been achieved, it has in fact turned into its opposite. Lacking any element of concretion, the view of the ethical as something formal, universally valid, and rational inevitably led to the complete atomization of human community and individual life, to unbounded subjectivism and individualism. Wherever the ethical is construed as apart from any determination by time and place, apart from the question of authorization, and apart from anything concrete, there life disintegrates into an infinite number of unrelated atoms of time, just as human community disintegrates into discrete atoms of reason. It is basically the same thing whether one understands the ethical as that which is strictly formal and universally valid, or as the "existential"
374   decision of the individual to be made ever and again, entirely anew in each "moment." The common foundation of both views is a destruction of the ethical by detaching it from its concrete determination. In fact, the ethical is not essentially a formal principle of reason, but a concrete relationship

---

10. ["See *DBWE* 6:287 (*Reader* 658): 'relationships based on obedience and dependence' and 'free responsibility,'" *DBWE* 6:373, n. 35.]

based on a command;[11] furthermore, formal reason is not a community-generating principle, but an atomizing one. Community consists only in the concrete and infinitely varied relationships in which human beings are responsible for one another. On the other hand, one must not simply throw overboard advances in understanding the ethical that were gained during the Enlightenment. Understood polemically, the Enlightenment remains correct in criticizing a system in which society fell into the privileged and the nonprivileged classes. The ethical is indeed related to universal human reason, and the orientation from above to below inherent in the ethical is indeed anything but a sanctioning of privileges. The Enlightenment was perfectly correct in pointing out that the ethical is not concerned with an abstract social order, with representatives of particular social classes, with "above" and "below" as such, but with *people*. It is consequently also correct in the passion with which it insists on the *equal dignity of all people* as ethical beings. It is incorrect only where it moves beyond these polemical statements and once again turns human beings into an abstraction with which to assail any human order in the name of the equality and dignity of human beings. It is incorrect when it turns human reason—the essence of which consists of the free perception and assertion of reality, which in this context means of concrete ethical statements—into a formal, abstract principle that dissolves and undermines all particular content. Against any attempt to misuse the ethical for the sanctioning of privileges, it is nevertheless important to keep the corrective of the Enlightenment in mind.

However, fear of the misuse of the ethical must not lead us simply to ignore the orientation from above to below that is inherent in the ethical. We cannot avoid the fact that the ethical demands a clear ordering of above and below. This means that above and below are not simply interchangeable depending on the individuals involved, their respective qualities and achievements. Being above does not consist in the subjective and personal value of the one who is above, but instead has its legitimization in a concrete, objective commission. The master craftsman remains the master of his apprentice, even if the apprentice is more talented, and the father remains the father of his son, even if the son is more worthy or competent. The authorization for ethical discourse remains with the master or the father, regardless of the subjective and personal side of the matter in question. The authorization belongs not to the person but to the office.

375

11. ["See *DBWE* 6:378 (*Reader* 678–679), where Bonhoeffer notes that the 'ethical' as a relationship based on a command differs from the commandment of God in that the latter 'not only prohibits and commands, but also gives permission,'" *DBWE* 6:374, n. 39.]

This implies at the same time that ethical discourse presupposes a certain duration and stability of these relationships of authority. Genuine ethical discourse involves more than a one-time pronouncement. It needs repetition and continuity; it demands time. This is precisely the burden, but also the dignity and credibility, of ethical discourse. One-time pronunciamentos [*pronouncements*] are nothing. The authorization for ethical discourse proves itself in loyalty, trustworthiness, duration, and repetition.

But all this is possible only on the basis of an inner affirmation of, and perseverance in, the relationship of above and below. Each is possible only in conjunction with the other. Only by affirming and persevering in being above is it possible to affirm and persevere in being below, and vice versa. Genuine ethical discourse ceases to exist, and ethical chaos is already breaking in, wherever one no longer dares to be above and where one "considers oneself too good" to be below, where being above seeks its rationale entirely from below—that is, where parents derive their authority from the trust of the children or a government's authority derives from its popularity—and, correspondingly, where being below is always seen merely as waiting in line for being above, that is, as what explodes any being above at all. The demand for an inner affirmation of, and perseverance in, being both above and below thus raises the crucial question *about the basis of the authorization* for ethical discourse; and with this question the ethical *reaches decisively beyond itself.*

While the exposition thus far may be understood—in our opinion, rightly so—as a general phenomenology of the ethical,[12] we have now encountered an ultimately decisive question that is beyond the ethical-phenomenological level. *What is the basis of the concrete authorization for ethical discourse?* Two answers immediately come to mind: either the authorization for ethical discourse is found positivistically in existing reality without any further attempt to interpret it, or one creates a system of orders and values within which authorization is ascribed to the parent, the master, the government. It is clear that the positivistic rationale is on shaky ground, since at any particular point it has no criterion beyond the given reality, which could always change. In addition, the positivistic rationale is bound to fail in its attempt to draw boundaries between the different authorities, such as government, parent, teacher, or church, which claim for themselves the authorization for ethical discourse. Instead, the actual *power* will come to be seen as the sole standard for *authorization* here. Positivism is thus unable to

---

12. ["See *DBWE* 6:366 (*Reader* 669), on the so-called ethical phenomenon ('the experience of the ought') . . . ," *DBWE* 6:376, n. 45.]

provide a rationale for the ethical. The approach that might initially seem more useful is the attempt to develop a system of authorities and orders. 377 This has been tried again and again by Christian philosophers, especially in the nineteenth century by the conservative Romantics, particularly Julius Stahl, and in the twentieth century by the Roman Catholic Max Scheler. Compared to the positivist approach, the advantage is obvious: here there are criteria that go beyond what is positively given for ordering and authorizing the authorities. These criteria are of a religious or, more precisely, of a Christian nature. The concrete authorities are divinely instituted; they are *direct manifestations of the divine will,* which demands submission. With such an approach one admittedly gains a certain independence from the shaky ground of what is positively and empirically given. On the other hand, however, the empirical positivism is replaced here by a metaphysical-religious positivism. For this reason alone, this approach will likewise fail to differentiate the different authorities and authorizations from one another without being arbitrary. Either the idea of the state, or that of parenthood, or that of the church becomes the dominant principle. The competitive struggle, which arises from the direct divine institution of the various authorities, is resolved by a more or less arbitrary decision in favor of the absolute claim of one of these authorities. Systematic construction or metaphysical deduction paralyzes real life.

Thus the question about the ground of the concrete authorization for ethical discourse still remains open. The question why the ethical must not be understood as a timeless principle, but instead as specific to time and place, therefore remains open as well. Finally, the question as to how and within what limits the "ethical" can become a topic also remains open.

We are thus led beyond the "ethical" to the only possible subject matter 378 of a "Christian ethic," namely, the *"commandment of God."*

In what was said about the "ethical" we have, perhaps unawares, hit upon bedrock, that is, upon a piece of the commandment of God itself.

The commandment of God is something different from what we have thus far described as the "ethical." It encompasses all of life. It is not only unconditional, it is also total. It not only prohibits and commands, but also gives permission. It not only binds but also sets free—in fact, it does so precisely by binding. Nevertheless, in a sense that still needs to be explained, the "ethical" belongs to the commandment. *The commandment is the sole authorization for ethical discourse.*

The commandment of God is the total and concrete claim of human beings by the merciful and holy God in Jesus Christ. Although at this point we cannot yet develop a general doctrine of the commandment of God, we will define those key points that are most important for our context.

The commandment of God is not, in distinction from the ethical, the most general summation of all ethical rules. It is not timeless and generally valid as opposed to being historical and temporal. It is not the principle as opposed to its application, not the abstract as opposed to the concrete, not the indeterminate as opposed to the determinate. If it were anything of the kind, it would have ceased to be the commandment of *God*. For in each case it would then be up to us to turn the indeterminate into the determinate, the principle into the application, the timeless into the temporal. At precisely the crucial point it would no longer be the commandment that is decisive, but instead our understanding, our interpretation, our application. Then the commandment of God would again have become our own choice.

God's commandment is God's speech to human beings. Both in its content and in its form, it is concrete speech to concrete human beings. God's
379   commandment leaves human beings no room for application and interpretation, but only for obedience or disobedience. God's commandment cannot be found and known apart from time and place; indeed, it can only be *heard* by one who is bound to a specific place and time. God's commandment is either utterly specific, clear, and concrete or it is not God's commandment.

Just as specifically as God spoke to Abraham and Jacob and Moses, and just as specifically as God spoke in Jesus Christ to the disciples, and to the congregations through the apostles, so God speaks just as specifically to us, or God does not speak at all. Does this mean that in every moment of our lives we could come to know the will of God through some kind of special, direct divine inspiration, that in every moment God would unmistakably and unambiguously mark a specific action, as willed by God, with the "accent of eternity"? No, this is not what it means. For the concreteness of the divine commandment consists in its historicity; it encounters us in historical form. Does this now mean that we are after all, with a final uncertainty, at the mercy of all sorts of claims that historical powers place on us, that with regard to God's commandment we actually grope around in the dark? No, this is not what it means, precisely because God makes the commandment heard in a specific, historical form.

380   The question has now become inevitable as to where, or rather in what historical form, God issues the commandment. For the sake of simplicity and clarity, and despite the danger of being seriously misunderstood, we will initially answer this question in the form of a thesis: *the commandment of God revealed in Jesus Christ is addressed to us in the church, in the family, in work, and in government.*

The thesis is based on the presupposition, which initially is not fully comprehensible but must always be kept in mind, that God's commandment always is and always remains the commandment of God revealed in Jesus Christ. There is no other commandment of God than the one God has actually revealed, and it pleased God to reveal it in Jesus Christ.

This means that the commandment of God does not arise out of the created world, but rather comes from above to below. It does not result from the actual claim made on human beings by earthly powers and laws, such as the instinct for self-preservation, hunger, sexuality, or political power, but instead stands beyond them, demanding and judging. The commandment of God institutes an irrevocable above and below on earth, independent of the actual relationship of these powers. Through this, it confers the authorization for ethical discourse of which we have spoken above, or, to put it more comprehensively, the authorization to proclaim the divine commandment.

Because the commandment of God is the commandment revealed in Jesus Christ, no individual authority among those authorized to proclaim the commandment can absolutize itself. Only insofar as church, family, work, and government mutually limit each other, insofar as each is beside and together with the others, upholding the commandment of God each in its own way, are they authorized from above to speak. None of these authorities can identify itself alone with the commandment of God. The sovereignty of the commandment of God proves itself precisely in ordering these authorities in a relationship of being with each other, beside each other, together with each other, and over against each other so that the commandment of God as the commandment revealed in Jesus Christ is upheld only in these multifaceted concrete relationships and limitations.[13]   381

The commandment of God as the commandment revealed in Jesus Christ is always a concrete speaking *to* someone, and never an abstract speaking *about* something or someone. It always addresses and claims the hearer in such a comprehensive and at the same time definitive way that it no longer permits the freedom of interpretation and application, but only the freedom of obedience or disobedience.

The commandment of God revealed in Jesus Christ embraces life as a whole. It does not merely guard, like the ethical, the boundaries of life that must not be crossed, but it is at the same time the center and fullness of life. It is not only ought, but also allowed. It not only prohibits, but also liberates us for authentic life and for unreflective doing. It not only interrupts the life

---

13. ["The totalitarian claim of the National Socialist regime eliminated the possibility that church, family, work, and government could mutually limit and foster one another, since everything was subjected to the power of the state, and was no longer supposed to have an independent status," *DBWE* 6:381, n. 60.]

process whenever it goes astray, but it accompanies and guides it without our needing to be consciously aware of it. The commandment of God becomes the daily divine guidance of our lives. To illustrate this with an example: in the relationship of children to their parents, God's commandment is not just the threatening and judging warning directed against children who rebel against their parents, but it meets children, and accompanies and guides them through all the innumerable situations in which they honor and love their parents in daily life. God's commandment exists not only in the solemn form of the Fourth Commandment, for example, but also in the form of everyday words, admonitions, and requests for some kind of concrete behavior and activity within the community of the family. This does not imply a fragmentation but, quite the contrary, the comprehensive unity of God's command and at the same time its consummate concreteness. It means that the commandment prevents life from dis-integrating into innumerable new beginnings, but instead gives it a clear direction, an internal steadiness, and a firm sense of security. The commandment of God becomes the element "in" which one lives, even without always being aware of it. The commandment as the element of life means freedom of movement and activity, freedom from fear to act or to make a decision. It means certainty, calm, confidence, equanimity, joy. I honor my parents, keep my marriage vows, and respect the life and property of others not because of a menacing "You shall not" at the boundaries of my life, but because I myself affirm the given realities of parents, marriage, life, and property that I find in the center and fullness of life as God's holy institution.[14] Only when the commandment not only threatens me as a transgressor of the boundaries but also convinces me and wins me over by its actual content does it free me from the anxiety and uncertainty when making a decision. When I love my wife and affirm marriage as instituted by God, then my marriage acquires an inner freedom and a confidence of how to live and act that no longer suspiciously observes every step I make nor calls my every action into question. The divine prohibition of adultery is then no longer the focal point of all I think and do in my marriage—*as if the meaning and purpose of marriage consisted in avoiding adultery!* Rather, marriage as kept and freely affirmed, which means moving beyond the prohibition of adultery, is actually the prerequisite for fulfilling the divine commission of marriage. Here the divine commandment has become permission to live married life freely and confidently.

382

---

14. ["... See Bonhoeffer's April 30, 1944, letter: 'not on the boundaries but in the center' (*DBWE* 8:366 [*Reader* 779–780])," *DBWE* 6:382, n. 64.]

The commandment of God is permission to live before God as a human being.

God's commandment is *permission*. It is distinguished from all human laws in that it *commands freedom*. It proves itself as *God's* commandment in   383
that it eliminates this contradiction, in that the impossible becomes possible, and in that it really commands what lies beyond anything that can be commanded, namely, freedom. This is the lofty aim of God's commandment. It is not any less costly. Permission, freedom, does not mean that God now concedes to human beings a field where, after all, they could exercise their own choice, free from God's commandment. Rather, this permission, this freedom, is in fact generated precisely by God's commandment; it is possible only through and within God's commandment. It is never detached from God's commandment. It remains *God's* permission. As such, and only as such, does it free us from the tormenting anxiety of how to decide and act in a particular case, and make us confident that we are personally led and guided by the divine commandment. The rejection by Kant and Fichte of the "permitted" as an ethical concept is appropriate if what is permitted is understood as that which is neutral, independent of, and indifferent toward the commandment of God. However, their rejection is mistaken if it seeks to eliminate the concept of God's permission, the permission that arises from God's commandment, in favor of a pure concept of duty that will always prove too narrow to encompass and support the whole of human life.

God's commandment permits human beings to live as human beings before God—as human beings, not merely as the makers of ethical decisions, as students of ethics. What this entails can best be expressed with the verses by Matthias Claudius entitled "Human Beings":

Conceived and nurtured—by women wondrously
They come and see and listen—oblivious to illusion
Have longings and desires—and weep their little tears
Despise and venerate—feel danger and delight   384
Believe, doubt, err, and teach—deem all and nothing true
Are building and destroying—and struggle evermore
Sleep, waken, grow, and wither—with brown or graying hair
And all of this continues at most for eighty years.[15]

---

15. ["Matthias Claudius's poem, published in *Der Wandsbecker Bote*, includes after 'graying hair': 'etc.' (Part 4, 470)," *DBWE* 6:384, n. 68.]

The temporality, the fullness, and the frailty of human life has found an incomparable expression here. It is *this* life we have in mind when speaking about the commandment of God, and it is precisely *this* life of which the "ethical" knows nothing. The "ethical" can always only seek to interrupt this life, to confront it anew at any given moment with the conflict between its duties. The "ethical" can always only make this life questionable to itself. It can only dissolve it into countless individual decisions. The *flow* of life from conception to the grave is incomprehensible to the ethical, since it is "pre-ethical." The motives of actions are inscrutable, everything we do is interwoven with something conscious and subconscious, natural and supernatural, with inclination and duty, with the egotistical and the altruistic, the intended and inevitable, the active and passive, so that each deed is simultaneously an act of enduring, something done to oneself,[16] just as each enduring is also a doing—all this is reprehensible and abominable to the "ethical." In all circumstances the "ethical" seeks clarity, straightforwardness, purity, a conscious awareness of human motives and deeds; it dissects the knotted growth of life. God's commandment allows human beings to be human before God. It lets the flow of life take its course, lets human beings eat, drink, sleep, work, celebrate, and play without interrupting those activities,[17] without ceaselessly confronting them with the question whether they were actually permitted to sleep, eat, work, and play, or whether they did not have more urgent duties. God's commandment does not make human beings the critics and judges of themselves and their deeds, but allows them to live and act with the certainty and confidence of being guided by the divine commandment. The self-tormenting and hopeless question about the purity of one's motives, suspicious self-observation, the blazing and wearisome light of ceaseless conscious awareness—all this has nothing to do with God's commandment, which grants freedom to live and act. Permission to live through God's commandment includes the fact that the roots of human life and action are hidden in darkness, that doing and enduring are inextricably intertwined. Light falls into this life only by taking hold of this divine permission, that is, only from above.

Vis-à-vis God's commandment, a human being is not Hercules standing in perpetuity at a crossroads, struggling forever to make the right decision, someone worn out by conflicting duties, again and again failing and

385

---

16. ["Regarding 'active and passive,' see *DBWE* 6:226; regarding 'doing' and 'enduring,' see *DBWE* 4:145 (*Reader* 502–503), and *DBWE* 6:336–338," *DBWE* 6:384, n. 70.]

17. ["See *DBWE* 6:370 (*Reader* 672), on the 'disruption' of all of life 'from its boundary' and *DBWE* 6:381 (*Reader* 679–716), which states that the commandment not only 'interrupts,' but also 'accompanies . . . ,'" *DBWE* 6:384, n. 72.]

starting anew.[18] Nor does God's commandment show itself only in those momentous, turbulent, and utterly conscious moments of crisis in life. Rather, vis-à-vis God's commandment human beings are allowed to be actually on the way (rather than always hesitating at a crossroads). They are allowed to know the proper decision as something that is truly behind them (and not just as something with which they are always faced). They are allowed, entirely without any inner conflict, to do one thing and not the other—which perhaps is equally urgent from the perspective of a theoretical ethic. They are allowed to have already moved past the beginning, and to be guided, accompanied, and guarded on their way by the commandment as by a good angel. And God's commandment itself can now give life unified direction and personal guidance, in the form of everyday seemingly small and insignificant words, sentences, hints, and aids.

386

The commandment's goal is not avoiding transgression, not the agony of ethical conflict and decision, but rather the freely affirmed, self-evident life in church, marriage, family, work, and state. The "ethical" merely identifies the limits formally and negatively, and thus can only become a topic at the boundary, and in a formal and negative way. God's commandment, on the other hand, is concerned with the positive content and with the freedom of human beings to affirm that positive content. God's commandment as a topic of a Christian ethic is thus possible only by simultaneously paying attention both to its positive content and to human freedom. Neither a casuistry that predetermines concrete cases at the expense of human freedom, nor a formal doctrine of freedom at the expense of the positive content,[19] can do justice to the commandment as the topic of a Christian ethic. While the final goal of the "ethical" was to delimit and create space for living together in the whole fullness of life, the commandment is concerned with "living together" itself in its concrete contents, and with the human freedom that is made possible in and through these contents. But this makes clear that God's commandment encompasses the "ethical" as well. The critical point here is that we do not claim the reverse, namely, that the ethical would also comprise the commandment. For in that case the commandment, treated as the secondary element, would be nothing more than the special case, the concrete "application," of the ethical, whereas the commandment in its concrete content and in the human freedom it enables is, in fact, the original and primary element. Out of its own content

---

18. ["See the line in the 1943 drama fragment: 'You can't start life all over every day' *DBWE* 7:67," *DBWE* 6:385, n. 74.]

19. ["See *DBWE* 6: 99–100 on 'formalism and casuistry' . . . ," *DBWE* 6:386, n. 77.]

it sets the boundary and creates the space within which it can be heard and fulfilled. The boundary originates from the center and fullness of the life lived with the commandment of God, not vice versa.

387   If now we finally replace the philosophical concept of the "ethical" with the biblical concept of the "law," the result is that commandment and law belong inextricably together, although they must also be distinguished from each other. It also follows that the law is included within the commandment, originating from it, and is to be understood from it.

Thus the following reflections naturally organize themselves into two parts: 1. The Concrete Commandment of God; 2. The Law.[20]

---

20. [*The manuscript ends here.*]

38. The Concrete Commandment
and the Divine Mandates

DBWE 6:388–408

This Ethics *essay marks the end point of Bonhoeffer's long engagement with the Lutheran doctrine of divine orders. Luther himself held that God created three orders to organize human life and maintain justice in the world: daily life (which included marriage and family as well as livelihood), worldly government, and the church.*[1] *During Bonhoeffer's lifetime, Lutheran theologians bent this doctrine in nationalist directions, arguing that the* Volk *(people, nation, or race) was an order of creation. Bonhoeffer himself drew on this way of thinking in an early Barcelona lecture, appealing to the divine order of* Volk *to justify war.*[2] *But by the early 1930s he became critical of such "orders of creation" and adopted instead the term "orders of preservation." The theological motivation for this shift is nicely captured in* Creation and Fall: *"All orders of our fallen world are God's orders of preservation that uphold and preserve us for Christ. They are not orders of creation but orders of preservation. They have no value in themselves; instead they find their end and meaning only through Christ."*[3] *Here he rejects the idea that God's will could be read directly from nature or history; fallen creation can be rightly understood only in its relationship to Christ. Bonhoeffer shifted terminology again in* Ethics *and related writings, speaking of four "divine mandates": marriage (and family), work (or culture), government, and church.*[4] *With the language of mandates, Bonhoeffer maintained the christological orientation of the orders of preservation but now emphasized God's command: mandates are the historical-social forms of God's command for ordering worldly life.*

---

1. [*Wright,* Martin Luther's Understanding of God's Two Kingdoms, *130–131.*]
2. [DBWE *10:371* (Reader *84–85*).]
3. [DBWE *3:140. See also,* DBWE *11:267–268.*]
4. [*In addition to the present essay, Bonhoeffer discusses mandates in* DBWE *16:502–528* (Reader *699–716*), DBWE *6:65–74, and 380–387* (Reader *678–684*).]

The doctrine of the divine orders has traditionally been a locus for dealing theologically with the relationship of church and state. In continuity with this, the next selection ("State and Church") treats government as a divine order. The present selection has implications for church-state issues especially in the discussion of the mandates as limited and mutually limiting. (They are with-one-another, for-one-another, and over-against-one-another, as Bonhoeffer puts it.) This framework sharply diverges from the totalitarian vision of the state articulated by National Socialism and accepted by the German Christians, where the church, and indeed all spheres of life, was to be subsumed under the authority of the state.

It seems that Bonhoeffer intended in this essay to treat all four divine mandates, but the manuscript includes only a discussion of the church. Bonhoeffer's arrest on April 5, 1943, interrupted his work at this point.[5]

388   The commandment of God revealed in Jesus Christ embraces in its unity all of human life. Its claim on human beings and the world through the reconciling love of God is all-encompassing. This commandment encounters us concretely in four different forms that find their unity only in the commandment itself, namely, in the church, marriage and family, culture, and government.

God's commandment is not to be found anywhere and everywhere, not in theoretical speculation or private enlightenment, not in historical forces or compelling ideals, but only where it gives itself to us. God's commandment can only be spoken with God's own authorization; and only insofar as God authorizes it can the commandment be legitimately declared. God's commandment is to be found not wherever there are historical forces, strong ideals, or convincing insights, but only where there are divine mandates which are grounded in the revelation of Christ. We are dealing with such mandates in the church, in marriage and family, in culture, and in government.

389   By "mandate" we understand the concrete divine commission grounded in the revelation of Christ and the testimony of scripture; it is the authorization and legitimization to declare a particular divine commandment, the conferring of divine authority on an earthly institution. A mandate is to be understood simultaneously as the laying claim to, commandeering of, and formation of a certain earthly domain by the divine command. The bearer of the mandate acts as a vicarious representative, as a stand-in for the one who issued the commission. Understood properly, one could also use the term "order" here, if only the concept did not contain the inherent danger

---

5. [DBWE *6:408, n. 70.*]

of focusing more strongly on the static element of order rather than on the divine authorizing, legitimizing, and sanctioning, which are its sole foundation. This then leads all too easily to a divine sanctioning of all existing orders per se, and thus to a romantic conservatism[6] that no longer has anything to do with the Christian doctrine of the four mandates. If these misinterpretations could be purged from the concept of order, then it would be very capable of expressing the intended meaning in a strong and convincing way. The concept of "estate," which has proven reliable since the time of the Reformation, also suggests itself here. However, in the course of history it has become so obscured that it simply can no longer be employed in its original purity. The word carries too many overtones of human favoritism and of privileges to allow us still to hear its original humble dignity. Finally, the concept of "office" has become so secularized and so closely connected to institutional-bureaucratic thinking that it no longer conveys the solemnity of the divine decree. Lacking a better word we thus stay, for the time being, with the concept of mandate. Nevertheless, our goal, through clarifying the issue itself, is to contribute to renewing and reclaiming the old concepts of order, estate, and office.

390

The divine mandates depend solely on God's *one* commandment as it is revealed in Jesus Christ. They are implanted in the world from above as organizing structures—"orders"—of the reality of Christ, that is, of the reality of God's love for the world and for human beings that has been revealed in Jesus Christ. They are thus in no way an outgrowth of history; they are not earthly powers, but divine commissions. Church, marriage and family, culture, and government can only be explained and understood from above,[7] from God. The bearers of the mandate are not commissioned from below, executing and representing particular expressions of the collective will of human beings. Instead, they are in a strict and unalterable sense God's commissioners, vicarious representatives, and stand-ins. This is true regardless of the particular historical genesis of a church, a family, or a government. Within the domain of the mandates, God's authorization has thus designated an irrevocable above and below.

391

---

6. ["Concerning the 'romantic conservatism' that idealizes the traditional orders and therefore prefers them to anything new, see *DBWE* 6:377 (*Reader* 677). Bonhoeffer also shies away from the term 'order,' presumably due to its use by Paul Althaus and Werner Elert, the Lutheran theologians in Erlangen. On Althaus, see Robert Ericksen, *Theologians under Hitler*, 79–119," *DBWE* 6:389, n. 4.]

7. ["See Bonhoeffer's rendering of John 19:11 in 'State and Church,' in his statement that the power of government is a 'gift from above' (*DBWE* 16:511 [*Reader* 703–704])," *DBWE* 6:390, n. 7.]

God's commandment therefore always seeks to encounter human beings within an earthly relationship of authority, within an order that is clearly determined by above and below. However, this above and below immediately requires a more precise definition: (1) It is not identical with an earthly power relation. Under no circumstances may the more powerful simply invoke the divine mandate in their dealings with the weaker. It is, on the contrary, part of the nature of the divine mandate to correct and order the earthly power relations in its own way. (2) It must further be emphasized that the divine mandate creates not only the above, but in fact also the below. Above and below belong together in an inseparable and mutually delimiting relationship that must still be more precisely defined at a later point. (3) It is true that above and below refer not to a relation between concepts and things, but between persons. However, it is a relation between the kind of people who submit to God's commission, and to it alone, regardless of whether they find themselves above or below. Even a master has a Master, and this fact alone makes him a master and authorizes and legitimizes him vis-à-vis the servant. Master and servant owe one another the respect that springs from their respective participation in God's mandate.

392 Abuse of being below is equal to and just as frequent as the abuse of being above that inflicts injury on the person below. Apart from personal misconduct, the abuse of being above and being below is inevitable when the grounding of both in God's mandate is no longer recognized. Being above is then understood, grasped, and unscrupulously exploited as an arbitrary favor of fate, just as being below is considered an unjust discrimination, and must correspondingly lead to outrage and rebellion. However, those who are below can become conscious of their inherent powers; they can reach the critical moment in which they feel, through a sudden act of insight and self-liberation, the dark forces of destruction, of negation, of doubt, and of rebellion converging upon themselves; in this moment, through these chaotic forces, they feel superior to anything that exists, to anything above. At that very moment the relationship between above and below has been turned on its head. There is no longer an authentic above and below. Instead, those above derive their authorization and legitimization solely from below, and those below regard those who are above—seen from their perspective—merely as the embodied claim of those who are below to get above. Thus those below become an ongoing and inevitable threat to those who are above. Such people can only maintain their position "above" by fomenting ever-increasing unrest below, while at the same time using terror against the rebellious forces at work below. At this stage of inversion and

dissolution the relation between above and below is one of deepest hostility, of mistrust, deception, and envy. In this atmosphere even the purely personal abuse of being above and of being below thrives as never before. Trembling before the forces of rebellion, the fact that an authentic order instituted from above had been possible at all must appear as what it actually is, a miracle. The authentic order of above and below lives out of faith in the commission from "above," in the "Lord" of "lords." Such faith alone   393
banishes the demonic powers,[8] which arise from below. When this faith breaks down, then the entire arrangement that has been implanted in the world from above collapses like a house of cards. Some then say that it was a deception of the people while others claim that it was a miracle. Both groups must nevertheless be astounded by the power of faith.

Only in their being with-one-another, for-one-another, and over-against-one-another do the divine mandates of church, marriage and family, culture, and government communicate the commandment of God as it is revealed in Jesus Christ. None of these mandates exists self-sufficiently, nor can one of them claim to replace all the others. The mandates are *with-one-another* or they are not divine mandates. However, in being with-one-another they are not isolated and separated from one another but oriented toward one another. They are *for-one-another* or they are not God's mandates. But in this being-with-one-another and being-for-one-another, each of them is also limited by the other, and, in the context of being-for-one-   394
another, this limitation is necessarily experienced as a being over-against-one-another. Where *being-over-against-one-another* is no longer present, God's mandate no longer exists.

Being above is thus limited in a threefold way, each of which works differently. It is limited by God who issues the commission, by the other mandates, and by the relation to those below. These limits at the same time also safeguard being above. This safeguard serves to encourage the exercise of the divine mandate, just as the limit is the warning not to transgress it. Safeguard and limit are two sides of the same coin. God safeguards by limiting, and encourages by warning.

We will now deal in sequence first with the commandment of God in each of the four mandates, and then with their being with-one-another, for-one-another, and over-against-one-another.

---

8. ["The opposition in Germany spoke of the demonic in Hitler and the Third Reich . . . ," *DBWE* 6:393, n. 17.]

The Commandment of God in the Church

In the church the commandment of God encounters us in two different ways: in the sermon and in private confession or church discipline, that is, publicly and secretly, addressed to the gathered hearers of the sermon and to the individual human being. Both forms of the divine commandment necessarily belong together. Where private confession or church discipline[9] have been lost, there God's commandment in the sermon is merely understood as a proclamation of general moral principles, which as such are void of any concrete claim. Where, on the other hand, public preaching recedes completely into the background due to the prominence of the confessional, there, although concretion is not in short supply, a dangerous, legalistic casuistry develops, which destroys the freedom of faith. Its inevitable consequence is the ceaseless hidden offering of unsolicited advice to the other divine mandates of family, culture, and government, and the destruction of the free being-with-one-another of the mandates in favor of making the church mandate absolute. There is no doubt that in these two options we have identified the weaknesses of the Protestant and the Roman Catholic churches. The Protestant church lost its concrete ethics when ministers saw themselves no longer permanently confronted with the questions and the responsibilities of the confessional.[10] With a mistaken appeal to Christian freedom, they retreated from the concrete proclamation of the divine commandment. Only by rediscovering the divine office of private confession will the Protestant church find its way back to a concrete ethics, which it possessed during the time of the Reformation. The Roman Catholic priest, through discussion of innumerable "cases"[11] in which he has to make a decision, is prepared throughout his entire studies for his office as father confessor. There is no doubt that this risks the danger of a legalistic and schoolmasterly distortion of the divine commandment. This

395

396

---

9. ["Regarding private confession and church discipline, see the index of subjects of *Discipleship*, under 'confession' (*DBWE* 4:355); both terms, *Beichte*, 'private confession,' and *Gemeindezucht*, 'church discipline,' are included in the subject index that Bonhoeffer personally created for the German original, *Nachfolge*. At the Finkenwalde seminary the candidates were introduced to the meaning of confession and encouraged to observe the practice of personal confession. Church discipline was a subject discussed in the last course at Finkenwalde during 1937 (see *DBWE* 14:815, 825–838)," *DBWE* 6:395, n. 22.]

10. ["See *Life Together*: 'confession is about admitting concrete sins. People usually justify themselves by making general confessions of sin' (*DBWE* 5:113) . . . ," *DBWE* 6:395, n. 23.]

11. ["On casuistry, see *DBWE* 6:99, n. 106," *DBWE* 6:395, n. 24.]

danger can be averted only through a rediscovery of the Christian office of preaching.

Common to both forms of the divine commandment in the church is the fact that they are a *proclamation of divine revelation. Proclamation* is the specific mandate given to the church. God wants a place at which, until the end of the world, God's word is again and again spoken, pronounced, delivered, expounded, and spread. The Word that in Jesus Christ came from heaven wants to come again in the form of human speech. The mandate of the church is the divine word. In this word God wills to be personally present. In the church God is determined to speak in person.

The church proclaims the word of the revelation of God in Jesus Christ. It is thus a word that does not arise out of a human being's own heart, mind, and nature, but that through God's will and mercy descends on human beings from heaven. By its coming it simultaneously establishes a clear counterpoint of above and below. Above there is the office of proclamation, below is the hearing congregation. In the place of God and Jesus Christ the bearers of the preaching office stand, with their proclamation, before the congregation. The preacher is not the mouthpiece of the congregation but instead, if we may use the expression for once, the mouthpiece of God vis-à-vis the congregation. They are authorized to teach, admonish, and comfort, to forgive sins, but also to retain sins. They are at the same time the shepherds, the pastors of the congregation. This office is directly instituted by Jesus Christ, and receives its legitimacy not through the will of the congregation, but through the will of Jesus Christ. It is instituted *within* the congregation, not *by* the congregation.[12] It is coexistent with the congregation. Where this office is fully exercised within the congregation, there all its other offices, which after all can only serve office of the divine word, come alive; for where the word of God governs alone, there faith and service are born. The congregation that awakes under the proclamation of the word of God will prove the authenticity of its faith by honoring the preaching office in its matchless glory and by serving it with all its might, rather than by appealing to its own faith and the priesthood of all believers,[13] thereby showing disrespect for the office, hindering it, or even seeking to make it dependent on the congregation. The preaching office's being above is protected from abuse and danger precisely by a genuine being below of the congregation, that is, by faith, prayer, and service, but not through an undermining and

397

---

12. ["See *DBWE* 4:230 . . . ," *DBWE* 6:397, n. 28.]

13. ["See *Sanctorum Communio* regarding 'the Lutheran doctrine of the priesthood of all believers' (*DBWE* 1:206)," *DBWE* 6:397, n. 29.]

overturning of the divine order and the congregation's wrongful seeking to be above.

The office of proclamation as witness to Jesus Christ is bound to Holy Scripture. Here we must dare to assert that scripture essentially belongs to the preaching office while the sermon belongs to the congregation. Scripture needs to be interpreted and preached. In its essence it is not a devotional book of the congregation. The interpreted sermon text belongs to the congregation and, starting from this basis, there is a "searching in the scriptures . . . to see whether these things were so" (Acts 17:11), as the sermon has proclaimed. Thus, as a borderline case there exists the necessity of contradicting the sermon on the grounds of Holy Scripture.[14] However, even this presupposes that Holy Scripture belongs in essence to the teaching office. When an individual Christian or a group of Christians take hold of Holy Scripture by appealing to the equal rights of all Christians, to their maturity in faith, and to the evidence of the biblical text, this is certainly not yet a sign of exceptional reverence and exceptional spiritual insight into the nature of divine revelation. Instead, it is the breeding ground of much audacity, disorder, rebellion, and spiritual confusion. The holiness of scripture is properly acknowledged by recognizing that it is a grace to be called to interpret and proclaim scripture, and that it is also a grace to be allowed just to be the hearer of the interpretation and proclamation. To say that the book of sermons and the prayer book are the chief books of the congregation, while Holy Scripture is the book of the preacher, may perhaps be an appropriate way of expressing the divine counterpoint of congregation and office. It must be clear, however, that these thoughts do not originate from an arrogant clerical presumption to instruct the masses, but from God's revelation itself.[15]

399   On the basis of Holy Scripture the preaching office proclaims Jesus Christ as the Lord and Savior of the world. There is no legitimate proclamation by the church that is not proclamation of Christ. The church does not have a twofold word, the one general, rational, and grounded in natural law and the other Christian—that is, it does not have one word for unbelievers and another for believers.[16] Only a pharisaical arrogance can

---

14. In a normal case, the examination of the sermon does not belong in the congregation but in the pastoral visitations by the church authorities. It is unhealthy if the congregation is compelled to listen to the sermon always with a critically examining ear.

15. It is self-evident that here we are not dealing with a prohibition to read the Bible, such as the Hindu prohibition of the fourth caste to study the Vedas; rather, we are concerned with the understanding of the intrinsically rightful place of scripture.

16. ["See *DBWE* 6:357, 'On the Possibility of the Church's Message to the World,' regarding the 'rejection of a double morality of the church,'" *DBWE* 6:399, n. 38.]

lead the church to withhold the proclamation of Christ from some but not from others. The word of the church is justified and authorized solely by the commission of Jesus Christ. Therefore any of its words that fail to take this authorization into account must be just empty chatter. For example, let us take the church's encounter with the government, whose mandate is certainly not to confess Christ. Instead, government should be challenged about very specific problems whose remedy is part of its divine mandate. In so doing, however, the church cannot simply cease to be church. Only by fulfilling its own mandate can it legitimately question the government about fulfilling its mandate. The church also does not have a twofold commandment at its disposal, one for the world and one for the Christian congregation. Instead, its commandment is the *one* commandment revealed in Jesus Christ, which it proclaims to the whole world.

The church proclaims this commandment by giving witness to Jesus Christ as the Lord and Savior of Christ's church-community and the world, thus calling everyone into community with Christ.

Jesus Christ, the eternal Son with the Father in eternity—this means that nothing created can be conceived and essentially understood in its nature apart from Christ, the mediator of creation. Everything has been created through Christ and toward Christ, and everything has its existence only in Christ (Col. 1:15ff.). Seeking to understand God's will with creation apart from Christ is futile.

Jesus Christ, the God who became human—this means that God has bodily taken on human nature in its entirety, that from now on divine being can be found nowhere else but in human form, that in Jesus Christ human beings are set free to be truly human before God. Now the "Christian" is not something beyond the human, but it wants to be in the midst of the human.[17] What is "Christian" is not an end in itself, but means that human beings may and should live as human beings before God. In becoming human, God is revealed as the one who seeks to be there not for God's own sake but "for us." To live as a human being before God, in the light of God's becoming human, can only mean to be there not for oneself, but for God and for other human beings.

Jesus Christ, the crucified Reconciler—this means, first, that by its rejection of Jesus Christ the entire world has become godless, and that no effort on its part can lift this curse from it. In the cross of Christ the worldliness of the world has once and for all received its identifying mark. However, Christ's

400

---

17. ["This point is further elaborated in the letters from prison. See Feil, *Theology of Dietrich Bonhoeffer*, 87f., 94; cf. 72–74," *DBWE* 6:400, n. 42.]

cross is the cross of the world's reconciliation with God. Therefore, precisely the godless world simultaneously stands under the identifying mark of reconciliation as freely instituted by God. The cross of reconciliation sets us free to live before God in the midst of the godless world,[18] sets us free to live in genuine worldliness. The proclamation of the cross of reconciliation frees us to abandon futile attempts to deify the world, because it has overcome the divisions, tensions, and conflicts between the "Christian" and the "worldly," and calls us to single-minded action and life in faith in the already accomplished reconciliation of the world with God. A life of genuine worldliness is possible only through the proclamation of the crucified Christ. Thus it is not possible in contradiction to the proclamation, and also

401   not beside it in some kind of autonomy of the worldly; but it is precisely "in, with, and under"[19] the proclamation of Christ that a genuinely worldly life is possible and real. The godlessness and godforsakenness of the world cannot be recognized apart from or in opposition to the proclamation of the cross of Christ, for the worldly will always seek to satisfy its unquenchable desire for its own deification. Where the worldly nevertheless establishes its own law *beside* the proclamation of Christ, there it falls completely under its own spell, and in the end must set itself in God's place. In both cases the worldly ceases to be worldly. Left to its own devices, the worldly is neither willing nor able to be only worldly, but it desperately and frantically seeks its own deification. Consequently it is precisely this decidedly and exclusively worldly life that becomes trapped in a half-hearted pseudo-worldliness. It lacks the freedom and courage for a genuine and full-blown worldliness, that is, the freedom and courage to let the world be what it really is before God, namely, a world that in its godlessness is reconciled with God. The substantive characteristics of this "genuine worldliness" we will have to discuss later. What is decisive here is only *that there is genuine worldliness only and precisely because of the proclamation of the cross of Jesus Christ.*

Jesus Christ, the risen and exalted Lord—this means that Jesus Christ has overcome sin and death, and is the living Lord to whom has been given all power in heaven and on earth. All worldly powers are subject to and bound

---

18. ["In 1933 Bonhoeffer stated in *Creation and Fall* that human beings who have fallen away from God must 'live before God without the life that comes from God' (*DBWE* 3:142). In a July 16, 1944, letter from prison he wrote: 'Before God, and with God, we live without God' (*DBWE* 8:479 [*Reader* 803]). See *DBWE* 6:122–123," *DBWE* 6:400, n. 43.]

19. ["The expression 'in, with, and under' is part of the Lutheran terminology used to speak of the 'real presence' of Christ in the bread and wine of the Lord's Supper . . . ," *DBWE* 6:401, n. 44.]

to serve Christ, each in its own way. The proclamation of Christ is now addressed to all creatures as the liberating call to come under the lordship of Jesus Christ. This proclamation is not subject to any earthly limitations; it is ecumenical, which means it encompasses the entire globe. The lordship of Jesus Christ is not a foreign rule, but the lordship of the Creator, Reconciler, and Redeemer. It is the lordship of the one through whom and toward whom all created being exists, indeed the one in whom alone all created being finds its origin, essence, and goal. Jesus Christ does not impose a foreign law on created being, but neither does Christ permit created being to have an autonomy apart from Christ's commandment. The commandment of Jesus Christ, the living Lord, sets created being free to fulfill its own law; that is the law inherent in it from its origin, essence, and goal in Jesus Christ. The commandment of Jesus Christ does not establish the rule of the church over government, nor the rule of government over family, nor of culture over government and church, or whatever other relationships of dominance may be conceivable here. To be sure, the commandment of Jesus Christ rules church, family, culture, and government. But it does so by simultaneously setting each of these mandates free to exercise their respective functions. Jesus Christ's claim to rule as it is proclaimed by the church simultaneously means that family, culture, and government are set free to be what they are in their own nature as grounded in Christ.[20] Only through this liberation, which springs from the proclaimed rule of Christ, can the divine mandates be properly with-one-another, for-one-another, and against-one-another, as we will have to discuss extensively at a later point.

We just said that the rule of Christ's commandment over all created being is not synonymous with the rule of the church. With this assertion we have touched upon a crucial problem of the church's mandate, which we can no longer avoid.

It is the mandate of the church to proclaim God's revelation in Jesus Christ. However, it is the mystery of this name that it denotes not merely an individual human being, but at the same time comprises all of human nature within itself. Jesus Christ can always only be proclaimed and witnessed to as the one in whom God has bodily taken on humanity. Jesus Christ is one in whom there is the new humanity, the community-of-God. In Jesus Christ the word of God and the community-of-God are inextricably bound together. Through Jesus Christ the word of God and the community-

---

20. Here the antagonism between heteronomy and autonomy is overcome and taken up into a higher unity, which we could call Christonomy.

of-God belong inseparably together. Thus, where Jesus Christ is proclaimed according to the divine mandate, there is also always a church-community. To begin with, this simply means that there are human beings who accept, believe, and simply allow themselves to receive the word of Christ, in contrast to others who do not accept but reject it. It means that there are human beings who allow themselves to receive what, from God's perspective, all human beings should actually receive; it means that there are human beings who stand vicariously in the place of all other human beings, of the whole world. To be sure, they are human beings who at the same time lead their worldly lives in family, culture, and government, and do so as those who through Christ's word have been set free for life in the world. However, gathering around the divine word, having been chosen by and living in this word, they now also constitute a corporate entity, a body in its own right that is separate from the worldly orders. This "corporate entity" is

404   now our subject, specifically and first of all with regard to its necessary distinction from the divine mandate of proclamation. The word of God, as it is proclaimed by virtue of the divine mandate, rules over and governs all the world. The "corporate entity" that comes into being around this word does not rule over the world, but only serves the fulfilling of the divine mandate. The law within this "corporate entity" can never and may never become the law of the worldly orders lest an alien rule be established. Conversely, the law of a worldly order can never and may never become the law of this corporate entity. The uniqueness of the divine mandate of the church thus consists in the fact that the proclamation of Christ's lordship over all the world needs to remain distinct from the "law" of the church as a corporate entity, while, on the other hand, the church as a corporate entity cannot be separated from the office of proclamation.

The church as a distinct corporate entity serves to fulfill the divine mandate and does so in a twofold way: *first,* in that everything in this corporate entity is oriented toward effectively proclaiming Christ to all the world— which means that the church-community itself is merely an instrument, a means to an end; *second,* in that by this action of the church-community on behalf of the world and in its stead, the goal of the divine mandate of proclamation and the beginning of its fulfillment has already been reached. Thus the church-community, precisely by seeking to be merely an instrument and a means to an end, has in fact become the goal and center of all that God is doing[21] with the world. The concept of vicarious representative

---

21. ["... On the church as both a means to an end and as an end in itself, see *DBWE* 1:261," *DBWE* 6:404, n. 59.]

action defines this dual relationship most clearly. The Christian community stands in the place in which the whole world should stand. In this respect it serves the world as vicarious representative; it is there for the world's sake. On the other hand, the place where the church-community stands is the place where the world fulfills its own destiny; the church-community is the   405 "new creation," the "new creature,"[22] the goal of God's ways on earth. In this dual vicarious representation, the church-community is in complete community with its Lord; it follows in discipleship the one who was the Christ precisely in being there completely for the world and not for himself.

The church as a distinct corporate entity is thus subject to a double divine purpose, to both of which it must do justice, namely, being oriented toward the world, and, in this very act, simultaneously being oriented toward itself as the place where Jesus Christ is present. As a distinct corporate entity, it is characteristic of the church to express the *un*limited message of Christ within the *de*limited domain of its own cultural and material resources, and it is precisely the unlimitedness of the message of Christ that calls people back into the delimited domain of the church-community.

The danger of Roman Catholicism is that it understands the church   406 essentially as an end in itself, at the expense of the divine mandate of proclaiming the word. Conversely, the danger of the Reformation is that it focuses exclusively on the mandate of proclaiming the word at the expense of attending to the church as a distinct domain and thus overlooks almost completely that the church is an end in itself, which consists precisely in its   407 being-for-the-world. Our Protestant services today suffer from a liturgical poverty and uncertainty. Church order and church law are weak. Genuine church discipline is almost completely lacking. Very widespread among Protestants is an inability even to understand the significance of disciplined practices, such as spiritual exercises,[23] asceticism, meditation,[24] and contemplation. There is a lack of clarity about the "profession of the ministry" and its special responsibilities. Finally, there is also a frightening confusion or arrogance on the part of countless Protestant Christians with regard to

---

22. ["For 'new creation' see 2 Cor. 5:17, καινὴ κτίσις. See *Discipleship*'s description of the church as 'the *"new human being"*' (*DBWE* 4:218)," *DBWE* 6:405, n. 60. *See also the references to the church as the "new humanity,"* DBWE *11:295–311*, DBWE *12:315, 323*, DBWE *5:55*, DBWE *6:403* (Reader *186–197, 274–275, 281, 534, 695*).]

23. [". . . see allusions to such practices in *DBWE* 4:46f. (*Reader* 461–462), 158–161," *DBWE* 6:407, n. 63.]

24. ["See *DBWE* 4:159 regarding 'daily meditation on the word of God.' See also *DBWE* 14:931–936," *DBWE* 6:407, n. 64.]

Christians who refuse to take an oath,[25] conscientious objectors,[26] etc. One only needs to think about and draw attention to these things in order to sense immediately where the deficiency of the Protestant church lies. Exclusive interest in the divine mandate of proclamation, and thus interest in the church's commission for the world, has resulted in overlooking the intrinsic connection between this commission and the church's own domain. This deficiency led to a necessary decline in the power, the fullness, and the richness of the proclamation itself, since it lacked fertile soil. Metaphorically speaking, the commission of proclamation has been planted in the church-community like a seed in the field. Unless the soil has been prepared the seed shrivels up and loses its inherent fruitfulness.

408

---

25. ["In a 1938 decree initiated by Dr. Friedrich Werner, in his capacity as director of the Evangelical Church Chancellery in Berlin, pastors were ordered to take a loyalty oath to Hitler. Only a very small minority refused to take the extremely controversial oath (see *DB-ER* 599–602)," *DBWE* 6:407, n. 66.]

26. ["After 1932–1933 Bonhoeffer himself was convinced that conscientious objection was legitimate, and he resolved to make that choice . . . ," *DBWE* 6:407, n. 67.]

39. THEOLOGICAL POSITION PAPER ON STATE AND CHURCH

DBWE 16:502–528

In this position paper, Bonhoeffer outlines the nature and tasks of the state as a divine mandate. That governing is a divine mandate means the authority to govern derives from God rather than from the people, "from above" rather than "from below." This clearly sets Bonhoeffer's concept of government against the National Socialist account of the state, which, as Bonhoeffer has argued since at least his essay on the Führer,[1] *derives its authority from below. Bonhoeffer's vision of government from above also challenges if not a democratic form of government then, certainly a democratic justification for it.*

Further limiting governing are the other mandates: marriage (and family), work (or culture), and especially the church.[2] In dealing with the various limits and duties of the church and government in relationship to one another, Bonhoeffer returns to a number of themes in "The Church and the Jewish Question"[3] from 1933.

Although Bonhoeffer's account of government as mandate does entail strict limits on government power, it also grants government a divine dignity Bonhoeffer found lacking in the American understanding of the state[4]: government has the God-given task of preserving the world for Christ.

---

1. [DBWE *12:268–282* (Reader *359–369*).]

2. [*For the relationship of the mandates to one another, see* DBWE *6:388–408* (Reader *685–698*).]

3. [DBWE *12:361–370* (Reader *370–378*).]

4. [DBWE *15:450–456.*]

503   **1. Conceptual**

The concept of the state is alien to the New Testament. It is of ancient
pagan origin. In the New Testament the concept of government[5] replaces
it. State means an ordered commonwealth; government is the power that
creates and upholds the order. In the concept of the state, those who govern
and those who are governed are combined; in the concept of government
only those who govern are meant. The concept of the polis [*city*], which
is constitutive for the concept of the state, has no necessary connection
with the concept of exousia [*government*]. In the New Testament the polis
504   is an eschatological concept, the future city of God, the new Jerusalem,
the divinely ruled heavenly commonwealth. Governing authority is not
fundamentally restricted to the earthly polis; it can reach beyond it (as it is
also present in the smallest form of community in the father-child, master-
servant relationship). Therefore, the concept of government includes no
definitive form of commonwealth, no definitive form of the state. Government is the power set in place by God to exercise worldly rule with
divine authority. Government is the vicarious representative action of God
on earth.[6] It can only be understood from above.[7] Government does not
emerge from the commonwealth; instead, it orders the commonwealth
505   from above. If it were exegetically correct to view government as an angelic
power, even this would refer only to its place between God and the world.
Theologically, only the concept of government, not of the state, is usable.
Yet in concrete reflection we cannot avoid, of course, the concept of the
state.

In the concept of the church, especially where its relation to government as well as to the state is to be clarified, we must differentiate between
the pastoral office and the congregation or the Christians. The pastoral
office is the power set in place by God to exercise spiritual rule with divine

----

5. ["... In *Ethics* as well as in 'State and Church,' Bonhoeffer identifies government as
one of the four mandates. The other three are marriage, work, and church. A mandate
is a divinely commissioned task, which is performed with 'authority' in an 'office.' For
more on government as one of the four mandates, cf. *DBWE* 16:518–521, 549–550; cf. also
DBWE 6:68–75, 388–408 (*Reader* 685–698)," *DBWE* 16:503, n. 5.]

6. ["...This idea of 'vicarious representative action' *(Stellvertretung)* shapes Bonhoeffer's reflection in the *Ethics* manuscript 'The Concrete Commandment and the Divine
Mandates' (*DBWE* 6:388–394 [*Reader* 686–689])," *DBWE* 16:504, n. 14.]

7. ["... on the understanding of government 'from above,' cf. above all *DBWE* 6:120–
121, 390–393 [*Reader* 687–689])," *DBWE* 16:504, n. 15.]

authority. It emerges not from the congregation but from God.[8] Whereas worldly and spiritual rule are to be strictly distinguished, Christians are still at the same time citizens; and citizens in turn, whether they are believers, are at the same time subject to the claim of Jesus Christ. Thus the relation of the pastoral office to government is different from the relation of Christians to government. This distinction needs to be kept in mind to avoid continual misunderstandings.

2. The Establishment of Government

A. *In Human Nature*

Classical antiquity, especially Aristotle, grounded the state in *human nature*. The state is the highest perfection of the rational nature of the human being; to serve the state is the highest purpose of human life. All ethics is political ethics. Virtues are political virtues. This grounding of the state has been taken over in principle by Catholic theology. The state emerges out of human nature. The capacity of the human being to live in community as well as the relationship between the ruler and the ruled are part of creation. Within the natural-created dimension, the state fulfills the destiny of human nature; it is the "highest manifestation of the natural communal character of human existence" (Schilling, *Moraltheologie*, vol. 2, 609). This Aristotelian and Thomistic teaching is found in somewhat modified form in Anglican theology. But it has also penetrated into modern Lutheranism. The connection between natural theology and incarnational theology among Anglicans (a dubious connection, now clearly recognized by young Anglo-Catholics and corrected by a theologia crucis [*theology of the cross*]) opens up the possibility of a peculiar natural-Christian grounding of the state. By way of Hegel and Romanticism modern Lutheranism has taken up the natural concept of the state. Here the state is the fulfillment not of the universal rational nature of humanity but of the creative will of God in the people. The state is essentially a people's state. The people fulfill a God-intended destiny in the people's state. What matters here is not the content of that destiny in its particulars. The ancient classical concept of the state lives on in the forms of the rational state, the people's state, the cultural state, the social state, and also finally and decisively the Christian

506

507

---

8. [". . . Cf. also in the *Ethics* manuscript 'The Concrete Commandment and the Divine Mandates' Bonhoeffer's statement that 'this office is directly instituted by Jesus Christ, and receives its legitimacy not through the will of the congregation, but through the will of Jesus Christ' (*DBWE* 6:397 [*Reader* 691–692])," *DBWE* 16:505, n. 17.]

508 state. The state is the fulfillment of certain given realities contained in it; indeed, in the final honing of this teaching it becomes the actual subject of these realities—thus of the people, of the culture, of the economy, of religion. It is "the real God" (Hegel). The understanding of the state as commonwealth is common to all these teachings; by that understanding the concept of government is obtained only in a difficult and roundabout way. Fundamentally, then, government also must be derived from human nature; and it is hence difficult to understand it at the same time as the coercive power that turns against the human being, for it is precisely in coercive power that the authority of the state is essentially different from the voluntary superordination and subordination that exists in every community. Wherever the state is derived from created human nature, the concept of government is dissolved and reconstructed from below, even where one does not at all intend this. Where the state becomes the fulfillment of all spheres of human life and culture, it forfeits its true dignity, its specific authority as government.

509 **B. In Sin**

Building on the thought of Augustine, the Reformation overcame the ancient classical concept of the state. It establishes the state not as a commonwealth in the created nature of the human being (although certain hints in this direction appear among the Reformers); instead, it establishes the state as government *in the fall.* Sin made the divine institution of government necessary. By means of the sword given to it by God, government is to protect human beings from the chaos that sin causes. It is to punish the criminal and preserve life. Thereby government is established as a coercive power *and* as guardian of an external justice. The Reformation takes both into account in the same way. Nevertheless, the development of thinking diverged along two paths. The first defined the concept of justice by means of the concept of coercive power and was led to the concept of the state governed by power. The second defined power by means of justice and arrived at the concept of the state governed by law. The first saw exousia only where there was power; the second saw it only where there was law. Thereby both diminished the Reformation concept of exousia.

510 Yet it remained common to both that they recognized the state not as the fulfillment of creaturely capacities but as an order of God established from above. The state is understood not from below—from the standpoint of the people, of the culture, etc.—but from above, that is, as government in the true sense. So in this way the original point of departure, both of the Reformation and of the Bible, was preserved. The state is thus not essentially a people's, cultural, etc. state. All these are merely possible, divinely permit-

ted forms of the political commonwealth that can be replaced by an abundance of other forms yet unknown to us. In distinction from the forms of commonwealth permitted by God, government is established and ordained by God alone. People, culture, social nature, etc. are world. Government is order equipped with divine authority in the world.[9] Government is not itself world, but of God. In addition, the concept of the Christian state is from this perspective untenable, for the governmental character of the state is independent of the Christian character of persons in government. Government exists also among non-Christians.

C. From the Standpoint of Christ

Especially from what has just been said, but also from the preceding discussion, it becomes clear that the establishment of the state in sin as well as in human nature leads to a concept of the state in itself and thus apart from its relation to Jesus Christ. Whether as an order of creation or an order of preservation, the state exists for itself, more or less independent of the revelation of God in Jesus Christ. Despite all the advantages of the second grounding over the first, even here this conclusion cannot be avoided. But now the question arises: from what standpoint can I say something theologically tenable—in contrast to a general Christian philosophy—concerning paradise or the fall, if not *from the standpoint of Jesus Christ*? Through Jesus Christ and for Jesus Christ all things are created (John 1:3; 1 Cor. 8:6; Heb. 1:2) and in particular also "thrones or dominions or rulers or powers" (Col. 1:16). Only in Jesus Christ does all this actually have its existence (Col. 1:17). Yet he is the same one who is "the head of . . . the church" (Col. 1:18). Insofar as the government instituted by God is intended and not some kind of philosophical concept of government, it is therefore under no circumstances possible to speak theologically of government apart from Jesus Christ nor, since he is indeed the head of his church, apart from the *church of Jesus Christ*. The true grounding of government is therefore Jesus Christ himself. The relation of Jesus Christ to government can be expressed in seven parts:

    1. As the mediator of creation, "through whom" government is also created, Jesus Christ is the only and necessary connection between government and the Creator; there is no immediate connection of government to God; Christ is its mediator.

511

---

9. ["In the *Ethics* manuscript 'The Concrete Commandment and the Divine Mandates' (*DBWE* 6:389 [*Reader* 686–687]), the 'conferring of divine authority' on an earthly institution is termed a 'mandate' (cf. *DBWE* 16:519–520, n. 85)," *DBWE* 16:510, n. 40.]

2. Like everything created, government also has "existence only in Jesus Christ," and hence its essence and being. If Jesus Christ did not exist, then nothing created would exist any longer; it would thus be destroyed in the wrath of God.

3. Along with everything created, government is oriented "toward Jesus Christ." Its purpose is Jesus Christ himself. It is supposed to serve him.

4. Because Jesus Christ has all power in heaven and on earth (Matt. 28:18), he is also the Lord of the government.

5. By the reconciliation on the cross Jesus Christ restored the relationship between government and God (Col. 1:20 τὰ πάντα [*all things*]).

6. Beyond this connection to Jesus Christ, which government has in common with everything created, government stands also in a special relation to Jesus Christ:

a) Jesus Christ was crucified by permission of the government.

b) The government, which recognized and openly bore witness to the innocence of Jesus (John 18:38; cf. also the role of Lysias, Felix, Festus, and Agrippa in the legal proceedings against Paul), thereby manifested its true nature.

c) The government that does not risk standing by its knowledge and judgment in exercising governmental power has abandoned its office under the pressure of the people. Therein lies no condemnation of the office as such, but only of the inadequate exercise of this office.

d) Jesus submitted to the government, yet reminded it that its power is not up to human discretion but is "given . . . from above" (John 19:11).

e) Jesus thereby bore witness that the government in the proper or improper execution of its office, precisely because it is power from above, 512 can only serve him. Absolving him from guilt and yet handing him over to be crucified, the government necessarily bore witness that it stands in the service of Jesus Christ. Thus precisely through the cross Jesus reclaimed his dominion over government (Col. 2:15), and at the end of all things "every ruler, government, and power" will be "sublated"[10] (in a double sense) through him.

7. As long as the earth exists, Jesus will always be at the same time the Lord of all government and the head of the church-community, without government and church-community ever becoming one. But in the end there will be a holy city (polis) without a temple, for God and the Lamb will themselves be the temple (Revelation 21), and the citizens of this city will

---

10. ["This standard translation of Hegel's term (*aufgehoben*, 'sublated') means both to overcome and to redeem. Cf. 1 Cor. 15:24," *DBWE* 16:512, n. 52.]

be believers from the community of Jesus in all the world, and God and the
Lamb will exercise dominion in this city. In the heavenly polis, state and
church will be one.

Only the grounding of government in Jesus Christ leads beyond groundings in natural law, which is where, finally, the groundings both in human
nature and human sin end up. The grounding in human nature sees in the
given realities of peoples, etc., the foundation of the state in natural law.
Imperialism and revolution—that is, external and internal revolution—draw
upon this to justify themselves. To limit the concept of power [*Eph. 1:21*] by
means of the concept of law, the grounding in sin must discern norms of
natural law and through these will have a more strongly conservative orientation. However, because the concept and the content of natural law are ambiguous (depending on whether it is obtained from various given realities or
from various norms), it does not suffice as the grounding of the state. Natural law can establish the tyrannical state as well as the state governed
by law, the people's state as well as imperialism, democracy as well as the
dictatorship.[11] We secure firm ground under our feet only by the biblical   513
grounding of government in Jesus Christ. If and to what extent then from
this standpoint a new natural law can be found is a theological question
that remains open.[12]

3. The Divine Character of Government

A. *In Its Being*

Government is given to us not as an idea or as a task but as reality, as
"existing" (αἱ δὲ οὖσαι, Rom. 13:1c). In its being it is a divine office. Persons in government are God's "liturgists," servants, vicarious representatives (Rom. 13:4). The being of government is independent of its having
come into being. Even if the path of human beings to governmental office
may again and again pass through guilt, even if guilt hangs on almost
every crown (Shakespeare's royal dramas), the being of government stands
beyond its earthly origination; for government is an order of God not in

---

11. ["For Bonhoeffer's refusal to ground ethics in 'natural law,' cf. his sketch in the
Ethics, 'On the Possibility of the Church's Message to the World' (*DBWE* 6:352–362) . . . ,"
DBWE 16:512, n. 55.]

12. ["On Bonhoeffer's own attempt to grasp 'the natural' 'in distinction from the
creaturely, in order to incorporate the fact of the fall into sin,' and 'in distinction from
the sinful, in order to incorporate the creaturely,' see the *Ethics* manuscript begun at
Ettal in December 1940, 'Natural Life,' in *DBWE* 6, esp. pp. 173–174 (*Reader* 632–633),"
DBWE 16:513, n. 56.]

its origination but in its being. Like everything that exists, government is also in a certain sense beyond good and evil—i.e., it has not only an office but also a historical being. Through an ethical failure it does not yet lose eo ipso [*of itself*] its divine dignity. "My country, right or wrong, my country" expresses this state of affairs. It is the historical relation of one entity to another, repeating itself in the relation of father to child, brother to brother, and master to servant, and in those cases becoming immediately

514 obvious. There is no ethical isolation of the son from the father; on the basis of actual being, there is even a necessary sharing and acceptance of the guilt of the father or the brother. There is no glory in standing in the ruined city of one's birth, under the assumption that you yourself at least have not become guilty. That is the self-glorification of the moralist over against history. The clearest expression for this dignity of government, which rests even in its historical being, is its power, the sword that it wields. Even where government becomes guilty, ethically assailable, its power is from God. It has its existence only in Jesus Christ, and through the cross of Christ is reconciled with God.

B. In Its Task

The being of government is connected with a divine task. Only in the fulfillment of its task is its being fulfilled. A complete apostasy from its task would call its being into question. However, by God's providence this complete apostasy is only possible as an eschatological event. There, under severe martyrdom, it leads to the church-community's complete separation from the government as the embodiment of the anti-Christ. The task of government consists in serving the dominion of Christ on earth by worldly exercise of the power of the sword and of the law. Government serves Christ inasmuch as it establishes and preserves an external righteousness by wielding the sword given to it, and it alone, in God's stead. In this it has not only the negative task of punishing the wicked but also the positive task

515 of commending the good as well as the godly (1 Pet. 2:14!). It is thereby granted, on the one hand, legal power, and, on the other hand, the right to educate for the good—that is, for outward justice. To be sure, how it practices this right to educate is a question that can be dealt with only in connection with government's relationships to the other divine orders. The frequently addressed question—namely, of what the good, the outward justice that government is to cultivate, consists in—is easily answered if one stays focused on the grounding of government in Jesus Christ. In any case, this good cannot stand in contradiction to Jesus Christ. The good consists in the existence of space for the final goal—the service to Jesus Christ—within every action of government. This refers not to an action

that is Christian but to an action that does not exclude Jesus Christ.[13] Government arrives at such an action when it takes the contents of the second table[14] as its measure in any given historical situation and decision. But how does government become aware of these contents? First of all, from the preaching of the church. In the case of a godless government, however, a providential correspondence exists between the contents of the second table and the law inherent in historical life itself.[15] The failure to observe the second table destroys the very life that government is supposed to protect. Thus the task of protecting life, rightly understood, leads inherently to the upholding of the second table. Is the state, then, grounded after all in natural law? No, for here we are speaking only about the government that does not understand itself and nevertheless can arrive providentially at the same decisive insights for its task that are revealed in Jesus Christ to the government that understands itself rightly. Thus, suffice it to say that here natural law is grounded in Jesus Christ.

Thus the task of government, whether or not it knows its true grounding, consists in establishing, by the power of the sword, an outward justice in which life is preserved and in this way remains open for Christ.

Does the government's task also include upholding the first table, i.e., the decision for the God and Father of Jesus Christ? We want to deal with this question in the section on government and church and here say only this: 516
the knowledge of Jesus Christ belongs to the destiny of all human beings, including those with governmental authority. To the task of government as such, however, belongs the praise and protection of the godly (1 Pet. 2:14), independent of the personal faith of the governmental authorities. Indeed, only in the protection of the godly does government fulfill its true task of serving Christ.

The task of government to serve Christ is at the same time its inescapable destiny. It serves Christ, whether knowingly or unknowingly, indeed, whether it is faithful or unfaithful to its task. It must serve him, whether it

---

13. [". . . cf. also Bonhoeffer's thoughts regarding William Paton's book in point 4 of 'The Church and the New Order in Europe': 'A worldly order that abides within the Decalogue will be open for Christ.' It 'is, to be sure, not "Christian," but it is a legitimate earthly order according to God's will' (*DBWE* 16:531–532)," *DBWE* 16:515, n. 67.]

14. ["Bonhoeffer is referring to the second table of the Decalogue," *DBWE* 16:515, n. 68.]

15. ["Cf. Bonhoeffer's comments in 'Church and World I' on the retrieval of ethical and humanistic values for the church when it is threatened with destruction (*DBWE* 6:339–341); cf. also point 4 of his 'Thoughts on William Paton' (see *DBWE* 16:531–532). On the theological basis for all this, cf. Bonhoeffer's reflections on the openness of the 'natural' for Christ (*DBWE* 6:171–178 [*Reader* 631–635])," *DBWE* 16:515, n. 70.]

wants to or not. If it desires not to, it serves the witness to the name of Christ through the suffering of the church-community. So close and inseparable is the relation of government to Christ. One way or another it cannot escape its task of serving Christ. It serves him by its existence.

C. In Its Claim

The claim that government has on the basis of its power and its task is the claim of God and binds the conscience. Government demands obedience "because of conscience" (Rom. 13:5), which can also be interpreted as "for the Lord's sake" (1 Pet. 2:13). Such obedience is combined with respect (Rom. 13:7; 1 Pet. 2:17). In the performance of the governmental task the demand for obedience is unconditional, qualitatively total, extending to conscience and bodily life. Faith, conscience, and bodily life are bound in obedience to the divine task of government. Uncertainty can emerge only where the content and the scope of the task of government become questionable. The Christian is not obliged and not able to prove in every single case the right of the governmental demand. The duty of Christians to obey binds them up to the point where the government forces them into direct violation of the divine commandment, thus until government overtly acts contrary to its divine task and thereby forfeits its divine claim. When in doubt, obedience is demanded, for the Christian does not bear the governmental responsibility. But if government oversteps its task at some point— e.g., by making itself lord over the faith of the church-community—then at this point it is indeed to be disobeyed for the sake of conscience and for the sake of the Lord. Yet it is not permissible to draw the sweeping conclusion from this offense that this government now has no further claim to obedience in any or even all other demands. Disobedience can only be a concrete decision in the individual case. Generalizations lead to an apocalyptic demonization of government. Even an anti-Christian government remains in a certain respect still government. It would therefore not be permissible to refuse to pay taxes to a government that was persecuting the church. Conversely, the act of obedience to government in its state functions—paying taxes, taking oaths, serving in the military—is always a proof that this government is still not understood apocalyptically. An apocalyptic understanding of a concrete government would have to entail total disobedience; for in that case every single act of obedience is manifestly connected with a denial of Christ (Rev. 13:7). Because in all decisions of the state the historical entanglement in the guilt of the past is incalculably large, it is for the most part not possible to judge the legitimacy of a single decision. Here

the venture of responsibility[16] must be risked. But the responsibility for   518
such a venture on the part of government can in concreto [*in the concrete*]
(i.e., apart from the general shared responsibility of individuals for political action) be borne only by the government. Even where the guilt of government is blatantly obvious, the guilt that gave rise to this guilt may not
be disregarded. The refusal to obey within a specific historical political
decision of the government, as well as this decision itself, can only be a venture of one's own responsibility. A historical decision cannot be completely
incorporated into ethical concepts. There is one thing left: the venture of
action.[17] That holds true for the government as well as for subjects.

4. Government and the Divine Orders in the World[18]

Government has the divine task of preserving the world with its God-given
orders in reference to Christ. It alone bears the sword for that purpose.
Every person is obligated to obey it.[19] But with its task and its claim it always
presupposes the created world. Government keeps what is created in its
order but cannot itself produce life; it is not creative. However, within the
world it governs it discovers two orders through which God the Creator
exercises creative power and upon which it is therefore by nature depen-   519
dent: *marriage* and *work*. We find both in the Bible, already in paradise,
attesting that they belong to God's creation, which exists through and
toward Jesus Christ. Even after the fall, i.e., in the form in which alone we
know them, both still remain divine orders of discipline and grace, because

---

16. ["Cf. the significance in Bonhoeffer's *Ethics* of the category of 'venture' *(Wagnis)*, which increases with his participation in the conspiracy against Hitler (*DBWE* 6:248, 257, 274, [*Reader* 637, 648] et passim). Cf. also 'After Ten Years' . . . (*DBWE* 8:41 [*Reader* 765–766]); cf. also *DBWE* 8:236 and 512–514 . . . ," *DBWE* 16:517, n. 78.]

17. ["This is one of the few places in Bonhoeffer's written work from the time of his participation in the conspiracy against Hitler that provides a glimpse of his own personal view of this participation," *DBWE* 16:518, n. 79.]

18. ["Bonhoeffer here takes up the theme of the 'orders of creation,' which since the mid-1920s had been the theological crystallization point of the conflicting understand-ings of the state . . . ," *DBWE* 16:518, n. 80.]

19. ["Bonhoeffer lifted portions of the following text verbatim, but also with char-acteristic changes, for his *Ethics* chapter titled 'Christ, Reality, and Good'; see *DBWE* 6:70–73. This refers to a passage that Bonhoeffer subsequently (in the second half of 1941, according to the hypothesis of the German editors of *DBW* 6) inserted into the chapter conceived in 1940; see *DBWE* 6:65, n. 67, and 68–69, n. 75," *DBWE* 16:518, n. 81.]

God desires to be revealed even to the fallen world as the Creator, and because God allows the world to exist in Christ and makes the world Christ's own. Marriage and work exist from the beginning under an appointed divine mandate that must be performed in faithful obedience to God. For this reason marriage and work have their own origin in God that is not established by government but is to be acknowledged by it. Through marriage bodily life is propagated, and human beings are procreated for the glorification and service of Jesus Christ. Yet that means marriage encompasses not only the place of procreation but also that of raising children to obey Jesus Christ. For the child its parents are God's representatives as the child's procreators and educators. Through work a world of values is created for the glorification and service of Jesus Christ. As in marriage, work is not divine creation out of nothing; rather it is the production of something new on the basis of the first creation—in marriage of new life, in work of new values. Work hereby encompasses the whole realm from agriculture, through trade and industry, to science and art (cf. Gen. 4:17ff.). Thus, for the sake of Jesus Christ a special right preserves marriage and with it the family and preserves work and with it economic life, culture, science, and art. That means government possesses for this realm only regulative but not constitutive significance. Marriage is contracted not by government but before government. Economic life, science, and art are not cultivated by government itself, but they are subject to its supervision and, within certain limits (not to be further specified here), to its control. But at no time does government become the subject of these spheres of work. Where it extends its authority beyond its own task, it will in the long run forfeit its true authority in these matters.

521   The order of the people is distinguished from the order of marriage and the order of work. According to scripture its origin lies neither in paradise nor in an explicit divine mandate. On the one hand (according to Genesis 10), the people is a natural consequence of the spread of the generations upon the earth. On the other hand (Genesis 11), it is a divine order that allows humanity to live in its disintegration and mutual misunderstanding, thereby reminding it that its unity lies not in its own absolute power but in God alone—i.e., in the Creator and Redeemer. But in scripture there is no special task of God for the people. Whereas marriage and work are divine offices, the people is historical reality that in a particular way points to the divine reality of the *one* people of God, to the church. Scripture provides no reference to the relationship of people and government; it does not call for a people's state; it knows of the possibility that various peoples can be unified under one government. It knows that the people grows from below, but that government is established from above.

520

5. Government and Church

Government is established for the sake of Christ. It serves Christ, and thereby it also serves his church. The reign of Christ over all government certainly in no way implies the reign of the church over government. But the same Lord whom government serves is the head of the church-community, the Lord of the church. Government's service to Christ consists in the exercise of its task to secure an outward justice by the power of the sword. In this respect it provides an indirect service to the church-community, which can only thus live a "quiet and peaceable life" (1 Tim. 2:2). By its service to Christ, government is essentially connected with the church. Where it properly fulfills its task, the church-community can live in peace; for government and church-community serve the same Lord.

A. The Claim of Government on the Church

The claim of government to obedience and respect extends to the church as well. With regard to the pastoral office, of course, government can insist only that this office not interfere with the worldly office but fulfill its own task, in which indeed the admonition to obey the government is included. The government has no power over this task itself, as it is exercised in the pastorate and in the office of church administration. Insofar as the pastoral office is a publicly practiced office, government is entitled to oversee that everything happens in good order—i.e., in accordance with outward justice. Only in this respect does it also have a say in how the office is staffed and configured. The pastoral office itself is not subordinate to government. Nevertheless, government has full claim to the obedience of members of the Christian community. It does not thereby position itself as a second authority alongside the authority of Christ; rather its own authority is only a form of the authority of Christ. In obedience to government the Christian obeys Christ. The Christian as citizen does not cease to be a Christian, but serves Christ in a different way. In this way the content of the legitimate governmental claim is already sufficiently determined as well. It can never lead the Christian against Christ; rather it helps Christians serve Christ in the world. In this way the person in government becomes for the Christian a servant of God.

B. The Claim of the Church on Government

The church has the task of calling the whole world to submit to the reign of Jesus Christ. It bears witness for government to their common Lord. It calls government officials to belief in Jesus Christ for the sake of their own salvation. It knows that in obedience to Jesus Christ the task of government

522

is properly executed. Its goal is not that government enact Christian politics, Christian laws, etc., but rather that it be genuine government in the sense of its particular task. The church is what first leads government to an understanding of itself. For the sake of the common Lord, it lays claim to the hearing of government, the safeguarding of public Christian proclamation against acts of violence and blasphemy, the safeguarding of church order against arbitrary encroachment, and the safeguarding of Christian life in obedience to Jesus Christ. The church can never abandon this claim. It must let it be publicly heard as long as government itself claims to recognize the church. Where, of course, government explicitly or actually stands against the church, the time can come when the church, while not relinquishing its claim, nevertheless no longer wastes its words. It knows very well that government, whether it performs its task properly or improperly, must always only serve its Lord and thereby the church as well. The government that refuses to safeguard the church thereby places the church all the more conspicuously under the protection of its Lord. Government that reviles its Lord bears witness thereby all the more resoundingly to the power of this Lord, who is praised in the church's martyrdoms.

C. The Ecclesial Responsibility of Government

The responsibility of government corresponds to the claim of the church. Here a reply needs to be given to the question of the government's stance in relation to the First Commandment. Must government come to a religious decision, or is its task religious neutrality? Is government responsible for the cultivation of true Christian worship, and does it have the right to prohibit other worship? Certainly government officials should also come to faith in Jesus Christ. However, the governmental office remains independent from religious decision. It is, nevertheless, the responsibility of the governmental office to safeguard, indeed to praise, the devout—i.e., to support the cultivation of religion. A government that overlooks this responsibility uproots true obedience and thus its own authority (France 1905).[20] The governmental office as such thereby remains religiously neutral and only inquires after its own task. It can, therefore, never become the subject of the founding of a new religion without dissolving itself. It safeguards any

---

20. ["In France the separation of church and state was introduced in 1905 . . . ," *DBWE* 16:523, n. 97.]

worship that does not undermine the governmental office. It makes sure that no antagonism that would endanger national order arises out of the diversity of forms of worship. It achieves this, however, not by suppression of worship, but by a clear observance of its own governmental task. It will then become clear that true Christian worship does not endanger this task but instead continually constitutes it anew. If persons in government are 524 Christian, then they must know that Christian proclamation occurs not by the sword but by the word. The sentence "Cuius regio, eius religio" [*whose realm, his religion*][21] was possible only under very particular political circumstances, namely, the agreement of the sovereigns to take in any who were expelled. As a principle it is incompatible with the governmental office. But if there should be a particular state of church crisis, then it would lie within the responsibility of Christians in government to make their power available at the request of the church to restore healthy conditions. That does not, however, mean that the government as such takes over functions of church governance. What is exclusively at stake is the restoration of proper order, in which the pastoral office can be practiced rightly and in which government and church can fulfill their respective tasks.[22] Government will maintain its commitment to the First Commandment by being government in the proper way, also exercising its governmental responsibility toward the church. But it does not have the office of confessing and proclaiming faith in Jesus Christ.

D. The Political Responsibility of the Church

If political responsibility is exclusively understood to mean governmental responsibility, then clearly only government has to bear this responsibility. However, if with this concept life in the polis is meant quite generally, then in a manifold sense we can speak of a political responsibility of the church as a response to the claim of government on the church. We distinguish here once more between the responsibility of the pastoral office and the responsibility of Christians. Part of the church's role as guardian is to call sin by name and to warn human beings of sin; for "Righteousness exalts a nation that is, temporally and eternally, but sin is a reproach to any people

---

21. [*"The formula adopted at the Religious Peace of Augsburg (1555), by which the princes of the Empire were to be permitted to settle whether the religion of their own lands should be R[oman] C[atholic] or Lutheran,"* Oxford Concise Dictionary of the Christian Church, 156.]

22. ["On Bonhoeffer's conceptions of the government's functions in the reconstitution of the church following the overthrow, see his draft 'End of the Church Struggle' (*DBWE* 16:574–580) and the corresponding constitutional provisions by Friedrich J. Perels (*DBWE* 16:580–583) . . . ," *DBWE* 16:524, n. 99.]

that is, a temporal and eternal reproach" (Prov. 14:34). If the church did not do that, then it would itself become implicated with the blood of the ungodly (Ezek. 3:17ff.). This warning against sin extends quite publicly to the church-community, and those who will not hear it bring judgment upon themselves. Thus, the purpose of the preacher is not to improve the world but to call it to faith in Jesus Christ, to bear witness to the reconciliation through him and his reign. The theme of proclamation is not the depravity of the world but the grace of Jesus Christ. It is the responsibility of the pastoral office to take seriously the proclamation of the kingly reign of Christ and through direct, respectful speech to make government aware of its failures and mistakes that necessarily threaten its governmental office. If the word of the church is in principle not accepted, then all that is left to it is enough political responsibility to establish and preserve at least among its own members the order of outward justice no longer present in the polis, thereby serving the government in its own way.

Is there a political responsibility of the *individual Christian?* Individual Christians can certainly not be held responsible for the government's actions, nor dare they make themselves responsible for them. But on the basis of their faith and love of neighbor, they are responsible for their own vocation and personal sphere of living, however large or small it is. Wherever this responsibility is faithfully exercised, it has efficacy for the polis as a whole. According to scripture there is no right to revolution, but there is a responsibility for all individuals to safeguard the purity of their offices and tasks in the polis. And thus in a genuine sense individuals serve government with their responsibility. No one, not even government itself, can take this responsibility from the people or forbid it from being a part of their lives in sanctification, for it derives from obedience to the Lord of the church and of government.

E. Conclusions

The various connections between government and church do not allow for the regulation of the relationship on the basis of a principle; neither the separation of state and church nor the state church form is in itself a solution of the problem. Nothing is more dangerous than drawing generalized theoretical conclusions from isolated experiences. The programmatic endorsement of the church's withdrawal from the world, from the connections with the state that still exist, under the impression of living in an apocalyptic time, is, in this sort of generality, only a somewhat nostalgic historical-philosophical interpretation of the times that, were it truly taken seriously, would necessarily lead to the most radical implications of Revelation 13.[23] By the same token, the vision and planning of a state church or church of the people can likewise originate out of the philosophy of history. No constitutional form can give suitable expression to proximity and distance in the relationship of government and church. Government and church are bound, and bound together, by the same Lord. Government and church are distinguished from each other in their task. Government and church have the same sphere of action, human beings. None of these relations may be isolated and in this way supply the ground for a certain constitutional form (thus, for example, arranged as state church, free church, church of the people); what matters is giving concrete room in every given form for the relationship actually established by God and entrusting the way it develops to the Lord over government and church.

6. The Form of the State and Church

In the doctrine of the state deriving from the Reformation as well as from Catholicism, the question concerning the form of the state is always secondary. As long as the government fulfills its task, the form under which it does so is not essential, at least for the church. But it is justified to ask which form of the state offers the best guarantee for the fulfillment of the government's task and therefore ought to be supported by the church. No form of the state is as such an absolute guarantee of a proper performance of the office of government. Only concrete obedience to the divine task justifies a form of the state. Nevertheless, some general guiding principles can be formulated to identify the forms of the state that offer relatively advantageous conditions for proper governmental action and thereby for a proper relationship between state and church; and precisely these relative differences can be of great import in practice.

I. The relatively best form of the state will be that in which it is most clear that government is from above, from God, and in which its divine origin shines through most brightly. A properly understood divine right of government in its glory and in its responsibility belongs to the essence of the relatively best form of the state (in distinction from the rest of Western royalty, the Belgian kings called themselves "de grâce du peuple" [*by the grace of the people*].

527

528

---

23. ["The implication is that the state is the 'beast rising out of the sea' (cf. Rev. 13:1) and that Christians must suffer martyrdom," *DBWE* 16:526, n. 102.]

II. The relatively best form of the state will see its power not compromised but sustained and secured

a) by a strict maintenance of outward justice,

b) by the right, grounded in God, of the family and of work,

c) by the proclamation of the gospel of Jesus Christ.

III. The relatively best form of the state will express its solidarity with its subjects not through a restriction of its divinely bestowed authority but through just action and true speech that joins it and its subjects in mutual trust. Here it will become apparent that what is best for government will also be best for the relationship of government and church.

40. Theological Position Paper on the Question of Baptism

DBWE 16:551–572

In 1942, Arnold Hitzer, a Confessing Church pastor, wrote a paper arguing against the practice of infant baptism. On the basis of the New Testament and in conversation with the Lutheran confessions, Hitzer called for the exclusive practice of adult, or believer, baptism. Bonhoeffer was commissioned to write this position paper in response.[1] While his argument is wide-ranging, its crux is a critique of Hitzer's concept of faith. Hitzer is right to tie baptism to faith, argues Bonhoeffer, but he errs in understanding faith too subjectively, too psychologically, and too individualistically. Faith should not be defined subjectively, with primary reference to the believer, but objectively as God's grace. And faith should not be understood psychologically, as something open to psychological examination, but theologically, as something disclosed in revelation. And finally, faith should not be defined with primary reference to the individual, since the faith of the church-community always precedes that of the individual. This understanding of faith, together with the biblical exegesis and interpretation of the Lutheran confessions, supports Bonhoeffer's conclusion that infant baptism is theologically justified, or, more precisely, that the rejection of infant baptism is not theologically justifiable.[2]

---

1. [DBWE *16:551, n. 1. Julius Schniewind was also commissioned to prepare a paper, which is why Bonhoeffer titles this a "co-report."*]

2. [*". . . On Bonhoeffer's understanding of infant baptism, see also* DBWE *1:240–242,* DBWE *2:159–161* (Reader *108–109*), DBWE *4:207–212,"* DBWE *16:551, n. 1.*]

551   **Co-report on the "Reflection on the Question of Baptism"**
                    in Reference to the Question of Infant Baptism

A. *The Testimony of Holy Scripture.*

The practice of infant baptism cannot be directly proven in the New Testament (NT), to be sure, but can nevertheless be seen as probable there. In

552   any case, its presence and justification can be disputed neither on exegetical nor on theological grounds.

I. *Exegetical.*

Matt. 28:19. The coordination of βαπτίζοντες [*baptizing*] with μαθητεύσατε
[*make disciples*] is, of course, linguistically possible but by no means necessary. The old reading, βαπτίσαντες [*having baptized*], which according
to Bengel's rule[3] cannot simply be disregarded, would preclude any such
coordination. We must keep open the possible interpretations that "baptizing" and "teaching" fulfill the μαθητεύειν [*to make disciples*], as well as that
baptizing here precedes teaching. The αὐτούς [*them*] might mean that a
smaller selection of the nations is referred to; further conclusions cannot
be drawn from this word. To understand μαθητεύειν exclusively as evangelization through preaching is not sufficiently established linguistically.

Mark 10:15. In the present context, a possible translation of the words ὡ
παιδίον is "*as* a child"; indeed, according to J. Jeremias *Infant Baptism in the
First Four Centuries*, this is the most likely translation.

Mark 10:14. Jesus promises the Reign of God to the children. The term
τοιούτων [*such as these*] does not mean that the promise refers to those who

553   in their frame of mind resemble children, but rather that the promise does
not belong only to these children brought here to Jesus but to all who are
like them, thus to all children, analogous to the beatitude given the poor,
cf. Lohmeyer, *Markuskommentar* [*Commentary on Mark*], pages 202ff.

Acts 16:40 says not that the "brothers and sisters" belong to Lydia's house
but at the most that they gathered there.

Acts 16:15, 33; 18:8; 1 Cor. 1:16; Acts 11:15 speak of the baptism of an
"entire household"—see the terms ἅπαντες, ὅλως, πᾶς. [*all, entire, every*]—
Leaving aside the improbability of the assumption that these households
were devoid of small children, it is impossible to exclude the "children"

---

3. ["In *Novum Testamentum Graece*, 379, § 10, Bengel asserts: 'Proclivi scriptioni prae-
stat ardua' (the more difficult reading is preferred over the easier reading)," *DBWE*
16:552, n. 6.]

of these households in principle since in fact those children already grown were also counted among the "children." So the only question remaining is that of their age. Nowhere is there any mention that small children did not count as part of the "household" or that they were to be excluded from the baptism. Besides, in light of the conception of the household within which an indivisible whole is understood, this idea is improbable (cf. also Matt. 10:13).

Col. 2:11. Baptism as περιτομὴ τοῦ Χριστοῦ [*circumcision of Christ*] would be an inappropriate designation if there were no infant baptism, since circumcision occurred on the eighth day after birth. It can in no way be asserted from scripture that the circumcision of children was based in their *natural* inclusion within the Israelite community of the *people*; it has   554
much more to do with the sign of the divine covenant that encompasses fathers and children. It is only for this reason that Paul can refer to baptism as περιτομὴ τοῦ Χριστοῦ, indeed, that circumcision can play such a great role in the NT's theological disputations in the first place.

Acts 2:39 . . . "for you, for your children." In light of the imminent expectation of the end, "children" is intended to refer not to the coming generations but to the sons and daughters of those being addressed here; cf. 2:17. The eschatological character of baptism as deliverance from the final judgment (2:40) makes a differentiation in the ages of the children improbable.

Statements about Children in General.
John is filled with the Holy Spirit in his mother's womb (Luke 1:15); at the encounter with the pregnant Mary "the child leaped in Elizabeth's womb" (Luke 1:41). The newborn Jesus is the Savior and Lord of the world (Luke 2:10 and 2:30–31). Children are brought to Jesus (Mark 10:13, the same expression, by the way, as with healing miracles 7:32, 8:22, thus with events of eschatological significance). The strong expressions, "the disciples spoke sternly to them," "rebuked them," cf. Mark 8:33; Jesus "was indignant," cf. Mark 7:34; the call of Jesus "to let" the children "come to him," cf. Matt. 11:28; not to "hinder" them, his taking them into his arms, cf. Mark 9:36 and Luke 2:28 (thus this refers to very small children) — in the face of the longed-for blessing signify an event of eschatological substance (cf. Lohmeyer, loc. cit.). The Reign of God belongs to the children (Mark 10:13–14); in Luke 18:15 we find in place of παιδία (child between the ages of eight days and twelve years) the term βρέφη (infants). There was no question of Jesus baptizing children, since the baptism with the Holy Spirit became possible only after Jesus' resurrection and ascension,   555
and John's baptism was superseded by the presence of Christ.—In Matt.

18:2–3 the disciples are given the example of a child, not in its frame of mind but in its being. The receiving of a child amounts to the receiving of Christ (Mark 9:37). Children cry in the temple, "Hosanna to the Son of David," and in this Jesus sees the fulfillment of Ps. 8:3 (Matt. 21:15–14). Here as well the eschatological character of the event is clear. Nowhere in the NT are children slighted in regard to salvation, the in-breaking reign of God; on the contrary, that kind of attempt by the disciples (!) runs up against the "indignation"—i.e., the outrage—of Jesus. Jesus' acceptance of children, like that of the blind, lame, poor, signifies an eschatological event of salvation. It occurs, therefore, precisely not on the basis of some sort of natural, psychologically understood innocence of children—a thoroughly modern idea—but rather as the miracle of God, who humbles the lofty and raises up the lowly. The "innocence" of children is a gift of Christ but never a natural state by means of which the gifts of Christ—such as baptism, for instance—become superfluous. The eschatological character of Jesus' acceptance of children calls instead for their baptism by the church.

Statements about Children in the Christian Church-Community.
In Eph. 6:1 and Col. 3:20, children are addressed under the obvious presupposition that they belong to the church-community—ἐν κυρίῳ [*in the Lord*]. (At the very least it remains questionable whether 1 John 3:12 and 14 do not belong in this category as well.) There is no reference elsewhere in the NT to unbaptized people belonging to the church-community. Yet there is also no mention that children should be baptized at a certain age; there is no exhortation along these lines to parents or children, which is most easily explained by the obvious presupposition of infant baptism. In any case, the argumentum e silentio [*conclusion drawn from silence*][4] can be applied more strongly in favor of infant baptism than against it. First Cor. 7:14 implies infant baptism more readily than not. If one views baptism as an act not of forgiveness of sins but of "sealing" for the last judgment, the conception that baptism is in fact superfluous because of the "holiness" of children is an impossible idea (apart from the fact that in the NT a gift of God's grace is never "superfluous"; otherwise even baptism might possibly be "superfluous" for faith). It is more the case that the holiness of children can serve as the very condition for baptism, that is, precisely as the suspension of the question of their maturity. The reference to Jewish laws for pros-

556

---

4. ["... Bonhoeffer uses the argument as follows: that infant baptism is not mentioned because it was taken for granted," *DBWE* 16:555, n. 29.]

elytes, according to which children born after their parents' conversion do not need to be baptized, because they are born in "holiness," is logically limited by the fact that even these children were circumcised. Christian baptism, however, is περιτομὴ τοῦ Χριστοῦ. The idea that children born before their parents' conversion needed to be baptized, whereas children born to Christian parents were not baptized, leads to the improbable and groundless conception of baptized and unbaptized persons existing as members of the Christian church-community.

II. Theological Considerations.

Baptism and Faith in the NT.

If infant baptism can be neither asserted nor disputed on purely exegetical grounds, perhaps a theological overview of other biblical statements will lead to further clarity.

1. *In the NT, baptism and faith are indissolubly connected.* As a result, the objective character of each is to be much more strongly emphasized than occurs in Hitzer's Observation. Baptism is the actual consummated transfer of the human being into the church-community of the end times and incorporation into the body of Christ by means of a physical action instituted by Christ. Within it occur the washing away of sin, being born again, dying and rising with Christ, conformation with the image of Christ, reception of the Holy Spirit, sealing within the eschatological church-community for the day of judgment. All of this occurs as Christ's own action toward his church (Eph. 5:26) apart from any cooperation and activity on the part of the person. Wherever the salvific gifts of baptism are referred to, hardly any attention is directed to the individual recipient or the personal "conditions" attached to receiving baptism; rather, the entire weight falls on the power inherent within the sacrament in its performance instituted by Christ, a power dependent on no human conditions, and on the entire church-community, the body of Christ, to whom this sacrament belongs. Indeed, in spite of all embarrassed interpretative attempts to evade it, 1 Cor. 15:29 speaks of a baptism on behalf of the dead (presumably Christians who had died unbaptized), a practice that Paul not only refuses to condemn but even uses as an argument against those who deny the resurrection of the dead. If baptism really is "being born again," resurrection from the dead (cf. also Eph. 5:14 in addition to Rom. 6:4), why shouldn't such a conception of baptism not lead to that sort of practice as an extreme expression of the power of the sacrament, albeit one not accepted by the church? The Pauline research of recent years has taught us to recognize this realism in Paul's thinking ever more clearly and has made impossible any reinterpretation into the "spiritual-moral" realm.

557

Now, of course, it can escape no one that baptism is brought constantly into the closest connection with faith (in addition to the passages named earlier, cf. esp. Rom. 6:8 and 11; Col. 2:12b; Gal. 3:26ff.); and although it is never explicitly asserted that only believers may be baptized, the connection between baptism and faith is an unarticulated presupposition whenever baptisms occur. Now, to be sure, the concept of faith requires clarification in a certain dimension from the very outset. In the "Observation" the predominant definition of faith as "personal faith," as "personal decision for Jesus," as "free decision of the individual," gives the biblical concept an almost imperceptible twist that is foreign to it and necessarily has dubious

558 consequences. At the very least it must be kept in mind that for Paul the formulation "my faith" or "I believe" never occurs (cf. the limitation of the "I believe" in Mark 9:24; according to Nestle, Acts 8:37 is a later, poorly attested addition!), that the noun "faith" is much more frequent in Paul than the verb "to believe" (in Gal., e.g., 15 to 2; cf. Lohmeyer, *Grundlagen paulinischen Theologie* [*Foundations of Pauline Theology*], 115ff.), that even "we believe" or "you [plural] believe" is relatively infrequent compared to the absolute use of the noun and the important modifier πίστις Χριστου [*faith in/of Christ*]. The formulations "faith came" and "faith was revealed" (Gal. 3:23, 25) are particularly striking. Faith is therefore first of all to be conceived objectively as revelation, event, grace, gift of God or Christ, through which the self is entirely superseded—"I . . . , no longer I" (Gal. 2:20!).—In faith we receive a share in an event in which God alone and wholly is the one acting, as Father, Son, and Holy Spirit (cf. 1 Cor. 12:3; Rom. 8:15, 26–27). Only because "faith came," "was revealed," do *we* believe as a church-community; and only when this is recognized may it be said, with the reservation of Mark 9:24, I believe, yet even then always in such a way that one's gaze rests at no time on one's own self but instead on the content of faith. It becomes clear even from this point that the concept of faith underlying the "Observation" places the accent in an unbiblical way on the "personal," on the self, on one's free decision; and it thereby considerably encumbers the problem of baptism and faith from the outset.

2. In reference to baptism the human person is purely passive. There is no self-baptism; but even the phrase "have oneself baptized," which occurs so strikingly often in the "Reflection," occurs in the NT only one single

559 time (Acts 22:16); the passive is used everywhere else. The person *is* baptized. The faith that receives baptism—and only in faith can baptism be received—can in no way be understood as an active cooperation in baptism; it is pure reception and only real in the very act of reception. For this reason faith is not an independent precondition that could be separated

from the reception of baptism. Without faith there is no salvation, no community with Christ. But faith does not create salvation, does not create the sacrament; rather, it receives them. The human being is also or rather precisely in faith purely passive in the face of salvation; indeed, faith is nothing short of the theological terminus that characterizes pure human passivity in the reception of salvation. This is the reason justification by grace alone is the same as justification by faith alone. "There is no trace of the view that the essence of faith for Paul or anywhere in the NT is self-surrender to God and Christ" (Cremer, *Biblico-theological Lexicon of New Testament Greek*).

3. Since faith always springs from the Word of God (Rom. 10:17), it can be portrayed psychologically only as a conscious, comprehending hearing of and responding to the Word of God. Confession of faith and decision of faith are—necessary—expressions, forms of faith, but they are not identical with faith itself. There are confessions of Christ and personal decisions for Christ that cannot stand before Christ (Matt. 7:21; Luke 9:57ff.; Matt. 26:33ff.). The essence of faith—independent of our psychological faculty of imagination! Faith is in fact not a psychological concept but a theological one!—is not conscious comprehending, responding, deciding, but the pure reception of salvation as it is revealed to us in Christ as the Word of God. The NT does not reflect further on the psychological possibilities of this reception. The NT has no interest in what is of great interest in the "Reflection." Only in allusions does it speak of possibilities of receiving salvation, which in any case do not issue in personal confession of faith and personal decision of faith. In Matt. 9:2, Jesus promises forgiveness of sins to the paralytic on account of the faith of those who carried him (even if αὐτῶν [*their*] were to refer *also* to the paralytic, which is hardly possible linguistically, it is noteworthy that it does not read αὐτοῦ [*his*]; cf. the healing miracles that result from the faith and intercession of others, esp. Mark 9:23; Matt. 8:13!). First Cor. 7:14 speaks of a sanctification of the unbelieving spouse by the believing one, a sanctification not conditioned by 560 personal faith. First Cor. 15:29 belongs in a special way in this context (see above), likewise the promise of salvation to the infants (Luke 18:15), the praise and thanks of Jesus for the revelation of God to the "immature" (cf. also Luke 9:49–50, where in connection with the acceptance of children John reports in the name of the disciples that they stopped someone from performing miracles in Jesus' name because he was not following Jesus— the same thing is apparently taking place in this lack of discipleship as with the children, namely, not consciously making a decision—to which Jesus answers, "Do not stop him," cf. Luke 18:16; "for whoever is not against us is for us"). Finally, thinking about people in corporate terms in the NT (cf.

Matt. 10:13 and the words about the cities in Matt. 11:20)[5] belongs here
as well. From all these passages emerges no more, but also no less, than
the warrant for the question whether it is permissible to withhold baptism
from children born to believing parents on the grounds that they lack the
psychological preconditions for a personal confession and decision.

4. The NT speaks explicitly only of the baptism of believers. Proclamation, repentance, faith, baptism is the sequence attested repeatedly. By
baptism the person who has come to faith is incorporated into the body
of Christ. The praxis of the NT thus solves the essential connection of
baptism and faith concretely through the predominant practice of adult
baptism. This corresponds to the mission situation. Yet, as we have seen,
it would be false to understand the essential unity of baptism and faith
exclusively as the temporal succession of personal confession of faith and
baptism. Baptism takes place only where there is faith. In the mission situation this means the conscious confession of faith by adults; since, however,
according to its nature even the confession of faith (which, by the way, is not
passed on with certainty anywhere in scripture) must not be understood
as a work, a psychological process, the question remains open whether
faith as pure reception could not also be the vicarious faith of the church-
community for its children and/or the faith of the young children of the
church-community themselves. In this case, of course, we must constantly
keep in mind that people are never baptized "in" their own faith; thus
children are also not baptized "in" the faith of the church-community or
their own faith but solely in the name of Jesus Christ. The New Testament
561   practice of the believer's baptism of adults can be understood theologically as merely one possible solution for the relationship of baptism and
faith, alongside which the possibility of infant baptism cannot be ruled out.
In any case, the *refusal* of infant baptism cannot be grounded in the New
Testament; this is true precisely because of the conception of faith in the
doctrine of justification. If we add to this insight, gained from the concept
of faith, the baptismal command and promise of Jesus as a sacramental
reality, and in addition come to the realization that every human being is
born in sin and stands in need of rebirth, then the theoretical possibility of
infant baptism becomes a concrete hope rooted in faith and a confidence,
in light of which the church-community believes itself no longer permitted
to withhold baptism from its children.

---

5. ["Cf. Bonhoeffer's understanding of the 'collective person' in *DBWE* 1:284, there
appealing also to Matt. 11:21ff. . . . ," *DBWE* 16:560, n. 57.]

B. On the Teaching of the Lutheran Confessional Writings.

1. The grounding of baptism is the baptismal command of Christ. This is universal. The gift of baptism is (summarized in the decisive concept of) rebirth. The efficacy of baptism rests on the command and promise of Christ. Baptism calls for faith as God's gift of grace. What does this mean in regard to infant baptism? How is infant baptism received in faith? Answer: through the faith of infants and through the faith of the church-community.

2. Child's faith: The primary objection is directed against its psychological impossibility. Against this the following can be said:

a) It is psychologically no less impossible to speak of the sin of infants,   562
as the doctrine of original sin does. Sin and faith are not psychological acts but real relationships to God.

b) Unlike the pietistic concept of faith, the Reformation concept is defined not psychologically but theologically. "Such faith, such 'clinging' and 'grasping,' is so completely a reception of grace that every psychological description of this process must be eliminated. Nor can the act of reception be bound to psychological presuppositions" (Schlink, *Theology of the Lutheran Confessions*, page 152).

c) The later Lutheran differentiation between fides directa and reflexiva, immediata and mediate [*direct and reflexive faith, immediate and mediate faith*],[6] exists for a theologically good reason, and protects against any psychologizing and law-oriented distortions of the concept of faith.

d) Luther does not make an autonomous theologumenon[7] out of a child's faith; rather he contradicts the false reasoning that attempts to assert its impossibility.

3. The faith of godparents: the primary objection is directed against the impossibility of vicarious representative faith. On this the following can be said:

a) The faith of the church-community always precedes the faith of the   563
individual; this is so in the double sense that the church-community administers baptism by faith in the command and promise of Christ and that it receives baptism in a faith that intercedes for the child to be baptized.

b) In intercession the faith of the church-community claims Christ's word for the child and is certain that God hears its prayers.

---

6. [". . . cf. also Bonhoeffer's appeal to the distinction between *fides directa*, 'direct faith,' and *fides reflexa*, 'reflexive faith' in *DBWE* 2:158–161 (*Reader* 107–109)," *DBWE* 16:562, n. 64.]

7. [*A theological opinion as opposed to a defined dogma.*]

c) The faith of the church-community baptizes the child not on the strength of the church-community's faith or the child's faith but on the strength of the word of Christ.

d) The faith of the church-community bears the children through intercession and Christian instruction on the basis of the baptism that has taken place.

e) The church-community cannot see any better into the hearts of adults, whom it receives in faith as members through baptism on the basis of their confession, than it can see into the hearts of children.

f) The faith of the church-community is not a work that it performs in place of the child; instead, it is pleading for, hoping for, and receiving the promises of Christ on behalf of the child—all of this brought about by the word of Christ.

g) The utilization of the Gospel text Mark 10:13ff. for infant baptism relies on the promise to children that it includes about the kingdom of heaven. On what basis would we want to be allowed to deny baptism to those to whom the kingdom of heaven belongs?

h) The argument of the confessional writings does not so much aim toward positive dogmatic proof of the necessity of infant baptism as it disputes the right to refuse infant baptism. "Vicarious representative" faith is meant to become an independent theologumenon no more than is a child's faith; rather the faith of the church-community, within which it dares to baptize children on account of Christ's promise, is not refuted; nor is it repudiated in biblicistic legalism as a heresy.

564   i) On the relation between a child's faith and the godparents' faith, let us note that the confessional writings name both alongside each other. Here the emphasis falls decisively on the godparents' faith, without which there can be no infant baptism. Here as well the faith of the church-community bears the faith of the individual. The unarticulated faith of the child is confessed publicly by the godparents.

k)[8] In the end a child's faith and the godparents' faith are only an expression for that objectivity of faith that was spoken of in the New Testament context. Because "*faith* came," "*faith* was revealed," people can, where this event has taken place, be baptized in faith and receive baptism in faith.

4. In strict terms, the theological reflection must therefore confine itself to opening the possibility of infant baptism. The doctrine of infant baptism is a borderline doctrine on which nothing further can be built systematically yet which as such has its own justification. This internal

---

8. ["No item 'j' occurs in the German original," *DBWE* 16:564, n. 76.]

limitation of theologically feasible assertions about infant baptism is crossed (even in the confessional writings) where an independent doctrine is advocated about the necessity of infant baptism for salvation and about the damnation of children who die unbaptized. Even in those places where it is applied to individual aspects of the reality of revelation, the concept of the necessity for salvation leads, of itself, to an intolerable rending of the entirety of salvation and a legalistic understanding of these particular dimensions. The biblical question is not what *must* necessarily take place for salvation but rather what *may* take place. But in the light of salvation, who would want to decline doing something that was permitted? The question of the salvation of those who have died can never be answered directly, even when we consider the baptized. It makes sense and is justified only in that, repeatedly, it refers the individual and the church-community entirely to God's grace—that is, to Christ, his word, and his sacrament. The casuistic thinking that has developed around the question of the necessity of baptism for salvation makes baptism into a human work.   565
It is equally false to declare infant baptism "unnecessary" for the salvation of children and to appeal glibly to the grace of God that "is greater than baptism," an appeal of which scripture contains not one word. In this context we must refute the charge that the confessional writings tie the grace of God too strongly to baptism, thereby granting baptism an independent stature alongside Christ. The authors of the confessional writings did not need to explicitly assert the fact that we are made holy not by faith in baptism but by faith in Christ. The confessional writings, however, correctly attest that God was pleased to "bind" God's grace to Christ—that is, to Word and sacrament—and that there has been no grace of God revealed to us apart from Word and sacrament; and the God who is supposedly "greater" than this grace, according to our own thoughts and wishes, is not the God of the Bible. Instead of longing for this sort of "greater" God, of whom surely we can know nothing, we should praise and utterly abide by the gracious nearness of God as it is given to us in the bond to Word and sacrament.

5. The confessional writings rightly resist the fanatics who forbid infant baptism; rather, on the basis of scripture and its "key," the doctrine of justification, they open the way for infant baptism. But above all, they repudiate as fanatical arrogance the idea that the baptism performed by the church in faith in the word of Christ and in his name is no baptism. The *validity* of baptism rests solely on the command and promise of Jesus Christ. The *benefit* of baptism depends on the faith that receives it. For this reason the opponents of infant baptism may never question its validity but at the most its benefit.

6. The confessional writings do not provide any further information about the chronological relationship of baptism and faith. They are content with having established their essential mutual unity. While adult baptism places faith chronologically prior to baptism, infant baptism leaves the question open. To be sure, the faith of the church-community precedes the baptism, but the child's initial faith as well as its later, conscious faith are effects of baptism. The faith of the church-community today is impossible to imagine without the institution of baptism that preceded it. On the other hand, those in the first church-community were already believers when they were baptized. Finally, however, the institution of baptism by Christ precedes the faith of the church-community as established at Pentecost. Thus, in the end (unless some arbitrarily chosen time period, such as, for instance, the baptism of the first church-community, is detached from the overall context) the question of the chronological relationship of baptism and faith comes down to the question of the chronological relationship of word and sacrament. But this question can no longer be theologically decided, since in Jesus Christ Word and sacrament are one. Even John 1:1 can no longer be separated from John 1:14. The argument that Christ first preached and only at the end of his life instituted the sacraments overlooks the fact that the bodily presence of the preaching Christ was itself already a sacrament and that the institution of the sacraments before his departure can only be understood as ensuring his ongoing bodily presence. Thus the question of the chronological relationship of Word and sacrament, of faith and baptism, cannot be solved theologically but only pedagogically-psychologically-practically. It is certainly inadmissible—in this the "Observation" is correct—to deduce the necessity of infant baptism from, e.g., the dogmatic concept of gratia praeveniens [*prevenient grace*],[9] to treat infant baptism as an illustration of a dogmatic proposition. Of course, it is equally impermissible to deduce the repudiation of infant baptism from some concept of the church-community. All that determines the truth or falsity of infant baptism are the biblical assertions about baptism that are opened by the key of the Holy Scripture, the message of justification by grace and faith alone. Yet if from this perspective infant baptism can be regarded as permissible, then subsequently the concept of, e.g., gratia praeveniens can rightly be cited as an illustration of infant baptism.

566

---

9. [" . . . [I]n the Lutheran baptismal theology, particularly of the nineteenth and twentieth centuries, the term refers to the grace of justification that precludes all human action . . . ," *DBWE* 16:566, n. 82.]

C. Baptism and Church-Community.

1. Just as in the mission situation the relationship of baptism and faith is resolved in the predominance of adult baptisms, in the situation of the church of the people this relationship is resolved predominantly in infant baptism. Both possibilities are given in the freedom and responsibility of   567
the church-community and will indeed be practiced according to the spiritual state of the church-community, according to the faith of the church-community, and according to its situation in the world. The misuse of baptism occurs just as much in places where infant baptism is practiced amid neglect of its strict relation to the faith of the church-community as in places where the faith of adults becomes a work on which the validity of the baptism is said to rest. Infant baptism always threatens to separate baptism from faith, just as adult baptism always threatens to destroy the baptismal grace founded in Christ's word alone. A misuse of infant baptism of the sort one can unmistakably observe in our church's past will therefore necessarily lead the church-community to an appropriate limitation of its practice and to a new appreciation of adult baptism.

2. In times of the church's secularization, the utter repudiation of infant baptism and the demand for the baptism and rebaptism of believers have been raised repeatedly as a battle cry for the renewal of the church as well as for the formation of a pure church-community of believers separated from the world. Never has this rallying cry renewed the church. Instead, it has led to innumerable splinter groups that in part led their own life on the periphery of the church and in part themselves returned again to infant baptism in the next generation. This observation is not a theological argument; it belongs, however, to the records of church history, which must be pondered by every responsible Christian who deals with these questions.

3. The historically speculative assertion that, along with the end in our time of the Constantinian epoch of church history, infant baptism, as a specific aspect of that epoch, had to fall away as well rests on the error that infant baptism was first introduced under Constantine. On the contrary, it is certain that Irenaeus, Tertullian, Hippolytus, and Origen (who traces it back to apostolic tradition) take infant baptism for granted as general practice. The Synod of Carthage of 251 gave advice regarding the question whether baptism should occur on the third or the eighth day following birth. The mark of the Constantinian epoch is not that the Christian   568
church-community baptized its children, but that baptism as such became a qualification for civic life; the problematic development lay not in infant baptism, but rather in this secular qualification of baptism. These should be clearly differentiated.

4. In a secularized church the longing for a pure, authentic, true, church-community of believers, separated from the world and prepared for battle, is very understandable; yet it is full of dangers: too easily an ideal church-community replaces the real church-community of God; too easily the pure church-community is understood as an achievement to be enacted by human beings; too easily Jesus' parables of the weeds among the wheat and of the fish net are overlooked; too easily it is forgotten that God loved the *world* and desires that *everyone* be saved; too easily a fallacious, legalistic biblicism displaces responsible theological reflection. The separation of the church-community from the world, the purity, readiness for battle, truthfulness of the church-community—these are not goals to be pursued directly in themselves but fruits that spontaneously follow an authentic proclama-

569 tion of the Gospel. Luther's Reformation came not from the attempt to realize a better, perhaps "original Christian" ideal of church-community, but rather from the new recognition of the gospel from Holy Scripture. It can only be a matter of orientation to the gospel today, not of the reestablishment of the original Christian church-community. Authentic church renewal will always be distinguished from fanaticism in that the former always takes its departure from the central and certain teachings of scripture. Now it is, of course, incontrovertible that the proper administration of the sacrament of baptism is a central requirement of scripture; however, following all that has already been said, the repudiation of infant baptism can certainly not be characterized as a central and certain teaching of Holy Scripture. Where, however, human thoughts—even the best, purest, and most pious—are made the point of departure for efforts at church renewal, there the church's cause, which rests solely on the clear and certain word of God, is threatened, especially if human thoughts repudiating the faith of the church pass themselves off as divine truth.

5. Particularly dubious in the given "Special Reflections on Baptism and Church-Community" are the following formulations: page 39: "Those who do not wish to step entirely over to Christ's side, to confess this and give expression to it by having themselves baptized, should remain outside! . . . Here a clear, full decision is required. Here the air becomes pure. This truthfulness makes the message credible and the witness of the church attractive to youth."

Here we find a rigorism and idealism—definitely attractive to youth—that all too directly identifies personal decisiveness with faith (see above), that quenches the dimly burning wick and breaks the bruised reed. The statement on page 38 that, subjectively regarded, one's belonging to the community of Jesus Christ rests on the free decision of the individual, on the capacity to act voluntarily, corresponds to this. Here, too, "free deci-

sion" is inserted in place of "faith" and thereby a dangerous distortion of   570
the biblical concept of faith is undertaken (see above). The introduction of
the unbiblical concept of "believer's baptism" and the striking, oft repeated
use of the reflexive form "have oneself baptized" also correspond to this
terminological and thereby at the same time objectively significant conceptual shift. All of this points in the same direction, toward a psychologi-
cal-activist thinking deviating from the Bible. "Decision for Christ"—itself
an unbiblical term—is the activist perversion of the passive character of
faith. Decision for Christ places the human person in the center of view.
"Faith" is entirely oriented upon its object, upon Christ. On page 37 infant
baptism is characterized as an infringement not only of the freedom of
the human being (where does *that* conception of freedom come from?
from idealism and liberal theology, not from the Bible), but also of God
in God's election by grace. This denies the universality of the salvific will
of God as it is attested in scripture; the grace of God is separated from the
means of grace (as we already observed above in another place), and the
church-community and world move clearly away from each other as those
chosen and damned from all eternity. What then, however, do we do with
John 3:16? The same relationship of church-community and world that
presented itself earlier on the psychological level as "personal decision" and
"indecisiveness" repeats itself here on the basis of an abstract doctrine of
double predestination and a corresponding freedom of God from God's   571
own means of grace, i.e., from God's revelation. In both cases the true relationship of church-community and world, which unfolds only in faith in
the revelation of God in the world and encompasses both John 3:16 and 1
John 2:17, is missed and brought into a false, one-dimensional formulation.
This may be more impressive, more attractive; but it makes the church of
God into an ideal of the pious.

6. The abolition of infant baptism is not an effective means of confronting the secularization of the church, because even "believer's baptism"
does not secure against severe relapses; indeed, experience has shown that
it is precisely the special emphasis on personal conversion experiences that
frequently leads to fanatical derailments and setbacks.

7. What is required of the Christian church-community today is not
the abolition of infant baptism but a correct Protestant baptismal discipline. Since infant baptism, where it is performed in faith (see above), thus
within the believing community, cannot be disallowed on the basis of scripture but may be gratefully adopted as a special gift of God's grace to the
believing community, the correct Protestant baptismal discipline will have
to direct its attention to the question of whether believing godparents and
parents as members of the church-community bring their child to baptism.

In the first place, positively, this discipline will take baptismal instruction for the church-community, godparents, and parents more seriously than previously; it will testify to the particular grace of infant baptism that dares not be thrown away like a cut-rate good; it will warn of the misuse of baptism and, if necessary, will refuse infant baptism in places where in its clear judgment baptism is being sought apart from faith. Yet in its refusal it will be guided not by some sort of rigorism but by God's love for the world and for his church-community.

8. How does the church respond to Christians who say they must refuse infant baptism in its entirety for reasons of faith? a) The church has no right on the basis of Holy Scripture to discipline believing members of the church-community who do not have their children baptized. b) The same is true in regard to pastors who take this stance relative to their own children. In both cases the church will perceive a practical indication of the seriousness of baptismal grace. c) The church cannot, however, allow its pastors to deny baptism to believing Christians who desire it for their children, because this denial cannot be justified from scripture. d) The church cannot allow its pastors to proclaim a doctrine, counter to scripture, about the impermissibility of infant baptism, whereas it cannot bar them from recommending adult baptism on biblical grounds. e) But under no circumstances can the church permit rebaptism, i.e., the declaration of the invalidity of the baptism performed by the church of Christ in faith in the word of Christ from time immemorial. In doctrine and practice rebaptism destroys the unity and the community of the church in that it views all those baptized as children as unbaptized, i.e., as not belonging to the body of Christ. This is where the dangerous aspect of the "Observation" lies, to which the church can say only No. Those who are rebaptized divorce themselves not only from the world but also from the church of Jesus Christ.

41. THEOLOGICAL POSITION PAPER ON THE *PRIMUS USUS LEGIS*

DBWE 16:584–601

Justification by grace through faith, arguably the central doctrine of the Lutheran theological tradition, leads directly into discussions about the use or purpose of "the law." That justification is through faith rules out the idea that the law's purpose is to prescribe the works by which people justify themselves. Rather, the law forces them to despair at their very inability to do so, and thereby drives them into the gracious arms of Christ, who has fulfilled the law for them. In addition to this spiritual or theological use, the law also has a civic or political use, namely the maintaining of order and restraining of sin in society. While Luther himself usually discussed only these two uses, the generations after him often added a third, where the law functions as a guide for living the Christian life. Thus Bonhoeffer inherited a tradition of speaking about three uses of the law, which the Lutheran confessions ordered thus: civic, theological, and moral. To speak of the first use of the law (primus usus legis), *then, is to discuss the law's civic use.*[1]

In response to the first reports of the deportation of the Jews, a Confessing Church council charged a committee with drafting a statement on the commandment, "Thou shalt not kill." Bonhoeffer, who sat on that committee, prepared this position paper on the broader question of preaching the law, specifically the first use of the law.[2] *This paper reflects his concern that the Lutheran confessions' presentation of the first use was open to being read in terms of natural law and therefore liable to misinterpretation in the direction of "a false theology of the orders." Against this, he was intent to emphasis the revealed nature of the law by closely tying it to the gospel. The first use of the law has its origin and goal in the gospel.*

---

1. [*See Lohse*, Martin Luther's Theology, *270–272; Gassmann et al.*, Historical Dictionary of Lutheranism, *178–179.*]

2. [DBWE *16:584, n. 1.*]

The Doctrine of the *Primus Usus Legis*
according to the Confessional Writings and Their Critique.

1. The *concept of the usus legis* is found in the headings to the section of the FC[3] de tertio usu legis, translated "Concerning the Third Use of the Law," and also in the Solida declaratio VI/1 in the Latin text; in the German text instead of the concept of *usus* we find that of the "benefit" of the law. In the Epitome we read that the law of God "has been given to people for three reasons" (corresponding to the Smalcald Articles, "Concerning the Law," page 311.[4]). From this we infer that the question regarding the *subject of the usus,* namely, whether it is God or the preacher, is, of course, not explicitly determined but nevertheless is to be answered with the sense that the subject is God. Epit. 7 also supports this: "Therefore, for both the repentant and the unrepentant, for the reborn and those not reborn, the law is and remains one single law, the unchangeable will of God. In terms of obedience there is a difference only in that those people who are not yet reborn do what the law demands unwillingly, because they are coerced (as is also the case with the reborn with respect to the flesh). Believers, however, do without coercion, with a willing spirit, insofar as they are born anew, what no threat of the law could ever force from them." Accordingly, the concept of the usus legis dare not mislead us into thinking primarily of different forms of preaching—that is, forms of using the law on the part of preachers—under different circumstances; but rather it has to do first with different effects of the one single law. In reference to their subject, these effects are to be understood equally as the free working of God on the human being and as belief and unbelief on the part of the person, so that the subject of the use of the law must be seen to be not the preacher but God, and then in addition, if so desired, the hearer of the sermon, the human being. Since, however, this question is not explicitly clarified in the confessional writings, dangerous ambiguities arise in the course of its delineation. Because of its decisive importance for the entire preaching of the law, the question of the subject of the usus had to be answered from the FC. If, that

585

---

3. ["... The following abbreviations are used below by Bonhoeffer: CA = Confessio Augustana (Augsburg Confession); AC = Apology of the Augsburg Confession; Smalc. Art. = Smalcald Articles; LC = Large Catechism; FC = Formula of Concord, which consists of two parts: Ep = Epitome; SDec = Solid Declaration; and NT = New Testament ...," *DBWE* 16:584, n. 1.]

4. ["... In the present text, the page and paragraph enumerations and the abbreviations for individual texts follow the 2000 Fortress Press edition of *Book of Concord* ...," *DBWE* 16:584, n. 1.]

is, the preacher or the church were the subject of the three usus, then there would be a preaching of the law for the world that would be significantly different from that for the congregation. The one would contain the demand of a civil-political-rational righteousness of works that would be cut off from the demand of the obedience of faith toward the triune God. The other would contain only an admonition to those who believe in Christ. But if God is the subject of the three usus, then there is *one* preaching of the law, which achieves different effects among unbelievers and believers. The preacher as the subject of the usus would know of an isolated preaching of   586
works; God as subject of the usus, by the preaching of the *one* law, works different effects in believers and unbelievers. Because the concept of the usus leaves this decisive preliminary question unresolved, its usefulness ought to be questioned (cf. below 12.).

2. The law of God is "a divine teaching in which the righteous, unchanging will of God revealed how human beings were created in their nature, thoughts, words, and deeds to be pleasing and acceptable to God. This law also threatens those who transgress it with God's wrath and temporal and eternal punishments" (SDec V/17). The law is "the commandments of the Decalogue, wherever they appear in the Scriptures" (AC IV/6). The proper office of the law is "reproving sin and teaching good works" (duplex usus? [*double use*]) (SDec V/18). The primus usus legis effects the establishment of a disciplina externa et honesta [*external discipline and respectability*] (SDec V/1) through threats and promises. The secundus usus [*second use*] effects the recognition of sin. The tertius usus [*third use*] serves the converted as a guiding principle of their action and as chastisement of the flesh still alive even in them. The conception that the distinction between the three usus has to do with a chronological sequence of proclamation or with two groups of persons to be differentiated from one another in principle (unbelievers and believers)[5] is at least not ruled out in the confessional writings, but in actual fact it cannot be sustained. The externa   587
disciplina still applies to believers, as do the threat and chastisement of the law to the extent a believer is still flesh ("For the old creature, like a stubborn, recalcitrant donkey, is also still a part of them, and it needs to be forced into obedience to Christ not only through the law's teaching, admonition, compulsion, and threat but also often with the cudgel

---

5. ["Cf. the distinction made in early Protestant dogmatics between the law's preservation of the unregenerated in external discipline and the regenerated, by contrast, both outwardly as well as inwardly—i.e., spiritually; cf. Schmid, *Doctrinal Theology of the Evangelical Lutheran Church*, 510," *DBWE* 16:586, n. 22.]

of punishments and tribulations," SDec VI/24); believers also still require the recognition of sin through the law. In addition, the primus usus itself contains the entire contents of the law, namely, the Decalogue in both tables, just as it also already contains threat and promise. The uncertainty as to whether the usus paedagogicus [*pedagogical use*][6] is to be accorded an independent significance, whether it, as a fourth usus, is to be placed between the politicus and elenchticus,[7] and the fact that the Smalc. Art. know of only a twofold usus legis (primus and secundus) make it clear that the differences between the usus legis must be understood not in chronological terms—and that means not with reference to groups of people that are different in principle—but instead with respect to their content. The primus usus defines the content of the law in reference to the establishment of certain external works; the secundus usus defines the relationship of the law to the person, in that the individual is led to the recognition of opposition to the law and of their condemnation; the tertius usus defines the law as a gracious help from God for doing the works commanded. The primus usus is the law as preaching about works; the secundus is the law as preaching about the recognition of sin; the tertius is the law as preaching about the fulfillment of the law. The proclamation of the law always contains all three elements. It works in different ways, depending on God's will and who the hearer is, bringing about the performance of external works, repentance, new obedience. Yet where the differentiation of the three usus misleads us, so that we understand these as distinctions of chronological sequence or of different preaching methods to address groups of persons thought to be different from one another in principle, the unity of the law of God is broken, and we face the question of the theological justification of the usus doctrine (see below 12.) in addition to the question treated under 1.) of the usefulness of the usus concept.

588   3. The primus usus is not treated consistently in the confessional writings. It does not receive any separate attention. We encounter its substance, with positive emphasis, in the polemic against the doctrine of monastic perfection, against the Catholic Church's claim to worldly rule, against the Enthusiasts, and in the doctrine of worldly rule; with negative emphasis, in the doctrine of justification by faith and the critique of righteousness of works connected with this in the doctrine of free will; we encounter it in

---

6. ["... i.e., the function of the law as a disciplinarian, or *Zuchtmeister,* for the sake of Christ; cf. Gal. 3:24," *DBWE* 16:587, n. 25.]

7. ["Cf. the fourfold use of the law as *usus politicus, elenchticus, paedagogicus* as well as *didacticus* in Schmid, *Doctrinal Theology of the Evangelical Lutheran Church,* 510," *DBWE* 16:587, n. 26.]

neutral systematic form in the debate regarding the tertius usus legis. The confessional writings are interested in the primus usus only in its relation to the gospel.

4. Definition: The primus usus legis is used "to maintain external discipline and respectability against dissolute, disobedient people." We shall now investigate the content, purpose, means of implementation, preacher, and hearer of the primus usus.

5. The *content* of the primus usus legis is the entire Decalogue with respect to the works it requires, combined with the threat and promise it contains. "Here we maintain that the law was given by God, in the first place, to curb sin by means of the threat and terror of punishment and also by means of the promise and offer of grace and favor" (Smalc. Art., "Concerning the Law"). In terms of its content, the entire law is contained within the primus usus legis (AC IV/8). The idea that the second table of the law might be preached without the first is found nowhere in the con-   589 fessional writings. On the contrary, such a division is criticized sharply throughout. Nevertheless, the first table already contains the indication that even the second table cannot be fulfilled by works alone, thus overcoming the primus usus (AC IV/8, 35, 130). The law, however, is not only contained in the Decalogue but permeates the entire NT.[8] "What could be a more sobering and terrifying demonstration and proclamation of the wrath of God against sin than the suffering and death of Christ, his Son? But as long as these things all proclaim God's wrath and terrify the human being, it is still not the proclamation of the gospel or of Christ, in the strict sense. It is instead the proclamation of Moses and the law *to the unrepentant*" (SDec V/12). Although the confessional writings do not assert this, and perhaps do not even intend it (they are able even to speak of a "sermon" without Christ—sine mentione Christi [*without mentioning Christ*] [SDec V/10], which can only be a reference to the primus usus), the

---

8. ["In the historical context in which he wrote, Bonhoeffer's comments in this document about the centrality of the law were a radical message that would not have been missed by his colleagues in the Confessing Church. The Institute for the Research and Removal of Jewish Influence on the Religious Life of the German People had been established in 1939, and by 1941 several regional churches had agreed to the segregation of 'non-Aryan Christians' through the establishment of separate congregations. In their sermons and theological writings, pastors and theologians of that era pointedly attacked 'the law' and 'legalism' as Judaic influences. In contrast, here Bonhoeffer is discussing the continued validity and centrality of the law of Moses in Christianity. For a more thorough discussion of this aspect of Bonhoeffer's thought, see Christine-Ruth Müller, *Dietrich Bonhoeffers Kampf*, 213–222," *DBWE* 16:589, n. 40. *For more on the Institute mentioned above, see Heschel,* The Aryan Jesus.]

preceding requires the conclusion that proclamation of the teaching and cross of Christ belongs also to the primus usus legis as preaching of the law. Yet insofar as the cross is always also proclamation of the gospel and, seen from this perspective, proclamation of the gospel is already contained even in the Decalogue, in the First Commandment, the primus usus legis can never be preached in abstract detachment from the gospel. Despite this, its proper nature is to require the works of the law that serve external discipline and respectability. By threatening punishment and by attracting people with the (earthly) blessings promised by God for an honorable

590   life, the works of the law are compelled out of people's fear or longing for happiness. This is where the exclusive orientation of the primus usus legis to bringing about *works*, that is, certain *conditions*, is expressed. From this perspective the "natural law innate to human hearts" can now also be characterized as the content of the lex [*law*] in its primus usus; this natural law "is in agreement with the Law of Moses or the Ten (!) Commandments" (AC IV/7). In all this the possibility of a lex naturae [*natural law*] deviating from the Decalogue and thereby introducing a conflict is not even considered; in any case, the sole standard is always the Decalogue. It is therefore the will *of God*, not of human beings, that takes effect in the primus usus as well as in the lex naturae. The organ through which the lex naturae comes into play is the ratio [*reason*]. Standing opposed to it are the demonic powers, evil impulses, and the devil, which are mightier than the ratio, so that even despite "valiant effort" the ratio only seldom prevails (AC XVIII/71–72). This makes clear that not every human urge can pass itself off as natural law. The Decalogue remains the final criterion. "God truly demands and desires this sort of outwardly honorable life, and for the sake of God's commands one would have to perform the same good works that are prescribed in the Ten (!) Commandments" (AC IV/22).

6. The *purpose of the primus usus* is the establishment of the iustitia civilis or rationis, carnis [*civil righteousness or the righteousness of reason, of the flesh*] (AC IV/22–24, XVIII/70). It consists of an honorable life in accord with the

591   Decalogue in its first and second tables (to talk about God, to display outward acts of worship and holy behavior, to honor one's parents, to refrain from stealing, AC XVIII/70). This lies "to some extent" within the ability of free will and of reason, although it is only rarely actualized (AC XVIII/72). It is rightfully praised by humans and by God; "we willingly give this righteousness of reason the praises it deserves, for our corrupt nature has no greater good than this, . . . God even honors it with temporal rewards" (AC IV/24). This means that all worldly life is subject to the Decalogue insofar as works are concerned. God desires the iustitia civilis from all people, even from Christians. This is said against the Enthusiasts, "who teach that

Christian perfection means physically leaving house and home, spouse and child" (CA XVI/4) and who thus wish to make the gospel into a new law for the world. By contrast, the truth is that the gospel "teaches an internal, eternal reality and righteousness of the heart, not an external, temporal one" (see above), that the gospel does not provide new laws regarding civil life (CA XVI/55). This statement about the gospel thus necessarily assumes the proclamation of the Decalogue for the establishment of iustitia civilis. Without this connection, such an assertion would itself be Enthusiastic. The confessional writings therefore assert that, in regard to the content of the law, the Decalogue contains the full teaching and the gospel contributes nothing additional.

7. As a *means for the implementation of the primus usus legis*, and thus for the establishment of iustitia civilis, "God provides law, regulates political authority, provides learned wise people who serve the government" (AC IV/22). Thus the government is placed under the law of God and in the service of God. The law of the Decalogue preached by the church is implemented by the government by means of force. The sword is given to the government for this purpose. To be sure, the confessional writings presuppose that reason will dictate to the government the same law as the Decalogue; thus they do not reckon with the possibility of an opposition in principle between the lex naturae and the Decalogue. Yet this does not signify a double grounding of government in natural law and revealed law; instead, it is only because both have been declared to be identical (see above, section 5) that natural law, reason, can be given as the basis for governmental action. Natural law can never claim divine authority against the Decalogue. Although, or rather because, the government has its origin in God's law as proclaimed by the church and serves it, it has its own worth over against the church that proclaims the gospel. It has this worth, not in a freedom from God's law or the Decalogue that is grounded in its own law, but in the obedience with which it brings about the implementation of God's law by means of its action. Insofar as it does God's will in this way, punishing evil and rewarding good, it glorifies its divine office, it has a claim to obedience, and rulers may have a clean conscience (AC XVI/65). The confessional writings laud the Protestant doctrine, which has restored to government its own worth over against the Roman human statutes. In this way, the doctrine of the iustitia civilis serves polemically to free and honor natural, worldly life under the Decalogue over against the Roman doctrine of the perfection of monastic life. Yet when a natural law asserts itself against the law of God in the Decalogue, when the power of government no longer wishes to serve the Decalogue (a case that the confessional writings do not consider), this perverted nature and reason cannot in that case lay claim to their own

592

divine law; instead, they must be placed under the law of God by means of proclamation. For the confessional writings the "natural" is determined solely by the Decalogue.[9]

593   8. The one proclaiming the primus usus legis is primarily the church, secondarily the government, head of the family, and master. The church proclaims the primus usus by preaching the entire law in all three usus, thus indirectly; the government proclaims the primus usus directly. The church proclaims the primus usus in the service of the gospel; the government proclaims it as an end in itself. The Decalogue belongs in the church *and* in city hall.[10]

9. Hearers of the primus usus legis are the "unbelievers, the unruly, and the disobedient." Thus it is *people*, not orders as such, who are being addressed. The orders belong instead, according to the confessional writings, more on the side of those doing the proclaiming. For the confessional writings there is no theological problem about *whether* to preach to unbelievers or about *what* to preach to them. Even the practical problem of reaching the unbelievers is assumed to be solved: some are reached by the church, others by the government. Although the confessional writings presumably understand unbelievers to refer to a certain group of persons, this conception founders insofar as, according to the confessions, even Christians themselves are still in the flesh and for this reason are in need of the primus usus legis just as fully as are unbelievers (cf. the New Testament vice lists). Conversely, the unruly, the non-Christians, also stand under the call of the gospel and fall under the proclamation of the law for the sake of the gospel. There is no proclamation *solely* for unbelievers, but only the sort that applies to unbelievers *as well*. A clear division into two groups of persons is theologically inappropriate. Although the confessional writings do not explicitly preclude this understanding, it nevertheless cannot be reconciled with their theological assertions.

10. *The primus usus and the gospel.*

a) The primus usus stands in tension with the gospel because it demands a righteousness of works and thereby makes people presumptuous (Smalc.
594   Art., "Concerning the Law"; SDec V/10). For this reason the iustitia civilis is sin and hypocrisy before the gospel (AC II/34, IV/35). "'Whatever does not proceed from faith is sin.' For a person must be acceptable to God before-

---

9. ["On Bonhoeffer's understanding of the 'natural,' see *DBWE* 6:171–178 (*Reader* 631–635)," *DBWE* 16:591, n. 68.]

10. ["Doctrine declaring that the claim God's law makes on the life of a Christian is obsolete," *DBWE* 14:432, n. 99. ". . . On Bonhoeffer's own repudiation of antinomianism, cf. '"Personal" and "Objective" Ethics,' *DBWE* 16:547, n. 40," *DBWE* 16:593, n. 69.]

hand . . . , before that person's works are at all pleasing to him" (SDec IV/8). The primus usus legis is "sublated"[11] (in the double sense of the word) by the gospel. It is broken and fulfilled. In following Jesus, the Sabbath is desecrated, father and mother are deserted, and God is obeyed more than are human beings; yet precisely in following him the sanctification of the feast day, the honoring of parents, and worldly obedience in faith are all the more truly fulfilled.

b) *The primus usus legis* is *related* to the gospel: 1.) through this use of the law arises the worldly order, which according to God's will preserves the world from disorder and arbitrariness; 2.) within this order human beings receive from God all good gifts of earthly life and are able to do good works through faith in the gospel. In the confessional writings this idea, that worldly orders are there for the sake of Christian life flowing from faith in the gospel, takes precedence over the conception that the orders serve as the presupposition for deliverance by the gospel. 3.) The government, which protects these orders, is concerned with the maintenance of the Christian proclamation—"God the Lord demands this of *all* kings and princes . . ." (AC XXI/44)—and, as God's order, is itself "preserved and defended by God against the devil" (AC VIII/50). 4.) Within the iustitia civilis, following the First Commandment means going to church, listening to the sermon,   595 listening to the gospel, and thinking about it to a certain extent; here one is not to "wait until God pours his gifts into them from heaven without means" (SDec II/53, 46, 24). The access to this "means," to the sermon, is the closest possible connection and sharpest distinction between primus usus and gospel. To be sure, within the primus usus this obedience remains external worship and sin. Yet precisely this itself becomes the "prerequisite" for faith in the gospel, even as it is simultaneously its most extreme contradiction. 5.) The gospel instructs us in gratitude for every worldly order in which it is found. It does not allow us to expect anything good from disorder. But it also calls us to the knowledge of Jesus Christ, through whom, for whom, and for whose sake all things are created.

c) *The primus usus legis cannot be separated from the proclamation of the gospel.* Because this use of the law applies to unbelievers and believers (Ep VI/6, SDec VI/9), because it is not a method of proclamation, but instead a dimension of the "one unchanging will of God," it cannot be separated from the other two usus. There is no Christian preaching of works with-

---

11. ["When Bonhoeffer uses *aufheben* in a technical Hegelian sense, it is often translated 'to sublate,' which means that the 'thesis' (here the *primus usus legis*) is both negated by and fulfilled in a new synthesis (here the gospel)," *DBWE* 16:594, n. 75.]

out preaching the recognition of sin and the fulfillment of the law. Yet the law cannot be preached without the gospel. To be sure, the confessional writings see law and gospel proclaimed differently in individual words of scripture ("In some places it communicates the law. In other places it communicates the promise concerning Christ . . . ," AC/5). Nevertheless, at the same time they perceive law and gospel bound together always, from the Decalogue to the preaching of the cross; and they teach that from the beginning both proclamations have existed "alongside each other"—that is, not sequentially (SDec V/23).[12] Thus, in the final analysis it is not the preacher but God alone who distinguishes law and gospel. Wherever the primus usus is isolated, it turns into moralistic preaching and ceases to be God's living word. It is clericalism and hypocrisy[13] to preach only works to a person or a group of persons and to be satisfied with their external fulfillment, while withholding the entire proclamation of the law and gospel. The cleric who spouts moralism can engender only hypocrites. The interpretation of the Decalogue in the Large Catechism is the best practical instruction in the right preaching of the primus usus.

596

d) *The primus usus has its origin and goal in the gospel.* Because the gospel is to be preached to all people, because Jesus Christ became human and died for the sins of all people, because he procured salvation for his enemies, the Christian proclamation is directed to all people with the call to faith. For this reason it has no *independent* interest in the establishment of a certain civic order. It calls for civic order, because it calls to faith. Because God in Christ loved human beings and the world, order should exist among human beings and in the world as well. Because human beings belong to God in grace, they should also obey God in works. Because a congregation is present, justice, peace, order should and can be present. Faith remains the prerequisite and origin of all works. Only from this perspective, however, is the gospel now also the goal of the primus usus. God desires external order not just because the gospel is present but in order that it may be present. Understood in this way, the primus usus has a "pedagogical" character on account of Christ (AC IV/22). Thus the sequence "gospel and law" as well as that of "law and gospel" has its own validity.[14] In the confessional writings

597

---

12. ["*Book of Concord*, 585 . . . ," *DBWE* 16:595, n. 94.]

13. ["Here Bonhoeffer uses *Pharisäismus*; see the discussion of the use of this term in *DBWE* 16:26–27," *DBWE* 16:596, n. 96.]

14. ["Here Bonhoeffer is referring to the debate sparked by Karl Barth's statement: 'I should like . . . to call attention to the fact that I shall not speak about "Law and Gospel" but about "*Gospel and Law*." The traditional order, "Law and Gospel," has a perfect right in its place. . . . It must not, however, define the structure of the whole teaching to be out

the second order is predominant. In both sequences, however, the gospel is the "proper" word of God.

e) *Primus usus and congregation.* In the primus usus unbelievers are addressed on the basis of their being called into the congregation. Apart from this calling, the church has no authority for the proclamation of the law. This assertion is not articulated by the confessional writings but is a necessary conclusion from the preceding material.

f) *Primus usus and the reign of Christ.* The confessional writings address the biblical teaching of the lordship of Jesus Christ over all earthly rulers and powers exclusively in the article on Christology, but not in connection with the doctrine of worldly orders.

11. *Some conclusions and questions.*

a. The proclamation of the primus usus extends as far as that of the gospel; it is therefore unlimited according to God's will. But it encounters a concrete internal limit in human unbelief and disobedience, an external limit in the power of a government to oppose the proclamation, to hinder it, and to deprive those who proclaim it of all worldly responsibility. As long as Christians stand in worldly responsibility, the orientation provided by the primus usus is part of their confession of Christ. The more the situation of Revelation 13 emerges through proclamation and the more Christians are not those who share responsibility for the injustice of the world but are themselves those who suffer injustice, the more the worldly responsibility laid on them by the primus usus will prove valid by obedient suffering and earnest discipline in the congregation. But even the congregation in the catacombs never has the universality of its mission taken from it. In preaching law and gospel, it professes this mission and thereby keeps alive its responsibility for the world. The congregation can never content itself with cultivating its own life; to do so means denying its Lord. Even in places where it can still preserve the iustitia civilis only among its own members, because its word is not received by the world, it does this in service to the world and as part of its universal mission. Its experience will be that the world is in trouble and that the reign of Christ is not of this world, but precisely here it will be   598 reminded of its mission to the world. Otherwise it would become a religious club. The mission of the congregation is not limited in principle. It will have to make its own decision in each case about how it implements this mission in light of the signs of the time. To understand itself too directly within the situation of Revelation 13 will always be a grave danger for the congregation

lined here' ('Gospel and Law,' in *Community, State, and Church*, 71); see p. 96 for Barth's defense of the sequence 'law and gospel,'" *DBWE* 16:596–597, n. 101.]

and the full scope of its mission. Apocalyptic proclamation can be a flight from the primus usus legis.[15] The congregation will neither compensate for the weakness of the word of God with religious fanaticism[16] nor confuse its own frailty with the weakness of the word.

b. In contrast to the other usus, in the confessional writings the primus usus is not given any explicit biblical grounding. Does this mean that it is unbiblical? 1. The Bible knows of no preaching of the primus usus detached from the gospel. 2. The Bible knows of no difference *in principle* between preaching to unbelievers and believers in the sense of a division between primus usus legis and gospel. 3. The Bible teaches, however, that the proclamation and the conduct of the congregation occur in responsibility for the world. There is absolutely no evasion of this responsibility; for God loved the world and desires that all people be helped. 4. The Bible's position regarding the orders of the world occurs primarily in concrete instructions to the congregation (Romans 13. Philemon. Tables of household duties. Vice lists). There is, however, also direct preaching to the governing authorities (Paul before Felix: about the resurrection of the dead, about faith in Christ, about righteousness, chastity, and future judgment Acts 24:14ff.; before Festus: reference to the political right of protection against arbitrariness 25:9ff.; before Agrippa 26:1ff.; John before Herod Matt. 14:4). In each case the issue is one of concrete obedience to the One to whom all power in heaven and on earth has been given.

c. The silence within the confessional writings as to the form of the proclamation of the primus usus—whether it is confined to sermon and instruction, that is, whether it may be directed to those who govern only through addressing the congregation, or also through direct public or private speaking to persons in government, whether it must contain the explicit reference to the gospel each and every time, whether it consists of directly naming concrete sin or the general proclamation of the law, whether it consists in the form of protest, warning, or request—this silence gives proclaimers who face these questions freedom for a concrete, responsible decision to the extent that their awareness of the subject they are pursuing and of the status in which they find themselves (as preachers, heads of households, rulers) is grounded in faith. In fact, there is concrete evidence from the Reformation period for all these possibilities.

599

---

15. ["Cf. 'Thoughts on William Paton's Book,' *DBWE* 16:528–529," *DBWE* 16:598, n. 108.]

16. ["Cf. *DBWE* 6:344: 'Isolated from each other, however, the exclusive claim leads to fanaticism and sectarianism, the all-encompassing claim to the secularization and capitulation of the church,'" *DBWE* 16:598, n. 109.]

d. The primus usus legis is just as far removed from moralistic preaching (which perceives its actual task as taking a position on events of the day, thereby attributing to worldly orders a significance in their own right and understanding the gospel only as a means to an end) as from the sermon that is "religious" in principle (which separates the gospel from a person's life in the world). Both forms of preaching are determined thematically and are thus an arbitrary curtailment and denial of the living Word of God that places us into concrete worldly responsibility. Instead of the false juxtaposition of political and religious themes, the true distinction and connection of law and gospel is to take its place in the sermon. A relatively sure sign of the false theme is the polemical apologetics that dominate these kinds of sermons; even the greatest religious or "prophetic" emphasis cannot conceal that the world and the human being, and not the Word of God, are the standard of proclamation. But with this false theme, the listener is deprived of both the claim and the comfort of Jesus Christ.

e. The primus usus signifies the interest on the part of Christian proclamation in the content of the law. It excludes a purely formal definition of the law. It refers not to the responsible person in a conflict of duties[17] but to the realization of certain conditions; not to the Christian within the worldly order but to the form of the worldly order according to the will of God.[18] In the realm of the iustitia civilis there is a possible and necessary cooperation between Christians and non-Christians in clarifying certain subjects and in advancing concrete tasks. Because of their fundamentally different foundations, the results emerging from this cooperation have the character not of the proclamation of the word of God but of responsible deliberation or demand on the basis of human perception.[19] This distinction must be preserved under all circumstances. Cooperation can be desired and promoted by both worldly and spiritual rule. Whether cooperation among Christians of different denominations in matters of the iustitia civilis can lead beyond this to common ecclesial proclamation depends on the unanimity of interpretation of the word of God in faith in Jesus Christ. While the concrete form taken within the proclamation relates primarily to the punishment of concrete sins, in the realm of responsible deliberation and demand this concreteness can and must arrive at positive results.

600

---

17. ["Cf. 'The Structure of Responsible Life,' *DBWE* 6:257–289 (*Reader* 636–659)," *DBWE* 16:599, n. 117.]

18. ["Cf. *DBWE* 6:163–166, 258–259 (*Reader* 625–628, 637–639) (regarding the establishment of certain 'conditions') . . . ," *DBWE* 16:599, n. 118.]

19. ["Cf. Bonhoeffer's phrase 'on the authority of responsible counsel' ('On the Possibility of the Word of the Church to the World,' *DBWE* 6:361)," *DBWE* 16:600, n. 119.]

12. *Critique of the usus doctrine* as found in the confessional writings.

a. The concept of the usus is misleading in respect to its subject.

b. The relation of the primus usus to unbelievers threatens to lead to a splintering of the unity of the law and of the wholeness of the proclamation.

c. The differentiation of the three usus ultimately lacks clarity. The primus usus itself contains an element of preaching that calls for repentance (the "threat"), just as the secundus and tertius usus contain an element of the primus usus. This lack of clarity is grounded in the distinction between groups of people that is connected with the usus doctrine and in an understanding of the usus, which has not been fully avoided, as different methods of proclamation.

d. The relationship of the preaching of the primus usus and natural law is not clear. In its present form, the doctrine of the primus usus can provide the impetus for a false theology of the orders.

e. A renewal of the usus doctrine would need either to portray the one law in its threefold form as preaching works, preaching recognition of sin, and preaching the fulfillment of the law (by Christ and faith), avoiding 601 distinctions made by the hearer; or (and) to treat the validity and effect of the entire law of God (in its threefold form) as a systematically separate question. More precisely, this is a question of its *validity* in the twofold perspective applying to unbelievers and believers and of its *effect* in the fourfold perspective as righteousness of works, discipline leading to Christ, despair, and gracious instruction. The vacillation of Lutheran dogmatics between duplex, triplex, and quadruplex usus legis [*double, triple, and quadruple use of the law*] can be explained by the mixing up of all these questions, the question of form being triple, the question of validity double, the question of effect quadruple. Every attempt to absorb one question within another necessarily leads to confusion. The concept of the usus, however, harbors the danger of such confusion within itself.

PART 7
Theology from Prison:
Worldly, Religionless Christianity

42. What Does It Mean
to Tell the Truth?

DBWE 16:601–608

On April 5, 1943, Bonhoeffer was arrested for his participation in the conspiracy to overthrow the Third Reich. He was sent first to Tegel military interrogation prison in Berlin, where he spent the next eighteen months, then to a Gestapo prison in Berlin for four more months. He was moved briefly to Buchenwald concentration camp outside Weimar and then to Flossenbürg near the present-day German-Czech border. He was executed there on April 9, 1945.[1]

Throughout these last two years of his life, Bonhoeffer remained remarkably productive. The concluding portion of this Reader *includes selections from his prison writings. In the unfinished essay below, Bonhoeffer asks, What makes speech true? He rejects a number of theories that ground truth in the intention of the speaker, the character of the speaker, the formal truth of the statement, and elsewhere. Instead, he argues, speech is true when it expresses reality. This makes telling the truth a sometimes complicated matter, since reality is complicated and, in its fallen state, contradictory. Speaking the truth can mean different things depending on the situation and the office of the speaker. This essay was no academic exercise, since Bonhoeffer composed it in prison as he was actively misleading his interrogators.[2] But it would be a mistake to read this essay as opportunistic rationalizing by a man under extreme pressure. Rather, this essay is a case study of the framework Bonhoeffer outlined in* Ethics, *where he rejected a series of competing ethical visions in favor of his own account of responsible action as that which accords with reality as it is structured by God's mandates.*

---

1. [DBWE *7:1, editor's introduction.*]
2. [DBWE *16:601, n. 1.*]

601 From the moment in our lives in which we become capable of speech, we are taught that our words must be true. What does this mean? What does "telling the truth" mean? Who requires this of us?

602 It is clear that initially it is our parents who order our relationship with them by demanding truthfulness;[3] and accordingly this demand is also related and limited initially—in the sense our parents intend it—to this closest circle of the family. We note further that the relationship expressed in this demand cannot simply be reversed. The truthfulness of the child toward parents is by its very nature something different from that of parents toward their child. While the life of the small child lies open to the parents and the child's word is to reveal all that is hidden and secret, the same cannot be true of the reverse relationship. In regard to truthfulness, therefore, the parents' claim on the child is something different from that of the child on the parents.

From this we can see immediately that "telling the truth" means different things, depending on where one finds oneself. The relevant relationships must be taken into account. The question must be asked whether and in what way a person is justified in demanding truthful speech from another. Just as language between parents and children is different, in accord with who they are, from that between husband and wife, between friend and friend, between teacher and student, between governing authority and subject, between enemy and enemy, so too is the truth contained in this language different.

The objection that arises immediately, however, that persons owe truthful speech not to this or that person but to God alone, is correct as long as we do not thereby disregard that even God is not a general principle but is the Living One who has placed me in a life that is fully alive and within this life demands my service. Those who say "God" are not allowed simply to cross out the given world in which I live; otherwise they would be speaking not of the God who in Jesus Christ came into the world but rather of some sort of metaphysical idol. This is precisely the point, namely, how I bring into effect in my concrete life, with its manifold relationships, the truthful speech I owe to God. The truthfulness of our words that we owe to God

603 must take on concrete form in the world. Our word should be truthful not in principle but concretely. A truthfulness that is not concrete is not truthful at all before God.

---

3. ["Cf. *DBWE* 4:128–131 on Matt. 4:33–37, under the heading 'Truthfulness,'" *DBWE* 16:602, n. 3.]

"Telling the truth" is therefore not a matter only of one's intention but also of accurate perception and of serious consideration of the real circumstances. The more diverse the life circumstances of people are, the more responsibility they have and the more difficult it is "to tell the truth." The child, who stands in only one life relationship, namely, that with his or her parents, does not yet have anything to ponder and weigh. But already the next circle of life in which the child is placed, namely, school, brings the first difficulties. Pedagogically it is therefore of the greatest importance that in some way—not to be discussed here—the parents clarify the differences of these circles of life to their child and make his or her responsibilities understandable.

Telling the truth must therefore be learned. This sounds repellent to those who believe that one's character alone must suffice, and that if this is blameless all the rest is child's play. Since it is the case, however, that the ethical cannot be detached from reality, the ever-greater capacity to perceive reality is a necessary component of ethical action.[4] But with reference to the issue we are discussing, action consists in speaking. *What is real is to be expressed in words.* This is what truthful speech consists of. Yet this assertion unavoidably contains the question of the "how" of language. What matters is the "right word" for any given circumstance. To discover this is a matter of long, earnest, and continual effort that is based in experience and the perception of reality. In order to say how something is real—i.e., to speak truthfully—one's gaze and thought must be oriented toward how the real is in God, and through God, and toward God.[5]

It is superficial to limit the problem of truthful speech to individual cases of conflict. Every word I speak stands under the stipulation that it be true; quite apart from the truthfulness of its content, the relationship it expresses between me and another person is already true or untrue. I can fawn over a person, or I can be overbearing, or I can dissimulate without expressing any material falsehood, and my word is nevertheless untrue because I am destroying and undermining the reality of the relationship between husband and wife, or supervisor and subordinate, etc. The single word is always a portion of an entire reality that seeks expression in the word. Depending on the person to whom I am speaking, the person who is questioning me, or what I am discussing, my word, if it seeks to be truthful, must vary. A truth-

604

---

4. ["Cf. Bonhoeffer's remarks on 'accordance with reality' in *DBWE* 6:222–224, and in *DBWE* 6:261–264 (*Reader* 639–248) et passim," *DBWE* 16:603, n. 6.]

5. ["Cf. *DBWE* 6:48: 'All things appear as in a distorted mirror if they are not seen and recognized in God. All that is—so to speak—given, all laws and norms, are abstractions, as long as God is not known in faith to be the ultimate reality,'" *DBWE* 16:603, n. 7.]

ful word is not an entity constant in itself but is as lively as life itself. Where this word detaches itself from life and from the relationship to the concrete other person, where "the truth is told" without regard for the person to whom it is said, there it has only the appearance of truth but not its essence.

The cynic is the one who, claiming to "tell the truth" in all places and at all times and to every person in the same way, only puts on display a dead idolatrous image of the truth. By putting a halo on his own head for being a zealot for the truth[6] who can take no account of human weaknesses, he destroys the living truth between persons. He violates shame,[7] desecrates the mystery, breaks trust, betrays the community in which he lives, and smiles arrogantly over the havoc he has wrought and over the human weakness that "can't bear the truth." He says that the truth is destructive and demands its victims, and he feels like a god over the feeble creatures and does not realize that he is serving Satan.

There is such a thing as Satan's truth. Its nature is to deny everything real under the guise of the truth. It feeds on hatred against the real, against the world created and loved by God. It gives the impression of carrying out God's judgment on the fall of the real into sin. But God's truth judges what is created out of love; Satan's truth judges what is created out of envy and hatred. God's truth became flesh in the world and is alive in the real; Satan's truth is the death of all that is real.[8]

605

The concept of the living truth is dangerous and arouses the suspicion that the truth can and may be adapted to the given situation, so that the concept of truth utterly dissolves, and falsehood and truth draw indistinguishably close to each other. Also, what was said about the necessary discernment of the real could be misunderstood in such a way that the measure of truth I am willing to say to the other person is determined by a calculating or pedagogical attitude toward him or her. It is important to keep this danger in mind. The only possible way to counteract it, however, is through attentive discernment of the relevant contents and limits that the real itself specifies for one's utterance in order to make it a truthful one. Yet the dangers inherent in the concept of living truth must never cause a person to forsake this concept in favor of the formal, cynical conception of truth.

---

6. ["On the 'tyrannical despiser of humanity,' see *DBWE* 6:84–87; cf. Bonhoeffer's own reflections on this text on December 5 and 15, 1943 (*DBWE* 8:215 and 223) . . . ," *DBWE* 16:604, n. 10.]

7. ["On shame as a 'sign of disunion' and as a seeking after 'covering,' see *DBWE* 6:303–307; in Bonhoeffer's letter to Eberhard Bethge on December 5, 1943, we read: 'God himself made clothing for human beings' (*DBWE* 8:228)," *DBWE* 16:604, n. 11.]

8. [". . . On Gen. 3:1–3, see *DBWE* 3:103–110 (*Reader* 243–248)," *DBWE* 16:605, n. 14.]

Let me try to illustrate this. Every word lives and has its home within a certain radius. The word spoken in the family is different from the word spoken at the office or in public. The word born in the warmth of personal relationship freezes in the cold air of public exposure. The word of command appropriate to a civil service position would break the bonds of trust in the family if spoken there. Every word should have and retain its own place. As a result of the increasing profligacy of public discourse in newspapers and the radio, the nature and limits of different words are no longer clearly perceived; in fact, what is distinctive about a personal word, for example, is nearly destroyed. Chatter has replaced authentic words. Words no longer have any weight. There is too much talking. Yet when the limits of different words blur together, when words become rootless, homeless, then what is said loses hold of the truth; indeed, at that point lying almost inevitably emerges. When the various orders of life no longer respect one another, then words become untrue. For example, a teacher asks a child in front of the class whether it is true that the child's father often comes home drunk. This is true, but the child denies it. The teacher's question brings the child into a situation that he or she does not yet have the maturity to handle. To be sure, the child perceives that this question is an unjustified invasion into the order of the family and must be warded off. What takes place in the family is not something that should be made known to the class. The family has its own secret[9] that it must keep. The teacher disregards the reality of this order. In responding, the child would have to find a way to observe equally the orders of the family and those of the school. The child cannot do this yet; he or she lacks the experience, the discernment, and the capacity for appropriate expression. In flatly saying no to the teacher's question, the response becomes untrue, to be sure; at the same time, however, it expresses the truth that the family is an order sui generis [*of its own kind*] where the teacher was not justified to intrude. Of course, one could call the child's answer a lie; all the same, this lie contains more truth—i.e., it corresponds more closely to the truth—than if the child had revealed the father's weakness before the class. The child acted rightly according to the measure of the child's perception. Yet it is the teacher alone who is guilty of the lie. By rebuking the questioner, an experienced person in the child's situation would also have been able to avoid a formal untruth in responding and thereby would have been able to find the "right word" in the situation. Lies on the part of children and inexperienced persons in general

606

---

9. ["Cf. Bonhoeffer's letter to Eberhard Bethge on December 5, 1943 . . . (*DBWE* 8:215)," *DBWE* 16:605, n. 15.]

The Bonhoeffer Reader

can frequently be traced back to their being placed in situations that they cannot fully fathom. For this reason it is questionable whether it makes sense to generalize and extend the concept of lying (which is and ought to be understood as something downright reprehensible) in such a way that it coincides with the concept of a formally untrue statement. Indeed, all of this demonstrates how difficult it is to say what lying really is.

The usual definition, according to which the conscious contradiction between thought and speech is a lie, is completely inadequate. For instance, this definition includes the most harmless April Fool's joke. The concept of the "jocose lie"[10] rooted in Catholic moral theology removes from the lie its decisive characteristics of gravity and malice (just as, in the other direction, it removes from the joke its decisive characteristics of innocent play and freedom), and for this reason it is most infelicitous. The joke has nothing at all to do with the lie and must not be reduced with it to a common denominator. If one then asserts that a lie is the conscious deception of others to their harm, this also would include, e.g., the necessary deception of the enemy in war or in analogous situations (of course, Kant declared that he was too proud ever to tell an untruth, yet at the same time he was compelled to extend this assertion ad absurdum by declaring that he would feel obliged to reveal truthful information on the whereabouts of a friend seeking refuge with him to a criminal in pursuit of the friend). If one characterizes this sort of behavior as a lie, then lying receives a moral consecration and justification that contradicts its meaning in every respect. This leads initially to the conclusion that lying is not to be defined formally by the contradiction between thought and speech. This contradiction is not even a necessary component of lying. In this respect speech that is thoroughly correct and incontestable is nevertheless a lie, such as if a notorious liar once tells "the truth" to throw people off,[11] or if a known ambiguity lurks beneath the appearance of correctness, or the decisive truth remains intentionally hidden. Hence, a deliberate silence can be a lie, even though, on the other hand, it certainly need not be one.

These reflections lead to the recognition that the essence of lying is found much deeper than in the contradiction between thought and speech. We could say that the person who stands behind what is said makes it into a

---

10. [*I.e., lies told in joking.*]

11. ["See *DBWE* 6:77: 'It is worse to be evil than to do evil. It is worse when a liar tells the truth than when a lover of truth lies,'" *DBWE* 16:607, n. 20.]

lie or the truth. Yet even this is not adequate; for a lie is something objective and must be determined accordingly. Jesus identifies Satan as the "father of lies" [*John 8:44*]. Lying is first of all the denial of God as God has been revealed to the world. "Who is the liar but the one who denies that Jesus is the Christ?" [*1 John 2:22*]. Lying is a contradiction of the word of God as it was spoken in Christ and in which creation rests. Consequently, lying is the negation, denial, and deliberate and willful destruction of reality as it is created by God and exists in God to the extent that it takes place through words and silence. Our word in union with the Word of God is intended to express what is real, as it is in God, and our silence is to be a sign of the boundary drawn around the word by what is real, as it is in God.

In the effort to articulate the real, we encounter it not as a unified whole but in a condition of disruption and self-contradiction, requiring reconciliation and healing. We find ourselves embedded in various orders of the real, all at the same time, and our word that strives for the reconciliation and healing of the real is nevertheless continually drawn back into the existing disunion and into contradiction. It can only fulfill its purpose of expressing the real, as it is in God, by drawing into itself the existing contradiction as well as the context of the real. The human word, if it is to be true, may not deny the fall into sin any more than the creative and reconciling word of God by which all division is overcome.[12] Cynics want to make their word true by always expressing the particular thing they think they understand without regard for reality as a whole. Precisely in this way they utterly destroy the real, and their word becomes untrue, even if it maintains the superficial appearance of correctness. "That which is, is far off, and deep, very deep; who can find it out?" (Eccl. 7:24).

608

How does my word become true? 1) By recognizing who calls on me to speak and what authorizes me to speak; 2) by recognizing the place in which I stand; 3) by putting the subject I am speaking about into this context.

These considerations tacitly depend on an earlier assumption, that speaking itself stands under certain conditions, that it does not accompany the natural course of one's life in a perpetual flow but has its own place, time, and mission, and therewith its limits.

1. Who or what authorizes or calls on me to speak? Whoever speaks without authorization or without being called upon is a windbag. Because what matters in respect to every word is the double relation to the other person

---

12. ["Cf. 'God's Love and the Disintegration of the World,' *DBWE* 6:309," *DBWE* 16:608, n. 23.]

and to a subject matter; this relation must be discernible in every word. An unconnected word is hollow; it contains no truth. This is an essential difference between thought and speech. Thought in itself has no necessary connection to the other person, but only to the subject matter. The claim that you are also allowed to say what you are thinking does not in itself authorize you to do so. Speaking includes the authorization and call given by the other person. Example: in my thoughts I can consider another person to be stupid, ugly, incompetent, corrupt, or alternatively to be clever or full of character; but it is something quite different whether I am justified in speaking this, what causes me to do so, and to whom I express it. Undoubtedly, a justification for speaking emerges from an office that has been bestowed on me. Parents can scold or praise their child, but in contrast the child is justified in doing neither toward his or her parents. A similar relation exists between teacher and students, although the rights of the teacher in regard to the child are more limited than those of the father. Thus the teacher, in criticizing or praising the student, is necessarily confined to certain particular mistakes or accomplishments, while, e.g., broad judgments as to character fall not to the teacher but to the parents. The justification for speech always lies within the boundaries of the concrete office that I fill. If these boundaries are crossed, the word becomes intrusive, arrogant, and, whether scolding or praising, harmful. There are persons who feel themselves called to "tell the truth," as they put it, to everyone who crosses their path.[13]

13. ["The manuscript breaks off at this point; points 2 and 3 are not developed," *DBWE* 16:608, n. 24.]

43. Speech of the Major

DBWE 7:167–170

While in prison, Bonhoeffer experimented for the first time with writing fiction, producing a short story as well as fragments of a drama and a novel.[1] Because these works of fiction focus on cultured middle-class family life in light of Christianity and clearly include autobiographical elements, they have generally been read as windows into the life of Bonhoeffer and his family. But the case can be made that these works are also theology in narrative form.[2]

This combination of autobiographical and theological reflection is on display in the brief excerpt from the novel printed below. The character of Harald von Bremer, also called "the major," recounts a childhood incident in which he and another schoolboy named Hans settled a rivalry. That fictional incident has been shown to resemble an episode from Bonhoeffer's own childhood, where he and another classmate competed for leadership of their class before setting their differences aside in friendship.[3] In the course of the major's reflection on this affair, Bonhoeffer presents a number of themes that run throughout his nonfiction theological work. The major's recollection that he and Hans learned to be "human beings who must live depending on, and relating to, each other, cooperating with each other side by side" summarizes the themes of mutuality and interpersonal encounter that are hallmarks of Bonhoeffer's theological anthropology.[4] And in reflecting on how such mutuality places "limits" on an individual's otherwise limitless aspirations, the major's speech resonates with Bonhoeffer's own thinking about the formation of personal and ethical identity.[5] Moreover, when the major suggests that these dynamics apply not only to individuals but to nations, he echoes Bonhoeffer in interpreting the individual person in close relationship to collective persons.

1. [*These are published in* DBWE 7.]
2. [*Clifford Green makes this case in* DBWE *7:1–12, editor's introduction. This introductory material is drawn from those pages.*]
3. [DBWE *7:151, n. 29.*]
4. [*See* DBWE *7:167, n. 110.*]
5. [*See* DBWE *7:168, n. 116.*]

167   "You have touched upon more questions than we can discuss over a cup of tea, Franz," said the uncle. "I think your teacher is right in many respects, especially in what he said about the 'great times' of history and about historiography. It's true that the history of successes has been written more or less completely, and there's probably not much of importance to be added. But now it's time—and this is a much more difficult task—to write the history of what has not succeeded, and the history of the victims of what has been called 'success.' To use your teacher's words, it's time to write the history not of the giants and demigods, but of human beings. I don't mean the history of the eternally restless and rebellious masses, gathering and building toward an explosion. They, too, are superhuman, though subterranean, mythic forces that are connected in some mysterious way with the great people of history who have succeeded. No, I mean the history of human beings who, tossed about between these forces, seek to live their lives in the middle of work and family, suffering and happiness.[6]

"I told you about Hans and myself. Both of us thought we were demigods, until we realized—or at least sensed—that we are human beings who must live depending on, and related to, each other, cooperating with each other side by side. And that was our good fortune. We became friends. Demigods have no friends, only tools which they use or discard according to whim. I distrust anyone who has no close friend. Either they're a demigod or, much worse, imagine they are. For me, the main issue for individuals and for peoples is whether or not they have learned to live with other human beings and peoples. That's more important to me than all their ideas, thoughts, and convictions.

168   "Your history teacher probably meant something like this. But I would not agree with him that what we learn from history and life is the need for compromise. People who speak that way are still focused only on ideas and therefore are continually resigning themselves to discovering that no idea prevails in life in pure form. They then call that compromise and see it as a sign of the imperfection and wickedness of the world.

"I look only at people and their task of living with other people, and I view succeeding at this very task as the fulfillment of human life and history. What your teacher considers a misfortune is in my view the only good fortune and happiness human beings have. They don't need to live with ideas, principles, doctrines, and morals, but they can live with one another, providing one another with limits. Precisely in so doing, they point one another toward their real task. This life alone is fruitful and human. You wouldn't

---

6. ["Cf. 'The View from Below' (*DBWE* 8:52 [*Reader* 774–775])," *DBWE* 7:167, n. 109.]

believe the change in Hans and me after the games back then—and the whole class as well. For weeks I was at Hans's bedside every day; that's when we got to know each other and began to see the world differently. I would almost say that only then did we become real human beings, each thanks to the other.

"But a new life began in the class, too. The spell that Hans's personality had cast on the class, which had been further strengthened by my arrival, was broken. The talents and personalities of our classmates could develop. Whereas before there had only been blind allegiance, now strong and healthy camaraderie began to grow. Even Meyer—who was to have been expelled from school, but thanks only to Hans's intervention had been given probation instead—sought to make friends again, though he had to start all over again at the bottom. Later he was removed from school for other unpleasant reasons.

"Hans remained the leader of the class until graduation, but now as *primus inter pares* [*first among equals*], and he never made a decision without first discussing it with me. So, was that a compromise between Hans and me? I wouldn't call it that, because that would devalue it. But the decisive thing was not what we both lost, namely our claim to live alone in the world as demigods, but what we gained, namely a humane life in community with another human being.[7]

169

"Now I believe the same thing holds true for nations, as well, and fundamentally for all historical movements. Let me put it a little differently from your history teacher. Like nature, history also develops an extra measure of strength in order to reach a modest but necessary goal. Look at the thousands of chestnuts promised us by the blossoms on the trees around us. How many of them will reach their goal of growing into new chestnut trees? Hardly one. Nature is prodigal in order to be sure. Similarly, we think the end results of the powerful movements of history, the great conflicts, revolutions, reformations, and wars, seem utterly disproportionate to the effort

---

7. ["See Bonhoeffer's relational concept of freedom as it had developed by 1932–1933: 'Only by being in relation with the other am I free. No one can think of freedom as a substance or as something individualistic' (*DBWE* 3:63 [*Reader* 222–223]). The beginning of this development is found in *Sanctorum Communio*, especially in Bonhoeffer's discussion of the 'active "being-for-each-other"' of the members of the church-community (*DBWE* 1:178ff). It is further developed in *DBWE* 2:87–89 in conversation with the work of Eberhard Grisebach, Friedrich Gogarten, and Hinrich Knittermeyer. See also the manuscript written in Geneva in early September 1941 about William Paton's book, *The Church and the New Order in Europe*: 'That is, freedom is in the first place not an *individual* right but a *responsibility*; freedom is not in the first place oriented toward the individual but toward the neighbor' (*DBWE* 16:532)," *DBWE* 7:169, n. 118.]

expended. History, too, is prodigal when it is concerned to preserve the human race. It expends the most uncanny effort to bring people to a single, necessary insight. Even though we see and bemoan the unfathomable disproportion between the seemingly meaningless, fruitless sacrifices and the very modest results, we must never underrate the importance of even the most modest result. It's like the one of every thousand chestnut trees that unnoticeably takes root in the ground and in turn promises to bear fruit. Of course it's a lame comparison; history and nature are two different things. But neither is subject to the maxim, 'All or nothing.'[8] Rather, both obey the law of the preservation, continuation, and fulfillment of life, even at the cost of great sacrifice and deprivation. If there is something to learn from history, I would not call it compromise, but love for life as it really is."

170

The major took a deep breath, leaned back in his cane chair, and looked out beyond the circle of good-looking, youthful figures toward the flowering chestnut trees.

"Harald, Harald," Frau von Bremer now spoke up, "that's the wisdom of old age, but it's not for young people. They want to hear something else."

"Maybe, my dear Sophie, that may be," the major answered calmly. "What harm does it do? Old people and young people, too, must live together and get along. Is there anything more perverse and repulsive than when older people mimic the speech of the young, saying what the young want to hear? They become contemptible, not only in their own eyes, but also in those of youth. They violate the order of life. Who, for example, would forbid Christoph," he added, smiling, "who I can tell has been dissatisfied with what I've been saying, from telling me just as honestly what he thinks, as I've said what I think? In fact, I very much want to hear his opinion, and I presume we do have a few minutes before we have to think of plans for the rest of the day. So, courage, Christoph!"

---

8. ["See *Ethics*, where 'the miracle of Christ's resurrection' is described as illuminating life; there 'One takes from life what it offers, not all or nothing, but good things and bad, important things and unimportant, joy and pain' (*DBWE* 6:91–92). Cf. also the same sentiment in the important letter of July 21, 1944, in *DBWE* 8:485f. (*Reader* 805–806)," *DBWE* 7:169–170, n. 122.]

44. LETTERS AND PAPERS
FROM PRISON

DBWE 8:37–52, 362–367, 372–373, 383–390,
393–397, 405–407, 425–431, 440, 446–448,
450–451, 455–458, 460–461, 475–482, 485–486,
489–495, 498–504, 514–516, 459–460

The editorial introduction in this section of the Reader *is spread through the texts rather than appearing all at the beginning. That is because the theological argument is not a systematic treatise but develops in letters as Bonhoeffer explores new ideas; it is also because other genres besides letters are found in this section. Nevertheless, the thematic focus binding the following texts together is Bonhoeffer's proposal for a worldly, nonreligious Christianity.*

AFTER TEN YEARS

At Christmas 1942, Bonhoeffer looked back over the decade since the beginning of the Hitler regime. "After Ten Years" was written not only for his closest friend, Eberhard Bethge, but also for his brother-in-law Hans von Dohnanyi, and for Hans Oster, a career military officer working with Dohnanyi in military intelligence. Since these two were leaders in the resistance conspiracy against Hitler, and Bonhoeffer was now himself a co-conspirator, we can imagine the charged personal, political, and ethical situation in which he wrote. In fact, his arrest was only three months away, on April 5, 1943.

When not on assignment for the resistance movement, Bonhoeffer was working on his Ethics, *a project he had begun in 1940. In fact, the section of "After Ten Years" headed "Who Stands Firm?" contains his analysis of failed ethical postures during that decade, an analysis that Bonhoeffer had first written in the* Ethics *manuscript under the heading "Ethics as Formation." Full of insights from the church and politi-*

761

cal struggle, "After Ten Years" thus forms a natural transition from Bonhoeffer's Ethics *manuscript to the provocative new theological project that he launched after a year in prison. Near the end of this section of the* Reader *is found an "Outline for a Book," in which Bonhoeffer began to present his thoughts in a more systematic way; unfortunately, the pages he managed to write did not survive.*

37   Ten years is a long time in the life of every human being. Because time is the most precious gift at our disposal, being of all gifts the most irretrievable, the thought of time possibly lost disturbs us whenever we look back. Time is lost when we have not lived, experienced things, learned, worked, enjoyed, and suffered as human beings. Lost time is unfulfilled, empty time. Certainly that is not what the past years have been. We have lost much, things far beyond measure, but time was not lost. Indeed, the insights and experiences we have gained and of which we have subsequently become aware are only abstractions from reality, from life itself. Yet just as the ability to forget is a gift of grace, so similarly is memory, the repetition of received teachings, part of responsible life. In the following pages I want to try to give an accounting of some of the shared experience and insight that have been forced upon us in these times, not personal experiences, nothing systematically organized, not arguments and theories, but conclusions about human experience—lined up side by side, connected only by concrete experience— that have been reached together in a circle of like-minded people. None of this is new; rather, it is something we have long been familiar with in times gone by, something given to us to experience and understand anew. One cannot write about these things without every word being accompanied by

38   the feeling of gratitude for the community of spirit and of life that in all these years was preserved and shown to be worthwhile.

Without Ground under One's Feet

Have there ever been people in history who in their time, like us, had so little ground under their feet,[1] people to whom every possible alternative open to them at the time appeared equally unbearable, senseless, and contrary to life? Have there been those who like us looked for the source of their strength beyond all those available alternatives? Were they looking entirely in what has passed away and in what is yet to come? And neverthe-

---

1. ["On the notion of 'ground under one's feet,' see the final paragraph of Bonhoeffer's sermon of May 8, 1932, on 2 Chron. 20:12 (*DBWE* 11:439–440); see also *DBWE* 7:67–69," *DBWE* 8:38, n. 2.]

less, without being dreamers, did they await with calm and confidence the successful outcome of their endeavor? Or rather, facing a great historical turning point, and precisely because something genuinely new was coming to be that did not fit with the existing alternatives, did the responsible thinkers of another generation ever feel differently than we do today?

Who Stands Firm?[2]

The huge masquerade of evil has thrown all ethical concepts into confusion. That evil should appear in the form of light, good deeds, historical necessity, social justice is absolutely bewildering for one coming from the world of ethical concepts that we have received. For the Christian who lives by the Bible, it is the very confirmation of the abysmal wickedness of evil.

The failure of *"the reasonable ones"*—those who think, with the best of intentions and in their naive misreading of reality, that with a bit of reason they can patch up a structure that has come out of joint—is apparent. With their ability to see impaired, they want to do justice on every side, only to be crushed by the colliding forces without having accomplished anything at all. Disappointed that the world is so unreasonable, they see themselves condemned to unproductiveness; they withdraw in resignation or helplessly fall victim to the stronger. 39

More devastating is the failure of all ethical *fanaticism*. The fanatic believes that he can meet the power of evil with the purity of a principle.[3] But like the bull in the arena, he attacks the red cape rather than the person carrying it, grows tired, and suffers defeat. He traps himself in the insignificant and ends up in the trap of the cleverer one.

The man of *conscience* has no one but himself when resisting the superior might of predicaments that demand a decision. But the dimensions of the conflict wherein he must make his choices are such that, counseled and supported by nothing but his very own conscience, he is torn apart. The innumerable respectable and seductive disguises by which evil approaches him make his conscience fearful and unsure until he finally settles for a salved conscience instead of a good conscience, that is, until he deceives his own conscience in order not to despair. That a bad conscience may be stronger and more wholesome than a deceived one is something that the man whose sole support is his conscience can never comprehend.

---

2. [*See* Ethics, DBWE *6:77–80.*]

3. ["On the critique of an ethics of principle, see *DBWE* 10:336–367, et passim, as well as *DBWE* 6:81–82 . . . ," *DBWE* 8:39, n. 5.]

The reliable path of *duty* seems to offer the escape from the bewildering plethora of possible decisions. Here, that which has been commanded is clutched as the most certain; the responsibility for what has been commanded lies with the one giving the command rather than the one who carries it out. However, duty is so circumscribed that there is never any room to venture that which rests wholly in one's own responsibility, the action that alone strikes at the very core of evil and can overcome it.[4] The man of duty will in the end have to do his duty also to the devil.

There is the one who determines to take a stand in the world by acting on his own *freedom*. He values the necessary action more highly than an untarnished conscience and reputation. He is prepared to sacrifice a barren principle to a fruitful compromise or a barren wisdom of mediocrity to fruitful radicalism.[5] Such a one needs to take care that his freedom does not cause him to stumble. He will condone the bad in order to prevent the worse and in so doing no longer discern that the very thing that he seeks to avoid as worse might well be better. This is where the basic material of tragedy is to be found.

In flight from public discussion and examination, this or that person may well attain the sanctuary of private *virtuousness*. But he must close his eyes and mouth to the injustice around him. He can remain undefiled by the consequences of responsible action only by deceiving himself. In everything he does, that which he fails to do will leave him no peace. He will either perish from that restlessness or turn into a hypocritical, self-righteous, small-minded human being.

Who stands firm? Only the one whose ultimate standard is not his reason, his principles, conscience, freedom, or virtue; only the one who is prepared to sacrifice all of these when, in faith and in relationship to God alone, he is called to obedient and responsible action. Such a person is the responsible one, whose life is to be nothing but a response to God's question and call. Where are these responsible ones?

The number **40** appears in the left margin beside the first paragraph.

---

4. [*A venture of responsibility to strike at the core of evil is a very good description of Bonhoeffer's own attitude to his participation in the conspiracy to kill Hitler. See also below, where Bonhoeffer answers his own question, "Who stands firm?": "Only the one who is prepared to sacrifice all of these [principles] when, in faith and in relationship to God alone, he is called to obedient and responsible action." For treatment of "The Structure of Responsible Life,"* see Ethics, DBWE *6:257–289* (Reader *637–659*).]

5. ["On 'compromise' and 'radicalism,' see *Ethics, DBWE* 6:153–159 (*Reader* 618–623)," *DBWE* 8:40, n. 7.]

Civil Courage

What really lies behind the lament about the lack of civil courage? In these years we have encountered much bravery and self-sacrifice but almost no civil courage anywhere, even among ourselves. Only an altogether naive psychology would trace this deficiency back simply to personal cowardice. The reasons behind this are quite different. In the course of a long history, we Germans have had to learn the need for obedience and the power thereof. We saw the meaning and greatness of our life in the subordination of all personal wishes and ideas under the commission that came to be ours. Our gaze was directed upward, not in slavish fear but in the free trust that beheld a career in the commission and a vocation in the career. The readiness to follow an order from "above" rather than one's own discretion arises from and is part of the justified suspicion about one's own heart. Who would contest that, in relation to obedience, commission, and career, the German has again and again accomplished the utmost in bravery and life commitment. But he safeguarded his freedom—where in the world was freedom spoken of more passionately than in Germany, from Luther to the philosophy of idealism?—by seeking to free himself from self-will in order to serve the whole: career and freedom were to him two sides of the same thing. However, in doing so he misjudged the world; he did not reckon with the fact that the readiness to subordinate and commit his life to the commission could be misused in the service of evil. When such misuse occurred, the exercise of the career itself became questionable, and all the basic moral concepts of the Germans were shaken. What became apparent was that Germans lacked still one decisive and fundamental idea: that of the need for the free, responsible action even against career and commission. In its place came the irresponsible lack of scruples, on the one hand, and self-tormenting scruples that never led to action, on the other. But civil courage can grow only from the free responsibility of the free man. Only today are Germans beginning to discover what free responsibility means. It is founded in a God who calls for the free venture of faith to responsible action and who promises forgiveness and consolation to the one who on account of such action becomes a sinner.[6]

41

---

6. [*See above, two notes previous.*]

On Success

Even though it is indeed not true that success also justifies the evil deed and the reprehensible means, it is similarly out of the question to regard success as something that is ethically wholly neutral. It so happens that historical success creates the ground on which alone life can go on. The question remains as to whether it is ethically more responsible to go to war like Don Quixote against a new age or, conceding one's defeat and freely consenting to it, finally to serve the new age. Success, after all, makes history, and the One who guides history always creates good from the bad over the head of the men who make history. It is a short circuit when the stickler for principle, thinking ahistorically and hence irresponsibly, simply ignores the ethical significance of success. It is good that for once we are forced to engage seriously the ethical problem of success. As long as the good is successful, we can afford the luxury of thinking of success as ethically irrelevant. But the problem arises once evil means bring about success. In the face of such a situation, we learn that neither the onlooker's theoretical critique and self-justification, that is, the refusal to enter into the arena of facts, nor opportunism, that is, disavowal and capitulation in the face of success, does justice to the task at hand. We may not and do not desire to act like offended critics or opportunists. Case by case and in each moment, as victors or vanquished, we desire to be those who are coresponsible for the shaping of history. The one who allows nothing that happens to deprive him of his coresponsibility for the course of history, knowing that it is God who placed it upon him, will find a fruitful relation to the events of history, beyond fruitless criticism and equally fruitless opportunism. Talk of going down heroically in the face of unavoidable defeat is basically quite nonheroic because it does not dare look into the future. The ultimately responsible question is not how I extricate myself heroically from a situation but how a coming generation is to go on living. Only from such a historically responsible question will fruitful solutions arise, however humiliating they may be for the moment. In short, it is much easier to see a situation through on the basis of principle than in concrete responsibility. The younger generation will always have the surest sense whether an action is done merely in terms of principle or from living responsibly, for it is their future that is at stake.

On Stupidity

Stupidity is a more dangerous enemy of the good than malice. One may protest against evil; it can be exposed and, if need be, prevented by use of force. Evil always carries within itself the germ of its own subversion in that it leaves behind in human beings at least a sense of unease. Against stupidity we are defenseless. Neither protests nor the use of force accomplish anything here; reasons fall on deaf ears; facts that contradict one's prejudgment simply need not be believed—in such moments the stupid person even becomes critical—and when facts are irrefutable they are just pushed aside as inconsequential, as incidental. In all this the stupid person, in contrast to the malicious one, is utterly self-satisfied and, being easily irritated, becomes dangerous by going on the attack. For that reason, greater caution is called for when dealing with a stupid person than with a malicious one. Never again will we try to persuade the stupid person with reasons, for it is senseless and dangerous.

If we want to know how to get the better of stupidity, we must seek to understand its nature. This much is certain, that it is in essence not an intellectual defect but a human one. There are human beings who are of remarkably agile intellect yet stupid, and others who are intellectually quite dull yet anything but stupid. We discover this to our surprise in particular situations. The impression one gains is not so much that stupidity is a congenital defect but that, under certain circumstances, people are *made* stupid or that they allow this to happen to them.[7] We note further that people who have isolated themselves from others or who live in solitude manifest this defect less frequently than individuals or groups of people inclined or condemned to sociability. And so it would seem that stupidity is perhaps less a psychological than a sociological problem. It is a particular form of the impact of historical circumstances on human beings, a psychological concomitant of certain external conditions. Upon closer observation, it becomes apparent that every strong upsurge of power in the public sphere, be it of a political or a religious nature, infects a large part of humankind with stupidity. It would even seem that this is virtually a sociological-psychological law. The power of the one needs the stupidity of the other. The process at work here   44 is not that particular human capacities, for instance, the intellect, suddenly atrophy or fail. Instead, it seems that under the overwhelming impact of rising power, humans are deprived of their inner independence and, more or less consciously, give up establishing an autonomous position toward the emerging circumstances. The fact that the stupid person is often stubborn

---

7. ["Like the section on the 'tyrannical despiser of human beings' in *Ethics* (*DBWE* 6:73 [*Reader* 611], 'He considers the people stupid and they become stupid'), the present section employs 'stupidity' as a psychological characteristic of Hitler and his followers," *DBWE* 8:43, n. 18.]

must not blind us to the fact that he is not independent. In conversation with him, one virtually feels that one is dealing not at all with him as a person, but with slogans, catchwords, and the like that have taken possession of him. He is under a spell, blinded, misused, and abused in his very being. Having thus become a mindless tool, the stupid person will also be capable of any evil and at the same time incapable of seeing that it is evil. This is where the danger of diabolical misuse lurks, for it is this that can once and for all destroy human beings.

Yet at this very point it becomes quite clear that only an act of liberation, not instruction, can overcome stupidity. Here we must come to terms with the fact that in most cases a genuine internal liberation becomes possible only when external liberation has preceded it. Until then we must abandon all attempts to convince the stupid person. This state of affairs explains why in such circumstances our attempts to know what "the people" really think are in vain and why, under these circumstances, this question is so irrelevant for the person who is thinking and acting responsibly. The word of the Bible that the fear of God is the beginning of wisdom declares that the internal liberation of human beings to live the responsible life before God is the only genuine way to overcome stupidity.

But these thoughts about stupidity also offer consolation in that they utterly forbid us to consider the majority of people to be stupid in every circumstance. It really will depend on whether those in power expect more from people's stupidity than from their inner independence and wisdom.

Contempt for Humanity?

The danger of allowing ourselves to be driven to contempt for humanity is very real. We know very well that we have no right to let this happen and that it would lead us into the most unfruitful relation to human beings. The following thoughts may protect us against this temptation: through contempt for humanity we fall victim precisely to our opponents' chief errors. Who-

45 ever despises another human being will never be able to make anything of him. Nothing of what we despise in another is itself foreign to us. How often do we expect more of the other than what we ourselves are willing to accomplish. Why is it that we have hitherto thought with so little sobriety about the temptability and frailty of human beings? We must learn to regard human beings less in terms of what they do and neglect to do and more in terms of what they suffer. The only fruitful relation to human beings—particularly to the weak among them—is love, that is, the will to enter into and to keep community with them. God did not hold human beings in contempt but became human for their sake.

Immanent Justice

It is one of the most astonishing experiences and also one of the most incontrovertible that evil—often in a surprisingly short span of time—proves itself to be stupid and impractical. That does not mean that punishment follows hard on the heels of each individual evil deed; what it does mean is that the suspension of God's commandments on principle in the supposed interest of earthly self-preservation acts precisely against what this self-preservation seeks to accomplish. One can interpret in various ways this experience that has fallen to us. In any case, one thing has emerged that seems certain: in the common life of human beings, there are laws that are stronger than everything that believes it can supersede them, and that it is therefore not only wrong but unwise to disregard these laws. This helps us understand why Aristotelian-Thomistic ethics elevated wisdom to be one of the cardinal virtues. Wisdom and stupidity are not ethically indifferent, as the neo-Protestant ethics of conscience wanted us to believe. In the fullness of the concrete situation and in the possibilities it offers, the wise person discerns the impassable limits that are imposed on every action by the abiding laws of human communal life. In this discernment the wise person acts well and the good person acts wisely.

There is clearly no historically significant action that does not trespass   46 ever again against the limits set by those laws. But it makes a decisive difference whether such trespasses against the established limit are viewed as their abolishment in principle and hence presented as a law of its own kind, or whether one is conscious that such trespassing is perhaps an unavoidable guilt that has its justification only in that law and limit being reinstated and honored as quickly as possible. It is not necessarily hypocrisy when the aim of political action is said to be the establishment of justice and not simply self-preservation. The world *is*, in fact, so ordered that the fundamental honoring of life's basic laws and rights at the same time best serves self-preservation, and that these laws tolerate a very brief, singular, and, in the individual case, necessary trespass against them. But those laws will sooner or later—and with irresistible force—strike dead those who turn necessity into a principle and as a consequence set up a law of their own alongside them. History's immanent justice rewards and punishes the deed only, but the eternal justice of God tries and judges the hearts.

Some Statements of Faith on God's Action in History

I believe that God can and will let good come out of everything, even the greatest evil. For that to happen, God needs human beings who let everything work out for the best. I believe that in every moment of distress God will give us as much strength to resist as we need. But it is not given to us in advance, lest we rely on ourselves and not on God alone. In such faith all fear of the future should be overcome. I believe that even our mistakes and short-comings are not in vain and that it is no more difficult for God to deal with them than with our supposedly good deeds. I believe that God is no timeless fate but waits for and responds to sincere prayer and responsible actions.

Trust

Few have been spared the experience of being betrayed. The figure of Judas, once so incomprehensible, is hardly strange to us. The air in which we live is so poisoned with mistrust that we almost die from it. But where we broke through the layer of mistrust, we were allowed to experience a trust hitherto utterly undreamed of. There, where we trust, we have learned to place our lives in the hands of others; contrary to all the ambiguities in which our acts and lives must exist, we have learned to trust without reserve. We now know that one can truly live and work only in such trust, which is always a venture but one gladly affirmed. We know that to sow and to nour-ish mistrust is one of the most reprehensible things and that, instead, trust is to be strengthened and advanced wherever possible. For us trust will be one of the greatest, rarest, and most cheering gifts bestowed by the life we humans live in common, and yet it always emerges only against the dark background of a necessary mistrust. We have learned to commit our lives on no account into the hands of the mean but without reserve into the hands of the trustworthy.

The Sense of Quality

When we lack the courage once again to establish a genuine sense of boundaries between human beings and personally to fight for them, we perish in an anarchy of human values. The impudence that has its being in the contempt for all such boundaries is just as much a mark of the rabble as the inward uncertainty, haggling, and courting the favor of the inso-lent; making common cause with rabble is the way toward rendering one-self rabble.[8] When one no longer knows what one owes oneself and others,

---

8. ["In relation to the key concepts of this section: 'rabble,' 'nobility,' 'order,' 'above and below,' see *DBWE* 7:26–31. Regarding 'above and below,' see also *DBWE* 6:372–373, 380 (*Reader* 673–674, 678–679), and *DBWE* 16:503–505 (*Reader* 700–701)," *DBWE* 8:47, n. 24.]

where the sense for human quality and the strength to respect boundaries cease to exist, chaos is at the door. When, for the sake of material comfort one tolerates impudence, one has already surrendered, there the floods of chaos have been permitted to burst the dam at the place where it was to be defended, and one becomes guilty of all that follows. In other times it may have been the task of Christianity to testify to the equality of all human beings; today it is Christianity in particular that should passionately defend the respect for human boundaries and human qualities. The misinterpretation that it is a matter of self-interest, or the cheap allegation that it is an antisocial attitude, must be resolutely faced. They are the perennial reproaches of the rabble against order. Whoever becomes soft and unsure here does not understand what is at issue, and presumably those reproaches may well apply to him. We are in the midst of the process that levels every rank of society. But we are also at the hour of a new sense of nobility being born that binds together a circle of human beings drawn from all existing 48 social classes. Nobility arises from and exists by sacrifice, courage, and a clear sense of what one owes oneself and others, by the self-evident expectation of the respect one is due, and by an equally self-evident observance of the same respect for those above and those below. At issue all along the line is the rediscovery of experiences of quality that have been buried under so much rubble, of an order based on quality. Quality is the strongest foe of any form of bringing everything to the level of the masses. Socially this means abandoning the pursuit of position, breaking with the star cult, an opening out upward and downward particularly in connection with the choice of one's friends, delight in private life, and courage for public life. Culturally the experience of quality signals a return from the newspaper and radio to the book, from haste to leisure and stillness, from distraction to composure, from the sensational to reflection, from the idol of virtuosity to art, from snobbery to modesty, from extravagance to moderation. Quantities compete for space; qualities complement one another.

Sympathy

We have to consider that most people learn wisdom only through personal experiences. This explains, *first*, the astonishing inability of most people to take any kind of preventive action—one always believes that he can evade the danger, until it is too late. *Second*, it explains people's dull sensitivity toward the suffering of others; sympathy grows in proportion to the increasing fear of the threatening proximity of disaster. There is some justification in ethics for such an attitude: one does not want to interfere with fate; inner calling and the power to act are given only when things have become serious. No one is responsible for all of the world's injustice and suffering, nor does one want to establish oneself as the judge of the world. And there is some justification also in psychology: the lack of imagination, sensitivity, and inner alertness is balanced by strong composure, unperturbed energy for work, and great capacity for suffering. From a Christian perspective, none of these justifications can blind us to the fact that what is decisively lacking here is a greatness of heart. Christ withdrew from suffering until his hour had come; then he walked toward it in freedom, took hold, and overcame it. Christ, so the Scripture tells us, experienced in his own body the whole suffering of all humanity as his own—an incomprehensibly lofty thought!—taking it upon himself in freedom. Certainly, we are not Christ, nor are we called to redeem the world through our own deed and our own suffering; we are not to burden ourselves with impossible things and torture ourselves with not being able to bear them. We are not lords but instruments in the hands of the Lord of history; we can truly share only in a limited measure in the suffering of others. We are not Christ, but if we want to be Christians it means that we are to take part in Christ's greatness of heart, in the responsible action that in freedom lays hold of the hour and faces the danger, and in the true sympathy that springs forth not from fear but from Christ's freeing and redeeming love for all who suffer. Inactive waiting and dully looking on are not Christian responses. Christians are called to action and sympathy not through their own firsthand experiences but by the immediate experience of their brothers, for whose sake Christ suffered.[9]

On Suffering

It is infinitely easier to suffer in obedience to a human command than in the freedom of one's very own responsible action. It is infinitely easier to suffer in community with others than in solitude. It is infinitely easier to suffer publicly and with honor than in the shadow and in dishonor. It is infinitely easier to suffer through putting one's bodily life at stake than

9. ["In the context of the first deportation of Jews from Berlin (October 18, 1941), see the reports composed by F. J. Perels and Bonhoeffer (*DBWE* 16:225–229). Hans von Dohnanyi made these available to Colonel Oster and General Beck 'in the hope that the military would either agree to intervene or accelerate its preparation for revolt' (*DB-ER*, 746). Cf. also Bethge, 'Dietrich Bonhoeffer and the Jews,' 72–77; C.-R. Müller, *Dietrich Bonhoeffers Kampf*, 303–320; Schreiber, *Friedrich Justus Perels*, 165–173; W. Meyer, *Unternehmung Sieben*, 7–11. In the church's confession of guilt in the chapter titled 'Guilt, Justification, Renewal' in *Ethics*, Bonhoeffer referred to the Jews 'for the first time as "brothers"'

to suffer through the spirit. Christ suffered in freedom, in solitude, in the shadow, and in dishonor, in body and in spirit. Since then, many Christians have suffered with him.

Present and Future

To this day, it seemed to us that developing a plan for our professional and personal life was one of the inalienable rights belonging to human life. That has come to an end. Through the weight of circumstances, we have been put into the situation where we must forgo "worrying about tomorrow." But there is a crucial difference as to whether this results from the free response of faith, as the Sermon on the Mount states, or is coerced subservience to the demands of the present moment. For most people the enforced renunciation of planning for the future means that they have succumbed to living only for the moment at hand, irresponsibly, frivolously, or resignedly; some still dream longingly of a more beautiful future and try thereby to forget the present. For us both of these courses are equally impossible. What remains for us is only the very narrow path, sometimes barely discernible, of taking each day as if it were the last and yet living it faithfully and responsibly as if there were yet to be a great future. "Houses and fields and vineyards shall again be bought in this land" [*Jer. 32:15*], Jeremiah is told to proclaim—in paradoxical contradiction to his prophecies of woe—just before the destruction of the holy city; in light of the utter deprivation of any future, those words were a divine sign and a pledge of a great, new future. To think and to act with an eye on the coming generation and to be ready to move on without fear and worry—that is the course that has, in practice, been forced upon us. To hold it courageously is not easy but necessary.

Optimism

It is more sensible to be pessimistic; disappointments are left behind, and one can face people unembarrassed. Hence, the clever frown upon optimism. In its essence optimism is not a way of looking at the present situation but a power of life, a power of hope when others resign, a power to hold

(Bethge, 'Nichts scheint mehr in Ordnung,' 36). The passage from *Ethics* reads: the church 'has become guilty of the lives of the weakest and most defenseless brothers and sisters of Jesus Christ' (*DBWE* 6:139). Regarding the development of that sentence, see *DBWE* 6:139 n. 25. See also Feil, 'Freundschaft—ein Thema der Theologie?,' 118–119," *DBWE* 8:49, n. 30.]

51 our heads high when all seems to have come to naught, a power to tolerate setbacks, a power that never abandons the future to the opponent but lays claim to it. Certainly, there is a stupid, cowardly optimism that must be frowned upon. But no one ought to despise optimism as the will for the future, however many times it is mistaken. It is the health of life that the ill dare not infect. There are people who think it frivolous and Christians who think it impious to hope for a better future on earth and to prepare for it. They believe in chaos, disorder, and catastrophe, perceiving it in what is happening now. They withdraw in resignation or pious flight from the world, from the responsibility for ongoing life, for building anew, for the coming generations. It may be that the day of judgment will dawn tomorrow; only then and no earlier will we readily lay down our work for a better future.

Peril and Death

In recent years we have become increasingly familiar with the thought of death. We ourselves are surprised by the composure with which we accept the news of the death of our contemporaries. We can no longer hate Death so much; we have discovered something of kindness in his features and are almost reconciled to him. Deep down we seem to feel that we are his already and that each new day is a miracle. It would not be correct to say that we die gladly—even though no one is unacquainted with that weariness, which ought not to be allowed to arise under any circumstances. We are too inquisitive for that, or, to put it more seriously, we would like to see something more of our scattered life's meaning. But we do not make of Death a hero either; life is too great and too dear for us to do so. Still more do we refuse to look for the meaning of life in danger; we are not desperate enough to do so and know too much of the treasures of life. We also know too well the fear for life and all the other destructive effects of unrelenting imperilment of life. We still love life, but I believe that Death can no longer surprise us. After what we have experienced in the war, we hardly dare acknowledge our wish that Death will find us completely engaged in the fullness of life, rather than by accident, suddenly, away from what really matters. It is not external circumstances but we ourselves who shall make of our death what it can be, a death consented to freely and voluntarily.

Are We Still of Any Use?

52 We have been silent witnesses of evil deeds. We have become cunning and learned the arts of obfuscation and equivocal speech. Experience has ren-

dered us suspicious of human beings, and often we have failed to speak to them a true and open word. Unbearable conflicts have worn us down or even made us cynical. Are we still of any use? We will not need geniuses, cynics, people who have contempt for others, or cunning tacticians, but simple, uncomplicated, and honest human beings. Will our inner strength to resist what has been forced on us have remained strong enough, and our honesty with ourselves blunt enough, to find our way back to simplicity and honesty?

The View from Below[10]

It remains an experience of incomparable value that we have for once learned to see the great events of world history from below, from the perspective of the outcasts, the suspects, the maltreated, the powerless, the oppressed and reviled, in short from the perspective of the suffering. If only during this time bitterness and envy have not corroded the heart; that we come to see matters great and small, happiness and misfortune, strength and weakness with new eyes; that our sense for greatness, humanness, justice, and mercy has grown clearer, freer, more incorruptible; that we learn, indeed, that personal suffering is a more useful key, a more fruitful principle than personal happiness for exploring the meaning of the world in contemplation and action. But this perspective from below must not lead us to become advocates for those who are perpetually dissatisfied. Rather, out of a higher satisfaction, which in its essence is grounded beyond what is below and above, we do justice to life in all its dimensions and in this way affirm it.

LETTER: APRIL 30, 1944

With the letter of April 30, 1944, Bonhoeffer launches the dispatches to his friend Eberhard Bethge that are often described as his "prison theology," or what Bethge himself calls in the biography "the new theology."[11] Bonhoeffer opens with the question: "what is Christianity," indeed, "who is Christ actually for us today" and in the future age? These are the letters that caused so much excitement, and consternation in some quarters, when they became widely known in the 1960s, and which have been debated ever since.

---

10. [*One of the very frequently quoted texts of Dietrich Bonhoeffer, this paragraph was not included in the first published version of "After Ten Years," though it was probably written about the same time. Cf.* DBWE *8:52, n. 37.*]

11. [DB-ER, *853–891.*]

There are three main topics in these letters, that run from April until the "Outline for a Book" in August 1944. The first topic, the critique of religion, appears in this letter. And the second topic, a "worldly, non-religious Christianity" to replace a "religious" Christianity, is already alluded to.[12] *The third topic, the "coming of age" of humanity, Bonhoeffer's summary of the change in human self-understanding since the Renaissance and the Enlightenment, will appear in a subsequent letter.*

Already it is obvious that understanding what Bonhoeffer means by "religion," and what he does not mean, is critical. Perhaps no issue has bedeviled Bonhoeffer interpretation more than this one. And yet it is not difficult to understand if we put aside our preconceptions and simply read what Bonhoeffer wrote. "Religion" for Bonhoeffer does not mean the church institution and its various beliefs and practices, as if a "religionless Christianity" would abandon congregations, clergy, worship, prayer, sacraments, the Bible—what people usually understand by religion. Bonhoeffer does not define religion by these forms, in an institutional way;[13] *he defines it, rather, in an operational or functional way—it is a certain* way of behaving, feeling, and thinking, a particular psychic posture. *Specifically, it is a way of trying to cope with human weaknesses, suffering, fears, and unsolved problems. Religion is governed and formed by human vulnerability. Accordingly, the essence of the "God" of religion is* power, *power to solve human problems; that is what Bonhoeffer calls the deus ex machina, or the "stopgap." He summarizes: "Human religiosity directs people in need to the power of God in the world, God as the deus ex machina."*[14]

Bonhoeffer's argument in these letters is, first, that modern people have outgrown the dependency of this psychic posture of religion—see below on "coming of age," adulthood, and autonomy. But, second, and even more importantly, such religion is simply not authentic Christianity. It is bad theology—a false idea of God, faith, and Christian life.[15] *Bonhoeffer's constructive proposal, therefore, is a* nonreligious, *worldly Christianity built on his well-established understanding of "Christ the center" of life.*[16]

---

12. [*See "religionless Christian," DBWE 8:363* (Reader 777–778).]

13. [*Bonhoeffer is not the prophet of the "spiritual but not religious" movement, though he might share some of its criticisms of institutional Christianity.*]

14. [DBWE *8:479* (Reader *803*).]

15. [*For a systematic analysis of the theology of* Letters and Papers from Prison, *see Clifford Green,* Bonhoeffer, *chap. 6.*]

16. [*See the 1933 Christology lectures* (DBWE *12:299–360, esp. 324–327* [Reader *261–313, 282–285*]). *See, in contrast to that Christology, Bonhoeffer's formal but critical references to religion as "metaphysics" and "inwardness" or "individualism"* (DBWE *8:364, 372–373* [Reader *778, 780–782*]). *Instead of these, Bonhoeffer wants a Christianity rooted in the social, historical world— a "worldly, non-religious Christianity."*]

How good it would be for us both, I feel, if we could live through this time 362
together and stand by each other. But it's probably even "better" that we
can't, but rather that each of us has to go it alone. It's hard for me not to be
able to help you in any way—except by thinking of you. I really do, every
morning and evening and when I read the Bible and often during the day
too. Please don't worry about me at all; I'm getting along uncommonly well;
you'd be surprised if you came to see me. People here keep saying to me—
and I'm very flattered by it, as you can see—that I "radiate such peace" and
that I'm "always so cheerful"—so that if I occasionally experience myself as
anything but, I suppose it's deceptive (which I don't really believe!).[17]

What might surprise or perhaps even worry you would be my theological thoughts and where they are leading, and here is where I really miss
you very much. I don't know anyone else with whom I can talk about them
and arrive at some clarity. What keeps gnawing at me is the question, what
is Christianity, or who is Christ actually for us today?[18] The age when we
could tell people that with words—whether with theological or with pious
words—is past, as is the age of inwardness and of conscience, and that
means the age of religion altogether. We are approaching a completely religionless age; people as they are now simply cannot be religious anymore.
Even those who honestly describe themselves as "religious" aren't really
practicing that at all; they presumably mean something quite different by
"religious." But our entire nineteen hundred years of Christian preaching and theology are built on the "religious a priori"[19] in human beings.
"Christianity" has always been a form (perhaps the true form)[20] of "reli- 363
gion." Yet if it becomes obvious one day that this "a priori" doesn't exist,

17. ["See the poem 'Who am I?,' *DBWE* 8:459–460 (*Reader* 816–817)," *DBWE* 8:362, n. 8.]

18. ["Cf. the 1933 Christology lectures in *DBWE* 12:302 (*Reader* 263–264): 'The question of "who" is the question about transcendence,'" *DBWE* 8:362, n. 10.]

19. [*The concept of the religious a priori was introduced into theology by Ernst Troeltsch and
appropriated by Bonhoeffer's doctoral supervisor, Reinhold Seeberg. For Bonhoeffer's early rejection
of it, see* DBWE 2:58.]

20. ["On 'Christianity' as the 'true' (form of) religion, see Barth, *Church Dogmatics*
1/2, § 17,3, p. 326: "religion is not always 'unfaith,' but '[t]here is a true religion: just
as there are justified sinners. . . . If we abide strictly by that analogy . . . we need have
no hesitation in saying that the Christian religion is the true religion,'" *DBWE* 8:363, n.
12. *Bonhoeffer, however, does not share with Barth the idea of a "true religion" but rather proposes
a religionless-worldly Christianity. That is because they have two different definitions of religion,
even though they share a basic critical attitude to "religion" as a human alternative to God's self-
revelation.*]

that it has been a historically conditioned and transitory form of human expression, then people really will become radically religionless—and I believe that this is already more or less the case (why, for example, doesn't this war provoke a "religious" reaction like all the previous ones?)—what does that then mean for "Christianity"? The foundations are being pulled out from under all that "Christianity" has previously been for us, and the only people among whom we might end up in terms of "religion" are "the last of the knights" or a few intellectually dishonest people. Are these supposed to be the chosen few? Are we supposed to fall all over precisely this dubious lot of people in our zeal or disappointment or woe and try to peddle our wares to them? Or should we jump on a few unfortunates in their hour of weakness and commit, so to speak, religious rape? If we are unwilling to do any of that, and if we eventually must judge even the Western form of Christianity to be only a preliminary stage of a complete absence of religion, what kind of situation emerges for us, for the church? How can Christ become Lord of the religionless as well? Is there such a thing as a religionless Christian? If religion is only the garb in which Christianity is clothed—and this garb has looked very different in different ages—what then is religionless Christianity? Barth, who is the only one to have begun

364   thinking along these lines, nevertheless did not pursue these thoughts all the way, did not think them through, but ended up with a positivism of revelation, which in the end essentially remained a restoration. For the working person or any person who is without religion, nothing decisive has been gained here. The questions to be answered would be: What does a church, a congregation, a sermon, a liturgy, a Christian life, mean in a religionless world? How do we talk about God—without religion, that is, without the temporally conditioned presuppositions of metaphysics, the inner life, and so on? How do we speak (or perhaps we can no longer even "speak" the way we used to) in a "worldly" way about "God"? How do we go about being "religionless-worldly" Christians, how can we be ἐκ-κλεσία [*church, literally those who are called out*], those who are called out, without understanding ourselves religiously as privileged, but instead seeing ourselves as belonging wholly to the world? Christ would then no longer be the object of religion, but something else entirely, truly lord of the world. But what does that mean? In a religionless situation, what do ritual and prayer mean? Is

365   this where the "arcane discipline,"[21] or the difference (which you've heard

---

21. [*For Bonhoeffer's other discussions of the "arcane discipline" (discipline of the secret), see* DBWE *11:285,* DBWE *4:45, and* DBWE *14:548, 526. See also* DBWE *8:356, n. 19 and* DBWE *4:54, n. 36 (Reader 468 n. 12).*]

about from me before) between the penultimate and the ultimate,[22] have new significance?

I have to stop for today so this letter can go off right now. I'll write more the day after tomorrow about this. I hope you understand more or less what I mean, and it's not boring you. Good-bye for now! It's not easy, always having to write without a response; you must forgive me if that makes it something of a monologue. I'm really not reproaching you for not writing—you have too much else to do!

Yours as ever, I think about you very much,

Dietrich

I have a little more time to write after all.

The Pauline question of whether περιτομή [*circumcision*] is a condition for justification is today, in my opinion, the question of whether religion is a condition for salvation. Freedom from περιτομή is also freedom from religion. I often wonder why my "Christian instinct" frequently draws me more toward nonreligious people than toward the religious,[23] and I am sure it's not with missionary intent; instead, I'd almost call it a "brotherly" instinct. While I'm often reluctant to name the name of God to religious people—because somehow it doesn't ring true for me there, and I feel a bit dishonest saying it (it's especially bad when other people start talking in religious terminology; then I clam up almost completely and feel somehow uncomfortable and in a sweat)—yet on some occasions with nonreligious people I can speak God's name quite calmly, as a matter of course. Religious people speak of God at a point where human knowledge is at an end (or sometimes when they're too lazy to think further), or when human strength fails. Actually, it's a deus ex machina [*God from the machine*][24] that they're always bringing on the scene, either to appear to solve insoluble problems or to provide strength when human powers fail, thus always exploiting human weakness or human limitations. Inevitably that lasts only until human beings become

366

---

22. ["On this, see *DBWE* 6:146–170 (*Reader* 613–630): 'Ultimate and Penultimate Things,'" *DBWE* 8:365, n. 20.]

23. ["See also Bonhoeffer's letter of June 25, 1942, to Bethge, *DBWE* 16:329: 'But I sense how an opposition to all that is "religious" is growing in me. Often into an instinctive revulsion—which is surely not good either. I am not religious by nature. But I must constantly think of God, of Christ; authenticity, life, freedom, and mercy mean a great deal to me,'" *DBWE* 8:366, n. 24.]

24. ["... In the ancient theater this was a figure who could be made to appear 'suddenly' with the help of a mechanical device and to solve problems 'supernaturally' ...," *DBWE* 8:366, n. 25.]

powerful enough to push the boundaries a bit further and God is no longer needed as deus ex machina. To me, talking about human boundaries has become a dubious proposition anyhow. (Is even death still really a boundary, since people today hardly fear it anymore, or sin, since people hardly comprehend it?) It always seems to me that we leave room for God only out of anxiety. I'd like to speak of God not at the boundaries but in the center, not in weakness but in strength, thus not in death and guilt but in human life and human goodness. When I reach my limits, it seems to me better not to say anything and to leave what can't be solved unsolved. Belief in the resurrection *is not* the "solution" to the problem of death. God's "beyond" is not what is beyond our cognition! Epistemological transcendence has nothing to do with God's transcendence.[25] God is the beyond in the midst of our lives. The church stands not at the point where human powers fail, at the boundaries, but in the center of the village. That's the way it is in the Old Testament, and in this sense we don't read the New Testament nearly enough in the light of the Old. I am thinking a great deal about what this religionless Christianity looks like, what form it takes, and I'll be writing you more about it soon. Here perhaps we in particular, midway between East and West, will be given an important task. Now I really have to close. How good it would be to have a word from you sometime about all this. It would really mean a lot to me, more than you can probably suppose. By the way, do read Prov. 22:11–12 sometime. This bars the way to all escapism in the guise of piety.

Wishing you the very, very best, with all my heart
yours, Dietrich

LETTER: MAY 5, 1944

372   A few more words about "religionlessness." You probably remember Bultmann's essay on "demythologizing the New Testament."[26] My opinion of

---

25. ["The Kantian concept of transcendence, understood as 'what is beyond our ability to know' (on Kant, see *DBWE* 8:450 [*Reader* 797]), had already been rejected in *Sanctorum Communio*, cf. *DBWE* 1:51 . . . ," *DBWE* 8:367, n. 28.]

26. [*The 1941 essay by the New Testament scholar Rudolf Bultmann, "New Testament and Mythology," generated great interest and controversy for several decades. Though some wanted to put Bultmann on trial for heresy, Bonhoeffer praised his "intellectual honesty" (DBWE 16:260), even though he thought that the crucial theological issue was the problem of "religion," not "mythology."*]

it today would be that he went not "too far," as most people thought, but rather not far enough. It's not only "mythological" concepts like miracles, ascension, and so on (which in principle can't be separated from concepts of God, faith, etc.!) that are problematic, but "religious" concepts as such. You can't separate God from the miracles (as Bultmann thinks); instead, you must be able to interpret and proclaim them *both* "nonreligiously." Bultmann's approach is still basically liberal (that is, it cuts the gospel short), whereas I'm trying to think theologically. What then does it mean to "interpret religiously"?

It means, in my opinion, to speak metaphysically, on the one hand, and, on the other hand, individualistically. Neither way is appropriate, either for the biblical message or for people today. Hasn't the individualistic question of saving our personal souls almost faded away for most of us? Isn't it our impression that there are really more important things than this question (—perhaps not more important than this *matter*, but certainly more important than the *question*!?)? I know it sounds outrageous to say that, but after all, isn't it fundamentally biblical? Does the question of saving one's soul even come up in the Old Testament? Isn't God's righteousness and kingdom on earth the center of everything? And isn't Rom. 3:24ff. the culmination of the view that God alone is righteous, rather than an individualistic doctrine of salvation? What matters is not the beyond but this world, how it is created and preserved, is given laws, reconciled, and renewed. What is beyond this world is meant, in the gospel, to be there *for* this world—not in the anthropocentric sense of liberal, mystical, pietistic, ethical theology, but in the biblical sense of the creation and the incarnation, crucifixion, and resurrection of Jesus Christ. Barth was the first theologian—to his great and lasting credit—to begin the critique of religion, but he then put in its place a positivist doctrine of revelation that says, in effect, "like it or lump it." Whether it's the virgin birth, the Trinity, or anything else, all are equally significant and necessary parts of the whole, which must be swallowed whole or not at all. That's not biblical. There are degrees of cognition and degrees of significance. That means an "arcane discipline" must be reestablished, through which the mysteries of the Christian faith are sheltered against profanation. The positivism of revelation is too easy-going, since in the end it sets up a law of faith and tears up what is—through Christ's becoming flesh!—a gift for us. Now the church stands in the place of religion—that in itself is biblical—but the world is left to its own devices, as it were, to rely on itself. That is the error. At the moment I am thinking about how the concepts of repentance, faith, justification, rebirth, and sanctification should

373

be reinterpreted in a "worldly" way—in the Old Testament sense and in the sense of John 1:14.[27] I'll write you more about it.

THOUGHTS ON THE DAY OF BAPTISM OF DIETRICH WILHELM RÜDIGER BETHGE, CA. MAY 16–18, 1944

Eberhard Bethge had married Bonhoeffer's niece, Renate Schleicher, on May 15, 1943, and Bonhoeffer had sent them a wedding sermon from his cell.[28] When their son was born they named him after Bonhoeffer, who sent this meditation for his godson's baptism. Anticipating the future world when the child had grown up, Bonhoeffer includes near the end some ideas from his new theological reflections.

383   You are the first of a new generation in our family. Never mind if your coming confuses us a little about our generational relationships, as we suddenly see ourselves moving earlier than expected into the second, third, and fourth generation. It's clear, nevertheless, that you are the eldest, you lead the procession of the next generation, and you will have the incomparable advantage of sharing a good part of your life with the third and fourth generations before you. Your great-grandfather will be able to tell you about

384   people he knew personally who were born in the eighteenth century; and some day, long after the year 2000, you will be the living bridge for your descendants to an oral tradition going back over 250 years—all that, of course, *sub conditione Jacobea* [*on the condition laid down by James (James 4:15)*], "if the Lord wishes, we will live." So your birth is a particular occasion for us to reflect on how times change, and to try to discern the outlines of the future.

The three names you bear point to three houses with which your life is, and should remain, inseparably linked. The house of your grandfather on your father's side[29] was a village parsonage. Simplicity and health, a communal and varied intellectual life, unpretentious enjoyment of the good things of life, in natural and un-self-conscious sharing with ordinary people and their work; a capacity for looking after oneself in practical matters and a

---

27. [*And the Word became flesh and lived among us. . . .*]
28. [DBWE *8:82–87.*]
29. ["Wilhelm Bethge," *DBWE* 8:384, n. 4.]

modesty founded on inner contentment; these are the enduring earthly values that found their home in the village parsonage and that you will find in your father. In all life's circumstances they will give you a firm foundation for living together with others and for genuine accomplishment and inner happiness.

The cosmopolitan culture of the old middle-class[30] tradition represented by your mother's home has created, in those who inherit it, a proud awareness of being called to high responsibility in public service, intellectual achievement and leadership, and a deep-rooted obligation to be guardians of a great historical heritage and intellectual tradition. This will endow you, even before you are aware of it, with a way of thinking and acting that you can never lose without being untrue to yourself.

It was a kind thought on your parents' part to have you named after a great-uncle, a pastor who is a good friend of your father's;[31] he is currently sharing the fate of many other good Germans and Protestant Christians, and so he has only been able to look on from afar as your parents married and you were born and baptized, but he has great confidence and joyful hopes for your future. He tries always to keep up the spirit—as he understands it—that is embodied in the home of his parents, your great-grandparents. He considers it a good omen for your future that this was the house where your parents first met, and he hopes that one day you will be aware of and thankful for its spirit and draw upon the strength that it gives.

The old village parsonage and the old middle-class house belong to a   385
world that will have vanished by the time you grow up. But the old spirit will survive the period of its misjudgment and its actual failure, and after a time of withdrawal, renewed inner reflection, probing, and healing will create new forms for itself. To be deeply rooted in the soil of the past makes life harder, but also richer and more vigorous. There are fundamental truths in human life to which it always returns sooner or later. We can't hurry it; we have to be able to wait. "God seeks out what has gone by," the Bible says (Eccl. 3:15).

In the coming years of upheaval, it will be the greatest of gifts to know that you are safe in a good home. It will be a bulwark against all dangers from without and within. The time when children arrogantly broke away

---

30. [". . . It is difficult to convey the meaning of *bürgerlich* in English today without some degree of misunderstanding. Although 'middle class' or 'bourgeois' are the dictionary translations, they do not convey the fact that the Bonhoeffer family was an upper-class family, in some sense aristocratic, and numbered among the leading citizens in Germany," *DBWE* 8:181, n. 22.]

31. [*I.e., Bonhoeffer himself.*]

from their parents will be past. The home will draw children back to their parents' care; it will be their refuge where they find counsel, calm, and clarity. You are fortunate in having parents who know from their own experience what a parental home can mean in stormy times. Amid the general impoverishment of spiritual life, you will find your parents' home a treasury of spiritual values and a source of inspiration. Music, as your parents understand and practice it, will bring you back from confusion to your clearest and purest self and perceptions, and from cares and sorrows to the underlying note of joy. Your parents' ability to cope with life will lead you early on to help yourself with your own hands and not to despise any manual task. Your parents' gift of gaining effortlessly the goodwill of others will bring you many friendships and help when needed. The devotional life of your home will not be noisy or wordy, but it will teach you to pray, to fear and love God above all, and to do the will of Jesus Christ gladly. "My child, keep your father's commandment, and do not forsake your mother's teaching. Bind them upon your heart always. . . . When you walk, they will lead you; when you lie down, they will watch over you; and when you awake, they will talk with you" (Prov. 6:20–22). "Today salvation has come to this house" (Luke 19:9).

———————————

386

I would wish you could grow up in the country; but it will no longer be the countryside where your father grew up. The big cities, where people expected everything life has to offer, every pleasure, where they swarmed together as if for a festival, have brought death and dying upon themselves with every imaginable horror, and women and children have become refugees fleeing these terrifying places. The age of big cities on our continent seems to be over. The Bible says Cain was the original founder of cities. Maybe there will still be some world-class metropolises, but their luster, seductive though it may be, will have something uncanny for Europeans, in any case.

On the other hand, the great migration out of the cities will change the countryside completely. The quiet and seclusion of country life has already been invaded by radio, cars, telephones, and the bureaucratic organization of almost all aspects of life. If millions of people who can't let go of the pace and expectations of city life move to the country, if whole industries are moved to rural areas, the urbanization of the countryside will progress rapidly and change the whole basic structure of rural life. There are just as few villages like those of thirty years ago left as there are idyllic South Sea islands. People long for solitude and quiet, but they will have a hard time finding it. Nevertheless, in this time of change, they will gain from having a plot of land under their feet from which to draw strength for a new, simpler, more natural and contented life of daily work and evening leisure. "There is great gain in godliness combined with contentment . . . if we have food and clothing, we will be content with these" (1 Tim. 6:6–7). "Give me neither poverty nor riches, feed me with the food that I need, or I shall be full, and deny you, and say 'Who is the LORD?' or I shall be poor, and steal, and profane the name of my God" (Prov. 30:8). "Flee from the midst of Babylon . . . she could not be healed. Forsake her, and let each of us go to our own country" (Jer. 51:6ff.).

We grew up with our parents' and grandparents' experience that each per-   387
son can and must plan, develop, and shape his own life, that there is a life work on which one must decide, and that he can and must pursue this with all his might. But from our own experience we have learned that we cannot even plan for the next day, that what we have built up is destroyed overnight. Our lives, unlike our parents' lives, have become formless or even fragmentary. Nevertheless, I can only say that I have not wanted to live in another time than ours, even though it tramples on our outward happiness. More clearly than in other ages, we realize that the world is in God's wrathful and merciful hands. In Jeremiah's words: "Thus says the Lord: I am going to break down what I have built, and pluck up what I have planted. . . . And you, do you seek great things for yourself? Do not seek them, for I am going to bring disaster upon all flesh, says the LORD; but I will give you your life as a prize of war in every place to which you may go" (chap. 45). If we come through the wreckage of a lifetime's acquired goods with our living souls intact, let us be satisfied with that. If the creation is being destroyed by its very Creator, what right have we to grumble about the destruction of our own work? It will be the task of our generation, not to "seek great things," but to save and preserve our souls out of the chaos, and to realize that this is the only thing we can carry as "booty" out of the burning house. "Keep your heart with all vigilance, for from it flow the springs of life" (Prov. 4:23). We shall have to bear our lives more than to shape them, to hope more than to plan, to hold out more than to stride ahead. But for you, the younger, newborn generation, we want to preserve that soul, which will empower you to plan and build up and give shape to a new and better life.

We have lived too much in our thoughts; we believed that by considering all the options of an action in advance we could ensure it, so that it would proceed of its own accord. We learned too late that it is not the thought but readiness to take responsibility that is the mainspring of action. Your generation will relate thought and action in a new way. You will only think about what you have to answer for in action. For us thought was in many ways a luxury afforded to onlookers; for you it will be entirely subordinated to action. "Not everyone who *says* to me, 'Lord, Lord,' will enter the kingdom of heaven, but only one who *does* the will of my Father in heaven" (Matt. 7:21).

388   For the greater part of our lives, pain was a stranger to us. Avoiding pain, as far as possible, was one of our subconscious guiding principles. Subtlety of feeling, intense awareness of one's own pain and that of others, are both the strength and the weakness of our way of life. Your generation will begin early having to bear privations and pain and having your patience severely tested, so you will be tougher and more realistic. "It is good for one to bear the yoke in youth" (Lam. 3:27).

We believed we could make our way in life with reason and justice, and when both failed us, we no longer saw any way forward. We have also over-estimated, time and again, the importance of reasonableness and justice in influencing the course of history. You who are growing up in the midst of a world war, which 90 percent of humankind doesn't want but for which they are giving their lives and goods, will learn from childhood on that this world is ruled by forces against which reason can do nothing. Thus your generation will deal with these powers more soberly and successfully. In our lives the "enemy" did not really exist. You know that you have enemies and friends, and what each means, enemy and friend, for your life. From childhood you will learn to fight your enemy in ways we never knew and to trust your friend unconditionally. "Do not human beings have a hard service on earth?" (Job 7:1). "Blessed be the LORD, my rock, who trains my hands for war, and my fingers for battle; my rock and my fortress, my stronghold and my deliverer, my shield, in whom I take refuge" (Ps. 144:1–2). "A true friend sticks closer than one's nearest kin" (Prov. 18:24).

Are we moving toward an age of colossal organizations and collective institutions, or will the desire of innumerable people for small, manageable, personal relationships be satisfied? Does the one have to exclude the other? Isn't it conceivable that it is precisely the vast scale of world organizations that allows more room for life at the personal level? A similar question is whether we are moving toward a time when the fittest will be selected, that is, toward a society ruled by aristocracy, or toward a uniformity in all outward and inward human living conditions. Although there has been a very far-reaching equalization of material and spiritual living conditions among human beings, the sense of quality, cutting across all levels of today's society 389   in seeking the human values of justice, achievement, and courage, could create a new selection of people, to whom the right to provide strong leadership will be given. We can give up our privileges without a struggle, recognizing the justice of history. Events and circumstances may arise that take precedence over our wishes and our rights. Then, not in embittered and barren pride, but consciously yielding to divine judgment, we shall prove ourselves worthy to survive by identifying ourselves generously and selflessly with the whole community and the suffering of our fellow human beings. "But any nation that will bring its neck under the yoke of the king of Babylon and serve him, I will leave on its own land, says the LORD, to till it and live there" (Jer. 27:11). "Seek the welfare of the city . . . and pray to the LORD on its behalf" (Jer. 29:7). "Come, my people, enter your chambers, and shut your doors behind you; hide yourselves for a little while until the wrath is past" (Is. 26:20). "For his anger is but for a moment; his favor is for a lifetime. Weeping may linger for the night, but joy comes with the morning" (Ps. 30:5).

You are being baptized today as a Christian. All those great and ancient words of the Christian proclamation will be pronounced over you, and the command of Jesus Christ to baptize will be carried out, without your understanding any of it. But we too are being thrown back all the way to the beginnings of our understanding. What reconciliation and redemption mean, rebirth and Holy Spirit, love for one's enemies, cross and resurrection, what it means to live in Christ and follow Christ, all that is so difficult and remote that we hardly dare speak of it anymore. In these words and actions handed down to us, we sense something totally new and revolutionary, but we cannot yet grasp it and express it. This is our own fault. Our church has been fighting during these years only for its self-preservation, as if that were an end in itself. It has become incapable of bringing the word of reconciliation and redemption to humankind and to the world. So the words we used before must lose their power, be silenced, and we can be Christians today in only two ways, through prayer and in doing justice among human beings. All Christian thinking, talking, and organizing must be born anew, out of that prayer and action. By the time you grow up, the form of the church will have changed considerably. It is still being melted and remolded, and every attempt to help it develop prematurely into a powerful organization again will only delay its conversion and purification. It is not for us to predict the day—but the day will come—when people will once more be called to speak the word of God in such a way that the world is changed and renewed. It will be in a new language, perhaps quite nonreligious language, but liberating and redeeming like Jesus's language, so that people will be alarmed and yet overcome by its power—the language of a new righteousness and truth, a language proclaiming that God makes peace with humankind and

390

that God's kingdom is drawing near. "They shall fear and tremble because of all the good and all the prosperity I provide for them" (Jer. 33:9). Until then the Christian cause will be a quiet and hidden one, but there will be people who pray and do justice and wait for God's own time. May you be one of them, and may it be said of you one day: "The path of the righteous is like the light of dawn, which shines brighter and brighter until full day" (Prov. 4:18).

LETTER: MAY 20, 1944

393   When you are in love, you want to live, above all things, and you hate every-thing that represents a threat to your life. You hate the memories of these last few weeks; you hate the blue sky that reminds you of them; you hate those planes, and so on. You want to live with Renate and be happy, as you have the right to be. And you have to live, for Renate's sake and for little Dietrich's (and even big Dietrich's). You have no right to talk the way your chief did the other night; on the contrary, that would be irresponsible on your part. You must sort that out with him quite calmly sometime. What is necessary goes without saying, but you could never follow that course just out of some personal emotion. However, there is a danger, in any pas-sionate erotic love, that through it you may lose what I'd like to call the

394   polyphony of life. What I mean is that God, the Eternal, wants to be loved with our whole heart, not to the detriment of earthly love or to diminish it, but as a sort of cantus firmus [*fixed melody*][32] to which the other voices of life resound in counterpoint.[33] One of these contrapuntal themes, which keep their *full independence* but are still related to the cantus firmus, is earthly love. Even in the Bible there is the Song of Solomon, and you really can't imagine a hotter, more sensual, and glowing love than the one spoken of here (cf. 7:6!). It's really good that this is in the Bible, contradicting all those who think being Christian is about tempering one's passions (where is there any such tempering in the Old Testament?). Where the cantus firmus is clear and distinct, a counterpoint can develop as mightily as it wants. The two are "undivided and yet distinct," as the Definition of Chalcedon says, like the divine and human natures in Christ. Is that perhaps why we are so

32. ["In a polyphonic composition, the primary, steady voice to which the other voices relate," *DBWE* 8:394, n. 7. *Following the Chalcedonian model Bonhoeffer cites here, the "fixed melody" would be the love of God, to which all earthly loves and activities are counterpoints.*]

33. ["An independent melodic line counter to the cantus firmus," *DBWE* 8:394, n. 8.]

at home with polyphony in music, why it is important to us, because it is the musical image of this christological fact and thus also our *vita christiana* [*Christian life*]? This idea came to me only after your visit yesterday. Do you understand what I mean? I wanted to ask you to let the cantus firmus be heard clearly in your being together; only then will it sound complete and full, and the counterpoint will always know that it is being carried and can't get out of tune or be cut adrift, while remaining itself and complete in itself. Only this polyphony gives your life wholeness, and you know that no disaster can befall you as long as the cantus firmus continues. Perhaps in these coming days you have together, but also in the days of separation that may follow, many things will be easier to bear. Please, Eberhard, don't fear and hate the separation, if it should come again, and all its dangers, but have confidence in the cantus firmus.

395

LETTER: MAY 21, 1944

I had just written the date of this letter, to be with you in my thoughts during these hours of preparation for the baptism and of the service itself,[34] and at that very moment the sirens began. Now I'm sitting in the sick bay, hoping that today at least you have been spared an air raid. What times these are! And what a baptism! What memories for years to come! What is important is to channel all these impressions, so to speak, the right way in one's mind; then they will just make you more defiant, harder, clearer, and that is good. A baptismal day like this doesn't allow for softer moods. When in the middle of a threatening air raid God sends out the call, the gospel call to God's kingdom through baptism, it's remarkably clear what this kingdom is and seeks. A kingdom stronger than war and danger, a kingdom of power and might, a kingdom that is eternal terror and judgment for some and eternal joy and righteousness for others. It is not a kingdom of the heart but reigns over the earth and the whole world, not a passing but an eternal kingdom that builds its own highway and calls on people to prepare its way; a kingdom for which it is worth risking our lives.

395

Now they've started shooting, but it doesn't seem to be getting too bad today. How I'd like to hear you preach in a few hours' time. Your sermons that I've heard—the last one was at Christmas—have always opened my eyes anew to the Bible and God's word. I'm hoping very much to hear something

396

---

34. [*The baptism of Dietrich Bethge.*]

about this sermon and the rest! I'd also like to hear your liturgy. Of course, I would wish that you could listen to the sermon yourself, but for Renate and the family it's certainly better this way. I can't think of anyone else who could do it as it should be done. For you it is a sacrifice, on one hand, and after all that has gone before, a significant intellectual accomplishment, which I very much admire, but, on the other hand, surely also a very special joy.

At eight this morning I heard, as a fine beginning for the day, a chorale prelude on "Was Gott tut, das ist wohlgetan" [*Whatever God ordains is right*]; I listened to it with thoughts of you and of my godchild! I hadn't heard an organ for a long time, and its sound was like a fortress in time of trouble. I'm particularly sorry that your letter in which you asked me to be godfather got lost. I am sure you said some kind, comforting, and encouraging words that would have done me good, and I would have been, and am, very grateful. Do you suppose it might still turn up? Or would you write me a few words to replace it? I suppose you'll also have to make an after-dinner speech today and will mention me. I'd like to hear what you said. Especially because we so seldom say such words to each other, one feels a hunger for them now and then. Do you understand that? Perhaps it's stronger than usual here in this isolation; we used to take everything for granted, and actually we still do—even so! By the way, here the other day did you find that "talking is harder" now than before? I didn't in the least; I'm just asking because you wrote something of the sort recently.

Perhaps you were surprised at yesterday's letter, which was meant to say something to *you* but, on the other hand, was so helpless itself. But isn't that the way it is? One is trying to help and is oneself the most in need of help. The part about the cantus firmus was actually written more for Renate's sake than yours, that is, more for the sake of your concord with each other 397 than as if I thought you didn't already know all that well enough. The image of polyphony is still following me around. In feeling some sorrow today at not being able to be with you, I couldn't help thinking that sorrow and joy, too, belong to the polyphony of the whole of life and can exist independently side by side.

LETTER: MAY 29, 1944

405   Weizsäcker's book on *The Worldview of Physics* continues to preoccupy me a
      great deal. It has again brought home to me quite clearly that we shouldn't
406   think of God as the stopgap for the incompleteness of our knowledge,

because then—as is objectively inevitable—when the boundaries of knowledge are pushed ever further, God too is pushed further away and thus is ever on the retreat. We should find God in what we know, not in what we don't know; God wants to be grasped by us not in unsolved questions but in those that have been solved. This is true of the relation between God and scientific knowledge, but it is also true of the universal human questions about death, suffering, and guilt. Today, even for these questions, there are human answers that can completely disregard God. Human beings cope with these questions practically without God and have done so throughout the ages, and it is simply not true that only Christianity would have a solution to them. As for the idea of a "solution," we would have to say that the Christian answers are just as uncompelling (or just as compelling) as other possible solutions. Here too, God is not a stopgap. We must recognize God not only where we reach the limits of our possibilities. God wants to be recognized in the midst of our lives, in life and not only in dying, in health and strength and not only in suffering, in action and not only in sin. The ground for this lies in the revelation of God in Jesus Christ. God is the center of life and doesn't just "turn up" when we have unsolved problems to be   407
solved. Seen from the center of life, certain questions fall away completely and likewise the answers to such questions (I'm thinking of the judgment pronounced on Job's friends!). In Christ there are no "Christian problems." Enough on this; I've just been interrupted again.

LETTER: JUNE 8, 1944

In the following letter, Bonhoeffer for the first time uses the notion of humanity's "coming of age" or adulthood (Mündigkeit) to summarize the historical process by which people have grown away from a "religious" posture with the result that "God" has become increasingly marginalized and subjectivized. It is the third of the three main organizing concepts in the prison theological letters, and the only one that is really new in his thinking. The metaphor of coming of age, becoming adult, refers to young adults who become independent of their parents, autonomous, and therefore responsible for their own lives.

By speaking of the world's "coming of age" or adulthood, Bonhoeffer does not imply humanity's historical progress to a higher moral stage but rather refers to the increase of knowledge, power, and organization by means of which human beings take more control of their lives and thereby become more autonomous. Bonhoeffer's use of the phrase "coming of age," his genealogy of the historical development, and his illustrations of this process in science, ethics, politics, law, philosophy, and even theology are drawn from the philosopher Wilhelm Dilthey (1833–1911), whose books he had been reading in prison.[35]

When Bonhoeffer writes of the "coming of age of the world," he is not making a global generalization about every society and all people on the planet. As the genealogy from Dilthey shows, this is a development that has occurred in Europe and North America in recent centuries, especially within the educated class of which people like the Bonhoeffer family were typical representatives; in the decades since World War II, this development has spread to other peoples and societies.

Note that, for Bonhoeffer, the "coming of age" movement he describes is not simply identical to secularization, namely, the processes by which science, government, and so forth develop their own rationale and rules, independent of church and religious interpretation. While this is partly involved, it does not lead Bonhoeffer to sketch a "secular" theology, but a nonreligious, "worldly" theology.[36] *Fundamentally, Bonhoeffer's words "adulthood" and "autonomy" refer to a change in human self-understanding, a change from a life posture of religious dependence to one of autonomy. This then leads Bonhoeffer to formulate his central question as "the claim of Jesus Christ on the world that has come of age."*[37]

425   You ask so many important questions about the thoughts that have preoccupied me lately that I'd be glad if I could answer them myself.[38] It's all still at a very early stage, and as usual I'm guided more by my instinct for responding to questions that may arise than being already clear about them. I'll try to describe my position from a historical angle. The movement toward human autonomy (by which I mean discovery of the laws by which the world lives and manages its affairs in science, in society and government, in art, ethics, and religion), which began around the thirteenth century (I don't want to get involved in disputing exactly when), has reached a certain completeness in our age. Human beings have learned to manage all important issues by themselves, without recourse to "Working hypothesis: God." In
426   questions of science or art, as well as in ethical questions, this has become a matter of course, so that hardly anyone dares rock the boat anymore. But in the last hundred years or so, this has also become increasingly true of

---

35. [*Dilthey*, Weltanschauung und Analyse. *See* DBWE *8:425–426, nn. 10 and 14. See also the letter of July 16 below, where Bonhoeffer follows Dilthey's account of the "one major development leading to the world's autonomy" (DBWE 8:475–477 and nn. 18–28).*]

36. [*For further discussion, see Clifford Green, "Bonhoeffer's Quest for Authentic Christianity," esp. 347–353, which deals with "Christian 'worldliness' beyond religion and secularism."*]

37. [*See letter of June 30, 1944, DBWE 8:451 (Reader 798).*]

38. [*A reference to Bethge's letter to Bonhoeffer of June 3, 1944, DBWE 8:411–414.*]

religious questions; it's becoming evident that everything gets along without "God" and does so just as well as before. As in the scientific domain, so in human affairs generally, "God" is being pushed further and further out of our life, losing ground.

The historical views of both Catholics and Protestants agree that this development must be seen as the great falling-away from God, from Christ, and the more they lay claim to God and Christ in opposing this, and play them off against it, the more this development considers itself anti-Christian. The world, now that it has become conscious of itself and the laws of its existence, is sure of itself in a way that it is becoming uncanny for us. Failures, things going wrong, can't shake the world's confidence in the necessity of its course and its development; such things are accepted with fortitude and sobriety as part of the bargain, and even an event like this war is no exception. In very different forms the Christian apologetic is now moving against this self-confidence. It is trying to persuade this world that has come of age that it cannot live without "God" as its guardian. Even after   427
we have capitulated on all worldly matters, there still remain the so-called ultimate questions—death, guilt—which only "God" can answer, and for which people need God and the church and the pastor. So in a way we live off these so-called ultimate human questions.

But what happens if some day they no longer exist as such, or if they are being answered "without God"? Here is where the secularized offshoots of Christian theology come in, that is, the existential philosophers and the psychotherapists, to prove to secure, contented, and happy human beings that they are in reality miserable and desperate and just don't want to admit that they are in a perilous situation, unbeknown to themselves, from which only existentialism or psychotherapy can rescue them. Where there is health, strength, security, and simplicity, these experts scent sweet fruit on which they can gnaw or lay their corrupting eggs. They set about to drive people to inner despair, and then they have a game they can win. This is secularized methodism.[39] And whom does it reach? a small number of intellectuals, of degenerates, those who consider themselves most important in the world and therefore enjoy being preoccupied with themselves. A simple man who spends his daily life with work and family, and certainly also with various stupid affairs, won't be affected. He has neither time nor inclination to be concerned with his existential despair, or to see his perhaps modest share of happiness as having "perilous," "worrisome," or "disastrous" aspects.

---

39. ["... Bonhoeffer's use of the term 'methodism' here refers to a form of pietism that he rejected, not the Methodist Church ...," *DBWE* 8:427, n. 16.]

I consider the attack by Christian apologetics on the world's coming of age as, first of all, pointless, second, ignoble, and, third, unchristian. Pointless—because it appears to me like trying to put a person who has become an adult back into puberty, that is, to make people dependent on a lot of things on which they in fact no longer depend, to shove them into problems that in fact are no longer problems for them. Ignoble—because an attempt is being made here to exploit people's weaknesses for alien purposes to which they have not consented freely. Unchristian—because it confuses Christ with a particular stage of human religiousness, namely, with a human law. More about this later, but first a few more words about the historical situation.

428

The question is Christ and the world that has come of age. The weakness of liberal theology was that it allowed the world the right to assign to Christ his place within it; that it accepted, in the dispute between church and world, the—relatively mild—peace terms dictated by the world. Its strength was that it did not try to turn back the course of history and really took up the battle (Troeltsch!), even though this ended in its defeat. Defeat was followed by capitulation and the attempt at a completely new beginning, based on "regaining awareness" of its own foundations in the Bible and the Reformation. Heim sought, along pietist-methodist lines, to convince individuals that they were confronted with the alternatives "despair or Jesus." He was winning "hearts." Althaus (continuing the modern positivist line in a strongly confessional direction) tried to regain from the world some room for Lutheran doctrine (ministry) and Lutheran ritual, otherwise leaving the world to its own devices. Tillich undertook the religious interpretation of the development of the world itself—against its will—giving it its form through religion. That was very brave, but the world threw him out of the saddle and galloped on by itself. He too thought he understood the world better than it did itself, but the world felt totally misunderstood and rejected such an insinuation. (The world *does* need to be understood in a better way than it does itself! but not "religiously," the way the religious socialists want to do.)

429

Barth was the first to recognize the error of all these attempts (which were basically all still sailing in the wake of liberal theology, without intending to do so) in that they all aim to save some room for religion in the world or over against the world. He led the God of Jesus Christ forward to battle against religion, πνευμα [*spirit*] against σάρξ [*flesh*]. This remains his greatest merit (the second edition of *The Epistle to the Romans*, despite all the neo-Kantian eggshells!). Through his later *Dogmatics* he has put the church in a position to carry this distinction in principle all the way through. It was not in his ethics that he eventually failed, as is often said—his ethical observations, so far as they exist, are as important as his dogmatic ones—but in the nonreligious interpretation of theological concepts he gave no concrete guidance, either in dogmatics or ethics. Here he reaches his limit, and that is why his theology of revelation has become positivist, a "positivism of revelation," as I call it.

To a great extent the Confessing Church now has forgotten all about Barth's approach and lapsed from positivism into conservative restoration. Its significance is that it holds fast to the great concepts of Christian theology, but it appears to be exhausting itself gradually in the process. Certainly these concepts contain the elements of genuine prophecy (which include the claim to the truth as well as mercy, as you mentioned) and of genuine ritual, and only to that extent does the message of the Confessing Church get attention, a hearing—and rejection. But both[40] remain undeveloped, remote, because they lack interpretation. Those who, like, for example, P. Schütz or the Oxford or Berneuchen movements, who long for "movement" and "life," are dangerous reactionaries, backward looking, because they want to go back before the beginnings of revelation theology[41] and seek "religious" renewal. They haven't understood the problem at all, so their talk is completely beside the point. They have no future whatsoever (except possibly the Oxford people, if only they weren't so lacking in biblical substance). As for Bultmann, he seems to have sensed Barth's limitation somehow, but misunderstands it in the sense of liberal theology, and thus falls into typical liberal reductionism (the "mythological" elements in Christianity are taken out, thus reducing Christianity to its "essence"). My view, however, is that the full content, including the "mythological" concepts, must remain—the New Testament is not a mythological dressing up of a universal truth, but this mythology (resurrection and so forth) is the thing itself!—but that these concepts must now be interpreted in a way that does not make religion the condition for faith (cf. the περιτομή [*circumcision*] in Paul!). Only then, in my opinion, is liberal theology overcome (which still determines even Barth, if only in a negative way), but at the same time the question it asks is really taken up and answered (which is *not* the case with the Confessing Church's positivism of revelation!). The fact that the world has come of age is no longer an occasion for polemics and apologetics, but is now actually better understood than it understands itself, namely, from the gospel and from Christ.

430

431

---

40. ["I.e., prophecy and worship," *DBWE* 8:430, n. 31.]
41. [*That is, the theology of Karl Barth.*]

Now to your question of whether the church has any "ground" left to stand on, or whether it is losing it altogether, and the other question, whether Jesus himself used the human "predicament" as a point of contact, so that "methodism," criticized above, is in the right.[42]

LETTER: JUNE 21, 1944

440   At the moment I'm reading the quite outstanding book by W. F. Otto, the classical philologist at Königsberg, on "the gods of [ancient] Greece." As he says at the end, it's about this "world of faith that arose from the riches and depth of existence rather than from its cares and longings."[43] Can you understand that this formulation, and the exposition that goes with it, have something I find very attractive, and that I am—*horribile dictu* [*horrible to say*]!—less offended by gods who are so portrayed than by certain forms of Christianity? that I almost believe I could claim these gods for Christ? For my current theological thinking, this book is very valuable. By the way, there's a good deal about Cardano in Dilthey.

LETTER: JUNE 27, 1944

446   At present I'm writing an exposition of the first three commandments.[44] I'm
447   finding the first one especially difficult. The usual interpretation of idolatry as "wealth, lust, and pride" doesn't seem at all biblical to me. That is moralizing. Idols are to be *worshipped*, and idolatry presupposes that people still worship something. But we don't worship anything anymore, not even idols. In that respect we're really nihilists.

A bit more on what we were thinking about the Old Testament. OT faith differs from other oriental religions in not being a religion of redemption. But Christianity is always characterized as a religion of redemption. Isn't there a cardinal error here, through which Christ is separated from the OT and interpreted in the sense of redemption myths? To the objection that redemption has a crucial importance in the OT as well (out of Egypt and

---

42. [*The letter concludes the following day without taking up these questions.*]

43. ["Otto, *Homeric Gods*, 287; trans. altered," *DBWE* 8:440, n. 9.]

44. ["See *DBWE* 16:633–644. In the Lutheran numbering of the Ten Commandments, the first concerns idolatry, whereas in the Reformed this is the second commandment," *DBWE* 8:446, n. 7.]

later out of Babylon, cf. Deutero-Isaiah), the reply is that this is redemption *within history*, that is, *this side* of the bounds of death, whereas everywhere else the aim of all the other myths of redemption is precisely to overcome death's boundary. Israel is redeemed out of Egypt so that it may live before God, as God's people on earth. The redemption myths look for an eternity outside of history beyond death. Sheol and Hades are not metaphysical constructs but rather images that present "what has been" on earth as still existing, but perceived in the present only in shadowy form. It is said to be decisive that in Christianity the hope of the resurrection is proclaimed, and that in this way a genuine religion of redemption has come into being. Now the emphasis is on that which is beyond death's boundary. And precisely here is where I see the error and the danger. Redemption now means being redeemed out of sorrows, hardships, anxieties, and longings, out of sin and death, in a better life beyond. But should this really be the essence of the proclamation of Christ in the Gospels and Paul? I dispute this. The Christian hope of resurrection is different from the mythological in that it refers people to their life on earth in a wholly new way, and more sharply than the OT. Unlike believers in the redemption myths, Christians do not have an ultimate escape route out of their earthly tasks and difficulties into eternity. Like Christ ("My God . . . why have you forsaken me?" [*Matt. 27:46; Ps. 22:1*]), they have to drink the cup of earthly life to the last drop, and only when they do this is the Crucified and Risen One with them, and they are crucified and resurrected with Christ. This-worldliness must not be abolished ahead of its time; on this, NT and OT are united. Redemption myths arise from the human experience of boundaries. But Christ takes hold of human beings in the midst of their lives. [448]

You see, I always come round to the same sort of thoughts. Now I have to substantiate them in detail out of the NT. That will follow somewhat later. This is enough for today! Farewell, Eberhard, God keep you every day!

Letter: June 30, 1944

Now I'll try to continue with the theological topics from where I stopped recently. My starting point was that God is being increasingly pushed out of a world come of age, from the realm of our knowledge and life and, since Kant, has only occupied the ground beyond the world of experience. On the one hand, theology has resisted this development with apologetics and taken up arms—in vain—against Darwinism and so on; on the other hand, it has resigned itself to the way things have gone and allowed God to function only as deus ex machina in the so-called ultimate questions, that [450] is, God becomes the answer to life's questions, a solution to life's needs and conflicts. So if anyone gives no evidence of such problems or refuses to lose self-control or be pitied over these things, then this person is really closed to talking about God; or else the man without such questions and so forth must have it proven to him that in truth he is up to his neck in such questions, needs, or conflicts, without admitting it or knowing it. If we succeed here—and existential philosophy and psychotherapy have worked out some very ingenious methods in this respect—then this man is open for God, and methodism can celebrate its triumphs. But if people cannot successfully be made to regard their happiness as disastrous, their health as sickness, and their vitality as an object of despair, then the theologians are at their wits' end. The person being dealt with either is a stubborn sinner of the most malignant kind or is living an existence of "bourgeois self-satisfaction," and the one is as far from salvation as the other. You see, this is the attitude that I am contending against. When Jesus made sinners whole, they were real sinners, but Jesus didn't begin by making every person into a sinner.

451 He called people from their sin, not into it. Certainly the encounter with Jesus turned all human values upside down. This is what happened at Paul's conversion, but his encounter with Jesus preceded the recognition of his sins. Certainly Jesus accepted people living on the margins of human society, prostitutes, and tax collectors, but certainly not only them, because he wanted to accept all humankind. Never did Jesus question anyone's health and strength or good fortune as such or regard it as rotten fruit; otherwise why would he have made sick people well or given strength back to the weak? Jesus claims all of human life, in all its manifestations, for himself and for the kingdom of God.

Of course, I have to be interrupted right at this point! Let me just quickly state, once again, the issue that concerns me: the claim of Jesus Christ on the world that has come of age.

LETTER: JULY 8, 1944

455 Now a few more thoughts on our topic. To present the biblical side of the matter needs more lucid thinking and concentration than I have today. Wait a few more days until it's cooler. I haven't forgotten either that I owe you something about interpreting biblical concepts nonreligiously. But for today, here are some preliminary remarks.

God's being pushed out of the world, away from public human existence, has led to an attempt to hang on to God at least in the realm of the "personal," the "inner life," the "private" sphere. And since each person has a "private" sphere somewhere, this became the easiest point of attack. What used to be the servants' secrets—to put it crudely—that is, the intimate areas of life (from prayer to sexuality)—became the hunting ground of modern pastors. In this way they resemble (even though their intentions are entirely different) the most evil of the tabloid journalists—remember the *Wahrheit* and the *Glocke?*[45]—who made public the intimate lives of prominent people. The intention of such journalism was societal, financial, and political blackmail; in the other case it's religious blackmail. Sorry, but I can't put it more sparingly. From a sociological viewpoint this is a revolution from below, a rebellion of the inferior. Just as the mean-spirited can only deal with eminent people when they can imagine them "in the bathtub" or in other embarrassing situations, it's the same here. There is a sort of evil satisfaction in knowing that every person has failings and weak spots. In my contact with the "outcasts" of society, the "pariahs," I have noticed repeatedly that the dominant motive in their judgment of other people is mistrust. Everything a person of high repute does, even the most selfless deed, is suspect from the outset. Such "outcasts," by the way, are found at all levels of society. In a flower garden they are only grubbing around for the dung on which the flowers grow. The less a person is connected to others, the more likely he will fall prey to this attitude. Among the clergy there is also a disconnectedness that we call being "holier-than-thou," that sort of prying into the sins of others in order to catch them out. It's as if you wouldn't know a fine house until you have found cobwebs in the remotest cellar, or you could appreciate a good play only after you saw how the actors behave behind the scenes. The same trend is found in novels of the last fifty years, which only think they have portrayed their characters honestly if they depict them in the marriage bed, and in movies, which have to have scenes of people undressing. To be clothed, veiled, pure, and chaste is considered a lie, a disguise, impure from the outset, which only gives proof of one's own impurity. This mistrust and suspicion as the basic attitude toward other people is the rebellion of the inferior. From a theological viewpoint the error is twofold: first, thinking one can only address people as sinners after having spied out their weaknesses and meanness; second, thinking that the essential nature of a person consists of his innermost, intimate depths and background, and calling this the person's "inner life." And precisely these most secret human places are to be the domain of God!

456

---

45. ["*Die Wahrheit* was published 1937 to 1938 in Berlin; *Glocke: Sozialistische Halb-monatzeitschrift* was published from 1915/16 to 1925 in Munich. Both were German tabloids," *DBWE* 8:455, n. 11.]

To the first assumption one must say that human beings are sinners, but that is a long way from saying they are mean. To put it tritely, does it make Goethe or Napoleon a sinner to say that they weren't always faithful husbands? It is not the sins of weakness but rather the sins of strength that matter. There is no need to go spying around. Nowhere does the Bible do this. (Strong sins: with a genius, hubris; for peasants, breaking the natural order [is the Decalogue perhaps a peasant ethic?]; the bourgeoisie, steering shy of free responsibility. Is that right?)

To the second assumption: the Bible does not know the distinction that we make between the outward and the inward life. How could it, actually? It is always concerned with the anthropos teleios, the *whole* human being, even in the Sermon on the Mount, where the Decalogue is extended into the "innermost" interior. The notion that a good "character" could take the place of all human goodness is completely unbiblical. The discovery of the so-called inner life dates from the Renaissance (probably from Petrarch). The "heart" in the biblical sense is not the inner life but rather the whole person before God. Since human beings live as much from their "outer" to their "inner" selves as from their "inner" to their "outer" selves, the assumption that one can only understand the essence of a human being by knowing his most intimate psychological depths and background is completely erroneous.

What I am driving at is that God should not be smuggled in somewhere, in the very last, secret place that is left. Instead, one must simply recognize that the world and humankind have come of age. One must not find fault with people in their worldliness but rather confront them with God where they are strongest. One must give up the "holier-than-thou" ploys and not regard psychotherapy or existential philosophy as scouts preparing the way for God. The intrusive manner of all these methods is far too unaristocratic for the Word of God to be allied with them. The Word of God does not ally itself with this rebellion of mistrust, this rebellion from below. Instead, it reigns.

So, now would be the time to speak concretely about the worldly interpretation of biblical concepts. But it's just *too* hot today! . . .

By the way, it would be very nice if you didn't throw away my theological letters but, since they are surely a burden for you to keep there, send them off to Renate from time to time. I might perhaps like to read them again later for my work. One writes some things in a more uninhibited and lively way in a letter than in a book, and in a conversation through letters I often have better ideas than when I'm writing for myself. But it's not important!— Incidentally, Mr. H. Linke, Berlin-Friedrichshagen, Wilhelmstr. 58 would be glad of a greeting from you from time to time.

CHRISTIANS AND HEATHENS

The poems Bonhoeffer began writing in Tegel prison in June 1944 are often highly autobiographical. But this poem, sent with a letter dated July 8, 1944, distills key themes from Bonhoeffer's theological reflections in the preceding letters. Stanza 1 presents "religion" as rooted in and shaped by human need, with God portrayed as the problem solver, the deus ex machina. The tables are turned in Stanza 2, where the power God of wishful human fantasy is replaced by the weak and crucified God. This is the God who, in Stanza 3, freely comes to humanity, giving not what humans had asked but what in their idolatry they really needed—forgiveness, for Christians and heathens alike.

1. People go to God when they're in need,   460
   plead for help, pray for blessing and bread,
   for rescue from their sickness, guilt, and death.
   So do they all, all of them, Christians and heathens.

2. People go to God when God's in need,   461
   find God poor, reviled, without shelter or bread,
   see God devoured by sin, weakness, and death.
   Christians stand by God in God's own pain.

3. God goes to all people in their need,
   fills body and soul with God's own bread,
   goes for Christians and heathens to Calvary's death
   and forgives them both.

LETTER: JULY 16, 1944

Now for a few more thoughts on our topic. I'm just working gradually toward   475
the nonreligious interpretation of biblical concepts. I am more able to see
what needs to be done than how I can actually do it. Historically there is just
one major development leading to the world's autonomy.[46] In theology it was

---

46. [*In the intellectual genealogy that follows, Bonhoeffer is again following Dilthey (for details, see the editorial notes on DBWE 8:475–477); the themes are the spread of human autonomy in all disciplines, and the consequent overcoming of the idea of God as a working hypothesis.*]

476	Lord Herbert of Cherbury who first asserted that reason is sufficient for religious understanding. In moral philosophy Montaigne and Bodin substitute rules for life for the commandments. In political philosophy Machiavelli separates politics from general morality and founds the doctrine of reason of state. Later H. Grotius, very different from Machiavelli in content, but following the same trend toward the autonomy of human society, sets up his natural law as an international law, which is valid *etsi deus non daretur*, "as

477	if there were no God." Finally, the philosophical closing line: on one hand, the deism of Descartes: the world is a mechanism that keeps running by itself without God's intervention; on the other hand, Spinoza's pantheism: God is nature. Kant is basically a deist; Fichte and Hegel are pantheists. In every case the autonomy of human beings and the world is the goal of thought. (In the natural sciences this obviously begins with Nicholas of Cusa and Giordano Bruno and their—"heretical"—doctrine of the infinity of the universe. The cosmos of antiquity is finite, as is the created world of medieval thought. An infinite universe—however it is conceived—is self-subsisting, "etsi deus non daretur." However, modern physics now doubts that the universe is infinite, yet without falling back to the earlier notions of

478	its finitude.) As a working hypothesis for morality, politics, and the natural sciences, God has been overcome and done away with, but also as a working hypothesis for philosophy and religion (Feuerbach!). It is a matter of intellectual integrity to drop this working hypothesis, or eliminate it as far as possible. An edifying scientist, physician, and so forth is a hybrid. So where is any room left for God? Ask those who are anxious, and since they don't have an answer, they condemn the entire development that has brought them to this impasse. I have already written to you about the various escape routes out of this space that has become too narrow. What could be added to that is the *salto mortale* [*death-defying leap*] back to the Middle Ages. But the medieval principle is heteronomy, in the form of clericalism. The return to that is only a counsel of despair, a sacrifice made only at the cost of intellectual integrity. It's a dream, to the tune of "Oh, if only I knew the road back, the long road to childhood's land!" There is no such way—at least not by willfully throwing away one's inner integrity, but only in the sense of Matt. 18:3, that is, through repentance, through *ultimate* honesty! And we cannot be honest unless we recognize that we have to live in the world— "etsi deus non daretur." And this is precisely what we do recognize—before God! God himself compels us to recognize it. Thus our coming of age leads us to a truer recognition of our situation before God. God would have us know that we must live as those who manage their lives without God. The

same God who is with us is the God who forsakes us (Mark 15:34!). The   479
same God who makes us to live in the world without the working hypothesis
of God is the God before whom we stand continually. Before God, and with
God, we live without God. God consents to be pushed out of the world and
onto the cross; God is weak and powerless in the world and in precisely
this way, and only so, is at our side and helps us. Matt. 8:17 makes it quite
clear that Christ helps us not by virtue of his omnipotence but rather by
virtue of his weakness and suffering! This is the crucial distinction between
Christianity and all religions. Human religiosity directs people in need to
the power of God in the world, God as deus ex machina. The Bible directs
people toward the powerlessness and the suffering of God; only the suffering God can help. To this extent, one may say that the previously described
development toward the world's coming of age, which has cleared the way
by eliminating a false notion of God, frees us to see the God of the Bible,
who gains ground and power in the world by being powerless. This will   480
probably be the starting point for our "worldly interpretation."

July 18[47]

Do you suppose that some letters have been lost due to the raids on Munich?
Did you get the one with the two poems? It was sent right at that time and
contained some more preliminary discussion on the theological topic. The
poem "Christians and Heathens" includes a thought that you will recognize here. "Christians stand by God in God's own pain"—that distinguishes
Christians from heathens. "Could you not stay awake with me one hour?"
Jesus asks in Gethsemane. That is the opposite of everything a religious person expects from God. The human being is called upon to share in God's
suffering at the hands of a godless world. Thus we must really live in that
godless world and not try to cover up or transfigure its godlessness somehow
with religion. Our lives must be "worldly," so that we can share precisely
so in God's suffering; our lives are *allowed* to be "worldly," that is, we are
delivered from false religious obligations and inhibitions. Being a Christian
does not mean being religious in a certain way, making oneself into something or other (a sinner, penitent, or saint) according to some method or
other. Instead it means being human, not a certain type of human being,

47. [*Continuation of the letter of July 16.*]

but the human being Christ creates in us. It is not a religious act that makes someone a Christian, but rather sharing in God's suffering in the worldly life. That is "μετανοια" [*conversion, turning around, or repentance*] not thinking first of one's own needs, questions, sins, and fears but allowing oneself to be pulled into walking the path that Jesus walks, into the messianic

481   event, in which Is. 53 is now being fulfilled! Hence "believe in the good news" and, in John, the reference to the "Lamb of God who takes away the sin of the world" [*John 1:29*] (by the way, J. Jeremias asserted recently that "lamb" in Aramaic can also be translated as "servant." That's really fine, in view of Is. 53!). This being pulled along into the—messianic—suffering of God in Jesus Christ happens in the NT in various ways: when the disciples are called to follow him, in table fellowship with sinners, through "conversions" in the narrower sense of the word (Zacchaeus), through the action of the woman "who was a sinner" (done without any confession of sin taking place) in Luke 7, through the healing of the sick (see above Matt. 8:17), through receiving the children. The shepherds stand at the manger just as do the wise men from the East, not as "converted sinners," but simply because they are drawn to the manger (by the star) just as they are. The centurion at Capernaum, who makes no confession of sin at all, is held

482   up as an example of faith (cf. Jairus). The rich young man is "loved" by Jesus. The courtier in Acts 8, Cornelius (Acts 10), are anything but persons in desperate straits. Nathanael is "an Israelite in whom there is no deceit" (John 1:47), and finally there are Joseph of Arimathea and the women at the tomb. The one thing they all have in common is their sharing in the suffering of God in Christ. That is their "faith." There is nothing about a religious method; the "religious act" is always something partial, whereas "faith" is something whole and involves one's whole life. Jesus calls not to a new religion but to life. But what is this life like? this life of participating in God's powerlessness in the world? I'll write about this next time, I hope. For today I'll just say this: if one wants to speak of God "nonreligiously," then one must speak in such a way that the godlessness of the world is not covered up in any way, but rather precisely to uncover it and surprise the world by letting light shine on it. The world come of age is more god-less and perhaps just because of that closer to God than the world not yet come of age. Forgive me, this is all still put terribly clumsily and badly; I'm very aware of this. But perhaps you are just the one to help me again to clarify and simplify it, if only by my being able to tell you about it, and to hear you, as it were, keep asking and answering me! . . .

LETTER: JULY 21, 1944[48]

This short greeting is all I want to send you today. I think you must be so often present in spirit with us here that you will be glad for every sign of life, even if our theological discussion takes a breather for a while. To be sure, theological thoughts do preoccupy me incessantly, but then there are hours, too, when one is content with the ongoing processes of life and faith without reflecting on them. Then the *Daily Texts*[49] simply make you happy, as I found especially to be the case with yesterday's and today's, for example. And then returning to the beautiful Paul Gerhardt hymns makes one glad to have them in the repertoire.

In the last few years I have come to know and understand more and more the profound this-worldliness of Christianity. The Christian is not a *homo religiosus* [*religious person*] but simply a human being, in the same way that Jesus was a human being—in contrast, perhaps, to John the Baptist. I do not mean the shallow and banal this-worldliness of the enlightened, the bustling, the comfortable, or the lascivious, but the profound this-worldliness that shows discipline and includes the ever-present knowledge of death and resurrection. I think Luther lived in this kind of this-worldliness. I remember a conversation I had thirteen years ago in America with a young French pastor.[50] We had simply asked ourselves what we really wanted to do with our lives. And he said, I want to become a saint (—and I think it's possible that he did become one). This impressed me very much at the time. Nevertheless, I disagreed with him, saying something like: I want to learn to have faith. For a long time I did not understand the depth of this antithesis. I thought I myself could learn to have faith by trying to live something like a saintly life. I suppose I wrote *Discipleship* at the end of this path. Today I clearly see the dangers of that book, though I still stand by it.[51] Later on I discovered, and am still discovering to this day, that one only learns to have faith by

485

486

48. [*This letter was written the day after the failed July 20, 1944, attempt to kill Hitler. That failure, and its implications for the future, prompts Bonhoeffer to look back over the course of his life, and to ask what it means to be a Christian in light of his latest theological reflections.*]

49. [*The annual* Moravian Daily Texts *that Bonhoeffer used were first published in 1730, and an English edition is still published by the Moravian Church in North America.*]

50. [*For Bonhoeffer's friendship with Jean Lasserre during his 1930–1931 postdoctoral year at Union Theological Seminary, see* DBWE *10:26–28, 37, n. 168, 40–43.*]

51. [*Regarding learning "to have faith by trying to live something like a saintly life" and renouncing "making something of oneself," see* DBWE 8:480 (Reader 803–804): *"Being a Christian does not mean being religious in a certain way, making oneself into something or other (a sinner, penitent, or saint) according to some method or other."*]

living in the full this-worldliness of life. If one has completely renounced making something of oneself—whether it be a saint or a converted sinner or a church leader (a so-called priestly figure!), a just or an unjust person, a sick or a healthy person—then one throws oneself completely into the arms of God, and this is what I call this-worldliness: living fully in the midst of life's tasks, questions, successes and failures, experiences, and perplexities—then one takes seriously no longer one's own sufferings but rather the suffering of God in the world. Then one stays awake with Christ in Gethsemane. And I think this is faith; this is metanoia. And this is how one becomes a human being, a Christian. (Cf. Jer. 45!) How should one become arrogant over successes or shaken by one's failures when one shares in God's suffering in the life of this world? You understand what I mean even when I put it so briefly. I am grateful that I have been allowed this insight, and I know that it is only on the path that I have finally taken that I was able to learn this. So I am thinking gratefully and with peace of mind about past as well as present things.

Perhaps you are surprised at such a personal letter. But when I feel like saying such things sometimes, who else should I say them to? Perhaps the time will come when I can speak to Maria this way, too; I do very much hope so. But I cannot put that burden on her yet.

May God lead us kindly through these times, but above all, may God lead us to himself.

LETTER: CA. JULY 27, 1944

489   Your formulation of our theological theme is very clear and simple. The question how there can be a "natural" piety is at the same time the question about "unconscious Christianity"[52] that preoccupies me more and more. The Lutheran dogmatists distinguished a *fides directa* [*direct faith*] from a *fides reflexa* [*reflective faith*].[53] They related that to the so-called faith of the infant at baptism.[54] I wonder if we are not here addressing a very wide-reaching problem. More about that, hopefully, soon.

---

52. ["... On this concept in Bonhoeffer, see *DBWE* 6:170, n. 111; *DBWE* 7:106, 225, n. 134 ... ," *DBWE* 8:489, n. 3.]

53. [*See* DBWE *2:157–161* (*Reader* 106–109); DBWE *4:153;* DBWE *16:562* (*Reader* 725).]

54. [*See* "... *DBWE* 2:159, n. 30; see also Bonhoeffer's theological opinion paper on the question of baptism (1942) in *DBWE* 16:561–566, esp. 561–562 (*Reader* 724–729, esp. 724–725) ... ," *DBWE* 8:489, n. 5.]

Notes I, Tegel, July–August 1944[55]   490

The expulsion of God from the world is the discrediting of religion
Living without God
But what if Christianity were not a religion at all? worldly nonreligious inter-
pretation of Christian concepts.
Christianity arises out of the encounter with a concrete human being: Jesus.
Experience of transcendence
educated people? Breakdown of Christian ethics.

No social ethics.
     Confessional matters.

"I believe only what I see."
God—not a relig. . . .[56]

Return to M.A.[57]

Notes II, Tegel, July–August 1944   491

Unconscious Christianity: Left hand doesn't know
                                   what the right hand is doing.
                                   Matt. 25.
                         Not knowing what to pray.
Motto: Jesus said to him: "What do you want me to do for you?" [*Mark 10:51*]

---

55. [". . . These notes—see *DBWE* 8:362–365 (*Reader* 777–779), regarding their
themes—contain key ideas and phrasing for the outline for a book (*DBWE* 8:499–504
[*Reader* 810–815]), which Bonhoeffer sent to Bethge on August 3, 1944; cf. *DBWE* 8:498,"
DBWE 8:490, n. 1.]

56. ["One word illegible, perhaps 'relationship.' (See *DBWE* 8:501 (*Reader* 813): 'Our
relationship to God is not a 'religious' one.)," *DBWE* 8:490, n. 6.]

57. ["Middle Ages. . . . Cf. *DBWE* 8:478 (*Reader* 802) ('*salto mortale* back to the Middle
Ages')," *DBWE* 8:490, n. 7.]

LETTER: JULY 28, 1944

491   You think that the Bible does not say much about health, happiness, strength, and so on. I have thought that over again very carefully. I'm sure it is not true of the OT in any case. The mediating theological concept in the
492   OT between God and the happiness, and so forth, of human beings is that of blessing, as far as I can see. Certainly in the OT, for instance among the patriarchs, the focus is not on happiness but on God's blessing, which itself encompasses all earthly good. This blessing is the addressing and claiming of earthly life for God, and it contains all God's promises. To regard the OT blessing as superseded by the NT would once again resemble the customary, overspiritualized view of the NT. But do you think it is an accident that the subject of sickness and death comes up in the context of the misuse of the Lord's Supper ("the cup of *blessing* . . ." 1 Cor. 10:16! 1 Cor. 11:30), or that Jesus restores people's health, or that when Jesus's disciples are with him they "lack nothing"? Now, should one oppose the cross with the OT blessing? That is what Kierkegaard did. This turns the cross and/or suffering into a principle, and this is precisely what gives rise to an unhealthy methodism that denies suffering its quality of contingency within divine providence. Incidentally, the person who receives blessing in the OT must also suffer much (Abraham, Isaac, Jacob, Joseph), but this never (as little as in the NT) leads to making happiness and suffering, blessing and the cross,
493   mutually exclusive. In this respect the difference between OT and NT may consist solely in the fact that in the OT the blessing also includes the cross and in the NT the cross also includes the blessing.

   To change the subject completely: not only action but suffering, too, is a way to freedom. In suffering, liberation consists in being allowed to let the matter out of one's own hands into the hands of God. In this sense death is the epitome of human freedom.[58] Whether the human deed is a matter of faith depends on whether people understand their own suffering as a continuation of their action, as a consummation of freedom. I find this very important and very comforting.

---

58. [*See Bonhoeffer's poem, 'Stations on the Way to Freedom,'* DBWE *8:512–514.*]

A Few Thoughts on Miscellaneous Topics, ca. August 1944

Giordano Bruno: "The sight of a friend can cause a strange shudder, since   494
no enemy can have such terrifying qualities as a friend"—Do you understand this? I am trying to but really do not understand it after all. Does the
"terrifying" refer to the danger of betrayal that is simultaneously inherent
in every intimate human relationship (Judas?)?

Spinoza: Affects are never overcome by reason but only by stronger
affects.

It is the advantage and the essence of the strong that they are able to pose
the great decisive questions and take clear positions on them. The weak
must always decide between alternatives that are not their own.

Presumably we are made in such a way that perfection is boring to us; I
do not know whether that was always the case. But I have no other way to
explain the fact that Raphael remains as distant and indifferent to me as   495
Dante's paradise. Likewise, neither eternal ice nor eternal blue sky appeals
to me. I seek "perfection" in what is human, living, earthly, that is, neither in
the Apollonian nor in the Dionysian or Faustian. It seems I am for the more
moderate climate in every direction.

August 3

That which is beyond[59] consists not of things infinitely distant but of things
closest at hand.

Ultimate seriousness is never without a dose of humor.

---

59. [*Translation corrected: In this sentence "das Jenseitige," literally "that which is beyond,"
means "the transcendent." See below DBWE 8:501 (Reader 813): "The transcendent is not the
infinite, unattainable tasks, but the neighbor within reach."*]

The essential thing about chastity is not a renunciation of pleasure but an all-encompassing orientation of life toward a goal. Where there is no such orientation, chastity inevitably deteriorates into the ridiculous. Chaste living is the prerequisite for clear and superior thoughts.

On the way to freedom death is the greatest of feasts.

Please forgive these demanding pearls of wisdom! They are fragments of conversations that never took place and as such they belong to you. When one is forced to exist only in one's own thoughts, as I am, one gets the most stupid thoughts, such as committing one's miscellaneous thoughts to writing!

LETTER: AUGUST 3, 1944

498   I've enclosed here an outline for a book. I don't know if you can get anything out of it, but I do think you will understand roughly what I mean. I hope that I can maintain the calm and strength it will take to write this work. The church must get out of its stagnation. We must also get back out into the fresh air of intellectual discourse with the world. We also have to risk saying controversial things, if that will stir up discussion of the important issues in

499   life. As a "modern" theologian[60] who has nevertheless inherited the legacy of liberal theology, I feel responsible to address these questions. There are probably not many among the younger generation who combine these two elements. How I need your help! But if we do have to be deprived of clarifying conversation, at least we are not deprived of prayer, which alone allows us to begin and do this kind of work.

---

60. [*That is, one who stood with Barth on the issue of transcendence and revelation while independently following his own course, which included "the legacy of liberal theology," as seen, for example, in his respect for Bultmann on demythologizing.*]

OUTLINE FOR A BOOK, AUGUST 3, 1944

In this book outline, Bonhoeffer shows how he planned a more systematic presentation of the ideas in the foregoing letters. He begins with the idea of humanity's coming of age, arguing that technical organization (science, insurance, bureaucracy, and so forth) leads to control of nature, but that greatly increased power in human hands presents a new menace. Nevertheless, such increase of human power and control negates the belief in "God" as deus ex machina, stopgap, or working hypothesis. This in turn leads to religionlessness, insofar as precisely that idea of "God" supported the degenerate "religious" mode of Christianity.

Defensive resistance to this development is found in Protestant pietism and Lutheran orthodoxy, and while the revelation theology of the Confessing Church provides a garrison against National Socialism, it does not nurture personal faith in Christ, nor provide theological grounding for science, art, and ethics.[61]

After this critical opening, chapter 2 takes up Bonhoeffer's positive proposal: worldly nonreligious Christianity, or nonreligious interpretation of biblical and theological concepts. It begins by introducing the theme of "worldliness," then devotes most of the chapter outline to two topics: God, and "what . . . we really believe." The paragraph on God collects ideas familiar from the letters, emphasizing particularly the theme of freedom for others first introduced in Sanctorum Communio: *"genuine transcendence" is found in a "relationship to God [which] is a new life in 'being there for others,' through participation in the being of Jesus." Authentic faith, accordingly, is not a matter of mere beliefs, but something that our lives depend on. As Bonhoeffer put it in* Discipleship, *only those who are obedient believe, and only those who believe are obedient.[62] Consequently, disputes between Protestants and Catholics, and between Lutherans and Reformed, are no longer real; they do not form lives shaped by the being of Jesus—here one should recall the prominence Bonhoeffer accorded the Sermon on the Mount. This emphasis on the integrity of faith and life, and the relativizing of creeds and denominations, should not ignore, however, the importance of beliefs drawn from the Bible that form Christian life: creation, fall, reconciliation, repentance, new life, eschatology.[63] How such understandings of God and Christian faith are to be embodied in worship is a subject simply announced to "follow later"!*

---

61. [*This summarizes an insight from* Ethics *about "reason, culture, humanity, tolerance, autonomy," which were under attack from barbarism, the irrational, and the arbitrary, finding anew their origin in Christ and the church; see* DBWE 6:339–341.]

62. [*See* DBWE 4:63 (Reader 539–540). *"Obedience" in* Discipleship *especially means following the commandments of Jesus in the Sermon on the Mount.*]

63. [DBWE 8:502 (Reader 814). *"Eschatology," the Greek word for what Bonhoeffer calls in a common theological phrase "last things," is the teaching about the ultimate redemption and consummation of all things in the Kingdom of God.*]

The third and final chapter concludes with practical implications for church life. Like Jesus, the being of the church is to be a "being for others" as the congregation of faith participates "in the worldly tasks of life in the community . . . [by] helping and serving."

Having accompanied Bonhoeffer through several years of work on his Ethics *manuscripts, Bethge naturally asks Bonhoeffer about the relation of this new book to his* Ethics. *The reply, widely ignored for the interpretation of* Ethics, *is that they are closely related: Bonhoeffer calls the book he has begun in prison the "shorter piece," and the* Ethics *the "larger work." Then he writes: "I guess the best way to describe them is that the shorter piece is in a certain sense a prologue to the larger work and, in part, anticipates it."*[64]

From the August 23 letter, we know that Bonhoeffer made real progress on the first chapter. Unfortunately, the text did not survive.

499   I would like to write an essay—not more than one hundred pages in length—with three chapters: 1. Taking Stock of Christianity; 2. What is Christian faith, really? 3. Conclusions.

500   In the first chapter I would describe

(a) The coming of age of the human being (as indicated earlier). Safeguarding human life against "accidents," "blows of fate"; if it is impossible to eliminate them, then at least the reduction of danger. The "insurance industry" as a Western phenomenon (to be sure, it depends on accidents, but its purpose is to make them less painful); its goal is to be independent of nature. Nature used to be conquered by the soul;[65] with us it is conquered through technological organization of all kinds. What is unmediated for us, what is given, is no longer nature but organization. But with this protection from the menace of nature, a new threat to life is created in turn, namely, through organization itself. Now the power of the soul is lacking! The question is: What will protect us from the menace of organization? The human being is thrown back on his own resources. He has learned to cope with everything except himself. He can insure himself against everything but other human beings. In the end it all comes down to the human being.

(b) The religionlessness of the human being come of age. "God" as working hypothesis, as stopgap for our embarrassments, has become superfluous (as indicated previously).

---

64. [DBWE *8:518.*]

65. ["'Soul' (*Seele*) implies both intellectual powers and emotional resources," *DBWE* 8:500, n. 4.]

(c) The Protestant church: pietism as a final attempt to preserve Protestant Christianity as religion; Lutheran orthodoxy, the attempt to save the church as an institution of salvation;[66] Confessing Church: revelation theology; a δόσ μοι ποῦ στῶ[67] standing against the world; with regard to it, an "objective" interest in Christianity. The arts, the sciences in search of their origin. Generally in the Confessing Church: Standing up for the "cause" of the church, and so on, but little personal faith in Christ. "Jesus" disappears from view. Sociologically: no impact on the broader masses; a matter for the lower and upper-middle classes. Heavily burdened by difficult, traditional ideas. Decisive: Church defending itself. No risk taking for others.

(d) Morals of the people. Sexual morality as example.

Chapter 2:   501

(a) Worldliness and God.

(b) Who is God? Not primarily a general belief in God's omnipotence, and so on. That is not a genuine experience of God but just a prolongation of a piece of the world. Encounter with Jesus Christ. Experience that here there is a reversal of all human existence, in the very fact that Jesus only "is there for others." Jesus's "being-for-others" is the experience of transcendence! Only through this liberation from self, through this "being-for-others" unto death, do omnipotence, omniscience, and omnipresence come into being. Faith is participating in this being of Jesus. (Becoming human, cross, resurrection.) Our relationship to God is no "religious" relationship to some highest, most powerful, and best being imaginable—that is no genuine transcendence. Instead, our relationship to God is a new life in "being there for others," through participation in the being of Jesus. The transcendent is not the infinite, unattainable tasks, but the neighbor within reach in any given situation. God in human form! Not as in oriental religions in animal forms as the monstrous, the chaotic, the remote, the terrifying, but also not in the conceptual forms of the absolute, the metaphysical, the infinite, and so on, either, nor again the Greek god—human form of the "God-human form of the human being in itself." But rather "the human being for others"! therefore the Crucified One. The human being living out of the transcendent.

---

66. ["Cf. Bonhoeffer's lecture at the preacher's seminary in Finkenwalde, winter 1935–1936: 'Visible Church in the New Testament,' *DBWE* 14:443: 'Wherever God's word and deed are torn asunder in this way, as happens in orthodoxy, the church of necessity turns into a religious institution in which there is no longer any defense against the pietistic, total dissolution of the concept of the church itself,'" *DBWE* 8:500, n. 7.]

67. [*The beginning of a Greek sentence that can be translated as, "Give me a place to stand, and I will move the earth" (Archimedes).*]

502   (c) Hence the interpretation of biblical concepts on this principle.
(Creation, fall, reconciliation, repentance, faith, *vita nova* [*new life*],[68] last
things.)

(d) Cultus. (Details to follow later, in particular on *cultus* and "religion"!)

(e) What do we really believe? I mean, believe in such a way that our lives
depend on it? The problem of the Apostles' Creed? What *must* I believe?
wrong question. Outdated controversies,[69] especially the interconfessional
ones; the differences between Lutheran and Reformed (and to some extent
Roman Catholic) are no longer real. Of course, they can be revived with
passion at any time, but they are no longer convincing. There is no proof for
this. One must simply be bold enough to start from this. The only thing we
can prove is that the Christian-biblical faith does not live or depend on such
differences. Barth and the Confessing Church have encouraged people to
entrench themselves again and again behind the notion of the "faith of the
Church" rather than asking and stating honestly what they really believe.
This is why even in the Confessing Church the breezes are blowing less than
freely. Saying that it depends not on me but on the church can be a cheap
503   clerical excuse and is always perceived that way outside the church. It is the
same with the dialectical claim that I do not have my faith at my disposal
and therefore cannot simply state what I believe. All these thoughts, justifiable though they might be in their place, do not absolve us from being
honest with ourselves. We cannot, like the Roman Catholics, simply identify
ourselves with the church. (Incidentally, this is probably the source of the
common opinion that Catholics are insincere.) Well, then, what do we really
believe? Answer: see (b), (c), and (d).

Chapter 3:

Conclusions: The church is church only when it is there for others. As
a first step it must give away all its property to those in need. The clergy
must live solely on the freewill offerings of the congregations and perhaps
be engaged in some secular vocation. The church must participate in the
worldly tasks of life in the community—not dominating but helping and
serving. It must tell people in every calling what a life with Christ is, what
it means "to be there for others." In particular, *our* church will have to confront the vices of hubris, the worship of power, envy, and illusionism as
the roots of all evil. It will have to speak of moderation, authenticity, trust,

---

68. ["'New Life in Paul' was the theme of Bonhoeffer's New Testament lecture at the
Finkenwalde preacher's seminary in the summer of 1936; see *DBWE* 14:605–625," *DBWE*
8:502, n. 19.]

69. ["On this and the following, see *DBWE* 16:84," *DBWE* 8:502, n. 22.]

faithfulness, steadfastness, patience, discipline, humility, modesty, contentment. It will have to see that it does not underestimate the significance of
the human "example" (which has its origin in the humanity of Jesus and is
so important in Paul's writings!); the church's word gains weight and power
not through concepts but by example. (I will write in more detail later about
"example" in the NT—we have almost entirely lost track of this thought.)
Further: revision of the question of "confession" (Apostolikum) [*Apostles'
Creed*]; revision of apologetics; revision of the preparation for and practice
of ministry.

504

All this is put very roughly and only outlined. But I am eager to attempt
for once to express certain things simply and clearly that we otherwise like
to avoid dealing with. Whether I shall succeed is another matter, especially
without the benefit of our conversations. I hope that in doing so I can be of
some service for the future of the church.

LETTER: AUGUST 21, 1944

*The letter of August 21, 1944 was one of the last Bonhoeffer wrote from Tegel prison.
The letter, and the poem "Who Am I?" that follows it, are both theological texts and
deeply personal statements of faith.*

*From Tegel Bonhoeffer was taken in October to the Gestapo prison on Prinz-
Albrecht-Strasse in Berlin, and from there in February to Buchenwald, in April to
Regensburg, and from there via Schönberg to Flossenbürg, where he was executed on
April 9, 1945. Eberhard Bethge published the first selection of the theological letters
from prison in 1951, after publishing the* Ethics *in 1948 on the third anniversary of
Bonhoeffer's death.*

A week from today is your birthday. I looked at the *Daily Texts* again and
meditated for a while on them. I think everything depends on the words "in
Him."[70] Everything we may with some good reason expect or beg of God is
to be found in Jesus Christ. What we imagine a God could and should do—
the God of Jesus Christ has nothing to do with all that. We must immerse
ourselves again and again, for a long time and quite calmly, in Jesus's life,
his sayings, actions, suffering, and dying in order to recognize what God
promises and fulfills. What is certain is that we may always live aware that

514

515

---

70. ["... The interpretative text from the *Daily Texts* for August 28, 1944, was 2 Cor.
1:20: 'For in him every one of God's promises is a "Yes ...,"'" *DBWE* 8:514, n. 3.]

God is near and present with us and that this life is an utterly new life for us; that there is nothing that is impossible for us anymore because there is nothing that is impossible for God; that no earthly power can touch us without God's will, and that danger and urgent need can only drive us closer to God. What is certain is that we have no claim on anything but may ask for everything; what is certain is that in suffering lies hidden the source of our joy, in dying the source of our life; what is certain is that in all this we stand within a community that carries us. To all this, God has said Yes and Amen in Jesus. This Yes and Amen is the solid ground upon which we stand. Again and again in these turbulent times, we lose sight of why life is really worth living. We think that our own life has meaning because this or that other person exists. In truth, however, it is like this: If the earth was deemed worthy to bear the human being Jesus Christ, if a human being like Jesus lived, then and only then does our life as human beings have meaning. Had Jesus not lived, then our life would be meaningless, despite all the other people we know, respect, and love. Perhaps we sometimes lose sight of the meaning and purpose of our calling. But can't one express that in the simplest form? The unbiblical concept of "meaning," after all, is only one translation of what the Bible calls "promise."

I sense how inadequate these words are to accomplish what they would like, namely, to reassure you and make you happy and secure in your loneliness. Surely this lonely birthday does not have to be a lost day if it becomes an occasion once again for you to lay the clear foundation you want for the rest of your life. It's often been a great help to me in the evening to think of all the people whose prayers I can count on, from the children to the grown-ups. I think I owe a debt of gratitude for God's protection in my life to the prayers of others known and unknown.

Something else: often the NT says, "be strong" (1 Cor. 16:13; Eph. 6:10; 2 Tim. 2:1; 1 John 2:14). Isn't human weakness (stupidity, immaturity, forget-
516 fulness, cowardice, vanity, corruptibility, vulnerability to temptations, etc.) a greater danger than wickedness? Christ makes human beings not only "good" but also strong. Sins of weakness are truly human sins; willful sins are diabolical (and thus also "strong"!). I must think about this some more. . . .

459 # WHO AM I?

Who am I? They often tell me
I step out from my cell
calm and cheerful and poised,
like a squire from his manor.

Who am I? They often tell me
I speak with my guards
freely, friendly and clear,
as though I were the one in charge.

Who am I? They also tell me
I bear days of calamity
serenely, smiling and proud,
like one accustomed to victory.

Am I really what others say of me?
Or am I only what I know of myself?
Restless, yearning, sick, like a caged bird,
struggling for life breath, as if I were being strangled,
starving for colors, for flowers, for birdsong,
thirsting for kind words, human closeness,
shaking with rage at power lust and pettiest insult,   460
tossed about, waiting for great things to happen,[71]
helplessly fearing for friends so far away,
too tired and empty to pray, to think, to work,
weary and ready to take my leave of it all?

Who am I? This one or the other?
Am I this one today and tomorrow another?
Am I both at once? Before others a hypocrite
and in my own eyes a pitiful, whimpering weakling?
Or is what remains in me like a defeated army,
Fleeing in disarray from victory already won?

Who am I? They mock me, these lonely questions of mine.
Whoever I am, thou knowest me; O God, I am thine!

---

71. ["Cf. the allusion in the accompanying letter *DBWE* 8:458, n. 25, to the anticipated coup attempt of July 20, 1944," *DBWE* 8:460, n. 4.]

APPENDIX

THE GERMAN CHURCH STRUGGLE AND RESISTANCE

Secondary Sources

Barnett, Victoria J. *For the Soul of the People: Protestant Protest against Hitler.* New York: Oxford University Press, 1992.

Bergen, Doris L. *Twisted Cross: The German Christian Movement in the Third Reich.* Chapel Hill: University of North Carolina Press, 1996.

Conway, John. *The Nazi Persecution of the Churches: 1944–1945.* London: Weidenfeld and Nicolson, 1968.

Ericksen, Robert P. *Theologians under Hitler: Gerhard Kittel, Paul Althaus, and Emanuel Hirsch.* New Haven: Yale University Press, 1985.

Gerlach, Wolfgang. *And the Witnesses Were Silent: The Confessing Church and the Jews.* Translated and edited by Victoria J. Barnett. University of Nebraska Press, 2000.

Helmreich, Ernst Christian. *The German Churches under Hitler: Background, Struggle, and Epilogue.* Detroit: Wayne State University Press, 1979.

Heschel, Susannah. *The Aryan Jesus: Christian Theologians and the Bible in Nazi Germany.* Princeton: Princeton University Press, 2008.

Hockenos, Matthew D. *A Church Divided: German Protestants Confront the Nazi Past.* Bloomington: Indiana University Press, 2004.

Hoffmann, Peter. *The History of the German Resistance, 1933–1945.* Translated by Richard Barry. Cambridge, MA: MIT Press, 1977.

Holtschneider, K. Hannah. *German Protestants Remember the Holocaust: Theology and the Construction of Collective Memory.* New Brunswick: Distributed by Transaction Publishers, 2001.

Jantzen, Kyle. *Faith and Fatherland: Parish Politics in Hitler's Germany.* Minneapolis: Fortress Press, 2008.

Scholder, Klaus. *The Churches and the Third Reich.* 2 vols. Translated by John Bowden. Philadelphia: Fortress Press, 1988.

Von Klemperer, Klemens. *German Resistance against Hitler: The Search for Allies Abroad, 1938–1945.* New York: Clarendon Press; Oxford: Oxford University Press, 1992.

From *DBWE*

Report on a Meeting of the Central Office for Ecumenical Youth Work, *DBWE* 11:170–176

Lecture in Ciernohorské Kúpele: On the Theological Foundation of the Work of the World Alliance, *DBWE* 11:356–369

Address at the International Youth Conference in Gland, *DBWE* 11:375–381

Draft for a Petition to the National Synod of the German Evangelical Church, Berlin, September 24, 1933, *DBWE* 12:175–176

Statement of the Berlin Pastors, "To the National Synod of the German Evangelical Church," Berlin, September 27, 1933, *DBWE* 12:181–183

Discussion Paper for the Ecumenical Conference in Dassel: The Concept of Confession from the Standpoint of the Concept of Truth, *DBWE* 12:282–285

The Church and the Jewish Question, *DBWE* 12:361–371 (*Reader* 370–378)

The Jewish-Christian Question as Status Confessionis, *DBWE* 12:371–374 (*Reader* 379–381)

The Bethel Confession (First draft and August version), *DBWE* 12:374–424

The Aryan Paragraph in the Church, *DBWE* 12:425–432 (*Reader* 382–388)

What Should a Student of Theology Do Today?, *DBWE* 12:432–435 (*Reader* 389–392)

Documents related to the Pastors' Conference in Bradford, *DBWE* 13:44–52

Telegram from the German Pastors in London to August Marahens and Hans Meiser, December 19, 1933, *DBWE* 13:57

Telegram from the German Protestant Pastors in London to the Reich Church Government, London, January 6, 1934, *DBWE* 13:77

Telegram from Friedrich Wehrhan to the Reich Church Government, London, January 7, 1934, *DBWE* 13:77

Documents related to a Conference with representatives of the Reich Church Government, *DBWE* 13:104–115

From the Report on the Fifth International Youth Conference, Fanø, *DBWE* 13:201–210

The secession of the German Evangelical Congregations in Great Britain from the Reich Church, *DBWE* 13:230–236

Letter from the German Evangelical Pastors' Association in Great Britain to all pastors abroad, London, November 1934, *DBWE* 13:255–257

Fanø Theses and Address: The Church and the Peoples of the World, *DBWE* 13:304–311 (*Reader* 393–397)

Report on the theological conference in Bruay-en-Artois, September 15, 1934, *DBWE* 13:310–313

Lecture on the theology of Karl Barth and the situation in Germany (transcript), *DBWE* 13:314–315

Assessment by Hans Schönfeld for the Ecumenical Advisory Committee of the Provisional Church Administration, Berlin, June 27, 1935, *DBWE* 14:62–63.

Manifesto "To Our Brothers in the Ministry," Berlin-Dahlem, July 30, 1935, *DBWE* 14:84–86.

From the Reich and Prussian Minister for Church Affairs to the Reich and Prussian Minister for Science, Training, and Public Education, Berlin, November 12, 1935, *DBWE* 14:118.

To the Brothers of the First Session, Finkenwalde, November 15, 1935, *DBWE* 14:119.

From the Preachers' Seminary to the Provisional Administration of the German Evangelical Church, Finkenwalde, February 28, 1936, *DBWE* 14:142–145.

From the Reich and Prussian Minister for Church Affairs to the Reich Church Committee, Berlin, June 22, 1936, *DBWE* 14:188.

Report of the Security Service of the Reichsführer SS–Regional Division Office North–to the Main Headquarters of the Security Service, June 23, 1936, *DBWE* 14:188–189.

To the Brothers of the First Two Sessions, Finkenwalde, June 24, 1936, *DBWE* 14:189–190.

Manifesto of the Seminary Brotherhood of the Confessing Church, Bloestau, Finkenwalde, Naumburg, June 1936, *DBWE* 14:190–191.

Circular letter to the Brothers of the First and Second Sessions, Finkenwalde, July 22, 1936, *DBWE* 14:213–220.

Excerpt "War and Peace" from a Report on the Theme of the World Church Conference in Oxford, 1937, Berlin, April 15, 1937, *DBWE* 14:297–299.

Lecture Course on Lutheran Confessional Writings, *DBWE* 14:335–337.

Essay on the Confessing Church and the Ecumenical Movement, August, 1935, *DBWE* 14:378–412 (*Reader* 398–414).

Bonhoeffer's sketch for his statement "From Barmen to Oeynhausen," *DBWE* 14:600–604.

Essay and Discussion on Church Communion, *DBWE* 14:656–697.

Bonhoeffer's Essay on Church Communion, June 1936, *DBWE* 14:656–678 (*Reader* 432–451).

Helmut Gollwitzer's response to Bonhoeffer's essay, October 1936, *DBWE* 14:678–689.

Bonhoeffer's questions concerning the essay discussion, October 1936, *DBWE* 14:689–697.

Letter from the Office of the Gestapo, Berlin, to Reich Church Minister Hanns Kerrl, Berlin, regarding closure of Preacher's Seminary in Finkenwalde, November 30, 1937, *DBWE* 15:19–20

Letter to the Finkenwalde brothers, Groß-Schlönwitz, December 20, 1937, *DBWE* 15:20–26

Lecture on the Path of the Young Illegal Theologians of the Confessing Church. Stettin, October 26, 1938, *DBWE* 15:416–437

BIBLIOGRAPHY

Althaus, Paul. *Der deutsche Stunde der Kirche* (The German hour of the church). 2nd ed. Göttingen: Vandenhoeck & Ruprecht, 1934.

———. *Der Geist der lutherischen Ethik im Augsburgischen Bekenntnis.* (The spirit of Lutheran ethics in the Augsburg Confession.) Munich: Chr. Kaiser Verlag, 1930.

Ames, E. S. "Liberalism Confirmed." *Christian Century* (March 22, 1939): 380–382.

Anselm. *Cur Deus Homo.* In *Basic Writings.* Translated and edited by Thomas Williams, 237–326. Indianapolis: Hackett, 2007.

Augustine. *Confessions* and *Enchiridion.* Translated and edited by Albert C. Outler. Philadelphia: Westminister, 1955.

———. *Saint Augustine: Anti-Pelagian Works.* Edited by Philip Schaff. New York: Christian Literature Company, 1887.

Barnett, Victoria J. *For the Soul of the People: Protestant Protest against Hitler.* New York: Oxford University Press, 1992.

Barth, Karl. *Church Dogmatics.* 4 vols. Edited by G. W. Bromily and T. F. Torrance. Edinburgh: T. & T. Clark, 1956–1975.

Vol. 1/1: *The Doctrine of the Word of God: Prolegomena to Church Dogmatics.* 2nd ed. Translated by G. W. Bromily. Edinburgh: T. & T. Clark, 1975.

Vol. 1/2: *The Doctrine of the Word of God: Prolegomena to Church Dogmatics.* Translated by G. T. Thomson and Harold Knight. Edinburgh: T. & T. Clark, 1956.

Vol. 2/2: *The Doctrine of God.* Translated by G. W. Bromily, J. C. Campbell, Iain Wilson, J. Strathearn McNab, Harold Knight, and R. A. Stewart. Edinburgh: T. & T. Clark, 1957.

———. *Die christliche Dogmatik im Entwurf* (Christian dogmatics in outline).

Vol. 1: *Die Lehre vom Worte Gottes: Prolegomena zur christlichen Dogmatik* (The doctrine of the Word of God: Prolegomena to Christian dogmatics). Munich, 1927. Also published in *Gesamtausgabe* (Collected works), vol. 2 (1927). Edited by G. Sauter. Zürich, 1982.

———. *The Epistle to the Romans.* Translated by Edwyn C. Hoskyns. London: Oxford University Press, 1960.

———. "Gospel and Law." In *Community, State and Church: Three Essays.* Edited by Will Herberg, 71–100. New York: Doubleday Anchor Books, 1960.

———. *The Word of God and the Word of Man.* Translated by Douglas Horton. New York: Harper & Brothers, 1957.

Barth, Karl, and Eduard Thurneysen. *Come, Holy Spirit: Sermons.* Translated by George W. Richards. Eugene, OR: Wipf & Stock, 2010.

Bengel, J. A. *Novum Testamentum Graece.* Tübingen, 1734.

Bergen, Doris L. *Twisted Cross: The German Christian Movement in the Third Reich.* Chapel Hill: University of North Carolina Press, 1996.

Bethge, Eberhard. *Dietrich Bonhoeffer: A Biography.* Edited and revised by Victoria J. Barnett. Minneapolis: Fortress Press, 2000.

———. "Dietrich Bonhoeffer and the Jews." In *Ethical Responsibility: Bonhoeffer's Legacy to the Churches.* Edited by John D. Godsey and Geffrey B. Kelly, 43–96. New York: Edwin Mellen, 1981.

———. "Nichts scheint mehr in Ordnung" (Nothing seems to be in order anymore). In *Ethik im Ernstfall: Dietrich Bonhoeffers Stellung zu den Juden und ihre Aktualität* (Ethics in the serious case: Dietrich Bonhoeffer's position on the Jews and its relevance). Edited by Wolfgang Huber and Ilse Tödt, 30–40. Munich: Chr. Kaiser Verlag, 1982.

Biedermann, Alois Emanuel. *Christliche Dogmatik* (Christian dogmatics). 2nd ed., revised. Berlin: G. Reimer, 1885.

Bonhoeffer, Dietrich. *The Collected Sermons of Dietrich Bonhoeffer.* Edited by Isabel Best. Minneapolis: Fortress Press, 2012.

———. *Dietrich Bonhoeffer Werke.* 17 vols. Edited by Eberhard Bethge et al. Munich: Chr. Kaiser/Gütersloher Verlagshaus, 1986–99.

Vol. 1: *Sanctorum Communio: Eine dogmatische Untersuchung zur Soziologie der Kirche.* Edited by Joachim von Soosten. Munich: Chr. Kaiser Verlag, 1986.

Vol. 2: *Akt und Sein: Transzendentalphilosophie und Ontologie in der systematischen Theologie.* Edited by Hans-Richard Reuter. Munich: Chr. Kaiser Verlag, 1988.

Vol. 3: *Schöpfung und Fall: Theologische Auslegung von Genesis 1–3.* Edited by Martin Rüter and Ilse Tödt. Munich: Chr. Kaiser Verlag, 1989.

Vol. 4: *Nachfolge.* Edited by Martin Kuske and Ilse Tödt. Munich: Chr. Kaiser Verlag, 1989; 2nd ed., Gütersloh: Chr. Kaiser/Gütersloher Verlagshaus, 1994.

Vol. 5: *Gemeinsames Leben: Das Gebetbuch der Bibel.* Edited by Gerhard Ludwig Müller and Albrecht Schönherr. Munich: Chr. Kaiser Verlag, 1987.

Vol. 6: *Ethik.* Edited by Ilse Tödt, Heinz Eduard Tödt, Ernst Feil, and Clifford Green. Munich: Chr. Kaiser Verlag, 1992; 2nd ed., Gütersloh: Chr. Kaiser/Gütersloher Verlagshaus, 1998.

Vol. 7: *Fragmente aus Tegel.* Edited by Renate Bethge and Ilse Tödt. Gütersloh: Chr. Kaiser/Gütersloher Verlagshaus, 1994.

Vol. 8: *Widerstand und Ergebung.* Edited by Christian Gremmels, Eberhard Bethge, and Renate Bethge, with Ilse Tödt. Gütersloh: Chr. Kaiser/Gütersloher Verlagshaus, 1998.

Vol. 9: *Jugend und Studium: 1918–1927.* Edited by Hans Pfeifer, with Clifford Green and Carl-Jürgen Kaltenborn. Munich: Chr. Kaiser Verlag, 1986.

Vol. 10: *Barcelona, Berlin, Amerika: 1928–1931.* Edited by Reinhard Staats and Hans Christoph von Hase, with Holger Roggelin and Matthias Wünsche. Munich: Chr. Kaiser Verlag, 1991.

Vol. 11: *Ökumene, Universität, Pfarramt: 1931–1932* (Ecumenical, academic, and pastoral work: 1931–1932). Edited by Eberhard Amelung and Christoph Strohm. Gütersloh: Chr. Kaiser/Gütersloher Verlagshaus, 1994.

Vol. 12: *Berlin: 1932–1933.* Edited by Carsten Nicolaisen and Ernst-Albert Scharffenorth. Gütersloh: Chr. Kaiser/Gütersloher Verlagshaus, 1997.

Vol. 13: *London: 1933–1935.* Edited by Hans Goedeking, Martin Heimbucher, and Hans-Walter Schleicher. Gütersloh: Chr. Kaiser/Gütersloher Verlagshaus, 1994.

Vol. 14: *Illegale Theologenausbildung: Finkenwalde 1935–1937.* Edited by Otto Dudzus and Jürgen Henkys, with Sabine Bobert-Stützel, Dirk Schulz, and Ilse Tödt. Gütersloh: Chr. Kaiser/Gütersloher Verlagshaus, 1996.

Vol. 15: *Illegale Theologenausbildung: Sammelvikariate: 1937–1940.* Edited by Dirk Schulz. Gütersloh: Chr. Kaiser/Gütersloher Verlagshaus, 1998.

Vol. 16: *Konspiration und Haft: 1940–1945.* Edited by Jørgen Glenthøj, Ulrich Kabitz, and Wolf Krötke. Gütersloh: Chr. Kaiser/Gütersloher Verlagshaus, 1996.

Vol. 17: *Register und Ergänzungen.* Edited by Herbert Anzinger and Hans Pfeifer, assisted by Waltraud Anzinger and Ilse Tödt. Gütersloh: Chr. Kaiser/Gütersloher Verlagshaus, 1999.

—————. *Dietrich Bonhoeffer Works.* Edited by Victoria J. Barnett, Wayne Whitson Floyd Jr., and Barbara Wojhoski. 17 vols. Minneapolis: Fortress Press, 1996–2013.

Vol. 1: *Sanctorum Communio: A Theological Study of the Sociology of the Church.* Edited by Clifford J. Green. Translated by Reinhard Krauss and Nancy Lukens. Minneapolis: Fortress Press, 1998.

Vol. 2: *Act and Being: Transcendental Philosophy and Ontology in Systematic Theology.* Edited by Wayne Whitson Floyd Jr. Translated by H. Martin Rumscheidt. Minneapolis: Fortress Press, 1996.

Vol. 3: *Creation and Fall: A Theological Exposition of Genesis 1–3*. Edited by John W. de Gruchy. Translated by Douglas Stephen Bax. Minneapolis: Fortress Press, 1996.

Vol. 4: *Discipleship*. Edited by Geffrey B. Kelly and John D. Godsey. Translated by Barbara Green and Reinhard Krauss. Minneapolis: Fortress Press, 2001.

Vol. 5: *Life Together* and *Prayerbook of the Bible*. Edited by Geffrey B. Kelly. Translated by Daniel W. Bloesch and James H. Burtness. Minneapolis: Fortress Press, 1996.

Vol. 6: *Ethics*. Edited by Clifford J. Green. Translated by Reinhard Krauss and Charles West, with Douglas W. Stott. Minneapolis: Fortress Press, 2004.

Vol. 7: *Fiction from Tegel Prison*. Edited by Clifford J. Green. Translated by Nancy Lukens. Minneapolis: Fortress Press, 2000.

Vol. 8: *Letters and Papers from Prison*. Edited by John W. de Gruchy. Translated by Isabel Best, Lisa E. Dahill, Reinhard Krauss, Nancy Lukens, with Barbara Rumscheidt, Martin Rumscheidt, and Douglas W. Stott. Minneapolis: Fortress Press, 2010.

Vol. 9: *The Young Bonhoeffer: 1918–1927*. Edited by Paul Matheny, Clifford J. Green, and Marshall Johnson. Translated by Mary Nebelsick, with Douglas W. Stott. Minneapolis: Fortress Press, 2001.

Vol. 10: *Barcelona, Berlin, New York: 1928–1931*. Edited by Clifford J. Green. Translated by Douglas W. Stott. Minneapolis: Fortress Press, 2008.

Vol. 11: *Ecumenical, Academic, and Pastoral Work: 1931–1932*. Edited by Victoria J. Barnett, Mark S. Brocker, and Michael B. Lukens. Translated by Anne Schmidt-Lange, with Isabel Best, Nicolas Humphrey, and Marion Pauck. Minneapolis: Fortress Press, 2012.

Vol. 12: *Berlin: 1932–1933*. Edited by Larry L. Rasmussen. Translated by Isabel Best and David Higgins, with Douglas W. Stott. Minneapolis: Fortress Press, 2009.

Vol. 13: *London: 1933–1935*. Edited by Keith Clements. Translated by Isabel Best, with Douglas W. Stott. Minneapolis: Fortress Press, 2007.

Vol. 14: *Theological Education at Finkenwalde: 1935–1937*. Edited by H. Gaylon Barker and Mark Brocker. Translated by Douglas W. Stott. Minneapolis: Fortress Press, 2013.

Vol. 15: *Theological Education Underground: 1937–1940*. Edited by Victoria J. Barnett. Translated by Victoria J. Barnett, Claudia D. Bergmann, Peter Frick, and Scott A. Moore, with Douglas W. Stott. Minneapolis: Fortress Press, 2012.

Vol. 16: *Conspiracy and Imprisonment: 1940–1945.* Edited by Mark S. Brocker. Translated by Lisa E. Dahill, with Douglas W. Stott. Minneapolis: Fortress Press, 2006.

Vol. 17: *Index.* Edited by Victoria J. Barnett and Barbara Wojhoski. Minneapolis: Fortress Press, 2014.

Book of Concord: The Confessions of the Evangelical Lutheran Church. Edited by Robert Kolb and Timothy J. Wengert. Translated by Charles Arand, Eric Gritsch, Robert Kolb, William Russell, James Schaaf, Jane Strohl, and Timothy J. Wengert. Minneapolis: Fortress Press, 2000.

Bousset, Wilhelm. "Der zweite Brief an die Korinther" (The Second Letter to the Corinthians). In *Die paulinischen Briefe und die Pastoralbriefe* (The Pauline letters and the Pastoral letters). Vol. 2 of *Die Schriften des Neuen Testaments* (The New Testament scriptures), edited by J. Weiss, W. Bousset, and W. Heitmuller, 3rd ed., 167–223. Göttingen: Vandenhoeck & Ruprecht, 1917.

Brown, F., S. R. Driver, and C. A. Briggs. *The New Brown-Driver-Briggs-Gesenius Hebrew and English Lexicon.* Peabody, MA: Hendricksen, 1979.

Brown, William Adams. *Church and State in Contemporary America: A Study of the Problems They Present and the Principles Which Should Determine Their Relationship.* New York: Charles Scribner's Sons, 1936.

Bultmann, Rudolf. "New Testament and Mythology." In *Kerygma and Myth.* Revised ed. Translated by Reginald H. Fuller, 1–44. New York: Harper & Row, 1961.

Calvin, John. *Institutes of the Christian Religion.* 2 vols. Edited by John T. McNeill. Translated by Ford Lewis Battles. Philadelphia: Westminster, 1960.

Cervantes Saavedra, Miguel de. *The Adventures of Don Quixote.* Translated by J. M. Cohen. New York: Penguin, 1950.

Chomjakow, Aleksej Stephanowic. "Die Einheit der Kirche" (The unity of the church). In *Östliches Christentum* (Eastern Christianity). Edited by N. Bubnoff and H. Ehrenberg, 2:1–27. Munich: C. H. Beck, 1925.

Claudius, Matthias. *Asmus omnia sua Secum portans oder Sämtliche Werke des Wandsbecker Boten* (Asmus carrying all his belongings with him, or, the complete works of the Wandsbeck courier). Berlin: Pantheon, 1941. 7 vols. Reprint of the 1st ed. (1775–1812). Munich, 1976.

Conway, John. *The Nazi Persecution of the Churches: 1944–1945.* London: Weidenfeld and Nicolson, 1968.

Cremer, Hermann. *Biblico-theological Lexicon of New Testament Greek.* 3rd ed. Translated from the second German edition by William Urwick. Edinburgh: T. & T. Clark, 1883; New York: Charles Scribner's Sons, 1895.

Cullen, Countee. *The Black Christ and Other Poems*. New York: G. P. Putnam's Sons, 1929.

Deißmann, Adolf. *Die neutestamentliche Formel "in Christo Jesu" untersucht* (An examination of the New Testament phrase "in Christ Jesus"). Marburg: N. G. Elwert, 1892.

DeJonge, Michael P. "Between Fundamentalism and Secularism: Bonhoeffer's Negotiation of Oppositional Pairs in *Ethics* and Its Precedent in *Act and Being*." In *Dietrich Bonhoeffer's Theology Today: A Way between Fundamentalism and Secularism?* Edited by John W. de Gruchy, Stephen Plant, and Christiane Tietz, 75–89. Gütersloh: Gütersloher Verlagshaus, 2009.

——. "Bonhoeffer the Theologian from the Perspective of Intellectual History." In *Interpreting Bonhoeffer: Historical Perspectives, Emerging Issues*. Edited by Clifford J. Green and Guy C. Carter, 197–204. Minneapolis: Fortress Press, 2013.

——. *Bonhoeffer's Theological Formation: Berlin, Barth, and Protestant Theology*. Oxford: Oxford University Press, 2012.

——. "God's Being Is in Time: Bonhoeffer's Theological Appropriation of Heidegger." *Dietrich Bonhoeffer Yearbook* 5 (2011/2012):121–135.

——. "The Presence of Christ in Karl Barth, Franz Hildebrandt, and Dietrich Bonhoeffer." *Dietrich Bonhoeffer Yearbook* 4 (2010): 96–115.

——. "Respecting Rights and Fulfilling Duties: Bonhoeffer's 'Formed Life' in Bioethical Perspective." In *Bonhoeffer and the Biosciences: An Initial Exploration*. Edited by Ralf K. Wüstenberg, Stefan Heuser, and Esther Hornung, 109–122. Frankfurt: Peter Lang, 2010.

Delitzsch, Franz. *A System of Biblical Psychology*. Translated by Robert Ernest Wallis. Edinburgh: T. & T. Clark, 1890.

Dilthey, Wilhelm. *Weltanschauung und Analyse des Menschen seit Renaissance und Reformation* (Worldview and analysis of humanity since the Renaissance and Reformation). Vol. 2 of *Gesammelte Schriften* (Collected works). 7th ed. Stuttgart: Teubner; Göttingen: Vandenhoeck & Ruprecht, 1964.

Dostoyevsky, Fyodor Mikhaylovich. *The Brothers Karamazov*. Translated by David McDuff. London: Penguin, 2003.

——. *Crime and Punishment*. Edited by George Gibian. Translated by Jessie Coulson. New York: Norton, 1975.

Ehrenberg, Hans, ed. *Credo Ecclesiam: Festgabe Wilhelm Zoellner zum 70.* (I believe in the church: Celebratory volume for Wilhelm Zoellner on his seventieth birthday). Gütersloh: Bertelsmann, 1930.

Erdmann, Karl Dietrich. *Die Zeit der Weltkriege* (The time of the world wars). Vol. 4 of *Handbuch der Deutschen Geschichte* (Handbook of German history). Edited by Bruno Gebhardt and Herbert Grundmann. Stuttgart: Klett-Cotta, 1978.

Ericksen, Robert P. *Theologians under Hitler: Gerhard Kittel, Paul Althaus, and Emanuel Hirsch*. New Haven: Yale University Press, 1985.

Feil, Ernst. "Freundschaft—ein Thema der Theologie?" (Friendship—a theme in theology?). In *Theologie und Freundschaft: Wechselwirkungen; Eberhard Bethge und Dietrich Bonhoeffer* (The reciprocity of theology and friendship: Eberhard Bethge and Dietrich Bonhoeffer). Festschrift for Eberhard Bethge. Edited by Christian Gremmels and Wolfgang Huber, 110–134. Gütersloh: Gütersloher Verlagshaus, 1994.

——. *The Theology of Dietrich Bonhoeffer*. Translated by Martin Rumscheidt. Minneapolis: Fortress Press, 1985.

Gassmann, Günther, Duane H. Larson, and Mark W. Oldenburg, eds. *Historical Dictionary of Lutheranism*. Lanham, MD, and London: Scarecrow, 2001.

Gerlach, Wolfgang. *And the Witnesses Were Silent: The Confessing Church and the Jews*. Translated and edited by Victoria J. Barnett. Lincoln: University of Nebraska Press, 2000.

Gerrens, Uwe. *Medizinisches Ethos und theologische Ethik: Karl und Dietrich Bonhoeffer in der Auseinandersetzung um Zwangssterilisation und "Euthanasie" im Nationalsozialismus* (Medical ethos and theological ethics: Karl and Dietrich Bonhoeffer in the controversy regarding forced sterilization and "euthanasia" under National Socialism). Munich: Oldenbourg, 1996.

Geß, Wolfgang Friedrich. *Das Dogma von Christi Person und Werk, entwickelt aus Christi Selbstzeugnis und den Zeugnissen der Apostel* (The dogma of the person and work of Christ, developed from Christ's own testimony and the testimonies of the apostles). Basel: C. Detloff, 1887.

Green, Clifford J. *Bonhoeffer: A Theology of Sociality*. Revised ed. Grand Rapids, MI: Eerdmans, 1999.

——. "Bonhoeffer's Quest for Authentic Christianity: Beyond Fundamentalism, Nationalism, Religion and Secularism." In *Dietrich Bonhoeffer's Theology Today: A Way between Fundamentalism and Secularism*. Edited by John W. de Gruchy, Stephen Plant, and Christiane Tietz, 335–353. Gütersloh: Gütersloher Verlagshaus, 2009.

——. "Pacifism and Tyrannicide: Bonhoeffer's Christian Peace Ethic." *Studies in Christian Ethics* 18.3 (December 2005): 31–47.

Harnack, Adolf von. *History of Dogma*, Vol. 4. Translated by E. B. Speiers. New York: Russell & Russell, 1958.

——. *Marcion: The Gospel of the Alien God*. Translated by John E. Steely and Lyle D. Bierma. Durham, NC: Labyrinth, 1990.

——. *What Is Christianity? Sixteen Lectures Delivered in the University of Berlin during the Winter Term, 1899–1900*. Translated by Thomas Bailey Saunders.

New York: Harper, 1957. Reprint, with an introduction by Rudolf Bultmann. Gloucester, MA: Peter Smith, 1978.

Hauptmann, Gerhart. *The Fool in Christ, Emanuel Quint: A Novel.* Translated
by Thomas Seltzer. New York: H. Fertig, 1976.

Haynes, Stephen R. *The Bonhoeffer Legacy: Post-Holocaust Perspectives.* Minneapolis: Fortress Press, 2006.

Hegel, Georg Wilhelm Friedrich. *Lectures on the Philosophy of Religion.* 3 vols.
Edited by Peter C. Hodgson. Translated by R. F. Brown, P. C. Hodgson,
and J. M. Stewart, with the assistance of J. P. Fitzer and H. S. Harris.
Berkeley: University of California Press, 1984–1987.

Heidegger, Martin. *Being and Time: A Translation of Sein und Zeit.* Translated
by Joan Stambaugh. Albany: State University of New York Press, 1996.

Helmreich, Ernst Christian. *The German Churches under Hitler: Background,
Struggle, and Epilogue.* Detroit: Wayne State University Press, 1979.

Henkys, Jürgen. *Dietrich Bonhoeffers Gefängnisgedichte: Beiträge zu ihrer Interpretation* (Dietrich Bonhoeffer's prison poems: Toward an interpretation).
Munich: Chr. Kaiser Verlag, 1986.

Heschel, Susannah. *The Aryan Jesus: Christian Theologians and the Bible in Nazi
Germany.* Princeton: Princeton University Press, 2008.

Hildebrandt, Franz. *EST: Das lutherische Prinzip* (EST: The Lutheran principle). Göttingen: Vandenhoeck & Ruprecht, 1931.

Hildebrandt, Horst, ed. *Die deutschen Verfassungen des 19. und 20. Jahrhunderts*
(The German constitutions of the 19th and 20th centuries). 11th ed.
Paderborn: Schöningh, 1979.

Hockenos, Matthew D. *A Church Divided: German Protestants Confront the Nazi
Past.* Bloomington: Indiana University Press, 2004.

Hoffmann, Peter. *The History of the German Resistance, 1933–1945.* Translated
by Richard Barry. Cambridge, MA: MIT Press, 1977.

Holl, Karl. *What Did Luther Understand by Religion?* Edited by James Luther
Adams and Walter F. Bense. Translated by Fred W. Meuser and Walter R.
Wietzke. Philadelphia: Fortress Press, 1977.

Holl, Karl, and Wolfram Wette, eds. *Pazifismus in der Weimarer Republik:
Beiträge zur historischen Friedensforschung* (Pacifism in the Weimar Republic: Contributions to historical peace reasearch). Paderborn: Schöningh,
1981.

Holtschneider, K. Hannah. *German Protestants Remember the Holocaust: Theology and the Construction of Collective Memory.* New Brunswick: Distributed
by Transaction Publishers, 2001.

Homer, *The Odyssey.* Translated by Robert Fagles. New York: Penguin, 1996.

Horton, Walter Marshall. "Between Liberalism and the New Orthodoxy."
Christian Century 56 (May 17, 1939): 637–640.

Huber, Ernst Rudolf, and Wolfgang Huber. *Staat und Kirche im 19. und 20. Jahrhundert. Dokumente zur Geschichte des deutschen Staatskirchenrechts* (State and church in the nineteenth and twentieth centuries. Documents on the history of German state-church law). Vol. 4: *Staat und Kirche in der Zeit der Weimarer Republik* (State and church in the time of the Weimar Republic). Berlin: Duncker & Humblot, 1988.

Hunsinger, George. *How to Read Karl Barth: The Shape of His Theology.* New York: Oxford University Press, 1991.

Ibsen, Henrik. *Brand: A Version for the Stage by Geoffrey Hill.* Translated by Inga-Stina Ewbank. London: Penguin, 1996.

Jantzen, Kyle. *Faith and Fatherland: Parish Politics in Hitler's Germany.* Minneapolis: Fortress Press, 2008.

Jeremias, Joachim. "ἀμνός ἀρήν ἀρνίον." (Lamb.) In *Theological Dictionary of the New Testament.* Edited by Gerhard Kittel, 1:338–341. Grand Rapids, MI: Eerdmans, 1964.

———. *Infant Baptism in the First Four Centuries.* Translated by David Cairns. Philadelphia: Westminster, 1960.

Kähler, Martin. *The So-Called Historical Jesus and the Historic Biblical Christ.* Translated by Carl E. Braaten. Philadelphia: Fortress Press, 1964.

Kant, Immanuel. *The Critique of Pure Reason.* Translated and edited by Paul Guyer and Allen W. Wood. Cambridge: Cambridge University Press, 1998.

Kattenbusch, Ferdinand. "Der Quellort der Kirchenidee" (The source of the idea of church). In *Festgabe von Fachgenossen und Freunden. A. von Harnack zum 70. Geburtstag dargebracht* (Celebratory volume presented to Adolf von Harnack from colleagues and friends on his 70th birthday), edited by Karl Holl, 143–172. Tübingen: J. C. B. Mohr, 1921.

Knittermeyer, Hinrich. "Transzendentalphilosophie und Theologie: Eine kritische Erinnerung zum 22. April 1924" (Transcendental philosophy and theology: A critical memory of April 22, 1924). *Christliche Welt* 38 (1924): 220–226, 258–267, 354–361, 408–413.

Kuske, Martin. *The Old Testament as the Book of Christ: An Appraisal of Bonhoeffer's Interpretation.* Translated by S. T. Kimbrough Jr. Philadelphia: Westminster, 1976.

Livingston, E. A., ed. *Oxford Concise Dictionary of the Christian Church.* 2nd ed., revised. Oxford: Oxford University Press, 2006.

Löhe, Wilhelm. *Three Books concerning the Church.* Translated by Edward T. Horn. Reading, PA: Pilger, 1908.

Lohmeyer, Ernst. *Das Evangelium des Markus* (The gospel of Mark). 10th ed. Göttingen: Vandenhoeck & Ruprecht, 1937.

———. *Grundlagen paulinischer Theologie* (Foundations of Pauline theology). Tübingen: J. C. B. Mohr, 1929.

Lohse, Bernhard. *Martin Luther's Theology: Its Historical and Systematic Development.* Translated and edited by Roy A. Harrisville. Minneapolis: Fortress Press, 1999.

Luther, Martin. *Luther's Works,* 55 vols. Vols. 1–30, edited by Jaroslav Pelikan. St. Louis: Concordia, 1958–1967. Vols. 31–55, edited by Helmut Lehmann. Philadelphia: Muhlenberg Press and Fortress Press, 1957–1967.

> *The Bondage of the Will. LW* 33:3–295.
>
> "Disputation concerning Man." *LW* 34:137–144.
>
> "Fourteen Consolations for Those Who Labor and Are Heavy Laden." *LW* 42:121–166.
>
> *Lectures on Galatians. LW* 26:4–358 and 27:4–149.
>
> *Lectures on Romans. LW* 25.
>
> "The Sacrament of Penance." *LW* 35:9–22.
>
> "The Sacrament of the Holy and True Body of Christ." *LW* 35:45–67.
>
> *Sermons I. LW* 51.
>
> "A Sermon on Preparing to Die." *LW* 42:99–115.
>
> *Table Talk. LW* 54.
>
> "Temporal Authority: To What Extent It Should Be Obeyed." *LW* 45, 75–129.

———. *Werke: Kritische Gesamtausgabe.* 58 vols. Weimarer Ausgabe. Weimar: H. Böhlau, 1883–.

Meier, Kurt. *Der evangelische Kirchenkampf: Gesamtdarstellung in drei Bänden* (The Protestant Church Struggle: Complete account in 3 vols.). Vol. 1: *Der Kampf um die "Reichskirche"* (The struggle over the "Reich church"). Göttingen: Vandenhoeck & Ruprecht, 1976.

Melanchthon, Philip. *The Loci Communes of Philip Melanchthon.* Translated by Charles Leander Hill. Boston: Meador, 1944.

Meyer, Dietrich, and Eberhard Bethge, eds. *Nachlaß Dietrich Bonhoeffer: Ein Verzeichnis; Archiv-Sammlung-Bibliothek.* (Dietrich Bonhoeffer's literary estate: A bibliographical catalog; Archive, collection, library). Munich: Chr. Kaiser Verlag, 1987.

Meyer, Winfried. *Unternehmen Sieben: Eine Rettungsaktion für vom Holocaust Bedrohte aus dem Amt Ausland/Abwehr im Oberkommando der Wehrmacht* (Operation Seven: A rescue action by the Military Intelligence Office in the High Command for those threatened by the Holocaust). Frankfurt: Hain, 1993.

Müller, Christine-Ruth. *Dietrich Bonhoeffers Kampf gegen die nationalsozialistische Verfolgung und Vernichtung der Juden* (Dietrich Bonhoeffer's fight against the National Socialist persecution and annihilation of the Jews). Munich: Chr. Kaiser Verlag, 1990.

Natorp, Paul. *Vorlesungen über praktische Philosophie* (Lectures on practical philosophy). Erlangen: Verlag der Philosophischen Akademie, 1925.

Naumann, Friedrich. *Briefe über Religion—mit Nachwort "Nach 13 Jahren"* (Letters on religion—with an afterword "After 13 years"). Berlin: Georg Reimer, 1917.

Nelson, F. Burton. "The Life of Dietrich Bonhoeffer." In *The Cambridge Companion to Dietrich Bonhoeffer*. Edited by John W. de Gruchy, 22–49. Cambridge: Cambridge University Press, 1999.

Niebuhr, Reinhold. *Beyond Tragedy: Essays on the Christian Interpretation of History*. New York: Charles Scribner's Sons, 1937.

———. *An Interpretation of Christian Ethics*. New York: Harper & Brothers, 1935.

———. *Moral Man and Immoral Society: A Study of Ethics and Politics*. New York: Charles Scribner's Sons, 1932.

Nietzsche, Friedrich. *The Antichrist*. In *The Portable Nietzsche*. Translated by Walter Kaufmann, 565–656. New York: Penguin Books, 1982.

———. *Beyond Good and Evil: Prelude to a Philosophy of the Future*. Translated and edited by Marion Faber. Oxford: Oxford University Press, 1998.

———. *Thus Spoke Zarathustra*. Translated by Walter Kaufmann. New York: Viking Press, 1966.

———. *The Will to Power*. Edited by Walter Kaufmann. Translated by Walter Kaufmann and R. J. Hollingdale. Reprint, New York: Vintage Books, 1968.

Otto, Walter F. *The Homeric Gods: The Spiritual Significance of Greek Religion*. Translated by Moses Hadas. New York: Octagon Books, 1978.

Paton, William. *The Church and the New Order*. London: SCM Press, 1941.

Pelikan, Jaroslav. *From Luther to Kierkegaard: A Study in the History of Theology*. St. Louis: Concordia, 1950.

Robinson, James M., ed. *The Beginnings of Dialectical Theology*. Vol. 1. Translated by Keith R. Crim and Louis De Grazia. Richmond, VA: John Knox, 1968.

Röhm, Eberhard. *Sterben für den Frieden. Spurensicherung: Hermann Stöhr (1898–1940) und die ökumenische Friedensbewegung* (Dying for peace. Tracing the path: Hermann Stöhr (1898–1940) and the ecumenical peace movement). Stuttgart: Calwer, 1985.

Rosenberg, Alfred. *The Myth of the Twentieth Century: An Evaluation of the Spiritual-Intellectual Confrontations of Our Age*. Ostara Publications, 2012.

Rumscheidt, Martin. "The Formation of Bonhoeffer's Theology." In *The Cambridge Companion to Dietrich Bonhoeffer.* Edited by John W. de Gruchy, 50–70. Cambridge: Cambridge University Press, 1999.

Schaeder, Erich. *Das Geistproblem der Theologie: Eine systematische Untersuchung* (A systematic examination of the spiritual problem of theology). Erlangen: Deichert, 1924.

Scheler, Max. *Man's Place in Nature.* Translated by Hans Meyerhoff. Boston: Beacon, 1961.

Schiller, Friedrich. *The Minor Poems of Schiller.* Edited by John Herman Merivale. London: W. Pickering, 1844.

Schilling, Otto. *Lehrbuch der Moraltheologie* (Compendium of moral theology). 2 vols. Vol. 2: *Spezielle Moraltheologie* (Special moral theology). Munich: Hüber, 1928.

Schlatter, Adolf von. *Die neue deutsche Art in der Kirche* (The new German kind in the church). Bethel bei Bielefeld: Anstalt Bethel, 1933.

Schlingensiepen, Ferdinand. *Dietrich Bonhoeffer, 1906–1945. Martyr, Thinker, Man of Resistance.* Translated by Isabel Best. London: T. & T. Clark, 2010.

Schlink, Edmund. *Theology of the Lutheran Confessions.* Translated by Paul F. Koehneke and Herber J. A. Bouman. Philadelphia: Muhlenberg, 1961.

Schmid, Heinrich. *The Doctrinal Theology of the Evangelical Lutheran Church.* Translated by Charles A. Hay and Henry E. Jacobs. 3rd ed., revised. Minneapolis: Augsburg, 1899.

Schmidt, Hans. *Die Erzählung von Paradies und Sündenfall* (The story of paradise and the fall). Tübingen: J. C. B. Mohr, 1931.

Schmidt, Traugott. *Der Leib Christi: Eine Untersuchung zum urchristlichen Gemeindegedanken* (The body of Christ: An examination of the early Christian concept of community). Leipzig: Deichert, 1919.

Scholder, Klaus. *The Churches and the Third Reich.* 2 vols. Translated by John Bowden. Philadelphia: Fortress Press, 1988.

Scholz, Heinrich. *Religionsphilosophie* (Philosophy of religion). 2nd ed. Berlin: Reuther & Reichard, 1922.

Schreiber, Matthias. *Friedrich Justus Perels: Ein Weg vom Rechtskampf der Bekennenden Kirche in den politischen Widerstand* (Friedrich Justus Perels: A path from the rights struggle of the Confessing Church into the political resistance). Munich: Chr. Kaiser Verlag, 1989.

Schürer, Emil. *Geschichte des jüdischen Volkes im Zeitalter Jesu Christi.* Vol. 3: *Das Judentum in der Zerstreuung und die jüdische Literatur.* 2nd ed., newly revised. Leipzig: J. C. Hinrichs, 1898. Translated by T. A. Burkill et al. as *The History of the Jewish People in the Age of Jesus Christ (175 BC–AD 135),* revised and edited by Geza Vermes and Fergus Millar. Edinburgh: T. & T. Clark, 1973.

Schweitzer, Albert. *The Quest of the Historical Jesus.* Translated by W. Montgomery, J. R. Coates, Susan Cupitt, and John Bowden. Minneapolis: Fortress Press, 2001.

Sperry, Willard L. "How My Mind Has Changed in This Decade." *Christian Century* (January 18, 1939): 82–84.

Spitz, Lewis W. *The Renaissance and Reformation Movements.* Chicago: Rand McNally, 1971.

Thomasius, Gottfried. *Christi Person und Werk: Darstellung der evangelisch-lutherischen Dogmatik vom Mittelpunkte der Christologie aus* (Christ's person and work: Presentation of evangelical Lutheran dogmatics from the center of Christology). Vol. 1: *Die Voraussetzungen der Christologie und die Person des Mittlers* (The presuppositions of Christology and the person of the mediator). Erlangen: T. Bläsing, 1886.

Tillich, Paul. *The Religious Situation.* Translated by H. Richard Niebuhr. New York: Meridian Books, 1956.

Tödt, Ilse, ed. *Dietrich Bonhoeffers Hegel-Seminar 1933: Nach den Aufzeichnungen von Ferenc Lehel* (Dietrich Bonhoeffer's Hegel seminar 1933: According to the notes of Ferenc Lehel). Munich: Chr. Kaiser Verlag, 1988.

Torquemada, Juan de. *Summa de ecclesia contra impugnatores potestatis summi pontificis* (Summary treatise concerning the church, against those who attack the supreme authority of the papacy). Rome: Eucharius Silber, 1489.

Uhl, Willo, ed. *Der Franckforter* ("Eyn deutsch Theologia") (A German theology). Bonn: A. Marcus und E. Weber, 1912.

United States Holocaust Memorial Museum. "Antisemitic Legislation, 1933–1939." In *Holocaust Encyclopedia.* http://www.ushmm.org/wlc/en/article.php?ModuleId=10007901.

Vilmar, August Friedrich Christian. *Zur neuesten Kulturgeschichte Deutschlands* (On the most recent history of German culture). Vol. 1: *Politisches und Sociales* (Political and social). Frankfurt and Erlangen: Heyder & Zimmer, 1858.

Vischer, Friedrich Theodor. *Auch Einer: Eine Reisebekanntschaft* (Someone too: A travel acquaintance). Frankfurt: Insel Verlag, 1987.

Von Klemperer, Klemens. *German Resistance against Hitler: The Search for Allies Abroad, 1938–1945.* New York: Clarendon; Oxford: Oxford University Press, 1992.

Weizsäcker, Carl Friedrich Freiherr von. *The World View of Physics.* Translated by Marjorie Grene. Chicago: University of Chicago Press, 1957.

Westcott, B. F., and F. J. A. Hort. *The New Testament in the Original Greek.* London: Macmillan; New York: Harper, 1895.

Wieman, Henry Nelson. "Some Blind Spots Removed." *Christian Century* (January 27, 1939): 116–118.

Wieman, Henry Nelson, and Walter Marshall Horton. *The Growth of Religion.* Chicago: Willett, Clark, 1938.

Wrede, William. *The Messianic Secret.* Translated by J. C. G. Grieg. Cambridge: J. Clarke, 1971.

Wright, William J. *Martin Luther's Understanding of God's Two Kingdoms: A Response to the Challenge of Skepticism.* Grand Rapids, MI: Baker Academic, 2010.

Young, Josiah. *No Difference in the Fare: Dietrich Bonhoeffer and the Problem of Racism.* Grand Rapids, MI: Eerdmans, 1998.

Zahn-Harnak, Agnes. *Adolf von Harnack.* 2nd ed. Berlin: Walter de Gruyter, 1951.

INDEX OF BIBLICAL REFERENCES

INDEX OF NAMES

BIOGRAPHICAL DETAILS about most of the persons listed here are given in the index of names of the *DBWE* volumes in the form of "biograms." The bibliography also gives information about the writings of many scholars named in this index.

THE NAME OF MARTIN LUTHER is mentioned by Bonhoeffer or in editors' notes innumerable times in this volume. This index selectively lists only pages where significant views of Luther are mentioned, as distinct from simple mentions of his name or references to one of his writings.

REFERENCES TO "JESUS CHRIST" as a theological subject are found in the subject index. This name index lists a selection of Bonhoeffer's frequent use of the name "Jesus" such as found, for example, in his Christology lectures, his *Discipleship* book, and the New Testament gospels.

Index of Subjects